✦ HOLLIES

HOLLIES

The Genus *Ilex*

Fred C. Galle

SCIENTIFIC ADVISOR: Dr. Theodore R. Dudley
TECHNICAL ADVISOR: Gene K. Eisenbeiss

Published in association with the Holly Society of America, Inc.

TIMBER PRESS
Portland, Oregon

To the late Dr. Theodore R. Dudley
for his untiring interest
and scientific approach
to the genus *Ilex*

References to products are not intended to be an endorsement
to the exclusion of other products that may have similar uses.

Reprinted 1998

Printed in Hong Kong

Timber Press, Inc.
The Haseltine Building
133 S.W. Second Avenue, Suite 450
Portland, Oregon 97204, U.S.A.

Library of Congress Cataloging-in-Publication Data

Galle, Fred C.
Hollies : the genus Ilex / Fred C. Galle.
p.   cm.
Includes bibliographical references (p.   ) and indexes.
ISBN 0-88192-380-X
1. Holly. I. Title
SB413.H7G34   1997
635.9′33271—dc20   96-31934
CIP

Contents

Color plates follow page 144.

Foreword

All too often the phrase "a definitive work" is used to describe a publication whose scope comprises some portion of the total subject. The dictionary, however, defines the word *definitive* as "designating a statement, such as a scholarly work, that can stand as the most complete and authoritative on its subject."

In 1901, after a purported two decades of research, Theodore Loesener published the first of his two-part monograph on the family Aquifoliaceae, to which the hollies belong, in *Nova Acta Academiae Ceasareae Leopoldino—Carolinae Germnicae, Naturae Curiosorium*. The work was written in Latin. Seven years later, part two was published in German by the same society. Almost a century has passed and the work still stands as the most comprehensive and definitive work on hollies. It is a basic reference for all researchers, if they are fortunate enough to locate a copy and can read or translate botanical Latin and scientific German.

So much more is known today about *Ilex* than was known in Loesener's time. The 60-million-year-old genus, with species presently exceeding 700 in number and found on every continent except Antarctica, is useful in manufacturing operations, furniture building, farming operations, medicine, horticulture, as a means for trapping a food source, and as the prime ingredient in producing a rare *eaux de vie*. Authoring a botanical work on such a group of plants does not fall within purview of a journalistic ghost writer or an undergraduate student. A definitive work mandates the efforts of a scholar, teacher, practitioner, and writer whose specialty encompasses a multidisciplinary approach to the genus. The author of this work, Fred C. Galle (pronounced like the word *galley*), has the requisite qualifications. The Holly Society of America was privileged when Fred assumed the task which required seven years of research, scientific selection, composition, and writing. Furthermore, this work has been reviewed and edited for botanical veracity by two of the foremost authorities on the genus: Dr. T. R. Dudley, principal scientist (deceased 1995), and G. K. Eisenbeiss, research horticulturist, both of the United States National Arboretum, Washington, D.C.

The Holly Society of America is proud to have had a small part in the generation of a definitive work, written in English, the modern scientific language. This work has the qualifications required to become the prime reference on hollies well into the next century.

Holly Society of America

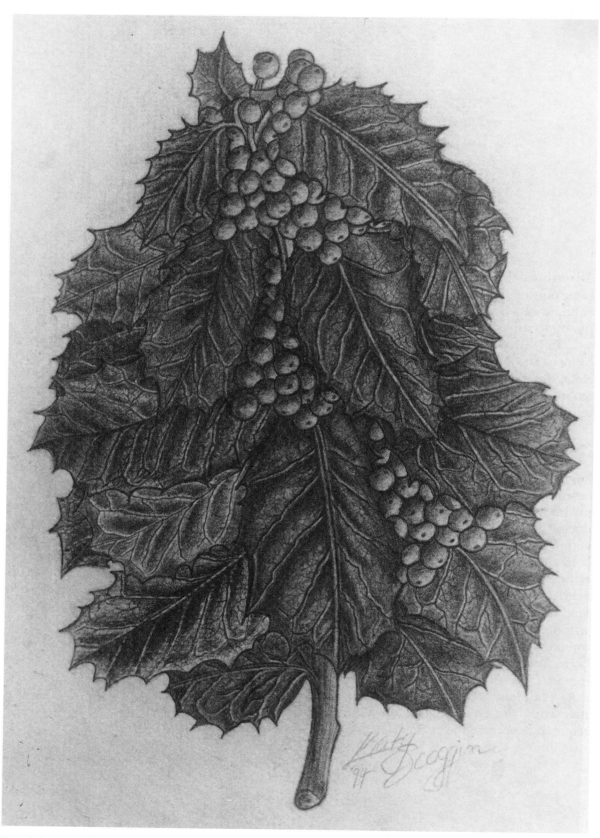

Pencil sketch of *Ilex* 'Emily Bruner' by Katy Scoggin.

Preface

A book of this nature cannot be written alone. There are many friends to acknowledge and thank. I especially want to thank plant lovers, associates, and the many new and old friends who helped along the way. I owe much to these friends from the Netherlands, Belgium, Ireland, Scotland, Isle of Wight, Australia, Canada, and the United States for endless correspondence, phone calls, visits, and patience in discussing hollies.

Many hours were spent discussing this project with Barton (Bart) Bauer before I finally accepted the challenge. I thought the work would be light since there were only some 450 species to research, but by the end of the project I had come across close to 800 species. Many of the original botanical descriptions needed to be translated from Latin. Thanks, Bart, for your friendly letters, support, and loan of slides and photographs.

The manuscript was reviewed frequently during its development. Special thanks are due the late Dr. Theodore Dudley and Gene Eisenbeiss for serving as scientific and technical advisers. Gene took on the additional task of reviewing the final manuscript, which required many long hours of work. Both men offered great assistance in obtaining reprints from the U.S.D.A. library at Beltsville, Maryland.

I also want to thank the nursery professionals and plant enthusiasts who answered my letters and responded to my phone calls about particular plants: Conard-Pyle Nursery, West Grove, Pennsylvania; Jim Cross, Environmentals Company, Cutchogue, New York; Tom Dodd Jr., Tom Dodd Nursery, Semmes, Alabama; Flowerwood Nursery, Mobile, Alabama; Bon Hartline, Anna, Illinois; Louisiana Nursery, Opelousas, Louisiana; Bob Simpson, Simpson Nursery Company, Vincennes, Indiana; Audrey Teasdale, Monrovia Nursery, Azusa, California; Philip Waldman, Roslyn Nursery, Dix Hills, New York; and Wight Nursery, Cairo, Georgia.

Reference libraries were very essential in tracking down many details on old and new species. I spent many days at the University of Georgia Research Library, where I was assisted by Arlene Luchsinger and her staff, and at Auburn University. The staff at the Troup-Harris-Coweta Regional Library in LaGrange, Georgia, assisted in obtaining obscure references on holly species. The New York Botanic Garden Library and staff helped find additional references. Thank you to each one for your help.

Thanks to Randy Allen, a longtime friend and former employee, now in LaGrange, Georgia, for the excellent ink drawings of leaf patterns, flowers, fruits, pyrenes, and other material. Randy even reproduced some of my sketches that had been misplaced.

I visited many public and private holly collections all over the country, following up with repeated visits and correspondence to get more information. Some of the gardens and arboreta staff visited were Bernheim Forest, Clermont, Kentucky; Callaway Gardens, Pine Mountain, Georgia; Clemson University Botanical Arboretum, Clemson, South Carolina; Dawes Arboretum, Newark, Ohio; Ebersole Holly Garden, Carthage, North Carolina; Hal Elmore, Holly Haven, Knoxville, Tennessee; Holden Arboretum, Mentor, Ohio; Huntington Botanical Gardens, San Marino, California; Missouri Botanical Garden, St. Louis; North Carolina University Arboretum, Raleigh; New Jersey Experimental Station, New Brunswick; Planting Fields Arboretum, Oyster Bay, New York; Scott Arboretum, Swarthmore College, Swarthmore, Pennsylvania; Tyler Arboretum, Lima, Pennsylvania; University Arboretum, Tuscaloosa, Alabama; U.S. National Arboretum, Washington, DC; and Washington Park Arboretum, Seattle, Washington. To all of these and many others unnamed here I owe thanks.

Taking and collecting photos was an endless task. Thanks to David Burnett, formerly with Planting Fields Arboretum, New York; Naud Burnett, Dallas, Texas; Edward Martin, Mississippi State University; Virginia Morell, Seattle, Washington, for use of slides from the late Bill Kosar and her generous support; Robert Ticknor, retired from Willamette Research Center, Aurora, Oregon, for color slides and general help; Franklin West, Pennsylvania; and the many other friends who provided help with the photos. Edward Lawrence, Alabama Botanic Garden, arranged to have his California colleague Howard Schorn send a fossil specimen to be photographed. Thank you to all.

I am grateful to Susyn Andrews, Royal Horticultural Society, for reading the lengthy section on English hollies and cultivars.

Several individuals have contributed chapters to this volume. Thanks to Harry William Dengler, College Park, Maryland, for his chapter on holly folklore; the late Alden Hopkins, Williamsburg, Virginia, for his chapter on holly topiaries; and Libby Oliver, Williamsburg, Virginia, for her chapter on decorating with hollies, with photographs by Gordon Chappell, Colonial Williamsburg Division of Landscape and Facilities.

Without the help of Bill Eardley, Springfield, Illinois, and Sam Smoot, Pine Mountain Valley, Georgia, this book would not have been written. Bill kept me in computers, and Sam got me out of many day-to-day challenges. Thanks.

Finally, I wish to thank my family: Erek Galle, Jamestown, Rhode Island, for redrawing my poor pencil sketches of landscape and planting suggestions; and my 13-year-old granddaughter Katy Scoggin, San Bernardino, California, for taking on the long task of my treasured pencil sketch of *Ilex* 'Emily Brunner'. Thanks to my wife, Betty, for her patience with my filing system; for tolerating my books, files, and papers scattered from the dining room table to the study; and for assisting me with the computer and printer. Thanks to my "silent" partner.

List of Abbreviations

A.G.M.	Award of Garden Merit (instituted by R.H.S. in 1921)
A.M.	Award of Merit (instituted by R.H.S. in 1988)
A.M.T.	Award of Merit after Trials at the R.H.S. Gardens, Wisley, England
F.C.C.	First Class Certificate (instituted by R.H.S. in 1859)
F.C.C.T.	First Class Certificate after Trials at the R.H.S. Gardens, Wisley, England
H.S.A	Holly Society of America
NA	U.S. National Arboretum, Washington, D.C.
PI	U.S. Plant Introduction [number]
PP	U.S. Plant Patent [number]
R.H.S.	Royal Horticultural Society, London
U.S.A.	United States of America
U.S.D.A.	United States Department of Agriculture

Color names are based on the Royal Horticultural Society Colour Chart (see Huse and Kelly 1984, Royal Horticulture Society 1990).

Hardiness zones are based on the U.S. Department of Agriculture Hardiness Zone Map of 1990.

◆ PART I

CHAPTER 1

Holly Folklore and Legends

Harry William Dengler[1]

There are few groups of trees and shrubs that possess such a fascinating and diverse background as do the plants belonging to the genus *Ilex* or, as they are more commonly called, hollies. Since the days of the Romans, the Greeks, the Druids, and the Indians of the Americas, holly has played an exciting part in medicine and magic, science and superstition, and legend and lore.

Much of our present-day folklore of medicines, superstitions, and Christmas customs comes from the practices and beliefs of the early Britons, which can be traced further to the Druids, an order of priests, teachers, philosophers, and astronomers of ancient Britain and Gaul, who lived some two thousand years ago. The Druids believed that the sun never deserted the holly tree (*Ilex aquifolium*) and therefore that the holly was a sacred plant. It was their custom to decorate the inside of their dwelling places with evergreens in which the woodland spirits would take refuge from the rigors of winter.

Holly has long been symbolic of Christmas. The name is believed to be a corruption of the word *holy,* although many historians differ on the point. William Turner, the earliest English writer on plants, in his herbal of 1568 called the tree *Holy* and *Holytree.* In parts of Italy, sprigs of holly were used to decorate mangers in commemoration of the infant savior. In Germany, holly is called *Christdorn,* the thorn woven into the crown of crucifixion. Legend has it that the berries of holly were once yellow, but, being stained from the wounds of Christ, have ever since remained red. Among the old Pennsylvania Dutch, the holly berry represented the blood of Christ issuing from His wounds, and the white flowers of the holly tree were symbolic of the purity in which He was conceived.

Stowe in his *Survey of London* (1598) wrote that every house, the parish churches, all the street corners, and the market places were decorated with holly at Christmas. Henry Mayhew estimated that 250,000 bunches of holly were sold in London in 1851. All the great nations of antiquity—the Assyrians, Egyptians, Persians, Greeks, and Romans—decorated their altars, their homes, and their bodies with flowers, and combined leaves and blossoms into wreaths and garlands. The composition of these floral decorations possessed deep significance and the plants involved had symbolic meaning, being varied according to the social standing of the wearer and the seasons of the year. In Rome, wreaths of holly were sent newlyweds as tokens of good wishes and congratulations.

The symbolism or language of flowers is almost as aged as that of speech itself. The ancient Chinese, Assyrian, and Egyptian races seemed to possess a simple but complete way of transmit-

---

[1]Harry W. Dengler is former extension forester at Maryland Extension Service, University of Maryland, College Park, and one of the founders of the Holly Society of America.

ting ideas and sentiments via floral arrangements. Each blossom and plant had its meaning, and these were ingeniously selected and composed to convey the message at hand—a practice much favored by suitors. Floral symbolism reached its zenith with the classic Greeks. In the old floral vocabularies, mistletoe represented the ability to overcome difficulties, while holly stood for foresight; a bouquet of the two plants carried this message: "By foresight you will surmount your difficulties."

Most people of antiquity celebrated an annual observance when the usual curbs on propriety and sobriety were considerably relaxed. During such occasions, the populace exhibited much merriment and indulged in passions that never would be tolerated at other periods of the year. These eruptions of human energy, often plunging into mad orgies of excesses, took place most commonly towards the end of the year and were usually associated with the beginning or ending of a sowing or harvesting season.

Of all such festivals, none is perhaps more widely known than that of the Saturnalia, which took place in December, the last month of the Roman year, about the time of our present Christmas. The Saturnalia commemorated the good King Saturn, god of sowing and husbandry, during whose reign no war was rife, the fields and flocks produced abundantly, no individuals were bound in slavery, and the world was a most pleasurable place in which to live. During the great feast of Saturnalia, the Romans sent holly boughs along with a gift to their friends as token of their good wishes and as emblems of the esteem in which they held them. It is from this custom that historians consider holly to be symbolic of goodwill and for this reason that we decorate our homes and churches with this colorful greenery during the holidays.

The holly, like other thorny plants, was believed in early Europe to repel all evil spirits. In its name, the witches perceived the word *holy,* and its spiny foliage and blood-red berries were suggestive of Christian associations. Pliny the Elder wrote that a holly tree planted about the house served as a counter-charm and kept away all evil spirits or enchantments and defended the house from lightning. Branches of holly were hung about the homes and stables, and cattle were said to thrive if a piece of holly was hung where it could be seen on Christmas Day.

Canes of holly were formerly highly prized in early England. Fast-growing, young shoots of holly made excellent walking sticks and were carried by maidens and matrons alike as protection against mad dogs, vicious beasts, and other perils of the day. As early as 507 B.C. Pythagoras wrote that if a staff made of holly is flung at a (mad) dog, the beast would lie quietly near it.

Henry Phillips in 1823, however, deemed quite credulous the old customs of his ancestors, who trusted branches of holly to defend them against witchcraft. "But this precaution," he wrote, "has become unnecessary, since old ladies have lost their charming powers, and the spells of the youthful fair are too agreeable to be driven from us by a rod of holly."

Many superstitions existed about bringing in the holly for Christmas. In Wales, if it was brought in before Christmas Eve, it was sure to cause family quarrels throughout the year. In parts of Germany and England, the prickly varieties were known as he-hollies, while the smooth-leaved kinds were called she-hollies. The type of holly brought into the household determined who was to dominate the home during the year. If the holly was smooth, the wife was in command; if the holly was prickly, the husband governed for the year. This later custom was brought to the New World and was known in the late nineteenth century among the Ulster Scots of Pennsylvania. Here, the belief existed, too, that if the holly was brought into the house in good weather, the wife would master the household for the ensuing year, but if brought in during rough weather, the husband would be the ruler.

Superstitions, too, existed regarding the removal of the holly after Christmas. In some parts of England, it was decidedly unlucky to leave holly up after New Year's Eve, or Twelfth Night (6 January, the final day of Christmas celebrations), lest the maidens of the household be visited by a ghost for each leaf in the decorations. Others said that a misfortune for each leaf would befall those unheeding this rule. The holly could not merely be thrown away but had to be burnt, else the ill luck would continue as though the holly had not been removed. Elsewhere in England, holly had to be taken down before Shrove Tuesday (Mardi Gras, the last day before Lent) and burnt on the same fire on which the pancakes were to be baked; misfortune was to be certain to befall anyone so unwise as not to heed this belief.

In some parts of England, the holly had to be saved until the following year to protect the house from lightning. In cottages with leaded-pane windows, it was essential that one pane of each window include a sprig of variegated holly in the holiday decorations. If the Christmas decorations were thrown away, a death in the family would occur before next Christmas. A sprig of holly from church decorations, however, was considered quite valuable and ensured its owner a year of good luck.

Among the early Anglicans of America, holly was kept in their churches until Good Friday to prevent the Christmas festivals from being forgotten. Berries from the Christmas holly were kept for good luck during the year in Louisiana.

Among the Chinese, *Ilex purpurea* (synonym *I. chinensis*), the Oriental holly, was much used for decorating temple-courts and large halls during their New Year festivals in February.

Legend has it in Brittany that when Christ was bearing His cross, a small bird attempted to relieve His sufferings by plucking thorns from His brow. The bird's breast became stained with blood and became known forever afterwards as robin redbreast. To this very day in England and Germany, it is considered unlucky to step on a holly berry, a favorite food of the robin, in recognition of the bird's charitable act.

Of all old English traditions, however, one of the most enchanting is that even the bees must be wished a Merry Christmas: a sprig of shiny green and bright red holly must adorn each hive.

Quite apart from the holly superstitions associated with Christmas are those related to divination, the pretended art of foreseeing future events by supernatural or magical means. Perhaps, to paraphrase Folkard, the most interested in this form of sorcery were those vain and silly maidens who no longer could endure the suspense of not knowing the names of their future husbands. There had to be three maidens for the magic to work. Off they would go to the house of the old witch, who would show them how to construct a witch's chain of holly, juniper, and mistletoe berries with an acorn at the end of each link, and how to wind these beads around a slender wand of wood. This was to be placed on the fire with magical sayings and, as the last acorn was burnt, each would see her future husband walk across the room.

A less expensive but more painful method of seeing a future husband in early England was for the maiden to place three pails of water on her bedroom floor. Upon retiring, she pinned three leaves of holly on her nightdress, opposite her heart. During her sleep, she would be awakened by three loud yells, followed by three coarse laughs; after this, the form of her future husband would be seen. The intensity of his love for the maiden was determined by whether or not the pails were disturbed. Unfortunately, this charm was only potent if carried out on Halloween, Midsummer Eve, New Year's Eve, and Christmas Eve

Another traditional form of foreseeing the future in parts of England consisted of collecting nine smooth-leaved (she-holly) leaves and placing them in a three-cornered handkerchief that had to be tied with nine knots. The knotted handkerchief was placed under the pillow and during sleep, pleasant dreams of the future were certain to ensue. For this spell to be fully effective the holly leaves had to be picked late on a Friday and the utmost care taken to maintain complete silence until the following morning.

A quaint fortune-telling superstition of England consisted of fixing little candles on holly leaves and placing them in a pan of water. If the leafy vessels floated, it was a sure sign that the project the person had in mind at the time would prosper. If, however, they sank, the person would do well to abandon the idea as soon as possible.

Native Americans of Pennsylvania regarded the holly as their "Red Badge of Courage" and the token of success in battle. They knew how to preserve and harden the berries without shrinkage or loss of the brilliant colors. The preserved berries were used as decorative buttons on vests, sleeves, trousers, and in their hair. Brisk trading in the berries occurred with tribes where holly did not grow naturally.

These Native American groups often painted or embroidered sprays of holly, like coats-of-arms, on their shields and jackets. Many legends were told about the holly connection with happier days and great victories. The spines of the leaves symbolized the fierceness of the warriors and their refusal to take insults from anyone; the toughness of wood indicated that they would never submit to their enemies. Since the leaves of holly do not readily fall off, the tree was an emblem of courage and everlasting life. Before going to war, these early Americans often pinned sprigs of holly on their clothes with great ceremony to speed their triumphant return in safety.

In the floral vocabulary of the ancients, holly symbolized "defense" and, strangely enough, eastern North American Indians planted holly about their cabins as "protectors," feeling that the trees kept away the evil spirits.

Among the many old and curious beliefs associated with healing was the idea that diseases could be transferred to trees and plants, especially by passing the patient through an arch or hoop of the branches, or through a cleft in the trunk of a tree. In almost every country of the world, this superstition could be found. In England, ruptured children, or those with rickets, were passed through fissures of tree trunks, often of holly. To ensure success, the tree could never before have been used for this purpose. The trunk was split from east to west; the youngster was passed through by a maiden and received by a boy on the other side. Sometimes this was repeated three times; sometimes, too the child had to be thrust through head first for the charm to work; at other times, the feet had to be the foremost part of the body. When the passing through ceremony was completed, the split that had been held open with wedges, was allowed to spring together, and the wound bound and plastered up with clay. As the gash gradually healed, so did the youngster's rupture in a like manner.

The largest-known American holly tree was similarly used to cure the rupture of a boy some forty years ago in North Carolina. The Russians used holly trees in a somewhat similar manner for curing tuberculosis.

Culpeper, in his pithy herbals of 1653, related that holly is governed by the planet Saturn and thus influences the "melancholy," a sediment of the blood whose receptacle was the spleen. The holly, like other Saturnine plants, was therefore considered "cold and dry in quality, fortifying the retentive faculty, and memory; makes men sober, solid, and staid, fit for study; stays the unbridled joys of lustful blood, stays the wandering thoughts; and reduces them home to the centre." Writing specifically about the virtues of the holly tree, Culpeper stated that the berries expel wind and are, therefore, good for the colic. If a dozen ripe berries were eaten in the morning before fasting, they purged the body of wastes. If, however, the berries were first dried and beaten into a powder, they bound the body and stopped bleeding and fluxes. The bark of the tree and also the leaves are exceptionally good, being used in fomentations for broken bones and for such members as are out of joint. Girarde, in his herbal of 1597, some fifty years earlier, had published Culpeper's remedies in language more picturesque than printable.

In more modern times, infusions, decoctions, and fomentations of holly were used for a wide assortment of human disorders. In England, a tea of holly bark was a cure for the cough. In France, a decoction of leaves and bark was considered equal to and sometimes better than quinine in the treatment of intermittent fever. A tea of holly leaves was a cure for measles by some North American Indian tribes, while an elixir of the leaves, bark, and wood was regarded by them as a specific against disease. A beverage of the berries pacified Cherokee women and curbed their urge for wandering. The juice of holly leaves was also good for pain in the side.

Native American women wore sprigs of holly during childbirth, believing them to ease the pain and to ensure the delivery of healthy offspring.

John Evelyn, in 1662, related that a posset made of milk and beer in which the most pointed holly leaves are boiled is certain to abate torments of colic when all else failed. Leaves of holly, he reported, when dried to a fine powder and drunk in white wine prevail against gall stones.

In England, an old cure for chilblains was to thrash them soundly with branches of holly; a rustic specific for whooping cough was to drink new milk out of a cup made from the wood of variegated holly. Followers of Zoroaster in Persia and India used an infusion of water and holly bark to sprinkle the faces of newborn children.

An old and quaint English cure for toothache concerns the belief that the pain was caused by the gnawing of little worms inside the tooth. The remedy for this was to hold a smoldering holly coal in the mouth so that the smoke could enter the cavity of the afflicted part. This promptly dispatched the tiny offenders and caused them to drop out of the tooth.

While all these remedies have been attributed to our familiar American and English Christmas hollies, other members of this same family have likewise contributed to the well-being of the world. In the far East, decoctions of the bark and leafy shoots of the familiar Chinese holly, *Ilex cornuta,* are commonly used as tonics, especially for the kidneys; the crushed seeds of this species are frequently used in medicines. Among the people of the Saint Helena Islands of South Carolina, a mixture of lard and *I. cassine,* mockingbird bush, is used as an ointment for smallpox. Farther northward, the berries and bark of *I. verticillata,* winterberry, the deciduous holly, have often been substituted for Peruvian bark in cases of intermittent fevers. The bark has also been used as a wash for gangrene and eruptions of the skin. *Ilex cassine* var. *cassine,* the dahoon holly, was used by the early settlers of North Carolina to purify the coastal swamp water and render it fit to drink.

Despite these varied and valued healing properties of holly and its contributions to the medicinal lore of the Old World, it is of interest to note two old Welsh superstitions: to pluck a sprig of holly in flower was a sure cause of death in the family of the picker, and holly must never be brought into a sick room for the patient was almost surely to suffer a relapse or die as a consequence.

Young branches of holly were cut by the Morbihan peasants in Europe and cured for hay. The stems were dried, bruised, and fed to cattle three times a day. Milk and butter from these holly-fed cows were said to be both wholesome and good.

In China the young shoots of *Ilex purpurea* are sometimes blanched and eaten in salads. Here, too, the limber twigs of the familiar Chinese holly, *I. cornuta,* are used as nose rings for cattle.

Palatable and stimulating is a tealike beverage called "maté," "yerba matá," or "Paraguay tea." Brewed from leaves of *Ilex paraguariensis,* one of several South American hollies, maté is an all purpose drink used by more than thirty million South Americans daily, principally in Paraguay and Argentina. An early South American Indian custom still practiced today is to serve visitors a gourd of maté. The chief sips some of the tea through a *bombilla* and passes the receptacle to the visitor, who drinks from the same tube. Everyone in camp partakes of the beverage until it is consumed. It is an act of unpardonable rudeness to refuse to drink any of the maté.

Maté is recognized by the chemists as a stimulant for the nerves and muscles as well as for the brain. During World War I, the British, French, and German armies found it to be a valuable stimulant in times of stress.

High in the eastern side of Ecuador's Andes, the Zapara and Jibaro Indians have used *guayusa* since pre-Columbian times. This tea is brewed from another South American holly, *Ilex guayusa,* related to but distinct from *I. paraguariensis.* In appearance *I. guayusa* is not unlike the old holly trees of England. While quite acceptable as a substitute for coffee or tea, the infusion, as brewed by these Indians, is so strong that it acts as an emetic. The *guayusa* pot is kept carefully covered and the brew simmered over a slow fire throughout the night. On rising in the morning, the Indians would drink enough to make them vomit, believing that the beverage conferred strength and swiftness to the hunter. Groves of this holly were planted about the villages of the Indians.

Since ancient times Native Americans in what became southern United States held in greatest esteem the celebrated "black drink" or "cassena," brewed from the toasted leaves of *Ilex vomi-*

toria, the yaupon of southeastern United States. This holly tea restored lost appetites, confirmed health, and gave its drinkers courage and agility in war. Accounts of the black drink ceremony were recorded as long ago as 1536. Participants in the ceremony gathered in the spring of the year, along the sea coast where the yaupon grew in abundance, some traveling several hundred miles to attend the rituals. The holly leaves were parched in earthenware vessels over fires and then boiled for a considerable period. While the leaves were brewing, the pot was kept carefully covered, but if by chance any women came into the vicinity while the pot was uncovered, the men threw the drink away, believing that some evil would be imparted to the beverage. No woman was allowed to move or walk about during the cooling and serving process and should, perchance, this occur, the men would throw the drink away, disgorge what they had already swallowed, and severely punish the transgressing female. At the same time, the men continually called out, "Who will drink? Who will drink?" Any woman within hearing distance of the shouts was obliged to remain motionless, even if standing on tiptoes, until the men had consumed their fill.

On other occasions, the cassine was used in ceremonies concerned with the well-being of the tribe. Sitting at the head of a semicircular bench, the chief, with his councilors and elders, accepted the blessing of those who were to partake of the drink. Having accepted a salutation from each brave starting with the eldest, the chief ordered the women to brew the drink.

Matters of importance to the tribe were discussed and debated by the priests, elders, and nobles of the tribe. No decisions were made until a number of councils had carefully deliberated the opinions and recommendations of the speakers. During the discussions, the chief was served the hot drink in a capacious shell. The chief, in turn, directed the rest to drink from the same vessel.

So esteemed did Native Americans hold this holly tea that no one was allowed to drink it during the council except those proved to be brave and courageous warriors. So strong was this beverage that it immediately threw the drinker into a deep sweat. Those whose stomachs rejected the beverage were not to be trusted to any difficult or warlike mission. The drink was believed to nourish and strengthen the body. Some sixty species of hollies yield leaves for beverage purposes.

It is interesting to note that the leaves of one holly frequently used for tea by people living on the Chinese-Tibetan border come from *Ilex yunnanensis* var. *eciliate,* which is related to *I. vomitoria* and has been used in a similar way as the hollies used by tribal groups in both North and South America since ancient times.

In old traditional English Shrovetide dances—the last merrymaking period before the observance of Lent—there often appeared a holly-boy and an ivy-girl. The holly was supposed to be male and to personify the steadfast and the holy, while the ivy, because of its clinging and embracing nature, was symbolical of a maiden love and friendship. In some areas of England it was traditional for the girls to make chains of holly to burn on Shrove Tuesday, the boys retaliating with ropes of ivy (Dallimore 1908).

The observance of May Day, with its poles and dances, has long been a traditional custom of the spring festivals of European peasants. This is a remnant of the ancient worship of the benevolent tree spirits and of the necessity each spring of paying homage to them to ensure the fertility of the fields and flocks in the coming year. Often, the spirit was represented by a pole, a freshly cut tree, a branch, a flower, a vegetable, a person, or some combination of the above, like a bough-bedecked mummer.

Jack-in-the-Green, so Sir James Frazer informed us, is the best-known example of the latter. Encased in a wickerwork covered with holly and ivy and surmounted by a crown of flowers and ribbons, he dances on May Day at the head of a troop of fellow chimney-sweeps, all collecting gifts of pennies. Here should be mentioned the preference of the chimney-sweeps for branches of holly in cleaning the chimneys of London, and the tradition that all flues must be cleaned by New Year's Eve to permit an easy exit for all household evils.

Of all the unusual customs concerning English hollies, perhaps none is more curious than the use of the bark in making birdlime. This mucilaginous substance was spread on branches and other places where birds were accustomed to roost. In the days before firearms, there was no easier way of trapping the ingredients for a tasty sparrow pot pie. Birdlime was also used for keeping snails, insects, and other vermin from climbing fruit trees and invading gardens. In some provinces of China, bark of the beautiful *Ilex latifolia* is used for the same purposes.

The bark of the holly was gathered in midsummer and boiled in spring water for twelve hours. On cooling, the inner green bark was separated from the rest and laid aside in a cool cellar for a fortnight, whence it became a perfect mucilage. It was then pounded fine in a mortar, washed in a stream of running water, boiled with a third part of capon or goose grease to prevent the birdlime from freezing in winter.

The folklore recorded here relates only to very few of the hundreds of hollies believed to occur in various parts of the world. As these species gradually become introduced to the Americas, and as their folklore successively becomes known, a most exciting story is surely to be unfolded.

CHAPTER 2

Landscaping with Hollies

Hollies have many fine qualities that make them an important group of both evergreen and deciduous plants in landscapes today (Plates 1 to 4). With proper selection they can become the main feature throughout the garden. They are versatile plants that can be used in a wide range of situations; dwarf hollies are suitable for bonsai, rock gardens, and facing taller shrubs; medium hollies are useful as foundation plants; and tall hollies make excellent screens, hedges, and wind breakers. However they are used, the year-round landscape appeal of hollies stems from their habit of growth, pleasing foliage, and ornamental berries.

It is important to know the size and shape of the numerous hollies. A wide range of plant forms is available, including shrubs of low density with cushionlike habit, larger shrubs with spreading and rounded habit, and upright pyramidal trees to 12 m (40 ft). or more high with loose to dense habit. Hollies come in every shape except as vines. Many are evergreen, but a few are deciduous and provide interesting contrast in the winter landscape.

Holly leaves are important features also and vary in color and texture. Most selected cultivars have bright dark olive-green foliage, but dull dark green to glossy green to grayish and variegated forms exists. Plants with variegated foliage can be used for contrast or to call attention to an area. There are numerous variegated English hollies (e.g., *Ilex aquifolium* 'Golden Milkboy', 'Golden Milkmaid', 'Ingramii', 'Silvary', 'Silver Milkboy', 'Silver Milkmaid', 'Silver Queen', and 'Wieman's Moonbrite'), one available American holly (*I. opaca* 'Steward's Silver Crown'), several yellow-variegated cultivars of Chinese holly (*I. cornuta* 'Cajun Gold', 'O. Spring', 'Sunrise'), and one attractive soft gray-green cultivar of Japanese holly (*I. crenata* 'Snowflake'). The spiny-leaved hollies are attractive in any season but are especially favored during Yuletide. Many excellent hollies have leaves without spines or leaves with only fine-serrated margins. Leaf texture varies from medium to coarse, and leaf size varies from small to large.

With proper selection, hollies provide colorful fruit for at least three to six months of the year and often longer (Plate 5). *Ilex crenata* (Japanese holly) with its many cultivars and *I. glabra* (inkberry) have black fruit while most of the other species have red fruit. Selected cultivars have yellow or orange fruit. The red fruit of *I. aquifolium* (English holly) and *I. cornuta* (Chinese holly) often persists (unless eaten by birds) into the late spring or late summer side-by-side the new developing green berries. Plants with attractive yellow berries are usually ignored by birds until all red-fruited plants have been stripped of their fruit. Yellow-fruited plants also are more showy on cloudy days than are their red counterparts. Some good yellow-fruited hollies include *I. aquifolium* 'Bacciflava', 'Berigold', 'Wieman's Yellow-pillar', and 'Yellow Beam'; *I. cornuta* 'D'Or'; *I. crenata* cultivars 'Butterball', 'Forty Niner', 'Honeycomb', 'Ivory Hall', 'Ivory Tower', 'Sir Echo', 'Sunshine', and the Watanabeana Group; and *I. opaca* cultivars 'Canary', 'Betty Nevison', and 'Princeton Gold'.

USING HOLLIES IN THE GARDEN

Selecting the right holly depends on knowing the hardiness of your area (and selecting a compatible plant) and the year-round characteristics of the plant. Make sure the plants are adapted to your area. It is disappointing to see the attractive small spiny-leaved *Ilex dimorphophylla* (Okinawan holly) sold in Atlanta, Georgia, and farther north (unless for bonsai) as the plants are only hardy in Zone 9. *Ilex opaca* (American holly) and *I. glabra* are the most cold hardy holly species up to Zone 5, and *I. aquifolium* (English holly) is hardy to Zone 7 and occasionally Zone 6. Deciduous hollies are hardy in Zones 4 to 9. Table 1 shows the hardiness range for selected evergreen holly species.

Table 1. Hardiness ranges for selected evergreen hollies.

SCIENTIFIC NAME	COMMON NAME	USDA ZONES
I. aquifolium	English holly	7, some in 6b to 8
I. cornuta	Chinese holly	(6b) 7 to 9
I. crenata	Japanese holly	6 to 9
I. latifolia	Lusterleaf holly	7 to 9
I. opaca	American holly	5a to 9b
I. pedunculosa	Long-stalked holly	5b to 8
I. purpurea	—	7b to 9
I. rotunda	—	8b to 9
I. vomitoria	Yaupon holly	7a to 9

The ultimate size and shape of a mature plant is most important in choosing or selecting for a particular site in the garden. For example, plants with small foliage often provide good contrast to plants with larger leaves and should be used in front of or at their side but never hidden behind a larger plant. This is a common mistake of many gardeners: placing a beautiful dwarf plant behind a tall, vigorous plant.

Hollies with variegated leaves can be used singly or in small groups of three to five plants. Avoid using contrasting plants alternately one by one; the effect can be busy and distracting. Background screen plantings do not need to be of the same cultivar, but select plants with the same quality of composition in leaves and plant form. Adding one or several yellow-fruited hollies of the same species in a screen or border planting adds spice and variety. Long screen barriers or hedgerows 30 m (100 ft.) or more do not need to be of the same plant, or in equal units of every 3 to 9 m (10 to 30 ft.). Avoid the blocky look by having different numbers of plants used together or stagger the plants to break a long, similar, and often monotonous look.

Because hollies produce beautiful clusters of colorful fruit in the fall and winter months, they should be placed in the garden where that fruit can best be displayed. Often red fruit in a darkened area does not show off against the dark green foliage. Such hollies need to be front lighted by the sun and placed near a picture window where they can be seen from within the house. Hollies with bright yellow to orange fruit show off better against the green foliage even in situations with overhead or back lighting.

When selecting hollies for the landscape, remember that these plants are dioecious. Each shrub or tree is either male (staminate) or female (pistillate). Only the female plants produce the fruit. For pollination to occur, however, there must be one male of the same species for several females. *Ilex latifolia* (lusterleaf holly) and *I. cornuta* (Chinese holly), for example, flower early in spring on old year wood and do not pollinate hollies such as *I. opaca* that flower in midspring to late spring on new growth. Some pollination by bees occurs between different holly species if the plants flower at the same time, but for best results have one male plant near by or in the background border of the garden for pollinating the female plants of the same species.

COMPANION PLANTS

I recall hearing a landscape architect say that he could design a beautiful house site with hollies, crape myrtles and a good groundcover like liriope. How monotonous! Even the most enthusiastic ilexophile would not find this very attractive. Numerous shrubs and small trees make excellent companions for deciduous and evergreen hollies, including species of *Abelia, Berberis* (barberry) *Buxus* (boxwood), *Camellia, Chaenomeles* (flowering quince), *Cotoneaster, Deutzia, Fothergilla, Forsythia, Hamamelis, Osmanthus, Rhododendron* (azaleas and rhododendrons), and *Vaccinium* (blueberry). *Prunus caroliniana* and *P. laurocerasus* (cherry laurel), *Elaeagnus pungens* and *E. multiflora,* and many other species provide good contrast through the seasons.

Hollies combine well with other broadleaved and narrow-leaved evergreens, including species of *Daphne, Juniperus* (juniper), *Leucothoe, Nandina, Pinus* (pine) *Pyracantha, Skimmia,* and *Taxus. Mahonia aquifolium* (Oregon grape), *M. bealei, Pieris floribunda* and *P. phillyreifolia* (American pieris), and *P. japonica* (Japanese pieris) are other good evergreen companions.

Among small flowering trees, good companions include *Cornus florida* (flowering dogwood), *C. kousa* (kousa dogwood), and their intraspecific hybrids; *Lagerstroemia indica* (crape-myrtle); *Oxydendrum arboreum* (sourwood); *Stewartia koreana, S. pseudo-camellia* (Japanese stewartia), and *S. sinensis;* and *Styrax japonicum* and *S. obassia.*

Ground covers for planting beneath hollies include *Hedera helix* (English ivy), *Liriope* species, *Pachysandra terminalis,* and *Sarcococca hookeriana* var. *humilis.*

Hollies are excellent background plants for an endless selection of perennials and bulbs including *Iris, Lilium* species (lily), *Narcissus* species (daffodils), and the colorful leaf forms of *Hosta* and *Ligularia* species.

An excellent companion for cut holly wreaths and arrangements is *Osmanthus heterophyllus* 'Variegatus' for its look-alike attractive variegated foliage.

FOUNDATION PLANTINGS

Hollies are important foundation plants, but must be carefully selected so as not to become overgrown and completely dominate the planting. Many cultivars of *Ilex opaca* (American holly) and the common yet beautiful *I. cornuta* 'Burfordii' become too large for a foundation planting but can be planted at the corner of a one-story building. *Ilex cornuta* 'Dwarf Burford', *I. cornuta* 'Anicet Delcambre', *I. opaca* 'Needlepoint', and the *I. cornuta* × *I. pernyi* hybrids are not as vigorous, however, and could be used as foundation plants. Other medium-size hollies include *I.* 'Elegance', *I.* 'Mary Nell', *I. myrtifolia, I.* 'September Gem', *I. vomitoria,* the Blue Hollies, China Boy®, and China Girl®. The American holly cultivars *I. opaca* 'Clarendon Spreading' and *I. opaca* 'Maryland Dwarf' are compact, broad shrubs seldom reaching 1.8 m (6 ft.) in twenty years. *Ilex aquifolium* 'Vera' is a slow-growing upright plant with good clusters of red fruit. For larger two-story homes and buildings, *I. aquifolium* cultivars, *I. cornuta* 'Burfordii', *I. latifolia, I. opaca* cultivars, *I. purpurea,* and *I. rotunda* are suitable where hardy. Figures 2-1 and 2-2 suggest foundation plantings for holly.

Foundation plantings of holly (and many other plants) often become leggy with age, yielding a massive crown or top. Two options are available for the concerned gardener. The first involves deheading the plant, often nearly to the ground, and starting over. The second option involves sculpturing the plants by limbing up and opening up the top to better display the trucks and branches.

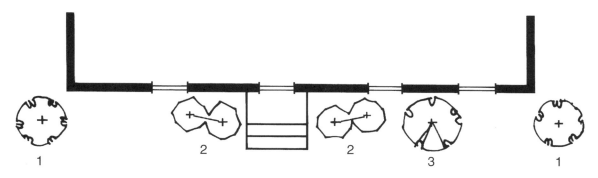

Figure 2-1. Suggested foundation planting with alternates. 1: *Ilex* 'September Gem', Blue Holly, China Girl, *I. cornuta* 'Dwarf Burford'; 2: *I. crenata* cultivars 'Beehive', 'Helleri', or 'Piccolo'; 3: *I. crenata* cultivars 'Hetzii' or 'Rotundifolia' or *I. glabra*. Drawing by Erek Galle.

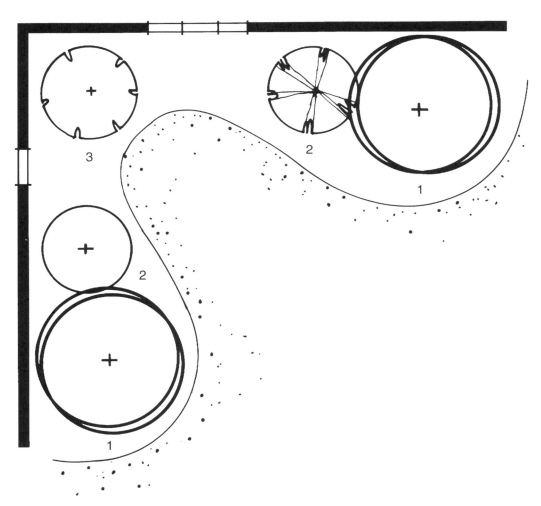

Figure 2-2. Suggested foundation planting. 1: *I. opaca* selections or *I. cornuta* 'Burfordii' or 'Dwarf Burford'; 2: *I. cornuta* 'O. Spring', *I. opaca* selections; 3: *I. × attenuata* 'Foster No. 2'. Drawing by Erek Galle.

MASSED PLANTINGS AND SPECIMEN PLANTS

Hollies lightly clipped or sheared make attractive informal masses or specimen plants (Plates 6, 7). They naturalize well in a woodland setting or, if sheared, adapt to a formal setting. Most hollies respond to pruning and there is no limit to creating living, green, sculptured forms appropriate to a given landscape (see Figure 2-3). Unfortunately, many of the Japanese hollies and dwarf forms of Chinese hollies (such as *Ilex cornuta* 'Carissa' and 'Rotunda') are planted in a mass setting but pruned individually like "green gum drops" when they would be best left to grow to a large green mass. The opposite misuse of hollies in the landscape is also seen, that is, spacing plants too close together so that they lose their identity in just a few years. These same plants might be divided and transplanted to other sections of the yard.

A good landscaped property goes beyond the usual foundation planting and repeats some of the same holly plants in a different setting. With selective care, collectors' gardens can have a display of many different plants complimenting each other. I recall seeing in Japan a large circular raised bed 7.5 to 9 m (25 to 30 ft.) in diameter that was planted with *Ilex crenata* 'Helleri'. Skillfully interplanted were about five plants with yellowish leaves like those of *I. crenata* 'Golden Heller'. The latter added a bit of spice to what might have been a mundane planting.

Many holly species and cultivars are excellent tree specimens or used in tall screens or hedges. They can be grown with foliage from the ground up or with the lower limbs removed to display the trunk. Many trees with multiple trunks are excellent with their trunks exposed (see Figure 2-4). The following species and cultivars are suggested for medium to large trees: *Ilex aquifolium, I. × altaclerensis, I. × attenuata, I. cornuta* 'Burfordii', *I. latifolia, I. opaca, I. purpurea, I. rotunda,* and *I. wilsonii.*

ESPALIERS

Many hollies can be trained as espaliers against a large brick wall or fence (Plate 8). Seldom seen but beautiful as espalier for a large wall is *Ilex latifolia* (lusterleaf holly). Other species to use include *I. aquifolium* (English holly), *I. cornuta* (Chinese holly), large cultivars of *I. crenata* (Japanese holly), *I. opaca* (American holly), and *I. vomitoria* (yaupon holly). Espaliered hollies can be very successful but require annual pruning. Root pruning also may be necessary every three to four years to restrict the plant's normal growth.

Hollies with multiple stems and a round-headed bushy form are better for espaliers than are the upright pyramidal hollies. *Ilex cornuta* 'Burfordii' (Figure 2-5) and *I. latifolia* are two possibilities for large walls. For smaller walls, the Blue hollies, *I. cornuta* 'Dwarf Burford', and hybrids of *I. cornuta* × *I. pernyi* are suitable.

HEDGES

Hollies can be pruned into tight hedges varying from 0.6 to 3 m (2 to 10 ft.) in height depending upon the species or cultivar selected (Figure 2-6). Cultivars of *Ilex crenata* such as 'Dwarf Pagoda', 'Helleri', 'Microphylla', and 'Morris Dwarf' are adaptable for very low hedges. *Ilex aquifolium, I. × attenuata* 'Foster No. 2', and *I. opaca* make excellent tall hedges or screens when planted on 4- to 6-ft. centers and pruned to keep tight.

It was customary, starting in the early 1800s, to enclose and subdivide gardens by hedges of holly, which had the added advantage of keeping cattle out. With proper pruning the red berries add to the display. Loudon (1844, p. 509) quoted Evelyn's description of hollies:

Figure 2-3. *Ilex crenata* in Japan. Photo by Fred Galle.

Figure 2-4. *Ilex crenata* in Japan. Photo by Fred Galle.

Figure 2-5. *Ilex cornuta* 'Burfordii' trained on a trellis at Monrovia Nursery, Azusa, California. Photo by Fred Galle.

I have seen hedges or, if you will, stout walls of holly, 20 feet in height, kept upright; and the gilded sort [variegated leaf type] budded low, and in two or three places one above another, shorn and fashioned into columns and pilasters, architecturally shaped, and at due distance; than which nothing can possibly be more pleasant, the berries adorning the entire column with scarlet festoons.

Holly hedges require some planning as to location, purpose, and height (Plates 9 to 11). A low hedge to outline beds requires a different kind of holly than a taller and larger hedge to divide garden areas or serve as a screen. Hedges should be planted 1.2 m (4 ft.) from a walkway if the height of the hedge will be maintained at about 1.5 m (5 ft.). Taller hedges, 0.6 to 3 m (8 to 10 ft.) in height, should be planted farther back from the walk. All hedges should be wider at the base than at the top. The wider space allows for sufficient light, air, and even moisture to the lower branches. Do not plant hedges or screens on a property line as overhanging branches or limbs on the abutting property can be cut or removed as the neighbor sees fit. When planted within your own property you have full control of the planting and can prune and maintain as you see fit.

Screen plantings are usually allowed to grow taller than hedges, into small to large trees. The same species or cultivar may be used, or a random planting of taller-growing hollies is also an effective screen. At Callaway Gardens, Pine Mountain, Georgia, a long unpruned hedge of *Ilex cornuta* 'Burfordii' backed by tall evergreen magnolias is used along a drive to screen the gardens from a highway. Elsewhere a massed planting of *I. cornuta* 'Burfordii' and *I. vomitoria* were used to screen a large parking area. At my home on a wooded property I am planting an informal screen

Figure 2-6. English holly hedge (*Ilex aquifolium*) near Christchurch University, New Zealand. Photo courtesy of Christchurch University.

using a number of holly species and their cultivars. This screen is not a row of individual plants but a mass of red- and yellow-fruited hollies, including *I. opaca* and its cultivar 'Dan Fenton', *I. × attenuata* and its cultivar 'Foster No. 2', *I. cornuta* and its cultivars 'Burfordii' and 'D'Or', and *I.* 'Emily Brunner'. As time permits, I hope to add several cultivars of English holly, *I. aquifolium*, to this informal screen. The possibilities are endless. Figures 2-7 to 2-9 suggest possible hedge or border plantings with holly, and Figures 2-10 and 2-11 suggest random border plantings.

DWARF HOLLIES

If garden space is limited, plant some of the unusual dwarfs and small hollies in irregular beds, in groups, or as a border planting in front of larger shrubs. *Ilex* 'Rock Garden' is a beautiful dwarf spiny-leaf holly and an excellent rare plant that should be used more often. In fifteen years, plants may reach only 0.3 to 0.5 m (12 to 18 inches) high and wide. Figure 2-12 suggests a planting that features holly gems.

Dwarf hollies can be sheared as low edging plants in formal or informal designs to separate various parts of the garden. These same hollies are excellent container or tub plants on decks, porches, or anywhere a portable holly is desired (Figure 2-13). Many shops and hotels are now planting fruiting specimens in containers near their entrances or outside picture windows where they can be seen from a dining room or lounge. Even large evergreen hollies such as *Ilex cornuta* 'Burfordii' are being used as permanent plantings in malls where they fill large circular and tapered

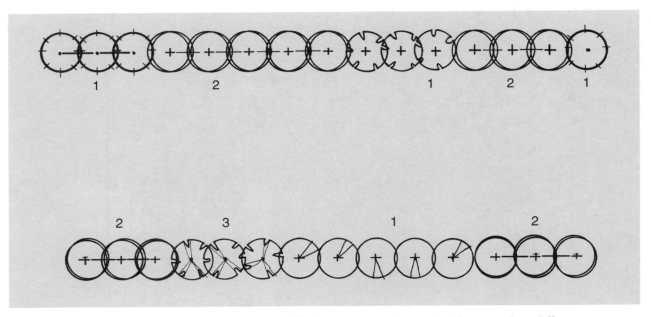

Figure 2-7. Suggested hedge or border planting. A blocky appearance is created with two or three different cultivars. 1: *I. opaca* cultivars with *I. aquifolium* cultivars; 2: *I. opaca* cultivars with *I. attenuata*; 3: *I aquifolium* with *I. altaclerensis*. Drawing by Erek Galle.

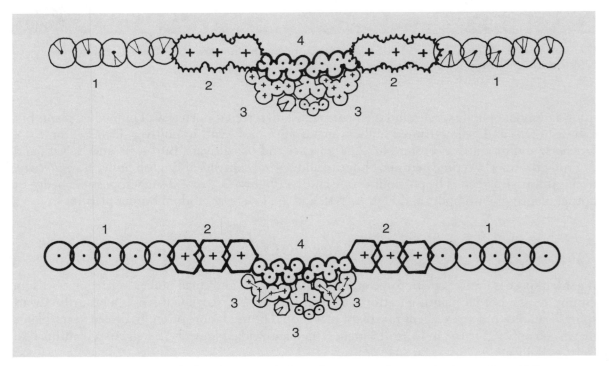

Figure 2-8. Suggested border or hedge planting with three alternates. 1: *I. opaca* selection or *I. aquifolium* selection; 2: *I. vomitoria* selection with *Camellia sasanqua* or *C. japonica*; 3: *I.* 'September Gem', China Boy, China Girl; 4: cultivars of *I. decidua* or *I. verticillata*. Drawing by Erek Galle.

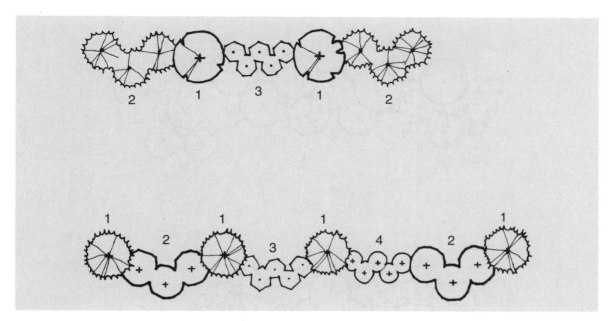

Figure 2-9. Suggested border planting. 1: *I. opaca* with *I. latifolia* or *I. aquifolium*; 2: *I. vomitoria* cultivars or Blue Holly selections; 3: *I.* 'October Gem' with China Girl or China Boy; 4: *I. crenata* 'Rotundifolia' with dwarf *I. crenata* cultivar. Drawing by Erek Galle.

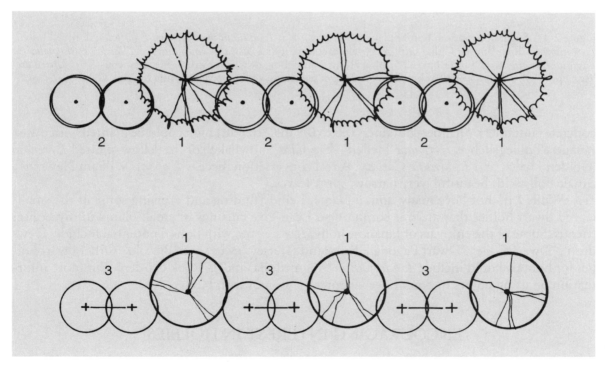

Figure 2-10. Suggested random border planting. 1: *Magnolia grandiflora* or *M. virginiana*; 2: *I. cornuta* 'Burfordii', *I. opaca* or *I. aquifolium* cultivars; 3: Alternates *I. latifolia, I. vomitoria, I. cornuta* × *I. pernyi* cultivars. Drawing by Erek Galle.

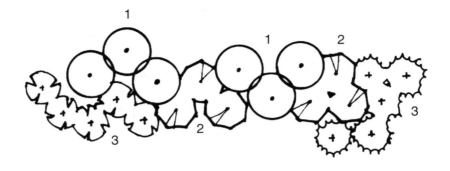

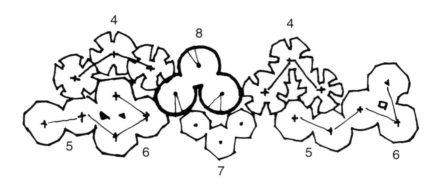

Figure 2-11. Suggested random border planting. 1: *I. opaca* or *I. aquifolium* selections, *I. latifolia*; 2: Blue Holly, *I. vomitoria*, China Boy, or China Girl; 3: *I. crenata* cultivars; 4: *I. opaca*, *I. aquifolium* or *I. latifolia*, *Magnolia virginia*, *I.* × *attenuata* 'Foster No. 2'; 5: Blue Holly, China Boy, or China Girl; 6: miscellaneous; 7: *I. verticillata* 'Red Sprite'; 8: *I. vomitoria* 'October Gem', *I. crenata* selections, or *I. glabra*. Drawing by Erek Galle.

concrete containers. Shallow containers 0.6 to 0.9 m (2 to 3 ft.) high could be planted with dwarf Japanese hollies such as *I. crenata* 'Helleri', *I. crenata* 'Snowflake', or the yellow-spotted *I. crenata* 'Golden Heller' and *I. cornuta* 'Carissa'. A real conversation piece is *I. opaca* 'William Hawkins', a male holly with beautiful, very narrow, spiny leaves.

　　While I do not have many bonsai plants, I enjoy finding and growing some of the small-leaved dwarf hollies that are not common so I can give cuttings or small plants to my bonsai friends. Some of the cultivars of Japanese holly, *Ilex crenata*, with bonsai potential include 'Dewdrop', 'Dwarf Cone', 'Dwarf Pagoda', 'Fairyland', 'Jersey Jewel', and 'Piccolo'. Other dwarf hollies for bonsai should include *I. aquifolium* 'Angustifolia' and *I.* 'Rock Garden'. For more information on using hollies in bonsai, see Chapter 5, "Bonsai with Holly."

ENCOURAGING INTEREST IN HOLLIES

As holly enthusiasts we should display in our gardens, whether as specimens plants or in combination with other plants, the tried and true holly species and cultivars along with the new introductions that are seldom seen or readily available. We should accept the role as ambassadors of the new and better holly cultivars and sound their praises far and wide. Many excellent holly cultivars that have been named and registered are slow to reach the marketplace. By displaying these hollies in our gardens we can create interest. In a small raised bed in my own garden are beautiful spec-

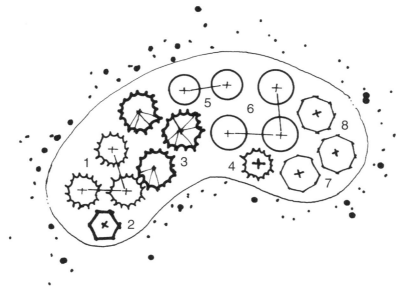

Figure 2-12. Suggested bed of holly gems. 1: *I. crenata* 'Beehive' or 'Dewdrop'; 2: *I. crenata* 'Piccolo'; 3: *I. crenata* 'Border Gem', 'Butterball', 'Helleri', or 'Snow Flake'; 4: *I.* 'Rock Garden'; 5: *I. cornuta* 'Carissa' or 'Rotunda'; 6: *I. cornuta* 'Carissa' or *I. crenata* 'Dwarf Pagoda'; 7: *I. crenata* 'Delaware Diamond'; 8: *I. crenata* 'Dan's Gold'. Other alternates include *I. crenata* 'Green Dragon', 'Green Pygmy', 'Pinocchio', 'Sky Pencil', and the Jersey Pigmy hybrids *I.* 'Jersey Globe', *I.* 'Jersey Jewel', *I.* 'Jersey Midget', *I.* 'Jersey Moppet', and *I.* 'Jersey Sprite'. Drawing by Erek Galle.

Figure 2-13. A portable holly in Japan. The roots of this specimen of *Ilex crenata* are wrapped in straw, so the plant can be moved wherever it is needed. Photo by Fred Galle.

imens of *I. crenata* 'Beehive', *I. crenata* 'Piccolo', and a small plant of the hybrid *I.* 'Rock Garden' for all my friends and visitors to see. These hollies are extremely rare in Georgia and should be in our local display garden and state botanical gardens for visitors and state nursery staff to see.

Displaying a potted holly specimen in your local library or at church and community functions will call attention to them. We should encourage and assist our public gardens and arboreta to have special holly days with walks, special programs, and perhaps even a plant sale. Sale plants can be grown from cuttings taken from a plant in the organization's collection, or from cuttings rooted and grown by a local nursery for resale by the sponsoring organization. It is hoped that the Arboreta Committee of the American Holly Society will develop a program to get more and better hollies available to the general gardening public. A source list of unusual hollies is available from the Secretary (see Appendix 1) or through a local holly chapter. Appendix 2 lists retail and wholesale holly nurseries in North America.

MY FAVORITE PLANTS

As a dedicated plantsman I enjoy all plants. When, therefore, I am asked to name my favorite plant, my reply is that it is the plant at which I am looking at the time. It could be an azalea just coming into flower or a holly with its attractive glossy foliage. Nonetheless, there are three hollies that I always enjoy. *Ilex latifolia* (lusterleaf holly) has large spiny, glossy leaves. Although it is too large for most gardens, it makes a handsome specimen in a large garden, and its large clusters of fragrant yellow flowers draw attention to the plant in the spring. *Ilex pedunculosa* (long-stalked holly) has wavy, glossy, entire leaves, which are a good background for the long pendulous peduncles bearing red fruits like small cherries. *Ilex vomitoria* (yaupon holly) has many uses in the landscape from the low compact 'Dwarf' to the pendulous 'Folsom's Weeping', the latter available in both male and female forms. It has both red-fruited cultivars (e.g., 'Gray's Greenleaf') and yellow-fruited cultivars (e.g., 'Saratoga Gold', 'Wiggins'). Yaupon holly is excellent in a woodland garden, for large massed plantings, as a tall pruned hedge, or as a small multitrunked specimen tree (Figure 2-14).

I enjoy all the hollies in my collection and value them as low-maintenance plants. With careful attention to the species and cultivars suitable and adaptable for your area, any gardener can enjoy these versatile landscape plants.

EVERGREEN HOLLIES FOR THE HOME LANDSCAPE

Hundreds of named hollies are registered but unfortunately never evaluated in a arboreta or a display garden, nor are they available in the nursery trade. The following list of outstanding evergreen hollies for the home landscape includes hardiness information and brief comments on the major groups (e.g., English, American, and Japanese hollies). M = male, F = female. For more detailed information, see the descriptions in Part II of this volume.

Ilex × altaclerensis
Many cultivars, often listed as *I. aquifolium,* leaves usually entire, glossy, usually upright pyramidal, some variegated forms, usually with red fruit, generally hardy in zones 6b to 8 or 9, heat tolerant, more vigorous in the West.

'Adaptable', to 3.5 m (12 ft.), leaves dark green, spines small, hardy. F.
'Balearica', to 3.5–5 m (12–15 ft.), leaves dark green, usually entire, growth vigorous. F.
'Balkans', 3.5 m (12 ft.) or more, leaves dark green, spiny, good fruiting, hardy. F.

Figure 2-14. Sculptured plant of yaupon holly (*Ilex vomitoria*) at Dallas Arboretum, Dallas, Texas. Photo by Naud Burnett.

'Camelliifolia', to 3.5 m (12 ft.) or more, leaves dark green, usually entire, also variegated forms. F.
'Cherryberry', to 3.5 m (12 ft.) or more, leaves dark green, usually entire, upright open. F.
'Eldridge', 3.5 m (12 ft.), leaves dark green, usually entire. F.
'Green Maid', 3–5 m (10–15 ft.), leaves dark green, twisted, usually entire, vigorous. F.
'J. C. van Tol', 3–3.5 m (10–12 ft.), leaves dark green, usually entire, free fruiting, hardy. F.
'Wieman's Favorite', 3.5 m (12 ft.) or more, leaves dark green, entire to two to four spines, hardy. F.

Ilex aquifolium, English holly
　　Many cultivars, leaves usually spiny, glossy, habit usually upright pyramidal, varying in vigor, some weeping, variegated forms, fruit red and some yellow, select for hardiness in East, more vigorous in the West.

'Amber', leaves dark green, usually entire, fruit orange and large. F.
'Angustifolia', 1.5–3 m (5–10 ft.), leaves small and narrow, spiny, habit compact, slow growing, often listed as male but red-fruited forms are available. M, F.
'Apricot Glow', 3.5 m (12 ft.) or more, leaves dark green, spiny, fruit orange with reddish blush. F.
'Argentea Marginata', 3 m (10 ft.) or more, leaves variegated, margins yellowish white, compact habit. F.

'Aurifodina', 3 m (10 ft.) or more, leaves variegated, dark green centers, margins streaked, blotches gray or yellowish green. F.

'Bacciflava', to 3.5 m (12 ft.), leaves subentire to spiny, fruit yellow. F.

'Beacon', 3.5 m (12 ft.) or more, leaves dark green, spiny, good fruit sprays. F.

'Beautyspra', 3.5 m (12 ft.) or more, leaves dark green, spiny, early ripening, good for cut and landscaping. F.

'Big Bull', 3.5 m (12 ft.) or more, leaves dark green, entire to one to three spines, good pollinator. M.

'Brownell's Special', 3 m (10 ft.) or more, leaves dark green, spiny, stems purplish, good fruiting. F.

'Covergirl', 1.5–3 m (5–10 ft.), leaves dark green, good fruiting, compact growth. F.

'Deletta', 1.5–3 m (5–10 ft.), leaves dark green, spiny, heavy fruiting, compact growth, hardy. F.

'Doug Barbour', 3 m (10 ft.) or more, leaves dark green, spiny, good pollinator, hardy. F.

'Escort', 3–3.5 m (10–12 ft.), leaves dark green, spiny, good pollinator. M.

'Ferox', to 3 m (10 ft.), leaves dark green, very spiny on margins and surface. M.

'Ferox Aurea', similar to 'Ferox', leaves with yellow margins. M.

'Firecracker', 1.8–3 m (6–10 ft.), leaves dark green, spiny, stems purplish, good fruiting. F.

'Flavescens', 1.8–3 m (6–10 ft.), leaves with yellow variegation, best in full sun. F.

'George Daniel', good pollinator, hardy. M.

Gold Coast™, 3 m (10 ft.) or more, leaves with dark green centers, irregular yellow margins, spiny. M.

'Hastata', 1.5–2.5 m (5–8 ft.), distinct leaves, spiny, stems purplish. M.

'Ingramii', 1.5–2.5 m (5–8 ft.), leaves dark green, whitish mottled and blotched on surface. M.

'Larry Peters', 1.8–3 m (6–10 ft.), leaves dark green, spiny, very hardy. M.

'Lewis', 3–3.5 m (10–12 ft.), leaves dark green, spiny, stems purplish. F.

'Lily Gold', 3–3.5 m (10–12 ft.), leaves variegated, margins yellow, stems purple. M.

'Lorne Peters', 1.8–3 m (6–10 ft.), leaves dark green, spiny, hardy. M.

'Pinto', to 3 m (10 ft.), leaves variegated, margins dark green, pale yellowish blotch in center, subentire, good fruiting. F.

'Rederly', 3 m (10 ft.) or more, leaves dark green, spiny, good fruiting. F.

'Ricker', 3–3.5 m (10–12 ft.), leaves dark green, spiny, compact columnar, hardy. F.

'Shortspra', 3–3.5 m (10–12 ft.), leaves dark green, spiny, compact habit, good fruiting. F.

'Silver Queen', 3–3.5 m (10–12 ft.), leaves variegated, margin yellowish. M.

Sparkler®, 3–3.5 m (10–12 ft.), leaves dark green, spiny, good fruiting. F.

'Wieman's Globe', leaves dark green, spiny. F.

'Wieman's Moonbrite', leaves variegated, yellow blotches, spiny. M.

'Wieman's Yellow-pillar', leaves dark green, spiny, fruit yellow. F.

'Willow Grove', to 3 m (10 ft.), leaves dark green, usually spiny, compact pyramidal habit. F.

'Wilsonii', 3.5 m (12 ft.) or more, leaves dark green, large, entire to subentire, popular. F.

'Winter Queen', to 3 m (10 ft.), leaves dark green, spiny, hardy. F.

'Yellow Beam', leaves dark green, spiny, fruit yellow. F.

Ilex × attenuata

Natural and artificial interspecific hybrids of *I. cassine* × *I. opaca* including *I. myrtifolia*. Large shrubs to trees, leaves variable usually entire or with small spines near apex. Fruit usually red, sometimes yellow. Some plants very similar to *I. opaca* but most not as hardy. Best used in Southeast, in zones 7 to 9. All good specimen plants for tall hedges, screens, and background plants.

'Alagold', 3 m (10 ft.) or more, similar to 'Foster No. 2', fruit yellow. F.

'Attakapa', 3 m (10 ft.) or more, leaves similar to but larger than those of 'East Palatka'. F.

'Bienville Gold', excellent yellow fruit, leaves similar to those of 'Foster No. 2', upright compact form. F.

'Big John', 3 m (10 ft.) or more, leaves similar to those of 'Foster No. 2', good pollinator. M.

'Blazer', 2.5–3 m (8–10 ft.), leaves entire, good fruiting. F.

'Eagleson', 3–3.5 m (10–12 ft.) or more, from Texas, leaves entire to small spines, compact upright habit. F.

'East Palatka', 3 m (10 ft.) or more, leaves large, usually entire, heavy fruiting, large tree with open spreading habit, good specimen. F.

'Fay-T,' 3 m (10 ft.) or more, leaves usually small, spiny, fruit abundant, pyramidal habit. F.

'Foster No. 2', 3 m (10 ft.) or more, leaves narrow, spines small, popular specimen plant or for screens and hedges. F.

'Gato', 3.5 m (12 ft.) or more, leaves broad, upright, pyramidal habit. F.

'Greenleaf,' 3 m (10 ft.), leaves broad, spines small, habit upright and vigorous, good fruiting, popular. F.

'Hoosier Waif', to 3.5 m (12 ft.), leaves large, subentire, habit upright, irregular, and bushy. F.

'Howard', to 3 m (10 ft.) or more, leaves broad, good fruiting, compact columnar habit. F.

'Hume No. 2', to 3 m (10 ft.) or more, leaves broad, good fruiting, compact columnar habit. F.

'Nasa', to 3 m (10 ft.) or more, leaves narrow-elliptic, good fruiting, habit upright pyramidal. F.

'Oriole', to 3 m (10 ft.), leaves narrow-elliptic, habit compact pyramidal, slow growing. F.

'Pawley's Island', to 3 m (10 ft.) or more, leaves broad, habit upright mounding. F.

'Savannah', 3 m (10 ft.) or more, leaves broad, good fruiting, popular, habit open pyramidal. F.

'Sunny Foster', to 3 m (10 ft.) or more, leaves with yellow blotches, best in full sun, attractive accent plant. F.

'Taber No. 3', 3 m (10 ft.) or more, leaves broad, good fruiting, habit upright open pyramidal. F.

Ilex buergeri

Large trees from China, leaves to 7.5 cm (3 in.) long, irregular serrate, fruit red, rare in cultivation.

Ilex cassine, Dahoon holly

Native to lower southeastern United States, large shrubs or small trees, leaves elliptic to broad elliptic, hardy zones 7b to 9.

'Tyron Palace', fruit yellow. F.

'Wild Robert', fruit red, habit compact pyramidal. F.

Ilex cornuta, horned or Chinese holly

Excellent for Southeast and West Coast, forms vary from compact shrubs to larger shrubs or small trees, leaves variable, hardy zones 6b to 9.

'Anicet Delcambre', leaves usually entire, tip spine, elliptic oblong, good red fruiting. F.

'Burfordii', leaves entire with tip spine; good red fruiting, large shrub to small tree, very popular but often too large for small properties. F.

'Cajun Gold', leaves green, usually entire with yellow blotches and markings, good accent plant, best in partial to full sun. F.

'Carissa', leaves often concave, entire; dwarf compact habit, popular landscape plant. F.

'D'Or', leaves usually entire, yellow fruit colors late October and persists until late spring. F.

'Dwarf Burford', leaves smaller, fruit red, habit dense and compact, slower growing than 'Burfordii', popular. F.

'O. Spring', leaves green, usually entire with yellow blotches and markings; good accent plant, best in partial to full sun. F.

'Rotunda', leaves spiny, fruit red, habit compact dwarf. F.

'Sunrise', leaves green, usually entire with yellow blotches and markings; good accent plant, best in partial to full sun. F.

Ilex crenata, Japanese holly

Popular landscape plants, leaves usually less than 2.5 cm (1 in.) long, dark green, can be sheared for height, fruit black, rarely yellow, hardy zones 6 to 9.

Dwarf male cultivars: 'Beehive', 'Black Beauty', 'Border Gem', 'Compacta', 'Delaware Diamond', 'Dwarf Cone', 'Green Dragon', 'Green Island', 'Kingsville Green Cushion', 'Mr. C.', 'Repandens'.

Dwarf female cultivars: 'Convexa', 'Dewdrop', 'Dwarf Pagoda', 'Fairyland', 'Golden Gem' (leaves yellow), 'Golden Heller,' 'Green Lustre', 'Helleri', 'Mariesii', 'Miss Muffet', 'Piccolo', 'Prides Tiny', 'Schwoebel's Compact'.

Moderate to tall male cultivars: 'Alan Seay', 'Cherokee', 'Glory, 'High Light', 'Highlander', 'Hoogendorn', 'Howard', 'Hunt Selection', 'Jersey Pinnacle', 'Luther Copeland', 'Major', 'Maxwell', 'Nakada', 'Noble Upright', 'Northern Beauty', 'Rotundifolia', 'Steed's Upright', 'William Jackson', 'Willowleaf'.

Moderate to tall female cultivars: 'Fastigiata', 'Hetzii', 'Sentinel'.

Yellow-berried cultivars (all female): 'Butterball', 'Forty Niner', 'Honeycomb', 'Ivory Tower', 'Sir Echo', 'Xanthocarpa'.

Yellow-leaved cultivars: 'Midas Touch' M., 'Snowflake' F.

Ilex dimorphophylla, Okinawan holly

Leaves elliptic quadrangular, spines very stiff, adult leaves rounded, fruit small red, habit upright, rare plant, excellent for bonsai, hardy zones 8b to 10. F.

Ilex glabra, inkberry

Native to North America, leaves dark bluish green, upright branching shrub, fruit usually black, hardier than Japanese holly, hardy zones 5 to 10.

'Ivory Queen', fruit white. F.

Nordic®, compact form, hardy to zone 4a. F.

'Princeton's Compact', compact form. F.

'Shamrock', compact upright form. F.

Ilex integra

Large tree, leaves usually entire, fruit large orange-red, hardy zones 8 to 10.

'Bancroft', small teeth near apex.

Ilex latifolia, lusterleaf holly

Leaves large (to 18 cm or 6 in. long) and elliptic, tall trees 10–15 m (30–50 ft.) high, fruit red in clusters, excellent specimen and background plant, hardy zones 7 to 10.

'Variegata', rare.

Ilex × meserveae, blue hollies

A group name for hybrids of *I. rugosa × I. aquifolium.* All plants are patented, hardy in zones

6 to 8, not heat tolerant, susceptible to root rot in the Southeast. Leaves dark green, spiny, fruit red.

Blue Angel®, compact upright habit, hardy zones 7 to 9. F.
'Blue Boy', compact upright habit, hardy zones 6b to 9. M.
'Blue Girl', broad upright, spreading habit, hardy zones 6a to 9. F.
Blue Maid®, upright spreading habit, hardy zones 6b to 9. F.
Blue Prince®, upright compact habit, hardy zones 6b to 9. M.
Blue Princess®, compact rounded habit, hardy zones 6b to 9. F.
Blue Stallion®, vigorous upright spreading habit. M.
Golden Girl® (*I. rugosa* × *I.* × *aquifolium*), yellow fruit, compact upright spreading habit, hardy zones 6 to 9. F.

Ilex myrtifolia
Pendulous selections and yellow-fruited forms available.

'Uncle Herb', leaves very dark green, small, and elliptic. M.

Ilex opaca, American holly
Upright pyramidal trees usually 9–15 m (30–50 ft.), only two dwarf types available, leaves dark green variable as to spines and glossiness, fruit usually red, occasionally orange to yellow. Excellent specimen trees, hedges, screens, espaliers, and background plants. Compact in full sun, more open in partial to full shade. Hardy zones 5 to 10.

Dwarf cultivars: 'Clarendon Spreading' and 'Maryland Dwarf'. Both female, under 0.9 m (3 ft.) after six to ten years, wider than tall, fruit red, excellent specimen plants or in a large border.

Cultivars with upright pyramidal form:
'Amy', leaves dark green, spiny, good fruiting, pyramidal habit. F.
'Andorra', leaves spiny, fruit red. F.
'Canary', leaves spiny, fruit yellow, abundant. F.
'Carolina No. 2', leaves dark green, spiny near apex, fruit abundant. F.
'Cave Hill', leaves dark green, spiny, good fruit display. F.
'Cheerful', leaves dark green, spiny, fruit red abundant. F.
'Christmas Carol', good fruit display, compact pyramidal habit. F.
'Clarissa', upper two-thirds of leaves is spiny, fruit red, extremely hardy. F.
'Croonenberg', leaves dark green, glossy, spiny, good display of fruit, compact pyramidal habit, slow to fill out when young. F.
'Cumberland', leaves dark green, very glossy, good fruit display. F.
'Dan Fenton', leaves dark green, glossy, spiny, good fruit display. F.
'Danny Allen', leaves dark green, red fruit abundant, conical habit. F.
'David', leaves small and oval, spiny, good pollinator. M.
'Diane', leaves dark green, spiny, reddish orange fruit abundant, stripped early by birds, vigorous, compact, wide spreading habit. F.
'Dr. Cribbs', leaves spiny, good pollinator, vigorous broad pyramidal habit. M.
'Farage', leaves dark green with small spines on upper half, red fruit persistent, broad pyramidal habit. F.
'Fred Anderson', leaves dark green, glossy, spiny, good pollinator, broad conical habit. M.
'Fruitland Nursery', fruit yellow, persistent, pyramidal habit. F.

'Galyean Gold', leaves spiny, fruit yellow. F.

'Girard's Male', leaves spiny, good pollinator, narrow upright habit. F.

'Gloucester', leaves dark green, glossy, spiny, red fruit, narrow upright habit. F.

'Goldie', leaves spiny, fruit yellow, abundant. F.

'Griscom', leaves dark green, spines small, fruit red. F.

'Hedgeholly', leaves dark green, spiny, good fruiting, dense compact plant, excellent for hedges. F.

'Janice Arlene', leaves dark green, spiny, reddish orange fruit abundant, shade tolerant. F.

'Jersey Knight', leaves dark green, spiny, good pollinator. M.

'Jersey Princess', leaves glossy, spiny, good fruit display. F.

'Johnson', leaves spiny, good fruit display, pyramidal habit. F.

'Judy Evans', leaves glossy, spiny, good fruit display. F.

'Lady Alice', leaves spiny, good fruit display, easily propagated. F.

'Lamp Post', leaves twisted, spiny, good fruit display, compact conical habit. F.

'Lenape Moon', leaves spiny, upper half of leaf, fruit yellow, pinkish blush. F.

'Mamie Eisenhower', leaves dark green, spiny, fruit deep reddish orange, abundant. F.

'Manig', leaves spiny, fruit reddish orange abundant. F.

'Martha's Vineyard', leaves spiny, fruit reddish orange, vigorous, conical habit. F.

'Mary P. Turner', leaves glossy, spiny, dense pyramidal habit. F.

'Menantico', leaves wavy, spiny, good fruit display. F.

'Merry Christmas', leaves spiny, good fruit display. F.

'Miss Helen', leaves spiny, fruit dark red abundant, broad pyramidal habit. F.

'Morgan Gold', leaves spiny, fruit yellow, abundant. F.

'Morris Arboretum', leaves spiny, fruit attractive orange yellow. F.

'Mrs. Santa', leaves spiny, fruit abundant, pyramidal habit. F.

'Nelson West', leaves narrow-elliptic, good pollinator. M.

'North Wind', leaves spiny, good pollinator, compact conical habit. M.

'Old Heavy Berry', leaves dark green spiny, fruit abundant, slow growing, conical habit. F.

'Perfection', leaves dark green, almost flat, fruit red abundant. F.

'Perfection Xanthocarpa', leaves spiny, fruit yellow, attractive. F.

'Princeton Gold', fruit yellow, persistent, good winter foliage, vigorous pyramidal habit. F.

'Satyr Hill', leaves spiny, fruit well spaced, attractive. F.

'September Fire', leaves twisted, spiny, fruit ripens early, conical habit. F.

'Southern Illinois University', leaves wavy spiny, fruit abundant. F.

'Susan Gregory', leaves wavy spiny, fruit orange attractive. F.

'Valentine', leaves spiny, fruit red, attractive. F.

'Valley Evergreen', leaves spiny usually on upper half of leaf, fruit attractive, conical habit. F.

'Vera', leaves twisted, short, fruit red, good for cut and wreaths. F.

'Warrior', leaves spiny, good pollinator. M.

'William Hawkins', leaves distinct, linear, spiny, compact slow growing pyramidal habit. M.

'Wyetta', leaves glossy, spiny, fruit reddish orange, dense, pyramidal habit. F.

Ilex paraguariensis, Paraguay tea

Large shrub or tree, leaves usually entire, fruit reddish brown, hardy zones 8b to 10, source of maté tea.

Ilex pedunculosa, long-stalked holly

Large shrub or small tree, leaves entire, attractive red fruit on long peduncles, open habit to pyramidal, suitable for specimen and espalier, hardy zones 5 to 8.

Ilex perado, Madeira holly

Leaves large (more than 7.5 cm or 3 in. long) with small dark green spines, large shrub to trees 10 m (30 ft.) tall, fruit red, upright pyramidal habit, hardy zones 8a to 9. Good specimen and background or screen planting.

Ilex pernyi, Pernyi holly

Leaves small (less than 2.5 cm or 1 in. long), fruit glossy red, habit upright open, 3–5 m (10–15 ft.) tall, hardy zones 5b to 8.

Ilex purpurea

Large tree, leaves large (10 cm or 4 in. long), fruit red in loose clusters, hardy zones 7b to 9. Beautiful specimen, screen or background planting.

Ilex rotunda

Large shrubs to trees, leaves glossy and entire, fruit red, hardy zones 8b to 10. Large specimen tree, screen or background planting.

'Romal'. F.
'Lord'. M.

Ilex rugosa

Small prostrate shrub, leaves 5 cm (2 in.) long, fruit red, hardy zones 5 to 7, heat tolerant.

Ilex spinigera

Leaves to 4.5 cm (1¾ in.) long, spiny, fruit red, large shrub, dense habit of growth, hardy zones 8 to 9.

Ilex sugerokii

Large shrub, leaves to 3.8 cm (1½ in.) long, fruit red, rare in cultivation, hardy zones 7 to 9.

Ilex vomitoria, yaupon holly

Leaves glossy green, to 3.8 cm (1½ in.) long, dwarf form, variable shrubs to small trees, popular landscape plant in southeastern United States, hardy zones 6b to 9. Good specimen, hedge or screen planting.

Dwarf cultivars:
'Dwarf', fruit rare, excellent foundation facing, low hedge, or foreground plant. F.
'Stokes Dwarf', compact habit, popular landscape plant. M.
'Straughan's Dwarf', similar to 'Stokes Dwarf' but more open, soft textured. M.

Other cultivars:
'Dare County', attractive orange fruit, specimen plant. F.
'Folsom's Weeping', upright weeping habit, red fruit. M or F.
'Gray's Greenleaf', leaves dark green, very heavy red fruiting. M.
'Hoskin Shadow', leaves large (to 4 cm or 1⅝ in. long), dark green, red fruit, hardy zone 6. F.
'Kathy Ann', upright spreading habit, fruit red. F.
'Lynn Lowery', leaves dark green, upright spreading habit. F.
'Nanyehi', red fruit, hardy zone 6. F.
'Pride of Houston', fruit red; upright habit. F.
'Tricolor', leaves variegated, irregular, blotched yellow, best in full sun. M.
'Wiggins', yellow fruit, upright spreading habit. F.

'Wildwood Blue', leaves bluish cast, compact pyramidal habit, abundant fruit. F.
'Will Fleming', narrow upright habit, branches fastigiate, suitable for hedges and screens. F.

Ilex wilsonii

Leaves entire, fruit red on young plants, upright pyramidal trees, suitable for specimen or background plant. M or F.

Ilex yunnanensis

Large shrub, leaves to 3.8 cm (1½ in.) long, red fruit ripening early, suitable background or border plants, hardy zones 5 to 8, rare. M or F.

Interspecific Hybrids

'Brilliant' (*I. ciliospinosa* × *I sikkimensis*), leaves dark green to 5 cm (2 in.) long, spiny, red fruit abundant, upright pyramidal habit. F.

'Brilliant' (*I. ciliospinosa* × *I. pernyi*), similar to above. F.

'Brighter Shines', (*I. cornuta* 'Burfordii' × *I. pernyi*), leaves angulate, fruit red, compact pyramidal habit, hardy zones 6 to 9. F.

China Boy® (*I. rugosa* × *I. cornuta*), leaves dark green, truncate, good pollinator, upright rounded, large shrub, hardy zones 6 to 9. M.

China Girl® (*I. rugosa* × *I. cornuta*), similar to China Boy, fruit red, compact upright, rounded habit, hardy zones 6 to 9. F.

'Doctor Kassab' (*I. cornuta* × *I. pernyi*), leaves convex with short spines, fruit red, hardy zones 7 to 9. F.

'Dorothy Lawton' (seedling of *I.* 'Brilliant'), leaves dark green and oblong, red fruit, compact pyramidal habit, hardy zones 7 to 9. F.

Dragon Lady® (*I. pernyi* × *I. aquifolium*), leaves quadrangular, entire or spiny, fruit red, upright pyramidal habit, hardy zones 6b to 9a. F.

Ebony Magic®, 1.5–3 m (5–10 ft.), leaves dark green, spiny, stems purplish, good fruiting, a Blue Holly seedling. F.

'Edward J. Stevens' (putative hybrid of *I. cornuta* × *I. aquifolium*), very similar to 'Nellie R. Stevens', good pollinator, hardy zones 6 to 9. M.

'Emily Bruner' (seedling of *I. cornuta* × *I. latifolia*), leaves dark green, to 11 cm (4⅜ in.) long, with ten to thirteen spines each side, fruit red, upright pyramidal habit, popular in Southeast, hardy zones 7 to 9. F.

'Ginny Bruner' (sibling of 'Emily Bruner'), leaves dark green, to 7 cm (2¾ in.) long, uneven spiny on margin, upright pyramidal habit, hardy zones 7 to 9. F.

'Hohman' (*I. cornuta* × *I. pernyi*). F.

'Hollowell' (putative hybrid of *I. aquifolium* × *I. cornuta*), leaves broad-elliptic, to 7.5 cm (3 in.) long, one to three spines, good pollinator, hardy zone 7. M.

'Jade' (*I.* × *koehneana*), leaves broad-elliptic, stems purple, good pollinator, pyramidal, hardy zones 6 to 9. M.

'John T. Morris' (*I. cornuta* 'Burfordii' × *I. pernyi*), leaves slightly squarish, good pollinator for 'Lydia Morris', upright pyramidal habit, hardy zones 6 to 9. M.

'Lassie' (*I.* × *koehneana*), leaves broad lanceolate, numerous small spines, upright pyramidal habit, hardy zones 6b to 9. F.

'Loch Raven' (*I.* × *koehneana*), leaves ovate-elliptic, to 10 cm (4 in.) long, good pollinator for 'Lassie', pyramidal habit. M.

'Lydia Morris', (*I. cornuta* 'Burfordii' × *I. pernyi*), leaves quadrangular, red fruit, upright pyramidal habit, hardy zones 6b to 9. F.

'Malcolm S. Whipple' (putative hybrid of *I. aquifolium* × *I. cornuta*), leaves ovate, to 5 cm (2 in.) long, good pollinator, broad conical habit, hardy zones 7 to 9. M.

'Mary Nell' (*I.* 'Red Delight' × *I. latifolia*), leaves flat, ovate, glossy, to 9 cm (3½ in.) long, short spines, fruit red, upright pyramidal habit, popular in Southeast, hardy zones 7 to 9. F.

'Nellie R. Stevens' (putative hybrid of *I. cornuta* × *I. aquifolium*), leaves oblong, to 9 cm (3½ in.) long, nearly entire, red fruit, pyramidal habit, popular in Southeast. F.

'Patricia Varner' (seedling of *I.* × *aquipernyi* × *I.* 'Brilliant'), leaves broad-elliptic, fruit red, compact pyramidal habit. F.

'Rock Garden' (*I.* × *aquipernyi* × *I.* 'Accent'), leaves broad-elliptic, to 4.5 cm (1¾ in.) long, spiny low compact habit, excellent rock garden or low facing plant, still uncommon. F.

'San Jose' (*I.* × *aquipernyi*), leaves broad-elliptic, fruit red, upright pyramidal habit, hardy zones 6b to 9.

'San Jose' (*I.* × *koehneana*), from California, larger leaves, red fruit, broad pyramidal habit, hardy zones 7b to 9. F.

'September Gem' (*I. ciliospinosa* × *I.* × *aquipernyi*), leaves elliptic, to 7 cm (2¾ in.) long, fruit orange-red, ripening in September, compact upright pyramidal habit, hardy zones 7 to 9. F.

'Shin Nien' (*I. opaca* × *I. cornuta*), leaves elliptic, to 6.5 cm (2½ in.) long, spiny, compact habit, hardy zones 6a to 9. M.

'Wieman's Pacific Queen' (putative hybrid of *I.* × *aquipernyi*), leaves ovate-lanceolate, to 4 cm (1⅝ in.) long, fruit reddish orange, compact columnar habit, hardy zones 7 to 9. F.

'Wirt L. Winn' (putative hybrid of *I.* × *koehneana*), leaves oblong-elliptic, to 10 cm (4 in.) long, small spines, fruit red, broad-pyramidal habit, hardy zones 6b to 9. F.

DECIDUOUS HOLLIES FOR THE HOME LANDSCAPE

Deciduous hollies have often been overlooked as attractive landscape plants, but are now being recognized for their contribution to late fall and winter beauty. Several species have been recognized as attractive native shrubs for birds and other wildlife (the fruit is an important source of food), but are seldom recommended as landscape plants. Yet, once seen in winter, their branches laden with abundant, brilliant red fruit and the ground covered with a fresh layer of snow, these hollies cannot be forgotten. Whether in home garden landscapes or in highway plantings, deciduous hollies are becoming popular.

There are thirty species of deciduous hollies native to China, Japan, and North America. The three most common species are *Ilex decidua* (possumhaw holly), *I. serrata* (Japanese winterberry), and *I. verticillata* (winterberry), along with their cultivars and the attractive hybrids of *I. serrata* and *I. verticillata*. Many under-utilized species also have landscape potential, such as *I. macrocarpa* with its large black fruit. Unfortunately many deciduous hollies are only seen in botanical gardens and arboreta. Very rarely are they listed commercially. For the holly enthusiast and private gardens they are collector's items and a challenge to start from seed. Native species, such as *I. ambigua, I. amelanchier, I. buswellii,* and *I. curtissii,* are available from nurseries growing native plants or specialty nurseries. Often they are sold as seedlings, so be sure to request pollinator plants.

Deciduous hollies play an important part in the winter landscape as they are more cold-hardy than the evergreen hollies. They are ideal as a mass planting or an individual plant with a good background of broadleaved or narrow-leaved evergreens. One of the first-named cultivars of *Ilex verticillata* was introduced in the 1960s as 'Winter Red', a colorful fruiting shrub for highway plantings. Deciduous hollies also can be used in screen plantings or as unclipped hedges. One dwarf form exists, *Ilex verticillata* 'Red Sprite', and one medium dwarf, *I. verticillata* 'Shaver', both of which can be used as facing plants in front of larger shrubs and in foundation plantings. The Japanese often plant deciduous hollies at the edge of a pool to get the reflection of the fruit in the water.

To assure good pollination one male plant is needed for every 10 to 20 female plants. The pollinator plants can be placed at the back of a mass planting or in a separate area of the garden, preferably within 15 m (50 ft.) of the female plants. Because holly species flower at various times, it is important to select male plants that flower at the same time as the female plants. Both the male and the female plants should be closely related. Thus *Ilex serrata* and *I. verticillata* in section *Prinos* make a good combination, as do *I. decidua* and *I. longipes* in section *Prinoides*. Pollination of plants between sections is not generally advised because fruit set from such crosses is often less abundant and seed is not always fertile. While the lack of fertile seed is not important for the home landscape, it is important for a botanic garden where seed is collected for distribution. *Ilex decidua* has been noted to set fruit when pollinated by *I. opaca* if they flower together, and there are reports of *I. verticillata* crossing with *I. opaca*. Table 2 shows flowering times for selected deciduous hollies.

Deciduous hollies are easy to establish in home landscapes in full sun or partial shade. They respond to good, well-drained soils, mulching, and fertilizing. Selected named cultivars are recommended for home landscapes as they are superior to wild-collected or seedling-grown plants.

Ilex verticillata and *I. serrata* produce flowers on new growth from mid- to late spring and are best pruned in late winter before new spring growth develops. *Ilex decidua* also produces flowers on new growth and on spur growth on old stems. When pruning *I. decidua* care should be taken not to remove all the spur growth.

The persistence of deciduous holly fruit has not been studied. In many areas fruit persistence depends on the population of birds and squirrels who often remove the red fruits before Christmas. Apparently the fruits of *I. serrata* and *I. verticillata* are palatable to birds and squirrels earlier than those of *I. decidua*. Some cultivars lose their brilliant red color, turning black, due to frost and cold weather and drop or are stripped by wildlife. More study on the retention of fruit is needed. Yellow holly fruit, unless darkened by cold, is rarely eaten by birds; thus it persists until early spring when robins appear.

Hollies are also useful indoors for their decorative cut branches. Cut branches can be held in unsealed plastic bags for several months (from October through January or February) in cool storage. Deciduous hollies also are excellent in bonsai.

Most deciduous hollies are medium to large shrubs to small trees with red fruit. A few selected species and cultivars are discussed below. For a complete list of deciduous hollies with their descriptions see Part II of this volume.

Ilex amelanchier, sarvis or swamp holly
  Leaves obovate, fruit red, velvety, upright spreading shrubs, hardy zones 6 to 9.

Ilex 'Bonfire', fruit red, hardy zones 5 to 9, rare but worth the search, good fruiting. F.

Ilex collina
  Early bloomer with *I. opaca* and *I. decidua*. Red fruit borne on long pedicels.

Ilex decidua, possum haw holly
  Often considered the showiest of all the deciduous hollies but not as common nor as winter hardy as *I. verticillata*. An upright spreading tall shrub to small tree with attractive gray to silvery branches. Indigenous to low woodlands and bottom land also in dry upland forest, in the southern states. Fruit persists until mid- or late winter unless eaten by birds. Flowers on new growth and on spurs of older branches, and will often be pollinated by *I. opaca* American holly. Natural hybrid

Table 2. Deciduous holly flowering dates. Collected by Robert C. Simpson, Vincennes, Indiana.

	MAY	JUNE

Key:
◇◇◇ 1991
◆◆◆ 1992
✥✥✥ 1993

I. decidua
  'Council Fire"
  'Pocahontas'
  'Sundance'
  'Warrens Red'
I. opaca cultivars
I. verticillata
  'Afterglow'
  'Alfred Anderson'
  'Aurantiaca'
  'Cacapon'
  'Christmas Cheer'
  'Earlibright'
  'Fairfax'
  'Jim Dandy' (male)
  'Maryland Beauty'
  'Quitsa'
  'Red Sprite'
  'Shortcake
  'Shaver'
  'Sunset'
  'Tiasquam'
  'Winter Gold'
  'Winter Red'
I. serrata
I serrata × *I. verticillata* hybrids
  'Bonfire'
  'Apollo' (male)
  'Autumn Glow'
  'Harvest Red'
  'Sparkleberry'

seedlings of *I. decidua* × *I. opaca* have been observed and collected from seedling beds by Fred Galle in Georgia and Bob Simpson in Indiana. These plants have spiny leaves similar to those of American Holly, but have a light thin texture and often turn a purplish color in the fall, and are semi-evergreen in the winter. Possum haw hollies are often found along fence rows. Bon Hartline of Anna, Illinois reports seeing native plants in the Mississippi river bottoms in Union Co., IL, in four feet of overflow water for up to three months with no damage.

A good landscape plant hardy in zones 6 to 9. Some cultivars are not readily available. 'Warren's Red', the first *I. decidua,* named and introduced in the late 1950s, is the standard to evaluate others. Other good female red-fruited cultivars are 'Council Fire', 'Pocahontas', 'Red Cascade', 'Red Escort', and 'Sentry', which defoliates early in the fall to display the fruit. Two good reddish-orange-fruited cultivars are 'Benton' and 'Hunter'. 'Byer's Golden', a good yellow-fruited cultivar has been difficult to propagate but is available and 'Finch's Golden' is to be introduced soon; both are female.

Ilex longipes, Georgia long-stalked holly
Noted for red fruit on long pedicels, to 5 cm (2 in.) long, hardy zones 6 to 9.

Ilex serrata, Japanese winterberry
Handsome plants known since ancient times in Japan and planted in their gardens, or by ponds for the spectacular display of red fruits in the fall and winter. Introduced to the United States in 1866 and to Kew Gardens in England in 1893.

Commonly variable shrubs 2–4 m (6–13 ft.) tall with grayish brown branches; usually found in moist sites in Kyushu, Shikoku, and Honshu, Japan, and Central China. Fruits usually red, color early in mid- to late summer and persist until winter.

Good landscape plants and should be used more often. Hardy in zones 5 to 8b. Both 'Leucocarpa' a cultivar from Japan with pale yellowish fruits and 'Xanthocarpa' with yellow fruits can be obtained in the United States. 'Sundrops' has yellow fruit. The Japanese have several other named cultivars usually based on the color of the fruits. These are not commonly grown in the United States. *Ilex serrata* is popular as bonsai plants in Japan and the cultivar 'Koshobai' is specially favored. It also makes an excellent specimen plant. It has very small elliptic to linear leaves 1.5–3.5 cm (¹⁹⁄₃₂–1⅜ in.) long, 0.5–1 mm (¹⁄₃₂–³⁄₆₄ in.) wide. The vivid red fruits are very small, flattened globose, 2 mm (¹⁄₁₆ in.) long, and 2–3 mm (¹⁄₁₆–⅛ in.) diameter. Small plants of 'Koshobai' are available.

Ilex serrata × *I. verticillata* hybrids
The first crosses of *I. serrata* × *I. verticillata* were made by the late William (Bill) Kosar and the late F. de Vos, at the U.S. National Arboretum in 1960. 'Apollo' (male) and 'Sparkleberry' (female). Similar crosses were made soon after by Dr. Elwin R. Orton Jr. at Rutgers University. Orton's selections, 'Autumn Glow' and 'Harvest Red', are both females. 'Harvest Red' has red fruit, is hardy in zones 5 to 9, is rare but worth the search, and has good fruiting. 'Autumn Glow' has attractive fall foliage of a pale blend of purple, red, yellow, and green until frost. All four of these hybrids are hardy in zone 5. 'Raritan Chief' a male is a cross of *I. verticillata* × (*I. verticillata* × *I. serrata*) selected by Orton for its low compact habit and good retention of foliage.

Hybrid crosses are still being evaluated and natural hybrids, such as 'Bonfire', a hybrid collected in the wild, grown by Bob Simpson in the 1950s, have been named and introduced. These hybrids resemble *I. serrata* more closely than *I. verticillata*. All are vigorous, slender branching shrubs producing an abundance of small red fruits, coloring in late summer and early fall, and attractive to birds. Discoloring of fruits occurs around −12°C (10°F). Good landscape plants and noted for the massive fruit displays. 'Sparkleberry" has red fruit, is hardy in zones 5 to 9, is rare but worth the search, and has good fruiting.

Ilex verticillata, winterberry or black alder

Winterberry, introduced to England in 1736. The most widespread holly species in North America, from Nova Scotia to western Ontario, Wisconsin, Minnesota, south to Alabama and Florida west to Missouri, Texas, and into Mexico. The native habitat is low woodlands and river bottoms and occasionally in dryer upland forest and along fence rows. Is excellent as a large shrub or small tree.

Usually medium to large shrubs to small trees to 4 m (13 ft.) tall. Leaves turn brown or black after frost hence the name black alder. Fruits usually red, but some yellow and orange, persist until early spring, but favored by birds and squirrels, and often are stripped in mid- to late December. Fruits blacken and shrivel with −12°C (10°F) temperatures and repeated thawing. Hardy in zones 4 to 9.

Robert Simpson of Vincennes, Indiana is a leading promoter, grower, and introducer of cultivars of deciduous hollies. 'Winter Red' is a most popular winterberry and serves as the standard to evaluate others. Many of the new cultivars have limited or only regional distribution. 'Earlibright' ripens early in September with large red fruits. Other red-fruited cultivars (all female) include 'Afterglow', 'Cacapon', 'Earlibright', 'Red Sprite', 'Stop Light', 'Sunset', 'Winter Red'. Yellow fruited cultivars include 'Winter Gold' a branch sport of 'Winter Red'.

Orange-fruited cultivars are also available starting with an old but still popular forma known as f. *aurantiaca,* a forma found in the wild in 1938. First reported as variety, later changed to a forma in 1949 by Rehder. Frequently listed incorrectly as a cultivar. Other orange fruited selections originating as seedlings or found in the wild include 'Afterglow', and 'Peter's Fireworks'. Using the yellow- and orange-fruited cultivars intermixed with the reds will give a riot of kaleidoscopic color on an overcast winter day. Cut branches heavy in fruit of winterberry have proven to be a good winter cash crop. Several cultivars used for this purpose include 'Christmas Gem', 'Maryland Beauty', and 'Winter Red'. 'Oosterwijk' the first *I. verticillata* cultivar named in Europe, described but not yet registered by Susyn Andrews, is a popular winter export crop in the Netherlands. Cut fruiting branches can be held in unsealed plastic bags in cold storage (October through January and February).

Bob Simpson has separated *Ilex verticillata* into two geographical groups, the Southern and Northern types (ecotypes of no botanical standing). He has noted that the Southern types such as 'Winter Red' have larger and more fleshy leaves, darker stems, faster growth, and show less suckering. Northern types such as 'Afterglow' have many lighter colored stems, smaller leaves of different shapes and textures. The Southern types such as 'Sunset', 'Winter Red' and 'Winter Gold' are late bloomers as compared to the earlier flowering Northern types.

CHAPTER 3

Holly Orcharding

When planning a new holly orchard in the East or Northwest it is important to very carefully consider every aspect of the business of holly orcharding, including the feasibility, labor, production cost, and consumer market.

PACIFIC NORTHWEST ORCHARDS

The culture of holly for Christmas in the United States started in the Northwest. John Wieman in Oregon started working with nursery growers in 1927 and for the Oregon State Board of Horticulture, State Department of Agriculture in 1931. He wrote (1961) a pamphlet on the history of English holly (*Ilex aquifolium*) in Oregon in which he gave a short report of some of the nurseries growing English holly and selling cut greens in the early 1900s.

About 1890, Gustav Teufel in Portland, Oregon, was one of the first to plant English holly for cutting (Plate 12). Bert and Frank Clark, Portland, Oregon, reported shipping commercial holly in the early 1900s: Ambrose Brownell and his father, George, of Milwaukie, Oregon, shipped cut holly to San Francisco and Los Angles in 1918. Small amounts of cut holly were shipped to Eastern markets around 1920. George Teufel, son of Gustav, and the Clark brothers, Bert and Frank, introduced silver variegated holly to the Eastern markets around 1925. Other nursery growers who grew English holly in the Northwest included Harold Bayley and son Jack, Portland, Oregon; R. H. Bodley, Portland, Oregon; H. F. Bleeg, Portland, Oregon; John and Julius Broetje, Portland, Oregon; E. P. Drew, Beaverton, Oregon; Frank Falco, Max Lorenz, and Mr. Bohmann of Wilsonville, Oregon; J. B. Kelly, Portland, Oregon; Ray Leach, Oregon; C. E. Moyer, southern Oregon; P. H. Peyran, Gig Harbor, Washington; J. B. Pilkinton, Portland, Oregon; L. E. Sickler, Gladstone, Oregon; John B. Stump and family, Monmouth, Oregon; and H. W. Strong and son Jack, Gresham, Oregon.

The first English hollies in the Northwest (1850–1910) were seedling plants originating in England or France. The French-English hollies (blue stem types of holly) were the commercial holly in Oregon and Washington to the 1940s. In the early 1930s seedling selections were observed and tested and many were later registered as named cultivars.

The commercial growers in the Northwest west of the Cascade Mountains ship more than 100 carloads of holly greens and manufactured items by rail, truck, and air from early November until two weeks before Christmas. There are more than 1500 acres of holly grown in the Northwest and they return a sizable income to the region's economy. The cut holly industry employs more than 1000 workers in the orchards, packing shed, storage, and shipping. Very few large orchards are being planted today, but small orchards of up to ten acres are being established close to local markets as a second income, often by young couples looking for additional family income.

Production of quality holly for Christmas requires as much or more attention than a nursery crop. Nutrition must be maintained at a high level; insects, diseases, and algae must be controlled; pruning, cutting and grading must be done on a regular basis; and plants must be protected from foraging birds and animals. Most holly research, including the testing and evaluating of new hybrids, was carried on by progressive growers and at the Oregon State University Experiment Station under the direction of Dr. Robert (Bob) Ticknor (retired), who has provided much information for this chapter.

English holly is ideally suited to the Pacific Northwest with its mild, moist winters and relatively cool summers. Holly is grown successfully along the coast in western Oregon and Washington. Due to the hot dry summers south of Douglas County, Oregon, more southern interior areas are generally unsuited. The southern coastal range for growing holly is not clear cut. There are some commercial orchards in the San Francisco Bay area and excellent specimen plants are found throughout the southern range where water is provided.

There are advantages to growing English holly in both the coastal and interior locations. The cool moist coastal air is conducive to development of fine holly foliage; however, it also delays tree maturity and berry production and is favorable for *Phytophthora* leaf spot and green algae growth on the foliage. Cultivars that grow well in the interior valleys are often not suited for the coastal regions.

The ideal site for a holly orchard is still an unanswered question. Good orchards are growing on level sites in the valley floor and on slopes with all possible exposures. Berry ripening is earlier on shaded northeastern slopes. The site should be protected from strong drying winds to prevent excessive desiccation for good foliage and berry production.

Soil drainage is important for most tree crops including holly which is not adapted to wet poorly drained sites. The orchard should be accessible at all seasons of the year and not exposed to seasonal floods. The site should be free of late spring frost that may damage flower production and kill back new terminal growth.

A deep fertile, well-drained soil is preferred over marginal soil types for maintaining good quality foliage and good berry production. Holly and many broadleaved evergreens respond to soils high in organic matter and retention of soil moisture throughout the summer. It is generally accepted that slightly acid soils, pH 6.0–6.5 are best. Holly orchards on acid soils below pH 6.0 benefit from liming along with cover crops.

Pollination is required for holly trees since the male and female flowers are borne on separate plants. Some cultivars set more berries than others in the absence of male trees. Some trees set parthenocarpic fruit, which often is small, not as abundant, and ripening later but often dropping earlier.

Studies by the Oregon Experiment Station in the mid 1940s proved conclusively that male trees are necessary in a holly orchard to provide adequate pollination and fruit set. Mature trees require one male plant for every 50 female fruit-bearing trees, but small female trees require more male trees, often one male for every 10 to 20 female trees. Male trees should be selected that produce large quantities of viable pollen and good desirable foliage for wreath making. In some locations bee activity is restricted by weather conditions and more pollinizer trees may be required.

Grafting or budding male scions into the orchard provides extra pollen. Bouquets of male flowers introduced to the orchard add pollen for the bees, and hives of bees placed in or near the orchard aid pollination. Too many male pollinizer trees may result in too heavy fruit production, which results in a loss of foliage and fruit color. English holly cultivars that mature poor colored fruits may be helped by providing adequate pollination; however, some cultivars ripen their fruits late and lose their commercial cut value.

Many English holly cultivars are suitable for orchard production while others are not. Some of the early orchards in the Northwest were planted with seedlings, while most cultivars used today were selected from these seedlings orchards. In general they are trees with attractive spiny, glossy leaves and early ripening large red fruit. Holly with late ripening fruit are limited to local markets for delivery just before Christmas.

There are several different markets for cut holly, each with its own requirements. Hollies with large leaves, such as *Ilex aquifolium* 'Coronation', *I. aquifolium* Teufel Hybrids, and *I. × altaclerensis* 'Wieman's Favorite', are used in flower arrangements. For small 1- to 2-pound boxes, the smaller-textured cultivars such as *I. aquifolium* 'Rederly' are used in home arrangements.

Many of the cultivars of *Ilex × altaclerensis* are preferred by some arrangers for the less spiny leaves. For wreaths the spiny crinkled leaf types are important. Often the berries used in wreaths do not come from cultivars that supply the foliage but are cut fruit sprays that are pinned in for the finished touch.

Fine-textured cultivars such as *Ilex aquifolium* 'Beacon' are useful for boutonnieres. The variegated foliage types are used for many purposes. More than 25 years ago George Teufel and others advised planting more variegated types for the cut industry. These are still in short supply.

The novelty hollies are less known and at present have limited use. The yellow-leaved types such as *Ilex aquifolium* 'Wieman's Moonbrite' and the yellow-berried types should be used for Halloween, Thanksgiving, golden wedding anniversaries and other functions.

Fruit ripening is very important when evaluating cultivars for the market industry. It is important to select early ripening cultivars for the cut industry to spread the harvesting period. Fruit ripening varies due to seasonal climatic conditions, age of trees, and varied growing conditions. Studies at Oregon State University indicate that the number of seeds affects the berry ripening. The more seed produced within the fruit, the earlier it ripens. Some cultivars ripen their fruits late and are of little commercial value as a cut product. These are best used for landscaping. The fruit of very early ripening cultivars may soften and turn dark in storage and shipping. Berry and leaf quality both go hand-in-hand when selecting commercial cut holly. Table 3 presents fruit-ripening dates for selected hollies.

Cultivars of *Ilex aquifolium* and *I. × altaclerensis* vary in their resistance to winter injury. Dr. Ticknor has observed that cultivars with early maturing berries were less damaged than their late maturing counterparts. Likewise variegated leaf forms, in an early November freeze of −25° (−14°F), were subject to more leaf scorch than solid green leaf forms. There is confusion on hardiness of holly cultivars throughout the United States. Most cultivars of *I. aquifolium* and *I. × altaclerensis* selected in the East are based on cold hardiness but cannot be compared with selections for the Northwest until they are tested under the same physiological conditions and exposed to the same low temperature conditions.

English hollies are not easily established, but with proper planting and care they are vigorous and easily managed. Before planting the soil should be well prepared with the addition of organic matter such as manures and cover crops. Weed control should be done before planting.

The planting distance depends on the cultivars and on the management of the established orchard. The general trend is toward closer planting and even hedgerow culture. Holly cultivars that are slow growing and early fruiting can be planted close together, 1.8 to 3 m (6 to 10 ft.) apart in the rows spaced 4.5 to 6 m (15 to 20 ft.) apart. This type of spacing requires annual pruning to keep plants in bounds. Rapid-growing cultivars can be grown in hedgerows if properly managed with spur-type renewal pruning.

Standard spacing of 4.5 to 6 m (15 to 20 feet) between trees is sufficient for most orchard operations such as spraying, cutting, and hauling based on equipment to be used. Young orchard plants can be kept in nursery rows until they are three to four years old and reach 0.9 to 1.2 m (3 to 4 ft.) high; then they should be planted out. Good balled or large container plants can be moved and planted in late fall or early spring. Irrigation may be required until plants are established if rainfall is lacking.

Standard soil management practices for orchard crops can be used or modified for the holly

Table 3. Blooming dates and berry ripening dates (i.e., dates to start commercial cuttings) of various hollies at Corvallis, Oregon, from 1957 to 1963. Plants are listed in the order in which fruit ripens.

Name	Date full bloom	Date end bloom	Average date ripening
Early season			
I. aquifolium 'Escort' (M)	1 May	28 May	—
I. aquifolium 'Dr. Huckleberry'	4 May	21 May	5 October
I. aquifolium 'Teufel's Hybrid'	8 May	21 May	7 October
I. aquifolium 'Bleeg Green'	6 May	19 May	11 October
I. aquifolium 'Little Bull' (M)	6 May	24 May	—
Mid-season			
I. aquifolium 'Coleman'	12 May	28 May	17 October
I. aquifolium 'Coronation'	7 May	22 May	17 October
I. opaca (M)	1 May	22 May	—
I. opaca 'Arden'	30 May	17 June	17 October
I. aquifolium 'Beacon'	8 May	24 May	18 October
I. aquifolium 'Yuleglow'	—	—	18 October
I. aquifolium 'Teufel's Silver Variegated'	6 May	24 May	19 October
I. aquifolium 'Beautyspra'	7 May	22 May	19 October
I. aquifolium 'Early Commercial'	9 May	24 May	21 October
I. aquifolium 'Rederly'	12 May	28 May	21 October
I. opaca 'Cardinal'	3 June	22 June	23 October
I. aquifolium 'Teufel's Greenstem'	9 May	23 May	23 October
I. aquifolium 'Pinto'	5 May	19 May	24 October
Late season			
I. aquifolium 'Silvary'	10 May	26 May	25 October
French-English group	7 May	23 May	30 October
Very late			
I. opaca 'Taber No. 3'	4 June	21 June	8 November
I. cornuta (F)	28 April	19 May	10 November

orchard. Low fallow or clean cultivation during the growing season followed by a cover crop during the fall and winter months is generally practiced by holly growers. Cover crops should be mowed or turned under in the spring to assist in maintaining soil fertility and organic matter, and in the winter months to control erosion. A proper cover crop facilitates orchard traffic during the harvest operation. Excessive cultivation should be avoided and be confined to controlling weeds. The use of irrigation, such as drip culture, should be explored with the use of a permanent legume or low-maintenance grass sod.

The Oregon Experiment Station conducted a survey of Oregon holly orchards (1960–1961) which revealed only two serious nutritional deficiency problems. Nitrogen was the most common deficiency problem, and boron was found below the critical level and even at the deficiency level on some cultivars in various soils in the Willamette Valley.

The following brief description of deficiency symptoms (based on Hoagland nutrient solutions) has been released by Oregon State University to help in diagnosing English holly nutritional problems.

Nitrogen deficiency   Smaller leaves than normal and overall pale yellow-green color; short growth restricted and no second growth.

Boron deficiency   Irregularly shaped reddish or purplish spots on upper leaf surface, beneath spots are watersoaked in appearance, enlarging to concentric rings bordered with yellow; stem tip dieback and defoliation.

Phosphorus deficiency	Leaves smaller than normal, dark green, basal leaves turn yellow and drop prematurely.
Potassium deficiency	Leaf tips and margins turn pale yellow, later developing reddish cast; symptoms very slow in developing.
Manganese deficiency	First on subterminal (2 or 3 from tips) leaves, very small measlelike spots between veins; increasing in number toward leaf tip and margins; margins become dark and necrotic with time.
Iron deficiency	Slow to develop; leaves develop typical interveinal chlorosis with entire leaves becoming yellow and chlorotic.
Sulfur deficiency	Leaves yellowing at tips of terminal leaves; some areas of leaves remain green.
Magnesium deficiency	Very slow to develop, lower leaves become chlorotic, developing at leaf tips and margins, progressing slowly.

Studies at Oregon State University have shown that holly leaves have the ability to supply organic and inorganic nutrients to new shoots expanding in spring and early summer, and at other times of the year. Their data showed two periods when this occurs, when leaf buds are rapidly expanding and in September and October when berries are enlarging and rapidly maturing. The seeds place a heavy demand on the leaves for phosphorus and nitrogen, which often brings about yellowing and premature drop. This shows it is best to apply nitrogen and phosphorus fertilizers in early spring and fall to maintain optimum growth. Maximum growth is not desirable, as the goal is to have the spray growth remain short and not exceed in length the two-year-old fruit-bearing wood, typically about 46 cm (18 in.).

The holly orchard as with other orchard crops requires constant attention to insect, disease, algae prevention and control. These problems are described in other chapters. Holly growers should be familiar with the identification and damage of these pests and be constantly alert to keep them under control.

HARVESTING

No rule can be set as to the age of holly to be cut for harvesting (Plate 13). This will depend upon the cultivars and growing conditions. Some cultivars can be lightly pruned in six to eight years to allow the trees to develop additional production surface. The early cutting of sprays can be combined with pruning to space branches and eliminate over crowding in the tree. Multistemmed trees do not permit the spacing of laterals or the development of the spur renewal system. Thus developing a cutting system where one-quarter to one-third of the berried sprays are cut off from the laterals each year leaves stubs with strong buds to renew shoot development. In two to three years the new shoots will be of a good length and berried to provide cutting material.

Topping central leaders and strong laterals is often necessary to force new growth on older wood. All new leaders should not be allowed to develop but spaced and trained for sufficient room for proper development.

Old trees may need to be revitalized with removal of old growth, promoting new vigorous sprays of good quality. Trees properly fertilized with ample moisture available are essential for producing good cutting material.

The amount of sprays to remove in a single harvest is debatable. Harvesting can begin when the berries are red ripe and can be held in good condition until they reach the consumer. The condition of the holly berries is important for the development of additional color, and size is stopped when removed from the tree. Holly trees tolerate severe cutting but heavy pruning takes the tree out of production for at least two to three years, depending on the vigor of the tree.

Continuous heavy cutting has a dwarfing effect on the tree. Tests at Oregon State University have shown that heavy annual cutting produces the greatest amount of marketable holly over a five-year period. Trees not trimmed heavily increase in size and quantity of foliage more rapidly and return large yields later. Some cultivars, however, fail to produce a good crop of berries each year, and it may be desirable to cut heavily in years of heavy berry production.

PRUNING

The central leader and main lateral branches should not be removed when harvesting sprays. Heading back may be necessary when trees get too tall or widespread, but heading back of young trees delays the expansion of its bearing surfaces. Removal of lower limbs around the base of a tree is debatable for they shade the ground, keep down weed growth, and prevent too close cultivation near the trunk. *Phytophthora ilicis,* however, can spread from the ground to the leaves by contact or splashing.

Harvesting of sprays should be distributed over the entire tree by removing branches from each branch system. When cutting of small laterals for sprays, leave a stub of several inches for future sprays to develop from latent buds. In dense growth, however, the lateral can be removed permanently, removing it flush at the origin on the main branch. This will not leave latent buds to develop, and new growth will be eliminated.

When harvesting, all unmarketable cuttings should be discarded in the field, eliminating the cost of hauling the material to the packing shed for grading. Pruning and harvesting should be combined into one operation to eliminate a follow up.

The tips of the previous season's terminal growth are used in making wreaths but heavy cutting of these tips from spray-producing trees is not recommended to avoid the loss of well-balanced sprays later on. Well-balanced sprays of branches, foliage, and berries give the highest return per pound and should be the main objective.

HANDLING CUT HOLLY

Cut holly is a perishable product and should be handled properly to prevent drying, defoliation, and browning of leaves and berries (Plates 14, 15). Exposing cut holly to dry air is detrimental to the fresh bright appearance.

The present practice of early harvesting of cut holly sprays increases the storage problems of the material. The cutting date depends on the date of berry maturity and the storage life of the different cultivars. Based on the last shipping date, around 10 December, the cutting of sprays starts about two to six weeks prior. Thus a storage period of two to six weeks is required for the product to reach the ultimate consumer in top quality condition. Depending on storage, wreath makers will start cutting sprigs around the first of November or earlier.

The harvesting of cut holly should be planned around the preservation of quality which is often lost by (1) withering, (2) mechanical injury, (3) defoliation, (4) browning of the leaves, and (5) disease. Cut holly should not be exposed to drying out from direct sunlight and/or from improper storage in heated rooms. Holly cut in warm dry weather should be moved within the hour to a cool moist place.

Avoid excessive rough treatment. Cut holly is often thrown from trees to large crates or canvas baskets. Most cultivars tolerate this treatment; excessive rough treatment, however, causes inconspicuous scratches and cracks on the leaves, which provide entry places for fungi and later become discolored areas during storage. The major fungi problem in holly storage in the Pacific Northwest is *Phytophthora ilicis*. Cutting or handling frozen holly should be avoided if temperatures are below 0°C (32°F). Defoliation of cut holly can be controlled by (1) partial drying, (2) hormone treatment, and (3) cold storage. Holly sprays after cleaning and hormone treatment should be partially dry before packing into porous packages.

Hormone treatment to prevent defoliation is successful if followed by proper storage temperatures below 4°C (40°F). Cold storage of cut holly reduces the rate of respiration. It is important to remember that cut holly is alive and to retain the best appearance it must be kept alive.

HORMONE DIP

The hormone used is alpha naphthaleneacetic acid (NAA). Tests at the Oregon Experiment Station recommend a minimum concentration of 40 ppm, with higher concentrations giving more effect and often needed where defoliation conditions are severe. High concentrations such as 120 ppm have caused injury to cut holly and may increase respiration rate and reduce the storage life of the holly. NAA is available in pure form from chemical supply companies or may be obtained in a commercial preparation for delaying apple drop. The pure form of NAA should be dissolved in alcohol (just enough to dissolve it) before adding it to water. One ounce of NAA to 200 gallons of water makes a solution of 37 ppm to which a wetting agent or spreader should be added for better wetting of the waxy holly leaves. The commercial preparation is easy to use: using four times the recommendation for apple drop makes a solution of 40 ppm. Pure NAA is stable up to two years in the original container. Once opened the container should be used immediately or stored in the dark. The signal word for NAA is *caution,* as the chemical belongs to toxicity category III.

Cut holly coming in from the orchard is dropped into a large vat of water (a mild cleaning agent may be added) and picked up by agitators to a rinse of clear water. It moves along a continuous rack over a sloping drain table (Plate 16) and is then dipped into the hormone solution and moved over another sloping drain table to collect the solution drip. The holly is not soaked in the solution, just merely passed through. Figures 3-1 and 3-2 show typical setups for processing cut holly.

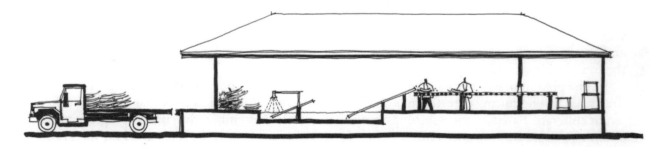

Figure 3-1. A diagrammatic sketch for a building in which cut holly is processed, from washing to hormone dip tank to sorting and grading. Drawing by Erek Galle.

One ton of washed or sprayed holly retains about 30 to 40 gallons of water after it has drained. That water goes through the NAA dip tank and dilutes the solution. Thus, the liquid level in the dip tank should be constantly monitored. For example, five tons of wet holly dipped in 400 gallons will reduce the concentration from 30 ppm to about 20 ppm. The solution can be brought

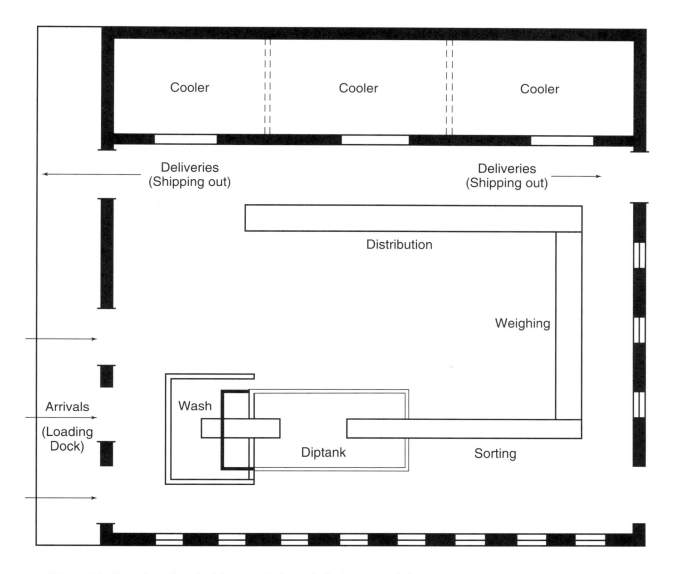

Figure 3-2. Flow chart for a building in which cut holly is processed, from washing to hormone dip to sorting and grading to packing to cold storage. Drawing by Erek Galle.

up to its original strength by adding one-third the amount of the hormone originally used. The solution should be kept as clean as possible and requires frequent renewal. A continuous flow system is advised, pumping the dip solution through filters plus screening out debris from the surface. The dip solution will deteriorate and must be constantly renewed. The rate of deterioration depends on aeration, temperature, and other factors. The solution should not be used longer than three to four days before renewal.

To reduce disease symptoms in stored cut holly, it is now common to add 25 to 30 ppm of copper to the dip solution. Copper does not dissolve at high pH, so the tank solution must be below 6.5 pH by adding nitric acid. The source of copper is copper sulfate or powdered blue stone (cupric sulfate pentahydrate or blue vitriol) at the rate of 1.6 oz. per gallon of water with 100 ppm of NAA. Check with your local county agents for a list of sensitive cultivars and other possible treatments.

PACKING

Cut holly should be drained to prevent the packages from dripping, but not packed dry. The holly is removed from the conveyor belt to a table, culled, trimmed, and packed by hand. Cut holly should be cleaned, dipped and packaged the same day it was cut from the orchard. The quality of cut holly during the storage period is effected by (1) humidity, (2) temperature, and (3) the presence of ethylene in the atmosphere.

Humidity is controlled by proper packaging. Commonly used cartons come in 5-, 10-, and 25-pound units. Smaller packages may be used for mail order. The cartons are often waxed inside and lined with a moisture barrier of polyethylene film, foil, or wax-lined paper and then sealed with gummed tape. With good storage the moisture in the packed holly will be retained for two weeks or longer.

Cut holly should be kept in cold storage. In tests conducted at Oregon State University cut holly remained in good condition 50 percent longer at 32°F than at 45°F. The packaged holly should be refrigerated but not exposed to temperature below freezing. If packages are frozen injury can be minimized by thawing slowly with careful handling (no shaking) of the packages.

Ethylene gas in minute quantities causes defoliation of holly leaves. Because this gas is produced from ripened fruits such as apples, pears, and bananas, holly should not be stored or shipped with these fruits. Other sources of ethylene contamination are leaky gas pipes and incomplete combustion of gas and oil.

Cut holly for wreaths can be stored in bulk, packaging carefully to avoid damaging or bruising. Most holly packages are not moisture-proof and not likely to maintain relative humidity near 100 percent. Storage tests at Oregon State University have shown both discoloration and defoliation to be more rapid at a relative humidity of 98 percent than at 85 percent. Some transparent wrapping materials have been reported to cause severe discoloration and defoliation, possibly in combination with high temperatures. The types of transparent materials should be checked or approved for this use.

ORCHARDS EAST OF THE MISSISSIPPI RIVER

For many years the source of cut holly in the eastern United States was from indigenous stands of wild trees, and the supply seemed bottomless. By the late 1920s, however, trees were ruthlessly vandalized and beautiful large female American hollies were cut down for the sources of boughs. Rapidly the sources of good hollies were being depleted.

The early pioneers of holly preservation and propagation in the East were Earle Dilatush of Pennsylvania; Wilfred Wheeler Jr. of Massachusetts; and Elizabeth C. White and Clarence W. Wolf of New Jersey. Selecting the best American hollies and giving them cultivar names was soon underway. Asexual propagation of American hollies and other species was undertaken by nursery growers. The cutting of native holly boughs and growing seedling trees was slowly surpassed by production from the selected cultivars and forms.

One of the first orchards in the Southeast in 1927 was the Van Cise orchard, Albany, Georgia, which produced *Ilex × attenuata* 'Howard'. Soon to follow was J. C. Penny's five-acre orchard at Penny Farms, Florida, which featured Dr. Hume's selections of *I. × attenuata*. In the late 1920s Clarence W. Wolf of Millville, New Jersey, president and co-founder of the Jersey Silica Sand Company and later first president of the Holly Society of America, started sending Christmas gifts of collected native holly to his customers. In the late 1930s he started a 68-acre private holly orchard. Soon more than 40 tons of berried holly sprays were sent out annually to his customers.

In the 1930s cut English holly grown in the Pacific Northwest was shipped to the East and the need for additional sources was not apparent. Orchards in the East, however, were nearer the large markets and thus had reduced shipping costs. This was an important factor in the mid 1940s when, due to the Second World War, shipping restrictions were placed on many non-essential agriculture crops. Many small eastern holly orchards and nurseries began supplying the local demand for cut holly during the holiday season.

Many of the basic preliminary problems of establishing a holly orchard in the East are similar to those in the Northwest. Picking a site is important. It is easier to avoid a poor location than to overcome it after a planting is established. Good air drainage is important to lessen the problems of late spring frost and frost pockets. Although holly grows on many different soil types, light sandy and stiff clay soils should be avoided. The ideal soil is fertile, loamy, and well-drained with the combined advantages of sandy and clay soils.

Most English holly cultivars are not reliably hardy for the Northeast and the Mid Atlantic areas. Occasionally some cultivars are hardy around Baltimore, Maryland, but further testing is required. The *Ilex × attenuata* cultivars available for growing in the Southeast such as 'East Palatka' and 'Howard' are not as much in demand as are the spiny-leaf cultivars of American holly. The following American holly cultivars are recommended for orcharding in the South:

FEMALE	MALE
'Arden'	'David'
'Cumberland'	'Jersey Knight'
'Dan Fenton'	'Makepeace'
'Eleanor'	'Silica King'
'Farage'	
'Hedgeholly'	
'Jersey Delight'	
'Jersey Princess'	
'Lady Alice'	
'Mamie Eisenhower'	
'Maurice River'	
'Menantico'	
'Miss Helen'	
'Natale'	
'Nelson West'	
'Old Heavy Berry'	
'Satyr Hill'	
'Vera'	

Male hollies should be planted in the orchard at a ratio of one male to 15 female plants to insure good pollination. Bee hives in or near the orchard when the plants are in flower are good insurance. Trees should be planted 6 to 7.5 m (20 to 25 ft.) apart or about 173 trees per hectare (70 trees per acre).

Novelty trees to be considered are the yellow-fruited forms of American holly, of which there are more than 50 cultivars. Not all of these are commercially available but some are listed in nursery catalogs, including 'Betty Nevison', 'Canary', 'Morgan Gold', and 'Princeton Gold'. 'Steward's Silver Crown', a patented plant with attractive variegated leaves, is available to add contrast and color to wreaths and arrangements.

In the Southeast the late Jackson (Jack) M. Batchelor, an active Holly Society of America member, after retiring from Hill Culture Division, Soil Conservation Service, U.S.D.A., started a nursery and holly orchard in Willard, North Carolina. Jack tested both holly species and cultivars for adaptability in his area. Most of the American holly cultivars were too slow or did not adapt. The *Ilex × attenuata* hybrids such as 'East Palatka', 'Howard', 'Hume No. 2', and 'Taber

No. 3' were suited for the Southeast, with 'Howard' proving to be the best for orcharding. *Ilex cornuta* 'Shangri La', a hybrid developed by Batchelor, showed good promise for commercial production. Strawberries were planted for six years in his young holly orchard for a quick cash crop; and Toulouse geese were used to control grass around the mulched trees. There is no information on the outcome of this orchard today.

Additional hollies to evaluate for the Southeast for orcharding and cut foliage include the following:

> *I.* × *attenuata* 'Alagold' (yellow fruit)
> *I.* × *attenuata* 'Eagleson'
> *I.* × *attenuata* 'Foster No. 2'
> *I.* × *attenuata* 'Savannah'
> *I. myrtifolia* (yellow- and red-fruited forms)
> *I. latifolia*
> *I. cornuta* 'Burfordii'
> *I. cornuta* 'D'Or' (yellow fruit)
> *I. cornuta* 'O. Spring' (variegated foliage)

A new project is underway in the tidewater area of Virginia to grow and promote English holly for the cut market. The project is the dream of J. Nelson Stuart of Reedville, Virginia, who has tested and evaluated plants for a number of years. At present 28 hectares (69 acres) are planted in the counties of North Thunderland, Lancaster, and Caroline, with the support of the Virginia Horticultural Research Station, Virginia Beach. The cultivars planted at present are *Ilex aquifolium* 'Escort' and *I.* × *altaclerensis* 'Green Maid'. Other cultivars are still being tested.

DECIDUOUS HOLLY ORCHARDS

Several nursery orchards are devoted to growing deciduous holly for cutting at Thanksgiving and Christmas season. Jenkins Florist, Mitchellville, Maryland, has marketed cut branches of deciduous holly for more than 30 years to the Washington, D.C., area. The two main cultivars grown of *I. verticillata* are 'Christmas Gem' and 'Maryland Beauty'. The plants were first spaced about 6 ft. apart, then 12 ft., and finally 20 ft. for mowing and use of equipment. David Jenkins continues to select superior seedlings from his own trees for future plantings.

The Mott Holly Farm, Kalamazoo, Michigan, is owned by Phil Mott, a third-generation grower of cut "Michigan Holly" (*Ilex verticillata*). Most of the Mott holly is grown in peat bogs. Three superior clones are grown. The orchard consists of approximately 37,000 plants, spaced 1.2 × 3 m (4 × 10 ft.) apart. The plants are cut on a three-year rotation for desirable fruit production. About 25 tons of holly are cut annually and shipped nationwide.

Robert Simpson of Simpson Nursery, Vincennes, Indiana, and Bon Hartline of Hartline Holly Nursery, Anna, Illinois, are the pioneers in selection, growing and promoting the use of deciduous hollies in the United States. Both have made important selections of *Ilex verticillata* and *I. decidua*. A partial list of deciduous holly recommended for orcharding is as follows:

> *I. decidua* cultivars
> 'Byer's Golden'
> 'Council Fire'
> 'Pocahontas'
> 'Red Cascade'
> 'Warren's Red'

I. serrata × *I. verticillata* cultivars
    'Autumn Glow'
    'Harvest Red'
    'Sparkleberry'

I. verticillata cultivars
    'Winter Red'
    'Winter Gold'
    'Maryland Beauty'
    'Christmas Gem'

CHAPTER 4

Hollies for Topiary

Alden Hopkins[1]

Topiarius—"an ornamental gardener, one skilled in fanciful landscape-gardening"—refers, of course, to the art of training and clipping trees or other plant material into fanciful, artificial shapes. It is a project requiring time and patience, the "art of a leisurely age." The landscape architect whose diploma from a professional graduate school may relate that he or she is a *magistri in arte topiaria* indicates the historical background of the modern practitioners and their reliance in part on the formality of Rome and the later great seventeenth- and eighteenth-century gardens, when formality in training plants was at its height. Today we are all trainers of plant material, yet with a far broader meaning than that of the *topiarius.*

The *opus topiarum,* popular ornamentation for the Roman garden, returned to fashion again in early Tudor times to remain a highly prized feature of gardens, large and small, for more than two hundred years. The Dutch appeared to be particularly fond of this ornament and developed a fine sense in its use in their flat canal-encompassed gardens. With the arrival of William and Mary in the seventeenth century, English gardens soon reflected the court interest in topiary work, one of the fancies of a king intensely interested in gardening. Hampton Court received his particular attention, and with the revisions undertaken by the two famous gardeners, George London and Henry Wise, the former superintendent of the Royal Gardens, much of the old design was removed and the yews in fashionable clipped shapes set out in the fountain garden. Many of these now long unclipped trees exist today as mere accents in that garden.

At the start of the eighteenth century, a gardening book, *The Theory and Practice of Gardening,* by Alexander Le Blond D'Argenville (1703), translated from French by John James of Greenwich, had considerable influence on the English garden design. In one chapter, he wrote of topiary work and its fashion:

> Heretofore they gave them a thousand extravagant forms, which are yet much in use in the gardens of Italy and Spain: some shaped out men on horseback, boars, stags, dogs; in short an entire Hunting-piece. Others cut them into Pyramids, Obelisks, Balls and scrolls—This practice still continues in Holland and Flanders, where these whimsical Designs are more in vogue than in any other country.

Soon after 1700, there arose a voluble reaction to these collections over which the gardeners with their shears had reigned so long. Topiary work had been carried to such extremes that little

---

[1]The late Alden Hopkins was resident landscape architect for Colonial Williamsburg, Virginia, for 20 years and specialist in period landscape design.

was free from the cutting and snipping. People were tiring of it all. This reaction was instigated, no doubt, in great part by the columnists of that day who recognized that the time was ripe for a complete reversal of fashion in gardening. The artists of picturesque and romantic landscapes were also in the fore with their back-to-nature paintings, illustrating the peace and simplicity of rustic surrounding unhampered by scythe and shears.

This rediscovery of the beauty of natural plant shapes in the garden, the freedom from "the work of the scissors upon every plant and bush," was heartily encouraged by Joseph Addison in his *Spectator* articles. He wrote (*Spectator 414,* 25 June 1712) that the British gardener, instead of humoring nature, loved to deviate from it as much as possible:

> I would rather look upon a tree in all its Luxuriance and Diffusion of Boughs and Branches, than when it is then cut and trimmed into a mathematical figure; and cannot best fancy that an orchard in flower looks infinitely more delightful than all the little labyrinths of the most finished Parterre.

These early years of the eighteenth century saw the beginning of the revolution in the use of topiary pieces. In 1713, at the same time Addison was criticizing, Alexander Pope broke out in poetry and derisive descriptions of the art and especially the abundance of work now cluttering many fashionable gardens. In the *Guardian,* he wittily quoted from a listed sale of nursery stock:

> Adam and Eve in yew, Adam a little shattered by the fall of the tree of knowledge in the great storm; Eve and the serpent very flourishing. St. George in box, his arm scarce long enough, but will be in condition to stick the dragon by next April; a green dragon of the same, with tail of ground ivy for the present. (N.B.—These two not sold separately.) Divers eminent poets in bay, somewhat blighted, to be disposed of a penny worth. A quickset bay, shot up into a porcupine, by its being forgot a week in rainy weather.

In all, this trend to extremes of topiary art, soon to cause its complete downfall, can be summed up in a further quote from Pope:

> We seem to make it our study to recede from nature, not only in the various tonsure of greens into the most regular and formal shapes—and are yet better pleased to have our trees in the most awkward figures of men and animals than in the most regular of their own.

Thus the topiary fad, fashionable for more than two hundred years, slowly passed away. Many gardens were completely torn apart to follow the new natural style so well publicized at Stowe. There were a few places, however, which escaped and, today, display antique specimens of yew topiary scattered and arranged throughout the plain parterres. Levens Hall and Packwood House still show their great clipped "Greens."

In the colonies, this art, so prized under William and Mary, held on for a considerable period after its termination in England. Here, too, its popularity was considerable and we have numerous records of topiary "greens" from New England to Virginia. The early years of the seventeenth century provided few references, but the eighteenth, with more prosperity, brought many. In Boston, yews were ordered from England in 1736 by Thomas Hancock, "100 small yew trees in the rough which I'd frame up here to my own fancy." It appears from this quotation that yew topiary in considerable quantity, perhaps for bordering a parterre, was planned for this new garden.

The most authentic evidence of the popularity and use of clipped evergreens in Virginia is the Bodleian Plate, believed made between 1733 and 1747. This copper plate engraving, discovered at Oxford's Bodleian Library, shows the several important public buildings of Williamsburg, the capital of the Colony. Among them the main building of the College of William and Mary is clearly illustrated. Here is discovered a wonderful display of topiary lining the three parallel entrance walks in an exact planned manner. Although these examples have long since disappeared, there is additional evidence of their having existed and that the impression created by the plate of this use of topiary is correct. A quotation from E. Hazard, who traveled in Virginia in 1777, gives one eye-witness proof of the use of topiary as ornament at the College: "At this Front of the College is large court yard, ornamented with gravel walks, trees cut into different forms, and grass." There is no indication of the kind of plant material, whether holly, box, yew, or other green.

An earlier reference to these topiary pieces at the College was made in 1732 by Reverend William Dawson, professor of divinity, in addressing the Bishop of London describing the various buildings and "the East front of the College, before which is a garden planted with evergreens kept in very good order."

With the College as a nearby example, there is little reason to doubt but that domestic yards and gardens held fashioned greens still in style there. We do know of one place, owned by Colonel John Curtis, an early student of botany and correspondent of many eminent European men of similar interests. In a letter to Peter Collinson in 1738, he wrote:

> I have had silver and gold hollies, yews, philereus, etc., come flourishing to me three feet high, the balls or standards having heads as big as a peck and the pyramids in full shape and are at this time flourishing in my garden; but every individual tree was put into a basket with earth and the basket and tree buried together the basket soon rotted so that the tree was never stunted in the least.

Of these evergreens so carefully planted and enjoyed so fully by Colonel Curtis, one yew still survives in this garden, now part of the Eastern State Hospital grounds. Of great size and age, and green rather than silver or gold, it has long since lost any of its former topiary appearance.

Though the keen interest and support of John D. Rockefeller Jr., the restoration of Williamsburg has been made possible. Research into the life, activity, and appearance of the city at the period of its greatest glory in the eighteenth century was one of the first requirements. Among these many lines of study, the first were concerned with architecture and landscape architecture, including the garden locations, pattern, ornamentation, and plant materials. In this new land, the first gardeners soon recognized the great abundance of native plants, collecting and sending them in a continuous stream to collectors and botanists in England. The native evergreen hollies were among these—American holly (*Ilex opaca*), yaupon holly (*I. vomitoria*), and dahoon holly (*I. cassine*).

The formation of "greens" in geometric and fanciful shapes is somewhat of an art in itself as anyone knows who has attempted, with shears in hand, to cut a way into a piece of boxwood or holly. In the selection of the basic plant or grouping of plants is the most important step. Many times a particularly odd-shaped plant may suggest an animal in general outline, or it may form a portion of a figure, which, with the addition of another, may result in the beginning of an amusing realistic form. By trimming here and drastically cutting there in another part of the plant, a ragged form may eventually appear. To undertake this, a study of the branching habit is necessary, for the more the plant is developed through natural pruning rather than by use of wire and forms, the easier the general maintenance will ultimately be. The use of artificial support was not neglected in the early years of topiary construction. From D'Argenville we learn that many times were used "Verdures, which are the few in number on account of the continual charge they require, as well as Wood and Wire for the constant Repair of their frames, as in their clipping four times a year." D'Argenville was quite correct, too, on the need for constant care in the clipping and the forming. At several recent restoration plantings in Virginia, there have been developed a peacock, a frog, a setting hen, and geometric forms—all started from a plant or grouping of plants which gave some semblance of these objects to commence with.

The formation of a geometric form in holly or other material is a much more simple project. For a tall interrupted cone, select a plant with a central trunk and side branches so arranged that a severe cutting back will still leave a sufficient number of branches to furnish the remaining basic form with new growth. It will require a number of years' growth before the piece is well filled in and takes shape. For other forms—pyramids, corkscrews, globe, and cylinders—the same careful selection and severe pruning are required. No forms and very few wires are necessary, if the plant to be formed is selected with care.

Other geometric forms may be made by the combination of several plants grouped around a center accent, or a series of repeating accents to form a screen or backdrop. A simple hedge, the lowest form of topiary work, can gradually be developed with the addition of knobs, points, waving variations, and swoops in profile into a most imaginative and interesting sight.

In Williamsburg, our selection of holly species for topiary work has been limited to those known before the year 1800. The section of the country is most fortunate to have at hand three native evergreen hollies of great beauty and ease of culture. The American holly fills the woods and from the earliest days was transferred into gardens for use as shade, natural accents, hedges, and topiary. The other two, yaupon and dahoon, are among the most beautiful evergreens. This is

Figure 4-1. *Ilex vomitoria* (yaupon holly) sheared seedlings at Colonial Williamsburg. Photo © Colonial Williamsburg Foundation. Used by permission.

Figure 4-2. *Ilex vomitoria* (yaupon holly) sheared at Colonial Williamsburg. Photo © Colonial Williamsburg Foundation. Used by permission.

especially true of the yaupon holly. Its ease of clipping into any form and its great beauty in its native growth, in foliage, and in glistening red berries make it outstanding among evergreen shrubs. Its native habitat covers the South from Virginia to Florida and west to Arkansas and Texas.

Topiary hollies in the restored gardens at Colonial Williamsburg serve as decorative garden features, as conversation pieces, and to create an atmosphere reminiscent of the eighteenth century.

CHAPTER 5

Bonsai with Holly

Bonsai, the art of growing potted dwarf trees, is an excellent and rapidly growing hobby in the United States (see Plate 17). There are active bonsai clubs throughout the country that hold monthly meetings, demonstrations, and shows. The U.S. National Arboretum in Washington, D.C., has an excellent permanent bonsai display, a collection of penjing plants from China, and an American collection. Other major gardens such as Brooklyn Botanic Gardens in New York have permanent displays of bonsai plants.

The word *bonsai* is a compound of two Chinese characters, sounded as "bon" and "sigh" in Japanese and meaning tray planting or plant in a pot or container. In China, where the word is pronounced as "pun" and "sigh," bonsai has been very popular since about 400 A.D. The art of bonsai began in China and was exported to Japan and then to the Western world. The Chinese word for bonsai is *penjing*, miniature landscape.

Bonsai combines horticultural techniques with a love of nature and an appreciation of the art form. The styles or types of bonsai are based on the shape of the tree trunk used, varying from a single straight trunk to cascading to double and forest groups. The Japanese recognize at least twelve styles, which, like fashions, change, while the Chinese recognize at least seven styles.

The stylized bonsai is an adaption of indoor-outdoor container growing with an emphasis on the art of pruning and training in a bonsai style. The dwarfing of a bonsai is not from poor soil or starvation, for a humus well-drained soil is important as is constant care in watering and a modest fertilization program.

A beginner will benefit by reading one or more of the excellent books on the subject and by studying the styles and forms of prized bonsai. A visit to a local bonsai club, display, or show is also helpful. Bonsai plants require daily care, often just a visual observation, but they cannot be ignored. Starting bonsai with a young seedling or beginner's kit, as advertised in magazines and catalogs, generally requires many years of developing and training and often ends with negative results and lack of interest. It is better to start by purchasing a young trained bonsai or by working with a nursery or greenhouse plant. Look for a plant that already has some character or bonsai form. This will seldom be a well-groomed and well-pruned plant but rather a misshaped, nearly neglected plant.

Bonsai are to look as old trees with many styles from formal, informal, to cascades. Thus it is best to select a plant that has some potential of developing. Choose one that shows a good trunk and branching low to the base. Many hollies have large leaves that would be out of proportion with a dwarf tree. Some plants such as boxwood and azaleas can be root pruned immediately and replanted to a small container. Many hollies, however, cannot be root pruned immediately and placed in a shallow pot due to their less fibrous root system. Hollies, therefore, need to go through training pots, gradually shifting to smaller pots over several years. Shallow and exposed roots are added features in a bonsai as well as the trunk and branching habit. The training and shaping is often created by wiring the trunk and branches and then carefully removing the wire before it becomes embedded in the stem.

Bonsai plants spend most of their lives in containers, so the selection of an authentic Japanese style is important. The shape, size, color, texture, and design are all important. The container is both functional and aesthetically important and should complement and be in harmony with the plant it holds.

GENERAL CARE AND INFORMATION

Most holly bonsai plants should be maintained outdoors, but can be displayed indoors for a short period of time without harm. Some species such as *Ilex dimorphophylla* (Okinawan holly), a subtropical plant, can be an indoor plant (Plate 18). The best place to maintain and display bonsai is on an attractive wood bench or table 0.9 to 1.2 m (3 to 4 ft.) high or on a deck, patio, or balcony. The ideal site for hollies receives morning sun and afternoon shade. Other bonsai plants, such as junipers and pines, tolerate full sun.

The potting soil or media should retain moisture, but have good drainage and aeration with a pH of 5.5 to 6.5. Good basic mixes are 1 to 2 parts perlite, 2 to 5 parts fine pine or redwood bark, 1 part each sphagnum peat moss and pumice rock *or* 1 part calcinated clay (cat litter).

The watering of a bonsai is very important and can never be neglected. More bonsai are lost due to improper watering than from all other causes. Generally a thorough watering, once a day during the spring, summer, and fall, is advised. If, however, the media is heavy and drains poorly, a daily water will kill the plant. Check the soil media of your plants and replace as necessary to improve the drainage.

Because bonsai are grown in a small amount of soil and watered frequently, it is necessary to replenish soil nutrients. Slow-release fertilizers are advised. Remember, you have a mass of roots confined in a small container so use fertilizer sparingly. It is best applied in early spring, with a second application, if necessary, in late spring or early summer.

Repotting, pruning, and trimming are important in keeping bonsai dwarf. Repotting should generally be done every two to three years, but the root system should be examined every year to determine if repotting is required. The best time is late winter or early spring. Fork out some of the soil and cut or trim some of the roots if necessary. Use your fingers or a small dibble to firm but not compact the new soil around the roots. Water and recheck to see if additional soil is necessary. Pruning and trimming also keep a bonsai dwarf. Remove the vigorous new growth in the spring and periodically throughout the growing season, but never remove *all* new growth.

Most holly bonsai require a winter dormant period. The kind of winter protection needed depends on the severity of the local winter weather, but in most areas where holly are grown, winter protection is necessary to ensure bonsai survival. Whatever the level of winter protection, it is important that the roots do not freeze. Some options for holly include the following:

1. Healed into the ground in a protected area, the pot covered with leaves.
2. In a cold frame or cold greenhouse.
3. In the closed window well of a basement.
4. In a storage shed or unheated garage. In subzero weather, protection of the container is important to not freeze the roots for any long period of time.

Check with members of a local bonsai club for their recommendations for winter protection. While the plants are in winter storage, check the root system for moisture and water when needed.

Tender bonsai plants such as *Ilex dimorphophylla* will not withstand temperatures below

−6°C (21°F). *Ilex myrtifolia* and *I. vomitoria* will not survive below −12°C (10°F). During the winter months when tender holly bonsai are indoors, they should be kept in a cool but lighted room and in a shallow tray of water to compensate for moisture loss.

The art and care of bonsai offers new challenges, requiring year-round attention. It is a fun hobby, but be careful—bonsaitis is very catching.

DWARF HOLLIES SUITABLE FOR BONSAI

Although many hollies have leaves too large for bonsai culture, many other species and cultivars are suitable though seldom used. The following list describes hollies that would make good bonsai.

Evergreen Hollies Suitable for Bonsai

Ilex aquifolium 'Angustifolia', red fruit, attractive, narrowly lanceolate, spiny leaves, narrow pyramidal habit.

Ilex cornuta, commonly used in China, a large plant with trunks 10–15 cm (4–6 in.) in diameter, fruit usually red.
'Dwarf Burford', leaves usually less than 5 cm (2 in.) long, compact habit, fruit red.
'Spiny', leaves less than 4 cm long, compact upright habit, fruit red.

Ilex cornuta × *I. pernyi* hybrids, moderate-sized leaves

Ilex crenata
'Beehive' (M), compact, mounding to 1 m (3 ft.).
'Butterball', yellow fruit.
'Delaware Diamond' (M), very dwarf, dense mounding habit, 30 cm (12 in.) high in 12 years, smallest-leaved Japanese holly.
'Dewdrop' (F), very dwarf, 10 cm (4 in.) high in 7 years.
'Dwarf Pagoda' (F), compact, upright horizontal growth.
'Fairyland' (F), dwarf, 15 cm (6 in.) in 7 years.
'Golden Heller', similar to 'Helleri' with yellow cast to leaves, some with yellow blotches.
'Green Dragon' (M), irregular growth, essentially upright, sibling of 'Dwarf Pagoda'.
'Helleri' (F), compact habit to 1 m (3 ft.) high.
'Piccolo' (F), low compact habit, 25 cm (10 in.) in 10 yrs.
'Rocky Creek' (M), branches upright, twisted, corkscrewlike.
'Snowflake' (F), leaves variegated, irregular yellowish white margin.
'Tee Dee' (F), compact, open habit, to 1 m (3 ft.) in 20 years.

Ilex dimorphophylla, red fruit, small narrow spiny leaves similar to Chinese holly only 3.5 cm (1⅜ in.) long, adult leaves entire, subtropical, tender at −7°C (20°F), indoor bonsai.

Ilex myrtifolia, red fruit, narrow-elliptic leaves to 4 cm (1⅝ in.) long, irregular upright habit; yellow-fruited cultivars available.

Ilex opaca 'William Hawkins' (M), originally from a witches broom, unusual leaves, very narrow spiny, compact low pyramidal habit.

Ilex pedunculosa, attractive red fruit on long pendulous peduncles to 5 cm (2 in.) long, leaves entire, to 7.5 cm (3 in.) long.

Ilex pernyi, red fruit, small spiny leaves to 3.5 cm (1⅜ in.) long, upright irregular habit.

Ilex rugosa, red fruit, irregular low prostrate shrub, leaves oblong to lanceolate, to 4 cm (1⅝ in.) long, rugose surface, must be in shade.

Ilex spinigera, red fruit, smaller leaves similar to English holly only 4 cm (1⅝ in.) long, rare.

Ilex sugerokii, red fruit, leaves serrate, ovate, to 3.8 cm (1½ in.) long, pyramidal habit.

Ilex vomitoria, red fruit.
'Dare County' orange fruit.
'Dwarf', slow to fruit.
'Folsom's Weeping', upright weeping habit.
'Stokes Dwarf', slow to fruit.
'Straughan's Dwarf', slow to fruit.
'Wiggins', yellow fruit.

Ilex yunnanensis, red fruit, leaves lanceolate, up to 3.8 cm (1½ in.) long, pyramidal habit.

Hybrids
Ilex 'Jersey Globe', red fruit, rare, low habit.
Ilex 'Jersey Jewel', red fruit, rare, low habit.
Ilex 'Jersey Midget', red fruit, low and dwarf habit.
Ilex 'Jersey Moppet', red fruit, rare, low and stout habit.
Ilex 'Jersey Sprite', red fruit, rare, leaves small and spiny, low and dwarf habit.
Ilex 'Rock Garden', red fruit, leaves to 2.5 cm (1 in.) long, low and dwarf habit.

Deciduous Hollies Suitable for Bonsai

Ilex decidua
'Byer's Golden', yellow fruit.
'Warren's Red', light gray stems and branches, red fruit.
'Red Cascade', light gray stems and branches, red fruit.
'Council Fire', light gray stems and branches, red fruit.

Ilex longipes, cherrylike red fruit, an uncommon species with long pendulous peduncles.
'Natchez Belle'.

Ilex serrata, red fruit, popular bonsai in Japan, attractive branching habit, leaves to 5 cm (2 in.) long.
'Koshobai', rare, small linear leaves to 3.5 cm (1⅜ in.) long, very small red fruit 3 mm (⅛ in.) in diameter.

Ilex serrata × *I. verticillata* hybrids
'Autumn Glow' (F)
'Bonfire' (F)
'Harvest Red' (F)
'Raritan Chief' (M)
'Sparkleberry' (F)

Ilex verticillata
forma *aurantiaca*, light orange fruit.
'Christmas Cheer', red fruit.
'Earlibright', red fruit.
'Red Sprite', large red fruit.
'Stop Light', red fruit.
'Winter Gold', yellowish pink fruit.
'Winter Red', red fruit.

CHAPTER 6

Decorating for Christmas with Holly

Libby Hodges Oliver[1]

A branch of holly adorned with a cluster of bright red berries evokes thoughts of Christmas as readily as Santa and Rudolph. *Ilex opaca* (American holly) projects the image all of us carry as the epitome of holly; however, other hollies will create bolder and varied looks for decorations. For example, *Ilex cornuta* 'Burfordii' (Chinese holly), with its large clusters of berries, makes a bright red statement, and, for delicate arrangements, *I. vomitoria* (yaupon holly), with its porcelain berries and neat small leaves, will last several days when cut and placed in water.

The deciduous hollies with long leafless branches of berries are sought after by florists and seen in the swanky New York hotel lobbies. They can be purchased if you do not grow them. *Ilex decidua* (possumhaw holly) and *I. verticillata* (winterberry) are often simply sold as "Ilex" in the trade.

Just a sprig of holly tucked behind a brass candlestick, or tied with a red ribbon to a sconce, or stuck on a window pane will put the finishing touch of Christmas decorating. Prints from the 1700s show the practice of sticking holly leaves on window panes (probably with beeswax). Today we have easy-to-apply adhesives with which to adhere the leaves. The red berries of holly can be seen to advantage by trimming a few leaves which may obscure the impact of the berries. Or, all the leaves can be trimmed away to leave just berries. This is a good way to use those stems with poor leaves and great berries. The stems with berries only can then be used individually in wreaths (see Figure 6-1, Plate 19) and arrangements or in clusters (see Figure 6-2, Plate 20). The clusters are made by wiring together 10 to 12 stems each 10 inches long. They can be used as accents tucked into pine roping at the corners of a doorway.

Of course, holly left out of water will dry out quickly. Conditioning the holly overnight by placing the stems in a bucket of water will extend the life of holly just as it will with other greens. In some areas of the country, the holly foliage will benefit from a bath to remove dust.

A basic arrangement of holly and mixed greens will last 2 to 3 weeks if cared for by recutting the stems and providing fresh water every 4 to 5 days. Flowers can be added when desired to give the arrangement a new look. Favorite flowers at Christmas include lilies, star of Bethlehem, and snowflake pompoms. For a less formal design, arrange holly in a basket with fresh fruit, okra, lotus pods, and cotton bolls. Red holly berries emphasize the color of a pomegranate or red apple, while green apples look sophisticated with variegated holly (see Plate 21).

All holly benefits from being arranged with needled evergreens to soften the density of the broadleaved holly. White pine, Leyland cypress (flat cedar), rosemary, and juniper have needled foliage which compliments holly.

---

[1] Libby H. Oliver is manager of floral services for Colonial Williamsburg Foundation, Virginia, where she is responsible for flower arrangements, dried materials, and Christmas decorations used in the exhibition buildings.

Figure 6-1. Steps in making a Christmas wreath to hang on a door. Drawing © Colonial Williamsburg Foundation. Used by permission.

New contraptions made with floral foam enable decorations to be placed on lamp posts, window sills, gates, and many places where they would have lasted only one or two days without the added source of water. The floral foam comes shaped in rings and swag or spray form. Try inserting holly stems into the foam for a mass of Christmas cheer which can be attached to your mailbox. Water can be poured into the foam every few days to keep it fresh. Figure 6-3 shows how a simple Christmas tree decoration can be made using a foam base and holly (see Plate 22).

Christmas decorations today are not always in the traditional red, white, and green. Golden colors are making the holiday festive too. Yellow-berried hollies are good options for arrangements requiring a golden touch.

The variegated *Ilex aquifolium* (English holly) has almost become as associated with Christmas as the standard American holly. The cream-edged variegated leaves reflect candlelight and look outstanding in photographs. They are often called Oregon holly since many of the commercial growers are located in that state.

Holly provides both shiny leaves and bright berries which are as important in decorating for Christmas as are mistletoe and poinsettias. With proper attention, a decoration of holly will last the entire holiday season.

Figure 6-2. Steps in preparing a garland of fruit and foliage to use as accents at the corner of a door. Drawing © Colonial Williamsburg Foundation. Used by permission.

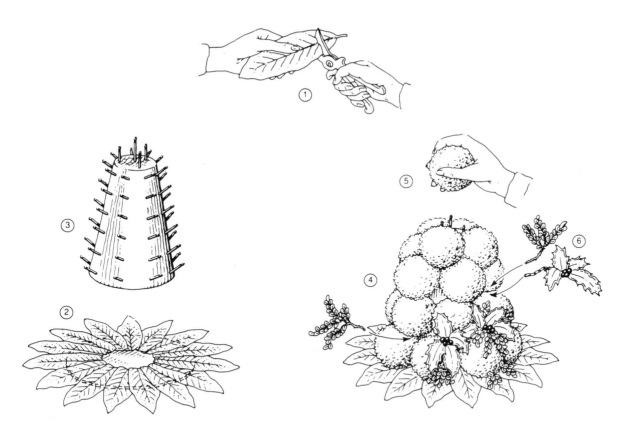

Figure 6-3. Using a foam or wood base to make a centerpiece of magnolia leaves, holly leaves, and holly berries for a Christmas table. Drawing © Colonial Williamsburg Foundation. Used by permission.

CHAPTER 7

Hollies in Art

Throughout history holly has been displayed in art. In many art museums there are excellent tapestries with holly leaves in the design. The use of holly for Christmas decorations is difficult to trace but probably a custom adopted from the Romans. Loudon (1844) in his book titled *Arboretum et Fruticetum Britannicum* reported that "using holly, with cut boughs of narrow-leaved evergreens such as spruce, fir, pine, hemlock and others were popular greens for decorating the home and church at Christmas seasons."

Another favorite tradition at the holiday season is sending cards to friends. The cards often in a subtle way display or show the interest of the sender with plants such as holly (Plate 23), ivy and others to wild life and general winter scenes. Our colorful wrapped gifts often display holly motif. Note paper and letterhead show plant art.

Many enthusiasts have collections of holly art in a multitude of styles and media, the range interest is unlimited. Beautiful hand painted china are collectors items and become family heirlooms (Plate 24).

Artists often do special holly portraits, such as Athos Menoboni and others, to block prints by Frances Mennen (Plates 25, 26). My special holly treasures are two watercolor paintings by my daughter for Christmas gifts when she was 13 and 14 years old, and a new treasure is a pencil drawing by my 13-year-old granddaughter (see page 10).

Holly jewelry is crafted in many styles and forms from gold and silver leaves to branches with berries, inlaid with tiny garnets or rubies, as stick pins and buckles (Plate 27).

Holly wood is a very good medium for carving (Plate 28) or turning and when properly cured is used for tool handles. The close white grain is very hard and often stained or dyed black to make piano keys. Fresh green wood is easier to carve and work, but care is required to keep the wood from checking or splitting when drying out. Many cabinet makers and wood hobbyists treat their fresh wood with polyethylene glycol (PEG). Danish oil is also recommended. Working with holly can offer year round pleasure.

◆ PART II

CHAPTER 8

Taxonomic History

The plant family Aquifoliaceae contains four genera: *Byronia, Ilex, Nemopanthus,* and *Phelline.* The genus *Ilex* is the largest, with 30 deciduous species and more than 780 evergreen species, and occurs worldwide in temperate, warm temperate, subtropical, and tropical climatic zones. *Byronia* Endlicher has about 25 species in Indonesia, Malaysia, the Philippines, the People's Republic of China and the Peruvian and Bolivian Andes. These species are the most primitive in the family and most are extremely rare. *Byronia anomala* is occasionally cultivated in Hawaii where it is native. Many authorities regard *Byronia* as a subgenus of *Ilex,* although there are some sound taxonomic justifications and characters to maintain it as a distinct genus. *Nemopanthus* Rafinesque (1819) is a monotypic genus. *Nemopanthus mucronatus* Trelease 1892, commonly called mountain holly or catberry, is an uncommon species outside New England and the Allegheny Mountains of West Virginia of the United States. It is rare even in botanic gardens and arboreta. *Phelline* La Billardière has about 10 endemic species in New Caledonia.

The family name, Aquifoliaceae, was erected by Bartling (1830) from *Aquifolium,* the pre-Linnean and classical name for holly. Specifically, *Ilex aquifolium* (English holly) means "having pointed or spiny leaves."

The genus *Aquifolium* was erected by Philip Miller (1734) and is now a synonym of *Ilex* Linnaeus (1753). Swiss botanist Augustin de Candolle erected the family name in French in 1813; however, in 1830 Friedrich Gottlieb Bartling was the first to publish Aquifoliaceae in the correct Latin format.

Ilex, the generic name, was erected by Carl Linnaeus in *Systema Naturae* (1735) and repeated in several of his works including *Species Plantarum* (1753), the starting point of modern botanical nomenclature. *Ilex* is the classical Latin name for the holly oak, *Quercus ilex,* an evergreen Mediterranean oak with hollylike spinose leaves.

The natural distribution of *Ilex* is cosmopolitan and occurs in the tropical, subtropical, warm temperate, and temperate climatic zones in all continents in both hemispheres. Fossil records indicate that progenitors of extant *Ilex* existed prior to the continental drift when there was one land mass named Gondwana. Fossil records contain about 250 species from all over the world, excluding Antarctica. Many of the fossil records are based on identification of pollen and pyrenes. Numerous fossil species are very similar to modern-day species, while other fossils originally thought to be *Ilex* may represent *Mahonia, Quercus, Myrica,* and other genera not closely allied to the Aquifoliaceae. Continued study and evaluation of the fossil records is necessary to understand the phylogeny, evolution, and current diversity of the genus. By applying a variety of geobotanical methods, Richard Pott (1990) of Germany constructed the immigration of *I. aquifolium* from the glacial refugal habitats of Spain to northwestern Europe during the Boreal and Atlantic periods. See Appendix 3 for more information on holly fossils.

The diversity of the genus *Ilex* is due to the very large distribution of the species indigenous to a vast array of microhabitats. The genus is genetically very fluid (plastic) leading to broad basal polymorphic species and population expressions. There are few fertilization barriers when different species are sympatric and flowering concurrently. This fact expands the phenotypic polymorphism.

There are three major geographic centers of current diversity for *Ilex*: two in the Old World and one in the New World. The richest and primary area in the world for *Ilex* diversity is the Sino-Japanese phytogeographic areas including Taiwan, Japan, China, Korea, Myanmar, and the Indo-China Peninsula with, at present, nearly 300 species including about 75 subspecies, varieties, and forms (infraspecific taxa). The second center is Latin America, especially South America and Brazil, with nearly 320 species and 55 infraspecific taxa. The third center is the Malay Peninsula and archipelagos (including Malaya, Indonesia, Borneo, New Guinea, the Philippines, Papua, and the Pacific Islands).

The three areas described above are thought to be the phytogenetic-paleological center of diversity and dispersal of the genus *Ilex*. There are really two or three such centers of evolution and concentric dispersal of the genus, presumably from one, now obscured, central trunk. In addition to the Malaysian area, the species of Latin America (with far more currently known species) demonstrated more affinity with species of North America than with those of Malaysia. Between eastern Asia (China, Japan, etc.) and southeastern North America there are numerous examples of counterpart congeneric species and affinities, such as *I. collina* Alexander (U.S.A.) with *I. geniculata* Maximowicz (Japan), and *I. macropoda* Miquel (China, Korea, and Japan) with *I. monticola* A. Gray (northeastern U.S.A.). Southeastern United States (and into Mexico) is the current center of diversity for deciduous species with approximately 15 species which probably were historically derived from southern migrating evergreen species during the Pleistocene period. With this kind of distribution pattern the genus clearly is of very ancient origin.

The other areas of the world having significant *Ilex* components are the Indo-Himalayan region with 42 species; North America with 23; Europe and Southwest Asia (Turkey, Iran, etc.) with 5; Africa with 2 or 3; and Australia, New Zealand, and New Caledonia with approximately 5. In addition there are 8 named, naturally occurring or cultivated interspecific hybrids.

Allowing for an adjustment factor of 10 percent due to the conspecific nature of some taxa and recognition of synonyms, the current number of species in the world approaches 800, considerably more than the 350 to 425 species given by most references. Accelerated rates of exploration in previously unknown or poorly studied areas such as Latin America, Malaysia, and China combined with taxonomic re-evaluation of the species already known in all geographic areas (leading to monographs and revisions) will without question increase the number of species recognized in the world. Dr. T. R. Dudley has predicted that by the year 2000 the number of *Ilex* species will exceed 800. For example, in China alone 40 plus species new to science were discovered, documented, and described between 1980 and 1989. The description and information on the *Ilex* species now recognized is found elsewhere in this volume. There is a serious need for continuous monographic treatment of the genus.

One of the areas of *Ilex* taxonomy needing further study is the division of the genus into subgenera, sections, and series. Theodor Loesener (1901) grouped species not completely classified under geographic regions where material was collected. This practice, while not satisfactory, keeps groups of hollies from Colombia, Venezuela, Philippines, Jamaica, and elsewhere together. Regrettably there are about 50 *Ilex* species lacking complete information of sections and series due to insufficient data. It is hoped that a young botanist might make it his or her life's study to review all the *Ilex* species and their placement into sections and series.

Two other attempts to organize the genus *Ilex* are worth noting here. Asa Gray (Fernald 1950) recognized three sections in the genus *Ilex*: section *Aquifolium* Gray, section *Prinoides* Gray, and section *Prinos* (Linnaeus) Gray. Krüssmann (1983–1986) divided the genus into two subgenera (one evergreen, one deciduous), each with two sections:

Genus *Ilex* Linnaeus
    Subgenus *Aquifolium* (Gray) Rehder
        Section *Aquifolium* Maximowicz
        Section *Lioprinus* Loesener
    Subgenus *Prinos* Loesener
        Section *Euprinus* Loesener
        Section *Prinoides* (De Candolle) Gray

Neither of these classifications is adequate for our current understanding of the genus, but there are still too many questions, particularly about the evergreen species, to propose a complete classification of the genus. This is due in part to the lack of complete information for some evergreen species and varieties. For example, the type of inflorescence, fruit, and pyrene are important in the classification of *Ilex*. Without complete information it is often impossible to place a species in the correct section and series. Plant explorers in South America in the last several years, following loggers and heavy equipment, collected herbarium material from fallen trees and shrubs. Today, the descriptions of new species often report only flowers with fruits being unknown, or immature. The chances of obtaining this information from autumn or winter collections and even finding the plants again is problematic.

The classification of evergreen hollies awaits further study as exemplified by the problem of the South American species. Prior to 1965 and following, many new holly collections resulting from expeditions into Venezuela, Guayana Highlands, and other areas in South America have accumulated. In 1965 Gabriel Edwin published a paper in which 22 new species and 7 varieties endemic to the Guayana Highlands were grouped into a new section *Guayanoilex* and two subsections and one series. Additional species collected later by others were added. Some species allied to others were transferred to the related sections. Most of these new taxa, which have been described by the late Julian Steyermark, John J. Wurdack, Jose Cuatrecasas, and others, do not conform to Edwin's section *Guayanoilex,* but may be temporarily placed here with species general to the area until more information is available.

Steyermark reported on the difficulties of studying the Venezuelan members of genus *Ilex*. Many of the new taxa are based on either fruiting material or on staminate or pistillate specimens only. Some of the descriptions by Edwin included references to a so-called black pubescence on various parts of the plant. It has now been verified that the black tricomes are only artifacts consisting of fungal hyphal threads. Thus the reference to the black pubescence in the Edwin descriptions has been omitted. Many of the taxa included in section *Guayanoilex* are similar to other species from South America. This presents a challenge to a young taxonomist to restudy the *Ilex* species from South America before all the living plant material in natural habitats are destroyed.

A problem awaiting resolution in section *Pseudoaquifolium* is the relationship of series *Rivulares* Y.-k. Li (1986) to series *Hanceanae, Microdontae,* and *Sideroxyloides,* all in section *Pseudoaquifolium.* A reinvestigation of all taxa in these series is needed to provide and prove and reassessment and reassignment of all species.

The following outline of *Ilex* species by sections and series summarizes the information currently known about relationships among the hollies. There are three subgenera (two evergreen and one deciduous), with sections and series. About 50 evergreen species are *insertu sedis,* that is, their taxonomic position is unknown.

Genus *Ilex* Linnaeus 1735. Evergreen or deciduous, low creeping to intermediate shrubs (rarely epiphytic) to large trees, usually dioecious, occasionally polygamodioecious; leaves usually alternate (four species from New Guinea with opposite leaves); buds small, usually with 3 outer scales; leaves petioled (if only obscurely), entire or serrate, often spiny; stipules minute; flowers actinomorphic, small, usually pale yellowish or greenish white, rarely pink or reddish, axillary, solitary, fascicled or borne in cymes, usually 4-merous or 5- to 9-merous, stamens usually 4–6, alternating with petals; petals small, connate at base, spreading, distinct; fruits bacco-drupes or berries, usually globose; pyrenes usually 4–6 per fruit though 1–18 are possible, smooth, striate, striate-sulcate, rugose or pitted. About 800 species in temperate, subtropical, and tropical regions in North and South America, Asia, Africa, and Australia.

Subgenus *Prinos* (Linnaeus) Loesener 1890. Deciduous shrubs or trees, branchlets with conspicuous lenticels on current season's growth; leaf margins serrate or crenulate, rarely subentire; female inflorescences solitary.

Section *Micrococca* (Loesener 1901) S.-y. Hu 1949. Deciduous large trees with conspicuous lenticels on current season's growth; leaves serrate; fruit small, globose, solitary in pubescent compound cymes or pseudoumbels; pyrenes 6–8, smooth, leathery.
Ilex micrococca Maximowicz 1881
Ilex micrococca f. *tsangii* T. R. Dudley 1980
Ilex polyneura (Handel-Mazzetti) S.-y. Hu 1949
Ilex polyneura var. *glabra* S.-y. Hu 1949

Section *Prinoides* (De Candolle) A. Gray 1856. Deciduous large shrubs or small trees; mature fruits red or black; pyrenes 4–9, rough, striate, stony.
Ilex aculeolata Nakai 1930
Ilex ambigua (Michaux) Torrey 1843
Ilex amelanchier M. Curtis *ex* Chapman 1860
Ilex asprella (Hooker & Arnott) Champion *ex* Bentham 1852
Ilex asprella var. *megalophylla* T. R. Dudley 1980
Ilex asprella var. *tapuensis* S.-y. Hu 1949
Ilex buswellii Small 1933
Ilex buswellii f. *channellii* (Edwin) T. R. Dudley, *comb. nov.*
Ilex collina Alexander 1940
Ilex collina f. *vantrompii* (Brooks) Core & Davis 1944
Ilex curtissii (Fernald) Small 1933
Ilex cuthbertii Small 1933
Ilex decidua Walter 1788
Ilex decidua var. *mulleri* Edwin *ex* T. R. Dudley, *var. nov.*
Ilex kiangsiensis (S.-y. Hu) C.-j. Tseng & B. W. Liu 1981
Ilex kusanoi Hayata 1911
Ilex longipes Chapman *ex* Trelease 1889
Ilex longipes f. *hirsuta* (Lundell) T. R. Dudley, *comb. & stat. nov.*
Ilex macrocarpa Oliver 1888
Ilex macrocarpa var. *reevesae* S.-y. Hu 1946
Ilex macropoda Miquel 1867
Ilex montana var. *mollis* (Gray) Britton 1867
Ilex monticola A. Gray 1856
Ilex poneantha Koidzumi 1928
Ilex tsoii Merrill & Chun 1930

Section *Prinos* (De Candolle) S.-y. Hu 1949. Deciduous large shrubs or small trees; female flowers and fruits solitary or in 2- to 3-flowered inflorescences; pyrenes 4–6, smooth.
Ilex geniculata Maximowicz 1881

Ilex laevigata (Pursh) A. Gray 1857
Ilex laevigata f. *herveyi* Robinson 1908
Ilex phyllobolos Maximowicz 1881
Ilex serrata Thunberg *ex* J. A. Murray 1784
Ilex serrata subsp. *cathayensis* T. R. Dudley 1991
Ilex verticillata (Linnaeus) A. Gray 1857
Ilex verticillata f. *aurantiaca* (Moldenke) Rehder 1949
Ilex verticillata f. *chrysocarpa* Robinson 1900
Ilex verticillata f. *hogdonii* Seymour 1969

Section *Pseudoprinos* S.-y. Hu 1949. Deciduous large shrubs or small trees, branches with spurs; lenticels conspicuous on current season's growth; leaves serrate; ovaries with capitate or cristate stigmas, with styles evident; fruits solitary, depressed globose; pyrenes 6–13, slightly impressed striate, woody.
Ilex fragilis Hooker 1875
Ilex fragilis f. *kingii* Loesener 1901
Ilex fragilis f. *subcoriacea* C.-j. Tseng 1981

Subgenus *Byronia* (Endlicher) Loesener 1897. Evergreen shrubs or trees with many branches and usually alternate leaves, except for 4 species with opposite leaves. Leaves thick and leathery when mature, rarely less than 5 cm (2 in.) long, margins entire or rarely finely serrate. Inflorescences solitary in leaf axils at base of new shoots, rarely panicled or fasciculate (as in *I. venulosa*), long peduncles, often 2–3 irregularly branched, occasionally umbelliform. Flowers dioecious, female flowers often numerous, male flowers usually singular, petals faintly ribbed, appearing with new foliage; ovaries 5 to 6 to 22 locules, with one compressed pyrene in each.

Opposite-leaved Species.
Ilex decussata Heine 1953
Ilex nitens Ridley 1926
Ilex oppositifolia Merrill 1939
Ilex zygophylla Merrill 1939

Section *Byronia* Loesener 1897.
Ilex alternifolia (Zollinger & Moritzi) Loesener 1901
Ilex anomala Hooker & Arnott 1832
Ilex anomala f. *taitensis* (A. Gray) Nadeaud *ex* Loesener 1901
Ilex arnhemensis (F. Mueller) Loesener 1901
Ilex arnhemensis subsp. *ferdinandii* (Harms) Pedley 1984
Ilex bogorensis Loesener 1901
Ilex celebensis Capitaine 1906
Ilex condorensis Pierre 1893
Ilex cymosa Blume 1827
Ilex dictyoneura Loesener 1901
Ilex eugeniaefolia Pierre 1893
Ilex excavata Pierre 1893
Ilex grandifolia Merrill 1934
Ilex harmandiana Pierre 1893
Ilex hypoglauca (Miquel) Loesener 1901
Ilex javanica Koorders & Valeton 1914

Ilex lacunosa (Miquel) Loesener 1901
Ilex laurocerasus Airy Shaw 1939
Ilex macrophylla Wallich 1875
Ilex marquesensis F. Brown 1935
Ilex pachyphylla Merrill 1915
Ilex pleiobrachiata Loesener 1901
Ilex polypyrena C.-j. Tseng & B. W. Liu 1981
Ilex sclerophylla Hooker f. 1875
Ilex sclerophylloides Loesener 1901
Ilex tavoyensis Balakrishnam 1967
Ilex teratopsis Loesener 1901
Ilex thorelii Pierre 1895
Ilex wallichii Steudel 1840

Section *Lioprinus* Loesener 1897.
   Series *Araliodes* Loesener 1897. Evergreen shrubs; leaves glabrous, not punctate, margins entire, with long, slender petioles 25–30 mm (1–2 in.) long; inflorescences solitary, peduncles long and slender; flowers 4-merous; fruits black; pyrenes unisulcate.
   Ilex loranthoides Martius 1861

   Series *Chinenses* S.-y. Hu 1949. Evergreen shrubs or trees; leaves usually crenate, serrate, some entire, stipules absent; inflorescences cymose or subumbelliform; fruits usually ellipsoidal, rarely globose; pyrenes 4–6, usually longitudinally and deeply unicanaliculate; endocarps leathery or slightly woody.
   Ilex atrata W. Smith 1917
   Ilex atrata var. *wangii* S.-y. Hu 1949
   Ilex cheniana T. R. Dudley 1988
   Ilex dasyphylla Merrill 1931
   Ilex dasyphylla var. *lichuanensis* S.-y. Hu 1980
   Ilex debaoensis C.-j. Tseng 1981
   Ilex editicostata H. H. Hu & Tang 1940
   Ilex ferruginea Handel-Mazzetti 1933
   Ilex ficifolia C.-j. Tseng f. *ficifolia* 1962
   Ilex ficifolia f. *daiyunshanensis* C.-j. Tseng 1981
   Ilex hirsuta C.-j. Tseng 1981
   Ilex huiana C.-j. Tseng 1981
   Ilex illustris Ridley 1920
   Ilex jinggangshanensis C.-j. Tseng 1981
   Ilex jiuwanshanensis C.-j. Tseng 1981
   Ilex kwangtungensis Merrill 1927
   Ilex lancilimba Merrill 1929
   Ilex litseaefolia H. H. Hu & Tang 1940
   Ilex longzhouensis C.-j. Tseng 1984
   Ilex lonicerifolia Hayata 1913
   Ilex lonicerifolia var. *hakkuensis* (Yamamoto) S.-y. Hu 1949
   Ilex machilifolia H.-w. Li *ex* Y.-r. Li 1985
   Ilex maclurei Merrill 1934
   Ilex manneiensis S.-y. Hu 1949
   Ilex matsudai Yamamoto 1925

Ilex melanophylla H. T. Chang 1959
Ilex pseudomachilifolia C.-y. Wu *ex* Y.-r. Li 1985
Ilex purpurea Hasskarl 1844
Ilex purpurea var. *pubigera* C.-y. Wu *ex* Y.-r. Li 1986
Ilex pyrifolia C.-j. Tseng 1981
Ilex quianlinshanensis C.-j. Tseng 1981
Ilex robusta C.-j. Tseng 1981
Ilex sterrophylla Merrill & Chun 1940
Ilex suaveolens (Léveillé) Loesener 1914
Ilex suaveolens var. *brevipetiola* W. S. Wu & Y. X. Luo 1992
Ilex tugitakayamensis S.-i. Sasaki 1931
Ilex unicanaliculata C.-j. Tseng 1981
Ilex xylosmaefolia C.-y. Wu *ex* Y.-r. Li 1986

Series *Crassifoliae* Loesener 1897. Evergreen shrubs or trees; leaves glabrous, serrate to serrulate, undersides punctate; inflorescences axillary, solitary; flowers usually 4-merous.
Ilex andicola Loesener 1901
Ilex anonoides Loesener 1901
Ilex crassifolia Hooker 1837
Ilex crassifolioides Loesener 1901
Ilex cuzcoana Loesener 1908
Ilex gabinetensis Cuatrecasas 1948
Ilex julianii Edwin 1963
Ilex karstenii Loesener 1901
Ilex microsticta Loesener 1905
Ilex obtusata (Turczaninow) Triana 1878
Ilex pustulosa Triana 1878
Ilex savannarum Wurdack 1961
Ilex scandens Cuatrecasas 1948
Ilex trachyphylla Loesener 1908
Ilex truxillensis Turczaninow 1858

Series *Dasyneurae* Loesener 1897. Evergreen shrubs or small trees; leaves glabrous, serrate to serrulate, densely reticulate, numerous minute punctate glands beneath; inflorescences axillary, solitary, branched; flowers 4-merous.
Ilex amboroica Loesener 1909
Ilex boliviana Britton *ex* Rusby 1893
Ilex boliviana var. *brittoniana* Loesener 1901
Ilex herzogii Loesener 1916
Ilex hippocrateoides Kunth 1824
Ilex retusa (Klotzsch) Loesener 1901

Series *Excelsae* Loesener 1898. Evergreen trees; leaves entire or serrate, seldom crenate or finely serrate, usually glabrous, rarely punctate; inflorescences usually solitary, distinct stalked peduncles, female inflorescences with 3 to many flowers; flowers usually 4- or 4- to 5-merous, seldom 6- to 8-merous.
Ilex brassii Merrill & Perry 1939
Ilex ledermannii Loesener 1924
Ilex schlechteri Loesener 1924

Series *Laxae* Loesener 1897. Evergreen shrubs or trees; leaves usually entire, some serrate or serrulate; inflorescences axillary, solitary, clearly open and laxly arranged, rarely fasciculate or umbelliform, peduncles usually long; female flowers usually in groups of 3; fruits globose; pyrenes 6–8, dorsally impressed, smooth or unisulcate.

Ilex amplifolia Rusby 1896
Ilex amygdalifolia Rusby 1893
Ilex costaricensis Donn & W. Smith 1914
Ilex gundiachiana Loesener 1912
Ilex macfadyenii (Walpers) Rehder 1921
Ilex macfadyenii subsp. *ovata* (Grisebach) D. H. Nicholson 1991
Ilex mattangicola Loesener 1901
Ilex moana Borhidi & Muniz 1970
Ilex mucronulata Cuatrecasas 1948
Ilex pseudobuxus (Reisseck) Loesener 1893
Ilex pseudobuxus f. *peduncularis* (Reisseck) Loesener 1901
Ilex sapotifolia Reisseck 1861
Ilex sebertii Panchon 1869
Ilex sellowii Loesener 1901
Ilex taubertiana Loesener 1901
Ilex tuerckheimii Loesener 1912
Ilex tuerckheimii var. *subalpina* Loesener 1912
Ilex vitiensis A. Gray 1857
Ilex zippeliana T. R. Dudley, *nom. nov.*

Series *Umbelliformes* (Loesener) S.-y. Hu 1949.

Ilex altiplana Steyermark 1988
Ilex annamensis Tardieu 1945
Ilex beccarianus Loesener 1901
Ilex excelsa (Wallich) Hooker 1875
Ilex excelsa f. *hypotricha* (Loesener) H. Hara 1971
Ilex fabrilis Pierre 1893
Ilex godajam (Colebrooke *ex* Wallich) Wallich
Ilex godajam f. *capitellata* (Pierre) Loesener 1901
Ilex loeseneri Tardieu 1945
Ilex macarenensis Cuatrecasas 1955
Ilex pedunculosa Miquel 1868
Ilex pedunculosa var. *senjoensis* (Hayashi) H. Hara 1954
Ilex rotunda Thunberg *ex* J. A. Murray 1784
Ilex rotunda var. *microcarpa* (Lindley *ex* Paxton) S.-y. Hu 1949
Ilex rotunda f. *xanthocarpa* Shin 1952
Ilex suichangensis C. Z. Zheng 1988
Ilex umbellulata (Wallich) Loesener 1901

Section *Paltoria* (Ruiz & Pavón) Maximowicz 1881. Evergreen shrubs to 5 m (16 ft.) tall; leaves serrate or crenate, rarely entire, lower surfaces glandular or punctate or epunctate; staminate inflorescences fasciculate on second-year growth, or solitary on current season's growth; female flowers usually solitary, rarely cymose, axillary on current season's growth, occasionally fasciculate in *I. triflora;* flowers usually 4-merous; fruits globose, 6–9 mm (7/32–11/32 in.) diameter; pyrenes usually 4, smooth or rarely rugose on dorsal surface, striate, esulcate.

Series *Buxifoliae* Loesener 1897. Evergreen shrubs; leaves small, usually entire, occasionally serrulate or crenulate near apex, glabrous, not punctate; inflorescences solitary in leaf axils, fasciculate, with 1–3 flowers; flowers 4-merous.

Ilex buxifolia Gardner 1845
Ilex buxifolioides Loesener 1901
Ilex congonhinha Loesener 1901
Ilex lindenii Loesener 1892
Ilex mandonii Loesener 1901

Series *Cassiniodes* (Loesener) S.-y. Hu 1949. Evergreen shrubs or trees, branchlets puberulent; leaves usually serrate, rarely entire; inflorescences solitary, axillary on new growth, male flowers cymose, 3- to 9-flowered, female flowers single or uniflorous; inflorescences rarely 3-flowered; flowers usually 4- to 6-merous; fruits red, globose, with pedicels usually 0.5–5 cm (³⁄₁₆–2 in.) long, rarely shorter; pyrenes 4–6, smooth, endocarps thick coriaceous or sublignescent.

Ilex × *attenuata* Ashe 1924
Ilex brandegeeana Loesener 1901
Ilex canariensis Poiret 1813
Ilex canariensis subsp. *azevinho* Solander & Lowe 1901
Ilex cassine Linnaeus 1753
Ilex cassine var. *angustifolia* Aiton 1789
Ilex cassine f. *aureo-bractea*
Ilex cassine var. *mexicana* (Turczaninow) Loesener 1901
Ilex coriacea (Pursh) Chapman 1860
Ilex cubana Loesener 1892
Ilex cumulicola Small 1924
Ilex dugesii Fernald 1895
Ilex flaveo-mollissima Metcalf 1923
Ilex gale Triana 1878
Ilex glabra (Linnaeus) A. Gray 1856
Ilex glabra f. *leucocarpa* Woods 1956
Ilex hakkuensis Yamamoto 1925
Ilex johnstonii Merrill 1950
Ilex kirinsanensis Nakai 1953
Ilex krugiana Loesener 1893
Ilex krugiana f. *pacipertensis* Loesener 1919
Ilex liebmannii Stanley 1931
Ilex ludianensis S.-c. Huang *ex* Y.-r. Li 1985
Ilex myrtifolia Walter 1788
Ilex nunezii Borhidi 1972
Ilex opaca Aiton 1789
Ilex opaca f. *subintegra* Weatherby 1921
Ilex opaca f. *xanthocarpa* Rehder 1907
Ilex poilanei Tardieu 1945
Ilex quercetorum I. M. Johnston 1938
Ilex rockii S.-y. Hu 1949
Ilex rubinervia Tardieu 1945
Ilex rubra Watson 1886
Ilex shennongjiaensis T. R. Dudley & S. C. Sun 1983
Ilex sugerokii Maximowicz 1881

Ilex sugerokii var. *brevipedunculosa* (Maximowicz) S.-y. Hu 1949
Ilex taiwanensis (S.-y. Hu) H.-w. Li 1963
Ilex turquinensis Alain 1953
Ilex uleana Loesener 1905
Ilex velutinulosa Cuatrecasas 1951
Ilex yunnanensis Franchet 1889
Ilex yunnanensis var. *brevipedunculata* S.-y. Hu 1946
Ilex yunnanensis var. *eciliate* S.-y. Hu 1949
Ilex yunnanensis var. *gentilis* (Franchet *ex* Loesener) Diels 1900
Ilex yunnanensis var. *parviflora* (Hayata) S.-y. Hu 1949
Ilex yunnanensis var. *paucidentata* S.-y. Hu 1949

Series *Polyphyllae* Loesener 1897. Evergreen shrubs or trees; leaves crenulate-serrulate or serrulate or crenate-serrate, small, usually 3 cm (1³⁄₁₆ in.) long, rarely 5 cm (2 in.) long, usually glabrous, undersides usually punctate; inflorescences axillary, solitary, rarely pseudopaniculate or fasciculate; flowers 4-merous, rarely 5-merous.
Ilex amara (Velloso) Loesener 1897
Ilex chamaedryfolia Reisseck 1861
Ilex colombiana Cuatrecasas 1948
Ilex cowanii Wurdack 1961
Ilex dumosa Reisseck 1861
Ilex elliptica Kunth 1818
Ilex ericoides Loesener 1901
Ilex glazioviana Loesener 1901
Ilex kunthiana Triana 1862
Ilex lechleri Loesener 1901
Ilex macbridiana Edwin 1965
Ilex maguirei Wurdack 1961
Ilex matthewsii Loesener 1901
Ilex minimifolia Loesener 1901
Ilex myricoides Kunth 1830
Ilex ovalis (Ruiz & Pavón) Loesener 1901
Ilex paltorioides Reisseck 1861
Ilex paruensis Steyermark 1988
Ilex phillyreifolia Reisseck 1861
Ilex stenophylla Steyermark 1951
Ilex suber Loesener 1885
Ilex trichoclada Loesener 1901
Ilex venezuelensis Steyermark 1951
Ilex virgata Loesener 1901
Ilex vitis-idaea Loesener 1901
Ilex weberbaueri Loesener 1905

Series *Rupicolae* Loesener 1897. Evergreen shrubs; leaves rigid, thick, crenate-serrate to crenulate-serrulate to serrulate, glabrous or rarely pilose, punctate or epunctate beneath, 2.5–5.5 cm (1–2⅛ in.) long; inflorescences axillary, solitary, single or lateral; flowers 4- to 5-merous or 5- to 7-merous.
Ilex caniensis Macbride 1926
Ilex farallonensis Cuatrecasas 1951
Ilex naiguatina Loesener 1901

Ilex praetermissa Kiew 1977
Ilex rupicola Kunth 1824
Ilex scopulorum Kunth 1824
Ilex scopulorum var. *caracasana* Loesener 1901
Ilex sessilifolia Triana 1872
Ilex sessilifolia var. *pearcei* Loesener 1901
Ilex suprema Cuatrecasas 1948
Ilex tahanensis Kiew 1978
Ilex uniflora Bentham 1846
Ilex uniflora var. *paramensis* Cuatrecasas 1949
Ilex uniflora f. *pastoensis* Loesener 1901

Series *Stigmatophorae* (Loesener) S.-y. Hu 1949. Evergreen shrubs or small trees, puberulent; leaves usually punctate beneath, margins crenate or serrate; inflorescences fasciculate, 1- to 7-flowered or solitary cymose; flowers usually 4-merous; fruits black, usually globose; pyrenes 4, smooth, striate, occasionally ridge on the back.
Ilex bonincola Makino 1917
Ilex bonincola var. *angustifolia* Nakai 1933
Ilex crenata Thunberg *ex* J. A. Murray 1784
Ilex crenata subsp. *fukasawana* (Makino) Murata 1972
Ilex crenata var. *hachijoensis* Nakai 1926
Ilex crenata f. *longipedunculata* S.-y. Hu 1949
Ilex crenata var. *multicrenata* C.-j. Tseng 1985
Ilex crenata var. *paludosa* (Nakai) Hara 1954
Ilex crenata f. *pendula* (Koidzumi) Hara 1954
Ilex crenata var. *thompsonii* (Hooker f.) Loesener 1901
Ilex crenata var. *tokarenensis* Hatusima 1971
Ilex crenata f. *tricocca* (Makino) Hara 1972
Ilex crenata f. *watanabeana* Makino 1914
Ilex matanoana Makino 1913
Ilex maximowicziana Loesener 1901
Ilex maximowicziana var. *kanehirae* (Yamamoto) Yamazaki 1987
Ilex nokoensis Hayata 1911
Ilex percoriacea Tuyama 1935
Ilex subcrenata S.-y. Hu 1951
Ilex szechwanensis Loesener 1901
Ilex szechwanensis var. *heterophylla* C.-y. Wu *ex* Y.-r. Li 1985
Ilex szechwanensis var. *huiana* T. R. Dudley 1984
Ilex szechwanensis var. *mollissima* C.-y. Wu *ex* Y.-r. Li 1985
Ilex triflora Blume 1826
Ilex viridis Champion *ex* Bentham 1852
Ilex yuiana S.-y. Hu 1951

Series *Vacciniifoliae* Loesener 1897. Evergreen shrubs or small trees; leaves usually entire, or with few serrulate teeth near the apex, lateral veins distinct, not punctate; inflorescences axillary, solitary or single laterals, rarely fasciculate; flowers usually 4-merous; pyrenes usually esulcate. Includes the three species of series *Racemosae* Loesener 1897: *I. confertifolia*, *I. havilandi*, and *I. orestes*.
Ilex alainii T. R. Dudley, *nom. nov.*
Ilex apicidens N. E. Brown 1906

Ilex apiculata Merrill 1934
Ilex asperula Martius *ex* Reisseck 1861
Ilex atabapoensis T. R. Dudley, *nom. nov.*
Ilex auricula S. Andrews 1983
Ilex azuensis Loesener 1913
Ilex baracoensis Borhidi 1979
Ilex brevipedicellata Steyermark 1988
Ilex celebesiaca Loesener 1901
Ilex charrascosensis T. R. Dudley, *nom. nov.*
Ilex confertifolia Merrill 1938
Ilex ekmaniana Loesener 1923
Ilex formonica Loesener 1919
Ilex gagnepainiana Tardieu 1945
Ilex gleasoniana Steyermark 1955
Ilex guianensis (Aublet) Kuntze 1891
Ilex guianensis var. *elliptica* Amshoff 1950
Ilex havilandi Loesener 1901
Ilex hypopsile Loesener 1901
Ilex impressa Loesener 1934
Ilex lohfauensis Merrill 1918
Ilex microwrightioides Loesener 1913
Ilex nummularia Reisseck 1861
Ilex obcordata Swartz 1797
Ilex orestes Ridley 1931
Ilex orestes var. *dulitensis* Airy Shaw 1939
Ilex organensis Loesener 1901
Ilex pseudoembelioides Loesener 1901
Ilex pseudovaccinium Reisseck *ex* Maximowicz 1881
Ilex pubipetala Loesener 1923
Ilex quitensis (Willdenow *ex* Roemer & Schultes) Loesener 1901
Ilex scutiiformis Reisseck 1861
Ilex sintenisii (Urban) Britton 1924
Ilex subavenia Alain 1962
Ilex subcordata Reisseck 1861
Ilex tectonica Hahn 1988
Ilex vacciniifolia Klotzsch 1848
Ilex vaccinoides Loesener 1912
Ilex walkeri Wight & Gardner 1858
Ilex walsinghamii R. Howard 1992

Subgenus *Aquifolium* Gray 1848
  Section *Aquifolium* Gray 1848
    Series *Aquifoliodes* (Loesener) S.-y. Hu 1949. Evergreen trees or shrubs; leaves coarsely serrate; inflorescences fasciculate, staminate fascicles 1- to 3-flowered, pistillate fascicles uniflorous; flowers 4-merous; fruits large, 6–12 mm (7/32–1/2 in.) diameter, with pedicels 2–12 mm (1/16–1/2 in.) long; pyrenes wrinkled, pitted, dorsal surfaces convex; endocarps stony.
    Ilex × altaclerensis (Loudon) Dallimore 1908
    Ilex aquifolium Linnaeus 1753
    Ilex × beanii Rehder 1922

Ilex centrochinensis S.-y. Hu 1949
Ilex clarkei Loesener 1901
Ilex colchica Pojarkova 1945
Ilex cornuta Lindley & Paxton 1850
Ilex dimorphophylla Koidzumi 1928
Ilex hylonoma S.-y. Hu & Tang 1940
Ilex hylonoma var. *glabra* S.-y. Hu 1949
Ilex integra Thunberg *ex* Murray 1787
Ilex integra var. *brachypoda* (S.-y. Hu) Hatusima 1971
Ilex × *kiusiana* Hatusima 1936
Ilex × *koehneana* Loesener 1919
Ilex leucoclada (Maximowicz) Makino 1905
Ilex perado Aiton 1792
Ilex perado subsp. *azorica* (Loesener) Tutin 1933
Ilex perado subsp. *iberica* (Loesener) S. Andrews 1985
Ilex perado var. *lopezlillo* (Kunkel) S. Andrews 1985
Ilex perado subsp. *platyphylla* (Webb & Berthelot) Tutin 1933
Ilex spinigera (Loesener) Loesener 1909
Ilex × *wandoensis* C. F. Miller 1982, *nom. nud.*
Ilex zhejiangensis C.-j. Tseng 1981

Series *Denticulatae* S.-y. Hu 1949. Evergreen trees or shrubs; leaves crenulate-serrate or serrate, rarely entire; inflorescences fasciculate, pseudopaniculate, or pseudoracemose, flowers 4-merous; male flowers connate at base, female flowers with separate petals; fruits globose, stigma with navel-like depression; pyrenes rugose or pitted, rarely palmately striate; endocarps hard.
Ilex chingiana Hu & Tang 1940
Ilex chingiana var. *puberula* S.-y. Hu 1949
Ilex densifolia Miquel 1857
Ilex denticulata Wallich 1830
Ilex kaushue S.-y. Hu 1949
Ilex kudingcha C.-j. Tseng 1981
Ilex latifolia Thunberg *ex* J. A. Murray 1784
Ilex latifolia f. *variegata* Makino 1940
Ilex nanningensis Handel-Mazzetti 1934
Ilex oblonga C.-j. Tseng 1981
Ilex occulta C.-j. Tseng 1981
Ilex perlata C. Chen & S.-c. Huang *ex* Y.-r. Li 1985
Ilex pubilimba Merrill & Chun 1940
Ilex suzukii S.-y. Hu 1949
Ilex trichocarpa H.-w. Li *ex* Y.-r. Li 1985
Ilex tsangii S.-y. Hu 1949
Ilex tsangii var. *quangxiensis* T. R. Dudley 1984

Series *Dipyrenae* S.-y. Hu 1949. Evergreen shrubs or trees, branchlets pubescent; juvenile leaves spinose, mature leaves often entire, apex ending in a spine; inflorescences pauci-fasciculate, 1- to 5-flowered; fruits red, ellipsoid or depressed-globose; pyrenes 2, occasionally 1–4, palmately striate, sulcate; endocarps woody.
Ilex bioritsensis Hayata 1911
Ilex chengkouensis C.-j. Tseng 1981

Ilex ciliospinosa Loesener 1911
Ilex dabieshanensis Kan Yao & Moa-Bin 1987
Ilex dipyrena Wallich 1820
Ilex dipyrena var. *leptocantha* (Lindley) Loesener 1900
Ilex euryoides C.-j. Tseng 1981
Ilex georgei Comber 1933
Ilex miguensis S.-y. Hu 1951
Ilex pernyi Franchet 1883
Ilex synpyrena C.-j. Tseng 1981
Ilex wenchowensis S.-y. Hu 1946
Ilex wugonshanensis C.-j. Tseng 1981

Series *Hookerianae* S.-y. Hu 1950. Evergreen trees or shrubs; leaves entire or crenate; inflorescences pseudoracemose, flowers 4-merous; fruits red; pyrenes 4, palmately striate, sulcate, and rugose; endocarps woody. Includes species from series *Rugosae* Loesener.
Ilex archboldiana Merrill & Perry 1934
Ilex curranii Merrill 1920
Ilex delavayi Franchet 1898
Ilex fargesii Franchet 1898
Ilex fargesii var. *brevifolia* S. Andrews 1986
Ilex fargesii subsp. *melanotricha* (Merrill) S. Andrews 1986
Ilex fargesii var. *parvifolia* (S.-y. Hu) S. Andrews 1986
Ilex gracilis C.-j. Tseng 1985
Ilex hookeri King 1886
Ilex intricata Hooker f. 1875
Ilex × *makinoi* Hara 1936
Ilex × *meserveae* S.-y. Hu 1940
Ilex nothofagifolia Kingdon-Ward 1927
Ilex revoluta Stapf 1894
Ilex rugosa F. Schmidt 1858
Ilex rugosa f. *hondoensis* (Yamazaki) T. R. Dudley 1987
Ilex rugosa f. *stenophylla* (Koidzumi) Sugimoto 1936
Ilex rugosa f. *vegeta* Hara 1945
Ilex xizangensis Y.-r. Li 1981

Series *Insignes* Loesener 1897. Evergreen trees or shrubs; leaves large, 9–20 cm (3½–8 in.) long, margins serrate or serrulate; inflorescences fasciculate, axillary, flowers 4-merous; pyrenes 4, striate, sulcate to rugose.
Ilex bartletti Merrill 1934
Ilex borneensis Loesener 1901
Ilex ketambensis T. R. Dudley 1983
Ilex kingiana Cockerell 1911
Ilex liana S.-y. Hu 1951
Ilex pseudo-odorata Loesener 1901
Ilex sikkimensis Kurz 1875

Series *Lemurensis* Loesener 1897. Evergreen trees or shrubs; leaves usually entire, rarely serrulate, glabrous, epunctate; inflorescences in leaf axils, fasciculate or solitary, female inflorescences with 1–3 flowers; flowers 4-merous; fruits globose; pyrenes striate-sulcate.

Ilex chapaensis Merrill 1940
Ilex embelioides Hooker f. 1875
Ilex gardneriana Wight 1832
Ilex guerreroii Merrill 1915
Ilex maingayi Hooker f. 1875
Ilex malabarica Beddome 1875
Ilex mitis (Linnaeus) Radlkofer 1885
Ilex sumatrana Loesener 1901
Ilex tadiandamolensis Murthy, Yoganarashimham, & Nair 1987
Ilex thwaitesii Loesener 1901
Ilex wightiana Wallich 1848
Ilex wightiana var. *cuspidata* Loesener 1901
Ilex zeylanica (Hooker f.) Maximowicz 1881

Series *Repandae* (Loesener) S.-y. Hu 1950. Evergreen trees or shrubs; leaves crenulate or serrate, rarely subentire or entire, epunctate; inflorescences axillary, fasciculate, male inflorescences rarely pseudopaniculate, female inflorescences pseudoracemose, rarely solitary; flowers 4-merous, rarely 5-merous; fruits 4–8 mm (⁵⁄₃₂–⁵⁄₁₆ in.) diameter; pyrenes small, palmately striate, usually sulcate dorsally on back, wrinkled and pitted on sides; endocarps usually stony (except in *I. cinerea*).
Ilex argentina Lillo 1911
Ilex austro-sinensis C.-j. Tseng 1985
Ilex brachyphylla (Handel-Mazzetti) S.-y. Hu 1950
Ilex buergeri Miquel 1868
Ilex chartacifolia C.-y. Wu *ex* Y.-r. Li 1985
Ilex chartacifolia var. *glabra* C.-y. Wu *ex* Y.-r. Li 1985
Ilex chuniana S.-y. Hu 1951
Ilex cinerea Champion 1852
Ilex cognata Reisseck 1868
Ilex confertiflora Merrill 1934
Ilex confertiflora var. *kwangsiensis* S.-y. Hu 1950
Ilex corallina Franchet 1886
Ilex corallina var. *macrocarpa* S.-y. Hu 1950
Ilex corallina var. *pubescens* S.-y. Hu 1950
Ilex corallina var. *wangiana* (S.-y. Hu) Y.-r. Li 1985
Ilex cupreonitens C.-y. Wu *ex* Y.-r. Li 1985
Ilex cyrtura Merrill 1941
Ilex dasyclada C.-y. Wu *ex* Y.-r. Li 1985
Ilex dianguiensis C.-j. Tseng 1985
Ilex dicarpa Y.-r. Li 1985
Ilex discolor Hemsley 1887
Ilex discolor var. *lamprophylla* (Standley) Edwin 1966
Ilex discolor var. *tolucana* (Hemsley) Edwin *ex* T. R. Dudley, *comb. & stat. nov.*
Ilex dunniana H. Léveillé 1911
Ilex fengqingensis C.-y. Wu *ex* Y.-r. Li 1984
Ilex ficoidea Hemsley 1886
Ilex formosae (Loesener) H. L. Li 1963
Ilex formosana Maximowicz 1881
Ilex gintungensis H.-w. Li *ex* Y.-r. Li 1985
Ilex glomerata King 1895

Ilex glomeratifolia Hayata 1913
Ilex graciliflora Champion 1852
Ilex grisebachii Maximowicz 1881
Ilex grisebachii var. *haitiensis* Loesener 1919
Ilex grisebachii var. *nipensis* Loesener 1923
Ilex guangnanensis C.-j. Tseng & Y.-r. Li 1985
Ilex guayusa Loesener 1901
Ilex hondurensis Standley 1938
Ilex hypaneura Loesener 1892
Ilex hypaneura var. *nudicalyx* Borhidi 1979
Ilex intermedia Loesener *ex* Diels 1900
Ilex kunmingensis H.-w. Li *ex* Y.-r. Li 1985
Ilex kunmingensis var. *capitata* Y.-r. Li 1985
Ilex ligustrina Jacques 1790
Ilex liukiensis Loesener 1901
Ilex loheri Merrill 1925
Ilex macrostigma C.-y. Wu *ex* Y.-r. Li 1985
Ilex marlipoensis H.-w. Li *ex* Y.-r. Li 1985
Ilex medogensis Y.-r. Li 1984
Ilex micropyrena C.-y. Wu *ex* Y.-r. Li 1985
Ilex minutifolia Macbride 1951
Ilex nannophylla Borhidi & Muniz 1976
Ilex ningdeensis C.-j. Tseng 1981
Ilex nitida (Vahl) Maximowicz 1881
Ilex nitida subsp. *bahiahondica* (Loesener) Borhidi 1971
Ilex nubicola C.-y. Wu *ex* Y.-r. Li 1984
Ilex nuculicava S.-y. Hu 1949
Ilex nuculicava f. *brevipedicellata* (S.-y. Hu) T. R. Dudley, *comb. & stat. nov.*
Ilex nuculicava f. *glabra* (S.-y. Hu) C.-j. Tseng 1981
Ilex odorata Hamilton 1825
Ilex paraguariensis St.-Hilaire 1822
Ilex paraguariensis var. *sincorensis* Loesener 1908
Ilex paraguariensis var. *vestita* (Reisseck) Loesener 1908
Ilex peiradena S.-y. Hu 1950
Ilex permicrophylla Merrill 1925
Ilex pingheensis C.-j. Tseng 1989
Ilex pingnanensis S.-y. Hu 1950
Ilex punctatilimba C.-y. Wu *ex* Y.-r. Li 1985
Ilex repanda Grisebach 1861
Ilex repanda var. *hypaneura* (Loesener) Edwin *ex* T. R. Dudley 1979, *comb. & stat. nov.*
Ilex robustinervosa C.-j. Tseng 1981
Ilex ruijinensis (C.-j. Tseng) T. R. Dudley 1985
Ilex socorroensis Brandegee 1910
Ilex subficoides S.-y. Hu 1949
Ilex subodorata S.-y. Hu 1950
Ilex tenuis C.-j. Tseng 1981
Ilex tetramera (Rehder) C.-j. Tseng 1981
Ilex tetramera var. *glabra* (C.-y. Wu *ex* Y.-r. Li) T. R. Dudley 1988
Ilex tonkiniana Loesener 1901
Ilex trista Standley 1926

Ilex uraiensis Yamamoto 1932
Ilex uraiensis var. *formosae* S.-y. Hu 1949
Ilex urbaniana Loesener 1892
Ilex urbaniana var. *riedlaei* (Loesener) Edwin *ex* T. R. Dudley, *comb. & stat. nov.*
Ilex valenzuelana Alain 1960
Ilex venosa C.-y. Wu *ex* Y.-r. Li 1984
Ilex volkensiana (Loesener) Kanehira & Hatusima 1936
Ilex wangiana S.-y. Hu 1950
Ilex warburgii Loesener 1901
Ilex warburgii var. *benguetensis* (Elmer) Loesener 1901
Ilex wattii Loesener 1901
Ilex yangchunensis C.-j. Tseng 1981

Section *Guayanoilex* Edwin 1965. Leaves punctate or epunctate beneath; fruits bacco-drupes, almost always large for the genus; pyrenes average size for the genus;, with U-shaped or broadly V-shaped dorsal surface not common in other species, dorsal smooth, uni-canaliculate, unisulcate; mesocarp usually large, starchy or glutinous. Species native to Guayana Highlands, Venezuela.

Subsection *Florigemmae* Edwin 1965
    Series *Axillariae* Edwin 1965. Leaves punctate or epunctate beneath; female flowers always axillary.
        Ilex archeri Edwin 1965
        Ilex ciliolata Steyermark 1988
        Ilex costata Edwin 1965
        Ilex fanshawei Edwin 1965
        Ilex gransabanensis Steyermark 1988
        Ilex huachamacariana Edwin 1965
        Ilex lasseri Edwin 1965
        Ilex paujiensis Steyermark 1988
        Ilex tepuiana Steyermark *ex* Edwin 1965
        Ilex tiricae Edwin 1965
        Ilex uaramae Edwin 1965

    Series *Lateraliae* Edwin 1965. Female flowers axillary or lateral.
        Ilex duidae Gleason 1931
        Ilex jauaensis Steyermark 1988
        Ilex magnifructa Edwin 1965
        Ilex marginata Edwin 1965

Subsection *Mixtigemmae* Edwin 1965. Leaves punctate beneath; female flowers and buds of mixed racemose; flower-bearing apex leafy or entirely flower bearing.
    Ilex abscondita Steyermark 1988
    Ilex amazonensis Edwin 1965
    Ilex aracamuniana Steyermark 1989
    Ilex lymanii Edwin 1965
    Ilex sessilifructa Edwin 1965
    Ilex sipapoana Edwin 1965
    Ilex subrotundifolia Steyermark 1951

Section *Lauroilex* S.-y. Hu 1950. Evergreen trees, branches glabrous; leaves thick, leathery, entire; inflorescences fasciculate or pseudopaniculate, compound or in threes, cymose or umbelliform, flowers 5- to 7-merous; fruits small, globose, 4 mm (⁵⁄₃₂ in.) diameter; pyrenes 5–7, small, smooth, dorsal surface 3-striate; endocarp leathery.
Ilex omeiensis H. H. Hu & Tang 1940
Ilex syzygiophylla C.-j. Tseng 1981
Ilex venulosa Hooker f. 1875
Ilex venulosa var. *simplicifrons* S.-y. Hu 1950

Section *Pseudoaquifolium* S.-y. Hu 1950.
Series *Chlorae* Loesener 1897. Evergreen shrubs and trees; leaves entire, glabrous, not punctate; inflorescences in leaf axils; flowers small, 4-merous, rarely 5-merous; fruits black with a bloom.
Ilex diospyroides Reisseck 1861
Ilex lundii Warming 1880
Ilex lundii f. *ignatiana* Loesener 1901
Ilex sapiiformis Reisseck 1861

Series *Daphnophyllae* Loesener 1897. Evergreen shrubs or trees; leaves entire or serrulate, usually acuminate, punctate or epunctate; inflorescences axillary, fasciculate; flowers usually 4-merous, rarely 5-merous.
Ilex caliana Cuatrecasas 1948
Ilex dioica (Vahl) Maximowicz 1881
Ilex laurina Kunth 1825
Ilex loretoica Loesener 1905
Ilex nervosa Triana & Plancheon 1872
Ilex nervosa var. *aequatoriensis* Loesener 1901
Ilex nervosa var. *glabrata* Steyermark 1951
Ilex yutajiensis Wurdack 1961

Series *Hanceanae* S.-y. Hu 1950. Evergreen shrubs, branchlets pubescent; leaves leathery or thin, margins entire, apices obtuse, retuse, or emarginate, punctate or epunctate; inflorescences paucifasciculate, cymose, with 1–3 flowers; fruits small, 3–5 cm (⅛–³⁄₁₆ in.) diameter, with pedicels 1–2 mm (¹⁄₃₂–¹⁄₁₆ in.) long; pyrenes 4, striate; endocarps leathery.
Ilex bidens C.-y. Wu *ex* Y.-r. Li 1984
Ilex chamaebuxus C.-y. Wu *ex* Y.-r. Li 1984
Ilex championii Loesener 1901
Ilex hanceana Maximowicz 1881
Ilex tamii T. R. Dudley, *nom. nov.*

Series *Ledifoliae* Loesener 1897. Evergreen shrubs or trees; leaves entire, glabrous, usually revolute, epunctate beneath; inflorescences axillary, fasciculate; flowers 4-merous.
Ilex schwackeana Loesener 1901

Series *Lihuaiensis* T. R. Dudley 1991
Ilex lihuaiensis T. R. Dudley 1991

Series *Longecaudatae* S.-y. Hu 1950. Evergreen shrubs or trees, branchlets glabrous or pubescent; leaves leathery, punctate, apices acuminate with acumens rarely obtuse or

retuse; inflorescences fasciculate, male inflorescences single or 3-flowered, female inflorescences single, 4-merous, rarely 5- to 6-merous, ovaries globose or elongated; fruits
small, globose, 3–5 mm (⅛–³⁄₁₆ in.) diameter; pyrenes 4, rarely 5, striate; endocarps
leathery.

Ilex chevalieri Tardieu 1945
Ilex goshiensis Hayata 1911
Ilex hayataiana Loesener 1941
Ilex kengii S.-y. Hu 1950
Ilex kengii f. *tiantangshanensis* C.-j. Tseng 1981
Ilex longecaudata Comber 1933
Ilex longecaudata var. *glabra* S.-y. Hu 1950
Ilex nitidissima C.-j. Tseng 1984
Ilex oligodenta Merrill & Chun 1930
Ilex retusifolia S.-y. Hu 1950
Ilex saxicola C.-j. Tseng & H. Liu 1984
Ilex strigillosa T. R. Dudley 1984
Ilex sublongecaudata C.-j. Tseng & S.-o. Liu *ex* Y.-r. Li 1984
Ilex wilsonii Loesener 1908
Ilex wilsonii var. *handel-mazzetti* T. R. Dudley 1984

Series *Megalae* Loesener 1897. Evergreen shrubs or trees; leaves usually entire, occasionally serrulate near apex, punctate or epunctate beneath; inflorescences in leaf axils, fasciculate, flowers 4-, 6-, or 8-merous, male flowers large, petals 2–3 to 3–4 mm (¹⁄₁₆–⅑
to ⅛–⁵⁄₃₂ in.) long; pyrenes esulcate and estriate. Combined with series *Pseudoebenaceae*
Loesener 1897.

Ilex brasiliensis (Sprengel) Loesener 1901
Ilex brasiliensis var. *parviflora* (Reisseck) Loesener 1901
Ilex cardonae Steyermark 1988
Ilex euryiformis Reisseck 1861
Ilex friburgensis Loesener 1901
Ilex glaucophylla Steyermark 1954
Ilex integerrima (Velloso) Loesener 1901
Ilex integerrima var. *ebenacea* (Reisseck) Loesener 1901
Ilex integerrima var. *schenckiana* Loesener 1901
Ilex longipetiolata Loesener 1901
Ilex longipilosa Steyermark 1988
Ilex megalophylla (Hemsley) Edwin *ex* T. R. Dudley, *comb. & stat. nov.*
Ilex pierreana Loesener 1901
Ilex psammophila Martius *ex* Reisseck 1861
Ilex pseudoebenacea Loesener 1901
Ilex pseudotheezans Loesener 1901
Ilex ptariana Steyermark 1952
Ilex skutchii Edwin *ex* T. R. Dudley 1993
Ilex tateana Steyermark 1951
Ilex theezans Martius 1983
Ilex theezans var. *acrodonta* (Reisseck) Loesener 1901
Ilex theezans var. *augustii* Loesener 1901
Ilex theezans var. *fertilis* (Reisseck) Loesener 1901
Ilex theezans var. *gracilior* (Warming) Loesener 1901
Ilex theezans var. *grandifolia* Loesener 1901

Ilex theezans var. *riedelii* (Loesener) Loesener 1901
Ilex velutina Martius *ex* Reisseck 1842
Ilex villosula Loesener 1901

Series *Micranthae* Loesener 1897. Evergreen shrubs or trees; leaves glabrous, entire, punctate or epunctate beneath; inflorescences in leaf axils, fasciculate; flowers usually 4-merous, rarely 5- to 6-merous, petals usually 2 mm (1/16 in.) long.
Ilex ardisiifrons Reisseck 1861
Ilex arimensis (Loesener) Britton & Willdenow 1930
Ilex belizensis Lundell 1937
Ilex berteroi Loesener 1892
Ilex blancheana W. Judd 1986
Ilex blanchetii Loesener 1901
Ilex brevipetiolata Steyermark & Wurdack 1957
Ilex cuyabensis Reisseck 1861
Ilex danielii Killip & Cuatrecasas 1925
Ilex daphnoides Reisseck 1861
Ilex duarteensis Loesener 1933
Ilex floribunda Reisseck 1881
Ilex floribunda var. *minor* Loesener 1901
Ilex gentlei Lundell 1945
Ilex glabella Steyermark 1988
Ilex goudotii Loesener 1901
Ilex guaiquinimae Steyermark 1988
Ilex harrisii (Loesener) Loesener 1899
Ilex inundata Poeppig *ex* Reisseck 1861
Ilex jelskii Zahlbruckner 1895
Ilex jenmanii Loesener 1901
Ilex micrantha Triana 1872
Ilex oliveriana Loesener 1901
Ilex petiolaris Poeppig 1852
Ilex pseudomacoucoua Loesener 1933
Ilex reisseckiana T. R. Dudley, *nom. nov.*
Ilex spruceana Reisseck 1861
Ilex tarapotina Loesener 1901
Ilex umbellata Klotzsch 1848
Ilex vismiifolia Reisseck 1861

Series *Microdontae* (Loesener) S.-y. Hu 1950. Evergreen shrubs or small trees, branches light gray; leaves leathery or thin, serrate or subentire, elliptic, oblong-oblanceolate or obovate-elliptic, apices acuminate or with long acumens; inflorescences fasciculate, subracemose or pseudopaniculate; fruits small, globose, 3–5 mm (1/8–3/16 in.) diameter; pyrenes 5–7, small, smooth, with one striate or none; endocarps leathery.
Ilex actidenticulata Steyermark 1988
Ilex brevicuspis Reisseck 1861
Ilex caaquazuensis Loesener 1901
Ilex cauliflora H.-w. Li *ex* Y.-r. Li 1984
Ilex cerasifolia Reisseck 1861
Ilex cerasifolia var. *glaziovii* (Warming) Loesener 1901
Ilex estriata C.-j. Tseng 1981

Ilex forrestii Comber 1933
Ilex forrestii var. *glabra* S.-y. Hu 1950
Ilex karuaiana Steyermark 1952
Ilex microdonta Reisseck 1861
Ilex summa Steyermark 1988
Ilex tsiangiana C.-j. Tseng 1981
Ilex wardii Merrill 1941

Series *Myrsinoides* Loesener 1897. Evergreen shrubs or trees; leaves glabrous, subentire to entire, punctate beneath; inflorescences axillary, multifasciculate, flowers 4- to 7-merous; ovaries usually 9-merous.
Ilex ardisioides Loesener 1901
Ilex epiphytica King 1895

Series *Prinifoliae* S.-y. Hu 1950. Evergreen shrubs or trees; leaves entire, rarely crenulate-serrate; inflorescences fasciculate; flowers 6- to 8-merous; pyrenes 6–8, rarely 4, striate, rarely sulcate; endocarps leathery, rarely woody.
Ilex hainanensis (Loesener) Merrill 1934
Ilex pubescens Hooker & Arnott 1833
Ilex pubescens var. *kwangsiensis* Handel-Mazzetti 1933
Ilex stewardii S.-y. Hu 1950
Ilex wuiana T. R. Dudley 1988

Series *Sideroxyloides* (Loesener) S.-y. Hu 1950. Evergreen shrubs or trees; leaves entire; inflorescences axillary, fasciculate, male inflorescences single or 3-flowered cymes, female inflorescences fasciculate, 1-flowered on pedicels; fruits globose, stigmas prominent, columnar or capitate, styles often distinct, calyces persistent, larger than 13 mm (½ in.) diameter; pyrenes 4–7, striate; endocarps leathery.
Ilex buxoides S.-y. Hu 1950
Ilex cochinchinensis (Loureiro) Loesener 1901
Ilex divaricata Martius *ex* Reisseck 1861
Ilex dolichopoda Merrill & Chun 1940
Ilex elmerrilliana S.-y. Hu 1950
Ilex englishii Lace 1914
Ilex fukienensis S.-y. Hu 1950
Ilex fukienensis f. *puberula* C.-j. Tseng & H. H. Lui 1981
Ilex guizhouensis C.-j. Tseng 1981
Ilex honbaensis Tardieu 1945
Ilex jiaolingensis C.-j. Tseng 1981
Ilex kobuskiana S.-y. Hu 1950
Ilex liangii S.-y. Hu 1949
Ilex memecylifolia Champion *ex* Bentham 1857
Ilex metabaptista Loesener var. *metabaptista* 1900
Ilex metabaptista var. *myrsinoides* (H. Léveillé) Rehder 1933
Ilex salicina Handel-Mazzetti 1933
Ilex shimeica Kwok 1963
Ilex sideroxyloides (Swartz) Grisebach 1857
Ilex sideroxyloides var. *occidentalis* (Macfadyen) Loesener 1899
Ilex sinica (Loesener) S.-y. Hu 1950
Ilex tutcheri Merrill 1918

Ilex verisimilis Chun & C.-j. Tseng 1981
Ilex vietnamensis T. R. Dudley, *nom. nov.*

Series *Vomitoriae* Loesener 1897. Evergreen, large shrubs or small trees; leaves crenulate; inflorescences fasciculate; flowers 4-merous; pyrenes 4, ribbed on back.
Ilex fuertensiana (Loesener) T. R. Dudley, *comb. nov.*
Ilex vomitoria Aiton 1789
Ilex vomitoria subsp. *chiapensis* (Sharp) E. Murray 1982
Ilex vomitoria f. *pendula* Foret & Solymosy 1960

Section *Thyrosprinus* Loesener 1897
Series *Brachythyrsae* Loesener 1897. Evergreen shrubs or trees; leaves densely serrate or serrulate, usually glabrous, punctate beneath; inflorescences in leaf axils, solitary, paniculate or racemose, flowers usually 4-merous, petals 2–3 mm (¹⁄₁₆–¹⁄₈ in.) long.
Ilex biserrulata Loesener 1901
Ilex oligoneura Loesener 1901
Ilex pseudothea Reisseck 1861
Ilex pseudothea var. *cipoensis* Loesener 1901
Ilex trichothyrsa Loesener 1901

Series *Spicatae* T. R. Dudley, *stat. nov.* Evergreen shrubs or trees; leaves papery or coriaceous, entire, glabrescent or pubescent, lower surfaces punctate or epunctate beneath; inflorescences paniculate or racemose, solitary or rarely borne singly and axillary; flowers small or minute, 4- to 6-merous; ovaries often numerous; fruits blackish.
Ilex baasiana Stone & Kiew 1984
Ilex brunnea Merrill 1915
Ilex chimantaensis T. R. Dudley, *nom. nov.*
Ilex chimantaensis var. *pygmaea* (Edwin) T. R. Dudley, *comb. nov.*
Ilex cissoidea Loesener 1901
Ilex clemensiae Heine 1953
Ilex cristata Merrill & Perry 1939
Ilex engleriana Loesener 1901
Ilex engleriana var. *halconensis* (Merrill) Loesener 1942
Ilex forbesi E. G. Baker 1923
Ilex foxworthyi Merrill 1910
Ilex gracilipes Merrill 1908
Ilex harmsiana Loesener 1901
Ilex malaccensis Loesener 1901
Ilex paucinervis Merrill 1920
Ilex pleurostachys Turczaninow 1858
Ilex pulogensis Merrill 1910
Ilex racemifera Loesener 1908
Ilex sarawaccensis Loesener 1901
Ilex scabridula Merrill & Perry 1941
Ilex spicata (Miquel) Blume 1894
Ilex stapfiana Loesener 1901
Ilex subcaudata Merrill 1915
Ilex wenzelii Merrill 1913

Series *Symplociformes* Loesener 1897. Evergreen shrubs or trees; leaves serrate or serrulate, glabrous, punctate beneath; inflorescences in leaf axils, paniculate or racemose, flowers usually 4-merous.
Ilex conocarpa Reisseck 1861
Ilex davidsei Steyermark 1988
Ilex symplociformes Reisseck 1861

Series *Thyrsiflorae* Loesener 1897. Evergreen shrubs or trees; leaves usually close together, usually serrulate, glabrous, punctate; inflorescences paniculate or racemose, axillary, fasciculate, flowers small, usually 4-merous, rarely 5- to 6-merous, petals 2 mm (1/16 in.) long.
Ilex affinis Gardner 1842
Ilex affinis var. *apollinis* (Reisseck) Loesener 1901
Ilex affinis var. *pachypoda* (Reisseck) Loesener 1901
Ilex affinis var. *rivularis* (Gardner) Loesener 1901
Ilex ampla I. M. Johnston 1938
Ilex amygdalina Reisseck *ex* Loesener 1901
Ilex angustissima Reisseck 1861
Ilex casiquiarensis Loesener 1901
Ilex fructiclipeata Cuatrecasas 1951
Ilex humbertii Cuatrecasas 1956
Ilex laureola Triana 1872
Ilex laureola var. *neglecta* Loesener 1901
Ilex macrolaurus Loesener 1901
Ilex martii Loesener 1901
Ilex martiniana D. Don 1832
Ilex nayana Cuatrecasas 1948
Ilex ovalifolia G. Meyer 1818
Ilex thyrsiflora Koltzsch 1861
Ilex thyrsiflora var. *schomburgkii* (Klotzsch) Loesener 1901
Ilex yurumanquiana Cuatrecasas 1948

Unclassified *Ilex* Species. Assignment of these species to section and series on alliance and relationship within the genus is not known to complete the classification. Many new taxa (and old) lack complete information on pistillate and staminate specimens, fruit color, and shape and condition of the pyrenes. Also missing in some cases is information on the habitat and other plants within the area; these are important notes to record when collecting specimens, but often are forgotten when mounting herbarium specimens.
Ilex anodonta Standley & Steyermark 1940
Ilex antonii Elmer 1913
Ilex barahonica Loesener 1913
Ilex bolivarensis Edwin 1965
Ilex brenesii Standley 1926
Ilex bullata Cuatrecasas 1948
Ilex chiriquensis Standley 1936
Ilex cookii Britton & P. Wilson 1926
Ilex daphnogenea Reisseck 1861
Ilex davidsoniae Standley 1936
Ilex eoa Alain 1960
Ilex florifera Fawcett & Rendle 1921

Ilex florsparva Cuatrecasas 1951
Ilex forturensis W. J. Hahn 1993
Ilex holstii Steyermark 1988
Ilex jamaicana Proctor 1967
Ilex jaramillara Cuatrecasas 1990
Ilex kleinii Edwin 1967
Ilex liesneri Steyermark 1985
Ilex magnifolia Cuatrecasas 1990
Ilex mamillata C.-y. Wu *ex* C.-j. Tseng 1985
Ilex marahuacae Steyermark 1988
Ilex maxima W. J. Hahn 1993
Ilex neblinensis Edwin 1965
Ilex neblinensis var. *wurdackii* Edwin 1965
Ilex nemorosa Rizzini 1975
Ilex pallida Standley 1926
Ilex parvifructa Edwin 1965
Ilex pernervata Cuatrecasas 1948
Ilex polita Steyermark 1988
Ilex pseudoumbelliformis T. R. Dudley, *nom. nov.*
Ilex puberula Proctor 1967
Ilex reticulata C.-j. Tseng 1984
Ilex rimbachii Standley 1937
Ilex soderstromii Edwin 1965
Ilex soderstromii var. *ovata* Edwin 1965
Ilex solida Edwin 1965
Ilex spinulosa Cuatrecasas 1948
Ilex stellata W. J. Hahn 1993
Ilex steyermarkii Edwin 1965
Ilex tardieublotii Tran Dirh Dai 1984
Ilex ternatiflora (C. H. Wright) R. Howard 1986
Ilex tonii Lundell 1968
Ilex valerii Standley 1926
Ilex vesparum Steyermark 1951
Ilex vulcanicola Standley 1925
Ilex williamsii Standley 1950
Ilex wurdackiana Steyermark 1988

CHAPTER 9

Morphological Characteristics
of the Genus *Ilex*

HABIT

The members of the genus *Ilex* are deciduous or evergreen trees or shrubs. Less than 30 species are deciduous and approximately 800 species are evergreen. They range in height from tall trees 15–20 to 30.5 m (50–65 to 100 ft.) such as *I. aquifolium*, *I. opaca*, and *I. rotunda* to creeping prostate plants only 1.5–2.5 cm (¹⁹⁄₃₂–1 in.) tall such as *I. georgei* and *I. intricata*, both from China. Most of the reported sizes of plants listed as large shrubs to small trees are based on the collector's report. In many areas the vegetation has been disturbed and cut back so that the actual habit of plants cannot be determined. In some cases the size of plants is given as low shrubs 1–2 m (3–6 ft.), such as *I. colombiana*, *I. cumulicola*, *I. longipilosa*, *I. tiricae*, *I. vitis-idaea*, and *I. weberbaueri*. One climbing shrub is listed, *I. scandens* from Colombia. Some species are described as epiphytic shrubs, including *I. baasiana*, *I. epiphytica*, *I. wenzelii*, and *I. wurdackiana*.

Branchlets

Ilex species are generally slow-growing plants with the annual growth being 5–15 cm (2–6 in.) long. The young branchlets are usually terete or angulate. Most are glabrous or pubescent with simple and straight hairs, while some are puberulent or minutely pubescent, scarcely visible to the naked eye. Pubescent hairs are usually rusty red or grayish to whitish. Occasionally some branchlets are rugose or warty and appear yellowish brown and corky. This excrescent growth is denser on first-year growth and varies from mere ridges to distinct warts.

Abbreviated Shoots or Spurs

Also called short shoots in the literature. Spurs or abbreviated shoots are found only within the deciduous-leaved subgenus *Prinos*. The spurs are 0.5–5 cm (⅜–2 in.) long, densely covered by persistent scars and bud scales of former inflorescences or leaves. Spurs are found on some species (e.g., *Ilex fragilis*, *I. decidua*).

Lenticels

Lenticels are found on all species. They are very conspicuous and obvious on the deciduous species and rarely visible on most evergreen species. Lenticels are usually conspicuous on first-year growth. They are usually elliptic, white, and slightly elevated on second-year growth. Mature trunks of *Ilex poneantha* and *I. amelanchier* are conspicuously white lenticellate.

Terminal Buds

Ilex species have a variety of interesting terminal buds. Some species (e.g., *I. atrata*) have large ovoid buds up to 1–2 cm (⅜–¾ in.) long with thick, coriaceous, and densely ciliate buds. Others have narrow conic, acute buds with loose scales, appearing naked. Some species have well-developed terminal buds, while others have no terminal buds, and still others have poorly developed buds. The presence or absence of the terminal buds, and their shape and size are often of taxonomic significance.

LEAVES

The size, shape, margin, and texture of *Ilex* leaves are important features in the classification of the species. In some cases, however, these features have been overemphasized and have thus added to the taxonomic confusion. For example, *I. crenata* and *I. viridis* are two closely related species that belong in the same section. Yet, due to differences in the size of the leaves and relative thickness, they were initially placed in different sections.

Leaf Size and Shape

Several species of *Ilex* have leaves more than 20 cm (8 in.) long such as *I. dolichopoda*, *I. ketambensis*, *I. kingiana*, and *I. sikkimensis*. *Ilex latifolia* has leaves up to 17 cm (6⅝ in.) long; however, 'Kurly Koe', a new *I. latifolia* hybrid from cultivation, is reported to have leaves up to 30 cm (12 in.) long. The species with the smallest leaves, only 5–15 mm (³⁄₁₆–¹⁹⁄₃₂ in.), is *I. intricata*. Several *I. crenata* cultivars have leaves less than 13 mm (½ in.) long: 'Border Gem', 'Delaware Diamond', 'Dwarf Pagoda', 'Green Dragon', and 'Mariesii'. In the majority of the species the leaves vary from 2 to 10 cm (¾ to 4 in.) long.

Leaf shape varies from suborbicular (e.g., *Ilex nothofagifolia*) to linear-lanceolate (e.g., *I. myrtifolia*), ovate to obovate (e.g., *I. verticillata*), or ovate (e.g., *I. sugerokii*). The unique leaves of *I. cornuta* are subquadrangular to quadrangular-oblong. The leaves of evergreen species are usually elliptic to oblong-elliptic, and the deciduous species are usually ovate or ovate-elliptic.

The age of the plants and environmental conditions can influence leaf size and shape. Vigorous sprouts of a young health plant may have leaves two to three times as large as the normal leaves. The position of the leaves on the branchlet may also effect the leaf shape. Often leaves at the base of the branchlet will change in width upward to the apex. Thus basal ovate leaves will become elliptic to even lanceolate toward the apex of the branchlet.

Leaf Texture

Ilex species show considerable variation in leaf texture. The leaves of some species are thick-coriaceous or leathery. Many species have shiny glabrous leaves (e.g., *I. aquifolium*, *I. latifolia*). Some species have such thick leaves that the lateral nerves are obscured (e.g., *I. elmerrilliana*). A few species have rugose upper surfaces due to the impressed veinlets (e.g., *I. intricata*). Some evergreen species have more chartaceous, paperlike leaves with distinct lateral nerves (e.g., *I. hookeri*). The leaves of subgenus *Prinos* are deciduous with prominent veins. The veinlets are so prominent in *I. tsoii* that the leaf surfaces are marked with distinct minute areolae.

Leaf Margins

About half of the *Ilex* species have serrate or crenulate margins. The teeth may be fine and aristate (e.g., *I. serrata*), coarse and remote (e.g., *I. latifolia*), or crenulate and often inconspicuous (e.g., *I. crenata, I. vomitoria*). About 40 percent of the species have entire leaves; the remainder have spinose leaves or leaves that are serrate in varying degrees. The margins of the spinose leaves in some species may change with age of the plant. In *I. aquifolium, I. cornuta, I. corallina,* and *I. dimorphophylla* the margins of the leaves change from spinose to subentire to entire as they develop from the juvenile to the mature stage.

Leaf Venation

All *Ilex* species have pinnate, netted veins. The midribs are usually impressed above and elevated beneath. The lateral nerves vary from 2 to 20 pairs. About 50 percent of the species have obscure lateral nerves. Venation in herbarium specimens is often affected by the method of preparation; specimens not dried properly often show more pronounced venation.

Leaf Apices and Bases

Nearly all the common apex variations are found in *Ilex*. The apices may be long caudate and acute, caudate and obtuse, acuminate and serrate, short acuminate and retuse, obtuse and retuse, emarginate, obcordate, and tricuspidate and spinose. Both the apices and the bases of leaves may vary with the size and shape of the blades and with the position of the leaves on a branchlet. Leaves on the lower portion of a twig may be ovate with rounded bases and acute apices, while leaves at the apex of the same twig may be elliptic with obtuse bases and acuminate apices.

Petioles

Most species of *Ilex* have canaliculate or grooved petioles, a few have flat or terete ones. The presence or absence of grooves on the upper surface of the petioles is often useful in separating species. The length of the petioles may vary from 2 to 25 mm (1/16 to 1 in.) depending on the species.

Stipules

Stipules are basal appendages of the petioles, 2 per leaf petiole. *Ilex* species are essentially stipulate. In 90 percent of the species the stipules are persistent and present after the leaves fall, often very minute. In some cases the stipules are obscure or absent by abortion. Usually the stipules are minute, callose, deltoid, and less than 1 mm (1/32 in.) long. Large stipules are found in *I. serrata* and are usually 2 mm (1/16 in.) long, pilose, and caducous.

Persistence

The duration (longevity) of leaves varies among the evergreen species. All species in subgenus *Prinos* have deciduous leaves that last one season. The leaves of some species do not remain after the first season, falling off after the terminal buds unfold in the spring. The leaves of *I. aquifolium* and *I. cornuta* persist on third-year growth. The longest lived leaves are persist through the fourth year (e.g., *I. bioritsensis, I. pernyi*).

INFLORESCENCES

In *Ilex* the fundamental organization of the inflorescences is a trichotomous axillary cyme. Through reduction or proliferation of the cymes, and as a result of the evolution of the shoot system, various types of inflorescences were evolved. Staminate plants of many species are cymose where the pistillate flowers are solitary.

Solitary Inflorescences

The solitary type of inflorescence is found only on species that flower on new growth (see Figure 9-1). They are nearly all axillary to a leaf and often associated with an adaxial dormant vegetative bud. The simplest type of solitary inflorescence consists of a cyme with one to three flowers. The peduncles are usually 5–10 mm (³⁄₁₆–⅜ in.) long and the pedicels are usually shorter than peduncles. Two examples are *Ilex serrata* and *I. decidua*.

By branch multiplication the cyme can evolve to a dichotomous compound cyme (e.g., *Ilex maclurei*) or a trichotomous compound cyme with long secondary axes and evidence of tertiary axes (e.g., *I. micrococca*). By reducing the number of flowers in a simple cyme a simple flower evolves with a long pedicel and two median or super median prophylla (e.g., *I. pedunculosa*). By reduction of the number of flowers and the length of the pedicels, a subsessile solitary fruit occurs on a short pedicel 2–3 mm (¹⁄₁₆–⅛ in.) long. With reduction of the secondary axes of a compound dichotomous cyme a pseudo-umbel may be evolved with peduncles 10–20 mm (⅜–¾ in.) long and many bracteoles at the base of the pedicels (e.g., *I. umbellulata*). If the pedicels are also reduced then a subcapitate inflorescence evolves (e.g., *I. tugitakayamensis*).

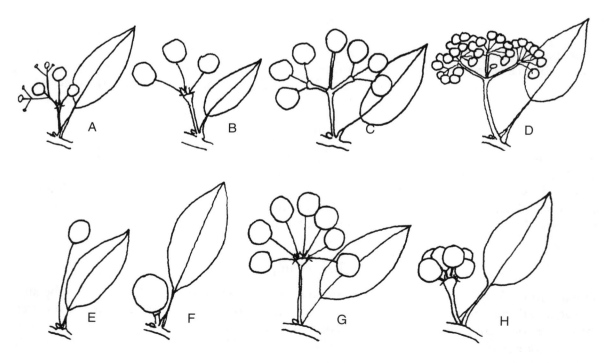

Figure 9-1. Types of solitary inflorescences in *Ilex*. A, B: simple cymes; C: dichotomous compound cyme; D: trichotomous compound cyme; E: long-pedunculate solitary flower; F: short-pedicellate solitary flower; G: pseudo-umbel; H: headlike inflorescence.

Fasciculate Inflorescences

The fasciculate types of inflorescence occur only on species flowering on second-year or older growth (Figure 9-2). They are axillary to old leaves and never have a dormant axillary bud at their bases. Shiu-ying Hu (1950) described eight fasciculate types, while most plant descriptions combine the variations and simply refer to a fasciculate inflorescence.

A sessile fascicle is the most common type with a basal collar formed of several persistent cartilaginous or leathery bud scales, and a short axis with or without an abortive terminal bud. A membranaceous scale subtends each of the 1- to 3-flowered individual branches (e.g., the staminate inflorescences of *I. ficoidea*). By multiplying the branches at the individual branches a fascicle with trichotomous cymes or pseudo-umbels may be evolved (e.g., *I. omeiensis, I. syzygiophylla, I. venulosa*).

With an increase in the number of flowers on the branches and the elongation of the central axis a pseudopaniculate inflorescence will evolve (e.g., the staminate inflorescences of *I. latifolia*). With a reduction in the number of flowers on the branches a loose fascicle or pseudoraceme of uniflorous cymes may develop. The pedicels each have one or two submedian prophylla (e.g., the flowers of *I. intermedia*). With the shortening of both axes and pedicels a compact fascicle of uniflowered pedicels, each having one or two basal prophylla may develop (e.g., the pistillate inflorescences of *I. corallina*). With a reduction in the number of individual flowers in a fascicle, paired fruits are produced (e.g., *I. hanceana, I. georgei*). A single-flowered condition results with continued reduction of the number of flowers (e.g., *I. chingiana*). The position of aborted flowers is indicated by the scar or scars at the base of the short fruiting pedicels.

Structure of the Inflorescences

Bud-scales
Fasciculate types of inflorescences develop from axillary buds. The bud-scales of these inflorescences are often persistent, cartilaginous, or coriaceous. It is often difficult to differentiate bud-scales from bracts because the change in texture is gradual.

Bracts
Bracts are the leaflike scales that enclose the individual branches of a fascicle. Bracteoles enclose the secondary or tertiary branches. Most bracts have stipplelike basal appendages. The shape and size of the appendages are important in classification. For example, species that have bracts with long slender, ciliate appendages belong in the same section.

Prophylla
Prophylla (or prophylls) are the scales on the pedicels that do not enclose flowers. They may be basal, superbasal, median, or supermedian on the pedicels. The insertion of the prophylla is often used as an auxiliary character for distinguishing species, but it is not always reliable. For example, *Ilex tetramera* is differentiated from *I. corallina* by its larger fruits, by its leaf texture, and by the minute prophylla which cover less than half of the fruiting pedicels. In contrast the prophylla of *I. corallina* reach the calyx.

Peduncles
Peduncles are the basal stalks of all the branched solitary types of inflorescences and those of the multiflorous individual branches of the fasciculate types. The peduncles of solitary inflorescences have no bracts at their bases, while the peduncles of fasciculate inflorescences all have basal bracts. The length of the peduncles of a species is a variable character and may be used to differentiate species. For example, *Ilex rotunda* is differentiated from *I. umbellulata* by its shorter peduncles 9–13

Figure 9-2. Types of fasciculate inflorescences in *Ilex*. A: fascicle with 1- to 3-flowered individual branches; B: fasciculate compound cymes; C: fasciculate pseudo-umbels; D: pseudopanicle; E: loose fascicle with uniflorous individual branches; F: compact fascicle with uniflorous individual branches; G: paired fruits; H: solitary fruit of a much reduced fascicle.

mm (¹¹⁄₃₂–½ in.) long, and *I. sterrophylla* is differentiated from its closely related species, *I. editi-costata,* by its shorter peduncles 3–6 mm (⅛–⁷⁄₃₂ in.) long.

Pedicels

Pedicels are the stalks (or penultimate branches) of either the solitary individual flowers or of the ultimate branches of compound inflorescences. *Ilex pedunculosa* has the longest pedicels of an evergreen species, 4–4.5 cm (1⅝–1¾ in.) long, while *I. longipes* has the longest pedicels of decid-uous species, more than 5 cm (2 in.) long. The average length of pedicels for *Ilex* species is 2–15 mm (⅛–¹⁹⁄₃₂ in.) long, with one or two prophylla at the base (basal), at the middle (median), or above the middle (submedian). The length of pedicels is usually a stable character and is used to distinguish species. *Ilex asprella* and *I. longipes* are differentiated from all other species of the decid-uous-leaved section *Prinos* by their long slender pedicels. The length of fruiting pedicels is a dependable character for distinguishing closely related species like *I. macropoda* and *I. tsoii.*

Central Axis

All fasciculate inflorescences types have a central axis. It may be very short or almost completely suppressed (e.g., *Ilex corallina, I. intricata*). It may be nearly as long as the inflorescence and appear pseudoracemose (e.g. *I. intermedia*) or pseudopaniculate (*I. latifolia*). The length of the central axis of different inflorescences on a single branch is variable and not a reliable character to distinguish species. As a subaxillary character it is useful in separating a variety from a species. For example, *I. confertiflora* var. *kwangsiensis* is differentiated from the species by its long central axis of 22 mm (¹³⁄₁₆ in.) long and its large leaves.

Secondary and Tertiary Axes

Compound cymes, both solitary and fasciculate, all have secondary, or sometimes tertiary axes. The presence or absence of secondary axes and their relative length are good distinguishing features. For example, *Ilex maclurei* differs from other Chinese *Ilex* species by having a secondary axis in the infructescence. *Ilex polyneura* is different from its close relative *I. micrococca* by having more lateral nerves in the leaves and by its shorter secondary axes that are shorter than the fruiting pedicels.

Sexual Dimorphism

All *Ilex* species are functionally dioecious, and the inflorescences of nearly all the species are sex-ually differentiated. Sometimes the word *polygamodioecious* is used to describe *Ilex* flowers. *Gray's Manual of Botany* (Fernald 1950) is one source that uses this word. Polygamodioecious simply means that pistils are present, though rudimentary and non-functional, in staminate flowers and that stamens occur in pistillate flowers but are rudimentary. Sex chromosomes are unknown, and there is no method of determining or predicting the sex of a plant without flowers or fruit. Usu-ally the staminate inflorescences are more prolific and the flowers more showy. The abundant flowering is due to the branching of the solitary inflorescences or the fascicle, or through special-ization of the shoot systems (e.g., *I. vomitoria*).

Prolific staminate inflorescences generally result from increased branching. In *Ilex serrata* the inflorescences are solitary, the pistillate flowers are usually solitary or occasionally a much reduced 2- or 3-flowered cyme with peduncles 1–1.5 mm (¹⁄₃₂–³⁄₆₄ in.) long, and the staminate inflorescences are cymose with 9 to 21 flowers and peduncles 3 mm (⅛ in.) long. In *I. purpurea* the pistillate cymes have peduncles 3–10 mm (⅛–⅜ in.) long, usually shorter than the leaf peti-oles, and are 3- to 7-flowered, the staminate cymose inflorescences usually have 21 or more flow-ers, and the peduncles, 4–14 mm (⁵⁄₃₂–¹⁷⁄₃₂ in.) long, always exceed the leaf petioles in length. In *I. latifolia* the fragrant staminate fascicles usually are so prolific that they appear pseudopaniculate. In *I. macrocarpa* the pistillate flowers are solitary and axillary, and the staminate flowers are 1- to

3-flowered, cymose, and often fasciculate. This condition is also common in *I. yunnanensis, I. crenata,* and related species. *Ilex asprella* has only solitary pistillate flowers and fasciculate staminate flowers on uniflorous individual branches.

The inflorescences of *Ilex* are usually inconspicuous. Pistillate inflorescences have fewer flowers than the staminate inflorescences and thus are less conspicuous than the staminate. Female plants in flower are less attractive to collectors. Many herbarium specimens represent only the staminate plant in flower and the pistillate in fruit, or report flowers and fruits as unknown. Many new species proposed by collectors lack sufficient material or collectors do not understand the significance of sexual dimorphism of certain species, such as *I. macrocarpa* with pistillate axillary flowers and staminate flowers 1 to 3 cymose or fasciculate, and consequently add to the proliferating of synonymy.

FLOWERS

The flowers of *Ilex* are usually small and inconspicuous. The majority of flowers when fully open are 5–6 mm (³⁄₁₆ in.) in diameter. The largest flowers of common evergreen species are only 9–10 mm (¹¹⁄₃₂–³⁄₈ in.) in diameter (e.g., *I. latifolia*). Two deciduous species, *I. macrocarpa* and *I. poneantha*, have large flowers 10–13 mm (³⁄₈–½ in.) in diameter, while the small flowers of *I. micrococca* are only 3–4 mm (⅛–⁵⁄₃₂ in.) in diameter.

More than 80 percent of the *Ilex* flowers are whitish, pale yellow, or pale greenish yellow; the others are pink to various shades of red to purplish pink. The flowers of *I. intricata* are brownish. The pistillate flowers of *I. lancilimba* are purplish pink and the staminate flowers greenish yellow. The color of flowers may vary with the habitat of the plant and age of the flowers. *Ilex yunnanensis* flowers have been reported as greenish yellow, yellowish white, pink to reddish pink. There appears to be some correlation of flower color with other characters of the various groups. All the species in the deciduous-leaved subgenus *Prinos* have whitish flowers except *I. serrata*, which has white to reddish pink flowers. Other sections may be based on flowers that are greenish white to yellowish white or pink to purplish pink. *Ilex aquifolium* has purplish streaks. Flowering specimens in herbaria are poorly represented and collection notes on flower color is generally lacking. Flower colors of named cultivars is generally lacking.

The fragrance of *Ilex* flowers is also often overlooked and not recorded. This feature should be noted and recorded for all species. The light fragrance is best observed in early morning and is very attractive to bees. *Ilex latifolia* and *I. aquifolium* are noted for their fragrance.

There are few records on the length of flowering period or on the time of flowering. The length of flowering varies from species to species about 10 days to two weeks. The peak of flowering also varies among species. Species that set their flower buds in midsummer on old wood are the first to flower in the spring, before species that flower on new growth in the spring. *Ilex cornuta* is one of the first hollies to flower in the spring—from mid-March to early April in central Georgia—and is often subject to damage by a late frost. *Ilex opaca* and *I. decidua* flower from mid-May to late May in central Indiana and is followed by early flowering types of *I. verticillata* in late May to mid-June. Some of the late flowering types of *I. verticillata* flower mid-June to late June. Flowers may be seen on *I. verticillata* the first week of August in Maine.

Calyx

The calyx in *Ilex* species is always persistent. At anthesis it is patelliform and after flowering it becomes explanate. The persistent calyx is small, 2–4 mm (¹⁄₁₆–⁵⁄₃₂ in.) in diameter. Many species have large calyces, measuring more than half that of the fruit. Others have small quadrangular calyces 2 mm (¹⁄₁₆ in.) in diameter. The indumentum of the calyx lobes is variable. With *I. triflora* the calyces may be either sparsely or densely pubescent. The cilia on the margins of the calyx lobes are quite constant and may be present or absent. The pubescent ciliate calyx of *I. verticillata* is one among several of the constant characteristics distinguishing that species from *I. laevigata,* which has a glabrous calyx.

Corollas

The size and shape of the corolla of the staminate flowers are constant. The petals are slightly united at the base and always rotate. The petal lobes are usually oblong, 2–3 mm (¹⁄₁₆–⅛ in.) wide or rarely larger. The pistillate flowers of some species are rotate and united, while in other species they are only slightly united. In some species the petals are only slightly united or appear lobed with distinct and separate lobes. The degree of fusion of the petals and the shape of the corolla and lobes seem to have serial or sectional significance.

Stamens and Staminodia

The stamens at full anthesis may be longer than, equal to, or shorter than the petal lobes. The anthers are usually oblong ovoid, 0.75–1 mm (¹⁄₆₄–¹⁄₃₂ in.) long. The shape of the anthers and the length of the stamens may change with the age of the flowers. The aborted stamens (staminodia) of pistillate flowers are always shorter than the petal lobes and bear rudimentary or aborted anthers that are usually glabrous or rarely hairy (e.g., *I. memecylifolia*).

Ovaries and Pistilloidia

The ovaries of female *Ilex* flowers have two to thirteen united or syncarpous carpels. At anthesis the ovaries are usually ovoid, 1–2 mm (¹⁄₃₂–¹⁄₁₆ in.) in diameter, and usually devoid of styles but with a discoid and lobed stigma (e.g., *I. opaca*) or peglike. The ovaries can also be slightly elevated with pointed mammiform stigmas (e.g., *I. kwangtungensis*), or they can be subglobose with a capitate stigma (e.g., *I. tsoii*). *Ilex fragilis* has cushion-shaped ovaries with evident styles and capitate or narrow-cristate stigmas. In *I. macrocarpa* the ovaries are ovoid, with evident styles and columnar stigmas. Usually the ovaries are glabrous, but a few species have sparsely pubescent ovaries and fruits.

After the fruits mature the presence of styles and the shape of the stigmas are constant characters in some species of *Ilex* and important in delineating species and sections. Columnar stigmas are characteristic of many species (e.g., *I. sideroxyloides*), while others have flat or slightly impressed navel-like stigmas (e.g., *I. chingiana, I. denticulata*).

The aborted ovaries of staminate flowers are called pistilloidia. These may be subglobose with obtuse or slightly impressed center, or pulvinate with a rostellate beak. The apices of the stigma *Ilex micrococca* are cleft or bifid. The presence or absence of a small beak on aborted ovaries is of serial and sectional significance. The aborted ovaries are usually always glabrous except in *I. brachyphylla.*

Modifications in the Sexes of Holly

Dioecism is a feature of the genus *Ilex*. All species bear staminate and pistillate flowers on different plants. Gene Eisenbeiss (pers. comm.) of the U.S. National Arboretum, Washington, D.C., reported seeing a pistillate plant of *I. cornuta* produce some perfect flowers and fruits. This was observed under controlled test, and the fruits from the perfect flowers were fertile. Reports of other perfect flowers in holly have not been officially documented. There are reports, particularly with *I. opaca* cultivars, of plants being asexual or parthenocarpic. Again there are no official reports or documentation.

I have observed a seedling staminate plant of *Ilex cornuta* at Callaway Gardens, Pine Mountain, Georgia, with a few scattered small red fruits each year. Unfortunately, the seeds were never checked; however, I have been told that fertile seeds collected from a staminate plant have produced some very strange seedlings unlike the parent plant.

The staminate plants of a species, without exception, produce larger and more branched inflorescences than do the pistillate plants of the same species. This has been observed in both evergreen and deciduous *Ilex* species.

The anthers of a pistillate flower are aborted and sterile. They are small and not fully developed, and the pollen sacs are often not present or are empty. The ovoid pistil is the functional organ of a pistillate flower. The rudimentary ovary of a staminate flower is sterile. It is low and small, cushion-shaped or pulvinate, and usually pinched-in at the center. The functional organs of a staminate flower are the stamens. The oblong-globose anthers are borne on short stalks or filaments, and the thecae or pollen sac is filled with pollen grains.

Some rudimentary ovaries of staminate flowers may develop small fruits. S.-y. Hu reported that staminate plants of *I. yunnanensis* Franchet in the Arnold Arboretum annually produce small red fruits. These fruits have no pyrenes or seed and are about one-fourth the size of normal fruits.

Off-season Flowers

Hollies generally bloom in spring. Off-season flowering is not uncommon in cultivated plants. Staminate plants of *Ilex cornuta* and female plants of *I. cornuta* 'Burfordii', *I. aquifolium* cultivars, and *I.* × *altaclerensis* cultivars have been observed flowering from early to mid fall, especially when a very hot and dry summer is followed by a cool moist fall. These off-season (fall) flowers may produce parthenocarpic development of the rudimentary ovaries. Similar conditions have been observed with spring-flowering pistillate plants of *I. aquifolium* that flower in the spring and are followed by staminate flowers in the fall. Usually the type of inflorescences and the size and shape of the fall-produced fruits are completely different from those of normal fruits. The fall fruits, produced by rudimentary ovaries of staminate plants, often remain on the plant until spring when staminate flowers normally appear. This condition is not seasonal but only recurs when all environmental conditions are right and often is not observed on the same plants from year to year. The environmental conditions are related to the weather, adequate soil moisture, soil fertility, and other factors.

FRUIT

In a botanical sense, the fruit of *Ilex* is not a berry nor is it a true drupe, though it is sometimes called a multiseeded drupe or bacco-drupe. All members of the genus have fleshy fruits (bacco-drupes), chartaceous exocarps, fleshy and often juicy mesocarps, distinct coriaceous, and woody or stony endocarps (pyrenes). Each endocarp contains a pyrene which in turn contains a seed coat and seed.

There is no single term for this type of fruit. In horticulture, a holly fruit is called a berry or a drupe. In 1825 De Candolle used the word *bacca* (berry). Later in 1862 Bentham and Hooker used the word *drupa* (drupe), as did Loesener in the early 1900s. The holly fruit might be called a drupelike berry or a berrylike drupe. In 1950 S.-y. Hu proposed the term *bacco-drupe,* which she defined as a fruit derived from a syncarpous ovary with chartaceous exocarp, fleshy mesocarp, and separated coriaceous, woody or stony endocarps (pyrenes) each containing a single seed. It is hoped that this term will be accepted in popular usage and in technical literature.

The fruit of *Ilex* develops from a superior ovary of a compound pistil. It is composed of two or more segments or carpels, usually four with one seed per carpel. The ovaries of *Ilex aquifolium,*

I. cornuta, and *I. opaca* are usually four-carpellate. As an ovary develops into a mature fruit, the outer layer of cells becomes the exocarp or epidermis and turns red, purplish black, or rarely yellow. The middle layers of cells, the mesocarp, are a uniform mixture of yellowish or bluish black flesh. A fleshy mesocarp is described as carnose, a mealy mesocarp as farinose-carnose, and a juicy mesocarp as succose-carnose. The inner layers of cells, the endocarp, develop into separate leathery (coriaceous), or woody (ligneous), or stony compartments. All these tissues are of maternal origin. Each endocarp (pyrene) has a locule containing a single seed.

Fruit Color

More than 80 percent of *Ilex* species have red fruit. S.-y. Hu reported that more than 95 percent of the Chinese *Ilex* species have red fruits. Many species from South America have black fruits, and a large number of species have no fruit color recorded. The fruit matures in autumn and persists for a long time, unless eaten by birds or animals, or until spring when the plant flowers again. Some species often hold the fruit until the second season. Red-fruited female species and cultivars are generally esthetically preferred for their attractive displays of fall fruit and are a striking sight in the landscape. They attract botanist attention for herbarium specimens, but many specimens are only collected in the spring or summer when the fruit is not mature. Even though black-fruited species are not as showy as red-fruited species they still attract attention. The black fruit of *Ilex asprella* is extended from the branches on long pedicels. *Ilex poneantha* and *I. macrocarpa* have large black fruits up to 16 mm or larger (⅝ in.) diameter. The fruit characters of size, shape, color, pedicels, persistent calyces, styles, and stigma are all helpful in distinguishing the species. Figure 9-3 shows various holly fruits.

Fruit Size and Shape

The average size of *Ilex* fruits is 6–8 mm (⁷⁄₃₂–⁵⁄₁₆ in.) in diameter. The largest fruits are usually in the deciduous-leaved section *Prinoides* and in evergreen species related to *I. aquifolium* and *I. denticulata. Ilex ketambensis* from North Sumatra has the largest fruit reported to date, 20–25 mm (¾–1 in.) in diameter, but unfortunately fruit color is unknown. The smallest red fruit of an evergreen species is produced by *I. liukiensis* from China and is only 3 mm (⅛ in.) in diameter. The smallest red-fruited holly is *I. serrata,* 'Koshobai', a garden cultivar with tiny fruits only 1.5 mm (³⁄₆₄ in.) in diameter.

The shape of holly fruit depends on its longitudinal and the transverse axes, and the width of the basal and apical ends of the fruit. Fruit is *globose* when the longitudinal and transverse axes are about the same. If the transverse axis is longer than the longitudinal axis and the apical and basal ends are flattened the fruit is *depressed globose* or *pomiform.* A fruit is *compressed globose* or *oblong* due to an undeveloped endocarp, and the length of one transverse axis is usually longer than the other. An *oblong* fruit is longer than broad, with the sides nearly or quite parallel. A fruit is *ellipsoid* when both ends are narrower than the middle, *ovoid* (egg-shaped) if the broadest portion is basal, or *pyriform* (pear-shaped or obovoid) with the broadest portion at the apical end.

Fruiting Pedicels

The length of the fruiting pedicels varies from 2–3 mm (¹⁄₁₆–⅛ in.) long (e.g., *I. crenata, I. corallina*) to 4–4.5 cm (1⅝–1¾ in.) long (e.g., *I. pedunculosa*). The length of fruiting pedicels can be used in distinguishing species, varieties, and cultivars. The orientation of the pedicels of various species of *Ilex* is quite constant. The pedicels of most species are upright, while those of *I. pedunculosa, I. asprella, I. geniculata, I. longipes, I. macrocarpa,* and *I. poneantha* curve downward or are pendant.

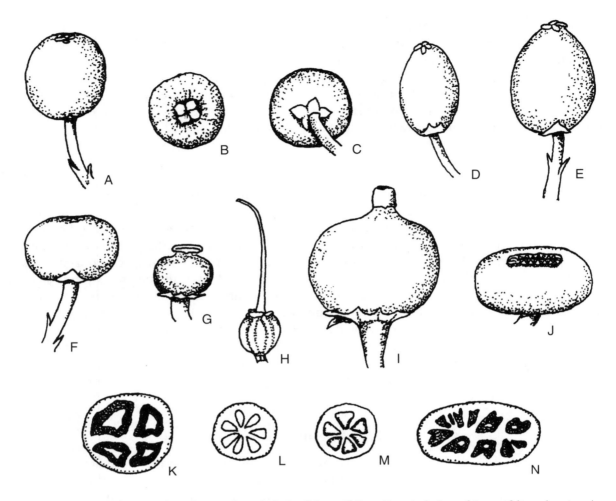

Figure 9-3. Fruit of *Ilex*. A: lateral view of single fruit of *I. aquifolium*; B: apical view of *I. aquifolium* showing 4 lobed disc-shaped stigma; C: basal view of *I. aquifolium* showing the quadrangular persistent calyx; D: ellipsoid fruit of *I. purpurea;* E: ovoid fruit of a form of *I. opaca* with prophylla on the pedicel; F: compressed-globose or pomiform fruit of *I. opaca*; G: subglobose fruit of *I. fragilis*; H: pendant fruit of *I. asprella* with elongate pedicel, ciliate calyx, and capitate stigma; I: large globose fruit of *I. macrocarpa*; J: compressed subglobose fruit of *I. anomala* with very short pedicel and navel-like stigma; K: cross section of *I. aquifolium* fruit, 4 carpellate, thick-walled endocarps; L: cross section of *I. glabra* fruit, 7 thin-walled endocarps; M: cross section of *I. verticillata* fruit, 6 thin-walled triangular endocarps; N: cross section of *I. anomala* fruit, 11 endocarps, 4 seeded and 7 empty. Redrawn by Randy Allen from Hume (1959).

Persistent Calyces

The size of persistent calyces after flowering, as well as the shape, number of lobes, and amount of hair on the calyces vary between species. The persistent calyces of evergreen species of *Ilex* are small, usually four-lobed, and appear squarish or quadrangular (e.g., *I. aquifolium*, *I. repanda*). *Ilex sideroxyloides* and related species are known for their large persistent calyces, which are more than half the diameter of the fruits. The deciduous species of *Ilex* usually have larger persistent calyces than do the evergreen species. The calyx-lobes of some species are obtuse, pubescent, and ciliate along the margins (e.g., *I. decidua*, *I. verticillata*). *Ilex laevigata* has glabrous calyx-lobes without cilia along the margins, and each lobe has a sharp, short, and stiff point, or apicule. The margins of the calyx-lobes may become torn or erose as the fruits mature. This erose condition of persistent calyces can be found on both deciduous and evergreen species.

Styles and Stigmas

The ovaries of *Ilex* species usually lack styles and the stigmas are sessile. The stigmas of mature fruits are constant within a series and sometimes within sections and are useful in distinguishing species. A fruit with a sessile stigma may have a four-lobed discoid remnant, or a plain navel-like mark at the apex. A short style is present in several deciduous species. The apical end of fruits may have capitate stigmas, columnar stigmas, or cristate stigmas. The presence or absence of styles and the shape of stigma remnants are helpful aids in identification of species. Figure 9-4 shows various stigmas and fruits of *Ilex*.

Pyrenes

The endocarp containing the seed of *Ilex* is called the pyrene. All *Ilex* pyrenes occur in one whorl embedded in a soft mesocarp. The abaxial surface or dorsal surfaces are much broader than the lateral or keeled adaxial surface. About 70 percent of *Ilex* species have four pyrenes. This indicates that the premature condition of the flower parts, including the ovaries, probably was four-merous. The species that have more than or less than four pyrenes are generally variable. Those with less than four pyrenes include *I. dipyrena* and related species. The number of pyrenes may be used to separate sections but is not entirely reliable. All species related to *I. aquifolium* have four pyrenes. Other species have more than four pyrenes, and still others have more than 10 pyrenes (e.g., *I. anomala*, *I. arnhemensis*, *I. malaccensis*, *I. pleiobrachiata*, *I. polypyrena*, *I. tavoyensis*, *I. thorelii*). Sometimes the pyrenes are fused partially or entirely. Figure 9-5 shows various holly pyrenes.

Pyrene Size and Shape

Ilex wardii has the smallest pyrenes, about 1.5 mm (³⁄₆₄ in.) long. The largest pyrenes belong to *I. chingiana* and are 15 mm (¹⁹⁄₃₂ in.) long. Those of *I. ketambensis* may possibly be longer. The size of pyrenes from other *Ilex* species are between these extremes.

Ilex pyrenes in cross section are usually triangular. Variations in the cross section may include oblong elliptic or suborbicular. The dorsal and lateral surfaces may be smooth and convex, and they may be ridged, reticulated, pitted, rugose, or uneven. The dorsal surfaces may be three-ridged and two-canaliculate, or they may be widely or narrowly U-shaped.

Pyrenes have various shapes such as oblong, oblong elliptic, elliptic, and (rarely) suborbicular obovate. The ends of the pyrenes are pointed or obtuse, rarely retuse.

Texture and Sculpturing of Pyrenes

The epidermis (covering) of pyrenes may be coriaceous or leathery (e.g., *Ilex crenata*), sublignescent (e.g. *I. rotunda*), woody or ligneous (e.g., *I. pernyi*), or even bony or stony (e.g. *I. latifolia*). The sculpturing of *Ilex* pyrenes is highly variable, but also important in distinguishing species. Two descriptive terms must be defined: striate and sulcate. Striate pyrenes have fine longitudinal lines, channels, or ridges; estriate pyrenes are without striations. Sulcate pyrenes have lengthwise grooves or furrows; esulcate pyrenes are without grooves or furrows.

1. The surface of the pyrenes may be smooth, or estriate and esulcate, free from any vascular bundles of the pericarp, and with coriaceous endocarps (e.g., *I. pedunculosa*, *I. serrata*, *I. verticillata*, *I. glabra*).

2. Striate and esulcate pyrenes may be coriaceous, with vascular bundles attached laterally to the surface (e.g., *I. longecaudata*).

3. Striate and esulcate pyrenes may have impressed striae on the dorsal surface that are smooth, coriaceous, with the vascular bundles slightly impressed into the endocarps, lateral surfaces usually smooth (e.g., *I. crenata*).

Figure 9-4. Stigmas and fruits of *Ilex*. A: discoid stigma of ovary of *I. serrata*; B: mammiform stigma of *I. kwangtungensis*; C: capitate stigma of *I. tsoii*; D: cristate stigma of *I. fragilis*; E: columnar stigma of *I. macrocarpa*; F: globose and pubescent rudimentary ovary of *I. brachyphylla*; G: rostellate rudimentary ovary of *I. micrococca*; H: large fruit of *I. macrocarpa* with columnar stigma; I: long pedicellate fruit of *I. asprella* with capitate stigma; J: large persistent calyx of fruit of *I. metabaptista*; K: small calyx of fruit of *I. ficoidea*; L: discoid stigma of *I. ficoidea*; M: large rugose pyrene of *I. chingiana* ×5; N: triangular smooth, thin endocarp of *I. pedunculosa*; O: 3-ridged, 2-caniculate pyrene of *I. macrophylla*; P, Q: U-shaped pyrene with smooth thin endocarp; R: triangular thick-walled stony pyrene of *I. subficoides*; S: thick-walled pyrene of *I. dipyrena*; T: suborbicular smooth pyrene of *I. georgei*; U: palmately striate and striate esulcate pyrene of *I. georgei* with slightly impressed striae; V: striate and sulcate pyrene of *I. ficoidea*. Drawing by Randy Allen.

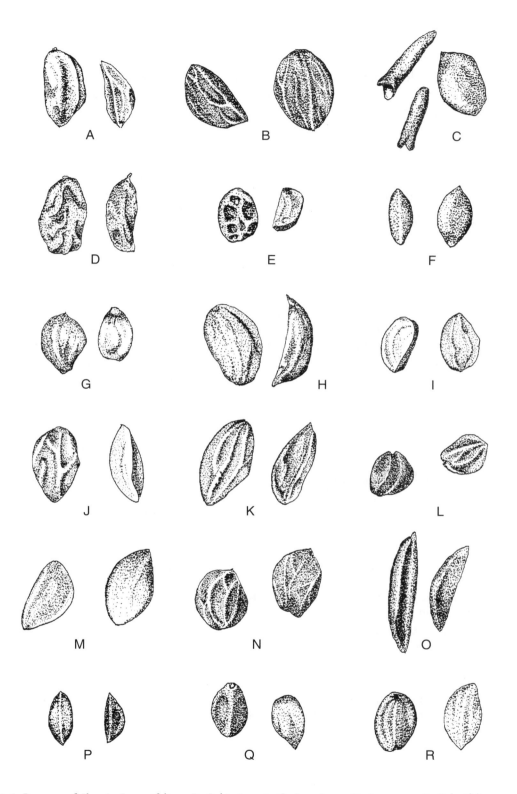

Figure 9-5. Pyrenes of *Ilex*. A: *I. aquifolium*; B: *I. bioritsensis*; C: *I. coriacea*; D: *I. cornuta*; E: *I. latifolia*;
F: *I. laevigata*; G: *I. longipes*; H: *I. macrocarpa*; I: *I. myrtifolia*; J: *I. opaca* 'Cumberland'; K: *I. opaca* 'Miss Helen';
L: *I. paraguariensis*; M: *I. pedunculosa*; N: *I. pernyi*; O: *I. purpurea*; P: *I. rotunda*; Q: *I. serrata*; R: *I. vomitoria*.
Drawing by Randy Allen.

4. Striate esculate coriaceous pyrenes may also have elevated striae, the vascular bundles clinging to the dorsal surfaces, lateral surfaces slightly striate (e.g., *I. vomitoria*).

5. Striate and sulcate sublignescent pyrenes may have three elevated vascular bundles evenly and longitudinally fused to the dorsal surfaces of the endocarps, lateral surfaces smooth (e.g., *I. rotunda*).

6. Palmately striate and sulcate woody pyrenes may have vascular bundles fused to the palmate ridges of the endocarps (e.g., *I. ficoidea*).

7. Rugose and pitted or wrinkled stony pyrenes may have irregularly branched and interveined vascular bundles, lateral surfaces rugose with short broken ridges (e.g., *I. cornuta*).

8. Unicanaliculate sublignescent or coriaceous pyrenes may be U-shaped in cross section (e.g., *I. lancilimba, I. purpurea*).

9. Three ridged and bicanaliculate stony pyrenes may have modified endocarps, with two deep canals on their dorsal surfaces (e.g., *I. macrocarpa*).

Various types of pyrenes are of sectional or serial significance. In the deciduous-leaved subgenus *Prinos,* section *Pseudoprinos* has smooth striate and esulcate pyrenes with impressed striae, while section *Micrococca* has unicanaliculate pyrenes. *Ilex purpurea* and its related species have unicanaliculate pyrenes; *I. rotunda* and its related species have three-striate and two-sulcate pyrenes; *I. crenata, I. glabra,* and their related species have smooth, striate esulcate, or estriate and esulcate pyrenes; and *I. aquifolium* and its related species have palmately striate and sulcate or rugose and pitted pyrenes.

Seeds

An *Ilex* seed enclosed by and including the endocarp is a pyrene. Many *Ilex* species exhibit a deep dormancy due partly to the hard endocarp and partly to conditions within the embryo. The seed contains an immature embryo within the endosperm and must complete its development after the fruit matures in the fall.

Modifications and Abnormalities of Holly Fruit

Abnormalities of the plant and environmental changes may produce modifications in the development of inflorescences and fruit structure. Poor plant vigor, which may result from old age, poor soil, lack of fertilizer, exposure, insufficient moisture, and late or early frost, can effect the development of inflorescences and fruit.

Insects and fungi attacks may cause deformities of the fruit such as being enlarged or unusually small and misshaped. Failure to color, discoloration, premature dropping, or failure to mature may be due to a pest or improper physiological conditions. The green fruits of *Ilex opaca* and *I. vomitoria* fail to turn red when infected by the maggot of the holly berry midge. Phytophthora leaf and twig blight of *I. aquifolium* can reduce fruit production. Proper diagnosis of the problem is the first step to discovering the cause and control. Contact your local county agent, state university, or the Holly Society of America.

Parthenocarpy in Holly

Parthenocarpy is the development of an ovary into mature fruit without fertilization and with infertile seed. This development is common among cultivated hollies. *Ilex cornuta* 'Burfordii' and

I. pernyi are known to fruit heavily without pollination. Parthenocarpic fruits often are not globose but pomiform with four prominent lobes. A cross section of the fruit usually shows empty locules.

CHEMICAL PROPERTIES

The natural chemical properties of *Ilex* species are seldom discussed in horticultural literature. A review is available in an article by F. Alikarides (1987) of the School of Medicine at the University of Athens, Greece. The following constituents are described: phenols and phenolic acid, phenyl propanoids, anthocyanins, flavones, terpenoids, sterols, purine alkaloids, amino acids, miscellaneous nitrogen compounds, fatty acids, alkanes and alcohols, carbohydrates, and vitamins and carotenoids. General and medicinal uses are discussed by Alikarides, followed by a large (154 sources) review of literature.

CHAPTER 10

Systematic Botany
The Classification and Naming of Plants

One has only to visit arboreta, read a nursery catalog, or review a book on plants to be aware of the Latin names given to plants. We soon learn that some plants have no common name and that others have so many common names they would not be recognized in the next state or in different parts of the world.

Latin has been referred to as a dead language. While seldom spoken it is read and does not change. It is accepted as the language for names in biological sciences worldwide and, of course, is the root language for many modern languages. Latin names often seem complicated but soon become familiar through practice as we work with our plants in the garden. Latin names become more important when we realize that they are recognized internationally. For example, the names Japanese holly or Inu-tsuge may not be recognized in some parts of the world, but *Ilex crenata,* the corresponding scientific name, is recognized worldwide (Figure 10-1). Scientific names thus are fundamental for any worldwide system of classification.

Classification or sorting is common to all people and things. Dogs, for example, are a group of animals different from cats and can be further subdivided into collies, terriers, spaniels, and others. Plants were classified by the early Greek philosopher Theophrastus (370–285 B.C.) into four major group: herbs, undershrubs, shrubs, and trees. Theophrastus, who is often called the Father of Botany, also developed the basic concepts of plant morphology. He noted the differences between flowering and non-flowering plants and was aware of many differences in plants, such as corolla types, inflorescences, ovary positions, and other structural features.

Today the Plant Kingdom is divided into divisions, which are composed of classes. Each class is subdivided into orders, which in turn are subdivided into plant families. The family is the smallest of the major classification categories and represents a more natural unit than the larger categories. It is the unit most frequently encountered in taxonomic studies. Each of the major divisions may be further subdivided, such as subclasses, suborders, subfamilies. Some families are further subdivided into tribes and subtribes. See Table 4 for a complete list of the currently accepted ranks.

A family can be composed of only one genus or of more than 100 genera. The holly family, Aquifoliaceae, is comprised of only four genera: *Byronia, Ilex, Nemopanthus,* and *Phelline.* A genus (or generic) name is a singular Latinized noun or a word treated as a noun. The initial letter of a genus name is always capitalized and the name is underlined or italicized. As a general rule, a genus name is spelled out the first time it appears in a paragraph, when it appears alone (not followed by a specific epithet), when it appears at the beginning of a sentence, or when confusion would result if the name were not spelled out. In all other cases, it is acceptable to abbreviate the

Figure 10-1. *Ilex crenata* (Japanese holly) in Japan, where it is known as inu-tsuge. Photo by Fred Galle.

Table 4. Series of ranks provided by *The International Code of Botanical Nomenclature* (Stafleu 1972). Note that names of ranks higher than genus are always written in roman type, while genus names and below are always written in italic type (or underlined). **Boldfaced** endings are common to all names in a given rank.

RANK OF TAXA: EXAMPLE

Division: Magnolia**phyta**
  Class: Magnoli**opsida**
    Subclass: Ros**idae**
      Order: Celastr**ales**
        Suborder: None
          Family: Aquifoli**aceae**
            Subfamily: None
              Tribe: None
                Subtribe: None
                  Genus: *Ilex*
                    Subgenus: *Prinos*
                      Section: *Prinos*
                        Subsection: None
                          Series: None
                            Species: *Ilex serrata*
                              Subspecies: *Ilex serrata* subsp. *cathayensis*
                            Variety: None
                          Forma: None
                            Cultivar: *I. serrata* 'Koshobai'

genus name by using only the initial capital letter. *Ilex,* for example, is often represented in this book by *I.*

A genus may be divided into subgenera, sections, subsections, and series based on continuous or discontinuous morphological characteristics. Eventually a genus is divided into species. In the case of the hollies, it is unfortunate that lack of adequate knowledge about the morphological features such as flowers, inflorescences, fruits, and pyrenes of many species has resulted in confusion with the current classification system.

Swedish botanist Carl Linnaeus (1707–1778), the Father of Taxonomy, replaced the complex polynomial plant name descriptions that were in use in his day with the binomial system set forth in *Species Plantarum* (1753). Since Linnaeus, the species name is a binomial formed by the genus name and the species epithet. To be "complete," all genus and/or species names must be followed by the author's name or by the name of the person(s) who formally published the plant name and description, or transferred the name from another genus, or changed the rank. For example, the complete name for English holly is *Ilex aquifolium* Linnaeus; the genus name is *Ilex,* the specific epithet is *aquifolium,* and the author is Carl Linnaeus. The author's name is often abbreviated, thus "L." or "Linn." can be used in place of "Linnaeus."

It is unfortunate that the three elements of a complete scientific name of a species—genus, species, and author—are seldom used in horticultural books. The author's name is a source of historical information. Frequently two author's names are given with the first name in parenthesis. For example, *Ilex verticillata* (Linnaeus) A. Gray was first described by Linnaeus (in 1753) as *Prinos verticillatus.* Later (in 1857), Asa Gray transferred this species to *Ilex,* so its name became *I. verticillata.* When a scientific name is published by two or more co-authors, the author citations are linked by an ampersand or the word *and. Ilex hylonoma* Hu & Tang 1940 was named by Hu and Tang in 1940. When the Latin word *ex* separates two author names, as in *I. decidua* var. *mulleri* Edwin *ex* T. R. Dudley, it indicates that the name was provided by Edwin, but was published for the first time by T. R. Dudley.

Specific epithets may be derived from various sources, including geographic locations, people names, plant characteristics, or even an arbitrary combination of letters. *Ilex praetermissa* Kiew (1977), for example, means "practically missed." Other examples of the origins of selected specific epithets are shown in Table 5. The *International Code of Botanical Nomenclature* (Stafleu 1972; hereafter referred to as the Botanical Code) recommends that all specific epithets be written with a small initial letter, even when they are derived from proper names.

NOMENCLATURE

Nomenclature (pronounced *no*-men-cla-tur) is the aspect and discipline of taxonomy dealing with correct names of botanical entities for taxa (known plants). Nomenclature is controlled and regulated by the Botanical Code. The term *taxon* (plural *taxa*) applies to any taxonomic group at any rank (e.g., family, genus, subgenus, species, subspecies, variety). By the eighteenth century, because the numbers of plants introduced and named, order and stability was necessary in plant nomenclature. Linnaeus proposed the first rules of naming plants in 1737 and again in 1751. In 1813 a set of rules on the process of assigning names was set forth by A. P. de Candolle in *Theorie elementaire de la botanique.* The rules later evolved into the *International Code of Botanical Nomenclature.*

Once a species new to science has been identified and characterized (1) a name is formulated and assigned; (2) a Latin description must be prepared; (3) a type specimen must be designated and a herbarium of deposit identified; and then (4) all these details must be published in any publication that is available to the botanical community. The name is not valid unless it is published with the above information in accordance with the Botanical Code. For information on the

Table 5. Origin of selected specific epithets.

GEOGRAPHICAL SOURCES
australis	south or southern
canadensis	from Canada; north or northern
colombiana	from Columbia
jamaicana	from Jamaica
montana	mountain
occidentalis	west or western
rivularis	brooklet or brook

PEOPLE NAMES
chuniana	for Woon-Young Chun
hookeri	for William Jackson Hooker
loeseneri	for Theodor Loesener
maximowicziana	for Carl Johann Maximowicz
merrillii	for Elmer Drew Merrill
steyermarkii	for Julian A. Steyermark
wurdackiana	for John L. Wurdack

PLANT CHARACTERISTICS
angustifolia	narrow
corallina	coral red
cornuta	horned, (leaves)
crenata	crenate
cristata	crested
ebenacea	ebony black
integra	entire margin
intricata	detailed
melanotricha	black hairs
opaca	white, not clear, opaque, or dull (not glossy)
paucinervis	few-nerved or few-veined
pedunculosa	long peduncles
serrata	serrate
spathulate	spoon-shaped
verticillata	in a whorled manner

OTHER
dubia	doubtful
geniculata	bent like a knee
medica	medicinal
tectonica	used for construction (from Greek *tektonikos*)
vesparum	covered with wasps

various type categories of the specimens (e.g., *holotype, isotype, lectotype*), see the glossary in this book and Article 7 of the Botanical Code. Two valuable references for plant names are *Index Kewensis* and *Kew Record of Taxonomic Literature Relating to Vascular Plants.* William T. Stearn's (1992) *Botanical Latin* is a very important reference for translating descriptions.

The style of a Latin description varies from describer to describer and is dependent on the describer's knowledge and use of Latin. Many times the description follows a general outline of tree or shrub, branches, and leaves, inflorescences, type and size, calyx, petioles, fruits, pyrenes, size and shape, and habitat. Association with other plants, while very important, is often not included in the original descriptions. It is evident that hollies are generally collected in the spring, as the descriptions often contain little or no information about the fruits and pyrenes. Rarely is a follow-up collection made to obtain this information.

SPECIES

A species (the word is both singular and plural) is a group of individual plants, which are fundamentally alike, indicating a high level of genetic affinity. The species concept cannot be defined in exact terms because different characteristics are used to define species of different genera. Species concepts are often criticized and are under continuing review and synthesis by botanists. When studying a population of native plants, one must take into account that no two plants are ever exactly alike genetically, except if the population is composed of layering root sprouts, or if it is rhizomatous or stoloniferous. The forces of nature and hereditary variances, all involved in evidence, are important in determining the phenotype of a species or phenotypes within a species (e.g., natural variability).

A distinct population of native plants is given a binomial name composed of the genus, and a species epithet (name) both in a Latinized format, plus the authority. American holly is named *Ilex opaca* Aiton and possumhaw holly is named *Ilex decidua* Walter.

SUBSPECIES, VARIETIES, AND FORMS

Natural variations found within a population of a species may be formally designated as subspecies, varieties, and forms. These terms are often confusing to horticulturists and gardeners. Unfortunately their usage is not uniform even among taxonomists.

A subspecies (abbreviated subsp.) is considered a major variation within the species and is often applied to geographically or ecologically distinct populations. The concept is seldom used with *Ilex,* although *I. arnhemensis* subsp. *ferdinandii* (Harms) Pedley 1984 from Australia and New Guinea is one example.

The term *variety* (abbreviated var.) is applied to a lesser variation of a species. The size and shape of leaves, glabrous or pubescent conditions, and plant habit are all variations that may be used to distinguish varieties.

The rank of forma (abbreviated f.) or form is used to designate more local, or sporadic minor variations, again of considerably lesser classification importance on individual plants. Fruit color is one example of a minor variation. In *Ilex, I. opaca* f. *xanthocarpa* Rehder 1901 still designates all yellow-fruited *I. opaca* occurring in the wild. It is doubtful if Rehder's original selection f. *xanthocarpa* is still commercially available. All the various yellow-fruited plants of *I. opaca* must not be given the cultivar name 'Xanthocarpa', but may be called f. *xanthocarpa*. Only the superior forms of yellow-fruited plants should be recognized with fancy cultivar (cultivated varieties) names such as 'Canary' or 'Yellow Jacquet' and must be clonally propagated to retain their cultivar name.

CLONES AND CULTIVARS

A plant grown from seed or dug in the wild, depending upon the variability of the particular species (variety or form), may not be identical to the parent plants or plants of the same species. Therefore, to preserve the horticulturally desirable features of a particular plant, such as a certain kind of fruit, leaf, or habit characteristic, that plant must be propagated vegetatively by cuttings, grafts, layers, divisions, or tissue culture. Such a plant and its propagations are known biologically as *clones* or nomenclaturally as *cultivars.*

A clone is a genetically uniform plant propagated by asexual or vegetative means. The term refers to a horticultural rather than a taxonomic (natural) distinction. The word generally is not used for a group of plants raised from seed, unless they are known to absolutely reproduce genetically true from seed. A cross of *Ilex cornuta* × *I. aquifolium* may produce 100 individual seedlings; each seedling is a different clone.

The term *cultivar,* as described in the *International Code of Nomenclature for Cultivated Plants* (Brickell et al. 1980; hereafter referred to as the Cultivated Code), denotes an assemblage of cultivated plants which can be distinguished by any character (morphological, cytological, or others), and which, when reproduced sexually or asexually, retain their distinguishing characteristics.

Horticulturists and nursery professionals often do not distinguish between the terms cultivar, variety, clone, and sometimes species. *Hortus Third* (Liberty Hyde Bailey Hortorium 1976) defines a cultivar thus: "A cultivar is a horticultural variety or race that has originated and persisted under cultivation not necessarily referable to a botanical species, and of botanical and horticultural importance, requiring a name." This definition is not accepted by every one. The *Ilex crenata* cultivars 'Mariesii' and 'Piccolo', when propagated vegetatively by cuttings, must be called clones or cultivars (or cultivated variety). This can be very confusing as a holly clone is a cultivar, but not all cultivated plants, such as fancy-named pansy plants (herbaceous, annuals, or perennials) grown from seed, are cultivars. A cultivar name is clearly distinguished by the abbreviation cv. before the capitalized name or, preferably, by enclosing it within single quotation marks.

PLANT PATENTS AND TRADEMARK PLANTS

Plant patents and trademark plants are not controlled by the Cultivated Code but are regulated in the United States by the Patent and Trademark Office of the Department of Commerce. The United States Congress enacted the Plant Patent Act in 1930, modifying the regular U.S. Patent Laws. This act protects hybridizers and introducers of new plants and safeguards their investment in producing and introducing a new plant. Similar protection laws exist in other countries.

Plant patents in the United States are guaranteed for 17 years and cannot be renewed (see Darke 1991, Munson 1988). A plant that is patented cannot be legally propagated without a license until the patent expires. Thus, if a 90- to 120-cm (3- to 4-ft.) tall patented plant is sold by a non-licensee on the day the plant's patent expires, it is obvious that an illegal act has been committed. Purchasing a patented plant from a non-legitimate source may also be guilty of patent infringement. Table 6 lists holly plant patents to June 1994.

Since 1981 plant names of the plant patents must have cultivar names. Plant patents constitute valid publication of cultivar names. Trademark names are not the same as cultivar names. Plant patents are nonrenewable, and anyone is free to propagate and sell a patented plant after the patent expires. The cultivar name in plant patents is of free use. The trademark names are not. The National Association of Plant Patent Owners (NAPPO) recommends reserving the use of single quotes exclusively for designating cultivar names, consistent with Article 29 of the 1980 edition of the Cultivated Code. Trademark names should not be enclosed in single quotes, but should always be followed by the appropriate trademark symbol, either ™ or ®. The NAPPO also recommends that consistent use of cultivar names in single quotes and trademark names with their appropriate symbol will help to avoid confusion.

A trademark may be a word, symbol, design, or combination of words and designs that identifies and distinguishes the goods or services of one party from those of another. Trademarks are enforceable indefinitely and can be renewed every 20 years. The Cultivated Code is strictly voluntary, promotes free use of cultivar names, and is not statutory. It refers to trademarks but cannot prohibit the practice of trademarking cultivars or names with a plant patent; however, Article 3 of the Cultivated Code states that "[a] cultivar name cannot, in general, be registered as trademark." Trademarks do not require registration, save for the proper use of the mark. Unregistered marks may use the trademark symbol (™) to indicate a claim of ownership. Registered trademarks offer legal advantages and allows the owner exclusive use of the registered symbol, a

Table 6. Holly plant patents to June 1994.

PATENT NUMBER	NAME OF PLANT	NON-PATENTED CULTIVAR, REGISTERED, OR TRADEMARKED NAME	DATE OF PATENT	INVENTOR	ASSIGNOR
817	*I. crenata*	'Green Island'	28 August 1946	John Franklin Styer	None
887	*I. crenata*	'Stokes'	25 October 1949	Warren E. Stokes	None
1749	*I. cornuta*	'Shangri La'	15 September 1958	Jackson M. Batchelor	None
1902	*I. crenata*	'Oconee River'	2 February 1960	Charles A. Rowland	None
2069	*I. crenata*	'Green Pygmy'	4 July 1961	Anthony M. Shammarello	None
2228	*I. cornuta*	'Cartwright Compact'	19 February 1963	Albert D. Cartwright	Cartwright Nursery
2229	*I. cornuta*	'Spiny'	9 February 1963	Albert D. Cartwright	Cartwright Nursery
2272	*I. crenata*	'Highlander'	6 August 1963	Norman H. Cole	None
2290	*I. cornuta*	'Willowleaf'	22 October 1963	Albert D. Cartwright	Cartwright Nursery
2434	*I. rugosa × I. aquifolium*	'Blue Girl'	11 August 1964	Kathleen K. Meserve	Jackson Perkins Company
2435	*I. rugosa × I. aquifolium*	'Blue Boy'	11 August 1964	Kathleen K. Meserve	Jackson Perkins Company
3168	*I. cornuta*	Berries Jubilee™	16 May 1972	Rowell B. Taylor Jr.	Monrovia Nursery Company
3187	*I. cornuta*	'Carissa'	23 May 1972	John R. Rears	Wight Nursery
3517	*I. aquifolium × I. rugosa*	Blue Prince®	12 March 1974	Kathleen K. Meserve	Conard-Pyle Company
3575	*I. opaca* 'Minard's Red'	—	18 June 1974	Armond V. Matsinger	A. Matsinger
3662	*I. aquifolium × I. rugosa*	Blue Angel®	17 December 1974	Kathleen K. Meserve	Conard-Pyle Company
3675	*I. rugosa × I. aquifolium*	Blue Princess®	7 January 1975	Kathleen K. Meserve	Conard-Pyle Company
3887	*I. crenata*	'Stokes'	25 October 1949	Warren E. Stokes	None
4146	*I. verticillata* 'Winter Red'	—	8 November 1977	Robert C. Simpson	Simpson Nursery
4180	*I. verticillata* 'Winter Red'	—	reissue[1] 13 February 1979	—	—
4367	*I. opaca* 'Steward's Silver Crown'	—	16 January 1979	T. Linwood Steward Jr.	None
4685	*I. aquifolium × I. rugosa* 'Mesid' Variety	Blue Maid®	7 April 1981	Kathleen K. Meserve	Conard-Pyle Company

capital *R* inside a circle (®). The use of the trademark indicates origin, but does not exclude others from propagating the trademarked plant. It does, however, prohibit use of another trademark for the same plant name. A plant patent restricts others from propagating and selling a patented plant without the patent holder's agreement.

The use of trademark names is not new to the nursery industry. For example, Star Roses™ from Conard Pyle Nursery, indicated origin but did not specify particular cultivars or roses. With hollies the use of a trademark in association with a patented cultivar 'Mesog' is now registered and sold as China Girl®. The same is true with China Boy® ('Mesdob') and Dragon Lady® ('Meschick'). These three China Hollies have different parentage than the Blue Hollies. Later, eight Blue Hollies (*Ilex × meserveae*) were patented and three had trade names. When the China and Blue Hollies were first introduced, the names Mesdob, Mesog, Mesid, Mesan, and others were thought to be Code (temporary identification) names and not cultivars. It soon followed in arti-

Patent number	Name of plant	Non-patented cultivar, registered, or trademarked name	Date of patent	Inventor	Assignor
4803	*I. rugosa ×* *I. cornuta* 'Mesdob'	China Boy®	19 January 1982	Kathleen K. Meserve	Conard-Pyle Company
4804	*I. × meserveae* 'Mesan' Variety	Blue Stallion®	19 January 1982	Kathleen K. Meserve	Conard-Pyle Company
4878	*I. rugosa × I. cornuta* 'Mesog'	China Girl®	17 August 1982	Kathleen K. Meserve	Conard-Pyle Company
4996	*I. aquifolium × I. pernyi* 'Meshick' Variety	Dragon Lady™	15 March 1983	Kathleen K. Meserve	Conard-Pyle Company
5004	*I. × meserveae*	Ebony Magic™	22 March 1983	Lester Demaline	Willoway Nursery
5143	*I. aquifolium* 'Monvilla'	Gold Coast™	22 November 1983	Rosendo Avila	Monrovia Nursery Company
6962	*I. glabra* 'Chamzin'	Nordic™	8 August 1989	James Zampini	Lake County Nursery Exchange
6978	*I. × altaclerensis*	'Wight Selection'	8 August 1989	Martin Langmaid	Weyerhauser Company
7652	*I. × meserveae* 'Mesgolg'	Golden Girl®	7 September 1991	Kathleen K. Meserve	Conard-Pyle Company
8537	*I.* 'Hefcup'[2]	Buttercup®	11 January 1994	Randy B. Hefner	Randy B. Hefner (Monrovia Nursery Company)
8792	*I.* 'Wyebec'	Becky Stevens®	21 June 1994	Norman G. Fischer	Wye Nursery
8873	*I. aquifolium* 'Limsi'	—	30 August 1994	Arie Blanken	Conard-Pyle Company
8779	*I. vomitoria* 'Condeaux'[3]	Bordeaux®	14 June 1994	Jerry B. Pittman	Flowerwood Nursery
8793	*I.* 'Wyeriv'	'River Queen'®	21 June 1994	Norman G. Fischer	Wye Nursery

[1]A statement in the abstract for patent no. 4146 claimed that "The hybrid is sterile." This abstract was struck from patent no. 4180 as 'Winter Red' is not a hybrid nor is it sterile.
[2]Sport of *I.* 'Nellie Stevens'
[3]Sport of 'Stokes Dwarf'

cles, manuals, and books that these trademark names of the China and Blue Hollies were seen incorrectly in single quotes. All have now been given registered trademark names as follows: Blue Angel®, Blue Boy®, Blue Girl®, Blue Maid®, Mesid®, Blue Prince®, Blue Princess®, Blue Stallion®, and Golden Girl® ('Mesgolg'). This is contrary to the intent of trademark law which is only to indicate origin. Both the Cultivated Code and trademark regulations do not apply a trademark to any particular cultivar. A trademark name must not be cultivar name. It is not the intent of this book to go into all the ramifications in this present situation; however, a system is needed to provide protection for the right of the developers and marketers of new plants, while preserving order and stability in nomenclature.

Presently there seems to be little concern or consideration for nomenclature stability, and trademarks have been confused with cultivar names by the nursery industry and the general public. In this book the names of trademark plants will appear in the cultivar list with corresponding cultivar names but will not be enclosed with single quotes as a cultivar name, since they are not cultivar names. (Trademark users should obtain competent legal advice on proper trademark use).

NAMING NEW CULTIVARS

Naming plant selections (cultivars) is a distinct responsibility and should be done with the goals of introducing markedly improved or quality plants and making them commercially available. A good name can serve to promote and sell the plant, be easy to remember, and have an attractive, euphonic sound. It is essential to avoid duplication of names and, as an aid to so doing, the name should be internationally registered. Following registration a complete description of the plant should be published. International registration automatically provides valid publication.

Information on specialized nomenclature problems relating to cultivated plants is available in the Cultivated Code (Brickell et al. 1980), which is formulated by the International Commission for the Nomenclature of Cultivated Plants of the International Union of Biological Sciences. The Commission also assigns registrations authorities for various genera.

The Holly Society of America, Inc., is the international registration authority for cultivated *Ilex*. Gene K. Eisenbeiss, horticulturist at the U.S. National Arboretum, Washington, D.C., serves as registrar for the Holly Society and is responsible for registering cultivar names in *Ilex* and maintaining a permanent registration file of these names. All registered cultivar names have been validly published with their appropriate descriptions and historical data in various publications of the Holly Society. A comprehensive list of names registered from 1958 to 1983 has been published (Eisenbeiss and Dudley 1983), and a new *Ilex* cultivar registration list is available for 1958 to 1993 (Eisenbeiss 1995). Information and registration applications (fee $5.00) are available from Gene Eisenbeiss, U.S. National Arboretum, 3501 New York Avenue NE, Washington, D.C. 20002.

The importance of registration is evident. Frequent confusion arose in the past from use of the same clonal name for plants of different origins. Breeders and introducers are not obligated to register their named hollies and, in the past, names of patented plants were not registered. These omissions only added to the problems for the growers and consumers, gardeners and taxonomists. As the value of registration is recognized and accepted, confusions, mistakes, and duplications of plant names may be prevented in the present and future and can also be corrected from the past.

GUIDE TO REGISTRATION OF HOLLY PLANTS

The Cultivated Code is an excellent reference in the naming of plants and should be in the hands of all breeders, introducers, and namers. Some of the general rules governing cultivar names are as follows:

1. New hollies should be introduced only as cultivars and should be vegetatively propagated.

2. New cultivar names published after 1 January 1959 must be fancy names in any modern language and not in Latin form.

3. Cultivar names, when following a botanical name, must be distinguished by the abbreviation cv. or enclosed in single quotes such as *I. aquifolium* 'Alaska', but not both. Two or more cultivars in *Ilex* are not permitted to have the same name in the same cultivar class (*Ilex* has only one cultivar class) after 1 January 1959.

4. Similar names which differ only slightly in spelling from existing names should be avoided.

5. New names should preferably consist of one or two words and must not consist of more than three words or elements; an abbreviation or numeral is counted as an element.

6. Cultivar names *cannot* be formed by combining parts of the Latin or species name, such as *I. crenajaponica*.

7. Names composed of abbreviations, numerals, or arbitrary sequence of letters should be avoided.

8. Proper names, such as Boston, Seattle, and so forth, should be avoided.

9. Words should be spelled out, not abbreviated, except for the abbreviation *Mrs.* Example: 'Kingsville Dwarf' not 'Kingsville Dwf'.

10. Names exaggerating the merits of the cultivar, which may become inaccurate through the introduction of future cultivars, must be avoided. Example: *Ilex* 'Earliest Red Berries' or *I.* 'Largest Fruit'.

11. Names that refer to some attribute likely to be common to other cultivars should be avoided. Example: 'Yellow Queen' but not 'Yellow Fruit.'

12. Cultivar names in languages using Roman letters should be left unchanged. Transliterated names from Cyrillic or other language are regarded as the original name. Example: *I. crenata* 'Nakada' and *I. crenata* 'Wiesmoor Silber'. However, cultivar names, **not** common names, originally formulated in a Roman alphabet may be transliterated or translated to Roman type.

13. New holly names are not recognized as legitimate under the Code unless their names and descriptions are validly published.

14. The parentage of new hybrid hollies should be given when known, with the female parent listed first. In some countries the parentage is often listed in reverse or in alphabetical order; in such cases the sex of each parent should be indicated. Example: *I. crenata* 'Green Dragon' ('Mariesii' × 'John Nosal') or ('John Nosal', male, × 'Mariesii', female).

15. The description should include the names of the originator and/or introducer, Holly Society of America registration number (H.S.A. 1-89), date of introduction, foliage description, fruit size and color, plant habit, hardiness, and any especially significant features that differentiate this plant from other cultivars.

With a little imagination we should never run out of suitable names. For stimulation we need only look at other International Plant Registers for ideas, such as the list of roses, narcissus, or hemerocallis. The important thing is to internationally **register new names to avoid confusion and duplication of names** so common in the past.

✦ PART III

CHAPTER 11

Deciduous Holly Species

Ilex aculeolata Nakai 1930 (synonyms *I. dubia* var. *hupehensis* Handel-Mazzetti 1933, *I. rhamnifolia* Merrill 1934, *I. aculeolata* var. *kiangsiensis* S.-y. Hu 1949).

Deciduous shrubs to 2 m (6 ft.) tall with brown branches, elongated spur branchlets and conspicuous lenticels; leaves obovate, 2–5 cm (¾–2 in.) long, 1–3 cm (⅜–1⅜ in.) wide, usually sparsely pubescent on both surfaces, margins coarsely serrate; fruits black, globose, 7 mm (¼ in.) diameter, solitary; pyrenes 4, deeply striate. Habitat: People's Republic of China, Hunan and Jiangxi provinces, and south to northern Guangdong and Guangxi provinces in woodland areas at 250–600 m (825–2000 ft.) elevation. Allied to *I. pubescens*.

Ilex ambigua (Michaux) Torrey 1843. Mountain holly, mountain winterberry (synonyms *Prinos ambiguus* Michaux 1803, *Synstima caroliniana* (Walter) Rafinesque 1838, *I. montana* var. *ambigua* (Torrey & Gray) Ashe 1864, *Synstima ambigua* (Michaux) Rafinesque *ex* S. Watson 1887, *Synstima caroliniana* (Walter) Trelease 1889).

Deciduous, large shrubs or small trees to 6 m (20 ft.) tall with glabrous purplish twigs; leaves elliptic, ovate, or suborbicular, 4–7 cm (1½–2¾ in.) long, serrulate or crenate-serrulate at least above the middle; fruits red, globose, 6–7 mm (³⁄₁₆–¼ in.) diameter, solitary, matures early but seldom persists after November; pyrenes ribbed. Habitat: United States, found in hammocks and sand hill areas with live oak, hawthorn, and hickory in the southern Coastal Plains area, from North Carolina to Florida, west into Alabama, Mississippi, Texas, and Arkansas. Hardy in zones 6 to 9b. Very variable growth habit; leaf size, shape, and pubescence; and fruit size. Allied to *I. decidua*.

Ilex amelanchier M. Curtis *ex* Chapman 1860. Sarvis or swamp holly (synonyms *Prinos dubia* G. Don 1832, *I. dubia* (G. Don) Britton, Stern, & Poggenburg 1888).

Deciduous, large shrubs to 6 m (20 ft.) tall, branches with both elongate and spur branchlets, slightly pubescent; leaves ovate to obovate, 4–8 cm (1½–3½ in.) long, finely serrate, pubescent beneath, dried leaves often persist in the fall; fruits solitary, dull red with a soft bloom, globose 7–10 mm (¼–⅜ in.) diameter, pedicels to 2 cm (¾ in.) long; pyrenes grooved. Habitat: southeastern United States, in shady swamps of the Coastal Plains from southern Virginia to northern Florida, west to Alabama, Mississippi and eastern Louisiana. Hardy in zones 6 to 9. This uncommon plant shows some affinity to *I. brandegeeana* from Mexico. Closest ally among North American species is *I. longipes*. Introduced in 1880. Plates 29, 30.

Ilex asprella (Hooker & Arnott) Champion *ex* Bentham 1852 var. *asprella* (synonyms *Prinos asprellus* Hooker & Arnott 1833, *I. oxyphylla* Miquel 1861).

Deciduous, large shrubs to 3 m (10 ft.) tall with slender branches and spurs, lenticels conspicuous; leaves ovate or ovate-elliptic, 3–7 cm (1³⁄₁₆–2¾ in.) long, 1.5–3 cm (⁹⁄₃₂–1³⁄₁₆ in.) wide, margins serrate, apices acute, finely pubescent above, glabrous beneath; flowers white, 4- to 5-lobed, solitary or in axillary umbels; fruits black, globose, 5–6 mm (³⁄₁₆–⁷⁄₃₂ in.) diameter, pedicels pendant, 2–3 cm (¾–1³⁄₁₆ in.) long; pyrenes 4–6, elliptic, 3-striate ridges. A common shrub in the coastal provinces of warm-temperate and subtropical climates. Habitat: southeastern People's Republic of China, Hong Kong, Vietnam. Common in Taiwan and the only deciduous species of *Ilex* in the Philippine Islands, where it occurs 1200–1900 m (3900–6300 ft.) elevation. Al-

Figure 11-1. *Ilex amelanchier.* Photo by Barton Bauer Sr.

lied to *I. longipes* of the southeastern United States. Introduced to the United States in 1960.

Ilex asprella var. *megalophylla* T. R. Dudley 1980.
Differs from variety *asprella* by larger leaves that are (5–)6–12 cm (2⅜–4¾ in.) long, (2–) 3–4 cm (1³⁄₁₆–1⅝ in.) wide; longer acumens, 1.5–2 cm (½–¾ in.) long; generally longer pedicels of the male flowers, 1–2 cm (⅜–¾ in.) long; and the usually shorter pedicels of the female flowers, 1–2 cm (⅜–¾ in.) long. Holotype from the Philippine Islands, Island of Negros.

Ilex asprella var. *tapuensis* S.-y. Hu 1949.
A large-fruited variety, 8–9 mm (⁵⁄₁₆–1¹⁄₃₂ in.) diameter. Habitat: People's Republic of China. Collected at Tapu, eastern Guangdong Province.

Ilex buswellii Small 1933 f. *buswellii.* Buswell's possumhaw holly (synonym *I. ambigua* (Michaux) Chapman 1860).
Deciduous, large shrubs to 3 m (10 ft.) tall, heav-

ily branched with dark purple glabrous twigs; leaves elliptic to ovate, 2–3 cm (¾–1¼ in.) long, margins serrulate above the middle; fruits shiny red, globose, 9–11 mm (¹¹⁄₃₂–1³⁄₃₂ in.) diameter; pyrenes ribbed. Habitat: United States. The southernmost native deciduous species in North America. Originally reported in hammocks along the Caloosahatchee River in Florida, near Fort Myers. Last reported site was in the Daytona Beach area, Lake County, Florida; area now destroyed. Possibly still on other island dunes and localities in Lake County such as Lake Harris. Hardy in zones 7 to 10.

Ilex buswellii f. *channellii* (Edwin) T. R. Dudley, *comb. nov.* (basionym *I. ambigua* f. *channellii* Edwin, *Rhodora* 59: 23. 1957).
This form differs from typical *I. buswellii* by having soft puberulent branches, with short soft, white hairs; leaves occasionally to 4 cm (1⅝ in.) long. Habitat: United States, very rare in Mississippi. Holotype: Jackson, Mississippi, 16 August 1953, *R. B. Channell 2440* (US); isotypes, NA, Duke.

Ilex collina Alexander 1940 f. *collina* (synonym *Nemopanthus collinus* (Alexander) Clark 1974).
Deciduous large shrubs or small trees 3–4 m (10–

Figure 11-2. *Ilex asprella* var. *asprella.* Drawing by Chien-chu Chen in *Illustrations of Native and Introduced Ligneous Plants of Taiwan* (1962) by Tang-shui Liu.

13 ft.) tall; leaves broadly elliptic to obovate, finely serrate with teeth ending in a small gland; fruits red, globose, 7–8 mm (¼–⁵⁄₁₆ in.) diameter, sometimes turbinate, pedicels 10–13 mm (⅜–½ in.) long. Habitat: United States; discovered first in West Virginia, then in Virginia in 1941 at high altitudes. Very rare, scattered distribution in West Virginia, southwestern Virginia, and isolated mountainous areas of North Carolina and Tennessee. Often confused with *I. longipes* and shows some affinity with *I. verticillata* in the United States due to the leaf margin and shape of the calyx lobes. Closest affinity is with *I. geniculata* in Japan. Incorrectly considered to be a species of *Nemopanthus.* Hardy in zone 3. Several cultivars have been registered (see the cultivar list).

Ilex collina f. *vantrompii* (Brooks) Core & Davis 1944 (synonyms *I. longipes* f. *vantrompii* Brooks 1940, *Nemopanthus collinus* f. *vantrompii* (Brooks) Clark 1974).

A yellow-fruited form from Cheat Mountain, West Virginia, named in 1940 for the discoverer, H. O. Van Tromp. Never rediscovered in the wild. Not known in cultivation. Female.

Ilex curtissii (Fernald) Small 1933. Curtiss's holly (synonym *I. decidua* var. *curtissii* Fernald 1902).

Deciduous, large shrubs or small trees to 5 m (15 ft.) tall, spreading branches, glabrous with elongated and spur branchlets; leaves thin, lanceolate to elliptic spathulate, 2–3.5 cm (¾–1⅜ in.) long, margin ob-scurely crenate; fruits red, globose, 4–5 mm (⁵⁄₃₂–³⁄₁₆ in.) diameter, borne singly or in small clusters. Habitat: southeastern United States in hammocks along the Suwannee River in Florida. Hardy in zones 7 to 10. Often regarded as a variety or synonym of *I. decidua,* but has consistently smaller leaves of thinner texture and longer pedicels. Plate 31.

Ilex cuthbertii Small 1933. Cuthbert's holly.

Deciduous, large shrubs or small trees to 5 m (15 ft.) tall, usually with densely pubescent twigs; leaves thick, obovate to elliptic, usually inconspicuously toothed, pubescent on both surfaces, but mainly on the bottom; fruits red, subglobose, singly or in pairs, 5–10 mm (⁵⁄₁₆–⅜ in.) diameter; pyrenes ribbed. Habitat: southeastern United States, in wooded areas of the Coastal Plains of Florida and Georgia. Hardy in zones 8 to 10. Rare. May only be a form or variety of *I. decidua.* Allied to *I. decidua* and *I. longipes.*

Ilex decidua Walter 1788 var. *decidua.* Possumhaw holly (synonyms *I. prinoides* Solander 1789, *I. aestivalis* Lamarck 1792, *I. tenuifolia* Salisbury 1796, *I. prionitis* Willdenow 1798, *Bumelia crenulata* Sprengel 1801, *Prinos deciduus* (Walter) De Candolle 1825, *I. decidua* var. *urbana* Wood 1861, *I. berberidifolia* Standley 1929).

Deciduous, large shrubs or small trees to 10 m (30 ft.) tall with light gray glabrous spreading

Figure 11-3. *Ilex curtissii.*

branches, both typical and short spurlike branchlets; leaves partly fascicled, elliptic to lanceolate or obovate, bases cuneate, 4–7 cm (1⅝–2¾ in.) long, 8–20 mm (⁵⁄₁₆–¾ in.) wide, glabrous dark green above and pubescent on midribs beneath, sharply serrate. There is an enormous variability in leaf shape, size, and texture, and in fruit size and color. Leaves turn yellow to orange in the fall; fruits shiny orange to red, occasionally yellow, solitary or in clusters of 3 on short spurs, globose 5–8 mm (³⁄₁₆–⁵⁄₁₆ in.) diameter, pedicels about 1 cm (⅜ in.) long; pyrenes ribbed. Fruit persisting into midwinter unless eaten by birds. Habitat: United States, usually found in low woodland and river bottoms, also in drier upland forest, steep slopes, and fence rows in the Southeast from Maryland, (Montgomery and Prince George's Counties), Virginia to Florida, west to Texas and Mexico. Also found in the central states of Indiana, Illinois, Arkansas, to Iowa. Hardy in zones 6 to 9. Allied to but distinct from *I. ambigua* and *I. longipes*. A good landscape plant and numerous selected cultivars available. Natural hybrids of *I. decidua* and *I. opaca* have been observed (see Figure 11-4). Introduced in 1760. Plate 32.

Ilex decidua var. *mulleri* Edwin *ex* T. R. Dudley, var. nov.

   Diagnosis: A typo differt laminis trinique pubescentibus, serrulis marginarum sine spinulis apicalibus peduncularis glabris.

   This new variety is well distinguished from typical *I. decidua* by a thick, stiff, and white indumentum covering both leaf surfaces, without

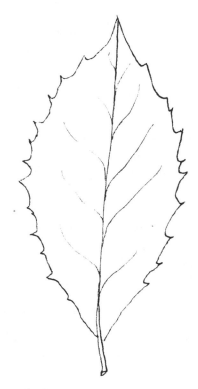

Figure 11-4. *Ilex decidua* × *I. opaca* natural hybrid.

spinulations or mucros on margins, and by glabrous peduncles. Holotype: Mexico, Nuevo Leon State Trail from La Trinidad to Potrero Redondo, Villa Santiago, basally branched shrubs to 3–6 m

Figure 11-5. *Ilex decidua* var. *decidua*. Photo by Barton Bauer Sr.

Figure 11-6. *Ilex decidua* var. *decidua*. Photo by Barton Bauer Sr.

(10–20 ft.) tall, scattered in pine-oak forest. *C. J. Muller 2946* (US); isotypes, MI, US.

Ilex fragilis Hooker 1875 f. *fragilis* (synonyms *I. burmanica* Merrill 1941, *I. opienensis* S.-y Hu 1946).

Deciduous large shrubs or small trees to 5 m (16 ft.) tall, with both elongated and spur branchlets; lenticels conspicuous; leaves serrate, ovate or ovate-elliptic, 5.5–14 cm (2⅛–5½ in.) long, 2.5–5.5 cm (1–2³⁄₁₆ in.) wide, rounded or obtuse at base, apices cuspidate, lateral veins 6–8 pairs, margins serrate; flowers 6- to 8-lobed, usually solitary and axillary to scales or basal leaves to elongated shoots, petioles 2–5 mm (¹⁄₁₆–³⁄₁₆ in.) long; fruits red, depressed globose, 4 mm (⁵⁄₃₂ in.) long, 5–6 mm (³⁄₁₆–³⁄₃₂ in.) diameter, persistent calyces; pyrenes 6-13, striate, woody. Habitat: Myanmar, eastern Himalayas, high mountains of Sikkim, People's Republic of China, borders of Sichuan, and Yunnan provinces, altitude 500–3000 m (4900–9900 ft.). A curious species unrelated to any other *Ilex*. Introduced to England by F. Kingdon Ward in the early 1900s. Cuttings were brought from English gardens to the U.S. National Arboretum by F. G. Meyer in 1957. Possibly hardy in zone 7b. The closest affinity is possibly with *I. monticola* of the United States. The leaves and ovaries of *I. fragilis* show a close relationship with *I. macrocarpa*; however, the latter has larger black fruit and strongly ridged pyrenes.

Ilex fragilis f. *kingii* Loesener 1901.

A form with leaves having a dense pubescence on upper and lower surfaces. Habitat: Eastern Himalayas, common in high mountains of Myanmar and adjacent People's Republic of China, Sichuan and Yunnan provinces.

Ilex fragilis f. *subcoriacea* C.-j. Tseng 1981.

A newer form differing from f. *fragilis* by having subcoriaceous leaves. (It is doubtful if a single very minor deviation of leaf texture should be recognized at any botanical rank, especially when based on only one specimen. T. R. Dudley 1984). Habitat: People's Republic of China, Sichuan and Yunnan provinces.

Ilex geniculata Maximowicz 1881. Furin holly, furinume modoki (synonym *I. geniculata* var. *glabra* Okuyama 1984).

Deciduous, large shrubs, 3–5 m (10–16 ft.) tall, with grayish brown slender branches; leaves glabrous or slightly pubescent, ovate to elliptic-ovate, 4–10 cm (1⅝–4 in.) long, 2.5–5 cm (1–2 in.) wide, acu-

Figure 11-7. *Ilex decidua* var. *decidua*. Photo by Fred Galle.

minate apices, bases rounded, sharply serrate, slightly pubescent beneath, yellow in the fall; fruits red, globose, 4 mm (5/32 in.) diameter, solitary or rarely 3 in loose cyme, on long nodding peduncles and pedicels, 1.5–3.5 cm (5/8–1 3/8 in.) long; pyrenes smooth. Habitat: Japan, mountainous areas of Honshu, Shikoku, and Kyushu Islands. Attractive shrubs with distinct pendulous red fruit. Hardy in zones 5 to 9. Introduced to Arnold Arboretum in 1894 by C. S. Sargent. E. H. Wilson quotes "I had never seen in fruit a shrub so lovely." Unfortunately not readily available." Closely allied to *I. collina* of the southern United States, a North American counterpart species. The specific name generally refers to a curious joint or "knee" on the terminal half of the pedicel.

Ilex kiangsiensis (S.-y. Hu) C.-j. Tseng & B. W. Liu 1981 (synonym *I. aculeolata* var. *kiangsiensis* S.-y. Hu 1949, cf. Dudley 1984).
    Deciduous, large shrubs or small trees, branchlets sparsely puberulent or glabrescent; leaves obovate-elliptic or elliptic, 5–8 cm (2–3 1/8 in.) long, 1.8–3.3 cm (1/2–1 5/16 in.) wide, apices shortly acuminate, bases cuneate or attenuate, both surfaces puberulent to glabrescent, margins entire below the middle, serrulate toward apices; fruits black, ellipsoid, 10–15 mm (3/8–1 9/32 in.) long, 6–8 mm (7/32–5/16 in.) diameter, solitary and axillary; pyrenes 4–5, dorsally striate. Habitat: People's Republic of China, localized in southern Jiangxi Province, near the border of Guangxi-Guangdong provinces. Allied to *I. aculeolata,* but differing with nearly glabrous branches and much longer ellipsoid fruits borne on longer pedicels.

Ilex kusanoi Hayata 1911 (synonym *I. taiwaniana* Hayata 1911).
    Deciduous, small trees with glabrous branches; leaves ovate, 4–6.5 cm (1 5/8–2 1/2 in.) long, 3–4 cm (1 3/16–3/8 in.) wide, glabrous on both surfaces; fruits red, globose, 6 mm (7/32 in.) diameter, single or in axillary clusters of 1–3; pyrenes ribbed. Habitat: Lanyu Island of Ryukyu and Taiwan only. Allied to *I. macropoda.*

Ilex laevigata (Pursh) A. Gray 1857 f. *laevigata.* Smooth winterberry (synonyms *Prinos laevigatus* Pursh 1814, *I. lanceolata* (Pursh) Chapman 1860).
    Deciduous, medium to large shrubs to 3 m (10 ft.) tall; leaves lanceolate-ovate to lanceolate, 3–6 cm (1 3/16–2 1/2 in.) long, finely serrulate, semiglossy above, slightly pubescent beneath; yellow in the fall; fruits red, often translucent depressed globose, 7–8 mm (1/4–5/16 in.) diameter, solitary on pedicels 2–5 mm (1/16–3/16 in.) long, calyx lobes glabrous; pyrenes smooth. Habitat: United States in swamps and low areas from Maine, New Hampshire, Pennsylvania,

and south to northern Georgia. Hardy in zones 4 to 9. Attractive fall yellow foliage. Introduced in 1812; fruit is often sparse and plants are very rare in cultivation. Allied to *I. verticillata.* Large-fruited *I. verticillata* have been erroneously sold as *I. laevigata.* One "authority" treats *I. laevigata* as a synonym of *I. verticillata,* an insupportable position.

Ilex laevigata f. *herveyi* Robinson 1908.
    A yellow-fruited botanical form. Collected by a Mr. Hervey along the Tauton River near Fall River, Massachusetts. Often incorrectly given the cultivar name 'Hervey'.

Ilex longipes Chapman *ex* Trelease 1889 f. *longipes.* Georgia long-stalked holly (synonyms *Nemopanthus canadensis* Gattinger 1887, *non* De Candolle, *I. decidua* var. *longipes* (Chapman *ex* Trelease) Ahles 1964).
    Deciduous, large shrubs or small trees to 3–6 m (10–20 ft.) tall, wide-spreading glabrous branches, short spurlike branchlets; leaves elliptic to elliptic-obovate, usually glabrous, 3–9 cm (1 3/16–3 1/2 in.) long, crenate-serrate teeth often tipped with appressed spinelike bristle; fruits shiny red, globose,

Figure 11-8. *Ilex kusanoi.* Drawing by Chien-chu Chen in *Illustrations of Native and Introduced Ligneous Plants of Taiwan* (1962) by Tang-shui Liu.

Figure 11-9. *Ilex laevigata* f. *laevigata.* Photo by Barton Bauer Sr.

7–10 mm (¼–⅜ in.) diameter, or larger, usually solitary on long pendant pedicels, 1.3–3.5 cm to 5 cm (½–1⅜ to 2 in.) long; pyrenes ribbed. Habitat: southern United States, usually in woods or rocky slopes in Tennessee, Alabama, Georgia, Florida, west to Mississippi, Louisiana, and Texas. Hardy in zones 6 to 9. The first cultivar 'Natchez Belle' was named in 1976 (see cultivar list). The status of *I. longipes* and *I. decidua* cause considerable confusion. Some believe the two species are conspecific or may include *I. longipes* as a variety of *I. decidua.* Allied to *I. asprella* and *I. decidua.*

> *Ilex longipes* f. *hirsuta* (Lundell) T. R. Dudley, *comb. & stat. nov.* (basionym *I. longipes* var. *hirsuta* Lundell, *Flora Texas* 3: 118. 1961).
> This form differs from typical *I. longipes* by having shorter, hirsute, fruiting pedicels and denser, coarser indumentum on the branchlets and on the somewhat smaller leaves. Holotype: Texas, Newton County, *L. C. Lundell & S. W. Geiser 11875* (MI); isotype, SMU.

Ilex macrocarpa Oliver 1888 var. *macrocarpa.* Heitzu-shu (synonyms *I. dubia* var. *hupehensis* Loesener (in part) 1901, *I. henryi* Loesener 1901, *I. macrocarpa* var. *trichophylla* Loesener 1901, *Celastrus salicifolia* H. Léveillé 1914, *Diospyros bodinieri* H. Léveillé 1914, *I. montana* var. *hupehensis* (Loesener) Fernald 1933, *I. macrocarpa* var. *brevipedunculata* S.-y. Hu 1946, *I. macrocarpa* var. *longipedunculata* S.-y. Hu 1946).
Deciduous trees to 30 m (98⅓ ft.) tall, gray-green glabrous branches, elongate and spur branchlets, conspicuous lenticels; leaves ovate to ovate-elliptic,

5–15 cm (2–6 in.) long, 3–7 cm (1³⁄₁₆–2¾ in.) wide, margins serrate; flowers 5- to 6-merous, 10–13 mm (⅜–½ in.) across; fruits black, solitary, orbicular-globose, large, 11–16 mm (⁷⁄₁₆–⅝ in.) diameter, persistent columnar stigma; pyrenes 6–7, deeply ribbed. Habitat: People's Republic of China, Vietnam; a widely distributed and variable species. Large cultivated specimens are found in England. Hardy in zone 7. Allied to *I. montana, I. monticola,* and especially to *I. poneantha.* Introduced by E. H. Wilson in 1907 to the Arnold Arboretum.

> *Ilex macrocarpa* var. *reevesae* S.-y. Hu 1946 (synonym *I. reevesae* S.-y. Hu 1946).
> Leaves and inflorescences characterized by the pubescent branchlets. Habitat: People's Republic of China, a very localized variety from Sichuan Province. Probably only a minor variant, probably a synonym of the species.

Ilex macropoda Miquel 1867. Ao-hada, ke-nashi-ao-hada (synonyms *I. costata* Blume *ex* Miquel 1881, *I. dubia* var. *hupehensis* Loesener (in part) 1901, *I. dubia* var. *macropoda* (Miquel) Loesener 1901, *I. dubia* var. *pseudomacropoda* Loesener 1901, *I. monticola* var. *macropoda* (Miquel) Rehder 1915, *I. macropoda* var. *pseudomacropoda* (Loesener) Nakai 1930, *I. montana* var. *macropoda* (Miquel) Fernald 1939, *I. macropoda* f. *pseudomacropoda* (Loesener) Hara 1956).
Deciduous trees to 13 m (43 ft.) tall, grayish brown glabrous branches, elongate and spur branchlets, conspicuous lenticels; leaves ovate or broad-elliptic, 4–8 cm (1⅝–3⅛ in.) long, 2.5–4.7 cm (1–1¾ in.) wide, glabrous above and pubescent beneath, sharply serrate; fruits vivid red, globose 5 mm (½ in.) diameter, solitary, pedicels 6–6.5 mm (⁷⁄₃₂–

Figure 11-10. *Ilex longipes* f. *longipes.* Photo by Barton Bauer Sr.

¼ in.) long; fruit color darkens after frost; pyrenes 5, striate. Habitat: Japan, a fairly common species in mountainous areas of Hokkaido, Honshu, Shikoku, and Kyushu; People's Republic of China, widely distributed in the Jiangxi, Zhejiang, and Fujian provinces; and in Korea. Closely related to *I. verticillata* and *I. monticola* of the United States. Hardy in zones 6 to 9.

Ilex micrococca Maximowicz 1881 f. *micrococca.* Tama mizuki, aka-mizuki, woho-sandzuki (synonyms *I. micrococca* var. *longifolia* Hayata 1913, *I. micrococca* f. *pilosa* S.-y. Hu 1949).

Deciduous trees to 20 m (65 ft.) tall, grayish brown branches, conspicuous lenticels; leaves ovate or ovate-elliptic, 7–13 cm (2¾–5⅛ in.) long, 3–5 cm (1³⁄₁₆–2 in.) wide, margins subentire or aristate-serrate, bases rounded, apices acuminate, 6–8 pairs of lateral veins; fruits red, small in axillary compound cymes, 3 mm (⅛ in.) diameter; pyrenes 6–8, elliptic, smooth. Habitat: Japan, People's Republic of China, Hainan Province, eastern and southern mainland, Taiwan, Vietnam. Possibly hardy in zone 8. Per Loesener, *I. micrococca* is allied to and transitional with *I. venulosa* Hooker.

Ilex micrococca f. *tsangii* T. R. Dudley 1980.
Differs from forma *micrococca* by fruit maturing yellow. Named for W. T. Tsang, the first to document a yellow-fruited variant from the wild.

Ilex monticola A. Gray 1856. Mountain holly (synonyms *I. ambigua* Torrey 1843, *I. montana* Torrey & Gray 1848 var. *montana, non* Grisebach 1860, *I. ambigua* var. *montana* (Torrey & Gray) Ashe 1864, *I. dubia sensu* Trelease & Loesener 1893, *I. dubia* var. *monticola* (Gray) Loesener 1901, *I. amelanchier* var. *monticola* (Gray) Loesener 1911, *I. ambigua* var. *monticola* (Gray) P. P. Wunderlin & Poppleton 1977).

Deciduous, large shrubs or small trees to 9 m (30 ft.) tall with slender glabrous branches; leaves variable, usually ovate-lanceolate to elliptic, in the southern range the leaves may be rounded, as broad as they are long, glabrous or with pubescence on the midribs below, sharply serrate, 6–20 cm (2⅜–6 in.) long; fruits vivid red, globose, 1 cm (⅜ in.) diameter, single or in axillary clusters; pyrenes ribbed. Habitat: U.S.A. in wooded mountain slopes from New York to Georgia and Alabama. Reported from Mexico in 1945 by A. J. Sharp in the following states: Chiapas, Puebla and Tamaulipas. Hardy in zones 5 to 9. A variable species and often given other species names including *I. dubia.* Allied to *I. fragilis* and *I. macropoda. Ilex monticola* is now considered to be the correct botanical name for *I. montana,* although the latter will probably continue to be used because of its

Figure 11-11. *Ilex micrococca* f. *micrococca.* Drawing by Chien-chu Chen in *Illustrations of Native and Introduced Ligneous Plants of Taiwan* (1962) by Tang-shui Liu.

long-term usage in the botanical and horticultural literature.

Ilex montana var. *mollis* (Gray) Britton 1867 (of dubious state and representing all the forms with pubescent leaves; synonyms *I. dubia* (Don) Britton 1800, *I. mollis* Gray 1867, *I. monticola* var. *mollis* (Gray) Britton 1894, *I. beadlei* Ashe 1897, *I. dubia* var. *mollis* (Gray) Loesener 1901, *I. dubia* f. *beadlei* (Ashe) Loesener 1901, *I. dubia* f. *grayiana* Loesener 1901, *I. beadlei* var. *laevis* Ashe 1924, *I. dubia* var. *beadlei* (Ashe) Rehder 1927, *I. montana* var. *beadlei* (Ashe) Fernald 1939, *I. montana* f. *rotundifolia* Woods 1951, *I. ambigua* f. *mollis* (Gray) H. E. Ahles 1964).

Leaves are usually smaller and less ovate than *I. monticola.* The extreme pubescent form was called *I. beadlei.* The pubescent expressions are usually found in the southern range of this species. This problem has not yet been resolved and needs more intensive study. Plate 33.

Ilex phyllobolos Maximowicz 1881. Hosoba-ume-modoki, miyama-ume-modoki (synonyms *I. nipponica* Makino 1900, *I. spathulata* Koidzumi 1925, *I. serrata* var. *nipponica* (Makino) Ohwi 1953, *I. nemotoi* Ohwi, *non* Makino 1965).

Deciduous shrubs or small trees to 3–6 m (10–20 ft.) tall, branches nearly glabrous; leaves oblanceolate to ovate, 4–13 cm (1½–5 in.) long, 1–2 cm (⅜–¾ in.) wide, margins with short mucronulate teeth, lightly pubescent on both surfaces while young; fruits red, globose, 5–6 mm (³⁄₁₆–⁷⁄₃₂ in.) diameter, solitary or 3 in subsessile cymes, pedicels very short, less than 6 mm (⁷⁄₃₂ in.) long; pyrenes 5, smooth. Habitat: Japan, found in moist sites in the mountains of Honshu. Allied to *I. decidua* in the United States and *I. serrata* in Japan.

Ilex polyneura (Handel-Mazzetti) S.-y. Hu 1949 var. *polyneura* (synonym *I. micrococca* var. *polyneura* Handel-Mazzetti 1933).

Deciduous trees to 20 m (65 ft.) tall with conspicuous lenticels; leaves oblong-elliptic, 8–15 cm (3⅛–6 in.) long, 3.5–6.5 cm (1⅜–2½ in.) wide, bases rounded or obtuse, apices acuminate, margins finely and sharply serrate, lateral veins 11–20 pairs, pubescent on lower surface; fruits red, globose, 4 mm (⁵⁄₃₂ in.) diameter, persistent calyces; pyrenes 7, elliptic, smooth. Habitat: People's Republic of China, western Yunnan and Xizang provinces, limited distribution, mountainous areas. Differs from *I. micrococca* by the greater number of veins, 11–20, on the leaves, larger inflorescences, and petioles channeled above.

Ilex polyneura var. *glabra* S.-y. Hu 1949.

This variety differs in having glabrous leaves and inflorescences. Habitat: People's Republic of China, reported only from southern and southwestern Yunnan Province.

Ilex poneantha Koidzumi 1928.

Deciduous, small trees, erect spreading habit, young branches dull brown, lenticellate, slightly pubescent; leaves glabrous, glossy above, elliptic-ovate to ovate, rarely oblong, 5–10 cm (2–4 in.) long, 4.5–6.5 cm (1¾–2⅜ in.) wide, bases rounded to obtuse, margins crenate, distinctly keeled, petioles 10–15 mm (⅜–¹⁹⁄₃₂ in.) long; staminate inflorescences fasciculate; pistillate white flowers 6- to 8-merous; fruits black, flattened globose, 13–16 mm (½–⅝ in.) diameter, 11–12 mm (⁷⁄₁₆–¹⁵⁄₃₂ in.) thick, prominent persistent columnar stigma, 2–3 mm (¹⁄₁₆–⅛ in.) long, solitary and spurlike clusters, pedicels 10–13 mm (⅜–½ in.) long. Habitat: endemic to Amami O-Shima Island of the Ryukyu Islands, Mount Yuwandake. Very closely allied to *I. macrocarpa*. Introduced to cultivation in the early 1980s. Hardy in Dare County, North Carolina, zone 8b. Plate 34.

Ilex serrata Thunberg *ex* J. A. Murray 1784 subsp. *serrata*. Japanese winterberry, ume-modoki (synonyms *I. sieboldii* Miquel 1866, *I. arguitidens* Miquel

Figure 11-12. *Ilex poneantha*. Photo by Barton Bauer Sr.

1868, *I. nemotoi* Makino 1900, *I. serrata* var. *arguitidens* (Miquel) Rehder 1900, *I. serrata* var. *sieboldii* (Miquel) Rehder 1900, *I. serrata* var. "sieboldii" Loesener 1901).

Deciduous, medium to large shrubs 2–4 m (6–13 ft.) tall, grayish brown branches with conspicuous lenticels; leaves elliptic to ovate-elliptic, 4–8 cm (1⅝–3 in.) long, 2.5 cm (1 in.) wide, sharply serrate, glabrous or sparsely pubescent on midribs, lateral veins 6- to 8- (to 10-) paired, petioles 6–8 mm (⁷⁄₃₂–⁵⁄₁₆ in.) long; flowers pale purple to white; fruits red, globose, 5 mm (³⁄₁₆ in.) diameter, solitary or in simple cymes; pyrenes 4–5, smooth. Habitat: Japan, common variable shrub in moist sites. Introduced

Figure 11-13. *Ilex poneantha*. Photo by Barton Bauer Sr.

to the United States in 1866, and to the Royal Botanic Gardens, Kew, England, in 1893. Hardy in zones 5 to 8b. Fruit colors early in late summer and persists into winter. A good bonsai plant; several botanical varieties and cultivars available. Allied to *I. verticillata* in the United States. Plates 35, 36.

Figure 11-15. *Ilex serrata* subsp. *serrata.* Photo by Barton Bauer Sr.

Figure 11-14. *Ilex serrata* subsp. *serrata.* Photo by Barton Bauer Sr.

Ilex serrata subsp. *cathayensis* T. R. Dudley 1991 (synonym *I. leiboensis* Z. M. Tan 1988).

Deciduous shrubs to 2 m (6.6 ft.) tall, branches blackish brown, black hirsute hairs, elliptic lenticels, pale yellow or whitish, branchlets pale yellowish green, hirsute; leaves elliptic or obovate-elliptic, 4–8.5 cm (1⅝–3⅜ in.) long, 2–5 cm (¾–2 in.) wide, bases cuneate, apices acute or short acuminate, lateral veins 4–6 paired, margins remotely serrulate, nearly entire, petioles slender, hirsute, 8–15 mm (5⁄16–19⁄32 in.) long; inflorescences unknown; infructescences axillary, solitary, 2- to 4-fruited, peduncles 3–9 mm (⅛–11⁄32 in.) long, hirsute, pedicels 2–7 mm (1⁄16–9⁄32 in.) long, short hirsute; fruits globose, 4–5 mm (5⁄32–3⁄16 in.) diameter, persistent calyces, 5-lobed; pyrenes 5, smooth. Habitat: People's Republic of China, Sichuan, Liaoning, and Xinjiang provinces, at 1250 m (4125 ft.) elevation, but not a restricted endemic.

Ilex serrata f. *leucocarpa* Beissner 1908, see *I. serrata* 'Leucocarpa' in Chapter 12.

Ilex serrata var. *subtilis* (Miquel) Yatabe 1892, see *I. serrata* 'Koshobai' in Chapter 12.

Ilex serrata f. *xanthocarpa* Rehder 1915, see *I. serrata* 'Xanthocarpa' in Chapter 12.

Figure 11-16. *Ilex serrata* subsp. *serrata.* Photo by Fred Galle.

Ilex tsoii Merrill & Chun 1930.

Deciduous, large shrubs or small trees to 4 m (13 ft.) tall, elongate and spur branchlets, conspicuous lenticels; leaves ovate or ovate-elliptic, 5–10 cm (2–4 in.) long, 3–5 cm (1³⁄₁₆–2 in.) wide, pubescent, margins serrate; fruits dark purple, globose, 6–8 mm (⁷⁄₃₂–⁵⁄₁₆ in.) diameter, pedicels 1–2 mm (¹⁄₁₆ in.) long; pyrenes 6, reticulate, sulcate. Habitat: People's Republic of China, in warm temperate southern and eastern area. Similar to *I. monticola* in the United States. Also allied to *I. fragilis*. Differs from *I. macropoda* in having very short pedicels.

Ilex verticillata (Linnaeus) A. Gray 1857 var. *verticillata*. Black alder, winterberry (synonyms *Prinos verticillatus* Linnaeus 1753, *P. confertus* Moench 1794, *P. gronovii* Michaux 1803, *P. padifolius* Willdenow 1809, *P. prunifolius* Desfontaines 1815, *P. ambiguus* Watson 1825, *non* Michaux, *I. verticillata* var. *padifolia* (Willdenow) Torrey & Gray 1878, *I. verticillata* var. *tenuifolia* (Torrey) Watson 1878, *I. verticillata* var. *cyclophylla* Robinson 1900, *I. bronxensis* Britton 1912, *I. verticillata* f. *fastigata* (E. Bicknell) Fernald 1922).

Deciduous, large shrubs or small trees, 4.6 m (15 ft.) tall; leaves elliptic or obovate to oblanceolate, 3.5–9 cm (1³⁄₈–3½ in.) long, 2–2.5 cm (¾–1 in.) wide, serrate or doubly serrate, usually pubescent below at least on the veins, leaves turn brown or black after frost; fruits usually red, globose, 6–8 mm (⁷⁄₃₂–⁵⁄₁₆ in.) diameter, on short pedicels, solitary or in pairs, seldom persisting after late November; calyx lobes pubescent; pyrenes smooth. Habitat: North America in swamps and low woodland areas, from Nova Scotia to western Ontario, Wisconsin, Minnesota, south to Alabama and Florida, west to Missouri and Texas. Extremely variable species in refer-

Figure 11-18. *Ilex verticillata* var. *verticillata*. Photo by Barton Bauer Sr.

Figure 11-19. *Ilex verticillata* var. *verticillata*. Photo by Fred Galle.

Figure 11-17. *Ilex verticillata* var. *verticillata*. Photo by Barton Bauer Sr.

ence to leaf shape and size, degree of pubescence or lack of pubescence, and growth habit. Introduced in 1736 and hardy in zones 3 to 9. A popular landscape plant for its attractive red fruit, holds its fruit longer than *I. decidua* and *I. serrata*. Some specialists believe there is a southern "type" (fewer but heavier stems, darker bark) and a northern "type" (slower growing, shorter, smaller leaves, earlier blooming), possibly ecotypes. Allied to *I. laevigata*. A.M. 1962. Plates 37, 38.

Ilex verticillata f. *aurantiaca* (Moldenke) Rehder 1949 (synonym *I. verticillata* var. *auarantiaca* Moldenke 1939).

A wild plant with orange fruit, first collected in 1938 by Harold N. Moldenke at the edge of swamp at Newfoundland, Morris County, New Jersey, and described by him as a variety in 1939. No intermediate forms observed; often listed incorrectly as a cultivar, 'Aurantiaca'. First published in *Revista Sudamericana De Botanica Marzo* (1939), no. 1–2. Leaves typical of northern type, fruits vivid orange, often with yellowish blush, globose, 6–8 mm (7/32–5/16 in.) diameter, usually single or 1–3 in cluster, persistent, not eaten by birds; flowers early; upright spreading, multistemmed shrub, slow growing, to 3 m (10 ft.) tall. Often listed incorrectly as a cultivar. Plate 39.

Ilex verticillata f. *chrysocarpa* Robinson 1900.

A wild form with yellow fruit, collected along the Tauton River, near Georgetown, Massachusetts. Often listed as a cultivar, 'Chrysocarpa'. Leaves typical; fruit yellow, globose, 6–8 mm (7/32–5/16 in.) diameter, sparse fruiting; upright spreading, multistemmed large shrub; hardy in zone 4. Availability limited.

Ilex verticillata f. *hogdonii* Seymour 1969.

A form differing from typical individuals with glabrous leaves having no translucent dots; from New Hampshire. Often confused with *I. laevigata* due to the completely glabrous leaves.

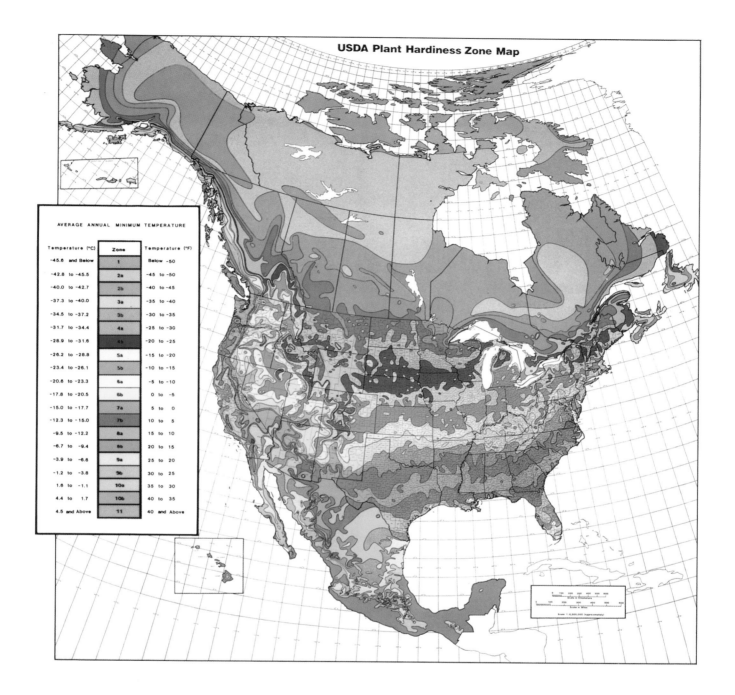

USDA Plant Hardiness Zone Map

AVERAGE ANNUAL MINIMUM TEMPERATURE

Temperature (°C)	Zone	Temperature (°F)
-45.6 and Below	1	Below -50
-42.8 to -45.5	2a	-45 to -50
-40.0 to -42.7	2b	-40 to -45
-37.3 to -40.0	3a	-35 to -40
-34.5 to -37.2	3b	-30 to -35
-31.7 to -34.4	4a	-25 to -30
-28.9 to -31.6	4b	-20 to -25
-26.2 to -28.8	5a	-15 to -20
-23.4 to -26.1	5b	-10 to -15
-20.6 to -23.3	6a	-5 to -10
-17.8 to -20.5	6b	0 to -5
-15.0 to -17.7	7a	5 to 0
-12.3 to -15.0	7b	10 to 5
-9.5 to -12.2	8a	15 to 10
-6.7 to -9.4	8b	20 to 15
-3.9 to -6.6	9a	25 to 20
-1.2 to -3.8	9b	30 to 25
1.6 to -1.1	10a	35 to 30
4.4 to 1.7	10b	40 to 35
4.5 and Above	11	40 and Above

HARDINESS ZONE
TEMPERATURE RANGES

°F	ZONE	°C
below −50	1	below −45
−50 to −40	2	−45 to −40
−40 to −30	3	−40 to −34
−30 to −20	4	−34 to −29
−20 to −10	5	−29 to −23
−10 to 0	6	−23 to −17
0 to 10	7	−17 to −12
10 to 20	8	−12 to −7
20 to 30	9	−7 to −1
30 to 40	10	−1 to 5

Plate 1. The holly collection at Bokrijk Arboretum, Houthalen, Belgium. Photo by Bokrijk Arboretum.

Plate 2. Variegated hollies at Bokrijk Arboretum, Houthalen, Belgium. Photo by Bokrijk Arboretum.

Plate 3. *Ilex opaca* collection at Bernheim Forest Arboretum, Clermont, Kentucky. Photo by Fred Galle.

Plate 4. Holly collection at Synoptic Garden. Photo by J. Knapp.

Plate 5. Hollies provide colorful fruit and foliage for the landscape. Photo by Fred Galle.

Plate 6. A sheared specimen of *Ilex vomitoria*. Photo by Fred Galle.

Plate 7. Collection of *Ilex vomitoria* at Colonial Williamsburg, Virginia. Photo by Jack Siebenthaler.

Plate 8. This portable holly screen at Monrovia Nursery consists of container plants trained as espaliers. Photo by Fred Galle.

Plate 9. A formal hedge of *Ilex vomitoria* at Brookgreen Gardens. Photo by Fred Galle.

Plate 10. A hedge of *Ilex opaca*. Photo by Fred Galle.

Plate 11. A Blue Holly hedge in winter. Photo by Fred Galle.

Plate 12. A holly orchard run by the Teufel family in Oregon. Photo by Fred Galle.

Plate 13. Harvesting cut holly at the Teufel holly farm in Oregon. Photo by Fred Galle.

Plate 14. Sacks for collecting the cut holly. Photo by Fred Galle.

Plate 15. Sacks of cut holly ready for hauling to the processing plant. Photo by Fred Galle.

Plate 16. Processing cut holly at the Teufel holly farm in Oregon. Photo by Fred Galle.

Plate 17. *Ilex crenata* 'Helleri' grown as a bonsai. Photo by Fred Galle.

Plate 18. *Ilex dimorphophylla,* Okinawan holly, is a subtropical plant that can be grown indoors as a bonsai. Photo by Fred Galle.

Plate 20. Clusters of holly berries accent at door at Colonial Williamsburg. Photo by Gordon Chappell.

late 19. A Christmas wreath on a door at Colo-
al Williamsburg. Photo by Gordon Chappell.

Plate 21. A mantle arrangement featuring variegated holly, lady apples, leyland cypress, and ivy. Photo by Gordon Chappell.

Plate 22. A holly centerpiece for a Christmas table. Photo by Gordon Chappell.

Plate 23. Christmas card with holly design. Photo by Fred Galle.

Plate 24. Hand-painted holly china. Photo by Barton Bauer Sr.

Plate 25. Holly portrait by Peggy Scoggin, 1964. Photo by Fred Galle.

Plate 26. Holly portrait. Photo by Barton Bauer Sr.

Plate 27. Holly jewelry. Photo by Barton Bauer Sr.

Plate 28. Carving of holly wood. Photo by Fred Galle.

Plate 29. *Ilex amelanchier*. Photo by Fred Galle.

Plate 30. *Ilex amelanchier*. Photo by Fred Galle.

Plate 31. *Ilex curtissii*. Photo by Fred Galle.

Plate 32. *Ilex decidua* var. *decidua*. Photo by Fred Galle.

Plate 33. *Ilex montana* var. *mollis*. Photo by Fred Galle.

Plate 34. *Ilex poneantha.* Photo by Fred Galle.　　Plate 35. *Ilex serrata* subsp. *serrata.* Photo by Fred Galle.

Plate 36. *Ilex serrata* subsp. *serrata.* Photo by Fred Galle.　　Plate 37. *Ilex verticillata* var. *verticillata.* Photo by Fred Galle.

Plate 38. *Ilex verticillata* var. *verticillata.*
Photo by J. Knapp.

Plate 39. *Ilex verticillata* f. *aurantiaca.* Photo by Fred Galle.

Plate 40. *Ilex decidua* 'Council Fire'. Photo by Robert Simpson.

Plate 41. *Ilex decidua* 'Pocahontas'. Photo by Robert Simpson.

Plate 42. *Ilex decidua* 'Red Cascade'. Photo by Robert Simpson.

Plate 43. *Ilex decidua* 'Warren's Red'. Photo by Robert Simpson.

Plate 44. *Ilex serrata* 'Koshobai'. Photo by Fred Galle.

Plate 45. *Ilex serrata* 'Sundrops'. Photo by Gene Eisenbeiss.

Plate 46. *Ilex verticillata* 'Afterglow'. Photo by Robert Simpson.

Plate 48. *Ilex verticillata* 'Earlibright'. Photo by Fred Galle.

Plate 47. *Ilex verticillata* 'Cacapon'. Photo by Robert Simpson.

Plate 50. *Ilex verticillata* 'Shaver'. Photo by Robert Simpson.

Plate 49. *Ilex verticillata* 'Red Sprite'. Photo by Fred Galle.

Plate 52. *Ilex verticillata* 'Sunset'. Photo by Fred Galle.

Plate 51. *Ilex verticillata* 'Stop Light'. Photo by Robert Simpson.

Plate 53. *Ilex verticillata* 'Winter Gold'. Photo by Robert Simpson.

Plate 55. *Ilex* 'Bonfire'. Photo by Fred Galle.

Plate 56. *Ilex* 'Sparkleberry'. Photo by Fred Galle.

Plate 54. *Ilex verticillata* 'Winter Red'. Photo by Robert Simpson.

Plate 57. *Ilex aquifolium* var. *aquifolium* (right) and *I. opaca* f. *opaca* (left) at Hillwood Museum. Photo by Hillwood Museum.

Plate 58. *Ilex bioritsensis*. Photo by Fred Galle.

Plate 59. *Ilex ciliospinosa*. Photo by J. Knapp.

Plate 60. *Ilex colchica*. Photo by Fred Galle.

Plate 61. *Ilex cornuta*. Photo by Fred Galle.

Plate 62. *Ilex crenata* var. *crenata* on Mount Kujū, Japan. Photo by Fred Galle.

Plate 63. *Ilex dimorphophylla.* Photo by Fred Galle.

Plate 64. *Ilex dipyrena.* Photo by Fred Galle.

Plate 65. *Ilex glabra* f. *glabra.* Photo by Fred Galle.

Plate 66. *Ilex glabra* f. *glabra.* Photo by Fred Galle.

Plate 67. *Ilex integra* var. *integra*. Photo by Fred Galle.

Plate 68. *Ilex latifolia*. Photo by Fred Galle.

Plate 69. *Ilex myrtifolia*. Photo by Fred Galle.

Plate 71. *Ilex paraguariensis*. Photo by William Kosar.

Plate 70. *Ilex opaca* f. *opaca*. Photo by Fred Galle.

Plate 72. *Ilex pedunculosa* var. *pedunculosa*. Photo by David Burnett.

Plate 74. *Ilex purpurea* var. *purpurea*. Photo by Fred Galle.

Plate 73. *Ilex pedunculosa* var. *pedunculosa*. Photo by Fred Galle.

Plate 75. *Ilex purpurea* var. *purpurea*. Photo by Fred Galle.

Plate 76. *Ilex rotunda* var. *rotunda*. Photo by Fred Galle.

Plate 77. *Ilex rugosa* f. *rugosa.* Photo by J. Knapp.

Plate 78. *Ilex vomitoria* subsp. *vomitoria.* Photo by Fred Galle.

Plate 79. *Ilex vomitoria* subsp. *vomitoria.* Photo by Fred Galle.

Plate 80. *Ilex wilsonii* var. *wilsonii.* Photo by Fred Galle.

Plate 81. *Ilex* × *altaclerensis* 'Green Maid'.
Photo by Gene Eisenbeiss.

Plate 82. *Ilex* × *altaclerensis* 'James G. Esson'. Photo by David Burnett.

Plate 83. *Ilex* × *altaclerensis* 'Nobilis Picta'. Photo by Fred Galle.

Plate 84. *Ilex* × *altaclerensis* 'Royal Red'. Photo
by William Kosar.

Plate 86. *Ilex aquifolium* 'Angustifolia'. Photo by Fred Galle.

Plate 85. *Ilex × altaclerensis* 'Wieman's Favorite'. Photo by Fred Galle.

Plate 87. *Ilex aquifolium* 'Argentea Marginata'. Photo by Fred Galle.

Plate 88. *Ilex aquifolium* 'Beacon'. Photo by David Burnett.

Plate 89. *Ilex aquifolium* 'Beautyspra'. Photo by Fred Galle.

Plate 90. *Ilex aquifolium* 'Dude'. Photo by Fred Galle.

Plate 91. *Ilex aquifolium* 'Earlygold'. Photo by William Kosar.

Plate 92. *Ilex aquifolium* 'Ferox Argentea'. Photo by Fred Galle.

Plate 93. *Ilex aquifolium* 'Firecracker'. Photo by William Kosar.

Plate 94. *Ilex aquifolium* 'Fisheri'. Photo by Fred Galle.

Plate 95. *Ilex aquifolium* 'Flavescens'. Photo by Fred Galle.

Plate 96. *Ilex aquifolium* 'Fructu Lutea'. Photo by David Burnett.

Plate 97. *Ilex aquifolium* Gold Coast®. Photo by Fred Galle.

Plate 98. *Ilex aquifolium* 'Golden Milkboy'. Photo by William Kosar.

Plate 99. *Ilex aquifolium* 'Hastata'. Photo by Fred Galle.

Plate 100. *Ilex aquifolium* 'Ingramii'. Photo by Fred Galle.

Plate 101. *Ilex aquifolium* 'Princess Pat'. Photo by U.S. National Arboretum.

Plate 102. *Ilex aquifolium* 'Pyramidalis'. Photo by Fred Galle.

Plate 103. *Ilex aquifolium* 'Rederly'. Photo by Fred Galle.

Plate 104. *Ilex aquifolium* 'Silvary'. Photo by Fred Galle.

Plate 105. *Ilex aquifolium* 'Teufel's Silver Variegated'. Photo by Fred Galle.

Plate 106. *Ilex aquifolium* 'Wieman's Yellow-pillar'. Photo by Fred Galle.

Plate 107. *Ilex aquifolium* 'Wil-Chris'. Photo by Fred Galle.

Plate 108. *Ilex aquifolium* 'Wilsonii'. Photo by Fred Galle.

Plate 109. *Ilex aquifolium* 'Yellow Beam'. Photo by U.S. National Arboretum.

Plate 110. *Ilex × attenuata* 'Alagold'. Photo by Fred Galle.

Plate 111. *Ilex* × *attenuata* 'Bienville Gold'. Photo by Fred Galle.

Plate 112. *Ilex* × *attenuata* 'East Palatka'. Photo by Fred Galle.

Plate 113. *Ilex* × *attenuata* 'Foster No. 2'.
Photo by U.S. National Arboretum.

Plate 114. *Ilex* × *attenuata* 'Greenleaf'. Photo by Fred Galle.

Plate 115. *Ilex* × *attenuata* 'Hume No. 2'. Photo by Fred Galle.

Plate 116. *Ilex × attenuata* 'Oriole'. Photo by Gene Eisenbeiss.

Plate 117. *Ilex × attenuata* 'Oriole'. Photo by Gene Eisenbeiss.

Plate 118. *Ilex × attenuata* 'Savannah'. Photo by Fred Galle.

Plate 119. *Ilex × attenuata* 'Sunny Foster'. Photo by William Kosar.

Plate 120. *Ilex × attenuata* 'Tanager'. Photo by Gene Eisenbeiss.

Plate 121. *Ilex cornuta* 'Anicet Delcambre'. Photo by Fred Galle.

Plate 122. *Ilex cornuta* 'Burfordii'. Photo by Fred Galle.

Plate 123. *Ilex cornuta* 'Burfordii'. Photo by Fred Galle.

Plate 124. *Ilex cornuta* 'Carissa'. Photo by Fred Galle.

Plate 125. *Ilex cornuta* 'D'Or'. Photo by Fred Galle.

Plate 126. *Ilex cornuta* 'Dwarf Burford'. Photo by Fred Galle.

Plate 127. *Ilex cornuta* 'Dwarf Burford'. Photo by Fred Galle.

Plate 128. *Ilex cornuta* 'Fine Line'. Photo by Ken Tilt.

Plate 130. *Ilex cornuta* 'Ira S. Nelson'. Photo by William Kosar.

Plate 129. *Ilex cornuta* 'Grandview'. Photo by William Kosar.

Plate 131. *Ilex cornuta* 'O. Spring'. Photo by Fred Galle.

Plate 132. *Ilex cornuta* 'Rotunda'. Photo by William Kosar.

Plate 133. *Ilex cornuta* 'Sunrise'. Photo by William Kosar.

Plate 134. *Ilex crenata* 'Convexa'. Photo by Fred Galle.

Plate 135. *Ilex crenata* 'Delaware Diamond'. Photo by Fred Galle.

Plate 136. *Ilex crenata* 'Dwarf Pagoda'. Photo by Fred Galle.

Plate 137. *Ilex crenata* 'Golden Heller'. Photo by Fred Galle.

Plate 138. *Ilex crenata* 'Helleri'. Photo by Fred Galle.

Plate 139. *Ilex crenata* 'Mariesii'. Photo by Fred Galle.

Plate 140. *Ilex crenata* 'Microphylla'. Photo by Fred Galle.

Plate 141. *Ilex crenata* 'Midas Touch'. Photo by Fred Galle.

Plate 142. *Ilex crenata* 'Piccolo'. Photo by Fred Galle.

Plate 143. *Ilex crenata* 'Sky Pencil'. Photo by Fred Galle.

Plate 144. *Ilex crenata* 'Snowflake'. Photo by Fred Galle.

Plate 146. *Ilex glabra* 'Chamzin'. Photo by Fred Galle.

Plate 145. *Ilex crenata* 'Twiggy'. Photo by Gene Eisenbeiss.

Plate 147. *Ilex glabra* 'Ivory Queen'. Photo by Fred Galle.

Plate 148. *Ilex glabra* 'Princeton's Compact'. Photo by Fred Galle.

Plate 150. *Ilex opaca* 'Canary'. Photo by Gene Eisenbeiss.

Plate 149. *Ilex opaca* 'B. & O.'. Photo by William Kosar.

Plate 151. *Ilex opaca* 'Christmas Snow'. Photo by Fred Galle.

Plate 152. *Ilex opaca* 'Clarendon Spreading'. Photo by Fred Galle.

Plate 153. *Ilex opaca* 'Cullowhee'. Photo by Fred Galle.

Plate 154. *Ilex opaca* 'Fire Chief'. Photo by Fred Galle.

Plate 155. *Ilex opaca* 'Manig'. Photo by David Burnett.

Plate 156. *Ilex opaca* 'Merry Christmas'. Photo by David Burnett.

Plate 157. *Ilex opaca* 'Miss Helen'. Photo by David Burnett.

Plate 158. *Ilex opaca* 'Nelson West'. Photo by Fred Galle.

Plate 159. *Ilex opaca* 'North Wind'. Photo by Fred Galle.

Plate 160. *Ilex opaca* 'Oak Grove No. 1'. Photo by Fred Galle.

Plate 161. *Ilex opaca* 'Steward's Silver Crown'. Photo by Fred Galle.

Plate 162. *Ilex opaca* 'William Hawkins'. Photo by Fred Galle.

Plate 163. *Ilex vomitoria* 'Dwarf'. Photo by Fred Galle.

Plate 164. *Ilex vomitoria* 'Gray's Greenleaf'. Photo by Fred Galle.

Plate 166. *Ilex* 'Adonis'. Photo by Gene Eisenbeiss.

Plate 165. *Ilex vomitoria* 'Saratoga Gold'. Photo by Fred Galle.

Plate 167. *Ilex* 'Agena'. Photo by Gene Eisenbeiss.

Plate 168. *Ilex* Becky Stevens™. Photo by Norman Fischer.

Plate 169. *Ilex* Blue Angel®. Photo by Conard-Pyle Nursery.

Plate 170. *Ilex* Blue Angel®. Photo by David Burnett.

Plate 171. Sport of *Ilex* 'Blue Boy'. Photo by Fred Galle.

Plate 172. *Ilex* Blue Maid®. Photo by Fred Galle.

Plate 173. *Ilex* Blue Prince®. Photo by Conard-Pyle Nursery.

Plate 174. *Ilex* Blue Princess®. Photo by Conard-Pyle Nursery.

Plate 175. *Ilex* Blue Stallion®. Photo by Conard-Pyle Nursery.

Plate 176. *Ilex* Buttercup™. Photo by Conard-Pyle Nursery.

Plate 177. *Ilex* 'Calina'. Photo by Fred Galle.

Plate 178. *Ilex* Cardinal™. Photo by Fred Galle.

Plate 179. *Ilex* 'Carolina Cone'. Photo by Fred Galle.

Plate 180. *Ilex* 'Cetus'. Photo by Fred Galle.

Plate 181. *Ilex* China Boy®. Photo by Conard-Pyle Nursery.

Plate 182. *Ilex* China Girl®. Photo by Conard-Pyle Nursery.

Plate 183. *Ilex* 'Clusterberry'. Photo by William Kosar.

Plate 184. *Ilex* 'Doctor Kassab'. Photo by William Kosar.

Plate 185. *Ilex* Dragon Lady®. Photo by Conard-Pyle Nursery.

Plate 186. *Ilex* 'Elegance'. Photo by Gene Eisenbeiss.

Plate 187. *Ilex* 'Emily Bruner'. Photo by Fred Galle.

Plate 189. *Ilex* Golden Girl®. Photo by Conard-Pyle Nursery.

Plate 188. *Ilex* Festive™. Photo by Flowerwood Nursery.

Plate 190. *Ilex* 'Honey Jo'. Photo by B. Cannon.

Plate 191. *Ilex* 'Hohman'. Photo by William Kosar.

Plate 192. *Ilex* 'John T. Morris'. Photo by Gene Eisenbeiss.

Plate 193. *Ilex* 'Martha Berry'. Photo by Ken Tilt.

Plate 194. *Ilex* 'Mary Nell'. Photo by William Dodd.

Plate 195. *Ilex* 'Miniature'. Photo by Gene Eisenbeiss.

Plate 196. *Ilex* 'Nellie R. Stevens'. Photo by Fred Galle.

Plate 197. *Ilex* 'Nellie R. Stevens'. Photo by Fred Galle.

Plate 199. *Ilex* River Queen™. Photo by Norman Fischer.

Plate 198. *Ilex* Oak Leaf™. Photo by Flowerwood Nursery.

Plate 200. *Ilex* 'Rock Garden'. Photo by Fred Galle.

Plate 201. *Ilex* 'Ruby'. Photo by William Kosar.

Plate 202. *Ilex* 'Scepter'. Photo by Gene Eisenbeiss.

Plate 203. *Ilex* 'September Gem'. Photo by Robert Ticknor.

Plate 204. *Ilex* 'Venus'. Photo by Gene Eisenbeiss.

Plate 205. *Ilex* 'Wirt L. Winn'. Photo by Fred Galle.

Plate 206. This larger holly was cut back heavily prior to transplanting. Photo by Fred Galle.

Plate 207. A large and wide holly prior to hatracking. Photo by Elwin Orton.

Plate 208. The same holly after hatracking. Photo by Elwin Orton.

Plate 209. The same holly one year after hatracking. Photo by Elwin Orton.

Plate 210. Cuttings of *Ilex aquifolium* in a nursery. Photo by Monrovia Nursery.

Plate 211. The holly test gardens at Clemson University. Photo by Fred Galle.

Plate 212. Leaf miner damage on holly leaves. Photo by Elwin Orton.

Plate 213. Scale on holly branch. Photo by Fred Galle.

Plate 214. Root girdling on holly. Photo by Elwin Orton.

Deciduous Holly Cultivars

Ilex collina 'Mary Randolph' (female; selection discovered along stream bank in Randolph County, West Virginia; moved to Morgantown, West Virginia, by O. M. Neal; named and registered H.S.A. 4-76 by Neal; original plant lost in a flood; rare in the trade).

Leaves broadly lanceolate, width equals length, rugose, veins prominently raised above and below, bases cuneate to attenuate, apices acuminate, sessile gland at tip, petioles 19 mm (¾ in.) long; fruits red, glossy, globose, to 13 mm (½ in.) diameter, flattened at base, fasciculate, pendulous peduncles 10–13 mm (⅜–½ in.) long, abundant; broadly upright compact habit, original plant 1.5 m (5 ft.) tall, 1 m (3 ft.) wide in 15 years; hardy in zone 3. First named cultivar of this species. Named in honor of Mrs. Jennings Randolph, descendent of Virginia Randolph of Revolutionary War fame.

Ilex collina 'Mary Staggers' (female; selection; an old shrub estimated 50 years old, discovered along stream bank in Randolph County, West Virginia, by O. M. Neal; named and registered H.S.A. 5-76 by Neal; original plant lost in a flood; rare in the trade).

Leaves broadly lanceolate, longer than wide, veins prominently raised above and below, glabrous to sparsely pilose in axils of veins below, bases cuneate to attenuate, apices acuminate, sessile gland at tip, petioles to 19 cm (¾ in.) long; fruits red, glossy, pyriform, tapers to the stigma, prominent sessile stigma, stalklike extension of fruit, 13 mm (½ in.) diameter, fasciculate, pendulous peduncles, 10–13 mm (⅜–½ in.) long; original plant estimated 50 years old, 2.4 m (8 ft.) tall, 3.7 (12 ft.) wide; hardy in zone 3. Named for wife of Harley Staggers, former West Virginia congressman. Selected for distinct fruit.

Ilex decidua 'Arkansas' (female; plant at Bernheim Forest; collected by T. Klein in Arkansas; provisional name not registered).

Leaves typical; fruits red. Not available at present.

Ilex decidua 'Benton' (female; seedling collected in Benton, Illinois, in 1970s and named by J. B. Hartline; not registered).

Fruits reddish orange. Availability doubtful.

Ilex decidua 'Byers Golden' (female; discovered about 1959 by M. D. Byers near Deposit, Alabama; named and published by T. R. Dudley; registered H.S.A. 11-69 and introduced by M. D. Byers, Byers Nursery).

Leaves typical; fruits vivid yellow 13A–13B, globose, 6.5 mm (¼ in.) diameter, persisting until spring; stiff upright habit, ascending branches. First named cultivar of *I. decidua* with yellow fruit. Availability is limited due to difficulty in propagation.

Ilex decidua 'Cascade', see 'Red Cascade'

Ilex decidua 'Council Fire' (female; synonyms 'H. B. Red', 'H. B. Late Red'; seedling collected in the wild about 1958 by J. B. Hartline; moved to Hartline Farm, Makanda, Illinois; named and registered H.S.A. 5-78 by Hartline).

Leaves dark green, narrower than most, dropping early to permit a good display of fruit; fruits vivid red 45A, glossy, globose, 6.5 mm (¼ in.) diameter, often persisting into 2nd fall; original plant multistemmed, well branched, compact habit, 5.6 m (18 ft.) tall, 3 m (10 ft.) wide in 25 years. Plate 40.

Ilex decidua 'Finch's Golden' (female; wild seedling found by Bill Finch in 1980s in Hale County near Union Town, Alabama; named by John Smith, not registered; propagated and introduced in 1991 by Magnolia Nursery; originally named, propagated, and distributed but not registered as 'Gold Finch', a later homonym of *I. opaca* 'Gold Finch').

Leaves typical; fruits brilliant yellow; propagates easily.

Ilex decidua 'Greenfield Tennessee' (female; seedling collected in Greenfield, Tennessee, in 1970s; named by J. Bon Hartline; not registered).

Fruits reddish orange. Not available.

Ilex decidua 'H. B. Dam' (female; original plant near dam on property of H. B. Hartline; named in 1980s by J. Bon Hartline; not registered).

Leaves typical; fruits large, dark red, darkening early; bark dark.

Ilex decidua 'Hunter' (female; plant at Hunter residence, Carbondale, Illinois; discovered in 1980s and named by J. Bon Hartline; not registered).

Leaves typical; fruits vivid reddish orange 44B, globose, 8–10 mm (5/16–3/8 in.) diameter, single and on fruiting spurs; more upright habit than most. Not available at present.

Ilex decidua 'Miller City' (female; discovered in 1980s in Miller City, Illinois; named by J. Bon Hartline; not registered).

Fruits reddish orange. Availability doubtful.

Ilex decidua 'Peach' (female; natural seedling discovered in 1980s by J. Giordano, north of Union Town, Alabama; not registered).

Leaves typical; fruits red with yellow blotch. Not available at present.

Ilex decidua 'Pocahontas' (female; chance seedling selected in a private garden in Pocahontas, Missouri; named and registered H.S.A. 4-77 by J. Bon Hartline).

Leaves typical, becoming yellow and dropping before 'Council Fire'; fruits vivid red 44A, globose, 7–11 mm (9/32–7/16 in.) diameter, good fruit retention; upright habit, original plant 5.9 m (16 ft.) tall, 3.7 m (12 ft.) wide in 15 years. Plate 41.

Ilex decidua 'Red Cascade' (female; synonym 'Cascade'; original seedling obtained from Warren and Son Nursery; selected 1965 by R. C. Simpson; named and introduced 1987, registered H.S.A. 14-88 by Simpson, Simpson Nursery).

Leaves very dark green, broad, glossy; fruits deep reddish orange 43A, globose to slightly truncate, 8 mm (5/16 in.) diameter, holds well in winter, single, older branches have fruiting spurs; upright spreading

habit, branches unusual intense white, not light gray as typical, original plant small tree, globe-shaped crown, 7.5 m (25 ft.) tall, 6 m (20 ft.) wide, distinct undulating horizontal branching; hardy in zone 6; defoliates early. Plate 42.

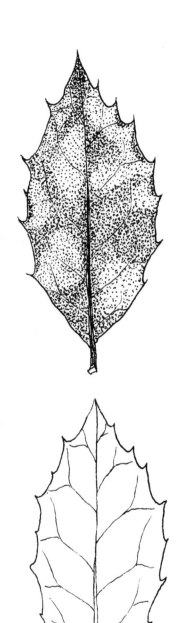

Figure 12-1. *Ilex decidua* 'Red Cascade'.

Ilex decidua 'Red Escort' (male; selected 1965 by R. C. Simpson from seedlings obtained from Warren and Son Nursery; named and introduced 1987; registered H.S.A. 13-88 by Simpson, Simpson Nursery).

Leaves typical, retain late in fall; original plant small tree, 7.5 m (25 ft.) tall, 6 m (20 ft.) wide in 25 years; hardy in zone 6. First male cultivar of this species to be named, introduced, and registered.

Ilex decidua 'Reed' (female; seedling collected 1952 by R. C. Simpson on property of W. C. Reed, Vincennes, Indiana; moved to Simpson Nursery; named by Simpson; not registered).

Fruits red, abundant; defoliates early.

Ilex decidua 'Sentry' (female; synonym 'Simpson No. 31'; selected from seedlings purchased about 1965 from Forest Keeling Nursery by R. C. Simpson; selected and distributed for evaluation in 1972; named, introduced in 1987, and registered H.S.A. 15-88 by Simpson, Simpson Nursery).

Leaves larger than most, defoliate earlier than average; fruits vivid red 45A, subglobose, 6.5 mm (¼ in.) long, 8 mm (⁵⁄₁₆ in.) diameter, single and 6–7 on fruiting spurs, pedicels purplish, 6.5 cm (¼ in.) long; original plant a small tree, columnar habit, 6 m (20 ft.) tall, 3 m (10 ft.) wide in 25 years; hardy in zone 6. Selected for columnar growth and early defoliation. Should be grown as a single stem small tree.

Ilex decidua 'Sundance' (female; seedling discovered in Cobden, Illinois; introduced about 1958 by J. Bon Hartline; not propagated or registered).

Leaves typical; fruits small, dark red, globose, 6–8 mm (³⁄₁₆–⁵⁄₁₆ in.) diameter, single; vigorous broad-spreading, bushy habit, rounded at maturity. Availability doubtful.

Ilex decidua 'Walton' (female; seedling discovered in 1970s by J. Bon Hartline on Ned Walton farm, Anna, Illinois; named and introduced by Hartline; not registered).

Leaves typical; fruits vivid red 45A, subglobose, 9 mm (¹¹⁄₃₂ in.) long, 1–3 in clusters; upright spreading habit. Availability doubtful.

Ilex decidua 'Warren's Red' (female; upright sport from seedling plant discovered and named by Otis Warren; introduced by Warren and Son Nursery in late 1950s; registered H.S.A. 16-88 by R. C. Simpson).

Leaves dark green, typical shape, very glossy, leaves retained later than most; fruits vivid red 45A, globose, 6–8 mm (⁷⁄₃₂–⁵⁄₁₆ in.) diameter, single and 2–6 on fruiting spurs, abundant, persistent; upright slightly branching habit, original plant a small tree, 7.5 m (25 ft.) tall, 6 m (20 ft.) wide; hardy in zone 6. One of the first cultivars of *I. decidua* cultivar to be named and introduced. Plate 43.

Ilex longipes 'Lagniappe' (female; seedling of *I. longipes* discovered in 1980s near Crosby, Mississippi; named by J. Giordano; not registered).

Selected and named for the large red pendulous fruits. Name in southern creole dialect means "something extra."

Ilex longipes 'Natchez Belle' (female; natural seedling of *I. longipes* discovered around 1967 by B. R. Hendrix at his residence, Hawthorne Manor, Crosby, Amity County, Mississippi, in a large colony of approximately 2000 plants; evaluated and selected in 1975 by Hendrix, T. R. Dudley, and G. Eisenbeiss; registered H.S.A. 9-76 by Hendrix).

Leaves broadly obovate, to 9.5 cm (3¾ in.) long, 4.5 cm (1¾ in.) wide, bases long and narrowly tapering, cuneate, apices acute, glabrous above, depressed veins and villous below, margins finely serrulate, petioles 8 mm (⁵⁄₁₆ in.) long, leaves yellow in fall, retain in winter; fruits vivid red 45A, glossy, globose to oblate, 8–15 mm (⁵⁄₁₆–¹⁹⁄₃₂ in.) diameter, pendulous pedicels 2–3.5 cm (¾–1⅜ in.) long, distinct large cherrylike fruits; original old plant 4 m (13 ft.) tall, 1 m (3 ft.) wide. First selection of *I. longipes* to be named and registered.

Ilex longipes 'Seven Sisters' (female; a naturally occurring clump of seven seedling female plants at Hawthorne Manor, Crosby, Amity County, Mississippi; named by J. M. Giordano; not registered).

Ilex serrata 'Dainagon' (origin Japan).
Description not available.

Ilex serrata 'Gemperi' (female; origin Japan; plants at Ebersole and Brookgreen Gardens).
Fruits red, striped yellowish white.

Ilex serrata 'Gosho Dainagon' (origin Japan).
Description not available.

Ilex serrata 'Hairosango' (origin Japan).
Description not available.

Ilex serrata 'Hatsuyuki' (female; synonym 'First Snow'; origin Japan).
Fruits yellowish white.

Ilex serrata 'Horai' (synonym 'Treasure has come'; origin Japan).
Description not available.

Ilex serrata 'Koshobai' (female; synonyms 'Kosho Umemodoki', *I. serrata* var. *subtilis*; first described in 1868 from a garden plant in Japan).

Leaves dark green, narrowly elliptic to linear, very small, 1.5–3.5 cm (19⁄32–1⅜ in.) long, 0.5–1 mm (1⁄32 in.) wide, curled downward; fruits vivid red 45A, very small, flattened, globose, 2 mm (1⁄16 in.) long, 2–3 mm (⅛ in.) diameter, pedicels 2–3 mm (1⁄16–⅛ in.) long. Popular as a bonsai plant and collector's plant. Plate 44.

Ilex serrata 'Leucocarpa' (female; synonyms 'Shiro-ume-modoki', 'Inu-ume', *I. serrata* f. *leucocarpa* Beissner; first described in 1908; given cultivar status by Ohwi 1965).

Leaves typical; fruits pale yellowish white.

Ilex serrata 'Rakusogu' (at Belgium Botanical Garden).

Fruits bicolor, red, yellowish white blush; flowers pink.

Ilex serrata 'Shirosango' (synonym 'White Coral').

Ilex serrata 'Sundrops' (female; open-pollinated seed of yellow-fruited *I. serrata* received from P. H. Kubota, Nikko, Tochigi Prefecture, Japan, U.S. National Arboretum No. 17021, PI 272055; origin from cultivated plant in Angyo, Seitami Prefecture, Japan; 9 plants grown—3 males and 6 females, of which 1 female had yellow fruit; named and registered H.S.A. 14-91 by G. Eisenbeiss; first yellow-fruited selection of *I. serrata* named in United States; introduced 1993).

Leaves atypical of species, extremely pubescent above, elliptic to ovate, to 10 cm (4 in.) long, 3.8 cm (1½ in.) wide; fruits light greenish yellow 5C, globose, 6 mm (7⁄32 in.) diameter, ripening in early September; compact spreading habit, original plant 2.4 m (7.9 ft.) tall, 4.8 m (15.8 ft.) wide; hardy in zone 5. Plate 45.

Ilex serrata 'Xanthocarpa' (female; synonyms 'Kimino Umemodoki', *I. serrata* f. *xanthocarpa* Rehder; first described in 1915).

Leaves typical; fruits yellow.

Ilex verticillata 'Afterglow' (female; selected from seedlings purchased in 1960 by R. C. Simpson of Simpson Nursery, Vincennes, Indiana; named and introduced in 1976; registered H.S.A. 2-88 by Simpson).

Leaves very glossy, typical of northern type, 6.5–7.5 cm (2½–3 in.) long; fruits vivid reddish orange 33B, slightly subglobose, 8 mm (5⁄16 in.) long, 9 mm (11⁄32 in.) diameter, 1–3 in clusters, may persist until spring; flowers early; multistemmed, slow growing compact, globe habit; original plant 3 m (10 ft.) tall and wide in 25 years; hardy in zone 4. Plate 46.

Ilex verticillata 'Alfred Anderson' (female; discovered about 1963 by R. K. Peters on roadside embankment, about 16 km (10 miles) northwest of Gettysburg, Adams County, Pennsylvania; root sprouts collected; original plant destroyed; named and registered H.S.A. 3-91 by Peters; propagated by Bull Valley Nursery).

Leaves elliptic to ovate, occasionally obovate, 6–8.5 cm (2⅜–3⅜ in.) long, 2–3 cm (¾–13⁄16 in.) wide, bases attenuate, apices acuminate, margins finely but unevenly serrate to doubly serrate, white hairs beneath, to pilose; fruits globose, deep reddish orange 43A, 6–8 mm (7⁄32–5⁄16 in.) diameter, single, peduncles 2–3 mm (1⁄16–⅛ in.) long, abundant, ripening in early October, persisting past December; original plants rounded, 2 m (6 ft.) tall and wide, ascending open habit; hardy to zone 5A.

Ilex verticillata 'Aquinnah' (female; seedling discovered at Barnard's Inn Farm by Mary L. Hill, Duke County, Massachusetts; named and registered H.S.A. 8-91 by Hill; distributed by Yew Dell and Simpson Nurseries; name is Native American word for "gay color by the seashore").

Leaves ovate, to 6 cm (2⅜ in.) long, 2.5 cm (1 in.) wide; fruits deep red 46A, glossy, depressed globose, 4 mm (5⁄32 in.) long, 8 mm (5⁄16 in.) diameter; upright, multistemmed, rounded habit, 1.8 m (6 ft.) tall, 1.5 m (4.9 ft.) wide. Selected for dark red, depressed, globose fruits.

Ilex verticillata 'Aurantiaca', see *I. verticillata* f. *aurantiaca* in Chapter 11.

Ilex verticillata 'Bright Horizon' (female; originally reported as a putative hybrid of *I. verticillata* × *I. laevigata*; seed collected 1958 in the wild from a compact plant of *I. verticillata* in North Tisbury, Massachusetts, by Polly Hill; selected and named 1969; registered H.S.A. 1-72 by Hill; later re-identified as *I. verticillata*; sibling of 'Earlibright').

Leaves typical of northern type, slightly smaller than average; fruits dark reddish orange, subglobose, 8–10 mm (5⁄16–⅜ in.) diameter, persistent, short pedicels 3 mm (⅛ in.) long; compact turbinate habit, herringbone branching; original plant 1.8 m (6 ft.) tall, 0.8 m (2½ ft.) wide in 12 years; hardy in zone 4.

Ilex verticillata 'Cacapon' (female; seedling of wild origin, West Virginia; grown at Horticulture Farm, University of West Virginia; selected 1955; named and registered H.S.A. 3-73 by O. M. Neal; U.S. PI 377678).

Leaves of northern type, dark green, glossy, waxy; fruits vivid red 44B, globose, 8 mm (5/16 in.) diameter; compact upright, turbinate habit; original plant 3.7 m (12 ft.) tall, 2.5 m (8 ft.) wide in 15 years. Similar to 'Fairfax' but more upright and slightly darker fruit. Same origin as 'Jackson' and 'Shaver', which see. Plate 47.

Ilex verticillata 'Christmas Cheer' (female; synonym 'Xmas Cheer'; originally listed as 'Xmas Cheer', then changed to 'Christmas Cheer'; origin unknown; introduced in late 1950s by Gulf Stream Nursery, Wachapreague, Virginia).

Leaves darker green than most; flowers early; fruits deep red 46A, globose, 6 mm (7/32 in.) diameter, maturing in September; compact habit. Also reported by some as a hybrid of *I. serrata* but never verified.

Ilex verticillata 'Christmas Gem' (female; seedling obtained from Gulf Stream Nursery, Wachapreague, Virginia, about 1960; selected 1968; named 1970 and registered H.S.A. 6-70 by C. L. Jenkins and Sons).

Leaves typical; fruits reddish orange, slightly ellipsoidal, heavy fruiting; original plant 1.8 m (6 ft.) tall, 2.5 m (8 ft.) wide. Selected for cut spray quality.

Ilex verticillata 'Chrysocarpa', see *I. verticillata* f. *chrysocarpa* in Chapter 11.

Ilex verticillata 'Compacta', see 'Red Sprite'.

Ilex verticillata 'Dwarf Male', see 'Jim Dandy'.

Ilex verticillata 'Earlibright' (female; synonym 'Earlybright'; originally reported as putative hybrid of *I. verticillata* × *I. laevigata*; collected in the wild on Martha's Vineyard, Massachusetts; moved to Barnard's Inn Farm by Polly Hill; named and registered H.S.A. 5-75 by Hill; later re-identified as *I. verticillata*).

Leaves typical of northern type; fruits vivid reddish orange, depressed globose, 10 mm (3/8 in.) long, 13–16 mm (1/2–5/8 in.) diameter, single; columnar habit, fastigiate branched; original plant 2.1 m (7 ft.) tall, 1.2 m (4 ft.) wide. Sibling of 'Bright Horizon', fruit ripens earlier. Plate 48.

Ilex verticillata 'Early Male', see 'Southern Gentleman'.

Ilex verticillata 'Fairfax' (female; selected 1947 by O. M. Neal in swamp at Reedsville, West Virginia; divided and moved to University of West Virginia Experiment Farm at Reedsville; named and registered H.S.A. 4-73 by Neal; U.S. PI 377679).

Leaves distinctly rugose; fruits vivid red 45A, globose, 8–10 mm (5/16–3/8 in.) diameter, heavy fruiting to 5 fruits per node, persistent; original plant 4.6 m (15 ft.) tall, 1 m (3 ft.) wide at approximately 30 years, more typically rounded in habit. Similar to 'Winter Red', but not common in trade.

Ilex verticillata 'Golden Verboom' (female; a seedling grown and introduced by K. Verboom, The Netherlands).

Ilex verticillata 'Jackson' (male; selected seedling from population of unknown origins at Horticulture Farm, University of West Virginia; named, introduced, and registered H.S.A. 5-73 by O. M. Neal, U.S. PI 377680).

Leaves typical; upright turbinate habit, original plant 3 m (10 ft.) tall, 1 m (3 ft.) wide in 15 years. Selected for dark green leaves and heavy pollen producer. First male of this species to be named and registered. Same origin as 'Cacapon' and 'Shaver', which see.

Ilex verticillata 'Jim Dandy' (male; synonym 'Dwarf Male', an illegitimate name under which this cultivar was introduced; chance seedling of collected liners purchased in 1966 from Exeter, New Hampshire, by Simpson Nursery; initial selection in 1985; named, introduced, and registered H.S.A. 3-92 by R. C. Simpson).

Leaves ovate to obovate, 7 cm (2¾ in.) long, 3 cm (1 3/16 in.) wide; flowers 5–6 petals; shrubs turbinate, 3 m (9 ft.), 2.1 m (6.6 ft.) wide, hardy in zone 4. Selected for slow growth, dense turbinate, compact habit, small leaves, early prolonged flowering period, and abundant flowers.

Ilex verticillata 'Jimmy Peters' (female; chance seedling; originated 1980 in garden of R. K. Peters; selected, named, and registered H.S.A. 3-88 by Peters).

Leaves typical; fruits vivid red, globose, 6.5 mm (¼ in.) diameter, single or 2–3 in fascicles, pedicels 2 mm (1/16 in.) long; original shrub multistemmed, columnar habit, fastigiate branching, 1.5 m (5 ft.) tall, 0.76 m (2½ ft.) wide in 8 years; hardy in zone 5a. Selected for early fruit ripening, early leaf drop, and columnar habit.

Ilex verticillata 'Jolly Red' (female; discovered in early 1960s in Bloomfield, Connecticut, by Lud Hoffman; named and introduced by Hoffman).

Leaves dark green, broadly elliptic, 7–8 cm (2¾–3 1/8 in.) long, 3.5–4.5 cm (1 3/8–1¾ in.) wide, margins serrate, petioles 15 mm (19/32 in.) long; fruits vivid red, 6–8 mm (7/32–5/16 in.) diameter, abundant.

Ilex verticillata 'Maryland Beauty' (female; seedling obtained in 1930 from Dreer Nursery by C. L. Jenkins; selected 1940; named 1968, introduced, and registered H.S.A. 5-70 by Jenkins and Sons, Mitchellville, Maryland).

Leaves typical of northern type; fruits dark red, heavy fruiting, ripen early in September, single and clusters around stems; plant 1.5 m (5 ft.) tall, 2.2 m (7 ft.) wide in 10 years. Selected for commercial cut sprays.

Ilex verticillata 'Nana', see 'Red Sprite'.

Ilex verticillata 'North Star' (male; synonym 'Simpson's Dwarf Male No. 1'; selected from 10 seedlings collected in New Hampshire by R. Simpson about 1960).

Dense rounded habit, slow growing. Selected for extended early, abundant flowers.

Ilex verticillata 'Oosterwijk' (female; selected seedling; selected and named 1984 by H. L. van de Laar from 10 seedlings selected 1950 for propagation by P. Oosterwijk, Boskoop, from seedlings of *I. verticillata* grown by D. van Wilgen of Boskoop, Netherlands, for more than 40 years).

Vigorous shrubs; fruits red, globose 8–9 mm (5/16–11/32 in.) diameter. Cut branches keep in cold storage for Christmas market in Aalesmeer and Boskoop. First *I. verticillata* cultivar named in Europe. Fruiting branches are exported to France, Italy, Sweden, Germany, and United States. Plants not available in United States.

Ilex verticillata 'Orange Beauty' (female; origin unknown; plant on estate of Albert Vesley, Rockford, Illinois; named by unknown person; not registered).

Fruit orange.

Ilex verticillata 'Peter's Fireworks' (female; discovered 1955 in swampy woodland west of Bendersville, Pennsylvania, by R. K. Peters; selected and named in 1987, registered H.S.A. 4-88 by Peters).

Leaves typical; fruits deep reddish orange 34A, subrotund, 8 mm (5/16 in.) long, 11 mm (7/16 in.) diameter, persistent. Selected for heavy large fruit and persistence.

Ilex verticillata 'Polycarpa' (female; plant at Tyler Arboretum; first listed in 1934 by Le-Mac Nursery).

Leaves elliptic, 6.5–8 cm (2½–3⅛ in.) long, 2–3 cm (¾–1³⁄₁₆ in.) wide, fruits vivid red 45A, flatting globose, 8–10 mm (5/16–3/8 in.) diameter, 6 mm (7/32 in.) thick, 1–3 in clusters; upright spreading habit. Availability doubtful.

Ilex verticillata 'Quansoo' (male; wild seedling selected in 1984 on Martha's Vineyard, Massachusetts, by Polly Hill; named and registered H.S.A. 6-86 by Hill).

Leaves typical; very floriferous male flowers; compact habit, ascending branches, numerous basal shoots; original plant 3.7 m (12 ft.) tall, 3 m (10 ft.) wide; very hardy and drought resistant. Good pollinator. Name is of Algonquin origin for a salt marsh and meadow near Chilmark, Martha's Vineyard, Massachusetts.

Ilex verticillata 'Quitsa' (female; seedling grown by Polly Hill; seed collected 1958; named and introduced 1984; registered H.S.A 3-86 by Hill).

Leaves typical; fruits vivid red 44A, globose, 6.5 mm (¼ in.) diameter, pedicels 4 mm (5/32 in.) long; upright growth, numerous vigorous basal stems; plant 2.1 m (7 ft.) tall, 1.8 m (6 ft.) wide in 28 years; reported to be very hardy and drought resistant. Name is of Algonquin origin for a place name near Gay Head, on Martha's Vineyard, Massachusetts.

Ilex verticillata 'Ralph E. Lincoln' (female; seedling grown by E. B. Seligmann; seed collected in northern Virginia, 1965–1970; named and registered H.S.A. 5-83 by Seligmann).

Leaves typical; fruits vivid red 45A, globose, 9 mm (11/32 in.) diameter, heavy fruiting, persistent; original plant 3 m (10 ft.) tall and wide in approximately 15 years, multistemmed with ascending branches.

Ilex verticillata 'Red Sprite' (female; synonyms 'Compacta', 'Macrocarpa', 'Nana', *I. verticillata* var. *nana* but never published; chance seedling discovered in the wild near Hampden Nursery, Hampden, Massachusetts, by P. A. Sicbaldi; named and registered H.S.A. 2-80 by L. J. Sicbaldi; first sold as 'Nana').

Leaves typical; fruits vivid red 45A, globose, slightly flattened at end, very large to 13 mm (½ in.) diameter, pedicels 3 mm (⅛ in.) long, single, abundant; dense globose, very compact habit, mature plants to 1–1.2 m (3–4 ft.) tall. Excellent dwarf plant with abundant large red fruits. Plate 49.

Ilex verticillata 'Rhett Butler' (male; selected seedling from plants received at Millcreek Nursery in 1950s or 1960s, date received and source forgotten; plants propagated and sold by Millcreek until 1976; original plant moved to W. Frederick residence, later destroyed; named and registered H.S.A. 1-91 by Frederick; propagation by Klehm Nursery available 1991).

Leaves ovate, to 6 cm (2⅜ in.) long, 3 cm (1³/₁₆ in.) wide, inflorescences cymose, 3-branched, 12-flowered; large shrubs to 3.6 m (11.8 ft.) high, 3 m (10 ft.) wide; hardy in zone 4. Reported as a possible hybrid. Good pollinator for 'Scarlett O'Hara'.

Ilex verticillata 'Scarlett O'Hara' (female; origin same as 'Rhett Butler'; named and registered H.S.A. 2-91 by W. Frederick; introduced by Klehm Nursery 1991).

Leaves elliptic, to 7.5 cm (3 in.) long, 2.8 cm (1⅛ in.) wide, bases cuneate, apices acuminate, margins usually serrate, occasionally double serrate; fruits deep reddish orange 42A, globose, 8 mm (⁵/₁₆ in.) diameter, reported heavy fruiting; large shrubs, 17 years old; ascending habit, dense branching, to 3.6 m (11.8 ft.) high, 3 m (10 ft.) wide; hardy in zone 4. Reported as a hybrid.

Ilex verticillata 'Shaver' (female; seedling grown at Horticulture Farm, University of West Virginia; selected about 1955; named and registered H.S.A. 6-73 by O. M. Neal, U.S. PI 377681).

Leaves of northern type, light green, thin texture, oblanceolate, 6.5 cm (2½ in.) long, 2 cm (¾ in.) wide; fruits vivid red 45A, globose, large to 13 mm (½ in.) diameter; original plant turbinate habit, 1.5 m (5 ft.) tall, 1 m (3 ft.) wide in 15 years. Same origin as 'Cacapon' and 'Jackson', which see. Plate 50.

Ilex verticillata 'Shortcake' (female; seedling grown by Polly Hill; named, introduced, and registered H.S.A. 5-86 by Hill).

Leaves typical; fruits vivid red 44A, globose, 6.5 mm (¼ in.) diameter, pedicels 1–2 mm (¹/₃₂–¹/₁₆ in.) long; semidwarf, upright branching, 1.5 m (5 ft.) tall, 1.06 m (3½ ft.) wide in 28 years. Reported to be very hardy and drought resistent.

Ilex verticillata 'Stop Light' (female; synonym 'Hopperton'; chance seedling selected 1985 at Hopperton Nursery by R. Simpson; registration pending).

Leaves of northern type, very dark green, concave, apices long pointed; fruits dark red, glossy, 8–13 mm (⁵/₁₆–½ in.) diameter, abundant; broadly upright habit, slow growing. Plate 51.

Ilex verticillata 'Sunset' (female; purchased seedling grown in Simpson Nursery; discovered 1960; named and introduced 1983 by R. Simpson; registered H.S.A. 11-88 by Simpson, Simpson Nursery).

Leaves of southern type, dark green, elliptic to narrowly lanceolate, to 13 cm (5 in.) long, 5 cm (2 in.) wide; fruits deep reddish orange to vivid red 43A and 45B, subglobose, 11 mm (⁷/₁₆ in.) diameter, 1–5 in clusters, abundant, not as persistent as 'Winter Red'; vigorous spreading habit; original plant multistemmed, wider than high, 2.4 m (8 ft.) high, 2.7 m (9 ft.) wide in 30 years; hardy in zone 4. Selected for vigorous spreading habit, large fruit, dark green foliage, and dark brown twig color. Plate 52.

Ilex verticillata 'Tiasquam' (female; seedling grown by Polly Hill; named and introduced 1984; registered H.S.A. 4-86 by Hill).

Leaves waxy, dark green; fruits vivid red 44A, globose to slightly flatting globose, 7–8 mm (⁹/₃₂–⁵/₁₆ in.) diameter, pedicels 3 mm (⅛ in.) long, ripening in early September, persistent; original plant 1.8 m (6 ft.) tall, 1.5 m (5 ft.) wide in 28 years. Reported to be very hardy and drought resistant. Named for river in Martha's Vineyard, Massachusetts.

Ilex verticillata 'Winter Gold' (female; yellow-fruited branch sport of 'Winter Red' discovered about 1983 by R. C. Simpson; selected and named 1987; introduced and registered H.S.A. 10-88 by Simpson, Simpson Nursery).

Leaves of southern type, typical in shape but lighter green than 'Winter Red'; fruits strong yellowish pink 32D, globose, 8–10 mm (⁵/₁₆–⅜ in.) diameter, single or 1–3 on peduncles; plant habit similar to 'Winter Red'; hardy in zone 4. Should be very popular due to the persistent colorful fruits not readily eaten by birds. Plate 53.

Ilex verticillata 'Winter Red' (female; selected from purchased seedlings in 1960; named and introduced 1977 by R. C. Simpson, PP 4143; reissued PP 29912 in 1979; registered H.S.A. 9-88 by Simpson, Simpson Nursery).

Leaves of southern type, dark green, glossy, elliptic lanceolate; fruits vivid red 45A, globose, 8–10 mm (⁵/₁₆–⅜ in.) diameter, abundant, persistent; flowers late; original plant multistemmed, erect, with rounded shape, 2.7 m (9 ft.) tall, 2.5 m (8 ft.) wide; hardy in zone 4. Very popular selection and standard for other selections. Cut branches can be held in unsealed plastic bags several months in cool storage (October–January/February). Plate 54.

Ilex verticillata 'Xmas Cheer', see 'Christmas Cheer'.

CHAPTER 13

Interspecific Deciduous Holly Hybrids

Ilex 'Apollo' (male; controlled cross of *I. serrata* × *I. verticillata* made in 1960 by W. F. Kosar; selected, named, and registered H.S.A. 2-78 by G. Eisenbeiss).

Leaves light green, new growth distinctly reddish, to 10 cm (4 in.) long, 7.5 cm (3 in.) wide, apices acuminate, veins distinctly depressed above, margins very finely serrate, similar to *I. serrata,* fall color light yellow; vigorous upright habit, multiple basal ascending branches, 3.7 m (12 ft.) tall and wide; hardy in zone 5. Good pollinator for sibling 'Sparkleberry'.

Ilex 'Autumn Glow' (female; controlled cross of *I. serrata* × *I. verticillata* by E. R. Orton Jr.; selected at Rutgers University; named and registered H.S.A. 7-69 by Orton).

Leaves light green, elliptic or elliptic-ovate, 3.8–6.5 cm (1½–2½ in.) long, 2–3.2 cm (¾–1¼ in.) wide, bases cuneate, apices acute, margins serrate; fruits vivid red, oval, 6 mm (⁷⁄₃₂ in.) diameter, persisting until mid-December, fruits more subject to sunburn than 'Harvest Red'; spreading habit or very broadly vase-shaped, 3.7 m (12 ft.) tall, 3 m (10 ft.) wide. Attractive fall foliage of pale blend of purple, red, yellow, and green until freezing temperatures.

Ilex 'Bonfire' (female; selected about 1957 from approximately 150 *I. serrata* seedlings grown at Simpson Nursery; named and introduced in 1983; registered H.S.A. 17-88 by R. C. Simpson, Simpson Nursery; punitive hybrid of *I. serrata* × *I. verticillata*).

Leaves elliptic to slightly lanceolate, to 12.5 cm (5 in.) long, 5 cm (2 in.) wide; fruits vivid red 45A, globose to slightly ovoid, 8 mm (⁵⁄₁₆ in.) diameter, single or 2–4 in clusters, persistent, pedicels 3 mm (⅛ in.) long, young plants fruit early; vigorous spreading habit, original plant 3.7 m (12 ft.) tall and wide in approximately 30 years; hardy in zone 5. Plate 55.

Ilex 'Carolina Cardinal' (female; plant at North Carolina State University Botanical Garden, received as gift in 1980s; named and introduced by NCSUBG; parent plant 1–1.3 m (3–4 ft.) tall, 2 m (6 ft.) wide; good display of fruit; available in 1994–1995).

Ilex 'Harvest Red' (female; controlled cross of *I. serrata* × *I. verticillata* made in 1960 by E. R. Orton Jr., Rutgers University; selected, named, and registered H.S.A. 8-69 by Orton).

Leaves elliptic or elliptic-ovate, 4.5–7 cm (1¾–2¾ in.) long, 2.5–3.2 cm (1–1¼ in.) wide, bases cuneate, apices acute, margins serrate; fruits vivid red, globose, 6.5 mm (¼ in.) diameter, do not sunburn, persisting until mid-December; very broadly vase-shaped habit, 5.1 m (6 ft.) tall, 1.8 m (6 ft.) wide in 9 years. Fall foliage dark purple until freezing temperatures. Styer Garden Award 1991.

Ilex 'Hopewell Grenadier' (female; controlled cross of (*I. serrata* × *I. verticillata*) 'Sparkleberry' × *I. serrata* made in 1979 by R. B. Rypma, Athens, Ohio; selected, named, and registered H.S.A. 4-91 by Rypma; introduced by Berryhill Nursery 1992).

Leaves elliptic, to 9 cm (3½ in.) long, 3.5 cm (1⅜ in.) wide, bases attenuate, apices acuminate, glabrous above, midrib beneath densely pubescent, margins more finely serrate than 'Hopewell Myte', petioles pale yellow to reddish, to 1.5 cm (¹⁹⁄₃₂ in.) long; fruits deep reddish orange 42A, fading to lighter red in February and March, globose, 7–8 mm (⁹⁄₃₂–⁵⁄₁₆ in.) diameter, single or fasciculate, 2–3 in cluster, pedicels red, 3 mm (⅛ in.) long; upright habit, original plant 3.1 m (10 ft.) tall in 12 years; hardy in zone 5.

Ilex 'Hopewell Myte' (female; controlled cross of ((*I. serrata* × *I. verticillata*) 'Sparkleberry' × *I. serrata*) made in 1980 by R. B. Rypma, Ohio University

Botanic Gardens; selected, named, and registered H.S.A. 18-88 by Rypma).

Leaves ovate to elliptic, to 6.6 cm (2⅝ in.) long, 3.5 cm (1⅜ in.) wide, bases rotund to attenuate, apices acuminate, margins serrate, petioles greenish yellow to red, 8 mm (⁵⁄₁₆ in.) long, branchlets very deep purplish red; fruits vivid red 45A, globose 6 mm (⁷⁄₃₂ in.) diameter, single to 2–3 in fascicles, pedicels reddish, 4 mm (⁵⁄₃₂ in.) long, good fruit display; dwarf, low spreading habit, original plant 0.6 m (2 ft.) tall, 1.2 m (4 ft.) wide, growth rate and habit similar to *I. opaca* 'Maryland Dwarf'; hardy in zone 5a. Named "Hopewell" for Native Americans who built the mounds near Hopewell, Ohio; "Myte" derived from Shakespearean poetic usage.

Ilex 'Raritan Chief' (male; controlled cross of *I. verticillata* × (*I. verticillata* × *I. serrata*) made in 1966 by E. R. Orton Jr., Rutgers University; selected, named, and registered H.S.A. 14-76 by Orton).

Leaves elliptic, 4.5–5.8 cm (1¾–2¼ in.) long, 1.9–2.8 cm (¾–⅞ in.) wide, bases cuneate, margins serrate, good green foliage color retained throughout growing season; low compact broad habit; original plant 1.5 m (5 ft.) tall, 2.5 m (8 ft.) wide in 10 years. Selected for compact habit and good retention of foliage. Good pollinator.

Ilex 'Sparkleberry' (female; controlled cross of *I. serrata* × *I. verticillata* made in 1961 by W. F. Kosar, U.S. National Arboretum; selected and named by Kosar; registered H.S.A. 2-73 by G. Eisenbeiss).

Leaves ovate to elliptic, to 7.5 cm (3 in.) long, margins finely serrate; fruits vivid red 44A, globose, 8–10 mm (⁵⁄₁₆–⅜ in.) diameter, pedicels 5 mm (³⁄₁₆ in.) long, single to 3 in fascicles, heavy fruiting, persistent; upright spreading habit; original plant 4.6 m (15 ft.) tall in 16 years; hardy in zone 5a. Received the Pennsylvania Horticultural Society's Gold Medal Plant Award 1988. Plate 56.

CHAPTER 14

Evergreen Holly Species

Ilex abscondita Steyermark 1988.

Evergreen shrubs or small trees to 3–5 m (10–16 ft.) tall; leaves broadly obovate, 5.5–9 cm (2⅛–3½ in.) long, 4–6 cm (1⅝–2⅜ in.) wide, punctate, bases cuneate, apices rotund, margins entire, revolute, petioles 7–13 mm (9/32–½ in.) long; inflorescences axillary, solitary, peduncles and pedicels minutely puberulent; fruits immature, ovoid, 7–9 mm (9/32–¹¹/32 in.) long, 6 mm (7/32 in.) diameter. Habitat: Venezuela, Amazonas, Cerro de la Neblina, at 1900 m (6300 ft.) elevation. Allied to *I. magnifructa* and *I. sipapoana*.

Ilex actidenticulata Steyermark 1988.

Evergreen, small trees, 3–8 m (10–26 ft.) tall; leaves lanceolate-elliptic or oblanceolate, 5–8.5 cm (2–3⅜ in.) long, 1.5–3 cm (¹⁹/32–1³/16 in.) wide, minutely punctate beneath, bases narrow-acute, apices acute to sharply acuminate, margins 1–3 slender acute teeth, upper one-fourth to one-third leaf, petioles 8–10 mm (⁵/16–⅜ in.) long; inflorescences axillary, solitary, fasciculate; fruits globose, 5 mm (³/16 in.) diameter; immature pyrenes dorsally canaliculate. Habitat: Venezuela. Allied to *I. karuaiana* and *I. microdonta*.

Ilex affinis Gardner 1842 var. *affinis, non* Reisseck 1861. Congonha (synonyms *I. affinis* f. *angustifolia* Reisseck 1861, *I. affinis* f. *brachyphylla* Loesener 1901, *I. affinis* var. *genuina* Loesener 1901, *I. affinis* f. *medica* (Reisseck) Loesener 1901, *I. affinis* f. *steno-thyrsa* Loesener 1901, *I. affinis* var. *valida* Loesener 1901).

Evergreen shrubs or small trees, leaves very variable, obovate-oblong or lanceolate to elliptic-lanceolate, 2.5–19 cm (1–4 in.) long, 6–38 mm (7/32–1½ in.) wide, punctate beneath, apices obtuse, with brief acumen, bases acute or cuneate, margins recurved, minutely serrulate, petioles 3.5–15 mm (9/64–¹⁹/32

in.) long; inflorescences axillary, solitary, racemose, flowers 4-merous; fruits red, globose, 3–5 mm (⅛–³/16 in.) diameter; pyrenes 4, striate, sulcate. Habitat: Brazil. Extremely polymorphic with many named variations, most of which will probably, at a later date, be treated as synonyms of the species. Allied to *I. amara, I. ovalifolia,* and *I. symplociformes*.

Ilex affinis var. *apollinis* (Reisseck) Loesener 1901 (synonym *I. apollinis* Reisseck 1861).

A variety differing from typical individuals with leaves obovate-elliptic or oblanceolate, 4–8.5 cm (1⅝–3⅜ in.) long, 1.3–2.6 cm (¹⁵/32–1 in.) wide, petioles 5 mm (³/16 in. long, apices obtuse or obtuse acuminate, bases narrow, margins recurved. Habitat: Brazil, Bahia State. Possibly a synonym of the species.

Ilex affinis var. *pachypoda* (Reisseck) Loesener 1901 (synonym *I. pachypoda* Reisseck 1861).

A variety differing from typical individuals with oblong or ovate-lanceolate leaves, 6.5–12 cm (2½–4¾ in.) long, 1.8–4 cm (¹¹/16–1⅝ in.) wide, margins recurved; inflorescences solitary, flowers 5- to 6-merous. Habitat: Brazil, Goiás State. Probably a synonym of the species.

Ilex affinis var. *rivularis* (Gardner) Loesener 1901 (synonyms *I. affinis* var. *latifolia* Reisseck 1861, *I. paraguariensis* var. *latifolia* Martius 1861, *I. rivularis* Gardner 1861).

A variety differing from typical individuals with oval or obovate leaves, usually 7–8 cm (2¾–3⅛ in.) long, 3–4 cm (1³/16–1⅝ in.) wide. Habitat: Brazil, Minas Gerais State. Probably a synonym of the species.

Ilex alainii T. R. Dudley, *nom. nov.* (basionym *I. victorinii* Alain, *Contrib. Ocas. Mus. Hist. Nat. Col. 'La Salle'* 12: 2. 1953; *non I. victorinii* Cheval 1951).

Evergreen trees or shrubs, glabrous, branchlets striate; leaves obovate-elliptic, often broadly elliptic or cuneate-obovate, 3.5–6 cm (1⅜–2⅜ in.) long, 1.3–2.8 cm (½–1¼ in.) wide, bases cuneate or narrow-cuneate, apices obtuse or emarginate, recurved, margins revolute, entire, petioles 2.5–4.5 mm (³⁄₃₂–¹¹⁄₆₄ in.) long; inflorescences axillary, 1- to 3- to 8-flowered; fruits globose, 5–7 cm (³⁄₁₆–⁹⁄₃₂ in.) diameter; pyrenes 4. Habitat: Cuba, Oriente Province, Moa Cayogan. Allied to *I. hypaneura*.

Ilex × altaclerensis (Loudon) Dallimore 1908 (synonyms *I. maderensis* Hort., *non* Lamarck 1791, *I. aquifolium* var. *altaclerensis* Loudon 1838, *I. perado* Hort., *non* Aiton 1792).

Includes all natural-occurring and artificial hybrids of *I. aquifolium* and *I. perado*. Evergreen, large shrubs or trees; leaves elliptic, 2–10 cm (2–4 in.) long, margins slightly undulate, entire to occasionally with spiny teeth; inflorescences axillary, fasciculate; fruits red. Often confused with *I. aquifolium* but the leaves are larger, usually entire, and with distinct winged petioles and grooves beneath. Many cultivars available; see descriptions in Chapter 15.

Ilex alternifolia (Zollinger & Moritzi) Loesener 1901 (synonyms *Viburnum alternifolia* Zollinger & Moritzi 1845, *I. densiflora* Zippelius *ex* Loesener 1901).

Evergreen shrubs, with erect branches, mature plants ascending and layering grayish branches, dense prominent lenticels; leaves elongate, 5–11.5 cm (5–4¼ in.) long, 2–5 cm (¾–2 in.) wide; fruit unknown. Habitat: Indonesia, Sumatra, Java.

Ilex altiplana Steyermark 1988.

Evergreen shrubs or trees 3–20 m (10–65 ft.) tall, branches minutely pubescent or glabrescent; leaves ovate or oblong-elliptic, 4–6 cm (1⅝–2½ in.) wide, bases acute, apices acute or acuminate, margins entire, petioles 3–7 mm (⅛–⁹⁄₃₂ in.) long; inflorescences axillary, solitary, 1- to 4-flowered; fruits subglobose, 4–5 mm (⁵⁄₃₂–³⁄₁₆ in.) diameter; pyrenes 4, trigonous, dorsally esulcate. Habitat: Venezuela, Bolivar: between San Ignacio de Yuruani and San Francisci do Yuruani, along small streams at 1200 m (3960 ft.) elevation. Allied to *I. macarenensis*.

Ilex amara (Velloso) Loesener 1897. Cauna, caunina (synonyms *Chomelia amara* Velloso 1835, *I. amara* var. *angustifolia* Reisseck 1861, *I. amara* var. *latifolia* Reisseck 1861, *I. amara* var. *longifolia* Reisseck 1861, *I. amara* f. *microphylla* Reisseck 1861, *I. paraguariensis* Reisseck 1861, *non* St.-Hilaire 1822, *I. brevifolia* Bonpland 1869, *I. crepitans* Bonpland 1883, *I. amara* f. *corcovadensis* Loesener 1901, *I.*

amara var. *crepitans* (Bonpland) Loesener 1901, *I. amara* f. *densiserrata* Loesener 1901, *I. amara* f. *humboldtiana* (Bonpland) Loesener 1901, *I. amara* f. *leucocalycoides* Loesener 1901, *I. amara* var. *muenteriana* Loesener 1901, *I. amara* f. *nigropunctata* (Miers) Loesener 1901, *I. amara* f. *ovalifolia* (Bonpland) Loesener 1901, *I. amara* var. *tijucensis* Loesener 1901, *I. amara* var. *bahiensis* Loesener 1908).

Evergreen, large shrubs or small trees; leaves variable, obovate or obovate-oblong or oblong-lanceolate to elliptic-lanceolate, 2.5–10 cm (1–4 in.) long, 0.6–3.9 cm (⁷⁄₃₂–1½ in.) wide, punctate beneath, apices obtuse with brief acumen, bases acute or cuneate, margins recurved, minutely serrulate, petioles 3.5–15 mm (⁹⁄₆₄–¹⁹⁄₃₂ in.) long; inflorescences axillary, solitary, racemose, flowers 4-merous; fruits red, globose, 3–5 mm (⅛–³⁄₁₆ in.) diameter; pyrenes 4, striate, sulcate. Habitat: Brazil. Extremely polymorphic. Allied to *I. affinis, I. chamaedryfolia, I. dumosa, I. virgata,* and *I. vitis-idaea*.

Ilex amazonensis Edwin 1965.

Evergreen small trees to 6–8 m (20–26 ft.) tall, branchlets puberulent; leaves broadly ovate, 5.3–7 cm (2³⁄₃₂–2¾ in.) long, 3–4.2 cm (1³⁄₁₆–1⅝ in.) wide, villose and punctate beneath, bases rotund to obtuse, apices shortly acuminate, acumens short, lance-triangular, margins entire, revolute, petioles 8–14 mm (⁵⁄₁₆–¹⁷⁄₃₂ in.) long; inflorescences axillary, fasciculate, pedunculate, flowers usually 5-merous; fruits black when dry, pyriform, 7 mm (⁹⁄₃₂ in.) long, 6 mm (⁷⁄₃₂ in.) diameter; pyrenes 4, narrow or wide triangulate, unisulcate or unicanaliculate, with or without marginal edges. Habitat: Venezuela, Amazonas, upper Canon Grande basin, at 1900 m (6270 ft.) elevation, Cerro de la Neblina, Rio Yatua.

Ilex amboroica Loesener 1909.

Evergreen shrubs, glabrous or partially so; leaves oblong or oblong-elliptic to ovate-oblong, 4.7–9 cm (1¹³⁄₁₆–3½ in.) long, 1.5–2.8 cm (¹⁹⁄₃₂–1⅛ in.) wide, bases cuneate or cuneate-obtuse, apices obtuse or obtuse-acuminate, punctate below, margins subcrenulate-serrulate, petioles 5–8 mm (³⁄₁₆–⁵⁄₁₆ in.) long; male inflorescences axillary, solitary, flowers 4-merous; fruits unknown. Habitat: Bolivia, on Monte Cerro Ambroro, 1300–1400 m (4390–4620 ft.) elevation. Allied to *I. boliviana* and *I. hippocrateoides*.

Ilex ampla I. M. Johnston 1938.

Evergreen, large trees to 22 m (72 ft.) tall, wide spreading crown, glabrous; leaves oblong or ovate-oblong, 16–18 cm (6⅜–7¹⁄₁₆ in.) long, 6–9.5 cm (2⅜–3¾ in.) wide, minutely punctate, bases rotund or subcordate, apices obtuse, margins remotely crenate, petioles 12–15 mm (¹⁵⁄₃₂–¹⁹⁄₃₂ in.) long; inflorescences axillary, solitary, short cylindrical-racemiform, 3 cm (1 3/16 in.) long, 20–30 flowers; fruits dark red, globose-ellipsoid, 4–5 mm (5/32–3/16 in.) long, 3–4 mm (1/8–5/32 in.) wide, pyrenes unknown. Habitat: Guatemala, Clomba Department Quezaltenango at 900 m (2970 ft.) elevation. Allied to *I. affinis.*

Ilex amplifolia Rusby 1896.

Evergreen, glabrous shrubs or small trees; leaves broadly oval, 8–15 cm (3 1/8–6 1/8 in.) long, 6.5–9 cm (2 1/2–3 3/4 in.) wide, bases rotund or subcuneate, apices briefly elongated, margins entire to minutely serrulate, petioles 7–9 mm (9/32–11/32 in.) long; inflorescences glabrous, axillary, solitary, branched, peduncles 6–22 mm (7/32–13/16 in.) long, pedicels 7–9 mm (9/32–11/32 in.) long; fruits unknown. Habitat: Bolivia, near Tipuani-Guana. Allied to *I. sapotifolia.*

Ilex amygdalifolia Rusby 1893 (synonym *I. andarensis* Rusby *ex* Loesener 1841).

Evergreen shrubs; leaves ovate-lanceolate to elliptic, glabrous, 8–19 cm (3 1/8–7 3/4 in.) long, 2.5–6.8 cm (1–2 11/16 in.) wide, bases rotund to obtuse, apices acuminate, margins entire, petioles 5–11 mm (3/16–3/8 in.) long; inflorescences axillary, 4- to 10-fasciculate, peduncles 9–25 mm (11/32–1 in.) long, pedicels 3–5 mm (1/8–3/16 in.) long; fruits dark purplish, globose, 5 mm (3/16 in.) diameter; pyrenes 4–5. Habitat: Bolivia, near Songa and in Sandillana, at 2300–2400 m (7590–7920 ft.) elevation. Allied to *I. amplifolia* and *I. sapotifolia;* may at a later date be regarded as conspecific.

Ilex amygdalina Reisseck *ex* Loesener 1901.

Evergreen shrubs or trees, branches ascending; leaves lanceolate, 6–8.7 cm (2 3/8–3 7/16 in.) long, 0.9–1.8 cm (11/32–11/16 in.) wide, apices narrow-obtuse, bases acute or cuneate-acute, margins recurved, remotely crenulate-serrulate to subentire, petioles 9–11 mm (11/32–7/16 in.) long; inflorescences axillary, paucifasciculate, pedicels 2–4 mm (1/16–5/32 in.) long, flowers 4- to 5-merous; fruits red, globose, 4–5 mm (5/32–3/16 in.) diameter; pyrenes 4–5, striate. Habitat: Peru. Allied to *I. affinis.*

Ilex andicola Loesener 1901.

Evergreen, small trees 3–7 m (10–23 ft.) tall; leaves glabrous, oval to elliptic or obovate, 6–7.5 cm (2 3/8–3 in.) long, 2.5–3.5 cm (1–1 3/16 in.) wide, bases obtuse to cuneate, apices usually rounded, margins recurved, subcrenulate to serrulate, petioles 9–10 mm (11/32–3/8 in.) long; inflorescences axillary, solitary, branched, 4- to 15-flowered, peduncles 10–18 mm (3/8–11/16 in.) long, pedicels 1–2 mm (1/32–1/16 in.) long; fruits unknown. Habitat: Bolivia, at high elevations 3000–3700 m (9,900–12,200 ft.). Allied to *I. crassifolia.*

Ilex angustissima Reisseck 1861.

Evergreen shrubs 1–2 m (3–6 ft.) tall; leaves linear-sublanceolate, 5–6 cm (2–2 3/8 in.) long, 3–8 mm (1/8–5/16 in.) wide, apices acute or obtuse to acute, bases narrow, margins recurved, remotely serrulate or subentire, petioles 4–7 mm (5/32–9/32 in.) long; inflorescences axillary, solitary, or fasciculate, flowers 4-merous; fruits unknown. Habitat: Brazil, Minas Gerais State. Allied to *I. affinis.*

Ilex annamensis Tardieu 1945.

Evergreen, small trees to 1.5–1.8 m (5–6 ft.) tall, branches glabrous, erect, lenticellate; leaves lanceolate or obovate, 7–9 cm (2 3/4–3 1/2 in.) long, 3 cm (1 3/16 in.) wide, bases cuneate or rotund, apices acute, margins entire, recurved, petioles 1–1.3 cm (3/8–1/2 in.) long, glabrous; male inflorescences solitary or 1- to 3-fasciculate, peduncles 1–1.3 cm (3/8–1/2 in.) long, pedicels 7 mm (9/32 in.) long; fruits globose, 6 mm (7/32 in.) diameter. Habitat: Vietnam, Annam. Allied to *I. excavata.*

Ilex anodonta Standley & Steyermark 1940. Cerezo.

Evergreen, large shrubs or trees to 12 m (40 ft.) tall, branches glabrous, dark brown, lenticels inconspicuous; leaves oblong or elliptic-oblong to obovate-oblong, 6.5–10 cm (2 1/2–4 in.) long, 2.5–3.8 cm (1–1 1/2 in.) wide, bases acute or subrotund, apices subacuminate or abruptly acute, stipules usually 3.5 mm (9/64 in.) long, fine-pointed, margins entire, glabrous, subrevolute, petioles 7–13 mm (9/32–1/2 in.) long; inflorescences axillary, fasciculate, pedicels 2.5 mm (3/32 in.) long, flowers 4-merous; fruits unknown. Habitat: Guatemala, Department San Marcos, top of ridge between Canjula and La Union Juarez, at 2000–3000 m (6600–9900 ft.) elevation.

Ilex anomala Hooker & Arnott 1832 f. *anomala.* Koawan, kowan, kawan, Hawaiian holly (synonyms *Byronia sandwicensis* Endlicher 1836, *Polystigma hookeri* Meissner 1840, *I. anomala* f. *sandwicensis* (Endlicher) Loesener 1901, *I. hawaiensis* S.-y. Hu 1967).

Evergreen trees to 14 m (56 ft.) tall, vigorous, upright branches, young branches dark gray-brown, mature dark gray; leaves oval to obovate-lanceolate to elliptic-lanceolate, 5–13 cm (2–5 1/8 in.) long, 3–5 cm (1 1/8–5 in.) wide, margins entire, finely recurved, bases narrowly to broadly cuneate, rarely obtuse, apices obtuse to rounded, densely veined, petioles 6–30 mm (7/32–1 3/16 in.) long, foliage dense, short internodes often 2–10 mm (1/16–3/8 in.) apart, stipules widely triangular; inflorescences solitary, axillary, long peduncles 15–50 mm (½–2 in.) long; corollas large 6–10 petals, calyces 4-merous; fruit black, subglobose to ellipsoidal, 4.5–5 mm (⁵⁄₃₂–³⁄₁₆ in.) long, 5–6 mm (³⁄₁₆–⁷⁄₃₂ in.) wide, ovaries 10–22 locules; pyrenes 10–18. Habitat: Tahiti, Polynesia. Allied to *I. harmandiana.*

Ilex anomala f. *taitensis* (A. Gray) Nadeaud *ex* Loesener 1901 (synonym *Byronia taitensis* A. Gray 1856).

Leaves obovate to narrowly lanceolate-elliptic; ovaries 12–14 locules, rarely 18. Habitat: Tahiti.

Ilex anonoides Loesener 1901.

Leaves evergreen, glabrous, broadly oval to broadly obovate, 11.5–18 cm (4⁷⁄₁₆–7⁵⁄₁₆ in.) long, 7.5–10.5 cm (3–4⅛ in.) wide, bases rounded, petioles 14–25 mm (¹⁷⁄₃₂–1 in.) long; inflorescences axillary, solitary, branched, 4- to 7-flowered, peduncles 6–17 mm (⁷⁄₃₂–2¹⁄₃₂ in.) long, pedicels 1 mm (¹⁄₃₂ in.) long; fruits grayish brown, globose, 5 mm (³⁄₁₆ in.) diameter; pyrenes 4. Habitat: Peru. Allied to *I. crassifolioides* and *I. pustulosa.*

Ilex antonii Elmer 1913. Masaliksik.

Evergreen, gnarled and ridged, small trees to 7 m (25 ft.) tall, branches from center, ascending, erect dense large shrubs; leaves flat, dark green, cuneiform, 1.5 cm (1⅜ in.) long, 7 mm (⁹⁄₃₂ in.) wide, apices truncate, rounded, distinctly emarginate, margins entire, petioles short; inflorescences usually solitary, occasionally 2–3 in cluster, pedicels 2–4 mm (¹⁄₁₆–⁵⁄₃₂ in.) long; fruits unknown. Habitat: Philippines, endemic in dense thickets, elfin forest, on high exposed ridges of Mount Calelan, at about 2400 m (7900 ft.) elevation. Named for son of Elmer.

Ilex apicidens N. E. Brown 1906.

Evergreen, glabrous shrubs, branches tuberculate, leaf scars obvious; leaves elliptic or obovate, 5–11 mm (³⁄₁₆–⁹⁄₃₂ in.) long, 4–7 mm (⁵⁄₃₂–⁹⁄₃₂ in.) wide, bases obtusely rotund or cuneate, apices rotund or emarginate, margins entire at base, revolute, 5–9 small teeth at apex, petioles 1–2 mm (¹⁄₃₂–¹⁄₁₆ in.) long; inflorescences axillary, solitary or 2- to 3-flowered pedunculate cymes, flowers 4-merous. Habitat: Venezuela, on summit of Mount Roraima, at 2600 m (8600 ft.) elevation. Allied to *I. obcordata.*

Ilex apiculata Merrill 1934.

Evergreen shrubs, branches angulate, glabrous; leaves elliptic to oblong-elliptic, 1–1.5 cm (⅜–¹⁹⁄₃₂ in.) long, 5–8 mm (³⁄₁₆–⁵⁄₁₆ in.) wide, bases acute, apices rotund, margins entire, rarely 1–2 serrate teeth near apex, petioles minutely pubescent, 1–2 mm (¹⁄₃₂–¹⁄₁₆ in.) long; flowers axillary, solitary, 4-

Figure 14-1. *Ilex aquifolium* var. *aquifolium.* Photo by Barton Bauer Sr.

merous; fruits ovoid, short beak, 4 mm (⁵⁄₃₂ in.) long; pyrenes 3. Habitat: Indonesia, Sumatra, Tapianoeli, summit of Dolok, Soceroegan, Habinsaran. Allied to *I. hanceana* and *I. walkeri.*

Ilex aquifolium Linnaeus 1753 var. *aquifolium.* English holly, common holly, European holly, Oregon holly, Christdorn, Christdorn, Holme, Hulst, Agrifolio, Ostrolist, Seiyo hiiragi (synonyms *Aquifolium* Haller Enum. Gotting. 1753, *A. ilex* Scopoli 1773, *I. aquifolium* var. *vulgaris* Aiton 1789, *A. spinosum* Gaertner 1791, *I. sempervirens* Salisbury 1796, *I. balearica* Desfontaines 1809, *I. vulgaris* J. Gray 1821, *I. chrysocarpa* Wender 1825, *I. crassifolia* Aiton *ex* Steudel 1837, *I. citriocarpa* Murray, *I. aquifolium* var. *integrifolia* Lange 1864, *I. aquifolium* var. *arbutifolia* Todaro 1884, *I. aquifolium* f. *arbutifolia* Loesener 1901, *I. aquifolium* f. *balearica* (Desfontaines) Loesener 1901, *I. aquifolium* f. *heterophylla* (Aiton) Loesener 1901, *I. aquifolium* f. *heterophylla* subf. *algarviensis* Loesener 1901, *I. aquifolium* f. *vulgaris* Loesener 1901, *I. aquifolium* var. *acubiforms* F. Gillot (or J. Gillier) 1904, *I. aquifolium* var. *algarviensis* Chodat 1909, *I. aquifolium* var. *barcinonae* Pau 1922, *I. aquifolium* var. *laetevirens* Sennen 1926, *I. montsenatense* Sennen 1936).

Evergreen, large shrubs or pyramidal trees to 15–25 m (50–80 ft.) tall, branchlets glabrous or minutely puberulent when young; leaves dark green, glossy, ovate or elliptic to oblong-ovate, 3–10 cm (1³⁄₁₆–4 in.) long, 2–5 cm (¾–2 in.) wide, margins wavy, spiny, leaves on old trees often entire, petioles pubescent, rarely winged, 5–16 mm (³⁄₁₆–⅝ in.) long; inflorescences axillary, fasciculate, flowers white, fragrant, 4-merous; fruits red, occasionally yellow, usually globose, 7–10 mm (⁹⁄₃₂–⅜ in.) diameter, usually in clusters; pyrenes usually 4, striate, sulcate, to rugose. Habitat: western and southern Europe, North Africa, and western Anatolia. Does not occur in China as often reported, unless cultivated. Hardy in zones 6b to 8a. Cultivated since ancient times. Numerous cultivars with green or variegated leaves are in cultivation; see descriptions in Chapter 15. Allied to *I. colchica, I. cornuta,* and *I. spinigera.* Plate 57.

> *Ilex aquifolium* var. *australis* Loesener 1982, see *I.* × *altaclerensis.*
>
> *Ilex aquifolium* var. *caspica* Loesener 1901, see *I. colchica.*
>
> *Ilex aquifolium* var. *chinensis* Loesener 1901, see *I. centrochinensis* S.-y. Hu 1949.
>
> *Ilex aquifolium* var. *nigricans* Goeppert 1911, see *I.* × *altaclerensis.*
>
> *Ilex aquifolium* var. *platyhylloides* (Chodat) Loesener 1908, see *I.* × *altaclerensis.*
>
> *Ilex aquifolium* f. *spinigera* Loesener 1901, see *I. spinigera.*

Ilex aracamuniana Steyermark 1989.

Evergreen trees 6–10 m (20–65 ft.) tall, glabrous throughout; leaves lanceolate to oblong-elliptic, 6.5–10 cm (2½–4 in.) long, 2–3.5 cm (¾–1⅜ in.) wide, dark punctate beneath, bases acute, apices acute, margins entire, leaves ascending at 45- to 60-degree angles; inflorescences solitary, axillary and lateral, winged by decurrent leaf bases; fruits subglobose, 8–10 mm (5⁄16–⅜ in.) diameter, pyrenes 5, trigonal, unisulcate dorsally. Habitat: Venezuela, Territory Federal Amazonas, Rio Negro, Cerro Araemuni summit, at 1550 m (5115 ft.) elevation. Allied to *I. huachamacariana* and *I. sipapoana.*

Ilex archboldiana Merrill & Perry 1934.

Evergreen trees to 15 m (50 ft.) tall, branchlets grayish white, pubescent, twigs dense; leaves obovate to elliptic, 1.5–3.5 cm (19⁄32–1⅜ in.) long, 1–2 cm (⅜–¾ in.) wide, glossy, bases broadly subcordate, apices obtuse to retuse, margins entire, slightly revolute, glabrous, petioles 5 mm (3⁄16 in.) long; inflorescences axillary, solitary, or 3–5 flowers cymose umbels, peduncles 6 mm (7⁄32 in.) long, pedicels 3 mm (⅛ in.) long; fruits red, subglobose, 4–5 mm (5⁄32–3⁄16 in.) diameter; pyrenes 4. Habitat: Papua New Guinea, in ridge forests, Mount Tata, Central Division. Allied to *I. revoluta.*

Ilex archeri Edwin 1965.

Evergreen shrubs 1.5–3 m (5–10 ft.) tall, branches pubescent; leaves usually obovate, 3.2–5.5 cm (1¼–2⅛ in.) long, 1.8–2.5 cm (11⁄16–1 in.) wide, villose and punctate beneath, bases acute or cuneate, apices orbiculate, obtuse, or slightly acute, margins entire, revolute, petioles villose, 5–9 mm (3⁄16–11⁄32 in.) long; inflorescences axillary, solitary, flowers 4- to 5-merous; fruits brown when dry, subglobose, 8 mm (5⁄16 in.) long, 6.5 mm (¼ in.) diameter; pyrenes 4, dorsally unisulcate. Habitat: Venezuela, Amazonas, near Cerro de la Neblina, Rio Yatua, at 1500–1700 m (4950–5600 ft.) elevation.

Ilex ardisiifrons Reisseck 1861.

Evergreen, glabrous, large shrubs or trees; leaves elliptic-oblong, or elliptic-lanceolate, 6.5–10 cm (2½–4 in.) long, 1.7–3 cm (21⁄32–1 3⁄16 in.) wide, apices obtuse, usually acuminate, bases acute or subcuneate-acute, margins entire, revolute, petioles 5–8 mm (3⁄16–5⁄16 in.) long; inflorescences axillary, fasciculate, flowers 4-merous, fruits black, subglobose, 7 mm (9⁄32 in.) long, 6 mm (7⁄32 in.) wide; pyrenes 4. Habitat: Brazil, Amazonas State, near the Japurá River. Allied to *I. vismiifolia.*

Ilex ardisioides Loesener 1901.

Evergreen, glabrous shrubs or trees; leaves obovate-elliptic or oblong-elliptic, 4.5–7.8 cm (1¾–3⅛ in.) long, 1.6–3.1 cm (⅝–1 3⁄16 in.) wide, punctate beneath, apices obtuse acuminate, acumen often obscure, bases cuneate, margins recurved, entire, petioles 6–8 mm (7⁄32–5⁄16 in.) long; inflorescences axillary, fasciculate, branched, flowers 4- to 5-merous; fruits black, globose, 6–7 mm (7⁄32–9⁄32 in.) diameter; pyrenes 4–5, unistriate. Habitat: Taiwan. Allied to *I. epiphytica.*

Ilex argentina Lillo 1911. Roble, pala de yuba.

Evergreen trees 12 m (40 ft.) tall, branches whitish, sulcate; leaves ovate, slightly acuminate, punctate margins serrate, entire near base; inflorescences axillary, fasciculate, few-flowered; fruits ellipsoid, calyces persistent. Habitat: Argentina, Province de Tucuma. Allied to *I. paraguariensis.*

Ilex arimensis (Loesener) Britton & Willdenow 1930 (synonym *I. guianensis* var. *arimensis* Loesener 1901).

Leaves usually entire, petioles 10–18 mm (⅜–11⁄16 in.) long; inflorescences 4- to 15-branched. Habitat: Bolivia and Trinidad. Allied to *I. jenmanii.*

Ilex arnhemensis (F. Mueller) Loesener 1901 subsp. *arnhemensis* (synonym *Byronia arnhemensis* F. Mueller 1882).

Evergreen shrubs or trees to 25 m (82 ft.) tall, erect stems, bark grayish; leaves glabrous, ovate-oblong to oblong, 8–12 cm (3⅛–4¾ in.) long, 4–7 cm

(1⅝–2¾ in.) wide, entire recurved margins, bases cuneate, apices usually obtuse to shortly acuminate, petioles 7–20 mm (9/32–¾ in.) long; inflorescences solitary, axillary, 3–7 umbelliform, flowers 6- to 8-merous; fruit globose to ellipsoid, 4 mm (5/32 in.) diameter; pyrenes 12–13. Habitat: northern Australia, along the Charlotte River in Arnhem Land, Australia, Papua New Guinea. Allied to *I. anomala.*

Ilex arnhemensis subsp. *ferdinandii* (Harms) Pedley 1984 (synonyms *I. peduncularis* F. Mueller 1870, *I. ferdinandii* Harms 1942).

Flowers 6-merous; fruits globose, prominent apical umbo; petals not persistent beneath fruits. Habitat: western Australia, understory in rain forest, and southern Papua New Guinea.

Ilex asperula Martius *ex* Reisseck 1861 (synonyms *I. asperula* var. *gracilipes* (Merrill) Loesener 1901, *I. asperula* var. *martiusiana* Loesener 1901, *I. asperula* var. *pyrenea* Loesener 1901).

Evergreen shrubs 2–2.5 m (6–8 ft.) tall, branchlets pubescent; leaves oval to ovate or obovate, 2.9–3.5 cm to 7.5 cm (13/32–1⅜ in. to 3 in.) long, 1.5–2.3 cm (19/32–⅞ in.) wide, apices rotund or obtuse, short-spined, bases obtuse or rotund, margins entire, revolute, petioles 2–5 mm (1/16–3/16 in.) long; inflorescences axillary, solitary, branched, 2- to 3-flowered, flowers usually 4-merous; fruits unknown. Habitat: Brazil. Allied to *I. brasiliensis, I. subcordata,* and *I. velutina.*

Ilex atabapoensis T. R. Dudley, *nom. nov.* (basionym *I. spathulata* Steyermark, *Ann. Missouri Bot. Garden* 75: 331. 1988; and homonym of *I. spathulata* Koidzumi 1925).

Evergreen shrubs to 2 m (6 ft.) tall, branchlets glabrous; leaves narrow-spathulate, 2.5–4.5 cm (1–1¾ in.) long, 0.5–1.2 cm (3/16–15/32 in.) wide, punctate below, bases narrowed and decurrent, apices rotund, emarginate, margins entire, revolute, below, petioles 5–8 mm (3/16–5/16 in.) long; inflorescences axillary, solitary, lateral, 1- to 2-flowered; fruits globose, 6 mm (7/32 in.) diameter, pedicels 10–12 mm (⅜–15/32 in.) long. Habitat: Venezuela, Amazonas, Department Atabapo, Cerro Marahuaka, slopes upstream from Rio Yameduaka, at 1225 m (4040 ft.) elevation. Allied to *I. gleasoniana.*

Ilex atrata W. Smith 1917 var. *atrata* (synonym *I. atrata* var. *glabra* C.-y. Wu *ex* Y.-r. Li 1985).

Evergreen trees with large terminal buds; leaves elliptic, 12–16 cm (4¾–6½ in.) long, 3.5–5 cm (1⅜–2 in.) wide, margins finely serrate or crenate-serrate, bases rounded, obtuse or broadly cuneate, apices acuminate, petioles 15–25 mm (9/16–1 in.) long; inflorescences simple cymes, axillary on new growth, peduncles 2–3 mm (1/16–⅛ in.) long, pedicels 5–8 mm (3/16–5/16 in.) long; fruits red, globose, 6 mm (7/32 in.) diameter, stigma with 4–5 lobes; pyrenes 5, smooth, estriate, esulcate. Habitat: People's Republic of China, rare species from Yunnan Province, in the Nan Tamai Valley. Allied to *I. kwangtungensis.*

Ilex atrata var. *wangii* S.-y. Hu 1949.

Differs from the species with peduncles longer than the pedicels, both puberulent. Habitat: southwestern People's Republic of China, Yunnan Province. Similar to *I. manneiensis.*

Ilex × attenuata Ashe 1924. Topel holly (synonyms *I. nettletoniana* R. H. Ferguson 1937, *I. topeli* Hort. 1937).

Natural hybrids between *I. opaca, I. cassine,* and *I. myrtifolia.* Large shrubs or small trees, pyramidal habit; leaves extremely variable, elliptic or oblanceolate to oblong-obovate, 4–10 cm (1⅝–4 in.) long, width variable, usually less than ⅓ of length, apices acuminate, one spine at apex, bases attenuate, margins entire or 1–5 small spines usually on upper half of leaf; inflorescences axillary, on new growth; fruits red, globose 6–8 mm (7/32–5/16 in.) diameter, usually in clusters; pyrenes smaller and usually more elongated than *I. opaca;* seed germinate first season. Habitat: United States, scattered in the wild in Florida, coastal regions of Georgia and North and South Carolina, especially in areas where at least the ranges of two of the three parent species overlap. Numerous cultivars now named from nursery-grown seedlings and collected plants.

Ilex auricula S. Andrews 1983.

Evergreen shrubs to 3 m (10 ft.) tall, branchlets softly pubescent when young; leaves orbiculate, rarely elliptic, pubescent, 0.5–1.2 cm (3/16–15/32 in.) long, 0.5–1.2 cm (3/16–15/32 in.) wide, strongly convex, strongly revolute, margins usually entire, leaf margins of flowering shoots occasionally with short divaricate spines, petioles 1–2 mm (1/32–1/16 in.) long; inflorescences on new growth, axillary, fasciculate, flowers 4-merous; fruits black, globose, 5–6 mm (3/16–7/32 in.) diameter; pyrenes 4, scarcely ridged. Habitat: Brazil, Bahia State in the Sierra do Sincorá, at 1300–1500 m (4300–4950 ft.) elevation. Allied to *I. nummularia,* and *I. scutiiformis,* and *I. subcordata.*

Ilex austro-sinensis C.-j. Tseng 1985.

Evergreen shrubs or trees 3–12 m (10–40 ft.) tall, branchlets striate, puberulent or glabrescent; leaves oblong or elliptic-oblong or ovate-elliptic, 5–10 cm (2–4 in.) long, 2–4 cm (¾–1⅝ in.) wide, apices acuminate, acumens 6–10 mm (7/32–⅜ in.) long, bases rotund or obtuse, margins revolute, remotely serrate or subentire, petioles puberulent, 5–10 mm (3⁄16–3⁄8 in.) long; inflorescences puberulent, axillary, fasciculate, 1- to 3-flowered cymose, flowers 4-merous; fruits ellipsoid, color unknown, stigmas persistent, thick-disciform or capitate. Habitat: People's Republic of China, Guangxi, Guangdong, and Hainan provinces. Allied to *I. corallina.*

Ilex azuensis Loesener 1913.

Evergreen trees, branches glabrous; leaves villose beneath, obovate to obcordate, 1.2–4 cm (15⁄32–15⁄8 in.) long, 0.8–2.5 cm (5⁄16–1 in.) wide, bases mostly acute or cuneate, apices obtuse, occasionally broadly acute, margins entire, little to very revolute, petioles usually glabrous, 3–6 mm (1⁄8–7⁄32 in.) long; flowers on new wood, axillary, solitary; fruits globose, pyrenes 4, smooth. Habitat: Dominican Republic, in forest on high ridges. Allied to *I. impressa.*

Ilex baasiana Stone & Kiew 1984.

Evergreen, epiphytic shrubs, branches slender elongated; leaves narrowly lanceolate, 3.5–8.5 cm (13⁄8–33⁄8 in.) long, 0.5–1.2 cm (3⁄16–15⁄32 in.) wide, bases acuminate, cuneate to very slightly decurrent, margins entire, slightly recurved, petioles 3–8 mm (1⁄8–5⁄16 in.) long; male inflorescences axillary, racemose, flowers 5-merous; fruits unknown. Unusual epiphytic shrubs with tuberous roots. Habitat: Malaysia, in montane rain forest toward summit of Gunung Ulu Kali, Genting Highlands, Pahang State. Named for P. Baas, now director of Ryksherbarium, Leiden. Allied to *I. wenzelii.*

Ilex baracoensis Borhidi 1979.

Evergreen shrubs, branches glabrous; leaves broadly obovate or suborbiculate to subcordate, 2.5–4.5 cm (1–13⁄4 in,) long, 1.8–4 cm (11⁄16–15⁄8 in.) wide, bases cuneate, apices rotund to truncate, margins with 4–6 inconspicuous teeth on each side, petioles 2–4 mm (1⁄16–5⁄32 in.) long, inflorescences axillary, umbellate, 3- to 4-flowered, flowers 4-merous; fruits unknown. Habitat: eastern Cuba. Allied to *I. hypaneura.*

Ilex barahonica Loesener 1913.

Evergreen trees, bark flaking, branchlets puberulent; leaves broadly elliptic or ovate, 2–3.3 cm (3⁄4–11⁄4 in.) long, 1–2.2 cm (3⁄8–13⁄16 in.) wide, bases and apices broadly acute to rarely subobtuse, bases decurrent, margins upper half, submicroscopically serrulate, petioles 1–3 mm (1⁄32–1⁄8 in.) long; female flowers axillary, fasciculate, 5- to 6-merous, pedicels very short, to 3 mm (1⁄8 in.) long; fruits unknown. Habitat: Dominican Republic, Santo Domingo, Barahona Province. Allied to *I. repanda.*

Ilex bartletti Merrill 1934.

Evergreen trees, glabrous, branches lenticellate, purplish brown; leaves oblong-ovate or elliptic-ovate, bases broadly acute or rotund, apices acuminate, margins apiculate-serrate, teeth acuminate, 1–1.5 mm (1⁄32–3⁄64 in.) long, incurved, prominent veins and reticulations impressed above, petioles 1.5–2 cm (19⁄32–3⁄4 in.) long; fruits depressed-globose, 5–6 mm (3⁄16–7⁄32 in.) diameter, axillary, solitary; pyrenes 7–8, sepals persistent. Habitat: Indonesia, Sumatra, East Coast, Deleng Si Bajak, Karolan. Allied to *I. kingiana.*

Ilex × *beanii* Rehder 1922 (synonyms *I. aquifolium* var. *elliptica* Nicholson 1894, *I. dipyrena* var. *elliptica* Dallimore 1908, *I. elliptica* (Dallimore) Bean 1914; parentage: *I. aquifolium* × *I. dipyrena*).

Evergreen trees; leaves broadly elliptic, bases cuneate to obtuse, apices acute, margins with 2–4 small spines on each side, usually on upper half of leaf; fruits red; flowers before *I. aquifolium.* Named for W. J. Bean, who first pointed out in the Royal Botanic Gardens, Kew, that this holly is very likely a hybrid between *I. aquifolium* × *I. dipyrena.*

Ilex beccarianus Loesener 1901.

Evergreen, large shrubs with ascending branches; leaves oval-oblong or obovate to sublanceolate or elliptic, 4.5–10 cm (13⁄4–4 in.) long, 1.5–4.5 cm (1⁄2–13⁄4 in.) wide, bases cuneate or acute, apices obtuse to acuminate, margins entire, recurved, petioles 7–9 mm (9⁄32–11⁄32 in.) long; fruits unknown. Habitat: Indonesia, Sarawak and Borneo. Allied to *I. excavata.*

Ilex belizensis Lundell 1937.

Evergreen, glabrous, tall trees 20–40 m (65–131 ft.) tall; leaves oblong-elliptic or broadly oblanceolate, 8–11.5 cm (31⁄8–41⁄2 in.) long, 0.5–2 cm (3⁄16–3⁄4 in.) wide, bases rotund, slightly decurrent or acute, apex acuminate, acumens obtuse, margins entire, slightly revolute; inflorescences axillary, fasciculate, 3–8 pedicels, minutely puberulent; fruits immature, drying black, ovoid or ellipsoid, 6–7 mm (7⁄32–9⁄32 in.) long, 5–6 mm (3⁄16–7⁄32 in.) diameter; pyrenes 5. Habitat: Belize, advancing forest on limestone plateau, near Valentim, El Oayo District. Allied to *I. guianensis.*

Ilex berteroi Loesener 1892 (synonyms *I. macoucoua* De Candolle 1825, *I. berteroi* var. *ovalifolia* Loesener 1912, *I. clementis* Britton & P. Wilson 1920, *I. berteroi* var. *buchiana* Loesener 1929).

Evergreen shrubs 1–3 m (3–10 ft.) tall; leaves obovate-elliptic or elliptic, 3–6 cm (13⁄16–23⁄8 in.) long, 1.1–2.1 cm (7⁄16–13⁄64 in.) wide, apices rotund, occasionally retuse, bases acute or subcuneate-acute, margins entire, revolute, petioles 5–8 mm (³⁄₁₆–⁵⁄₁₆ in.) long; inflorescences fasciculate in leaf axils, glabrous, 1- to 3-flowered, flowers 4-merous, peduncles 3 mm (⅛ in.) long; fruits unknown. Habitat: Dominican Republic. Allied to *I. guianensis.*

Ilex bidens C.-y. Wu *ex* Y.-r. Li 1984.
      Evergreen trees to 15 m (50 ft.) tall, branchlets light gray, angulate-sulcate, densely puberulent, older branches with semiorbicular, elevated lenticels; leaves obovate, 1.5–2.8 cm (¹⁹⁄₃₂–1⅛ in.) long, 1–1.5 cm (⅜–¹⁹⁄₃₂ in.) wide, apices truncate or emarginate, bases obtuse, margins entire with 1 (–2) denticulate teeth on each side near apex, midveins densely puberulent and elevated on upper surface, petioles 2–4 mm (¹⁄₁₆–⁵⁄₃₂ in.) long; inflorescences axillary and fasciculate on new and 2nd-year growth, 2–3 cymose or single, pedicels 2–3.5 mm (¹⁄₁₆–⁹⁄₆₄ in.) long, flowers very small; fruits unknown. Habitat: People's Republic of China, Yunnan Province. Allied to *I. chamaebuxus* and *I. championii.*

Ilex bioritsensis Hayata 1911 (synonyms *I. veitchii* Veitch 1912, *I. pernyi* var. *veitchii* (Veitch) Bean 1914, *I. diplosperma* S.-y. Hu 1946).
      Evergreen shrubs or small trees to 10 m (33 ft.) tall, branchlets glabrescent or sparsely puberulent; leaves ovate or quadrangular, dark olive green, glossy, 2.5–6 cm (1–2⅜ in.), usually 3 cm (1³⁄₁₆ in.) long, 1.5–3.5 cm (¹⁹⁄₃₂–1⅜ in.), usually 2 cm (¾ in.) wide, apices acuminate, acumens 5–15 mm (³⁄₁₆–¹⁹⁄₃₂ in.) long, bases rotund or truncate, margins sinuate, 3–4 strong spines on each side, petioles 3 mm (⅛ in.) long, leaves persist on 4th-year wood; inflorescences axillary and fasciculate on 2nd-year growth; fruits red, ellipsoid, 8–10 mm (⁵⁄₁₆–⅜ in.) long, pedicels 2 mm (¹⁄₁₆ in.) long, glabrous; pyrenes 2, palmately 8–10 striate. Habitat: first recorded from Taiwan, Bioritsu. Also indigenous in southwestern People's Republic of China, Hubei, Guizhou, Sichuan, and Yunnan provinces. Allied to *I. pernyi.* Plate 58.

Ilex biserrulata Loesener 1901.
      Evergreen, glabrous shrubs or tree; leaves oblong, oblong-elliptic to lanceolate, 8–11.5 cm (3⅛–4½ in.) long, 1.9–3 cm (¾–1³⁄₁₆ in.) wide, apices acuminate, acumens 10–20 mm (⅜–¾ in.) long, bases acute, margins recurved, coarsely serrate or double serrate, petioles 7–10 mm (⁹⁄₃₂–⅜ in.) long; inflorescences axillary, solitary, racemose, flowers 4-merous; fruits unknown. Habitat: Brazil. Allied to *I. amara.*

Ilex blancheana W. Judd 1986.
      Evergreen shrubs or small trees to 4 m (13 ft.) tall, branchlets pubescent; leaves elliptic to slightly obo-

Figure 14-2. *Ilex bioritsensis.* Drawing by Chien-chu Chen in *Illustrations of Native and Introduced Ligneous Plants of Taiwan* (1962) by Tang-shui Liu.

vate, 1.5–2.9 cm (¹⁹⁄₃₂–1¼ in.) long, 1.1–2 cm (⁷⁄₁₆–¾ in.) wide, bases broadly cuneate, apices obtuse to slightly retuse, rarely acute, margins entire, slightly revolute, conspicuously veined, petioles 4–6 mm (⁵⁄₃₂–⁷⁄₃₂ in.) long; inflorescences axillary, fasciculate, 3- to 9-flowered, flowers 4-merous; fruits unknown. Habitat: southern Haiti; high elevations of cloud forest along the River Blands, south of Morne la Visti, Massif de la Selle. Similar to *I. berteroi.*

Ilex blanchetii Loesener 1901 (synonym *I. vismiifolia* Reisseck 1861).
      Evergreen, glabrous shrubs, 1.5–2.5 m (5–8 ft.) tall; leaves broadly oval or broadly ovate, 3–8 cm (1³⁄₁₆–3⅛ in.) long, usually 5 cm (2 in.) long, 3.5 cm (1⅜ in.) wide, apices obtuse or rotund, bases obtuse or rotund, margins entire, recurved, petioles 2–5 mm (¹⁄₁₆–³⁄₁₆ in.) long; inflorescences axillary, fasciculate, branched, flowers 4-merous, peduncles 1 mm (¹⁄₃₂ in.) long, pedicels 1 mm (¹⁄₃₂ in.) long; fruits unknown. Habitat: Brazil, Bahia State, near Bahiam; a coastal species near dunes. Allied to *I. micrantha* and *I. spruceana.*

Ilex bogorensis Loesener 1901 (synonym *Prinos cymosa* var. *minor* Miquel 1859).

Evergreen shrubs, upright spreading to rounded habit, grayish branches; leaves thin-leathery, elliptic to oblong-elliptic to elliptic-lanceolate, 9–13 cm (3½–5⅛ in.) long, 3–4 cm (1³⁄₁₆–1⅝ in.) wide, margins entire, recurved, bases crenate, apices obtuse to acuminate, 5–12 mm (³⁄₁₆–¹⁵⁄₃₂ in.) long, petioles 8–11 mm (⁵⁄₁₆–⁷⁄₁₆ in.) long; inflorescences solitary in leaf axils, peduncles 7–20 mm (⁹⁄₃₂–¾ in.) long; fruit unknown. Habitat: Indonesia, Sumatra, Java. Allied to *I. alternifolia*.

Ilex bolivarensis Edwin 1965.

Evergreen, large shrubs to 3 m (10 ft.) tall, branchlets pubescent; leaves obovate, occasionally spathulate-obovate, 2.6–3.5 cm (1–1⅜ in.) long, 1.3–1.7 cm (½–²¹⁄₃₂ in.) wide, punctate beneath, bases acute or subspathulate, apices rotund or acuminate, margins entire, petioles 3–5 mm (⅛–³⁄₁₆ in.) long; fruits purplish black, ovoid, 7 mm (⁹⁄₃₂ in.) long, 5 mm (³⁄₁₆ in.) diameter, pyrenes 4, smooth. Habitat: Venezuela, Bolivar State, at 2150 m (7095 ft.) elevation.

Ilex boliviana Britton *ex* Rusby 1893 var. *boliviana* (synonyms *I. boliviana* var. *acutata* Loesener 1901, *I. boliviana* var. *rusbyana* Loesener 1901).

Evergreen shrubs; leaves prominently reticulate, ovate to oval to ovate-elliptic, 2.4–4.3 cm (⅞–1¹¹⁄₁₆ in.) long, 1–2.3 cm (⅜–⅞ in.) wide, bases obtuse to rounded, apices obtuse to acuminate, margins serrulate-crenulate, punctate beneath, petioles 2–4.5 mm (¾–1¾ in.) long; inflorescences axillary, solitary, branched, 7- to 31-flowered; fruits black, subglobose, 4 mm (⁵⁄₃₂ in.) wide. Habitat: Bolivia. Allied to *I. hippocrateoides*.

Ilex boliviana var. *brittoniana* Loesener 1901.

This variety differs from typical individuals with densely hairy branches and inflorescences; leaves sparsely pubescent on midribs beneath. Habitat: Bolivia. This variety may represent no more than natural variation and may eventually be treated as a synonym of the species.

Ilex bonincola Makino 1917.

Evergreen shrubs, glabrous, branchlets slender, angulate striate when dry; leaves alternate, elliptical or elliptic-oblong, 2.5–6 cm (1–2⅜ in.) long, 2–3 cm (¾–1³⁄₁₆ in.) wide, bases acute, apices obtuse, submarginate, serrate, narrowly subrevolute at apex, midribs prominent beneath, veinlets reticulate, petioles canaliculate, 7–15 mm (⁹⁄₃₂–¹⁹⁄₃₂ in.) long. Habitat: Japan, Bonin Islands, south Honshu. Allied to *I. matanoana*.

Ilex bonincola var. *angustifolia* Nakai 1933.

A variety with narrow-elliptic leaves. Habitat: Japan, Bonin Islands.

Ilex borneensis Loesener 1901.

Evergreen, glabrous shrubs, branchlet striate, angulate; leaves elliptic or oblong-elliptic, 15–22 cm (6–8¾ in.) long, 5–7.5 cm (2–2¾ in.) wide, bases usually acute, apices obtuse, usually with short spine at tips, margins serrulate, petioles 15–30 mm (¹⁹⁄₃₂–1³⁄₁₆ in.) long; inflorescences fasciculate, axillary; fruits red, globose, 6–7 mm (⁷⁄₃₂–¹¹⁄₃₂ in.) diameter; pyrenes 4. Habitat: Indonesia, Borneo, on Mount Mattang. Allied to *I. pseudo-odorata*.

Ilex brachyphylla (Handel-Mazzetti) S.-y. Hu 1950 (synonym *I. ficoidea* var. *brachyphylla* Handel-Mazzetti 1933).

Evergreen, small trees to 4 m (13 ft.) tall, branchlets glabrous; leaves oblong-ovate, 5–9 cm (2–3½ in.) long, 2–3.5 cm (¾–1⅜ in.) wide, apices obtuse, abruptly acuminate, acumens 10–12 mm (⅜–¹⁵⁄₃₂ in.) long, bases rotund or obtuse, margins serrate, petioles 6–9 mm (⁷⁄₃₂–¹¹⁄₃₂ in.) long; inflorescences axillary and fasciculate on 2nd-year growth, flowers 4-merous; fruits unknown. Habitat: People's Republic of China, great lakes region of Hunan Province. Allied to *I. ficoidea*.

Ilex brandegeeana Loesener 1901 (synonym *I. triflora* Brandegee 1894, *non* Blume 1826).

Small trees to 15 m (50 ft.) tall, branches densely pubescent; leaves elliptic to ovate to elliptic-lanceolate, 3–8.5 cm (1³⁄₁₆–3⅜ in.) long, 1.3–2.5 cm (¹⁵⁄₃₂–1 in.) wide, apices acute, bases obtuse to subrounded, margins recurved, entire to occasionally serrulate denticulate; inflorescences axillary, solitary, 1- to 3-flowered, flowers 5- to 6-merous; fruits unknown. Habitat: Mexico, Baja California. Allied to *I. cassine* and *I. rubra*.

Ilex brasiliensis (Sprengel) Loesener 1901 var. *brasiliensis* (synonyms *Rhamnus brasiliensis* Sprengel 1825, *I. coronaria* Reisseck 1861, *I. pubiflora* Reisseck 1917).

Evergreen, pubescent, large shrubs to 6 m (20 ft.) tall; leaves obovate or obovate-lanceolate, variable in size, usually 2–6 cm (¾–2⅜ in.) long, 1.5 cm (¹⁹⁄₃₂ in.) wide, apices obtuse or rotund, apiculate, bases obtuse or acute, margins usually entire, revolute, petioles 5–8 mm (³⁄₁₆–⁵⁄₁₆ in.) long; inflorescences fasciculate in leaf axils, flowers usually 4- to 5-merous; fruits black, ellipsoid, 4.5–5.5 mm (¹¹⁄₆₄–¹³⁄₆₄ in.) diameter; pyrenes 5–6, striate. Habitat: Brazil and Paraguay. Allied to *I. theezans*.

Ilex brasiliensis var. *parviflora* (Reisseck) Loesener 1901 (synonyms *I. pubiflora* var. *angustifolia* Reisseck 1861, *I. pubiflora* var. *latifolia* Reisseck 1861).

A variety with smaller leaves, 2–5 cm (¾–2 in.)

long, 1.5 cm (19/32 in. wide; inflorescences pedunculate. Habitat: Brazil, Paraná State.

Ilex brassii Merrill & Perry 1939.

Evergreen, large trees, to 20 m (65 ft.) tall, branches terete; leaves elliptic, 5–9 cm (2–3½ in.) long, 3–5.5 cm (1 3/16–2⅛ in.) wide, bases rotund or obtuse, apices short, broadly acuminate to obtuse, margins entire, petioles 10 mm (⅜ in.) long; male inflorescences axillary, paniculate, flowers 4-merous; fruits unknown. Habitat: New Guinea, Papua, Gaima, lower Fly River, around margins of sago swamps in rain forest. Allied to *I. ledermannii.*

Ilex brenesii Standley 1926.

Evergreen shrubs or small trees; leaves oblong-lanceolate or lanceolate-oblong, 6–8 cm (2⅜–3⅛ in.) long, 1.5–2.3 cm (19/32–⅞ in.) wide, apices acuminate, bases acute or subobtuse, margins entire, long petioles 2.5 cm (1 in.) long; inflorescences axillary, branched, flowers 4- to 7-merous; fruits unknown. Habitat: Costa Rica.

Ilex brevicuspis Reisseck 1861. Orelha de mico.

Evergreen trees to 8 m (26 ft.) tall, branchlets rugose, puberulent, minute sparse lenticels; leaves oval or ovate or elliptic or lanceolate-oblong, 5–8 cm (2–3⅛ in.) long, 1.7–3.4 cm (21/32–1⅜ in.) wide, apices acuminate, bases obtuse or acute, margins recurved, entire or scarcely serrulate near apex, petioles 6–11 mm (7/32–7/16 in.) long; inflorescences axillary, fasciculate or pseudopaniculate, 3- to 7-branched, peduncles 3–12 mm (⅛–15/32 in.) long, pedicels 1.5–3 mm (3/64–⅛ in.) long, flowers 4- to 5-merous; fruits red, ellipsoid, 3 mm (⅛ in.) long, 2.5 mm (3/32 in.) wide; pyrenes 4, rugose, obscure striate. Habitat: Brazil. Allied to *I. cerasifolia* var. *glaziovii, I. microdonta,* and *I. sapotifolia.*

Ilex brevipedicellata Steyermark 1988.

Evergreen trees 15 m (50 ft.) tall; leaves oblong-obovate, 4–7 cm (1⅝–2¾ in.) long, 2.5–3.5 cm (1–1⅜ in.) wide, black punctate beneath, bases acute, apices rotund, often emarginate at apex, margins entire, revolute, glabrous; inflorescences axillary, solitary, lateral; fruits suborbiculate, rotund, 1.5 mm (3/64 in.) wide, 0.5 mm (1/64 in.) long. Habitat: Venezuela, Amazonas, Department Atabapo, Cerro Marahuaka, forested slopes along eastern branch of Cano Negro. Allied to *I. gleasoniana* and *I. sessilifructa.*

Ilex brevipetiolata Steyermark & Wurdack 1957.

Evergreen tree to 10 m (33 ft.) tall, branches striate-subsulcate, slightly pilose; leaves entire, oval or subovate, 4–6 cm (1⅝–2⅜ in.) long, 2.8–4.2 cm (1⅛–1 11/16 in.) wide, apices obtuse or subrotund, bases subobtuse or rotund, slightly punctate below; petioles short, 1–2 mm (1/32 in.) long, slightly rugose; inflorescences axillary, solitary, 1- to 3-flowered; fruits globose, 5 mm (3/16 in.) diameter, pyrenes 4, rarely 5. Habitat: Venezuela, Bolivar, small forest slopes of Uaipán-tepui at 1400 m (4620 ft.) elevation, in vicinity of "Misia Kathy Camp." Allied to *I. duidae* and *I. spruceana.*

Ilex brunnea Merrill 1915.

Evergreen, epiphytic shrubs, glabrous, branches somewhat angled, pale green; leaves oblong-ovate to elliptic-lanceolate, glossy, 3–5 cm (1 3/16–2 in.) long, 1.4–3 cm (17/32–1 3/16 in.) wide, bases acute or acuminate, apices blunt acuminate, margins entire, minutely densely punctate beneath, few scattered large, dark glands, petioles 5 mm (3/16 in.); male inflorescences racemose, axillary, solitary, rarely 2, 2- to 6-fasciculate, many-flowered, pedicels to 5 mm (3/16 in.) long, bracteoles, flowers 4- to 5-merous. Habitat: Philippines, Luzon, Tayabas, Mount Pular. Allied to *I. engleriana* var. *halconensis.*

Ilex buergeri Miquel 1868. Shii-mochi, Hizen mochi (synonyms *I. subpuberula* Miquel 1866, *I. buergeri* var. *subpuberula* (Miquel) Loesener 1901, *I. ficoidea sensu* Rehder 1933).

Evergreen, large trees to 15 m (50 ft.) tall, branchlets pubescent, bark smooth, gray; leaves ovate-oblong or lanceolate, 5–8 cm (2–3⅛ in.) long, 1.5–2.5 cm (19/32–1 in.) wide, apices obtuse, gradually acuminate, rarely acute, acumens 7–12 mm (9/32–15/32 in.) long, bases rotund or obtuse, rarely cuneate, margins loosely and irregularly serrate, petioles 6–12 mm (7/32–15/32 in.) long; inflorescences axillary and fasciculate on 2nd-year growth; flowers 4-merous, yellow-green, fragrant; fruits red, globose or subglobose, 4.5–6 mm (11/64–7/32) diameter; pyrenes 4, wrinkled, sulcate. Habitat: first recorded from Japan, also in People's Republic of China, temperate coastal and central provinces. Introduced to United States in 1960. Allied to *I. ficoidea.*

Ilex bullata Cuatrecasas 1948.

Evergreen trees, branches rugose, minutely pilose; leaves obovate or obovate-elliptic, 3–6 cm (1 3/16–2⅜ in.) long, 1.5–3.2 cm (19/32–1¼ in.) wide, punctate beneath, bases cuneate to attenuate, apices obtuse or acuminate, or acute, margins revolute, concave, prominently swollen between veins beneath, petioles 3–5 mm (⅛–3/16 in.) long; inflorescences axillary, umbellate; fruits small; pyrenes 4. Habitat: Colombia, near Department del Valle, western Cordillera along Digua and San Juan rivers. Distinct from other Colombian species with concave leaves, prominent bullate swelling veins beneath and depressed on upper surfaces.

Figure 14-3. *Ilex buergeri*. Photo by Barton Bauer Sr.

Ilex buxifolia Gardner 1845, *non* Hance 1876.

Evergreen shrubs to 2 m (6 ft.) tall, branches glabrous; leaves oblong-obovate to sublanceolate, 1.5–1.8 cm (19/32–11/16 in.) long, 3–8 mm (1/8–5/16 in.) wide, apices acute, small apicule, bases acute, margins entire, recurved, petioles 1.5–4 mm (3/64–5/32 in.) long; inflorescences in leaf axils, fasciculate, flowers usually 4-merous; fruits black, globose, 3.5–4.5 mm (7/64–3/16 in.) diameter, pedicels 3–5 mm (1/8–3/16 in.) long; pyrenes 4. Habitat: Brazil, Rio de Janeiro State. Allied to *I. congonhinha*.

Ilex buxifolioides Loesener 1901.

Evergreen shrubs, branchlets glabrous; leaves elliptic-oblong or obovate-oblong, 0.4–1.2 cm (5/32–15/32 in.) long, 3–6 mm (1/8–6/32 in.) wide, bases acute to obtuse, apices obtuse, minute apiculate, margins recurved, entire or with 1–3 minute crenate-serrulate teeth, petioles 0.5–2.5 mm (1/32–3/32 in.) long; inflorescences axillary, solitary, flowers 5-merous; fruits black, ellipsoid, 10 mm (3/8 in.) long, 8 mm (5/16 in.) diameter; pyrenes 5, sulcate. Habitat: Bolivia, Yungas Mountains, at 3700–4000 m (12,200–13,200 ft.) elevation. Allied to *I. buxifolia* and *I. mandonii*.

Ilex buxoides S.-y. Hu 1950.

Evergreen trees, branchlets pubescent; leaves elliptic or obovate-elliptic or subrhomboidal, 2.5–4.5 cm (1–1¾ in.) long, 1–2 cm (3/8–3/4 in.) wide, apices obtuse and notched, bases cuneate, margins entire, punctate beneath, petioles 4–5 mm (5/32–3/16 in.) long; inflorescences axillary on 2nd-year growth, fasciculate, pedicels 5 mm (3/16 in.) long, flowers 4- to 5-merous; fruits red, globose, 4 mm (3/16 in.) diameter, calyces persistent, stigmas elevated; pyrenes 4,

reticulate-striate. Habitat: People's Republic of China, endemic to Guangdong and Guangxi provinces. Allied to *I. tutcheri*.

Ilex caaquazuensis Loesener 1901. Caa-na.

Evergreen trees to 8–10 m (26–33 ft.) tall, branchlets striate, angulate, lenticels present; leaves oval or ovate, 3–4.5 cm (13/16–1⅝ in.) long, 1.2–2 cm (15/32–3/4 in.) wide, apices acute or obtuse, with sharp tip, bases cuneate-obtuse or cuneate-acute, margins recurved, entire or 1–2 sparse serrulate teeth near apex, petioles 4–7 mm (5/32–9/32 in.) long; inflorescences axillary, fasciculate, female inflorescences 1–3 pedunculate, flowers 4-merous; fruits black, globose, 5 mm (3/16 in.) diameter; pyrenes 4, striate. Habitat: Paraguay, in forest near Caaquazu. Allied to *I. brevicuspis* and *I. microdonta*.

Ilex caliana Cuatrecasas 1948.

Evergreen, large trees to 30 m (98 ft.) tall, branchlets minutely hirsute; leaves oblong, elliptic-lanceolate or lanceolate, 10–20 cm (4–8 in.) long, 3.5–5 cm (1⅜–2 in.) wide, punctate beneath, bases attenuate or slightly obtuse, margins crenate-serrulate, recurved, petioles hirsute, 10–15 mm (3/8–19/32 in.) long; inflorescences axillary, fasciculate, flowers 4-merous; fruits 6 mm (7/32 in.) diameter; pyrenes 4. Habitat: Colombia, Department del Valle, Western Cordilleras, near Rio Cali, at more than 2000 m (6600 ft.) elevation. Allied to *I. laurina*.

Ilex canariensis Poiret 1813 subsp. *canariensis*. Keebino, acebino (synonyms *I. balearica* Hort., *I. canariensis* var. *typica* Loesener 1901).

Large shrubs or small tree 3–7 m (10–23 ft.) tall, upright pyramidal habit; leaves ovate-oblong to lanceolate, 3.5–11 cm (1⅜–4 in.) long, 1.5–4.5 cm (19/32–1¾ in.) wide, apices acute, bases obtuse to cuneate-obtuse, margins entire, rarely denticulate-serrulate, petioles 7–15 mm (9/32–19/32 in.) long; inflorescences axillary, solitary, fasciculate, flowers usually 4-merous; fruits dark red, glossy, subglobose to ellipsoid 10 mm (3/8 in.) wide, peduncles 10–15 mm (3/8–19/32 in.) long, pedicels 4–5 mm (5/32–3/16 in.) long; pyrenes 4, sulcate. Habitat: Spain, Madeira and the Canary Islands. Allied to *I. coriacea*.

Ilex canariensis subsp. *azevinho* Solander & Lowe 1901 (synonyms *I. maderensis* Willdenow 1813, *I. aestivales* Bush 1826, *I. canariensis* var. *azevinho* Loesener 1901, *I. azevinho* Solander & Lowe 1922).

A variety differing from typical individuals with leaves smaller, oblong lanceolate to lanceolate, to 6 cm (2⅜ in.) long, 2 cm (3/4 in.) wide. At a later date this variety may be sunk into synonymy of the species.

Figure 14-4. *Ilex canariensis* subsp. *canariensis*. Photo by Barton Bauer Sr.

Ilex caniensis Macbride 1926.

Evergreen shrubs 1.5–2 m (5–6 ft.) tall; leaves elliptic or elliptic-oblong or obovate, pubescent, 3–4.5 cm (1³⁄₁₆–1¾ in.) long, 2–2.5 cm (¾–1 in.) wide, bases usually rotund, apices obtuse-rotund, apices acute, mucronulate; inflorescences axillary, 1- to 3-flowered, peduncles 2 mm (¹⁄₁₆ in.) long, pedicels 1–2 mm (¹⁄₃₂–¹⁄₁₆ in.) long, flowers 5- to 6-merous; fruits unknown. Habitat: Peru, grassy slopes, Cani, Department of Huanuco. Allied to *I. uniflora*.

Ilex cardonae Steyermark 1988.

Evergreen trees, branches glabrous; leaves oblong-elliptic, 11–13 cm (4³⁄₈–5⅛ in.) long, 3.5–4.5 cm (1³⁄₈–1¾ in.) wide, bases and apices acute, margins obscurely repand and crenulate, petioles 6–8 mm (⁷⁄₃₂–⁵⁄₁₆ in.) long; male inflorescences axillary, solitary, pedunculate, 3- to 5-flowered, flowers 4-merous; fruits unknown. Habitat: Venezuela, Amazonas, Rio Castanho, at 100–140 m (330–460 ft.) elevation. Allied to *I. tateana*.

Ilex casiquiarensis Loesener 1901 (synonym *I. affinis* Reisseck 1861, *non* Gardner 1842).

Evergreen shrubs or trees; leaves obovate-oblong, 6.5–12.5 cm (2³⁄₈–5 in.) long, 1.9–3.5 cm (¾–1³⁄₈ in.) wide, apices acuminate, bases acute or subcuneate, margins recurved, remotely crenulate, petioles 6–9 mm (⁷⁄₃₂–1¹⁄₃₂ in.) long; inflorescences usually in leaf axils, paucifasciculate, rarely solitary; fruits unknown. Habitat: Venezuela, near San Carla, along the Casiquiare and Negro rivers. Allied to *I. laureola*.

Ilex cassine Linnaeus 1753 var. *cassine*. Dahoon holly (synonyms *I. cassine* var. *latifolia* Aiton 1784, *I. pri-*noides Willdenow 1798, *Aquifolium carolinesse* Catesby *ex* Duhamal 1807, *I. chinensis* Sims 1814, *I. laurifolia* Nuttall 1822, *I. chinensis* De Candolle 1825, *I. dahoon* var. *laurifolia* (Nuttall) Nuttall 1832, *I. ramulosa* Rafinesque 1837, *Ageria germinata* Rafinesque 1838, *A. heterophylla* Rafinesque 1838, *A. obovata* Rafinesque 1838, *A. palustris* Rafinesque 1838, *Prinos cassinoides* Hort. *ex* Steudel 1841, *I. dahoon* var. *grandiflora* Koch 1853, *I. lanceolata* Grisebach 1866, *I. phillyreifolia* Hortor *ex* Dippel 1892, *I. cassine corymbosia* W. T. Miller, *I. cassinaefolia* Loesener 1901, *I. castaneifolia* Hort. *ex* Loesener 1901).

Evergreen, large, very variable shrubs or small trees to 10 m (33 ft.) tall, branchlets usually pubescent, branches smooth gray; leaves oblanceolate or elliptic, rarely obovate, usually glossy, 4–10 cm (1⅝–4 in.) long, 1–3.5 cm (³⁄₈–1³⁄₈ in.) wide, apices usually acute, bases acute, rarely obtuse, margins somewhat revolute, entire, occasionally sparsely tooth, pubescent beneath, petioles 2–12 mm (¹⁄₁₆–½ in.) long; inflorescences axillary, males in cymes, females solitary or 3-flowered cymes, flowers 4-merous; fruits usually red, sometimes orange to yellow, globose, 5–7 mm (³⁄₁₆–⁹⁄₃₂ in.) diameter, peduncles 7–10 mm (⁹⁄₃₂–³⁄₈ in.) long; pyrenes 4, reticulate, shallow pitted. Habitat: United States, Coastal Plains along streambanks, swamps, and hammocks, usually in acid soils from North Carolina to Florida, Louisiana, and Texas, to Mexico and Cuba. Hardy in zones 7b to 10. Introduced to England in 1726 by Mark Catesby. Many varieties and cultivars are available and more often seen in gardens than is the species. The leaves have been used with those of *I. vomitoria* for making a strong herbal tea. Natural hybrids between *I. opaca* and *I. cassine,* known as *I.* ×

attenuata, are sometimes found where the two species occur.

Ilex cassine var. *angustifolia* Aiton 1789 (synonyms *I. aquifolium carolinianum* Duhamal 1755, *I. angustifolia* Willdenow 1809, *I. cassinoides* Link 1821, *I. cassinoides* Du Mont 1821, *I. ligustrina* Elliott 1824, *I. watsoniana* Spach 1834, *I. dahoon* var. *ligustrum* (Elliott) Woods 1870, *I. dahoon* var. *angustifolia* (Willdenow) Torrey & Gray 1878).

A botanical variety with narrow-linear-lanceolate leaves, 6–9 cm (2⅜–3 in.) long, 8–17 mm (⁵⁄₁₆–²¹⁄₃₂ in.) wide, usually entire. Habitat: United States, Coastal Plains, along swamps, streambanks, and hammocks, from Florida to Louisiana and southern Virginia. More common in gardens than the species.

Ilex cassine f. *aureo-bractea.*

Fruit yellow. Plant found in 1928 by L. LeBruce in Georgetown, South Carolina, and moved to Brookgreen Gardens, South Carolina.

Ilex cassine var. *mexicana* (Turczaninow) Loesener 1901 (synonyms *Pileostegia mexicana* Turczaninow 1859, *I. mexicana* (Turczaninow) Black 1880, *I. lanceolata* Grisebach 1888, *I. cassine* f. *glabra* Loesener 1894, *I. cassine* f. *hirtella* Loesener 1898).

Branches glabrous, except slightly pubescent at apex; leaves elliptic-lanceolate, 9 cm (3 in.) long, 2.1–2.3 cm (²⁵⁄₃₂–⅞ in.) wide, apices slightly acuminate, bases obtuse, petioles 5–6 mm (³⁄₁₆–⁷⁄₃₂ in.) long; fruits red. Habitat: Mexico, reported in Veracruz State near Orizaba.

Ilex cauliflora H.-w. Li *ex* Y.-r. Li 1984.

Evergreen shrubs to 5 m (16 ft.) tall, branchlets angulate-sulcate, glabrous; leaves elliptic-lanceolate or oblong-elliptic, 6–9.5 cm (2⅜–3½ in.) long, 2.5–4 cm (1–1⅝ in.) wide, apices acuminate or long-acuminate, bases obtuse or subrotund, margins serrulate, petioles 1–1.2 cm (⅜–1⁵⁄₃₂ in.) long; inflorescences axillary, borne only in axils of leaf scars on 2nd-year growth, umbellate, glabrous, 5- to 10-fascicled, peduncles 1 mm (¹⁄₃₂ in.) long, pedicels 3–4 mm (⅛–⁵⁄₃₂ in.) long; fruits red, globose 3 mm (⅛ in.) diameter, calyces persistent, stigmas capitate; pyrenes 4, 4- to 5-striate. Habitat: People's Republic of China, Yunnan Province. A unique species with small fruits borne in axillary fascicles of one leaf scar on 2nd-year growth. Fruits have capitate stigmas. Allied to *I. microdonta.*

Ilex celebensis Capitaine 1906.

Evergreen shrubs or small trees, branches upright; leaves entire or obscure undulate; peduncles with few flowers, 5 petals; fruits globose; pyrenes 5. Habitat: Indonesia, Celebes Islands. Allied to *I. anomala* and *I. cymosa.*

Ilex celebesiaca Loesener 1901.

Evergreen shrubs with dense foliage; leaves ovate to ovate-elliptic, 1–2.2 cm (⅜–1³⁄₁₆ in.) long, 5–11 mm (9³⁄₁₆–⁷⁄₁₆ in.) wide, apices obtuse or acute, small

Figure 14-5. *Ilex cassine* var. *cassine.* Photo by Barton Bauer Sr.

spine at apex, bases cuneate to cuneate-subrotund, margins usually entire, recurved, midrib depressed above, petioles 1–3 mm (¹⁄₃₂–⅛ in.) long; inflorescences axillary; fruits unknown. Habitat: Indonesia, Celebes Islands. Allied to *I. walkeri*.

Ilex centrochinensis S.-y. Hu 1949 (synonyms *I. aquifolium* var. *chinensis* Loesener 1901, *I. dipyrena* var. *leptocantha* Loesener 1900).

Evergreen shrubs to 3 m (10 ft.) high, branchlets slender, angulate, sparsely pubescent or glabrescent; leaves elliptic-lanceolate, rarely ovate-elliptic, 5–9 cm, usually 6–7 cm (2–3½ in., usually 2⅜–2¾ in.), 1.5–2.8 cm (¹⁹⁄₃₂–1⅛ in.) wide, bases obtuse or rarely rotund, apices acuminate, margins spinose-dentate, 4–10 spines on each side, 2–4 mm (¹⁄₁₆–⁵⁄₃₂ in.) long; inflorescences axillary, fasciculate, on 2nd-year growth, flowers 4-merous; fruits red, globose, 6–7 mm (⁷⁄₃₂–⁹⁄₃₂ in.) diameter; pyrenes 4, wrinkled and pitted all over, endocarps stony. Habitat: People's Republic of China, endemic to the Hubei and Sichuan provinces, where the Yangtze River cuts through limestone mountains and forms deep gorges; also in the *Metasequoia* area of southwestern Hubei. Found as a shrub along roadsides, streams, and woodland areas, at 500–700 m (1650–2300 ft.) elevation. Allied to *I. aquifolium*.

Most material offered as *I. centrochinensis* is *I. ciliospinosa*. Very rare, if at all, in the United States, but reported in England and Australia in 1925 is U.S.D.A. Plant PI No. 62723 from England, originally labeled as *I. fargesii*, and in 1928 introduced from France, PI No. 78144, also under the same name. In the 1940s both PI plants were changed to *I. ciliospinosa*. In 1949 *I. ciliospinosa* PI No. 62723 was mistakenly identified as *I. centrochinensis*. Unfortunately, soon after both PI No. 62723 and PI No. 78144 were listed under the incorrect name of *I. centrochinensis*. Dudley (1984a) confirmed in detail that the early distributions of PI No. 62632 and PI No. 78144 were indeed, *I. ciliospinosa,* and not *I. centrochinensis*.

Ilex cerasifolia Reisseck 1861 var. *cerasifolia* (synonyms *I. lagoensis* Warming 1880, *I. cerasifolia* var. *lagoensis* (Warming) Loesener 1901).

Evergreen shrubs 2.5–4 m (8–13 ft.) tall, branchlets sulcate or striate, lenticels present; leaves oblong or oblong-lanceolate, 6.5–9 cm or 9–12 cm (2½–3½ in. or 3½–4¾ in.) long, 2.2–3 cm or 3–4.5 cm (¹³⁄₁₆–1³⁄₁₆ in. or 1³⁄₁₆–1¾ in.) wide, apices acuminate, acumens 5–15 mm (³⁄₁₆–¹⁹⁄₃₂ in.) long, bases acute or subcuneate acute, margins recurved, serrulate near apex, petioles 5–10 mm (³⁄₁₆–⅜ in.) long; inflorescences axillary, solitary, fasciculate, flowers 4-merous; fruits red, globose, 4.5–5.5 mm (¹¹⁄₆₄–

¹³⁄₆₄ in.) diameter; pyrenes 4, rarely 5, sulcate, striate. Habitat: Brazil. Allied to *I. microdonta*.

Ilex cerasifolia var. *glaziovii* (Warming) Loesener 1901 (synonym *I. glaziovii* Warming 1880).

A variety with pilose branches, petioles, and inflorescences; leaves entire or subentire, shiny above. Habitat: Brazil, Rio de Janeiro State. This taxon may not warrant botanical recognition.

Ilex chamaebuxus C.-y. Wu *ex* Y.-r. Li 1984.

Evergreen, large shrubs or small trees to 3 m (10 ft.) tall, branchlets light gray, angular-sulcate, densely puberulent; leaves obovate, 12–18 mm (¹⁵⁄₃₂–1¹⁄₁₆ in.) long, 6–18 mm (⁷⁄₃₂–1¹⁄₁₆ in.) wide, apices cordate, bases obtuse or wide-cuneate, margins entire, petioles 2–4 mm (¹⁄₁₆–⁵⁄₃₂ in.) long; male inflorescences cymose or forked or single, fasciculate, peduncles 2–3 mm (¹⁄₁₆–⅛ in.) long, pedicels 0.5–1.5 mm (¹⁄₆₄–³⁄₆₄ in.) long; female flowers and fruits unknown. Habitat: People's Republic of China, Yunnan Province. Very similar to *I. championii*. Possibly with the study of more adequate material this species may be a variety or *I. championii* or *I. bidens* (T. R. Dudley).

Ilex chamaedryfolia Reisseck 1861. Congonhinha (synonyms *I. chamaedryfolia* var. *mugiensis* Loesener 1901, *I. chamaedryfolia* var. *typica* Loesener 1901).

Evergreen shrubs, usually 2 m (6 ft.) tall, dense erect; leaves obovate or elliptic-oblong, 2–3 cm (¾–1³⁄₁₆ in.) long, 10–12 mm (⅜–½ in.) wide, sparsely punctate beneath, apices obtuse or rotund, bases narrow-acute, margins recurved, lower half entire, crenulate toward apex, petioles 1–2.5 cm (⅜–1 in.) long; inflorescences axillary, solitary on new growth, pseudopaniculate, flowers 4-merous; fruits black, globose or ellipsoid, 3–4 mm (⅛–⁵⁄₃₂ in.) long, 2.7–3.7 mm (³⁄₁₆–⁷⁄₆₄ in.) wide, peduncles 3–4 mm (⅛–⁵⁄₃₂ in.) long, pedicels 2–6 mm (¹⁄₁₆–⁷⁄₃₂ in.) long; pyrenes 5, striate, sulcate. Habitat: Brazil, Minas Gerais State. Allied to *I. dumosa* and *I. glazioviana*.

Ilex championii Loesener 1901 (synonym *I. memecylifolia* var. *nummularifolia* Champion *ex* Bentham 1852).

Evergreen shrubs or trees to 12 m (40 ft.) tall, branchlets puberulent or glabrescent; leaves ovate or obovate, rarely obovate-elliptic, 2–4.5 cm (¾–1¾ in.) long, 1.5–2.5 cm (¹⁹⁄₃₂–1 in.) wide, glabrous and punctate beneath, apices abruptly acuminate or rotund, notched or emarginate, bases obtuse, margins entire, puberulent above, petioles 4–5 mm (⁵⁄₃₂–³⁄₁₆ in.) long; inflorescences axillary on 2nd-year growth, fasciculate; fruits red, paired, globose, 3–4 mm (⅛–⁵⁄₃₂ in.) diameter, calyces persistent; pyrenes 4, 3-

striate. Habitat: People's Republic of China, Gui-zhou, Guangxi, and Guangdong provinces. First discovered in Hong Kong and described as a variety of *I. memecylifolia*. Allied to *I. lohfauensis*.

Ilex chapaensis Merrill 1940 (synonyms *I. howii* Merrill & Chun 1938, *I. megistocarpa* Merrill 1940).

Evergreen, small trees 5–6 m (16–20 ft.) tall, branches lenticellate; leaves ovate or elliptic, 6 cm (2⅜ in.) long, 2.5 cm (1 in.) wide, bases cuneiform or acute, apices acute or attenuate, margins entire, undulate, recurved; inflorescences axillary, solitary, paucifasciculate, male flowers 1–3, 5- to 7-merous, female flowers 1–4, 6-merous; fruits unknown. Habitat: Vietnam (Indochina), Chapa. Allied to *I. wightiana*.

Ilex charrascosensis T. R. Dudley, *nom. nov.* (basionym *I. paucinervis* Alain 1960, invalid name, and homonym of *I. paucinervis* Merrill 1920).

Evergreen, glabrous shrubs; leaves ovate or elliptic to suborbiculate, 1.6–2.8 cm (⅝–1⅛ in.) long, 1–2.3 cm (⅜–⅞ in.) wide, bases usually rotund, apices rotund to obtuse, veins prominent and branched to margins, margins slightly recurved; inflorescences axillary, 1- to 3-flowered, peduncles 1–2.5 mm (1/32–3/32 in.) long, pedicels 1.5 mm (3/64 in.) long, flowers 4-merous; fruits unknown. Habitat: Cuba, Oriente Province, Charrascos, Sierra de Cristal. Allied to *I. obcordata*.

Ilex chartacifolia C.-y. Wu *ex* Y.-r. Li 1985 var. *chartacifolia*.

Evergreen trees to 10 m (33 ft.) tall, branchlets angulate-sulcate, puberulent, lenticels on 2nd- and 3rd-year growth; leaves wide-elliptic or oblong, 8–10 cm (3⅛–4 in.) long, 3.5–5 cm (1⅜–2 in.) wide, apices abruptly acuminate, bases cuneate, margins slightly crenulate-serrulate, petioles 1–1.5 cm (⅜–19/32 in.) long; inflorescences axillary on 2nd-year growth, pseudoracemose, peduncles thick, pedicels puberulent, 5 mm (3/16 in.) long; fruits red, globose, 6 mm (7/32 in.) diameter, calyces persistent; pyrenes 4, palmately sulcate and striate. Habitat: People's Republic of China, Yunnan Province. Allied to *I. dunniana*.

Ilex chartacifolia var. *glabra* C.-y. Wu *ex* Y.-r. Li 1985.

A variety differing from typical individuals with glabrous branchlets, terminal buds, petioles and midveins. Habitat: People's Republic of China, Yunnan Province. It is doubtful if the described glabrous condition of this variety is discernable on a population basis, and accordingly probably does not warrant botanical recognition. (T. R. Dudley).

Ilex chengkouensis C.-j. Tseng 1981.

Evergreen trees, branches pubescent, angulate; leaves oblong, 3.5–6.5 cm (1⅜–2½ in.) long, 1.5–3.5 cm (19/32–1⅜ in.) wide, apices narrowly truncate, terminating with spines, bases truncate or subcordate, margins sinuate, revolute, 2–4 spinose on each side; inflorescences axillary, 1- or 2-fasciculate, pedicels 2 mm (1/16 in.) long; fruits red, subglobose, 9 mm (11/32 in.) diameter; pyrenes 4, palmately striate, sulcate. Habitat: People's Republic of China, Sichuan Province. Allied to *I. pernyi*.

Ilex cheniana T. R. Dudley 1988 (synonym *I. congesta* H.-w. Li *ex* Y.-r. Li 1985, *non* Reisseck 1861).

Evergreen, small trees to 5 m (15 ft.) tall, branchlets blackish striate, sparsely pubescent, conspicuous elliptic lenticels; leaves elliptic, 9–11 cm (3½–4¼ in.) long, 4–5 cm (1⅝–2 in.) wide, bases suborbicular, subobtuse, apices acuminate, margins sparsely serrate, petioles 6–10 mm (7/32–⅜ in.) long; flowers unknown; infructescences 3-fruited cymose, puberulent, axillary, on new growth, peduncles 5–6 mm (3/16–7/32 in.) long, pedicels 5 mm (3/16 in.) long; fruits red, globose, 1 cm (⅜ in.) diameter, persistent calyces; pyrenes 4, dorsally wide unisulcate. Habitat: People's Republic of China, Yunnan Province, Longling, Yunlongshan. Named for C. Chen, the original collector of this species. Allied to *I. xylosmaefolia*.

Ilex chevalieri Tardieu 1945.

Evergreen trees 12 m (40 ft.) tall, branches slender, large lenticels; leaves elliptic or ovate-elliptic, 3.5–4 cm (1⅜–1⅝ in.) long, 2 cm (¾ in.) wide, bases acute, apices acuminate, acumens 1 cm (⅜ in.) long, margins entire, petioles 7–8 mm (9/32–5/16 in.) long; flowers unknown; fruits solitary or paired, globose, 3 mm (⅛ in.) diameter; pyrenes 4, dorsally sulcate. Habitat: Vietnam, Annam, Nha Trang. Trees not attacked by termites. Allied to *I. poilanei* and *I. wilsonii*.

Ilex chimantaensis T. R. Dudley, *nom. nov.* (basionym *I. sulcata* Edwin, *Mem. N.Y. Bot. Gard.* 12(3). 1965, which is a later homonym of *I. sulcata* Wallich 1827).

Evergreen trees to 9 m (30 ft.) tall, branchlets sparsely puberulent; leaves narrowly obovate, 2.8–7 cm (1⅛–2¾ in.) long, 0.9–4 cm (11/32–1⅝ in.) wide, epunctate or occasionally punctate beneath, bases acute or cuneate to subspathulate, apices abruptly acuminate, acumen 0.5–2 mm (1/64–1/16 in.) long, margins entire, petioles 6.5–11 mm (¼–7/16 in.) long; inflorescences axillary or lateral, solitary, pedunculate, flowers 5-merous; fruits dark red, globose, 8–10 mm (5/16–⅜ in.) diameter; pyrenes of 2 sizes (large and small), canaliculate. Habitat: Venezuela, Bolivar, at 2120 m (7000 ft.) elevation.

Ilex chimantaensis var. *pygmaea* (Edwin) T. R. Dudley, *comb. nov.* (basionym *I. sulcata* var. *pygmaea* Edwin, *Mem. N.Y. Bot. Gard.* 12(3): 141. 1965).

A variety differing from typical plants in having smaller leaves, usually 2.8–3.5 cm (1⅛–1⅜ in.) long, 0.9–1.7 cm (¹¹⁄₃₂–²¹⁄₃₂ in.) wide. Habitat: Venezuela, Bolivar.

Ilex chingiana Hu & Tang 1940 var. *chingiana*.

Evergreen, glabrous trees to 12 m (40 ft.) tall; leaves oblong-elliptic, rarely oblanceolate, 11–14 cm (4⅜–5½ in.) long, 4.5 cm (1¾ in.) wide, apices acuminate, bases obtuse, margins remotely serrate, petioles 10–15 mm (⅜–¹⁹⁄₃₂ in.) long; inflorescences small, fasciculate, usually only 1 fruit maturing, flowers 4-merous; fruits red, globose, 15 mm (¹⁹⁄₃₂ in.) diameter, stigma navel-like; pyrenes 4, reticulate-striate, wrinkled and pitted. Habitat: endemic to People's Republic of China, Guangxi Province, mixed forests. Allied to *I. nuculicava*.

Ilex chingiana var. *puberula* S.-y. Hu 1949.

A variety with narrowly oblanceolate leaves, bases cuneate, terminal buds and petioles puberulent. Habitat: People's Republic of China, Guangxi Province. This variety may well fall unto the natural variations of the species and be referred into synonym of the species.

Ilex chiriquensis Standley 1936.

Evergreen trees, glabrous; leaves rotund-elliptic or broadly cuneate-obovate, 3.5–6 cm (1⅜–2⅜ in.) long, 3.5 cm (1⅜ in.) wide, sparse black punctate beneath, bases obtuse or broadly cuneate, apices broadly rotund to submarginate, margin entire below middle, obscurely and remotely appressed crenate toward apices, petioles canaliculate, 8–12 mm (⁵⁄₁₆–¹⁵⁄₃₂ in.) long; inflorescences axillary, fasciculate, pedicels 3 mm (⅛ in.) long; fruits unknown. Habitat: Panama, in rain forest, Bajo Chorro, Boquette District, Province Chiriqui, at 1800 m (5940 ft.) elevation. Leaves unlike other species from southern Central America, being unusually wide, broadly rounded at apex, and with few veins. Allied to *I. davidsoniae*.

Ilex chuniana S.-y. Hu 1951.

Evergreen, small trees; leaves lanceolate, rarely narrow-elliptic. 3–3.5 cm (1³⁄₁₆–1⅜ in.) long, ⁹⁄₃₂–15 mm (¹¹⁄₃₂–¹⁹⁄₃₂ in.) wide, bases acute or acuminate, apices obtuse, margins crenate, midribs impressed, petioles canaliculate, 3–5 mm (⅛–³⁄₁₆ in.) long, minute persistent stipules; inflorescences pauci-fasciculate, axillary, pedicels 2 mm (¹⁄₁₆ in.) long, prophylls 2; fruits red, subglobose-ellipsoid, 5.5 mm (⁷⁄₃₂ in.) long, 4.5 mm (¹¹⁄₆₄ in.) diameter, pedicels 2 mm (¹⁄₁₆ in.) long, sparsely puberulent, calyces persistent; pyrenes 4, striate. Habitat: People's Republic of China, tropical forest of Hunan Province, at 1000 m (3300 ft.) elevation. Named for T. W. Chun, director of the Botanical Institute Sun Yat-sen University, Guangzhan, People's Republic of China. Allied to *I. peiradena*.

Ilex ciliolata Steyermark 1988.

Evergreen small trees to 5 m (16 ft.) tall, branches minutely puberulent; leaves elliptic-ovate to oblong-ovate, 4.5–6.5 cm (1¾–2½ in.) long, 2–3.2 cm (¾–1¼ in.) wide, obscurely and minutely punctate beneath, bases acute to subacute, apices acute, obtuse or rotund, margins entire, lower midribs minutely puberulent, midribs above and marginal upper surface puberulent, petioles 4–7 mm (⁵⁄₃₂–⁹⁄₃₂ in.) long; male inflorescences axillary, solitary, lateral, peduncles and pedicels minutely puberulent; fruits globose, 4 mm (⁵⁄₃₂ in.) diameter. Habitat: Venezuela, Bolivar, north of El Pauji on trail to Uaiparu at 800–900 m (2600–2970 ft.) elevation. Allied to *I. chimantaensis* and *I. steyermarkii incertu sedia*.

Ilex ciliospinosa Loesener 1911 (synonym *I. bioritsensis* var. *ciliospinosa* (Loesener) Comber 1933).

Evergreen, large shrubs or small trees to 7 m (23 ft.) tall, branchlets densely pubescent; leaves pubescent, elliptic or ovate-elliptic, 3.5–7.5 cm (1⅜–3 in.) long, 1–2.5 cm (⅜–1 in.) wide, apices shortly acuminate or acute, acumens 3–5 mm (⅛–³⁄₁₆ in.) long, bases rotund, rarely obtuse, margins serrate, 4–6 spines on each side, petioles 2–3 mm (¹⁄₁₆–⅛ in.) long, leaves persist on 4th-year wood; inflorescences axillary, paucifasciculate, fascicles 2- to 5-flowered, flowers 4-merous; fruits red, globose, 10 mm (⅜ in.) diameter, pedicels 2–3.5 mm (¹⁄₁₆–⁹⁄₆₄ in.) long; pyrenes 1–4, usually 2. Habitat: People's Republic of China, western Hubei, Sichuan, and adjacent provinces. Introduced in 1908 before described and named. Allied to *I. bioritsensis* and *I. dipyrena*. Plate 59.

Ilex cinerea Champion 1852. Gray holly, muttchagii (synonym *I. cinerea* var. *faberi* Loesener 1901).

Evergreen shrubs or small trees to 6 m (20 ft.) tall, branchlets minutely pubescent; leaves lanceolate, 7–15 cm (2¾–6 in.) long, 2–4 cm (¾–1⅝ in.) wide, apices acute or shortly acuminate, acumens 4–8 mm (⁵⁄₃₂–⁵⁄₁₆ in.) long, bases rotund or obtuse, margins minutely crenate or serrate, teeth dark, petioles 2–4 mm (¹⁄₁₆–⁵⁄₃₂ in.) long; inflorescences axillary and fasciculate on 2nd-year growth, males 3- to 9-flow-

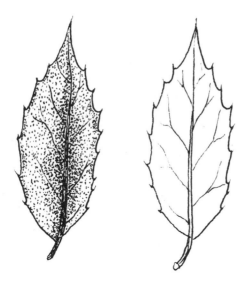

Figure 14-6. *Ilex ciliospinosa*. Drawing by Randy Allen.

ered, females uniflorous; fruits red, globose, 7 mm (9/32 in.) diameter, persist until next season, calyces persistent; pyrenes 4, dorsal surface palmately striate, sides wrinkled, rugose. Habitat: Hong Kong. Erroneously reported from various provinces in southern People's Republic of China and Vietnam. Allied to *I. formosana*.

Ilex cissoidea Loesener 1901.
    Evergreen, small trees; leaves ovate-elliptic or ovate, 7–14 cm (2¾–5½ in.) long, 2.5–4.2 cm (1–1 5/32 in.) wide, apices obtuse acuminate, acumen

Figure 14-7. *Ilex ciliospinosa*. Photo by Barton Bauer Sr.

usually 12 mm (15/32 in.) long, bases rotund or cordate, margins entire, recurved, petioles 6–13 mm (7/32–15/32 in.) long; inflorescences in leaf axils, 2- to 3-fasciculate, flowers 4-merous; fruits black, globose, 2 mm (1/16 in.) diameter; pyrenes 5–7. Habitat: Borneo, Malaysia, Sarawak district. Allied to *I. spicata*.

Ilex clarkei Loesener 1901.
    Evergreen, glabrous, shrubs or small trees; leaves lanceolate-elliptic, rarely ovate-elliptic, 5–9 cm (2⅛–3½ in.) long, 2.2–3 cm (¾–1 3/16 in.) wide, bases cuneate, apices usually acuminate, margins entire, slightly recurved, petioles 8–15 mm (5/16–19/32 in.) long; inflorescences fasciculate, axillary; fruits red, globose, 7–8 mm (9/32–5/16 in.) diameter; pyrenes 2. Habitat: southern India, at 2600–3000 m (8550–9900 ft.) elevation. Allied to *I. aquifolium* and *I. dipyrena*.

Figure 14-8. *Ilex ciliospinosa*. Photo by Barton Bauer Sr.

Ilex clemensiae Heine 1953.
    Evergreen, epiphytic shrubs, glabrous; leaves elliptic, 6–10 cm (2⅜–4 in.) long, 2.5–5.5 cm (1–2⅛ in.) wide, margins entire, revolute, minute punctate, apicules 1 mm (1/32 in.) long, petioles 3–4 mm (⅛–5/32 in.) long; inflorescences axillary, peduncles 1 mm (1/32 in.) long, 10-flowered, pedicels 1–3 mm (1/32–⅛ in.) long, flowers purplish, 5-merous; fruits dark purple, 8 mm (5/16 in.) diameter; pyrenes 5. Habitat: Malaysia, northern Borneo, on Mount Kinabalu at 1212–1515 m (4000–5000 ft.) elevation. Allied to *I. wenzelii*.

Ilex cochinchinensis (Loureiro) Loesener 1901 (synonyms *Hexadica cochinchinensis* Loureiro 1793, *I. ardisioides* Loesener 1901, *I. cleyeroides* Hayata 1913, *I. oligadenia* Merrill & Chun 1940).

Evergreen trees to 9 m (30 ft.) tall, branchlets angulate puberulent below terminal buds, minute lenticels; leaves elliptic or oblong-elliptic, 9–16 cm (3¾–6⅜) long, 2.5–4.5 cm (1–1¾ in.) wide, apices acute or obtuse, acuminate, acumens 3–10 mm (⅛–⅜ in.) long, bases obtuse or cuneate, margins entire, punctate beneath, petioles 7–10 mm (9⁄32–⅜ in.) long, canaliculate; inflorescences axillary on 2nd-year growth, fasciculate; fruits red, globose, 5–6 mm (3⁄16–7⁄32 in.) diameter, pedicels 8–9 mm (5⁄16–11⁄32 in.) long; pyrenes 4–5, smooth. Habitat: People's Republic of China, Hainan Province in subtropical forest, southern Taiwan, and northern Vietnam. Allied to *I. dolichopoda* and *I. salicina*.

Ilex cognata Reisseck 1868.
　　Evergreen, glabrous trees, branchlets striate, subsulcate; leaves elliptic or elliptic-oblong, 10–13 cm (4–5⅛ in.) long, 3.8–5 cm (1½–2 in.) wide, apices briefly acuminate, bases acute, margins recurved, subcrenulate-serrulate, petioles 6–10 mm (7⁄32–⅜ in.) long; inflorescences axillary, 5-fasciculate, flowers 4- to 5-merous; fruits unknown. Habitat: Brazil. Allied to *I. nitida* and *I. paraguariensis*.

Ilex colchica Pojarkova 1945 (synonyms *I. hyrcana* Pojarkova 1945, *I. stenocarpa* Pojarkova 1945, *I. imerethica* Pojarkova 1965, *I. colchica* subsp. *imerethica* (Pojarkova) Pojarkova 1983).
　　Evergreen, large shrubs or small trees, 3–6 m (18–26 ft.) tall; leaves elliptic, 5–11.5 cm (1–4½ in.) long, 3–3.5 cm (13⁄16–1⅜ in.) wide, keeled, bases obtuse, apices acuminate, margins spinose, 3–6 spines on each side, petioles 5–8 mm (3⁄16–5⁄16 in.) long; flowers 4-merous, on 2nd-year growth; fruits deep reddish orange, globose, 8–10 mm (⅜–5⁄16 in.) diameter, 2–5 in clusters; pyrenes 4. Hardy in zone 7b, possibly zone 7a. Habitat: Bulgaria and Transcaucasia to Black Sea region of Turkey, east to the Caucasus. Introduced to U.S. National Arboretum in 1966 by seed from the Caucasus, and then ten years later from the Varna District of Bulgaria on the Black Sea. Plate 60.

Ilex colombiana Cuatrecasas 1948.
　　Evergreen shrubs to 2 m (6 ft.) tall, young branchlets erect, scarcely hirsute, later glabrous; leaves broadly ovate, rigid, 3.5–6.5 cm (1⅜–2½ in.) long, 2.5–5 cm (1–2 in.) wide, bases rotund, apices attenuate, margins entire, petioles small, 0.5–0.8 mm (1⁄64–1⁄32 in.) long; inflorescences axillary, solitary, branched; fruits oblong-globose, 6–7 mm (7⁄32–9⁄32 in.) long; pyrenes 4. Habitat: Colombia, Department del Cauca, Central Cordillera, Cabeceras del Pio Palo, at 3300–3350 m (10,900–11,055 ft.) elevation. Allied to *I. minimifolia*.

Figure 14-9. *Ilex cochinchinensis*. Drawing by Chien-chu Chen in *Illustrations of Native and Introduced Ligneous Plants of Taiwan* (1962) by Tang-shui Liu.

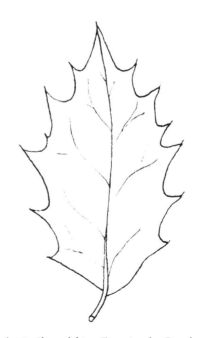

Figure 14-10. *Ilex colchica*. Drawing by Randy Allen.

Ilex condorensis Pierre 1893.

Evergreen, large, glabrous shrubs, branches grayish brown, lenticels dense; leaves smooth, oval to oblong-elliptic to oblong-lanceolate, 12–15 cm (4¾–6⅛ in.) long, 2.3–5.5 cm (⅝–2⅛ in.) wide, entire recurved margins, bases obtuse or acute, apices obtuse to acuminate, pedicels 12–16 mm (¹⁵⁄₃₂–⅝ in.) long; inflorescences solitary in leaf axils, branched, 6 petals; fruits depressed-globose, 5–6 mm (³⁄₁₆–⁷⁄₃₂ in.) diameter; pyrenes 6. Habitat: southern Vietnam. Allied to *I. hypoglauca*.

Ilex confertiflora Merrill 1934 var. *confertiflora*.

Evergreen shrubs or small trees to 3.5 m (12 ft.) tall, branchlets glabrous; leaves oblong, 7–10 cm (2¾–4 in.) long, 2 cm (¾ in.) wide, apices abruptly acuminate, acumens triangular, 2–5 mm (¹⁄₁₆–³⁄₁₆ in.) long, bases usually rotund, margins finely serrate, teeth dark, petioles thick, 7–10 mm (⁹⁄₃₂–⅜ in.) long; inflorescences axillary and fasciculate on 2nd-year growth, puberulent; fruits red, globose, 5 mm (³⁄₁₆ in.) diameter, pedicels 1.5–2 mm (³⁄₆₄–¹⁄₁₆ in.) long, calyces persistent; pyrenes 4, palmately striate, rugose, wrinkled. Habitat: People's Republic of China, Guangdong Province, its coastal islands, and Vietnam. Allied to *I. cinerea* and *I. ficoidea*.

Ilex confertiflora var. *kwangsiensis* S.-y. Hu 1950.

A variety differing from typical individuals with larger leaves, longer acumens, and female inflorescences having prominent rachises to 22 mm (¹³⁄₁₆ in.) long. Habitat: People's Republic of China, Guangxi Province.

Ilex confertifolia Merrill 1938.

Evergreen, glabrous shrubs or small trees; leaves oblong-obtuse, 1 cm (⅜ in.) long, 3–5 mm (⅛–³⁄₁₆ in.), margins revolute, veins obsolete; inflorescences axillary, racemes, 4- to 6-flowered, pedicels 2 mm (¹⁄₁₆ in.) long; ovaries 4–6 locules. Habitat: northern Borneo, Sarawak, on Mount Marud, exposed areas at 2400 m (7920 ft.) elevation. Allied to *I. havilandi*.

Ilex congonhinha Loesener 1901. Congonhinha.

Evergreen, glabrous, small trees; leaves oblong to oblanceolate, 1.2–3.2 cm (¹⁵⁄₃₂–1¼ in.) long, 4–8 mm (⁵⁄₃₂–⁵⁄₁₆ in.) wide, apices acute, minutely spined, bases acute, margins revolute, entire, occasionally serrate near apex, petioles 1.7–4 mm (³⁄₆₄–⁵⁄₃₂ in.) long; inflorescences axillary, paucifasciculate, flowers 4- to 5-merous; fruits black, globose 3–3.5 mm (⅛–⁷⁄₆₄ in.) diameter; pyrenes 4. Habitat: Brazil, Minas Gerais State. Allied to *I. buxifolia*.

Ilex conocarpa Reisseck 1861. Congonha, catuabe do mato (synonyms *I. conocarpa* var. *brevipetiolata* Loe-

sener 1901, *I. conocarpa* var. *genuina* Loesener 1901, *I. conocarpa* var. *senaei* Loesener 1901, *I. conocarpa* var. *tripuhyensis* Loesener 1901).

Evergreen, large shrubs or trees, to 10 m (33 ft.) tall; leaves oblong or narrowly lanceolate, usually 8–12 cm (3⅛–4¾ in.) long, 2.5–4 cm (1–1⅝ in.) wide, apices acute or acuminate, bases cuneate or acute, margins recurved, serrate or densely serrulate, petioles 5–20 mm (³⁄₁₆–¾ in.) long; inflorescences axillary, paniculate, flowers 4-merous, petals 2.75–4 mm (⁷⁄₆₄–⁵⁄₃₂ in.) long; fruits grayish brown when dry, ovoid to globose 6 mm (⁷⁄₃₂ in.) long, 4 mm (⁵⁄₃₂ in.) wide; pyrenes 4, striate. Habitat: Brazil, Bahia State, and Venezuela. Allied to *I. symplociformes*.

Ilex cookii Britton & P. Wilson 1926.

Evergreen shrubs or small trees 2–6 m (6–20 ft.) tall, branches with lenticels; leaves elliptic, 2–4.5 cm (¾–1¾ in.) long, 1–2.2 cm (⅜–⅞ in.) wide, apices acute or acuminate, bases cuneate or rotund, margins entire, slightly recurved, petioles 3–6.5 mm (⅛–¼ in.) long; inflorescences axillary, fasciculate, flowers 4- to 5-merous; fruits globose, 5 mm (³⁄₁₆ in.) diameter, color unknown; pyrenes 5. Habitat: Puerto Rico, Cerro de Punta, endangered plant, at 1212–1330 m (4000–4390 ft.) elevation.

Ilex corallina Franchet 1886 var. *corallina*. Fan cha shu (synonyms *I. corallina* var. *loeseneri* H. Léveillé 1914, *I. corallina* var. *aberrans* Handel-Mazzetti 1933).

Evergreen, glabrous trees to 10 m (33 ft.) tall, branchlets slender, lenticels minute; leaves ovate or ovate-elliptic or ovate-lanceolate, 5–13 cm (2–5⅛ in.) long, 1.5–5 cm (¹⁹⁄₃₂–2 in.) wide, apices acute or shortly acuminate, bases rotund or obtuse, margins in juvenile forms spinosely toothed, teeth dark, apiculate, adult leaf margins crenate-serrate, petioles 4–9 mm (⁵⁄₃₂–¹¹⁄₃₂ in.) long; inflorescences axillary and fasciculate on 2nd-year growth, subsessile, males 3-flowered cymes, females solitary; fruits purplish red, subglobose, 3 mm (⅛ in.) long, 4 mm (⁵⁄₃₂ in.) diameter, pedicels 2–3 mm (¹⁄₁₆–⅛ in.) long; pyrenes 4, rugose, palmately striate and sulcate. Habitat: People's Republic of China, Yunnan, Sichuan, Guizhou, and Hubei provinces, in mixed forest at 600–2000 m (2000–6600 ft.) elevation. One specimen collected at Kwang-yun in Sichuan Province represents the most northern limit for *Ilex* in People's Republic of China (Hu 1949). Allied to *I. buergeri*, *I. cinerea*, *I. ficoidea*, and *I. warburgii*. Sometimes confused with *I. centrochinensis*.

Ilex corallina var. *macrocarpa* S.-y. Hu 1950.

A variety differing from typical individuals with larger fruits 6 mm (⁷⁄₃₂ in.) diameter; pyrenes larger, 3.5–5 mm (⁹⁄₆₄–³⁄₁₆ in.) long. Habitat:

People's Republic of China, Yunnan Province, in the southern range of the species.

Ilex corallina var. *pubescens* S.-y. Hu 1950.

A variety differing from typical individuals with pubescent branchlets, terminal buds and midribs. Usually found at lower elevations with the species. Habitat: People's Republic of China, Yunnan Province. This variety may later be proven to represent natural variation and be regarded as a synonym of the species.

Ilex corallina var. *wangiana* (S.-y. Hu) Y.-r. Li 1985 (synonym *I. wangiana* S.-y. Hu 1950).

A variety differing from typical individuals with puberulent or glabrescent fruits, hairy disciform or subcapitate stigmas. Habitat: People's Republic of China, Yunnan Province, in the Ichang Gorge.

Ilex coriacea (Pursh) Chapman 1860. Large gallberry, sweet gallberry (synonyms *Prinos coriacea* Pursh 1814, *I. angustifolia* var. *ligustrifolia* De Candolle 1832, *Ennepta atomaria* (Nuttall) Rafinesque 1838, *E. coriacea* (Pursh) Rafinesque 1838 *I. lucida* Torrey & Gray 1878).

Evergreen, large shrubs to 4 m (13 ft.) tall, branches glabrous or slightly pubescent; leaves dark green, obovate to elliptic, 5–10 cm (2–4 in.) long, 1.5–3.5 cm ($^{19}/_{32}$–1$^3/_8$ in.) wide, apices acute, bases usually obtuse, margins entire or occasionally with appressed teeth on upper half of leaf, petioles 3–9 mm ($^1/_8$–1$^{1}/_{32}$ in.) long; inflorescences axillary, on new growth, males fasciculate, females usually solitary, flowers 6- to 9-merous; fruits variable, usually black to reddish brown, glossy, globose, 6–10 mm ($^7/_{32}$–$^3/_8$ in.) diameter, juicy, maturing early and removed by birds; pyrenes 6–9, smooth. Habitat: United States, Coastal Plains from southern Virginia to Florida, Texas, and Mexico. Hardy in zones 7 to 10. Allied to *I. glabra* with larger leaves and more open habit of growth; not as desirable a landscape plant. Source of a light clear honey.

Ilex cornuta Lindley & Paxton 1850. Horned holly, Chinese holly (synonyms *I. furcata* Lindley 1854, *I. fortunei* Lindley 1857, *I. cornuta* f. *gaetena* Loesener 1901, *I. cornuta* var. *fortunei* (Lindley) S.-y. Hu 1949).

Evergreen, large shrubs or small trees, branchlets glabrous; leaves dark olive green, glossy, quadrangular-oblong, rarely ovate, 3–8 cm, usually 5–6 cm (1$^1/_{16}$–3$^1/_8$, usually 2–2$^3/_8$ in.) long, 2–4 cm ($^3/_4$–1$^5/_8$ in.) wide, bases rotund or truncate, apices acute or shortly acuminate, tip with strong spine, 1 spine in each corner of the rectangular leaves, margins entire, or 1–3 spines on the sides, leaves often entire with 1

Figure 14-11. *Ilex coriacea.* Photo by Barton Bauer Sr.

terminal spine on mature plants, petioles 4–8 mm ($^5/_{32}$–$^5/_{16}$ in.) long, leaves persist on 3rd-year growth; inflorescences axillary and fasciculate on 2nd-year growth, flowers yellowish white, 4-merous; fruits usually red, rarely yellow, globose, 8–10 mm ($^5/_{16}$–$^3/_8$ in.) diameter; pyrenes 4, wrinkled, pitted, rugose all over, endocarps bony. Habitat: People's Republic of China, coastal and hilly regions of lower Yangtze provinces to western Hubei and Shandong provinces; also Korea. Plants found in mixed woody areas along stream banks and mountains slopes. Allied to *I. aquifolium.* Commonly cultivated in the southeastern United States and in the west coast, also in Europe. Hardy in zone 6b. Many cultivars available, 'Burfordii' the most common; see descriptions in Chapter 15. Hybrids of *I. cornuta* with other species are listed and described in Chapter 16.

Ilex cornuta was first introduced to England from China by Robert Fortune in 1846. The Fortune introduction (as f. *fortunei*) was spineless or nearly so, similar to 'Burfordii', as documented by herbarium specimens collected by Fortune in China. The bark, leaves, and fruits of this species are used in herbal medicine for their tonic value. Reported to be a remedy for diseases of the kidney. Seed oil has been used

Figure 14-12. *Ilex coriacea*. Photo by Barton Bauer Sr.

in China for soap manufacturing; a dye and gum are extracted from the bark. This species is also a host for scale insects that produce a wax, collected and highly prized by the Chinese in earlier days. Plate 61.

Ilex costaricensis Donn & W. Smith 1914.

Evergreen shrubs, branchlets glabrous; leaves broadly elliptic, occasionally elliptic-obovate, 3–6.5 cm (1³⁄₁₆–2½ in.) long, 1–3.5 cm (³⁄₈–1³⁄₈ in.) wide, bases acute, apices acute, short-acuminate or cuspidate, margins entire, revolute, petioles 1.5–2 cm (¹⁹⁄₃₂–¾ in.) long; inflorescences on new growth, axillary, solitary, usually pedunculate, 3-flowered cymes; fruits unknown. Habitat: Costa Rica. Allied to *I. guianensis*.

Ilex costata Edwin 1965.

Evergreen shrubs to 2 m (6 ft.) tall, branchlets pubescent; leaves oval to broadly ovate or obovate to elliptic, 3.8–6.5 cm (1½–2½ in.) long, 2.5–3.8 cm (1–1½ in.) wide, punctate beneath, bases acute to cuneate, apices acute to short acuminate, margins entire, petioles 2–3.5 mm (¹⁄₁₆–⁹⁄₆₄ in.) long; inflorescences axillary, fasciculate, flowers 4- to 5-merous; fruits red, globose; pyrenes 4–5, unicaniculate. Habitat: Guyana, shrub savannahs at 1100 m (3630 ft.) elevation, Kemarang River, Parkariana Mountains.

Ilex cougesta H.-w. Li *ex* Y.-r. Li 1985.

Evergreen shrubs to 5 m (16 ft.) tall; leaves evergreen, leathery, elliptic, 7–9 cm (2¾–3½ in.) long, 4–5 cm (1⅝–2 in.) wide, margin partially serrated; pedicels 5 mm (³⁄₁₆ in.) long, pubescent; petioles 6–10 cm (2¾–4 in.) long, pubescent; flowers unknown; fruits red, globose, 1 cm (³⁄₈ in.) in diameter; fruit cluster 3-fruit cymose; pyrenes 4, with 1 sulcate in cross section, V form. Habitat: People's Republic

of China, Yunnan Province, near Longling, Yunlongshan, in woody mountains. Allied to *I. xyolosmaefolia*.

Ilex cowanii Wurdack 1961.

Evergreen trees to 18 m (60 ft.) tall, branchlets minutely hirsute; leaves elliptic, 4.5–6 cm (1¾–2⅜ in.) long, 2–3 cm (¾–1³⁄₁₆ in.) wide, bases acute, apices acute or narrow-obtuse, mucronate, margins serrulate, petioles 5–8 mm (³⁄₁₆–⁵⁄₁₆ in.) long; inflorescences axillary, solitary, branches 1- to 3-flowered, flowers usually 4-merous; fruits unknown. Habitat: Venezuela, Amazonas, dense woodland along Cano de Dios at 1800 m (5940 ft.) elevation. Allied to *I. myricoides*.

Ilex crassifolia Hooker 1837, *non* Aiton *ex* Steudel 1837.

Evergreen trees, branches pubescent; leaves broadly elliptic to ovate-oblong, 5–7.5 cm (2–3 in.) long, 3–4.5 cm (1³⁄₁₆–1¾ in.) wide, bases cuneate to obtuse or rotund, apices mostly rotund, minute apiculate, punctate below, margins recurved, entire, petioles 8–11 mm (⁵⁄₁₆–⁷⁄₁₆ in.) long; male inflorescences, fasciculate, pedunculate, peduncles to 7 mm (⁹⁄₃₂ in.) long, 3–7 subsessile flowers, flowers 4- to 5-merous, female flowers solitary. Habitat: Peru, Chachapoyas. Allied to *I. crassifolioides* and *I. scopulorum*.

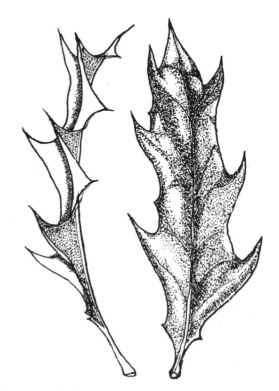

Figure 14-13. *Ilex cornuta*. Drawing by Randy Allen.

Figure 14-14. *Ilex cornuta.* Photo by Barton Bauer Sr.

Ilex crassifolioides Loesener 1901.

Evergreen, small trees to 6 m (20 ft.) tall; leaves obovate to broadly oval, 7–10.5 cm (2¾–4⅛ in.) long, 2.7–6.5 cm (1¹⁄₁₆–2½ in.) wide, bases usually cuneate-rounded to rounded, apices obtuse to rounded, margins recurved, crenulate-serrulate, petioles 7–14 mm (⁹⁄₃₂–¹⁷⁄₃₂ in.) long; inflorescences axillary, solitary, single branches, peduncles 2–6 mm (¹⁄₁₆–⁷⁄₃₂ in.) long, pedicels 1–2 mm (¹⁄₃₂–¹⁄₁₆ in.) long; fruits unknown. Habitat: Peru near Tarapoto on Mount Campara at 1700 m (5600 ft.) elevation. Allied to *I. crassifolia.*

Ilex crenata Thunberg *ex* J. A. Murray 1784 var. *crenata.* Japanese holly, boxleaf holly, inu-tsuge, muttcha-gara (synonyms *Celastrus adenophylla* Miquel 1867, *I. elliptica* Siebold *ex* Miquel 1867, *I. luzonica* Rolfe 1886, *I. crenata* f. *luzonica* (Rolfe) Loesener 1901, *I. crenata* var. *typica* Loesener 1901, *I. fauriei* Gandoger 1918).

Evergreen shrub, extremely variable from low spreading or low dwarf compact shrubs to fastigiate, upright, small trees to 5 m (16 ft.) tall, densely branched, puberulent, lenticels sparse; leaves glabrous, close together and 3–10 mm (⅛–⅜ in.) apart,

even on 2nd-year growth, usually dark olive green, dull or glossy, rarely variegated, obovate or ovate or oblong-elliptic, 1–2.5 cm (⅜–1 in.) long, rarely larger, 0.5–1.5 cm (³⁄₁₆–¹⁹⁄₃₂ in.) wide, punctate beneath, bases obtuse, acute or crenate, apices rounded, obtuse or subacute, margins crenate-serrate, usually 6–10 teeth on each side, punctate beneath, margins usually flat or occasionally convex-bullate, short petioles 2–3 mm (¹⁄₁₆–⅛ in.) long, canaliculate, puberulent; staminate inflorescences solitary, axillary, 1- to 7-flowered cymose or subumbellate, on current year's branchlets, pistillate inflorescences axillary, solitary or 2- to 3-flowered cymose, rarely pseudo-fasciculate on 2nd-year wood, pedicels 4–6 mm (⁵⁄₃₂–⁷⁄₃₂ in.) long, 1–2 submedial prophylls, flowers white, rotate, 4-merous, female corollas ovate, 3–4 mm (⅛–⁵⁄₃₂ in.) long, male corollas 1.5–2 mm (³⁄₆₄–¹⁄₁₆ in.) long; fruits black, rarely yellow, globose, 6–8 mm (⁷⁄₃₂–⁵⁄₁₆ in.) diameter; pyrenes 4, smooth, striate, esulcate. Habitat: Japan, People's Republic of China, in Fujian and Zhejiang provinces, coastal regions of Korea, Kuril, Sakhalin Islands, Taiwan, Philippines, and the Himalayas.

In Honshu and Kyushu, Japan, the species grows wild from sea level to 1000 m (3300 ft.) and shows tremendous variability with local populations. In the north in Hokkaido, Japan, the species is a low growing shrub in deep forests, at elevations below snowline. Many cultivars from Japan, Europe and North America. Introduced to Europe about 1864. Hardy in zones 6a to 10. The nomenclature (Dudley and Eisenbeiss 1992) of forms, varieties, and cultivars are now less confusing, and new cultivars are still being introduced; see descriptions in Chapter 15. Plate 62.

Ilex crenata f. *fastigiata* (Makino) Hara 1958, see *I. crenata* 'Fastigiata' in Chapter 15.

Ilex crenata var. *fastigiata* Makino 1917, see *I. crenata* 'Fastigiata' in Chapter 15.

Ilex crenata subsp. *fukasawana* (Makino) Murata 1972. Tsukushi inu-tsuge (synonym *I. crenata* var. *fukasawana* Makino 1972).

Evergreen shrubs with branches prominently angulate; leaves oblong, 2.5–4 cm (1–1⅝ in.) long, thin-textured, margins crenate; fruits 3-sided. Habitat: Japan, southern Kyushu. Sometimes listed as a cultivar.

Ilex crenata var. *hachijoensis* Nakai 1926.

A variety differing from typical individuals with leaves oval, bordered reddish purple; fruit pedicels 6–10 mm (⁷⁄₃₂–⅜ in.) long. Habitat: India, Bhutan.

Ilex crenata var. *latifolia* (synonyms 'Grandifolia', f. *latifolia,* 'Latifolia', 'Major', 'Major Fortunei', 'Rotundifolia', *I. elliptica, I. fortunei*).

Figure 14-15. *Ilex crenata* var. *crenata*. Drawing by Chien-chu Chen in *Illustrations of Native and Introduced Ligneous Plants of Taiwan* (1962) by Tang-shui Liu.

A dubious variety based on cultivated material, numerous synonyms, and inadequate descriptions; 'Latifolia' origin in Japan, introduced in 1865 to Netherlands.

Ilex crenata f. *longipedunculata* S.-y. Hu 1949.

Evergreen, large shrubs; leaves oblong or obovate-elliptic or obovate, 2–3 cm (¾–1³⁄₁₆ in.) long, 1–1.5 cm (⅜–¹⁹⁄₃₂ in.) wide, inflorescences cymose, peduncles 10–12 mm (⅜–½ in.) long, pedicels 2–3 mm (¹⁄₁₆–⅛ in.) long. Habitat: People's Republic of China, Shandong Province.

Ilex crenata var. *multicrenata* C.-j. Tseng 1985.

A new variety differing from the typical species with glabrescent young branches; leaves very strongly crenate, 13–15 teeth on each side. Habitat: People's Republic of China, Guangxi Province.

Ilex crenata var. *paludosa* (Nakai) Hara 1954. Hai-inu-tsuge (synonyms *I. radicans* Nakai 1930, *I. crenata* subsp. *radicans* (Nakai) Tatewaki 1933,

I. crenata f. *microphylla* Tatewaki 1933, *I. crenata* var. *radicans* (Nakai) Murai 1935, *I. paludosa* Nakai *ex* Honda & Tobita 1941, *I. paludosa* Nakai *ex* Honda & Tobita 1944, *I. radicans* var. *paludosa* Nakai 1944, *I. crenata* var. *radicans* (Nakai) Ohwi 1953).

Similar to typical species, but with low, creeping stems and branches; leaves broadly elliptic, bases obtuse, apices rotund. Northernmost limits in wet swampy places and on beaches of Honshu and Hokkaido, Japan; Siberia, formerly U.S.S.R.; Sakhalin Island. Should not be listed as a cultivar.

Ilex crenata f. *pendula* (Koidzumi) Hara 1954 (synonym *I. crenata* var. *pendula* Koidzumi 1939).

A form with weeping branches. Habitat: Japan, collected on Mount Rokkō, Settsu Province.

Ilex crenata var. *thompsonii* (Hooker f.) Loesener 1901 (synonyms *I. thompsonii* Hooker f. 1875. Collected 1965 on Mount Tongler, West Bengal, India, at 2424 m (8000 ft.) by F. de Vos & E. Corbett as *I. intricata* Hooker, PI 307276, later identified as *I. thompsonii*).

Leaves obovate-oblanceolate, 1.3–2.5 cm (½–1 in.) long; subacute or apiculate serrulate. Habitat: Nepal, Bhutan, India, West Bengal, and Sikkim, at 3000–3300 m (9,900–11,000 ft.) elevation. Additional critical study is needed.

Ilex crenata var. *tokarenensis* Hatusima 1971.

A variety with leaves smaller than typical individuals, 1–2 cm (⅜–¾ in.) long, with fewer teeth. Habitat: Japan, Tokara Island.

Ilex crenata f. *tricocca* (Makino) Hara 1972 (synonym *I. crenata* var. *tricocca* Makino 1941).

A form with fruits borne in threes. Habitat: Japan.

Ilex crenata f. *watanabeana* Makino 1914.

A form with yellow fruits. Habitat: southern Japan and Okinawa. Named for Toyodzi Watanabe, noted Japanese botanist. Originally collected in the wild by Chushiro Harada, in town of Uematsu-Cho, Nischikuma-Gum District, Hagano-Ken Prefecture, Japan. Makino's 1914 description was based on a plant from Harada's garden. In 1956 John L. Creech obtained a plant from the Kyushu Agriculture Experiment Station, Kurume Fukuoka, Japan, for the U.S. Department of Agriculture. In 1966 E. Griffith and H. Hyland recorded the plant in the U.S.D.A. plant inventory 164:45: *I. crenata* (fruits yellow) PI 231948, but not identified as *I. crenata* f. *watanabeana* in PI inventories or in Glenn Dale distributions. The *I. crenata* (PI 231948) and its seed *I. crenata* (PI 231948-S) were propagated and widely distributed from Glenn Dale and as U.S. National Arboretum 10815. It is generally agreed that all named selections of yellow-fruited *I. crenata* originating in the United States are plants or seedlings of this plant, *I. crenata* (PI 231948). Often listed incorrectly as a cultivar. Fruits greenish yellow. Habitat: southern Japan and Okinawa. For additional information, see Watanabeana Group in Chapter 15.

Figure 14-16. *Ilex crenata* f. *watanabeana.* Photo by Barton Bauer Sr.

Ilex cristata Merrill & Perry 1939.

Evergreen trees, branches grayish; leaves ovate, 2–3.5 cm (¾–1³⁄₁₆ in.) long, 0.9–1.3 cm (¹¹⁄₃₂–½ in.) wide, bases usually cuneate, apices obtuse acuminate, margins entire, serrations near apex, petioles 2 mm (¹⁄₁₆ in.) long; inflorescences small, axillary, solitary; fruits depressed ovoid to subglobose, 3 mm (⅛ in.) diameter; pyrenes small. Habitat: New Guinea. Allied to *I. spicata.*

Ilex cubana Loesener 1892 (synonyms *I. montana* Grisebach 1859, *I. cubana* var. *turguinica* Loesener 1901, *I. cubana* var. *viburnica* Loesener 1933).

Evergreen shrubs; leaves ovate, 3.5–5 cm (1⅜–2 in.) long, 2.5–3.5 cm (1–1⅜ in.) wide, apices rounded, bases cuneate to obtuse, margins entire, petioles 5–10 mm (³⁄₁₆–⅜ in.) long; inflorescences axillary, solitary, on new growth, flowers usually 4-merous; fruits brownish black, globose, 4–5 mm (⁵⁄₃₂–³⁄₁₆ in.) diameter; pyrenes 5. Habitat: eastern Cuba. Allied to *I. coriacea.*

Ilex cumulicola Small 1924. Dune holly (synonyms *I. arenicola* Ashe 1924, *I. opaca* var. *arenicola* (Ashe) Ashe 1925, *I. arenicola* f. *sebringensis* McFarlin 1932, *I. pygmaea* McFarlin 1932).

Evergreen, large shrubs or small trees to 8 m (26 ft.) tall, pale gray to whitish fastigiated branches; leaves narrow-elliptic, 2.5–4.5 cm (1–1¾ in.) long, 2–2.5 cm (¾–1 in.) wide, apices acuminate, margins slightly revolute, small spines pointed forward; inflorescences axillary, on new growth; fruits red, globose 7–8 mm (⁹⁄₃₂–⁵⁄₁₆ in.) diameter, crushed fruit has fragrance of ripe pineapples; pyrenes 5–6. Habitat: Florida, endemic to the interior dunes around Lake Jackson near Sebring, northern limits in Clay County near Kingsley Lake; also abundant in the Olala National Forest, and in Lake County. Hardy in zones 8 to 10. Allied to *I. cassine* and *I. opaca. Ilex* × *attenuata* 'Fort McCoy' may be a named cultivar. Some evidence is accumulating to indicate that *I. cumulicola* is a hybrid if so, it eventually will be referred to *I.* × *attenuata.*

Ilex cupreonitens C.-y. Wu *ex* Y.-r. Li 1985

Evergreen, glabrous, small trees 5–6 m (16–20 ft.) tall, branchlets glandular-lenticellate; leaves oblong-elliptic, 6.5–10 cm (2⅜–4 in.) long, 2.5–4 cm (1–1⅝ in.) wide, apices long-acuminate, bases obtuse or subrotund, margins moderately serrate, petioles 10–12 mm (⅜–¹⁵⁄₃₂ in.) long; inflorescences fasciculate; fruits red, globose, 5 mm (³⁄₁₆ in.) diameter, calyces persistent, stigmas thick-discoid; pyrenes 4, striate, sulcate. Habitat: People's Republic of China, Yunnan Province. Allied to *I. subodorata.*

Ilex curranii Merrill 1920.

Evergreen, large shrubs to 3 m (10 ft.) tall, branches glabrous; leaves ovate, glossy, 1–1.5 cm (⅜–¹⁹⁄₃₂ in.) long, 0.7–1.2 cm (⁹⁄₃₂–¹⁵⁄₃₂ in.) wide, bases acute to rotund, apices short and bluntly acuminate, margins crenate, often with incurved tip, petioles 2–4 mm (¹⁄₁₆–⁵⁄₃₂ in.) long; inflorescences axillary, solitary or occasionally 2–3 in fascicles; fruits black, subglobose, 5 mm (³⁄₁₆ in.) diameter; pyrenes 4; Habitat: Philippines, Luzon, mossy forest on Mount Pulog about 2500 m (8250 ft.) elevation. Allied to *I. rugosa* and similar to *I. buergeri.*

Figure 14-17. *Ilex cumulicola.* Photo by Barton Bauer Sr.

Ilex cuyabensis Reisseck 1861. Congonha (synonym *Labatia conica* Velloso 1836, *I. conica* Radlkofer 1887).

Evergreen trees 3–7 m (10–23 ft.) tall, branches with lenticels; leaves elliptic or obovate-elliptic, 7–12 cm ($2\frac{3}{4}$–$4\frac{3}{4}$ in.) long, 2.7–4.7 cm ($1\frac{1}{16}$–$1\frac{7}{8}$ in.) wide, apices obtuse or acuminate, bases obtuse or cuneate-obtuse, margins entire, recurved, petioles 8–12 mm ($\frac{5}{16}$–$\frac{15}{32}$ in.) long; inflorescences axillary, fasciculate, branched, flowers 4-merous; fruits unknown. Habitat: Brazil, Mato Grosso State, along the Guaporé River. Allied to *I. floribunda, I. guianensis,* and *I. inundata.*

Ilex cuzcoana Loesener 1908.

Evergreen shrubs to 2 m (6 ft.) tall; leaves ovate or oval, 5.3–6 cm ($1\frac{3}{16}$–$2\frac{3}{8}$ in.) long, 1.5–2.4 cm ($\frac{19}{32}$–1 in.) wide, apices acuminate, bases obtuse to subcrenate, margins usually serrulate, petioles 3–6 mm ($\frac{1}{8}$–$\frac{7}{32}$ in.) long; inflorescences axillary, solitary, branched, 3–15 small flowers, flowers 4-merous; fruits unknown. Habitat: Peru, near Urubamba, sparsely distributed on steep slopes at 2100–2200 m (6900–7260 ft.) elevation. Allied to *I. crassifolia.*

Ilex cymosa Blume 1827. Kisekkal, jaloto on, mensirah, timah-timah (synonyms *I. singaporiana* Wallich 1832, *Prinos cymosa* Hasskarl 1844, *I. cymosa* var. *cumingiana* Rolfe 1884, *I. philippinensis* Rolfe 1884, *I. fletcheri* Merrill 1907, *I. koordersiana* Loesener *ex* Koorders 1913).

Evergreen large shrubs or trees to 17 m (55 ft.) tall, bark whitish, lenticellate; leaves elliptic to obovate-elliptic, margins entire, recurved, 6–13 cm ($2\frac{3}{8}$–$5\frac{1}{8}$ in.) long, 2.5–5 cm (1–2 in.) wide, bases rounded to crenate-obtuse, apices usually obtuse, petioles 5–15 mm ($\frac{3}{16}$–$\frac{1}{2}$ in.) long; inflorescences in axils of leaves, cymose; fruits globose to ellipsoidal, 2.5–5 mm ($\frac{1}{16}$–$\frac{3}{16}$ in.) diameter, shiny, black, in clusters of 7–10; pyrenes 7–10, striate. Habitat: Malaysia, Indonesia, Sumatra, Java, Philippines. Allied to *I. thorelii.*

Ilex cyrtura Merrill 1941.

Evergreen trees to 12 m (40 ft.) tall, branchlets glabrous or very sparsely pubescent; leaves elliptic-oblong or obovate-elliptic, 6–11 cm ($2\frac{3}{8}$–$4\frac{3}{8}$ in.) long, 2–4 cm ($\frac{3}{4}$–$1\frac{5}{8}$ in.) wide, apices often curved, acumens 1.5–2.2 cm ($\frac{19}{32}$–$\frac{13}{16}$ in.) long, bases obtuse or cuneate, margins serrate, petioles slender, 8–12 mm ($\frac{5}{16}$–$\frac{15}{32}$ in.) long; inflorescences axillary and fasciculate on 2nd-year growth, pubescent, flowers 4-merous; fruits red, globose, 6 mm ($\frac{7}{32}$ in.) diameter, pedicels 5–9 mm ($\frac{3}{16}$–$\frac{11}{32}$ in.) long; pyrenes 4, rugose, palmately striate. Habitat: first recorded from Myanmar, Adung Valley, Bhutan; later collected in People's Republic of China, Guizhou and Guangxi provinces. Introduced to England by G. Forrest in the late 1920s. Allied to *I. ficoidea.*

Ilex dabieshanensis Kan Yao & Moa-Bin 1987.

Evergreen, glabrous trees to 5 m (16.5 ft.) tall; leaves ovate-oblong to ovate-elliptic, 5.5–8 cm ($2\frac{1}{8}$–$3\frac{1}{8}$ in.) long, 2–4 cm ($\frac{3}{4}$–$1\frac{5}{8}$ in.) wide, apices short-acuminate, acumens 5–8 mm ($\frac{3}{16}$–$\frac{5}{16}$ in.) long, tip spines 1–2 mm ($\frac{1}{32}$–$\frac{1}{16}$ in.) long, margins straight, 6–10 short and thin spines on each side, petioles glabrous, 5–8 mm ($\frac{3}{16}$–$\frac{5}{16}$ in.) long; inflorescences fasciculate, axillary; fruits subglobose to ellipsoid, 4–5 mm (5⁄32–3⁄16 in.) diameter, long pedicels 2 cm (3⁄4 in.) long, pyrenes 2, 3.5 mm (9⁄64 in.) long, 3 mm (1⁄8 in.) wide, dorsal surface palmately striate and sulcate. Habitat: People's Republic of China, Dabieshan mountain range, Anhui Province. Allied to *I. bioritsensis.*

Ilex danielii Killip & Cuatrecasas 1925.

Evergreen trees; leaves obovate-elliptic, 4–7 cm (1 5⁄8–2 3⁄4 in.) long, 1.7–3.5 cm (5⁄8–1 3⁄8 in.) wide, bases obtuse or attenuate, apices rotund or obtuse, margins smooth, revolute; fruits solitary, depressed rotund, 6 mm (7⁄32 in.) diameter, pyrenes 5–6. Habitat: Colombia, Antioguia and San Vicente. Allied to *I. guianensis.*

Ilex daphnogenea Reisseck 1861 (synonym *I. laurina* Klotzsch 1849, *non* Kunth 1825).

Evergreen, glabrous tree; leaves elliptic or elliptic-oblong, 11–16 cm (4–6 1⁄2 in.) long, 4–5.5 cm (1 5⁄8–2 1⁄8 in.) wide, apices obtuse acuminate, bases acute or cuneate-acute, margins entire, recurved, petioles 11–17 mm (7⁄16–21⁄32 in.) long; inflorescences axillary, fasciculate, branched, flowers 4-merous; male peduncles 7–17 mm (9⁄32–21⁄32 in.) long, male pedicels 1 mm (1⁄32 in.) long; fruits unknown. Habitat: Guyana near the Essequibo River. Allied to *I. jenmanii* and *I. umbellata.*

Ilex daphnoides Reisseck 1861.

Evergreen shrubs or trees, branches lenticellate; leaves elliptic or elliptic-lanceolate, 4.3–7.5 cm (1 3⁄16–3 in.) long, 1.1–2.6 cm (7⁄16–2 in.) wide, apices obtuse or subacute, apiculate, bases cuneate-acute or acute, margins entire, recurved, petioles 6–11 mm (7⁄32–7⁄16 in.) long; inflorescences axillary, subsessile, flowers 4-merous; fruits unknown. Habitat: Brazil. Allied to *I. vismiifolia.*

Ilex dasyclada C.-y. Wu *ex* Y.-r. Li 1985.

Evergreen shrubs 1.8–2.5 m (6–8 ft.) tall, branchlets slender, angulate-sulcate, rarely puberulent; leaves oblong or oblong-elliptic, 7.5–9 cm (3–3 1⁄2 in.) long, 2.2–3.5 cm (13⁄16–1 3⁄8 in.) wide, apices acuminate, bases obtuse, margins inconspicuously to moderately serrate, glabrous, petioles 5–8 mm (3⁄16–5⁄16 in.) long; inflorescences cymose; fruits (immature) globose, 3–4 mm (1⁄8–5⁄32 in.) diameter, calyces persistent, pedicels 1–2 mm (1⁄32–1⁄16 in.) long; pyrenes immature. Habitat: People's Republic of China, Yunnan Province, in forest at 1600 m (5300 ft.) elevation. Allied to *I. pingnanensis.*

Ilex dasyphylla Merrill 1931 var. *dasyphylla* (synonym *I. fulveo-mollissima* Metcalf 1932).

Evergreen trees to 9 m (30 ft.) tall, branchlets pubescent, lenticels numerous, inconspicuous; leaves pubescent, ovate or ovate-elliptic or ovate-lanceolate, 3–9 cm (1 3⁄16–3 1⁄2 in.) long, 1.3–2.4 cm (7⁄16–1 in.) wide, bases obtuse, rarely rounded, apices acuminate, rarely acute, margins entire, short petioles 4–5 mm (5⁄32–3⁄16 in.) long; inflorescences cymose, solitary and axillary on new growth, peduncles slender, 4–5 mm (5⁄32–5⁄16 in.) long, pedicels 2 mm (1⁄16 in.) long, petals red; fruits red, globose, 5–6 mm (3⁄16–7⁄32 in.) diameter; pyrenes 4–5, unicanaliculate on back. Habitat: southeastern People's Republic of China, Fujian, Guangdong, and Guangxi provinces. Allied to *I. purpurea.*

Ilex dasyphylla var. *lichuanensis* S.-y. Hu 1980.

A variety differing from typical individuals with dense ferruginous long hairs on branchlets, leaves, and inflorescence; fruits small, 4–5 mm (5⁄32–3⁄16 in.) diameter, persistent hirsute sepals. Habitat: People's Republic of China, Guangdong and Guangxi provinces.

Ilex davidsei Steyermark 1988.

Evergreen trees to 18 m (26 ft.) tall, branchlets minutely puberulent, glabrescent; leaves elliptic-oblong or narrow-elliptic, 4–7.5 cm (1 5⁄8–3 in.) long, 1.5–3 cm (19⁄32–1 3⁄16 in.) wide, punctate beneath, bases acute to subacute, apices with prolonged obtuse acumens, 5–12 mm (3⁄16–15⁄32 in.) long, margins 2–4 remote crenulations on each side, petioles 5–8 mm (3⁄16–5⁄16 in.) long; inflorescences axillary, solitary, elongated racemose, 1.2–1.5 cm (15⁄32–19⁄32 in,) long; fruits unknown. Habitat: Venezuela, Amazonas, Department Rio Negro, lower part of the Rio Baria, inundated forests along rivers. Allied to *I. conocarpa* and *I. symplociformes.*

Ilex davidsoniae Standley 1936.

Evergreen, small trees, glabrous; leaves oblong-elliptic, 9.5 cm (3 3⁄4 in.) long, 4.5 cm (1 3⁄4 in.) wide, bases obtuse, apices abruptly acuminate, acumens obtuse, margins coarse crenate, 14 teeth on each side, pedicels canaliculate, 4–7 mm (3⁄16–9⁄32 in.) long; inflorescences axillary, numerous, umbellate, peduncles short, pedicels 3–5 mm (1⁄8–3⁄16 in.) long; immature fruits ellipsoid-globose, 4 mm (5⁄32 in.) long. Habitat: Panama, in rain forest, Bajo Chorro, Boquette District, Province Chiriqui, at 1800 m (5940 ft.) elevation. Allied to *I. chiriquensis.*

Ilex debaoensis C.-j. Tseng 1981.

Evergreen trees to 10 m (33 ft.) tall, branchlets brownish, angulate, 2nd-year branches subterete, with lenticels; leaves ovate or elliptic, 5–6.5 cm (2–2 1⁄2 in.) long, 2–2.5 cm (3⁄4–1 in.) wide, apices acuminate, acumens triangular and widely cuneate, decurrent at base, margins remotely crenulate, slightly revolute, petioles 1.7–1.9 cm ($^{21}/_{32}$–$^3/_4$ in.) long; inflorescences solitary, axillary, 3-fruited cymes; fruits red, obovoid-ellipsoid, 9 mm ($^{11}/_{32}$ in.) long, 6 mm ($^7/_{32}$ in.) diameter; pyrenes 5. Habitat: People's Republic of China, Guangxi Province. Allied to *I. ferruginea*.

Ilex decussata Heine 1953.

Evergreen trees; leaves opposite or decussate, lanceolate or obovate-elliptic, 5 cm (2 in.) long, 1.5 cm ($^{19}/_{32}$ in.) wide, bases long-cuneate, margins entire, petioles decurrent, 7–10 mm ($^9/_{32}$–$^3/_8$ in.) long; inflorescences cymose umbellate, axillary, peduncles 2.5–4 cm (1–1$^5/_8$ in.) long, pedicels 1 mm ($^1/_{32}$ in.) long, male flowers 4-merous, female flowers and fruits unknown. Habitat: Indonesia and Malaysia, on Mount Kinabalu at 1818–4090 m (6,000–13,500 ft.) elevation. Allied to *I. oppositifolia*.

Ilex delavayi Franchet 1898 (synonyms *I. delavayi* var. *exalta* Comber 1933, *I. delavayi* var. *comberiana* S.-y. Hu 1950, *I. delavayi* var. *linearifolia* S.-y. Hu 1950).

Evergreen, glabrous shrubs or trees to 9 m (30 ft.) tall; branchlets pubescent, often appear warty; leaves elliptic-lanceolate, usually 4–5 cm (1$^5/_8$–2 in.) long, 1–2 cm ($^3/_8$–$^3/_4$ in.) wide, apices obtuse or acute, bases acute or cuneate, margins crenulate-serrate, petioles slender, 10–15 mm ($^3/_8$–$^{19}/_{32}$ in.) long; inflorescences axillary on 2nd-year growth, 2- to 5-fasciculate, flowers 4-merous; fruits red, globose, 5 mm ($^3/_{16}$ in.) diameter, pedicels 2–4 mm ($^1/_{16}$–$^5/_{32}$ in.) long; pyrenes 4, palmately striate, sulcate. Habitat: People's Republic of China, endemic to mountains of northwestern Yunnan and southeastern Xizang provinces, just above Tibet, in mixed forests at 3540 m (11680 ft.) elevation. Allied to *I. intricata*.

Ilex densifolia Miquel 1857.

Evergreen trees to 10 m (33 ft.) tall, branchlets puberulent, striate; leaves ovate to elliptic, 3.5–6.5 cm (1$^3/_8$–2$^1/_2$ in.) long, 1.8–3 cm (1$^1/_{16}$–1$^3/_{16}$ in.) wide, apices subacute, acuminate, acumens 4–6 mm ($^5/_{32}$–$^7/_{32}$ in.) long, bases rotund, margins recurved, serrulate; inflorescences axillary, fasciculate, flowers 4-merous; fruits unknown. Habitat: Indonesia, Java. Allied to *I. denticulata*.

Ilex denticulata Wallich 1830 (synonym *I. nilagirica* Miquel *ex* Hooker f. 1875, *I. denticulata* f. *insularis* Loesener 1901, *I. denticulata* Thwaites 1860).

Evergreen, glabrous trees to 12 m (40 ft.) tall; leaves oval-elliptic or elliptic-oblong, 5–10 cm (2–4 in.) long, 2.5–3.7 cm (1–1$^1/_4$ in.) wide, apices short, abruptly acuminate or obtuse, acumens 3–8 mm

($^1/_8$–$^5/_{16}$ in.) long, bases obtuse or cuneate, margins densely and irregularly denticulate-serrate, petioles stout, 10–13 mm ($^3/_8$–$^{15}/_{32}$ in.) long; inflorescences axillary, fasciculate or pseudoracemose, central axil 5–10 mm ($^3/_{16}$–$^3/_8$ in.) long, pedicels 6–10 mm ($^7/_{32}$–$^3/_8$ in.) long, flowers 4-merous; fruits red, globose or depressed-globose, 6–7 mm ($^7/_{32}$–$^9/_{32}$ in.) diameter; pyrenes 4, irregularly striate sulcate, wrinkled, pitted. Habitat: People's Republic of China, southwestern Yunnan Province. First recorded from Nilghiri Hills, India. Allied to *I. latifolia*.

Ilex dianguiensis C.-j. Tseng 1985 (synonym *I. vacciniifolia* C.-y. Wu *in exsiccata, non* Stapf 1894).

Evergreen shrubs 3.5 m (11 ft.) tall, branchlets angulate, glabrous; leaves elliptic or obovate-elliptic, 4–6 cm (1$^5/_8$–2$^3/_8$ in.) long, 1.5–2.5 cm ($^{19}/_{32}$–1 in.) wide, apices abruptly acuminate, bases decurrently attenuate, margins crenulate, glabrous, petioles 8–11 mm ($^5/_{16}$–$^7/_{16}$ in.) long; inflorescences axillary, 6- to 9-fasciculate or racemose; fruits globose, 5 mm ($^3/_{16}$ in.) diameter, pedicels 6–7 mm ($^7/_{32}$–$^9/_{32}$ in.) long; pyrenes 4, palmately striate, sulcate. Habitat: People's Republic of China, Guizhou and Yunnan provinces. Allied to *I. cyrtura* and possibly a synonym of it.

Ilex dicarpa Y.-r. Li 1985.

Evergreen shrubs 5 m (16 ft.) tall, branchlets angulate-sulcate, grooves puberulent or glabrescent; leaves oblong or elliptic, 8–10 cm (3$^1/_8$–4 in.) long, 3.5–4 cm (1$^3/_8$–1$^5/_8$ in.) wide, apices short acuminate, bases widely cuneate, margins inconspicuously crenate-serrate or subentire, petioles 6–7 mm ($^7/_{32}$–$^9/_{32}$ in.) long; inflorescences axillary and fasciculate on 2nd-year growth; fruits globose, 4–6 mm ($^5/_{32}$–$^7/_{32}$ in.) diameter, usually in pairs, pedicels 5–6 mm ($^3/_{16}$–$^7/_{32}$ in.) long; pyrenes 4. Habitat: People's Republic of China, Xinjiang Province. Allied to *I. intermedia*.

Ilex dictyoneura Loesener 1901.

Evergreen, glabrous trees 4–5 m (13–16 ft.) tall, branches erect, pale gray; leaves broadly ovate to oblong-obovate, 9–12 cm (3$^1/_2$–4$^3/_4$ in.) long, 3.4–6.5 cm (1$^3/_8$–2$^1/_2$ in.) wide, margins entire, slightly recurved, bases cuneate, apices obtuse to acuminate, 5–10 mm ($^3/_{16}$–$^3/_8$ in.) long, petioles 10–13 mm ($^3/_8$–$^1/_2$ in.) long; inflorescences at base of new growth, peduncles 19–24 mm ($^3/_4$–1 in.) long; fruit unknown. Habitat: northern Vietnam. Allied to *I. pleiobrachiata*.

Ilex dimorphophylla Koidzumi 1928. Okinawan holly.

Evergreen shrubs, branchlets glabrous; new leaves

on young shoots dark green, glossy, elliptic to narrowly rectangular, 1.5–3.5 cm (¹⁹⁄₃₂–1⅜ in.) long, 5–7 mm (³⁄₁₆–⁹⁄₃₂ in.) wide, margins undulate, wavy, 3–8 sinuate-dentate spines on each side, bases obtuse to slightly truncate, apices with elongate tip spines, slightly recurved, petioles 1–3 mm (¹⁄₃₂–⅛ in.) long, adult leaves on mature plants obovate-elliptic or broadly elliptic, 1–3.5 cm (⅜–1⅜ in.) long, 7–17 mm (⁹⁄₃₂–²¹⁄₃₂ in.) wide, bases obtuse, margins entire, petioles 0.5–3 mm (¹⁄₆₄–⅛ in.) long, leaves persist on 3rd-year growth; inflorescences axillary and fasciculate on 2nd-year growth; fruits red, globose, 3 mm (⅛ in.) diameter. Habitat: Japan, endemic Liukiu Island, Amami O-Shima, Mount Yuwandake. Hardy in zones 8b-10. Allied to *I. cornuta*. Hybrids between *I. dimorphophylla* and *I. cornuta* are showing great promise and fruiting in the Philadelphia, Pennsylvania, area. Plate 63.

Ilex dioica (Vahl) Maximowicz 1881. Citronniermontagne (synonyms *Prinos dioicus* Vahl 1798, *I. dioica* var. *gracilior* Loesener 1892, *I. fasciculata* Turczaninow 1958, *I. dioica* var. *fendleri* Loesener 1901).

Evergreen shrubs or small trees; leaves oval or ovate to elliptic, 7–13 cm (2¾–5⅛ in.) long, 3.5–8 cm (1⅜–3⅛ in.) wide, punctate beneath, apices slightly acuminate, rarely obtuse or rotund, bases obtuse or cuneate obtuse, margins revolute, serrulate-crenulate, petioles 10–20 mm (⅜–¾ in.) long; inflorescences axillary, plurifasciculate, branched, flowers 4-merous; fruits black, subglobose, 4 mm (⁵⁄₃₂ in.) diameter; pyrenes 4. Habitat: Caribbean Islands, Mount Serrat, Martinique, and Grenada. Allied to *I. laurina, I. nervosa,* and *I. nitida.*

Ilex diospyroides Reisseck 1861.

Evergreen trees, branches glabrous, lenticels present; leaves ovate-elliptic or suboval or oblong, 6–12 cm (2⅜–4¾ in.) long, 2.6–4.8 cm (2–1⅞ in.) wide, apices obtuse, minute apicules usually 11 mm (⁷⁄₁₆ in.) long, bases obtuse or cuneate-obtuse, margins entire, recurved, petioles 6–12 mm (⁷⁄₃₂–¹⁵⁄₃₂ in.) long; inflorescences fasciculate in leaf axils, branched, flowers 4-merous; fruits black, ellipsoid 8–11 mm (⁵⁄₁₆–⁷⁄₁₆ in.) long, 5–8 mm (³⁄₁₆–⁵⁄₁₆ in.) wide; pyrenes 4. Habitat: Venezuela, near Rio Casiquiare. Allied to *I. lundii* and *I. sapiiformis.*

Ilex dipyrena Wallich 1820 var. *dipyrena*. Himalayan holly, caulah (Nepal), diusa, gumshing, kundar (synonyms *I. dentonii* Hort. *ex* Loudon 1838, *I. cunninghamii* Hort. *ex* Loesener 1901, *I. monopyrena* Watt *ex* Loesener 1901, *I. dipyrena* var. *paucispinosa* Loesener 1908, *I. dipyrena* var. *elliptica* Dallimore 1914, *I. dipyrena* var. *connexiva* W. Smith 1917, *I. bioritsensis* var. *integra* Comber 1933).

Figure 14-18. *Ilex dimorphophylla*. Photo by Barton Bauer Sr.

Evergreen trees, branches minutely puberulent; leaves elliptic-oblong, shiny, 4–10 cm (1⅝–4 in.) long, 2–4 cm (¾–1⅝ in.) wide, apices shortly acuminate, acumens 3–10 mm (⅛–⅜ in.) long, terminated by sharp spines 2 mm (¹⁄₁₆ in.) long, bases rotund to obtuse, margins entire or subentire, with few spines or spinose, to 14 spines on each side, petioles 4–6 mm (⁵⁄₃₂–⁷⁄₃₂ in.) long; inflorescences axillary and fasciculate on 2nd-year growth, flowers 2- to 4-merous; fruits red, globose, 6–9 mm (⁷⁄₃₂–¹¹⁄₃₂ in.) diameter, pedicels 1–3 mm (¹⁄₃₂–⅛ in.) long; pyrenes 1–4, usually 2, subpalmately striate, sulcate. Habitat: southwestern People's Republic of China, common and widespread species in Yunnan Province, India, and Myanmar. First described from Nepal. Allied to *I. aquifolium, I. clarkei,* and *I. kingiana.* Plate 64.

Ilex dipyrena var. *leptocantha* (Lindley) Loesener 1900 (synonym *I. leptocantha* Lindley 1854).

A variety with thin leaves, midribs engraved or furrowed on top. Habitat: People's Republic of China, Ichang Gorge.

Ilex discolor Hemsley 1887 var. *discolor*. Limoneillo.

Evergreen trees, branchlets puberulent or glabrescent, striate, angulate; leaves broadly obovate or obovate-elliptic or elliptic, 2.8–4.5 cm (1¹⁄₁₆–1¾ in.) long, 1.1–2.1 cm (⁷⁄₁₆–¾ in.) wide, apices obtuse or subrotund, minute apiculate, bases obtuse or cuneate, margins serrulate, revolute, petioles 4–5 mm (⁵⁄₃₂–³⁄₁₆ in.) long; inflorescences axillary, fasciculate, flowers 4-merous; fruits unknown. Habitat: Mexico, Chiapas State, east of Nabogame. Allied to *I. repanda.*

Ilex discolor var. *lamprophylla* (Standley) Edwin 1966.

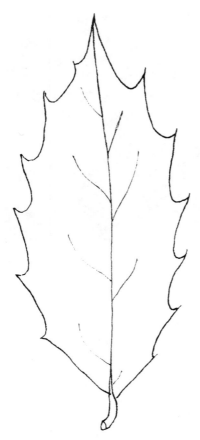

Figure 14-19. *Ilex dipyrena*. Drawing by Randy Allen.

A variety with glabrous leaves, elliptic, 5–10 cm (2–4 in.) long; fruits oval, 5 mm (³⁄₁₆ in.) diameter. Habitat: Guatemala, El Salvador, Nicaragua, and Costa Rica.

Ilex discolor var. *tolucana* (Hemsley) Edwin *ex* T. R. Dudley, *comb. & stat. nov.* (basionym *I. tolucana* Hemsley, *Biol. Centr. Am. Bot.* 1. 1878; synonyms *I. californica* Brandegee 1886, *I. tolucana* var. *bourgaevi* Loesener 1901, *I. tolucana* var. *californica* (Brandegee) Loesener 1901, *I. tolucana* var. *liebmanii* Loesener 1901).

A variety with glabrous branchlets, leaves usually smaller than typical individuals, lanceolate-elliptic, 1.5–2.5 cm (¹⁹⁄₃₂–1 in.) long. Habitat: Mexico, Guatemala, Honduras, and El Salvador on open sites.

Ilex divaricata Martius *ex* Reisseck 1861.
Evergreen shrubs or trees; leaves obovate or obovate-elliptic, 5–10 cm (2–4 in.) long, 3–4 cm (1³⁄₁₆–1⅝ in.) wide, apices rotund, often notched, bases cuneate, margins entire, recurved, petioles 9–

15 mm (¹¹⁄₃₂–¹⁹⁄₃₂ in.) long; inflorescences axillary, fasciculate, branched, flowers 4-merous; fruits unknown. Habitat: Venezuela, Colombia, and Brazil. Allied to *I. sideroxyloides*.

Ilex dolichopoda Merrill & Chun 1940.
Evergreen, small trees to 7 m (23 ft.) tall, branchlets minutely puberulent, lenticels inconspicuous; leaves oblong or obovate-oblong, 18–25 cm (7³⁄₁₆–10 in.) long, 6–7 cm (2⅜–2¾ in.) wide, apices acute, bases rotund, margins entire, petioles 8–10 mm (⁵⁄₁₆–⅜ in.) long; inflorescences axillary on 2nd-year growth, fasciculate, fascicles 9- to 16-flowered, pedicels 2.8–3.2 cm (1⅛–1¼ in.) long; fruits red, subglobose, 8 mm (⁵⁄₁₆ in.) diameter; pyrenes 5–6, 3-striate. Habitat: People's Republic of China, endemic to Hainan Province at 600 m (2000 ft.) elevation. Allied to *I. cochinchinensis*.

Ilex duarteensis Loesener 1933.
Evergreen, medium trees, glabrous, branches subrotund, longitudinal folded striations; leaves ovate or oval or obovate, 7–12 cm (2¾–4¾ in.) long, 4–6 cm (1⅝–2⅜ in.) wide, bases obtuse or rotund, apices rotund, rarely obtuse or acuminate, petioles 10–15 mm (⅜–¹⁹⁄₃₂ in.) long; inflorescences axillary, fasciculate, peduncles 3 mm (⅛ in.) long, pedicels 5–6 mm (³⁄₁₆–⁷⁄₃₂ in.) long; fruits unknown. Habitat: Cuba and Dominican Republic, Duarte, in mountains at 700 m (2300 ft.) elevation. Allied to *I. tarapotina*.

Ilex dugesii Fernald 1895. Naranjillo.
Evergreen shrubs, branches pubescent; leaves ovate to obovate-oblong, 3.5–6 cm (1⅜–2⅜ in.) long, 1.6–2.7 cm (⅝–1¹⁄₁₆ in.) wide, apices acuminate, recurved mucros, bases acute to obtuse, margins recurved, denticulate-serrate, petioles 6–9 mm (⁷⁄₃₂–¹¹⁄₃₂ in.) long; inflorescences axillary, solitary on new growth, flowers 4-merous; fruits reddish, glossy, globose, 7–8 mm (⁹⁄₃₂–⁵⁄₁₆ in.) diameter; pyrenes 4, sulcate. Habitat: Mexico. Allied to *I. rubra*. May eventually prove to be synonymous with *I. rubra*.

Ilex duidae Gleason 1931.
Evergreen, bushy, glabrous shrubs to 2 m (6 ft.) tall; leaves broadly elliptic or subobovate-oblong, 5–8 cm (2–3⅛ in.) long, 3.5–5.5 cm (1⅜–2⅛ in.) wide, punctate beneath, bases rotund, apices rotund, minute apiculate tip, margins entire, subrevolute, petioles stout, 3 mm (⅛ in.) long; inflorescences axillary, flowers 5-merous; fruits unknown. Habitat: Venezuela, Cerro Duida, on Savannah hills and ridge crest at 1025–1200 m (3380–3960 ft.) elevation; also in Colombia and Guyana.

Ilex dumosa Reisseck 1861. Caa-Chiri, Congonhas minda (synonyms *I. dumosa* var. *guaranina* Loesener 1901, *I. dumosa* var. *gomezii* Loesener 1901, *I. dumosa* var. *montevidensis* Loesener 1901, *I. dumosa* var. *mosenii* Loesener 1901).

Evergreen shrubs or small trees, branchlets pubescent; leaves elliptic to obovate-oblong, 3.5–6 cm (1⅜–2⅜ in.) long, 12–15 mm (¹⁵⁄₃₂–¹⁹⁄₃₂ in.) wide, sometimes punctate beneath, apices obtuse, acuminate, bases narrow-acute, margins recurved, crenulate, petioles 3–9 mm (⅛–¹¹⁄₃₂ in.) long; inflorescences axillary, solitary, on new growth, branched, flowers usually 4-merous; fruits black, subglobose, 5 mm (³⁄₁₆ in.) diameter, peduncles 3–7 mm (⅛–⁹⁄₃₂ in.) long, pedicels 1–4 mm (¹⁄₃₂–⁵⁄₃₂ in.) long; pyrenes 4, striate, sulcate. Habitat: Brazil and Paraguay. Allied to *I. amara* and *I. chamaedryfolia*.

Ilex dunniana H. Léveillé 1911 (synonyms *I. subrugosa* Loesener 1911, *I. latifolia* var. *fangii* Rehder 1930, *I. latifolia* var. *subrugosa* (Loesener) H. H. Hu & Tang 1940, *I. chieniana* S.-y. Hu 1946, *I. fangii* (Rehder) S.-y. Hu 1946, *I. intermedia* var. *fangii* (Rehder) S.-y. Hu 1950).

Evergreen trees to 10 m (33 ft.) tall, branchlets glabrous, conspicuous lenticels; leaves oblong-elliptic or ovate-oblong, 6–10 cm (2⅜–4 in.) long, 2–4 cm (¾–⅝ in.) wide, apices obtuse, acuminate, acumens 5–10 mm (³⁄₁₆–⅜ in.) long, bases obtuse or acute, margins serrate, teeth dark, petioles 10–15 mm (⅜–¹⁹⁄₃₂ in.) long; inflorescences axillary on 2nd-year growth, females pseudoracemose; fruits red, globose, 5–6 mm (³⁄₁₆–⁷⁄₃₂ in.) diameter; pyrenes 4, palmately striate, sulcate on back, rugose and wrinkled on sides. Habitat: People's Republic of China, southwestern Sichuan Province, at 1800–2000 m (5900–6600 ft.) elevation. Allied to *I. intermedia*.

Ilex editicostata H. H. Hu & Tang 1940.

Evergreen shrubs or small trees to 6 m (20 ft.) tall, stout branches; leaves glabrous, lanceolate, 5–12 cm (2–4¾ in.) long, 2–4 cm (¾–1⅝ in.) wide, bases cuneate, apices acuminate, margins entire, petioles 12–26 mm (¹⁵⁄₃₂–1 in.) long; inflorescences cymose, with 1–3 fruits, peduncles pubescent, 3–6 mm (⅛–⁷⁄₃₂ in.) long, pedicels 4–7 mm (⁵⁄₃₂–⁹⁄₃₂ in. long; fruits red, globose, 9–10 mm (¹¹⁄₃₂–⅜ in.) diameter, persistent calyces; pyrenes 4–6, shallow unicanaliculate on dorsal surface. Habitat: People's Republic of China, Zhejiang, Guizhou, and Jiangxi provinces, in forests, at 600–700 m (1980–2300 ft.) elevation. Allied to *I. maclurei*.

Ilex ekmaniana Loesener 1923 (synonym *I. ekmaniana* var. *regnelliana* Loesener 1923).

Evergreen shrubs, branches glabrous; leaves obo-vate or elliptical-obovate, 1.8–3.5 cm (¹¹⁄₁₆–1⅜ in.) long, 0.7–2.5 cm (⁹⁄₃₂–1 in.) wide, bases usually cuneate, occasionally obtusely rotund, apices rotund, retuse, margins entire, recurved, petioles 2–4 mm (¹⁄₁₆–⁵⁄₃₂ in.) long; inflorescences on new wood, axillary, or lateral, flowers 4- to 5-merous; fruits red, subglobose to globose, usually 5–6 mm (³⁄₁₆–⁷⁄₃₂ in.) diameter; pyrenes usually 4, smooth. Habitat: Cuba, on dry sites at 575–1120 m (1900–3700 ft.) elevation.

Ilex elliptica Kunth 1818.

Evergreen shrubs; leaves elliptic or suboval, 1.9–3.5 (¾–1⅜ in.) long, 1.1–2 cm (⁷⁄₁₆–¾ in.) wide, bases rotund, margins recurved, entire at base, serrulate near apex, petioles 1–2 mm (¹⁄₃₂–¹⁄₁₆ in.) long; inflorescences axillary, flowers 5-merous; fruits subglobose, 8 mm (⁵⁄₁₆ in.) diameter; pyrenes 4. Habitat: Peru, near Contomasa. Allied to *I. kunthiana*.

Ilex elmerrilliana S.-y. Hu 1950 (synonym *I. memecylifolia sensu* Rehder 1929).

Evergreen shrubs or small trees to 5 m (16 ft.) tall, branchlets glabrous, lenticels inconspicuous; leaves elliptic or oblong-elliptic, 5–9 cm (2–3½ in.) long, 2–3.5 cm (¾–1⅜ in.) wide, apices abruptly acuminate, acumens 6–8 mm (³⁄₁₆–⁵⁄₁₆ in.) long, bases cuneate or acute, margins entire, petioles 4–8 mm (⁵⁄₃₂–⁵⁄₁₆ in.) long; inflorescences pseudofasciculate, flowers 5- to 8-merous; fruits red, globose, 5 mm (³⁄₁₆ in.) diameter, calyces persistent styles prominent; pyrenes 6–7, smooth. Habitat: People's Republic of China, Anhui and Fujian provinces. Allied to *I. memecylifolia*.

Ilex embelioides Hooker f. 1875.

Evergreen, small trees; leaves ovate-oblong to oblong-elliptic, 3–6.5 cm (1³⁄₁₆–2⅜ in.) long, 0.8–2.2 cm (⁵⁄₁₆–⅞ in.) wide, apices obtuse with minute spine, bases crenate or acute, margins entire, occasionally minutely serrulate, petioles 3–8 mm (⅛–⁵⁄₁₆ in.) long; inflorescences axillary, males fasciculate, female small, pedicellate umbels, flowers 4-merous; fruits bluish black, globose 3–4 mm (⅛–⁵⁄₃₂ in.) diameter; pyrenes 4, striate. Habitat: eastern India, also Thailand, eastern Bengal, Mount Khasia, common at Churra, at 910–1210 m (3000–4000 ft.) elevation. Allied to *I. malabarica*.

Ilex engleriana Loesener 1901 var. *engleriana*.

Evergreen, large shrubs or trees, glabrous; leaves usually oblong-lanceolate 5.8–8 cm (2⁵⁄₁₆–3⅛ in.) long, 2.2–3.3 cm (⅞–1⁵⁄₁₆ in.) wide, apices obtuse acuminate, acumens 5–7 mm (³⁄₁₆–⁹⁄₃₂ in.) long, bases cuneate, margins entire, recurved, petioles 7–10 mm (⁹⁄₃₂–⅜ in.) long; male inflorescences paniculate, axillary, solitary, flowers 4-merous; fruits unknown. Habitat: western Sumatra on Mount Singalan at 2800 m (9200 ft.) elevation. Allied to *I. laurifolia* and *I. spicata*.

Ilex engleriana var. *halconensis* (Merrill) Loesener 1942 (synonyms *Embelia halconensis* Merrill 1907, *I. halconensis* Merrill 1910, *I. apoensis* var. *glandulosa* Elmer 1919).

Evergreen shrubs or small trees to 10 m (33 ft.) tall, branches dark gray, slender, lenticellate; leaves oblong-ovate, 5–7 cm (2–2¾ in.) long, 1.5–3 cm (¹⁹/₃₂–1³/₁₆ in.) wide, entire, glandular-punctate beneath, petioles 6–8 mm (⁷/₃₂–⁵/₁₆ in.) long; racemes axillary, solitary, 3–4 cm (1³/₁₆–1⅝ in.) long, few-flowered, pedicels 4–5 mm (⁵/₃₂–³/₁₆ in.) long, flowers usually 6-merous; fruits unknown. Habitat: Philippines, on exposed ridges in mossy forest, at 1000–2000 m (3300–6600 ft.) elevation.

Ilex englishii Lace 1914.
Evergreen, large shrubs; leaves oblong, elliptic-oblong or oblong-lanceolate, 6–11 cm (2⅜–4.8 in.) long, 2–4.5 cm (¾–1¾ in.) wide, bases cuneate, apices acute to slightly rotund, margins entire, petioles 0.5–1.5 mm (¹/₆₄–³/₆₄ in.) long, canaliculate; male inflorescences, axillary, solitary, cymose, umbelliform or racemose; fruits (immature) depressed globose, 3–4 mm (⅛–⁵/₃₂ in.) diameter, calyces persistent. Habitat: Vietnam, Myanmar Plateau at 1500 m (4950 ft.) elevation. Allied to *I. cochinchinensis* and *I. macrophylla*.

Ilex eoa Alain 1960.
Evergreen shrubs 2–2.5 m (6.6–8.2 ft.) tall, branches glabrous, powdery gray; leaves obovate or obovate-oblong, 1.6–2.5 cm (⅝–1 in.) long, 0.9–1.9 cm (¹¹/₃₂–¾ in.) wide, bases obtuse to cuneate, apices rotund or retuse to truncate, margins entire, slightly recurved, petioles 3–4 mm (⅛–⁵/₃₂ in.) long; inflorescences axillary, fasciculate, pedicels usually 2.5 mm (³/₃₂ in.) long, bracteate, flowers 4-merous; fruits unknown. Habitat: Cuba, Province Oriente, Charrascal del Saca Lengua, Sierra de Cristal.

Ilex epiphytica King 1895.
Evergreen shrubs, often epiphytic; leaves oval-elliptic, 3–6.8 cm (1³/₁₆–2⅝ in.) long, 2–3.5 cm (¾–1⅜ in.) wide, punctate beneath, apices rotund or obtuse, minute or obsolete apiculate, bases obtuse or broadly cuneate, margins revolute, subentire, minutely undulate and serrulate near apex, petioles 3–7 mm (⅛–⁹/₃₂ in.) long; inflorescences axillary, solitary, fasciculate, flowers 5- to 7-merous; fruits black, ovoid, 5–6 mm (³/₁₆–⁷/₃₂ in.) diameter; py-

renes 5–7. Habitat: Malaysia, near Malacca and Sarawak district of Borneo. Allied to *I. ardisioides*.

Ilex ericoides Loesener 1901.
Evergreen shrubs; leaves oval, 5–13 mm (³/₁₆–¹⁵/₃₂ in.) long, 4–7 mm (⁵/₃₂–⁹/₃₂ in.) wide, close together, apices obtuse, usually apiculate, bases crenate, acute, margins revolute, serrulate, petioles 1–2 mm (¹/₃₂–¹/₁₆ in.) long; inflorescences axillary, solitary on new growth, branched, flowers 4-merous; fruits black, ellipsoid, 4.5 mm (¹¹/₆₄ in.) long, 4 mm (⁵/₃₂ in.) wide, pedicels 1 mm (¹/₃₂ in.) long; pyrenes 4, striate. Habitat: Peru. Allied to *I. lechleri* and *I. subcordata*.

Ilex estriata C.-j. Tseng 1981.
Evergreen shrubs, branchlets angulate, puberulent or glabrescent; leaves elliptic or oblong-elliptic, rarely ovate-elliptic, 7–8.5 cm (2¾–3⅜ in.) long, 3 cm (1³/₁₆ in.) wide, apices abruptly acuminate, acumens 1–1.5 cm (⅜–¹⁹/₃₂ in.) long, bases obtuse, margins subentire, petioles 4–6 mm (⁵/₃₂–⁷/₃₂ in.) long, puberulent or glabrescent; inflorescences axillary, 4- to 5-fasciculate; fruits red but blackish when dry, globose, 3 mm (⅛ in.) diameter, pedicels 4–6 mm (⁵/₃₂–⁷/₃₂ in.) long; pyrenes 4, smooth. Habitat: People's Republic of China, Sichuan and Yunnan provinces. Allied to *I. wardii*.

Ilex eugeniaefolia Pierre 1893. Trambui.
Evergreen, large trees to 18 m (60 ft.) tall, branches glabrous, lenticels sparse; leaves oblong or oval-oblong, 6.5–11 cm (2½–4⅜ in.) long, 2.8–4.5 cm (1⅛–1¾ in.) wide, bases crenate to obtuse, apices obtuse-acuminate, margins recurved, entire, petioles 8–11 mm (⁵/₁₆–⁷/₁₆ in.) long; inflorescences on new growth, flowers usually 7-merous; fruit color unknown, ellipsoid, 4 mm (⁵/₃₂ in.) long, 3–4 mm (⅛–⁵/₃₂ in.) diameter; pyrenes 8–12, striate or sulcate. Habitat: southern Vietnam. Allied to *I. cymosa*.

Ilex euryiformis Reisseck 1861.
Evergreen shrubs, branches pubescent; leaves elliptic or lanceolate, usually 4–6 cm (1⅝–2⅜ in.) long, 2 cm (¾ in.) wide, apices obtuse or acuminate, bases obtuse or acute, margins revolute, entire at base, usually serrulate near apex, petioles 5–10 mm (³/₁₆–⅜ in.) long; inflorescences fasciculate in leaf axils, pubescent, flowers 4-merous; fruits unknown. Habitat: Brazil, Minas Gerais State. Allied to *I. brasiliensis*.

Ilex euryoides C.-j. Tseng 1981.
Evergreen, small trees, branchlets densely pubescent, angulate; leaves ovate or elongate-ovate, rarely ovate-lanceolate, 2–3 cm (¾–1³/₁₆ in.) long, 1–1.5 cm (⅜–¹⁹/₃₂ in.) wide, apices triangular, terminating with short spines, bases obtuse, midribs pubescent

above, margins serrulate, 4–8 serrations on each side, petioles 3–4 mm (⅛–⁵⁄₃₂ in.) long, densely pubescent; inflorescences axillary, 3- to 4-fasciculate; fruits red, subglobose, 5–5.5 mm (³⁄₁₆ in.) diameter; pyrenes 2, smooth or palmately striate, sulcate. Habitat: People's Republic of China, Hubei Province. Allied to *I. pernyi*.

Ilex excavata Pierre 1893.
Evergreen, large glabrous shrubs to 3–4 m (10–13 ft.) tall; leaves oval to oval-oblong, 6–11 cm (2⅜–4¼ in.) long, 2.9–5 cm (1⅛–2 in.) wide, bases rotund to cuneate, apices acuminate, margins entire, recurved, petioles 7–13 mm (⁹⁄₃₂–½ in.) long; inflorescences, axillary, solitary, peduncles 8–10 mm (⁵⁄₁₆–⅜ in.) long, pedicels 2–5 cm (¹⁄₁₆–³⁄₁₆ in.) long; fruits red(?), globose, 7 mm (⁹⁄₃₂ in.) diameter; pyrenes 4–5, longitudinally impressed. Habitat: southern Vietnam, on Mount Dink near Baria. Allied to *I. condorensis*.

Ilex excelsa (Wallich) Hooker 1875 f. *excelsa*. Sas swa, tumari (synonyms *Cassine excelsa* Wallich 1824, *I. doniana* De Candolle 1825, *I. elliptica* D. Don 1825, *I. nepalinsis* Sprengel 1827, *I. exsulca* Wallich 1830, *I. saysia* Hamilton *ex* Loesener 1901).
Evergreen trees to 10 m (33 ft.) tall, branchlets glabrous, angulate; leaves close together, elliptic or oblong-elliptic, 5–10 cm (2–4 in.) long, 2–3.5 cm (¾–1⅜ in.) wide, bases cuneate to obtuse, apices acuminate, margins entire, slender petioles 10–12 mm (⅜–¹⁵⁄₃₂ in.) long; inflorescences solitary, cymose, 3–7 flowers, peduncles 5–12 mm (³⁄₁₆–¹⁵⁄₃₂ in.) long, puberulent, pedicels 3–4 mm (⅛–⁵⁄₃₂ in.) long; fruits red, ovoid-ellipsoid, 5 mm (³⁄₁₆ in.) diameter; pyrenes 4–6, usually 5, smooth or 2- or 3-striate, esulcate. Habitat: southern People's Republic of China, Guangxi and Yunnan provinces; also found in Bhutan, Nepal, Vietnam, and the Himalayan region of India. Plants in cultivation. Allied to *I. rotunda* and *I. umbellulata*.

Ilex excelsa f. *hypotricha* (Loesener) H. Hara 1971 (synonym *I. excelsa* var. *hypotricha* (Loesener) S.-y. Hu 1949).
This form differs from typical individual by its puberulent branchlets and the puberulent lower leaf surfaces. Habitat: People's Republic of China, Yunnan Province, and India, Bhutan, and East Bengal. At a later date this form may prove to be synonymous with the species, an expression of the natural range of variations.

Ilex fabrilis Pierre 1893. Bui, caybui (synonym *I. fabrilis* var. *ellipsoidea* Loesener 1901).
Evergreen trees to 15–20 m (50–65 ft.) tall; leaves

oval to oblong, 7–12 cm (2¾–4¼ in.) long, 2.5–5 cm (1–2 in.) wide, glabrous, margins entire, recurved, petioles 6–15 mm (⁷⁄₃₂–½ in.) long; inflorescences glabrous, umbelliform 7–15 flowers, peduncles 4–16 mm (⁵⁄₃₂–⅝ in.) long, pedicels 2–4 mm (¹⁄₁₆–⁵⁄₃₂ in.) long; fruits red, ovoid to ellipsoid, 4–5.3 mm (⁵⁄₃₂–³⁄₁₆ in.) long, 3–4 mm (⅛–⁵⁄₃₂ in.) wide; pyrenes 5–8, 3- to 4-striate, 3-sulcate. Habitat: South Vietnam, Saigon, in delta areas along the Mekong River. Allied to *I. umbellulata*.

Ilex fanshawei Edwin 1965.
Evergreen shrubs to 3 m (10 ft.) tall, branches glabrous; leaves obovate or broadly elliptic-ovate, 5.3–9 cm (2⅛–3½ in.) long, 2.8–4.2 cm (1⅛–1¹¹⁄₁₆ in.) wide, punctate beneath, bases acute to cuneate, apices usually acute, margins entire, revolute, petioles 7–14 mm (⁹⁄₃₂–¹⁷⁄₃₂ in.) long; inflorescences axillary, fasciculate, flowers 4-merous; fruits dark red, globose, 4–5 mm (⁵⁄₃₂–³⁄₁₆ in.) diameter; pyrenes 4–5, unicanaliculate, dorsally striate and sulcate. Habitat: Guyana, savannah woodlands, Kaieteur Plateau.

Ilex farallonensis Cuatrecasas 1951.
Evergreen, small trees, branches pale green, glabrous; leaves obovate-elliptic, or elliptic, 2–4.5 cm (¾–1¾ in.) long, 1.7–3 cm (⅝–1³⁄₁₆ in.) wide, bases obtuse-cuneate, apices rotund or obtuse, margins slightly revolute, minutely dentate, 3–4 teeth on each side, petioles thick, sulcate, 5 mm (³⁄₁₆ in.) long; female inflorescences axillary, fasciculate, peduncles 4–6 mm (⁵⁄₃₂–⁷⁄₃₂ in.) long, flowers 4-merous; fruits elliptic, 5 mm (³⁄₁₆ in.) long, 4 mm (⁵⁄₃₂ in.) wide, very short apiculate. Habitat: Colombia, Department del Valle, Cordillera Occidental, Los Farallones de Cali, Quebrada del Raton Mina El Diamante at 2950–3000 m (753–9900 ft.) elevation. Allied to *I. caniensis*.

Ilex fargesii Franchet 1898 subsp. *fargesii* (synonyms *I. fargesii* var. *megalophylla* Loesener 1911, *I. franchetiana* Loesener 1911, *I. fargesii* var. *angustifolia* C. Y. Chang 1981).
Evergreen, glabrous, small trees to 7 m (23 ft.) tall; leaves oblanceolate or oblong-elliptic, or lanceolate, 7–14 cm (2¾–5½ in.) long, 1.2–4 cm (¹⁵⁄₃₂–1⅝ in.) wide, bases cuneate or obtuse, apices acuminate, rarely acute, acumens 5–10 mm (³⁄₁₆–⅜ in.) long, margins usually entire at base, serrate above, petioles 10–25 mm (⅜–1 in.) long; inflorescences axillary, fasciculate or paniculate, flowers 4-merous, fragrant; fruits red, globose, 4–6 mm (⁵⁄₃₂–⁷⁄₃₂ in.) diameter, pedicels 2 mm (¹⁄₁₆ in.) long; pyrenes 4, palmately striate, sulcate. Habitat: Myanmar and People's Republic of China, Yunnan, Sichuan, Hu-

bei, and Xizang provinces at 900–3350 m (2,970–11,050 ft.) elevation. Introduced by E. H. Wilson to England in the early 1900s and then to Arnold Arboretum in 1910. Hardy in zone 5b. Allied to *I. hookeri.*

Ilex fargesii var. *brevifolia* S. Andrews 1986.

Evergreen shrubs to 4 m (13 ft.) tall, usually glabrous; leaves elliptic to elliptic-lanceolate, 6–7.3 cm (2⅜–2⅞ in.) long, 1.9–2.5 cm (¾–1 in.) wide, margins serrate, upper two-thirds of leaf. Habitat: People's Republic of China western Hubei Province.

Ilex fargesii subsp. *melanotricha* (Merrill) S. Andrews 1986 (synonyms *I. franchetiana sensu* Comber 1933, *non* Loesener 1911, *I. melanotricha* Merrill 1941).

Evergreen trees to 12 m (40 ft.) tall, branches glabrous, often with hairylike black sooty mold (thus the name *melanotricha*); leaves broadly oblanceolate to oblong-elliptic, (7.4–) 8.7–12 (–13.4) cm ((3–) 3⁷⁄₁₆–4¾ (–5⁹⁄₃₂ in.)) long, (2.1–) 2.9–4 (–4.2) cm ((½–) 1³⁄₁₆–1⅝ (–1¹¹⁄₁₆ in.)) wide, apices acuminate, never falcate, acumens 5–16 mm (⅜–⅝ in.) long, bases usually obtuse, margins serrate. Habitat: First recorded from Myanmar, also limited distribution in People's Republic of China, Yunnan and Xizang provinces at 1830–3350 m (6,000–11,050 ft.) elevation. Introduced to England by G. Forrest, and from England to the United States by F. G. Meyer in 1959. It is hardly tenable that the recognition of a taxon at specific or subspecific rank should be based on the presence of fungi on the leaves. The black hairs on the leaves are spore-bearing structures of a fungi belonging to the family Stibaceae. The fungus is rarely found on *I. fargesii* subsp. *fargesii.* Some *Ilex* specialists do not agree that *I. franchetiana* is a synonym of *I. fargesii,* but is a related species. Yet, on the other hand, *I. fargesii* is very polymorphic, and it may well be proven that var. *brevifolia* and var. *parvifolia* are but minor variants and actually synonyms of this multifaceted species.

Ilex fargesii var. *parvifolia* (S.-y. Hu) S. Andrews 1986 (synonym *I. franchetiana* var. *parvifolia* S.-y. Hu 1946).

A variety differing from typical individuals with smaller subcoriaceous leaves, 3–6 cm (1³⁄₁₆–2⅜ in.) long, 1.5–2.5 cm (¹⁹⁄₃₂–1 in.) wide, margins usually serrate throughout. Habitat: People's Republic of China, western Sichuan Province.

Ilex fengqingensis C.-y. Wu *ex* Y.-r. Li 1984.

Evergreen, small trees 5–7 m (16–23 ft.) tall, branchlets angulate, densely puberulent; leaves oblong-elliptic, 3–6 cm (1³⁄₁₆–2⅜ in.) long, 1.3–2 cm (⅓–¾ in.) wide, apices obtuse or short-acuminate, bases wide-cuneate or obtuse, margins undulate, sparingly serrate, veins reticulate, conspicuous on both sides, petioles 5–8 mm (³⁄₁₆–⁵⁄₁₆ in.) long, puberulent; female inflorescences fasciculate, uniflorous, flowers 4-merous; fruits globose, 4-angulate, 4 mm (⁵⁄₃₂ in.) diameter, pedicels 1–3 mm (¹⁄₃₂–⅛ in.) long; pyrenes 4, dorsally palmate, laterally sulcate, striate. Habitat: People's Republic of China, Yunnan Province, at 2800 m (9200 ft.) elevation. Allied to *I. corallina.*

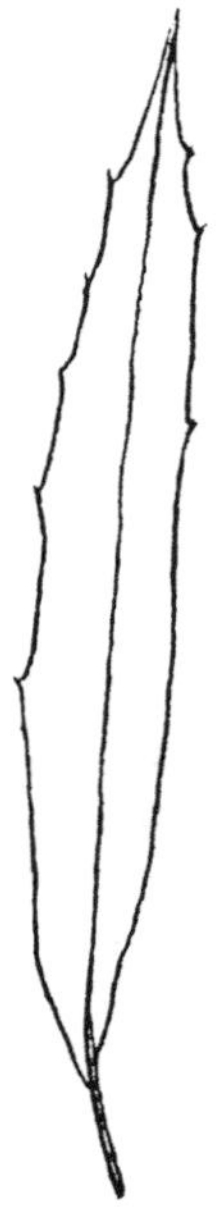

Figure 14-20. *Ilex fargesii* subsp. *fargesii.* Drawing by Randy Allen.

Ilex ferruginea Handel-Mazzetti 1933.

Evergreen, large shrubs or trees, branchlets pubescent, lenticels sparse; leaves persistent on 3rd-year growth, ovate to ovate-elliptic, 2.5–5 cm (1–2 in.) long, 1.5–3.5 cm (¹⁹⁄₃₂–1⅜ in.) wide, bases truncate or rounded, apices shortly acuminate, margins remotely crenate-serrate, short petioles 4 mm (⁵⁄₃₂ in.) long; inflorescences 3-flowered cymes, axillary on new growth, villose, peduncles 5–7 mm (³⁄₁₆–⁹⁄₃₂ in.) long, pedicels 5–9 mm (³⁄₁₆–¹¹⁄₃₂ in.) long; fruits red, globose, 5–7 mm (³⁄₁₆–⁹⁄₃₂ in.) diameter, persistent calyces; pyrenes 5, broadly unicanaliculate on back. Habitat: southern and southwestern People's Republic of China, Guangdong and Yunnan provinces. Allied to *I. kwangtungensis.*

Ilex ficifolia C.-j. Tseng f. *ficifolia* 1962.

Evergreen, glabrous shrubs, branchlets blackish

or red, turning grayish brown 2nd year; leaves elliptic or oblong-elliptic, 4–7 cm (1⅝–2¾ in.) long, 1.5–3 cm (¹⁹⁄₃₂–1³⁄₁₆ in.) wide, glabrous, apices acute or shortly acuminate, occasionally obtuse, bases cuneate or wide-cuneate, margins obscurely crenulate, revolute, petioles 5–6 mm (³⁄₁₆–⁷⁄₃₂ in.) long; inflorescences axillary, solitary, cymose, with 1–3 fruits, flowers 5-merous; fruits red, globose, 6 mm (⁷⁄₃₂ in.) diameter, calyces persistent; pyrenes 5. Habitat: People's Republic of China, Fujian Province. Allied to *I. suaveolens.*

Ilex ficifolia f. *daiyunshanensis* C.-j. Tseng 1981.
A form with pubescent petioles, pedicels, and peduncles. Habitat: People's Republic of China, Fujian Province. This form may only be a very minor variant demonstrating natural variation and not requiring botanical recognition.

Ilex ficoidea Hemsley 1886 (synonyms *I. cinerea sensu* Maximowicz 1881, *I. buergeri* var. *glabra* Loesener 1908, *I. arisanensis* Yamamoto 1925).
Evergreen trees to 8 m (26 ft.) tall, branchlets glabrous; leaves oblong-ovate or elliptic, 5–9 cm (2–3½ in.) long, 1.5–3.5 cm (¹⁹⁄₃₂–1⅜ in.) wide, apices obtuse to abruptly acuminate, acumens to 15 mm (¹⁹⁄₃₂ in.) long, bases obtuse or rotund, margins irregularly crenate-serrate, petioles 10–15 mm (⅜–¹⁹⁄₃₂ in.) long; inflorescences axillary and fasciculate on 2nd-year growth, males 1- to 3-flowered cymose, females uniflorous, flowers 4-merous; fruits red, globose or subglobose, 5–7 mm (³⁄₁₆–⁹⁄₃₂ in.) diameter, pedicels 2–3 mm (¹⁄₁₆–⅛ in.) long; pyrenes 4, palmately striate, sulcate, rugose, wrinkled. Habitat: common tree of eastern Asia, including eastern People's Republic of China, Taiwan, Hong Kong, Vietnam, and the Liukiu Island of Japan. Allied to *I. buergeri.*

Ilex flaveo-mollissima Metcalf 1923.
Evergreen shrubs or trees; leaves ovate, ovate-lanceolate to lanceolate, 4–6.5 cm (1⅝–2½ in.) long, 1.5–2 cm (1³⁄₁₆–¾ in.) wide, bases obtuse to rotund, apices long acuminate, margins subentire, occasionally 1–2 distinct serrations above middle, dense villose above, dense yellow-orange villose beneath, petioles 2–4 mm (¹⁄₁₆–⁵⁄₃₂ in.) long, dense yellow villose; inflorescences axillary, solitary, 1- to usually 3-flowered, flowers 4-merous; fruits immature, glabrous, distinct conical projection. A distinct species diagnosed by abundant yellowish villose pubescence. Habitat: People's Republic of China, central Fujian Province. Allied to *I. yunnanensis.*

Ilex floribunda Reisseck 1881 var. *floribunda* (synonyms *I. cuyabensis* Reisseck 1861, *I. floribunda* var. *typica* Loesener 1901).

Figure 14-21. *Ilex ficoidea.* Drawing by Chien-chu Chen in *Illustrations of Native and Introduced Ligneous Plants of Taiwan* (1962) by Tang-shui Liu.

Evergreen shrubs 1–2 m (3–6 ft.) tall, occasionally small trees, branches ascending; leaves oval or subovate, 7–13.5 cm (2¾–5³⁄₁₆ in.) long, 2–5 cm (¾–2 in.) wide, apices obtuse or acuminate, bases cuneate or cuneate obtuse, margins entire, recurved, petioles 4–12 mm (⁵⁄₃₂–¹⁵⁄₃₂ in.) long; inflorescences in leaf axils, fasciculate, branched, flowers usually 4-merous; fruits unknown. Habitat: Brazil, Bahia State, near Victoria. Allied to *I. cuyabensis, I. petiolaris,* and *I. vismiifolia.*

Ilex floribunda var. *minor* Loesener 1901.
A variety with leaves smaller than typical individuals, oval or oblong-oval, 5–8 cm (2–3⅛ in.) long, 2–3.5 cm (¾–1⅜ in.) wide, apices briefly acuminate. Habitat: Brazil.

Ilex florifera Fawcett & Rendle 1921.

Evergreen trees to 13 m (43 ft.) tall; leaves roundish elliptic, usually 6–10 cm (2⅜–4 in.) long, 4.5–8.5 cm (1¾–3⅜ in.) wide, apices rotund to emarginate at apex, bases rotund to truncate, margins entire; inflorescences axillary, many-flowered, flowers 4-merous, rank scented; fruits globose to ovate, 3 mm (⅛ in.) diameter, color unknown. Habitat: Jamaica, endemic in woodlands on limestone at 393–606 m (1300–2000 ft.) elevation.

Ilex florsparva Cuatrecasas 1951.

Evergreen trees, branches flexible, glabrous, pale green; leaves obovate, 8–12 cm (3⅛–4¾ in.) long, 5–7 cm (1⅝–2¾ in.) wide, sparsely and minutely dark brown punctate beneath, bases cuneate, apices rotund, abrupt apiculate, margins entire or obsoletely crenate, petioles 2–4 mm (1/16–5/32 in.) long, distinct prominent veins, forming slightly bullate surface; flowers 4-merous, minute, cymes on short pedicels, or axillary, solitary or fasciculate, peduncles 2–5 mm (1/16–3/16 in.) long, minutely pubescent, pedicels 1–2 mm (1/32–1/16 in.) long, petals 1.5 mm (3/64 in.) long; fruits unknown. Habitat: Colombia, Department del Valle, Calima River, La Trojita, at 50 m (165 ft.) elevation. Allied to *I. bullata.*

Ilex forbesi E. G. Baker 1923.

Evergreen, large trees, branches sparsely hairy; leaves elliptic or ovate-elliptic, 10–12 cm (4–4¾ in.) long, 4–6 cm (1⅝–2⅜ in.) wide, bases cuneate, apices acute, margins entire, petioles 10–12 mm (⅜–15/32 in.) long; inflorescences branched, 3–13 flowers; fruits black, ellipsoid, 5–8 mm (3/16–5/16 in.) long, 4–6 mm (5/32–7/32 in.) wide; pyrenes 6. Habitat: Papua New Guinea, at 506 m (2000 ft.) elevation. Allied to *I. maingayi.*

Ilex formonica Loesener 1919.

Evergreen, medium-sized trees, glabrous; leaves broadly obovate, rarely suborbicular, 0.8–1.3 cm (5/16–½ in.) long, 5–8 mm (3/16–5/16 in.) wide, bases acute or cuneate-obtuse to subrotund, apices rotund, often apiculate, margins entire; inflorescences axillary, solitary, flowers 4-merous, pedicels of single flowers 3–4 mm (⅛–5/32 in.) long; fruits globose, 5 mm (3/16 in.) diameter, stigmas prominent, swollen-capitate, pyrenes 4. Habitat: Haiti, massif de Hotte, Torbec, at 2225 m (7342 ft.) elevation. Allied to *I. obcordata.*

Ilex formosae (Loesener) H. L. Li 1963 (synonyms *I. mertensii* var. *formosae* Loesener 1901, *I. uraiensis* var. *formosae* (Loesener) S.-y. Hu 1949).

Evergreen trees, branchlets glabrous; leaves obovate, 2.5–4.5 cm (1–1¾ in.) long, 1.5–2.5 cm (19/32–1 in.) wide, apices rotund or obtuse, margins remotely crenulate; inflorescences axillary on old wood; fruits fasciculate, color unknown, globose, 10–12 mm (⅜–15/32 in.) diameter; pyrenes 4. Habitat: Taiwan, endemic to southern tip. Allied to *I. warburgii.*

Ilex formosana Maximowicz 1881 (synonyms *Lindera glauca* sensu H. Léveillé 1914, *I. ficoidea* sensu Rehder 1927, *I. rarasanensis* S.-i. Sasaki 1931, *I. mutchagara* sensu Kanehira 1936, *I. kelungensis* Loesener 1939, *I. formosana* var. *macropyrenea* S.-y. Hu 1950).

Evergreen trees to 12 m (40 ft.) tall, branchlets glabrous or glabrescent; leaves elliptic or oblong-lanceolate, 6–9.8 cm (2⅜–3⅝ in.) long, 1.9–3.3 cm (¾–15/16 in.) wide, apices acuminate, acumens 7–12 mm (9/32–15/32 in.) long, bases cuneate or rarely obtuse, margins remotely, minutely crenulate-serrulate, petioles 5–9 mm (3/16–11/32 in.) long; inflorescences axillary and fasciculate on 2nd-year growth, pubescent, males 3-flowered cymose, females uniflorous, flowers 4-merous; fruits red, subglobose, 4 mm (5/32 in.) long, 5 mm (3/16 in.) diameter, pedicels 2–3 mm (1/16–⅛ in.) long; pyrenes 4, palmately striate, sulcate, rugose, wrinkled. Habitat: Taiwan and People's Republic of China, Yunnan Province. Allied to *I. ficoidea.* Not to be confused with *I. formosae,* a Taiwan endemic.

Ilex forrestii Comber 1933 var. *forrestii* (synonyms *I. corallina* sensu Anonymous 1924, *I. odorata* sensu Anonymous 1929, *I. odorata* var. *tephrophylla* sensu Comber 1933).

Evergreen shrubs or trees to 7 m (23 ft.) tall, branchlets light gray, puberulent, rugose, lenticels small, sparse; leaves oblong-lanceolate or elliptic or obovate-elliptic, usually 8–9 cm (3⅛–3½ in.) long, 3 cm (1 3/16 in.) wide, apices acuminate, acumens 10–15 mm (⅜–19/32 in.) long, bases obtuse or rarely cuneate, margins entire lower half, upper half subentire, crenulate or serrate, midribs impressed, puberulent above, petioles 5–12 mm (3/16–15/32 in.) long; inflorescences axillary, subsessile, on 2nd-year growth, fasciculate, puberulent, male inflorescences often pseudopaniculate, flowers 4-merous; fruits red, globose, 3–5 mm (⅛–3/16 in.) diameter, calyces persistent; pyrenes 5–7, smooth. Habitat: People's Republic of China, Yunnan Province. Endemic to small area where 3 large Asiatic rivers—the Yangtze, Mekong, and Salween—run parallel and form deep gorges among high mountain ranges. *Ilex forrestii* is found in thickets and mixed forests at 2500–2800 m (8250–9200 ft.) elevation. Allied to *I. corallina* and *I. wardii.*

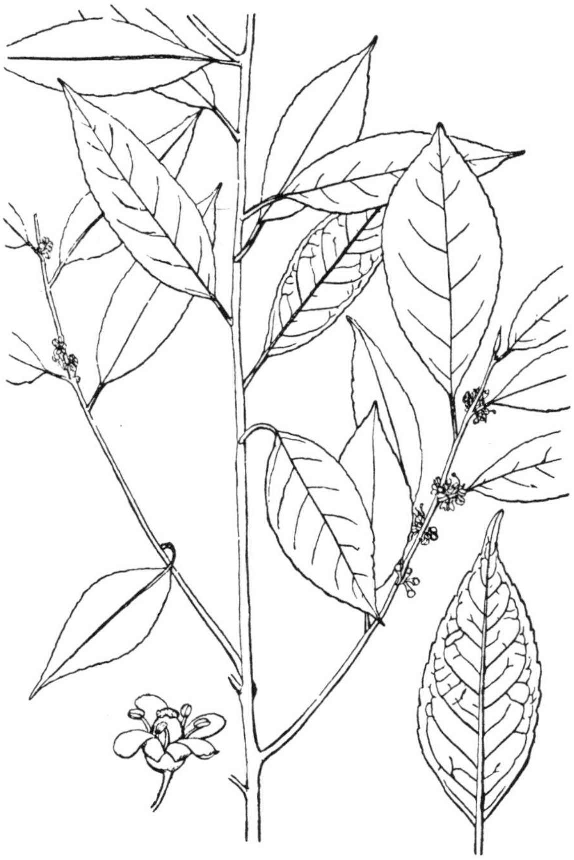

Figure 14-22. *Ilex formosana.* Drawing by Chien-chu Chen in *Illustrations of Native and Introduced Ligneous Plants of Taiwan* (1962) by Tang-shui Liu.

Ilex forrestii var. *glabra* S.-y. Hu 1950.

A variety differing from typical individuals with glabrous branches. Habitat: People's Republic of China, Yunnan Province. May not warrant any botanical recognition. Only further study and collections will resolve this and other similar cases.

Ilex forturensis W. J. Hahn 1993 (synonym *I. ignicola* Steyermark 1988).

Evergreen, small trees to 6 m (20 ft.) tall, branchlets minutely puberulent or glabrescent; leaves elliptic-oblong, 5.5–8 cm (2⅛–3⅛ in.) long, 2.5–3.5 cm (1–1⅜ in.) wide, bases acute or subacute, apices obtuse or subacute, margins entire, petioles 5–9 mm (3⁄16–11⁄32 in.) long; inflorescences axillary, solitary, lateral; fruits subovoid, 7–8 mm (9⁄32–5⁄16 in.) long, 5 mm (3⁄16 in.) wide, pedicels puberulent, 3–4 mm (⅛–5⁄32 in.) long; pyrenes 4, trigonous, dorsally broadly unisulcate, sulcations sharply angled. Habitat: Venezuela, Amazonas State, Department Rio Negro, Cerro Aratitiyope, south-southwest of Ocamo at 990–1100 m (3270–3630 ft.) elevation.

Ilex foxworthyi Merrill 1910.

Evergreen trees, branches glabrous; leaves ovate to elliptic-ovate, 4–9 cm (1⅝–3½ in.) long, 2.5–5 cm (1–2 in.) wide, bases broadly acute, apices blunt acuminate, margins entire, recurved, dense foliage, minutely punctate beneath, petioles 10 mm (⅜ in.) long; inflorescences pubescent, axillary, solitary, flowers 5- to 6-merous; fruits unknown. Habitat: Philippines, Luzon, on Mount Banahao, endemic to mossy forest at 1400–2100 m (4600–6900 ft.) elevation. Allied to *I. engleriana* var. *halconensis* and *I. spicata.*

Ilex friburgensis Loesener 1901.

Evergreen shrubs, lenticels conspicuous; leaves elliptic or obovate, 4.5–8.5 cm (1¾–3⅜ in.) long, 2–3.5 cm (¾–1⅜ in.) wide, apices rotund or obtuse, apiculate, bases obtuse or acute, margins recurved, usually entire, occasionally serrulate near apex, petioles 10–18 mm (⅜–11⁄16 in.) long; inflorescences pseudopaniculate in leaf axils, flowers 4- to 5-merous; fruits unknown. Habitat: Brazil, Rio de Janeiro State, near Nova Friburgo. Allied to *I. theezans.*

Ilex fructiclipeata Cuatrecasas 1951.

Evergreen, glabrous shrubs, branches brown, erect, slightly angulate; leaves oblong-elliptic, 7–9 cm (2¾–3½ in.) long, 2.8–3.7 cm (1⅛–17⁄16 in.) wide, sparsely brown punctate beneath, bases cuneate, apices attenuate, obtuse apiculate, margins recurved, subentire, obsolete, remote crenulate; inflorescences paniculate, axillary, fasciculate, racemiform, peduncles 1.5 mm (3⁄64 in.) long, pedicels 1–2 mm (1⁄32–1⁄16 in.) long; fruits purplish, globose, 3 mm (⅛ in.) diameter. Habitat: Colombia, Comisaria del Vaupés. Allied to *I. affinis* and *I. laureola.*

Ilex fuertensiana (Loesener) T. R. Dudley, *comb. nov.* (basionym *I. caroliniana* var. *fuertensiana* Loesener, in Urban, *Symbol. Antill.* 1: 272. 1912).

Evergreen shrubs or small trees to 6 m (18 ft.) tall, branchlets brown or yellow gray, pubescent, leaves elliptic-obovate, rarely lanceolate-obovate, 1.7–3.2 cm (11⁄16–1¼ in.) long, 0.8–1.5 cm (5⁄16–19⁄32 in.) wide, usually punctate beneath, bases acute or cuneate, decurrent, apices obtuse to subacute, short acuminate, margins usually revolute, serrulate-crenulate or denticulate, petioles puberulent, 2–4.5 mm (1⁄16–3⁄16 in.) long; inflorescences axillary, usually on new wood, fasciculate, peduncles puberulent, 2–4 mm (1⁄16–5⁄32 in.) long, pedicels forming cymose inflorescences; fruits dry, purple black, ellipsoid to subglobose, 6.5–7.5 mm (¼–9⁄32 in.) long, 5 mm (3⁄16 in.)

diameter; pyrenes 4, 3- to 5-ridged, striate sulcate. Habitat: Haiti and Dominican Republic, in forest, at 1600–2300 m (5280–7590 ft.) elevation. Allied to *I. vomitoria.*

Ilex fukienensis S.-y. Hu 1950 f. *fukienensis.*

Evergreen, glabrous shrubs to 4 m (13 ft.) tall; leaves ovate-oblong to lanceolate, 5.5–10 cm (2 3/16–4 in.) long, 1.5–3.5 cm (19/32–1⅜ in.) wide, apices acuminate, acumens 8–15 mm (5/16–19/32 in.) long, bases rotund or obtuse, margins entire, petioles 4–7 mm (5/32–9/32 in.) long; inflorescences axillary, fasciculate, pedicels 5 mm (3/16 in.) long, flowers 4-merous; fruits unknown. Habitat: People's Republic of China, endemic to central Fujian Province at 900 m (3000 ft.) elevation. Allied to *I. elmerrilliana.*

Ilex fukienensis f. *puberula* C.-j. Tseng & H. H. Lui 1981.

A form differing from typical individuals with puberulent branchlets and pedicels. Habitat: People's Republic of China, Fujian Province. Possibly not meriting botanical recognition.

Ilex gabinetensis Cuatrecasas 1948.

Evergreen, small trees to 8–10 m (26–33 ft.) tall, young branchlets pubescent, later glabrous; leaves elliptic or elliptic-oblong, 4–9 cm (1⅝–3½ in.) long, 2–4.5 cm (¾–1¾ in.) wide, bases rotund, apices slightly attenuate, obtuse or rotund, margins serrate-crenate, petioles 10–16 mm (⅜–⅝ in.) long; inflorescences axillary, solitary, pedunculate, flowers 4-merous; fruits immature; pyrenes 4. Habitat: Colombia, Western Cordillera, Caquetá. Allied to *I. crassifolia* and *I. crassifolioides.*

Ilex gagneipainiana Tardieu 1945.

Evergreen, small trees 5 m (16 ft.) tall, branches pubescent, striate-sulcate; leaves ovate or lanceolate, 2.6 cm (1⅛ in.) long, 1 cm (⅜ in.) wide, bases decurrent, apices acute or acuminate, acumens 3–4 mm (⅛–5/32 in.) long, margins entire or toothed near apex, punctate, petioles hirsute, 5 mm (3/16 in.) long; fruits red, solitary or 2- to 3-fasciculate, pedicels hirsute, 1 cm (⅜ in.) long; pyrenes 4, sulcate. Habitat: Vietnam, Tonkin. Allied to *I. vacciniifolia.*

Ilex gale Triana 1878.

Evergreen, large shrubs or small trees; leaves elliptic to elliptic-lanceolate, 4–5 cm (1⅝–2 in.) long, 1–2 cm (⅜–¾ in.) wide, apices obtuse, bases acute to cuneate, margins recurved, entire, petioles 7–17 mm (9/32–15/32 in.) long; inflorescences axillary, solitary, branched, flowers 5-merous; fruits, dark red to purplish, globose, peduncles 5–10 mm (3/16–⅜ in.) long, pedicels 2–3.5 mm (¾–1⅜ in.) long. Habitat: Colombia, near Ocana at altitude of 1300 m (4290 ft.). Allied to *I. amygdalina* and *I. cassine.*

Ilex gardneriana Wight 1832. Korharatu.

Evergreen, large shrubs or small trees; leaves ovate-lanceolate, 5–10 cm (2–4 in.) long, 2.1–4 cm (¾–1⅝ in.) wide, apices caudate, acuminate, bases rotund, margins entire, petioles 10–19 mm (⅜–¾ in.) long; inflorescences branched, flowers 4-merous; fruits unknown, peduncles 3–10 mm (⅛–⅜ in.) long, pedicels 3–5 mm (⅛–3/16 in.) long. Habitat: western peninsula India, Nilghiri Hills at Sisparah Ghat. Allied to *I. wightiana.*

Ilex gentlei Lundell 1945.

Evergreen, small trees 12.5 cm (4⅝ in.) diameter, twigs stout, densely puberulent; leaves obovate or oblanceolate or elliptic, 4–12.5 cm (1⅝–4⅝ in.) long, 1.7–6.5 cm (21/32–2½ in.) wide, bases decurrent, apices acute, obtuse or abruptly short-acuminate, margins entire, petioles stout, canaliculate, sparsely puberulent; female inflorescences axillary, puberulent, angulate, to 6 mm (7/32 in.) long; fruits subglobose, 7 mm (9/32 in.) diameter. Habitat: Belize, Toledo District. Allied to *I. belizensis* and *I. guianensis.*

Ilex georgei Comber 1933 (synonyms *I. pernyi* var. *manipurensis* Loesener 1901, *I. pernyi* sensu Loesener 1911, *non* Franchet 1883, *I. georgei* var. *rugosa* Comber 1941).

Evergreen shrubs to 6 m (20 ft.) tall, branchlets pubescent; leaves lanceolate to ovate-lanceolate, shiny, 2–4.5 cm (¾–1⅝ in.) long, 0.7–1.5 cm (9/32–19/32 in.) wide, apices acuminate, acumens 10 mm (⅜ in.) long, bases rotund or cordate, margins recurved, subentire, 4–7 spines on each side, petioles 1–2 mm (1/32–1/16 in.) long, leaves persist on 4th-year growth; inflorescences axillary and fasciculate on 2nd-year growth, flowers 4-merous; fruits red, obovate to ellipsoid, 4–6 mm (5/32–7/32 in.) long, 3–4 mm (⅛–5/32 in.) wide, usually paired, pedicels 2 mm (1/16 in.) long, pubescent; pyrenes 1–2, 7- to 9-striate, shallowly sulcate. Habitat: People's Republic of China, western and southwestern Yunnan Province and adjacent Myanmar, found in dense thickets on dry slopes at 1800–2700 m (5900–8900 ft.) elevation. Originally introduced by George Forrest to England. Cuttings were introduced from England to the United States by F. G. Meyer in 1957 and 1959. Allied to *I. ciliospinosa.*

Ilex gintungensis H.-w. Li *ex* Y.-r. Li 1985.

Evergreen, glabrous shrubs or trees 4–10 m (13–33 ft.) tall, branchlets slender, angulate-sulcate; leaves oblong-elliptic or ovate-elliptic, 7–11 cm

(2¾–4⅜ in.) long, 2.5–4 cm (1–1⅝ in.) wide, apices long acuminate, bases obtuse or rotund, margins moderately serrulate, petioles 5–8 mm (3⁄16–5⁄16 in.) long; inflorescences axillary and fasciculate on 2nd-year growth, males cymose, females uniflorous; fruits red, globose, 6 mm (7⁄32 in.) diameter, pedicels 4–5 mm (5⁄32–3⁄16 in.) long, calyces persistent; pyrenes 4, palmately striate, sulcate. Habitat: People's Republic of China, Yunnan Province, at 1800 m (5900 ft.) elevation. Allied to *I. wattii.*

Ilex glabella Steyermark 1988.

Evergreen trees, branchlets glabrous; leaves oblong-lanceolate, 10–15 cm (4–6 in.) long, 4.5–6 cm (1¾–2⅜ in.) wide, bases rotund, apices obtuse to acute, subacuminate, margins entire, petioles 10–11 mm (⅜–7⁄16 in.) long; male inflorescences subterminal, in upper leaf axils, fasciculate, umbellate; fruits unknown. Habitat: Venezuela, Amazonas, Department Rio Negro, Cerro de la Neblina. Allied to *I. reisseckiana* and *I. tarapotina.*

Ilex glabra (Linnaeus) A. Gray 1856 f. *glabra.* Inkberry, gallberry (synonyms *Prinos glabra* Linnaeus 1753, *I. angustifolia* var. *ligustrifolia* De Candolle 1825, *Ennepta myricoides* Rafinesque 1838, *Winterlia glabra* (Linnaeus) Moench *ex* Koch 1853, *I. glabra* var. *austrina* Ashe 1924).

Evergreen shrubs 1–3 m (3–10 ft.) tall, velvety pubescent branchlets, often stoloniferous forming dense clumps; leaves variable in color from light to dark olive green, glossy, obovate to elliptic, 2–5 cm (¾–2 in.) long, 1.5–2 cm (19⁄32–¾ in.) wide, apices obtuse, mucronulate, bases acute to cuneate, margins sparsely toothed toward the apex, petioles 3–6 mm (⅛–7⁄32 in.) long; inflorescences axillary on new growth, males often branched, females often solitary, flowers 5- to 8-merous; fruits usually black, rarely white, globose, 6–10 mm (7⁄32–⅜ in.) diameter, pedicels 2–4 mm (1⁄16–5⁄32 in.) long, immature fruits often purplish red changing to black; pyrenes 5–8, smooth. Habitat: Canada, Nova Scotia, United States, Coastal Plains, south to Florida and west to Texas and Missouri. Hardy in zones 5 to 10. Introduced in 1759. Allied to *I. coriacea* and *I. vomitoria.* Good source for a light clear gallberry honey. Extremely variable shade tolerant plants exist throughout its range; some forms have purplish red winter leaf color. Selected cultivars are available for general landscaping; see descriptions in Chapter 15. A red-fruited plant in Florida was reported by J. K. Small, but is not currently named. Plates 65, 66.

Ilex glabra f. *leucocarpa* Woods 1956.

A botanical form with white fruit selected in northern Florida. Cultivar 'Ivory Queen', with white fruit, was selected by C. Wolfe in New Jersey; it is a superior plant and commercially available. Incorrectly listed as cultivar 'Leucocarpa'.

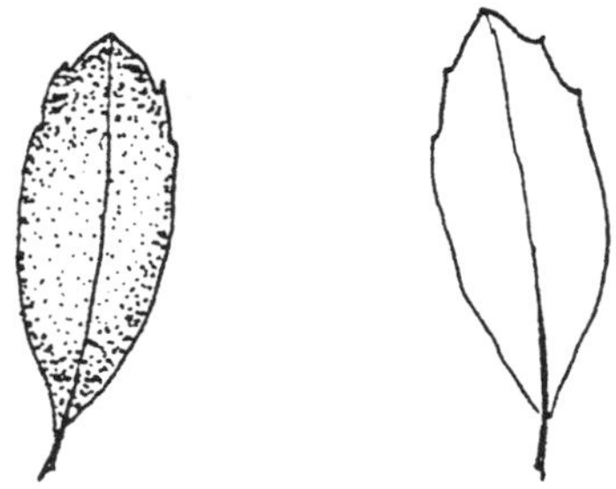

Figure 14-23. *Ilex glabra* f. *glabra.* Drawing by Randy Allen.

Ilex glaucophylla Steyermark 1954.

Evergreen, large shrubs to 3 m (10 ft.) tall; leaves glabrous, broadly elliptic to elliptic-obovate, 8–11 cm (3⅛–4⅜ in.) long, 2.5–5.3 cm (1–2⅛ in.) wide, bases acute to subcuneate, apex abruptly short, cuspidate, margins nearly entire, few spines, tipped serrations near apex, petioles decurrent, glabrous, 13–22 mm (½–13⁄16 in.) long; male inflorescences fasciculate on new growth, axillary, solitary, branched, peduncles 10–17 mm (⅜–11⁄16 in.) long, pedicels very short, 1–2 mm (1⁄32–1⁄16 in.) long, flowers 4- to 5-merous; fruits unknown. Habitat: Venezuela, wet woods, Estado Miranda, at 1200 m (3960 ft.) elevation. Allied to *I. parvifructa* and *I. ptariana.*

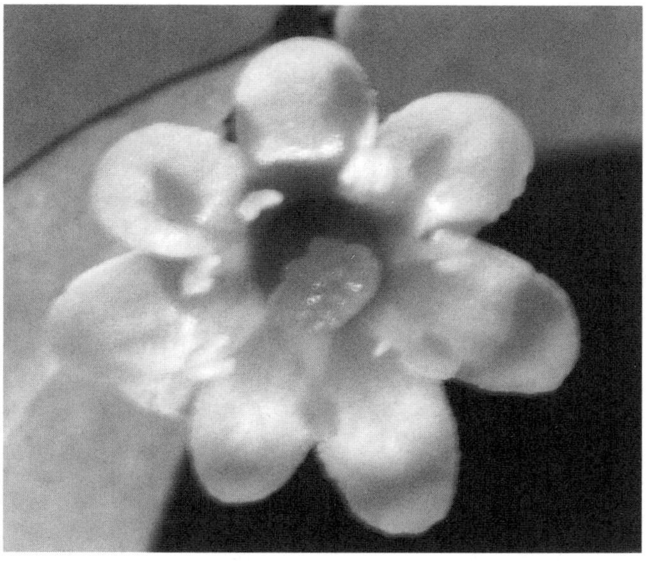

Figure 14-24. *Ilex glabra* f. *glabra.* Photo by Barton Bauer Sr.

Ilex glazioviana Loesener 1901.
Evergreen shrubs; leaves ovate to obovate-elliptic, 1.3–2.5 cm (¹⁵⁄₃₂–1 in.) long, 7–11 mm (⁹⁄₃₂–⁷⁄₁₆ in.) wide, apices obtuse to rotund, bases acute, margins recurved, 2–3 serrulate teeth on each side, petioles 2–3.5 mm (⅛–⁷⁄₆₄ in.) long; inflorescences axillary, solitary on new growth, subfasciculate, 1- to 3-flowered, flowers 4-merous; fruits unknown, single pedicels 3–6 mm (⅛–⁷⁄₃₂ in.) long, 1- to 3-fruited peduncles 2 mm (¹⁄₁₆ in.) long. Habitat: Brazil, Rio de Janeiro State, in the highest sections of the Orgãos Mountains. Allied to *I. chamaedryfolia* and *I. paltorioides*.

Ilex gleasoniana Steyermark 1955.
Evergreen shrubs, branchlets minutely pubescent; leaves obovate-oblong, 2–3.2 cm (¾–1¼ in.) long, 0.8–1.3 cm (⁵⁄₁₆–½ in.) wide, minute punctate beneath, bases narrow, apices rotund, briefly mucronate, margins entire, slightly revolute, petioles 3–5 mm (⅛–³⁄₁₆ in.) long; inflorescences axillary, solitary; fruits unknown. Habitat: Venezuela, Amazonas, on summit of Mount Duida. Allied to *I. apicidens*.

Ilex glomerata King 1895.
Evergreen trees to 12 m (40 ft.) tall, branchlets glabrous or glabrescent; leaves oblong or oblong-elliptic, 6–12 cm (2⅜–4¾ in.) long, 2–3.5 cm (¾–1⅜ in.) wide, apices acuminate, acumens 8–15 mm (⁵⁄₁₆–¹⁹⁄₃₂ in.) long, bases obtuse or cuneate, rarely rotund, margins serrate, petioles 8–15 mm (⁵⁄₁₆–¹⁹⁄₃₂ in.) long; inflorescences axillary and fasciculate on 2nd-year growth, flowers 4-merous; fruits red, globose, 7–8 mm (⁹⁄₃₂–⁵⁄₁₆ in.) diameter, pedicels 1–3 mm (¹⁄₃₂–⅛ in.) long, calyces persistent; pyrenes 4, palmately striate, sulcate, wrinkled, pitted. Habitat: Malaya, Perak, Indonesia, Java, Tenasserim, Myanmar; Vietnam, and People's Republic of China, Guangxi Province. Allied to *I. subficoides*.

Ilex glomeratifolia Hayata 1913. Arisan-soyogo.
Evergreen trees, branches glabrous; leaves oblong lanceolate, 9 cm (3½ in.) long, 2.8 cm (1⅛ in.) wide, bases acute or cuneate-acute, apices acuminate, or caudate-acuminate, acumens 1 cm (⅜ in.) long, margins subentire or obscurely serrulate, petioles 10 mm (⅜ in.) long; male inflorescences axillary, pedicels glabrous, 1.5 mm (³⁄₆₄ in.) long; fruits elliptic or subglobose, 6 mm (⁷⁄₃₂ in.) long, 5 mm (³⁄₁₆ in.) diameter; pyrenes 4. Habitat: Taiwan, Arisan. Allied to *I. formosana*.

Ilex godajam (Colebrooke *ex* Wallich) Wallich f. *godajam* 1839. Gadajam (synonyms *I. rotunda* Thunberg *ex* J. A. Murray 1791, not 1784, *Prinos godajam* Colebrooke *ex* Wallich 1832, *I. godajam* var. *genuina* Kurz 1875).

Evergreen trees to 8 m (26 ft.) tall, branchlets pubescent; leaves ovate or oblong, 5–8 cm (2–3⅛ in.) long, 2.5–4.5 cm (1–1¾ in.) wide, bases rounded, apices obtuse or very short acuminate, margins entire, midribs puberulent above, and pilose or glabrescent beneath, slender petioles 10–15 mm (⅜–½ in.) long; inflorescences umbelliform 3–13 flowers, axillary on new growth, peduncles 10–13 mm (⅜–½ in.) long, pedicels 2–5 mm (¾–2 in.) long; fruits red, globose, small, 3.5 mm (⁹⁄₆₄ in.) diameter; pyrenes 5–6, 3-striate, 2-sulcate. Habitat: People's Republic of China, Hunan Province, Vietnam, and Bhutan in India. Allied to *I. excelsa* f. *hypotricha*, *I. rotunda*, and *I. umbellulata*. Most likely this form will eventually become a synonym of the species.

Ilex godajam f. *capitellata* (Pierre) Loesener 1901 (synonym *I. capitellata* Pierre 1893).
This form differs from typical individuals with branchlets minutely pubescent and leaves beneath sparsely pubescent. Habitat: Vietnam, the plains of Ahopeu.

Ilex goshiensis Hayata 1911. Tsuge-mochi (synonyms *I. hanceana sensu* Hayata 1913, *I. hanceana* f. *rotundata* Makino *ex* Yamamoto 1925).
Evergreen shrubs or small trees to 6 m (20 ft.) tall, branchlets puberulent; leaves suborbicular or broadly elliptic, 2.8–4.8 cm (1⅛–1⅞ in.) long, 1.5–2.5 cm (¹⁹⁄₃₂–1 in.) wide, apices obtuse or retuse, acuminate, acumens 5 mm (³⁄₁₆ in.) long, bases acute, margins entire, petioles 4–8 mm (⁵⁄₃₂–⁵⁄₁₆ in.) long; inflorescences axillary, fasciculate, 1- to 3-flowered cymose, pedicels 3–5 mm (⅛–³⁄₁₆ in.) long, flowers 4- to 5-merous; fruits red, globose, 4 mm (⁵⁄₃₂ in.) diameter, calyces persistent, stigmas elevated; pyrenes 4, 3-striate. Habitat: northern and central Taiwan, southern Japan, the Ryukyu Island and People's Republic of China, Hainan Island. Allied to *I. oligodenta*.

Ilex goudotii Loesener 1901.
Evergreen, small trees, branches pubescent; leaves oval or oval-oblong to elliptic-oblong, 6.5–8.5 cm (2½–3⅜ in.) long, 2.6–4 cm (1–1⅝ in.) wide, apices somewhat obtuse or acuminate, bases cuneate obtuse, margins entire, recurved, petioles 6–12 mm (⁷⁄₃₂–¹⁵⁄₃₂ in.) long; inflorescences fasciculate in leaf axils, flowers usually 5-merous; male peduncles 3–5 mm (⅛–³⁄₁₆ in.) long, male pedicels 1–2 mm (¹⁄₃₂–¹⁄₁₆ in.) long; fruits unknown. Habitat: Colombia. Allied to *I. floribunda*.

Ilex graciliflora Champion 1852, *non* Johnston 1938.
Evergreen trees to 6–9 m (20–30 ft.) tall; leaves obovate or oblong-elliptic, 2.7–5 cm (1¹⁄₁₆–2 in.)

long, 1.3–3.5 cm (19/32–1 3/8 in.) wide, apices obtuse, rarely acute, or retuse, bases obtuse or acute, margins minutely and remotely serrulate, rarely subentire, petioles 10–15 mm (3/8–19/32 in.) long; inflorescences axillary and fasciculate on 2nd-year growth, puberulent, flowers 4-merous, female inflorescences uniflorous, pedicels 4–6 mm (5/32–7/32 in.) long; fruits red, globose, 5–6 mm (3/16–7/32 in.) diameter, persistent; pyrenes wrinkled, rugose, irregularly striate, sulcate. Habitat: endemic Hong Kong and nearby islands. Allied to *I. ficoidea.*

Ilex gracilipes Merrill 1908, *non* Johnston 1938.

Evergreen, small trees to 3–4 m (10–13 ft.) tall, glabrous, branchlets lenticellate; leaves oblong-ovate to elliptic-ovate, 2.5–5 cm (1–2 in.) long, 1–3 cm (3/8–1 3/16 in.) wide, bases acute, apices long-acuminate, margins apiculate denticulate, minutely punctate beneath, petioles slender, 5 mm (3/16 in.) long or less; inflorescences axillary, 1- or 2- to 4-flowered fascicles, flowers 3- to 5-merous; fruits subglobose or ovoid, 5–6 mm (3/16–7/32 in.) long, 15 longitudinal ridges; peduncles 2–3 cm (3/4–1 3/16 in.) long. Habitat: Philippines, Luzon, on Mount Taplaco and Mount Mariveles. Allied to *I. spicata.*

Ilex gracilis C.-j. Tseng 1985 (synonym *I. franchetiana* S.-y. Hu 1950).

Evergreen, small trees 8 m (26 ft.) tall, branchlets irregularly striate, pubescent; leaves elliptic or oblong-elliptic, 7–9 cm (2 3/4–3 1/2 in.) long, 2.2–3.5 cm (13/16–1 3/8 in.) wide, apices abruptly acuminate, acumens 1–1.5 cm (3/8–19/32 in.) long, bases obtuse or acute, margins crenulate, glabrous, petioles 1 cm (3/8 in.) long, pubescent; inflorescences axillary, 4- to 5-fasciculate or short racemes; fruits (immature) subglobose or ellipsoid-globose, 5 mm (3/16 in.) long, 4 mm (5/32 in.) diameter, pedicels 3.5–4 mm (9/64–5/32 in.) long, pubescent; pyrenes 4, palmately striate, slightly sulcate. Habitat: People's Republic of China, Yunnan Province. Allied to *I. fargesii.*

Ilex grandifolia Merrill 1934.

Evergreen, glabrous trees, branches lenticellate, dark brown; leaves oblong, 16–25 cm (6 1/4–9 3/4 in.) long, 6–8 cm (2 3/8–3 1/8 in.) wide, bases broadly rotund, apices acuminate, margins entire, petioles 1–2 cm (3/8–3/4 in.) long; inflorescences cymose, axillary, multiple flowers, peduncles 3–5 cm (1 3/16–2 in.) long, pedicels 1.5–2.5 cm (19/32–1 in.) long; fruits depressed-globose, 3 mm (1/8 in.) diameter, 14 locules. Habitat: Indonesia, east coast of Sumatra, Asahan, Adian Bolon, along the Toba trail, north of the Asahan River, between Adian Langge and Si Martoloe. Allied to *I. wallichii.*

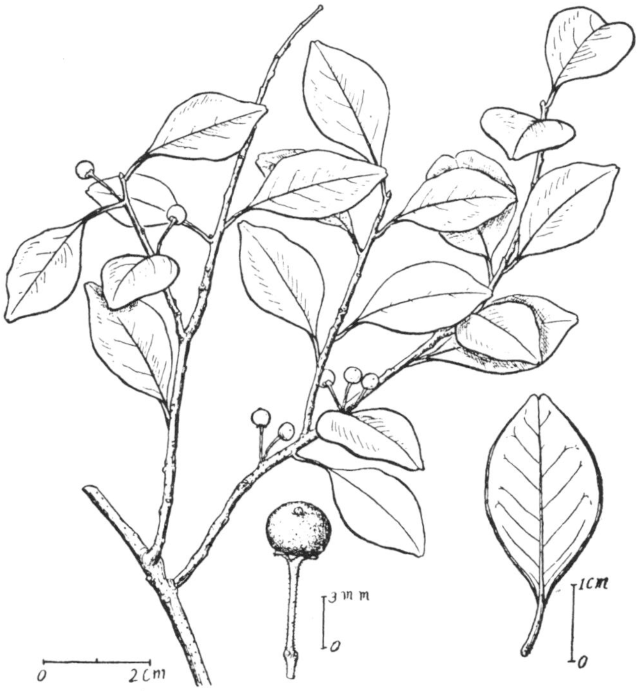

Figure 14-25. *Ilex goshiensis.* Drawing by Chien-chu Chen in *Illustrations of Native and Introduced Ligneous Plants of Taiwan* (1962) by Tang-shui Liu.

Ilex gransabanensis Steyermark 1988.

Evergreen shrubs to 1.5 m (5 ft.) tall, branchlets glabrous; leaves obovate-oblong or oblong-ovate, 5–9.5 cm (1–3 3/4 in.) long, 3.5–5 cm (1 3/8–2 in.) wide, punctate beneath, bases obtuse to subacute, apices rotund, obtuse or subobtuse, margins entire, glabrous, petioles 9–13 mm (11/32–1/2 in.) long; inflorescences axillary, lateral, solitary or fasciculate, pedunculate; fruits smooth. Habitat: Venezuela, Bolivar, on road between Ikabaru to Santa Elena. Similar to *I. tepuiana, I. fanshawei,* and *I. solida incertu sedia.*

Ilex grisebachii Maximowicz 1881 var. *grisebachii* (synonym *I. dioica* Grisebach 1861, *non* Bello 1883).

Evergreen trees, branchlets glabrous; leaves obovate, rarely ovate, 5.5–9 cm (2 1/8–3 1/2 in.) long, 2.5–4 cm (1–1 5/8 in.) wide, apices obtuse or rotund, bases obtuse or acute, margins minute or obscurely crenulate-serrulate, petioles 4–8 mm (5/32–5/16 in.) long; inflorescences axillary, 2- to 6-fasciculate, flowers 4-merous; fruits black, globose, 4 mm (5/32 in.) diameter; pyrenes 4, striate, sulcate. Habitat: Cuba. Allied to *I. dioica, I. nitida,* and *I. repanda.*

Ilex grisebachii var. *haitiensis* Loesener 1919.

A variety with smaller leaves, 1.5–3.5 cm (19/32–1 3/8 in.) long, 1–1.6 cm (3/8–5/8 in.) wide.

Habitat: Haiti. May later be regarded as a synonym of the species.

Ilex grisebachii var. *nipensis* Loesener 1923.

A variety with minutely pubescent stems; midribs only slightly impressed. Habitat: Cuba. Possibly to be treated as a synonym of the species.

Ilex guaiquinimae Steyermark 1988.

Evergreen trees, branchlet glabrous; leaves broadly oblong, 10–16 cm (4–6½ in.) long, 6.5–8 cm (2½–3⅛ in.) wide, punctate beneath, bases acute to subacute, apices rotund, margins entire, petioles 10–18 mm (⅜–11/16 in.) long; inflorescences axillary, solitary, lateral, pedunculate; fruits globose, 5 mm (3/16 in.) diameter; pyrenes dorsally broad, 1 sulcate. Habitat: Venezuela, Bolivar, Cerro Guaiquinima at 730–900 m (2400–2970 ft.) elevation. Allied to *I. jenmanii.*

Ilex guangnanensis C.-j. Tseng & Y.-r. Li 1985.

Evergreen, glabrous trees to 15 m (50 ft.) tall, branchlets angulate-striate; leaves oblong or oblong-elliptic, rarely elliptic-lanceolate, 4–8 cm (1⅝–3⅛ in.) long, 1.5–2.5 cm (19/32–1 in.) wide, apices long-acuminate or sickle-shaped, bases obtuse or wide cuneate, margins undulate, conspicuously serrate, petioles slender, 5–8 mm (3/16–5/16 in.) long; inflorescences axillary, fasciculate, 4-merous; fruits color unknown, globose, 6 mm (7/32 in.) diameter, calyces persistent; pyrenes 4, palmately striate, sulcate. Habitat: People's Republic of China, Yunnan Province. Allied to *I. cyrtura.*

Ilex guayusa Loesener 1901. Guayusa (synonym *I. guayusa* var. *utilis* Moldenke 1933).

Evergreen shrubs or trees, branchlets glabrous; leaves oblong or oblong-elliptic, 10–13 cm (4–5⅛ in.) long, 3.8–5 cm (1½–2 in.) wide, apices acute or acuminate, bases acute or subcuneate-obtuse, margins crenate-serrate, petioles 7–8 mm (9/32–5/16 in.) long; flowers and fruits unknown. Habitat: Ecuador and Peru. Allied to *I. nitida* and *I. paraguariensis.* One of the several species used for yerba de maté, an herbal drink made from the dried fermented leaves.

Ilex guerreroii Merrill 1915.

Evergreen shrubs or small trees, glabrous, branches stout, pale gray; leaves oblong to narrow-oblong-elliptic, glossy, 5–7 cm (2–2¾ in.) long, 1.5–2.8 cm (⅝–1⅛ in.) wide, bases decurrent-acuminate, apices acute, slightly acuminate or obtuse, margins entire, or sometimes obscurely crenate, petioles 5–10 mm (3/16–⅜ in.) long; pistillate inflorescences axillary, fasciculate, pedicels 4 mm (5/32 in.) long, bracteoles ovate, acuminate at basal end, flowers 4-merous, fruits immature. Habitat: Philippines, Luzon, Rizal, mountains near San Mateo. Allied to *I. sumatrana.*

Ilex guianensis (Aublet) Kuntze 1891 var. *guianensis.* Macoucou (synonyms *Macoucoua guianensis* Aublet 1775, *I. acuminata* Willdenow 1798, *I. macoucoua* Persoon 1805, *I. macoucoua* Klotzsch 1848, *I. bumelioides* Grisebach 1857, *I. cumanensis* Turczaninow 1858, *I. obcordata* Triana 1872, *I. occidentalis* Hemsley 1879, *I. guianensis* var. *macoucoua* (Persoon) Loesener 1901, *I. occidentalis* var. *maestrana* Loesener 1901, *I. occidentalis* var. *rotundifolia* Loesener 1901, *I. panamensis* Standley 1925, *I. guianensis* var. *cuencinsis* Loesener 1930).

Evergreen, large shrubs or trees 5–8 m (16–26 ft.) tall; leaves obovate-oblong to oval-oblong, 6–13 cm (2⅜–5⅛ in.) long, 2–5 cm (¾–2 in.) wide, apices rotund or obtuse, rarely acuminate, bases acute or cuneate-acute, margins entire, revolute, rarely serrulate, petioles 4–15 mm (5/32–19/32 in.) long; inflorescences in leaf axils, fasciculate, branched, flowers 4-merous; fruits black, ellipsoid, 6 mm (7/32 in.) long, 4.2 mm (11/64 in.) wide; pyrenes usually 4. Highly variable. Habitat: West Indies, Belize, Mexico, Colombia, Venezuela, and Guyana. Highly variable and widespread polymorphic. Allied to *I. cuyabensis, I. inundata,* and *I. umbellata.*

Ilex guianensis var. *elliptica* Amshoff 1950. Sekrepatoe-wiwirie, wajam moesesamoer.

A variety with leaves elliptical-oblong, shortly acuminate, petioles to 10 mm (⅜ in.) long. Habitat: Jamaica.

Ilex guizhouensis C.-j. Tseng 1981.

Evergreen shrubs or trees, branchlets slender, glabrous; leaves elliptic-oblong, 5–9 cm (2–3½ in.) long, 2–2.5 cm (¾–1 in.) wide, apices acuminate, acumens 8–13 mm (5/16–½ in.) long, bases obtuse, margins subentire, petioles 5–8 mm (3/16–5/16 in.) long, glabrous; inflorescences axillary, fasciculate; fruits black when dry, globose, 4 mm (5/32 in.) diameter, pedicels 2–3 mm (1/16–⅛ in.) long; pyrenes 4, palmately striate, slightly sulcate. Habitat: People's Republic of China, Guizhou Province. Allied to *I. fukienensis.*

Ilex gundiachiana Loesener 1912.

Evergreen, glabrous shrubs, branches slightly angulate; leaves oblong or oval-oblong to obovate, 3.5–7 cm (1⅜–2¾ in.) long, 1.8–3.5 cm (11/16–1⅜ in.) wide, bases acute or cuneate, rarely obtuse, apices obtuse or rotund, margins remotely serrulate or subcrenulate-serrulate, petioles 4–7 mm (5/32–9/32 in.) long; inflorescences solitary, flowers 5-merous; fruits ovoid, 6 mm (7/32 in.) long, 4–5 mm (5/32–3/16 in.) wide; pyrenes 6, striate. Habitat: Cuba, Oriente Province, Camp La Gloria. Allied to *I. tuerckheimii.*

Ilex hainanensis (Loesener) Merrill 1934 (synonym *I. rotunda* var. *hainanensis* Loesener 1901).

Evergreen, small trees to 5 m (16 ft.) tall, branchlets angulate, ridged, sparsely puberulent; leaves broadly elliptic-obovate or ovate-oblong, 3–7 cm (1 1/16–2 3/4 in.) long, 1.5–2.5 cm (19/32–1 in.) wide, apices short acuminate, acumens 3–7 mm (1/8–9/32 in.) long, tip acute or mucronate, bases obtuse, margins usually entire, rarely 1–2 teeth near apex, petioles 5–10 mm (3/16–3/8 in.) long; inflorescences axillary on 2nd-year growth, fasciculate or pseudopaniculate, female inflorescences 1- to 3-flowered cymose, peduncles 1–3 mm (1/32–1/8 in.) long, pedicels 3 mm (1/8 in.) long, flowers 5- to 6-merous, petals pink; fruits red, subglobose-ellipsoid, 4 mm (5/32 in.) long, 3 mm (1/8 in.) diameter; pyrenes usually 5, dorsal surface rough, canaliculate, sides smooth. Habitat: People's Republic of China, Hainan Island and high mountains of southeastern Guangxi Province. Allied to *I. pubescens.*

Ilex hakkuensis Yamamoto 1925. Nagaha-nindo-machinoki.

Evergreen plants, branches dark purple, lenticellate; leaves linear-lanceolate or lanceolate-elliptic, 8–10 cm (3 1/8–4 3/4 in.) long, 2–3 cm (3/4–1 3/16 in.) wide, bases acute, apices acuminate, margins entire, recurved, petioles 1.5–3 mm (3/64–1/8 in.) long; inflorescences axillary, umbellate, peduncles glabrous, 6–9 cm (2 3/8–3 1/2 in.) long. Habitat: Taiwan, Hakku, at 3000 m (9900 ft.) elevation. Allied to *I. shennongjiaensis, I. sugerokii,* and *I. yunnanensis.*

Ilex hanceana Maximowicz 1881 (synonym *I. buxifolia* Hance 1876, *non* Gardner 1845).

Evergreen shrubs, branchlets slender, pubescent, ridged; leaves obovate or obovate-oblong, 3.5 cm (1 3/8 in.) long, 1–2 cm (3/8–3/4 in.) wide, apices acuminate or obtuse or rotund, rarely retuse, bases obtuse or cuneate, margins entire, puberulent above, glabrous beneath, petioles 2–5 mm (1/16–3/16 in.) long; inflorescences axillary on 2nd-year growth, paucifasciculate, pubescent, flowers 4-merous; fruits red, globose, 5 mm (3/16 in.) diameter, calyces persistent, pedicels 1.5 mm (3/64 in.) long; pyrenes 4, long striate. Habitat: localized in Hong Kong. Allied to *I. lohfauensis.*

Ilex harmandiana Pierre 1893. Bui.

Evergreen, small trees, young branches glabrous, old branches grayish; leaves oval to subelliptic, 8–11 cm (3 1/8–4 3/8 in.) long, 3.5–5 cm (1 3/8–2 in.) wide, entire recurved margins, bases cuneate-obtuse to cuneate, apices short to obtuse or acuminate; inflorescences solitary in leaf axils, umbelliform, peduncles 8–18 mm (5/16–3/4 in.) long; 18–22 locules in ovaries; fruits unknown. Habitat: southern Vietnam, in Laos near the Mekong River near Attopen. Allied to *I. anomala.*

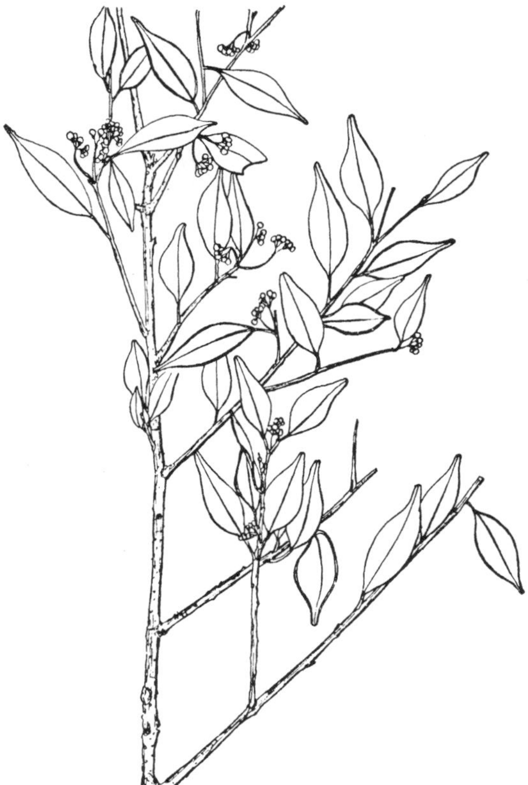

Figure 14-26. *Ilex hanceana.* Drawing by Chien-chu Chen in *Illustrations of Native and Introduced Ligneous Plants of Taiwan* (1962) by Tang-shui Liu.

Ilex harmsiana Loesener 1901.

Evergreen shrubs, glabrous; leaves usually oblong lanceolate, 5.5–8.5 cm (2 1/8–3 3/8 in.) long, 2–3.3 cm (3/4–1 5/16 in.) wide, apices obtuse with reflexed acumens 5–10 mm (3/16–3/8 in.) long, bases acute or broadly cuneate, margins entire, recurved, petioles 1–2 mm (1/32–1/16 in.) long; inflorescences in leaf axils, racemose, pedicels 1–2 mm (1/32–1/16 in.) long, flowers 5-merous; fruits black, globose, small 2.5–3 mm (3/32–1/8 in.) diameter; pyrenes 5–6. Habitat: Malaysia, western Borneo, on Mount Tiangladgin at 1000 m (3300 ft.) elevation. Allied to *I. spicata.*

Ilex harrisii (Loesener) Loesener 1899 (synonym *I. guianensis* var. *harrisii* Loesener 1899).

Evergreen shrubs or trees, branchlet glabrous, lenticellate; leaves oblong to obovate or oval-oblong, 3–6 cm (1 3/16–2 3/8 in.) long, 2.5–3.5 cm (1–1 3/8 in.) wide, bases cuneate, apices shortly acuminate, margins entire, petioles 11–19 mm (7/16–3/4 in.) long; inflorescences axillary, 4- to 8-fasciculate, flowers 4- to 5-merous; fruits unknown. Habitat: Jamaica. Allied to *I. guianensis.*

Ilex havilandi Loesener 1901 (synonyms *I. vaccinii-folia* Stapf 1894, *non* Koltzsch 1848, *I. vacciniifolia* var. *camptoneura* Stapf 1894, *I. vacciniifolia* var. *subenervis* Stapf 1894).

Evergreen shrubs, usually glabrous; leaves close together on the stem, obovate or obovate-elliptic, 1–1.7 cm (⅜–2¹⁄₃₂ in.) long, 5–9 mm (³⁄₁₆–¹¹⁄₃₂ in.) wide, apices rotund, often obtuse, bases cuneate, margins entire, recurved; inflorescences in leaf axils, pedicels 3–4 mm (⅛–⁵⁄₃₂ in.) long, flowers 4-merous; fruits unknown. Habitat: Borneo, on Mount Kinabalu, at 2900 m (9570 ft.) elevation. Allied to *I. walkeri.*

Ilex hayataiana Loesener 1941.

Evergreen, large trees to 12 m (40 ft.) tall, branchlets pubescent, lenticels conspicuous; leaves elliptic or ovate-elliptic, 2–5 cm (¾–2 in.) long, 1–2 cm (⅜–¾ in.) wide, apices acuminate, acumens 5–10 mm (⁵⁄₁₆–⅜ in.) long, bases obtuse or acute, margins entire, midrib elevated and pubescent above, petioles 4–7 mm (⁵⁄₃₂–⁹⁄₃₂ in.) long; inflorescences axillary on 2nd-year growth, fasciculate or pseudofasciculate, flowers 4-merous; fruits red, subglobose, 4 mm (⁵⁄₃₂ in.) diameter, pedicels 5–7 mm (³⁄₁₆–⁹⁄₃₂ in.) long; pyrenes 4, 3-striate. Habitat: central and northern Taiwan at 2300–3000 m (7600–9900 ft.), and Japan, Ryukyu Islands. Allied to *I. wilsonii.*

Ilex herzogii Loesener 1916.

Evergreen, glabrous shrubs; leaves obovate to obovate-oblong, 3.5–6.5 cm (1⅜–2½ in.) long, 2–3 cm (¾–1³⁄₁₆ in.) wide, bases cuneate to obtuse, apices obtuse or acuminate, rarely rotund; margins recurved, remotely serrulate near apex, petioles 7–10 mm (⁹⁄₃₂–⅜ in.) long; inflorescences axillary, solitary, flowers 4- to 5-merous; fruits globose, 4–5 mm (⁵⁄₃₂–³⁄₁₆ in.) diameter; pyrenes 4–5. Habitat: Brazil, near Tres Cruces, at 1500 m (4950 ft.) elevation. Allied to *I. myricoides.*

Ilex hippocrateoides Kunth 1824, *non* Triana & Plancheon 1833 (synonym *Prinos obtusatus* Willdenow 1818).

Evergreen, glabrous trees; leaves broadly oblong to oblong-lanceolate, 4–6 cm (1⅝–2⅜ in.) long, 1.4–2.3 cm (¹⁷⁄₃₂–⅞ in.) wide, bases acute, apices obtuse or acuminate, densely reticulate, margins with small teeth, serrulate, petioles 6–7 mm (⁷⁄₃₂–⁹⁄₃₂ in.) long; inflorescences axillary, solitary, 3- to 7-flowered, male flowers 4-merous, female flowers and fruits unknown. Habitat: Peru. Allied to *I. boliviana* and *I. truxillensis.*

Ilex hirsuta C.-j. Tseng 1981.

Evergreen, small trees 3.5–6 m (11–20 ft.) tall,

branchlets reddish brown hirsute; leaves elliptic to oblong-elliptic, rarely ovate-elliptic, 6–7 cm (2⅜–2¾ in.) long, 2.5–4 cm (1–1⅝ in.) wide, apices acute or short-acuminate, rarely obtuse, bases acute, densely hirsute on both surfaces, margins serrulate, remotely revolute, petioles 1.5 cm (¹⁹⁄₃₂ in.) long, hirsute; inflorescences cymes with 1–3 fruits, solitary, axillary, flowers 5-merous; fruits red, subglobose or ellipsoid-globose, 6 mm (⁷⁄₃₂ in.) diameter; pyrenes 4–5. Habitat: People's Republic of China, Hubei and Hunan provinces. Allied to *I. ficifolia* and *I. lonicerifolia.*

Ilex holstii Steyermark 1988.

Evergreen, large shrubs to 4 m (14 ft.) tall, branchlets glabrous; leaves lanceolate, 5.5–8 cm (2⅛–3⅛ in.) long, 1.3–2.5 cm (½–1 in.) wide, bases acute or subacute, apices acuminate, mucros 0.5 mm (¹⁄₆₄ in.) long, margins entire, petioles 6–10 mm (⁷⁄₃₂–⅜ in.) long; inflorescences axillary, solitary, lateral; fruits globose, 4–6 mm (⁵⁄₃₂–⁷⁄₃₂ in.) diameter, pedicels solitary or in twos, 4–7 mm (⁵⁄₃₂–⁹⁄₃₂ in.) long; pyrenes 4, trigonous, dorsally broadly unisulcate. Habitat: Venezuela, Amazonas, Department Rio Negro, Cerro Aratitiyope. Allied to *I. macarenensis* and *I. oliveriana.*

Ilex honbaensis Tardieu 1945.

Evergreen trees, branches glabrous, erect or ascending, lenticellate; leaves ovate or oblong, 7–9 cm (2¾–9½ in.) long, 3.5–4 cm (1⅜–1⅝ in.) wide, bases acute, apices acute, margins entire, recurved, petioles canaliculate, 6–10 mm (⁷⁄₃₂–⅜ in.) long; female inflorescences solitary or fasciculate, few-flowered, pyrenes 6, 2-sulcate. Habitat: Vietnam, Annam, Nha Trang. Allied to *I. cochinchinensis.*

Ilex hondurensis Standley 1938.

Evergreen trees 4.5–7.5 m (15–25 ft.) tall, trunks 7.5–20 cm (3–7.5 in.) diameter, glabrous; leaves oval or rotund-ovate, 5–6.5 cm (2–2½ in.) long, 3–4.5 cm (1³⁄₁₆–1¾ in.) wide, bases rotund or obtuse, apices broadly rotund or obtuse, margins remotely and obscurely appressed-crenate, sometimes entire; female inflorescences axillary, fasciculate, pedicels 4 mm (⁵⁄₃₂ in.) long; fruits immature, globose, 2.5 mm (³⁄₃₂ in.) diameter. Habitat: Honduras, edge of ravine near El Achate, hills above plains, Department Comayagua at 1800 m (5940 ft.) elevation. Allied to *I. discolor* var. *tolucana.*

Ilex hookeri King 1886.

Evergreen, glabrous trees to 18 m (60 ft.) tall; leaves elliptic or obovate-elliptic, 5–10 cm (2–4 in.) long, 2–4.5 cm (¾–1¾ in.) wide, apices acute or shortly acuminate, acumens 5 mm (³⁄₁₆ in.) long, bases obtuse or rotund, margins finely serrate, teeth apiculate, petioles 12–20 mm (15⁄32–3⁄4 in.) long; inflorescences axillary and fasciculate on 2nd-year growth, flowers 4-merous; fruits red, globose, 6 mm (7⁄32 in.) diameter; pyrenes 4, palmately striate, sulcate. Habitat: People's Republic of China, northwestern Yunnan Province; Myanmar; India, Bhutan and Sikkim. Introduced in the United States from England by F. G. Meyer in 1957. Allied to *I. fargesii.*

Ilex huachamacariana Edwin 1965.

Evergreen large shrubs or small trees to 8 m (26 ft.) tall, branchlets pubescent; leaves narrowly obovate to obovate, 3–6.5 cm (13⁄16–21⁄2 in.) long, 0.8–2.5 cm (5⁄16–1 in.) wide, punctate beneath, bases acute, subspathulate to attenuate, apices acute, margins entire, petioles 2.8–5 mm (11⁄4–3⁄16 in.) long; inflorescences axillary, solitary, pedunculate, flowers 5-merous; fruits dark red, subglobose to globose, 7–9 mm (9⁄32–11⁄32 in.) long, 7–8 mm (9⁄32–5⁄16 in.) diameter; pyrenes 5, unicanaliculate, marginal ridges. Habitat: Venezuela, Amazonas, Cerro Huachamacari, Rio Cunucunuma, at 1800 m (5900 ft.) elevation.

Ilex huiana C.-j. Tseng 1981 (synonym *I. angulata* var. *longipedunculata* S.-y. Hu 1949, *I. angulata* S.-y. Hu 1949).

Evergreen shrubs 2–3 m (6–10 ft.) tall, branchlets angulate, puberulent or glabrescent; leaves elliptic, rarely obovate, 2.5–5 cm (1–2 in.) long, 1–2 cm (3⁄8–3⁄4 in.) wide, apices acuminate or acute, bases acute, glabrous above except for puberulent midribs, margins entire or serrulate toward apex, petioles 5 mm (3⁄16 in.) long; female inflorescences cymose, 1- to 3-flowered, peduncles 5 mm (3⁄16 in.) long, single pedicels 9–12 mm (11⁄32–15⁄32 in.) long; fruits red, ellipsoid, 9–10 mm (11⁄32–3⁄8 in.) long, 5–6 mm (3⁄16–7⁄32 in.) diameter; pyrenes 5, dorsally wide-canaliculate. Habitat: People's Republic of China, Guangdong and Hainan provinces. Allied to *I. huiana* and *I. purpurea.*

Ilex humbertii Cuatrecasas 1956.

Evergreen plants, stems grayish brown, leaves ovate-elliptic to obovate-oblong, 6–8 cm (23⁄8–31⁄8 in.) long, 3.5–4.5 cm (13⁄8–13⁄4 in.) wide, punctate, bases obtuse, apices rotund, margins slight wavy, crenate; male inflorescences axillary, multiflorous, paniculate, peduncles 1.5–5 cm (19⁄32–2 in.) long, pedicels 4–10 in umbels; fruits unknown. Habitat: Colombia, Vaupés River, at 350 m (1150 ft.) elevation. Allied to *I. affinis, I. laureola,* and *I. martiniana.*

Ilex hylonoma S.-y. Hu & Tang 1940 var. *hylonoma* (synonym *I. intermedia sensu* S.-y. Hu 1946, *non* Loesener 1891).

Evergreen, small to medium trees, 4–10 m (13–33 ft.) tall, branchlets glabrescent; leaves elliptic or oblong-elliptic, 6–12 cm (23⁄8–43⁄4 in.) long, 2.4–4.5 cm (1–13⁄4 in.) wide, minutely pubescent above, rugose beneath, bases acute or obtuse, apices shortly acuminate, tips mucronate, margins coarsely and sharply serrate, occasionally with short spines, petioles 8–14 mm (5⁄16–17⁄32 in.) long; inflorescences axillary and fasciculate on 2nd-year growth, flowers 4-merous; fruits red, ellipsoid or subglobose, 10–13 mm (3⁄8–1⁄2 in.) diameter; pyrenes 4, irregularly wrinkled, pitted, endocarps bony. Habitat: western People's Republic of China, first reported from Sichuan Province's sacred Mount Omei, in mixed forests at 900–1700 m (3000–5600 ft.) elevation. Allied to *I. centrochinensis.*

Ilex hylonoma var. *glabra* S.-y. Hu 1949.

Evergreen trees to 10 m (33 ft.) tall, branchlets glabrous; leaves glabrous, thick texture, lanceolate or oblanceolate or ovate-lanceolate or elliptic, 6–10 cm (23⁄8–4 in.) long, 1.8–4.2 cm (3⁄4–15⁄8 in.) wide; fruits red, ellipsoid or subglobose, 8–10 mm (5⁄16–3⁄8 in.) diameter, pedicels 2–3 mm (1⁄16–1⁄8 in.) long. Habitat: People's Republic of China, over a wider range than typical individuals, from coastal Zhejiang Province west to Hunan Province and south to Guangxi Province.

Ilex hypaneura Loesener 1892 var. *hypaneura* (synonym *I. repanda* Grisebach 1861).

Evergreen shrubs or small trees; leaves oblong-elliptic or elliptic-lanceolate, 3.5–4.5 cm (3⁄8–13⁄16 in.) wide, apices obtuse, bases acute or cuneate, margins entire, revolute, petioles 4–6 mm (5⁄32–7⁄32 in.) long; inflorescences axillary, fasciculate, flowers 4-merous; fruits subglobose, 3–5 mm (1⁄8–3⁄16 in.) diameter, color unknown; pyrenes 4. Habitat: Cuba. Allied to *I. repanda.*

Ilex hypaneura var. *nudicalyx* Borhidi 1979.

A variety with glabrescent inflorescences and glabrous calyces. Habitat: Cuba. This variety may be regarded as a synonym of the species after more study.

Ilex hypoglauca (Miquel) Loesener 1901 (synonym *Prinos hypoglaucus* Miquel 1860).

Evergreen shrubs, young branches pubescent; leaves glabrous, elliptic to ovate, 11 cm (41⁄4 in.) long, 4.2 cm (15⁄8 in.) wide, entire, recurved margins; inflorescences solitary in leaf axils, peduncles branched; fruits unknown. Habitat: Indonesia, island of Bangka, off east coast of Sumatra. Allied to *I. alternifolia.*

Ilex hypopsile Loesener 1901.

Evergreen, small shrubs; leaves oval to ovate-oblong, 3.5–6 cm (1⅜–2⅜ in.), 1.6–3.3 cm (⅝–1 5/16 in.) wide, pubescent, apices rotund or obtuse, bases acute to subcuneate, margins entire, recurved, petioles 4–8 mm (5/32–5/16 in.) long; inflorescences at base of new growth, branched, flowers 4-merous; fruits unknown. Habitat: Brazil, Goiás State, on serpentine mountains. Allied to *I. asperula* and *I. scutiiformis.*

Ilex illustris Ridley 1920.

Evergreen shrubs or small trees with small buttresses; leaves obovate to narrow-oblong, 8–12 cm (3⅛–4¾ in.) long, 3.5–4 cm (1⅜–1⅝ in.) wide, bases acute to obtuse, apices acute or retuse, margins minutely toothed, more conspicuous near apex, petioles 10 mm (⅜ in.) long; inflorescences small umbels; fruits red, ovoid, 14 mm (17/32 in.) long, 8–10 mm (5/16–⅜ in.) diameter, pyrenes 4. Habitat: Malaysia. Allied to *I. purpurea.*

Ilex impressa Loesener 1934.

Evergreen, small trees, branches glabrous; leaves ovate, oval, rarely obovate, 2–4 cm (¾–1⅝ in.) long, 1–1.8 cm to 3 cm (⅜–11/16 to 1 3/16 in.) wide, bases and apices rotund, margins entire, recurved, petioles 4–5 mm (5/32–3/16 in.) long; male flowers small, axillary, densely fasciculate, 4- to 5-merous; fruits unknown. Habitat: Dominican Republic, Azua Province, Sierra de Occoa, at 1300 m (4290 ft.) elevation. Allied to *I. azuensis.*

Ilex integerrima (Velloso) Loesener 1901 var. *integerrima.* Cauna (synonyms *Prinos integerrima* Velloso 1827, *I. integerrima* var. *typica* Loesener 1901).

Evergreen shrubs or small trees; leaves obovate or elliptic, 8–12 cm (3⅛–4¾ in.) long, 3.5–4.5 cm (1⅜–1¾ in.) wide, apices rotund or obtuse, bases cuneate, margins usually entire, revolute or recurved, petioles 1.5–2.5 mm (3/64–3/32 in.) long; inflorescences fasciculate in leaf axils, flowers 4- to 5-merous, petals 3–3.5 mm (⅛–7/64 in.) long; fruits black, ovoid 10–12 mm (⅜–15/32 in.) long, 7–8 mm (9/32–5/16 in.) wide; pyrenes 5–6, sulcate. Habitat: Brazil, near Goiás. Allied to *I. longipetiolata, I. psammophila,* and *I. theezans.*

Ilex integerrima var. *ebenacea* (Reisseck) Loesener 1901 (synonyms *I. glabra* Velloso 1831, *I. ebenacea* Reisseck 1861).

A variety with obovate or obovate-elliptic leaves, 8–16 cm (3⅛–6½ in.) long, 3.5–6.5 cm (1⅜–2 in.) wide, petioles 2–3 mm (1/16–⅛ in.) long; male inflorescences 3-flowered, petals 3–3.5 mm (⅛–7/64 in.) long. Habitat: Brazil, Goiás State.

Ilex integerrima var. *schenckiana* Loesener 1901.

A variety with leaves obovate-elliptic, 8–13 cm (3⅛–5⅛ in.) long, 3.5–5 cm (1⅜–2 in.) wide; male inflorescences 1-flowered, petals 4–4.5 mm (5/32–11/64 in.) long. Habitat: Brazil, Minas Gerais State.

Ilex integra Thunberg *ex* Murray 1787 var. *integra.* Mochi-no-ki (Japan) (synonyms *Othera japonica* Thunberg 1783, *I. asiatica* Sprengel 1826, *I. othera* Sprengel 1826, *Prinos integra* (Thunberg *ex* Murray) Hooker & Arnott 1838, *I. bessonii* Hort. *ex* Lavallée 1877, *I. integra* var. *leucocarpa* Maximowicz 1881, *I. integra* var. *typica* Maximowicz 1881, *I. integrifolia* Hort. *ex* Gardner 1894, *I. japonica* Hort. *ex* Loesener 1901, *I. integra* f. *ellipsoidea* (Okamoto) Ohwi 1953).

Evergreen, small trees, 5–8 m (16–26 ft.) tall, branchlets glabrous; leaves obovate to obovate-elliptic, 4–7 cm (1⅝–2¾ in.) long, 1.5–2.5 cm (19/32–1 in.) wide, bases usually crenate, apices short-acuminate, acumens 5 mm (3/16 in.) long, margins usually entire, petioles 1–1.5 mm (1/32–3/64 in.) long; inflorescences axillary and fasciculate on 2nd-year growth, flowers 4-merous; fruits orangish to reddish orange, globose or oblong-ellipsoid, 10–18 mm (⅜–11/16 in.) diameter, pedicels 9–15 mm (11/32–19/32 in.) long; pyrenes 4, rugose, striate, sulcate, endocarps stony. Habitat: Japan, Liukiu Islands, Okinawa, and Korea, in woodland areas, low mountains, especially near the sea. Hardy in zones 6b to 9. Allied to *I. aquifolium.* Plate 67.

Ilex integra var. *brachypoda* (S.-y. Hu) Hatusima 1971 (synonym *I. brachypoda* S.-y. Hu 1953).

A variety differing from typical individuals with sessile or very short pedicels only 1–3 mm (1/32–⅛ in.) long. Habitat: Japan and Okinawa.

Ilex intermedia Loesener *ex* Diels 1900.

Evergreen trees, branchlets minutely puberulent or glabrescent; leaves oblong-elliptic or ovate-elliptic or obovate-elliptic, 6–12.5 cm (2⅜–5 in.) long, 2.4–4.5 cm (1–1¾ in.) wide, apices obtuse, acute or very shortly acuminate, bases cuneate, obtuse or rarely rotund, margins remotely crenulate or coarsely serrate, petioles 11–16 mm (7/16–⅝ in.) long; inflorescences fasciculate or pseudopaniculate, flowers 4-merous; fruits red, depressed-globose, 4 mm (5/32 in.) long, 5 mm (3/16 in.) diameter, calyces persistent; pyrenes small, palmately striate. Habitat: People's Republic of China, endemic to the *Metasequoia* area in Hubei Province, Lichuan Xian border. Allied to *I. graciliflora* and *I. integra.*

Ilex intricata Hooker f. 1875 (synonym *I. intricata* f. *macrophylla* Comber 1933).

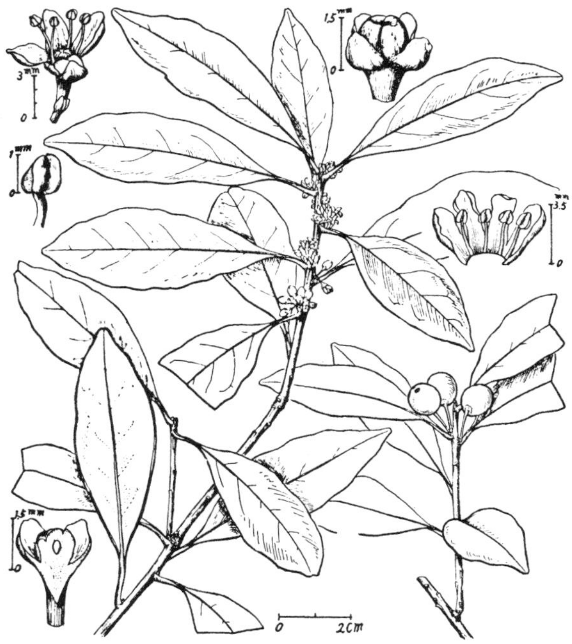

Figure 14-27. *Ilex integra* var. *integra.* Drawing by Chien-chu Chen in *Illustrations of Native and Introduced Ligneous Plants of Taiwan* (1962) by Tang-shui Liu.

Evergreen, glabrous, low, prostate shrubs; leaves small, obovate-elliptic, 5–15 mm (3/16–19/32 in.) long, 3–8 mm (1/8–5/16 in.) wide, shiny, apices obtuse or rotund, bases cuneate, margins serrate, 3–6 teeth on each side, petioles 1–2 mm (1/32–1/16 in.) long; inflorescences axillary on 2nd-year growth, paucifasciculate, fascicles with 1–3 flowers, flowers 4-merous, petals reddish to pale brown; fruits red, globose, 5 mm (3/16 in.) diameter; pyrenes 4, palmately striate, sulcate. Habitat: first described from material collected in northern India; Darjiling, Sikkim and Bhutan; also People's Republic of China, in northwestern Yunnan and southeastern Xizang provinces. Forms low, dense, matted masses on rocky slopes. Seeds were sent to England by F. Kingdom Ward in 1931 from Myanmar. Allied to *I. delavayi.* Related to and often confused with *I. nothofagifolia.*

Ilex inundata Poeppig *ex* Reisseck 1861 (synonyms *I. riparia* Reisseck 1861, *I. macoucoua* Poeppig *ex* Loesener 1901).

Evergreen, glabrous shrubs; leaves oval or oval-oblong, 7–11 cm (2 3/4–4 1/8 in.) long, 2.7–5.2 cm (1 1/16–2 1/6 in.) wide, apices obtuse or acuminate, acumens 6–12 mm (7/32–15/32 in.) long, bases obtuse or acute, margins entire, recurved, petioles 8–12 mm (5/16–15/32 in.) long; inflorescences axillary, 5- to 10-fasciculate, branched, flowers 4-merous; fruits red, ellipsoid; pyrenes 4, smooth. Habitat: Brazil, Amazonas and Para states, and Colombia. Allied to *I. umbellata.*

Ilex jamaicana Proctor 1967.

Evergreen trees to 7 m (23 ft.) tall; leaves obovate, 3–7 cm (1 3/16–2 3/4 in.) long, 1.5–3 cm (19/32–1 3/16 in.) wide, apices bluntly acuminate, bases cuneate, midribs prominent beneath, margins usually entire, petioles 4–8 mm (5/32–5/16 in.) long; inflorescences axillary, solitary or fasciculate, flowers 4- to 5-merous; fruits globose, 5 mm (3/16 in.) diameter, color unknown. Habitat: Jamaica, endemic in wet mossy woodlands on limestone at 758 m (2500 ft.) elevation.

Ilex jaramillara Cuatrecasas 1990 (synonym *I. khasiana* Purkayastha 1938; see *Rev. Acad. Colombo Cienc. Exact. Fis. Nat.* 67: 631. 1990).

Evergreen, small trees, young branches pubescent, lenticels present; leaves elliptic-oblong, 6–12.5 cm (2 3/8–5 in.) long, 3–4.5 cm (1 3/16–1 3/4 in.) wide, apices long-acuminate, mucronate tips, bases rotund to acute, margins serrate-crenate, pubescent, oblong midribs, petioles 10–16 mm (3/8–15/32 in.) long; inflorescences axillary, solitary, branched, flowers 4-merous; fruit ovoid-globose, 6 mm (7/32 in.) long, 4 mm (5/32 in.) wide, color unknown; pyrenes 4. Habitat: India, Assam, Khasi Hills, at 1212–1818 m (4000–6000 ft.) elevation.

Ilex jauaensis Steyermark 1988.

Evergreen, large shrubs to 4 m (14 ft.) tall, branchlets glabrous; leaves oblong-obovate, 4–5.5 cm (1 3/4–2 1/8 in.) long, 2–3 cm (3/4–1 3/16 in.) wide, punctate beneath, bases acute to subacute, apices rotund, retuse, margins entire, petioles 5 mm (3/16 in.) long; inflorescences axillary, solitary, 1-flowered, lateral; fruits subglobose, 9–10 mm (11/32–3/8 in.) diameter, pedicels 13–14 mm (1/2–17/32 in.) long; pyrenes trigonous, prominent marginal ridges. Habitat: Venezuela, Bolivar, Mesta de Jaua, Cerro Jaua in forest along tributary of Rio Marajano at 1750–1800 m (5775–5940 ft.) elevation. Similar to *I. chimantaensis* and *I. tiricae.*

Ilex javanica Koorders & Valeton 1914.

Evergreen, large trees to 35 m (115 ft.) tall; leaves elliptic to obovate, 6.5–10 cm (2 1/2–4 in.) long, 2.8–4.5 cm (1 1/8–1 3/4 in.) wide, bases acute or subattenuate, apices obtuse or acute-acuminate, distinct mucronate, margins entire, petioles 3–7 mm (1/8–9/32 in.) long; inflorescences axillary, solitary, 2- to 5-flowered, peduncles 10–12 mm (3/8–15/32 in.) long; fruits globose. Habitat: Indonesia, Java. Allied to *I. alternifolia.*

Ilex jelskii Zahlbruckner 1895.

Evergreen, pubescent, large shrubs or trees; leaves oval or elliptic-ovate, 5.5–8 cm (2⅛–3⅛ in.) long, 2–3.5 cm (¾–1⅜ in.) wide, apices acute or acuminate, bases obtuse or cuneate-obtuse, margins entire, recurved, petioles 8–13 mm (5/16–19/32 in.) long; inflorescences axillary, 5- to 10-fasciculate, branched, flowers 4- to 5-merous; fruits black, ovoid; pyrenes 4. Habitat: Peru, near Tombillo. Allied to *I. micrantha.*

Ilex jenmanii Loesener 1901.

Evergreen, large shrubs or small trees 6–10 m (20–33 ft.) tall; leaves oval or oval-oblong, 9.5–13.5 cm (3¾–5 5/16 in.) long, 3.3–6.5 cm (1 5/16–2⅜ in.) wide, apices acuminate or acute, bases cuneate-obtuse or obtuse, margins entire, recurved; inflorescences axillary, fasciculate, branched, flowers 4- to 5-merous; fruits subglobose; pyrenes 4, smooth. Habitat: Guyana near Demerara. Allied to *I. daphnogenea.*

Ilex jiaolingensis C.-j. Tseng 1981.

Evergreen trees to 30 m (98 ft.) tall, branchlets angulate, pubescent; leaves narrow-elliptic or elliptic-lanceolate, 4.5–6 cm (1¾–2⅜ in.) long, 1.4–2.1 cm (17/32–¾ in.) wide, apices acuminate, acumens 5–10 mm (3/16–⅜ in.) long bases cuneate, margins entire, petioles 5–7 mm (3/16–9/32 in.) long; inflorescences axillary on current, 2nd-, and 3rd-year growth, 5- to 6-fasciculate, single, flowers 4-merous, pubescent ovaries; fruits unknown, probably red and pubescent. Habitat: People's Republic of China, Guangdong Province. Distinct from related species by the pubescent ovaries.

Ilex jinggangshanensis C.-j. Tseng 1981.

Evergreen, small trees 5 m (16 ft.) tall, young branchlets blackish, angulate, pubescent; leaves elliptic-lanceolate or elliptic, 6–10 cm (2⅜–4 in.) long, 2–3 cm (¾–1 3/16 in.) wide, apices acuminate, bases cuneate, glabrous, midribs pubescent, margins inconspicuously serrulate or subentire, petioles 5–6 mm (3/16–7/32 in.) long, densely pubescent; inflorescences cymose, with 1–2 fruits, solitary, axillary, peduncles 6–10 mm (7/32–⅜ in.) long, pedicels 5–6 mm (3/16–7/32 in.) long, both pubescent; fruits red, globose, 5 mm (3/16 in.) diameter, calyces persistent; pyrenes 4. Habitat: People's Republic of China, Jiangxi Province. Allied to *I. purpurea.*

Ilex jiuwanshanensis C.-j. Tseng 1981.

Evergreen, large shrubs 4 m (13 ft.) tall, young branchlets blackish purple, glabrous; leaves linear-lanceolate 11–13 cm (4⅜–5⅛ in.) long, 1.1–2.3 cm (7/16–⅞ in.) wide, apices long acuminate, acumens 1 cm (⅜ in.) long, decurrent into tip, glabrous, margins entire, petioles 1 cm (⅜ in.) long, flat and winged; inflorescences cymose, with 1–3 fruits, solitary, axillary, peduncles 7 mm (9/32 in.) long, pedicels 2–4 mm (1/16–5/32 in.) long; fruits red, globose, 7 mm (9/32 in.) diameter; pyrenes 5, smooth or wide canaliculate. Habitat: People's Republic of China, Guangxi Province. Allied to *I. lancilimba.*

Ilex johnstonii Merrill 1950 (synonym *I. gracilipes* I. M. Johnston 1938, *non* Merrill 1908).

Evergreen shrubs 2.5–3.5 m (8⅕–11⅘ ft.) tall, upright spreading, branches minutely pubescent; leaves ovate or lanceolate, 3–5 cm (1 3/16–2 in.) long 13–24 mm (½–15/16 in.) wide, bases obtuse or acute, apices acute or briefly acuminate, petioles minutely pubescent, 3–6 mm (1 3/16–7/32 in.) long; margins obscurely undulate, entire or sparsely dentate near apex, revolute; inflorescences solitary, single flowers, flowers and fruits on new growth; fruits immature, subglobose, 4 mm (5/32 in.) diameter, 6 locules. Habitat: Guatemala, Soloma, Department Huehuetenango, at 2200 m (7260 ft.) elevation. Allied to *I. coriacea.*

Ilex julianii Edwin 1963.

Evergreen trees, glabrous, to 15 m (50 ft.) tall, older wood dark to light gray, striate, lenticels raised; leaves usually elliptic-oblong, 6–10 cm (2⅜–4 in.) long, 2–6 cm (¾–2⅜ in.) wide, bases rotund-obtuse, apices acute to tapered-acuminate, acumens lance-triangular, margins serrulate occasionally serrulate-denticulate, decurrent petioles 7–11 mm (9/32–7/16 in.) long; male inflorescences axillary, on old wood, plurifasciculate, to 10–16 flowers per fascicle, flowers usually 4-merous, peduncles 6–10 mm (7/32–⅜ in.) long, branched cymose, 3 pedicels; fruits unknown. Habitat: Venezuela, Distrito Federal, cloud forest on Fila Maestra, near Estado Aragua border at 2000–2200 m (6600–7260 ft.) elevation. Allied possibly to *I. retusa.*

Ilex karstenii Loesener 1901.

Evergreen; leaves obovate-elliptic, 9–12 cm (3½–4¾ in.) long, 4–5 cm (1⅝–2 in.) wide, bases usually acute, apices obtuse to acute, margins crenulate-serrulate; inflorescences axillary, solitary, branched, usually 5-flowered, peduncles 10–14 mm (⅜–17/32 in.) long, pedicels 3–4 mm (⅛–5/32 in.) long; fruits black, slightly depressed-globose, 4–5 mm (5/32–3/16 in.) diameter. Habitat: Colombia, near Popayán. Allied to *I. anonoides.*

Ilex karuaiana Steyermark 1952. Tarebi-yek.

Evergreen trees to 8–13 m (26–33 ft.) tall, branchlets glabrous; leaves ovate or lanceolate-elliptic, 5–9 cm (2–3½ in.) long, 1.3–4 cm (½–1⅝ in.) wide, obscurely punctate or epunctate beneath, bases acute, apices acute, acuminate, or subcuspidate, cuneate, margins remotely appressed serrulate, petioles 5–7 mm (3⁄16–9⁄32 in.) long; inflorescences axillary, fasciculate, subumbellate, 5- to 12-flowered; fruits subglobose, 4.5 mm (11⁄64 in.) diameter, pedicels 2.5–4 mm (3⁄32–5⁄32 in.) long. Habitat: Venezuela, Bolivar, in dense forest at base of Ptari-tepui along Rio Karuai at 1220 m (4025 ft.) elevation. Allied to *I. brevicuspis.*

Ilex kaushue S.-y. Hu 1949.

Evergreen trees, branches densely puberulent; leaves oblong or oblong-elliptic, 10–18 cm (4–7 3⁄16 in.) long, 4.5–7.5 cm (1 3⁄4–3 in.) wide, apices acute or briefly acuminate, bases obtuse or cuneate, margins serrate or doubly serrate, petioles slender 20–22 mm (3⁄4–13⁄16 in.) long, pubescent; inflorescences fasciculate or pseudoracemose, pedicels 8 mm (5⁄16 in.) long; fruits red, subglobose or ellipsoid, 11 mm (15⁄32 in.) long, 9–10 mm (11⁄32–3⁄8 in.) diameter, pubescent; pyrenes 4, reticulate striate, and sulcate, wrinkled and pitted. Habitat: People's Republic of China, endemic to Hainan Province. Allied to *I. latifolia.*

Ilex kengii S.-y. Hu 1950 f. *kengii.*

Evergreen trees to 10–12 m (33–40 ft.) tall, branchlets glabrous, lenticels numerous; leaves elliptic or ovate-elliptic, 4.5–11 cm (1 3⁄4–4 3⁄8 in.) long, 2–5 cm (3⁄4–2 in.) wide, punctate beneath, apices acuminate, acumens 10–15 mm (3⁄8–19⁄32 in.) long, bases obtuse, margins entire, petioles 7–13 mm (9⁄32–1⁄2 in.) long; inflorescences axillary on 2nd-year growth, pseudofasciculate, peduncles 3–8 mm (1⁄8–5⁄16 in.) long, pedicels 4–5 mm (5⁄32–3⁄16 in.) long, flowers 4-merous; fruits red, globose, 3 mm (1⁄8 in.) diameter; pyrenes 4, 5- to 6-striate. Habitat: People's Republic of China, mixed forest in Zhejiang, Guizhou, and Guangxi provinces. Allied to *I. longecaudata* and *I. wilsonii.*

Ilex kengii f. *tiantangshanensis* C.-j. Tseng 1981.

A form with puberulent branchlets, petioles, leaf midveins, and pedicels. Habitat: People's Republic of China, Guizhou and Guangxi provinces. Possibly not meriting botanical recognition.

Ilex ketambensis T. R. Dudley 1983.

Evergreen trees to 15 m (50 ft.) tall, branchlets reddish brown, puberulent, remotely scattered minute stellate and simple hairs; leaves lanceolate, 17–21 cm (6 3⁄4–8 1⁄4 in.) long, glossy, glabrous, bases cuneate, attenuate into petioles, apices acuminate, acumens 5–10 mm (3⁄16–3⁄8 in.) long, margins narrowly revolute, entire and sinuate, rarely minutely, and irregularly serrulate at apex, petioles grooved, 1–1.5 cm (3⁄8–19⁄32 in.) long; female inflorescences axillary, solitary, pedicels 4–10 mm (5⁄32–3⁄8 in.) long, glabrous; fruits ovoid, 20–25 mm (3⁄4–1 in.) diameter, color unknown, largest recorded fruit size to date (1983) for the genus, calyces persistent; pyrenes 4, dorsal surface tri-ribbed. Habitat: Indonesia, Sumatra, north, apparently endemic to Mount Ketambe in Gunung Leuser National Reserve. Allied to *I. borneensis.*

Ilex kingiana Cockerell 1911 (synonyms *I. insignis* Hooker f. 1875, *I. nobilis* Gumbleton 1887).

Evergreen, glabrous, small trees to 10 m (33 ft.) tall, branchlets glabrous, thick, grooved; leaves elliptic or elliptic-oblong, 10–23 cm (4–9 3⁄16 in.) long, 5–8 cm (2–3 1⁄8 in.) wide, bases cuneate to obtuse, apices acute, with short acumens, margins recurved, usually remotely serrulate to serrate, or spiny denticulate, petioles 9–25 mm (11⁄32–2 in.) long; inflorescences fasciculate, axillary; fruits red, globose or ellipsoidal, 6–10 mm (7⁄32–3⁄8 in.) diameter; pyrenes 1–4, striate, sulcate. Habitat: India, near Sikkim, Darjiling and Bhutan, at 2000–3000 m (6600–9900 ft.) elevation. Allied to *I. dipyrena, I. latifolia,* and *I. pseudo-odorata.*

Ilex kirinsanensis Nakai 1953.

Evergreen, low shrubs 0.5 m (20 in.) tall, branches lenticellate; leaves glandular, punctate beneath, elliptic or ovate-elliptic to oblong to obovate-oblong, margins crenate, inconspicuous serrulate; fruits globose, dark purple, 8–11 mm (5⁄16–7⁄16 in.) wide, peduncles 5–6 mm (3⁄16–7⁄32 in.) long. Habitat: Taiwan, Etjigo Province, on Mount Kirinzan. Allied to *I. sugerokii* var. *brevipedunculata.*

Ilex × *kiusiana* Hatusima 1936. Narihira mochi.

Naturally occurring hybrids of *I. buergeri* × *I. integra.* Evergreen shrubs to 4 m (14 ft.) tall; leaves 6–9 cm (2 3⁄8–3 1⁄2 in.) long; inflorescences peduncled, pedicels 6–8 mm (7⁄32–5⁄16 in.) long; fruits unknown. Habitat: Japan, northern Kyushu.

Ilex kleinii Edwin 1967.

Evergreen, small trees to 6 m (20 ft.) tall, glabrous; leaves elliptic, 2.5–4.5 cm (1–1 3⁄4 in.) long, 10–16 mm (3⁄8–5⁄8 in.) wide, apices mucronate, margins serrate, dentate, petioles 8–10 mm (5⁄8–3⁄8 in.) long; inflorescences solitary, 4–7 flowers, peduncles long, 3.2 cm (1 1⁄4 in.) long, pedicels 8–10 mm (5⁄16–3⁄8 in.) long, flowers 4-merous. Habitat: Brazil, Santa Catarina.

Ilex kobuskiana S.-y. Hu 1950.

Evergreen shrubs or small trees to 20 m (65 ft.) tall, branchlets glabrous; leaves ovate or oblong-elliptic, 4.5–9 cm (1 3⁄4–3 1⁄2 in.) long, 1.5–4 cm (1 3⁄16–1 5⁄8 in.) wide, apices obtuse or retuse, abruptly acuminate, acumens 5–7 mm (³⁄₁₆–⁹⁄₃₂ in.) long, bases rotund or obtuse, margins entire, petioles 9–12 mm (¹¹⁄₃₂–¹⁵⁄₃₂ in.) long; inflorescences axillary and fasciculate on 2nd-year growth, flowers 5- to 6-merous; fruits red, globose ovoid, 4 mm (⁵⁄₃₂ in.) diameter, calyces persistent; pyrenes 6, striate. Habitat: People's Republic of China, Hainan and eastern Guangdong provinces. Allied to *I. wilsonii*.

Ilex × koehneana Loesener 1919.
Natural or artificial hybrids of *I. aquifolium × I. latifolia*; first reported from cultivation in Florence, Italy, by Joseph Gaeta. Evergreen trees to 18 m (60 ft.) tall; leaves very variable, usually elliptic, 10–16 cm (4–6½ in.) long, 5.8–8 cm (2¼–3⅛ in.) wide, bases cuneate to obtuse, apices acuminate, margins spiny, petioles 10–16 mm (⅜–⅝ in.) long; inflorescences axillary, on old wood, flowers usually 4-merous; fruits red. A great many artificial hybrids that are usually intermediate between the two parents exist. See interspecific evergreen holly list in Chapter 16.

Figure 14-28. *Ilex × koehneana*. Photo by Barton Bauer Sr.

Ilex krugiana Loesener 1893 f. *krugiana*. Krug's holly (synonyms *I. montana* G. Garden & Brace 1889, *I. macoucoua* G. Garden & Brace 1889, *I. krugiana* f. *pacipertensis* Loesener 1919).
Evergreen trees 8–10 m (26–33 ft.) tall, branchlets glabrous, lenticels present; leaves ovate or ovate-elliptic, 5.5–9.5 cm (2⅛–3¾ in.) long, 2–4 cm (¾–1⅝ in.) wide, apices acute or acuminate, bases subrotund or obtuse, margins recurved, entire, petioles 10–22 mm (⅜–¹³⁄₁₆ in.) long; inflorescences axillary, 1- to 3-fasciculate, 1- to 3-flowered, flowers 4-merous; fruits black, globose, 4–5 mm (⁵⁄₃₂–³⁄₁₆ in.) diameter, pedicels 10 mm (⅜ in.) long; pyrenes 4.

Habitat: United States, Florida, Dade County, Haiti, and other islands of the Caribbean. Allied to *I. brevicuspis*.

Ilex krugiana f. *pacipertensis* Loesener 1919.
A form with large leaves, 6.5–11 cm (2½–4⅜ in.) long, 2.8–4.4 cm (1⅛–1²⁹⁄₃₂ in.) wide, margins entire or with very small teeth. Habitat: Haiti.

Ilex kudingcha C.-j. Tseng 1981.
Evergreen trees 6–20 m (20–65 ft.) tall, branchlets glabrous, angulate, gray brown; leaves oblong-elliptic or lanceolate-elliptic, 14–28 cm (5½–11 in.) long, 6–8 cm (2⅜–3⅛ in.) wide, apices shortly acuminate or obtuse, bases attenuate, margins serrulate, serrations slightly obtuse, black-apiculate, petioles 1.7–2 cm (²¹⁄₃₂–¾ in.) long, winged, glabrous; male inflorescences axillary, pseudopaniculate, fasciculate, branched, female inflorescences pseudoracemose, branched, peduncles stout, 4–6 mm (⁵⁄₃₂–⁷⁄₃₂ in.) long, pedicels stout, 8–10 mm (⁵⁄₁₆–⅜ in.) long; fruits red, globose, 1–1.2 cm (⅜–¹⁵⁄₃₂ in.) diameter; pyrenes 4, reticulate striate, and sulcate. Habitat: People's Republic of China, Guangxi and Guangdong provinces. Called "poor man's tea," leaves used for a hot season drink. Allied to *I. kaushue*.

Ilex kunmingensis H.-w. Li *ex* Y.-r. Li 1985 var. *kunmingensis*.
Evergreen, glabrous shrubs 2 m (6 ft.) tall, branchlets angulate-sulcate; leaves obovate-oblong or elliptic-lanceolate, rarely elliptic, 5.5–7.5 cm (2⅛–3 in.) long, 1.7–2.5 cm (²¹⁄₃₂–1 in.) wide, apices abruptly acuminate or long-acuminate, bases wide-cuneate, margins sparingly serrate, petioles 5–9 mm (³⁄₁₆–¹¹⁄₃₂ in.) long; flowers unknown; fruits (immature) subglobose, 4 mm (⁵⁄₃₂ in.) diameter, pedicels 2–3 mm (¹⁄₁₆–⅛ in.) long, calyces persistent, stigmas thick-disciform; pyrenes 4, smooth. Habitat: People's Republic of China, Yunnan Province, at 2100–2300 m (6900–7600 ft.) elevation. Allied to *I. corallina*.

Ilex kunmingensis var. *capitata* Y.-r. Li 1985.
A variety differing from typical individuals by having larger leaves, 5–8 cm (2–3⅛ in.) long, 2–3 cm (¾–1³⁄₁₆ in.) wide, sparsely puberulent fruiting pedicels, 3.5–5 mm (1⅜–2 in.) long, and by capitate stigmas. Habitat: People's Republic of China, Yunnan Province.

Ilex kunthiana Triana 1862. Palo mulato (synonyms *I. paltoria* Kunth 1824, *I. elliptica* Willdenow 1830, *I. kunthiana* f. *funckii* Loesener 1901, *I. kunthiana* f. *genuiana* Loesener 1901, *I. kunthiana* f. *purdiaei* Loesener 1901).

Evergreen shrubs, dense erect habit; leaves oval or obovate to narrowly elliptic-lanceolate, 1.8–3.2 cm (¹¹⁄₁₆–1⁹⁄₃₂ in.) long, 6–16 mm (⁷⁄₃₂–⅝ in.) wide, occasionally punctate beneath, apices obtuse or rotund, bases obtuse or rotund, margins recurved, entire at base, serrulate toward apex, petioles 2–4 mm (¹⁄₁₆–⁵⁄₃₂ in.) long; inflorescences axillary, solitary, fasciculate, flowers 4-merous or 4- to 5-merous; fruits ellipsoid; pyrenes unknown. Habitat: Colombia, near Bogota, at 3000 m (9900 ft.) elevation, and Venezuela. Allied to *I. ovalis*.

Ilex kwangtungensis Merrill 1927. Guangdong holly (synonyms *I. kwangtungensis* var. *pilosior* Handel-Mazzetti 1933, *I. kwangtungensis* var. *pilosissima* Handel-Mazzetti 1933, *I. shweliensis* Comber 1933, *I. latifrons* Chun 1934, *I. latifrons* var. *pilosissima* (Handel-Mazzetti) Chun 1934, *I. phanerophlebia* Merrill 1934).

Evergreen, small trees to 9 m (30 ft.) tall, branchlets puberulent; leaves persistent on 3rd-year growth, ovate-elliptic or oblong or lanceolate, 7–16 cm (2¾–6⅜ in.) long, 3–6 cm (1³⁄₁₆–2⅜ in.) wide, bases rounded or obtuse, apices acuminate, margins subentire, or minutely serrate, slightly recurved, curly villose beneath, and along midrib, petioles 10–18 mm (⅜–1¹⁄₁₆ in.) long; inflorescences axillary on new growth, 3- to 7-flowered cymes, pubescent, flowers pink or red; fruits red, ellipsoid, 12 mm (¹⁵⁄₃₂ in.) long, 9 mm (¹¹⁄₃₂ in.) diameter, persistent calyces; pyrenes 4, smooth, deep and broadly canaliculate. Habitat: southeastern People's Republic of China, Zhejiang, Fujian, Guangdong, and Hainan provinces. Allied to *I. purpurea*.

Ilex lacunosa (Miquel) Loesener 1901 (synonym *Prinos lacunosa* Miquel 1857).

Evergreen, small trees to 5 m (16 ft.) tall, young branches pubescent; leaves oval to elliptic, 2.5–6.5 cm (1–2½ in.) long, 1.3–3.5 cm (½–1⅜ in.) wide, margins, entire to very minute serrulate, recurved, bases rounded, apices rounded with small protrusion; inflorescences axillary, peduncles branched, 5–6 petals; fruits depressed-globose to ovoid; pyrenes 8–12. Habitat: Indonesia, north Sumatra in mountainous region at 1000 m (3300 ft.) elevation, in Batak Province, also near Tamahurung and Goedrin-baru. Allied to *I. cymosa*.

Ilex lancilimba Merrill 1929.

Evergreen trees to 10 m (33 ft.) tall, yellowish-pubescent branchlets; leaves glabrous, lanceolate, 8–14 cm (3⅛–5½ in.) long, 2–4 cm (¾–1⅝ in.) wide, bases cuneate or obtuse, apices acute or shortly acuminate, margins entire, petioles 15–25 mm (¹⁹⁄₃₂–1 in.) long; inflorescences axillary, 3-flowered cymes, peduncles 2 mm (¹⁄₁₆ in.) long, pedicels 1–2 mm (¹⁄₃₂–¹⁄₁₆ in.) long, staminate flowers pink to purplish, pistillate flowers greenish white; fruits red, globose, usually solitary, 10–12 mm (⅜–¹⁵⁄₃₂ in.) diameter, persistent calyces; pyrenes 4, dorsally broadly canaliculate, widely U-shaped in cross section. Habitat: southeastern People's Republic of China, Guangdong and Hainan provinces, in forests in tropical regions, at 1130 m (3730 ft.) elevation. Allied to *I. tugitakayamensis* of Taiwan.

Ilex lasseri Edwin 1965.

Evergreen trees, branches subglabrous; leaves obovate or cuneate-obovate to elliptic-obovate, 7–9 cm (2¾–3½ in.) long, 2.2–4.2 cm (1³⁄₁₆–1¹¹⁄₁₆ in.) wide, punctate beneath, bases attenuate, spathulate, apices rotund to obtuse, margins entire, revolute, petioles 3.8–5 mm (1½–³⁄₁₆ in.) long; inflorescences axillary, solitary, flowers 4-merous; fruits red, ovoid, 7 mm (⁹⁄₃₂ in.) long, 4 mm (⁵⁄₃₂ in.) diameter; pyrenes 4, unicanaliculate, marginal ridges. Habitat: Venezuela, Oparuma woods, Kavanayen.

Ilex latifolia Thunberg *ex* J. A. Murray 1784. Lusterleaf holly, tara yo, noko ko (synonyms *I. macrophylla* Blume 1825, *non* Wallich 1875, *I. tarajo* Hort. *ex* Goeppert 1854, *I. terago* Anonymous 1859).

Evergreen, glabrous, large trees to 20 m (65 ft.) tall; leaves thick, shiny above, oblong or ovate-oblong, 8–17 cm (3⅛–6¾ in.) long, 4.5–7.5 cm (1¾–3 in.) wide, apices obtuse or shortly acuminate, acumens 3–6 mm (⅛–⁷⁄₃₂ in.) long, bases rotund, margins serrate, petioles thick, 15–20 mm (¹⁹⁄₃₂–¾ in.) long; inflorescences axillary on 2nd-year growth, pseudopaniculate, sessile, 1- to 3-flowered, flowers 4-merous, yellow, fragrant, peduncles 2 mm (¹⁄₁₆ in.) long, uniflorous pedicels 5–8 mm (³⁄₁₆–⁵⁄₁₅ in.) long; fruits red, globose, 7 mm (⁹⁄₃₂ in.) diameter; pyrenes 4, wrinkled, pitted, 3 distinct ridges. Habitat: first recorded in Japan, also native to People's Republic of China, in coastal provinces, reported in Zhejiang and Shandong provinces. Allied to *I. denticulata*. Introduced to Europe by Philipp Franz von Siebold in 1840. Hardy in zones 7b to 10. Wood used for turning, bark for making bird lime, and leaves as a substitute for tea. Selected cultivars have been named in Japan. Plate 68.

Ilex latifolia f. *variegata* Makino 1940.
A form with variegated leaves. Best described as a cultivar. Uncommon in the United States.

Ilex laureola Triana 1872 var. *laureola* (synonym *I. laureola* var. *genuina* Loesener 1901).
Evergreen trees to 12 m (40 ft.) tall, branches pen-

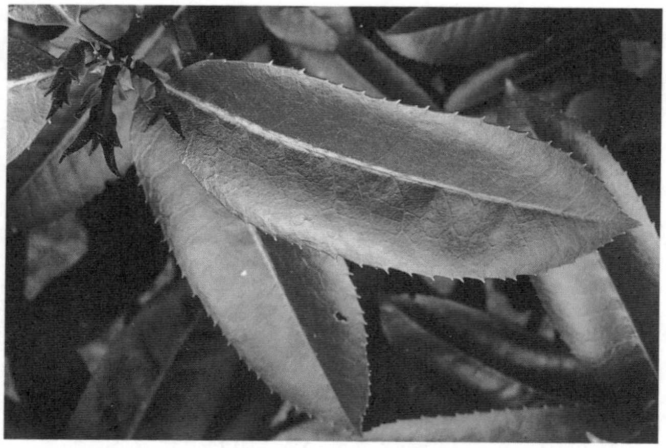

Figure 14-29. *Ilex latifolia.* Photo by Barton Bauer Sr.

dulous; leaves elliptic-oblanceolate, 6.3–14 cm (2½–5½ in.) long, 2.7–5.5 cm (1⅙–2 in.) wide, apices rotund or obtuse and acuminate, bases cuneate-obtuse, margins recurved, subentire or remotely crenulate, petioles 1.7–2.5 cm (²¹⁄₃₂–2 in.) long; inflorescences axillary, fasciculate, 1- to 3-flowered, flowers 4-merous; fruits black (brown), ovoid or ellipsoid 2–2.5 mm (¹⁄₁₆–³⁄₃₂ in.) diameter; pyrenes 4, striate. Habitat: Colombia, near Bogota, Venezuela and Guyana. Allied to *I. affinis.*

Ilex laureola var. *neglecta* Loesener 1901.

A variety differing from the typical species with thick leaves, 1.7–2.5 cm (²¹⁄₃₂–1 in.) long. Habitat: Guyana. Probably at a later date this variety will be regarded as a synonym of the species.

Ilex laurina Kunth 1825, *non* Klotzsch 1849 (synonym *I. daphnogenea* Reisseck).

Evergreen shrubs or trees; leaves lanceolate or elliptic lanceolate, 16–20 cm (6⅜–8 in.) long, 4–5.5 cm (1⅝–2⅛ in.) wide, punctate beneath, apices acuminate, acumen 15 mm (¹⁹⁄₃₂ in.) long, bases acute or cuneate acute, margins recurved, minutely serrulate, petioles 14–17 mm (¹⁷⁄₃₂–²¹⁄₃₂ in.) long; inflorescences axillary, plurifasciculate, branched, flowers 4-merous; fruits unknown. Habitat: tropical South America, possibly from Venezuela, Colombia, or Ecuador. Allied to *I. dioica.*

Ilex laurocerasus Airy Shaw 1939. Kunyatangbukit (synonym *Byronia laurocerasus*).

Evergreen, small trees 2–5 m (6.6–16 ft.) tall; leaves large, 13–25 cm (5⅛–9⅞ in.) long, 5.5–9.3 cm (2⅛–3⅝ in.) wide, bases rotund, often distinctly cordate, apices short-acuminate, margins entire, revolute, petioles very short, nearly sessile; male flowers white, 4- to 5-merous; female flowers and fruits unknown. Habitat: Indonesia, Ulu Koyan, sandy rain forest at 800–900 m (2640–2970 ft.) elevation. Allied to *I. hypoglauca.*

Ilex lechleri Loesener 1901.

Evergreen shrubs, branches upright spreading; leaves oval or ovate to oblong-oval, 1.5 cm (¹⁹⁄₃₂ in.) long, 6–11 mm (⁷⁄₃₂–⁷⁄₁₆ in.) wide, punctate beneath, usually glabrous, apices obtuse or rotund, bases obtuse or acute, margins crenulate-serrulate, petioles 2–3 mm (¹⁄₁₆–⅛ in.) long; inflorescences axillary, solitary, pedunculate, 1- to 3-flowered, flowers 4-merous; fruits unknown. Habitat: Peru. Allied to *I. ovalis* and *I. trichoclada.*

Ilex ledermannii Loesener 1924 (synonyms *I. ledermannii* var. *elliptica* Loesener 1924, *I. ledermannii* var. *ovalis* Loesener 1924).

Evergreen, large shrubs or small trees to 2 m (6 plus ft.) tall; leaves broadly oval or usually elliptic, or oblong-elliptic, 8–14 cm (3⅛–5½ in.) long, 4–8 cm (1⅝–3⅛ in.) wide, margins entire, recurved, bases rotund or obtuse, rarely cuneate, apices obtuse, or usually acuminate; inflorescences axillary, solitary, peduncles 10–20 cm (⅜–¾ in.) long; fruits unknown. Habitat: New Guinea, Papua, Sepik-Gibiet. Allied to *I. brassii.*

Ilex leucoclada (Maximowicz) Makino 1905. Hime mochi (synonym *I. integra* var. *leucoclada* Maximowicz 1881).

Evergreen, small shrubs, branches glabrous, yellowish gray, ascending from a long creeping base; leaves narrow-oblong or broadly oblanceolate or narrow-obovate-oblong, 8–15 cm (3–6 in.) long, 2–4 cm (¾–1⅝ in.) wide, bases acute, apices acute with obtuse tips, margins entire or crenate-serrate on upper margins, petioles 1–1.5 mm (¹⁄₃₂–³⁄₆₄ in.) long; inflorescences axillary; fruits red, globose. Habitat: Japan, Hokkaido and Honshu, in mountain woodlands. Allied to *I. integra.*

Ilex liana S.-y. Hu 1951.

Evergreen trees, stout branches, large buds, elliptic lenticels; leaves glabrous, ovate-oblong, rarely ovate, 5–9 cm (2–3½ in.) long, 4.5–5.5 cm (1¾–2⅛ in.) wide, bases rotund, apices acute, margins crenulate, midribs impressed, 17–18 veins, petioles glabrous, 2 cm (¾ in.) long; inflorescences pseudo-paniculate, axillary, solitary, 1- to 3-flowered, pedicels 5–6 mm (³⁄₁₆–⁷⁄₃₂ in.) long, 2 prophylls; fruits red, globose, 9 mm (¹¹⁄₃₂ in.) diameter, calyces persistent; pyrenes 4, pilose, palmately striate, sulcate to rugose. Habitat: People's Republic of China, Yunnan Province. Allied to *I. sikkimensis.*

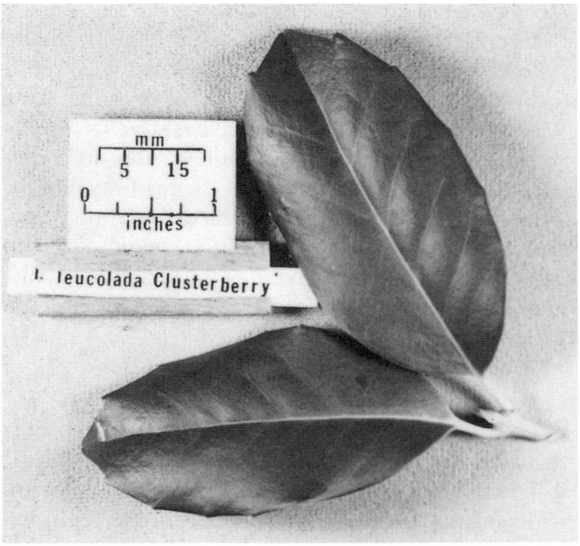

Figure 14-30. *Ilex leucoclada.* Photo by Barton Bauer Sr.

Ilex liangii S.-y. Hu 1949 (synonym *I. hanceana sensu* Merrill & Chun 1934).

Evergreen shrubs, branches plicate, rugose, ridged; leaves oblong-elliptic, 2–5 cm (¾–2 in.) long, 1–2.5 cm (⅜–1 in.) wide, bases obtuse or cuneate, apices obtuse, rotund or retuse, glabrous, margins entire, petioles 4–5 mm (5⁄32–3⁄16 in.) long; inflorescences paucifasciculate on 2nd-year growth, flowers 4-merous; fruits red, globose, 5 mm (3⁄16 in.) diameter; pyrenes 4, 3- to 4-striate. Habitat: People's Republic of China, Hainan Province.

Ilex liebmannii Stanley 1931.

Evergreen shrubs or trees, branchlets minutely pubescent; leaves lanceolate or elliptic-lanceolate, 4.5–5 cm (1¾–2 in.) long, 1–2 cm (⅜–¾ in.) wide, bases acute to obtuse, apices acuminate, margins entire, petioles minutely pubescent, 6–8 mm (7⁄32–5⁄16 in.) long; female inflorescences axillary, solitary, umbellate, 2- to 3-flowered, peduncles slender, 4–13 mm (5⁄32–½ in.) long; fruits subglobose, 3.5 mm (9⁄64 in.) long. Habitat: Mexico: Petlapa, Veracruz State. Allied to *I. cassine* var. *mexicana.*

Ilex liesneri Steyermark 1985.

Evergreen shrubs 1–2 m (3–6 ft.) tall; leaves narrow-elliptic-lanceolate, 4.5–9 cm (1¾–3½ in.) long, 0.5–1.5 cm (3⁄16–19⁄32 in.) wide, sparsely punctate beneath, bases acute, apices long attenuate, margins remotely crenulate-serrulate, 5–13 depressed crenulations on each side, petioles 5–15 mm (3⁄16–19⁄32 in.) long; inflorescences axillary, solitary, cymose, pedunculate, usually 7-flowered, flowers 4-merous; fruits subglobose or ovoid-subglobose, 7 mm (9⁄32 in.) diameter; pyrenes 4–5, dorsally costate. Habitat: Venezuela, Federal Amazonas Territory.

Ilex ligustrina Jacques 1790 (synonyms *I. minutiflora* Richard 1845, *non* Macbride 1951, *I. ligustrina* var. *parviflora* Grisebach 1861, *I. ligustrina* var. *minutiflora* (Richard) Loesener 1892, *I. ligustrina* f. *ekmanii* Loesener 1901, *I. ligustrina* f. *moestrana* Loesener 1901).

Evergreen shrubs or trees, branchlets glabrous; leaves obovate or obovate-oblong, 2.2 to 3.5–6 cm (13⁄16 to 1⅜–2⅜ in.) long, 0.8–2.8 cm (5⁄16–2⅛ in.) wide, apices obtuse or obtuse and notched, bases acute, margins serrulate or crenulate near apex, petioles 1–4 mm (1⁄32–5⁄32 in.) long; inflorescences axillary, 4- to 6-fasciculate, flowers 4-merous; fruits subglobose, 7 mm (9⁄32 in.) diameter; pyrenes 4, striate, sulcate. Habitat: Cuba. Allied to *I. cassine* and *I. grisebachii.*

Ilex lihuaiensis T. R. Dudley 1991 (synonym *I. rivularis* Y.-k. Li 1986, *non* Gardner 1861).

Evergreen shrubs to 2 m (6 ft.) tall, branchlets angulate, buds yellowish brown, branches dark brown, pubescent, angulate later grayish brown; leaves elliptic or obovate-elliptic, (0.7–) 1–3.5 cm ((9⁄32–) ⅜–1⅜ in.) long, (0.4–) 0.7–1.7 cm ((5⁄32–) 9⁄32–⅝ in.) wide, epunctate below, bases cuneate, epunctate below, apices emarginate, notched 0.5–1 mm (1⁄64–1⁄32 in.) deep, margins entire, slightly revolute, petioles 3–9 mm (⅛–11⁄32 in.) long, canaliculate; inflorescences axillary, fasciculate or subfasciculate, male cymes 1- to 3-flowered, peduncles puberulent, 3–6 mm (⅛–7⁄32 in.) long, pedicels puberulent, 4–8 mm (5⁄32–5⁄16 in.) long, female flowers solitary, 6–9 mm (7⁄32–11⁄32 in.) long, flowers 5- to 6-merous, rarely 7-merous, pedicels 6–9 mm (7⁄32–11⁄32 in.) long; fruits red, compressed-globose, 3 mm (⅛ in.) diameter, fruits are smallest of all evergreen species; pyrenes 5–6, rarely 7, dorsal surface tristriate. Habitat: People's Republic of China, Guizhou Province, Libo, Lihua, and Weilao, along streams. Allied to *I. championii* and *I. lohfauensis.*

Ilex lindenii Loesener 1892 (synonym *I. berteroi* Loesener 1892).

Evergreen shrubs; leaves oval, 3–3.5 cm (1 1⁄16–1⅜ in.) long, 1.5–1.8 cm (19⁄32–11⁄16 in.) wide, apices rotund, bases obtuse, margins entire, revolute, petioles 4–6 mm (5⁄32–7⁄32 in.) long; inflorescences axillary, 1- to 3-flowered, fasciculate, flowers 4-merous; fruits red to dark red, subglobose, 4–5 mm (5⁄32–3⁄16 in.) long, 4 mm (5⁄32 in.) wide. Habitat: Cuba. Allied to *I. mandonii.*

Ilex litseaefolia H. H. Hu & Tang 1940 (synonym *I. editicostata* var. *litseaefolia* H. H. Hu & Tang 1941).

Evergreen shrubs to 4 m (13 ft.) tall; leaves elliptic or ovate, 4–7.5 cm (1⅝–3 in.) long, 1.6–3.2 cm (⅝–1¼ in.) wide; inflorescences cymose, peduncles 4–5 mm (5/32–3/16 in.) long, pedicels 2–3 cm (1/16–⅛ in.) long; fruits red, globose, 4–7 mm (5/32–9/32 in.) diameter; pyrenes 6–8, occasionally 5, shallow-canaliculate. Habitat: southeastern People's Republic of China, Zhejiang and Guizhou provinces, at 800–1200 m (2640–3960 ft.) elevation. Allied to *I. editicostata.*

Ilex liukiensis Loesener 1901. Ryukyu-mochi, kuta-mutcha-gara (synonym *I. mertensis* Maximowicz 1885).

Evergreen, glabrous shrubs or small trees to 8 m (26 ft.) tall, branchlets striate, angulate; leaves obovate or oblong-elliptic, 3–7.5 cm (1 3/16–3 in.) long, 1.8–3.5 cm (11/16–1⅜ in.) wide, apices short-acuminate, bases acute, margins crenulate, petioles 8–14 mm (5/16–17/32 in.) long; inflorescences axillary and fasciculate on 2nd-year growth; fruits red, globose, 6–8 mm (7/32–5/16 in.) diameter, pedicels 9–14 mm (11/32–17/32 in.) long; pyrenes 4, rugose, striate. Habitat: Japan, Honshu, Okinawa, the Bonin and Liukiu Islands. Allied to *I. formosana* and *I. graciliflora.*

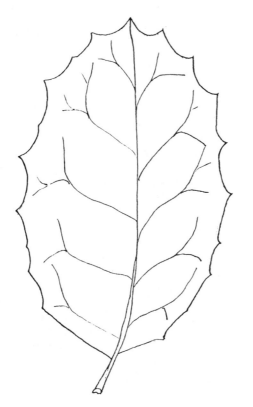

Figure 14-31. *Ilex liukiensis.* Drawing by Randy Allen.

Ilex loeseneri Tardieu 1945.

Evergreen trees 7–8 m (23–26 ft.) tall, branches yellowish, striate, sulcate, small lenticels; leaves elliptic or ovate-elliptic, 6–10 cm (2⅜–4 in.) long, 3.2–4 cm (1¼–1⅝ in.) wide, bases acute, apices abort acuminate, margins undulate, obscurely dentate, petioles canaliculate, 1.5–2 mm (3/64–1/16 in.) long; inflorescences axillary, fasciculate, 1- to 5-flowered, peduncles 1 cm (⅜ in.) long, pedicels 2.3 cm (⅞ in.) long, sepals 6; pyrenes 6, dorsally excavate. Habitat: Vietnam, massif du Phan si pan. Allied to *I. excavata.*

Ilex loheri Merrill 1925.

Evergreen trees, glabrous, branchlets rugose, irregularly angulate; leaves oblong to oblong-elliptic, 9–13 cm (3½–5⅛ in.) long, 3–6 cm (1 3/16–2⅜ in.) wide, bases acute, apices blunt, acuminate, acumens 1–1.5 mm (1/32–3/64 in.) long, margins distinctly and obscurely undulate-crenate, each crenulation with distinct black glands; inflorescences axillary, fasciculate, 2- to 3-flowered, flowers 4-merous, rachises to 5 mm (3/16 in.) long, bracts oblong-ovate, acuminate, 1–2 mm (1/32–1/16 in.) long, bracteoles similar but smaller; fruits unknown. Habitat: Philippines, Luzon, Rizal, Bento. May only be a large-leafed variant of *I. buergeri.*

Ilex lohfauensis Merrill 1918 (synonyms *I. hanceana* var. *anhweiensis* Loesener *ex* Rehder 1927, *I. hanceana* var. *lohfauensis* (Merrill) Chun 1934).

Evergreen, pubescent shrubs to 2 m (6 ft.) tall, branchlets densely pubescent; leaves oblong, rarely obcordate, 1–2.5 cm (⅜–1 in.) long, 5–12 mm (3/16–15/32 in.) wide, apices emarginate or obcordate, ciliate at apex, bases cuneate or rotund, pubescent, margins entire, often ciliate, hirsute above, pilose on both surfaces, petioles 1–2 mm (1/32–1/16 in.) long; inflorescences axillary and fasciculate on 2nd-year growth, 1- to 3-flowered, flowers usually 4-merous; fruits red, globose, 3.5 mm (9/64 in.) diameter, pedicels 1 mm (1/32 in.) long; pyrenes 4, smooth, 3-striate. Habitat: People's Republic of China, common in warm temperate and subtropical climates, southeastern Anhui and Jiangxi provinces, at 200–600 m (660–2000 ft.) elevation. Allied to *I. hanceana.* This taxon is clearly allied to *I. hanceana* and at a later date, after evaluating additional material, might be better regarded as *I. hanceana* var. *lohfauensis* (Merrill) Chun (1934).

Ilex longecaudata Comber 1933 var. *longecaudata.*

Evergreen trees to 9 m (30 ft.) tall, branchlets slender, lenticels sparse; leaves ovate-elliptic to elliptic, 4–9 cm (1⅝–11/32 in.) long, 10–25 mm (⅜–1 in.) wide, punctate beneath, apices narrow-caudate, acumens 7–20 mm (⁹⁄₃₂–¾ in.) long, tip sharp pointed, bases obtuse or rotund, margins entire, petioles slender, 6–12 mm (⁷⁄₃₂–¹⁵⁄₃₂ in.) long; inflorescences axillary on 2nd-year growth, fasciculate or pseudoracemose, puberulent, pedicels 2–3 mm (¹⁄₁₆–⅛ in.) long, flowers 4- to 5-merous; fruits red, globose, 3–4 mm (⅛–⁵⁄₃₂ in.) diameter, stigmas elevated, styles evident; pyrenes 5, 3-striate. Habitat: People's Republic of China, endemic to Yunnan Province at 1400–2700 m (4600–8900 ft.) elevation. There seems to be some affinity with *I. crenata, I. embelioides,* and *I. triflora.*

Ilex longecaudata var. *glabra* S.-y. Hu 1950.
A variety differing from typical individuals with thick leathery leaves and with lateral veins obscure; glabrous petioles and pedicels; smaller calyces, prominent stigmas, and shorter styles; pyrenes 4. Habitat: People's Republic of China, Yunnan Province.

Ilex longipetiolata Loesener 1901 (synonym *I. integerrima* var. *longipetulata* Hochreutiner 1941).
Evergreen trees, glabrous; leaves oblong or oval-oblong, 5.5–10 cm (2⅛–4 in.) long, 3–4 cm (1³⁄₁₆–1⅝ in.) wide, apices acuminate, bases cuneate-obtuse or cuneate-acute, margins entire, revolute, petioles 2.7–4.3 cm (1¹⁄₁₆–1¹¹⁄₁₆ in.) long; inflorescences fasciculate in leaf axils, flowers 4- to 5-merous; fruits black, depressed-ovoid, 7–9 mm (⁹⁄₃₂–¹¹⁄₃₂ in.) diameter; peduncles 6 mm (⁷⁄₃₂ in.) long, pedicels 2 mm (¹⁄₁₆ in.) long; pyrenes 4–5. Habitat: Brazil, Mount Alto Machahe near Nova Friburgo. Allied to *I. integerrima* and *I. psammophila.*

Ilex longipilosa Steyermark 1988.
Evergreen shrubs 1.5 m (5 ft.) tall, branches densely hirtellous with spreading hairs to 0.5 mm (¹⁄₆₄ in.) long; leaves cuneiform-obovate or suborbiculate-ovate, 4–7 mm (1⅝–2¾ in.) long, 2.5–5.5 cm (1–2⅛ in.) wide, minutely punctate beneath, bases cuneate, apices rotund, abruptly apiculate, margins usually entire, rarely 1–2 minute toothlike projections, slightly revolute, petioles densely hirtellous, 3–7 mm (⅛–⁹⁄₃₂ in.) long; inflorescences axillary, solitary, lateral, cymose or paniculate, peduncles 4–9 mm (⁵⁄₃₂–¹¹⁄₃₂ in.) long, pedicels 1.5–2 mm (³⁄₆₄–¹⁄₁₆ in.) long, flowers 4-merous; fruits unknown. Habitat: Venezuela, Bolivar, south of El Pauji, nonforested southern slope and summit of El Abismo, at 800–1050 m (2600–3465 ft.) elevation. Allied to *I. maguirei, I. velutina,* and *I. villosula.*

Ilex longzhouensis C.-j. Tseng 1984.
Evergreen trees to 12 m (40 ft.) tall, new branchlets dense reddish brown villose, 2nd-year growth loosely pubescent, lenticels subelevated orbicular or

elliptic; leaves pubescent, ovate-elliptic, rarely ovate, 5–8 cm (5–3⅛ in.) long, 2.5–3.5 cm (1–1⅜ in.) wide, bases obtuse or rotund, apices short-acuminate, margins repand-crenulate, petioles 2–5 mm (¹⁄₁₆–³⁄₁₆ in.) long; flowers unknown; infructescences cymose, single, axillary, with 1–3 fruits, peduncles 3–5 mm (⅛–³⁄₁₆ in.) long, pedicels 2–3 mm (¹⁄₁₆–⅛ in.) long, both dense reddish brown villose; fruits red, subglobose, 6.5 mm (¼ in.) diameter; pyrenes 5, dorsally unicanaliculate. Habitat: People's Republic of China, Guangxi Province, in open forest at 550 m (1800 ft.) elevation. Resembles *I. ferruginea.*

Ilex lonicerifolia Hayata 1913 var. *lonicerifolia.*
Evergreen, small trees, branchlets densely pubescent, lenticels few; leaves variable in size, oblong, oblong-elliptic, rarely ovate-elliptic, 8–11 cm (3⅛–4¼ in.) long, 2–4.5 cm (¾–1¾ in.) wide, bases obtuse, rarely rounded, apices short acuminate, rarely acute, sometimes rounded, margins entire, petioles 4–8 mm (⁵⁄₃₂–⁵⁄₁₆ in.) long; inflorescences axillary on new growth, subumbelliform, peduncles 1–2 cm (⅜–¾ in.) long, pubescent, pedicels 4–6 mm (⁵⁄₃₂–⁷⁄₃₂ in.) long; fruits red, ovoid-globose, 5–7 mm (³⁄₁₆–⁹⁄₃₂ in.) diameter, borne singly or in clusters, persistent calyces; pyrenes 5–6, concave on dorsal surface. Habitat: central and northern Taiwan, in forests, at 700–1000 m (2300–3300 ft.) elevation. Allied to *I. purpurea.*

Ilex lonicerifolia var. *hakkuensis* (Yamamoto) S.-y. Hu 1949 (synonym *I. hakkuensis* Yamamoto 1925).
Evergreen trees, branchlets glabrous, lenticels conspicuous; leaves oblong-elliptic, 5–11 cm (2–4¼ in.) long, 2–4.5 cm (¾–1¾ in.) wide, bases obtuse, apices acuminate, margins entire. Habitat: Taiwan.

Ilex loranthoides Martius 1861.
Evergreen, glabrous shrubs; leaves sub-rhomboid to ovate, 7–12 cm (2¾–4¾ in.) long, 3–4 cm (1³⁄₁₆–1⅝ in.) wide, bases obtuse to acute, apices acuminate, acumens 9–30 mm (¹¹⁄₃₂–1³⁄₁₆ in.) long, margins thick, entire, petioles 30–40 mm (1³⁄₁₆–1⅝ in.) long; inflorescences solitary, axillary, glabrous, open and loose branching, long slender peduncles 20–30 mm (¾–1³⁄₁₆ in.) long, pedicels 2–9 mm (¹⁄₁₆–¹¹⁄₃₂ in.) long, flowers 4-merous; fruits black, subglobose, 4 mm (⁵⁄₃₂ in.) long, 3.5 mm (⁷⁄₆₄ in.) wide; pyrenes 4, unisulcate. Habitat: southern Brazil.

Ilex loretoica Loesener 1905.
Evergreen, glabrous shrubs to 3 m (10 ft.) tall; leaves elliptic or obovate-elliptic, 12–18.5 cm (4¾–7⅜ in.) long, 5–9 cm (2–3½ in.) wide, apices obtuse or rotund, bases obtuse, margins recurved, re-

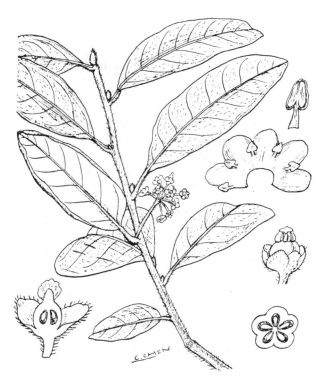

Figure 14-32. *Ilex lonicerifolia* var. *lonicerifolia*. Drawing by Chien-chu Chen in *Illustrations of Native and Introduced Ligneous Plants of Taiwan* (1962) by Tang-shui Liu.

motely serrulate, petioles 2–6 mm (¹⁄₁₆–⁷⁄₃₂ in.) long; inflorescences axillary, multifasciculate, branched, flowers 4-merous; fruits unknown. Habitat: Peru, Loreto region, at 1500–1600 m (4950–5280 ft.) elevation. Allied to *I. nervosa*.

Ilex ludianensis S.-c. Huang *ex* Y.-r. Li 1985.
Evergreen shrubs 1.5–3 m (5–10 ft.) tall, branchlets angulate, densely tomentose; leaves ovate or ovate-elliptic, 4–5 cm (1⅝–2 in.) long, 1.8–2.6 cm (1¹¹⁄₁₆–2 in.) wide, densely tomentose beneath, bases rotund, or rarely wide cuneate, apices acuminate, margins sparsely serrate, petioles 3–5 mm (⅛–³⁄₁₆ in.) long; inflorescences axillary, solitary; fruits red, globose, 7–8 mm (⁹⁄₃₂–⁵⁄₁₆ in.) diameter, pedicels densely tomentose, 1–1.3 cm (⅜–½ in.) long, persistent calyces; pyrenes 5. Habitat; People's Republic of China, Yunnan Province, mountain forests at 1400 m (4600 ft.) elevation. Allied to *I. yunnanensis*.

Ilex lundii Warming f. *lundii* 1880 (synonym *I. lundii* f. *claussemiana* Loesener 1901).
Evergreen, small trees; leaves obovate or oval or elliptic, 6.5–10 cm (2½–4 in.) long, 2.5–4 cm (1–1⅝ in.) wide, apices acuminate, mucros 1–3 mm

(¹⁄₃₂–⅛ in.) long, bases obtuse or acute, margins entire, recurved, petioles 6–15 mm (⁷⁄₃₂–¹⁹⁄₃₂ in.) long; inflorescences fasciculate in leaf axils, 1- to 3-flowered pedunculate, flowers 4- to 6-merous; fruits black, subglobose, 3.5 mm (⁷⁄₆₄ in.) long, 3 mm (⅛ in.) wide; pyrenes unknown. Habitat: Brazil, Minas Gerais State. Allied to *I. sapiiformis*.

Ilex lundii f. *ignatiana* Loesener 1901.
A form with leaves pubescent beneath on midribs and veins. Habitat: Brazil, Minas Gerais State. This forma probably does not merit formal botanical recognition.

Ilex lymanii Edwin 1965.
Evergreen shrubs to 4 m (13 ft.) tall, branchlets sparsely puberulent; leaves obovate or broadly elliptic-obovate, 5–5.6 cm (2–2⅛ in.) long, 2–3.5 cm (¾–1⅜ in.) wide, punctate beneath, bases acute or acuminate, apices obtuse or orbiculate, retuse or acute short acumens, rarely retuse, margins entire, revolute, petioles more than 5 mm (³⁄₁₆ in.) long; inflorescences axillary, solitary, racemose, flowers usu-

Figure 14-33. *Ilex lonicerifolia* var. *hakkuensis*. Drawing by Chien-chu Chen in *Illustrations of Native and Introduced Ligneous Plants of Taiwan* (1962) by Tang-shui Liu.

ally 5-merous; fruits brown when dry, ellipsoid, 8 mm (5/16 in.) long, 6.5 mm (1/4 in.) diameter; pyrenes 5, dorsally unicaniculate, marginal ridges. Habitat: Venezuela, Amazonas, infrequent at 1800 m (5900 ft.) elevation in Cerro Guanay.

Ilex macarenensis Cuatrecasas 1955.
Evergreen, small to large trees, glabrous, branches grayish brown; leaves elliptic-lanceolate, 5–9.5 cm (2–3¾ in.) long, 2–3.5 cm (¾–1⅜ in.) wide, bases attenuate-cuneate, apices narrow-acute, cuspidate, margins entire, petioles glabrous, 7–12 mm (9/32–15/32 in.) long; inflorescences axillary, solitary or cymose or fasciculate, pedicels glabrous or hirsute, 5–8 mm (3/16–5/16 in.) long; fruits immature, globose, 5 mm (3/16 in.) diameter; pyrenes 4. Habitat: Colombia, Meta. Allied to *I. umbellulata*.

Ilex macbridiana Edwin 1965.
Evergreen shrubs, 1.5–4 m (5–13 ft.) tall, branchlets glabrous, lenticels elliptic; leaves mostly obovate to elliptic-obovate, 2–3.5 cm (3.4–1⅜ in.) long, 0.9–1.6 cm (11/32–5/8 in.) wide, margins entire, bases usually cuneate, apices variable, broadly acute to acute, or obtuse, usually reddish punctate beneath; male inflorescences axillary, fasciculate on new wood, flowers 4-merous; fruits unknown. Habitat: Peru, Department de Amazonas, Chachapoyas Province, at 2400–2450 m (7920–8025 ft.) elevation. Allied to *I. lechleri* and *I. ovalis*. Named for J. Francis Macbride.

Ilex macfadyenii (Walpers) Rehder 1921 var. *macfadyenii*. Acebo de sierra (synonyms *Prinos montana* Swartz 1788, *P. lanceolata* Macfadyen 1837, *I. montana* var. *occidentalis* Walpers 1848, *I. montana* (Swartz) Grisebach 1860, *I. montana* (Swartz) Grisebach 1880, *I. montana* var. *orientalis* Loesener 1892, *Prinos macfadyenii* Walpers 1892, *I. subtriflora* (Grisebach) Loesener 1892, *I. macfadyenii* var. *domingensis* Loesener 1901, *I. macfadyenii* var. *hermineri* Edwin 1964).
Evergreen, small trees to 10 m (33 ft.) tall, branches pubescent, grayish brown; leaves pubescent, narrowly ovate to lanceolate, 2–4.5 cm (¾–1¾ in.) long, 1.5–2.5 cm (½–1 in.) wide, bases rounded, apices acute to long acuminate, margins sharply serrate on upper two-thirds of leaf, petioles 2–7 mm (1/16–9/32 in.) long; inflorescences solitary, usually fasciculate, peduncles 7–16 mm (9/32–5/8 in.) long, pedicels 3–5 mm (1/8–3/16 in.) long; fruits red, globose, 5–7 mm (3/16–8/32 in.) diameter; pyrenes 5–7, laterally compressed. Habitat: rare tree of the West Indies usually in the upper montane forests, Cuba, Jamaica, Martinique, Lesser Antilles, St. Kitts, Nevis, Guadeloupe, and Dominica. This species honors James

Macfadyen (1798–1850), a Scottish and Jamaican botanist, and author of an early flora of Jamaica.

Ilex macfadyenii subsp. *ovata* (Grisebach) D. H. Nicholson 1991. In *Smithsonian Contrib. Bot.* 77: 26.
Description not available.

Ilex machilifolia H.-w. Li *ex* Y.-r. Li 1985.
Evergreen trees to 10–20 m (33–65 ft.) tall, branchlets yellowish brown, angulate; leaves oblong-elliptic, 10–16 cm (4–6½ in.) long, 4–6 cm (1⅝–2⅜ in.) wide, bases usually wide-cuneate, apices acuminate, margins entire, petioles thick, 1.5–2 cm (7/16–¾ in.) long; flowers unknown; infructescences simple, unbranched, cymose, glabrous, peduncles 5–9 mm (3/16–11/32 in.) long, pedicels 10 mm (⅜ in.) long; fruits red, globose, 1 cm (⅜ in.) diameter, persistent calyces; pyrenes 5, deeply sulcate on dorsal surfaces. Habitat: People's Republic of China, Yunnan Province, mixed woodlands at 1800–2000 m (5900–6600 ft.) elevation. Allied to *I. editicostata*.

Ilex maclurei Merrill 1934.
Evergreen, small trees or shrubs to 4 m (13 ft.) tall, lenticels small, inconspicuous; leaves oblong or oblong-elliptic 9–19 cm (3½–7½ in.) long, 3.5–8.5 cm (1⅜–3⅜ in.) wide, bases obtuse or rounded, apex very obtuse or rounded, margins entire; flowers not seen; infructescences 2–3 dichotomous, peduncles 7–9 fruits, glabrous, 8–16 mm (5/16–11/16 in.) long, pedicels 3–6 mm (1/8–7/32 in.) long with 2 basal prophylla; fruits black, globose, 6–7 mm (7/32–9/32 in.) wide, stigma mammiform; pyrenes 4, U-shaped in cross section, deeply caniculate. Habitat: People's Republic of China, Guangdong Province, and Vietnam. Allied to *I. thorelii*.

Ilex macrolaurus Loesener 1901.
Evergreen shrubs or trees, branches glabrous; leaves oblong-elliptic or obtuse-oblong, 15–20 cm (6–8 in.) long, 4.5–6.8 cm (1¾–2⅝ in.) wide, apices obtuse or acuminate, acumens 1.4–2.5 cm (17/32–1 in.) long, bases acute, margins recurved, remotely serrulate or subentire, petioles 10–20 mm (⅜–¾ in.) long; inflorescences axillary, fasciculate, branched, flowers 4-merous; fruits unknown. Habitat: Ecuador, near Panure, along the Uaupés River. Allied to *I. laureola*.

Ilex macrophylla Wallich 1875.
Evergreen trees to 18 m (60 ft.) tall, branches widely spreading; leaves entire, 10–17 cm (3⅞–6⅝ in.) long, 3.8–6.8 cm (1½–2½ in.) wide, bases rotund or cuneate-obtuse, usually cuneate, apices obtuse, often short-acuminate, petioles 8–16 mm (5/16–5/8 in.) long; inflorescences axillary, male flowers 4-

merous; fruits globose, 4.5 mm (5⁄32 in.) diameter; pyrenes 7–9. Habitat: Malaysia. Allied to *I. alternifolia* and *I. pleiobrachiata.*

Ilex macrophylla var. *angustata* Loesener 1901, see *I. wallichii* Steudel 1840, *non* Hooker f. 1875.

Ilex macrophylla var. *ovata* Loesener 1901, see *I. wallichii* Steudel 1840, *non* Hooker f. 1875.

Ilex macrostigma C.-y. Wu *ex* Y.-r. Li 1985.
Evergreen, glabrous shrubs, branchlets angulate-sulcate; leaves elliptic or oblong-lanceolate, 4.5–8.5 cm (1¾–3⅜ in.) long, 1.8–2.5 cm (11⁄16–1 in.) wide, apices acuminate or long-acuminate, bases obtuse or wide-cuneate, margins sparingly to moderately serrulate, petioles 5–8 mm (3⁄16–5⁄16 in.) long; female inflorescences axillary, fasciculate, pedicels 2–3 mm (1⁄16–⅛ in.) long; fruits unknown. Habitat: People's Republic of China, Yunnan Province. Allied to *I. tetramera.*

Ilex magnifolia Cuatrecasas 1990. (See *Rev. Acad. Colombo Cienc. Exact. Fis. Nat.* 67: 633. 1990).

Ilex magnifructa Edwin 1965.
Evergreen small trees to 6 m (20 ft.) tall, branches glabrous; leaves broadly ovate to broadly elliptic or elliptic-ovate, 7–8.3 cm (2¾–3¼ in.) long, 3.8–5 cm (1½–2 in.) wide, punctate beneath, bases obtuse or orbiculate, apices obtuse, orbiculate, margins entire, revolute, petioles 2–4 mm (1⁄16–5⁄32 in.) long; inflorescences axillary, solitary, lateral, flowers 4-merous; fruits red, subglobose, 8–9 mm (5⁄16–11⁄32 in.) long, 6 mm (7⁄32 in.) diameter, pedicels 2.5–3.2 cm (1¼ in.) long; pyrenes 4, unicanaliculate. Habitat: Venezuela, Amazonas, along streamsides at 1250 m (4125 ft.) elevation.

Ilex maguirei Wurdack 1961.
Evergreen shrubs 0.5–2 m (1½–6 ft.) tall, young branchlets villose, later glabrous; leaves ovate-elliptic, 1.5–2.5 cm (19⁄32–1 in.) long, 1–2 cm (⅜–15⁄32 in.) wide, sparsely punctate beneath, bases rotund, apices obtuse or rotund, minute apiculate, margins revolute, entire, petioles 2–4 mm (1⁄16–5⁄32 in.) long; inflorescences axillary, solitary, 1- to 3-flowered, flowers 4-merous; fruits red-brown, broadly elliptic, 6–11 mm (7⁄32–7⁄16 in.) long. Habitat: Venezuela. Similar to *I. venezuelensis.*

Ilex maingayi Hooker f. 1875.
Evergreen, small trees 6–10 m (20–33 ft.) tall, old trees to 27 m (90 ft.) tall; leaves elliptic to elliptic-oblong, 9–16 cm (3–6⅜ in.) long, 2.8–5 cm (1⅛–2 in.) wide, glabrous, apices obtuse, acuminate, bases cuneate, margins entire, recurved, petioles 10–18 mm (⅜–11⁄16 in.) long; inflorescences solitary in leaf axils, branched, flowers 5- to 6-merous; fruits deep red, ellipsoid 5–7 mm (3⁄16–9⁄32 in.) long, 4.5–5.5 mm (5⁄32–13⁄64 in.) wide, peduncles 3–8 mm (⅛–5⁄16 in.) long, pedicels 1–2 mm (1⁄32–1⁄16 in.) long; pyrenes 4–6, striate, sulcate. Habitat: endemic to Malaysia, near Penang. Allied to *I. spicata* and *I. zeylanica.*

Ilex × *makinoi* Hara 1936. O-tsuru tsuge (synonyms *I. rugosa* var. *fauriei* Loesener 1901, *I. fauriei* (Loesener) Makino 1928, *non* Gandoger 1918).
A natural and wild-occurring hybrid of *I. leucoclada* × *I. rugosa,* differing from *I. rugosa* by all parts being larger, branchlets scarcely punctate, leaves narrow-oblong, 5–7 cm (2–2¾ in.) long, apices acute, impressed nerves and veinlets less prominent. Habitat: Japan, Hokkaido and Honshu.

Ilex malabarica Beddome 1875 (synonym *I. wightiana* Dalzell & Gibbs, *non* Wallich 1848).
Evergreen, large trees, branches glabrous; leaves narrow-elliptic-oblong, 4.5–9.5 cm (1¾–3¾ in.) long, 1.4–3.5 cm (17⁄32–1⅜ in.) wide, apices acute, acuminate, bases acute or cuneate, margins entire, recurved, petioles 4–8 mm (5⁄32–5⁄16 in.) long; inflorescences fasciculate in leaf axils, 3- to 5-flowered, flowers 5- to 6-merous; fruits red, depressed-globose, 3–4 mm (⅛–5⁄32 in.) diameter; pyrenes 6. Habitat: India, near Bombay. Allied to *I. metabaptista* and *I. wightiana.*

Ilex malaccensis Loesener 1901.
Evergreen shrubs 3–5 m (10–15 ft.) tall; leaves ovate or oval to elliptic, 6.5–13 cm (2½–5⅛ in.) long, 3.5–5 cm (1⅜–2 in.) wide, bases rotund, apices acuminate, margins entire, recurved; inflorescences racemose, axillary, female flowers 4- to 6-merous; fruits ovoid; pyrenes 10–16. Habitat: Malaysia, Maingay; Borneo, Sarawak. Allied to *I. spicata.*

Ilex mamillata C.-y. Wu *ex* C.-j. Tseng 1985, *non* C.-y. Wu *ex* Y.-r. Li 1985.
Evergreen shrubs or small trees 3–10 m (10–22 ft.) tall, branchlets glabrous, grayish white, densely lenticellate; leaves elliptic or elongate-elliptic or oblong-elliptic, rarely ovate-elliptic, 6–10 mm (2⅜–4 in.) long, 2–3.5 cm (¾–1⅜ in.) wide, bases obtuse or cuneate, apices acute or obtuse, rarely short-acuminate or emarginate, tips mucronulate, glabrous above except midribs, puberulent below, inconspicuous punctate, margins entire conspicuous veins above, petioles 3–7 mm (⅛–9⁄32 in.) long; inflorescences axillary, 1- to 3-flowered, fasciculate on new, 2nd-, or 3rd-year growth; fruits red, globose, 5 mm (3⁄16 in.) diameter, persistent calyces, stigmas mam-

miform or columnar; pyrenes 5, striate. Habitat: People's Republic of China, Guangxi Province.

Ilex mandonii Loesener 1901.

Evergreen, glabrous shrubs; leaves obovate or broadly oval, 7–14 mm (9/32–17/32 in.) long, 4–8 mm (5/32–5/16 in.) wide, apices rotund or obtuse, small spines, bases acute or cuneate obtuse, margins entire, occasionally 1–3 crenulate teeth near apex, petioles 1–2 mm (1/32–1/16 in.) long; inflorescences axillary, solitary, branched, flowers 4-merous; fruits black, globose or broadly ovoid, 8–9 mm (5/16–11/32 in.) diameter; pyrenes 5. Habitat: Brazil. Allied to *I. buxifolioides.*

Ilex manneiensis S.-y. Hu 1949 (synonym *I. manneiensis* var. *glabra* C.-y. Wu *ex* Y.-r. Li 1985).

Evergreen trees to 9 m (30 ft.) tall, branchlet yellowish-pubescent, numerous lenticels on new growth; leaves elliptic, 8–16 cm (3⅛–6½ in.) long, 2–4.5 cm (¾–1¾ in.) wide, bases rounded to cuneate, apices acuminate, margins entire, yellow-pubescent to glabrescent above, yellow-tomentose beneath; inflorescences solitary, axillary, 3-flowered cymes, pubescent peduncles 5–7 mm (3/16–9/32 in.) long, pedicels 2–3 mm (1/16–1/8 in.) long; fruits red, globose, 9 mm (11/32 in.) diameter, persistent calyces; pyrenes 5–6, back U-shaped, widely unicanaliculate. Habitat: southwestern People's Republic of China, Yunnan Province. Similar to *I. atrata* and *I. lancilimba.*

Ilex marahuacae Steyermark 1988.

Evergreen, small trees to 4 m (14 ft.) tall, branches glabrous; leaves ovate or oblong-ovate, 6.5–11 cm (2½–4⅜ in.) long, 2.5–4.5 cm (1–1¾ in.) wide, bases rotund to obtuse, apices obtuse to acutely acuminate, acumen 8–10 mm (4/16–3/8 in.) long, margins entire, petioles 6–8 mm (7/32–5/16 in.) long; inflorescences axillary, solitary, 2- to 3-flowered, flowers 4-merous; fruits globose, 5 mm (3/16 in.) diameter; pyrenes 4, trigonous, smooth. Habitat: Venezuela, Amazonas State, Cerro Marahuaka, forested slopes along east branch of Cano Negro.

Ilex marginata Edwin 1965.

Evergreen small trees 6–8 m (20–26 ft.) tall; branches glabrous; leaves usually ovate or elliptic-ovate, 7.5–10.5 (3–4⅛ in.) long, 3.8–4.2 cm (1½–1¹¹/₁₆ in.) wide, epunctate, bases usually cuneate, apices variable, acuminate or acute to rotund or retuse, margins entire, revolute, petioles 11–14 mm (7/16–17/32 in.) long; inflorescences axillary, solitary, flowers 5- to 6-merous; fruits brown when dry, ovoid-globose, 8–9 mm (5/16–11/32 in.) long, 7–12 mm (9/32–15/32 in.) diameter; pyrenes 5–6, uni-

canaliculate. Habitat: Venezuela, Bolivar, at 2125–2300 m (7010–7600 ft.) elevation.

Ilex marlipoensis H.-w. Li *ex* Y.-r. Li 1985.

Evergreen, glabrous trees 5–15 m (16–50 ft.) tall, branchlets angulate-sulcate, glabrous; leaves oblong-elliptic, 8–13 cm (3⅛–5⅛ in.) long, 3.5–4.5 cm (1⅜–1¾ in.) wide, margins moderately serrulate, petioles 8–10 mm (5/16–3/8 in.) long; inflorescences axillary, cymose, fasciculate; fruits (immature) subglobose, 5–6 mm (3/16–7/32 in.) long, 3.5–4.5 mm (9/64–11/64 in.) wide, calyces persistent, stigmas thick-disciform, pedicels 2–4 mm (1/16–5/32 in.) long; pyrenes 4, palmately striate, sulcate. Habitat: People's Republic of China, Yunnan Province. Allied to *I. wattii.*

Ilex marquesensis F. Brown 1935.

Evergreen trees; leaves ovate or obovate-lanceolate, 7 cm (2¾ in.) long, 3 cm (1³/₁₆ in.) wide, stipules minute, triangulate, 0.5–1 mm (1/64–1/32 in.) long, bases cuneate, apices acuminate or subacuminate, margins incurved, entire at base, 2–6 callous crenately incurved teeth at apex; inflorescences short cymes, usually 2.5 cm (1 in.) long, peduncles usually 15 mm (19/32 in.) long, pedicels usually 2 mm (1/16 in.) long; fruits black, subglobose, 5 mm (3/16 in.) long, 6 mm (7/32 in.) broad, crowned by 10–18 lobed stigmatic disks. Habitat: Marquesas Islands in Southeast Pacific. Allied to *I. anomala.*

Ilex martii Loesener 1901.

Evergreen shrubs, branches puberulent; leaves obovate or elliptic, 5.7–9 cm (2³/₁₆–3½ in.) long, 2.5–4 cm (1–1⅝ in.) wide, apices obtuse or subrotund, bases acute or obtuse, margins recurved, densely serrulate, petioles 6–10 mm (7/32–3/8 in.) long; inflorescences axillary, paniculate, flowers 4-merous; fruits black, globose, 6 mm (7/32 in.) diameter; pyrenes 4. Habitat: Brazil, near Diamantina. Allied to *I. affinis.*

Ilex martiniana D. Don 1832. Mapirinoeloe, kakotaro (synonyms *I. martiana* Walpers 1842, *I. lanceolata* Koltzsch 1848, *non* Grisebach 1888, *I. paniculata* Turczaninow 1858).

Evergreen shrubs or trees; leaves oval or ovate-oblong to elliptic, 8–9 cm (3⅛–3½ in.) long, 1.8–5 cm (1¹¹/₁₆–2 in.) wide, apices acuminate or acute, bases obtuse or rotund, margins recurved, densely serrulate or crenulate, petioles 4–12 mm (5/32–15/32 in.) long; inflorescences axillary, fasciculate or paniculate, flowers 4-merous; fruits red, globose, 3.5 mm (7/64 in.) diameter; pyrenes 4, smooth. Habitat: Guyana and Trinidad. Allied to *I. affinis.*

Ilex matanoana Makino 1913.

Evergreen, low shrubs, branchlets angulate, glabrous; leaves obovate or oblong-obovate, 0.8–3.2 cm (5⁄16–1¼ in.) long, 0.5–1.8 cm (3⁄16–11⁄16 in.) wide, bases cuneate, apices mucronate or obtuse and emarginate at apex, margins entire, not punctate, petioles 1.5–8 mm (3⁄64–5⁄16 in.) long; inflorescences solitary, pedicellate, flowers 4-merous; fruits unknown. Habitat: Japan, Bonin Island, south of Honshu. Allied and similar to *I. crenata,* but leaves not punctate. Named in honor of Migaki Matano, director of Imperial Museum.

Ilex matsudai Yamamoto 1925 (synonym *I. lonicerifolia* var. *matsudai* (Yamamoto) Yamamoto 1933).

Evergreen, glabrous trees, branches with conspicuous lenticels; leaves oblong-elliptic, 4–9.5 cm (1⅝–3¾ in.) long, 2.5–4 cm (1–1⅝ in.) wide, apices very shortly and broadly acuminate, rarely obtuse, acumens 3–5 mm (⅛–3⁄16 in.) long, bases acute, rarely obtuse, margins entire, recurved, petioles 8–15 mm (5⁄16–19⁄32 in.) long; inflorescences axillary, solitary, on new growth, cymose, flowers 4- to 5-merous; fruits red, ellipsoid, 8–10 mm (5⁄16–⅜ in.) long, 6–8 mm (7⁄32–5⁄16 in.) wide, peduncles 3–11 mm (⅛–7⁄16 in.) long, pedicels 5 mm (3⁄16 in.) long; pyrenes 4–5, smooth, dorsally deeply and widely unicanaliculate in cross section. Habitat: Taiwan. Allied to *I. maclurei.*

Ilex mattangicola Loesener 1901.

Evergreen shrubs or small trees, spreading, erect, glabrous branches; leaves usually obovate, 5.5–10 cm (2⅛–4 in.) long, 2–3.8 cm (¾–1½ in.) wide, bases cuneate, apices usually short, obtuse or acuminate, margins entire, recurved, petioles 8–11 mm (5⁄16–7⁄16 in.) long; inflorescences 1- to 3-flowered, peduncles 7 mm (9⁄32 in.) long; fruits red, globose to ellipsoid 7.5–9 mm (5⁄16–11⁄32 in.) diameter; pyrenes usually 7. Habitat: Borneo, Mount Mattang at 1000 m (3300) altitude. Allied to *I. zippeliana.*

Ilex matthewsii Loesener 1901.

Evergreen shrubs or trees; leaves broadly oval to suboval, 1.6–3 cm (⅝–13⁄16 in.) long, 8–16 mm (5⁄16–⅝ in.) wide, apices rotund, minute apiculate, bases obtuse or subrotund, margins recurved, serrulate, petioles 3–5 mm (⅛–3⁄16 in.) long; inflorescences axillary, solitary, pedunculate, 3- to 7-flowered, flowers 4-merous; fruits unknown. Habitat: Peru, near Chachapoyas. Allied to *I. ovalis.*

Ilex maxima W. J. Hahn 1993. In *Novon* 3(1): 43. 1993.

Description not available.

Figure 14-34. *Ilex matanoana.* Drawing by Chien-chu Chen in *Illustrations of Native and Introduced Ligneous Plants of Taiwan* (1962) by Tang-shui Liu.

Ilex maximowicziana Loesener 1901 var. *maximowicziana.* Nagaba inu tsuge, mucha gira (synonyms *I. crenata* var. *scoriatulum* Yamamoto 1925, *I. scoriatulum* Koidzumi 1929).

Evergreen trees to 10 m (33 ft) tall, branchlets ridged, lenticels obscure; leaves elliptic or broadly elliptic, 2–4.5 cm (¾–1¾ in.) long, 1.3–2.3 cm (½–⅞ in.) wide, apices acute or short-acuminate, bases acute or cuneate, margins crenulate-serrate, petioles 7–10 mm (9⁄32–⅜ in.) long; inflorescences axillary, 1- to 3-fasciculate, flowers 4-merous; fruits black, globose, 8 mm (5⁄16 in.) diameter, pedicels 7 mm (9⁄32 in.) long, calyces persistent; pyrenes 4, 5-striate. Habitat: Taiwan and Ryukyu Islands of Japan. Allied to *I. liukiensis* and *I. triflora.*

Ilex maximowicziana var. *kanehirae* (Yamamoto) Yamazaki 1987 (synonyms *I. mutchagara* Makino 1913, *I. crenata* var. *kanehirae* Yamamoto 1925, *I. crenata* var. *scoriarum* W. Smith 1925, *I. kanehirae* (Yamamoto) Koidzumi 1929, *I. scoriatula* Koidzumi 1929, *I. mutchagara* var. *kanehirae* (Yamamoto) Masumune 1935, *I. triflora* var. *kanehirae* (Yamamoto) S.-y. Hu 1949, *I. crenata* var.

mutchagara (Makino) Ohwi 1953, *I. fosbergiana* S.-y. Hu 1971, *I. maximowicziana* var. *mutchagara* (Makino) Hatusima 1975).

Evergreen shrubs, intermediate between *I. triflora* and *I. crenata*; leaves oblong or obovate or oblong-elliptic, apices rotund or obtuse; inflorescences fasciculate; fruits black, globose, 5–6 mm (³⁄₁₆–⁷⁄₃₂ in.) diameter. Habitat: People's Republic of China, Fujian Province near the Zhejiang border; also Japan, Amami-O-Shima Island, the Ryukyu Islands, and Taiwan. This variety has certainly made the rounds as noted by the number of synonyms and still needs further study.

Ilex medogensis Y.-r. Li 1984.

Evergreen trees 8 m (26 ft.) tall, branchlets grayish, angulate, glabrous; leaves elliptic or obovate-elliptic, 10–12 cm (4–4¾ in.) long, 4–5 cm (1⅝–2 in.) wide, apices abruptly long-acuminate, bases subrotund or wide-cuneate, margins slender, 1–1.5 cm (³⁄₈–¹⁹⁄₃₂ in.) long; female inflorescences axillary, fasciculate, branched, peduncles 1 mm (¹⁄₃₂ in.) long, pedicels 1 mm (¹⁄₃₂ in.) long; fruits ovoid, 5–6 mm (³⁄₁₆–⁷⁄₃₂ in.) diameter, calyces persistent, stigmas usually capitate; pyrenes 4. Habitat: People's Republic of China, Xizang Province. Allied to *I. tetramera*.

Ilex megalophylla (Hemsley) Edwin *ex* T. R. Dudley, *comb. & stat. nov.* (basionym *I. grandis* Reisseck, *Mart. Fl. Bras.* 11, part I: 47. 1861, which is a later homonym of *I. grandis* Hort. Hannover *ex* Decaisne 1853; synonym *I. grandis* var. *magnifica* Loesener).

Evergreen, glabrous large shrubs or small trees; leaves obovate or elliptic-oblong, 11–22 cm (4–8¾ in.) long, 3.8–7 cm (1¾–2¾ in.) wide, apices obtuse or rotund, minute apiculate, bases cuneate, margins entire, recurved, petioles 1.5–2 cm (¹⁹⁄₃₂–¾ in.) long; inflorescences fasciculate in leaf axils, flowers 4- to 7-merous; fruits black, ovoid 5–7 mm (³⁄₁₆–⁹⁄₃₂ in.) diameter; pyrenes unknown. Habitat: Brazil. Allied to *I. theezans*.

Ilex melanophylla H. T. Chang 1959.

Evergreen shrubs, branchlets rounded, glabrous, becoming black, 2nd-year wood brownish; leaves papery or subpapery, ovate or ovate-elliptic, 6–10 cm (2⅜–4 in.) long, 3–4 cm (1³⁄₁₆–1⅝ in.) wide, bases obtuse or cuneate, apices obtuse or subacute, lateral veins reticulate, conspicuous above, margins remotely crenate, petioles glabrous 6–8 mm (⁷⁄₃₂–⁵⁄₁₆ in.) long; flowers not seen; infructescences cymose, axillary, solitary, with 1–2 fruits, peduncles 5–8 mm (³⁄₁₆–⁵⁄₁₆ in.) long, becoming black, pedicels 1–1.4 cm (³⁄₈–¹⁷⁄₃₂ in.) long, calyces persistent, slender, 3 mm (⅛ in.) diameter, stigma persistent; pyrenes 4, 5–6 mm (³⁄₁₆–⁷⁄₃₂) long, dorsally canaliculate. Habi-

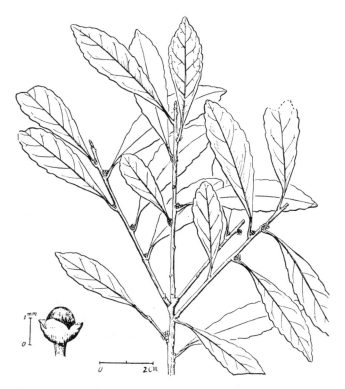

Figure 14-35. *Ilex maximowicziana* var. *kanehirae*. Drawing by Chien-chu Chen in *Illustrations of Native and Introduced Ligneous Plants of Taiwan* (1962) by Tang-shui Liu.

tat: People's Republic of China, Guangdong Province. Allied to *I. purpurea*.

Ilex memecylifolia Champion *ex* Bentham 1857 (synonym *I. memecylifolia* var. *oblongifolia* Loesener 1901).

Evergreen shrubs to 2 m (6 ft.) tall, branchlets puberulent; leaves ovate-oblong or obovate, 3.5–8.5 cm (1⅜–3⅜ in.) long, 1.4–3.5 cm (¹⁷⁄₃₂–1⅜ in.) wide, apices abruptly acuminate, acumens 2–8 mm (¹⁄₁₆–⁵⁄₁₆ in.) long, bases cuneate, margins entire, petioles 5–7 mm (³⁄₁₆–⁹⁄₃₂ in.) long; inflorescences fasciculate, males branched, females single flowers, pedicels 6–8 mm (⁷⁄₃₂–⁵⁄₁₆ in.) long, flowers 4- to 6-merous, fragrant; fruits red, globose, 6 mm (⁷⁄₃₂ in.) diameter, calyces persistent; pyrenes 4–5, reticulate striate. Habitat: People's Republic of China, Guangxi Province, Hong Kong, and Vietnam. Allied to *I. elmerrilliana*.

Ilex × *meserveae* S.-y. Hu 1940.

Artificial hybrids of *I. rugosa* × *I. aquifolium*, first produced in the early 1950s by K. K. Meserve of St. James, Long Island, New York. See Blue Holly

Group in Chapter 16. Evergreen shrubs 1–3 m (3–10 ft.) tall, branches sparsely puberulent; leaves ovate or elliptic, 2–6 cm (¾–2⅜ in.) long, 1.3–3.5 cm (½–1⅜ in.) wide, bases rotund, obtuse or acute, apices usually acute, margins spinose, 4–8 spines on each side, petioles 3–5 mm (⅛–3⁄16 in.) long; inflorescences axillary, fasciculate, flowers 4-merous; fruits red or yellow, usually globose, 8–10 mm (5⁄16–⅜ in.) diameter; pyrenes 4. At least 8 cultivars have been named.

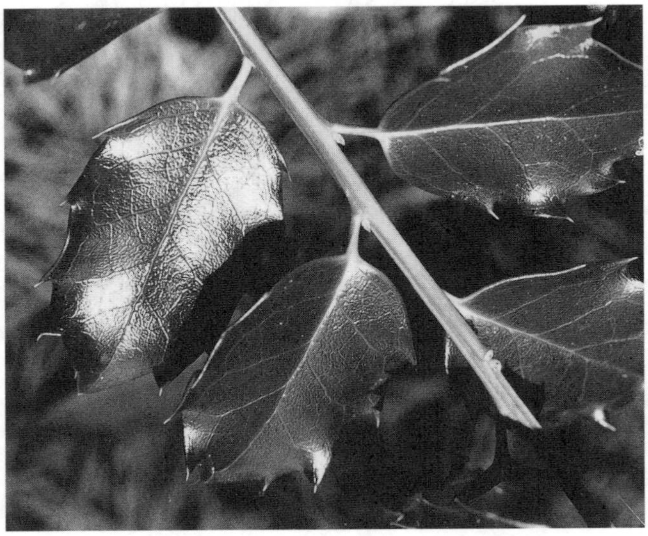

Figure 14-36. *Ilex × meserveae.* Photo by Barton Bauer Sr.

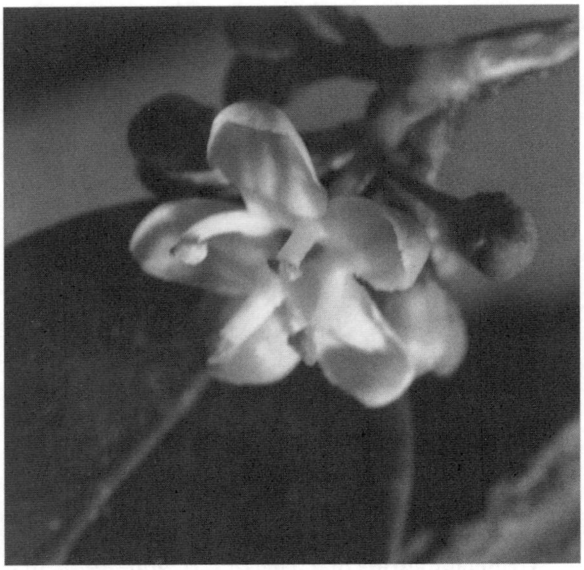

Figure 14-37. *Ilex × meserveae.* Photo by Barton Bauer Sr.

Ilex metabaptista Loesener var. *metabaptista* 1900.

Evergreen, large shrubs to 4 m (13 ft.) tall, branchlets pilose, lenticels present; leaves lanceolate to oblanceolate, 3–8 cm (1 3⁄16–3⅛ in.) long, 5–15 mm (3⁄16–19⁄32 in.) wide, apices acute or obtuse, minutely apiculate, bases acute or cuneate, margins entire, pilose, petioles 3–8 mm (⅛–5⁄16 in.) long; inflorescences axillary, sessile on 2nd-year growth, fasciculate, 5- to 6-merous, female inflorescences single, rarely 2–3 cymose; fruits red, ovoid-ellipsoid, 5–6 mm (3⁄16 in.) long, 4–5 mm (5⁄32–3⁄16 in.) diameter, calyces persistent; pyrenes 5–8, striate. Habitat: People's Republic of China, a narrow band extending north and south along the borders of Hubei, Hunan, Guizhou, and Guangxi provinces. Allied to *I. salicina.*

Ilex metabaptista var. *myrsinoides* (H. Léveillé) Rehder 1933 (synonyms *Maesa myrsinoides* Léveillé 1812, *Myrsine feddei* Léveillé 1912, *Embelia cavaleriei* H. Léveillé 1914, *I. fargesii* var. *bodinieri* Loesener 1914).

A variety differing from typical individuals with less puberulent branchlets, leaves, and inflorescences. Change is gradual. Habitat: People's Republic of China, western range of the species in Guizhou Province. Should possibly be considered a form rather than a variety, or probably not worthy of botanical recognition.

Ilex micrantha Triana 1872.

Evergreen, large shrubs, lenticels minute; leaves oval or ovate to ovate-elliptic, 7–10 cm (2¾–4 in.) long, 3–4 cm (1 3⁄16–1⅝ in.) wide, apices acuminate, bases obtuse or cuneate obtuse, margins entire, recurved, petioles 10–15 mm (⅜–19⁄32 in.) long; inflorescences fasciculate in leaf axils, flowers 4-merous; fruits unknown. Habitat: Colombia, near Canca and Papayan at 1000 m (3300 ft.) elevation. Allied to *I. blanchetii.*

Ilex microdonta Reisseck 1861.

Evergreen, glabrous shrubs or trees; leaves oval-oblong or oblong-lanceolate, 4–6.5 cm (1⅝–2½ in.) long, 1.6–2.2 cm (⅝–13⁄16 in.) wide, apices acute or subacuminate, bases acute or subcuneate, acute, margins recurved, serrulate near apex, petioles 9–15 mm (11⁄32–19⁄32 in.) long; inflorescences axillary, fasciculate, solitary, flowers 4-merous; fruits black, ellipsoid or globose, 4–5 mm (5⁄32–3⁄16 in.) long, 3.5–4.5 mm (9⁄32–11⁄64 in.) wide; pyrenes 4. Habitat: Brazil. Allied to *I. brevicuspis* and *I. cerasifolia* var. *glaziovii.*

Ilex micropyrena C.-y. Wu *ex* Y.-r. Li 1985.

Evergreen shrubs 2.5 m (8 ft.) tall, branchlets angulate-sulcate; leaves oblong-lanceolate, rarely oblong-elliptic, 8–12 cm (3⅛–4¾ in.) long, 2.5–4.2 cm (1–1¹¹⁄₁₆ in.) wide, apices acuminate, bases obtuse or wide cuneate, margins moderately serrulate, petioles 8–12 mm (⁵⁄₁₆–¹⁵⁄₃₂ in.) long; inflorescences axillary, pseudoracemose; fruits globose, 5 mm (³⁄₁₆ in.) diameter, stigmas thinly disciform, pedicels 5–7 mm (³⁄₁₆–⁹⁄₃₂ in.) long; pyrenes 4, small, palmately striate, sulcate. Habitat: People's Republic of China, Yunnan Province. Allied to *I. dunniana*.

Ilex microsticta Loesener 1905.

Evergreen, glabrous shrubs; leaves obovate to obovate-elliptic, 7–10.5 cm (2¾–4³⁄₁₆ in.) long, 3.5–5.5 cm (1⅜–2⅛ in.) wide, bases cuneate, apices rounded, margins serrulate, petioles 8–13 mm (⁵⁄₁₆–½ in.) long; inflorescences axillary, solitary, branched, peduncles 8–20 mm (⁵⁄₁₆–¾ in.) long, pedicels 2–3 mm (¹⁄₁₆–⅛ in.) long; fruits unknown. Habitat: Peru, near Huanuco. Allied to *I. crassifolioides*.

Ilex microwrightioides Loesener 1913 (synonym *I. microwrightioides* var. *calvescens* Loesener 1913).

Evergreen trees, branches spreading or erect; leaves broadly ovate or broadly oval-oblong to obovate, 0.7–1.6 cm (⁹⁄₃₂–⅝ in.) long, 5–9 mm (³⁄₁₆–¹¹⁄₃₂ in.) wide, bases obtuse, rotund or acute, apices rotund, subacuminate, apiculate, 0.7–1.6 cm (⁹⁄₃₂–⅝ in.) long, margins entire, petioles 2 mm (¹⁄₁₆ in.) long; inflorescences axillary, solitary, male inflorescences fasciculate, peduncles sparsely hirsute, flowers 4-merous; fruits ellipsoid, 3 mm (⅛ in.) long, 2 mm (¹⁄₁₆ in.) wide; pyrenes 4. Habitat: Dominican Republic, Province Azua, El Tetero, at 1350 m (4455 ft.) elevation. Allied to *I. walkeri*.

Ilex miguensis S.-y. Hu 1951.

Evergreen shrubs, branches glabrous; leaves elliptic, 1.5–3 cm (¹⁹⁄₃₂–1³⁄₁₆ in.) wide, 0.7–1.5 cm (⁹⁄₃₂–¹⁹⁄₃₂ in.) wide, bases acute, rarely obtuse, apices acute, spinulose, margins remotely serrate, toothlike, weakly spinose, glabrous, stipules minute, persistent; inflorescences paucifasciculate, axillary; fruits red, subglobose, pyrenes woody, palmately striate, not sulcate. Habitat: People's Republic of China, southern Xinjiang Province, rare, undergrowth, upper forests of Rong-to Valley at 3300–3600 m (10,890–11,880 ft.) elevation. Allied to *I. georgei*.

Ilex minimifolia Loesener 1901.

Evergreen, large shrubs, well-branched; leaves small, broadly oval or ovate-oblong, 4–7 mm (⁵⁄₃₂–⁷⁄₃₂ in.) long, 2–5 mm (¹⁄₁₆–³⁄₁₆ in.) wide, apices obtuse, bases rotund to acute, margins slightly recurved, entire at base, 1–3 serrulate near apex, petioles 8–18 mm (⁵⁄₁₆–¹¹⁄₁₆ in.) long; inflorescences axillary, solitary, pedicels 2–3.5 mm (¹⁄₁₆–⁷⁄₆₄ in.)

long; fruits unknown. Habitat: Bolivia. Allied to *I. lechleri*.

Ilex minutifolia Macbride 1951 (synonym *I. microphylla* Hooker 1832, *non* Hort. *ex* Regel 1866).

Evergreen, low-branched shrubs, young branches puberulent to glabrous; leaves suborbiculate or ovate or oval, 7–11 cm (2¾–4⅜ in.) long, 5–7 cm (2–2¾ in.) wide, black-punctuate beneath bases obtuse or rotund, apices often minutely apiculate, margins nearly plane, slightly glossy, petioles 0.75–1.5 mm (¹⁄₆₄–³⁄₆₄ in.) long; inflorescences axillary, solitary, males 3-flowered, females solitary, male peduncles 3 mm (⅛ in.) long pedicels rarely 3 mm (⅛ in.) long, flowers 4-merous; fruits subglobose; pyrenes 4, dorsally convex, striate and sulcate, Habitat: Peru, Amazonas, Chachapoyas. Allied to *I. ligustrina*.

Ilex mitis (Linnaeus) Radlkofer 1885. Wilpeer & Without (synonyms *Sideroxylon mite* Linnaeus 1767, *Leucoxylon laurinum* E. Meyer 1843, *I. capensis* Harvey & Sonder 1860, *Prinos lucida* Aiton 1861, *I. mitis* f. *camerunensis* Loesener 1901, *I. mitis* f. *monticola* (Tulasne) Loesener 1901, *I. mitis* f. *kilimandscharica* Loesener 1901).

Highly variable, evergreen large shrubs or trees to 30 m (100 ft.) tall; leaves elliptic to oblanceolate, 3–14 cm (1³⁄₁₆–5 in.) long, 1.3–4 cm (¹⁵⁄₃₂–1⅝ in.) wide, apices obtuse or rotund, with minute apicules, bases cuneate or acute, margins recurved, entire, occasionally remotely denticulate, petioles 4–5 mm (⁵⁄₃₂–³⁄₁₆ in.) long; inflorescences in leaf axils, branched, flowers usually 4-merous; fruits purplish brown, globose 3–5 mm (⅛–³⁄₁₆ in.) diameter, peduncles 1–8 mm (¹⁄₃₂–⁵⁄₁₆ in.) long, pedicels 2–5 mm (¹⁄₁₆–³⁄₁₆ in.) long; pyrenes 4–6. Habitat: Africa, in mountainous forest at 1363–2727 m (4500–9000 ft.). The only *Ilex* in Africa, somewhat rare in Kenya. Allied to *I. malabarica* and *I. metabaptista*.

Ilex moana Borhidi & Muniz 1970.

Evergreen shrubs, 3–4 m (10–13 ft.) tall, old branches glabrous, striate; leaves glabrous, usually orbiculate to suborbiculate to broadly elliptic, 2–3 cm (¾–1³⁄₁₆ in.) long, 1.5–2.5 cm (¹⁹⁄₃₂–1 in.) wide, bases rotund, apices obtuse or rotund, mucronulate, margins entire, recurved, apex frequently with 2–4 teeth; petioles 4–5 mm (⁵⁄₃₂–³⁄₁₆ in.) long; inflorescences lateral or axillary, usually 3 flowers, peduncles 5–7 mm (³⁄₁₆–⁹⁄₃₂ in.) long, pedicels 2–4 mm (¹⁄₁₆–⁵⁄₃₂ in.) long; fruits unknown. Habitat: Cuba, Oriente Province, region de Moa, Sierra de la Iberia. Allied to *I. macfadyenii* (Walpers) Rehder.

Ilex mucronulata Cuatrecasas 1948.

Evergreen trees to 20 m (5 ft.) high; leaves elliptic

to obovate-elliptic or ovoid-elliptic, 6–12 cm (2⅜–4¾ in.) long, 3–6 cm (1⅜–2⅜ in.) wide, bases attenuate, apices usually apiculate, minute mucros, margins entire, revolute, petioles 6–10 mm (⁷⁄₃₂–⅜ in.) long; inflorescences axillary, 1- to 3-flowered cymes, flowers 4-merous; fruits dark red, 10 mm (⅜ in.) diameter; pyrenes 4. Habitat: Colombia, Department del Valle, Quebrada, Ba San Joaquin, at low elevations. Allied to *I. amygdalifolia*.

Ilex myricoides Kunth 1830. Quinti (synonyms *Prinos myricoides* Willdenow *ex* Roemer & Schultes 1824, *Myginda myricoides* Willdenow 1828, *I. hippocrateoides* Triana & Plancheon 1833, *I. myricoides* f. *euryterophylla* Loesener 1901, *I. myricoides* f. *genuiana* Loesener 1901, *I. myricoides* var. *meridensis* Loesener 1901, *I. myricoides* var. *polyphylla* (Bentham) Loesener 1901, *I. myricoides* var. *trianiana* Loesener 1901).

Evergreen shrubs or trees; leaves oblong to oblong-obovate, 1.4–4.7 cm (¹⁷⁄₃₂–1¹¹⁄₁₆ in.) long, 8–22 mm (⁵⁄₁₆–¹³⁄₁₆ in.) wide, apices obtuse with small spine, bases acute, margins recurved, crenulate, petioles 2.5–7 mm (³⁄₃₂–⁹⁄₃₂ in.) long; inflorescences axillary, solitary, 3-flowered, pedunculate, flowers 4-merous, peduncles 5–7 mm (³⁄₁₆–⁹⁄₃₂ in.) long; fruits unknown. Habitat: Colombia, Ecuador, and Venezuela. Allied to *I. lechleri* and *I. matthewsii*.

Ilex myrtifolia Walter 1788. Myrtleleaf holly (synonyms *I. rosmarinifolia* Lamarck 1728, *I. angustifolia* De Candolle 1825, *I. cassine* var. *myrtifolia* (Walter) Sargent 1889, *I. cassine* var. *myrtifolia* (Walter) Chapman 1889, *I. cassine* var. *ligustrifolia* (Pursh) Dyzol 1892, *I. cassine* var. *parvifolia* (Koch) Schelle 1907).

Large shrubs or small trees 4–7 m (13–23 ft.) tall, branches gray, smooth, irregular, slightly pubescent; leaves dark olive green, elliptic or linear, 1–4 cm (⅜–1⅝ in.) long, 8–10 mm (⁵⁄₁₆–⅜ in.) wide, apices apiculate, bases acute to cuneate, margins slightly revolute, short petioles 2–5 mm (¹⁄₁₆–³⁄₁₆ in.) long; inflorescences axillary, solitary on new growth, solitary or branched, flowers 4-merous; fruits red, rarely yellow, globose, 6–8 mm (⁷⁄₃₂–⁵⁄₁₆ in.) diameter, pedicels 2–5 mm (¹⁄₁₆–³⁄₁₆ in.) long; pyrenes 4, smooth. Habitat: United States, Coastal Plains, in swamps and cypress ponds of North Carolina, to Florida and Louisiana. Hardy in zones 7 to 10. Allied to *I. cassine* and often listed as a variety of it. Frequently used as a background plant in the landscape. Plate 69.

Ilex myrtifolia f. *lowei*, see *I. myrtifolia* 'Lowei' in Chapter 15.

Ilex naiguatina Loesener 1901.
Evergreen shrubs; leaves elliptic to obovate, 2.2–

Figure 14-38. *Ilex myrtifolia*. Drawing by Randy Allen.

4.7 cm (¹³⁄₁₆–1¹³⁄₁₆ in.) long, 1.2–2.5 cm (½–1 in.) wide, apices rotund, bases obtuse to subacute, margins recurved, densely serrulate near apex, punctate beneath; inflorescences axillary, solitary on new growth, branched, 3-flowered, flowers 4- to 5-merous; fruits, ovoid or depressed-globose, 5 mm (³⁄₁₆ in.) diameter, peduncles 7–15 mm (⁹⁄₃₂–¹⁹⁄₃₂ in.) long; pyrenes 5. Habitat: Venezuela, Mount Naiguata near Caracas at 2500 m (8250 ft.) elevation. Allied to *I. uniflora*.

Ilex nanningensis Handel-Mazzetti 1934.
Evergreen, large trees to 20 m (65 ft.) tall, densely pubescent; leaves elliptic, rarely lanceolate, 5–8 cm (2–3⅜ in.) long, 1.5–3.5 cm (¹⁹⁄₃₂–1⅜ in.) wide, apices short or gradually acuminate, acumens broadly deltoid, 5–12 mm (³⁄₁₆–¹⁵⁄₃₂ in.) long, bases obtuse or cuneate, margins crenate-serrate, midribs impressed, pubescent above, petioles 7–10 mm (⁹⁄₃₂–⅜ in.) long, leaves persist on 4th-year wood; inflorescences axillary and fasciculate on 2nd-year growth, flowers 4-merous, yellow, fragrant, pedicels 6–8 mm (⁷⁄₃₂–⁵⁄₁₆ in.) long; fruits red, subglobose, 8 mm (⁵⁄₁₆ in.) long, 10 mm (3.8 in.) diameter; pyrenes 4, rugose, reticulate-striate. Habitat: People's Republic of China, possibly endemic, mountains between Guangxi and Guangdong provinces, and Vietnam. Allied to *I. subficoides*.

Ilex nannophylla Borhidi & Muniz 1976.
Evergreen shrubs to 2 m (6 ft.) tall, young branches glabrous and angulate; leaves orbiculate to broadly ovate, 0.5–1.3 cm (³⁄₁₆–½ in.) long, 0.3–1 cm (⅛–⅜ in.) wide, bases obtuse to rotund, apices usually acute or briefly acuminate, margins recurved, 1–3 dentate teeth near apex, petioles 1–2 mm (¹⁄₃₂–¹⁄₁₆ in.) long; flowers and fruits unknown. Habitat: Cuba, Oriente Province, at 1800 m (5940 ft.) elevation.

Ilex nayana Cuatrecasas 1948.
Evergreen, large trees, branchlet glabrous; leaves

Figure 14-39. *Ilex myrtifolia.* Photo by Barton Bauer Sr.

elliptic-oblong, 6–10 cm (2⅜–4 in.) long, 2–4 cm (¾–1⅝ in.) wide, bases usually cuneate, apices acute or acuminate, margins entire, petioles 5–10 mm (³⁄₁₆–⅜ in.) long; inflorescences axillary, racemose or pseudoumbellate, flowers 4-merous; fruits unknown. Habitat: Colombia, Department del Valle, and along Naya river. Allied to *I. laureola.*

Ilex neblinensis Edwin 1965 var. *neblinensis.*
Evergreen shrubs or small trees to 8 m (26 ft.) tall, branches glabrous; leaves broadly ovate or broadly obovate, 2.5–5 cm (1–2 in.) long, 2–2.8 cm (¾–1¼ in.) wide, punctate beneath, bases acute or cuneate, apices obtuse to rotund, occasionally retuse, margins entire, revolute, petioles 6–9 cm (⁷⁄₃₂–¹¹⁄₃₂ in.) long; inflorescences axillary, solitary, lateral, fasciculate, flowers usually 5-merous; fruits brown when dry, ovoid, 9–10 mm (¹¹⁄₃₂–⅜ in.) long, 7–8 mm (⁹⁄₃₂–⁵⁄₁₆ in.) diameter; pyrenes 3–4, striate. Habitat: Venezuela, Amazonas State, along east escarpment of upper Canon Grande basin, at 2100 m (6930 ft.) elevation.

Ilex neblinensis var. *wurdackii* Edwin 1965.
A variety differing from the type with larger and wider leaves, 6.5–8.5 cm (2½–3⅜ in.) long, 3.5–4.5 cm (1⅜–1¾ in.) wide. Habitat: Venezuela.

Ilex nemorosa Rizzini 1975 (synonym *I. uniflora* Rizzini 1974, *non* Fawcett & Rendle 1921).
Evergreen, small trees to 6 m (20 ft.) tall, branches glabrous; leaves obovate-oblong to obovate-elliptic, 5–9 cm (2–3½ in.) long, 3–6 cm (1³⁄₁₆–2⅜ in.) wide, bases broadly cuneate to obtuse, apices rotund, margins entire, petioles 10–15 mm (⅜–¹⁹⁄₃₂ in.)

long; inflorescences axillary, single; fruits unknown. Habitat: Brazil, Bahia State, humid forest.

Ilex nervosa Triana & Plancheon 1872 var. *nervosa* (synonym *I. nervosa* var. *genuina* Loesener 1901).
Evergreen shrubs or trees; leaves oval or elliptic to subovate, 10–17 cm (4–6¾ in.) long, 5.5–7.5 cm (2⅛–3 in.) wide, pubescent beneath, apices short acuminate, bases obtuse, margins recurved, entire or minutely serrulate, petioles 10–15 mm (⅜–¹⁹⁄₃₂ in.) long; inflorescences axillary, multifasciculate or paniculate, branched, flowers 5-merous; fruits unknown. Habitat: Colombia, near Bogota, at 2000–2500 m (6600–8250 ft.) elevation. Allied to *I. dioica.*

Ilex nervosa var. *aequatoriensis* Loesener 1901 (synonym *I. aequatoriensis* Loesener 1892).
A variety with smaller leaves and petioles 10–13 mm (⅜–¹⁵⁄₃₂ in.) long. Habitat: South America.

Ilex nervosa var. *glabrata* Steyermark 1951. Jagua negro.
A variety with leaves glabrous beneath. Habitat: Venezuela, above Tabay, Merida State, at 2285–9050 m (7500–9050 ft.) elevation.

Ilex ningdeensis C.-j. Tseng 1981.
Evergreen trees, branchlets brownish, angulate, densely black-puberulent; leaves obovate-elliptic or elliptic or oblong, 4–6 cm (1⅝–2⅜ in.) long, 2–2.7 cm (¾–1¹⁄₁₆ in.) wide, glandular punctuate beneath apices obtuse or rotund, or abruptly short-acuminate, bases decurrent and obtuse, margins crenulate, petioles 6–8 mm (⁷⁄₃₂–⁵⁄₁₆ in.) long, puberulent, canaliculate; inflorescences axillary, 4-fasciculate, branched, pedicels 5 mm (³⁄₁₆ in.) long; fruits red, globose, 10

mm (³⁄₈ in.) diameter; pyrenes 4, rugose, sulcate, sides striate, sulcate. Habitat: People's Republic of China, Fujian Province. Allied to *I. formosae*.

Ilex nitens Ridley 1926.

Evergreen, small trees; leaves opposite, oblong-elliptic, obtuse to elliptic-lanceolate, 9–9.5 cm (3½–3¾ in.) long, 3.5–4.2 cm (1³⁄₈–1¹¹⁄₁₆ in.) wide, margins entire, petioles stout, 1 cm (³⁄₈ in.) long; inflorescences axillary, short racemes, 1 cm (³⁄₈ in.) long, bracts at base, corolla tubes distinct, stigmas. Habitat: Malaysia, Pahang State, Gunung Benom, at 1818 m (6000 ft.) elevation. Allied to *I. wenzelii*.

Ilex nitida (Vahl) Maximowicz 1881 subsp. *nitida*.
Cuero de sapo, citronnien, bois petit Jean (synonyms *Prinos nitida* Vahl 1798, *I. macoucoua* Stapf 1861, *I. dioica* Bello 1883, *I. nitida* f. *integrifolia* Loesener 1892, *I. nitida* f. *ovalifolia* Loesener 1908).

Evergreen, glabrous shrubs or trees 5–20 m (16–65 ft.) tall, branchlets striate, angulate, lenticels present; leaves elliptic to obovate-elliptic, 5.5–14 cm (2⅛–5½ in.) long, 2–5 cm (¾–2 in.) wide, apices obtuse or rotund, shortly acuminate, bases acute or obtuse, margins crenulate serrate, rarely subentire, petioles 7–15 mm (⁹⁄₃₂–¹⁹⁄₃₂ in.) long; inflorescences axillary, fasciculate, flowers usually 4-merous; fruits red, ovoid, 7–8 mm (⁹⁄₃₂–⁵⁄₁₆ in.) long; pyrenes 4, 5-striate, 4-sulcate. Habitat: Mexico, Cuba, Puerto Rico, Montserrat, Guadeloupe and Martinique. Allied to *I. cognata*.

Ilex nitida subsp. *bahiahondica* (Loesener) Borhidi 1971 (synonym *I. nitida* var. *bahiahondica* Loesener 1923).

A subspecies with obovate to oval leaves, margins entire to subentire. Habitat: Cuba.

Ilex nitidissima C.-j. Tseng 1984.

Evergreen, small trees to 6 m (20 ft.) tall, branchlets angulate, puberulent or glabrescent; leaves elliptic or oblong-elliptic, rarely ovate-elliptic, 5.5–9 cm (2⅛–3 in.) long, 2.7–4 cm (1¹⁄₁₆–5.8 in.) wide, apices acuminate, bases obtuse or cuneate, rarely subrotund, margins subentire, occasionally remotely and inconspicuously serrate, petioles 6–8 mm (⁷⁄₃₂–⁵⁄₁₆ in.) long, puberulent; inflorescences axillary, 2- to 4-fasciculate; fruits red, globose, 5 mm (³⁄₁₆ in.) diameter, pedicels 8–10 mm (⁵⁄₁₆–³⁄₈ in.) long; pyrenes 4, smooth. Habitat: People's Republic of China, Hunan Province. Allied to *I. longecaudata*.

Ilex nokoensis Hayata 1911.

Evergreen shrubs, stems gray, lenticels black pilose, branches spreading, gray turning reddish, short hirsute; leaves oblong-ovate or obovate, 2.5 cm (1 in.) long, 1.3 cm (½ in.) wide, bases acute or cuneate to acute, apices rotund-obtuse or obtuse, occasionally callose-mucronate. Very similar to *I. crenata,* differing by having impressed veins on upper surface, margins obtusely crenate, petioles 2 mm (¹⁄₁₆ in.) long. Habitat: Japan, Nokosan, 2727 m (9000 ft.) elevation. Allied to *I. crenata*.

Ilex nothofagifolia Kingdon-Ward 1927 (synonyms *I. intricata* Hooker f. var. *oblata* W. E. Evans 1921, *I. oblata* (Evans) Comber 1933, *I. intricata sensu* Merrill 1941, *non* Hooker f. 1875).

Evergreen, glabrous, small trees to 6 m (20 ft.) tall, branchlets with long longitudinal rows of corky warts; leaves broadly elliptic, 7–14 mm (⁹⁄₃₂–¹⁷⁄₃₂ in.) long, 6–10 mm (⁷⁄₃₂–³⁄₈ in.) wide, apices obtusely cuspidate, bases obtuse, margins serrate, 4–7 teeth on each side, petioles slender, 4–5 mm (⁵⁄₃₂–³⁄₁₆ in.) long; inflorescences axillary on 2nd-year growth, paucifasciculate, petals pale green; fruits red, depressed globose, 3 mm (⅛ in.) long, 4 mm (⁵⁄₃₂ in.) diameter, usually solitary, pedicels 3 mm (⅛ in.) long; pyrenes 4, back 3- to 4-striate, sides smooth. Habitat: first recorded from Myanmar, and later collected in People's Republic of China, Yunnan Province, at 2300–3000 m (6600–9900 ft.) elevation. Species epithet first published as "nothofagacifolia"; correction was made in 1930 by F. Kingdon-Ward. Allied to *I. delavayi* and *I. intricata*.

Ilex nubicola C.-y. Wu *ex* Y.-r. Li 1984.

Evergreen shrubs or trees, branchlets angulate, sulcate; leaves oblong or wide-lanceolate or narrow-elliptic, 7–9 cm (2¾–3½ in.) long, 2–3.2 cm (¾–1¼ in.) wide, apices acuminate or long-acuminate, bases wide-cuneate, margins moderately wavy, denticulate, veins conspicuous on both surfaces, petioles 8–10 mm (⁵⁄₁₆–³⁄₈ in.) long; male inflorescences cymose, pseudopaniculate, flowers 4-merous; female flowers and fruits unknown. Habitat: People's Republic of China, Yunnan Province, at 2500 m (8200 ft.) elevation. Allied to *I. tetramera*.

Ilex nuculicava S.-y. Hu 1949 f. *nuculicava* (synonyms *I. cinerea* var. *nuculicava* Merrill 1928, *I. nuculicava* var. *auctumnalis* S.-y. Hu 1949).

Evergreen trees to 9 m (30 ft.) tall, branches puberulent or glabrescent; leaves oblong-elliptic, 8–13.5 cm (3⅛–5¼ in.) long, 2.2–4.5 cm (⅞–1¾ in.) wide, marked with black dots, apices short-acuminate, acumens 5–10 mm (³⁄₁₆–³⁄₈ in.) long, bases obtuse, margins subentire, undulate, minutely crenate, petioles 9–15 mm (¹¹⁄₃₂–¹⁹⁄₃₂ in.) long; inflorescences axillary and fasciculate on 2nd-year growth, branched, flowers 4-merous; fruits red, globose, 10 mm (³⁄₈ in.) diameter, pedicels 5–6 mm (³⁄₁₆–⁷⁄₃₂ in.)

long; pyrenes 4, palmately striate and sulcate, wrinkled, pitted. Habitat: People's Republic of China, endemic to Hainan Province, in woods at 500–1800 m (1650–5900 ft.) elevation. Allied to *I. cinerea*.

Ilex nuculicava f. *brevipedicellata* (S.-y. Hu) T. R. Dudley, *comb. & stat. nov.* (basionym *I. nuculicava* var. *brevipedicellata* S.-y. Hu, *Jour. Arnold Arboretum* 30: 387. 1949).

A form differing from typical individuals with much shorter fruiting pedicels, 2 mm (¹⁄₁₆ in.) long. Habitat: People's Republic of China, Hainan Province.

Ilex nuculicava f. *glabra* (S.-y. Hu) C.-j. Tseng 1981 (synonym *I. nuculicava* var. *glabra* S.-y. Hu 1949).

A form differing from typical individuals with glabrous buds, branchlets, and inflorescences. Habitat: People's Republic of China, Hainan Province.

Ilex nummularia Reisseck 1861, *non* Franchet & Savatier 1876.

Evergreen shrubs to 2 m (6.5 ft.) tall, branches pubescent; leaves broadly oval or ovate, 1.1–2.4 cm (⁷⁄₁₆–²⁹⁄₃₂ in.) long, 8–19 mm (⁵⁄₁₆–¹⁵⁄₁₆ in.) wide, apices rotund with short point, bases rotund, margins entire, recurved, occasionally small serrulate teeth near apex, petioles 2 mm (¹⁄₁₆ in.) long; inflorescences at base of new growth, fasciculate, flowers 4-merous; fruits unknown. Habitat: Brazil. Allied to *I. scutiiformis* and *I. subcordata*.

Ilex nunezii Borhidi 1972.

Evergreen, branched shrubs 1–2 m (3–6 ft.) tall, young branchlets minutely pubescent; leaves broadly triangular or ovate, 1–2 cm (³⁄₈–3.4 in.) long, bases truncate, rotund or subcordate, apices gently narrowed, obtuse, veins obsolete or conspicuous, margins entire; inflorescences axillary or terminal, pubescent, 1–3 corymbose, peduncles pubescent, 3–4 mm (¹⁄₈–⁵⁄₃₂ in.) long, pedicels 2–3 mm (¹⁄₁₆–¹⁄₈ in.) long; flowers 4-merous; fruits subglobose, yellowish brown; pyrenes 4. Habitat: Cuba, Oriente Province, Sierra Maestra on Mount Pico Suecia, at 1720 m (5676 ft.) elevation. Named in honor of Antonio Nunez, president, Academy of Science of Cuba, 1972. Allied to *I. turquinensis* and at a later date may be regarded as conspecific since both are from the same locality and habitat.

Ilex obcordata Swartz 1797, *non* Triana 1862 (synonym *I. cuneifolia* Hooker 1840, *I. shaferi* Britton & P. Wilson 1920).

Evergreen shrubs 1–3 m (3–10 ft.) tall, to slender dense crowned tree to 10 m (33 ft.) tall, twigs ridged below petioles; leaves obovate, 2 cm (¾ in.) long, 1 cm (³⁄₈ in.) wide, apices rotund, small pointed, bases acute or cuneate, margins entire, revolute, petioles 2–4 mm (¹⁄₁₆–⁵⁄₃₂ in.) long; male inflorescences 2- to 3-flowered, female flowers solitary, 4- to 6-merous; fruits red, globose, 4–5 mm (⁵⁄₃₂–³⁄₁₆ in.) diameter; pyrenes 4–6. Habitat: Jamaica, in woodland and exposed thicket, at 1210–2240 m (4000–7400 ft.) elevation. Allied to *I. pseudovaccinium* and *I. walkeri*.

Ilex oblonga C.-j. Tseng 1981.

Evergreen trees to 20 m (65 ft.) tall, branchlets purple-gray, angulate, terminal buds puberulent or glabrescent, elliptic lenticels; leaves oblong-elliptic or elliptic, rarely ovate-elliptic, 7.5–9.5 cm (3–3¾ in.) long, 2.7–3.6 cm (1¹⁄₁₆–1³⁄₈ in.) wide, glabrous, glandular punctate beneath, apices long acuminate or merely acuminate, bases attenuate-obtuse or obtuse, rarely rotund, glabrous, glandular punctate beneath, margins remotely crenulate, petioles 8–15 mm (⁵⁄₁₆–¹⁹⁄₃₂ in.) long; inflorescences axillary, 2- to 4-fasciculate, pedicels 2–4 mm (¹⁄₁₆–⁵⁄₃₂ in.) long, pubescent; fruits red, oblong or obovoid-oblong, 4–4.5 mm (⁵⁄₃₂–¼ in.) long, 3 mm (¹⁄₈ in.) diameter; pyrenes 4, irregularly striate and sulcate, occasionally rugose and channeled. Habitat: People's Republic of China, Guangxi Province. Allied to *I. nanningensis*.

Ilex obtusata (Turczaninow) Triana 1878 (synonym *Prinos obtusata* Turczaninow 1858, *non* Willdenow 1818).

Evergreen; leaves oval 6–9 cm (2³⁄₈–3½ in.) long, 5–6 cm (2–2³⁄₈ in.) wide, bases subrounded, apices obtuse to rounded, margins crenulate-serrulate, reticulate beneath, petioles 7–9 mm (⁹⁄₃₂–¹¹⁄₃₂ in.) long; inflorescences axillary, solitary, branched, 5- to 7-flowered, peduncles 9–12 mm (¹¹⁄₃₂–¹⁵⁄₃₂ in.) long, pedicels 2 mm (¹⁄₁₆ in.) long; fruits unknown. Habitat: Colombia, Pamplona Province, near LaBaya at 2600–2700 m (8600–8900 ft.) elevation. Allied to *I. crassifolioides*.

Ilex occulta C.-j. Tseng 1981.

Evergreen shrubs to 2 m (6 ft.) tall, branchlets slender, angulate, dark brown, puberulent to glabrescent; leaves elliptic or obovate-elliptic, rarely obovate, 3–4.5 cm (1³⁄₁₆–1¾ in.) long, 1.4–1.6 cm (¹⁷⁄₃₂–⁵⁄₈ in.) wide, glandular, punctate beneath, apices obtuse or subrotund, bases decurrently cuneate or cuneate-attenuate into petioles, margins subentire, subrevolute, petioles 5 mm (³⁄₁₆ in.) long, narrowly winged; inflorescences axillary, 2- to 3-fasciculate, pedicels 3–4 mm (¹⁄₈–⁵⁄₃₂ in.) long; fruits small, red, globose, 5–6 mm (³⁄₁₆–⁷⁄₃₂ in.) diameter, surface verrucose with small gall-like structures; pyrenes 4, rugose, sulcate. Habitat: People's Republic of China, Guangxi Province. Very different and diverse from all other known species of Chinese *Ilex*. Possibly with some affinity to *I. suzukii*.

Ilex odorata Hamilton 1825 (synonyms *Myrsine theifolia* Wallich 1832, *I. theifolia* Hooker 1875, *I. odorata* var. *teymanii* Loesener 1901).

Evergreen, small trees; leaves elliptic-oblong or lanceolate, 5–9.5 cm (2–3¾ in.) long, often longer, 1.2–3.5 cm (½–1⅜ in.) wide, bases acute or cuneate-obtuse, apices acuminate, acumens 5–17 mm (³/₁₆–²¹/₃₂ in.) long, margins minutely serrate, petioles 5–10 mm (³/₁₆–⅜ in.) long; inflorescences axillary, fasciculate, flowers 4-merous; fruits black, globose, 4–6.5 mm (⁵/₃₂–¼ in.) diameter; pyrenes 4. Habitat: India, southern Himalaya Mountains, at 1000–1700 m (3300–5600 ft.) elevation. Allied to *I. denticulata* and *I. glomerata*.

Ilex oligodenta Merrill & Chun 1930 (synonym *I. wilsonii sensu* Merrill 1934).

Evergreen, puberulent shrubs to 2 m (6 ft.) tall, branchlets slender, puberulent, lenticels numerous, conspicuous; leaves oblong-elliptic or oblong-lanceolate, 3–7.5 cm (1³/₁₆–3 in.) long, 1–2 cm (⅜–¾ in.) wide, apices gradually acuminate, acumens 7–15 mm (⁹/₃₂–¹⁹/₃₂ in.) long, bases obtuse, margins entire, occasionally 1–2 teeth near apex, puberulent, petioles 3–6 mm (⅛–⁷/₃₂ in.) long; inflorescences axillary, male inflorescences 3- to 7-flowered cymose, female inflorescences single, flowers 4-merous; fruits unknown. Habitat: People's Republic of China, Guangdong Province. Allied to *I. fukienensis* and *I. wilsonii*.

Ilex oligoneura Loesener 1901.

Evergreen shrubs or trees; leaves obovate-cuneate, 2.7–5 cm (1¹/₁₆–2 in.) long, 1.3–2.1 cm (¹⁵/₃₂–²⁵/₃₂ in.) wide, apices rotund, bases acute, margins recurved, subentire at base, minutely serrulate near apex, petioles 3–5 mm (⅛–³/₁₆ in.) long; inflorescences axillary, solitary, sessile or fasciculate, flowers usually 4-merous; fruits unknown. Habitat: Brazil. Allied to *I. amara* and *I. theezans*.

Ilex oliveriana Loesener 1901.

Evergreen, glabrous, large shrubs or trees; leaves lanceolate or oblanceolate, 4.5–7 cm (1¾–2¾ in.) long, 1.1–1.7 cm (⁷/₁₆–²¹/₃₂ in.) wide, apices acute or acute-acuminate, bases acute, margins entire, recurved, petioles 3–5 mm (⅕–³/₁₆ in.) long; inflorescences axillary, fasciculate, branched, flowers 4-merous; fruits black, globose 5 mm (³/₁₆ in.) diameter; pyrenes 4. Habitat: Venezuela and Guyana near Roraima at 1170 m (3860 ft.) elevation. Allied to *I. umbellata*.

Ilex omeiensis H. H. Hu & Tang 1940 (synonym *I. omeiensis* S.-y. Hu 1946).

Evergreen shrubs or small trees to 10 m (33 ft.) tall, branchlets glabrous; leaves broadly elliptic to oblong-elliptic, 10–20 cm (4–8 in.) long, 4–7 cm (1⅝–2¾ in.) wide, apices short-acuminate, acumens 5–10 mm (³/₁₆–⅜ in.) long, bases obtuse or rotund, margins entire, midribs impressed above, prominent beneath, lateral veins 6–8 pairs, petioles 13–20 mm (½–¾ in.) long; inflorescences axillary, females umbelliform, peduncles 7–12 mm (⁹/₃₂–¹⁵/₃₂ in.) long, pedicels 5–7 mm (³/₁₆–⁹/₃₂ in.) long, flowers 6- to 7-merous; fruits red, globose, 4 mm (⁵/₃₂ in.) diameter; pyrenes 6–7, 3-striate; endocarps smooth, leathery. Habitat: People's Republic of China, only from Mount Omei in western Sichuan Province, in mixed forests at 1500 m (4950 ft.) elevation. Allied to *I. venulosa*.

Ilex opaca Aiton 1789 f. *opaca*. American Holly, white holly (synonyms *I. aquifolium* Marsh 1785, *I. canadense* Marshall 1785, *I. laxifolia* Lamarck 1789, *I. quercifolia* Meerburgh 1798, *I. americana* Lamarck 1802, *I. opaca* var. *laxifolia* (Lamarck) Nuttall 1818, *Ageria opaca* (Aiton) Rafinesque 1838, *I. canadensis* Hort. *ex* Don 1853–1854, *I. prinifolia* Lavallée 1877, *I. opaca* var. *prinifolia* (Lavallée) Lavallée 1921).

Evergreen trees to 15 m (50 ft.) or more tall, young branchlets puberulent, branches spreading, usually forming a conical to pyramidal habit; leaves usually dark olive green, elliptic to elliptic-lanceolate to oval, 5–10 cm (2–4 in.) long, 3–6 cm (1³/₁₆–2⅜ in.) wide, rarely entire with only one apicule or spine, usually with 3–6 or more spines on each side, margins often revolute or recurved, flat to wavy, generally keeled, petioles 6–12 mm (⁷/₃₂–⅜ in.) long; inflorescences axillary on new growth, males in cymes, females solitary, 1–3 on peduncle, flowers 4-merous; fruits red, orange, or yellow, globose to ellipsoid, 8–12 mm (⁵/₁₆–⅜ in.) diameter, often persisting until spring or longer; pyrenes 4, striate, sulcate. Habitat: eastern United States, from eastern Massachusetts to Pennsylvania, West Virginia, south to Florida, west to Texas and Missouri, north to Tennessee and Indiana. Hardy in zones 6 to 10. Common understory tree in mixed hardwood forest; found in various sites from dry wood to edge of creeks and ravines and in swamps. Introduced in 1744. Allied to *I. cassine*, *I. myrtifolia*, and *I. rubra*.

In the United States no tree is more familiar to the general public than *I. opaca*. It was first described by Solander in Aiton's *Hortus Kewensis I* in 1789 and, while in question, some still only cite Aiton as the authority. Numerous hybrids of *I. opaca* are found in the wild where *I. cassine* and *I. myrtifolia* overlap. These hybrid plants are now listed as *I.* × *attenuata* and differ from *I. opaca* by having thinner leaves, more lanceolate to oblanceolate, usually flat, with spines near the apex, and consistent attenuate base.

Numerous cultivars are named and registered; see descriptions in Chapter 15. Some old varieties and forms are given cultivar names in *Hortus III,* but it is doubtful if plants are still available. Plate 70.

Ilex opaca var. *acuminata* Beissner 1903, see 'Acuminata'.

Ilex opaca subsp. *cumicola* (Nobs) Muir 1882, see *I. cumulicola.*

Ilex opaca var. *cumicola* (Aiton) Rose 1925, see *I. cumulicola.*

Ilex opaca var. *floribunda* Demcker 1904, see 'Floribunda'.

Ilex opaca var. *globosa* Beissner 1903, see 'Globosa'.

Ilex opaca var. *integra* Woods 1970, see *I.* × *attenuata.*

Ilex opaca var. *latifolia* Beissner 1903, see 'Latifolia'.

Ilex opaca var. *laxifolia* (Lamarck) Nuttall 1818, see *I. opaca.*

Ilex opaca var. *macrodon* Beissner 1903, see 'Macrodon'.

Ilex opaca var. *prinifolia* Lavallée 1821, see *I. opaca.*

Ilex opaca f. *subintegra* Weatherby 1921 (synonym *I. opaca* var. *subintegra* (Weatherby) Rehder 1923).

A botanical form with entire leaves or nearly so with usually one spine at the apex. Discovered in the wild by C. T. Jones near Mashpee, Massachusetts. Both male and female plants occur in the wild. The forma occurs throughout the range of species.

Ilex opaca f. *xanthocarpa* Rehder 1907.

A botanical form with yellow fruits. At least 50 or more plants have been found in the wild or grown as seedlings from yellow-fruited plants and given cultivar names. Some have incorrectly been named 'Xanthocarpa', with no source of origin. Others have been given fancy cultivar names such as 'Betty Nevison', 'Boyce Thompson Xanthocarpa', 'Yellow Berry', and 'Yellow Jacket' (see Chapter 15 for descriptions of named cultivars).

Ilex oppositifolia Merrill 1939.

Evergreen trees 12–18 m (40–60 ft.) tall; leaves opposite, sessile, elliptic to oblong-elliptic, 11–18

Figure 14-40. *Ilex opaca* f. *opaca.* Photo by Barton Bauer Sr.

cm (4⅜–7¼ in.) long, 6–11 cm (2⅜–4⅜ in.) wide, bases rotund to cordate, apices rotund or briefly acuminate, margins entire; inflorescences cymose umbellate, flowers usually 4-merous; fruits red, globose, 5–6 mm (³⁄₁₆–⁷⁄₃₂ in.) diameter; pyrenes 7–8. Habitat: Malaysia, on Mount Kinabalu, on forested ridges 1200–1500 m (4000–5000 ft.) elevation. Originally thought to be a celastraceous plant, *Microtropis* species. Allied to *I. zygophylla.*

Figure 14-41. A 50-year-old specimen of *Ilex opaca* at Tyler Arboretum, Lima, Pennsylvania. Photo by Franklin West.

Ilex orestes Ridley 1931 var. *orestes.*
Evergreen, small trees; leaves oblong-obovate, 3–5 cm (1³⁄₁₆–2 in.) long, 1–2 cm (³⁄₈–³⁄₄ in.) wide, bases narrow, apices retuse, densely punctate above, 5-paired veins beneath, nearly inconspicuous, petioles stout, 2 mm (¹⁄₁₆ in.) long; inflorescences axillary, pubescent, racemes; fruits small, globose. Habitat: Borneo, Sarawak, Santubong, Baoge Mountains. Allied to *I. havilandi.*

Ilex orestes var. *dulitensis* Airy Shaw 1939.
A variety with small leaves, rarely 2–3 cm (³⁄₄–1³⁄₁₆ in.) long, 1–2 cm (³⁄₈–³⁄₄ in.) wide, conspicuous pustulate verruculose beneath, veins above usually invisible. Habitat: Borneo.

Ilex organensis Loesener 1901.
Evergreen shrubs, branches pubescent; leaves oval-oblong, pubescent, 2–4.5 cm (³⁄₄–1³⁄₄ in.) long, 9–20 mm (¹¹⁄₃₂–³⁄₄ in.) wide, apices obtuse or rotund, usually with small point at apex, bases obtuse or acute, margins entire, revolute, petioles 3–6 mm (¹⁄₈–⁷⁄₃₂ in.) long; inflorescences axillary, solitary, pubescent, branches 1- to 3-flowered, flowers 4-merous; fruits black, globose, 5 mm (³⁄₁₆ in.) diameter; pyrenes 4. Habitat: Brazil, Orgãos Mountains. Allied to *I. asperula.*

Ilex ovalifolia G. Meyer 1818. Bakrabakaro (synonym *I. brexiaefolia* Hort. *ex* Houttuyn *ex* Goeppert 1852).
Evergreen, glabrous shrubs or small trees; leaves oval or obovate, 6–10.5 cm (2³⁄₈–4¹⁄₈ in.) long, 2.8–4 cm (2¹⁄₈–1⁵⁄₈ in.) wide, apices obtuse or briefly acuminate, bases cuneate-obtuse, margins recurved, densely subcrenulate-serrate, petioles 5–7 mm (³⁄₁₆–⁹⁄₃₂ in.) long; inflorescences axillary, paniculate, flowers 4-merous; fruits unknown. Habitat: French Guiana near Cayenne. Allied to *I. affinis.*

Ilex ovalis (Ruiz & Pavón) Loesener 1901 (synonyms *Paltoria ovalis* Ruiz & Pavón 1794, *I. paltoria* Persoon 1805).
Evergreen shrubs to 4 m (13 ft.) tall; leaves oval to suborbiculate, 1.5–2 cm (¹⁹⁄₃₂–³⁄₄ in.) long, 8–12 mm (⁵⁄₁₆–¹⁵⁄₃₂ in.) wide, apices rotund, bases obtuse or acute, margins recurved, crenulate-serrate, punctate beneath, petioles 2–2.5 mm (¹⁄₁₆–³⁄₃₂ in.) long; inflorescences axillary, solitary on new growth, 3-flowered, pedunculate, flowers 4-merous; fruits unknown. Habitat: Peru. Allied to *I. lechleri* and *I. matthewsii.*

Ilex pachyphylla Merrill 1915.
Evergreen trees to 10 m (33 ft.) tall, glabrous, branches stout, dark; leaves elliptic to obovate-elliptic, glossy, 5–10 cm (2–4 in.) long, 2.5–6 cm (1–2³⁄₈ in.) wide, bases somewhat narrowed, acute or slightly decurrent-acuminate, apices rotund to obtuse, slightly retuse, margins entire, revolute; inflorescences cymose, axillary, pseudoterminal, 2–5 cm (³⁄₄–2 in.) long, many-flowered, pedicels pubescent; flowers 5-merous; young fruits narrowly ovoid. Habitat: Philippines, Luzon, Tayabas, in mossy forest, Mount Bimuang, back of Infanta at 980 m (3234 ft.) elevation. Allied to *I. cymosa.*

Ilex pallida Standley 1926.
Evergreen shrubs 1.5–3 m (5–10 ft.) tall, branches densely puberulent; leaves oblong-elliptic or elliptic, 4–9 cm (1⁵⁄₈–3½ in.) long, 1.7–4 cm (2¹⁄₃₂–1⁵⁄₈ in.) wide, bases obtuse, apices acuminate, leaves do not blacken when dry, margins remotely serrulate, petioles stout, 5–7 mm (³⁄₁₆–⁹⁄₃₂ in.) long; inflorescences axillary, solitary, branches 2- to 3-flowered; fruits unknown. Habitat: Costa Rica, endemic in forests northeast of San Iairo de Heredia and Dota. Similar to *I. discolor* var. *lamprophylla.*

Ilex paltorioides Reisseck 1861. Congonha.
Evergreen shrubs 1–2 m (3–6 ft.) tall; leaves ovate or obovate, 1–2.3 cm (³⁄₈–⁷⁄₈ in.) long, 8–13 mm (⁵⁄₁₆–¹⁵⁄₃₂ in.) wide, apices obtuse or rotund, bases acute, margins recurved, crenulate-serrulate, petioles 1.5–3 mm (³⁄₆₄–¹⁄₈ in.) long; inflorescences axillary, solitary on new growth, usually single flowers, flowers 4-merous; fruits black, ellipsoid or globose, 3.5–4 mm (⁷⁄₆₄–⁵⁄₃₂ in.) diameter; pyrenes 4. Habitat: Brazil. Allied to *I. virgata* and *I. vitis-idaea.*

Ilex paraguariensis St.-Hilaire 1822 var. *paraguariensis.* Mate, Paraguay tea, yerba maté, yerba de maté, congonha, orelha de burro, caaquazu (synonyms *I. mate* St.-Hilaire 1824, *Rhamnus quitensis* Sprengel 1828, *I. curtibensis* Miers 1861, *I. domestica* Reisseck 1861, *I. sorbilis* Reisseck 1861, *I. theaezans* Bonpland 1861, *I. vestita* Reisseck 1861, *I. congonhas* Liais 1878, *I. curtibensis* var. *gardneriana* Miers 1880, *I. paraguariensis* D. Don 1882, *I. bonplandiana* Muenter 1883, *I. paraguayensis* Morong & Britton 1892).
Evergreen, highly variable, large shrubs or trees to 8 m (26 ft.) tall, branchlets glabrescent or puberulent; leaves obovate or elliptic-obovate, 3–14 cm (1³⁄₁₆–5½ in.) long, 0.8–6.5 cm (⁵⁄₁₆–2½ in.) wide, leaves often larger, to 25 cm (10 in.) long, 15 cm (6 in.) wide, apices obtuse or rotund, or obtuse to acuminate, bases cuneate or narrow-acute, margins recurved, coarsely crenate on upper two-thirds of leaf, petioles 5–19 mm (³⁄₁₆–³⁄₄ in.) long; inflorescences axillary and fasciculate on new growth, males pseudopaniculate, females usually solitary, flowers usually 4-merous; fruits dark reddish brown, globose or ellipsoid, to 5–7 mm (³⁄₁₆–⁹⁄₃₂ in.) diameter; py-

renes 4, striate, sulcate. Habitat: Paraguay, adjacent Argentina, and Brazil. The primary source of yerba de maté, an herbal drink made from the dried fermented leaves, is obtained both in the wild and from cultivated trees. Many cultivars are grown in South America. Allied to *I. cognata*. Plate 71.

Ilex paraguariensis var. *sincorensis* Loesener 1908.
A variety of evergreen shrubs 1–3 m (3–10 ft.) tall, differing from typical individuals with broadly elliptic leaves, and large red fruits, to 10 mm (3⁄8 in.) long. Habitat: Brazil, Minas Gerais State.

Ilex paraguariensis var. *vestita* (Reisseck) Loesener 1908.
A variety with branches, leaves, and inflorescences pubescent; calyces dense, gray-brown pubescent to hairy, male peduncles lax, usually 8 mm (5⁄16 in.) long. Habitat: Brazil, Minas Gerais State.

Ilex paruensis Steyermark 1988.
Evergreen shrubs to 2 m (6 ft.) tall, branchlets minutely pubescent; leaves broadly obovate, 2.5–3.5 cm (1–13⁄8 in.) long, 1.5–2.2 cm (19⁄32–13⁄16 in.) wide, densely black punctate above, bases acute, apices rotund, minute mucronulate tips, margins entire, midribs minutely puberulent below, petioles 2 mm (1⁄16 in.) long; inflorescences axillary, lateral, solitary or fasciculate, 1- to 3-flowered; fruits globose, 3 mm (1⁄8 in.) diameter, pedicels 1–3 mm (1⁄32–1⁄8 in.) long. Habitat: Venezuela, Amazonas, Department Atabapo, Serrania sel Paru, at 1100 m (3630 ft.) elevation. Allied to *I. vacciniifolia*.

Ilex parvifructa Edwin 1965.
Evergreen shrubs or small trees; leaves usually obovate, 4.5–5.8 cm (13⁄4–21⁄4 in.) long, 2.2–2.6 cm (13⁄16–1 in.) wide, bases cuneate or acute, apices usually acute, margins entire, slightly revolute, petioles 7–9 m (9⁄32–11⁄32 in.) long, inflorescences axillary, solitary, pedunculate, flowers 4-merous; fruits pale brown when dry, globose, 4 mm (5⁄32 in.) diameter; pyrenes 4, striate. Habitat: Venezuela, Bolivar State, woodlands along watercourse, North Valley, Cerro Guaiquinima, at 1600–1700 m (5280–5610 ft.) elevation.

Ilex paucinervis Merrill 1920.
Evergreen shrubs or small trees, glabrous; leaves oblong-elliptic to oblong, 2–4 cm (3⁄4–15⁄8 in.) long, 1–1.8 cm (3⁄8–11⁄16 in.) wide, bases acute, apices obtuse, distinctly retuse, pitted above but not glandular, margins entire, petioles 2–4 mm (1⁄16–5⁄32 in.) long; inflorescences axillary, solitary, racemes, 5- to 10-flowered, flowers 5-merous; fruits brown when dry, ovoid or globose, 3 mm (1⁄8 in.) diameter. Habitat: endemic to Philippines, Luzon, in forest at 1000 m (3300 ft.) elevation. Allied to *I. spicata*.

Ilex paujiensis Steyermark 1988.
Evergreen, small trees to 4 m (14 ft.) tall, branchlets glabrous; leaves obovate, 6.5–11 cm (23⁄8–43⁄8 in.) long, 2.5–4.5 cm (1–13⁄4 in.) wide, strongly black punctate beneath, bases, cuneate, apices rotund, occasionally retuse, margins entire, glabrous, petioles 5–10 mm (3⁄16–3⁄8 in.) long; inflorescences axillary, solitary, lateral; fruits globose, 6 mm (7⁄32 in.) diameter, pedicels 2–3 mm (1⁄16–1⁄8 in.) long. Habitat: Venezuela, Amazonas, south of El Pauji. Allied to *I. gransabanensis*.

Ilex pedunculosa Miquel 1868 var. *pedunculosa*. Long-stalked holly, soyogo (synonyms *I. pedunculosa* f. *continentalis* Loesener *ex* Diels 1901, *I. purpurea* Hasskarl var. *leveilleana* Loesener 1914, *I. impressivena* Yamamoto 1925, *I. morii* Yamamoto 1925, *I. pedunculosa* f. *genuina* Loesener 1927, *I. fujisanensis* Hort. *ex* Sakata).
Evergreen, large shrubs or small trees to 10 m (33 ft.) tall, branches glabrous, bark greenish gray, smooth; leaves ovate-elliptic to elliptic, 4–8 cm (15⁄8–31⁄8 in.) long, 2.5–3.5 cm (1–13⁄8 in.) wide, apices acuminate to abruptly acute at apex, bases rounded or obtuse, margins entire, petioles slender, 1–2 cm (3⁄8–3⁄4 in.) long; inflorescences axillary, peduncled cymes on new growth, flowers 4-merous, solitary, rarely 3-flowered; fruits red, globose, 7–8 mm (9⁄32–5⁄16 in.) diameter, nodding on long slender pedicels 4–4.5 cm (15⁄8–13⁄4 in.) long; pyrenes 5, smooth. Hardy in zones 6 to 9. Habitat: Kyushu and Honshu, Japan, central and eastern People's Republic of China, Taiwan, and Korea. Common tree in gardens in Japan and China, foliage used in decorations. Introduced by Charles S. Sargent from Japan to the Arnold Arboretum in 1893 and later by E. H. Wilson from China. Popular for its attractive red pendulous fruits. Allied to *I. rotunda*. Plates 72, 73.

Ilex pedunculosa f. *aurantiaca* (Koidzumi) Ohwi 1953, see *I. pedunculosa* 'Aurantiaca' in Chapter 15.

Ilex pedunculosa var. *aurantiaca* Koidzumi 1934, see *I. pedunculosa* 'Aurantiaca' in Chapter 15.

Ilex pedunculosa var. *senjoensis* (Hayashi) H. Hara 1954. Takane-soyogo (synonym *I. senjoensis* Hayashi 1952).
Low shrubs with long, creeping, sparsely branched stems; flowers 6-merous. Habitat: Japan, Shinano Province, high mountains of Honshu, on Mount Senjo.

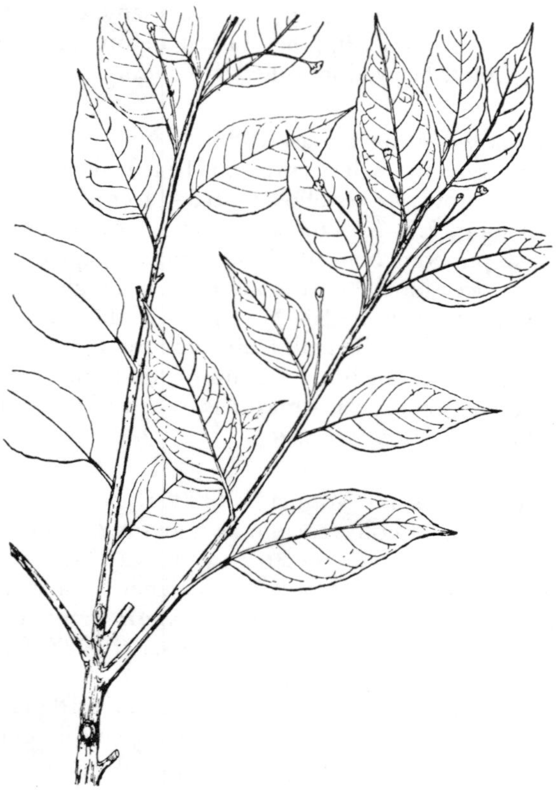

Figure 14-42. *Ilex pedunculosa* var. *pedunculosa.* Drawing by Chien-chu Chen in *Illustrations of Native and Introduced Ligneous Plants of Taiwan* (1962) by Tang-shui Liu.

Ilex pedunculosa f. *variegata* (Nakai) Ohwi 1953, see *I. pedunculosa* 'Variegata'.

Ilex pedunculosa var. *variegata* Nakai *ex* Makino 1925, see *I. pedunculosa* 'Variegata'.

Ilex peiradena S.-y. Hu 1950.

Evergreen, glabrous shrubs to 2 m (6 ft.) tall, branchlets slender, striate, rugose; leaves lanceolate, 4–7.5 cm (1⅝–3 in.) long, 1.2–2 cm (15⁄32–¾ in.) wide, apices short-acuminate, acumens 5–8 mm (3⁄16–5⁄16 in.) long, bases cuneate, margins subentire or minutely glandular-crenulate, petioles 6–10 mm (7⁄32–⅜ in.) long; inflorescences axillary and fasciculate on 2nd-year growth, flowers 4-merous; fruits yellow in July, subglobose, 3 mm (⅛ in.) long, 4 mm (5⁄32 in.) diameter, pedicels to 5 mm (3⁄16 in.) long, calyces persistent; pyrenes 4, palmately striate, sulcate, sides wrinkled, pitted, rugose. Habitat: People's Republic of China endemic to high mountains on the border of Guangxi and Guangdong provinces, and Vietnam. Allied to *I. ficoidea.* Leaves similar to those of *I. metabaptista.*

Ilex perado Aiton 1792 subsp. *perado* (synonyms *I. maderensis* Lamarck 1724, *I. crassifolia* Meerburgh 1798, *I. perado* var. *obtusa* De Candolle 1825, *I. microphylla* Hort. *ex* Regel 1866, *I. perado* var. *maderensis* (Lamarck) Loesener 1901, *I. perado* var. *maderensis* subvar. *genuina* Loesener 1901).

Evergreen, small trees to 5 m (16 ft.) tall; leaves obovate to ovate or oblong, rarely orbicular or elliptic, occasionally bullate, 6–8 cm (2⅜–3⅛ in.) long, 4–5.5 cm (1⅝–2⅛ in.) wide, sucker and seedling leaves often larger, margins usually entire, or with very small spines, pointing forward near apex, petioles usually glabrous; fruits red, usually globose, 7–10 mm (9⁄32–⅜ in.) diameter.

Ilex perado subsp. *azorica* (Loesener) Tutin 1933 (synonyms *I. perado* sensu Seubert 1844, *I. perado* var. *azorica* Loesener 1901, *I. azorica* (Loesener) Gandoger 1918, *I. perado* f. *umbrosa* P. C. Silva & Q. J. P. Silva 1974).

Evergreen shrubs; leaves orbicular or ovate or oblong, 3–6.5 cm (1 3⁄16–2½ in.) long, 2.5–5 cm (1–2 in.) wide, margins flat, usually entire, or appressed spines, pedicels 3–9 mm (⅛–11⁄32 in.) long, usually glabrous; fruits red, usually globose, 8–9 mm (5⁄16–11⁄32 in.) diameter; pyrenes usually 4. Habitat: Azores Islands.

Ilex perado subsp. *iberica* (Loesener) S. Andrews 1985 (synonyms *I. aquifolium sensu* Auett, *non* Willkomm & Lange 1877, *I. perado* var. *iberica* Loesener 1901).

Evergreen trees; leaves ovate to ovate-oblong, 8–9.5 cm (3⅛–3¾ in.) long, 4–5.5 cm (1¾–2⅛ in.) wide, flat, usually entire, or rarely very small

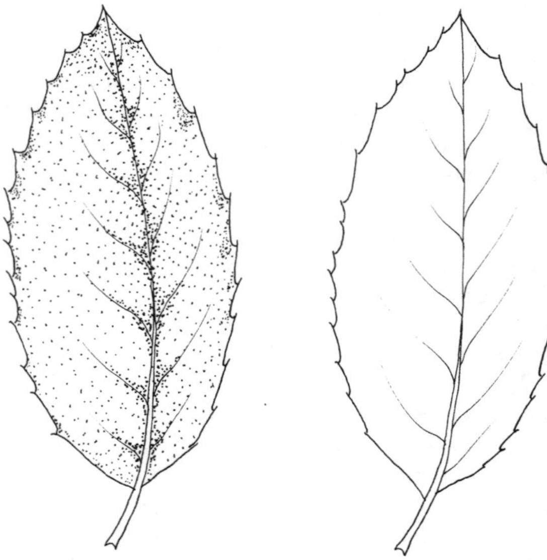

Figure 14-43. *Ilex perado.* Drawing by Randy Allen.

spinose, petioles pubescent, 10–24 mm (⅜–⅞ in.) long, sometimes winged; fruits red, globose, 9–10 mm (¹¹⁄₃₂–⅜ in.) diameter; pyrenes usually 4. Habitat: Spain and Portugal, Iberian Peninsula.

Ilex perado var. *lopezlillo* (Kunkel) S. Andrews 1985 (synonyms *I. platyphylla* subsp. *lopezlillo* Kunkel 1977, *I. perado* subsp. *lopezlillo* (Kunkel) Hansen & Sunding 1979).

Evergreen trees, branches glabrous; leaves elliptic-oblong, flat, to 11.2 cm (4½ in.) long, 5.7 cm (2³⁄₁₆ in.) wide, margins entire, petioles 14–20 mm (¹⁷⁄₃₂–¾ in.) long, usually glabrous, always winged; fruits red, globose, 7–10 mm (⁹⁄₃₂–⅜ in.) diameter; pyrenes usually 4. Habitat: Spain, Canary Islands only.

Ilex perado subsp. *platyphylla* (Webb & Berthelot) Tutin 1933 (synonym *I. platyphylla* Webb & Berthelot 1842).

Evergreen trees to 15 m (50 ft.) tall; leaves broadly ovate or obovate or oblong, rarely elliptic, 10–13 cm (4–5⅛ in.) long, 6–8.5 cm (2⅜–3⅜ in.) wide, sucker leaves larger, margins flat, entire to partly spiny, pointing forward, petioles usually pubescent, 8–16 mm (⁵⁄₁₆–⅝ in.) long, occasionally winged; fruits red, globose, 8–10 mm (⁵⁄₁₆–⅜ in.) diameter; pyrenes usually 4. Habitat: Spain, Tenerife and Gomera.

Ilex percoriacea Tuyama 1935. Atuba-motinoki.
Evergreen, small trees, branches glabrous; leaves oblong-elliptic to oblanceolate-oblong, 6.5–9.5 cm (2½–3½ in.) long, 1.7–2.8 cm (²¹⁄₃₂–1⅛ in.) wide, bases cuneate to narrow-cuneate, apices usually obtuse, margins entire, petioles 14–19 mm (¹⁷⁄₃₂–¾ in.) long, 5-angulate; fruits dull red, globose, 3 mm (⅛ in.) diameter. Habitat: endemic to Bonin Islands. Allied to *I. bonincola*.

Ilex perlata C. Chen & S.-c. Huang *ex* Y.-r. Li 1985.
Evergreen shrubs or trees, branchlets thick, purple black; leaves very large, elliptic or oblong, (20–) 30–36 cm ((8–) 12–14 in.) long; 9–13 cm (3½–5⅛ in.) wide, apices acuminate or falcate-acuminate, bases obtuse or wide-cuneate, margins moderately serrate, serrations bent back strongly and abruptly, glabrous above, densely velutinous and pubescent beneath, petioles 1.8–2.5 cm (¹¹⁄₁₆–1 in.) long; inflorescences axillary, cymose-paniculate, or fasciculate, puberulent; flowers purplish red, 4-merous; fruits red, subglobose, 9 mm (¹¹⁄₃₂ in.) long, 8 mm (⁵⁄₁₆ in.) diameter; pyrenes 4, rugose, striate, granular scaly. Habitat: People's Republic of China, Yunnan Province. Allied to *I. latifolia* and *I. purpurea*.

Ilex permicrophylla Merrill 1925.
Evergreen shrubs or small trees 3–4 m (10–13 ft.)

tall, branchlets and pedicels minutely cinereous-puberulent, branches gray, glabrous; leaves elliptic, 1–1.5 cm (⅜–¹⁹⁄₃₂ in.) long, 5–7 mm (³⁄₁₆–⁹⁄₃₂ in.) wide, bases and apices acute, margins entire, petioles 1–1.5 mm (¹⁄₃₂–³⁄₆₄ in.) long; flowers axillary, solitary, 4- to 5-merous, pedicels puberulent, 2–3 mm (¹⁄₁₆–⅛ in.) long, bibracteolate; fruits globose, 2–2.5 mm (¹⁄₁₆–³⁄₃₂ in.) diameter; pyrenes 3–4, calyces persistent, puberulent. Habitat: Philippines, Luzon, Benguet, Mount Baudan, and between Mankayan and Baguio, in mossy forests, at 2100 m (6930 ft.) elevation. Curiously similar to *I. yunnanensis* var. *parvifolia*. Allied to *I. hanceana*.

Ilex pernervata Cuatrecasas 1948.
Evergreen trees, branches glabrous; leaves obovate-elliptic to elliptic-oblong, 3.5–11 cm (1⅜–4⅜ in.) long, 2.2–6 cm (1¼–2⅜ in.) wide, bases attenuate, cuneate, or rotund, apices rotund to slightly obtuse-attenuate, margins entire, petioles 4–16 mm (⁵⁄₃₂–⅝ in.) long; inflorescences axillary, cymose; fruits 10–12 mm (⅜–¹⁵⁄₁₆ in.) diameter; pyrenes 6–7. Habitat: Colombia, Department del Valle, San Francisco, along Putomayo River at high elevations.

Ilex pernyi Franchet 1883. Perny's holly.
Evergreen shrubs or small trees to 8 m (26 ft.) tall, branchlets pubescent; leaves dark olive-green, ovate or ovate-lanceolate, 1.3–2.5 cm (¹⁵⁄₃₂–1 in.) long, 5–14 mm (³⁄₁₆–¹⁷⁄₃₂ in.) wide, broadest between the 2 anterior spines, apices triangularly acuminate, acumens 12–14 mm (⅜–¹⁷⁄₃₂ in.) long, terminated by strong spine, 3 mm (⅛ in.) long, bases rotund or truncate, margins sinuate, dentate, 1–3 (usually 2) spines on each side, the 2 anterior spines strongest, petioles very short 2 mm (¹⁄₁₆ in.) long, leaves persist on 4th- to 5th-year growth, crowded close together, appearing sessile; inflorescences axillary and fasciculate on 2nd-year growth, flowers 4-merous; fruits red, globose or depressed-globose, 7–8 mm (⁹⁄₃₂–⁵⁄₁₆ in.) diameter, pedicels 2 mm (¹⁄₁₆ in.) long; pyrenes 4, palmately striate, sulcate. Habitat: endemic to central People's Republic of China in the Qinling Shan Mountains, from Gansu to Shaanxi provinces, limited by climatic barrier; from Gansu down to the foothills of Huang shan in Anhui Province. Introduced to England by E. H. Wilson in 1900, and to the Arnold Arboretum in 1908 and 1917. Hardy in zones 5b to 9. See descriptions of *I. pernyi* cultivars in Chapter 16. Allied to *I. bioritsensis* and *I. georgei*.

Ilex petiolaris Poeppig 1852 (synonym *I. parviflora* Bentham 1852).
Evergreen trees to 8 m (26 ft.) tall; leaves oval-oblong to obovate-oblong, 6.3–12 cm (2½–4¾ in.) long, 2.5–5 cm (1–2 in.) wide, apices obtuse, acuminate, bases cuneate or cuneate acute, margins entire,

Figure 14-44. *Ilex pernyi*. Drawing by Randy Allen.

recurved, petioles 10–19 mm (⅜–¾ in.) long; inflorescences in leaf axils, fasciculate, branched, flowers small, 4-merous; fruits dark brown (dried), depressed globose, 4 mm (⁵⁄₃₂ in.) long, 4.5 mm (¹¹⁄₆₄ in.) wide, peduncles 4–9 mm (⁵⁄₃₂–¹¹⁄₃₂ in.) long, pedicels 1.5–3 mm (³⁄₆₄–⅜ in.) long; pyrenes 4, unisulcate. Habitat: northern Brazil, Amazonas State, along the Rio Negro near Barra. Allied to *I. floribunda, I. umbellata,* and *I. vismiifolia.*

Ilex phillyreifolia Reisseck 1861 (synonym *I. phillyreifolia* var. *typica* Loesener 1901).
    Evergreen shrubs, heavily branched; leaves ovate, 1.5–2.8 cm (¹⁹⁄₃₂–1⅛ in.) long, 7–18 mm (⁹⁄₃₂–¹¹⁄₁₆ in.) wide, apices obtuse or rotund, bases obtuse or rotund, margins recurved, crenulate-serrulate, petioles 1–2.5 mm (¹⁄₃₂–³⁄₃₂ in.) long; inflorescences axillary, solitary on new growth, 3-flowered, pedunculate, flowers 4- to 5-merous; fruits brownish black, globose, 3.5 mm (⁷⁄₆₄ in.) diameter; pyrenes 4. Habitat: Brazil. Allied to *I. kunthiana* and *I. myricoides.*

Figure 14-45. *Ilex pernyi*. Photo by Barton Bauer Sr.

Ilex pierreana Loesener 1901 (synonym *Melathallus diospyrifolius* Pierre 1893).
    Evergreen, glabrous large shrubs or trees; leaves elliptic or oblong-elliptic, 2.2–2.7 cm (¹³⁄₁₆–2⅙ in.) long, 6–9 cm (2⅜–3 in.) wide, apices obtuse, minutely mucronulate, bases cuneate or cuneate and subacute, margins entire, revolute, petioles 2–2.5 cm (¾–1 in.) long; inflorescences fasciculate in leaf axils, flowers 6- to 8-merous, petals 5–5.5 mm (³⁄₁₆–¹³⁄₆₄ in.) long; fruits unknown. Habitat: Brazil. Allied to *I. megalophylla.*

Ilex pingheensis C.-j. Tseng 1989.
    Evergreen shrubs 2–3 m (6–9 ft.) tall, branches slender, angulate, lenticels glabrous; leaves oblong-lanceolate or elliptic-lanceolate, 3.5–6 cm (1⅜–2⅜ in.) long, 1.5–2.5 cm (¹⁹⁄₃₂–1 in.) wide, bases cuneate, apices acuminate to long-acuminate, margins remotely serrulate, petioles slender, 4–7 mm (⁵⁄₃₂–⁹⁄₃₂ in.) long; fruits purplish, subglobose, 5 mm (³⁄₁₆ in.) diameter. Habitat: People's Republic of China, Fujian Province, in open woodlands at 900 m (2970 ft.) elevation. Allied to *I. corallina.*

Ilex pingnanensis S.-y. Hu 1950.
    Evergreen, small trees, branchlets pubescent; leaves oblong or oblong-elliptic, 5–12 cm (2–4¾ in.) long, 2.2–3.2 cm (¹³⁄₁₆–1¼ in.) wide, apices acuminate, acumens 8–14 mm (⁵⁄₁₆–¹⁷⁄₃₂ in.) long, bases obtuse, margins subentire, or minutely crenulate-serrulate, petioles 5–7 mm (³⁄₁₆–⁹⁄₃₂ in.) long; inflorescences axillary and fasciculate on 2nd-year growth; fruits red, globose, 6 mm (⁷⁄₃₂ in.) diameter, pedicels 2 mm (¹⁄₁₆ in.) long; pyrenes 4, palmately striate, sulcate, wrinkled, pitted. Habitat: People's Republic of China, eastern Guangxi Province. Allied to *I. formosana.* Often mistaken for *I. nanningensis,* but has smaller fruits, and larger leaves.

Ilex pleiobrachiata Loesener 1901.
    Evergreen, large shrub with spreading to erect grayish branches, dense conspicuous lenticels; leaves glabrous, oval to ovate, 6–11 cm (2⅜–4¼ in.) long, 2.7–5.4 cm (1¹⁄₁₆–5⅛ in.) wide, margins entire, recurved, petioles 7–12 mm (⁹⁄₃₂–¹⁵⁄₃₂ in.) long; inflorescences solitary in leaf axils, peduncles 9–22 mm (¹¹⁄₃₂–¹³⁄₁₆ in.) long, branched; mature fruit unknown; pyrenes 10. Habitat: Indonesia, Java. Allied to *I. anomala.*

Ilex pleurostachys Turczaninow 1858. In *Bull. Soc. Imp. Mosc.* 1858. 31: 436.
    Description not available.

Ilex poilanei Tardieu 1945.
    Evergreen trees 7–8 m (23–26 ft.) tall, branches

glabrous, spreading or erect, dense lenticels; leaves elliptic or ovate, 6–8 cm (2⅜–3⅛ in.) long, 3–3.5 cm (1³⁄₁₆–1⅜ in.) wide, bases decurrent, acute, apices acuminate, margins entire, recurved, petioles glabrous, 6 mm (7⁄32 in.) long; inflorescences axillary, solitary or with 2–3 flowers; fruits globose, 4 mm (5⁄32 in.) diameter; pyrenes 6, sulcate. Habitat: southern Vietnam, Annam to Nha Trang and Ninh Hoa. Allied to *I. rubinervia.*

Ilex polita Steyermark 1988.

Evergreen shrubs 2 m (6 ft.) tall, branches glabrous; leaves ovate or oblong or elliptic-oblong, glossy, 4–7.5 cm (1⅝–3 in.) long, 1.8–4.5 cm (11⁄16–1¾ in.) wide, bases obtuse or rotund, apices obtuse or rotund, margins entire, revolute, petioles 4–10 m (5⁄32–⅜ in.) long; inflorescences axillary, solitary, lateral, pedunculate, flowers 4-merous; fruits unknown. Habitat: Venezuela, Bolivar State, Auyántepui between escarpment and Guayaraca River.

Ilex polypyrena C.-j. Tseng & B. W. Liu 1981.

Evergreen trees to 6 m (20 ft.) tall, branchlets brownish, bark whitish; leaves obovate-elliptic, 6–8.5 cm (2½–3⅜ in.) long, 2.5–4.3 cm (1–1⁵⁄₁₆ in.) wide, apices rotund or obtuse, bases cuneate or cuneate-obtuse, glossy, glabrous, margins entire, petioles 1–1.8 cm (⅜–11⁄16 in.) long; inflorescences solitary, axillary, cymes dichotomously branched, 6-fruited; fruits dark purplish red, obovoid to globose, 7 mm (9⁄32 in.) diameter, calyces persistent; pyrenes 10–12, unisulcate. Habitat: People's Republic of China, Guangxi Province, Shiwan Large Mountain Range, Mount Tsaobi. Allied to *I. thorelii.* This is one of the most primitive species of subgenus *Bryonia,* which had not been previously reported from the People's Republic of China.

Ilex praetermissa Kiew 1977.

Evergreen shrubs usually 1–1.5 m (4–5 ft.) tall, branches lenticellate; leaves oblong-elliptic, 4.5–5.5 cm (1⅗–2⅛ in.) long, 1.5–2.5 cm (19⁄32–1 in.) wide, bases decurrent, apices obtuse or occasionally retuse, margins entire, petioles 5 mm (3.16 in.) long; inflorescences axillary, solitary or occasionally 2–3 cymes, flowers 4- to 5-merous; fruits purplish, ovoid, 6–7 mm (7⁄32–9⁄32 in.) long, 5 mm (3⁄16 in.) diameter; pyrenes 4–5. Habitat: Malaysia, Klang Gates Ridge, on the sides of dry quartzite ridges. Rare inconspicuous shrubs, thus specific name. Allied to *I. tahanensis.*

Ilex psammophila Martius *ex* Reisseck 1861.

Evergreen, glabrous, large shrubs or small trees to 8 m (26 ft.) tall; leaves oval or obovate or oblong, usually 7–10 cm (2¾–4 in.) long, 3–4 cm (1³⁄₁₆–1⅝ in.) wide, apices obtuse often acuminate, bases cuneate or cuneate-obtuse, margins entire, recurved, petioles 8–15 mm (5⁄16–19⁄32 in.) long; inflorescences fasciculate in leaf axils, flowers usually 5-merous; fruits brownish black, ovoid, 9 mm (11⁄32 in.) long, 7–8 mm (9⁄32–5⁄16 in.) wide; pyrenes 5–6, sulcate. Habitat: Venezuela and Brazil. Allied to *I. integerrima, I. longipetiolata,* and *I. lundii.*

Ilex pseudobuxus (Reisseck) Loesener 1893 f. *pseudobuxus* (synonym *I. pseudobuxus* f. *reissecki* Loesener 1901).

Evergreen shrubs to 4 m (13 ft.) tall; leaves close together, obovate to obovate-elliptic, 2–6 cm (¾–2⅜ in.) long, 0.9–3.5 cm (11⁄32–1⅜ in.) wide, bases acute or cuneate, apices rotund or obtuse, often with minute spine, margins rarely entire, occasionally serrulate, petioles 3–7 mm (1³⁄₁₆–2¾ in.) long; inflorescences axillary, glabrous, solitary, single or 3–7 flowers, peduncles 0.7–2 cm (9⁄32–¾ in.) long, pedicels 2–4 mm (1⁄16–5⁄32 in.) long; fruits dark violet, globose, 3.5–5.5 mm (⅛–7⁄32 in.) diameter; pyrenes 4. Habitat: Brazil, Espirito Santo, between Campos, Vitteria, and São Paulo. Allied to *I. macfadyenii.*

Ilex pseudobuxus f. *peduncularis* (Reisseck) Loesener 1901 (synonym *I. peduncularis* Reisseck 1861).

This form differs from the species with leaflike petioles on new branches and inflorescences pubescent to hairy. Habitat: Brazil, São Paulo State. May be a synonym of the species.

Ilex pseudoebenacea Loesener 1901.

Evergreen, large shrubs or small trees to 3–7 m (10–23 ft.) tall; leaves elliptic or suboval, 5–7 cm (2–2¾ in.) long, 1.7–3.8 cm (21⁄32–1¼ in.) wide, punctate beneath, apices obtuse or rotund, bases rotund or obtuse, margins recurved, remotely serrulate near apex, petioles 2–8 mm (1⁄16–5⁄16 in.) long; inflorescences at base of new growth, axillary, solitary, 1- to 3-flowered, pedunculate, flowers 4- to 5-merous; fruits black, globose or oval, 10 mm (⅜ in.) long, 7.5 mm (9⁄32 in.) wide; pyrenes 4–5, striate, sulcate. Habitat: Bolivia, near Hauycanis, and in Peru at 3340 m (9,900–11,000 ft.) elevation. Allied to *I. integerrima* var. *ebenacea.*

Ilex pseudoembelioides Loesener 1901.

Evergreen shrubs, branches pubescent; leaves oval or ovate-oblong, 1.7–4.3 cm (21⁄32–1½ in.) long, 4–17 mm (5⁄32–21⁄32 in.) wide, apices obtuse, acute acumens, 5–10 mm (3⁄16–⅜ in.) long at apex, bases cuneate or cuneate obtuse, margins entire, recurved, petioles 2–4 mm (1⁄16–5⁄32 in.) long; inflorescences at base of new growth, axillary, solitary, flowers 5-merous; fruits unknown. Habitat: Indonesia, Celebes Islands. Allied to *I. celebesiaca* and *I. embelioides.*

Ilex pseudomachilifolia C.-y. Wu *ex* Y.-r. Li 1985.

Evergreen trees to 10 m (33 ft.) tall, branchlets purplish black, lenticels small and conspicuous; leaves elliptic to obovate-elliptic, 15–18 cm (6⅛–7⁷⁄₁₆ in.) long, 5–7 cm (2–2¾ in.) wide, glabrous, bases wide-cuneate or obtuse, apices acuminate, margins scarcely undulate, slightly serrate, petioles 1.8–2 cm (⅝–¾ in.) long; flowers unknown; infructescences branched, cymose, axillary, peduncles 7–12 mm (⁹⁄₃₁–¹⁵⁄₃₂ in.) long, pedicels 3–7 mm (⅛–⁹⁄₃₂ in.) long; fruits red, ovoid globose (juvenile) persistent calyces. Habitat: southwestern People's Republic of China, Yunnan Province. Closely resembling *I. machilifolia* and may only be a variety or synonym of it.

Ilex pseudomacoucoua Loesener 1933.

Evergreen, glabrous trees, branches longitudinally striate, lenticels tuberculate, stipules persistent, deltoid; leaves lanceolate or oblong to ovate, 5–8 cm (2–3⅛ in.) long, 2.5–3 cm (1–1⅜ in.) wide, bases acute or obtuse, apices somewhat obtuse, often obsoletely acuminate, margins entire, recurved, petioles slender; inflorescences axillary, fasciculate, flowers 4- to 5-merous; fruits and male flowers unknown. Habitat: Dominican Republic, Santo Domingo Province, near Curenca. Allied to *I. guianensis* and *I. inundata.*

Ilex pseudo-odorata Loesener 1901.

Evergreen, small trees, branchlets angulate; leaves oval to obovate-lanceolate or elliptic-lanceolate, 9–20 cm (3½–7½ in.) long, 3.5–7.5 cm (1⅜–3 in.) wide, bases obtuse to rotund, apices short-acuminate, margins recurved, serrulate, petioles 8–18 mm (⁵⁄₁₆–¹¹⁄₁₆ in.) long; fruits red. Habitat: India, Himalaya Mountains, at 1000–2000 m (3300–6600 ft.) elevation. Allied to *I. kingiana* and *I. latifolia.*

Ilex pseudothea Reisseck 1861 var. *pseudothea* (synonym *I. pseudothea* var. *genuina* Loesener 1901).

Evergreen shrubs or trees; leaves oblong or oval to ovate-oblong, 3.5–4.5 cm (1⅜–1¾ in.) long, 1.3–2.6 cm (¹⁵⁄₃₂–2 in.) wide, apices obtuse or acute acuminate, bases acute or obtuse, margins recurved, densely serrulate or crenulate, petioles 3–6 mm (⅛–⁷⁄₃₂ in.) long; inflorescences axillary, paniculate or racemose, flowers 4-merous; fruits globose, 4–5 mm (⁵⁄₃₂–³⁄₁₆ in.) diameter, color unknown; pyrenes 4. Habitat: Brazil. Allied to *I. amara.*

Ilex pseudothea var. *cipoensis* Loesener 1901.

A variety with leaf margins crenulate or crenulate-serrulate, veins distinctly reticulate, apices with no acumens. Habitat: Brazil, Minas Gerais State.

Ilex pseudotheezans Loesener 1901.

Evergreen shrubs; leaves obovate, 4.5–9.5 cm (2⅛–3¾ in.) long, 2.5–5 cm (1–2 in.) wide, apices rotund or obtuse, minutely mucronate, bases acute or subcuneate, margins entire, recurved, petioles 2–7 mm (¹⁄₁₆–⁹⁄₃₂ in.) long; inflorescences fasciculate in leaf axils, 3- to 7-flowered, flowers 4-merous; fruits unknown. Habitat: Brazil, Goiás State, on serpentine rock. Allied to *I. brasiliensis, I. friburgensis,* and *I. theezans.*

Ilex pseudoumbelliformis T. R. Dudley, *nom. nov.* (basionym *I. attenuata* Steyermark, *Ann. Missouri Bot. Gard.* 75(1): 322. 1988, which is a later homonym of *I.* × *attenuata* Ashe 1924).

Evergreen trees 12 m (40 ft.) tall; leaves oblong-elliptic or broadly elliptic-lanceolate, 1–2 cm (⅜–¾ in.) long, 3–5 mm (⅛–³⁄₁₆ in.) wide, punctate beneath, bases obtuse or subacute, apices long attenuate, obtuse or acuminate, margins 7–10 crenulations on each side, petioles 7–14 mm (⁹⁄₃₂–¹⁷⁄₃₂ in.) long; inflorescences axillary, peduncles and pedicels minutely puberulent; fruits globose, 5–6 m (³⁄₁₆–⁷⁄₃₂ in.) diameter; pyrenes trigonous, 3–4 dorsally costate. Habitat: Brazil, Amazonas State, Sierra Pirapucu, at 1250 m (4100 ft.) elevation.

Ilex pseudovaccinium Reisseck *ex* Maximowicz 1881 (synonyms *I. scutiiformis* Warming 1879, *non* Reisseck 1861, *I. pseudovaccinium* var. *diminuta* (Reisseck) Loesener 1901, *I. pseudovaccinium* var. *scutiiformioides* Loesener 1901, *I. pseudovaccinium* var. *typica* Loesener 1901).

Evergreen shrubs to 1.5 m (4.9 ft.) tall, branches pubescent; leaves oval or ovate or subovate, 0.7–3 cm (⁹⁄₃₂–1³⁄₁₆ in.) long, 0.6–2.2 cm (⁷⁄₃₂–⅞ in.) wide, apices rotund or obtuse, small point at apex, bases rotund or obtuse, margins entire, recurved, occasionally slightly serrated near apex, petioles 1–5 mm (¹⁄₃₂–³⁄₁₆ in.) long; inflorescences axillary, solitary at base of new growth, branches 3- to 7-flowered, flowers usually 4-merous; fruits, broadly ovoid, 4 mm (⁵⁄₃₂ long, 3.5 mm (1⅜ in.) wide, peduncles 6 mm (⁷⁄₃₂ in.) long, pedicels 1–2 mm (¹⁄₃₂–¹⁄₁₆ in.) long; pyrenes 3. Habitat: Brazil, Goiás State, on Mount Ilacolumi. Allied to *I. scutiiformis.*

Ilex ptariana Steyermark 1952.

Evergreen, large shrubs or trees to 6.5–13 m (21–43 ft.) tall, branches glabrous; leaves obovate or elliptic-oblong, 4–9 cm (1⅝–3½ in.) long, 2–5 cm (¾–2 in.) wide, punctate beneath, bases narrow-subacute or narrow-obtuse, apices rotund or obtuse, leaves of female plants narrower than on male plants, margins entire, slightly revolute, petioles 6–10 mm (⁷⁄₃₂–⅜ in.) long; male inflorescences axillary, solitary, pedicels 16–28 mm (⅝–1⅛ in.) long; fruits unknown. Habitat: Bolivia and Venezuela, between Cave Rock and base of high sandstone bluffs, Ptaritepui, at 2285–2405 m (7540–7940 ft.) elevation. Allied to *I. integerrima*.

Ilex puberula Proctor 1967.
    Evergreen shrubs or trees to 10 m (33 ft.) tall; leaves narrow-ovate, 1–3 cm (⅜–1³⁄₁₆ in.) long, 0.5–1.5 cm (³⁄₁₆–¹⁹⁄₃₂ in.) wide, apices acute, bases rotund to cuneate, margins serrate, petioles to 5 mm (³⁄₁₆ in.) long; inflorescences axillary, solitary, flowers 5- to 6-merous; fruits subglobose, 3 mm (⅛ in.) long, color unknown. Habitat: Jamaica, endemic and rather local at St. Andrews Port, in open woodlands and steep slopes, at 1212–1515 m (4000–5000 ft.) elevation.

Ilex pubescens Hooker & Arnott 1833 var. *pubescens* (synonym *I. trichoclada* Hayata 1913).
    Evergreen shrubs to 3 m (10 ft.) tall, branchlets subquadrangular, rugose, puberulent; leaves elliptic or obovate-elliptic, usually 2–5 cm (¾–2 in.) long, 1–2.5 cm (⅜–1 in.) wide, apices acute or shortly acuminate, acumens 3–7 mm (⅛–⁹⁄₃₂ in.) long, tip cuspidate, bases obtuse, margins sharp or slightly serrate or entire, petioles 2.5–5 mm (1–2 in.) long; inflorescences axillary on 2nd-year growth, female inflorescences fasciculate, 1- to 3-flowered cymes, flowers 6- to 8-merous, petals pink; fruits red, globose, 4 mm (⁵⁄₃₂ in.) diameter; pyrenes usually 6, 3-striate. Habitat: southeastern People's Republic of China, and Taiwan, wide distribution in warm temperate and subtropical climates. Allied to *I. hainanensis* and *I. serrata*.

Ilex pubescens var. *kwangsiensis* Handel-Mazzetti 1933.
    This variety differs from typical individuals by having larger leaves and apices abruptly acuminate, numerous prominent veins; fruits smaller. Habitat: People's Republic of China, Guangdong Province.

Ilex pubilimba Merrill & Chun 1940 (synonym *I. hirsuticarpa* Tardieu 1945).
    Evergreen, pubescent trees to 15 m (50 ft.) tall; leaves elliptic, 3–7 cm (1³⁄₁₆–2¾ in.) long, 1.3–2.5 cm (¹⁵⁄₃₂–1 in.) wide, apices shortly acuminate, acumens 3–10 mm (⅛–⅜ in.) long, bases rotund, obtuse or cuneate, margins crenate-serrate, midribs impressed and pubescent above, petioles 1.5–3.5 mm (³⁄₆₄–⁹⁄₆₄ in.) long; inflorescences axillary and fasciculate on 2nd-year growth, flowers 4-merous; fruits red, depressed-globose, 7 mm (⁹⁄₃₂ in.) diameter, pubescent, pedicels 3–4 mm (⅛–⁵⁄₃₂ in.) long; pyrenes 4, rugose. Habitat: People's Republic of China, Hai-

Figure 14-46. *Ilex pubescens.* Drawing by Chien-chu Chen in *Illustrations of Native and Introduced Ligneous Plants of Taiwan* (1962) by Tang-shui Liu.

nan Province, in parts of southern Vietnam and Cambodia. Allied to *I. nanningensis*.

Ilex pubipetala Loesener 1923.
    Evergreen shrubs, branches erect or spreading; leaves obovate to oblong or sublanceolate-elliptic, 1.3–2.5 rarely to 3 cm (½–1 rarely to 1³⁄₁₆ in.) long, 0.5–1.1 cm (³⁄₁₆–⁷⁄₁₆ in.) wide, bases cuneate or narrow-acute, apices obtuse or rotund, conspicuous apiculate, petiole decurrent, 2–5 mm (¹⁄₁₆–³⁄₁₆ in.) long; male inflorescences axillary, paucifasciculate, 1- to 3-flowered, flowers 4-merous; fruits unknown. Habitat: Cuba, Oriente Province, Sierra de Nipe, at 1000 m (3300 ft.) elevation. Allied to *I. ekmaniana, I. hypaneura*, and *I. quitensis*.

Ilex pulogensis Merrill 1910. Papatak (synonym *I. apoensis* Elmer 1913).
    Evergreen, erect or parasitic shrubs or trees 4–20 m (13–65 ft.) tall, branches glabrous; leaves elliptic-ovate, 2.5–5 cm (1–2 in.) long, 1–2 cm (⅜–¾ in.) wide, bases cuneate, apices acuminate, margins entire, petioles 5 mm (³⁄₁₆ in.) long; inflorescences axillary, solitary, racemose, 8–15 flowers, flowers 5-merous; fruits globose, 3–3.5 mm (⁷⁄₆₄–⅛ in.) di-

ameter; pyrenes 5. Habitat: Philippines, mossy forest at 2000–2300 m (6600–7600 ft.) elevation. Allied to *I. spicata*.

Ilex punctatilimba C.-y. Wu *ex* Y.-r. Li 1985.
    Evergreen shrubs or small trees 3–5 m (10–16 ft.) tall, branchlets blackish, angulate, glabrous; leaves oblong-lanceolate, 8–10 cm (3⅜–4 in.) long, 2.5–3 cm (1–1³⁄₁₆ in.) wide, glandulous-punctate beneath apices acuminate, bases subrotund or obtuse, margins serrate, petioles dark, 12–15 mm (¹⁵⁄₃₂–¹⁹⁄₃₂ in.) long; male inflorescences umbellate, axillary, pseudo-paniculate, flowers 4-merous; fruits unknown. Habitat: People's Republic of China, Yunnan Province. Allied to *I. peiradena*.

Ilex purpurea Hasskarl 1844 var. *purpurea*. Tun-ching (winter green, in China), wan-sho-hong (everlasting red, in China), nanami-no-ki (in Japan), Kashi holly (synonyms *I. chinensis* Sims 1819, *I. old-hamii* Miquel 1867, *I. lucida* Blume *ex* Miquel 1870, *I. myriadenia* Hance 1883, *I. purpurea* var. *oldhamii* (Miquel) Loesener 1900, *I. purpurea* var. *myriade-nia* (Hance) Loesener 1901, *Callicarpa cavaleriei* Léveillé 1911, *Embelia rubro-violacea* Léveillé 1912, *Celastrus bodinieri* Léveillé 1914, *Symplocos courtoisii* Léveillé 1916, *I. chinensis* var. *glabra* S.-y. Hu 1959, *I. myriadenia* H. Hara 1983, *non* Hance 1893).
    Evergreen, large glabrous trees to 15 m (50 ft.) tall, branches smooth dark gray; leaves glabrous, elliptic, lanceolate or rarely oval, 5–11 cm (2–4¼ in.) long, 2–4 cm (¾–1⅝ in.) wide, margins crenate, rarely serrate, bases obtuse or cuneate, apices acuminate, petioles 8–10 mm (⁵⁄₁₆–⅜ in.) long; inflorescences solitary, axillary on new growth, 7- to 15-flowered cymes, peduncles 4–14 mm (⁵⁄₃₂–¹⁷⁄₃₂ in.) long, pedicels 2 mm (¹⁄₁₆ in.) long, flowers purplish pink or red; fruits shiny red, ellipsoid, 10–12 mm (⅜–¹⁵⁄₃₂ in.) long, 6–8 mm (⁷⁄₃₂–⁵⁄₁₆ in.) wide, prominent persistent stigma; pyrenes 4–5, dorsally U-shaped, smooth, deeply unicanaliculate. Habitat: People's Republic of China, in 13 provinces including Hainan Province, from sea level in the east to 2000 m (6600 ft.) elevation in the west and Vietnam. In Japan on Honshu, Shikoku, and Kyushu Islands. Long in cultivation and hardy in zones 8b to 10. Extensively used as an ornamental tree. Fruiting branches used in decorations from December to February, which includes the Chinese New Year. First introduced to England in 1810. There has been considerable confusion regarding the correct name of this species. The current opinion is that *I. pur-purea* Hasskarl is the correct name for what has been known for decades as *I. chinensis* Sims (*fide* S.-y. Hu 1949) and the latter is thought to be a later synonym of *I. cassine*. Plates 74, 75.

Figure 14-47. *Ilex purpurea* var. *purpurea*. Photo by Barton Bauer Sr.

Ilex purpurea var. *pubigera* C.-y. Wu *ex* Y.-r. Li 1986.
    New variety differing from the typical variety by having thicker leaves; larger globose fruits that are occasionally borne singly; and by having puberulent buds, infructescences, petioles, and midveins of upper surfaces of leaves. Habitat: People's Republic of China, Yunnan Province. May prove to be a synonym of the species, which is highly variable.

Ilex pustulosa Triana 1878.
    Evergreen; leaves glabrous, oval, 10–15 cm (4–6⅛ in.) long, 6–8 cm (2⅜–3⅛ in.) wide, bases rounded, margins serrulate, petioles 10–20 mm (⅜–¾ in.) long; inflorescences axillary, solitary, glabrous, branched, peduncles 8–11 mm (⁵⁄₁₆–⁷⁄₁₆ in.) long, pedicels 1.5–2 mm (³⁄₆₄–¹⁄₁₆ in.) long; fruits black, globose, 3.5–4 mm (⁷⁄₆₄–⁵⁄₃₂ in.) diameter; pyrenes 4, linear subsulcate. Habitat: Colombia, Bogota Province, near Fusagasuga at 2000 m (6600 ft.) elevation. Allied to *I. anonoides*.

Ilex pyrifolia C.-j. Tseng 1981.
    Evergreen, large shrubs to 2 m (10 ft.) tall, branchlets striate, glabrous, lenticels oblong; leaves wide-elliptic, 4–6.5 cm (1⅝–2½ in.) long, 3–4 cm (1³⁄₁₆–1⅝ in.) wide, bases rotund or obtuse, apices acuminate, acumens mucronate, margins serrulate, serrations black apiculate, petioles 7–8 mm (⁹⁄₃₂–⁵⁄₁₆ in.) long, canaliculate; fruits globose, 7 mm (⁹⁄₃₂ in.) diameter, cymes 2-fruited, peduncles 4 mm (⁵⁄₃₂ in.) long, pedicels 3 mm (⅛ in.) long; pyrenes 4, endocarps bony. Habitat: People's Republic of China, Sichuan Province. Allied to *I. purpurea*.

Ilex quercetorum I. M. Johnston 1938.

Evergreen trees, often with multiple trunks, 15 m (50 ft.) tall, branches brownish, puberulent; leaves lanceolate, 5–8 cm (2–3⅛ in.) long, 1.8–2.2 cm (11/16–13/16 in.) wide, bases acute, apices acuminate, margins entire, revolute, petioles canaliculate, 3–5 mm (⅛–3/16 in.) long, inflorescences axillary, solitary, pedicels brown puberulent, 8–13 mm (5/16–½ in.) long; fruits red, globose 8–10 mm (5/16–⅜ in.) diameter, pyrenes bisulcate. Habitat: Guatemala, Nebai, Department Quich in oak forest at 1860 m (6138 ft.) elevation. Allied to *I. pedunculosa.*

Ilex quianlinshanensis C.-j. Tseng 1981.

Evergreen trees, branchlets angulate, puberulent; leaves elliptic or oblong-elliptic, 5–9 cm (2–3½ in.) long, 2.5–3.5 cm (1–1⅜ in.) wide, apices short-acuminate, bases cuneate, midribs puberulent, margins inconspicuously serrulate, petioles 5 mm (3/16 in.) long, narrowly winged; inflorescences axillary, solitary; fruits black when dry, ellipsoid, 1 cm (⅜ in.) long, 7 mm (9/32 in.) diameter; pyrenes 4, widely canaliculate. Habitat: People's Republic of China, Guizhou Province. Allied to *I. huiana* and *I. purpurea.*

Ilex quitensis (Willdenow *ex* Roemer & Schultes) Loesener 1901 (synonyms *Rhamnus quitensis* Willdenow *ex* Roemer & Schultes 1820, *I. bumelioides* Kunth 1825).

Evergreen trees to 4–6 m (13–20 ft.) tall, branches pubescent; leaves obovate to ovate-oblong to obovate-elliptic, 1.6–4 cm (⅝–2⅜ in.) long, 0.8–1.4 cm (5/16–17/32 in.) wide, glabrous, apices rotund to subobtuse, bases acute or cuneate, margins recurved, entire or sharply serrulate, petioles 4–6 mm (5/32–7/32 in.) long; inflorescences axillary, solitary, paucifasciculate, flowers 4- to 5-merous; fruits dark bluish black, ellipsoid, 5 mm (3/16 in.) long, 3.5 mm (7/64 in.) wide, pedicels 5–10 mm (3/16–⅜ in.) long; pyrenes 4–5, sulcate. Habitat: Ecuador, near Loxa, at 2060 m (6800 ft.) elevation. Allied to *I. vacciniifolia.*

Ilex racemifera Loesener 1908.

Evergreen shrubs or trees; leaves ovate-elliptic to ovate-oblong, 5–8.5 cm (2–3⅛ in.) long, 2.2–3.2 cm (13/16–1¼ in.) wide, bases broadly cuneate to subrotund, apices acuminate, acumens 7–10 mm (9/32–⅜ in.) long, margins entire, recurved, petioles 2–4 mm (1/16–5/32 in.) long; inflorescences axillary, solitary, racemose, flowers 5-merous; fruits unknown. Habitat: Philippines, endemic in forest on Mindanao Island near Davao at 300–700 m (990–2300 ft.) elevation. Allied to *I. spicata.*

Ilex reisseckiana T. R. Dudley, *nom. nov.* (basionym *I. andarensis* Rusby *ex* Loesener, *Nov. Acta Acad. Caes. Leop Carol.* 78: 901. 1892, *nom. illegit.*).

Evergreen shrubs or trees, branches dark with minute lenticels; leaves oval to elliptic, 8–13 cm (3⅛–5⅛ in.) long, 3–5.5 cm (1 3/16–2⅛ in.) wide, apices acute or obtuse or acuminate, acumens 7–12 mm (9/32–15/32 in.) long, bases obtuse or rotund, margins entire, recurved, petioles 7–11 mm (9/32–7/16 in.) long; inflorescences in leaf axils, fasciculate, 3- to 7-branched, flowers usually 4-merous; fruits unknown. Habitat: Peru, on Mount Andara, Venezuela, Bolivar. Allied to *I. vismiifolia.* This new name commemorates Siegfried Reisseck (1819–1871), a great *Ilex* specialist who wrote the formidable account of *Ilex* for *Flora Brasiliensis* (published 1840–1906) by Carl F. P. von Martius.

Ilex repanda Grisebach 1861 var. *repanda* (synonym *I. repandoides* Loesener 1923).

Evergreen, glabrous trees, branchlets subangulate; leaves obovate or obovate-elliptic, 4.5–6 cm (1¾–2⅜ in.) long, 2–3.5 cm (¾–1⅜ in.) wide, apices rotund or obtuse, bases acute or cuneate-acute, margins serrulate-crenulate, revolute, petioles 5–7 mm (3/16–9/32 in.) long; inflorescences axillary, males 3- to 8-fasciculate, females solitary, flowers 4-merous; fruits red, globose to ellipsoid, 5–6 mm (3/16–7/32 in.) long, 4.5 mm (11/64 in.) diameter; pyrenes 4, striate, sulcate. Habitat: Cuba. Allied to *I. nitida.*

Ilex repanda var. *hypaneura* (Loesener) Edwin *ex* T. R. Dudley 1979, *comb. & stat. nov.* (basionym *I. hypaneura* Loesener, *Nov. Acta Acad. Caes. Leop. Carol.* 78. 1892. In vol. 89, part I, 315–316; part II, 65, 154, 194, 196. 1908).

A variety with minutely pubescent branchlets; leaves oblong, elliptic or elliptic-lanceolate, 3.5–4.5 cm (1⅜–1¾ in.) long, 1–2.2 cm (3/6–13/16 in.) wide, bases acute or cuneate, apices obtuse, rarely subrotund; inflorescences axillary, fasciculate, flowers 4-merous; fruits subglobose, 3 mm (⅛ in.) diameter; pyrenes 4. Habitat: Cuba and the Bahamas.

Ilex reticulata C.-j. Tseng 1984.

Evergreen shrubs to 2 m (6.6 ft.) tall, branches striate, brownish, with slightly elliptic lenticels; leaves elliptic, 5–5.7 cm (2–2¼ in.) long, 3–3.2 cm (1 3/16–1¼ in.) wide, glabrous on both surfaces, bases cuneate-obtuse, apices acute or short-acuminate, margins remotely serrate, conspicuous reticulate venation, petioles 4–5 mm (5/32–3/16 in.) long; inflorescences unknown; fruits red, axillary, solitary, 5 mm (3.16 in.) diameter, persistent calyces. Habitat: People's Republic of China, Guangxi Province, Yangshuo, Xanning Sham, in forest.

Ilex retusa (Klotzsch) Loesener 1901, *non* Turczaninow 1858 (synonyms *I. retusa* f. *brunnescens* Loesener 1901, *I. retusa* f. *genuiana* Loesener 1901, *I. retusa* var. *subpunctata* Loesener 1901, *I. retusa* f. *glabra* Steyermark 1957, *I. retusa* f. *major* Steyermark 1957).

Evergreen shrubs; leaves close together, 0–15 mm (0–¹⁹⁄₃₂ in.) apart, oval to obovate-elliptic, 1.5–4.7 cm (¹⁹⁄₃₂–1¹³⁄₁₆ in.) long, 2.5 cm (2 in.) wide, bases rounded to obtuse, apices rounded, margins finely serrate, petioles 2–4.5 mm (¹⁄₁₆–⁵⁄₃₂ in.) long; inflorescences pubescent, axillary, solitary, branched, peduncles 4–8 mm (⁵⁄₃₂–⁵⁄₁₆ in.) long, pedicels 1–2 mm (¹⁄₃₂–¹⁄₁₆ in.) long; fruits unknown. Habitat: Colombia and Guyana near Roraima. Allied to *I. boliviana* and *I. hippocrateoides*.

Ilex retusifolia S.-y. Hu 1950.

Evergreen shrubs, branchlets pubescent, lenticels present; leaves broadly elliptic, 5–7 cm (2–2¾ in.) long, 2–3 cm (¾–1³⁄₁₆ in.) wide, punctate beneath, apices very short, retuse, bases obtuse, margins entire, pubescent on both surfaces, petioles 8–12 mm (⁵⁄₈–¹⁵⁄₃₂ in.) long; inflorescences axillary and fasciculate on 2nd-year growth, single flowers, pedicels 4–5 mm (⁵⁄₃₂–³⁄₁₆ in.) long, flowers usually 5-merous; fruits unknown. Habitat: People's Republic of China, endemic to tropical forests of southwestern Guangxi Province. Allied to *I. wilsonii*.

Ilex revoluta Stapf 1894, *non* Tam 1963.

Evergreen shrubs, branchlets puberulent to glabrescent; leaves obovate or obovate-elliptic, 2–3.5 cm (¾–1³⁄₈ in.) long, 0.8–1.6 cm (⁵⁄₁₆–⁵⁄₈ in.) wide, apices obtuse or subacute, short spine, bases cuneate or acute, margins serrulate, revolute, petioles 2–5 mm (1¹⁄₁₆–³⁄₁₆ in.) long; inflorescences axillary, solitary, flowers 4-merous; fruits black purplish, globose, 5 mm (³⁄₁₆ in.) diameter; pyrenes 4. Habitat: Indonesia, Borneo, on Mount Kinabalu, 3600–3700 m (11,900–12,200 ft.) elevation. Allied to *I. archboldiana* and *I. rugosa*.

Ilex rimbachii Standley 1937.

Evergreen trees to 15 m (50 ft.) tall, branches spreading, pubescent, young branchlets velvety hairy, bark gray, medium-sized round warts; leaves broadly ovate to oval to ovate-oval, 3.5–4.5 cm (1³⁄₈–1¾ in.) long, 2–3.5 cm (¾–1³⁄₈ in.) wide, bases rotund, apices rotund to apiculate or obtuse, margins subentire or remote appressed spinose-serrate, petioles to 3 mm (⅛ in.) long, inflorescences axillary, peduncles 5–8 mm (³⁄₁₆–⁵⁄₁₆ in.) long, densely pilose; fruits dark red, globose, 6 mm (⁷⁄₃₂ in.) diameter. Habitat: Honduras, in forest region above Balsapampa, at 2600 m (8580 ft.) elevation.

Ilex robusta C.-j. Tseng 1981 (synonym *I. editicostata* var. *chowii* S.-y. Hu 1949).

Evergreen shrubs, branches glabrous; leaves stiff, elliptic or oblong-elliptic, 6.5–8 cm (2½–3⅛ in.) long, 3–4 cm (1³⁄₁₆–1⅝ in.) wide, apices short-acuminate, bases decurrently obtuse or cuneate, glabrous, margins entire, subrevolute, petioles 1–1.5 cm (⅜–¹⁹⁄₃₂ in.) long, 3 mm (⅛ in.) wide, flat and widely winged; inflorescences cymose, 3-fruited, solitary, axillary, flowers 6-merous, peduncles 1–1.2 cm (⅜–¹⁵⁄₃₂ in.) long, pedicels 4–5 mm (⁵⁄₃₂–³⁄₁₆ in.) long; fruits red, globose, 6 mm (⁷⁄₃₂ in.) diameter; pyrenes 6, surfaces flat or widely canaliculate. Habitat: People's Republic of China Guangxi Province. Allied to *I. lancilimba*.

Ilex robustinervosa C.-j. Tseng 1981.

Evergreen shrubs 2–3.5 m (6–12 ft.) tall, branchlets striate, glabrous; leaves ovate-oblong, rarely wide-ovate, 11–14 cm (4⅜–5½ in.) long, 5–7 cm (2–2¾ in.) wide, apices briefly acuminate, rarely rotund, bases rotund, margins subentire, slightly revolute, petioles 10–15 mm (⅜–¹⁹⁄₃₂ in.) long; female inflorescences axillary, fasciculate, or pseudoracemose, flowers 4-merous; fruits globose, 4.5 mm (1¾ in.) diameter, pedicels 5–6 mm (³⁄₁₆–⁷⁄₃₂ in.) long; pyrenes 4, striate, sulcate. Habitat: People's Republic of China, Guangdong Province. Allied to *I. dunniana*.

Ilex rockii S.-y. Hu 1949 (synonym *I. intricata sensu* Handel-Mazzetti 1933, *non* Hooker f. 1875).

Small shrubs 1–2 m (3–6 ft.) tall, distinct pubescent branches; leaves obovate-oblong, 1–2.5 cm (⅜–1 in.) long, 6–14 mm (⁷⁄₃₂–¹⁷⁄₃₂ in.) wide, apices rounded to obtuse, rarely subacute, bases cuneate, margins crenulate-serrate, 3–6 teeth prominent on upper half of leaf, petioles 2 mm (¹⁄₁₆ in.) long, leaves close together, persist even on 4th-year growth; inflorescences solitary, axillary, at base of new growth, flowers red, usually 5-merous; fruits red, globose, 5–7 mm (³⁄₁₆–⁹⁄₃₂ in.) diameter, pedicels 3–4 mm long; pyrenes 5, smooth. Habitat: People's Republic of China, in high mountains of northwestern Yunnan Province. A low alpine plant at altitudes of 4000–4330 m (13,200–14,290 ft.). Closely allied to *I. crenata*, *I. intricata* Hooker, and *I. yunnanensis*.

Ilex rotunda Thunberg *ex* J. A. Murray 1784 var. *rotunda*. Bacho, kurogane-mochi (synonyms *I. laevigata* Blume & Miquel 1870, *I. siroki* Cleyer & Koch 1872, *I. kosunensis* Yamamoto 1925, *I. sasakii* Yamamoto 1925).

Evergreen, large trees to 20 m (65 ft.) tall, branches grayish brown; leaves glabrous, elliptic to broadly elliptic, 4–9 cm (1⅝–3½ in.) long, 2–4 cm

(¾–1⅜ in.) wide, bases cuneate or obtuse, apices acute or short-acuminate, margins entire, slightly recurved, petioles 10–20 mm (⅜–¾ in.) long; inflorescences cymose or umbelliform, usually 4–8 flowers, solitary, axillary on new growth, peduncles 9–13 mm (¹¹⁄32–½ in.) long, pedicels 4–8 mm (⁵⁄32–⁵⁄16 in.) long; fruits red, globose or broadly ellipsoid 6–8 mm (⁷⁄32–⁵⁄16 in.) diameter; pyrenes 5–7, 3-striate, 2-sulcate on dorsal surface. Habitat: southern People's Republic of China, Zhejiang, Hunan, Guangdong, and Guangxi provinces; Honshu, Shikoku, and Kyushu Islands in Japan; Taiwan; Korea; Vietnam. First described from Japan and frequently cultivated in Asian gardens. In United States, popular in Florida winter killed in middle Georgia. Hardy in zones 9 to 10. Collections from Korea may prove hardier. Allied to *I. excelsa* and *I. pedunculosa*. Plate 76.

Figure 14-48. *Ilex rotunda* var. *rotunda*. Drawing by Chien-chu Chen in *Illustrations of Native and Introduced Ligneous Plants of Taiwan* (1962) by Tang-shui Liu.

Ilex rotunda var. *microcarpa* (Lindley *ex* Paxton) S.-y. Hu 1949 (synonym *I. microcarpa* Lindley *ex* Paxton 1855).

This variety differs from typical individuals by having puberulent peduncles and pedicels; fruits are usually smaller; pyrenes shorter and less sulcate. Habitat: southern People's Republic of China, Jiangxi Province. Allied to *I. excelsa*. This variety was first introduced to England in 1848–1850 by Robert Fortune on his second trip to China; possibly collected south of Shanghai in the vicinity of Ning-po near Hangzhou of Zhejiang. This variety may eventually prove to be a synonym of the species.

Ilex rotunda f. *xanthocarpa* Shin 1952. Kimino, kuroganemochi.

A form with yellow fruit. Not common in the United States.

Ilex rubinervia Tardieu 1945.

Evergreen, large shrubs to 2 m (6 ft.) tall, branches erect, glabrous; leaves lanceolate, 8–10 cm (3⅛–4 in.) long, 2.5–3.2 cm (1–1¼ in.) wide, bases recurrent, cuneate or oblique, apices short-acuminate, margins entire, recurved, petioles 1–1.5 cm (⅜–¹⁵⁄32 in.) long, canaliculate, glabrous; fruits axillary, solitary or 3- to 4-fasciculate, globose, 6 mm (⁷⁄32 in.) diameter; pyrenes 4. Habitat: southern Vietnam, Annam to Nha Trang and Ninh Hoa. Allied to *I. pedunculosa*.

Ilex rubra Watson 1886.

Evergreen, small trees 4–7 m (13–23 ft.) tall, branchlets slightly pubescent; leaves oval to oblong-lanceolate, 4.5–6 cm (1⅝–2⅜ in.) long, 1.6–2.6 cm (⅝–1 in.) wide, apices acute to acuminate, bases slightly acute, margins revolute, entire to serrate, petioles 7–11 mm (⁹⁄32–⁷⁄16 in.) long; inflorescences solitary, flowers 4-merous; fruits red, globose, 7–8 mm (⁹⁄32–⁵⁄16 in.) diameter; pyrenes 4, striate, sulcate. Habitat: Mexico. Allied to *I. cassine* and *I. opaca*.

Ilex rugosa F. Schmidt 1858 f. *rugosa*. Tsuru Tsuge.

Evergreen, glabrous, low shrubs, branchlets angulate, minutely punctate; leaves broadly lanceolate to ovate-oblong, 2–3.5 cm (¾–1⅜ in.) long, 5–15 mm (³⁄16–¹⁹⁄32 in.) wide, apices acute, but with ob-

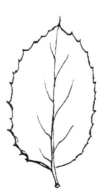

Figure 14-49. *Ilex rubra*. Drawing by Randy Allen.

tuse tips, bases obtuse, margins serrate, petioles 2–5 mm (¹⁄₁₆–³⁄₁₆ in.) long; inflorescences axillary, fasciculate, flowers usually 4-merous; fruits red, globose, 5 mm (³⁄₁₆ in.) diameter; pyrenes usually 4, striate, sulcate. Habitat: Japan, coniferous woods on the northern islands of Sakhalin and Siberia. Introduced to England in 1895. Hardy in zone 5b, but not heat tolerant. Allied to *I. intricata* and *I. nothofagifolia*. Plate 77.

Ilex rugosa f. *hondoensis* (Yamazaki) T. R. Dudley 1987 (synonym *I. rugosa* var. *hondoensis* Yamazaki).

A form with narrow-oblong or oblong leaves 1.5–4 cm (¹⁵⁄₃₂–1⅝ in.) long, 0.5–1.3 cm (³⁄₁₆–½ in.) wide. Habitat: Japan, in central and northern Honshu.

Ilex rugosa f. *stenophylla* (Koidzumi) Sugimoto 1936. Hosoba-tsuru-tsuge (synonyms *I. stenophylla* Koidzumi 1923, *I. rugosa* var. *stenophylla* (Koidzumi) Sugimoto 1936, *I. rugosa* var. *stenophylla* (Koidzumi) Tatewaki 1940).

A form with very narrow leaves, usually lanceolate to broadly linear. Habitat: Japan.

Ilex rugosa f. *vegeta* Hara 1945. Maruba-tsuru-tsuge (synonym *I. rugosa* var. *vegeta* Hara 1936).

A form with larger leaves to 4 cm (1⅝ in.) long, 2.3 cm (⅞ in.) wide. Habitat: Japan.

Ilex ruijinensis (C.-j. Tseng) T. R. Dudley 1985 (synonym *I. formosana* var. *ruijinensis* C.-j. Tseng 1981).

Evergreen trees, branchlets glabrous; very similar to *I. formosana* except for the hairy pubescent fruits. Habitat: People's Republic of China, Jiangxi Province, Ruijin Xian. Allied to *I. formosana*.

Ilex rupicola Kunth 1824 (synonyms *I. orbicularis* Willdenow 1830, *I. rupicola* var. *pleormera* Loesener 1904).

Evergreen trees with upright branches; leaves broadly oval or suborbiculate, 2.6–3 cm (1–1³⁄₁₆ in.) long, 1.7–2.5 cm (²¹⁄₃₂–1 in.) wide, apices rotund or obtuse, bases rotund, margins recurved, crenate-serrate, petioles 2–3 mm (¹⁄₁₆–⅛ in.) long; inflorescences axillary, solitary, 3- to 7-flowered pedunculate, flowers 4-merous, peduncles 7–10 mm (⁹⁄₃₂–⅜ in.) long, pedicels 1 mm (¹⁄₃₂ in.) long; fruits unknown. Habitat: Ecuador, near Saraguro. Allied to *I. scopulorum* and *I. uniflora*.

Ilex salicina Handel-Mazzetti 1933.

Evergreen shrubs, branchlets glabrescent; leaves linear-lanceolate, 4.5–11 cm (1¾–4⅜ in.) long, 9–23 mm (¹¹⁄₃₂–⅞ in.) wide, apices obtuse, acuminate, bases cuneate, margins entire, recurved, punctate beneath, petioles 6–10 mm (⁷⁄₃₂–⅜ in.) long; inflorescences axillary on 2nd-year growth, pseudofasciculate, terminal buds usually aborted, puberulent, flowers 4- to 6-merous; fruits red, globose, 6 mm (⁷⁄₃₂ in.) diameter, calyces persistent; pyrenes 4–6, smooth with single ridge. Habitat: People's Republic of China, endemic to the tropical rain forest along the Guangdong and Guangxi provinces, and Vietnam borders. Allied to *I. metabaptista*.

Ilex sapiiformis Reisseck 1861.

Evergreen shrubs; leaves oval or obovate, 5–7.5 cm (2–3 in.) long, 2–4 cm (¹⁄₁₆–⁵⁄₃₂ in.) wide, apices obtuse or rotund, bases cuneate, margins entire, recurved, petioles 8–12 mm (⁵⁄₁₆–¹⁵⁄₃₂ in.) long; inflorescences fasciculate in leaf axils, branched, flowers

Figure 14-50. *Ilex rugosa* f. *rugosa*. Photo by Barton Bauer Sr.

4-merous; fruits unknown. Habitat: Brazil, Pernambuco State. Allied to *I. guianensis* and *I. lundii.*

Ilex sapotifolia Reisseck 1861 (synonym *I. regnelliana* Maximowicz 1881).

Evergreen, small trees to 8 m (26 ft.) tall; leaves oblong-elliptic to elliptic, 12–14 cm (4 3/4–5 1/2 in.) long, 4 cm (1 5/8 in.) wide, bases usually obtuse, rarely acute, apices short-acuminate, margins recurved, usually serrulate near the apex, rarely entire, petioles 12–20 mm (1/2–3/4 in.) long; inflorescences axillary, solitary, fasciculate, usually 3-flowered, peduncles 10–25 mm (3/8–1 in.) long, single peduncles usually 3–6 mm (1/8–7/32 in.) long, pedicels 10 mm (3/8 in.) long; fruits grayish brown, oval to globose, usually 6 mm (7/32 in.) long, 5 mm (3/16 in.) wide; pyrenes 4–5. Habitat: Brazil, Rio de Janeiro State. Allied to *I. amygdalifolia* and *I. brevicuspis.*

Ilex sarawaccensis Loesener 1901.

Evergreen, glabrous shrubs; leaves obovate or obovate-elliptic, 11–15.5 cm (4 3/8–6 3/16 in.) long, 4.8–8 cm (1 7/8–3 1/8 in.) wide, apices rotund or obtuse, acuminate or subacute, bases broadly cuneate, margins entire, recurved, petioles 10–12 mm (3/8–15/32 in.); inflorescences axillary, racemose, rachis 6, 6–17 mm (7/32–21/32 in.) long, pedicels 6–8 mm (7/32–5/16 in.) long; fruits black, globose, 4–5 mm (5/32–3/16 in.) diameter; pyrenes 9. Habitat: Malaysia, western Borneo, near Santubong. Allied to *I. spicata.*

Ilex savannarum Wurdack 1961 (synonym *I. savannarum* var. *morichei* Edwin 1965).

Evergreen shrubs 1–2 m (3–6 ft.) tall, branches glabrous; leaves obovate, 4.5–6 cm (1 3/4–2 3/8 in.) long, 1.5–2.5 cm (19/32–1 in.) wide, bases cuneate, decurrent, apices rotund to slightly retuse, margins obscurely crenate-serrulate, punctate beneath, petioles 1–3 mm (1/32–1/8 in.) long; inflorescences racemose, to 9-flowered, flowers 4-merous; fruits globose, 5 mm (3/16 in.) diameter; pyrenes 4. Habitat: Venezuela; Rio Guiania, Sabana Elvenado on left bank of Cano Pimichin above Pimichin at low elevation. Allied to *I. retusa* Loesener.

Ilex saxicola C.-j. Tseng & H. Liu 1984.

Evergreen shrubs to 3 m (10 ft.) tall, branchlets slender, angulate, puberulent, lenticels present; leaves widely elliptic, 4–5.5 cm (1 5/8–2 1/8 in.) long, 2–3.5 cm (3/4–1 3/8 in.) wide, apices obtuse or rotund, bases obtuse, margins entire, petioles 4–6 mm (5/32–7/32 in.) long, inflorescences axillary, fasciculate; fruits red, globose, 4 mm (5/32 in.) diameter, pedicels 5–9 mm (3/16–11/32 in.) long; pyrenes 4–5, palmately striate. Habitat: People's Republic of China, Guangxi Province. Allied to *I. goshiensis.*

Ilex scabridula Merrill & Perry 1941.

Evergreen, twisted shrubs, long pendulous reddish brown branches, minutely scabrous; leaves glabrous, ovate to oblong, 3–7 cm (1 3/16–2 3/4 in.) long, 1.4–3 cm (17/32–1 3/16 in.) wide, bases obtuse to rotund, apices acuminate or acute, acumens 5–10 mm (3/16–3/8 in.) long, apiculate below, margins entire or remotely serrate near apex, punctate below, petioles 2.5–4 mm (3/32–5/32 in.) long; inflorescences solitary, axillary, racemose; fruits black, ellipsoid, 3 mm (1/8 in.) long, 3.5 mm (9/64 in.) diameter. Habitat: Irian Jaya, in mossy forest in valleys, with liana type vegetation at 2800–2900 m (9240–9570 ft.) elevation. Allied to *I. spicata.*

Ilex scandens Cuatrecasas 1948.

Evergreen, climbing shrubs; leaves ovoid-elliptic, 7–13 cm (9/32–5 1/8 in.) long, 2.5–5.5 cm (1–2 1/8 in.) wide, bases cuneate, apices obtuse, apiculate, margins crenate-serrate; inflorescences axillary, racemose, flowers 5-merous; fruits unknown. Habitat: Colombia. Leaves similar to *I. karstenii.* May at some future date be treated as a synonym of *I. karstenii.*

Ilex schlechteri Loesener 1924.

Evergreen, small trees, glabrous; leaves oval or oblong, 6–8 cm (2 3/8–3 1/8 in.) long, 3.7–5.5 cm (1 7/16–2 1/8 in.) wide, margins entire, recurved, bases obtuse or subrotund, apices obtuse or obtuse-acuminate, margins reticulate, petioles short; inflorescences pseudopaniculate, 5–11 mm (3/16–7/16 in.) long, flowers 5-merous; fruits unknown. Habitat: New Guinea, Papua, in woods near Djamu-Klamm. Allied to *I. ledermannii.*

Ilex schwackeana Loesener 1901.

Evergreen, large shrubs or trees; leaves obovate-elliptic, 2.5–5 cm (1–2 in.) long, 1.5 cm (1 3/16 in.) wide, apices rotund or excised, bases cuneate, margins entire, revolute, petioles 3–5 mm (1/8–3/16 in.) long; inflorescences axillary, fasciculate, rarely solitary, flowers 4-merous; fruits blackish, subglobose; pyrenes 4. Habitat: Brazil, Rio de Janeiro State, on Mount Alto-macha near Nova Friburgo. Allied to *I. vacciniifolia.*

Ilex sclerophylla Hooker f. 1875.

Evergreen shrubs, branches pubescent; leaves elliptic-oblong, 13–17 cm (5 1/8–6 3/4 in.) long, 4.5–6 cm (1 3/4–2 3/8 in.) wide, glabrous, apices obtuse, acuminate, bases cuneate-obtuse, margins entire, recurved, petioles 16–20 mm (5/8–3/4 in.) long; inflorescences axillary, solitary, branched, 3-flowered, flowers 4- to 5-merous; fruits unknown, peduncles 6–11 mm (7/32–7/16 in.) long, pedicels 1–1.5 mm

(¹⁄₃₂–³⁄₆₄ in.) long. Habitat: Malaysia on Mount Ophir near Malacca, Borneo, in Sarawak Province. Allied to *I. macrophylla* and *I. pleiobrachiata*.

Ilex sclerophylloides Loesener 1901.

Evergreen shrubs, branches erect to spreading, pale to whitish branches; leaves glabrous, oval to subelliptic, 7.5–11 cm (3–4¼ in.) long, 3.4–4.8 cm (1¹¹⁄₃₂–1⅞ in.) wide, margins entire, recurved, bases crenate to crenate-obtuse, apices rounded, petioles 9–11 mm (¹¹⁄₃₂–⁷⁄₁₆ in.) long; inflorescences on young branches, cymes, peduncles 7- to 15-branched, flowers 4-merous; fruits globose, 6 mm (⁷⁄₃₂ in.) diameter, pedicels 5 mm (3.16 in.) long; pyrenes 5–7. Habitat: Malaysia, Indonesia. Allied to *I. cymosa* and *I. eugeniaefolia*.

Ilex scopulorum Kunth 1824 var. *scopulorum* (synonyms *I. crassifolia* (Willdenow) *ex* Roemer & Schultes 1818, *I. scopulorum* var. *crassifolia* (Willdenow) Loesener 1901).

Evergreen trees with upright branches, lenticels present; leaves obovate-elliptic or oval or suborbiculate, 2.4–5.5 cm (¹⁵⁄₁₆–2⅛ in.) long, 1.3–3.1 cm (¹⁵⁄₃₂–1³⁄₁₆ in.) wide, apices rotund or subobtuse, bases rotund or subcuneate-obtuse, margins recurved, punctate beneath, bases entire, serrulate or subcrenulate-serrulate near apex, petioles 2–7 mm (¹⁄₁₆–⁹⁄₃₂ in.) long; inflorescences axillary, solitary, pedunculate, 1- to 7-flowered, flowers 4- to 5-merous; fruits globose, 10 mm (⅜ in.) diameter, peduncles 5–14 mm (³⁄₁₆–¹⁷⁄₃₂ in.) long, pedicels 2–6 mm (¹⁄₁₆–⁷⁄₃₂ in.) long; pyrenes 6, unisulcate. Habitat: Ecuador, at 3500 m (11550 ft.) elevation, and in western Venezuela.

Ilex scopulorum var. *caracasana* Loesener 1901 (synonym *I. crassifolia* Triana 1854, *non* Hooker 1837).

A variety with thicker leaves, male inflorescences 1- to 3-flowered, females single, flowers 5- to 7-merous; fruits large, 10 mm (⅜ in.) diameter. Habitat: Venezuela, near Caracas.

Ilex scutiiformis Reisseck 1861 (synonyms *I. scutiiformis* var. *genuina* Loesener 1901, *I. scutiiformis* var. *hilariana* Loesener 1901, *I. scutiiformis* f. *loeseneri* (Schwacke) Loesener 1901, *I. scutiiformis* f. *magnifolia* Loesener 1901, *I. scutiiformis* var. *senaeana* Loesener 1901).

Evergreen shrubs to 2 m (6 ft.) tall, branches pubescent; leaves oval or subelliptic, usually 3 cm (1³⁄₁₆ in.) long, 2 cm (¾ in.) wide, apices obtuse or rotund, bases rotund or obtuse, margins usually entire, revolute, petioles 1.5–4 mm (³⁄₆₄–⁵⁄₃₂ in.) long; inflorescences axillary, solitary on new growth, branches 3- to 15-flowered, flowers 4-merous; fruits black, glo-

bose, 4 mm (⁵⁄₃₂ in.) diameter; pyrenes 4. Habitat: Brazil. Allied to *I. asperula*.

Ilex sebertii Panchon 1869 (synonym *I. neocaledonica* Maximowicz 1881).

Evergreen, glabrous shrubs or trees; leaves glabrous, usually obovate to obovate-elliptic, 3.5–11 cm (1⅜–4¼ in.) long, 1.2–4.5 cm (⁷⁄₁₆–1¾ in.) wide, bases cuneate to acute, apices rounded or obtuse, margins recurved, entire, petioles 10–25 mm (⅜–1 in.) long; inflorescences axillary, solitary, slightly pubescent, branched, 1- to 3-flowered, peduncles 5–13 mm (³⁄₁₆–½ in.) long, pedicels 4–8 mm (⁵⁄₃₂–⁵⁄₁₆ in.) long; fruits grayish brown, globose 5.5–8 mm (³⁄₁₆–⁵⁄₁₆ in.) diameter; pyrenes 4–6. Habitat: New Caledonia on serpentine substrates. This species hyperaccumulates nickel from the substrata, and its sap may be blue. Allied to *I. zippeliana*.

Ilex sellowii Loesener 1901.

Evergreen shrubs, young branches pubescent, erect; leaves ovate to obovate, 3.5–5.5 cm (1³⁄₁₆–2⅛ in.) long, 1.6–2.5 cm (⅝–1 in.) wide, bases cuneate, apices obtuse or rounded, with one small spine, margins slightly ciliate, petioles 3–8 mm (⅛–⁵⁄₁₆ in.) long; inflorescences axillary, solitary, 1- to 3-flowered, peduncles 7–11 mm (⁹⁄₃₂–⁷⁄₁₆ in.) long, pedicels 3–5 mm (⅛–³⁄₁₆ in.) long; fruits grayish brown, globose, 4–5 mm (⁵⁄₃₂–³⁄₁₆ in.) diameter; pyrenes 4. Habitat: Brazil. Allied to *I. pseudobuxus*.

Ilex sessilifolia Triana 1872 var. *sessilifolia* (synonym *I. sessilifolia* var. *genuina* Loesener 1901, *I. pavonii* Loesener 1901).

Evergreen shrubs with yellowish olive-green villose branches; leaves ovate to ovate-elliptic, 3–5.2 cm (1³⁄₁₆–2 in.) long, 1.3–2.9 cm (¹⁵⁄₃₂–1⁵⁄₃₂ in.) wide, villose beneath, apices rotund or obtuse, bases obtuse, margins revolute, densely serrulate, petioles 4–7 mm (⁵⁄₃₂–⁹⁄₃₂ in.) long; inflorescences 3- to 7-branched, flowers 4-merous; fruits ellipsoid, 6 mm (⁷⁄₃₂ in.) long, 5 mm (³⁄₁₆ in.) wide; pyrenes 4. Habitat: Colombia, Peru, and Bolivia, at 2600–4000 m (8,580–13,200 ft.) elevation. Allied to *I. scopulorum* and *I. uniflora*.

Ilex sessilifolia var. *pearcei* Loesener 1901.

Leaves glabrous, slight pubescent on midribs beneath. Habitat: Peru and Bolivia at high elevations. This variety may later prove to be synonymous with the species.

Ilex sessilifructa Edwin 1965.

Evergreen small trees, branchlets sparsely puberulent; leaves obovate or subspathulate-obovate, 4.5–5.7 cm (1¾–2⅛ in.) long, 2–3 cm (3.4–1³⁄₁₆ in.) wide, punctate beneath, bases acute or acute, subspathulate, apices usually acute and retuse, margins entire; inflorescences axillary, solitary, pedicellate, flowers 4-merous; fruits dark red to reddish purple, globose to subglobose, 4.5–5 mm (¹¹⁄₆₄–³⁄₁₆ in.) long, 3 mm (⅛ in.) diameter, pedicels 4.5 mm (¹¹⁄₆₄ in.) long or less; pyrenes 4, triangular, dorsally unicanaliculate. Habitat: Venezuela, Amazonas, in lowland and slope forests at 650 m (2150 ft.) elevation, Cerro de la Neblina, Rio Yatua.

Ilex shennongjiaensis T. R. Dudley & S. C. Sun 1983.
Evergreen, small trees to 10 m (33 ft.) tall, branchlets reddish brown, puberulent to glabrescent; leaves elliptic-ovate, 2.5–4 cm (1–1⅝ in.) long, 1.5–2.5 cm (¹⁹⁄₃₂–1 in.) wide, apices acute to subobtuse, shortly mucronulate, mucro 2.5 mm (³⁄₃₂ in.) long, bases short attenuate or truncate, occasionally briefly cuneate, margins serrulate crenulate; inflorescences axillary, solitary, pedicels 5.5–12 mm (³⁄₁₆–¹⁵⁄₃₂ in.) long; fruits dark red, ovate, 8–12 mm (⁵⁄₁₆–¹⁵⁄₃₂ in.) long, glossy, calyces persistent; pyrenes 4–5, sulcate, ribbed. Habitat: People's Republic of China, western Hubei Province, Shennongjia Forest District. Allied to *I. sugerokii* and *I. yunnanensis*.

Ilex shimeica Kwok 1963.
Evergreen trees to 11 m (36 ft.) tall, branches brownish, lenticellate; leaves broadly oblong to elliptic, 7.5–9.5 cm (3–3¾ in.) long, 3.5–5.5 cm (1⅜–2⅛ in.) wide, bases rotund, apices obtuse or briefly acuminate, margins entire, petioles 1.2 mm (¹⁄₃₂ in.) long; inflorescences fasciculate, or umbellate; fruits subglobose to pyriform, 4–5 mm (⁵⁄₃₂–³⁄₁₆ in.) diameter, 2–6, peduncles 3–8 mm (⅛–⁵⁄₁₆ in.) long, pedicels 5–7 mm (³⁄₁₆–⁹⁄₃₂ in.) long; pyrenes 4–5, 2- to 4-striate. Habitat: People's Republic of China, near Lingshu and Hsian. Allied to *I. kobuskiana*.

Ilex sideroxyloides (Swartz) Grisebach 1857 var. *sideroxyloides*. Bois-citron, citronnier, bois fourni, tisitron, bois gris, cogolin (synonyms *I. myrtifolia* Lamarck 1732, *Prinos sideroxyloides* Swartz 1788, *I. macoucoua* De Candolle 1825, *Xylopia martinicensis* Sprengel 1825, *Myrsine rapanea* Siebold 1836, *I. sideroxyloides* f. *eggersii* Loesener 1901, *I. sideroxyloides* f. *jamaicensis* Loesener 1901, *I. sideroxyloides* f. *vulgaris* Loesener 1901).
Evergreen trees 6–15 m (20–50 ft.) tall, branches with sparse lenticels; leaves obovate or obovate-oblong or cuneate-obovate, 3.5–12 cm (1⅜–4¾ in.) long, 1.5–5 cm (¹⁹⁄₃₂–2 in.) wide, apices obtuse or rotund, often retuse, bases cuneate or cuneate acute, margins recurved, entire, petioles 5–17 mm (³⁄₁₆–²¹⁄₃₂ in.) long; inflorescences axillary, mostly solitary or branched, flowers 4- to 7-merous; fruits black, globose, 5–7 mm (³⁄₁₆–⁹⁄₃₂ in.) diameter; pyrenes

4–7, unisulcate. Habitat: Puerto Rico, Dominican Republic, Jamaica and adjacent islands. Allied to *I. divaricata*.

Ilex sideroxyloides var. *occidentalis* (Macfadyen) Loesener 1899 (synonyms *I. occidentalis* Macfadyen 1837, *I. sideroxyloides* f. *portoricensis* Loesener 1892).
A variety with obovate or cuneate-obovate or elliptic leaves, petioles 6–10 mm (⁷⁄₃₂–⅜ in.) long; flowers mostly fasciculate, axillary. Habitat: Puerto Rico.

Ilex sikkimensis Kurz 1875 (synonyms *I. odorata* Hooker f. 1875, *non* Hamilton 1825, *I. sikkimensis* var. *coccinea* Comber 1933).
Evergreen trees 10–17 m (33–56 ft.) tall, branchlets striate, sulcate; leaves elliptic to obovate-elliptic, 12–20 cm (4¾–8 in.) long, 3–6.5 cm (1³⁄₁₆–2½ in.) wide, bases rotund to cuneate, apices acute-acuminate, margins serrate, petioles 19–30 mm (¾–1³⁄₁₆ in.) long; inflorescences fasciculate, axillary, flowers fragrant, 4-merous; fruits red, globose, 4–4.5 (⁵⁄₃₂–¹¹⁄₆₄ in.) diameter; pyrenes 4, rugose, sulcate. Habitat: India, Bhutan, Sikkim, at 2000–3340 m (6,600–11,000 ft.) elevation. Hardy in zones 8b to 9. Allied to *I. pseudo-odorata*. Kurz (1875) based his description on a yellow-fruited variant from the wild, but the fruits probably had not matured.

Ilex sinica (Loesener) S.-y. Hu 1950 (synonym *I. malabarica* var. *sinica* Loesener 1908).
Evergreen, small trees to 8 m (26 ft.) tall, branchlets light gray, lenticels conspicuous; leaves oblong or oblong-elliptic, usually 7–10 cm (2¾–4 in.) long, 2.5–4 cm (1–1⅝ in.) wide, apices acuminate, acumens 5–20 mm (³⁄₁₆–¾ in.) long, bases obtuse, margins entire, puberulent on both surfaces, petioles 5–8 mm (³⁄₁₆–⁵⁄₁₆ in.) long; inflorescences fasciculate, pedicels 5–6 mm (³⁄₁₆–⁷⁄₃₂ in.) long, flowers 4- to 5-merous; fruits red, globose, 4 mm (⁵⁄₃₂ in.) diameter, calyces persistent, styles evident; pyrenes 6, striate. Habitat: People's Republic of China, subtropical southwestern Yunnan and Guangxi provinces. Allied to *I. memecylifolia*.

Ilex sintenisii (Urban) Britton 1924.
Evergreen shrubs or small trees to 5 m (16 ft.) tall; leaves obovate or elliptic, 1–2.7 cm (⅜–1⅛ in.) long, 0.6–2 cm (¼–¾ in.) wide, bases acute, apices rotund, apex notched, margins entire, midribs depressed above, petioles 3–6.5 mm (⅛–¼ in.) long; inflorescences axillary, solitary, flowers 4- to 5-merous; fruits globose, 5 mm (³⁄₁₆ in.) diameter, color unknown; pyrenes 4–5. Habitat: eastern Puerto Rico, known only from high mountains at 909 m (3000 ft.) elevation. Allied to *I. vacciniifolia*.

Ilex sipapoana Edwin 1965.

Evergreen large shrubs or small trees to 8 m (26 ft.) tall, branchlets dark puberulent; leaves variable, obovate or elliptic-obovate or subspathulate or elliptic-ovate, 6–8.5 cm (2⅜–3⅜ in.) long, 2.5–3.8 cm (1–1½ in.) wide, bases usually acute to cuneate, apices usually orbiculate, retuse, punctate beneath, petioles 6–9 mm (7/32–11/32 in.) long; inflorescences axillary, solitary, flowers 4- to 5-merous; fruits brown when dry, subglobose or ovoid, 7–8 mm (9/32–5/16 in.) long, 6–7 mm (7/32–9/32 in.) diameter; pyrenes 4–5, dorsally unicanaliculate, marginal ridges. Habitat: Venezuela, Amazonas, in marshes at 1500 m (4950 ft.) elevation, Cerro Sipapo.

Ilex skutchii Edwin *ex* T. R. Dudley 1993.

Evergreen, large trees to 40 m (131 ft.) tall, branches glabrous, current branches puberulent, gray-brown to black, striate, stipules deciduous, leaves glabrous, elliptic, occasionally ovate-elliptic, 7–10.5 cm (2¾–4⅛ in.) long, 2.6–3.6 cm (1⅛–3⅝ in.) wide, bases usually acute, decurrent, apices acute to acuminate, 1–1.5 mm (1/32–3/64 in.) long, margins entire, revolute, petioles puberulent, narrowly winged, 8–18 mm (5/16–11/16 in.) long; male inflorescences axillary, fasciculate, pedunculate, 3- to 7-flowered, cymose or subumbelliform, peduncles 3–9 mm (⅛–11/32 in.) long, pedicels 1.5–3 mm (1/16–⅛ in.) long, both puberulent; fruits red, globose, usually 4–5 mm (5/32–7/32 in.) diameter, pyrenes 4, 3-ribbed, 3-striate. Habitat: Costa Rica, from Heredia to San Jose. Allied to *I. ptariana* from Venezuela.

Ilex socorroensis Brandegee 1910.

Evergreen, large shrubs to trees 10 m (33 ft.) tall, stems brown-striped; leaves obovate, 3–5 cm (1 3/16–2 in.) long, 2–3.2 cm (¾–1¼ in.) wide, bases narrowed into short petioles, apices rotund, margins crenate-dentate; fruits oblong, conical, apiculate, pedicels 6 mm (7/32 in.) long; pyrenes 4–6. Habitat: Mexico, endemic to Isla Socorro, State of Puebla near Oaxaca border. Allied to *I. nitida*.

Ilex soderstromii Edwin 1965 var. *soderstromii*.

Evergreen trees to 4–20 m (14–65 ft.) tall, branchlets puberulent; leaves lanceolate or narrowly obovate to ovate, 5–7.5 cm (2–3 in.) long, 2.8–3.5 cm (1⅛–1⅜ in.) wide, bases cuneate, apices acute, punctate beneath, margins entire, revolute, petioles 6–12 mm (7/32–15/32 in.) long; inflorescences axillary, multifasciculate, pedunculate, flowers 4- to 5-merous; fruits brown when dry, ovoid, 5 mm (3/16 in.) long, 4 mm (5/32 in.) diameter; pyrenes 4, dorsally 2-striate, 2-sulcate. Habitat: Guyana at 430 m (1420 ft.) elevation.

Ilex soderstromii var. *ovata* Edwin 1965.

A variety with leaves longer and broader than typical individuals, broadly ovate, 9–9.5 cm (3½–3¾ in.) long, 5.3–6 cm (2 1/16–2⅜ in.) wide. Habitat: Guyana.

Ilex solida Edwin 1965.

Evergreen, large shrubs to 3 m (10 ft.) tall, branchlets puberulent; leaves usually ovate, occasionally broadly ovate or elliptic, 6.5–8.5 cm (2½–3⅜ in.) long, 3.2–4 cm (1¼–1⅝ in.) wide, bases subacute to obtuse, apices orbiculate, obtuse, margins entire, punctate beneath, petioles 2–4 mm (1/16–5/32 in.) long; inflorescences axillary, solitary, lateral, flowers 4-merous; fruits black, ellipsoid, 7 mm (9/32 in.) long, 4–5 mm (5/32–3/16 in.) diameter; pyrenes 4, usually smooth. Habitat: Venezuela, Bolivar State, at 1880–1950 m (6200–6440 ft.) elevation.

Ilex spicata (Miquel) Blume 1894. Kisekkal (synonyms *Prinos spicata* Miquel 1859, *Pseudehretia paniculata* Turczaninow 1864, *I. malaccensis* Loesener 1901, *I. spicata* var. *blumeana* Loesener 1901, *I. spicata* f. *cuneura* Loesener 1901, *I. spicata* f. *subenervia* Loesener 1901, *I. spicata* var. *typica* Loesener 1901).

Evergreen, glabrous shrubs, lenticels present; leaves usually oblong-lanceolate, 5–11 cm (2–4⅜ in.) long, 2.2–4.8 cm (⅞–1⅞ in.) wide, apices acuminate, mucro 6–13 mm (7/32–15/32 in.) long, bases rotund or cuneate, margins entire, revolute, petioles 7–14 mm (9/32–17/32 in.) long; inflorescences axillary, racemose 1–4 cm (⅜–1⅝ in.) long, pedicels 1–2 mm (1/32–1/16 in.) long; fruits black, globose-ellipsoid 4–5 mm (5/32–3/16 in.) long, 3 mm (⅛ in.) wide; pyrenes 6–8. Habitat: Indonesia, Java, Borneo, on Mount Kinabalu at 2300–2400 m (7590–7900 ft.) elevation, Sumatra, Mount Singulary, and in northwestern Irian Jaya near Bamoi. Allied to *I. zeylanica*.

Ilex spinigera (Loesener) Loesener 1909 (synonym *I. aquifolium* f. *spinigera* Loesener 1901).

Evergreen, dense large shrubs or small trees to 4 m (13 ft.) high, branchlets pubescent; leaves elliptic-ovate, 3–4.5 cm (1⅜–1¾ in.) long, 1.6–2.5 cm (⅝–2 in.) wide, glossy, undulate, keeled, pubescent, bases cuneate to obtuse, apices reflexed, acuminate, margins revolute, 2–4 sharp spines on each side, petioles 2–3 mm (1/16–⅛ in.) long; fruits red, globose to ellipsoid, 6–10 mm (7/32–⅜ in.) diameter, 8–10 mm (5/16–⅜ in.) long; pyrenes 4. Habitat: northern Iran, endemic of relict forest, at 600 m (2000 ft.) elevation. Allied to *I. aquifolium* and *I. colchica*.

Ilex spinulosa Cuatrecasas 1948.

Evergreen trees to 10 m (33 ft.) tall, branches hirsute, densely upward, forming nearly flat top; leaves

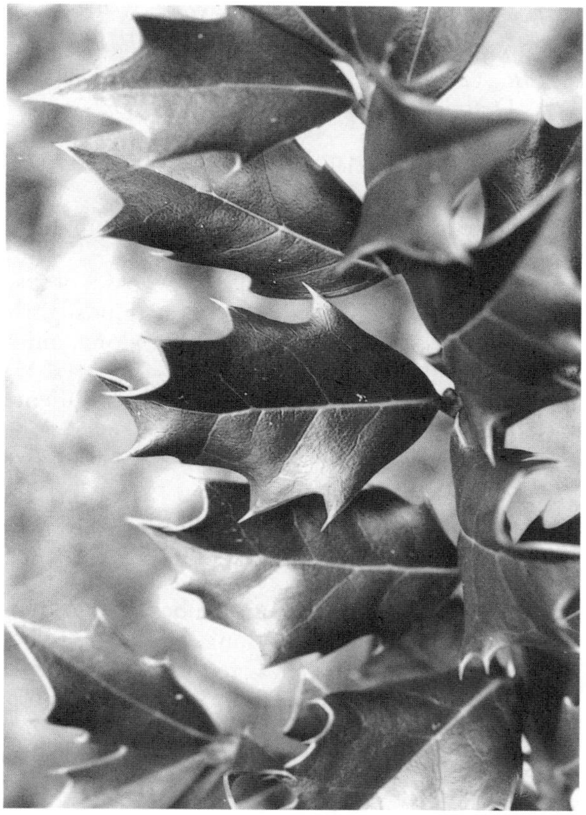

Figure 14-51. *Ilex spinigera.* Photo by Barton Bauer Sr.

ovate or oval-elliptic, hirsute beneath, bases rotund, apices attenuate, margins revolute, denticulate-serrate, 2–4 spines on each side, petioles 1–2 mm ($\frac{1}{32}$–$\frac{1}{16}$ in.) long; inflorescences axillary, solitary, branched; fruits ovoid, 4 mm ($\frac{5}{32}$ in.) long; pyrenes 1–2. Habitat: Colombia, Department del Valle, Cordillera, Los Farallones, Alto del Buey.

Ilex spruceana Reisseck 1861 (synonym *I. spruceana* var. *guianensis* Loesener 1901).

Evergreen large shrubs or trees; leaves usually oval, 6–8 cm ($2\frac{3}{8}$–$3\frac{1}{8}$ in.) long, 2.2–5.8 cm ($1\frac{3}{8}$-–$2\frac{1}{4}$ in.) wide, apices obtuse, bases acute or cuneate–acute, margins entire, recurved, petioles 5–11 mm ($\frac{3}{16}$–$\frac{7}{16}$ in.) long; inflorescences branched, flowers 4-merous; fruits black, ellipsoid, 7–8 mm ($\frac{9}{32}$–$\frac{5}{16}$ in.) long, 5–6 mm ($\frac{3}{16}$–$\frac{7}{32}$ in.) wide, peduncles 3–4 mm ($\frac{1}{8}$–$\frac{5}{32}$ in.) long, pedicels 3–5 mm ($\frac{1}{8}$–$\frac{3}{16}$ in.) long; pyrenes 4. Habitat: Venezuela, along the Rio Casiquiare. Allied to *I. blanchetii.*

Ilex stapfiana Loesener 1901.

Evergreen, glabrous shrubs or trees, lenticels present; leaves oblong, 8–13.5 cm ($3\frac{1}{8}$–$5\frac{5}{16}$ in.) long, 3–4 cm ($1\frac{3}{16}$–$1\frac{5}{8}$ in.) wide, apices obtuse-acuminate, mucro 10–13 mm ($\frac{3}{8}$–$\frac{15}{32}$ in.) long, bases cuneate, margins entire, recurved, petioles 5–8 mm ($\frac{3}{16}$–$\frac{5}{16}$ in.) long; inflorescences in leaf axils, racemose 2–4 cm ($\frac{3}{4}$–$1\frac{5}{8}$ in.) long, or fasciculate, pedicels 1–1.5 mm ($\frac{1}{13}$–$\frac{3}{64}$ in.) long, flowers 4-merous; fruits unknown. Habitat: Malaysia, Borneo, Sarawak district. Allied to *I. spicata.*

Ilex stellata W. J. Hahn 1993. In *Novon* 3(1): 41. Panama. (Supplement 20).

Ilex stenophylla Steyermark 1951.

Evergreen shrubs to 2.7–3.8 m (9–12 ft.) tall, branchlets densely pubescent: leaves narrow-oblanceolate or narrow-oblanceolate-elliptic, 2–4.5 cm ($\frac{3}{4}$–$1\frac{3}{4}$ in.) long, 0.8–1.5 cm ($\frac{5}{16}$–$\frac{19}{32}$ in.) wide, punctate beneath, bases acute, apices rotund or obtuse, margins crenulate-serrulate, petioles 2–3 mm ($\frac{1}{16}$–$\frac{1}{8}$ in.) long; male inflorescences axillary, subumbellate, 7- to 12-flowered, females unknown. Habitat: Venezuela, Bolivar, moist exposed sand bluffs near Cano Negro, at 1095–1520 m (3600–5000 ft.) elevation. Allied to and *I. affinis* and *I. dumosa.*

Ilex sterrophylla Merrill & Chun 1940 (synonym *I. sauveolens* var. *sterrophylla* (Merrill & Chun) Chang 1959).

Evergreen, large trees to 15 m (50 ft.) tall, branches glabrous, lenticels numerous; leaves glabrous, ovate to elliptic, 5–8 cm (2–$3\frac{1}{8}$ in.) long, 2–4 cm ($\frac{3}{4}$–$1\frac{5}{8}$ in.) wide, bases cuneate to sub-round, decurrent, apices acuminate, margins entire; inflorescence axillary, 3-flowered cymes, peduncles 12–23 mm ($\frac{15}{32}$–$\frac{7}{8}$ in.) long, pedicels 5–8 mm ($\frac{3}{16}$–$\frac{5}{16}$ in.) long, petals white; fruits red, ellipsoid, 7–9 mm ($\frac{9}{32}$–$\frac{11}{32}$ in.) long, persistent calyces; pyrenes 4, smooth, shallow concave on back. Habitat: southeastern People's Republic of China, Guangdong and Hainan provinces. Allied to *I. suaveolens,* which has serrate leaves. Often misidentified as *I. pedunculosa,* which has unistriate pyrenes, and as *I. purpurea,* which often has crenulate leaves.

Ilex stewardii S.-y. Hu 1950.

Evergreen shrubs or small trees to 8 m (26 ft.) tall, branchlets minutely puberulent; leaves lanceolate, oblong-lanceolate or oblong-elliptic, 5–8.5 cm (2–$3\frac{3}{8}$ in.) long, 1.4–3 cm ($\frac{17}{32}$–$1\frac{3}{16}$ in.) wide, apices long-acuminate, acumens 8–15 mm ($\frac{5}{16}$–$\frac{19}{32}$ in.) long, tip cuspidate or mucronate, bases acute or acuminate, margins entire, occasionally slightly serrate near apex, petioles 5–8 mm ($\frac{3}{16}$–$\frac{5}{16}$ in.) long; inflorescences fasciculate or pseudopaniculate, 1- to 5-flowered, flowers 6- to 7-merous, peduncles 3–7 mm ($\frac{1}{8}$–$\frac{9}{32}$ in.) long, pedicels 3–5 mm ($\frac{1}{8}$–$\frac{3}{16}$ in.) long;

fruits red, ovoid-subglobose, 4 mm (5/32 in.) long, 3 mm (1/8 in.) diameter; pyrenes 6, rough, 3-striate. Habitat: People's Republic of China, endemic to high mountains between Guangdong and Guangxi provinces, and Vietnam. Allied to *I. hainanensis.*

Ilex steyermarkii Edwin 1965.

Evergreen, small trees 4.5–6 m (15–20 ft.) tall, branchlets puberulent; leaves usually obovate, 4–5.5 cm (1 5/8–2 1/8 in.) long, 1.4–2.2 cm (17/32–13/16 in.) wide, bases acute or cuneate, apices usually acute, margins entire, revolute, punctate beneath, petioles 6–9 mm (7/32–11/32 in.) long; inflorescences axillary, solitary or lateral, flowers 4-merous; fruits pale brown when dry, globose, 5–6 mm (3/16–7/32 in.) diameter, pedicels 2–5 mm (1/16–3/16 in.) long; pyrenes 4, smooth. Habitat: Venezuela, Bolivar State, at 1700 m (5600 ft.) elevation. Named for botanist Julian Steyermark.

Ilex strigillosa T. R. Dudley 1984.

Evergreen, small trees to 8.5 m (28 ft.) tall, branchlets blackish, dense puberulent, with light gray sharp stiff hairs; leaves elliptic, 4–7.5 cm (1 5/8–3 in.) long, 1–2 cm (3/8–3/4 in.) wide, shiny, apices acuminate, acumens 5–10 mm (3/16–3/8 in.) long, bases acute to attenuate, margins entire or subentire, with conspicuous indentations, upper half with minute obvious black glands, 3–4 mm (1/8–5/32 in.) apart, petioles 7–10 mm (9/32–3/8 in.) long, densely puberulent; inflorescences axillary, fasciculate, 1- to 4-branched, peduncles short, 1 mm (1/32 in.) long; fruits red, globose-quadrangular, 2.5–3 mm (3/32–1/8 in.) long, 1.5–2 mm (3/64–1/16 in.) diameter, densely grayish white puberulent of minute, erect and appressed hairs; pyrenes 4, striate, pitted. Habitat: People's Republic of China, Guangxi Province. Allied to *I. kengii.* Distinct with hairy fruits.

Ilex suaveolens (Léveillé) Loesener 1914 var. *suaveolens* (synonym *Celastrus suaveolens* Léveillé 1914).

Evergreen trees, branches glabrous, lenticels numerous but inconspicuous; leaves glabrous, elliptic or lanceolate, 5–10 cm (2–4 in.) long, 2.5–4 cm (1–1 5/8 in.) wide, bases rounded, obtuse or cuneate, apices acuminate, margins crenate-serrate, occasionally subentire, pedicels 15–30 mm (19/32–3/4 in.) long; inflorescences subumbelliform, rarely cymose, solitary, axillary on new growth, long peduncles, glabrous, 15–35 mm (19/32–1 3/8 in.) long, petals pinkish; fruits red, compressed-globose, 5–6 mm (3/16–7/32 in.) diameter; pyrenes 4–5, smooth, estriate, esulcate. Habitat: southeastern People's Republic of China, Zhejiang, Guizhou, and Guangdong provinces. Allied to and perhaps intermediate between *I. purpurea* and *I. sterrophylla.*

Ilex suaveolens var. *brevipetiola* W. S. Wu & Y. X. Luo 1992. In *Bull. Bot. Res. North-East. Forest. Inst.,* 12(1): 123, China (Supplement 2 C).

Description not available.

Ilex subavenia Alain 1962 (synonym *I. coriacea* Alain 1960).

Evergreen shrubs, glabrous; leaves oblong-obovate to oblong-oblanceolate, 2.5–7 cm (1–2 3/4 in.) long, 1.4–2.7 cm (17/32–1 1/16 in.) wide, bases obtuse to cuneate, apices obtuse to rotund, margins slightly recurved, petioles 5–6 mm (3/16–7/32 in.) long; inflorescences axillary, solitary, pedicels 3–4 mm (1/8–5/32 in.) long; fruits unknown. Habitat: Cuba, Oriente Province, Sierra de Cristal. Similar to *I. hypaneura.*

Ilex subcaudata Merrill 1915.

Evergreen, erect shrubs or small trees, glabrous, branches slender; leaves ovate-elliptic, glossy, 5–7 cm (2–2 3/4 in.) long, 2–3.5 cm (3/4–1 3/8 in.) wide, bases acuminate, apices abruptly subcaudate-acuminate, acumens 1 cm (3/8 in.) long, blunt, somewhat falcate, margins entire, slightly recurved, petioles 3–4 mm (1/8–5/32 in.) long; male inflorescences racemose, solitary or in pairs, axillary, 3–5 cm (1 3/16–2 in.) long, 10 to 20 flowers, pedicels 4–5 cm (1 5/8–2 in.) long, flowers 4-merous, rarely 5-merous; fruits unknown. Habitat: Philippines, Luzon, Rizal, mountains back of San Mateo. Allied to *I. spicata.*

Ilex subcordata Reisseck 1861 (synonyms *I. subcordata* f. *nummularioides* Loesener 1901, *I. subcordata* f. *silveirae* Loesener 1901, *I. subcordata* f. *typica* Loesener 1901).

Evergreen shrubs to 2 m (6 ft.) tall, branches pubescent; leaves oval to subcordate to orbiculate, 1.3–2.6 cm (15/32–1 in.) long, 0.8–1.9 cm (5/16–3/4 in.) wide. apices acute, bases rotund or cordate, margins usually entire, revolute, petioles 1–2 mm (1/32–1/16 in.) long; inflorescences axillary, solitary at base of new growth, simple or branched, 1- to 3-flowered, flowers usually 4-merous; fruits black, globose, 5 mm ((3/16 in.) diameter; pyrenes 4. Habitat: Brazil. Allied to *I. scutiiformis.*

Ilex subcrenata S.-y. Hu 1951 (synonym *I. oblata sensu* Chun 1940, *non* Comber 1933).

Evergreen, dense shrubs, branches slender, pubescent; leaves broadly elliptic, 5–12 mm (3/16–15/32 in.) long, 4–9 mm (5/32–11/32 in.) wide, pubescent, punctate below, bases obtuse or rotund, apices obtuse or acute, petioles pilose, 2 mm (1/16 in.) long, stipules deltoid, persistent; male inflorescences subfasciculate, rare, axillary, solitary, 1- to 3-flowered, peduncles 3–4 mm (1/8–5/32 in.) long, pedicels pilose, 1.5–4 mm (3/64–5/32 in.) long; fruits unknown. Habitat: People's Republic of China, northern Guangxi Province, near Yao-shan in dense shady sites. Allied to *I. crenata*. This taxon may eventually prove to be a minor variant of *I. crenata*, not meriting botanical rank as a species.

Ilex suber Loesener 1885 (synonym *I. phillyreifolia* var. *leucocalyx* Loesener 1901).

Evergreen shrubs; leaves oval or ovate, 1.6–3.2 cm (⅝–1¼ in.) long, 9–19 mm (¹¹⁄₃₂–¹⁵⁄₁₆ in.) wide, apices rotund or subobtuse, apices rotund or subobtuse, bases crenate, obtuse, margins serrulate, rarely entire, petioles 1–2 mm (¹⁄₃₂–¹⁄₁₆ in.) long; inflorescences axillary, solitary on new growth, puberulent, branched, flowers 4-merous; fruits olive-brown when dried, globose, 3.5 mm (⁷⁄₆₄ in.) diameter; pyrenes 4. Habitat: Brazil, near Goiás State, in the serpentine mountains of Balisa. Allied to *I. phillyreifolia*.

Ilex subficoides S.-y. Hu 1949 (synonym *I. cinerea sensu* Groff 1939, *non* Champion 1852).

Evergreen trees to 15 m (50 ft.) tall, branchlets glabrous; leaves ovate or oblong-elliptic, 7–10 cm (2¾–4 in.) long, 3 cm (1³⁄₁₆ in.) wide, apices abruptly acuminate, acumens 7–16 mm (⁹⁄₃₂–⅝ in.) long, bases obtuse, margins minutely crenate, undulate, teeth marked with black spots, petioles 5–12 mm (³⁄₁₆–¹⁵⁄₃₂ in.) long; inflorescences axillary and fasciculate on 2nd-year growth, flowers 4-merous; fruits red, globose, 10–12 mm (⅜–¹⁵⁄₃₂ in.) diameter, pyrenes 4, wrinkled, pitted. Habitat: People's Republic of China; Jiangxi, Guangdong, Guangxi, and Hainan provinces, in mixed forest south of latitude 25° north. Possibly allied to *I. ficoidea* and *I. nuculicava*.

Ilex sublongecaudata C.-j. Tseng & S.-o. Liu *ex* Y.-r. Li 1984.

Evergreen shrubs to 2 m (6 ft.) tall, branchlets angulate, puberulent; leaves elliptic or oblong-elliptic, 4–6 cm (1⅝–2⅜ in.) long, 15–22 mm (¹⁹⁄₃₂–¹³⁄₁₆ in.) wide, glabrous beneath, apices long-acuminate, acumens 5–10 mm (³⁄₁₆–⅜ in.) long, bases obtuse, margins entire, midribs puberulent, petioles 4–6 mm (⁵⁄₃₂–⁷⁄₃₂ in.) long; inflorescences axillary and fasciculate on 2nd-year growth; fruits red, globose, 3.5–4 mm (⁹⁄₆₄–⁵⁄₃₂ in.) diameter, pedicels 2.5–4.5 mm (³⁄₃₂–¹¹⁄₆₄ in.) long, calyces persistent; pyrenes 4–5, 3- to 4-striate. Habitat: People's Republic of China, Yunnan Province. Allied to *I. longecaudata*.

Ilex subodorata S.-y. Hu 1950 (synonym *I. francheti-ana sensu* Comber 1933).

Evergreen trees to 12 m (40 ft.) tall, branchlet glabrous; leaves elliptic-lanceolate or oblanceolate,

6–9 cm (2⅜–3½ in.) long, 2–3 cm (¾–1³⁄₁₆ in.) wide, apices acuminate, acumens 5–12 mm (³⁄₁₆–¹⁵⁄₃₂ in.) long, bases cuneate, margins strongly serrate, teeth apiculate, petioles 8–12 mm (⅜–¹⁵⁄₃₂ in.) long; inflorescences axillary and fasciculate on 2nd-year growth; fruits red, depressed-globose, 4 mm (⁵⁄₃₂ in.) long, 5 mm (³⁄₁₆ in.) diameter, pedicels 1–2 mm (¹⁄₃₂–¹⁄₁₆ in.) long, calyces persistent; pyrenes 4, palmately striate, sulcate, rugose. Habitat: People's Republic of China, endemic western Yunnan Province. Allied to *I. odorata* and *I. tetramera*.

Ilex subrotundifolia Steyermark 1951 (synonym *I. brevipetiolata* Steyermark & Wurdack 1957).

Evergreen shrubs 1.3–2.8 m (4–9 ft.) tall, branchlets glabrous; leaves broadly ovate to suborbiculate, 2–6 cm (¾–2⅜ in.) long, 2–5.6 cm (¾–2¼ in.) wide, minutely punctate beneath, bases rotund, apices rotund or truncate, margins entire, revolute, petioles 4–5 mm (⁵⁄₃₂–³⁄₁₆ in.) long; inflorescences axillary, solitary; fruits globose, 4 mm (⁵⁄₃₂ in.) diameter; pyrenes 4, unicanaliculate, unequal or uneven triangular. Habitat: Venezuela, Bolivar, rocky uneven ground, Kavanayen, Rio Karuai Ilu-tepui, Cerro Sipapo at 1220–2500 m (4025–8250 ft.) elevation.

Ilex sugerokii Maximowicz var. *sugerokii* 1881. Akatsuge, kuro-soyogo (synonyms *I. sugerokii* f. *longipedunculosa* Maximowicz 1881, *I. sugerokii* subsp. *longipedunculosa* (Maximowicz) Makino 1913).

Large shrubs to 5 m (16 ft.) tall, branchlets puberulent; leaves ovate or ovate-elliptic, 2–4 cm (¾–1⅝ in.) long, 1–2.8 cm (⅜–1⅛ in.) wide, apices acute or shortly acuminate, bases rounded or obtuse, margins serrate on upper half of leaf, persistent on 4th-year growth, petioles 4–7 mm (⁵⁄₃₂–⁹⁄₃₂ in.) long; inflorescences solitary, axillary on new growth, flowers 4- to 6-merous; fruits red, globose, 5–6 mm (³⁄₁₆–⁷⁄₃₂ in.) diameter, or larger, pedicels slender, 3.5 cm (1⅜ in.) long; pyrenes 4–6, smooth. Habitat: Japan, endemic to the Fujiyama region. Hardy to zone 7. Allied to *I. rotunda*. Introduced by E. H. Wilson to

Figure 14-52. *Ilex sugerokii* var. *sugerokii*. Drawing by Randy Allen.

the Arnold Arboretum in 1914 and 1925, in 1961 by J. L. Creech to the U.S. National Arboretum.

Ilex sugerokii var. *brevipedunculosa* (Maximowicz) S.-y. Hu 1949. Akami-no-inu-tsuge (synonyms *I. sugerokii* f. *brevipedunculosa* Maximowicz 1881, *I. taisanensis* Hayata 1911, *I. sugerokii* subsp. *brevipedunculosa* (Maximowicz) Makino 1913, *I. euryaefolia* Mori & Yamamoto 1932).

A botanical variety with short pedicels 10–15 mm (3⁄8–1⁄2 in.) long; larger fruits, red, 7–8 mm (9⁄32–5⁄16 in.) diameter. Locally abundant in high mountains of Hokkaido and Honshu, Japan, and southern and central Taiwan. Similar to *I. yunnanensis* with densely pubescent branchlets and leaf margins that are completely serrated to the base.

Ilex suichangensis C. Z. Zheng 1988.

Evergreen trees to 10 m (33 ft.) tall, glabrous, branchlets moderate brown, angulate, glabrous, 2nd-year branchlets ashy brown, terete, lenticellate, elliptic; leaves long elliptic, 14–22 cm (5½–8¾ in.) long, 5–8 cm (2–3⅛ in.) wide, bases cuneate, apices long acuminate, acumens 1.5–2.5 cm (19⁄32–2 in.) wide, margins entire, veins prominent, petioles robust, thick, 3–3.5 cm (1 3⁄16–1⅜ in.) long; male and female inflorescences unknown; infructescences cymose or subumbelliform, 5- to 6-fruited, solitary, axillary, peduncles 12–20 mm (15⁄32–¾ in.) long, pedicels 8–10 mm (5⁄16–⅜ in.) long; fruits ellipsoid, (9–) 10–15 mm ((11⁄32–) 12⁄32–19⁄32 in.) long, 7–10 mm (9⁄32–⅜ in.) diameter, calyces persistent; pyrenes 5–6, dorsal surface 3- to 4-striate. Habitat: People's Republic of China, Zhejiang Province, Suichang, Ji-Xia, Chukeng-ao, at 1200 m (3960 ft.) elevation growing at margins of forests. Allied to *I. umbellulata.*

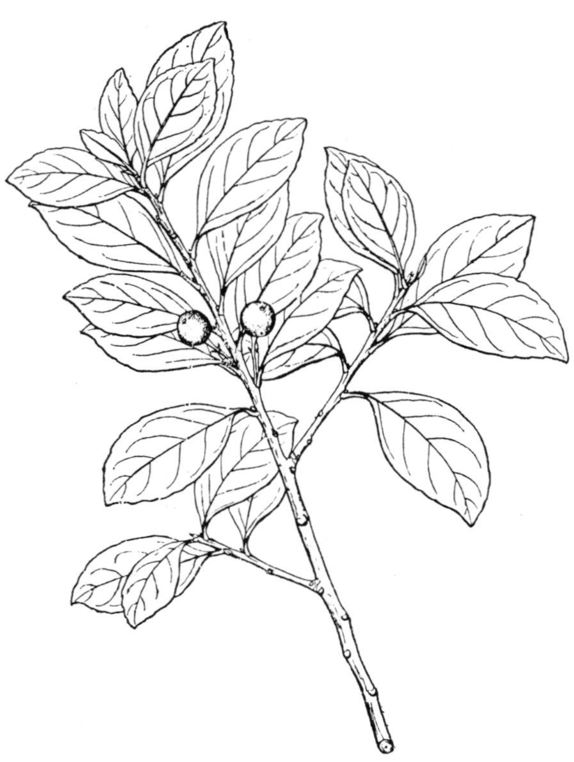

Figure 14-53. *Ilex sugerokii* var. *brevipedunculosa.* Drawing by Chien-chu Chen in *Illustrations of Native and Introduced Ligneous Plants of Taiwan* (1962) by Tang-shui Liu.

Ilex sumatrana Loesener 1901.

Evergreen, glabrous, large shrubs or small trees; leaves obovate-oblong or oval-oblong, 4–6.5 cm (1⅝–2⅜ in.) long, 1.6–2.5 cm (⅝–1 in.) wide, apices obtuse or rotund, acuminate, bases crenate, margins entire, recurved, petioles 6–11 mm (7⁄32–7⁄16 in.) long; inflorescences axillary, fasciculate, solitary flowers 4-merous; fruits unknown. Habitat: Indonesia, western part of Sumatra, Mount Singalar at 1800 m (5900 ft.) elevation. Allied to *I. thwaitesii.*

Ilex summa Steyermark 1988.

Evergreen shrubs to 3 m (10 ft.) tall, branchlets glabrous; leaves ovate, 2.5–4.5 cm (1–1¾ in.) long, 1.4–1.6 cm (17⁄32–⅝ in.) wide, black punctate above and beneath, bases rotund or broadly obtuse, apices apiculate or subacute, margins with 3–5 acute or setulose teeth, strongly revolute, petioles 3–6 mm (⅛–7⁄32 in.) long; inflorescences axillary, solitary, lateral, pedunculate; fruits globose, 6–7 mm (7⁄32–9⁄32 in.) diameter, pedicels 4–6 mm (5⁄32–7⁄32 in.) long; pyrenes 4, trigonous, dorsally unisulcate. Habitat: Venezuela, Bolivia: District Piar, Camarcaibarei-tepui at 2400 m (7900 ft.) elevation. Allied to *I. actidenticulata.*

Ilex suprema Cuatrecasas 1948.

Evergreen, small trees to 8 m (26 ft.) tall; leaves broadly ovate, 1–2 cm (⅜–¾ in.) long, 0.6–1.5 cm (7⁄32–19⁄32 in.) wide, bases cuneate, apices rotund, margins crenate-serrate, petioles 1–2 mm (1⁄32–1⁄16 in.) long; inflorescences axillary, solitary, or cymes of 2–3 flowers, flowers 5-merous; fruits black, globose, 8 mm (5⁄16 in.) diameter; pyrenes 5–6. Habitat: Colombia, Department del Valle, western Cordillera, La Laguna, at 3300–3500 (10,890–11,550 ft.) elevation. Allied to *I. uniflora.*

Ilex suzukii S.-y. Hu 1949.

Evergreen shrubs, branches glabrous, axillary buds large; leaves entire, elliptic, 2.5–4 cm (1–1⅝ in.) long, 1.5–2.2 cm (19⁄32–13⁄16 in.) wide, bases acute or cuneate, apices obtuse or very sharply acu-

minate, acumens 3 mm (1/8 in.) long, leaves persist on 4th-year growth; flowers unknown, infructescences axillary on 2nd-year growth paucifasciculate, fascicles with 2 or 3 fruits, pedicels glabrous, 4 mm (5/32 in.) long, with 2 minute deltoid prophylla at the base; fruits globose, 5 mm (3/16 in.) diameter; pyrenes 4, palmately striate and sulcate. Habitat: Taiwan. Allied to *I. mertensii.* This species often mistaken as *I. hanceana.*

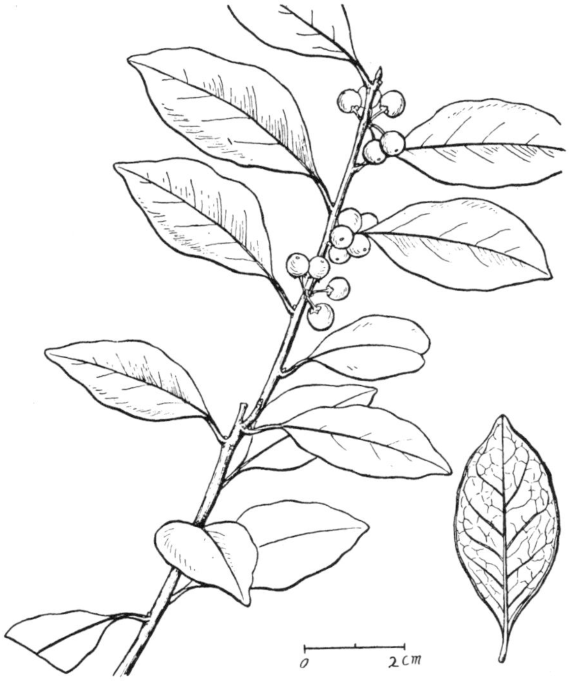

Figure 14-54. *Ilex suzukii.* Drawing by Chien-chu Chen in *Illustrations of Native and Introduced Ligneous Plants of Taiwan* (1962) by Tang-shui Liu.

Ilex symplociformes Reisseck 1861.

Evergreen, glabrous shrubs, branches ascending or slightly spreading; leaves narrow-ovate-elliptic or elliptic, usually 8–11 cm (3 1/8–4 3/8 in.) long, 2.2–3.2 cm (13/16–1 1/8 in.) wide, apices gradually acuminate, bases obtuse or acute, margins recurved, serrate or serrulate, petioles 7–13 mm (9/32–15/32 in.) long; inflorescences axillary, spikelike paniculate, flowers usually 4-merous; fruits unknown. Habitat: Brazil, near Jacobina. Allied to *I. conocarpa.*

Ilex synpyrena C.-j. Tseng 1981.

Evergreen shrubs, branchlets angulate, pubescent or glabrescent; leaves oblong-elliptic, 7 cm (2 3/4 in.) long, 2–2.5 cm (3/4–1 in.) wide, apices acute, bases decurrently acuminate, midribs puberulent above, margins entire, revolute, petioles 3–4 mm (1/8–5/32 in.) long, puberulent, winged; inflorescences axillary, 2- to 3-fasciculate; fruits red, globose, 10 mm (3/8 in.) diameter, pedicels very short; pyrenes 1–2, if 2 then connate, or fused into 1 or 2 units (a very rare condition in *Ilex*), striate, sulcate. Habitat: People's Republic of China, Yunnan Province. This species is not validly published, lacking locality and collector information. Apparently from only one herbarium specimen at the Institute of Botany, Academia Sinica, Beijing (PE). Should be re-published with a more adequate designation of collectors and locality of the holotype specimen. Allied to *I. kingiana* and *I. perryana.*

Ilex syzygiophylla C.-j. Tseng 1981.

Evergreen shrubs or trees to 25 m (82 ft.) tall, branchlets angulate, glabrous, lenticels present; leaves elliptic 7–10 cm (2 3/4–4 in.) long, 3–5 cm (1 3/16–2 in.) wide, apices acuminate, acumens 7–10 mm (9/32–3/8 in.) long, bases usually cuneate, margins entire, subrevolute, petioles 1–1.5 cm (3/8–19/32 in.) long; inflorescences axillary or borne laterally at bases of new branchlets, fasciculate, cymes or umbels 2- to 4-fruited, peduncles 4–5 mm (5/32–3/16 in.) long, pedicels 4–5 mm (5/32–3/16 in.) long; fruits red, globose, 5 mm (3/16 in.) diameter; pyrenes 5, striate. Habitat: People's Republic of China, Guangdong Province. Allied to *I. omeiensis* and *I. venulosa.*

Ilex szechwanensis Loesener 1901 var. *szechwanensis* (synonyms *I. szechwanensis* f. *angustata* Loesener 1901, *I. szechwanensis* f. *calva* Loesener *ex* Diels 1901, *I. szechwanensis* f. *puberula* Loesener 1901, *I. crenata* Thunberg var. *scoriarum* W. Smith 1917).

Evergreen shrubs 1–5 m (3–16 ft.) tall, sometimes low and creeping, branches puberulent; leaves punctate, ovate-elliptic or ovate-oblong, 3.5–7 cm (1 3/8–2 3/4 in.) long, 2–4 cm (3/4–1 5/8 in.) wide, bases usually obtuse, apices acuminate, acumens 3–5 mm (1/8–3/16 in.) long, margins serrate, rarely crenate or entire, petioles 4–6 mm (5/32–7/32 in.) long; male inflorescences 1- to 7-flowered cymes, solitary, axillary, pistillate inflorescences solitary, axillary, peduncles 8–10 mm (5/16–3/8 in.) long, fruits black, usually globose, 7–8 mm (9/32–5/16 in. diameter; pyrenes 4, smooth, striate, slightly impressed. Habitat: People's Republic of China, Guangdong, Guizhou, and Yunnan provinces. Allied to and intermediate between *I. crenata* and *I. triflora.*

Ilex szechwanensis var. *heterophylla* C.-y. Wu *ex* Y.-r. Li 1985.

A variety differing from typical individuals by having smaller, ovate or ovate-elliptic leaves, often 2–3.5 cm (3/4–1 3/8 in.) long, and 1–1.5 cm (3/8–1/2 in.) wide, sometimes smaller and larger leaves intermixed (on same branches and branchlets), smaller leaves 0.6–1 cm (7/32–3/8 in.) long, 0.4–0.8 cm (5/32–5/16 in.) wide, larger leaves 4–5 cm (1 5/8–2 in.) long, 1.8–2.2 cm (11/16–13/16 in.) wide; leaf margins sparsely crenate-serrate; leaf apices acuminate. Habitat: People's Republic of China, Yunnan Province, Maguan.

Ilex szechwanensis var. *huiana* T. R. Dudley 1984.

A variety differing from typical individuals with smaller leaves, 2–4.5 cm (3/4–1 3/4 in.) long, 1–2 cm (3/8–3/4 in.) wide; margins minutely crenate (not serrate) on upper half of leaf; stipules large, 2–2.5 cm (3/4–1 in.) long; petioles shorter, 2–5 mm (1/16–3/16 in.) long; flowers pink; fruits yellow. Habitat: People's Republic of China, Yunnan Province.

Ilex szechwanensis var. *mollissima* C.-y. Wu. *ex* Y.-r. Li 1985.

A variety differing from typical individuals with densely puberulent branches; smaller leaves and mid veins on upper surface densely pubescent; flowers and fruits smaller. Habitat: People's Republic of China, Yunnan Province, Pingbain. This variety and variety *heterophylla* by the same author may well prove to be synonyms of the species; it is beginning to appear that these varieties demonstrate normal natural variations caused by unusual and perhaps abnormal environmental conditions.

Ilex tadiandamolensis Murthy, Yoganarashimham, & Nair 1987.

Evergreen trees to 10 m (33 ft.) tall, young branches pubescent, later glabrous; leaves elliptic-lanceolate, glabrous, 3.5–9 cm (1 3/8–3 1/2 in.) long, 1.2–2.8 cm (15/32–1 1/8 in.) wide, bases attenuate, apices acute or emarginate, margins entire, petioles 3–8 mm (1/8–5/16 in.) long; inflorescences axillary, panicled cymose, pedicels 2–5 mm (1/16–3/16 in.) long; fruits ovoid. Habitat: India, Karnataka, evergreen forest of Tadiandamoi at 2000 m (6600 ft.) elevation. Allied to *I. malabarica.*

Ilex tahanensis Kiew 1978 (synonym *I. rupicola* Ridley 1915, *non* Kunth 1824).

Evergreen shrubs or small tree; leaves elliptic to oblong, 5–6.5 cm (2–2 1/2 in.) long, 2.5–3.8 cm (1–1 1/2 in.) wide, bases rotund, apices subacute, margins entire; inflorescences simple cymes, peduncles 1 cm (3/8 in.) long, flowers 4- to 5-merous; fruits globose; pyrenes 4. Habitat: Malaysia, rare mountain shrubs, near Padang, and other areas; from G. Tahan & G. Radong.

Ilex taiwanensis (S.-y. Hu) H.-w. Li 1963 (synonym *I. pedunculosa* var. *taiwanensis* S.-y. Hu 1949).

Large shrubs, branchlets minutely puberulent; leaves ovate to oblong, 1.5–3 cm (19/32–1 3/16 in.) long, 1–1.6 cm (3/8–5/8 in.) wide, apices acute, margins entire, petioles 7–9 mm (9/32–11/32 in.) long; inflorescences axillary, solitary, pedicels 11–14 mm (7/16–17/32 in.) long; fruits red. Endemic to northern Taiwan. Allied to *I. pedunculosa* and *I. yunnanensis.*

Ilex tamii T. R. Dudley, *nom. nov.* Nan-chiao (basionym *I. revoluta* Tam, *Acta Phytotax. Sin.* 8: 356. 1963, which is a later homonym of *I. revoluta* Stapf 1894).

Evergreen, small tree 4–8 m (13–26 ft.) tall, glabrous, branches angulate; leaves obovate, 4.5–5.5 cm (1 3/4–2 1/8 in.) long. 2–2.5 cm (3/4–1 in.) wide, bases cuneate or mucro-cuneate, decurrent, apices rotund or obtuse, punctuate, margins entire, revolute, petioles 3–4 mm (1/8–5/32 in.) long; inflorescences axillary, solitary; fruits globose, 6 mm (7/32 in.) diameter, pedicels 5 mm (3/16 in.) long; pyrenes 4, 1- to 2-striate and sulcate. Habitat: People's Republic of China, Hainan Province, near Hsuangehi-Na; Wanning Hsian, on mountain peaks, rare. Allied to *I. championii.*

Ilex tarapotina Loesener 1901.

Evergreen shrubs usually 3 m (10 ft.) tall, branches puberulent; leaves ovate to oblong to sublanceolate, 8.5–10.5 cm (3 3/8–4 1/8 in.) long, 2.5–3.5 cm (1–1 3/8 in.) wide, apices acuminate, acumens 8–15 mm (5/16–19/32 in.) long, bases cuneate to obtuse, margins entire, recurved, petioles 8–12 mm (5/16–15/32 in.) long; inflorescences axillary, fasciculate, branched, flowers usually 4-merous; peduncles 5–11 mm (3/16–7/16 in.) long, pedicels 1–2 mm (1/32–1/16 in.) long; fruits unknown. Habitat: Peru, rocky hillsides along the Rio Mayo near Tarapoto. Allied to *I. reisseckiana.*

Ilex tardieublotii Tran Dirh Dai 1984. In Nguyen Tier Ban, ed., *Fl. Taybguyen. Enum.* 45, *nov. nom.,* without replaced synonym ref.: *I. merrillii* Tardieu. (Supplement 20).

Ilex tateana Steyermark 1951.

Evergreen shrubs 2.8–3.3 m (9–11 ft.) tall, branches glabrous; leaves elliptic-oblong, 13–18 cm (5 1/8–7 1/4 in.) long, 4.5–7.5 cm (1 3/4–3 in.) wide, punctate, bases obtuse, apices rotund, margins obscure crenulate, petioles 6–9 mm (7/32–11/32 in.) long; male inflorescences axillary, fasciculate, flowers 4-merous; female plants not observed. Habitat: Venezuela, Amazonas, near Cano Negro, at 1095–1520 m (3600–5000 ft.) elevation. Allied to *I. laurina* and *I. pierreana.*

Ilex taubertiana Loesener 1901.

Evergreen, glabrous, large shrubs or small trees; leaves oval-elliptic to lanceolate, 6–8 cm (2⅜–3⅛ in.) long, 1.2–2.5 cm (15⁄32–2 in.) wide, bases obtuse to cuneate-obtuse, apices acute or acuminate with 1 cm (⅜ in.) spine, margins recurved, usually subdenticulate-serrulate toward apex, petioles 10–18 mm (⅜–11⁄16 in.) long; inflorescences glabrous, axillary, solitary, single or branched, long peduncles 14–30 mm (17⁄32–1 3⁄16 in.) long, pedicels 4–8 mm (5⁄32–5⁄16 in.) long; fruits grayish brown, depressed-globose, 4.5 mm (7⁄32 in.) diameter; pyrenes 4. Habitat: Brazil, Rio de Janeiro State, near Nova Friburgo on Mount Alto-macha. Allied to *I. sapotifolia.*

Ilex tavoyensis Balakrishnam 1967 (synonym *I. wallichii* Hooker f. 1875, *non* Steudel 1840).

Evergreen trees usually 4–5 m (13–16 ft.) to 15 m (50 ft.) tall, branches whitish, erect to ascending; leaves wide oval to elliptic, 5–12 cm (2–4¾ in.) long, 3–5.5 cm (1 3⁄16–2⅛ in.) wide, entire recurved margins, bases rounded to wide-cuneate, obtuse, rarely cuneate, apices rounded to obtuse or acuminate, petioles 7–13 mm (9⁄32–½ in.) long; inflorescences solitary in leaf axils, peduncles 9–20 mm (11⁄32–¾ in.) long, secondary pedicels 3–9 mm (⅛–11⁄32 in.) long; fruits depressed-ovoid, 4.5–6.5 mm (3⁄16–¼ in.) long, 6.5–7 mm (¼–9⁄32 in.) wide; pyrenes 12–14, striate. Habitat: southern Malaysia, Tenasserim near Tavoy. Allied to *I. cymosa.*

Ilex tectonica Hahn 1988. San Juan macho, sibuc cha, power stick (Belize) camibar, areno (Nicaragua), San Juan campano, San Juan arenillo (Honduras).

Evergreen trees to 45 m (148 ft.) tall, more than 1 m (3.3 ft.) diameter at breast height, trunks reported to be buttressed, mature stems pale brownish gray, new stems drying black or dark brown, white, oval lenticels; leaves elliptic, 7–10 cm (2¾–4 in.) long, 3.5–4.5 cm (1⅜–1¾ in.) wide, bases acute, slender-attenuate, apices short-caudate, margins usually entire, occasionally minutely spinose near apex, petioles thick, 4–8 mm (5⁄32–5⁄16 in.) long; inflorescences axillary, branched, flowers 4- to 5-merous; fruits red, ovoid, 5–6 mm (3⁄16–7⁄32 in.) long, 4 mm (5⁄32 in.) diameter; pyrenes crescent-shaped, triangular in cross section. Habitat: Belize, Honduras, and Nicaragua, in tall moist forest, also among pines in drier mixed forest. Utilized for timber; specific epithet from Greek *tecktonikos* (used for construction). Allied to *I. belizensis* and *I. guianensis.*

Ilex tenuis C.-j. Tseng 1981.

Evergreen trees to 7 m (23 ft.) tall, branchlets black to brownish, angulate, glabrous; leaves elliptic or obovate-elliptic, 5–8 cm (2–3⅛ in.) long, 2.4–3 cm (1–1 3⁄16 in.) wide, glandular punctate beneath, apices short-acuminate, rarely obtuse, bases attenuate, glabrous, margins remotely serrulate, serrations blackish apiculate, petioles 5–7 mm (3⁄16–9⁄32 in.) long, glabrous, canaliculate; inflorescences axillary, 2- to 4-fasciculate, pedicels 6 mm (7⁄32 in.) long; fruits red, globose, 1–1.1 cm (⅜–7⁄16 in.) diameter; pyrenes 4, rugose, striate, sulcate. Habitat: People's Republic of China, Guangdong Province. Allied to *I. ningdeensis.*

Ilex tepuiana Steyermark *ex* Edwin 1965.

Evergreen trees to 10 m (33 ft.) tall, branchlets glabrous; leaves lanceolate-obovate to broadly obovate, 5–7 cm (2–2¾ in.) long, 2.5–4 cm (1–1⅝ in.) wide, punctate beneath, bases cuneate to slightly spathulate, apices variable, acuminate or acute, retuse, margins entire, slightly revolute, petioles 2–5 mm (1⁄16–3⁄16 in.) long; inflorescences, axillary, solitary, flowers 4-merous; fruits black, subglobose; pyrenes 4, unicanaliculate. Habitat: Venezuela, Bolivar, between Ptari-tepui and Sororopán-tepui, at 1600 m (5300 ft.) elevation; also in Guyana.

Ilex teratopsis Loesener 1901.

Evergreen trees to 3–7 m (10–23 ft.) tall, branches glabrous, growth strong and upright; leaves glabrous, obovate to ovate or wide-oval, 8.8–15.5 cm (2½–6¼ in.) long, 5.5–8 cm (2⅛–3⅛ in.) wide, margins recurved, serrulate, bases rounded to subcrenulate, apices rounded, petioles 10–16 mm (⅜–⅝ in.) long; inflorescences solitary in leaf axils, long peduncles 16–26 mm (⅝–1 in.) long; fruits black, depressed-globose, 6–8 mm (9⁄32–5⁄16 in.) diameter; pyrenes 4. Habitat: Bolivia and Peru at 3000–3340 m (9,000–11,020 ft.) elevation. Allied to *I. anonoides.*

Ilex ternatiflora (C. H. Wright) R. Howard 1986 (synonym *Quiina ternatiflora* C. H. Wright 1868).

According to Howard (1986), Charles Wright described this species as *Quiina ternatiflora* in the *Anales de la Academia Ciencias Medicas Fisicasy Naturales Habana* (5: 204. 1868). This was the only report of the family Quiinaceae from Cuba. However, in the *Flora de Cuba* Brother Alain stated the species was of a questionable taxonomic position. A poor herbarium specimen was found at the New York Botanical Gardens, consisting of one leaf and some dissected flower parts. The sheet was annotated as *Ilex,* not Quiinaceae, by J. M. Pires in 1950, who was working on the family Quiina. It is hoped that additional collections of this species in Cuba will be made in the future.

Ilex tetramera (Rehder) C.-j. Tseng 1981 var. *tetramera* (synonyms *I. tephrophylla* (Loesener) S.-y. Hu

1950, *I. odorata* Hamilton *ex* D. Don var. *tephrophylla* Loesener 1880, *Symplocos tetramera* Rehder 1916).

Evergreen trees to 10 m (33 ft.) tall, branchlets glabrous or glabrescent; leaves oblong-elliptic, 6–9.5 cm (2⅜–3¾ in.) long, 1.5–3.5 cm (¹⁹⁄₃₂–1⅜ in.) wide, apices acuminate, acumens 8–12 mm (⁵⁄₁₆–¹⁵⁄₃₂ in.) long, bases obtuse or rotund, margins minutely crenulate or subentire, petioles 4–8 mm (⁵⁄₃₂–⁵⁄₁₆ in.) long; inflorescences axillary and fasciculate on 2nd-year growth, or subracemose, male peduncles and pedicels puberulent; fruits red, globose, 5–6 mm (³⁄₁₆–⁷⁄₃₂ in.) diameter, pedicels 1–3 mm (¹⁄₃₂–⅛ in.) long, calyces persistent; pyrenes 4, palmately striate, sulcate, sides wrinkled and pitted. Habitat: People's Republic of China, Guangxi Province. Allied to *I. formosana*.

Ilex tetramera var. *glabra* (C.-y. Wu *ex* Y.-r. Li) T. R. Dudley 1988 (synonym *I. tephrophylla* var. *glabra* C.-y. Wu *ex* Y.-r. Li 1985).

A variety differing from typical individuals by male flowers being borne on longer, glabrous pedicels 5 mm (³⁄₁₆ in.) long; leaves 7–9 cm (2¾–3½ in.) long, 2–2.5 cm (¾–1 in.) wide. Habitat: People's Republic of China, Yunnan Province, Menghai, Manyuan.

Ilex theezans Martius 1983 var. *theezans*. Cauna, pao d'azeile, yerba (synonyms *Achras coriacea* (Sprengel *ex* Martius) Loesener 1901, *I. theezans* var. *acrodonta* subvar. *hieronymiana* Loesener 1901, *I. theezans* var. *leptophylla* Loesener 1901, *I. theezans* var. *pachyphylla* Loesener 1901, *I. theezans* var. *warmingiana* Loesener 1901, *I. theezans* f. *glabra* Loesener 1901, *I. theezans* f. *puberula* Loesener 1901).

Evergreen shrubs or trees, lenticels present; leaves variable, ovate or obovate or obovate-elliptic, usually pubescent, 3–11.5 cm (1³⁄₁₆–4³⁄₁₆ in.) long, 1.2–5.5 cm (¹⁵⁄₃₂–2⅛ in.) wide, apices rotund or obtuse, bases cuneate to obtuse, margins entire, revolute, petioles 5–14 mm (³⁄₁₆–¹⁷⁄₃₂ in.) long; inflorescences fasciculate in leaf axils, 3- to 7-flowered, flowers 4- to 5-merous; fruits brownish black, ellipsoid or globose 4 mm (⁵⁄₃₂ in.) long, 5–8 mm (³⁄₁₆–⁵⁄₁₆ in.) wide; pyrenes 4–6, sulcate. Habitat: Brazil and Argentine. Allied to *I. brasiliensis* and *I. integerrima*.

Ilex theezans var. *acrodonta* (Reisseck) Loesener 1901 (synonyms *Prinos serratus* Velloso 1825, *I. acrodonta* Reisseck 1861, *I. acrodonta* var. *angustifolia* Reisseck 1861, *I. acrodonta* var. *latifolia* Reisseck 1861).

A variety with leaves obovate, 5–8 cm (2–3⅛ in.) long, 2–3 cm (¾–1³⁄₁₆ in.) wide, apices obtuse or acute, bases cuneate; fruits usually globose. Habitat: southern Brazil. With more study,

this variety may be treated as a synonym of the species.

Ilex theezans var. *augustii* Loesener 1901.

A variety with leaves obovate-oval or elliptic, 3–6 cm (1³⁄₁₆–2⅜ in.) long, 1.9–2.7 cm (¾–2¹⁄₁₆ in.) wide, apices rotund or obtuse, bases cuneate or cuneate obtuse, margins usually entire, occasionally serrulate near apex. Habitat: Brazil, Rio de Janeiro State. With more study, this variety may be treated as a synonym of the species.

Ilex theezans var. *fertilis* (Reisseck) Loesener 1901. Cauna amarga, cauna de folhas largas, caa-na (synonyms *I. gigantea* Bonpland *ex* Meirs 1860, *I. fertilis* Reisseck 1892).

Evergreen trees to 24 m (80 ft.) tall; leaves obovate or obovate-oblong, 5.5–8.5 cm (2⅛–3⅜ in.) long, 2–4 cm (¾–1⅝ in.) wide, apices obtuse or rotund, bases cuneate, petioles 3–6 mm (⅛–⁷⁄₃₂ in.) long; flowers rarely 6-merous; fruits globose. Habitat: southern Brazil, woodlands near Santa Cruz, and in Argentina near Paraná.

Ilex theezans var. *gracilior* (Warming) Loesener 1901 (synonyms *I. acrodonta* var. *angustifolia* Reisseck 1861, *I. fertilis* var. *gracilior* Warming 1879).

A variety with leaves smaller than typical individuals, obovate or obovate-elliptic, 3.5–5 cm (1⅜–2⅛ in.) long, 1–1.5 cm (⅜–¹⁹⁄₃₂ in.) wide, apices obtuse or acute, or acuminate, bases narrow; flowers 4- to 5-merous; fruits globose. Habitat: Brazil, Rio de Janeiro State.

Ilex theezans var. *grandifolia* Loesener 1901.

A variety with leaves larger than typical individuals, obovate or broadly suboval, 8–11.5 cm (3⅛–4³⁄₁₆ in.) long, 4–5.5 cm (1⅝–2⅛ in.) wide, apices obtuse, bases cuneate, margins usually entire, with 1–3 or 1–5 obscure teeth. Habitat: Brazil, Santos.

Ilex theezans var. *riedelii* (Loesener) Loesener 1901 (synonyms *I. ebenacea* Reisseck 1861, *I. fertilis* Warming 1879, *non* Reisseck 1892, *I. riedlaei* Loesener 1892).

Large shrubs or small trees to 4 m (13 ft.) tall, branches dark green angulate; leaves obovate or obovate-elliptic, 4–7.5 cm (1⅝–3 in.) long, 2–3 cm (¾–1³⁄₁₆ in.) wide, apices rarely mucronulate, bases cuneate, margins entire, remotely serrulate near apex; flowers 4- to 6-merous; fruits globose, stigmas prominent. Habitat: Brazil, rocky plains near Piedade, in Venezuela, Dominican Republic, and Puerto Rico.

Ilex thorelii Pierre 1895. Buiba vo.
Evergreen, glabrous trees to 12 m (40 ft.) tall;

leaves oval to obovate, 7–10.5 cm (2¾–4 in.) long, 3.5–4.6 cm (1⅜–1⅝ in.) wide, margins entire, recurved bases cuneate, rarely cuneate-obtuse, apices rounded; inflorescence solitary in leaf axils, long peduncles 17–22 mm (⅝–⅞ in.) long, branched pedicels 2–4 mm (1/16–5/32 in.) long; fruits subovoid, 5 mm (3/16 in.) long, 7 mm (9/32 in.) wide; pyrenes 10–12, one longitudinal furrow. Habitat: southern Indonesia. Allied to *I. eugeniaefolia* and *I. wallichii* Steudel.

Ilex thwaitesii Loesener 1901 (synonyms *I. walkeri* Thwaites 1860, *I. walkeri* var. *major* Wight & Gardner 1875).

Evergreen, small trees, branches glabrous; leaves obovate or broadly elliptic, 3.3–5.3 cm (1 7/32–2⅛ in.) long, 1.5–2.5 cm (19/32–1 in.) wide, apices rotund, apiculate, bases cuneate or cuneate-obtuse, margins recurved, entire, occasionally 1–2 small teeth near apex, petioles 5–10 mm (3/16–⅜ in.) long; inflorescences fasciculate in leaf axils, flowers to 4- to 6-merous; fruits color unknown, globose 4–4.5 mm (5/32–11/64 in.) diameter, peduncles 3–5.5 mm (⅛–13/64 in.) long; pyrenes 4–5. Habitat: India, Mount Pulney. Allied to *I. wightiana*.

Ilex thyrsiflora Koltzsch 1861 var. *thyrsiflora* (synonym *I. thyrsiflora* var. *genuina* Loesener 1901).

Evergreen shrubs; leaves oval or oval-oblong, 4.5–8 cm (1¾–3⅛ in.) long, 2–6.5 cm (¾–2½ in.) wide, apices acute or acuminate, bases rotund or obtuse, margins recurved, remotely serrulate, petioles 5–10 mm (3/16–⅜ in.) long; inflorescences axillary, solitary, fasciculate, branched, flowers 4-merous; fruits black, ellipsoid, 3 mm (⅛ in.) long, 2.5 mm (3/32 in.) wide; pyrenes 4. Habitat: Guyana and Belize. Allied to *I. martiniana*.

Ilex thyrsiflora var. *schomburgkii* (Klotzsch) Loesener 1901 (synonym *I. schomburgkii* Koltzsch 1861).

A variety differing from typical individuals with oval to oblong leaves, bases cuneate-obtuse or acute; inflorescences solitary. Habitat: Guyana. Probably will be sunk into synonymy of the species at a later date.

Ilex tiricae Edwin 1965.

Evergreen shrubs 0.5–1 m (1½–4 ft.) tall, branches ascending; leaves broadly ovate to ovate, rarely obovate, 3.5–5.5 cm (1⅜–2⅛ in.) long, 3–3.5 cm (1 3/16–1⅜ in.) wide, bases cuneate to orbiculate, apices shortly acuminate, acumens 0.1–2 mm (1/64–1/16 in.) long, margins entire to occasionally ⅛ to ⅔ of margins remotely serrulate, petioles 7–10 mm (9/32–⅜ in.) long; inflorescences axillary, solitary, flowers 6-merous; fruits dried, brown to mahogany, ovoid to subglobose, 10 mm (⅜ in.) long, 7 mm (9/32 in.) diameter; pyrenes 6, broadly canaliculate, marginal ridges. Habitat: Venezuela, Bolivar, shrubby thickets bordering swamps along east branch of headwaters of Rio Tirica, at 2120 m (7000 ft.) elevation.

Ilex tonii Lundell 1968.

Evergreen shrubs or small trees, glabrous, branches slender; leaves lanceolate, 5.5–9 cm (2⅛–3½ in.) long, 1.8–4 cm (11/16–1⅝ in.) wide, sparsely pubescent beneath, then glabrous, bases acute, apices acuminate-attenuate, margins crenate-serrulate, teeth incurved, blunt; inflorescences axillary, fasciculate, pedicels slender, to 1.5 cm (19/32 in.) long, minutely pubescent; young fruits glabrous, subglobose. Habitat: Mexico, Chiapas State, on grassy slopes with *Quercus* at 1787 m (5900 ft.) elevation.

Ilex tonkiniana Loesener 1901.

Evergreen shrubs, branchlets glabrous; leaves narrow-elliptic or oval-elliptic, 8–13 cm (5/16–½ in.) long, 2.2–4 cm (13/16–1⅝ in.) wide, bases obtuse or subrotund, apices obtuse or subacute, margins recurved, serrulate-crenulate, petioles 8–11 mm (5/16–7/16 in.) long; inflorescences axillary, fasciculate, flowers 4-merous; fruits unknown. Habitat: Vietnam, Tonkin. Allied to *I. cinerea* and *I. warburgii*.

Ilex trachyphylla Loesener 1908.

Evergreen; leaves ovate, oval to obovate, 5.5–9 cm (2⅛–3½ in.) long, 3.3–6.5 cm (1 5/16–2½ in.) wide, bases rounded, apices often notched, margins often remotely serrulate, petioles 2–4 mm (1/16–5/32 in.) long; inflorescences axillary, solitary, branched, peduncles 3–6 mm (⅛–7/32 in.) long; usually 1 pyrene, rarely 5–6. Habitat: Peru. Allied to *I. obtusata* and *I. sessilifolia*.

Ilex trichocarpa H.-w. Li *ex* Y.-r. Li 1985.

Evergreen, small trees to 4 m (13 ft.) tall, branchlets greenish to light brown, puberulent, angulate; leaves obovate-oblong or oblong-lanceolate, 8–10 cm (3⅛–4 in.) long, 2–3 cm (¾–1 3/16 in.) wide, apices acuminate, bases cuneate, margins moderately serrate, reticulate on both surfaces, petioles 5–10 mm (3/16–⅜ in.) long; inflorescences axillary; fruits red, ovoid-globose, 10 mm (⅜ in.) long, 8 mm (5/16 in.) diameter, densely puberulent; pyrenes 4. Habitat: People's Republic of China, Yunnan Province. Allied to *I. strigillosa* and closely resembles *I. kaushue*. At a later date this may be placed as a geographic subspecies of *I. kaushue*.

Ilex trichoclada Loesener 1901.

Evergreen shrubs 2–3.3 m (6–11 ft.) tall; leaves broadly ovate or oval, 6–13 mm (7/32–15/32 in.) long,

4–8 mm (⁵⁄₃₂–⁵⁄₁₆ in.) wide, apices rotund, bases rotund or obtuse, margins recurved, 3–4 serrulate on each side, petioles 2 mm (¹⁄₁₆ in.) long; inflorescences axillary, solitary, fasciculate, flowers 4-merous, peduncles 1–2.5 mm (¹⁄₃₂–³⁄₃₂ in.) long, pedicels 2 mm (¹⁄₁₆ in.) long; fruits unknown. Habitat: Bolivia, at 3600–4000 m (11,880–13,200 ft.) elevation. Allied to *I. lechleri*.

Figure 14-55. *Ilex trichoclada*. Drawing by Chien-chu Chen in *Illustrations of Native and Introduced Ligneous Plants of Taiwan* (1962) by Tang-shui Liu.

Ilex trichothyrsa Loesener 1901.

Evergreen shrubs or trees; leaves elliptic or obovate to lanceolate-elliptic, 2–6.5 cm (³⁄₄–2½ in.) long, 1–1.9 cm (³⁄₈–³⁄₄ in.) wide, apices obtuse or subacute, slightly acuminate, bases usually acute, margins recurved, slightly crenulate-serrulate, petioles 4–7 mm (⁵⁄₃₂–⁹⁄₃₂ in.) long; inflorescences axillary, paniculate, flowers 4-merous; fruits unknown. Habitat: Brazil. Allied to *I. amara*.

Ilex triflora Blume 1826 (synonyms *I. lobbiana* Rolfe 1884, *I. horsfieldii* (Miquel) Loesener 1901, *I. triflora* var. *acutata* Loesener 1901, *I. triflora* var. *horsfieldii* (Miquel) Loesener 1901, *I. triflora* var. *kurziana* Loesener 1901, *I. triflora* var. *lobbiana* (Rolfe) Loesener 1901, *I. triflora* var. *kangiana* Loesener 1901, *I. griffithii* (Hooker) Loesener 1902, *I. triflora* var. *javensis* Loesener 1914, *I. polyphylla* Ridley 1915, *I. triflora* var. *longifolia* Ridley 1915, *I. theicarpa* Handel-Mazzetti 1933, *I. fleuryana* Tardieu 1945).

Evergreen shrubs or small trees, zigzag pubescent branches; leaves pubescent, oblong-elliptic to ovate, often on 3rd-year growth, close together, 2–13 mm (¹⁄₁₆–½ in.) apart, 3–9 cm (1³⁄₁₆–3½ in.) long, 2.5 cm (1 in.) wide, bases rounded or obtuse, apices acute or very short acuminate, margins minutely serrate, punctate beneath, petioles 2–9 mm (¹⁄₁₆–¹¹⁄₃₂ in.) long; inflorescences pubescent, fasciculate, axillary, flowers pinkish, 4-merous, pedicels 6–14 mm (⁷⁄₃₂–¹⁷⁄₃₂ in.) long; fruits black, globose or ellipsoid, 7–8 mm (⁹⁄₃₂–⁵⁄₁₆ in.) long, 7 mm (⁹⁄₃₂ in.) diameter; pyrenes 4, smooth, striate. Habitat: People's Republic of China, Guangxi Province and numerous other southern provinces, Taiwan, Vietnam Tonkin, India, Malay Peninsula, Indonesia, Sumatra, Java, and Borneo. Allied to *I. crenata* and *I. liukiensis*.

Ilex trista Standley 1926.

Evergreen shrubs or trees 3–12 m (10–40 ft.) tall, nearly glabrous; leaves broadly elliptic or obovate-elliptic, 2.5–4 cm (1–1⅝ in.) long, 2–3 cm (³⁄₄–1³⁄₁₆ in.) wide, bases rotund or obtuse, apices rotund, margins coarsely crenate, about 7 crenations on each side, short petioles; fruits unknown. Habitat: Costa Rica, only in cold wet forest, from Canton de Dota at 2100–3000 m (6930–9900 ft.) elevation. Allied to *I. discolor* var. *lamprophylla*.

Ilex truxillensis Turczaninow 1858 (synonym *I. modesta* Reisseck *ex* Loesener 1901).

Evergreen; leaves close together, only 5–10 mm (³⁄₁₆–³⁄₈ in.) apart, elliptic-oblong to elliptic-lanceolate, 5–8.5 cm (2–3⅜ in.) long, 1.8–2.6 cm (²⁹⁄₃₂–2 in.) wide, bases obtuse to acute, apices obtuse to acute, margins remotely crenate-serrulate, petioles 5–11 mm (³⁄₁₆–⁷⁄₁₆ in.) long; inflorescences axillary, solitary, branched, 1- to 7-flowered, peduncles 8–10 mm (⁵⁄₁₆–³⁄₈ in.) long, pedicels 1–2 mm (¹⁄₃₂–¹⁄₁₆ in.) long; fruits unknown. Habitat: Venezuela, mountains near Trujillo at 3000 m (9900 ft.) elevation. Allied to *I. crassifolia* and *I. hippocrateoides*.

Ilex tsangii S.-y. Hu 1949 var. *tsangii*.

Evergreen, glabrous trees to 8 m (26 ft.) tall; leaves ovate-elliptic or elliptic, 5–8 cm (2–3⅛ in.) long, 2–3 cm (³⁄₄–1³⁄₁₆ in.) wide, apices acuminate, acumens 10–15 mm (³⁄₈–¹⁹⁄₃₂ in.) long, bases acute or cuneate, margins remotely crenulate or subentire, petioles slender, 10–16 mm (³⁄₈–⁵⁄₈ in.) long; inflorescences axillary and fasciculate on 2nd-year growth; fruits yellow in July, depressed-globose, 5 mm (³⁄₁₆ in.) long, 6 mm (⁷⁄₃₂ in.) wide; pyrenes 4, irregularly rugose, sulcate. Habitat: People's Republic of China, endemic to northeastern Guangdong Province. Allied to *I. graciliflora* Champion. This yellow-fruited variant was designated and described as the type of the species. All yellow-fruited plants of *I. tsangii* must be known as the var. *tsangii,* even though it is thought to be a variant, and may be of random and scattered occurrence. The red-fruited variety, var. *quangxiensis,* is much more common throughout the natural distribution range.

Ilex tsangii var. *quangxiensis* T. R. Dudley 1984.
A variety differing from typical individuals with smaller narrow-elliptic leaves, 2.5–5 cm (1–2 in.) long, 1–1.6 cm (³⁄₈–⁵⁄₈ in.) wide; smaller fruits red, 3–4 mm (¹⁄₈–⁵⁄₃₂ in.) diameter; pedicels 1.5–2.5 mm (³⁄₆₄–³⁄₃₂ in.) long. Habitat: People's Republic of China, Guangdong Province.

Ilex tsiangiana C.-j. Tseng 1981.
Evergreen shrubs or trees, branchlets angulate, glabrous; leaves narrow-oblong or elliptic-oblong, 3.5–5.5 cm (1³⁄₈–2¹⁄₈ in.) long, 1.5–2 cm (¹⁹⁄₃₂–³⁄₄ in.) wide, apices short-acuminate, rarely obtuse, bases obtuse, margins crenulate, petioles 7–10 mm (⁹⁄₃₂–³⁄₈ in.) long; inflorescences axillary, 1- to 3-fasciculate; fruits red, globose, 3–4 mm (¹⁄₈–⁵⁄₃₂ in.) diameter, pedicels 4–5 mm (⁵⁄₃₂–³⁄₁₆ in.) long; pyrenes 5, longitudinally semistriate. Habitat: People's Republic of China, Yunnan Province. Allied to *I. forrestii.*

Ilex tuerckheimii Loesener 1912 var. *tuerckheimii* (synonym *I. tuerckheimii* var. *constanza* Loesener 1912).
Evergreen shrubs, 1–1.5 m (3–5 ft.) high, pubescent branches erect or spreading, lenticellate; leaves broadly oval to nearly suborbiculate, usually oval-oblong, 1.5–4.2 cm (¹⁹⁄₃₂–1¹¹⁄₁₆ in.) long, 0.7–2.7 cm (⁹⁄₃₂–1¹⁄₈ in.) wide, bases rotund or obtuse, apices broadly subdeltoid or somewhat obtuse or acute, margins remotely serrulate near apex, recurved, petioles 1.5–5 mm (¹⁄₃₂–³⁄₁₆ in.) long; inflorescences axillary, solitary, male 2–3 flowers, peduncles 3–4 mm (¹⁄₈–⁵⁄₃₂ in.) long; fruits black. Habitat: Dominican Republic, Hispaniola. Allied to *I. macfadyenii* and *I. yunnanensis.*

Ilex tuerckheimii var. *subalpina* Loesener 1912.
Leaves small, 1.5–3 cm (¹⁹⁄₃₂–1³⁄₁₆ in.) long, 7–1.8 mm (⁹⁄₃₂–1¹⁄₁₆ in.) wide, petioles 1.5–3 mm (¹⁹⁄₃₂–1³⁄₁₆ in.) long. Habitat: Dominican Republic, Hispaniola. A distinct and consistent taxon that may at a later date be regarded as a subspecies of *I. tuerckheimii.*

Ilex tugitakayamensis S.-i. Sasaki 1931.
Evergreen, robust trees, glabrous branchlets, lenticels lacking; leaves glabrous, elliptic or oblong-elliptic, 10–14 cm (4–5½ in.) long, 3–5 cm (1³⁄₁₆–5 in.) wide, bases acute, apices short-acuminate, margins entire, petioles 2–2.5 mm (¹⁄₁₆–³⁄₃₂ in.) long; inflorescences subumbelliform, puberulent, solitary, axillary on new growth, peduncles 8–9 mm (⁵⁄₁₆–1¹⁄₃₂ in.) long, umbels 5- to 7-flowered; fruit red, ellipsoid-globose, 5–7 mm (³⁄₁₆–⁹⁄₃₂ in.) long, 5 mm (³⁄₁₆ in.) across, stigma navel-like; pyrenes 4–6, dorsally flattened or slightly concave. Habitat: Taiwan, rare tree on Mount Tugitaka. Allied to *I. lancilimba.*

Ilex turquinensis Alain 1953.
Evergreen shrubs 2–3 m (6–10 ft.) tall, branchlets puberulent; leaves obovate or suborbiculate to elliptic, 1–4 cm (³⁄₈–1⁵⁄₈ in.) long, 7–22 mm (⁹⁄₃₂–⁷⁄₈ in.) wide, bases cuneate, apices rotund to obtuse, margins recurved, slightly denticulate near apex; inflorescences 1- to 3-flowered, axillary, flowers 4-merous; fruits globose, 3–4 mm (¹⁄₈–⁵⁄₃₂ in.) diameter. Habitat: Cuba, Oriente Province, Cumbre de la Maestra. Allied to *I. cubana* and, perhaps at a later date, to be treated as conspecific, since these two taxa are from the same locality and habitat.

Ilex tutcheri Merrill 1918.
Evergreen, large shrubs to 4 m (13 ft.) tall; leaves obcordate or obovate, rarely obovate-elliptic, 3–6 cm (1³⁄₁₆–2³⁄₈ in.) long, 1.3–2.5 cm (½–1 in.) wide, apices rotund, retuse, bases acute or cuneate, margins entire, recurved, punctate beneath, petioles 4–8 mm (⁵⁄₃₂–⁵⁄₁₆ in.) long; inflorescences axillary and fasciculate on 2nd- and 3rd-year growth, flowers 4- to 6-merous; fruits red, globose, 5 mm (³⁄₁₆ in.) diameter, pedicels 5-10 mm (³⁄₁₆–³⁄₈ in.) long, calyces persistent; pyrenes 5–6, smooth, 2- to 3-striate. Habitat: People's Republic of China, eastern Guangdong Province. Allied to *I. championii* and *I. memecylifolia.*

Ilex uaramae Edwin 1965.
Evergreen shrubs to 2 m (6 ft.) tall, branchlets puberulent; leaves obovate to subspathulate-obovate, 2.8–5 cm (1¹⁄₈–2 in.) long, 1.6–2.2 cm (⁵⁄₈–1³⁄₁₆ in.) wide, bases acute, cuneate or subspathulate, apices shortly acuminate, acumens less than 0.5 mm (¹⁄₆₄ in.) long, margins entire, petioles puberulent, 5 mm (³⁄₁₆ in.) long; inflorescences axillary, solitary, 2- to 3-pedunculate; fruits brown when dry, subglobose, 5 mm (³⁄₁₆ in.) long, 6 mm (⁷⁄₃₂ in.) diameter; pyrenes 5—4 dorsally unisulcate without marginal ridges and 1 dorsally unicanaliculate with marginal ridges. Habitat: Venezuela, Bolivar, valley of savannah of Rio Uarama tepui, north of Tuepa at 1220 m (4000 ft.) elevation.

Ilex uleana Loesener 1905.

Evergreen shrubs 1–2 m (3–6 ft.) tall; leaves obovate to obovate-elliptic, 4–6 cm (1⅝–2⅜ in.) long, 1.5–2.5 cm (19⁄32–1 in.) wide, apices rotund, often with short acumen, bases cuneate, margins entire, recurved, petioles 4–7 mm (5⁄32–9⁄32 in.) long; inflorescences axillary, solitary, rarely fasciculate, branched, flowers 4-merous; fruits black, globose, 4–6 mm (5⁄32–7⁄32 in.) diameter; pyrenes 4. Habitat: Brazil. Allied to *I. cubana, I. daphnoides, I. gale,* and *I. pseudobuxus.*

Ilex umbellata Klotzsch 1848 (synonyms *I. humirioides* Reisseck 1861, *I. umbellata* var. *genuina* Loesener 1901, *I. umbellata* var. *humirioides* (Reisseck) Loesener 1901, *I. umbellata* var. *megaphylla* Loesener 1908).

Evergreen trees, branches pubescent; leaves oval or obovate-oblong, 8.5–11 cm (3⅜–4⅜ in.) long, 3–6.5 cm (1 3⁄16–2½ in.) wide, apices obtuse or acuminate, bases cuneate or cuneate-acute, margins entire, recurved, petioles 9–16 mm (11⁄32–⅝ in.) long; inflorescences axillary, fasciculate, branched, flowers 4-merous; fruits unknown. Habitat: Venezuela, Guyana near Roraima and Tapakuma along the Demerara River. Allied to *I. daphnogenea, I. guianensis, I. inundata,* and *I. jenmanii.*

Ilex umbellulata (Wallich) Loesener 1901 (synonyms *Ehretia umbellulata* Wallich 1824, *Pseudehretia umbellulata* (Wallich) Turczaninow 1863, *I. sulcata* Wallich 1875, *I. tonkinensis* Pierre 1895, *I. umbellulata* var. *megaphylla* Loesener 1908).

Evergreen, large trees to 15 m (50 ft.) tall, branchlets glabrous; leaves persistent on 3rd-year growth, oblong, 7–15 cm (2¾–6⅛ in.) long, 5–6 cm (2–2⅜ in.) wide, bases round or obtuse, apices obtuse or very short-acuminate, margins entire, slender petioles 8–15 mm (5⁄16–½ in.) long; inflorescences subumbelliform, axillary at base of new growth, peduncles 18–30 mm (11⁄16–1 3⁄16 in.) long, pedicels 6–10 mm (7⁄32–⅜ in.) long, both puberulent; fruits red, globose, 6 mm (7⁄32 in.) diameter; pyrenes 6–10, compressed-suborbiculate in outline, 3-striate, 1- to 2-sulcate on dorsal surface. Habitat: originally described from India, Silhet and Assam; also occurs in People's Republic of China, southwestern Yunnan Province in mixed forest at 780–1350 m (2575–4450 ft.) elevation and in Vietnam. Allied to *I. godajam.*

Ilex unicanaliculata C.-j. Tseng 1981.

Evergreen trees 4–8 m (13–26 ft.) tall, young branchlets brownish, angulate, pubescent or glabrescent, 2nd-year branches subterete, densely lenticellate, glabrous; leaves oblong or elliptic-oblong, 6.5–11 cm (2⅜–4⅜ in.) long, 3–4 cm (1 3⁄16–1⅝ in.) wide, glabrous except puberulent along midribs above, apices acute, bases obtuse or rotund, margins entire; inflorescences branched, cymose or umbellate, 5- to 6-fruited, solitary, axillary, peduncles 8 mm (5⁄16 in.) long, pubescent, pedicels 3–4 mm (⅛–5⁄32 in.) long, puberulent; fruits red, globose, 4 mm (5⁄32 in.) diameter; pyrenes 5–7. Habitat: People's Republic of China, Yunnan Province. Allied to *I. rotunda.*

Ilex uniflora Bentham 1846 var. *uniflora* (synonym *I. uniflora* f. *pittayensis* Loesener 1901).

Evergreen trees, branches glabrous; leaves broadly oval-elliptic or obovate, 2.5–4 cm (1–1⅝ in.) long, 1.2–2.7 cm (15⁄32–1 1⁄16 in.) wide, apices mucronulate, bases rotund or obtuse, margins serrulate or subcrenate-serrate, not punctate beneath, petioles 2–5.5 cm (¾–2⅛ in.) long; inflorescences axillary, solitary on new growth, 3-flowered pedunculate, flowers 5- or rarely 6-merous; fruits unknown, peduncles 5–9 mm (3⁄16–11⁄32 in.) long, pedicels 3 mm (⅛ in.) long. Habitat: Colombia. Allied to *I. sessilifolia.*

Ilex uniflora var. *paramensis* Cuatrecasas 1949.

A variety with small, crowded leaves, ovate to obovate to elliptic-oblong, 1.8–2.2 cm (11⁄16–13⁄16 in.) long, 0.7–1.4 cm (9⁄32–17⁄32 in.) wide. Habitat: Colombia.

Ilex uniflora f. *pastoensis* Loesener 1901.

Leaf petioles 2–4 mm (1⁄16–5⁄32 in.) long; inflorescences slender, flowers smaller than typical individuals, petals slender. Habitat: Colombia, near Pasto.

Ilex uraiensis Yamamoto 1932 var. *uraiensis* (synonyms *I. glomeratifolia sensu* Yamamoto 1925, *non* Hayata 1913, *I. mutchagara sensu* S.-i. Sasaki 1930, *non* Kanehira 1936, *I. uraiana* Hayata *ex* Kanehira 1936, *I. kelungensis sensu* Kanehira & Hatusima 1939, *non* Loesener 1901).

Evergreen large trees to 25 m (82 ft.) tall, branchlets minutely puberulent or glabrescent; leaves elliptic to obovate-elliptic, 3.5–10 cm (1⅜–4 in.) long, 1.2–3.5 cm (15⁄32–1⅜ in.) wide, apices abruptly acuminate, acumens 3–8 mm (⅛–5⁄16 in.) long, bases cuneate, margins remotely crenate or serrate, petioles 6–10 m (7⁄32–⅜ in.) long; inflorescences axillary and fasciculate on 2nd- and 3rd-year growth, flowers 4-merous; fruits red, globose, 10–11 mm (⅜–7⁄16 in.) diameter, pedicels 6–8 mm (7⁄32–5⁄16 in.) long, pubescent; pyrenes 4, irregularly striate, wrinkled. Habitat: northern Taiwan, near Uraisha and Sozan. Allied to *I. mertensii.*

Ilex uraiensis var. *formosae* S.-y. Hu 1949 (synonyms *I. mertensii* var. *formosae* Loesener 1901, *I. uraiensis* var. *macrophylla* S.-y. Hu 1953).

A variety differing from typical individuals

with glabrous branches; leaves obovate, 2.5–4.5 cm (1–1¾ in.) long, 1.5–2.5 cm (13⁄16–1 in.) wide, apices rotund; fruiting pedicels glabrous, 5–10 mm (3⁄16–3⁄8 in.) long. Habitat: Taiwan.

Ilex urbaniana Loesener 1892 var. *urbaniana*. Caerode sapo.

Evergreen shrubs or small trees, branchlets rugose, lenticels present; leaves oval or ovate, 4.5–8 cm (1¾–3 in.) long, 3.5–4.5 cm (1⅜–1¾ in.) wide, bases obtuse or cuneate-obtuse, apices rotund, margins revolute, entire, petioles 5–9 mm (3⁄16–11⁄32 in.) long; inflorescences axillary, fasciculate; fruits unknown. Habitat: Puerto Rico. Allied to *I. dunniana*.

Ilex urbaniana var. *riedlaei* (Loesener) Edwin *ex* T. R. Dudley, *comb. & stat. nov.* (basionym *I. riedlaei* Loesener, *Bot. Jahrb.* 15: 317. 1892).

A variety with leaves obovate, broader than long; calyx-lobes shorter than tube. Habitat: Puerto Rico.

Ilex vacciniifolia Klotzsch 1848.

Evergreen shrubs; leaves oval or oblong-ovate, 2.4–3.7 cm (1–7⁄16 in.) long, 1–1.9 cm (3⁄8–3⁄4 in.) wide, apices usually rotund, bases usually acute, margins entire, revolute, petioles 4–6 mm (5⁄32–7⁄32 in.) long; inflorescences axillary, solitary, 1- to 3-flowered, flowers 4-merous; fruits unknown. Habitat: Guyana. Allied to *I. asperula*.

Ilex vaccinoides Loesener 1912.

Evergreen shrubs or trees to 13 m (43 ft.) tall; leaves broadly obovate or obovate-elliptic or narrow-elliptic, rarely oblong-elliptic, 1.4–3.5 cm (17⁄32–1⅜ in.) long, 0.6–2 cm (7⁄32–3⁄4 in.) wide, bases cuneate or acute, apices rotund, briefly apiculate, margins usually entire, recurved, or serrulate near apex, petioles 2.5–6 mm (3⁄32–7⁄32 in.) long; inflorescences axillary, single, lateral or fasciculate, 1- to 3-flowered, peduncles 6–7 mm (7⁄32–9⁄32 in.) long, pedicels of single flowers 6 mm (7⁄32 in.) long, flowers 4-merous; fruits unknown. Habitat: Jamaica, near Monkey Hill at 1934 m (6382 ft.) elevation. Allied to *I. obcordata*.

Ilex valenzuelana Alain 1960.

Evergreen shrubs, branches minutely pilose; leaves elliptic to oblong-elliptic, 3–4.5 cm (13⁄16–1¾ in.) long, 1.5–2.1 cm (19⁄32–25⁄32 in.) wide, bases rotund to obtuse, apices rotund, margins serrulate, recurved or flat, glabrous, veins impressed above; inflorescences axillary, fasciculate, 1- to 3-flowered, male flowers rare, peduncles 3 mm (1⁄8 in.) long, pedicels 1.5 mm (3⁄64 in.) long, flowers 4- to 5-merous; fruits unknown. Habitat: Cuba, Oriente Province, del Arroyo Peladero, Venezuela, Sierra Maestra. Allied to *I. hypaneura* and *I. repanda*.

Figure 14-56. *Ilex uraiensis* var. *formosae*. Drawing by Chien-chu Chen in *Illustrations of Native and Introduced Ligneous Plants of Taiwan* (1962) by Tangshui Liu.

Ilex valerii Standley 1926.

Evergreen trees 4.5 m (15 ft.) tall, glabrous; leaves elliptic-oblong to broadly lanceolate-oblong or elliptic, 5–8.5 cm (2–3⅜ in.) long, 3–4 cm (13⁄16–1⅝ in.) wide, bases broadly rotund, apices abruptly acute or acuminate, margins entire; inflorescences axillary, branched 3- to 6-flowered, peduncles 1.8–2.5 cm (11⁄16–1 in.) long; fruits unknown. Habitat: Costa Rica, northeast of San Isidro de Heredia at 2300 m (7600 ft.) elevation. Very distinct species in Costa Rica with long petioles, entire leaves, and long pedunculate inflorescences. Named for Professor Juvenal Valerio of Costa Rica.

Ilex velutina Martius *ex* Reisseck 1842 (synonym *I. velutina* var. *pyrenea* Loesener 1895).

Evergreen, large shrubs; leaves oval or elliptic 4–6.5 cm (1⅝–2½ in.) long, 1.6–3.5 cm (5⁄8–1⅜ in.) wide, apices obtuse or rotund, apiculate, bases rotund or obtuse, margins entire, thick, revolute, petioles 2–4 mm (1⁄16–5⁄32 in.) long; inflorescences solitary or fasciculate in leaf axils, flowers 4- to 5-merous; fruits unknown. Habitat: Brazil, Pernambuco and Bahia states. Allied to *I. brasiliensis*.

Ilex velutinulosa Cuatrecasas 1951.

Evergreen shrubs, branches minutely tomentose; leaves obovate-elliptic or oblong-elliptic, 3–5.5 cm (1³⁄₁₆–2¹⁄₈ in.) long, 1.8–2.4 cm (¹¹⁄₃₂–¹⁵⁄₁₆ in.) wide, bases obtuse, crenulate, apices rotund, margins slightly thickened, revolute, or crenate-serrate; female inflorescences axillary, fasciculate, peduncles minutely hirsute, 5–7 mm (³⁄₁₆–⁹⁄₃₂ in.) long; fruits elliptic, velvety, 7 mm (⁹⁄₃₂ in.) long, 5 mm (³⁄₁₆ in.) wide. Habitat: Colombia, Department Santander, mountains east of Las Vegas at 3000–3300 m (9,900–10,890 ft.) elevation. Allied to *I. gale*.

Ilex venezuelensis Steyermark 1951.

Evergreen shrubs to 2.8 m (9 ft.) tall, branches densely pubescent; leaves narrow-oblong or narrow-elliptic-oblong, 1.5–2.9 cm (¹⁹⁄₃₂–1¹⁄₈ in.) long, 0.6–1 cm (7–³⁄₈ in.) wide, usually brown punctate beneath, bases obtuse, apices obtuse or rotund, margins entire, revolute, petioles 3–4 mm (¹⁄₈–⁵⁄₃₂ in.) long, inflorescences axillary, solitary, pedicels puberulent, 7–13 mm (⁹⁄₃₂–¹⁄₂ in.) long; fruits unknown. Habitat: Venezuela, Amazonas, on the high moist summit of Cerro Duida, at 1820–2075 m (6000–6850 ft.) elevation. Allied to *I. chamaedryfolia* and *I. vacciniifolia*.

Ilex venosa C.-y. Wu *ex* Y.-r. Li 1984.

Evergreen shrubs or small trees to 5 m (16 ft.) tall, branchlets angulate, glabrous, lenticellate; leaves glabrous, oblong-elliptic or wide-lanceolate, 7–12 cm (2³⁄₄–4³⁄₄ in.) long, 2.5–4.3 cm (1–1³⁄₄ in.) wide, apices long-acuminate, bases obtuse, 8–9 lateral veins reticulate on both surfaces, petioles 8–10 mm (⁵⁄₁₆–³⁄₈ in.) long; female inflorescences pseudoracemose; fruits ellipsoid, 9 mm (¹¹⁄₃₂ in.) long, 6 mm (⁷⁄₃₂ in.) diameter, pedicels 1–2 mm (¹⁄₃₂–¹⁄₁₆ in.) long, calyces persistent; pyrenes 4, palmately striate, sulcate. Habitat: People's Republic of China, Yunnan Province, at 2100 m (6900 ft.) elevation. Allied to *I. formosana*.

Ilex venulosa Hooker f. 1875 var. *venulosa*.

Evergreen, glabrous shrubs or small trees to 8 m (26 ft.) tall, branches with conspicuous white lenticels; leaves ovate or oblong-elliptic, 10–20 cm (4–8 in.) long, 3–6.5 cm (1³⁄₁₆–2¹⁄₂ in.) wide, apices acuminate, acumens very narrow, 2–3 cm (³⁄₄–1³⁄₁₆ in.) long, bases obtuse or rotund, margins entire, midribs prominent beneath, sulcate above, lateral veins 15–22 on each side, petioles 1.3–2.2 cm (¹⁄₂–¹³⁄₁₆ in.) long; inflorescences axillary, females 3 cymose, or subumbelliform, peduncles 7–12 mm (⁹⁄₃₂–¹⁵⁄₃₂ in.) long, pedicels 2–3 mm (¹⁄₁₆–¹⁄₃ in.) long; fruits red, globose, 3–4 mm (¹⁄₈–⁵⁄₃₂ in.) diameter, calyces persistent; pyrenes 5–7, 3-striate. Habitat:

People's Republic of China, Yunnan Province, India, Myanmar. First described from a specimen collected in northern India. Allied to *I. omeiensis*.

Ilex venulosa var. *simplicifrons* S.-y. Hu 1950.

A variety with more compact inflorescences, reduced cymes, fewer flowers, shorter peduncles, 2 mm (¹⁄₈ in.) long. Habitat: People's Republic of China, Yunnan Province, and India, Khasia Hills.

Ilex verisimilis Chun & C.-j. Tseng 1981.

Evergreen shrubs or small trees, branchlets striate, glabrous; leaves elliptic or elliptic lanceolate, 8–15 cm (3¹⁄₈–6 in.) long, 3–4.5 cm (1³⁄₁₆–1³⁄₄ in.) wide, apices long acuminate, acumens 1–2 cm (³⁄₈–³⁄₄ in.) long, bases decurrently obtuse or attenuate, margins entire, glabrous, punctate beneath, petioles 1.3–1.5 cm (¹⁄₂–¹⁹⁄₃₂ in.) long; inflorescences axillary on new growth, flowers 6-merous, stigmas nipple-like; fruits red, globose, 5 mm (³⁄₁₆ in.) diameter; pyrenes 6, striate. Habitat: People's Republic of China, wetland woods and along brooks in valleys of Guangdong, Guangxi, and Hunan provinces. Allied to *I. elmerrilliana* and *I. tutcheri*.

Ilex vesparum Steyermark 1951.

Evergreen shrubs or small trees, 2.8–10 m (9–33 ft.) tall; leaves ovate, 3.5–11 cm (1³⁄₈–4³⁄₈ in.) long, apices acuminate or cuspidate, acumens 3–6 mm (¹⁄₈–⁷⁄₃₂ in.) long, bases rotund, margins entire or remotely adpressed-serrulate, petioles 10–30 mm (³⁄₈–1³⁄₁₆ in.) long; male inflorescences axillary, fasciculate, pedunculate, 7-flowered, flowers 5- to 6-merous. Habitat: Venezuela, above Santa Cruz, on ridge leading to summit Cerro Peonia. Resembles *I. jenmanii* and *I. macfadyenii*. Name given for abundance (millions) of wasps densely covering branches and stems of the trees, giving the appearance of festoons of moss or liverworts suspended from the bark.

Ilex vietnamensis T. R. Dudley, *nom. nov.* (basionym *I. merrillii* Tardieu, *non* Syst., ed. Humbert, 12: 122. 1945, which is a later homonym of *I. merrillii* Briquet 1919; synonym *I. asprella*).

Evergreen, small trees to 3 m (10 ft.) tall, branches glabrous, angulate; leaves oblong or elliptic, 7–11 cm (2³⁄₄–4³⁄₈ in.) long, 4 cm (1⁵⁄₈ in.) wide, bases cuneate, apices acute or brief acuminate, margins entire, petioles canaliculate, glabrous, 1.5–2 cm (1³⁄₈–³⁄₄ in.) long; female inflorescences axillary, solitary or fasciculate; fruits rugose, warty, stigmas subcapitate, forming prominent crown on fruit; pyrenes 4, 2-sulcate. Habitat: Vietnam, Province du Darae. Allied to *I. memecylifolia*.

Ilex villosula Loesener 1901.

Evergreen, pubescent shrubs; leaves obovate or elliptic-obovate, 3–4.5 cm (1³⁄₁₆–1¾ in.) long, 1.5–2.2 cm (¹⁵⁄₃₂–⅞ in.) wide, apices rotund, bases acute or cuneate-acute, margins entire, revolute, petioles 3–4 mm (⅛–⁵⁄₃₂ in.) long; inflorescences at base of new growth, in leaf axils, solitary, flowers 4- to 5-merous; fruits unknown. Habitat: Peru, near Yambrasbamba. Allied to *I. velutina*.

Ilex virgata Loesener 1901 (synonym *I. chamaedryfolia* Warming 1879, *non* Reisseck 1861).
Evergreen shrubs, branchlets puberulent; leaves spathulate or obovate, 1.4–2.5 cm (¹⁷⁄₃₂–1 in.) long, 6–10 mm (⁷⁄₃₂–⅜ in.) wide, apices obtuse, often notched, bases cuneate, margins recurved, crenate-serrate, petioles 3–5 mm (⅛–³⁄₁₆ in.) long; inflorescences axillary, solitary on new growth, branched (pseudoracemes), puberulent, flowers 4-merous, pedicels 3–5 mm (⅛–³⁄₁₅ in.) long; fruits unknown. Habitat: Brazil, mountain near Nova Friburgo. Allied to *I. chamaedryfolia, I. paltorioides,* and *I. vitis-idaea*.

Ilex viridis Champion *ex* Bentham 1852 (synonym *I. triflora* var. *viridis* (Champion) Loesener 1901).
Evergreen shrubs or small trees to 5 m (16 ft.) tall, branches sub-quadrangular, sparsely pubescent; leaves ovate or obovate or broadly elliptic, 2.5–7 cm (1–2¾ in.) long, 1.5–3 cm (¹⁹⁄₃₂–1³⁄₁₆ in.) wide, bases cuneate, margins slightly recurved, crenate-serrate, usually 12–15 teeth on each side, punctate beneath; inflorescences solitary, axillary, pedicels 12–15 mm (½–¹⁹⁄₃₂ in.) long; fruits black, globose or depressed globose, 8 mm (⁵⁄₁₆ in.) long, 7 mm (⁹⁄₃₂ in.) diameter; pyrenes 4, rugose-striate. Habitat: first described from Hong Kong, also found in the People's Republic of China, Anhui Province, among others in southern and coastal China and Vietnam. Allied to *I. triflora*.

Ilex vismiifolia Reisseck 1861 (synonym *I. celastroides* Klotzsch 1849).
Evergreen shrubs or trees, branches puberulent; leaves ovate to obovate-oblong, usually 8 cm (3⅛ in.) long, 3 cm (1³⁄₁₆ in.) wide, apices obtuse or slightly acuminate, bases usually cuneate, margins entire, recurved, petioles 5–9 mm (³⁄₁₆–¹¹⁄₃₂ in.) long; inflorescences axillary, fasciculate, branched, flowers small, 4-merous; fruits brownish purple, globose 5 mm (³⁄₁₆ in.) diameter; pyrenes 4, unisulcate. Habitat: Guyana and northern Brazil along the Uaupés River near Panure, Brazil. Allied to *I. floribunda, I. guianensis, I. petiolaris,* and *I. reisseckiana*.

Ilex vitiensis A. Gray 1857.
Evergreen, large shrubs or trees; leaves glabrous, broadly oval to nearly rounded, 4–6 cm (1⅝–2⅜ in.) long, 1.7–3.2 cm (²¹⁄₃₂–1¼ in.) wide, bases broadly cuneate, apices long acuminate, 4–9 mm (⁵⁄₃₂–¹¹⁄₃₂ in.) long, margins entire, recurved, petioles 7–17 mm (⁹⁄₃₂–¹⁷⁄₃₂ in.) long; inflorescences singular, on new growth, pseudopanicles to fasciculate, peduncles 10–15 mm (⅜–½ in.) long, pedicels 3 mm (⅛ in.) long; fruit color unknown; pyrenes 8, unisulcate. Habitat: Fiji, Vevu and Tavuni Islands. Allied to *I. zippeliana*.

Ilex vitis-idaea Loesener 1901. Congonha.
Evergreen, low shrubs, branches with dense lenticels; leaves oval or obovate-oblong to elliptic-oblong, glabrous, 3–3.5 cm (1³⁄₁₆–1⅜ in.) long, 8–22 mm (⁵⁄₁₆–¹³⁄₁₆ in.) wide, apices obtuse or rotund, small spine at apex, bases acute or cuneate, margins recurved, acute serrulate, petioles 2–4 mm (¹⁄₁₆–⁵⁄₃₂ in.) long; inflorescences axillary, solitary on new growth, branched, flowers 4-merous; fruits black, subglobose, 3.5–4 mm (⁷⁄₆₄–⁵⁄₃₂ in.) diameter, branched pedicels 2–3 mm (¹⁄₁₆–⅛ in.) long, single pedicels 4 mm (⁵⁄₃₂ in.) long. Habitat: Brazil, Goiás State. Allied to *I. paltorioides* and *I. phillyreifolia*.

Ilex volkensiana (Loesener) Kanehira & Hatusima 1936 (synonym *I. mertensii* var. *volkensiana* Loesener 1921, in *Botanical Magazine* 599. 1936.)
No description.

Ilex vomitoria Aiton subsp. *vomitoria* 1789. Yaupon, cassina, cassinea (synonyms *Cassine peragua* Linnaeus 1753, *I. cassine* Linnaeus 1753, *Prinos glaber* Linnaeus 1762, *Cassine paragua* (Linnaeus) Miller 1768, *C. caroliniana* Lamarck 1785, *I. cassine* (Linnaeus) Walter 1788, *I. floridana* Lamarck 1791, *I. cassena* Michaux 1803, *I. religiosa* Barton 1812, *I. atramentaria* Barton 1826, *Hierophyllus cassine* (Linnaeus) Rafinesque 1830, *Ageria cassena* (Linnaeus) Rafinesque 1838, *Oreophila myrtifolia* Schelle 1849, *I. peragua* (Linnaeus) Trelease 1889, *I. caroliniana* (Lamarck) Loesener 1891).
Evergreen, large shrubs or small trees to 9 m (30 ft.) tall, usually multiple trunks, stiff pubescent branches, bark light gray; leaves ovate to oblong or elliptic, 1.5–4.5 cm (¹⁹⁄₃₂–1¾ in.) long, 1–2 cm (⅜–¾ in.) wide, apices obtuse or rotund, bases obtuse, margins crenate, petioles 3–5 mm (⅛–³⁄₁₆ in.) long; inflorescences axillary on 2nd-year wood, fasciculate or single, branched, flowers 4-merous; fruits red, rarely yellow, globose, 5–8 mm (³⁄₁₆–⁵⁄₁₆ in.) diameter, glossy, semitranslucent; pyrenes 4, ribbed on back. Habitat: mostly coastal areas of United States from southeastern Virginia to Florida west to Texas and Arizona. Hardy in zones 7a to 10. Allied to *I. cassine*. The number of synonyms indicates the confusion about this plant among early taxonomists. Leaves contain caffeine. Native Americans used

dried leaves to make a bitter tea called black drink; the very strong brew was used as a ceremonial and medicinal drink (causing vomiting when drunk to excess). Plates 78, 79.

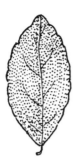

Figure 14-57. *Ilex vomitoria* subsp. *vomitoria*. Drawing by Randy Allen.

Ilex vomitoria subsp. *chiapensis* (Sharp) E. Murray 1982 (synonym *I. vomitoria* var. *chiapensis* Sharp 1950).

A subspecies differing from typical individuals with loosely pubescent leaves and longer hairs on the branchlets. Habitat: Mexico, Chiapas State, near San Gregorio, at 1666 m (5500 ft.) elevation. Collected in the wild in Chiapas State, Mexico; plants not winter hardy at U.S. National Arboretum.

Ilex vomitoria f. *pendula* Foret & Solymosy 1960.

Upright pendulous habit, branches often drooping 6 or more ft.; leaves typical, fruits vivid red, globose, 6–7 mm (⁷⁄₃₂–⁹⁄₃₂ in.) diameter; very popular landscape plant in the Southeast. A pendulous branched large shrub found in 1952 near Folsom, Louisiana. Also given a cultivar name 'Folsom's Weeping'. Both female and male plants are available. Seedlings are usually pendulous. 'Pendula' and other pendulous types have been named as cultivars; For a complete list of cultivars of *I. vomitoria,* see Chapter 15.

Ilex vulcanicola Standley 1925.

Evergreen shrubs to 1–3 m (3–10 ft.) tall, branchlets pubescent; leaves elliptic to oval, 1.5–3 cm (¹⁹⁄₃₂–¼₆ in.) long, 1.2–1.7 cm (¹⁵⁄₃₂–²¹⁄₃₂ in.) wide, bases broadly cuneate, apices rotund or obtuse, margins remotely and shallowly crenate on upper two-thirds of leaf, teeth tipped with minute incurved mucros, punctate beneath; inflorescences axillary, fasciculate; fruits subglobose, 4 mm (⁵⁄₃₂ in.) diameter; pyrenes 4, smooth. Habitat: Costa Rica, endemic in wet forest of the slopes of the central volcanoes at 2000–

2700 m (6600–8900 ft.) elevation. Reported at times to be epiphytic.

Ilex walkeri Wight & Gardner 1858 (synonym *I. walkeri* var. *emarginella* (Turczaninow) Loesener 1901).

Evergreen, densely branched shrubs or small trees; leaves obovate or broadly elliptic, 1.4–3.2 cm (¹⁷⁄₃₂–1¼ in.) long, 0.5–1.8 cm (³⁄₁₆–1¹⁄₁₆ in.) wide, apices rotund, usually with short spine, bases broadly cuneate to acute, margins recurved, entire, rarely serrulate near apex, distinct lateral veins beneath, petioles 2–5 mm (¹⁄₁₆–³⁄₁₆ in.) long; inflorescences axillary, solitary, fasciculate, flowers 4- to 6-merous; fruits black, ellipsoid or subglobose, 4 mm (⁵⁄₃₂ in.) long, 3.5 mm (⁹⁄₆₄ in.) wide, peduncles of single flowers 3.5–5 mm (⁹⁄₆₄–³⁄₁₆ in.) long, pedicels 1–2.5 mm (¹⁄₃₂–³⁄₃₂ in.) long; pyrenes 4–5. Habitat: Sri Lanka, Pulney Mountains, at 1515–2425 m (5000–8000 ft.) elevation. Allied to *I. mandonii.*

Ilex wallichii Steudel 1840. Medang, tulok, bulan, gading (synonyms *I. macrophylla* Hooker f. 1872, *I. macrophylla* var. *angustata* Loesener 1901, *I. macrophylla* var. *ovata* Loesener 1901, *I. venulosa* var. *nervulosa* Loesener 1901).

Evergreen trees to 17 m (55 ft.) tall, branches glabrous; leaves elliptic-oblong to obovate-oblong, 10–17.5 cm (4–7 in.) long, 3.8–6.8 cm (1½–2⅝ in.) wide, bases rotund to cuneate-obtuse, apices obtuse, acuminate, margins entire, petioles 8–16 mm (⁵⁄₁₆–⅝ in.) long; inflorescences axillary, solitary, flowers 4- to 6-merous, fruit color unknown, globose, 4.5 mm (¹¹⁄₆₄ in.) diameter; pyrenes 7–9, sulcate. Habitat: Singapore, Thailand, Malaysia, Indonesia, Vietnam. Allied to *I. pleiobrachiata.*

Ilex walsinghamii R. Howard 1992 (synonym *I. wrightii* Loesener 1901).

Evergreen shrubs, young branches usually pubescent; leaves obovate, 2–3.8 cm (¾–1½ in.) long, 1–2.2 cm (⅜–⅞ in,) wide, apices rotund, bases obtuse or cuneate obtuse, margins entire, revolute, petioles 1.5–3 mm (³⁄₆₄–³⁄₁₆ in.) long; inflorescences axillary, solitary, flowers 4-merous; fruits black, ovoid; pyrenes 4, sulcate. Habitat: eastern Cuba. Allied to *I. organensis.*

Ilex × *wandoensis* C. F. Miller 1982, *nom. nud.*

Naturally occurring putative hybrid, first reported as *I. integra* × *I. cornuta*, but more likely *I. cornuta* × *I. integra.* Found as a potted plant by C. Ferris Miller, dug from the wild in the village of Wando, reported from Taehuksan Island, South Korea. Specimen at U.S. National Arboretum, Washington, D.C.

Evergreen, dense shrubs or small trees to 5 m (16 ft.) high; leaves oval, 3.5–5 cm (1⅜–2 in.) long, 2.5–3.5 cm (1–1⅜ in.) wide, bases cuneate, apices attenuate, margins subentire to spinose, 1–3 spines on each side, petioles 5–6 mm (³⁄₁₆–⁷⁄₃₂ in.) long; inflorescences axillary and fasciculate on 2nd-year growth; fruits red, ellipsoid, 9–11 mm (¹¹⁄₃₂–⁷⁄₁₆ in.) long, 9 mm (¹¹⁄₃₂ in.) diameter; pyrenes intermediate. Habitat: Korea, Wando and Chindo Islands, steep hillsides. Many native plants have been moved by South Koreans to gardens; may be extinct on Chindo Island. Allied to *I. cornuta* and *I. integra*. Hybrid also artificial, prior to being recognized in the wild; see 'Semala' in Chapter 16.

Ilex wangiana S.-y. Hu 1950.

Evergreen, pubescent shrubs to 3 m (10 ft.) tall, branchlets angulate, ridged, sulcate; leaves ovate-elliptic, 4–7 cm (1⅝–2¾ in.) long, 1.4–2.5 cm (¹⁷⁄₃₂–1 in.) wide, apices obtuse, shortly acuminate, acumens 4–7 mm (⁵⁄₃₂–⁹⁄₃₂ in.) long, bases obtuse or rotund, pubescent on both surfaces, margins serrate or crenate-serrate, teeth dark, petioles 5–7 mm (³⁄₁₆–⁹⁄₃₂ in.) long; inflorescences axillary and fasciculate on 2nd-year growth; fruits red, globose, 3–4 mm (⅛–⁵⁄₃₂ in.) diameter, pedicels 2–3 mm (¹⁄₁₆–⅛ in.) long, calyces persistent; pyrenes 4, palmately striate, sides rugose, sulcate. Habitat: People's Republic of China, endemic in the Mekong Valley of northwestern Yunnan Province. Allied to *I. corallina*. Named after the collector C. W. Wang.

Ilex warburgii Loesener 1901 var. *warburgii*.

Evergreen shrubs to 4 m (13 ft.) tall, branchlets glabrous, lenticels obscure; leaves oblong-elliptic to broadly elliptic, 4–8.5 cm (1⅝–3⅜ in.) long, 2.4 cm (1 in.) wide, apices abruptly acuminate, acumens 8–15 mm (⁵⁄₁₆–¹⁹⁄₃₂ in.) long, bases obtuse or rotund, margins crenulate-serrate, petioles 8–15 mm (⁵⁄₁₆–¹⁹⁄₃₂ in.) long; inflorescences axillary, fasciculate or subracemose; fruits globose, 5–6 mm (³⁄₁₆–⁷⁄₃₂ in.) diameter, pedicels 4–8 mm (⁵⁄₃₂–⁵⁄₁₆ in.) long, calyces persistent; pyrenes 4, striate, sulcate. Habitat: Taiwan, and the Liukiu Islands of Japan. Allied to *I. glomerata*.

Ilex warburgii var. *benguetensis* (Elmer) Loesener 1901 (synonym *I. benguetensis* (Loesener) Elmer 1913).

A variety differing from typical individuals by being a large tree 20 m (65 ft.) tall; leaves oblongish, to 10 cm (4 in.) long, 3 cm (1³⁄₁₆ in.) wide, margins entire. Habitat: Philippines, northern Luzon.

Ilex wardii Merrill 1941.

Evergreen shrubs to 2 m (6 ft.) tall, branchlets

Figure 14-58. *Ilex* × *wandoensis*. Photo by Barton Bauer Sr.

light gray, puberulent; leaves elliptic or obovate-elliptic, usually 4–6 cm (1⅝–2⅜ in.) long, 1–3 cm (⅜–1³⁄₁₆ in.) wide, apices acuminate, acumens 10–15 mm (⅜–¹⁹⁄₃₂ in.) long, bases rotund or obtuse, margins sharply serrate, teeth dark and sharp tipped

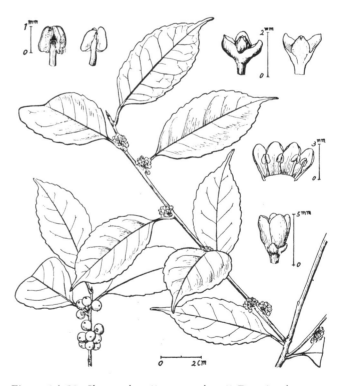

Figure 14-59. *Ilex warburgii* var. *warburgii*. Drawing by Chien-chu Chen in *Illustrations of Native and Introduced Ligneous Plants of Taiwan* (1962) by Tang-shui Liu.

(apiculate), midribs impressed, puberulent above, petioles 5–7 mm (³⁄₁₆–⁹⁄₃₂ in.) long; inflorescences axillary on 2nd-year growth, fasciculate, subsessile, flowers 4- to 5-merous, fragrant; fruits red, globose, 3–4 mm (⅛–⁵⁄₃₂ in.) diameter, pedicels 3–4 mm (⅛–⁵⁄₃₂ in.) long, calyces persistent, styles nipplelike; pyrenes 6, smooth, 1 long striate. Habitat: Myanmar and western People's Republic of China, Yunnan Province, on the western flank of the Tali Mountain Range. Allied to *I. forrestii*.

Ilex wattii Loesener 1901.

Evergreen, glabrous trees to 8 m (26 ft.) tall, branchlets angulate, striate, lenticels inconspicuous; leaves elliptic or elliptic-lanceolate, 6–11 cm (2⅜–4⅜ in.) long, 2–3.5 cm (¾–1⅜ in.) wide, apices acuminate, acumens 1–2 cm (⅜–¾ in.) long, bases obtuse or rarely rotund, margins serrate, reticulate on both surfaces, petioles 5–10 mm (³⁄₁₆–⅜ in.) long; inflorescences axillary and fasciculate on 2nd-year growth; flowers 4-merous; fruits red, subglobose, 6 mm (⁷⁄₃₂ in.) long, 7 mm (⁹⁄₃₂ in.) diameter, pedicels 2–3 mm (¹⁄₁₆–⅛ in.) long, calyces persistent; pyrenes 4, palmately 5-striate, sulcate, sides rugose, striate. Habitat: first described from India, Manipur; common also in People's Republic of China, southwestern Yunnan Province. Allied to *I. tetramera*.

Ilex weberbaueri Loesener 1905.

Evergreen, low shrubs; leaves ovate-oblong to obovate-oblong, 0.7–1.4 cm (⁹⁄₃₂–¹⁷⁄₃₂ in.) long, 3–9 mm (⅛–¹¹⁄₃₂ in.) wide, apices rotund to subacute, bases cuneate or cuneate-obtuse, margins recurved, crenulate-serrulate, 2–4 teeth on each side, petioles 1.5–3 mm (³⁄₆₄–⅛ in.) long; inflorescences axillary, solitary, branched, flowers 4-merous; fruits unknown. Habitat: Peru, near Junin, at 3000–3100 m (9900–10,230 ft.) elevation. Allied to *I. glazioviana*, *I. ovalis*, and *I. paltorioides*.

Ilex wenchowensis S.-y. Hu 1946.

Evergreen shrubs to 2 m (6 ft.) tall, branchlets pubescent; leaves ovate, 3–4.8 cm (1³⁄₁₆–1¹⁵⁄₁₆ in.) long, 1.2–2.5 cm (¹⁵⁄₃₂–1 in.) wide, apices acuminate, spinose, bases truncate or rotund, margins serrate, 3–7 spines on each side, midribs slightly depressed, pubescent, petioles 2 mm (¹⁄₁₆ in.) long, leaves persist on 3rd-year growth; inflorescences axillary and fasciculate on 2nd-year growth, flowers 4-merous; fruits red, depressed-globose, 5–6 mm (³⁄₁₆–⁷⁄₃₂ in.) long, 8 mm (⁵⁄₁₆ in.) diameter, pedicels 4–5 mm (⁵⁄₃₂–³⁄₁₆ in.) long; pyrenes 4, striate, sulcate. Habitat: People's Republic of China, southeastern Zhejiang Province. Allied to *I. pernyi* and *I. wugonshanensis*. Confused with *I. zhejiangensis*.

Ilex wenzelii Merrill 1913. Katagdo.

Evergreen, glabrous shrubs to 2 m (6 ft.) tall, epiphytic or pseudoepiphytic; leaves ovate, 5–7 cm (2–2¾ in.) long, 3–4 cm (1³⁄₁₆–1⅝ in.) wide, bases broadly rotund or abruptly contracted and slightly decurrent-acuminate, apices acuminate, acumen to 1 cm (⅜ in.) long, margins entire, petioles 1–1.5 cm (⅜–¹⁹⁄₃₂ in.) long; male inflorescences axillary, solitary, racemose or subfasciculate, 4- to 10-flowered, flowers 4- to 5-merous; fruits globose, 3.5–4 mm (⁹⁄₆₄–⁵⁄₃₂ in.) diameter; pyrenes 4–5. Habitat: endemic to Philippines, Leyte and Mindanao islands, in primary forest to 1100 m (3630 ft.) elevation. Allied to *I. spicata*.

Ilex wightiana Wallich 1848 var. wightiana. Orlo (synonym *I. wightiana* var. *peninsularis* Hooker f. 1875).

Evergreen, large trees to 17 m (56 ft.) tall, often with large trunks to 2 m (6 ft.) diameter; leaves elliptic to elliptic-oblong, 3.5–8.5 cm (1³⁄₅–3⅜ in.) long, 1.3–3.3 cm (¹⁵⁄₃₂–1⁷⁄₃₂ in.) wide, glabrous, apices obtuse or acute, acuminate, bases rotund to cuneate, reticulate beneath, margins entire, recurved, petioles 5–15 mm (³⁄₁₆–¹⁹⁄₃₂ in.) long; inflorescences axillary, solitary, paniculate, small flowers 5- to 6-merous; fruits grayish brown (when dry), globose 3.5–4 mm (⁷⁄₆₄–⁵⁄₃₂ in.) diameter, peduncles 2.5–10 mm (³⁄₃₂–⅜ in.) long, pedicels 3–7 mm (⅛–⁹⁄₃₂ in.) long; pyrenes 5–6. Habitat: India, also in southern and central Sri Lanka and Vietnam. Allied to *I. gardneriana* and *I. minutifolia*.

Ilex wightiana var. cuspidata Loesener 1901.

A variety differing from typical individuals with apices long, acuminate tips 8 mm (⁵⁄₁₆ in.) long. Habitat: Vietnam, Tonkin Province. This variety may well prove to be a very minor variant and synonym of the species.

Ilex williamsii Standley 1950.

Evergreen trees 4–15 m (13–50 ft.) tall, glabrous; leaves broadly obovate to ovate, occasionally broadly elliptic, 3–6 cm (1³⁄₁₆–2⅜ in.) long, 2.4 cm (1 in.) wide, bases broadly crenate, apices rotund, brief spiculate, margins entire, petioles 1 cm (⅜ in.) long; fruits globose, 5 mm (³⁄₁₆ in.) diameter. Habitat: Honduras, Department Morazan del Verra ale Uyca, at 2000 m (6600 ft.) elevation.

Ilex wilsonii Loesener 1908 var. wilsonii (synonym *I. memecylifolia* var. *plana* Loesener 1908).

Evergreen, glabrous trees to 10 m (33 ft.) tall; leaves oval or obovate-oblong, 3–6.5 cm (1³⁄₁₆–2½ in.) long, 1.5–3.5 cm (¹⁹⁄₃₂–1⅜ in.) wide, apices obtuse, abruptly acuminate, acumens 6–8 mm (⁷⁄₃₂–⁵⁄₁₆ in.) long, bases obtuse or rotund, margins entire, petioles 5–9 mm (³⁄₁₆–¹¹⁄₃₂ in.) long; inflorescences axillary and fasciculate on 2nd-year growth, males 3- to 5-flowered cymose, females single, pedicels 4–7 mm (⁵⁄₃₂–⁹⁄₃₂ in.) long, flowers 4-merous; fruits red in late summer, globose, calyces persistent; pyrenes 4, 3-striate. Habitat: People's Republic of China, first reported from western Hubei Province, but actually a widespread species along the Yangtze River from Sichuan Province southeast to the central and coastal provinces of Anhui and Zhejiang. Introduced into England in 1926 and into the United States before 1937. Hardy in zones 6 to 9. Allied to *I. kobuskiana*. Plate 80.

Ilex wilsonii var. *handel-mazzetti* T. R. Dudley 1984.

This variety differs from typical individuals with longer male flower peduncles, 8–15 mm (⁵⁄₁₆–¹⁹⁄₃₂ in.) long; petals fimbriate-erose, and minutely ciliolate; shorter female flower pedicels, 2–3 mm (¹⁄₁₆–¹⁄₈ in.) long. Habitat: People's Republic of China, Hunan Province.

Ilex wugonshanensis C.-j. Tseng 1981.

Evergreen shrubs to 2 m (6 ft.) tall, branchlets puberulent or glabrescent, angulate; leaves oblong-ovate or oblong-lanceolate or narrow-oblong, 4.5–6 cm (1³⁄₄–2³⁄₈ in.) long, usually 2–2.5 cm (³⁄₄–1 in.) wide, apices triangular, terminating in a spine, bases obtuse or subrotund, margins serrate, usually 2–3 spines on each side, each terminating with a spine, petioles 3–9 mm (¹⁄₈–¹¹⁄₃₂ in.) long, densely or sparsely puberulent; inflorescences axillary, fasciculate, uniflorous, flowers 4-merous; fruits red, globose, 6–7 mm (⁷⁄₃₂–⁹⁄₃₂ in.) diameter; pyrenes palmately striate, sulcate. Habitat: People's Republic of China, Jiangxi Province. Allied to *I. wenchowensis*.

Ilex wuiana T. R. Dudley 1988 (synonym *I. mamillata* C.-y. Wu *ex* Y.-r. Li 1985).

Evergreen trees to 12 m (40 ft.) tall, branchlets light gray, angulate, puberulent or glabrescent; leaves oblong-elliptic, 4–8 cm (1⁵⁄₈–3¹⁄₈ in.) long, 1.3–3.2 cm (¹⁄₂–1¹⁄₄ in.) wide, apices acuminate or short-acuminate, bases obtuse or wide-cuneate, margins entire or sparingly and inconspicuously serrate toward apex, veins moderately conspicuous on both surfaces, petioles 5–8 mm (³⁄₁₆–⁵⁄₁₆ in.) long; inflorescences axillary, fasciculate, with 1–4 fruits, pedicels 3–8 mm (¹⁄₈–⁵⁄₁₆ in.) long; fruits red, subglobose, 5–6.5 mm (³⁄₁₆–¹⁄₄ in.) diameter, persistent calyces with 6 lobes; pyrenes 6, 3-striate, 2-sulcate. Habitat: People's Republic of China, Yunnan Province at 1200 m (4000 ft.) elevation. Allied to *I. cochinchinensis*.

Ilex wurdackiana Steyermark 1988.

Evergreen, epiphytic shrubs, branchlets puberulent; leaves broadly obovate or oblong-lanceolate, 4–10.5 cm (1⁵⁄₈–4¹⁄₈ in.) long, 2–6 cm (³⁄₄–2³⁄₈ in.) wide, bases rotund to subcordate, apices acute to acuminate, margins entire, strongly punctate beneath, petioles 1–3 mm (¹⁄₃₂–¹⁄₈ in.) long; inflorescences axillary, solitary, lateral, flowers 4-merous; fruits ovoid, subglobose, 2.5–3 mm (³⁄₃₂–¹⁄₈ in.) long, 3 mm (¹⁄₈ in.) diameter, pedicels 2.5–4 mm (³⁄₃₂–⁵⁄₃₂ in.) long. Habitat: Venezuela, Bolivar State, endemic to regions of the Cerro Venamo and the tributaries of the Venamo and Cuyuní rivers. Named for John J. Wurdack.

Ilex xizangensis Y.-r. Li 1981.

Evergreen shrubs to 1 m (3 ft.) tall, branchlets angulate, glabrous; leaves oblong or oblong-elliptic or oblong-oblanceolate, 7–10 mm (⁹⁄₃₂–³⁄₈ in.) long, 2–3 mm (¹⁄₁₆–¹⁄₈ in.) wide, apices obtuse, bases cuneate, margins crenate-serrate, glabrous, petioles 2–3 mm (¹⁄₁₆–¹⁄₈ in.) long; inflorescences axillary and fasciculate on 2nd-year growth, flowers 4-merous; pedicels 5 mm (³⁄₁₆ in.) long; fruits unknown. Habitat: People's Republic of China, Xizang Province, Medog, Xian. Allied to *I. intricata*.

Ilex xylosmaefolia C.-y. Wu *ex* Y.-r. Li 1986.

Evergreen, small trees 4–6 m (13–20 ft.) tall, branchlets grayish with appressed yellowish tomentose; leaves elliptic-lanceolate or oblong-elliptic, 7–9 cm (2³⁄₄–3¹⁄₂ in.) long, 2–3.2 cm (³⁄₄–1⁷⁄₃₂ in.) wide, bases obtuse, apices acuminate or long-acuminate, margins sparingly crenate serrate, petioles 3–5 mm (¹⁄₈–³⁄₁₆ in.) long; inflorescences cymose, yellowish tomentose; fruits unknown. Habitat: People's Republic of China, Yunnan Province. Allied to *I. ferruginea*. Originally published as *I. xylosmifolia*.

Ilex yangchunensis C.-j. Tseng 1981.

Evergreen shrubs, branchlets angulate, glabrous; leaves narrow-elliptic or narrow-oblong-elliptic, 7–9 cm (2³⁄₄–3¹⁄₂ in.) long, 2.5 cm (1 in.) wide, apices short acuminate or obtuse, bases obtuse or attenuate, margins inconspicuously crenulate, petioles 1–1.3 cm (³⁄₈–¹⁄₂ in.) long; inflorescences axillary, 1- to 3-fasciculate; fruits maturing yellowish (probably immature), globose, 1 cm (³⁄₈ in.) diameter, pedicels 1.2–1.3 cm (¹⁵⁄₃₂–¹⁄₂ in.) long; pyrenes 4, irregularly striate, sulcate. Habitat: People's Republic of China, Guangdong Province. Allied to *I. nuculicava*.

Ilex yuiana S.-y. Hu 1951.

Evergreen shrubs, branches slender, densely pubescent; leaves elliptic, 1–3 cm (³⁄₈–1³⁄₁₆ in.) long, 0.8–1.4 cm (⁵⁄₁₆–¹⁷⁄₃₂ in.) wide, bases obtuse or acute, apices acute cuspidate, pubescent, punctate below, petioles 3–4 mm (¹⁄₈–⁵⁄₃₂ in.) long, densely

258 ◆ EVERGREEN HOLLY SPECIES

pubescent, stipules 1 mm (¹⁄₃₂ in.); inflorescences axillary, solitary, fruiting pedicels pubescent, 10–12 mm (³⁄₈–¹⁵⁄₃₂ in.) long; fruits depressed, subglobose, 5–7 mm (³⁄₁₆–⁹⁄₃₂ in.) diameter, calyces pubescent; pyrenes 4, endocarps leathery. Habitat: People's Republic of China, apparently limited to the Kiukiang Valley of northwestern Yunnan Province, at 1350–2300 m (4455–7590 ft.) elevation. Allied to *I. triflora*.

Ilex yunnanensis Franchet 1889 var. *yunnanensis*. Shu cha tze.

Shrubs or small trees to 5 m (16 ft.) tall, branchlets villose; leaves ovate or ovate-lanceolate, 2–3.5 cm (³⁄₄–1³⁄₈ in.) long, 1–2 cm (³⁄₈–³⁄₄ in.) wide, apices acute, mucronate, bases rounded or obtuse, margins recurved, crenulate-serrate, teeth often aristate, pubescent below on midribs when young; inflorescences solitary, axillary on new growth, flowers 4-merous, usually white but reported to be pink to red on snow range of northwestern Yunnan and western Hubei; fruits red, globose, 5–6 mm (³⁄₁₆–⁷⁄₃₂ in.) diameter, nodding pedicels 8–14 mm (⁵⁄₁₆–¹⁷⁄₃₂ in.) long; pyrenes 4, smooth. Common to the mountains of western People's Republic of China. Introduced by E. H. Wilson in 1911 to the Arnold Arboretum. Hardy in zone 5. The local name shu cha tze means "water tea" or the tea growing by the water. Along the Sino-Tibetan border, people collect the leaves and use them as a substitute for tea. Allied to *I. sugerokii*. Male plants collected in northwestern Hubei Province at 2500 m (8250 ft.) elevation produce flowers under cultivation in Washington, D.C., that were consistently red or pink.

Figure 14-60. *Ilex yunnanensis* var. *yunnanensis*. Drawing by Randy Allen.

Ilex yunnanensis var. *brevipedunculata* S.-y. Hu 1946.

This botanical variety has short pedicels usually 3–6 mm (¹⁄₈–⁷⁄₃₂ in.) long; flowers purplish red; fruit red, nodding. Habitat: People's Republic of China, Guizhou Province, at 2600–3600 m (8,580–11,880 ft.) elevation.

Ilex yunnanensis var. *eciliate* S.-y. Hu 1949.

A botanical variety differing from typical individuals with elliptic leaves 1–2.8 cm (³⁄₈–1¹⁄₈ in.) long, 4–12 mm (⁵⁄₃₂–¹⁵⁄₃₂ in.) wide, apices acute to obtuse, bases acute; flowers 4- to 6-merous, calyces eciliate. Habitat: People's Republic of China, Sichuan Province.

Ilex yunnanensis var. *gentilis* (Franchet *ex* Loesener) Diels 1900 (synonym *I. gentilis* Franchet *ex* Loesener 1901).

A botanical variety with leaves ovate or oblong, apices obtuse or rarely subacute, bases rounded, margins crenate; flowers 4-merous, rarely 5- to 7-merous. Habitat: People's Republic of China, Sichuan and Hubei provinces.

Ilex yunnanensis var. *parviflora* (Hayata) S.-y. Hu 1949 (synonym *I. parviflora* Hayata 1911).

A botanical variety with small leaves, oblong-lanceolate, 1.1–2 cm (⁷⁄₁₆–³⁄₄ in.) long, 6 mm (⁷⁄₃₂ in.) wide, margins serrate with aristate teeth. Habitat: central and southwestern Taiwan, at 2500–3300 m (8,250–10,900 ft.) elevation, and in People's Republic of China, Yunnan Province.

Ilex yunnanensis var. *paucidentata* S.-y. Hu 1949.

The leaves of this botanical variety are thicker and more rigid than those of typical individuals, leaves ovate-lanceolate, 2–3.5 cm (³⁄₄–1³⁄₈ in.) long, 1–1.5 cm (³⁄₈–¹⁹⁄₃₂ in.) wide, margins entire, spineless except for a terminal weak spine. Habitat: People's Republic of China, Yunnan Province.

Ilex yurumanquiana Cuatrecasas 1948.

Evergreen trees; leaves obovate-elliptic to elliptic-oblong, 9–15 cm (3½–6 in.) long, 4.5–7.5 cm (1¾–3 in.) wide, bases attenuate and cuneate, apices attenuate, subapiculate or obtuse, margins slightly wavy, obscurely crenate, minute teeth are separate and pointing forward, petioles 5–10 mm (³⁄₁₆–³⁄₈ in.) long; male inflorescences axillary, cymose; fruits unknown. Habitat: Colombia, Department del Valle, along Yurumangu River. Allied to *I. affinis* and *I. laureola*.

Ilex yutajiensis Wurdack 1961.

Evergreen, glabrous shrubs to 2 m (6 ft.) tall; leaves elliptic-oblong, 7–9 cm (2¾–3½ in.) long, 5–6 cm (2–2³⁄₈ in.) wide, bases rotund, apices rotund to subretuse, margins remote crenulate-serrulate, 5–7 mm (⁹⁄₃₂–¹¹⁄₃₂ in.) long; inflorescences axillary, 5- to 6-fasciculate; fruits globose; pyrenes 4. Habitat: Venezuela, Amazonas, Cerro Yutaje, Rio Manapiare, at 1500 m (4950 ft.) elevation. Allied to *I. loretoica*.

Ilex zeylanica (Hooker f.) Maximowicz 1881. Andun-wenna (synonyms *I. wightiana* Thwaites 1848, *non* Wallich 1848, *I. wightiana* var. *zeylanica* Hooker f. 1875).

Figure 14-61. *Ilex yunnanensis* var. *parvifolia.* Drawing by Chien-chu Chen in *Illustrations of Native and Introduced Ligneous Plants of Taiwan* (1962) by Tang-shui Liu.

Evergreen shrubs or trees, lenticels present; leaves usually ovate-elliptic, 6–11 cm (2⅜–4⅜ in.) long, 2.9–4.5 cm (1⅛–1¾ in.) wide, apices acute acuminate, bases cuneate, margins entire, recurved, petioles 6–12 mm (7/32–15/32 in.) long; inflorescences in leaf axils, paniculate, subsessile, 10–40 mm (⅜–1½ in.) long, 3- to 7-flowered pedunculate, flowers 5- to 6-merous; fruits black, globose 3.5–4.5 mm (7/64–11/64 in.) diameter; pyrenes 6, 3- to 4-striate. Habitat: southern and central Sri Lanka (Ceylon) at 1330 m (4390 ft.) elevation. Allied to *I. maingayi* and *I. spicata.*

Ilex zhejiangensis C.-j. Tseng 1981.

Evergreen shrub or small tree, 2–4 m (6–13 ft.) tall, branchlets puberulent or glabrescent, angulate; leaves ovate-elliptic or elliptic, rarely ovate, 3–6 cm (1³⁄₁₆–2⅜ in.) long, 1.5–3 cm (¹⁹⁄₃₂–1³⁄₁₆ in.) wide, bases rotund or obtuse, apices triangular, rarely obtuse, puberulent along midveins above, margins remotely serrate, 4–7 on each side, black apiculate, petioles 4–5 mm (5/32–3/16 in.) long; inflorescences axillary, fasciculate, solitary; fruits red, subglobose, 7–8 mm (9/32–5/16 in.) diameter, pedicels 4–8 mm (5/32–5/16 in.) long; pyrenes 4, irregularly rugose, sulcate. Habitat: People's Republic of China, Zhejiang Province. Probably allied to *I. centrochinensis,* but appears to be more like a hybrid of *I. cornuta* possibly with *I. centrochinensis* or another species.

Ilex zippeliana T. R. Dudley, *nom. nov.* (synonyms *I. laurifolia* Zippelius, *Am. Journ. Sci.* 1822; *non I. laurifolia* Nuttall 1822; *I. cymosa* var. *laurifolia* Zippelius 1827).

Evergreen, large shrubs or small trees, spreading to erect branches with dense lenticels; leaves glabrous, oblong, 4.7–9.4 cm (2–3¹¹⁄₁₆ in.) long, 1.9–3.7 cm (¾–1⁷⁄₁₆ in.) wide, bases cuneate, apices rotund to obtuse, margins entire, recurved, petioles 10–20 mm (⅜–¾ in.) long; inflorescences axillary, solitary, cymes with 9–15 flowers, peduncles 7–13 mm (⁹⁄₃₂–½ in.) long, pedicels 1–3 mm (¹⁄₃₂–⅛ in.) long; fruits red, globose, small 2.75–3 mm (³⁄₃₂–⅛ in.) diameter; pyrenes very small. Habitat: Philippines and Amboina, Indonesia. Allied to *I. cymosa* and *I. sebertii.*

Ilex zygophylla Merrill 1939.

Evergreen shrubs to 4.5 m (15 ft.) tall, branchlets and inflorescences sparsely puberulent; leaves opposite, elliptic, 2–4 cm (¾–1⅝ in.) long, 1.2–1.5 cm (⅜–¹⁹⁄₃₂ in.) wide, bases rotund, margins entire, revolute, petioles 1.5–3 mm (³⁄₆₄–⅛ in.) long; male inflorescence laterally cymose umbellate, flowers purple, 4- to 5-merous; fruits unknown. Habitat: North Borneo, Mount Kinabalu in mossy forest above 2400 m (7900 ft.) elevation. Distributed as a *Microtropis* species. Allied to *I. oppositifolia.*

CHAPTER 15

Evergreen Holly Cultivars

Ilex × altaclerensis Cultivars

For many years a hybrid group of large, broad-leaved hollies was included under *Ilex aquifolium* before separated out under *I. × altaclerensis*. In 1838 Loudon first used the epithet *altaclerensis* to describe Highclere holly, a variety of *I. aquifolium* said to have originated in the gardens of Highclere, the estate of the Earls of Carnarvon, near Newbury, Berkshire, England. *Ilex aquifolium* var. *altaclerensis* Hort. ex Loudon was said to be a cross between *I. aquifolium* and *I. perado*. Today *I. × altaclerensis* includes many similar but variable clones in which the following taxa are known to have played their parts: *I. perado* Aiton subsp. *perado* (*I. maderensis* Lamarck, non Hort.), *I. perado* Aiton subsp. *platyphylla* (Webb & Berthelot) Tutin var. *platyphylla* (*I. platyphylla* Webb & Berthelot), and *I. aquifolium* Linnaeus (*I. balearica* Desfontaines non Hort.).

For clarification of the complex problems with *Ilex × altaclerensis* (Hort. ex Loudon) Dallimore, I am indebted to Susyn Andrews of the Royal Botanic Gardens, Kew. Andrews also pointed out that the correct spelling for this group of cultivars should be *I. × altaclerensis* and not *altaclarensis* as spelled by Rehder. According to Ekwall (1960), the latinized name of Highclere, going back to 1270, was Alta Clera, which would give the adjective *altaclerensis*.

In general the plants in this group are large pyramidal evergreen shrubs or trees. The leaves are usually larger than those of *Ilex aquifolium*, being 6–14 cm (2⅜–5½) in. long, 5–7 cm (2–2¾ in.) wide. The leaf surfaces are flat and occasionally twisted but not undulate or wavy. The margins are entire or with small regular (sometimes irregular), dentate teeth. The flowers and fruits are also somewhat larger.

Andrews has divided the *I. × altaclerensis* clones into six groups (see below).

More than 50 cultivars formerly listed as *Ilex aquifolium* selections are now classified as hybrids and listed here as *I. × altaclerensis* cultivars. Some of these 50 are still listed under *I. aquifolium*. Many of the cultivars selected and named in the United States and Europe have not been placed in any group. Table 7 lists cultivars of *I. aquifolium* and *I. altaclerensis* that were published without description and other data. Most of the names are valid. The names were from catalogs, arboreta lists, and miscellaneous sources with little to no descriptions and background information.

BALEARICA GROUP
Leaves green, ovate to elliptic, to 7–9 cm (2¾–3 in.) long, margins entire to spiny, stems green, olive green to purplish above; all plants female, with abundant large fruit, some very free fruiting; vigorous trees with upright branches.
'Balearica'
'Moria', possibly a branch sport of 'Balearica'
'Purple Shaft', a branch sport of 'Balearica'

BELGICA GROUP
Leaves green to variegated, lanceolate, elliptic-lanceolate to elliptic-oblong, margins entire to spiny, stems green to yellowish green, some with yellowish streaks; all plants female.
'Belgica' (synonym *I. perado* Hort., non Aiton; Dutch holly)
'Belgica Aurea' (synonyms *I. perado* 'Aurea', 'Silver Sentinel')

CAMELLIIFOLIA GROUP
Hybrids with one parent being the typically spiny *Ilex aquifolium* or its ovate-leaved, often non-spiny variant in the Mediterranean. Leaves green or variegated, usually elliptic to elliptic oblong, to 9–13 cm

(3–5⅛ in.) long, margins usually entire or 1–3 spines on each side, flat or twisted, stems and petioles purplish above green below; all plants female.
    'Barterberry'
    'Camelliifolia' (synonyms 'Heterophylla Major', 'Magnifica')
    'Camelliifolia Variegata', branch sport of 'Camelliifolia'
    'James G. Esson'
    'Marnockii'

HENDERSONII GROUP
All are branch sports of 'Hendersonii'. Leaves dull green or variegated, usually oblong-ovate, to 9–11 cm (3–4⅜ in.) long, margins usually entire, rarely with spines, stems and petioles green; all plants female.
    'Golden King'
    'Hendersonii'
    'Howick' (synonym 'Hendersonii Variegata')
    'Lady Valerie'
    'Lawsoniana'
    'Ripley Gold'

HODGINSII GROUP
All are branch sports of 'Hodginsii'. Leaves green or variegated, ovate to ovate-oblong, margins entire to spiny, to 8–12 cm (3⅛–4¾ in.) long; stems green to greenish purple to purplish black; all plants male.
    'Hodginsii' (synonyms 'Altaclerensis', 'Nobilis', 'Shepherdii')
    'Nobilis Picta' (synonym 'Nobilis Variegata')

MADERENSIS GROUP
Leaves green, broadly ovate to elliptic, to 9–11 cm (3–4⅜ in.) long, margins entire to spiny, stems green to olive green to purplish above; all plants male.
    'Atrovirens'
    'Jermyns'
    'Maderensis'
    'Nigrescens'

'Adaptable' (female; chance seedling selected 1968, named and registered H.S.A. 2-75 by J. S. Wieman; female parent very hardy from New York).
    Leaves dark olive green, oval, to 8.3 cm (3¼ in.) long, 2 cm (¾ in.) wide, margins slightly wavy, numerous small spines, petioles 6 mm (7/32 in.) long; fruits red, rounded and slightly tapered, 11 mm (7/17 in.) long, 10 mm (⅜ in.) diameter, pedicels 5 mm (3/16 in.) long; habit ovoid. Selected for hardiness in container after prolong freeze in 1972.

'Atkinsonii' (male; introduced in the early 1900s by Fisher, Son, and Sibray).
    Leaves dark black green, broadly ovate-oblong, corrugated, 10–12 cm (4–4¾ in.) long, 5–7 cm (2–2¾ in.) wide, bases obtuse to rotund, margins slightly twisted at apex, 6–10 small spines, tip spines slightly reflexed, petioles stout, 10 mm (⅜ in.) long; stems green.

'Atrovirens' (male; synonyms *I. platyphylla maderensis atrovirens, I. maderensis atrovirens*; possibly a sport of 'Nigrescens'; first sold in England in 1855; Maderensis Group).
    Leaves dark olive green, broadly ovate, to 9 cm (3½ in.) long, 7 cm (2¾ in.) wide, 5–6 large spines, pointing forward, petioles and stems purplish above; robust habit. Rare in cultivation.

'Atrovirens Variegata' (male; synonym *I. platyphylla maderensis variegata*; old English cultivar; Maderensis Group).
    Leaves variegated, margins dark olive green, irregular yellow blotch mixed with pale green in center, ovate or obovate, 6.5–7.5 cm (2½–3 in.) long, 3.8–5.8 cm (1½–2¼ in.) wide, margins occasionally slightly wavy, 5–6 spines, stems reddish purple.

'Balearica' (female; synonyms *I. platyphylla* var. *balearica, I. aquifolium* var. *balearica*, 'Green Plane'; old cultivar in England introduced in the mid 1800s; Balearica Group).
    Leaves dark olive green, glossy, broadly ovate to broadly elliptic, 6.5–9 cm (2½–3½ in.) long, 2.5–4.5 cm (1–1¾ in.) wide, margins usually entire, occasionally 2–4 small spines, petioles reddish, 10–12 mm (⅜–15/32 in.) long, stems green or olive green; fruits red, globose to pyriform, 10 mm (⅜ in.) diameter, 3–5 in clusters, pedicels reddish, 10–13 mm (⅜–½ in.) long; vigorous grower.

'Balkans' (male and female selections named; from seed collected in the wild in Yugoslavia 1934 by E. Anderson and grown at Missouri Botanical Gardens; named and introduced by A. Brownell; no records available from Missouri Botanical Gardens; origin of name of female selection unknown).
    Leaves dark olive green, glossy, oval to broadly elliptic, 5.5–7.5 cm (2⅛–3 in.) long, 3–4 cm (1 3/16–1⅝ in.) wide, concave, bases cuneate to rotund, 5–9 spines on each side, wavy, tip spines slightly reflexed, petioles 10–13 mm (⅜–½ in.) long; fruits vivid red 45A, globose, 8 mm (5/16 in.) diameter, abundant, pedicels 8 mm (5/16 in.) long. Reported a cold hardy selection. See 'Marshall Tito'.

'Barterberry' (female; discovered about 1960 by Douglas Weguilin, on Barters Farm Nursery, England; named in 1982 by G. P. Brown, North Newton Nursery; introduced and listed in the catalog of Barters Farm Nursery; Camelliifolia Group).

Table 7. Questionable cultivar names of *Ilex aquifolium* and *I.* × *altaclerensis*.

'Aebelo'	Selected by C. Pederson, Bogense, Denmark
'Bailey's Red' (female)	Introduced by H. L. Pearcy Nursery, Salem, Oregon
'Besse Selection'	Plant at North Willamette Research and Extension Center, Canby, Oregon
'Beadles'	From Biltmore estate, *I.* × *altaclerensis*
'Bodley's Bleeg'	Old selection, plant from Oregon University, Corvallis, Oregon
'Citrocarpa' (female)	Discovered & named by Satteins von Kaufm. Heinr.
'Coleman' (female)	Coleman Nursery, Oregon, introduced 1940
'Curtiss Strain'	Biltmore estate, robust, winter killed 1985
'Ebony Male'	Lake County, New Perry, Ohio
'Elizabeth Hall'	Plant originally from New York Botanic Garden, *I.* × *altaclerensis*
'Gold Lady'	Plant at Bokrijk Arboretum, *I.* × *altaclerensis* type
'Golden Beauty' (male)	Introduced 1941 by W. P. Clarke, California, variegated foliage
'Golden Beau' (male)	Introduced by G. Teufel, leaves with yellow margin
'Green Knight' (male)	Introduced by A. Brownell in 1950
'Illicifolium'	Leaves short, spiny, stems purple
'Kamo' (male)	Media-Picta type, Roslyn Nursery, Dix Hill, New York
'Lees Dark Silver'	At U.S. National Arboretum, received from England, died
'Lem's Silver' (female)	Named by H. Hohman, cuttings received from Haf den Lenn, Seattle, Washington, believed to be 'Silvary'
'Levy'	Plant at Tyler Arboretum, before 1974
'Lillian Stricklen' (female)	Plant at Towson Nursery, selected & named 1963 by S. McLean for Mrs. G. Stricklen of Towson Nursery
'Mahlstede'	Plant at Horton Nursery, Painesville, Ohio, U.S. National Arboretum plant dead
'Nolls'	Plant at Angelica Nursery, 1958
'Parade'	Plant at Biltmore estate, 1960, winter killed 1985
'Perkins No. 1'	Plant at Tyler Arboretum, also at Swarthmore College, before 1985
'Plantifolia'	Hesse Nursery, Germany, leaves nearly entire
'Shady Lady' (female)	Named by A. Brownell
'Silver Star' (female)	Named by A. Brownell, Argentea Medio-Picta type
'Silver Tip'	Plant at Biltmore estate, winter killed 1980s
'Smithiana' (male, but also listed as a female)	Old cultivar, 1863, from England, leaves narrow often entire
'Souder Special'	Mrs. Archer
'Syracuse' (male)	Named by W. Wheeler, before 1960, no information
'Valiant'	Was on trial at U.S. National Arboretum
'Vanguard'	Was on trial at U.S. National Arboretum
'Varigold'	Plant at Strybing Arboretum, 1987
'Vera'	Plant from Clarendon Gardens, 1957
'Viceroy'	On trial at U.S. National Arboretum
'Vinedale'	On trial at U.S. National Arboretum
'Viola'	Named by W. Wheeler
'Willy No. 2'	Holly Haven Nursery

Leaves similar to 'Camelliifolia', dark green, elliptic, glossy, flat, margins nearly entire; fruits red, very large. Selected for large crop of fruits.

'Beadles' (old cultivar from the United States).
No information available, doubtful if plants are still available.

'Belgica' (female; synonyms Dutch Holly, *I. perado*, *I. belgica*, *I. aquifolium* var. *belgica*; old cultivar; first recorded sale in 1874; Belgica Group).
Leaves dark olive green, glossy, elliptic to elliptic oblong, flat, 7–10 cm (2¾–4 in.) long, 2.5–4.5 cm

(1–1¾ in.) wide, bases cuneate to obtuse, margins variable, entire, or with a few spines to 5–8 spines on each side, petioles 10–15 mm (⅜–¹⁹⁄₃₂ in.) long, stems green or yellowish green; fruits reddish orange, globose to slightly ellipsoid, 10 mm (⅜ in.) diameter, pedicels 8–10 mm (⁵⁄₁₆–⅜ in.) long; pyramidal habit.

'Belgica Aurea' (female; synonyms *I. perado* 'Aurea', 'Silver Sentinel'; raised in Netherlands by Koster and Son and exhibited in 1908; Belgica Group).
Leaves variegated, dark green center shading to gray-green, margins pale yellow, elliptic-lanceolate,

7–10 cm (2¾–4 in.) long, 3.5–4.5 cm (1⅜–1¾ in.) wide, very flat, margins variable, usually entire to occasional spines on upper half of leaf, petioles 10–13 mm (⅜–½ in.) long, stems green with yellow streaks; fruits red, sparse to seldom fruiting. Certificate of Recommendation in 1908, Boskoop, Netherlands.

'Camelliifolia' (female; synonyms *I. camelliifolia*, 'Camelliaefolia', 'Heterophylla', 'Laurifolium Longifolium'; earliest record of sales was 1865; Camelliifolia Group).

Leaves dark olive green, glossy, elliptic oblong, 7–13 cm (2¾–5 in.) long, 3–4.5 (1³⁄₁₆–1¾ in.) wide, bases rotund, margins usually entire, or 3–5 small spines on upper half of leaf, petioles 10 mm (⅜ in.) long, stems purplish; flower buds pale pink opening to white; fruits dark red, globose, 10 mm (⅜ in.) diameter, abundant. A.G.M. 1931.

'Camelliifolia Variegata' (female; sport of 'Camelliifolia'; first recorded sale in 1865; Camelliifolia Group).

Leaves variegated, dark green centers marbled gray-green, margins yellow, occasionally some leaves half or entirely yellow; fruits red but sparse. Not common; mature specimen at Edinburgh Botanic Garden.

'Captain Royal' (male; named and introduced by A. Brownell in the 1950s).

Leaves dark olive green, oval to broadly elliptic, margins usually entire, occasionally 1–3 small spines near apex, stems green.

'Cherryberry' (female; synonym 'Birdproof'; named and introduced by A. Brownell in the 1950s).

Leaves dark olive green, ovate to elliptic, 5.5–6 cm (2⅛–2⅜ in.) long, 3–3.8 cm (1⅜–1½ in.) wide, bases cuneate to rotund, margins wavy, usually entire, occasionally 2–4 erratic small spines near apex, tip spines reflexed, petioles 8 mm (⁵⁄₁₆ in.) long, stems green; fruits red.

'Colburn' (female; plant at Scott Arboretum; introduced by C. Beadle, Biltmore Nursery, Ashville, North Carolina).

Leaves dark olive green, ovate to elliptic, 4.5–6 cm (1¾–2⅜ in.) long, 2–3 cm (¾–1³⁄₁₆ in.) wide, bases cuneate to rotund, margins wavy, 2–4 small spines usually on upper half of leaf, tip spines reflexed, petioles stout, 8–10 mm (⁵⁄₁₆–⅜ in.) long; stems green; fruits red.

Dutch Hybrid Group or Pacific Northwest Hybrids.

Group names applied to English hollies in the Pacific Northwest differing from the spiny leaf forms associated with the Christmas season. Leaves dark green, usually flat, and entire; fruits usually larger, uniformly globose, early ripening, produced abundantly. See *I. aquifolium* Pacific Northwest Hybrid Group

'Dr. Huckleberry' (female; seedling selected on Wilmarth place at Brighton, Oregon; tested at North Willamette Experimental Research and Extension Center, Canby, Oregon, as O.S.C. No. 25 in the 1950s).

Leaves dark olive green elliptic, 9–11 cm (3½–4⅜ in.) long, 3.5–4 cm (1⅜–1⅝ in.) wide, margins wavy, usually entire, occasionally few spines near apex, petioles 10 mm (⅜ in.) long, stems dark; fruits deep reddish orange 43A, globose, 10 mm (⅜ in.) diameter, early ripening, pedicels reddish, 10 mm (⅜ in.) long. Good orchard tree.

'Eldridge' (female; discovered on Long Island, New York, about 1900; introduced by J. W. Batchelor).

Leaves dark olive green, elliptic to broadly elliptic, 7–9 cm (2¾–3½ in.) long, 4–5 cm (1¾–2 in.) wide, bases obtuse, margins usually entire, occasionally with few spines near apex, petioles stout, 10 mm (⅜ in.) long, stems green to purple; fruits deep reddish orange 43A, globose to pyriform, 10 mm (⅜ in.) diameter, pedicels reddish, 10 mm (⅜ in.) long.

'Emerald Elegance' (female; origin unknown).

Leaves dark olive green, glossy, elliptic, 6–7 cm (2⅜–2¾ in.) long, 2–2.5 cm (¾–1 in.) wide, leaves usually entire, flat or apex slightly curved down, margins occasionally with 1, rarely 2 small spines, on each side of upper one-third of leaf, petioles 10–20 mm (⅜–¾ in.) long; fruits vivid red, fruiting on young plants; upright pyramidal habit; hardy in zone 7. Selected for attractive foliage and fruit.

'Father Charles' (male; origin doubtful, possible from H. Hohman, Kingsville Nursery, in 1951 catalog).

Very similar to 'Camelliifolia'.

'Fisheri', see *I. aquifolium.*

'Golden King' (female; synonyms 'Aurea Rex', 'Hodginsii Aurea', 'Hodgin's Golden', 'King Edward VII'; sport of 'Hendersonii'; discovered in 1884 by J. Munro at Bangholm Nursery, Scotland; distributed in 1898; Hendersonii Group).

Leaves variegated, glossy dark green centers mottled gray green, irregular margins broad yellow, or yellowish white on older leaves, oblong-ovate, to 10 cm (4 in.) long, 6.5 cm (2½ in.) wide, margins usually entire, rarely 1–2 small spines near apex; stems green; fruits red. A.M. and F.C.C. 1898, A.G.M. 1969.

'Green Maid' (female; named and introduced in 1940 by A. Brownell).

Leaves dark olive green, elliptic, 5.5–8 cm (2⅛–3⅛ in.) long, 2.5–3 cm (1–1³⁄₁₆ in.) wide, bases rotund, margins twisted, entire to 1–2 spines near apex, petioles 8–10 mm (⁵⁄₁₆–⅜ in.) long, stems green; fruits deep reddish orange 43A, globose, 8–10 mm (⁵⁄₁₆–⅜ in.) diameter, pedicels 6–8 mm (⁷⁄₃₂–⁵⁄₁₆ in.) long; early ripening; vigorous dense habit. Often listed as *I. aquifolium*. Plate 81.

'Green Plane' (name given by A. Brownell; see 'Balearica').

'Hedge Row' (male; origin as seedling found by M. S. Whipple, plant on Long Island, New York, in the 1980s; specimen sent for description and identification).

Leaves dark olive green, elliptic, 3–6.5 cm (1³⁄₁₆–2½ in.) long, 1–2 cm (⅜–¾ in.) wide, slightly keeled, bases cuneate to obtuse, apices acuminate, margins undulate, 5–8 spines on each side, petioles dark, 8–10 mm (⁵⁄₁₆–⅜ in.) long; stems purplish above.

'Hendersonii (female; raised by T. Hodgins in early 1800s; distributed by Lawson Company, Edinburgh, Scotland, around 1846; Hendersonii Group).

Leaves dull olive green, oblong-ovate, 9–11 cm (3½–4⅜ in.) long, 4–6 cm (1⅝–2⅜ in.) wide, bases obtuse to rotund, veins depressed, margins slightly wavy, usually entire, occasionally 1–2 small spines near apex, petioles 10 mm (⅜ in.) long, stems green with faint purplish flush; fruits brownish red, globose, 8–10 mm (⁵⁄₁₆–⅜ in.) diameter, 3–5 in clusters, pedicels 6 mm (⁷⁄₃₂ in.) long.

'Heterophylla', see *I. aquifolium* 'Heterophylla'.

'Hodginsii' (male; synonyms 'Shepherdii', 'Nobilis', 'Altaclerensis'; raised by T. Hodgins in early 1800s; sent to J. Shepherd, curator of Liverpool Botanical Garden, before 1836; propagated and distributed by Fisher, Son, and Sibray; Hodginsii Group).

Leaves dark black green, broadly elliptic to ovate, 7.5–10 cm (3–4 in.) long, 3.5–5 cm (1⅜–2 in.) wide, bases obtuse to rotund, margins usually entire, occasionally few spines near apex, petioles 10–13 mm (⅜–½ in.) long; stems purple-black above, purplish green below; flower buds, purplish pink opening white. A.G.M. 1969.

'Hodginsii Aurea', see 'Golden King'.

'Hohman', see *I. aquifolium*.

'Howick' (female; synonym 'Hendersonii Variegata'; sport of 'Hendersonii'; named by S. Andrews; original plant at Howick estate in Northumberland, England, in the 1980s; Hendersonii Group).

Leaves variegated, dull olive green in center, occasionally mottled gray green, margins narrow band of pale yellowish white, oblong-ovate, to 9 cm (3½ in.) long, 5 cm (2 in.) wide, margins recurved, somewhat bullate, usually entire, occasionally with erratic spines near apex, petioles flushed pink; stems green, occasionally streaked yellow, flushed pink when young; fruits reddish orange, sparse.

'J. C. van Tol', see *I. aquifolium* 'J. C. van Tol'.

'James G. Esson' (female; seedling selection of *I.* × *altaclerensis* 'Eldridge' raised by J. G. Esson, superintendent of the Mrs. Roswell Eldridge estate, Great Neck, Long Island, New York; grown for several years at The New York Botanical Gardens; named by T. H. Everett in 1949; introduced to England by Hillier Nursery; Camelliifolia Group).

Leaves dark green, glossy, broadly ovate, 6–11 cm (2⅜–4⅜ in.) long, 3–5 cm (1³⁄₁₆–2 in.) wide, bases rotund to truncate, apices prolonged, margins wavy, usually 4–5 spines on each side, occasionally entire to sub entire, petioles purplish, 6–8 mm (⁷⁄₃₂–3⁵⁄₁₆ in.) long, stems purple-green; fruits vivid red 45A, globose to slightly ellipsoid, 6–10 mm (⁷⁄₃₂–⅜ in.) diameter, abundant, pedicels 6–8 mm (⁷⁄₃₂–⁵⁄₁₆ in.) long; vigorous rapid growth. Plate 82.

'Jermyns' (male; found at Jermyns House, Winchester, England, when purchased by Sir Harold Hillier in 1952; named by R. Lancaster in mid 1960s; Maderensis Group).

Leaves dark olive green, glossy, elliptic, to 10 cm

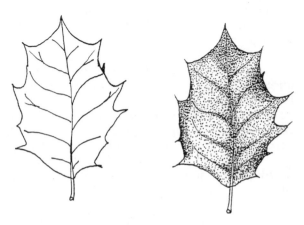

Figure 15-1. *Ilex* × *altaclerensis* 'James G. Esson'. Drawing by Randy Allen.

(4 in.) long, 4.8 cm (1⅞ in.) wide, margins usually entire, petioles yellow, stems brownish green; vigorous, broadly columnar habit. Good hedge plant.

'Lady Valerie' (female; sport of 'Golden King' discovered 1976 by Neil Murray on the property of the late Sir Basil Goulding at Dargle Gleen County, Wicklow, Ireland; named and introduced by Murray for Lady Valerie Goulding; Hendersonii Group).

Leaves variegated, dark olive green margins, irregular yellow blotches in center, broadly elliptic, to 9 cm (3½ in.) long, 4.5 cm (1¾ in.) wide, margins twisted, usually entire. occasionally some very small spines on one or both sides; fruits red. Similar to 'Lawsoniana' but with more twisted leaves.

'Laura Barnes' (female; origin unknown; plant at Tyler Arboretum, not *I. aquifolium* 'Laura Barnes' from Barnes Arboretum).

Leaves dark olive green, elliptic, 6.5–8.5 cm (2½–3⅜ in.) long, 2.5–3.5 cm (1–1⅜ in.) wide, bases cuneate to obtuse, apices acute, margins flat, variable, mature leaves entire to subentire, young tip leaves usually spiny, 5–8 spines on each side, petioles 10–16 mm (⅜–⅝ in.) long, stems green; fruits red, elliptic to elongate pyriform, 10–13 mm (⅜–½ in.) long, 8 mm (⁵⁄₁₆ in.) diameter, pedicels reddish, 5 mm (³⁄₁₆ in.) long; dense upright habit.

'Lawrence White', see *I aquifolium* 'Lawrence White'.

'Lawsoniana' (female; sport of 'Hendersonii'; origin from T. Hodgins Nursery in the 1800s; grafts sent to Lawson Company, Edinburgh, Scotland, before 1869 and distributed soon afterward; Hendersonii Group).

Leaves variegated, dark olive green margins, irregular mottling of lighter green and yellow in center, mature leaves have yellowish white mottling, broadly elliptic, to 11 cm (4⅜ in.) long, 6.5 cm (2½ in.) wide, margins usually entire, stems green, streaked yellow; fruits red, sparse. Often reverts back to green 'Hendersonii'.

'Leach Strain' (female; introduced by Perkins de Wilde Nursery in the 1950s).

Fruits red, large; compact pyramidal growth. Reported to be a hardy strain.

'Louise' (female; seedling of 'Teufel's'; selected 1948; registered H.S.A. 9-59 by G. Teufel).

Leaves dark olive green, glossy, oval, 5–7 cm (2–2¾ in.) long, 2.5–3 cm (1–1³⁄₁₆ in.) wide, bases obtuse to rotund, margins usually entire, rare spines near apex, margins twisted and curved, petioles 8–10 mm (⁵⁄₁₆–⅜ in.) long, stems green; fruits deep reddish orange 43A, globose, 12 mm (¹⁵⁄₃₂ in.) diameter, pedicels 8–10 mm (⁵⁄₁₆–⅜ in.) long; good clusters; hardy to −18°C (0°F).

'Maderensis' (male; old cultivar; first reference in 1854; Maderensis Group).

Leaves dark green, glossy, broadly ovate, 7.5–11 cm (3–4⅜ in.) long, 6–7 cm (2⅜–2¾ in.) wide, margins vary from entire to spiny, spines pointing forward, stems green. Susyn Andrews reports this as being the male counterpart of 'Balearica'.

'Maderensis Variegata'

Plants in the trade as *I. × altaclerensis* 'Maderensis Variegata' should be listed as *I. aquifolium* 'Maderensis Variegata', which see.

'Marnockii' (female; chance seedling at Fisher, Son, and Sibray around 1875; Camelliifolia Group).

Leaves dark olive green, glossy, elliptic oblong, 5–8 (–11) cm (2–3⅛ (–4⅜) in.) long, 2.5–3.5 (–5) cm (1–1³⁄₁₆ (–2) in.) wide, margins usually entire or occasionally erratic spines, twisted in the middle, stems dark black above, purplish below; flower buds purplish pink, opening white; fruits vivid red, globose, 10 mm (⅜ in.) diameter, pedicels 5–6 mm (³⁄₁₆–⁷⁄₃₂ in.) long.

'Marshall Tito' (male; synonym 'Balkans Male'; origin from seed collected in the wild in Yugoslavia in 1934 by E. Anderson of Missouri Botanic Garden; named by A. Brownell; introduced by Missouri Botanic Garden).

Leaves dark olive green, ovate to elliptic, 6.5–7.5 cm (2½–3 in.) long, 2.5–5 cm (1–2 in.) wide, bases obtuse to cuneate, tip leaves vigorous usually spiny, margins flat to wavy, 8–10 spines pointing forward, occasionally subentire or with 1–5 small spines near apex, petioles stout, 7–10 mm (⁹⁄₃₂–⅜ in.) long, stems purplish. See also 'Balkans'.

'Moira' (female; possibly a branch sport of 'Balearica' named by S. Andrews; Balearica Group).

Leaves dark olive green, ovate to rarely elliptic, to 7.5 cm (3 in.) long, 4 cm (1⅝ in.) wide, concave, margins entire, rarely with an odd spine, stems olive green; fruits vivid red.

'Moorei' (male; introduced by Fisher, Son, and Sibray between 1930 and 1947).

Leaves dark olive green, glossy, broadly ovate, to 10 cm (4 in.) long, 6.5 cm (2½ in.) wide, margins with 6–8 long divaricate spines pointing forward, veins prominent, stems greenish purple.

'Morris No. 1' (female; origin from the Morris Arboretum, Philadelphia, Pennsylvania; plant at Tyler Arboretum).

Leaves dark olive green, broadly elliptic, 6–8 cm (2⅜–3⅛ in.) long, 3–4.2 cm (1³⁄₁₆–1¹¹⁄₁₆ in.) wide, bases cuneate to obtuse, apices acute, margins usually entire, occasionally with small spines on upper one-third of leaf, petioles 8–10 mm (⁵⁄₁₆–⅜ in.) long, stems green; fruits red, ellipsoid, 10 mm (⅜ in.) long, 8 mm (⁵⁄₁₆ in.) diameter, pedicels 8–10 mm (⁵⁄₁₆–⅜ in.) long.

'Mundy' (male; introduced in 1898 by Fisher, Son, and Sibray).

Leaves dull olive green, ovate-oblong, concave, to 10.5 cm (4⅛ in.) long, 7 cm (2¾ in.) wide, with 9–11 spines on each side, occasionally subentire to entire, petioles yellow-green, stems green; flower buds purple.

'N. F. Barnes' (female; old cultivar from England; introduced by Fisher, Son, and Sibray after 1930).

Leaves dark green, glossy, elliptic, 5–6.5 cm (2–2⅜ in.) long, 2–3 cm (¾–1³⁄₁₆ in.) wide, bases obtuse, margins flat to slightly wavy, 5–10 small spines pointing forward, petioles 10 mm (⅜ in.) long; stems purple; fruits vivid red 45A, globose, 8–10 mm (⁵⁄₁₆–⅜ in.) diameter, pedicels 8–10 mm (⁵⁄₁₆–⅜ in.) long.

'Nigrescens' (male; synonyms *I. aquifolium* var. *nigrescens*, *I. aquifolium* var. *nigricans*, *I. balearica* var. *nigrescens*, *I. maderensis* var. *nigrescens*; first reference of sales around 1845; Maderensis Group).

Leaves dark olive green, ovate to broadly elliptic, to 10 cm (4 in.) long, 6.5 cm (2½ in.) wide, bases rotund, margins usually entire to subentire with 1–3 spines near apex, occasionally branches with leaves very spiny, 5–9 small spines pointing forward, petioles 8 mm (⁵⁄₁₆ in.) long, stems olive green.

'Nobilis Picta' (male; branch sport of 'Hodginsii', old cultivar first distributed before 1879; Hodginsii Group).

Leaves with dark green margins, irregular large blotches of brilliant yellow 11A, to yellow green in center, 6–10 cm (2⅜–4 in.) long 3–5 cm (1³⁄₁₆–2 in.) wide, margins usually entire, occasionally spines near apex, petioles 10–13 mm (⅜–½ in.) long. Rare in cultivation, reverts freely. Plate 83.

'Oak Vale' (female; old cultivar; chance seedling discovered by G. Cunningham and Son Nursery, England, before 1908).

Leaves dark green, uniform shaped, 7.5–9 cm (3–3½ in.) long, 4.5–5 cm (1¾–2 in.) wide, apices acute, margins flat, moderate spines; stems purplish above, green below.

'Platyphylla' (female; the epithet *platyphylla* has been applied to various hybrid hollies of the *Ilex × altaclerensis* group, causing confusion with *I. perado* var. *platyphylla* of the Canary Islands; possibly introduced by Fisher, Son, and Sibray).

Leaves dark green, glossy, broadly ovate, to 10 cm (4 in.) long, 6.5 cm (2½ in.) wide, margins variable from entire to 4–6 small spines on each side, stems green; fruits red.

'Post Office' (female; seedling planted in 1874 at the Pioneer Post Office in downtown Portland, Oregon; named and introduced by A. Brownell; Balearica Group).

Leaves dark olive green, margins usually entire or with scattered few spines; fruits red.

'Purple Shaft' (female; branch sport of 'Balearica'; named by R. Lancaster in 1965; Balearica Group).

Leaves dark green, glossy, ovate to oblong-ovate, to 9 cm (3½ in.) long, 4.5 cm (1¾ in.) wide, margins usually with a few spines, petioles purplish, stems greenish purple above, green beneath; fruits vivid red, free fruiting; vigorous growing.

'Ripley Gold' (female; sport of 'Golden King' discovered 1980 by T. Sparkes in garden in village of North Ripley, Hampshire, England; original tree lost; named and introduced by Sparkes; Hendersonii Group).

Leaves variegated, dark olive green margins, irregular yellow blotches in center, broadly elliptic, margins twisted, usually entire, leaves keep golden color in shade; fruits red. Similar to 'Lawsoniana' but like 'Lady Valerie' with twisted leaves.

'Royal Red' (female; named and introduced in the 1950s by A. Brownell).

Leaves dark olive green, oval to elliptic, 5–7 cm (2–2¾ in.) long, 2.5–3 cm (1–1³⁄₁₆ in.) wide, bases cuneate, margins usually entire, occasionally 1–3 small spines near apex, stems green; fruits vivid red, globose, 10–13 mm (3⁄8–1⁄2 in.) diameter, pedicels 6 mm (7⁄32 in.) long. Plate 84.

'Shepherdii', see *I.* × *altaclerensis* 'Hodginsii'.

'Silver Sentinel' (female: synonym 'Belgica Aurea'; reported from Koster and Son before 1908 as 'Belgica Aurea'; grown in England for many years as *I. perado* 'Variegata'; also reported as sport of 'Balearica'; registered H.S.A. 3-72; offered for sale by H. Hillier in 1972; improved selection of 'Belgica Aurea'; Belgica Group).

Leaves variegated, dark green with light green and gray markings in center, conspicuous irregular light yellow margins, occasionally streaked darker yellow toward center, elliptic, 8–10 cm (3–4 in.) long, 4.5 cm (1 3⁄4 in.) wide, bases cuneate, margins vary from entire to 4 spines on each side; fruits red, ovoid, long pedicels. Reported one of best variegated clones in England.

'Tatnall School' (male; from Tatnall School campus, Wilmington, Delaware; selected for hardiness; named and introduced by Millcreek Nursery in the 1980s).

Leaves dark olive green, elliptic, 5–7.5 cm (2–3 in.) long, 2.5–3.5 cm (1–1 3⁄8 in.) wide, bases cuneate, margins usually entire, tip leaves occasionally with 1–4 small spines on upper half of leaf, petioles 13–18 mm (1⁄2–11⁄16 in.) long; stems purple.

'Teufel's Hybrid', see *I. aquifolium.*

'W. J. Bean' (female; introduced in the 1920s by Fisher, Son, and Sibray; named for William Jackson Bean, curator of the Royal Botanic Gardens, Kew, England).

Leaves broadly elliptic, 8–10 cm (3 1⁄8–4 in.) long, 3.5–4 cm (1 3⁄8–1 5⁄8 in.) wide, margins wavy, 3–5 spines on each side, usually on upper two-thirds of leaf, tip spines reflexed, petioles 10–13 mm (3⁄8–1⁄2 in.) long, stems green; fruits vivid red 45A, ellipsoid, 14 mm (17⁄32 in.) long, 11 mm (7⁄16 in.) diameter, pedicels reddish, 8 mm (5⁄16 in.) long; compact, slow growing.

'Whittingtonensis', see *I. aquifolium.*

'Wieman's Favorite' (female; synonym 'Favorite'; selected about 1933; named and registered H.S.A. 8-76 by J. S. Wieman).

Leaves dark olive green, glossy, elliptic, 9–11.5 cm (3 1⁄2–4 1⁄2 in.) long, 5–6 cm (2–2 3⁄8 in.) wide, bases cuneate, margins flat to slightly wavy, 1–5 variable spines on each side, petioles 14 mm (17⁄32 in.) long; fruits red, glossy, ovoid, 13 mm (1⁄2 in.) long, 11 mm (7⁄16 in.) diameter, pedicels 13 mm (1⁄2 in.) long; oval habit, horizontal branching. Produces excellent flat sprays, popular for commercial packing. Plate 85.

'Wieman's Hedge-row' (male; seedling of *I.* × *altaclerensis* selected in 1974; named and registered H.S.A. 8-82 by J. S. Wieman).

Leaves dark olive green, ovate to narrow-elliptic, to 11 cm (4 3⁄8 in.) long, 7 cm (2 3⁄4 in.) wide, bases cuneate, keeled, slightly curved, subentire, 2–6 spines each side, strong tip spines, petioles 8 mm (5⁄16 in.) long; stems green; compact horizontal branching. Selected for hedges with moderate pruning.

'Wilsonii', see *I. aquifolium* 'Wilsonii'.

'Wight's Selection' (female; discovered 1980 by Marty Langmaid at Wight Nursery in a purchased lot of 'Wirt L. Winn' plants; introduced by Wight Nursery; PP No. 6978 still under testing for introduction; may later be given trademark name).

Leaves moderate yellow-green, dark red in winter, ovate to oblong-lanceolate, 6–9 cm (2 3⁄8–3 1⁄2 in.) long, 2.5–4.5 cm (1–1 3⁄4 in.) wide, bases obtuse, apices acute-cuspidate, margins variable, entire or 1–16 spines, petioles 1–1.5 cm (3⁄8–19⁄32 in.) long, young stems purplish; fruits vivid red 44A, globose 8–10 mm (5⁄16–3⁄8 in.) diameter; heat tolerant in the Southeast, hardy in zone 7A, possibly 6B. Upright pyramidal habit. At present under evaluation.

'Winter King' (male; selected, named, and introduced in 1955 by A. Brownell).

Similar to 'Winter Queen'. Selected for winter hardiness. Produces pollen on young plants.

'Winter Queen' (female; selected named and introduced in 1955 by A. Brownell).

Leaves dark olive green, oblong to broadly elliptic, 5–7.5 cm (2–3 in.) long, 3–4.5 cm (1 3⁄16–1 3⁄4 in.) long, bases rotund, margins wavy, 2–4 spines on each side, usually entire, 1–2 small spines near apex, occasional branches with spiny wavy leaves, 3–6 spines on each side, petioles 10 mm (3⁄8 in.) long, stems green; fruits dark reddish orange 43A, globose to slightly pyriform, 12 mm (3⁄8 in.) diameter, pedicels reddish, 6 mm (7⁄32 in.) long. Selected for winter hardiness.

'Yocum' (female; synonym 'Yokum'; origin unknown, possibly from Wilmat Nursery in the 1960s).

Leaves dark olive green, elliptic, keeled, slightly twisted, 4–5.5 cm (1 5⁄8–2 1⁄8 in.) long, 2–2.8 cm (3⁄4–1 1⁄4 in.) wide, bases obtuse to rotund, apices acuminate, margins usually entire, rarely 1 small single spine at apex or 1 small spine on each side of apex, petioles 8 mm (⁵⁄₁₆ in.) long, stems purplish; fruits vivid reddish orange 44B, globose to slightly pyriform, 8 mm (⁵⁄₁₆ in.) diameter, pedicels reddish, 3–5 mm (⅛–³⁄₁₆ in.) long, 1–4 in clusters.

Ilex aquifolium (English Holly) Cultivars

English hollies are the best known and most useful of all hollies. *Ilex aquifolium* is native to southern and western Europe, including Albania, Austria, Balearic Islands, Belgium, Bulgaria, Corsica, Denmark, France, Germany, Great Britain, Greece, Ireland, Italy, Yugoslavia, Luxembourg, Netherlands, Norway, Portugal, Romania, Sardinia, Sicily, North Africa, Spain, Sweden (where it is thought now to be extinct), and Turkey. In Britain it was originally found wild throughout, except in northeastern Scotland. It has many common names such as common Holly, Oregon holly, acebo, acebo spum, agrifolio, houx, holme, honx, stickpalm, hulst, Christdorn, Christtorn, ostrolist, seyo-hiiragi (Japan).

English hollies are evergreen trees to 25 m (75 ft.) high. They are heavily branched and usually form a dense pyramidal habit of growth. Some are narrow upright to columnar, a few are rounded, and some are weeping or with pendulous branches. The evergreen leaves are extremely variable in size and shape, varying from 2.5–7.5 cm (1–3 in.) long and 1–6.5 cm (⅜–2½ in.) wide. The margins are usually with spines and undulate or wavy. Adult foliage at the tops of large mature trees is often with entire margins. The dark olive green foliage is noted for its gloss or sheen and the extreme diversity of variegated patterns in the leaves. The small, white, fragrant flowers are borne in the leaf axils on old growth and often subject to late frost damage. The typical fruits are red, 5–10 mm (³⁄₁₆–⅜ in.) diameter, or larger. Yellow to orange fruits are usually rare.

The variegated forms of English holly are divided into two major groups, Argentea Group (yellow white-silver) and Aurea Group (yellow), which are further divided into subgroups depending on the location of the variegation as follows:

Argentea Medio-Picta
  Yellow white (silver) variegation in center of leaf
Argentea Marginata
  Yellow white (silver) variegation on margin
Aurea Medio-Picta
  Yellow (golden) variegation in center of leaf
Aurea Marginata
  Yellow (golden) variegation on margin

'Ferox' (hedgehog holly) is reported to be the oldest known cultivar. The origin is doubtful, but was thought to have been found in the wild in France in 1635. George London introduced it from France to England in the mid 1600s. Unfortunately, the origin and records of many old cultivars are no longer available for this would have been interesting reading.

One of the first collections of holly cultivars was that of T. Rench (also spelled Wrench), a nurseryman in Fulham, Middlesex, England, during the later part of the reign of Charles II, 1670–1685. Another early collection was developed by George London, also at Fulham, about the end of the seventeenth century. London and Wise (1706) wrote, "We have great varieties of hollies in England and have brought them to more perfection than they are in any other part of the World." Philip Miller (1731) recognized 33 varieties, now referred to as cultivars. In 1770 William Hanbury mentioned 42 cultivars (sorts); the greater proportion were variegated, and only eight were green-leaved. Evelyn's (1662) book *Silva* named 36 cultivars.

The grouping of hollies based on their foliage dates from John Loudon in 1838. He noted the large number of variegated hollies in London nurseries and grouped these as follows:

albo-marginatum	white-edged-leaved
aurea marginata	gold-edged-leaved
albo-pictum	white spotted-leaved
aureo-pictum	gold-spotted-leaved

Loudon also included the "silver-blotched" and "gold-blotched" hollies.

The first mention of a yellow-fruited holly, 'Fructu-lutea', was by William Cole (1657), who listed three sorts of holly:

1. The holly without prickles
2. The holly with prickled leaves
3. The holly with yellow berries

Cole also mentioned the yellow berried holly as having been found near Wardour Castle, in Wiltshire, England.

The earliest and most important work on English hollies is *The Common Holly and its Varieties* by Thomas Moore, published in a series of fourteen articles in the *Gardeners Chronicle*, London, 1874–1876 and again in 1880. Moore described 153 cultivars, and due to the full descriptions and completeness, these articles have become known as *Moore's Monograph*.

In 1908 W. Dallimore, foreman of the arboretum in the Royal Botanic Gardens, Kew, added an important contribution to hollies in his book *Holly,*

Yew and Box. Many of his descriptions and leaf illustrations of the English holly cultivars were from *Moore's Monograph.* Dallimore clarified the English holly "variety" descriptions and names of previous authors, and included information on other *Ilex* species. He placed some large broad-leaved hollies under *I. platyphylla* and some as hybrids. The latter, generally from hybrids of *I. aquifolium* × *I. perado,* are now included under the epithet *I.* × *altaclerensis.* More than fifty Loudon hybrids were formerly listed under *I. aquifolium* and included many cultivars such as 'Camelliifolia', 'Hendersonii', 'Marnockii', 'Platyphylla', 'Wilsonii', and 'W. J. Bean'.

For many years American horticulturists looked to England and Europe for the attractive cultivars of English holly. Many of the old cultivars described by Moore and Dallimore are still found today by the same or with new names. The holly collection at the Royal Botanic Gardens, Kew, England, still has some of the best cultivars and hybrids. Now, however, many cultivars have been named in the United States, and in the Pacific Northwest, many English hollies have been selected for orcharding and landscape use.

English hollies were first introduced to Oregon from England and France in the 1850s as seed and small rooted plants. Pacific Northwest growers began shipping holly for Christmas in the early 1900s to the local markets in Oregon, Washington, and California and later to the East.

The planting of holly orchards soon followed. The early orchards were composed mainly of seedlings of the green-leaved and blue-stemmed types. By 1925 the shift toward variegated hollies became very popular as cut material for the holiday season. Holly growers in Oregon, Washington, and British Columbia met in the early 1930s and in 1931 formed a trade association, The Oregon Holly Growers Association. Unfortunately this group was disbanded in 1991.

The selection of English holly cultivars in the United States started in the Northwest in the 1930s, and still continues in the East. Many of the early English holly cultivars from England were, unfortunately, renamed with "fancy names." Ambrose Brownell of Brownell Farms, Milwaukie, Oregon, was one of the promoters and prime introducers of English holly to the East and Northwest. He was noted for his "fancy named" plants, adding even further to the confusion and proliferation of names. For more information on the early history of English holly in the United States, see Wieman (1961). John Wieman, one of the early pioneers on the West Coast, was the first to register an English holly cultivar in the United States in 1959 with the Holly Society of America.

In the late 1960s Ray Leach was advising growers to increase production of the variegated trees to produce the 25-percent berried variegated holly needed to fill orders. In the 1980s the Florist Telegraphic Delivery Service started featuring variegated holly in its Christmas advertising, making the demands for variegated foliage even greater. There is still a shortage of good variegated cut holly cultivars and selected green cultivars for cut and general landscape demand.

The Washington Park Arboretum, Seattle, Washington, and the Oregon State University, North Willamette Experimental Research and Extension Center near Canby, Oregon, have excellent collections of English hollies. In the Midwest and Northeast selections are often based on cold hardiness. In the Southeast collections are often based on heat tolerance. For arboreta in these areas see the list of official holly arboreta and experimental holly test centers in Appendix 4.

In general English holly is hardy in zone 7, and many cultivars are now listed as being hardy in zone 6. The variegated hollies are popular in the Northwest both for orcharding and landscaping, and some are approved for the Northeast. Most variegated English hollies have resulted from sports of green-leaved types and often tend to revert back. This is common especially on the Medio Picta types, where the variegation occurs in the center of the leaves. The reverted green-leaved branches should be cut out. The marginal variegated groups rarely revert back to solid green leaves.

'Alaska' (female; synonym 'Aprather'; selected and introduced by H. and D. Nissen before 1960).

Leaves dark olive green, glossy, elliptic, 3–6 cm (1³⁄₁₆–2³⁄₈ in.) long, 3–4 cm (1³⁄₁₆–1⁵⁄₈ in.) wide, resembling the species, margins undulate, 5–7 coarse spines on each side; fruits vivid red; very narrow habit of growth; very winter hardy. Received Silver Medal in 1967 from the Netherlands.

'Alcicornis' (male; old plant from Scotland; selected by Lawson Nursery before 1874).

Leaves dark olive green, oblong-obovate, 9 cm (3½ in.) long, 4.5 cm (1¾ in.) wide, bases cuneate and entire, margins with 3–5 narrow stiff very long spines, 16 mm (⅝ in.) long; young bark green.

'Alice' (female; synonym 'Wheeler No. 1', 'Whitney No. 1'; seedling on G. G. Whitney estate, Woods Hole, Massachusetts; selected and named by W. Wheeler; see Whitney Holly Group).

No description available.

'Altaclerensis', see *I.* × *altaclerensis.*

Figure 15-2. *Ilex aquifolium* 'Alaska'. Photo by Hans-Georg Buchtmann.

'Amber' (female; selected, named, and introduced in the 1950s by Hillier and Sons Nursery, England).
Leaves dark green, glossy, elliptic, 5–6 cm (2–2⅜ in.) long, 3–4 cm (1³⁄₁₆–1⅝ in.) wide, usually entire, or few spines on upper half of leaf; fruits large, moderate orange, persistent.

'Ammerland' (female; sport of 'Camelliifolia'; selected in 1970 by H. Bruns in his nursery).
Leaves dark olive green, glossy, broadly elliptic, 4–8 cm (1⅝–3⅛ in.) long, 3–4 cm (1³⁄₁₆–1⅝ in.) wide, shows no characteristic of *I. perado*, 5–8 strong spines on each side, venation distinct, midribs light green, stems dark purple; fruits dark red, large; vigorous compact, broadly columnar habit; hardy to −22°C (−8°F). Possibly a cultivar of *I. × altaclerensis*.

'Angustifolia' (synonyms 'Ananassifolia', 'Myrtifolia Stricta', 'Petit' (male), 'Petite' (female), 'Pernettyifolia', var. *serrata*; known since 1789; usually reported as male, however female plants are available in England and the United States).
Leaves dark olive green, lanceolate or lanceolate-ovate, 3.5–6 cm (1⅜–2⅜ in.) long, 1–2 cm (³⁄₁₆–¾ in.) wide, long narrow entire apices, 5–7 small spines on each side, pointed forward; leaves quite variable; fruits vivid red 45A, globose to depressed globose, 5 mm (³⁄₁₆ in.) diameter, 4 mm (⁵⁄₃₂ in.) long, stems green or purplish; narrow pyramidal habit. Plate 86.

'Angustifolia Albo-Marginata' (synonym 'Serratifolia Albo Marginata'; old cultivar in late 1800s).
Leaves like 'Angustifolia' with margins yellowish white, heavier at apices.

'Angustimarginata Aurea' (new epithet by Susyn Andrews; male; name invalid; synonyms 'Angustifolia Aurea Marginata', 'Aurea Angustifolium', 'Myrtifolia Elegans'; old cultivar from England, known since 1863; not a form of 'Angustifolia' and not to be confused with 'Angustifolia' or 'Myrtifolia Aurea').
Leaves variegated, dark green, marked pale green, slender irregular yellow margins, elliptic oblong, 3.8–5.8 cm (1½–2¼ in.) long, to 2.5 cm (1 in.) wide, apices acuminate, stems usually purplish.

'Apricot' (female; origin in England; reported by Susyn Andrews to be a cultivar separate from 'Apricot Glow').
Fruits orange.

'Apricot Glow' (female; synonyms 'Apricot', 'Wieman's Apricot Glow'; open-pollinated seedling from a yellow-fruited seedling; selected 1965 by J. S. Wieman; registered H.S.A 2-86 by Wieman; sibling of 'Yellow Beam').
Leaves dark olive green, very glossy, ovate to broadly lanceolate, to 13.6 cm (5³⁄₁₆ in.) long, to 8.2 cm (3³⁄₁₆ in.) wide, bases rotund to truncate, margins thicker and lighter than blade, undulate, 6–10 lateral spines on each side, stout tip spine reflexed downward, petioles 11 mm (⁷⁄₁₆ in.) long, stems purplish; fruits strong orange 25B, with reddish blush, globose, 16 mm (⅝ in.) diameter, pedicels 5 mm (³⁄₁₆ in.) long; fruits orange, to 6 in cluster, color very distinct and effective in the landscape; conical habit, medium tall grower.

'Arbutifolia' (W. Paul; old cultivar from England, 1863).
Leaves dark green, glossy, lanceolate, 6 cm (2⅜ in.) long, 2.5 cm (1 in.) wide, margins slightly undulate, numerous spines, stems purple. Similar to 'Ciliata Major' but with narrower leaves.

'Argentea Longifolia' (male; synonyms 'Longifolia Argentea'; old cultivar from England before 1875).
Leaves elliptic to ovate, 6–7.5 cm (2⅜–3 in.) long, margins irregular, narrow, yellowish white;

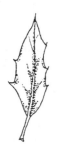

Figure 15-3. *Ilex aquifolium* 'Angustifolia'. Drawing by Randy Allen.

young foliage pink. Similar to 'Argentea-marginata' but with purple young stems.

'Argentea Marginata' (female; synonyms 'Albo-Marginata', 'Argentea Marginata Major', 'Argenteo Variegata', 'Broad Silver', 'Lee's Dark Silver', 'Rough-Leaved Silver', 'Silver Beauty' (U.S.A.), 'Silver Princess' (U.S.A.), 'Silver Variegated'; old cultivar from England introduced before 1770).
  Leaves dark olive green, margins yellow white, broadly elliptic, 5.5–7.5 cm (2⅛–2¾ in.) long, 3–4 cm (1³⁄₁₆–1⅝ in.) wide, bases cuneate, 5–7 spines on each side, flat to slightly wavy, young foliage pink; fruits vivid red 45A, ellipsoid, 10 mm (⅜ in.) long, 8 mm (⁵⁄₁₆ in.) diameter, pedicels reddish, 6 mm (⁷⁄₃₂ in.) long, stems light green. A.G.M. 1969. Plate 87.

'Argentea Marginata Elegantissima', see 'Elegantissima'.

'Argentea Marginata Erecta' (female; synonym 'Argentea Erecta'; old cultivar from England).
  Leaves mottled green center, broadly yellow-white margin, 5 cm (2 in.) long; spines; fruits red.

Argentea Marginata Group
  The most common of the hollies with yellowish white (silver) margins. Leaves variable among cultivars, dark green, margins irregular yellowish white, broadly ovate, 5–7.5 cm (2–3 in.), long, 3–4 cm (1³⁄₁₆–1⅝ in.) wide, spines irregular, usually numerous or occasionally nearly entire; fruits red. Names in trade include 'Argentea Marginata', 'Silvary', 'Silver Princess', 'Silver Queen', 'Teufel's Silver Variegated'.

'Argentea Marginata Latifolia', see 'Silver Queen'.

'Argentea Marginata Major', see 'Argentea Marginata'.

'Argentea Marginata Pendula' (female; synonyms 'Albomarginata Pendula', 'Argentea Pendula', 'Pendula Argentea', 'Pendula Argenteomarginata', 'Pendula Tricolor', 'Pendula Variegata', 'Perryana Major', 'Perry's Weeping', 'Silver Beauty', 'Silver Weeping'; introduced in 1859 by Messrs. Perry of Banbury, Oxford, England).
  Well-known red-fruiting cultivar of weeping habit, stems purplish, slow growing, low mounding form; leaves dark olive green, blotched gray-green, margin irregular yellowish white, ovate or ovate-oblong, 6.5–7.5 cm (2½–3 in.) long, large conspicuous spines.

'Argentea Marginata Stricta' (synonym 'Lurida Variegata'; origin unknown, from England).

Leaves broadly ovate, to 7.5 cm (3 in.) long, dark green center, blotched pale green and gray, broadly yellow margins, spines pointed forward; pyramidal habit, to 9.5 m (30 ft.) tall.

Argentea Medio-Picta Group
  Leaves dark olive green at the margins, large irregular yellowish white blotch in the center or lower half of leaf, elliptic to ovate, 3.8–5 cm (1½–2 in.) long, bases cuneate, spines 5–7 on each side, wavy, reverting green foliage should be pruned out; young stems green. Includes 'Silver Milkboy', female (first reported flowers in 1988), 'Silver Milkmaid', female, date of origin unknown.

'Argentea Regina', see 'Silver Queen'.

'Ashford' (female; parent tree at Ashford's Farm, Thurloxton, Somerset, England; discovered, named, and introduced by G. P. Brown in the 1980s).
  Leaves dark olive green, broadly elliptic, 6.5–7.5 cm (2½–3 in.) long, 3.8–5 cm (1½–2 in.) wide, strong spines on each side, young foliage red; fruits red; vigorous upright habit. Similar to 'Broomfield'.

'Astoria', see 'Beacon'.

'Atkinson', see *I. × altaclerensis* 'Atkinson'.

'Atlas' (male; seedling selected and introduced in 1961 by Proefstation voor de Boomwerkerij).
  Leaves dark green, glossy, broadly elliptic, margins undulate, 2–6 spines on each side, stems green; dense compact, pyramidal habit, to 5–6 m (16–20 ft.) tall.

'Atrovirens Variegata', see *I. × altaclerensis* 'Atrovirens Variegata'.

Aurea Marginata Group
  A large group of female hollies with variegated leaves with yellow margins. Leaves dark olive green with gray-green mottling, margins irregular yellow edge, moderately narrow, usually strongly developed near apex, usually oblong-ovate, 6.5–7.5 cm (2½–3 in.) long, 3.8 cm (1½ in.) wide, spines stout, wavy, stems purple; dense compact habit; not free fruiting.

'Aurea Marginata Ovata', see 'Ovata Aurea'.

'Aurea Marginata Pendula' (female; synonym 'Aurea Pendula', 'Gold Weeping', 'Pendula Aurea Marginata', 'Waterer's Golden Weeping'; from Waterer's Nursery, England, about 1875).
  Leaves variegated, margins brilliant yellow 11A,

dark green centers, oval to elliptic, 4.5–5 cm (1¾–2 in.) long, 2–2.5 cm (¾–1 in.) wide, bases obtuse, margins usually flat, 5–7 spines on each side, petioles 5–6 mm (³⁄₁₆–⁷⁄₃₂ in.) long, stems purplish; fruits vivid red 45A, globose, 6–8 mm (⁷⁄₃₂–⁵⁄₁₆ in.) diameter, pedicels reddish, 6–8 mm (⁷⁄₃₂–⁵⁄₁₆ in.) long; pendulous habit of growth.

Aurea Medio-Picta Group

An attractive group of selections that originated as sports on green-leaved types. Leaves vary as to size, coloration, and spines and are irregularly marked with a large yellowish blotch in the center that often occupies more than half of the surface, while the margins are an irregular glossy dark green. Under various names such as 'Golden Butterfly' (female); 'Golden Milkmaid' (female); 'Golden Milkboy' (male); 'Harlequin' (female).

'Aurea Picta Latifolia' (synonym 'Aurea Medio-Picta Latifolia').

A selected clone form 'Golden Milkmaid', known before 1876, leaves large and flattened.

'Aurea Regina', see 'Golden Queen'.

'Aurifodina' (female; synonyms 'Bicolor', 'Muricata'; old cultivar from England, first introduced in 1863, known as smudge holly).

Leaves variegated, dark olive green in center, heavily streaked or blotched with gray or yellowish green, turning light brownish yellow in winter, margins irregular yellowish green, ovate or oblong-ovate, 4.5–6.5 cm (1¾–2½ in.) long, 2–2.5 cm (¾–1 in.) wide, margins fairly flat, spiny, stems reddish green; fruits red.

'Bacciflava' (female; synonyms 'Chrysocarpa', 'Frutu Luteo', 'Xanthocarpa'; very old cultivar, first mentioned in 1775 by Richard Weston in *Flora Anglicana*, England; earliest reference to a yellow-fruited *I. aquifolium* is 1657, both 'Bacciflava' and 'Frutu Luteo' have been known for a long time and are impossible to tell apart).

Leaves dark olive green, elliptic, 6.5–8 cm (2½–3⅛ in.) long, 2.5–3 cm (1–1³⁄₁₆ in.) wide, bases obtuse, 3–5 spines on each side, often subentire, petioles 10 mm (⅜ in.) long, stems green; fruits brilliant greenish yellow 7B, globose, 8 mm (⁵⁄₁₆ in.) diameter, 3–5 in clusters.

'Baden' (female; introduced in early 1960s by Heatherfells Nursery, Andover, Massachusetts).

Leaves dark olive green, margins spiny; fruits red; erect growth. Selected for hardiness.

'Balearica', see *I. × altaclerensis* 'Balearica'.

'Balkans', see *I. × altaclerensis* 'Balkans'.

'Barnes' (male; sport of 'Angustifolia'; selected by H. G. Mattoon).

Leaves small, quadrangular shaped, 5–7 divaricate spines on each side; good pollinator.

'Barbarossa' (female; cross of 'Cottage Queen' × 'Little Bull' in 1956 by M. A. Nosal; selected, named, and registered H.S.A. 5-71 by Nosal).

Leaves dark olive green, glossy, oval to broadly elliptic, 6–7 cm (2⅜–2¾ in.) long, 3.5–4 cm (1⅜–1⁹⁄₁₆ in.) wide, bases rotund, apices acuminate, tip spines reflexed, margins undulate, 6–8 spines on each side, petioles 10 mm (⅜ in.) long; fruits vivid red 44A, globose to slightly pyriform, 8–10 mm (⁵⁄₁₆–⅜ in.) diameter; pyramidal habit.

'Bayley's Pride' (female; from Bayley Orchard; plant at North Willamette Experimental Research and Extension Center, Canby, Oregon).

Leaves dark green, glossy, margins spiny; fruits red, abundant; upright pyramidal habit.

'Beacon' (female; synonym 'Astoria'; selected 1946 in Astoria, Oregon, by J. S. Wieman; registered H.S.A. 10-61 by Wieman).

Leaves dark olive green, glossy, ovate, 4–6.5 cm (1⅝–2½ in.) long, 2–2.5 cm (¾–1 in.) wide, bases rotund to truncate, apices acuminate, tip spines reflexed, margins undulate, 5–8 strong spines on each side, petioles stout, 5–8 mm (³⁄₁₆–⁵⁄₁₆ in.) long, stems purplish; fruits vivid red 45A, globose, 8–10 mm (⁵⁄₁₆–⅜ in.) diameter, pedicels reddish, 8 mm (⁵⁄₁₆ in.) long; fruits ripen early, consistent fruiting; pyramidal habit. Good for sprays and boutonnieres. Plate 88.

'Beadle's Spiny Leaf' (female; from Ten Oaks Nursery in the 1960s).

Leaves dark green, glossy, margins spiny; fruits red, abundant.

'Beads of Gold' (female; seedling selected by J. van Alphen, Voorschoten, Netherlands; grown for a number of years; named in 1987; distributed by Darthuizer Nursery).

Leaves dark green, glossy; fruits yellow; compact, large pyramidal shrub, 5–7 m (16–23 ft.) high. Reported similar to 'Bacciflava'.

'Beautyspra' (female; discovered about 1930 at Wieman Nursery, Knappa-Swensen, Oregon, by J. S. Wieman; registered H.S.A. 11-61 by Wieman).

Leaves dark olive green, glossy, elliptic, 5–6.5 cm

(2–2½ in.) long, 1.5–2.5 cm (¹⁹⁄₃₂–1 in.) wide, margins wavy, 5–6 spines on each side, petioles 5–7 mm (³⁄₁₆–⁹⁄₃₂ in.) long; fruits vivid red 45A to 46A, globose, 6–8 mm (⁷⁄₃₂–⁵⁄₁₆ in.) diameter, pedicels 5–8 mm (³⁄₁₆–⁵⁄₁₆ in.) long; fruit ripens early. Recommended for orcharding and landscaping. Plate 89.

'Beetii' (old cultivar, before 1808, selected at Handsworth Nursery, England).
    Leaves dark olive green, glossy, short and wide, nearly oval, about 3.8 cm (1½ in.) long, 4.5 cm (1¾ in.) wide, margins thick, 3–4 long divaricate spines on each side. Distinct short blunt leaves. Reported no longer in cultivation.

'Belgica', see *I.* × *altaclerensis* 'Belgica'.

'Bella' (reported sport of 'J. C. van Tol'; from Germany; reported by Susyn Andrews to be intermediate stage of reversion from 'Angustifolia').

'Berigold' (female; synonym 'Bacciflava'; named and introduced by A. Brownell in the 1960s).
    Leaves dark olive green, broadly elliptic, 5–6 cm (2–2⅜ in.) long, 3 cm (1³⁄₁₆ in.) wide, bases obtuse, margins recurved, wavy, 3–5 spines on each side, occasionally subentire, petioles 10 mm (⅜ in.) long, stems green; fruits brilliant greenish yellow 3A, depressed globose, 7 mm (⁹⁄₃₂ in.) long, 9 mm (¹¹⁄₃₂ in.) diameter, pedicels 8 mm (⁵⁄₁₆ in.) long.

'Berlicum Beauty' (female; seedling discovered in 1984 by C. Esveld; original seedling found in a large bed of holly in a public park in Berlicum, Netherlands; to be introduced).
    Leaves dark green, glossy, sharp spines, stems green; fruits red, elongated or ellipsoid, abundant, persist until spring; pyramidal habit, 5–7 m (16–23 ft.) high.

'Berystede' (male; seedling origin, possibly from Clarendon Gardens in the 1960s).
    Leaves dark olive green, oval, 6.5 cm (2½ in.) long, 7–9 spines on each side. Very similar to 'Colburn'.

'Betty Brite' (female; synonym 'Gold Nugget'; mutation of 'Early Cluster'; selected and registered H.S.A. 1-86 by J. S. Wieman).
    Leaves variegated light gray green inside wide irregular vivid yellow 13B margins, broadly oval, to 13.2 cm (5⅛ in.) long, 8 cm (3⅛ in.) wide, 3–8 irregular divaricate spines on each side, tip spines reflexed, occasional small elliptic entire leaves, reversion to green is minimal; fruits dark red 46A, globose, 11 mm (⁷⁄₁₆ in.) diameter, to 8 in clusters, pedi-

Figure 15-4. *Ilex aquifolium* 'Bella' from Germany. Photo by Hans-Georg Buchtmann.

cels 11 mm (⁷⁄₁₆ in.) long. Recommended for tub and patio plants.

'Bicolor', see 'Aurifodina'.

'Big Bull' (male; synonym 'Teufel's Big Bull'; selected and introduced by Teufel Nursery in the 1960s).
    Leaves dark olive green, elliptic to broadly elliptic to oval, 5–7 cm (2–2¾ in.) long, 3–3.5 to 5 cm (1³⁄₁₆–1⅜ to 2 in.) wide, margins slightly wavy, entire to 1–3 spines on each side, upper half of leaf, petioles 10–13 mm (⅜–½ in.) long, stems green. Possibly a cultivar of *I.* × *altaclerensis*.

'Black Forest' (female; introduced about 1963 by Heatherfells Nursery, Andover, Massachusetts).
    Leaves dark green, margins spiny; fruits red; selected for hardiness.

'Bleeg Green' (male; from H. F. Bleeg Nursery; plant at North Willamette Experimental Research and Extension Center, Canby, Oregon).
    Leaves dark olive green, glossy, margins with many spines.

'Bonanza' (female; named and introduced by A. Brownell in the 1960s).
    Leaves dark olive green, elliptic to broadly elliptic, 5–6.5 cm (2–2½ in.) long, 2–3 cm (¾–1³⁄₁₆ in.) wide, bases rotund, margins wavy, 3–5 spines on each side, some leaves entire, petioles 6–8 mm (⁷⁄₃₂–⁵⁄₁₆ in.) long, stems purplish; fruits vivid red 45A, globose, 8–10 mm (⁵⁄₁₆–⅜ in.) diameter, pedicels 8 mm (⁵⁄₁₆ in.) long.

'Boulder Beau' (male; seedling of 'Boulder Creek'; selected and named by H. L. Elmore in the 1980s).

Leaves dark olive green, elliptic, 6–7.5 cm (2⅜–3 in.) long, 2–3 cm (¾–1³⁄₁₆ in.) wide, bases obtuse, margins undulate, 8–10 large spines on each side, tip spines reflexed, petioles 10–13 cm (⅜–½ in.) long; stems purplish.

'Boulder Creek' (female; introduced in 1957 by Leonard Coates Nursery; plant at the North Willamette Research and Extension Center, Canby, Oregon).

Leaves dark olive green, glossy, elliptic to oblong elliptic, 4.5–6 cm (1¾–2⅜ in.) long, 2.5–3 cm (1–1³⁄₁₆ in.) wide, bases cuneate to obtuse, margins wavy, 4–7 spines on each side, tip spines slightly reflexed, petioles 10–13 mm (⅜–½ in.) long; fruits vivid red 45A, globose, 8 mm (⁵⁄₁₆ in.) diameter, abundant, pedicels 5 mm (³⁄₁₆ in.) long.

'Bronze' (female; synonym 'Flavescens', which see; introduced by W. C. Slocock, Goldsworth Nursery; imported to United States by A. Brownell in the 1950s).

'Broomfield' (female; original tree in church yard at Broomfield, Quantock Hills, near Taunton, Somerset, England; discovered, named, and introduced by G. P. Brown in the 1980s).

Leaves dark olive green, broadly elliptic, strong spines on each side; fruits red. Similar to 'Ashford' but with green foliage.

'Brownell's Silver Princess' (name given by A. Brownell in the 1960s; synonym 'Silvary', which see).

'Brownell's Special' (female; selected and introduced by A. Brownell in or before 1960s).

Leaves dark olive green, glossy, elliptic to oval, 6–7 cm (2⅜–2¾ in.) long, 3–3.5 cm (1³⁄₁₆–1⅜ in.) wide, bases obtuse to rotund, margins reflexed, 6–9 spines on each side, stems purplish; fruits vivid red, depressed globose, 10 mm (⅜ in.) long, 12 mm (¹⁵⁄₃₂ in.) diameter, pedicels pinkish, 7–11 mm (⁹⁄₃₂–⁷⁄₁₆ in.) long; heavy bearer.

'Butler' (female; selected by A. N. Adams; introduced around 1954 by Ten Oaks Nursery).

Leaves dark olive green, glossy, margins spiny; fruits dark red, large.

'Callison' (female; selected by N. A. Callison in late 1940s; plant at North Willamette Research and Extension Center, Canby, Oregon).

Leaves moderate olive green, elliptic to oval, 5–6 cm (2–2⅜ in.) long, 2.5–3.5 cm (1–1⅜ in.) wide, bases obtuse to rotund, margins wavy, slightly twisted, entire to 1–3 small spines on each side, upper half of leaf; fruits deep reddish orange 43A, 10 mm (⅜ in.) diameter, pedicels 6–8 mm (⁷⁄₃₂–⁵⁄₁₆ in.) long; good fruit clusters.

'Camelliifolia', see *I. × altaclerensis*.

'Campus Variegated' (female; seedling on Oregon State University campus, Corvallis, Oregon, propagated by horticulture students in late 1940s; plant also at North Willamette Experimental Research and Extension Center, Canby, Oregon).

Leaves variegated, dark olive green, margins vivid yellow, 12A, oval 5–6 cm (2–2⅜ in.) long, 3–3.5 cm (1³⁄₁₆–1⅜ in.) wide, bases obtuse to rotund, margins nearly flat, subentire to 1–4 spines on each side, upper half of leaf, petioles 8 mm (⁵⁄₁₆ in.) long; fruits vivid red 45A, globose, 8–10 mm (⁵⁄₁₆–⅜ in.) diameter, pedicels reddish, 8 mm (⁵⁄₁₆ in.) long.

'Canadian Gold' (male?; seedling discovered in 1978 by G. Bock in a planting in Vancouver, British Columbia, Canada; introduced to Boskoop, Netherlands, by C. Klijn and Company).

Leaves variegated, golden yellow, broadly oval, 4–6 cm (1⅝–2⅜ in.) long, 2–4 cm (¾–1⅝ in.) wide, margins flat, sparsely spined. Better yellow foliage than 'Flavescens'; excellent winter hardiness.

'Captain Berggreen' (female; introduced around 1974 by the late E. Pederson).

Leaves dark olive green, glossy, elliptic, 6–8 cm (2⅜–3⅛ in.) long, 3–4 cm (1³⁄₁₆–1⅝ in.) wide, margins wavy, 5–7 strong spines on each side, petioles stout, slightly purple, 8–10 mm (⁵⁄₁₆–⅜ in.) long, stems purplish; fruits dark red, globose, 9–10 mm (¹¹⁄₃₂–⅜ in.) diameter, pedicels 5–6 mm (³⁄₁₆–⁷⁄₃₂ in.) long; strong upright pyramidal habit; hardy to −20°C (−4°F).

'Captain Bonneville' (male; found near Bonneville Dam in Oregon; introduced by A. Brownell in the 1960s).

Leaves dark olive green, oval to broadly elliptic, 6.5–8.5 cm (2½–3⅜ in.) long, 3–4 cm (1³⁄₁₆–1⅝ in.) wide, bases rotund, margins undulate, 4–6 strong spines on each side, petioles 10–12 mm (⅜–½ in.) long, stems green.

'Carpenello' (female; origin unknown; introduced around 1950s by Perkins de Wilde Nursery).

Leaves dark green, small spines; fruits red.

'Chambers' (female; plant at Washington Park Arboretum, Seattle, Washington, obtained from W. B. Clarke Nursery in 1952; listed in Clarke's catalog 1948).

Leaves dark olive green, elliptic, 6.5–8 cm (2½–3⅛ in.) long, 2.5–3.5 cm (1–1⅜ in.) wide, bases obtuse to rotund, margins wavy, 5–7 spines on each side, tip spines reflexed, stems purple; fruits deep reddish orange 43A, globose, 10 mm (⅜ in.) diameter, pedicels 6–8 mm (7⁄32–5⁄16 in.) long.

'Chameleon' (female; volunteer seedling described by J. S. Wieman in 1977; named and registered H.S.A.3-85 by Wieman).

Leaves dark olive green, ovate, large, 8.3 cm (3¼ in.) long, 6.5 cm (2½ in.) wide, margins unevenly divaricate, 4–7 sharp spines on each side, deeply rounded sinuses, 1 cm (⅜ in.) between spines, tip spines reflexed down, often twisted, stems dark extending into petioles and leaf blade, petioles dark, 6 mm (7⁄32 in.) long; fruits deep reddish orange 43A, elongate, 13 mm (½ in.) long, 11 mm (7⁄16 in.) diameter, pedicels 5 mm (3⅙ in.) long, fasciculate 1–4 branched; oval habit, erect branches; original plant at 8 years 2.1 m (7 ft.) tall, 1.5 m (5 ft.) wide. Hardy in zone 7a. Selected because of distinctive leaf coloration.

'Charlie Olivet' (female; selected from among 600 seedlings by Charlie Olivet before 1950; plant moved to University Maryland Experiment Station, Montgomery County, Maryland, for testing in the 1960s).

Selected for cold hardiness.

'Cherryberry', see *I.* × *altaclerensis* 'Cherryberry'.

'Christmas Eve' (female; selected from seedling tree in Tacoma, Washington, by W. E. De Mille; plant at North Willamette Experimental Research and Extension Center, Canby, Oregon).

Leaves moderate to dark olive green, oval, 6–7 cm (2⅜–2¾ in.) long, 3.5–4.5 cm (1⅜–1¾ in.) wide, bases obtuse to rotund, margins wavy, subentire to 2–4 spines on each side, stems purple, petioles 8–10 mm (5⁄16–⅜ in.) long; fruits deep reddish orange 43A, globose, 10–12 mm (⅜–½ in.) diameter, pedicels reddish, 8 mm (5⁄16 in.) long; good fruit clusters.

'Ciliata' (male; synonym 'Ciliata Minor'; old cultivar from England before 1826).

Leaves dark olive green, glossy, often tinged olive brown, ovate or lanceolate, 3–4 cm (1 3⁄16–1⅝ in.) long, rarely longer, 1.4–2 cm (½–¾ in.) wide, 5–9 small spines pointing forward, like fringe, on each side; stems dark purple.

'Ciliata Major' (female; old cultivar before 1863 from England).

Leaves dark olive green, ovate-elliptic, to 9 cm (3½ in.) long, 4 cm (1⅝ in.) wide, flattish, 5–9 spines pointing forward on each side, base usually entire, occasionally leaves entire; stems purplish.

'Clarendon Type C' (female; probably introduced by Clarendon Gardens; plant at Ebersole Gardens).

Leaves dark olive green, oval to elliptic, 4.5–6 cm (1¾–2⅜ in.) long, 2–3.2 cm (¾–1¼ in.) wide, bases obtuse to truncate, apices acuminate, tip spines reflexed, margins undulate, wavy, 5–7 spines on each side, petioles 5–7 mm (3⁄16–9⁄32 in.) long, stems purplish; fruits red, globose.

'Clouded Gold' (synonym 'Flavescens', which see; imported by A. Brownell in or before 1960).

'Colburn', see *I.* × *altaclerensis* 'Colburn'.

'Cookii' (female; synonym 'Obscura'; old cultivar from England before 1863).

Leaves variegated, dark green, marbled and spotted gray green, conspicuous small speckling, narrow yellowish green margins, ovate, 3–5 cm (1 3⁄16–2 in.) long, 2–3 cm (¾–1 3⁄16 in.) wide, margins flat, distinct but weak spines, stems purple; fruits reddish orange, free fruiting.

'Cornish Cream' (sex and origin unknown, from Europe; Argentea Marginata Group);

Leaves variegated, dark green margins, large irregular yellow blotch in center, ovate, 3.5 cm (1⅜ in.) long, 2.5 cm (1 in.) wide, margins undulate, 4–5 spines on each side, bases obtuse to nearly truncate, petioles 6 mm (7⁄32 in.) long. Similar to 'Somerset Cream'.

'Coronation' (female; synonym 'Leach's 600'; selected by R. Leach; plant at North Willamette Research and Extension Center, Canby, Oregon).

Leaves dark olive green elliptic, 5.5–8 cm (2⅛–3⅛ in.) long, 3–3.5 cm (1 3⁄16–1⅜ in.) wide, bases cuneate to obtuse, margins with 3–5 spines on each side, often entire or with 1–3 spines near apex, petioles 10 mm (⅜ in.) long, stems purplish; fruits deep reddish orange 43A, ellipsoid, 12 mm (½ in.) long,

8–10 mm (⁵⁄₁₆–³⁄₈ in.) diameter, pedicels reddish; good fruit clusters.

'Cottage Queen' (female; seedling selected 1930 by E. A. Nosal; seed from Cottage Gardens; named and registered H.S.A. 10-70 by M. A. Nosal).

Leaves dark dull green, ovate-elliptic, 5–7 cm (2–2¾ in.) long, 2.5–4 cm (1–1⅝ in.) wide, bases obtuse to rotund, apices acute, margins irregularly wavy, spines variable, long pointed, usually 4–6 on each side, rarely subentire, petioles 10 mm (³⁄₈ in.) long, stems green; fruits vivid red 45A, pyriform, 10–12 mm (³⁄₈–¹⁵⁄₃₂ in.) diameter, 1–6 in cluster, pedicels reddish, 3–5 mm (⅛–³⁄₁₆ in.) long; broadly conical habit, 3.7 m × 3 m (12 × 10 ft.) wide in 40 years; hardy to −29°C (−20°F).

'Covergirl' (female; synonym 'Wieman's Covergirl'; origin confusing; plant owned by A. M. Erickson; seedling selection 1949 by J. S. Wieman; named and registered H.S.A. 3-64).

Leaves dark olive green, small, 3.8 cm (1½ in.) long, 2 cm (¾ in.) wide; fruits vivid red, good clusters; compact dense, broad mounding habit.

'Crassifolia'. Leather-leaf holly (female; synonym 'Serrata'; old selection from England first described in 1770).

Leaves dark olive green, lanceolate, 4.5–6 cm (1¾–2⅜ in.) long, 1–1.5 cm (³⁄₈–½ in.) wide, thick and leathery, margins wavy, slightly twisted, 5–10 spines on each side, deeply undulated, tip spines reflexed downward, petioles 4–6 mm (⁵⁄₃₂–⁷⁄₃₂ in.) long, stems purplish; fruits flattened globose; slow growing. Some consider this cultivar grotesque and unattractive; others, however, find the leaves most unusual and interesting.

'Crinkle Green Sport', see 'Crinkle Variegated'.

'Crinkle Variegated' (female; synonyms 'Crinkle Green Sport', 'Wieman's Crinkle Variegated'; origin as a mutation on a silver variegated plant; selected, named, and registered H.S.A. 10-76 by J. S. Wieman).

Leaves variegated, irregular yellow blotch in the center, margins dark olive green, elliptic, 9.5 cm (3¾ in.) long, 4.5 cm (1¾ in.) wide, margins wavy, 6–8 strong spines on each side, often perpendicular to margin, petioles 13 mm (½ in.) long; fruits red; broadly conical habit with upright branches.

'Crispa' (male; synonyms 'Calamistrata', 'Contorta', 'Tortuosa'; an old selection first described in 1838; reported as a sport of 'Ferox').

Leaves dark olive green, glossy, extremely variable,

elliptic, 5–6 cm (2–2⅜ in.) long, 2.5–3 cm (1–1³⁄₁₆ in.) wide, leaves spirally twisted and contorted, margins thickened usually entire, occasionally 1–2 small spines near apex, tip spines twisted, reflexed downward, petioles 6–8 mm (⁷⁄₃₂–⁵⁄₁₆ in.) long; stems purplish.

'Crispa Aurea-Picta' (male; synonyms 'Contorta Aurea Picta', 'Crispa Aurea Maculata', 'Marginata Aureo Picta', 'Tortuosa Aureo-Picta'; an old selection from England before 1854; reported as a sport of 'Ferox Aurea').

Leaves twisted and contorted as in 'Crispa', dark olive green with the center marbled pale gray green and vivid yellow 15B, the yellow predominately near the base, stems purplish.

'Daddy O' (male; plant at Scott Arboretum, Swarthmore, Pennsylvania, and U.S. National Arboretum).

Leaves dark olive green, glossy, elliptic, 5.5–6 cm (2⅛–2⅜ in.) long, 2.5 cm wide (1 in.) wide, margins wavy, 4–5 spines each side, 1-year spines relaxed; petioles 10 mm (³⁄₈ in.) long; abundant flowers.

'Dandy' (male; synonym 'Manly Gold'; selected and introduced by J. S. Wieman in the late 1960s; similar to 'Flavescens').

Leaves variegated. Good pollinator for 'Moonbrite' and 'Night Glow'.

'Dapper' (male; chance seedling discovered by J. S. Wieman at his residence; introduced about 1978; named 1989; registered H.S.A. 3-94).

Leaves variegated, dark centers 131A, narrow light yellow 12C, margins, ovate to elliptic, to 6 cm (2⅜ in.) long, to 5 cm (2 in.) wide, tips aristate, reflexed down, bases truncate; broadly conical habit, slow growing, parent tree 2.1 m (78 in.) tall, 0.15 m (6 in.) wide. Possibly hardy in zone 7. May be suitable for container culture and bonsai.

'Davis' (female; origin unknown; possibly from Clarendon Gardens in the 1960s).

Leaves slender; fruits red, globose; compact habit.

'Decatur' (sex and origin unknown; plant at Holly Haven Nursery, Knoxville, Tennessee).

Leaves dark olive green, elliptic to broadly elliptic, 5.5–6.5 cm (2⅛–2½ in.) long, 2.5–3 cm (1–1³⁄₁₆ in.) wide, bases cuneate to obtuse, margins undulate, 7–10 spines on each side, petioles 8–10 mm (⁵⁄₁₆–³⁄₈ in.) long, stems purplish.

'Deletta' (female; chance seedling discovered about 1939; registered H.S.A 8-88 by R. K. Peters; introduced by Bull Valley Nursery, Aspers, Pennsylvania;

sibling to 'Winter Green' H.S.A. 1-87 and 'New Brunswick').

Leaves dark olive green, glossy, elliptic, curved, 5–7.6 cm (2–3 in.) long, 2–3.5 cm (¾–1⅜ in.) wide, tip spines reflexed downward, bases rotund, apices acuminate, tip spines reflexed, margins undulate, 7–8 stout spines evenly spaced on each side, petioles 6.5 mm (¼ in.) long; young twigs and petioles reddish on upper surface when mature; fruits vivid reddish orange 44A, obovoid, 11 mm (⁷⁄₁₆ in.) long, 5 mm (³⁄₁₆ in.) diameter, fasciculate 2–5 on peduncles 5 mm (³⁄₁₆ in.) long, heavy fruiting; original tree approximately 10 years old, broadly compact, conical, 1.8 m (6 ft.) tall, 1.2 m (4 ft.) wide; hardy in zone 6.

'Deluxe' (female; selected in 1935 by G. Teufel).

Leaves dark olive green, broadly elliptic, 7–9 cm (2¾–3½ in.) long, 4–5 cm (1⅝–2 in.) wide, bases cuneate, margins wavy, entire or with a few spines near apex, petioles 10–12 mm (⅜–½ in.) long, stems green; fruits deep reddish orange 43A, globose, 10–12 mm (⅜–½ in.) diameter, pedicels reddish, 10 mm (⅜ in.) long. Selected for orchards and landscaping.

'Dickinson' (male; origin unknown; plant at Scott Arboretum, Swarthmore, Pennsylvania; received from Clarendon Gardens in 1957).

Leaves dark olive green, oblong to elliptic, 5–7 cm (2–2¾ in.) long, 3–3.5 cm (1³⁄₁₆–1⅜ in.) wide, bases rotund, margins wavy, usually entire, rarely 1–2 small spines near apex, tip spines reflexed, petioles stout, 10–13 mm (⅜–⅓ in.) long, stems dark. Possibly *I. × altaclerensis*.

'Donningtonensis' (male; old cultivar said from and introduced by Fisher, Son, and Sibray; earliest reference 1861).

Leaves black green, narrow-oblong to lanceolate, often with lance-shaped or sicklelike apices, to 5 cm (2 in.) long, 1.3–2 cm (½–¾ in.) wide, bases occasionally with falcate lobes on young plants, margins usually entire, occasionally 1–5 erratic strong divaricate spines, stems purple. Uncommon in United States.

'Doralee Creek' (male; origin unknown, records lost; plant at North Carolina State University Arboretum).

Leaves dark olive green, glossy, oblong to elliptic, 4–5.5 cm (1⅝–2⅛ in.) long, 1.5–2.5 cm (¹⁹⁄₃₂–1 in.) wide, bases obtuse to truncate, apices acute, tip spines reflexed, usually twisted, margins undulate, 5–6 strong spines on each side, petioles stout, 8 mm (⁵⁄₁₆ in.) long, stems green; vigorous, pyramidal habit.

'Doug Barbour' (male; volunteer seedling about 1976 in garden of R. K. Peters; female parent 'Martha Lower', sibling of 'Deletta', 'Mary Peters', 'New Brunswick', 'Winter Green'; selected, named, and registered H.S.A. 7-89 by Peters; introduced 1990).

Leaves dark olive green, flat, ovate to elliptic, to 9.5 cm (3¾ in.) long, 4 cm (1⅝ in.) wide, bases cuneate to obtuse, tip spines reflexed, 7–9 spines on each side, petioles 10 mm (⅜ in.) long; conical dense habit; original tree 1.4 m (4 ft.) tall, 0.9 m (3 ft.) wide, in 14 years; hardy in zone 5b.

'Dr. Davis' (female; synonym 'Dr. Davis Silver Variegated', illegitimate name with 4 elements; origin unknown; named by Dr. Davis).

Leaves variegated, light yellow 10A margin, center dark green, oval to elliptic, 5–6 cm (2–2⅜ in.) long, 2.2–3 cm (¹³⁄₁₆–1³⁄₁₆ in.) wide, bases cuneate to obtuse, margins wavy, twisted, 5–6 spines on each side, petioles 10 mm (⅜ in.) long, stems green; fruits vivid red 45A, ellipsoid, 10 mm (⅜ in.) long, 8 mm (⁵⁄₁₆ in.) diameter, pedicels 8 mm (⁵⁄₁₆ in.) long.

'Dr. Huckleberry', see *I. × altaclerensis* 'Dr. Huckleberry'.

'Drew's Early' (female; synonym 'Drew's Early'; origin Drew's Nursery, Beaverton, Oregon).

Leaves elliptic to broadly elliptic, 5–7 cm (2–2¾ in.) long, 2.5–3.2 cm (1–1¼ in.) wide, bases obtuse to rotund, margins wavy, 5–6 spines on each side, tip spines reflexed, petioles 8–10 mm (⁵⁄₁₆–⅜ in.) long, stems purplish; fruits deep reddish orange 43A, globose, 8 mm (⁵⁄₁₆ in.) diameter, pedicels reddish, 8 mm (⁵⁄₁₆ in.) long.

'Dude' (male; synonym 'Wieman's Dude'; sport discovered in Gresham, Oregon, about 1935 by J. S. Wieman; named and registered H.S.A. 12-61 by Wieman).

Leaves variegated with yellow margin, center dark green to pale green, elliptic 4.5–9 cm (1¾–3½ in.) long, 2–3 cm (¾–1³⁄₁₆ in.) wide, bases cuneate to obtuse, margins undulate, 4–6 spines on each side, petioles 4–6 mm (⁵⁄₃₂–⁷⁄₃₂ in.) long, stems purplish; produces abundant pollen. Plate 90.

'Duke of Windsor' (male; before 1980; old plants grown on Long Island, New York; information and plant specimen from M. S. Whipple).

Leaves dark olive green, elliptic, 3.5–4.5 cm (1⅜–1¾ in.) long, 1.3–2 cm (½–¾ in.) wide, bases obtuse, apices acuminate, tip spines reflexed, margins undulate, 7–8 spines on each side, petioles 5 mm (³⁄₁₆ in.) long, stems green.

'Dumbarton Oaks' (female; origin unknown; plants at Dumbarton Oaks Gardens, Washington, D.C., and Planting Fields Arboretum).

Leaves dark olive green, elliptic, curved, 3–5 cm (1³⁄₁₆–2 in.) long, 1.3–2 cm (½–¾ in.) wide, bases obtuse, apices acute, tip spines slightly reflexed, margins undulate, distinct light yellowish white edge, 4–6 small spines on each side, petioles 5–6 mm (³⁄₁₆–⁷⁄₃₂ in.) long; fruits not observed.

Dutch Hybrid Group, see Pacific Northwest Hybrids below.

'Early Cluster' (female; synonyms 'Cluster', 'Wieman's Early Cluster'; introduced by J. S. Wieman in the 1960s).

Leaves dark olive green, elliptic to ovate-elliptic, 4–7.5 cm (1⅝–3 in.) long, 2–3.5 cm (¾–1⅜ in.) wide, bases obtuse to rotund, apices acute, tip spines reflexed, margins undulate, 4–8 strong spines on each side, petioles stout, 8–10 mm (⁵⁄₁₆–⅜ in.) long, stems green; fruits red, early, in good clusters.

'Early Commercial' (female; seedling in Bayley Orchard; possibly same as 'Firecracker' named by A. Brownell).

Leaves dark olive green, elliptic, 6.5–8 (2½–3⅛ in.) long, 2.5–3 cm (1–1³⁄₁₆ in.) wide, bases cuneate, margins wavy, 2–4 spines on each side, usually on upper half of leaf, occasionally subentire to entire, petioles reddish, 8–10 mm (⁵⁄₁₆–⅜ in.) long; fruits dark reddish orange 43A, globose, 8 mm (⁵⁄₁₆ in.) diameter, pedicels 6–8 mm (⁷⁄₃₂–⁵⁄₁₆ in.) long, good fruit clusters.

'Earlygold' (female; marginal variegated sport of 'Zero'; introduced and registered H.S.A. 8-59 by G. Teufel).

Leaves variegated, dark olive green, margins yellow, similar to 'Lily Gold' in foliage and color; fruits vivid red, early ripening. Reported to be hardiest form of Aureo-Marginata Group. Plate 91.

'Echo' (female; sport of 'Angustifolia'; introduced by A. Brownell in or before 1960).

Leaves dark olive green, elliptic, 4.5–5.5 cm (1¾–2⅛ in.) long, 2–2.5 cm (¾–1 in.) wide, bases cuneate, margins variable, wavy, 2–4 spines on each side, petioles 8–10 mm (⁵⁄₁₆–⅜ in.) long; fruits red, globose, 6–8 mm (⁷⁄₃₂–⁵⁄₁₆ in.) diameter.

'Eldridge', see *I.* × *altaclerensis* 'Eldridge'.

'Elegantissima' (male; synonym 'Argentea Marginata Elegantissima'; old cultivar from England before 1863).

Leaves variegated, dark green with gray-green mottling in center, undulate margins yellowish white, wavy, oblong to elliptic, 5–6.5 cm (2–2½ in.) long, numerous spines, young foliage pink, stems green, streaked with white.

'Erwin Seedling' (female; plant at North Willamette Research and Extension Center, Canby, Oregon).

Leaves dark olive green, elliptic, 5.5–6 cm (2⅛–2⅜ in.) long, 2.5–3 cm (1–1³⁄₁₆ in.) wide, margins wavy, 5–6 spines on each side, petioles 5–6 mm (³⁄₁₆–⁷⁄₃₂ in.) long; fruits vivid red 45B, globose, 10 mm (⅜ in.) diameter, pedicels 4–5 mm (⁵⁄₃₂–³⁄₁₆ in.) long.

'Escort' (male; synonym 'Brownell's Escort'; selected and introduced in 1935 by A. Brownell).

Leaves dark olive green, broadly elliptic, 6.5–7 cm (2½–2¾ in.) long, 2–3 cm (¾–1³⁄₁₆ in.) wide, bases rotund to truncate, margins undulate, 5–6 spines on each side, petioles 8–10 mm (⁵⁄₁₆–⅜ in.) long; stems dark green. Good pollinizer. Often listed as a clone of *I.* × *altaclerensis*.

'Evangeline' (female; synonyms 'Hazel's Wheeler Ax', 'Whitney Ax'; registered H.S.A. 15-60 by J. K. Lilly; Whitney Holly Group; originated on G. G. Whitney estate, Woods Hole, Massachusetts).

Leaves dark olive green, oval, 5–6 cm (2–2⅜ in.) long, 3–3.5 cm (1³⁄₁₆–1⅜ in.) wide, bases obtuse, margins slightly wavy, variable, entire to 3–5 spines on each side, near apex, tip spines slightly reflexed; petioles 6–8 mm (⁷⁄₃₂–⁵⁄₁₆ in.) long, stems green; fruits vivid red 45A, globose, 8 mm (⁵⁄₁₆ in.) diameter; pedicels reddish, 5 mm (³⁄₁₆ in.) long; reported very hardy.

'Father Charles', see *I.* × *altaclerensis* 'Father Charles'.

'Favorite', see *I.* × *altaclerensis* 'Wieman's Favorite'.

'Ferox' (sterile male; synonym 'Echinata'; the oldest identifiable holly cultivar still in cultivation, first reference in 1635; conflicting reports as to origin. one found in the wild in France and introduced to England by J. C. Loudon, also mentioned by P. Miller in 1731 as coming from Canada; described in 1640 by J. Parkinson as "a holly with leaves wholly prickly").

Leaves dark olive green, ovate-oblong, 5–7 cm (2–2¾ in.) long, 2–2.5 cm (¾–1 in.) wide, margins recurved, wavy, 5–7 spines, recurved surface covered with short, sharp, erect, spines, petioles 5 mm (³⁄₁₆ in.) long; stems purplish.

'Ferox Argentea' (sterile male; synonyms 'Echinatum Argentea Marginata', 'Ferox Argentea Mar-

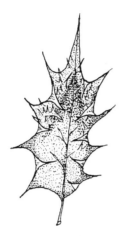

Figure 15-5. *Ilex aquifolium* 'Ferox'. Drawing by Randy Allen.

ginata'; old cultivar in England; first reported in 1662).

Leaves variegated with yellowish white margin; size, shape, and spines same as 'Ferox'; most spines yellowish white; stems purplish. Plate 92.

'Ferox Aurea' (sterile male; synonym 'Ferox Aureapicta'; old English cultivar before 1760).

Leaves similar to 'Ferox', margins dark olive green, conspicuous yellow green blotch in center near the base; stems purplish.

'Firecracker' (female; synonym 'Brownell's Firecracker'; selected and introduced in 1935 by A. Brownell).

Leaves dark olive green, elliptic, 7–8 cm (2¾–3⅛ in.) long, 3–3.5 cm (1³⁄₁₆–1⅜ in.) wide, margins wavy, 4–6 spines on each side, tip spines reflexed, petioles 10 mm (⅜ in.) long, stems purplish; fruits deep reddish orange 43A, ellipsoid, 10 mm (⅜ in.) long, 8 mm (⁵⁄₁₆ in.) diameter, pedicels reddish, 10 mm (⅜ in.) long; early abundant producer. Possibly the same as 'Early Commercial'. Plate 93.

'Firelight' (female; named and introduced by A. Brownell; description from Brownell catalog 1950; Dutch Hybrid Group).

Leaves slender, soft; fruits red. Similar to 'Platyphylla Pallida'.

'Fisheri' (male; old cultivar selected and introduced before 1863 by Fisher, Son, and Sibray, but never mentioned in its catalogs).

Leaves dark olive green, ovate, about 6.5 cm (2½ in.) long, 3.2 cm (1¼ in.) wide, apices acuminate, margins wavy, 2–6 large spines on each side, occasionally entire, stems usually green. Plate 94.

'Fisher's Island' (male; origin unknown, one of 3 male plants used by K. Meserve for hybridizing of *I.* × *meserveae*).

No plant or description available.

'Flavescens' (female; synonyms 'Aurantiaca', 'Bronze', 'Lutescens', 'Moonlight'; old cultivar from England; earliest reference 1861).

Leaves with variable yellow variegation, margins irregular brilliant yellow 12B, often extending over the upper half of leaf, broadly elliptic, 5–7 cm (2–2¾ in.) long, 2.5–3 cm (1–1³⁄₁₆ in.) wide, petioles 6–8 mm (⁷⁄₃₂–⁵⁄₁₆ in.) long, new leaves often entirely yellow, stems green; fruits deep reddish orange 43A, globose, 8 mm (⁵⁄₁₆ in.) diameter, 3–6 in clusters; pedicels reddish, 8 mm (⁵⁄₁₆ in.) long. Plate 95.

'Foxii' (male; old cultivar from England before 1863).

Leaves dark olive green, ovate to broadly elliptic, 6–8 cm (⁷⁄₃₂–⁵⁄₁₆ in.) long, 2.5–3 cm (1–1³⁄₁₆ in.) wide, bases cuneate to obtuse, margins often entire or 2–4 well-spaced spines on each side, tip spines reflexed, petioles 10–12 mm (⅜–½ in.) long, stems purplish. Resembles a long-spined 'Ovata'.

French-English Group

A group of variable hollies, variation depending on the source of propagating stock. Originally selected and propagated in the United States by P. H. Peyran of Hollycroft Gardens, Gig Harbor, Washington, from English hollies obtained in France. Trees fairly rapid growing with purplish stems and dark blue or purplish wood. Fruits red, flattened globose, late ripening. Many plants of this group tend to produce a high percentage of parthenocarpic fruits.

'Friesland' (female; discovered 1988 in South-Friesian beech forest by H.-G. Buchtmann).

Leaves dark olive green, glossy, elliptic, 5–9 cm (2–3½ in.) long, 2–3.5 cm (¾–1⅜ in.) wide, bases cuneate to obtuse, tip spines reflexed, margins undulate, 6–8 spines on each side, young stems purplish; fruits red; winter hardy.

'Fructo Alba' (female; synonyms 'Leucocarpa', var. *leucocarpa*; first reported in 1706, also 1719, 1754, 1872, 1892, 1915; detailed search made in 1970, late 1970s, and early 1980s but not found to date).

Fruit reported to be white.

'Fructu Aurantiaca' (female; synonyms 'Orange Berry', 'Orange Gem'; old cultivar from England before 1863).

Leaves dark green, glossy, elliptic, 5–7 cm (2–2¾ in.) long, 2.5–3 cm (1–1³⁄₁₆ in.) wide, 2–5 irregular spaced spines on each side, on upper half of leaf, occasionally subentire, tip spines reflexed, petioles 8–10 mm (⁵⁄₁₆–³⁄₈ in.) long, stems green or slightly purple; fruits vivid orange 25A, some blushed red, globose, 10–12 mm (³⁄₈–½ in.) diameter, pedicels 6–8 mm (⁷⁄₃₂–⁵⁄₁₆ in.) long; not free fruiting.

'Fructu Lutea' (female).

Leaves dark green, ovate to elliptic, 3.5–5 cm (1³⁄₈–2 in.) long, 1.8–2.5 cm (1¹⁄₁₆–1 in.) wide, bases obtuse to truncate, apices acute, tip spines reflexed, margins undulate, wavy, 3–5 (–7) strong spines on each side, petioles 5–8 mm (³⁄₁₆–⁵⁄₁₆ in.) long; fruits

Figure 15-6. *Ilex aquifolium* 'Friesland'. Photo by Hans-Georg Buchtmann.

brilliant yellow 13A, globose to slightly pyriform, 8 mm (⁵⁄₁₆ in.) diameter, color often blackens quickly after first heavy frost in United States, pedicels 5 mm (³⁄₁₆ in.) long. Plate 96.

Fructu Lutea Group

Earliest reference to a yellow-fruited English holly was discovered near Wardour Castle in Wiltshire, England, in 1657. 'Fructu Lutea' and 'Bacciflava' are the two epithets most commonly used today. It is impossible to tell them apart; both have dark green spiny leaves, green stems and petioles, rarely purplish; fruit color varies from pale yellow (almost cream) to brilliant yellow; reported in England to be retained for 2 seasons.

'George Daniel' (male; selected surviving seeding started by G. D. Peters from cut Oregon holly in 1980; named and registered H.S.A. 6-88 by R. K. Peters for G. D. Peters; introduced by Bull Valley Nursery, Aspers, Pennsylvania).

Leaves dark olive green, elliptic, 5–7.5 cm (2–3 in.) long, 2–3.75 cm (¾–1½ in.) wide, tip spines reflexed, bases rotund to truncate, apices acute, tip spines reflexed, margins undulate, 4–10 stout spines evenly spaced on each side, petioles green, 8 mm (⁵⁄₁₆ in.) long; young stems reddish on upper side; hardy in zone 6 to −18°C (0°F).

'Globe', see 'Wieman's Globe'.

'Gloria' (synonyms 'Wheeler No. 5', 'Whitney No. 5'), see Whitney Holly Group.

'Goldburst' (female; branch mutation of 'Wieman's Greenspread' discovered in 1978 by J. S. Wieman; registered H.S.A. 2-85 by Wieman).

Leaves variegated, irregular yellow streaking more or less in center, variable light green boarding yellow, margins dark green, broadly elliptic to ovate, 3.8 cm (1½ in.) long, 3.2 cm (1¼ in.) wide, margins undulate, 2–7 spines on each side, tip spines strongly reflexed, twisted to one side, petioles 11 mm (⁷⁄₁₆ in.) long, stems purplish; fruits vivid reddish orange 41A, globose to slightly elongate, 10 mm (³⁄₈ in.) diameter, 1–5 in clusters, pedicels 6.5 mm (¼ in.) long; broadly conical habit, erect branches.

Gold Coast™ (male; trademark for 'Monvilla'; variegated sport of 'Little Bull' discovered 1977 by R. Avila at Monrovia Nursery; PP No. 5143 by Monrovia Nursery).

Leaves variegated, center dark olive green, irregular margins of vivid greenish yellow 7A, narrow-elliptic to oblong elliptic, 2.5–4.5 cm (1–1¾ in.) long, 1.6–2 cm (⁵⁄₈–¾ in.) wide, bases cuneate, margins slightly wavy, 5–8 spines on each side, tip spines reflexed, petioles 5–7 mm (³⁄₁₆–⁹⁄₃₂ in.) long; stems dark purple; compact habit. Good pollinator. Plate 97.

'Goldedge' (female; synonym 'Golden Edge Variegated'; selected and introduced by J. S. Wieman before 1960).

Leaves variegated, margins vivid yellow 12A, dark green centers, elliptic, 5–6.5 cm (2–2½ in.) long, 2–2.5 cm (¾–1 in.) wide, bases obtuse, margins vary from entire to 3–5 spines on each side, tip spines twisted, reflexed, petioles 8 mm (⁵⁄₁₆ in.) long; fruits vivid red, ellipsoid to pyriform, 10 mm (³⁄₈ in.) long, 8 mm (⁵⁄₁₆ in.) diameter, pedicels reddish, 8–10 mm (⁵⁄₁₆–³⁄₈ in.) long.

'Golden Beauty' (no description or source).

'Golden Butterfly' (female; named and introduced by A. Brownell before 1960).

Figure 15-7. *Ilex aquifolium* 'Goldfrucht'. Photo by Hans-Georg Buchtmann.

Leaves variegated, irregular strong greenish yellow 153B, blotch in center, margins dark green, elliptic to broadly elliptic, 5–6.5 cm (2–2½ in.) long, 2.5–3.5 cm (1–1³⁄₈ in.) wide, margins wavy, 5–6 spines on each side, petioles 6 mm (⁷⁄₃₂ in.) long, stems green; fruits vivid red 45A, globose, 10 mm (³⁄₈ in.) diameter, good clusters.

'Golden Gate' (female; synonym 'Aurea Marginata Ovata'; introduced by A. Brownell before 1960).

Leaves variegated, margins irregular, pale yellow 13B, center dark olive green, oval, 5–6 cm (2–2³⁄₈ in.) long, 3.5–4 cm (1³⁄₈–1⁵⁄₈ in.) wide, 7–8 small spines on each side, stems purplish; fruits red, globose, 8 mm (⁵⁄₁₆ in.) diameter, pedicels 8 mm (⁵⁄₁₆ in.) long.

'Golden King' see *I.* × *altaclerensis* 'Golden King'.

'Golden Milkboy' (male; synonym 'Gold Milkboy').

Leaves variegated, large irregular, blotch of light yellow 10A, in the center, narrow irregular margins dark green, broadly elliptic to oval, flattened, 5.5–7.5 cm (2⅛–3 in.) long, 3–4.2 cm (1¹⁄₁₆–1¹¹⁄₁₆ in.) wide, bases cuneate to rotund, 4–5 spines on each side, petioles 10 mm (³⁄₈ in.) long; leaves close together around the stem. Also reported female. Plate 98.

'Golden Milkmaid' (female; synonyms 'Aurea Medio-Picta', 'Aurea Picta Spinosa', 'Gold Milkmaid'; old English selection before 1760).

Leaves variegated, large irregular blotch of greenish yellow in the center, margins irregular dark green, ovate to broadly elliptic, 5–6 cm (2–2³⁄₈ in.) long, 2.5–3 cm (1–1³⁄₁₆ in.) wide, bases cuneate to rotund, margins slightly wavy, 4–6 spines on each side, petioles 6 mm (⁷⁄₃₂ in.) long, stems purplish; fruits red, globose, 8 mm (⁵⁄₁₆ in.) diameter, pedicels 4–5 mm (⁵⁄₃₂–³⁄₁₆ in.) long.

'Golden Queen' (male; synonyms 'Aurea Regina', 'Elegans Aurea Marginata', 'Golden Variegated'; old popular cultivar from England before 1867; best gold-striped leaves).

Leaves large, variegated, dark olive green with pale and gray-green shading, broadly yellow margins, broadly ovate, 6.5–9 cm (2½–3 in.) long, 3.8–5 cm (1½–2 in.) wide, occasionally yellow on one side of midrib to completely yellow, margins spiny; stems green streaked yellow; vigorous habit. A.G.M. 1969.

'Golden van Tol' (female; sport of 'J. C. van Tol' discovered by W. Ravenstein and Sons, Boskoop, Netherlands, 1960).

Leaves variegated, dark green centers, margins yellow. Received F.C.C. 1969 at Boskoop.

'Gold Flash' (female; synonym 'Bosgold', the original name in the Netherlands; a branch sport of 'J. C. van Tol' discovered 1978; grown by Th. J. Nienwesteeg, Netherlands).

Leaves variegated, dark green, irregular yellow blotched in center, often reverts back to green, elliptic, margins entire to sparsely spined; fruits red, abundant, no pollination required; very hardy.

'Goldfrucht' (female; seedling discovered in 1958 in Berno Carstens Nursery; Fructu Lutea Group).

Leaves dark green, broadly bright green midribs, broadly elliptic, 5–7 cm (2–2¾ in.) long, 3 cm (1³⁄₁₆ in.) wide, 7–9 large spines on each side, prominent raised midribs, stems dark purple; fruits vivid yellow, light reddish blush, globose, 10 mm (³⁄₈ in.) diameter; dense compact, conical habit; original plant 5 m (16 ft.) tall in 30 years; good winter hardiness, withstood −28°C (−19°F).

'Goliath' (male; I. aquifolium; origin unknown; named by K. Meserve; used in hybridizing Blue Hollies; not the same as the female I. × meserveae 'Goliath').

Leaves dark olive green, elliptic or rarely obovate, 5–8 cm (2–3 in.) long, 2.4–4.2 cm (1–1¹¹⁄₁₆ in.) wide, 4–9 spines on each side.

'Graecean' (female; plant received from Edinburgh Botanic Garden, 1960; plant at U. S. National Arboretum, NA 15333, U.S. PI 267246).

Leaves dark green, glossy, slightly curved, broadly elliptic, 7.5–9 cm (3–3½ in.) long, 3.5–4 cm (1³⁄₈–1⁵⁄₈ in.) wide, 5–7 spines on each side, petioles 7–8 mm (⁹⁄₃₂–⁵⁄₁₆ in.) long, stems green; fruits red, globose to oval, 10 mm (³⁄₈ in.) diameter, single or to 3 in cluster; vigorous, upright open habit.

'Grandis' (male; old cultivar; introduced by Fisher, Son, and Sibray before 1867).

Leaves variegated, dark olive green in center, with gray-green markings, margins yellowish white, oval to broadly elliptic, to 7 cm (2¾ in.) long, and 5 cm (2 in.) wide, rather flat, margins spiny; stems purplish black.

'Green Maid', see I. × altaclerensis 'Green Maid'.

'Green Pillar' (female; seedling of unknown origin; named and registered H.S.A 3-71 by Hillier and Sons Nursery, Winchester, England).

Leaves dark green, elliptic, 7.5 cm (3 in.) long, 5 cm (2 in.) wide, bases cuneate, tips aristate, margins undulate, 6 large even spaced spines on each side, stems green; fruits red, obovoid to globose; medium sized tree 6–8 m (20–26 ft.) tall, slow growing, fastigiate habit.

'Green Plane', see I. × altaclerensis 'Balearica'.

'Green Sentinel' (female; found by John Bond, keeper of the Valley and Savill Gardens, Windsor Great Park, England, 1950s.

Leaves dark green; stems green; fruits red; slow growing, fastigiate habit.

'Green Shadow' (female; introduced in the 1950s by A. Brownell).

Leaves variegated, light green in center, margins distinct deep green; fruits red. See 'Misty Green' with leaves dark green center and lighter margins.

Green Stem Group

A name given to group of I. aquifolium cultivars with green young stems (not purplish). Attempts to sort all I. aquifolium cultivars by color of stems has not been satisfactory.

'Handsworthensis' (male; synonym I. spinosissma; old cultivar from England; introduced by Fisher, Son, and Sibray before 1863; plant at U.S. National Arboretum received from Hillier and Sons Nursery, 1958; NA 11259, U.S. PI 232707; occasionally listed as 'Handsworth').

Leaves dark green, glossy, ovate, 4.5 cm (1¾ in.) long, 2.2 cm (1³⁄₁₆ in.) wide, margins undulate, large spines pointing forward; upright dense habit. Appears to be slow growing.

'Handsworth New Silver' (female; synonyms 'Grandis Argentea Marginata', 'Handsworth Silver', 'Silverboy' (Brownell), 'Silver Plane'; old cultivar introduced by Fisher, Son, and Sibray before 1850).

Leaves variegated, dark green with gray green spots in center, margins distinct yellowish white, elliptic oblong, 6.5–9 cm (2½–3 in.) long, 2.5–3.5 cm (1–1³⁄₈ in.) wide, margins nearly flat, 10–12 large spines on each side, young foliage pink; stems purplish; fruits red. A.G.M. 1969.

'Harlequin' (female; introduced by A. Brownell before 1960).

Leaves variegated, pale green to dark olive green margins, irregular greenish yellow blotch in center, elliptic, 5–6.5 cm (2–2½ in.) long, 2–2.5 cm (¾–1 in.) wide, bases obtuse to rotund, margins undulate, 5–7 spines on each side, tip spines reflexed; fruits vivid red 45A, globose, 8 mm (⁵⁄₁₆ in.) diameter, pedicels reddish, 6–8 mm (⁷⁄₃₂–⁵⁄₁₆ in.) long.

'Harpune' (female; sport of 'Alaska' discovered in 1978 by H. Hachmann in Barnstedt, Holstein, Germany).

Leaves dark green, glossy, narrowly lanceolate, to 6 cm (2⅜ in.) long, 5–10 mm (³⁄₁₆–⅜ in.) wide, margins variable, subentire or sparsely spined or wide distinct serrations, arrow or spearlike, suggesting a harpoon; stems purplish; fruits red, seldom or sparse fruiting; vigorous growth; good winter hardiness.

Figure 15-8. *Ilex aquifolium* 'Harpune'. Photo by Hans-Georg Buchtmann.

'Hascombensis' (origin unknown; plant in Charles Musgrove garden, Hascombe, Surrey, England, before 1860).

Leaves reported identical to 'Angustifolia'; dense compact slow growing, pyramidal habit. Plant not common.

'Hastata' (male; synonyms var. *kewensis,* 'Latispina Minor', 'Latispina Nana', 'Latispina Pygmaea'; old cultivar introduced by Fisher and Holmes before 1863).

Leaves dark olive green, distinct hastate shape, 2–3 cm (¾–1³⁄₁₆ in.) long, 1.3 cm (½ in.) wide, margins undulate, 1–2 large spines on each side, near base, upper half entire, forming bluntish lobe or hastate look; stems purplish; dense slow growing. Plate 99.

'Haverbeck' (sport discovered 1987 in private garden by G. Horstmann, Schneverdingen, Germany).

Leaves variegated, irregular yellowish white margins, surface marbled yellowish white, gray and green, broadly elliptic, 5–6 cm (2–2⅜ in.) long, 3–4 cm (1³⁄₁₆–1⅝ in.) wide, 6–9 forward-pointed spines, branches dark purple.

'Helen Corbit' (female; seedling of 'Teufel's Hybrid'; probable male parent of 'Big Bull'; selected and registered H.S.A. 6-63 by J. D. Corbit Jr.).

Leaves dark green, variable, entire to densely spinose, margins nearly flat to very wavy; fruits red, glossy, prolific; broadly conical habit.

'Hendersonii', see *I. × altaclerensis* 'Hendersonii'.

'Henny' (female; discovered before 1980 by Schiphorst).

Leaves light to dark green, dull, 4–6 cm (1⅝–2⅜ in.) long, 3–4 cm (1³⁄₁₆–1⅝ in.) wide, margins spiny, stems purplish; fruits red, abundant; upright broad habit. Good hedge plant; not widely propagated or available.

'Heterophylla Aureomarginata' (male; old cultivar from England, before 1864; often called Egham holly).

Leaves dark green, splashed with yellow, margins yellow, broadly elliptic, 6.5–10 cm (2½–4 in.) long, 4.5–5 cm (1¾–2 in.) wide, margins usually entire or with a few sporadic strong spines, occasionally leaves half yellow.

'Heterophylla Aurea Picta' (male; synonym 'Pictum'; old selection from England before 1866).

Leaves dark green margins, often blotched pale gray green with irregular yellow blotch in center, ovate to elliptic, 6.5 cm (2½ in.) long, margins flat, usually entire; stems green.

Heterophylla Group

A group consisting of plants with narrow leaves mostly entire. Includes male and female plants. Not a recognized group, as true cultivars of *I. aquifolium* often have both spiny and entire leaves on the same plant.

'Hodginsii', see *I. × altaclerensis* 'Hodginsii'.

'Hohman' (female; origin unknown, plant at Scott Arboretum from Wilmat Nursery before 1950).

Leaves dark olive green, elliptic, 5–6.5 cm (2–2½ in.) long, 2–3 cm (¾–1³⁄₁₆ in.) wide, bases cuneate to slightly truncate, margins undulate, wavy, 5–8 strong spines on each side, very rarely subentire with 1–3 spines near the base, tip spines reflexed, petioles 5–8 mm (³⁄₁₆–⁵⁄₁₆ in.) long, stems brownish; fruits red. Also reported as a clone of *I. × altaclerensis*.

'Hollycroft Jack' (male; selected and named by Mrs. A. B. Thacher, Long Island, New York, before 1950).

Leaves dark olive green, oval to broadly elliptic, 6–8 cm (2³⁄₈–3⅛ in.) long, 3.5–4.5 cm (1³⁄₈–1¾ in.) wide, bases rotund, margins slightly wavy, 5–7 spines on each side, petioles 10 mm (³⁄₈ in.) long.

'Hollycroft Jill' (female; selected and named by Mrs. A. B. Thacher, Long Island, New York, before 1950).

Leaves dark olive green, elliptic to broadly elliptic, 4.5–6.5 cm (1¾–2½ in.) long, 2.5–3 cm (1–1³⁄₁₆ in.) wide, bases obtuse, margins undulate, 7–8 spines on each side, tip spines reflexed, petioles 8 mm (³⁄₈ in.) long, stems purplish; fruits red.

'Ilda' (female; selected from plants collected from nurseries and private collections; after 20 years' evaluation, introduced by Institution for Landscape Planteopformering Station, Lunderskov, Denmark, in the late 1980s).

Leaves dark green, elliptic, 5–7 cm (2–2¾ in.) long, 2.5–3.5 cm (1–1³⁄₈ in.) wide, bases obtuse, margins with few spines, stems green; fruits reddish orange, globose, 10 mm (³⁄₈ in.) diameter, mature in autumn, persisting until Christmas; vigorous broadly pyramidal habit. Easily propagated. Selected for cold hardiness. Similar to 'Pyramidalis' with wider leaves.

'Ilman' (male; same origin as 'Ilda').

Leaves dark green, glossy, elliptic, 5–9 cm (2–3½ in.) long, 3–4.5 cm (1³⁄₁₆–1¾ in.) wide, bases cuneate, apices attenuate, margins undulate, 5–7 large spines on each side; vigorous pyramidal habit. Good pollinator for 'Ilda' and 'Ils'; easily propagated. Selected for cold hardiness.

'Ils' (female; same origin as 'Ilda').

Leaves dark green, glossy, elliptic, 5–8 cm (2–3⅛ in.) long, 2.5–3.5 cm (1–1³⁄₈ in.) wide, tip leaves often subentire, bases cuneate to obtuse, apices attenuate, margins wavy, 4–6 spines on each side, stems purplish above, light green below; fruits dark red, clusters slightly flattened globose, 10 mm (³⁄₈ in.) long, 2–5 in clusters; vigorous broadly pyramidal habit. Easily propagated. Selected for cold hardiness.

'Inermis' (female; synonym 'Intermedia'; plant at U.S. National Arboretum received 1960 from Edinburgh Botanic Garden; NA 15335; U.S. PI 267248).

Leaves dark green, slightly glossy, broadly elliptic 7–9 cm (2¾–3½ in.) long, 3–4 cm (1³⁄₁₆–1⅝ in.) wide, usually flat, margins, 2–3 spines to 7 spines on each side, petioles 10–15 mm (³⁄₈–¹⁹⁄₃₂ in.) long; fruits red, globose, 8 mm (⁵⁄₁₆ in.) diameter, pedicels to 8 mm (⁵⁄₁₆ in.) long; vigorous upright habit.

'Ingramii' (male; synonyms 'Ingram', 'Polkadot', 'Silver Dust'; old cultivar from England before 1875).

Leaves variegated, dark olive green, somewhat mottled and rugose, irregular small whitish blotches over entire top surface, markings freckly with no distinct pattern, elliptic–ovate, 3 cm (1³⁄₁₆ in.) long, 1.3 cm (½ in.) wide, margins grayish white, slightly wavy, 8–10 small spines on each side, petioles 8 mm (⁵⁄₁₆ in.) long; young foliage pink. Plate 100.

'Integrifolia' (female; synonyms 'Rotundifolia', 'Senescens'; old cultivar from England before 1817).

Leaves dark olive green, elliptic, 6–7.5 cm (2³⁄₈–3 in.) long, 2.5–3 cm (1–1³⁄₁₆ in.) wide, margins subentire, occasionally some leaves with 4–6 small spines, tips slightly reflexed, petioles 8–10 mm (⁵⁄₁₆–³⁄₈ in.) long, stems green; fruits deep reddish orange 43A, globose, 8–10 mm (⁵⁄₁₆–³⁄₈ in.) diameter, pedicels pink, 6 mm (⁷⁄₃₂ in.) long, 3–5 in clusters.

'Irving' (female; seedling selected in the 1940s in P. Irvine's garden).

Leaves dark olive green, elliptic, 6–8 cm (2³⁄₈–3⅛ in.) long, 2.5–4 cm (1–1⅝ in.) wide, bases cuneate, margins undulate, 2–6 spines on each side, occasionally entire or spines on upper half of leaf, tips reflexed, petioles 10–15 mm (³⁄₈–¹⁹⁄₃₂ in.) long, stems darkish; fruits dark reddish orange 43A, globose to ellipsoid, 10–12 mm (³⁄₈–¹⁵⁄₃₂ in.) long, 8–10 mm (⁵⁄₁₆–³⁄₈ in.) diameter, pedicels 8–10 mm (⁵⁄₁₆–³⁄₈ in.); good clusters of fruit. Selected for early ripening.

'J. C. van Tol' (female; synonyms 'Laevigata Polycarpa', 'Polycarpa'; old cultivar from the Netherlands about 1895; introduced in 1904 by van Tol).

Leaves dark olive green, oval to elliptic, 5–7 cm (2–2¾ in.) long, 2.5–3 cm (1–1³⁄₁₆ in.) wide, bases cuneate to obtuse, margins recurved, usually entire, slightly bullate, impressed veins, petioles 8–10 mm (⁵⁄₁₆–³⁄₈ in.) long, stems green; fruits vivid red 45A, globose, 8–10 mm (⁵⁄₁₆–³⁄₈ in.) diameter, pedicels 8 mm (⁵⁄₁₆ in.) long; free fruiting; broadly pyramidal habit, very hardy. A.G.M. 1969.

'James G. Esson', see *I. × altaclerensis* 'James G. Esson'.

'Jermyns', see *I. × altaclerensis* 'Jermyns'.

'John Michalak' (female; selected named and registered H.S.A. 7-72 by M. A. Nosal; from a cross made in 1942 by E. A. Nosal).

Leaves dark olive green, elliptic, 5.8 cm (2¼ in.) long, 3 cm (1³⁄₁₆ in.) wide, margins undulating, 5–6 stout spines on each side; stems purplish; fruits red, pyriform, 10 mm (³⁄₈ in.) diameter; broad mounding habit; original tree 1.8 × 2.5 wide, (6 × 8 ft.) in 30 years.

'Kuhl's Variegated' (sex unknown; origin at Roslyn Nursery, 1980s).

Leaves variegated, deep yellow centers, dark green margins, size and shape; upright pyramidal habit; winter hardy to −21°C (−5° F), hardier than most variegated hollies.

'Lady Baltimore' (female; 45-year-old tree in Baltimore Park, now destroyed; named and distributed by Mrs. L. M. Lewis before 1969; registered H.S.A. 9-69 by R. L. Baker; plant at U.S. National Arboretum).

Leaves dark olive green, oval to elliptic, margins flat, 6–7 spines on each side; fruits dark red, globose, persist throughout winter.

'Langport' (sex unknown; discovered in late 1970s by G. P. Brown; plant at U.S. National Arboretum; medio-picta type).

Leaves variegated, broadly elliptic to ovate, 3.5–4 cm (1³⁄₈–1⁵⁄₈ in.) long, 2–2.5 cm (¾–1 in.) wide, dark green margins, streaked with yellowish green stripes and blotches in center; 4–6 spines on each side, reverts readily. Reported to be discontinued.

'Larry Peters' (male; chance seedling discovered about 1979 and registered H.S.A. 7-88 by R. K. Peters; parentage believed to be 'Martha Lower' × 'New Brunswick'; sibling of 'Winter Green' H.S.A. 1-87 and 'Deletta' H.S.A. 8-88).

Leaves dark olive green, very glossy, bronze in winter, elliptic to narrow-elliptic, 6.6 cm (2⁵⁄₈ in.) long, to 3.7 cm (1½ in.) wide, bases obtuse, tip spines reflexed, margins wavy, 6–11 stout spines evenly spaced on each side, petioles reddish, 6.5 mm (¼ in.) long; young stems reddish; original tree 10 years old, dwarf broadly conical, 0.76 m (2½ ft.) tall and wide; hardy in zone 6 to −24°C (−12°F).

'Latispina' (female; synonyms 'Latispina Major', 'Trapeziformis'; old distinct cultivar from England before 1845, possibly a sport of 'Crispa').

Leaves dark olive green, elliptic to quadrate, 3.5–4.5 cm (1³⁄₈–1¾ in.) long, 2.5–3 cm (1–1³⁄₁₆ in.) wide, bases usually rotund, apex entire, cuneate, margins twisted, undulate, 2–4 large spines usually recurved on each side; stems purplish.

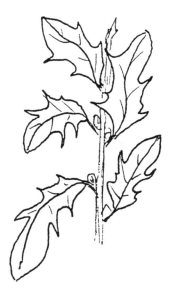

Figure 15-9. *Ilex aquifolium* 'Latispina'. Drawing by Randy Allen.

'Laura Barnes' (female; stray branch of cut holly in box of English holly obtained around 1930 from England; discovered by Laura Barnes and Phil Livingston, named by Livingston for Barnes, founder of Barnes Arboretum, Philadelphia, Pennsylvania; plant at Barnes Arboretum).

Leaves dark olive green, glossy, ovate to elliptic, 6.5–9 cm (2½–3½ in.) long, 3.8–5 cm (1½–2 in.) wide, bases and apices acuminate, margins usually flat, occasionally with slight twist, 5–10 spines on each side, petioles to 13 mm (½ in.) long; fruits vivid red, pyriform, 11 mm (⁷⁄₁₆ in.) long, 10 mm (³⁄₈ in.) diameter, pedicels 5 mm (³⁄₁₆ in.) long; pyramidal habit of growth. Not to be confused with a plant at Tyler Arboretum with same name and entire or subentire leaves, but listed as a cultivar of *I. × altaclerensis*.

'Laurifolia' (male; synonym 'Laurel Leaf'; an old cultivar from England before 1823).

Leaves dark black green, elliptic 6.5–8 cm (2½–3⅛ in.) long, 2.5–4 cm (1–1⁵⁄₈ in.) wide, margins usually entire, occasionally 1–3 small spines near apex, twisted near apex, tip spines reflexed, petioles 10–13 mm (³⁄₈–½ in,) long, stems purplish; very floriferous. Good pollinator.

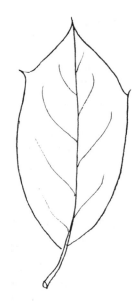

Figure 15-10. *Ilex aquifolium* 'Laurifolia'. Drawing by Randy Allen.

'Laurifolia Aurea' (male; synonym 'Aurea Longifolia'; sport of 'Laurifolia'; earliest sale in 1867).

Leaves variegated, dark black green centers, margins thin yellow edge; deep purple twigs. F.C.C. 1883.

'Laurifolia Fructo Lutea' (synonym 'Laurifolia Silinermis'; origin unknown; earliest reference in 1867 nursery catalog).

Similar to 'Pyramidalis Fructo Lutea' but with yellow fruits and green stems.

'Lawrence White' (male; origin unknown; one of 3 male plants used by K. Meserve for hybridizing of *I. × meserveae*).

Leaves dark green, oblong, strongly spined, stems purplish, puberulent; peduncles and pedicels pilose, calyces lobes ciliate. Doubtful if plants still available.

'Lawsoniana', see *I. × altaclerensis* 'Lawsoniana'.

'Lee Mead' (female; plant at North Willamette Experimental Research and Extension Center, Canby, Oregon).

Leaves dark olive green, oval, 4.5–6.5 cm (1¾–2½ in.) long, 2–2.5 cm (¾–1 in.) wide, bases rotund to cuneate, margins undulate, 4–6 spines on each side, twisted, tip spines reflexed, petioles 8 mm (⁵⁄₁₆ in.) long, stems purplish; fruits dark reddish orange 43A, globose, 8–10 mm (⁵⁄₁₆–⅜ in.) diameter, pedicels reddish, 8 mm (⁵⁄₁₆ in.) long.

'Lee's Dark Silver' (female; original plant at W. Fromow and Sons Nursery and introduced by the nursery in the 1960s; Argentea Marginata Group).

Leaves large; fruits red.

'Lems Silver' (female; temporary name given by H. Hohman to cuttings received from Haf den Lem, Seattle, Washington; believed to be synonym of 'Silvary', which see).

'Leo Sanders' (female; plant at North Willamette Research and Extension Center, Canby, Oregon, 1970s).

Leaves dark olive green, elliptic, 5–7 cm (2–2¾ in.) long, 2–2.5 cm (¾–1 in.) wide, bases cuneate, margins undulate, 3–6 spines on each side, tip twisted, reflexed, petioles 8–10 mm (⁵⁄₁₆–⅜ in.) long; fruits vivid red 44A, ellipsoid, 8–10 mm (⁵⁄₁₆–⅜ in.) long, 8 mm (⁵⁄₁₆ in.) diameter, pedicels reddish, 8 mm (⁵⁄₁₆ in.) long; good clusters.

'Lewis' (female; cuttings from a tree in town of Delight, between Baltimore and Reisterstown, Maryland; named and introduced before 1967 by S. McLean).

Leaves dark olive green, oblong, 4.5–6 cm (1¾–1⅜ in.) long, 2.5–3 cm (1–1³⁄₁₆ in.) wide, bases obtuse to rotund, margins undulate, wavy, 3–6 spines on each side, tip spines reflexed, petioles 8–10 mm (⁵⁄₁₆–⅜ in.) long, stems slightly purplish above; fruits dark red, large, abundant, pedicels 5–8 mm (³⁄₁₆–⁵⁄₁₆ in.) long; upright habit.

'Lichtenthalii' (female; synonym 'Lichtenthal'; old cultivar from Austria around 1880).

Leaves dark olive green, pale green along midribs and margins, narrow-oblong, to 10 cm (4 in.) long, 3.8 cm (1½ in.) wide, margins spiny, distinct with 1 small spine on each side at the base, stems purple; fruits red, shy fruiting; slow dense, compact growth.

'Lillibet' (female; sport of 'Angustifolia'; introduced by A. Brownell in the 1960s).

Leaves dark olive green, broader than those of 'Angustifolia'; fruits red; low spreading habit.

'Lilliput' (male; sport of 'Angustifolia'; introduced by A. Brownell in the 1960s for its similarity to 'Lillibet').

Leaves dark olive green, elliptic, 3–3.5 cm (1³⁄₁₆–1⅜ in.) long, 1–1.5 cm (⅜–¹⁹⁄₃₂ in.) wide, bases cuneate, margins flat, 4–7 spines on each side, usually evenly spaced, petioles 5 mm (³⁄₁₆ in.) long, stems purplish. Similar to 'Angustifolia' but with evenly spaced spines to the apex.

'Lily Gold' (male; sport of green-leaved tree; selected by G. Teufel in the 1960s).

Leaves variegated, dark glossy green centers, margins yellow, elliptic to ovate, 5.5–6.5 cm (2⅛–2½ in.) long, 3–4 cm (1³⁄₁₆–1⅝ in.) wide, bases obtuse, 6–9 divaricate spines on each side, petioles dark, stems purplish.

'Limsi' (female; Siberia trademark name in Europe; chance seedling of *I. aquifolium*; discovered by Arie Blanken in his nursery, Boskoop, Netherlands; PP No. 8873, August 1994; introduced in United States by Conard-Pyle Nursery).

Leaves dark green, glossy, elliptic, 5–8 cm (2–3⅛ in.) long, 3–5 cm (1³⁄₁₆–2 in.) wide, single apical spine, margins undulate, spiny variable from 1–14 spines on leaf; petioles usually 9 mm (¹¹⁄₃₂ in.) long, stems yellow green 148A; fruits vivid red 45A, 8–10 mm (⁵⁄₁₆–⅜ in.) diameter, very abundant. dense upright and pyramidal habit, cold hardy in zone 6, more tolerant than J. C. van Tol cultivars ('Bella', 'Gold Flash', 'Golden van Tol', 'J. C. van Tol', 'Lunn van Tol', 'Silver van Tol') and 'Pyramidalis'.

'Little Bull' (male; mutation of 'Angustifolia'; selected by G. Teufel in the 1960s).

Leaves dark olive green, lanceolate to elliptic, 2–3.5 cm (¾–1³⁄₁₆ in.) long, 1–2 cm (⅜–¾ in.) wide, bases cuneate, margins slightly wavy, 4–7 small spines on each side, petioles 5 mm (³⁄₁₆ in.) long, stems purplish; compact habit of growth. Good pollinizer.

'Longspra' (female; synonym 'Wieman's Longspra'; selected by J. S. Wieman about 1925).

Leaves dark olive green, glossy, elliptic, 5–7 mm (2–2¾ in.) long, 2.5–3.5 cm (1–1⅜ in.) wide, bases obtuse to rotund, margins undulate, wavy, usually 4–5 spines on each side, occasionally subentire with 1–2 sporadic spines, petioles 8 mm (⁵⁄₁₆ in.) long, stems dark green; fruits vivid red 45A, globose, 10 mm (⅜ in.) diameter, pedicels 5 mm (³⁄₁₆ in.) long, 1–3 in clusters; rapid growing; very hardy. Orchard type tree.

'Lorne Peters' (male; volunteer seedling around 1978, in garden of R. K. Peters; selected, named and registered H.S.A. 5-89 by Peters; introduced in 1990).

Leaves dark olive green, glossy, ovate to elliptic, to 7.6 cm (3 in.) long, 3.8 cm (1½ in.) wide, bases cuneate to truncate, tip spines reflexed, margins wavy, 5–8 spines, pointing forward, on each side, petioles 10 mm (⅜ in.) long, stems purplish; conical habit; original tree 1.8 m (6 ft.) high, 0.9 m (3 ft.) wide in 12 years; hardy in zone 5b.

'Louise', see *I. × altaclerensis* 'Louise'.

'Lunn van Tol' (female; sport of J. C. van Tol); origin G. G. Whitney estate, Woods Hole, Massachusetts; named by W. Wheeler in the 1960s).

Leaves dull light green, subentire; fruits red, ovoid.

'Lutescens', see *I. aquifolium* 'Flavescens'.

'Maculaska' (female; sport of 'Alaska'; propagated 1988; introduced 1991 by E. Stührenberg in his nursery, Wiesmoor, Germany; name illegitimate with Latin and English combined).

Leaves variegated, large yellow irregular blotches, narrow-elongate, 9–11 spines on each side; original plant 50 cm (20 in.) high; no winter damage in a protected area.

'Madam' (female; introduced around 1977 by the late E. Pederson).

Leaves dark olive green, glossy, elliptic, 4.5–5.5 cm (1⅝–2⅛ in.) long, 2.5–3 cm (1–1³⁄₁₆ in.) wide, margins undulate, 5–8 spine on each side, petioles thin, 5–10 mm (³⁄₁₆–⅜ in.) long, stems green; fruits red, globose, 9–10 mm (¹¹⁄₃₂–⅜ in.) diameter, pedicels 7–8 mm (⁹⁄₃₂–⁵⁄₁₆ in.) long; broadly pyramidal habit, wide angle branching; hardy to −20° (−4°F).

'Madame Briot' (female; synonyms 'Aurea Latifolia', 'Aurea Regina Nigra'; origin in France; first described 1866).

Leaves large, variegated, dark olive green center, wide irregular brilliant yellow 8A, margins, broadly oblong-ovate, 6.5–8.5 cm (2½–3⅜ in.) long, 3–4 cm (1³⁄₁₆–1⅝ in.) wide, bases rotund to truncate, margins slightly wavy, 6–8 spines on each side, tips reflexed, petioles 8 mm (⁵⁄₁₆ in.) long, stems purplish; fruits vivid red 45A, globose, 8 mm (5⅙ in.) diameter, pedicels reddish, 8 mm (⁵⁄₁₆ in.) long; fruits well. A.G.M. 1969.

'Maderensis', see *I. × altaclerensis* 'Maderensis'.

'Maderensis Variegata' (male; synonyms 'Maderensis Picta', *I. × altaclerensis* 'Maderensis Variegata'; old cultivar from England before 1868).

Leaves variegated, margins dark green, irregular yellowish blotch mixed with pale green in center, oval to obovate, 6.5–7.5 cm (2½–3 in.) long, 3.8–5.8 cm (1½–2¼ in.) wide, margins slightly wavy, spines evenly spaced; stems purplish.

'Malmborg' (female; origin unknown, possibly named for G. Malmborg by S. McLean; listed by McLean Nursery, 1960s).

Leaves dark olive green, elliptic, 5–6 cm (2–2⅜ in.) long, 2–2.5 cm (¾–1 in.) wide, bases cuneate to obtuse, margins wavy, 6–10 spines on each side, occasionally subentire, 2–3 small spines on upper half of leaf, petioles 5–7 mm (³⁄₁₆–⁹⁄₃₂ in.) long; fruits red, glossy, pyriform, 8 mm (⁵⁄₁₆ in.) long, 8 mm (⁵⁄₁₆ in.) diameter, pedicels 5–6 mm (³⁄₁₆–⁷⁄₃₂ in.) long; broad-spreading habit, slow to develop a leader.

'Manly Gold', see 'Dandy'.

'Marginata Bicolor'(female; planted in 1959 at Washington Park Arboretum, Seattle, Washington).
Leaves variegated, dark olive green in center, irregular vivid greenish yellow 7A margins, elliptic, 6–8 cm (2⅜–3⅛ in.) long, 2.5–3.2 cm (1–1¼ in.) wide, bases cuneate, margins flat or slightly wavy at apex, 4–6 spines usually on upper half of leaf, petioles 6–8 mm (⁷⁄₃₂–⁵⁄₁₆ in.) long, stems green; fruits vivid red 45A, globose, 8–10 mm (⁵⁄₁₆–⅜ in.) diameter, pedicels reddish, 8 mm (⁵⁄₁₆ in.) long.

'Marijo' (female; origin from private estate in Willow Grove, Pennsylvania; registered H.S.A. 4-64 by B. H. Brockley).
Leaves dark olive green, glossy, elliptic, 5–7 cm (2–2¾ in.) long, 1.8–2.8 cm (¹¹⁄₁₆–1⅛ in.) wide, bases obtuse, apices acuminate, tip spines slightly reflexed, margins slightly wavy, 6–8 spines on each side, petioles 7 mm (⁹⁄₃₂ in.) long; fruits red, large; herring bone habit of branching; symmetrical upright conical habit.

'Marnockii', see *I. × altaclerensis* 'Marnockii'.

'Martha Lower' (female; unnamed seedling purchased early 1950s by R. K. Peters from Boyers Nursery, Ardentsville, Pennsylvania, operated by Martha Lower; named by Peters; thought to be female parent of 'Deletta', 'Mary Peters', 'New Brunswick', and 'Winter Green', all registered by Peters; original tree killed in winter of 1977–1978 at −28°C (−19°F)).

'Martin' (female; chance seedling; origin Nazareth, Pennsylvania; 25- to 30-year-old seedling registered H.S.A. 7-67 by L. K. Zeigler).
Leaves dark green; fruits red; broadly conical habit.

'Mary Peters' (female; origin about 1976; volunteer seedling discovered about 1979 by R. K. Peters; female parent believed to be 'Martha Lower'; selected, named, and registered H.S.A. 6-89 by Peters; introduced in 1990; sibling of 'Deletta', 'New Brunswick', 'Winter Green').

Leaves dark olive green, glossy, oval to elliptic, 4.5–6.5 cm (1¾–2½ in.) long, 2–4 cm (¾–1⅝ in.) wide, bases cuneate to truncate, apices acuminate tip spines reflexed, margins thickened, recurved, wavy, 3–8 spines on each side, petioles 5–8 mm (³⁄₁₆–⁵⁄₁₆ in.) long, stems green; fruits strong pink 49A, prolate, 11 mm (⁷⁄₁₆ in.) long, 10 mm (⅜ in.) diameter, 2–3 in clusters; ovoid habit; original tree 2–7 m (9 ft.) high, 2.1 m (7 ft.) wide in 14 years; very hardy, survived winter 1977–1978 at −34°C (−29°F).

'Medio-picta', see Milkmaid Hollies.

'Microphylla' (synonym 'Angustifolia Minor'; 1874, plant at Bokrijk Arboretum, Belgium; received from Rosemoor Gardens, England, in the 1980s).
Leaves green, glossy, lanceolate, flat, 2.5–3.5 cm (1–1⅜ in.) long, distinct spines, stems purplish; small shrub with compact habit.

'Mildebrann' (female; seedling discovered near Stord, Norway; introduced by Norwegian Arboretum, Milde, Norway, in the 1980s).
Leaves dark green, glossy; fruits red, annual; vigorous habit; 8-year-old plants 2.5 m (8.2 ft.) high, 1.6 m (5.2 ft.) wide.

'Mildegave' (female; seedling discovered in Stord, Norway; introduced by Norwegian Arboretum, Milde, Norway, in the 1980s).
Leaves dark green; fruits reddish orange, large, produced on young plants, ripen early; vigorous broadly pyramidal habit; 8-year-old plants 2.2 m (7.2 ft.) high, 1.6 m (5.2 ft.) wide.

'Mildeglede' (female; seedling discovered in Stord, Norway; introduced by Norwegian Arboretum, Milde, Norway, in the 1980s).
Leaves dark green; fruits reddish orange, red with orange blotch, large, abundant; vigorous habit; 8-year-old plants 2.3 m (7.5 ft.) tall, 1.4 m (4.6 ft.) wide.

'Mildegubbe' (male; seedling discovered in the 1980s near Nedstrand, Ryfylle, Norway).
Leaves dark green, variable usually entire; flowers abundant; vigorous habit; 8-year-old plants 1.7 m (5.6 ft.) tall, 1.4 m (4.6 ft.) wide. Good pollinator.

'Mildegull' (female; possible garden escape or seedling; discovered near Fjosanger, Norway, by Bergen, in the 1980s).
Leaves dark green, spiny; fruits yellow, large, annual; vigorous habit; 8-year-old plants 1.8 m (5.9 ft.) tall, 1.4 m (4.6 ft.) wide.

Milkmaid Hollies

Often a group name for a variegated holly. Leaves dark green on margins, large central blotch of yellowish white. 'Golden Milkmaid' and 'Silver Milkmaid' are popular cultivars. See also 'Aurea Media Picta' and 'Aurea Picta Latifolia'.

'Miller Selection' (female; selected by P. Miller in 1947; plant at North Willamette Research and Extension Center, Canby, Oregon).

Leaves dark olive green, elliptic, 6–8 cm (2⅜–3⅛ in.) long, 2.5–3.5 cm (1–1⅜ in.) wide, bases cuneate to obtuse, margins wavy, 3–6 spines on each side, tips reflexed, petioles 10–12 mm (⅜–¹⁵⁄₃₂ in.) long, stems green; fruits vivid red 45A, globose, 10–12 mm (⅜–¹⁵⁄₃₂ in.) diameter, pedicels reddish, 8–10 mm (⁵⁄₁₆–⅜ in.) long.

'Mistgold' (male; named and introduced in the 1960s by A. Brownell).

Leaves variegated, dark olive green centers, greenish yellow margins, elliptic, 5–6.5 cm (2–2½ in.) long, 2.5–3 cm (1–1³⁄₁₆ in.) wide, bases cuneate to obtuse, margins wavy, 2–9 spines on each side, tip spines reflexed; stems green.

'Misty Green' (female; named and introduced in the 1960s by A. Brownell).

Leaves two tones of green: center dark green, margins lighter green; fruits red. See 'Green Shadow' with light green center, margins dark green.

'Monstrosa' (male; old cultivar from England; listed in an 1845–1853 catalog by Fisher, Son, and Sibray).

Leaves dark olive green, 5.5–7.5 cm (2⅛–3 in.) long, 2–2.5 cm (¾–1 in.) wide, bases cuneate to rotund, margins undulate, 4–5 spines on each side, usually pointed downward, tip spines reflexed, petioles 8 mm (⁵⁄₁₆ in.) long; stems dark green or purple; shy flowering; very dense growth.

'Monticello' (female; origin unknown; possibly from Angelica Nursery; plant received at Callaway Gardens in 1960, records destroyed in fire).

Leaves dark olive green, oval to broadly elliptic, 4.5–6 cm (1¾–2⅜ in.) long, 2–3 cm (¾–1³⁄₁₆ in.) wide, bases obtuse to rotund, margins undulate, 5–7 strong spines on each side, tips reflexed, petioles stout, 4–6 mm (⁵⁄₃₂–⁶⁄₃₂ in.) long; stems green; fruits vivid red 45A, pyriform, 10 mm (⅜ in.) long, 8 mm (⁵⁄₁₆ in.) diameter, pedicels reddish, 5 mm (³⁄₁₆ in.) long.

'Moonbrite', see 'Wieman's Moonbrite'.

'Moonglow', see 'Wieman's Moonbrite'.

'Moonlight' (female; synonym 'Flavescens', which see; renamed by A. Brownell in 1960).

'Moorei', see *I. × altaclerensis* 'Moorei'.

'Morochan' (sex unknown; seedling origin, from M. S. Whipple).

Leaves moderate olive green, oval to elliptic, 3–5.5 cm (1⅜–2⅛ in.) long, 1.6–2.5 cm (⅝–1 in.) wide, bases obtuse, apices acuminate, tip spines reflexed, margins undulate, 5–9 small spines on each side, petioles dark, 8 mm (⁵⁄₁₆ in.) long.

'Moyer's Autumn' (selected by Mr. Moyer in Oregon).

No description available.

'Moyer's Boutonniere' (female; selected by Mr. Moyer in Oregon; plant at North Willamette Experimental Research and Extension Center, Canby, Oregon, in the 1950s).

Leaves dark olive green, elliptic, 4–4.5 cm (1⅝–1¾ in.) long, 2–2.5 cm (¾–1 in.) wide, bases obtuse, margins wavy, 2–3 spines usually on upper two-thirds of leaf, occasionally entire, tips reflexed, petioles 8–10 mm (⁵⁄₁₆–⅜ in.) long, stems green; fruits deep reddish orange 43A, globose, 8 mm (⁵⁄₁₆ in.) diameter, pedicels reddish, 6–8 mm (⁷⁄₃₂–⁵⁄₁₆ in.) long.

'Moyer's Male' (selected by Mr. Moyer in Oregon).

No description available.

'Mrs. Goefrey Whitney' (named by W. Wheeler; Whitney Holly Group, which see).

No description available.

'Mrs. Pilkington' (female; plant at North Willamette Experimental Research and Extension Center, Canby, Oregon, in the 1950s).

Leaves dark olive green, elliptic, 5–7 cm (2–2¾ in.) long, 2–3.5 cm (¾–1⅜ in.) wide, bases cuneate to obtuse, margins wavy, 4–5 spines on each side, tips reflexed, petioles 8 mm (⁵⁄₁₆ in.) long; fruits red, globose, 10 mm (⅜ in.) diameter, pedicels reddish, 8 mm (⁵⁄₁₆ in.) long.

'Mundy', see *I. × altaclerensis* 'Mundy'.

'Munford Selection' (female; seedling selected by C. Munford; plant at North Willamette Experimental Research and Extension Center, Canby, Oregon, in the 1950s).

Leaves dark olive green, elliptic, 6–8 cm (2⅜–3⅛ in.) long, 3–3.5 cm (1³⁄₁₆–1⅜ in.) wide, bases obtuse, margins occasionally entire to 1–4 spines on each side, often on upper half of leaf, petioles reddish, 10 mm (⅜ in.) long, stems purplish; fruits deep reddish orange 43A, globose, 10 mm (⅜ in.) diameter, pedicels reddish, 8–10 mm (⁵⁄₁₆–⅜ in.) long, good clusters.

'Muricata', see 'Aurifodina'.

'Myrtifolia' (male; old cultivar from England before 1830).

Leaves dark green, glossy, flat, ovate-lanceolate, 3–3.8 cm (1³⁄₁₆–1½ in.) long, 1.3–1.6 cm (½–⅝ in.) wide, margins usually 6–8 spines, pointed forward, on both sides, stems green or purplish; slow growth, small shrub.

'Myrtifolia Aurea' (male; synonym 'Myrtifolia Aureo Marginata'; old cultivar from England; earliest reference 1863).

Leaves small, variegated, dark olive green with pale green marking in center, irregular yellow margins, stems purplish; slow growing, small tree.

'Myrtifolia Aurea Maculata' (male; old cultivar from England; earliest reference 1875).

Leaves dark olive green with pale green shading on margins, irregular blotch of deep yellow in center, stems purplish; slow dense growth, small shrub.

'N. F. Barnes', see I. × altaclerensis 'N. F. Barnes'.

'N.Y.B.G. No. 2' (female; origin New York Botanical Gardens).

Leaves dark olive green, glossy, elliptic to ovate-elliptic, 4.5–6.5 cm (1¾–2½ in.) long, 2–3 cm (¾–1³⁄₁₆ in.) wide, bases cuneate to obtuse, apices acute, tip spines slightly reflexed, margins nearly flat, to slightly recurved, 3–6 spines on each side, petioles 8–10 mm (⁵⁄₁₆–⅜ in.) long, stems dark green; fruits vivid red 45A, globose to slightly pyriform, 10–12 mm (⅜–¹⁵⁄₃₂ in.) long, 10 mm (⅜ in.) diameter, pedicels reddish, 5–6 mm (³⁄₁₆–⁷⁄₃₂ in.) long; compact pyramidal habit.

'N.Y.B.G. No. 698' (male; origin New York Botanical Gardens).

Leaves dark olive green, elliptic, 5–6.5 cm (2–2½ in.) long, 2.5–3 cm (1–1³⁄₁₆ in.) wide, bases cuneate to obtuse, margins flat, subentire to 1–5 small spines on each side, petioles 8–10 mm (⁵⁄₁₆–⅜ in.) long; stems purplish.

'Nantucket Whaler' (sex unknown; plant originally from Oregon; selected by Tony Gould in the 1980s at Craig estate, Nantucket Island, Massachusetts).

Leaves dark green, elliptic, small, numerous spines; stems purplish.

'Nashankie' (female; synonym 'Teufel's Greenstem'; introduced before 1960 by G. Teufel; plant at Callaway Gardens from Biltmore estate).

Leaves dark olive green, glossy, elliptic, 7–8.5 cm (2¾–3⅜ in.) long, 2.5–3.8 cm (1–1½ in.) wide, bases obtuse, margins undulate, wavy, 7–8 spines on each side, petioles 10, stems green; fruits vivid red 45A, globose, 10 mm (⅜ in.) diameter, pedicels 8–10 mm (⁵⁄₁₆–⅜ in.) long.

'New Brunswick' (discovered by T. Dilatush; introduced in 1954; not the same as Peters' plant described below).

No description available.

'New Brunswick' (male; origin about 1976; volunteer seedling in garden of R. K. Peters; female parent 'Martha Lower'; selected and named by Peters; sibling of 'Deletta', 'Doug Barbour', 'Winter Green').

Leaves dark olive green, glossy, elliptic, 5–8 cm (2–3⅛ in.) long, 2.5–4 cm (1–1⅝ in.) wide, bases cuneate, apices acuminate, tip spines reflexed, margins undulate, 3–6 spines on each side, occasionally subentire, petioles 8–10 mm (⁵⁄₁₆–⅜ in.) long; stems green, purplish on upper surface; hardy to −24°C (−12°F). Good pollinator.

'Night Glow' (female; cross 'Flavescens' × 'Dude', by J. S. Wieman; named and registered H.S.A. 7-76 by Wieman).

Leaves green, suffused yellow variegations, sometimes large random yellow spots, especially in upper portion of leaf, increased yellowing of leaves toward short apex, often smaller leaves entirely yellow, elliptic, variable in size to 5.8 cm (2¼ in.) long, 2.8 cm (1¼ in.) wide, margins undulate, to 9 strong spines on each side, petioles 7 mm (⁹⁄₃₂ in.) long; fruits orange, globose, 10 mm (⅜ in.) diameter, pedicels 3 mm (⅛ in.) long; conical habit, fastigiate branching; 0.92 m (3 ft.) high, 0.76 mm (2½ ft.) wide in 8 years. Sibling to 'Moon Glow' with smaller leaves and conical habit.

'Nigrescens', see I. × altaclerensis 'Nigrescens'.

'Nigricans' (male; introduced before 1870 by L. Van Houtte).

Leaves dark green, ovate or lanceolate, rarely elliptic, 3–5 cm (1³⁄₁₆–2 in.) long, about 2–3 cm (¾–1³⁄₁₆ in.) wide, margins slightly wavy to flat, fine spines, rarely entire, stems and petioles dark brown violet; upright spreading shrubs to 4–5 m (13–16 ft.) high. Similar to 'Angustifolia' but with larger purplish leaves. Rare in cultivation.

'Nobilis', see *I. × altaclerensis* 'Nobilis'.

'Noss' (female; seedling origin selected in the 1960s by W. J. Dauber).
Fruits red, abundant; pyramidal habit; hardy.

'Oak Vale', see *I. × altaclerensis* 'Oak Vale'.

'Olive Smith' (female; seedling from tree in Plainfield, New Jersey; named and registered H.S.A. 17-60 by H. B. Smith; tree at New York Botanical Gardens given in 1964 by H. B. Smith and his wife).
Leaves dark green, glossy, spiny; fruits vivid red; compact pyramidal habit.

'Orange Beauty' (female; origin Hillier Arboretum, Hampshire, England, in the late 1980s).
Similar to 'Apricot Glow', which see.

'Orange Gem' (selection of 'Fructo Aurantiaca'; named by A. Brownell in the 1950s).
Fruits orange.

'Oregon' (sex unknown; origin unknown; plant at Tyler Arboretum).
Leaves dark olive green, elliptic, 4–5.5 cm (1¾–2 in.) long, 2–3 cm (¾–1³⁄₁₆ in.) wide, bases rotund to truncate, apices acute, margins wavy, 7–9 spines on each side, petioles stout, reddish, 6–8 mm (⁷⁄₃₂–⁵⁄₁₆ in.) long; stems purplish; fruits not seen.

'Oregon Favorite' (female; planted 1968 at Washington Park Arboretum, Seattle, Washington).
Leaves dark olive green, broadly elliptic, 7–12 cm (2¾–4¾ in.) long, 3.5–6.5 cm (1⅜–2½ in.) wide, bases cuneate, margins wavy, 3–5 spines on each side, petioles 10–13 mm (⅜–½ in.) long; fruits deep reddish orange 43A, ellipsoid, 10 mm (⅜ in.) long, 8 mm (⁵⁄₁₆ in.) diameter, pedicels 10 mm (⅜ in.) long.

'Oregon Majesty' (female; named and introduced by A. Brownell in 1958).
Leaves dark olive green, ovate, 5–6.5 cm (2–2½ in.) long, 2.5–3.8 cm (1–1½ in.) wide, bases rotund, margins undulate, wavy, 2–6 spines on each side, occasionally with 2–3 spines on upper half of leaf, tip spines reflexed, petioles stout, 8–10 mm (⁵⁄₁₆ in.) long; stems purplish; fruits red.

'Oregon Select' (female; synonym 'Sawyer Selection'; named and introduced around 1948 by K. Sawyer; plant at U.S. National Arboretum).

'Oregon Select Variegated' (female; probably a sport of 'Oregon Select'; plant at North Willamette Experimental Research and Extension Center, Canby, Oregon, obtained from Mrs. Harold Richen).
Leaves variegated, yellowish white margins.

'Ovata' (male; old cultivar, possibly from England before 1854).
Leaves dark green, ovate, 4–5 cm (1⅝–2 in.) long, 2–2.5 cm (¾–1 in.) wide, bases rotund, margins flat, small spines, 6 on each side, very distinct, shallow scallops, petioles 6 mm (⁷⁄₃₂ in.) long, stems purple; slow compact grower.

'Ovata Aurea' (male; synonyms 'Aurea Marginata Ovata', 'Golden Gate (U.S.A.)', 'Ovata Aurea Marginata'; sport of 'Ovata'; 1874).
Described by Hillier and Sons Nursery as "one of the brightest and neatest variegated hollies"; very similar to 'Ovata', leaves variegated, dark olive green with brilliant yellow margin; stems reddish purple; slow growing.

Pacific Northwest Hybrid Group
A proposed new group name to include many hybrid seedlings of English holly, *I. × altaclerensis,* and possible mutations that originated on the U.S. Pacific Northwest Coast. The parental background is unknown and may never be unraveled. At present many selections (named and numbered) have entire or nearly spineless leaves are included in *I. × altaclerensis,* Dutch Hybrid Group, or Pacific Northwest Hybrid Group. It is questionable if this new proposed group will help settle the many problems of these hybrids.

'Painted Lady' (female; named and introduced by A. Brownell in the 1950s).
Leaves dark olive green, becoming splotched with red and purple in fall, persist through the winter; fruits red.

'Path-O-Gold' (named and introduced by A. Brownell). See *I. × altaclerensis* 'Pyramidalis Aureamarginata'.

'Pendula' (female; synonym *I. aquifolium* var. *pendula*; old cultivar found in a garden in Derby, England, and described by Loudon in 1842).
Leaves dark olive green, elliptic, 5–6.5 cm (2–2½ in.) long, 3–3.5 cm (1³⁄₁₆–1⅜ in.) wide, bases rotund, margins wavy, 6–8 spines on each side, tip spines reflexed; stems usually purplish; fruits vivid red 45A, globose, 8–10 mm (⁵⁄₁₆–⅜ in.) diameter, pedicels reddish, 8–10 mm (⁵⁄₁₆–⅜ in.) long; pendulous branches forming a dense conical shape.

There are four variegated selections previously described as sports of 'Pendula'. 'Argentea Marginata Pendula', 'Aurea Marginata Pendula', 'Weeping Golden Milkmaid', and 'Weeping Silver Milkmaid'.

'Peters' (female; date unknown; specimen at Scott Arboretum, Swarthmore, Pennsylvania; received from Perkins de Wilde Nursery).

Leaves dark olive green, ovate-elliptic, 4–6.5 cm (1⅝–2½ in.) long, 2–2.5 cm (¾–1 in.) wide, bases obtuse to rotund, apices acute, tip spines slightly reflexed, margins undulate, wavy, 2–7 spines on each side, occasionally uneven, 2 on one side, 5–6 on other, petioles stout, 8 mm (5/16 in.) long; fruits vivid red 45A, pyriform, 13 mm (½ in.) long, 10 mm (⅜ in.) diameter, pedicels reddish, 5 mm (3/16 in.) long; upright pyramidal habit.

'Petit' (male type of 'Angustifolia', which see; named by A. Brownell).

'Petite' (female type of 'Angustifolia', which see; named by A. Brownell).

'Phantom Gold' (male; Flavescens type; named and introduced by A. Brownell in the 1950s).

Leaves variegated, lower leaves dark olive green with faint yellow blotching, ovate-elliptic, 5–6.5 cm (2–2½ in.) long, 2–3.5 cm (¾–1⅜ in.) wide, tip leaves smaller often entirely vivid greenish yellow 7A, or irregularly blotched light green to greenish yellow, elliptic, 4–5 cm (1⅝–2 in.) long, 2 mm (¾ in.) wide, margins undulate, wavy 3–5 spines on each side, petioles 5 mm (3/16 in.) long; stems green.

'Pinto' (female; synonym 'Wieman's Pinto'; sport of 'Early Cluster'; discovered in 1935; named and registered H.S.A. 10-59 by J. S. Wieman).

Leaves variegated, dark olive green glossy margins, pale green to vivid yellow 12A, irregular blotch in center, occasionally small green leaves at stem tips, elliptic, 6–8 cm (2⅜–3⅛ in.) long, 2.5–4 cm (1–1⅝ in.) wide, bases cuneate to obtuse, margins subentire to 1–2 spines near apex, twisted, tip spines reflexed, petioles 8–10 mm (5/16–⅜ in.) long; stems purplish; fruits deep reddish orange 43A, globose, 8–10 mm (5/16–⅜ in.) diameter, pedicels 6–8 mm (7/32–5/16 in.) long; good clusters.

'Pixie' (female; branch sport of 'Angustifolia' propagated by R. Leach in the 1960s).

Leaves dark olive green, narrow-elliptic to lanceolate, 3.5–5 cm (1⅜–2 in.) long, 1.2–1.8 cm (15/32–11/16 in.) wide, bases cuneate to obtuse, margins entire to 2–4 spines on each side, twisted, petioles slender, 10 mm (⅜ in.) long, stems dark; fruits vivid red

44A, globose, 6 mm (7/32 in.) diameter, pedicels reddish, 6–8 mm (7/32–5/16 in.) long; good clusters.

'Polkadot' (named by A. Brownell), see 'Ingramii'.

'Princess Pat' (female; named and introduced by A. Brownell in the 1950s).

Leaves dark olive green, broadly elliptic, 5–7 cm (2–2¾ in.) long, 2–3.5 cm (¾–1⅜ in.) wide, bases obtuse, apices acute, margins undulate, 3–5 spines on each side, tip spines reflexed, petioles 8–10 mm (5/16–⅜ in.) long, stems purplish; fruits vivid red, globose, 10–12 mm (⅜–15/32 in.) diameter, 1–6 in clusters; upright pyramidal habit. Plate 101.

'Proud Mary' (female; variegated sport discovered by Kenneth McQuage in 1993 at his residence, Baltimore, Maryland; named and registered H.S.A. 2-95 by McQuage; propagated by McLean Nursery).

Leaves ovate, to 6 cm (2⅜ in.) long, 3 cm (1 3/16 in.) wide, curved, slightly keeled, margins variable, entire to 1–4 spines, sometimes 1–2 spines near tips, yellow 12C, often green centers with irregular borders yellow to yellow-green 146B, petioles to 8 mm (3/16 in.) long, leaf variegations irregular; fruits vivid red 45B, to 1 mm (⅜ in.) diameter, borne singly or fasciculate, 2–4 fruits on pedicels 3 mm (⅛ in.) long; hardy in zone 7.

'Pyramidalis' (female; old cultivar from C. B. van Nes, Netherlands, around 1885).

Leaves dark olive green, elliptic, 6–8 cm (2⅜–3⅛ in.) long, 2.5–3 cm (1–1 3/16 in.) wide, bases cuneate, margins usually entire, rarely 1–2 spines, often only on one side, petioles 10 mm (⅜ in.) long, stems green; fruits vivid red 45A, globose to slightly ellipsoid, 8–10 mm (5/16–⅜ in.) diameter, 1–4 in cluster, parthenocarpic, free fruiting; narrow conical, upright habit. Recommended for cut holly. A.G.M. 1969. Plate 102.

'Pyramidalis Aureamarginata' (female; synonym 'Path-O-Gold'; first reported 1910 by Van der Kraats, Netherlands).

Leaves variegated, margins yellow, dark green centers; stems green; fruits vivid red; very hardy. Leaf form and plant habit like 'Pyramidalis'.

'Pyramidalis Compacta' (female; plant at Callaway Gardens; no records obtained, possibly from Jackson-Perkins, West Grove, Pennsylvania, 1960s).

Very similar to 'Pyramidalis', but doubtful if it has a more compact habit of growth.

'Pyramidalis Fructu Lutea' (female; origin Hillier and Sons Nursery; first reported in the 1960s).

Leaves like 'Pyramidalis'; fruits yellow, conical plant habit. A.M. 1985.

'Rahden' (male; seedling discovered 1985 by Hans-Georg Buchtmann in a farmer's garden in Germany).

Leaves dark green, glossy, distinct lateral venation, broadly elliptic to oval, to 8 cm (3 in.) long, 6 cm ($2\frac{3}{8}$ in.) wide, often as wide as long, bases rotund to nearly truncate, margins wavy, 7–12 stout spines on each side, stems purplish; vigorous pyramidal habit; original plant 3 m (10 ft.) high; good winter hardiness.

'Recurva' (male; synonym 'Serratifolia Compacta'; old cultivar before 1844 from England).

Leaves dark olive green, elliptic, 3.5–5 cm ($1\frac{3}{8}$–2 in.) long, 1.5–1.8 cm ($\frac{19}{32}$–$\frac{11}{16}$ in.) wide, bases truncate, margins wavy, twisted, 5–8 spines on each side, long reflexed tip spines, petioles 8 mm ($\frac{5}{16}$ in.) long; stems usually purplish; slow compact habit of growth.

'Rederly' (female; synonyms 'Brownell's Rederly', 'Weiman's Sickler'; originated from a Sickler seedling, 50-year-old tree in Bailey Orchard; moved to Brownell Farms, Milwaukie, Oregon, in 1945; named and introduced by A. Brownell).

Leaves dark olive green, elliptic to oval, 4.5–5 cm ($1\frac{3}{4}$–2 in.) long, margins undulate, 4–5 spines on each side, petioles 8 mm ($\frac{5}{16}$ in.) long, stems green; fruits vivid red, globose, 10–11 mm ($\frac{3}{8}$–$\frac{7}{16}$ in.) diameter, 3–5 in cluster. Cultivar name is a combination of "red' and "early." Plate 103.

'Red Top' (male; chance seedling discovered 1968 in Darthuizer Nursery).

New leaves purplish red, stems purplish; open pyramidal habit. Introduced with 'Atlas', a superior selection; limited distribution.

'Ricker' (female; origin Takoma Park, Maryland; cuttings given to E. A. Hollowell in 1936 by P. L. Ricker, president of the Wild Flower Society; registered H.S.A. 4-63 by Hollowell).

Leaves dark olive green, elliptic to broadly elliptic, 6–8 cm ($2\frac{3}{8}$–$3\frac{1}{8}$ in.) long, 3–3.5 cm ($1\frac{3}{16}$–$1\frac{3}{8}$ in.) wide, bases rotund to truncate, margins wavy, 4–8 spines on each side, tip spines reflexed, petioles 6 mm ($\frac{7}{32}$ in.) long, stems dark; fruits vivid red 45A, globose, 10–13 mm ($\frac{3}{8}$–$\frac{1}{2}$ in.) diameter, pedicels reddish, 10 mm ($\frac{3}{8}$ in.) long; compact branching habit, columnar form; some perfect flowers observed. Selected for winter hardiness.

'Riverton' (male; selected in the 1940s in a yard in Riverton, Oregon; plant at North Willamette Experimental and Extension Center, Canby, Oregon).

Leaves dark olive green, obovate-elliptic, 5–7 cm (2–$2\frac{3}{4}$ in.) long, 2.5–3.5 cm (1–$1\frac{3}{8}$ in.) wide, bases rotund, margins wavy, 2–5 spines on each side, tip spines reflexed, petioles 8–10 mm ($\frac{5}{16}$–$\frac{3}{8}$ in.) long, stems dark purplish.

'Robert Brown' (male; seedling origin 1930 from California; selected and registered H.S.A. 8-70 by E. A. Nosal).

Leaves dark olive green, glossy, elliptic, 7.5–8.5 cm (3–$3\frac{3}{8}$ in.) long, 2.5–3.5 cm (1–$1\frac{3}{8}$ in.) wide, bases acuminate, margins wavy, 5–7 spines on each side, petioles stout, 8–11 cm ($\frac{5}{16}$–$\frac{7}{16}$ in.) long, stems purplish; globose to conical habit. Selected from 500 seedlings surviving 29°C (–20°F).

'Robinsoniana' (male; synonym 'Robinson'; old cultivar from England; introduced by Fisher, Son, and Sibray; earliest reference 1908).

Leaves dark olive green, elliptic, 7.5 cm (3 in.) long, 2.5 cm (1 in.) wide, margins undulate, long spines some straight from margin, others pointing up or down at right angles to leaf.

'Royal Red', see *I.* × *altaclerensis* 'Royal Red'.

'Rubricaulis Aurea' (female; synonyms 'Aurea Marginata', 'Aurea Marginata Rotundifolia', 'Bromeliaefolia', 'Farmers Variegated Holly'; a continental cultivar known in England before 1867).

Leaves variegated, dark olive green centers, very thin variegated margins, light yellow 10A, oval, 5–6 cm (2–$2\frac{3}{8}$ in.) long, 3.5–4 cm ($1\frac{3}{8}$–$1\frac{5}{8}$ in.) wide, bases rotund to truncate, leaves flat, 4–8 small red spines on each side, petioles 6 mm ($\frac{7}{32}$ in.) long, stems reddish brown; fruits vivid red 45A, globose, 10–12 mm ($\frac{3}{8}$–$\frac{15}{32}$ in.) diameter, pedicels reddish, 6–10 mm ($\frac{7}{32}$–$\frac{3}{8}$ in.) long.

'Sadie's Deluxe' (female; origin unknown; possible seedling; plant in S. Scudder garden, Mill Neck, New York).

Leaves dark olive green, broadly elliptic, 6.5–9 cm ($2\frac{1}{2}$–$3\frac{1}{2}$ in.) long, 3–4 cm ($1\frac{3}{16}$–$1\frac{3}{4}$ in.) wide, bases obtuse to slightly truncate, margins undulate, 6–10 spines on each side, petioles stout, 10–13 mm ($\frac{3}{8}$–$\frac{1}{2}$ in.) long, stems dark; fruits vivid red 45A, globose, 10 mm ($\frac{3}{8}$ in.) diameter, pedicels 8–10 mm ($\frac{5}{16}$–$\frac{3}{8}$ in.) long; vigorous pyramidal habit.

'Sally Hubbard' (female; registered H.S.A. 4-65 by S. F. Hubbard).

Leaves dark olive green, glossy; broadly conical habit. Selected for winter hardiness, retains green foliage in Willow Grove, Pennsylvania.

'San Gabriel' (female; origin unknown; listed by Hines Nursery, California, in 1966; plant at H. Elmore's Holly Haven Nursery).

Leaves dark olive green, lanceolate to elliptic, 4–5.5 cm (1⅝–2⅛ in.) long, 1.3 cm (½ in.) wide, bases cuneate, margins undulate, wavy, 5–7 spines on each side, tip spines reflexed, petioles 6–8 mm (7/32–5/16 in.) long, stems purplish; fruits vivid red 45A, ellipsoid, 10 mm (⅜ in.) long, 8 mm (5/16 in.) diameter, pedicels reddish, 6 mm (7/32 in.) long.

'Satan Leaf' (female; seedling selected and named by S. Scudder, from her property in Mill Neck, New York; moved to Planting Fields Arboretum in 1974).

Leaves dark olive green, broadly elliptic, 7–9 cm (2¾–3½ in.) long, 3.5–5 cm (1⅜–2 in.) wide, flat, usually 3–5 spines on each side, occasionally entire or with 1 spine at base, petioles 8–10 mm (5/16–⅜ in.) diameter; fruits red, pedicels 3–4 mm (⅛–5/32 in.) long.

'Scotch' (female; synonyms 'Golden Scotch', 'Regina Versicolor'; origin unknown; old cultivar presumably from England; plant at H. Elmore garden).

Leaves variegated, dull dark olive green centers, margins light yellow 10A, elliptic, 4.5–6 cm (1¾–2⅜ in.) long, 2–3 cm (¾–1 3/16 in.) wide, bases cuneate to obtuse, margins slightly wavy, 3–5 spines on each side, petioles 10–13 mm (⅜–½ in.) long, stems green; fruits deep reddish orange 43A, 8 mm (5/16 in.) diameter; pedicels reddish, 6 mm (7/32 in.) long; heavy fruiting.

'Scotch Gold' (male; Aurea Marginata type imported from England; named and introduced by A. Brownell in the 1950s).

Leaves variegated, dark olive green centers, large irregular greenish yellow margins, elliptic, 4.5–6.5 cm (1¾–6½ in.) long, 2–2.5 cm (¾–1 in.) wide, bases obtuse, margins undulate, wavy, 4–8 spines on each side, petioles 8 mm (5/16 in.) long; stems purplish.

'Scotica' (female; synonym 'Marginata'; old cultivar from England before 1830).

Leaves dark olive green, oval to elliptic, 5–7 cm (2–2¾ in.) long, 2.5–4 cm (1–1⅝ in.) wide, margins slightly twisted, entire, occasionally 1 single spine near apex and 1 erratic spine, petioles 8–12 mm (5/16–15/32 in.) long, stems purplish; fruits deep reddish orange 43A, shy fruiting, pedicels reddish, 5–7 mm (3/16–9/32 in.) long.

'Scotica Aurea' (female; sport of 'Scotica'; old cultivar from England; earliest reference 1863).

Leaves variegated, very similar in shape to those of 'Scotica', dark green centers, broad yellow margins, often more pronounced near the apex.

'Scotica Aurea Picta' (female; sport of 'Scotica'; old cultivar; reported from the Chestnut Nursery; earliest reference 1876).

Leaves variegated, very similar in shape to those of 'Scotica', irregular yellow blotch in center to greenish yellow, margins dark olive green.

'Serratifolia' (male; old cultivar from England around 1850, possibly from Durdham Down Nursery, Bristol, England).

Leaves dark green, glossy, lance-shaped to broad, 3–4 cm (1 3/16–1⅝ in.) long, 1.3–2.1 cm (½–13/16 in.) wide, apex elongated, keeled, 6–8 prominent spines on each side, pointing outward (not forward), apex slightly recurved (not as much as 'Recurva'), stems green or purplish; compact small shrub, dense habit. Often mistaken for 'Angustifolia', and 'Myrtifolia'. Not common in United States.

'Serratifolia Aurea Maculata' (male; old cultivar from England before 1876).

Leaves variegated, dark olive green margins, irregular yellow blotches in center.

'Sharpy' (female; origin unknown; introduced in United States before 1975; introduced to Boskoop, Netherlands by Le Feber and Company, Netherlands).

Leaves dark green, sharp spines, stems green; fruits red; vigorous upright shrub.

'Shepherdii', see *I.* × *altaclerensis* 'Hodginsii'.

'Shortspra' (female; synonym 'Wieman's Shortspra'; introduced by J. S. Wieman in the 1960s).

Leaves dark olive green, elliptic to broadly elliptic, 6–8 cm (2⅜–3⅛ in.) long, 3–3.5 cm (1 3/16–1⅜ in.) wide, bases cuneate to rotund, margins undulate, wavy, 4–6 spines on each side, petioles 8 mm (5/16 in.) long, stems green; fruits vivid red 45A, globose, 8–10 mm (5/16–⅜ in.) diameter, pedicels 5–8 mm (3/16–5/16 in.) diameter; compact upright habit. Good orchard and landscape plant.

'Silvary' (female; synonyms 'Argentea Marginata', 'Brownell's Silvary', 'Silver Broadleaf', 'Silver Princess'; original plant in a garden in Portland, Oregon, probably from England, propagated by G. Teufel; named and introduced 1935 by A. Brownell).

Leaves variegated, dark olive green centers, even margins of yellowish white, oval to elliptic, 4.5–6 cm (1¾–2⅜ in.) long, 2.3–3.5 cm (1–1⅜ in.) wide, bases obtuse to truncate, petioles 10 mm (⅜ in.)

long; stems purplish; fruits vivid red, globose to el-lipsoid, 10 mm (⅜ in.) diameter, pedicels 4 mm (⁵⁄₃₂ in.) long. Plate 104.

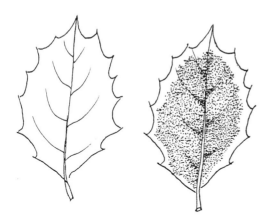

Figure 15-11. *Ilex aquifolium* 'Silvary'. Drawing by Randy Allen.

'Silver 900' (female; from R. Leach in 1956; plant at North Willamette Experimental Research and Extension Center, Canby, Oregon).
    Leaves variegated, margins light yellow 10A, centers dark olive green elliptic, 4–5.5 cm (1⅝–2⅛ in.) long, 2–2.5 cm (¾–1 in.) wide, bases cuneate to obtuse, margins slightly curved, 4–6 spines on each side, petioles 10 mm (⅜ in.) long stems green; fruits vivid red 44A, globose, 8 mm (⁵⁄₁₆ in.) diameter, pedicels 8 mm (⁵⁄₁₆ in.) long.

'Silverboy' (named by A. Brownell), see 'Handsworth New Silver'.

'Silver Broadleaf' (female; introduced from England), see 'Silvary'.

'Silver Charm' (female; synonym 'Argentea Marginata Erecta'; named by A. Brownell; very similar to 'Handsworth New Silver').
    Leaves variegated, margins pale yellowish white, wavy, spiny; fruits red. No specimens available, but could be same as 'Handsworth New Silver'.

'Silver Dust', see 'Ingramii'.

'Silver Edge' (female; synonym 'Wieman's Silver Edge'; introduced by J. S. Wieman in the 1960s).
    Leaves variegated, dark olive green centers, distinct irregular margins of pale yellowish white, oval to elliptic, 4–5 cm (1⅝–2 in.) long, 2.2–2.5 cm (¹³⁄₁₆–1 in.) wide, bases cuneate to obtuse, margins wavy, 4–6 spines on each side, petioles 5 mm (³⁄₁₆

in.) long, stems green; fruits deep reddish orange 43A, pyriform, 10 mm (⅜ in.) long, 8 mm (⁵⁄₁₆ in.) diameter, pedicels 5 mm (³⁄₁₆ in.) long.

'Silver King' (male; 'Argentea Regina'; type named by A. Brownell; generally agreed to be the same plant as 'Silver Queen', which see).

'Silver Milkboy' (female; introduced and named by Hillier and Sons Nursery; date not known).
    Leaves variegated, irregular pale yellow blotch in center to light green, margins dark olive green; seldom flowering; first reported as male, now confirmed as female, fruits red, very sparse.

'Silver Milkmaid' (female; synonyms 'Albo Picta', 'Argentea Media Picta'; old cultivar from England before 1820).
    Leaves variegated, irregular pale yellow 12D blotch in center to light green, margins dark olive green, elliptic, 4–5.5 cm (1⅝–2⅛ in.) long, 2.5–3 cm (1–1³⁄₁₆ in.) wide, bases cuneate, margins undulate, twisted, 4–5 spines on each side, tip spines reflexed, petioles 8 mm (⁵⁄₁₆ in.) long, stems green; fruits deep reddish orange 43A, globose, 8 mm (⁵⁄₁₆ in.) diameter, pedicels reddish, 8 mm (⁵⁄₁₆ in.) long. See 'Argentea Marginata'.

Silver Milkmaid Group
    A group name proposed for 'Argentea Media Picta' plants with pale yellow (cream) blotch in center of leaves. Variegation often reverts back to green.

'Silver Plane' (named by A. Brownell), see 'Handsworth New Silver'.

'Silver Princess' (named by A. Brownell), see 'Argentea Marginata' and 'Silvary'.

'Silver Queen' (male; synonyms 'Argentea Latifolia', 'Argentea Purpurea', 'Argentea Regina', 'Silver King' (U.S.A.); old cultivar from England known since 1863; Brownell listed a female 'Silver Queen', which is not correct).
    Leaves variegated, broad and irregular yellowish white margins, center dark olive green, faintly marbled gray green, broadly ovate, 7 cm (2¾ in.) long, 4.5 cm (1¾ in.) wide, young leaves pink; stems purplish; slow to develop a leader, being shrubby at an early age, later to 4–6 m (13–20 ft.) high.

'Silver Sentinel', see *I.* × *altaclerensis.* 'Belgica Aurea'.

'Silver Trim' (female; plant at North Willamette Experimental Research and Extension Center, Canby, Oregon, from R. Leach, 1956).

Leaves variegated, margins pale yellow 10A, centers dark olive green, broadly elliptic, 5–6.5 cm (2–2⅜ in.) long, 2.5–3 cm (1–1³⁄₁₆ in.) wide, bases cuneate to obtuse, margins wavy, 5–6 spines on each side, tip spines reflexed, petioles 8–10 mm (⁵⁄₁₆–⅜ in.) long, stems green; fruits vivid red 44A, globose, 8 mm (⁵⁄₁₆ in.) diameter, pedicels reddish, 6–8 mm (⁷⁄₃₂–⁵⁄₁₆ in.) long.

'Silver van Tol' (female; sport of 'J. C. van Tol'; introduced 1977 by B. Blanken, Boskoop, Netherlands).
Leaves variegated, variable, green centers, glossy, margins pale yellowish white, elliptic, 4–6 cm (1⅝–2⅜ in.) long, 3–4 cm (1³⁄₁₆–1⅝ in.) wide, slightly convex, more than 'J. C. van Tol'; fruits reddish orange. A.M. 1977.

'Silver Weeping' (female; named and introduced by A. Brownell in the 1950s). See 'Argentea Marginata Pendula'.

'Smithiana' (male; old cultivar introduced about 1863 by W. Paul; also listed as a female).
Leaves elliptic, 7.5–9 cm (3–3½ in.) long, 3–4.5 cm (1³⁄₁₆–1¾ in.) wide, bases cuneate to obtuse, margins flat, recurved, nearly entire, occasional spines near acuminate apex, petioles 10 mm (⅜ in.) long; stems green or purple.

'Somerset Cider' (female; discovered in Vaggs Hill Nursery, Somerset, England; named by G. P. Brown in the 1980s; Fructu Lutea Group).
Leaves dark green; fruits yellowish white, distinct reddish blotch on sunny side. Similar to 'Yellow Beam' and 'Bacciflava'.

'Somerset Cream' (female; branch sport of an old 'Argentea Marginata' tree at Great House Farm, North Newton, Somerset, England; discovered, named, and introduced by G. P. Brown in the 1980s).
Leaves variegated, margins green, irregular yellowish white blotches in center, margins divaricate, strong spines on each side, stems green; fruits red, numerous; upright pyramidal habit. See 'Silver Milkmaid'.

Sparkler® (female; synonym 'Monler'; origin Hunt's Nursery; introduced and trademarked around 1964 by Monrovia Nursery).
Leaves dark olive green, glossy, elliptic to narrow-elliptic, 4–5 cm (1⅝–2 in.) long, 1.8–2.2 cm (¹¹⁄₁₆–¹³⁄₁₆ in.) wide, bases cuneate to obtuse, margins slightly wavy, 6–8 spines on each side, tip spines reflexed, petioles 5–6 mm (³⁄₁₆–⁷⁄₃₂ in.) long; fruits vivid red 45A, globose, 8–10 mm (⁵⁄₁₆–⅜ in.) diameter, pedicels 5 mm (³⁄₁₆ in.) long; good clusters of fruit borne at an early age.

'Special' (female; introduced in 1940 by A. Brownell).
Leaves dark olive green, large, well-spined; fruits red, large, good producer; fast growing.

'Spiny Leaf' (female; introduced by Kingsville Nursery around 1950).
Leaves dark olive green, elliptic, 3.5–6 cm (1⅜–2⅜ in.) long, 2–2.5 cm (¾–1 in.) wide, bases cuneate to rotund, margins undulate, wavy, usually 5–8 stout spines on each side, tip spines reflexed, petioles 8 mm (⁵⁄₁₆ in.) long; stems green.

'Squire' (male; synonym 'Whitney No. 19', originally selected by W. Wheeler; seedling from Pennsylvania in 1925, grown on G. G. Whitney estate, Woods Hole, Massachusetts; registered H.S.A. 2-59 by J. K. Lilly).
Leaves narrow-elliptic.

'St. George' (male; synonym 'Whitney No. 108', originally selected by W. Wheeler; sibling of 'Squire'; registered H.S.A. 3-59 by J. K. Lilly).
Leaves dark olive green, glossy, oblong.

'Stanford White' (sex unknown; from Standford estate, Nisseguoge, New York).
Leaves variegated, margins dark olive green large irregular blotches in center, brilliant yellow green 154C, elliptic, 5–7 cm (2–2¾ in.) long, 2–3 cm (¾–1³⁄₁₆ in.) wide, bases cuneate to obtuse, apices acute, margins flat, 6–7 small spines on each side, petioles 6–8 mm (⁷⁄₃₂–⁵⁄₁₆ in.) long.

'Starker's Flat Spray'
No description available.

'Starker's Glossy Leaf'
No description available.

'Starker's Silver' (female; plant at North Willamette Experimental Research and Extension Center, Canby, Oregon).
Leaves variegated, margins light yellow 16D, centers dark olive green, oval to broadly elliptic, 6–8 cm (2⅜–3 in.) long, 2.5–3 cm (1–1³⁄₁₆ in.) wide, margins slightly wavy, 6–7 spines on each side, petioles 8 mm (⁵⁄₁₆ in.) long, stems green; fruits red, globose, 10 mm (⅜ in.) diameter, pedicels 6–8 mm (⁷⁄₃₂–⁵⁄₁₆ in.) long.

'Starker's Velvet Leaf'
No description available.

'Stührenberg Silber' (male; sport of 'Angustifolia'; discovered 1988 on 'Angustifolia' by E. Stührenberg).

Leaves larger than those of 'Angustifolia', variegated, dark green with large irregular light yellowish white blotched, spotted with small green dots, flat broadly elliptic, very attractive; upright pyramidal habit.

'Sunnybrooke' (male; named and introduced by A. Brownell before 1953).

Leaves dark olive green, elliptic, 5–7 mm (2–2¾ in.) long, 2–2.5 cm (¾–1 in.) wide, bases cuneate to obtuse, margins with 4–5 spines on each side, occasionally subentire with 1–2 spines near apex, petioles 10 mm (⅜ in.) long.

'Sunnyside' (female; named and introduced by A. Brownell before 1953).

Leaves dark olive green, glossy, elliptic, 5–6 cm (2–2⅜ in.) long, 2–2.5 cm (¾–1 in.) wide, bases cuneate to obtuse, margins undulate, 5–6 spines on each side, tip spines reflexed, petioles 10 mm (⅜ in.) long, stems dark purple; fruits vivid red 45A, globose, 8–10 mm (⁵⁄₁₆–⅜ in.) diameter, pedicels 5 mm (³⁄₁₆ in.) long.

'T. H. Everett' (male; origin New York Botanical Garden; named for Tom H. Everett before 1973).

Leaves dark olive green, glossy, elliptic, 6–8.5 cm (2⅜–3⅜ in.) long, 2.5–3.5 cm (1–1⅜ in.) wide, bases obtuse to rotund, apices acuminate, tip spines reflexed, margins undulate, variable, subentire to 1–7 spines on each side, petioles stout, 10–13 mm (⅜–½ in.) long; stems green; pyramidal habit. Good pollinator.

'Tatnall School', see *I. × altaclerensis* 'Tatnall School'.

'Teufel's' (female; synonym 'Teufel's Hybrid'; introduced in 1950 by G. Teufel).

Leaves dark olive green, broadly elliptic, 6–8 cm (2⅜–3⅛ in.) long, 3–4 cm (1³⁄₁₆–1⅝ in.) wide, bases rotund, margins wavy, entire to 2–4 small spines on each side, tip spines slightly reflexed, petioles 10 mm (⅜ in.) long, stem dark green; fruits vivid red 45B, globose, 10 mm (⅜ in.) diameter, pedicels 8 mm (⁵⁄₁₆ in.) long. Possibly a cultivar of *I. × altaclerensis*.

'Teufel's Deluxe' (female; named and introduced by G. Teufel before 1960).

Leaves dark olive green, elliptic, 5–7 cm (2–2¾ in.) long, 2.5–3 cm (1–1³⁄₁₆ in.) wide, bases obtuse, margins wavy, twisted, subentire to 2–4 spines on each side, tip spines reflexed, petioles 10 mm (⅜ in.) long; fruits deep reddish orange 43A, globose, 10 mm (⅜ in.) diameter, pedicels reddish, 6–8 mm (⁷⁄₃₂–⁵⁄₁₆ in.) long. Possibly a cultivar of *I. × altaclerensis*.

Teufel Hybrids

In addition to the 5 Teufel hybrids described here, the following are without descriptions. 'Teufel's Falco', 'Teufel's French' (female), 'Teufel's French Hybrid', 'Teufel's Green' (female), 'Teufel's Silvertip', 'Teufel's Weeping', and 'Teufel's Yellowberry'. Some may be *I. × altaclerensis* hybrids.

'Teufel's Large Berry' (female; introduced by G. Teufel before 1960).

Leaves dark olive green, oval to broadly elliptic, 5.5–6.5 cm (2⅛–2½ in.) long, 3–3.5 cm (1³⁄₁₆–1⅜ in.) wide, bases cuneate to obtuse, margins wavy, entire to 1–3 spines on each side, on upper one-third of leaf, tip spines reflexed, petioles 10 mm (⅜ in.) long; fruits deep reddish orange 43A, ellipsoid to globose, 10–12 mm (⅜–¹⁵⁄₃₂ in.) diameter, in good clusters, pedicels 6–8 mm (⁷⁄₃₂–⁵⁄₁₆ in.) long.

'Teufel's Silver Variegated' (female; introduced by G. Teufel before 1960).

Leaves variegated, margins light yellow 10A, dark olive green centers, elliptic, 5–6.5 cm (2–2½ in.) long, 2.5–3 cm (1–1³⁄₁₆ in.) wide, bases obtuse to rotund, margins slightly wavy, 6–7 spines on each side, tip spines reflexed, petioles 10 mm (⅜ in.) long; fruits vivid red 44A, globose, 8 mm (⁵⁄₁₆ in.) diameter, in good clusters, pedicels reddish, 8 mm (⁵⁄₁₆ in.) long. Plate 105.

'Teufel's Special' (female; introduced by G. Teufel, in the 1960s; small plant at Tyler Arboretum).

Leaves dark olive green, elliptic to ovate, 5–7 cm (2–2¾ in.) long, 2.5–4 cm (1–1⅝ in.) wide, bases cuneate to rotund, apices acute, margins undulate, 4–6 spines on each side, petioles reddish, 10 mm (⅜ in.) long; stems purplish; fruits not seen.

'Thornton' (female; 30-year-old tree discovered in 1962 on a farm north of Warneck, Maryland; named and registered H.S.A 6-65 by L. F. Livingston).

Leaves dark olive green, glossy, foliage green year round; very hardy.

'Tiger' (female; original tree in park at Wellington, Somerset, England; discovered and named by G. P. Brown in the 1980s; not introduced).

Leaves green, spiny; fruits yellow, 4 distinct red lines separating the quarters; strong upright habit.

'Tortuosa', see 'Crispa'.

'Trapeziformis', see 'Latispina'.

'Tremough' (female; 50-year-old-tree; found at abandoned home near Wytheville, Virginia; named and registered H.S.A. 5-63 by S. J. Kincer).

Leaves dark olive green, glossy, elliptic, 4–5 cm (1⅝–2 in.) long, 2–2.5 cm (¾–1 in.) wide, margins undulate 4–5 spines on each side, small tip leaves with 7–8 small spines on each side, petioles 5 mm (³⁄₁₆ in.) long, stems purplish; fruits red, globose, abundant; broad habit; withstanding −18°C (0°F).

'Tricolor' (female; Callaway Gardens; graft made in 1953, records of scion wood lost in fire).

Leaves variegated, margins light greenish yellow 8B, dark olive green centers, some tip leaves completely yellow; oval, 4.5–6 cm (1¾–2⅜ in.) long, 3–3.5 cm (1³⁄₁₆–1⅜ in.) wide, nearly flat, 5–7 spines on each side, stems reddish brown; fruits red, globose, 6 mm (⁷⁄₃₂ in.) diameter, pedicels 5–6 mm (³⁄₁₆–⁷⁄₃₂ in.) long.

'20 Below' (female; selected in Oregon in the late 1960s by R. Leach).

Leaves dark olive green, elliptic, 5.5–6.5 cm (2⅛–2½ in.) long, 2.5–3 cm (1–1³⁄₁₆ in.) wide, bases cuneate to obtuse, entire, to 2–4 spines on each side, tip spines reflexed, margin wavy, petioles 8 mm (⁵⁄₁₆ in.) long; fruits deep reddish orange 43A, globose, 8 mm (⁵⁄₁₆ in.) diameter, pedicels 8 mm (⁵⁄₁₆ in.) long, good fruit clusters.

'Vaggs Hill Yellow' (female; parent tree in Vaggs Hill Nursery, Yeovil, Somerset, England; discovered before 1977, named and introduced by G. P. Brown).

Fruits yellow, heavy clusters. Similar to 'Bacciflava'.

'Victoria' (male; synonyms 'Aurea Marginata Latifolia', 'Aurea Regina Nigra'; old cultivar from England, known before 1880).

Leaves variegated, dark green, elliptic, 5–6.5 cm (2–2½ in.) long, 2.5 cm (1 in.) wide, spines variable, stems usually purplish green, three types of foliage. (1) dark green, pale margins and pale blotching, stems green; (2) dark green, marbled blotching, broad yellow irregular margin; (3) entire twigs with yellow leaves, occasionally blotches of pale green.

'Viking' (male; origin, open-pollinated seedling of 'Donningtonensis' from K. Meserve, 1958; plant at U.S. National Arboretum; selected and named by R. J. Fleming, 1982).

Leaves olive green, glossy, elliptic 5–6 cm (2–2⅜

in.) long, 2.5–3 cm (1–1³⁄₁₆ in.) wide, margins wavy 4–5 spines each side; petioles stout, 8–9 mm (⁵⁄₁₆–¹¹⁄₃₂ in.) long; abundant flowers.

'Vineland' (male; open-pollinated seedling of 'Donningtonensis' from K. Meserve, 1958; selected and named by R. J. Fleming, 1982; plant at U.S. National Arboretum possibly a cultivar of *I.* × *altaclerensis*).

Leaves dark olive green, glossy, elliptic, 5.5–6 cm (2⅛–2⅜ in.) long, 2.5–3 cm (1–1³⁄₁₆) wide, curved, variable, nearly entire to 4 spines on each side, tips reflexed; petioles 10 mm (⅜ in.) long; stems dark green; flowers abundant.

'Virginia Nosal' (female; origin, seed from Cottage Gardens in 1930; selected and introduced before 1960 by E. A. Nosal; registered H.S.A. 9-70 by M. A. Nosal).

Leaves dark olive green, glossy, very large, variable, often strong divaricate spines, sometime spineless, stem purplish; fruits dark red, pyriform, 6 in cluster; broadly conical habit, hardy to −29°C (−20°F).

'Vreeland' (male; plant at Callaway Gardens; received in 1958 from T. Dilatush).

Leaves dark olive green, ovate, 6.5–8 cm (2½–3⅛ in.) long, 3–5 cm (1³⁄₁₆–2 in.) wide, bases rotund, margins usually entire or 1–4 spines on each side, petioles stout, 10 mm (⅜ in.) long, stems purplish. Possibly a clone of *I.* × *altaclerensis*.

'W. J. Bean', see *I.* × *altaclerensis* 'W. J. Bean'.

'Walton's Male' (male; possibly introduced by Millcreek Nursery in the 1960s).

Leaves dark olive green, elliptic, 5–5.8 cm (2–2¼ in.) long, 2–2.5 cm (¾–1 in.) wide, bases cuneate to obtuse, margins undulate, wavy, 5–6 spines on each side, tip spines reflexed, petioles 8 mm (⁵⁄₁₆ in.) long, stems purplish.

'Watereriana' (male; synonyms 'Nana Aurea Variegata', 'Waterer's Gold Striped', 'Waterer's Male'; old cultivar from Waterer's Nursery, Knap Hill, England, before 1863).

Leaves variegated, dark olive green mottled with greenish yellow and gray-green sectional stripes, irregular yellow margins, occasionally leaves half to entirely yellow, oval to elliptic, 4–4.5 cm (1⅝–1¾ in.) long, 2–3.5 cm (¾–1⅜ in.) wide, margins entire to 2–4 spines on each side, top leaves often entire, petioles 8 mm (⁵⁄₁₆ in.) long; stems green striped greenish yellow; dense compact, slow growing.

'Watereriana Compacta' (synonym 'Waterer's Green').

Compact dense habit of growth.

'Waterer's Dwarf Golden' (synonyms *I. nana, I. nanum,* possibly 'Watereriana'; origin unknown).

'Waterer's Green' (male; old cultivar from England; plant at Bokrijk Arboretum, Belgium).

Leaves moderate olive green, slightly variegated, very narrow irregular, whitish margins, 4–5 cm (1⅝–2 in.) long, 2.5 cm (1 in.) wide, irregular small spines, 1–3 on each side, upper half of leaf, branches dark purple; upright pyramidal habit.

Figure 15-12. *Ilex aquifolium* 'Waterer's Green'. Photo by Hans-Georg Buchtmann.

'Weeping Golden Milkmaid' (female; synonyms 'Aurea Picta Pendula', 'Pendula Aurea Picta'; old English cultivar per S. Andrews; plant at Royal Botanical Garden, Kew, England, 1975).

Leaves variegated, irregular greenish yellow, blotching in center of leaf; distinct weeping habit.

'Wheeler No. 4' (female; synonym 'Whitney No. 4'; introduced by W. Wheeler; see Whitney Holly Group).

Leaves dark olive green, elliptic, 5.5–8 cm (2⅛–3⅛ in.) long, 2.5–3.5 cm (1–1⅜ in.) wide, bases cuneate to obtuse, margins undulate, usually 3–6 spines on each side, occasionally subentire, petioles 8–13 mm (5/16–½ in.) long; stems green; fruits red, globose, 8 mm (5/16 in.) diameter, pedicels reddish, 6–8 mm (6/32–5/16 in.) long.

'Whipple's Seedling No. 5' (female; seedling discovered by the late M. Whipple in his garden in St. James, New York; planned to name and register).

Leaves dark olive green, ovale to oval, 5.5–7.5 cm (2⅛–3 in.) long, 4 cm (1⅝ in.) wide, bases truncate, apices acute, tip spines reflexed, margins undulate, 4–5 widely spaced spines on each side, petioles 7–10 mm (9/32–⅜ in.) long; stems purplish; fruits red, globose.

'Whitesail' (female; synonym 'Osgood'; seedling selection of 'Handsworth New Silver'; named and introduced by J. S. Wieman in the 1960s).

Leaves variegated, margins pale yellowish white, dark olive green centers, elliptic, 5–7 cm (2–2¾ in.) long, 1.5–2.5 cm (19/32–1 in.) wide, bases cuneate, usually 4–5 spines on each side, petioles 8 mm (5/16 in.) long; stems purplish.

Whitney Holly Group

A collective name given to 6 of the best female hollies on G. G. Whitney estate, Woods Hole, Massachusetts; selected by W. Wheeler from 100 seedlings purchased around 1925 or 1931 from a nursery in Pennsylvania or New York. Cold hardy to −29°C (−20°F). Wheeler numbered them 1 through 5 and AX (outside garden), then later renamed some of them. 'Evangeline' registered H.S.A. 15-60 by J. K. Lilly. See *I.* × *altaclerensis* 'Father Charles', also in the Wheeler and Whitney Group and 'Mrs. Goefrey Whitney'.

'Wheeler No. 1' = 'Whitney No. 1', synonym 'Alice'
'Wheeler No. 2' = 'Whitney No. 2'
'Wheeler No. 3' = 'Whitney No. 3'
'Wheeler No. 4' = 'Whitney No. 4'
'Wheeler No. 5' = 'Whitney No. 5', synonym 'Gloria'
'Wheeler AX' = 'Whitney AX', syn 'Hazel', 'Evangeline'

'Whittingtonensis' (male; old cultivar from England; introduced by Fisher, Son, and Sibray; earliest reference 1863).

Leaves dark olive green, lanceolate or elliptic-ovate, 6.5–7.5 cm (2½–3 in.) long, 1.6–2.5 cm (⅝–1 in.) wide, margins recurved, wavy, 5–7 stiff spines, often unequally spaced. Similar to 'Donningtonensis' but with more spines and lighter green leaves. Can be confused with 'Robinsoniana'.

'Wieman's Beacon', see 'Beacon'.

'Wieman's Beautyspra', see 'Beautyspra'.

'Wieman's Brightbush' (female; synonyms 'Brightbush', 'Pinto'; sport of 'Wieman's Globe'; selected about 1945 and registered H.S.A. 8-84 by J. S. Wieman).

Leaves variegated, center blotched and streaked brilliant yellow, irregularly banded light green, margins irregularly marked dark olive green, variable, ovate to elliptic to obovate, 5.5–7 cm (2⅛–2¾ in.) long, 3.5–4.5 cm (1⅜–1¾ in.) wide, bases cuneate to attenuate, margins undulate 4–7 large spines on each side, tip spines reflexed, twisted, petioles pale yellow, flat, 1–1.3 cm (⅜–½ in.) long; stems purplish; fruits vivid red 44A, globose to pyriform, 14 mm (17/32 in.) diameter, 1–5 in clusters, pedicels 13 mm (½ in.) long.

'Wieman's Chief' (male; synonym 'Chief'; introduced by J. S. Wieman in the 1960s).

Leaves dark olive green, ovate-elliptic, 4.5–6.5 cm (1¾–2½ in.) long, 2.5–3 cm (1–1 3/16 in.) wide, bases obtuse to rotund, margins undulate, wavy, 5–6 spines on each side, tip spines reflexed, petioles 10–13 mm (⅜–½ in.) long; stems dark green, abundant male flowers; hardy.

'Wieman's Crinklegreen' (female; seedling selected, named, and registered H.S.A. 7-82 by J. S. Wieman).

Leaves dark olive green, ovate to obovate, 6.7 cm (2⅝ in.) long, 3.2 cm (1¼ in.) wide, margins strongly divaricate, 4–6 spines on each side, tip spines often off-centered, strongly reflexed, often cantered to one side, petioles 7 mm (9/32 in.) long; fruits vivid red 45A, globose, 10 mm (⅜ in.) diameter, pedicels 5 mm (3/16 in.) long, 6 per cluster; low conical habit. Selected for Christmas pot plants.

'Wieman's Dude', see 'Dude'.

'Wieman's Early Cluster', see 'Early Cluster'.

'Wieman's Favorite', see *I.* × *altaclerensis* 'Wieman's Favorite'.

'Wieman's Globe' (female; synonym 'Globe'; seedling selected at Knappa-Swensen, Oregon; named and registered H.S.A. 14-61 by J. S. Wieman).

Leaves dark olive green, elliptic, 4.5–6.5 cm (1¾–2½ in.) long, 2.2–3 cm (13/16–1 3/16 in.) wide, bases cuneate to rotund, margins undulate, wavy, 4–7 spines on each side, petioles 6–8 cm (7/32–5/16 in.) long; stems green; fruits vivid red 45A, globose to ellipsoid, 10 mm (⅜ in.) long, 8 mm (5/16 in.) diameter, pedicels reddish, 8 mm (5/16 in.) long; compact rounded habit.

'Wieman's Greenspread' (female; chance seedling discovered 1970 by J. S. Wieman; named and registered H.S.A. 6-82 by Wieman).

Leaves dark olive green, glossy, ovate to narrow-elliptic, variable in size to 9 cm (3½ in.) long, 4.5 cm (1¾ in.) wide, flat wavy margins, divaricate, thick almost revolute, 2–6 large, stout spines pointing forward, petioles 10 mm (⅜ in.) long; stems green; fruits red, globose, 11 mm (7/16 in.) diameter, pedicels 5 mm (3/16 in.) long. Good landscape plant, with shrubby, compact, fastigiate branching.

'Wieman's Hedge-row', see *I.* × *altaclerensis* 'Wieman's Hedge-row'.

'Wieman's Ivory' (female; named and introduced by J. S. Wieman in the 1970s).

Leaves variegated, light green, wide-varying margin of pale yellowish white; fruits red.

'Wieman's Longspra', see 'Longspra'.

'Wieman's Low-spread' (female; chance seedling discovered in Portland, Oregon, about 1972 and registered H.S.A. 9-84 by J. S. Wieman).

Leaves dark olive green, ovate, variable in size, 4.5–7.3 cm (1¾–2⅛ in.) long, 2.5–4.5 cm (1–1¾ in.) wide, bases obtuse to truncate, margins undulate, wavy, 8–10 spines on each side, tip spines reflexed, petioles 8–10 mm (5/16–⅜ in.) long, stems purplish; fruits vivid reddish orange 44B, pyriform, 11 mm (7/16 in.) long, 13 mm (½ in.) diameter, good clusters, pedicels 10–13 mm (⅜–½ in.) long; low spreading habit.

'Wieman's Moonbrite' (male; synonyms 'Moonbrite', 'Moonglow'; controlled cross of 'Flavescens' × 'Duke' in 1966 by J. S. Wieman; registered H.S.A. 3-75 by Wieman).

Leaves variegated, green with large blotches of suffused yellow usually at apex, to tip leaves entirely yellow, elliptic, 8–9.5 cm (3–3¾ in.) long, 5 cm (2 in.) wide, margins thickened, undulate, 7–8 large spines on each side, tip spines reflexed, petioles 6 mm (7/32 in.) long; conical compact habit. First cultivar of 'Flavescens' type to be selected, named, and registered from controlled hybridization.

'Wieman's Pinto', see 'Pinto'.

'Wieman's Sickler', see 'Rederly'

'Wieman's Yellow Beam', see 'Yellow Beam'.

'Wieman's Yellowberry', see 'Wieman's Yellow-pillar'.

'Wieman's Yellow-pillar' (female; synonym 'Wieman's Yellowberry'; chance seedling discovered about 1967; named and registered H.S.A. 9-82 by J. S. Wieman).

Leaves dark olive green, broadly ovate to broadly obovate, to 7 cm (2¾ in.) long, 3.2 cm (1¼ in.) wide, 2–7 strong spines on each side, tip spines reflexed; fruits vivid yellow 13B, globose to slightly elongate, 10 mm (⅜ in.) diameter, to 6 in clusters, pedicels 7 mm (9/32 in.) long; columnar habit. Plate 106.

'Wietmarschen' (female; seedling discovered in 1963 in a large stand of *I. aquifolium* by P. Germer).

Leaves deep dark green, glossy, elliptic, 6–8 cm (2⅜–3⅛ in.) long, 2.5–4 cm (1–1⅝ in.) wide, subentire 1–3 spines on each side, often only 1 spine, spines 10 mm (⅜ in.) long, petioles 10 mm (⅜ in.) long; fruits light red, globose, 8–10 mm (5/16–⅜ in.) diameter, numerous, colors early, persist until new fruit appears; dense upright habit; propagates readily; hardy to −22°C (−8°F).

'Wil-Chris' (female; synonym 'Mallett'; selected around 1949 in Oregon by Bob Mannle; named by Will Curtis and Dr. Davis, in late 1970s).

Leaves dark olive green, elliptic to broadly elliptic, 6–8 cm (2⅜–3⅛ in.) long, 2.5–3 cm (1–1 3/16 in.) wide, bases rotund to truncate, margins wavy, 5–6 spines on each side, tip spines reflexed, petioles dark, 6–8 mm (7/32–5/16 in.) long, stems purplish; fruits deep reddish orange 43A, globose, 6–8 mm (7/32–5/16 in.) diameter, pedicels reddish, 6–8 mm (7/32–5/16 in.) long. Plate 107.

'William Hubbard' (male; named and registered H.S.A. 5-65 by S. F. Hubbard, Mechanicsville, Pennsylvania).

Similar to 'Sally Hubbard'. Selected for winter hardiness.

'Willow Grove' (female; plant in Tyler Arboretum from W. Germain, Horsham (near Willow Grove), Pennsylvania).

Leaves dark olive green, elliptic, 5.8–7 cm (2⅛–2¾ in.) long, 2.5–3.5 cm (1–1⅜ in.) wide, bases obtuse, apices acute, margins variable, entire to spiny, 1–9 spines on each side, petioles 8–10 mm (5/16–⅜ in.) long; stems green; fruits red, ellipsoid, 8–10 mm diameter, pedicels reddish, 6 mm (7/32 in.) long, sparse fruiting; compact pyramidal habit. Possibly a cultivar of *I. × altaclerensis*.

'Wilsonii' (female; chance seedling from Fisher, Son, and Sibray in early 1890s; introduced from England in 1899).

Leaves dark olive green, glossy, broadly ovate, 10–12 cm (4–4¾ in.) long, 6–8 cm (2⅜–3 in.) wide, bases cuneate to rotund, prominent light green midribs, margins slightly wavy, occasionally subentire or 6–9 spines on each side, pointing forward, petioles stout, 10 mm (⅜ in.) long, stems green; fruits vivid red 45A, globose to slightly ellipsoid, 10 mm (⅜ in.) diameter, abundant; vigorous compact pyramidal habit. Popular old cultivar. F.C.C. 1899, A.G.M. 1969. Plate 108.

'Winter Green' (female; chance seedling discovered by R. K. Peters about 1976; female parent thought to be 'Martha Lower'; named in 1986 and registered H.S.A. 1-87 by Peters).

Leaves dark olive green, glossy, variable, elliptic to broadly ovate, 5–7.5 cm (2–3 in.) long, 3–5 cm (1 3/16–2 in.) wide, bases rotund, keeled, curved, margins slightly wavy, 5–7 spines on each side, tip spines reflexed, occasionally leaves subentire, petioles 6–10 mm (7/32–⅜ in.) long, stems green; fruits vivid red 44A, globose to slightly pyriform, 13 mm (½ in.) long, 10 mm (⅜ in.) diameter, pedicels reddish, 4–6 mm (5/32–7/32 in.) long; conical habit; 2.8 m (8 ft.) tall, 1.2 m (4 ft.) wide in 10 years; hardy in zone 5, survived −32°C (−28°F) in 1978.

'Winter King' (male; named and introduced in 1955 by A. Brownell).

Leaves dark olive green, oval, 4.5–6.5 cm (1¾–2½ in.) long, 2.5–3.5 cm (1–1⅜ in.) wide, bases obtuse to rotund, margins subentire, occasionally 2–3 small spines on upper half of leaf, petioles stout, 10–13 mm (⅜–½ in.) long, stems green. Possibly a clone of *I. × altaclerensis*.

'Winter Queen' (female; named and introduced by A. Brownell in the 1950s).

Leaves dark olive green, glossy, elliptic, keeled, 5–6 cm (2–2⅜ in.) long, 2–3 cm (¾–1 3/16 in.) wide, bases obtuse, apices acuminate, tip spines reflexed, margins undulate, 2–4 spines on each side, occasionally subentire, petioles 8 mm (5/16 in.) long, stems green; fruits vivid red 45A, globose to slightly pyriform, 10–13 mm (⅜–½ in.) diameter, 1–3 in clusters, pedicels reddish, 5 mm (3/16 in.) long.

'Wreath Berry' (female; origin possibly from Clarendon Gardens early in the 1960s).

Leaves smooth; fruits red, large. No other description available. Possibly a clone of *I. × altaclerensis*.

Xanthocarpa (female; name given by some to plants with yellow fruits; Fructu Lutea Group; should not be used further as a cultivar name).

'Yellow Beam' (female; synonym 'Wieman's Yellow Beam'; chance seedling of yellow-berried plant; selected, named, and registered H.S.A. 9-76 by J. S. Wieman).

Leaves dark olive green, broadly elliptic, 4.5–7 cm (1¾–2¾ in.) long 2.5–4 cm (1–1⅝ in.) wide, bases obtuse to rotund, margins wavy, 8–9 stout spines on each side, petioles 6.5 mm (¼ in.) long; fruits vivid yellow 12A, globose, 8–10 mm (5⁄16–⅜ in.) diameter, good clusters, pedicels 6–8 mm (7⁄32–5⁄16 in.) long; oval habit horizontal branching. Firm fruit, resists bruising, popular for commercial packing. Plate 109.

'Yocum' (synonym 'Yokum'), see *I.* × *altaclerensis* 'Yocum'.

'Yonkers' (female; large plant at Boyce Thompson Institute; named about 1941 by W. Wheeler).

Leaves dark olive green, elliptic, 4.5–6 cm (1¾–2⅜ in.) long, 2–2.8 cm (¾–1¼ in.) wide, bases obtuse to truncate, margins undulate, 4–6 spines on each side, petioles 8–10 mm (5⁄16–⅜ in.) long, stems dark; fruits vivid red, globose, 8–10 mm (5⁄16–⅜ in.) diameter, pedicels reddish, 5 mm (3⁄16 in.) long.

'Yule Glow' (female; synonym 'Yuleglow'; origin unknown; plant at North Willamette Research and Extension Center, Canby, Oregon).

Leaves dark olive green, glossy, broadly elliptic, 5–6.5 cm (2–2⅜ in.) long, 3–3.5 cm (1 3⁄16–1⅜ in.) wide, bases cuneate to obtuse, margins twisted, undulate, 4–6 spines on each side, tip spines reflexed, petioles 8–10 mm (5⁄16–⅜ in.) long, stems green; fruits vivid red 45A, globose, 10 mm (⅜ in.) diameter, good clusters, pedicels reddish, 8 mm (5⁄16 in.) long.

'Zella' (female; origin unknown, possibly Wilmat Nursery before 1954; plant growing at Scott Arboretum, Swarthmore, Pennsylvania).

Leaves dark olive green, broadly elliptic to oval, keeled, 4–5.5 cm (1⅝–2⅛ in.) long, 2.2–3.5 cm (1 3⁄16–1⅜ in.) wide, bases rotund, apices acuminate, tip spines reflexed, margins undulate, 3–5 spines on each side, petioles 5 mm (3⁄16 in.) long; fruits vivid red 45A, globose, 8 mm (5⁄16 in.) diameter, 1–3 in clusters, pedicels reddish, 3–5 mm (⅛–3⁄16 in.) long.

'Zelta's Elite' (female; synonym 'Crinkle Green Sport'; sport of 'Crinkle Variegated' discovered by J. S. Wieman in 1980 and named for his daughter; registered H.S.A. 2-94 by Wieman).

Twigs purplish brown; leaves variegated, oval-elliptic, keeled, dark green center 131A, variably streaked light green, margins irregular yellow 8w 8A, tips aristate, bases cuneate to truncate, margins yellow with 2–7 variable stout, divaricate, spines on each side, tip spines reflexed down, sometimes twisted, 4–5 cm (1⅝–2 in.) long, 2–2.5 cm (¾–1 in.) wide, bases rotund, petioles 8 mm (5⁄16 in.) long; fruits red 45B, ovoid-obovoid, to 9 mm (11⁄32 in.) long, 8 mm (5⁄16 in.) wide, singly or in fascicles of 2–3, pedicels 6 mm (7⁄32 in.) long. Hardiness unknown, only tested in coastal Oregon and San Mateo, California, possibly hardy in zone 7. Selected for outstanding gold-marginated, variegated leaves.

'Zero' (female; synonym 'Teufel's Weeping'; selected by G. Teufel before 1960).

Leaves dark olive green, broadly elliptic, 6–8 cm (2⅜–3 in.) long, 3–3.5 cm (1 3⁄16–1⅜ in.) wide, bases rotund to slightly truncate, margins recurved, wavy, 5–7 spines on each side, petioles 6–8 mm (7⁄32–5⁄16 in.) long, stems purplish; fruits deep reddish orange, 43A, globose, 8 mm (5⁄16 in.) diameter, pedicels reddish, 6–8 mm (7⁄32–5⁄16 in.) long; vigorous, upright weeping habit. Hardy, hence the name 'Zero'.

'Zimmerman No. 1' (origin unknown; plant at Callaway Gardens obtained from Wells Nursery, Bridgeton, New Jersey).

Doubtful if available.

'Zimmerman No. 2' (female; origin unknown; plant at Callaway Gardens obtained from Wells Nursery, Bridgeton, New Jersey).

Leaves dark olive green, broadly elliptic, 5–7 cm (2–2¾ in.) long, 3–3.5 cm (1 3⁄16–1⅜ in.) wide, bases obtuse to rotund, margins wavy, 6–8 spines on each side, petioles 8 mm (5⁄16 in.) long; fruits vivid red, globose, 10 mm (⅜ in.) diameter, pedicels 6 mm (7⁄32 in.) long. Doubtful if available.

Ilex × *attenuata* Cultivars

Ilex × *attenuata* was the first interspecific hybrid of holly established from North American native plants. Willard Ashe determined this hybrid based on native hollies collected near Mossyhead Post Office, Walton County, Florida (hybrid plants no longer found in this area). Ashe described it in 1924 as an interspecific hybrid of *I. cassine* and *I. opaca*. *Ilex cassine* is extremely variable in leaf size and form and, in 1924, included var. *angustifolia* and var. *myrtifolia*. Today many references and specialists list *I. myrtifolia* at the specific rank. Many authorities include the Foster Hybrid Group and other hybrids of *I. myrtifolia* × *I. opaca* under *I.* × *attenuata*; however, it is best to list *I.* × *attenuata* as an interspecific hybrid of *I. cassine × I. opaca,* which in the broadest sense includes *I. myrtifolia.* This is the view adopted in the present volume.

Theodor Loesener (1901) noted intermediate forms of *Ilex cassine × I. opaca* and of *I. myrtifolia × I. cassine,* but he did not assign Latin names. Alfred Rehder (1940) reported that *I. × attenuata* was first cultivated in 1933 and that *I. topeli* Hort. (of garden origin) was the name first used. He placed *I. topeli* in synonymy to *I. × attenuata.* Eisenbeiss (1973) reported that *I. topeli* was listed in two different nursery catalogs in 1922.

Ilex × attenuata is a naturally occurring and artificial hybrid involving *I. cassine × I. opaca,* and *I. myrtifolia × I. opaca.* The range of natural occurring hybrids is within the areas where the three species occur. This is roughly confined to the coastal areas of South Carolina, North Carolina, southern Georgia, Florida, Alabama, Mississippi, and Louisiana. Artificial hybrids result from controlled crosses or from seedlings of plants where two or more of the parental taxa grow near by. It is of interest to point out that no natural narrow-leaved hybrids such as in the Foster Hybrid Group have been reported in the wild. I have seen, in natural uniform populations of *I. myrtifolia,* plants of *I. opaca* nearby. Ted Dudley (pers. comm.) also reported observing one stand of *I. myr-*

tifolia in Lake County, Florida, with *I. opaca* in the vicinity.

Ilex × attenuata and its numerous cultivars usually have entire leaves, or nearly so with only small spines usually on the upper half of the leaf, and attenuate leaf bases. There are entire leaf forms of *I. opaca* f. *subintegra,* and those found are in the wild outside the range of *I. cassine* and *I. myrtifolia. Ilex opaca* found in the range of *I. cassine* and *I. myrtifolia* can usually be distinguished by the characteristics listed in Table 8. It should be noted that no clear cut description of *I. × attenuata* exists due to the natural variability within each of the three species.

In the 1940s the Foster Hybrid Group was introduced by the late E. E. Foster of Foster Nursery, Bessemer, Alabama. The five or six cultivars introduced were chance hybrids from a plant similar to *Ilex cassine* var. *angustifolia* or *I. myrtifolia* pollinated by a nearby cultivar of *I. opaca.* There is still speculation as to the identity of the female parent plant. The late Joseph McDaniel reported on the Foster Hybrids, but unfortunately did not get to see the original parent plants before they were removed. I visited Foster in the mid 1950s, saw the parent plant, and later described it as *I. cassine* var. *angustifolia,* a narrow-leaved variety. At that time I had no experience with *I. myrtifolia,* which the plant could have

Table 8. Variations between *I. opaca, I. cassine, I. myrtifolia,* and *I. × attenuata.*

I. opaca	*I. × attenuata*	*I. cassine*	*I. myrtifolia*
Leaves usually heavy to moderate, strong spines; f. *subintegra* with entire leaves.	Leaves entire, or only spines on upper ½ of leaf.	Leaves sublanceolate to elliptic, 2.5–3.8 cm (1–1½ in.) long, margins usually entire.	Leaves elliptic to linear, 4–10 cm (1½–4 in.) long, margins usually entire.
Leaves of heavier texture.	Leaves thinner.	Leaves moderate texture.	Leaves moderate to heavy texture.
Leaf bases cuneate to rotund, apices cuneate to acute; often margins spinose to base.	Leaf bases and apices usually attenuate.	—	—
Flowers borne on new growth.	Flowers later, just following *I. opaca.*	—	—
Fruit ripens mid November to early December.	Fruit ripens mid to late November, before *I. opaca.*	—	—
Seed germination 1–2 years.	Seed germination usually 3–6 months.	—	—
Winter hardy, zones 5–6.	Usually less winter hardy, to zone 7, rarely zone 6a.	—	—
Pyrenes longer 6–9.25 mm (7/32–1 1/32 in.).	Pyrenes shorter, 3.9 mm (4/25 in), rarely to 6 mm (7/32 in.).	—	—
Young twigs thick, fruits typically borne singly.	Young twigs thin, fruit borne on cymes of 2–3 fruits.	—	—
Fruits typically large.	Fruits typically smaller.	—	—

very well been. This again points up the difficulty in getting correct information when specimens and data are not recorded.

Unfortunately my many early notes and correspondence on holly were moved after retiring and later lost or destroyed. I am only aware of five Foster Hybrids: No. 1, 2, 3, and 5, females, and No. 4, male. McDaniel reported a No. 6, male, but unfortunately there are no records or source of this plant. Both 'Foster No. 2' and 'Foster No. 3' are heavy fruiting and very similar in leaf shape; both were propagated in the late 1950s and 1960s and sold as Foster Holly. It is now generally agreed that 'Foster No. 2' is a very important commercial holly in the eastern United States.

Foster did not grow any F2 seedlings from his hybrids. This work was done by the late Philip Brosemer in Huntsville, Alabama, who produced numerous extremely variable F2 and F3 seedlings. Some of these plants were sold as "Foster Seedlings" or "Foster Hollies." Brosemer's nursery unfortunately was subdivided and discontinued. Some of his best Foster Seedlings were purchased by the late Geddes Douglas, Brentwood, Tennessee, who plans to name and register some of them. He had some ten or more numbered selections, two yellow-fruited plants, an orange-fruited plant, and some with very narrow linear leaves. Again there are no records of these plants being named. I visited Douglas several times and in 1975 was given some of these numbered plants for Callaway Gardens. Unfortunately most of these plants were destroyed, but two plants of 'Foster No. 2' (males) survived at my home.

The late Al Scherff of the now defunct Athens Nursery in Georgia had some of the Brosemer Foster Seedlings, but there are no records to determine if these were the same as the Douglas plants. I have two yellow-fruited plants and several unlabeled plants from Scherff for evaluation. It would be interesting to know if the relatively newly introduced 'Alagold' and 'Blazer' are from the original Brosemer seedlings or seedlings of them.

The first reported controlled crosses of *Ilex myrtifolia* or *I. cassine* var. *myrtifolia* × *I. opaca* were made by Henry Skinner while at the Morris Arboretum in Philadelphia, Pennsylvania. These plants, not introduced, were very similar to 'Foster No. 2' but with very wavy leaves. W. F. (Bill) Kosar continued breeding the Skinner hybrids at the U.S. National Arboretum. He produced F2 and F3 progenies with leaves more like 'Foster No. 2' than the original Skinner F1 hybrids (see 'Oriole' and 'Tanager').

In 1960 Bill Kosar made controlled crosses of *Ilex cassine* × *I. opaca* 'Jersey Knight'. Some of these plants, none introduced, are still growing at the U.S. National Arboretum. All are compact but of weak

tree habit. The leaves, similar to those of 'East Palatka', are larger than those of the female *I. cassine* parent and equal or larger in length than those of the male *I. opaca* parent. The terminal leaves are consistently obovate to oblanceolate and attenuate at the base.

O. M. Neal at West Virginia University, Morgantown, West Virginia, also made crosses in the late 1950s and early 1960s of *Ilex cassine* × *I. opaca*, and *I. myrtifolia* × *I. opaca* (e.g., 'Erma Byrd', 'Hallie Carrico', 'Monongahelia', 'Mountain State').

The study of *Ilex* × *attenuata*, the Foster hollies, and many others is incomplete. As pointed out by G. K. Eisenbeiss there is still need for additional field study of *I. cassine*, its natural variations, and its named varieties. Due to the increasing disturbance of natural areas the need is urgent.

'Alagold' (female; open-pollinated seedling of 'Foster No. 2' discovered in 1965 by J. A. Webb; introduced in 1979 by Webb and Rainbow Nursery; named and registered H.S.A. 1-83 by C. Pounders).

Leaves dark olive green, elliptic to narrow-elliptic, 3–4.5 cm (1³⁄₁₆–1¾ in.) long, 1–1.8 cm (¾–1¹⁄₁₆ in.) wide, bases cuneate to slightly obtuse, apices acute, margins usually entire, occasionally 1–3 small spines near apex, petioles 6.5–7 mm (¼–⁹⁄₃₂ in.) long; fruits brilliant orange yellow 17B, globose, 6.5 mm (¼ in.) diameter, pedicels 2–5 mm (¹⁄₁₆–³⁄₁₆ in.) long; compact pyramidal habit, 3 × 1.2 m (9 × 4 ft.) in approximately 15 years; hardy in zone 7. Plate 110.

'Attakapa' (female; volunteer tree growing at Louisiana Nursery; named and introduced in the 1960s by K. Durio).

Leaves moderate olive green, elliptic to elliptic-ovate, 5–8.5 cm (2–3⅜ in.) long, 2.5–3.2 cm (1–1¼ in.) wide, bases cuneate, apices acute, margins usually entire, rarely 1 spine on each side near apex, petioles reddish, 10–13 mm (⅜–½ in.) long; fruits red, globose, 6 mm (⁷⁄₃₂ in.) diameter, 1–2 in clusters, pedicels 5 mm (³⁄₁₆ in.) long; tall upright cone-shaped tree. Leaves larger and more oblong than those of 'East Palatka'.

'Betty Hills' (female; introduced in late 1950s; registered H.S.A. 1-59 as *I. opaca* by Hills Nursery; not the same as 'Pawley's Island').

Leaves moderate to dark green, elliptic to elliptic-obovate, 5–8 cm (2–3⅛ in.) long, 2.8–4 cm (1⅛–1⅝ in.) wide, slightly curved, bases attenuate, apices acute to obtuse, tip spines reflexed, margins usually entire, occasionally 1–2 very small spines near apex, petioles dark, 8–10 mm (⁵⁄₁₆–⅜ in.) long; fruits vivid red 45A, globose, 5–7 mm (³⁄₁₆–⁹⁄₃₂ in.) diameter,

1–5 in clusters, abundant, peduncles 8–10 mm (⁵⁄₁₆–³⁄₈ in.) long, pedicels 2–3 mm (¹⁄₁₆–¹⁄₈ in.) long, ripen early, persist; columnar, pyramidal habit.

'Bienville Gold' (female; chance seedling discovered and named by Tom Dodd in the 1980s; introduced in 1995; named for colonizer, the governor of Louisiana and founder of the city of New Orleans).
    Leaves dark green; yellow fruits; description incomplete. Plate 111.

'Big John' (male; seedling of 'Foster No. 2' discovered by J. A. Webb; introduced in 1980).
    Pollinator for 'Alagold' and 'Blazer'.

'Blazer' (female; open-pollinated seedling of 'Foster No. 2' discovered in 1965 by J. A. Webb; introduced in 1980 by Webb and Rainbow Nursery; named and registered H.S.A. 2-83 by C. Pounders).
    Leaves dark olive green, broadly elliptic to broadly obovate, 2.5–4.5 cm (1–1¾ in.) long, 1.3–2.5 cm (½–1 in.) wide, bases cuneate to obtuse, apices acute, prominent tip spines, petioles 2–5 mm (¹⁄₁₆–³⁄₁₆ in.) long; fruits vivid red 46B, globose, 8 mm (⁵⁄₁₆ in.) diameter, pedicels 2–5 mm (¹⁄₁₆–³⁄₁₆ in.) long, 6–7 fruits on short spurs; upright open branching habit, 1.8 × 0.92 m (6 × 3 ft.) in approximately 15 years.

'Buxton' (female; discovered in the 1980s by B. Bauers Jr. on Hatteras Island, North Carolina).
    Original tree multistemmed, 5 m (16 ft.) high; margins entire.

'Eagleson' (female; chance seedling discovered about 1966 at Eagleson Nursery; selected, named, and registered H.S.A. 6–72 by T. Eagleson).
    Leaves dark olive green, oblong to narrow-elliptic, to 6.5 cm (2½ in.) long, 2.5 cm (1 in.) wide, margins undulate, 1–4 small spines near apex, or occasionally entire; fruits red, globose; vigorous compact columnar habit, 3.7 × 2.7 m (12 × 9 ft.) in 8 years.

'East Palatka' (female; original tree found in East Palatka, Florida; named and introduced by H. Hume around 1926).
    Leaves moderate olive green, oval elliptic, 4.5–6.5 cm (1¾–2½ in.) long, 1.8–2.5 cm (¹¹⁄₁₆–1 in.) wide, bases cuneate, apices obtuse, small tip spines, margins nearly flat, usually entire, rarely 1–2 very small spines near apex, petioles 8–10 mm (⁵⁄₁₆–³⁄₈ in.) long; fruits vivid red 45A, globose, 6–8 mm (⁷⁄₃₂–⁵⁄₁₆ in.) diameter, 1–3 on peduncles, 8–10 mm (⁵⁄₁₆–³⁄₈ in.) long, pedicels 2–3 mm (¹⁄₁₆–¹⁄₈ in.) long, abundant; upright open spreading pyramidal habit; hardy in zones 7. Plate 112.

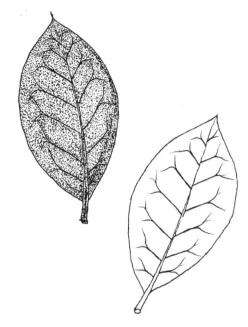

Figure 15-13. *Ilex × attenuata* 'East Palatka'. Drawing by Randy Allen.

'Edna Jean' (female; volunteer seedling discovered in 1976 by Mrs. R. N. Reams in Rockwood, Tennessee; moved to Oak Ridge, Tennessee; named and registered H.S.A. 1-89 by M. H. Albert for his mother; possible hybrid of *I. cumulicola* × *I. opaca* or *I. × attenuata* × *I. cumulicola*).
    Leaves dark green, obovate, 6.24 cm (2¼ in. long), 4.5 cm (1¾ in.) wide, bases attenuate to slightly rotund, apices acuminate, distinctly curled laterally, margins revolute, nearly touching ventrally, 1–4 coarse short spines on each side, upper two-thirds of leaf, petioles dark red, 9.5 mm (³⁄₈ in.) long; fruits vivid red 45B, globose, 10 mm (³⁄₈ in.) diameter, single, pedicels 3 mm (¹⁄₈ in.) long; original tree pyramidal, at 14 years 3.7 m (12 ft.) high, 2.5 m (8 ft.) wide; hardy in zone 7, survived −32°C (−24°F) with no injury.

'Erma Byrd' (female; *I. × attenuata* × *I. opaca* cross made about 1958; selected 1972; registered H.S.A. 8-73 by O. M. Neal).
    Leaves dark olive green, obovate, to 6.5 cm (2½ in.) long, 2.5 cm (1 in.) wide, bases attenuate, slightly keeled, margins 3–6 moderate spines on each side, usually on upper half of leaf; fruits vivid red, globose to slightly elongate, 10 mm (³⁄₈ in.) diameter, pedicels 6 mm (⁷⁄₃₂ in.) long, abundant, persist to next season; pyramidal habit, 3.7 × 1.8 m (12 × 8 ft.) wide in 15 years; hardy in zone 6a. Named for wife of West Virginia Senator Robert C. Byrd.

'Fay-T' (female; synonym 'Foret B'; selected in 1958 by J. Foret from seedlings; introduced and named in 1991 by Foret).

Leaves dark olive green, obovate-elliptic, 5.5–7 cm (2⅛–2¾ in.) long, 2.5–3.5 cm (1–1⅜ in.) wide, bases attenuate, apices broadly cuneate, reflexed, slightly keeled, margins recurved, usually 1–2 spines on each side, occasionally 3 spines, rarely 4, petioles 8–10 mm (5⁄16–⅜ in.) long; fruits vivid red, globose, 7–8 mm (9⁄32–5⁄16 in.) diameter, abundant; pyramidal habit.

Foster Hybrid Group

A name given to a group of chance seedlings of *I. cassine* × *I. opaca* or *I. myrtifolia* × *I. opaca,* grown and introduced in the 1940s by E. E. Foster. There are 5, possibly 6, numbered selections. Plants of this group introduced by others include 'Big John', 'Blazer', 'Foster Sparkler', and 'Alagold', which see.

'Foster No. 1' (female; Foster Hybrid Group, see 'Foster No. 2').

Leaves dark olive green, elliptic, 3–4.5 cm (1 3⁄16–1¾ in.) long, 1.1–1.5 cm (7⁄16–19⁄32 in.) wide, bases cuneate, apices acute, margins twisted, entire to 1–3 small spines on each side, upper half of leaf, occasionally all or 3 spines on one side, petioles 5 mm (3⁄16 in.) long; fruits vivid red 45A, globose to ovoid, 5–6 mm (3⁄16–7⁄32 in.) diameter, pedicels 5 mm (3⁄16 in.) long; upright pyramidal small tree. Old specimen 30 plus years at Tom Dodd Nursery, 13 m (45 ft.) tall, 6 m (20 ft.) wide. Similar to 'Foster No. 2'.

'Foster No. 2' (female; synonym 'Fosteri'; grown and introduced in the 1940s by E. E. Foster).

Leaves dark olive green, elliptic to obovate-elliptic, slightly keeled and curved, 3–7.5 cm (1 3⁄16–3 in.) long, 1.3–2 cm (½–¾ in.) wide, bases cuneate, apices acuminate, margins 1–5 spines on each side, occasionally wavy, petioles dark, 5 mm (3⁄16 in.) long; fruits vivid red 45A, globose to slightly pyriform 10 mm (⅜ in.) long, 6–8 mm (7⁄32–5⁄16 in.) diameter, single to 2–3 per peduncle, abundant; upright narrow pyramidal habit; hardy in zone 6b. A very popular landscape plant and best known of the Foster Hybrid Group. Plate 113.

'Foster No. 3' (female: Foster Hybrid Group, see 'Foster No. 2').

Leaves moderate to dark olive green, elliptic to obovate-elliptic, 3.5–5 cm (1⅜–2 in.) long, 1.3–3 cm (½–1 3⁄16 in.) wide, margins slightly convex, 2–5 small spines on each side, usually on upper two-thirds of leaf, petioles 4–6 mm (5⁄32–7⁄32 in.) long; fruits vivid red 45A, slightly pyriform, 10 mm (⅜ in.) long, 8 mm (5⁄16 in.) diameter, pedicels 8 mm (5⁄16 in.) long. Very similar to 'Foster No. 2'.

Figure 15-14. *Ilex* × *attenuata* 'Foster No. 2'. Photo by Fred Galle.

'Foster No. 4' (male; Foster Hybrid Group, see 'Foster No. 2').

Leaves dark olive green, elliptic, 2.8–4.5 cm (1⅛–1¾ in.) long, 1–1.8 cm (⅜–11⁄16 in.) wide, bases cuneate, apices acuminate, margins flat to slightly wavy, 1–3 small spines on each side, usually upper half of leaf, petioles 3–5 mm (⅛–3⁄16 in.) long; upright pyramidal habit. Not common.

'Foster No. 5' (female; Foster Hybrid Group, see 'Foster No. 2').

Leaves more like an elongated *I. opaca,* moderate green, thin texture.

'Foster No. 6' (male; Foster Hybrid Group, see 'Foster No. 2').

Reported by the late J. McDaniel; no other information available.

'Foster Sparkler' (introduced by C. Pounders in the 1980s).

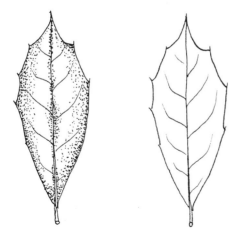

Figure 15-15. *Ilex × attenuata* 'Foster No. 2'. Drawing by Randy Allen.

Leaves dark olive green, elliptic to oval elliptic, keeled, 3–4 cm (1³⁄₁₆–1⅝ in.) long, 1.5–2 cm (¹⁹⁄₃₂–¾ in.) wide, bases cuneate to obtuse, apices acute, tip spines, margins subentire, 1–2 small spines on each side, upper one-third of leaf, petioles dark, 3 mm (⅛ in.) long.

'Gato' (female; gift plant given to K. Durio; named and introduced by Durio in the 1970s).
Leaves moderate olive green, elliptic, 5–7 cm (2–2¾ in.) long, 2–3.5 cm (¾–1⅜ in.) wide, bases cuneate, apices acute, margins entire at base, 4–5 small spines on each side, upper two-thirds of leaf, petioles 10–13 mm (⅜–½ in.) long; fruits red, ellipsoid, 6–8 mm (⁷⁄₃₂–⁵⁄₁₆ in.) diameter, pedicels 6 mm (⁷⁄₃₂ in.) long; upright pyramidal habit.

'Greenleaf' (female; synonyms 'Nick's', 'Peace'; selected by S. Peace; introduced by Greenleaf Nursery in the 1970s).
Leaves moderate olive green, elliptic, 5–5.5 cm (2–2⅛ in.) long, 3 cm (1³⁄₁₆ in.) wide, curved, 5–6 small spines on each side, petioles 10 mm (⅜ in.) long; fruits vivid red 44A, globose, 6–8 mm (⁷⁄₃₂–⁵⁄₁₆ in.) diameter, singly to 2–3 in cyme, good abundant clusters; upright irregular vigorous habit. Popular in commercial nurseries. The *International Checklist of Cultivated Ilex* (Dudley and Eisenbeiss 1973) was in error in rejecting the name 'Greenleaf', often listed as an *I. opaca* but now considered by most authorities as *I. × attenuata*. Plate 114.

'Hallie Carrico' (female; synonym 73-6; original tree in Horticulture Farm, West Virginia University, Morgantown, West Virginia; selected, named, and registered H.S.A. 1-76 by O. M. Neal).

Leaves dark bluish green, ovate to broadly elliptic, to 5.8 cm (2¼ in.) long, 3.8 cm (1½ in.) wide, curved, keeled, bases cuneate to narrow-acuminate, apices cuneate to acuminate, margins wavy, 5–7 spines on each side; fruits red, subglobose, 8 mm (⁵⁄₁₆ in.) diameter, 10 mm (⅜ in.) long, single, pedicels 13 mm (½ in.) long, persistent, often lasting 2 years; pyramidal habit, 4.6 × 2.5 m (15 × 8 ft.) wide in 15 years; hardy in zone 5; roots easy and flowers same time as *I. opaca* in Morgantown. Named for a distinguished teacher in Raleigh County, West Virginia.

'Hoosier Waif' (female; discovered on flood plain of Sewell Run, Monroe County, Indiana, by R. B. Rypma; moved in 1974 to Chillicothe, Ohio; also growing at Athens, Ohio; registered H.S.A. 19-88 by Rypma).
Leaves moderate olive green, elliptic to obovate-elliptic, 5–7.5 cm (2–3 in.) long, 2–2.8 cm (¾–1⅛ in.) wide, bases attenuate, apices obtuse, with tip spines, margins recurved, subentire, 1–5 small spines on each side, upper half of leaf, occasionally entire, petioles dark, 8–10 mm (⁵⁄₁₆–⅜ in.) long; fruits vivid reddish orange 44B, globose to slightly pyriform, 6–8 mm (⁷⁄₃₂–⁵⁄₁₆ in.) diameter, pedicels 5–8 mm (³⁄₁₆–⁵⁄₁₆ in.) long, single to 2–3 on peduncles, abundant; bushy growth, weak terminal leaders, branches with strong drooping habit, good for hedges and foundation plantings; hardy to −29°C (−20°F). The name "Hoosier Waif" means "poor lost plant north of its natural range."

'Howard' (female; original tree from Howard Farm near Macclenny, Florida; selected in the 1930s; named and introduced by H. Hume).
Leaves dark olive green, broadly elliptic, 6–7 cm (2⅜–2¾ in.) long, 2.5–3 cm (1–1³⁄₁₆ in.) wide, curved, convex, often slightly twisted, nearly entire, occasionally 1–3 spines on each side, near apex, petioles 5–7 mm (³⁄₁₆–⁹⁄₃₂ in.) long; fruits vivid red 45A, globose, 8 mm (⁵⁄₁₆ in.) diameter, pedicels 10 mm (⅜ in.) long, abundant, 1–3 on pedicel; compact columnar habit, vigorous, densely branched.

'Hume No. 1' (female; synonyms 'Humei', 'Humei No. 1'; origin unknown; named and introduced by H. Hume).
Leaves moderate olive green, elliptic, slightly keeled, 6–8 cm (2⅜–3⅛ in.) long, 2.5–3.5 cm (1–1⅜ in.) wide, bases cuneate, apices acute, tip spines slightly reflexed, margins nearly entire, occasionally 1 spine, often on only one side, near apex, petioles 10–13 mm (⅜–½ in.) long; fruits red; open pyramidal habit.

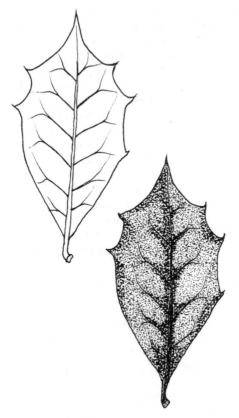

Figure 15-16. *Ilex × attenuata* 'Howard'. Drawing by Randy Allen.

'Hume No. 2' (female; original tree at Glen Saint Mary Nursery, Glen Saint Mary, Florida; named and introduced by H. Hume; in propagation since 1909).

Leaves moderate olive green, obovate to broadly elliptic, 4.5–8.5 cm (1¾–3⅛ in.) long, 2–3.8 cm (¾–1½ in.) wide, bases cuneate, apices acuminate, tip spines slightly reflexed, margins usually entire, occasionally 1–2 small spines on upper half of leaf, petioles 10–13 mm (⅜–½ in.) long; fruits vivid red 45A, globose, 8 mm (5⁄16 in.) diameter, 1–8 in clusters, peduncles 8–10 mm (5⁄16–⅜ in.) long, pedicels 2–3 mm (⅛–⅛ in.) long, abundant; upright, open, broadly pyramidal habit. Plate 115.

'Jill' (female; origin unknown; plant at Swarthmore College from J. R. Frorer holly collection and now lost; descriptions from herbarium specimens).

Leaves green, elliptic to elliptic-obovate, 3.5–6.5 cm (1⅜–2½ in.) long, 2–2.5 cm (¾–1 in.) wide, margins subentire, 2–3 remote teeth near apex, petioles 5–8 mm (3⁄16–5⁄16 in.) long; fruits red, globose, 6–8 mm (7⁄32–5⁄16 in.) diameter, pedicels 5 mm (3⁄16 in.) long; plant may not now be available.

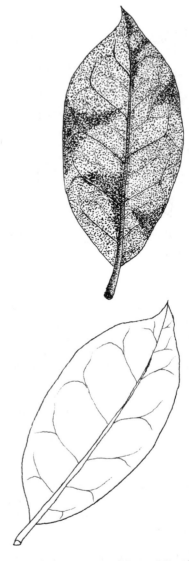

Figure 15-17. *Ilex × attenuata* 'Hume No. 2'. Drawing by Randy Allen.

'Kerns' (female; selected by Kern's nursery in the 1960s).

Leaves moderate olive green, elliptic, 5–6.5 cm (2–2½ in.) long, 2–2.5 cm (¾–1 in.) wide, keeled, curved, nearly entire, 1–2 small spines near apex, petioles 1 cm (⅜ in.) long; fruits vivid red 44A, globose, 8–10 mm (5⁄16–⅜ in.) diameter; vigorous grower.

'Marilyn' (female; chance seedling discovered by Clarence E. Hubbuch in 1976; named and registered H.S.A. 3-94 by Hubbuch for his late wife; to be introduced in 1997).

Leaves ovate to elliptic, 5 cm (2 in.) long, 2 cm (¾

in.) wide, many leaves smaller, leaf tips aristate, slightly reflexed down, slightly twisted, bases strongly acuminate, margins variable, entire to 1–2 moderate spines on each side, petioles 8 mm (5/16 in.) long; fruits reddish orange 34B, globose, to 8 mm (5/16 in.) diameter, borne singly, pedicels brownish, 3 mm (⅛ in.) long; original plant dense habit, 2.7 m (9 ft.) tall, 2.4 m (6 ft.) wide, hardy zone 6, withstood −31°C (−24°F) in 1994.

'Monongahelia' (female; selected seedling from controlled cross *I. myrtifolia* × *I. opaca* by O. M. Neal; named and registered H.S.A. 2-66 by Neal).

Leaves dark green, margins somewhat revolute, undulate and twisted, 2–5 spines on each side; fruits red, persist 3 winter. Similar to Foster Hybrids but more hardy.

'Mountain State' (male; synonym 73-7; *I. myrtifolia* × *I. opaca* controlled cross made in 1956; named and registered H.S.A. 2-76 by O. M. Neal).

Leaves olive green, narrow-elliptic, to 5.8 cm (2½ in.) long, 2.2 cm (1³/16 in.) wide, bases narrow-cuneate, apices cuneate, margins flat or wavy, 3–6 small spines on each side; conical habit, original tree 6.1 m (20 ft.) tall in 20 years; hardy in zone 5. Similar to Foster Hybrid Group but considerably hardier.

'Nasa' (female; a Foster seedling grown in Huntsville, Alabama; selected in the 1970s by J. A. Webb, named by T. Dodd Jr.).

Leaves dark olive green, linear to narrow-elliptic, 2.5–5 cm (1–2 in.) long, 0.5–1 cm (3/16–⅜ in.) wide, bases and apices attenuate, midribs depressed, margins recurved, entire to 1 very small spine, on one or both sides, near apex, petioles dark, 4–5 mm (5/32–

3/16 in.) long; fruits vivid red 45A, globose, 5 mm to rarely 8 mm (3/16–5/16 in.) diameter, pedicels reddish 3 mm (⅛ in.) long; upright pyramidal habit.

'Oreola' (plant at VanDusen Botanical Garden, Vancouver, British Columbia, Canada).

No description available.

'Oriole' (female; selected from F2 population of *I. myrtifolia* × *I. opaca* cross made at U.S. National Arboretum; registered H.S.A. 4-66 by W. F. Kosar; sibling of 'Tanager').

Leaves dark olive green, elliptic to elliptic-obovate, 2.5–4 cm (1–1⅜ in.) long, 0.8–1.5 cm (5/16–19/32 in.) wide, bases cuneate, apices acute, margins with 1–3 very small spines on a side, upper one-third of leaf, tip leaves often entire, petioles 5–7 mm (3/16–9/32 in.) long; fruits vivid red 46B, ovoid, 10 mm (⅜ in.) long, 8–9 mm (5/16–11/32 in.) diameter, pedicels 6–8 mm (7/32–5/16 in.) long; upright, spreading, compact habit, slow growing, fine textured; original plant 1 m (3 ft.) high in 9 years, mature plant 20+ years 5.5 m (18 ft.) tall, 2.5 m (8 ft.) wide. Plates 116, 117.

'Parkway' (female; seedling collected by C. Pounders in Alabama; plant at U.S. National Arboretum).

Leaves dark olive green, very similar to those of 'Foster No. 2'; fruits slightly larger than those of 'Foster No. 2'.

'Pawley's Island' (female; introduced by Hammock Shop Nursery, Pawley's Island, South Carolina, in the 1970s).

Leaves moderate olive green, elliptic to elliptic-obovate, 4–5 cm (1⅝–2 in.) long, 2–3 cm (¾–1³/16 in.) wide, slightly keeled and curved, bases attenu-

Figure 15-18. *Ilex × attenuata* 'Oriole'. Photo by Barton Bauer Sr.

ate, apices acute, to obtuse, tip spines reflexed, margins subentire to 1–4 spines on each side, usually upper two-thirds of leaf, petioles dark, 6–8 mm (⁷⁄₃₂–⁵⁄₁₆ in.) long; fruits vivid red 45A, globose, 5–7 mm (³⁄₁₆–⁹⁄₃₂ in.) diameter, ripen early; upright rounded, mounded habit.

'Pembroke' (female; seedling of 'East Palatka'; introduced around 1955 by Goochland Nursery; no longer in production).
    Leaves dark olive green, elliptic, 6.5–7 cm (2½–2¾ in.) long, 3.5 cm (1⅜ in.) wide, bases cuneate to obtuse, curved, flat to slightly convex, 2–3 spines on upper one-third of leaf, petioles 8–12 mm (⅜–½ in.) long; fruits red, globose.

'Ro Val' (male; seedling selected in Louisiana in early 1970s by W. A. Roach and E. Vallot).
    Leaves moderate dark green, elliptic to elliptic-obovate, 6.5–9 cm (2½–3½ in.) long, 2–3.5 cm (¾–1⅜ wide, occasionally larger, flat, bases attenuate to cuneate, margins subentire to 3–5 very small spines, usually upper two-thirds of leaf, petioles dark, 10–15 mm (⅜–¹⁹⁄₃₂ in.) long; young stems brownish; upright open habit.

'Rosalind Sarver' (female; synonyms 'Mrs. Sarver', 'Mrs. Sauer'; discovered by Descanso Nursery; origin Sarver Nursery; Sarver moved from Texas to San Marcos, California; origin of seed possibly from Texas).
    Leaves moderate olive green, elliptic, 6–8 cm (2⅜–3⅛ in.) long, 3–3.5 cm (1³⁄₁₆–1⅜ in.) wide, keeled, curved, 4–5 small spines on each side, upper two-thirds of leaf, petioles dark, 10 mm (⅜ in.) long; fruits vivid red 48B, globose, 8–11 mm (⁵⁄₁₆–⁷⁄₁₆ in.) diameter, pedicels 6–10 mm (⁷⁄₃₂–⅜ in.) long, singly and 2–3 in clusters, abundant fruiting. Reported in California to set fruit without pollination, fruits sterile. Used as street tree in California; tolerates drought and moderately alkaline soils.

'Savannah' (female; found in late 1960s by W. H. Robertson in Savannah, Georgia).
    Leaves moderate olive green, broadly elliptic, 5–8.5 cm (2–3⅜ in.) long, 2–6 cm (¾–2⅜ in.) wide, slightly keeled and curved, bases cuneate, apices acuminate, margins nearly flat, 2–4 small spines on each side, on upper two-thirds of leaf, petioles dark, 8–10 mm (⁵⁄₁₆–⅜ in.) long; fruits vivid red 45A, globose to slightly ovoid, 8–10 mm (⁵⁄₁₆–⅜ in.) diameter, 1–3 in clusters, peduncles reddish, 10 mm (⅜ in.) long, pedicels 3 mm (⅛ in.) long; upright open, pyramidal. Popular in Savannah city parks and throughout the Southeast. Plate 118.

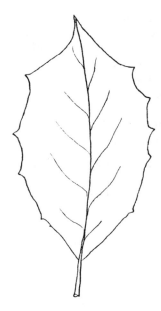

Figure 15-19. *Ilex × attenuata* 'Rosalind Sarver'. Drawing by Randy Allen.

'Sunny Foster' (female; variegated leaf mutation of 'Foster No. 2'; discovered in 1964 by W. F. Kosar at the U.S. National Arboretum; named and registered H.S.A. 1-82 by G. K. Eisenbeiss).
    Leaves dark green, with non-marginal light yellow 10A blotches, on upper half to one-third of leaf, barely noticeable on young leaves, in dense shade often absent, elliptic, 3.5–4.5 cm (1⅜–1¾ in.) long, 1–1.6 cm (⅜–⅝ in.) wide, bases cuneate, apices acuminate, margins 1–3 small spines on each side, upper

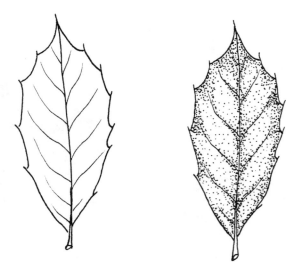

Figure 15-20. *Ilex × attenuata* 'Savannah'. Drawing by Randy Allen.

half of leaf, petioles 5–6 mm (³⁄₁₆–⁷⁄₃₂ in.) long; fruits vivid red 44A, ellipsoid, 8 mm (⁵⁄₁₆ in.) long, 7–8 mm (⁹⁄₃₂–⁵⁄₁₆ in.) diameter, 1–3 in cluster, pedicels 4–5 mm (⁵⁄₃₂–³⁄₁₆ in.) long. Very similar to 'Foster No. 2'. Attractive accent tree in direct sunlight. Plate 119.

'Taber' (female; selected by G. L. Taber; named by H. Hume around 1910–1920).
Fruits red, large; narrow upright habit.

'Taber No. 2' (female, origin unknown; selected by G. L. Taber; named by H. Hume).
Leaves dark olive green, small, elliptic to narrowly obovate, tapered at both ends, margins usually entire, occasionally 1–3 small spines on each side of leaf, upper half of leaf; fruits red.

'Taber No. 3' (female; synonym 'Tabor No. 3'; exact origin unknown, probably young seedling from Tennessee; grown at Glen Saint Mary Nursery, Glenn Saint Mary, Florida; named and introduced by H. Hume).
Leaves dark olive green, elliptic, curved, 6–8 cm (2³⁄₈–3¹⁄₈ in.) long, 3–4.5 cm (1³⁄₁₆–1³⁄₄ in.) wide, margins flat to convex, 1–2 spines on each side, on upper one-third of leaf, tip spines reflexed, petioles 10–16 mm (³⁄₈–⁵⁄₈ in.) long; fruits vivid red 45A, ellipsoid, 9–10 mm (¹¹⁄₃₂–³⁄₈ in.) long, 8 mm (⁵⁄₁₆ in.) diameter, abundant; upright open, pyramidal habit.

'Taber No. 4' (female; synonym 'Tabor No. 4'; selected by H. Hume).
Leaves dull dark green, curved; fruits red, large; upright pyramidal, branches with slightly dropping habit.

'Tanager' (female; selected seedling from F2 population of interspecific hybrid *I. myrtifolia* × *I. opaca* cross made by W. F. Kosar at the U.S. National Arboretum; named and registered H.S.A. 3-65 by Kosar; sibling of 'Oriole').
Leaves dark olive green, elliptic, to 4.5 cm (1³⁄₄ in.) long, 1.3 cm (½ in.) wide, bases cuneate, apices acuminate, margins spinose; fruits red; slow growing, compact upright habit; hardy in zone 7a. Plate 120.

'Topeli' (female; native *I.* × *attenuata*; collected in 1931 by J. A. Topel on Penbroke Jones estate, Wilmington, North Carolina; specimen sent to Rehder and named *I. topeli*).
Leaves moderate olive green, elliptic to obovate-lanceolate, 4.5–7.5 cm (1³⁄₄–3 in.) long, 1.3–2.2 cm (½–¹³⁄₁₆ in.) wide, bases cuneate, apices acuminate, small tip spines reflexed, margins usually entire, petioles dark, 8 mm (⁵⁄₁₆ in.) long, young stems purplish;

fruits vivid red 45A, globose, 5–6 mm (³⁄₁₆–⁷⁄₃₂ in.) diameter, 1–3 in cluster; upright pyramidal, pendulous branches.

Ilex cassine Cultivars

'Baldwin' (female; origin unknown; form of *I. cassine* var. *angustifolia*).
Leaves moderate olive green, elliptic to obovate-elliptic, 3–6 cm (1³⁄₁₆–2³⁄₈ in.) long, 1.3–2.5 cm (½–1 in.) wide, bases cuneate, apices acuminate, margins entire, flat, petioles dark, 6–8 mm (⁷⁄₃₂–⁵⁄₁₆ in.) long; fruits vivid red 45A, globose, 6–8 mm (⁷⁄₃₂–⁵⁄₁₆ in.) diameter, 1–2 in clusters, peduncles 8–13 mm (⁵⁄₁₆–½ in.) long; small trees, upright pyramidal habit.

'Bryanii' (female; synonym *I. cassine* var. *bryanii*; discovered in 1938 by Tarbox and Blake near Myrtle Beach, South Carolina; moved to Brookgreen Gardens).
Leaves moderate olive green, elliptic, 4.5–6.5 cm (1³⁄₄–2½ in.) long, 1.5–3 cm (¹⁹⁄₃₂–1³⁄₁₆ in.) wide, petioles and young stems purplish; fruits vivid yellow 13A, globose to slightly ovate, 6 mm (⁷⁄₃₂ in.) diameter; small upright spreading tree.

'Tortifolia' (female; synonym *I. cassine* var. *angustifolia* f. *tortifolia*; discovered in 1933 in Horry County, South Carolina, by F. G. Tarbox Jr.).
Leaves dark green, linear lanceolate to elliptic, somewhat twisted, 3.5–6 cm (1³⁄₈–2³⁄₈ in.) long, 1–2 cm (³⁄₈–³⁄₅ in.) wide, margins with small spines upper half of leaf, twisted; fruits red, globose, 4–6 mm (⁵⁄₃₂–⁷⁄₃₂ in.) diameter, 1–3 in cluster.

'Tyron Palace' (female; seedling of *I. cassine* var. *angustifolia* plants at Tyron Palace, New Bern, North Carolina; obtained about 1950 from Greenbriar Nursery).
Leaves moderate olive green, linear, 3.5–6.5 cm (1³⁄₈–2½ in.) long, 8–10 mm (⁵⁄₁₆–³⁄₈ in.) wide, young stems purplish; fruits yellow.

'Wild Robert' (female; wild seedling of *I. cassine* var. *angustifolia* discovered about 1981 on rice patty dike in Colleton County, South Carolina, by Earle Marvin; named and introduced by Marvin, Wildwood Nursery).
Leaves dark olive green, elliptic to slightly elliptic-obovate, 3–5 cm (1³⁄₁₆–2 in.) long, 1.3–2 cm (½–³⁄₄ in.) wide, bases cuneate, apices acute, margins usually entire, occasionally 1–3 very small spines, upper one-third of leaf, petioles dark, 6–8 mm (⁷⁄₃₂–⁵⁄₁₆ in.)

long; fruits vivid red 45B, globose, 5–6 mm (3/16–7/32 in.) diameter, single, pedicels 5–8 mm (3/16–5/16 in.) long; upright compact pyramidal habit. Named for Marvin's father, Robert.

'Willow Leaf' (sex unknown; mentioned in *Hortus III*).
No description available.

Ilex coriacea (Large Gallberry Holly) Cultivars

Large (or sweet) gallberry holly was first described in 1814 by Frederick T. Pursh as *Prinos coriacea* and later changed to *Ilex coriacea* in 1860 by Alvin Chapman. It is native in North America to the Coastal Plains and lower Piedmont, from southern Virginia to Florida, Texas, and Mexico. The species is a source of light clear honey.

Large gallberry hollies are evergreen shrubs to 4 m (13 ft.) tall. They are taller and have a more open habit of growth than *Ilex glabra*. The leaves are dark green, obovate to elliptic, and larger than those of *I. glabra*, 5–10 cm (2–4 in.) long, 1.5–3.5 cm (19/32 –1⅜ in.) wide. The male inflorescences are fasciculate and axillary, female flowers are usually singular. The fruits are usually black to reddish brown.

Ilex coriacea is hardy in zones 7 to 10. It is not as winter hardy as *I. glabra* nor as popular as a landscape plant. Only two cultivars are known.

'Brookgreen' (female; cuttings collected in woods from native plants at Brookgreen Gardens; plant at Ebersole Gardens).
Leaves dark green, elliptic to obovate, 5–7 cm (2– 2¾ in.) long, 2–3 cm (¾–1 3/16 in.) wide, margins minutely spiny, upper half of leaf, petioles dark, 5–7 mm (3/16–9/32 in.) long; fruit black, 7–8 mm (9/32–5/16 in.) diameter; large upright spreading, multistem habit.

'Georgia Wine' (female; native plant collected around 1984 in Burke County, Georgia, by nurseryman Bill Craven; selected for winter foliage color; named for the late Louis Owen, a Georgia nurseryman; introduced by Twisted Oaks Nursery; described and published for first time).
Leaves dark olive green, obovate, 4–6 cm (1⅝– 2⅜ in.) long, 1.5–2.2 cm (19/32–13/16 in.) wide, 1–3 remote teeth near apex, petioles 6–8 mm (7/32–5/16 in.) long, terminal buds reddish brown; fruits black, abundant; leaves glossy dark grayish reddish brown 200B in late fall and winter; upright spreading habit, original plant burned over, 1.5–1.6 m (5–6 ft.) tall and wide. Also listed in nurseries as *I. glabra*.

Ilex cornuta (Chinese Holly) Cultivars

Chinese (or horned) holly and its numerous cultivars are very popular landscape plants in the southeastern United States. The species is native to both the People's Republic of China and Korea. In China *Ilex cornuta* grows in the hilly regions of the lower Yangtze provinces, where it is common on the hilly slopes of Ningpo, Hangzhou River, Suzhou, Nanjing, and westward to Ichang and Changsha. In Korea it is limited to sites near the sea, sometimes in the first zone of vegetation above the high tide line. Its common names in Korea and China are much more descriptive than its English common names. In Korea it is known as tiger spine tree, and in China it is called bony thorn, tiger thorn, cat thorn, and eight-angled thorn.

Robert Fortune in 1846 introduced *Ilex cornuta* to England from plants collected near Shanghai. The species was described and named by John Lindley and Sir Joseph Paxton in 1850. Following its introduction to England it was introduced to Germany, France, Switzerland, and to the United States in the late 1890s.

Chinese hollies are evergreen shrubs or small trees to 7.5 m (25 ft.) tall. The leaves are extremely variable and polymorphic in shape, varying from cordate to oblong and entire to quadrangular and spinose. Like many Asiatic spinose holly species, mature plants of *Ilex cornuta* often have entire leaves or leaves with only one or two spines near the apices. It is not uncommon to see large mature plants with spinose leaves at the base, and entire leaves at the top of the plant. The leaves are usually dark olive green and glossy, 3–8 cm (1 3/16–3⅛ in.) long, 2–4 cm (¾–1⅝ in.) wide, persisting on 3-year growth. The first cultivars introduced had green foliage but were soon followed by variegated foliage types including 'O. Spring', 'Sunrise', 'Cajun Gold'.

The fruits are typically vivid red, globose, 8–10 mm (5/16–⅜ in.) diameter, and borne in abundant fascicular clusters. Two important yellow-fruited cultivars are 'Avery Island' and 'D'Or'.

The light yellow flowers are axillary, fasciculate, and borne on 2-year growth. They open very early in the spring and are often subject to frost damage.

Heavy fruit production often results in yellow foliage in late summer and early fall. This can be corrected by applying additional nitrogen fertilizer when the discoloration is first noted. Cyclic biannual fruiting and decline in hardiness are also associated with heavy fruiting. Again, additional fertilizer applications in mid summer will help flower bud initiation, and flower and fruit development for the next season.

Chinese hollies are popular landscape plants with

more than 50 cultivars introduced. They are hardy in zone 7a and, in selected protected sites, in zone 6b. *Ilex cornuta* 'Burfordii', one of the first Chinese cultivars to be named, has been popular since its introduction in 1935. Unfortunately, due to its ultimate large size, it has outgrown its usefulness for today's smaller home properties. For the small home foundation planting, 'Anicet Delcambre', 'Dwarf Burford', and other compact Chinese hollies are replacing 'Burfordii'. Both 'Carissa' and 'Rotunda' are popular dwarf plants for a low compact foundation planting or low hedge. *Ilex cornuta* 'Rotunda' was first reported as sterile, but mature plants 25 years old and older are producing red fruit. It is now projected that in the mid to late 1990s 'Carissa' also will be reported having fruit.

Ilex cornuta has numerous medicinal uses in China. The dried leaves are officially called "Folium Ilicis cornutae" and are prescribed for fever with cough, pain in the back and knees, dizziness, and ringing in the ears. The bark is used to cure lumbago and rheumatism, and as a tonic for liver and kidney aliments. The seed oil has been used in the manufacturing of soap, and the flexible young branchlet are used by farmers to make nose-rings for cattle. In China, wax is gathered from the scale insect that infests *I. cornuta*.

Table 9 lists Chinese holly cultivars lacking complete descriptions. The names were gleaned from nursery catalogs, plant lists, and arboreta and test gardens. The U.S.D.A. Plant Introduction Station at Beltsville, Maryland, sent out numbered plants for testing and evaluation: U.S. No. 198277, U.S. PI 195133, U.S. PI 198274, and U.S. PI 65860.

'Aglo' (female; seedling from seed collected about 1955 at Shayne, Louisiana; grown, selected, and named by G. Posy; registered H.S.A. 1-77 by C. S. Britt; sibling of 'Olga').

Leaves dark olive green, square or blocky shaped, 5–7.7 cm (2–3 in.) long, 3.8–5 cm (1½–2 in.) wide, 3 marginal spines each side, strong tip spines reflexed down, petioles 3 mm (⅛ in.) long; fruits vivid red, globose, 10 mm (⅜ in.) diameter, in clusters, pedicels 18 mm (¹¹⁄₁₆ in.) long; compact conical habit; hardy in zone 7; original tree 6.1 m (20 ft.) tall, 2.3 m (7½ ft.) wide in approximately 18 years.

'Anicet Delcambre' (female; synonyms 'Needle Point', 'Willowleaf'; seedling selected in 1957 by A. Delcambre, I. S. Nelson, and J. Foret at Jungle Gardens; seed originally from U.S. Department of Agriculture; named for Delcambre, a foreman at Tabasco Plant, Avery Island, Louisiana).

Leaves dark olive green, linear elliptic to elliptic oblong, slightly convex, 5–8.5 cm (2–3⅜ in.) long, 2–2.5 cm (¾–1 in.) wide, bases rotund, apices acuminate, petioles 10–13 mm (⅜–½ in.) long; fruits vivid red 45A, globose, 6–8 mm (⁷⁄₃₂–⁵⁄₁₆ in.) diameter, pedicels 8 mm (⁵⁄₁₆ in.) long, 2–8 in clusters; upright, compact rounded habit. Plate 121.

'Anna Mae' (female; seedling raised at Grandview Nursery; selected and registered H.S.A. 7-60 by S. Solymosy).

Leaves dark olive green, glossy, oval to broadly elliptic, convex, 6–7.5 cm (2⅜–3 in.) long, 3.5–4.5 cm (1⅜–1¾ in.) wide, bases obtuse to rotund, apices acuminate to single tip spine, margins entire occa-

Table 9. Cultivars of *Ilex cornuta* (Chinese holly) without complete descriptions.

NAME	SOURCE
'Anderson'	Clarendon Gardens catalog
'Baueri'	From George Bauer of California
'Big Leaf'	Plant at Scientist Cliffs, Maryland
'Britt'	Seedling of 'Burfordii' found in Tarboro, North Carolina, by Dave Beard & Bill Steiner; plant at Scientist Cliffs, Maryland
'Burfordii Globe'	Origin unknown
'Cooledge'	Monrovia Nursery list, possibly Cooledge Nursery
'Giant Beauty'	Source unknown
'Grand Beauty'	Monrovia Nursery list
'Hitchcock'	Will Rodgers Park, Oklahoma City, Oklahoma
'J. B. Wight'	Received from Verhalen Nursery; smaller than 'Burfordii', internodes shorter, more compact
'Lindbergi'	Lindberg Gardens, Asheville, North Carolina
'Memphis Queen'	Cartwright Nursery
'Tall'	Will Rodgers Park, Oklahoma City, Oklahoma; name from Art Johnson
'Tustin' (female)	Hines Nursery catalog 1975
'Walderi'	McClintock, California; Monrovia Nursery test list

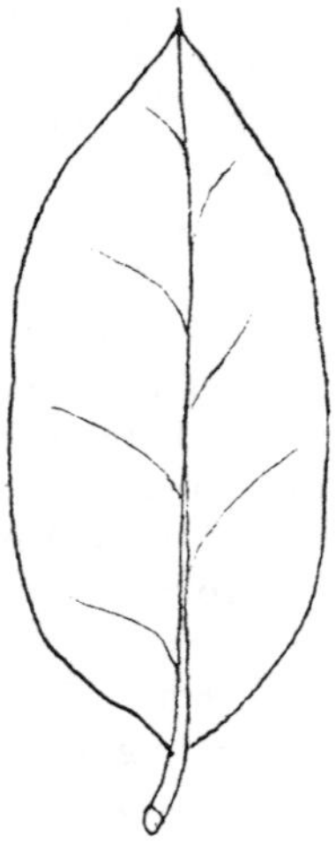

Figure 15-21. *Ilex cornuta* 'Anicet Delcambre'. Drawing by Randy Allen.

sionally 1–2 spines at apex, petioles 8 mm (5⁄16 in.) long; fruits vivid red 45A, globose, 10 mm (3⁄8 in.) diameter, pedicels 8–10 mm (5⁄16–3⁄8 in.) long; upright compact habit.

'Avery Island' (female; synonym 'Chinese Yellow'; seedling selected in late 1940s; named by E. A. McIlhenny from a hedge row at Jungle Gardens).

Leaves dark olive green, glossy, variable, large leaves quadrangular, 7–9 cm (2¾–3½ in.) long, 3.5–5 cm (1⅜–2 in.) wide, 7 spines (3 apical, 2 basal, 2 lateral), single-spined leaves entire, usually 1 apical spine, occasionally 3 apical spines; fruits light yellow, globose, 6.5 mm (¼ in.) diameter, abundant; loose upright growth habit.

'Azusa' (female; origin Monrovia Nursery before 1959; plant at Callaway Gardens obtained in 1961 from Monrovia Nursery).

Leaves dark olive green, irregular quadrangular, convex, 4–5 cm (1⅝–2 in.) long, 2–2.5 cm (¾–2 in.) wide, bases obtuse to truncate, apices acuminate, tip spine reflexed, 2 top marginal spines to 4.5 cm (1¾ in.) across, 2 basal spines, petioles 6 mm (7⁄32 in.) long.

Berries Jubilee™ (female; synonyms 'Greer', 'Taylor'; origin Taylor's Nursery; trademark and PP No. 3168 by Monrovia Nursery).

Leaves dark olive green, glossy, quadrangular to nearly square, 5–7.5 cm (2–3 in.) long, 3–4.5 cm (1⅝–1¾ in.) wide, bases truncate to squarish, 1 spine at each of 4 corners, tip spines strongly reflexed, occasionally additional small spines on margins, petioles 5 mm (3⁄16 in.) long; fruits vivid red 45A, globose, 11–13 mm (7⁄16–½ in.) diameter, abundant, pedicels 5–7 mm (3⁄16–9⁄32 in.) long; compact mounding habit.

'Big Dan' (male; plant at Ebersole Gardens; origin unknown; could be a hybrid of *I. cornuta*).

Leaves dark olive green, quadrangular, flat to slightly convex, 4–6.5 cm (1⅝–2⅜ in.) long, 2–2.8 cm (¾–1⅛ in.) wide, bases rotund, apices acuminate, margins with 2–3 widely spaced spines on each side, petioles 6–8 mm (7⁄32–5⁄16 in.) long; upright pyramidal habit. Leaves not typical.

'Bostic' (female; selected by Mrs. L. Bostic; registered H.S.A. 8-60 by S. Solymosy).

Leaves dark olive green, oblong to obovate-oblong, 6–7.5 cm (2⅜–2¾ in.) long, 3–4 cm (1 3⁄16–1⅝ in.) wide, bases rotund, apices acuminate, tip spines reflexed, margins entire, usually 1 spine on each side near apex, petioles 8 mm (5⁄16 in.) long; fruits vivid red 45A, globose, 8–10 mm (5⁄16–3⁄8 in.) diameter.

'Bracey' (female; unknown purchased seedling; original plant in garden of Gwney Bracey, Southern Pines, North Carolina; named by F. Ebersole).

Leaves dark olive green, glossy, quadrangular, 4–7 cm (1⅝–2¾ in.) long, 2.5–3.5 cm (1–1⅜ in.) wide, bases rotund to truncate, apices acuminate, tip spines usually reflexed, 2 top marginal spines, usually 2 basal marginal spines, petioles 5 mm (3⁄16 in.) long; fruits vivid red 45A, globose to slightly pyriform, 10 mm (3⁄8 in.) diameter, pedicels 10–13 mm (3⁄8–½ in.) long; upright compact spreading habit.

'Brawley' (female; plant thought to be *I. pernyi,* sent to Callaway Gardens in 1954 for identification, changed to *I. cornuta*; named 'Brawley' for record by F. Galle).

Leaves dark olive green, quadrangular, 3.5–5.5 cm (1⅜–2⅛ in.) long, 2–3 cm (¾–1 3⁄16 in.) wide, bases obtuse to truncate, apices acuminate, tip spines reflexed, margins basal spines 1 on each side, top spines on each side, rarely entire, petioles 5 mm (3⁄16 in.) long; fruits vivid red 45A, globose, 6–8 mm (7⁄32–5⁄16 in.) diameter, abundant; compact upright habit.

'Burfordii' (female; synonyms *I. burfordii* Howell Nursery Catalog 1935, *I. cornuta* var. *burfordii* De France, National Horticulture Magazine 1934; the most important and popular of *I. cornuta* cultivars with many conflicting stories on origin; seeds of *I. cornuta,* possibly from or by way of England, sent from U.S. Department of Agriculture in early 1900s to T. W. Burford of West View Cemetery; two plants survived on the cemetery grounds; nursery-man W. L. Monroe obtained cuttings of these plants for propagation in 1920 and agreed to name the plant 'Burfordii'; Howell Nursery often erroneously reported as the introducer).

Leaves dark olive green, glossy, obovate to obovate-oblong, convex, bullate, 4.5–8 cm (1¾–3⅛ in.) long, 2.5–4.5 cm (1–1¾ in.) wide, bases rotund, apices obtuse or short acuminate, small tip spines, margins usually entire, or rarely with 2 small spines at corners of apex, petioles 5–7 mm (³⁄₁₆–⁹⁄₃₂ in.) long; fruits vivid red 45A, globose to slightly ellipsoid, 10–13 mm (⅜–½ in.) diameter, abundant, 3–8 in clusters; compact, upright spreading habit, mature plants often 6 m (20 ft.) tall or taller; hardy in zone 7A. Very popular plant in the Southeast. Plates 122, 123.

'Burfordii Nana', see 'Dwarf Burford'.

'Burford Sport', see 'RPV Special'.

'Burford Yellowleaf', see 'Sunrise'.

'Cajun Gold' (female; mutation of 'Burfordii'; selected at Grandview Nursery; registered 9-60 by S. Solymosy).

Leaves green with yellow markings of broad bands and blotches, margins usually entire.

'Cario' (male; a plant on a parkway in Cario, Illinois, used by J. McDaniel in 1964 to produce the hybrid cultivar 'Joe McDaniel'; name not registered).

Leaves very similar to those of 'Burfordii'.

'Carissa' (female; bud mutation of 'Rotunda' discovered by R. Bears at Wight Nursery; named and registered H.S.A. 4-72; PP No. 3187 by Wight Nursery).

Leaves dark olive green, glossy, elliptic, 5–7 cm (2–2¾ in.) long, 2–3 cm (¾–1³⁄₁₆ in.) wide, bases cuneate, apices acuminate, long terminal spines, margins entire, often concave, petioles 5 mm (³⁄₁₆ in.) long; fruits not observed on original plant (see 'Rotunda'); dwarf compact rounded habit. Popular dwarf landscape plant. Plate 124.

'Carolina Sentinel' (female; origin unknown; plant at North Carolina State University Arboretum; reported as a hybrid of *I.* × *attenuata* but now looks like a hybrid of *I. cornuta* with fasciculate inflorescences, peduncles, and pyrenes).

Leaves dark green, glossy, elliptic, 3–5 cm (1³⁄₁₆–2 in.) long, 1.5–2.5 cm (¹⁹⁄₃₂–1 in.) wide, slightly curved, margins usually 1–2 small spines on upper half of leaf, bases rotund to broadly acuminate, tip

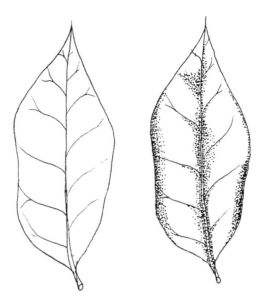

Figure 15-22. *Ilex cornuta* 'Carissa'. Drawing by Randy Allen.

spine broadly acuminate; fruits vivid red, globose, 7–8 mm (⁹⁄₃₂–⁵⁄₁₆ in.) diameter, fasciculate, in clusters; upright broadly pyramidal habit; hardy in zone 7a, possibly zone 6.

'Cartwright Compacta' (female; open-pollinated seedling grown at Cartwright Nursery; selected and named in 1961 by A. D. Cartwright Sr.; PP No. 2228).

Leaves dark olive green, glossy, oblong, slightly convex, 4–7 cm (1⅝–2¾ in.) long, 2–3 cm (¾–1³⁄₁₆ in.) wide, bases obtuse to rotund, apices acuminate, small tip spines, margins entire, petioles 6–8 mm (⁷⁄₃₂–⁵⁄₁₆ in.) long; fruits vivid red 45A, globose, 8–11 mm (⁵⁄₁₆–⁷⁄₁₆ in.) diameter, 3–8 in clusters, abundant; dense broad compact, upright habit; hardy in zone 6b.

'Casey's Dwarf' (female; origin unknown; plant at Callaway Gardens from Clarendon Gardens in 1958).

Leaves dark olive green, oblong to obovate-oblong, convex, 3.5–5 cm (1⅜–2 in.) long, 1.3–2.5 cm (½–1 in.) wide, bases rotund, apices obtuse, tip spines slightly reflexed, margins usually entire, rarely 1 spine on each side, near apex, petioles 5 mm (³⁄₁₆ in.) long; fruits vivid red 45A, globose, 8 mm (⁵⁄₁₆ in.) diameter, 1–4 in clusters, pedicels 8 mm (⁵⁄₁₆ in.) long; compact upright spreading habit.

'Clarendon Bat Wing' (female; synonym 'Bat Wing'; discovered at Clarendon Gardens by F. W. Howe about 1945 and named by him; introduced by T. Howe about 1962; original plant died, plant at Ebersole Gardens; registered H.S.A. 2-92 by P. Joseph).

Leaves dark olive green, extremely variable, oval or obovate or quadrangular to triangular, 3–4.5 cm (1³⁄₁₆–1¾ in.) long, 2.5–4 cm (1–1⅝ in.) wide, bases rotund, apices acuminate, rounded leaves convex, often entire, 1 tip spine, most leaves with 2 top marginal spines to 4.5 cm (1¾ in.) across, tip spines usually reflexed, occasionally other small spines, hence the name "bat wing," petioles 3–5 mm (⅛–³⁄₁₆ in.) long; fruits vivid red, 45A, globose, 10–12 mm (⅜–¹⁵⁄₃₂ in.) diameter, pedicels pinkish, 8–10 mm (⁵⁄₁₆–⅜ in.) long, single to very heavy clusters; upright rounded habit, multistemmed; hardy in zone 7.

'D'Or' (female; original plant at Mrs. Carl Singletary's garden, Columbus, Georgia; purchased as 'Burfordii' from Hogansville Nursery, Hogansville, Georgia; had very poor growth, replaced and moved to back yard; yellow fruit observed by F. Galle in 1954; named by Mrs. Singletary; reported to H.S.A. by F. Galle but not yet registered).

Leaves dark olive green, glossy, oblong to obovate-oblong, convex, bullate, 5–7 cm (2–2¾ in.) long, 2.5–4 cm (1–1⅝ in.) wide, bases obtuse to rotund, apices acuminate, tip spines, margins usually entire, occasionally 1–2 spines near apex, foliage on cut back plants often quadrangular, 4 spines, 1 at each corner, petioles 6 mm (⁷⁄₃₂ in.) long; fruits vivid yellow 13A, globose, 10–13 mm (⅜–½ in.) diameter, good clusters, pedicels 8–10 (⁵⁄₁₆–⅜ in.) long; hardy in zone 7b. Reported not to color in cold areas. In central Georgia, fruit colors in late October to early November and persists until late spring. Plate 125.

'Dazzler' (female; synonyms 'Bakersfield', 'Walderi'; discovered in Fresno, California, by Mr. Walder; propagated by Monrovia Nursery).

Leaves dark olive green, glossy, terminal leaves oval to obovate, convex, 5–8 cm (2–3⅛ in.) long, 3–4 cm (1³⁄₁₆–1⅝ in.) wide, bases rotund, tip spine at apex; basal leaves quadrangular, 5 cm (2 in.) long, 2 cm (¾ in.) wide, 1 spine at each corner of base, apex with 1 reflexed terminal spine and 1 spine at each apex corner, petioles 8 mm (⁵⁄₁₆ in.) long; fruits vivid red 45A, globose, 13–15 mm (½–¹⁹⁄₃₂ in.) diameter, prolific, pedicels 5–7 mm (³⁄₁₆–⁹⁄₃₂ in.) long. Selected for large clusters of large red fruits.

'Delcon' (male; introduced around 1980 by Warren County Nursery; origin doubtful; cuttings possibly from Cartwright Nursery).

Leaves dark olive green, glossy, oblong to slightly oblong-ovate, 3.5–5 cm (1⅜–2 in.) long, 1.6–2.5 cm (1⅝–1 in.) wide, bases usually rotund, apices acuminate, short tip spines, margins entire, revolute, slightly convex, petioles 4–6 mm (⁵⁄₃₂–⁷⁄₃₂ in.) long; slow compact growth, broadly ovate and upright habit, good hedge plant; survived −29°C (−20°F) in 1984. Differs from 'Anicet Delcambre' and 'Willowleaf' being male and from leaves smaller, oblong to oblong-ovate.

'Dodd Special' (female; selected and introduced by T. Dodd; plant at Callaway Gardens).

Leaves dark olive green, irregular quadrangular, convex, apices acuminate, tip spines reflexed, margins 2 basal spines at each corner, 2 top spines at corner, 4–6.5 cm (1⅝–2⅜ in.) across, petioles 6 mm (⁷⁄₃₂ in.) long; fruits vivid red 45A, globose, 8 mm (⁵⁄₁₆ in.) diameter, pedicels 8–10 mm (⁵⁄₁₆–⅜ in.) long; vigorous upright spreading habit.

'Dr. James Foret' (female; seedling in hedgerow at Jungle Gardens; selected in 1957 by A. Delcambre, I. S. Nelson, and J. Foret; named for the latter).

Leaves dark olive green, quadrangular oblong, to 3.8 cm (1½ in.) long, 1.3 cm (½ in.) wide, margins usually flat, usually 1 tip spine, occasionally 5-spined, apex 3-spined; fruits vivid red, glossy, globose, 6.5 mm (¼ in.) diameter, compact clusters; compact rounded habit.

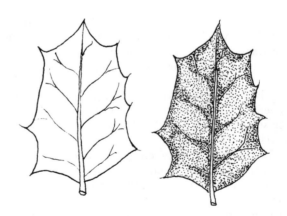

Figure 15-23. *Ilex cornuta* 'Dr. James Foret'. Drawing by Randy Allen.

'Dr. John Creech' (female; seedling in hedgerow at Jungle Gardens; selected in 1957 by A. Delcambre, I. S. Nelson, and J. Foret; named for John L. Creech of the U.S. National Arboretum).

Leaves dark olive green, quadrangular oblong, to 5 cm (2 in.) long, 2 cm (¾ in.) wide, margins with distinct light yellowish edge, 7-spined, 3 strong spines at apex, tip spine reflexed, outer spines curved upward, lateral spines in opposite directions; fruits red, globose, 6.5–9 mm (¼–¹¹⁄₃₂ in.) diameter; large shrub, compact growth habit.

'Dr. R. A. Young' (female; seedling in hedgerow at Jungle Gardens; selected in 1957 by A. Delcambre, I. S. Nelson, and J. Foret; named for R. A. Young, who worked with the late E. A. McIlhenny).

Leaves moderate to light olive green, linear-obovate, apices acute, base widening to 1.9 cm (¾ in.) wide, to 6.5 cm (2½ in.) long, 1.3 cm (½ in.) wide, margins slightly twisted, single tip spines; fruits vivid red, glossy, globose, 13 mm (½ in.) diameter in loose clusters; compact upright habit.

'Dwarf Burford' (female; synonyms 'Burfordii Compacta', 'Burfordii Nana'; discovered in 1947 among cutting-grown plants at Ferger Landscape Company; selected, named, and registered H.S.A. 2-58 by J. Ferger).

Leaves dark olive green, glossy, oval to oval oblong, convex, slightly bullate, 4–5 cm (1⅝–2 in.) long, 2–2.5 cm (¾–1 in.) wide, bases rotund, apices obtuse, 1 small tip spine, margins entire, petioles 5 mm (³⁄₁₆ in.) long; fruits vivid red 45A, globose, 8 mm (⁵⁄₁₆ in.) diameter, abundant, pedicels 5–7 mm (³⁄₁₆–⁹⁄₃₂ in.) long; compact dense habit, slower growing than 'Burfordii'. Plates 126, 127.

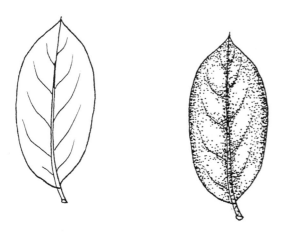

Figure 15-24. *Ilex cornuta* 'Dwarf Burford'. Drawing by Randy Allen.

'E. A. McIlhenny' (female; seedling in hedgerow at Jungle Gardens; selected in 1957 by A. Delcambre, I. S. Nelson, and J. Foret; named for the late E. A. McIlhenny of Jungle Gardens).

Leaves dark olive green, glossy, pandurate, quadrangular oblong, to 7.5 cm (3 in.) long, 3.8 cm (1½ in.) wide, nearly flat, margins mostly 5-spined; fruits

vivid red, globose, 11 mm (⁷⁄₁₆ in.) diameter, in tight clusters; compact vigorous, large shrub, semi-upright habit.

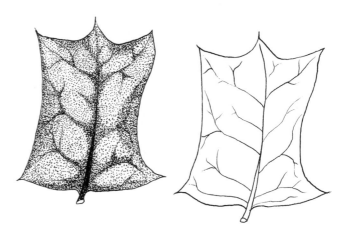

Figure 15-25. *Ilex cornuta* 'E. A. McIlhenny'. Drawing by Randy Allen.

'Femina Spreading' (female; plant at Ebersole Gardens; origin Robbins Nursery; name illegitimate due to Latin form).

Leaves moderate olive green, oval to quadrangular, 4–6 cm (1⅝–2⅜ in.) long, 2.5–3.5 cm (1–1⅜ in.) wide, bases rotund to truncate, apices acuminate, tip spines reflexed, margins variable entire to 1–2 marginal top spines, bases spineless to 2 marginal spines; fruits vivid red 45A, globose, 8–10 mm (⁵⁄₁₆–⅜ in.) diameter, good clusters; upright compact rounded habit.

'Fine Line' (female; origin unknown; plant at the display garden at Magnolia Gardens and Nursery in the 1980s).

Leaves dark olive green, extremely variable, oblong to obovate to quadrangular, 3.5–6 cm (1⅜–2⅜ in.) long, 2–3 cm (¾–1⅜ in.) wide, bases rotund, apices acute, margins with attractive distinct, translucent edge, entire to 2–3 spines on late summer growth, petioles 5 mm (³⁄₁₆ in.) long; fruits vivid red 45A, globose, 8 mm (⁵⁄₁₆ in.) diameter, fascicles 1–5 in clusters, pedicels 5–10 mm (³⁄₁₆–⅜ in.) long; upright compact, columnar habit. Plate 128.

'Floralia' (female; seedling found in South Carolina; selected and registered H.S.A. 12-59 by P. F. Henderson; said to have been pollinated by *I. opaca* and share its habit and gray bark, but this never confirmed).

'Foster's Compact' (female; origin unknown; plant at Callaway Gardens from Patterson Nursery in 1959).

Leaves dark olive green, glossy, obovate to quadrangular, convex, 3.5–6 cm (1⅜–2⅜ in.) long, 2–2.5 cm (¾–1 in.) wide, bases rotund to truncate, apices acuminate, tip spines reflexed, 2 top marginal spines 4–6 cm (1⅝–2⅜ in.) across, 2 basal corner spines; fruits red, globose; compact habit.

'Frank Bailey' (female; original plant on grounds of Bailey Arboretum; named for previous owner of farm estate and registered H.S.A. 1-73 by M. A. Nosal).

Leaves dark olive green, oblong, 5–7.5 cm (2–3 in.) long, 2.5 cm (1 in.) wide, usually 5 spines, apical spines strongly depressed, tip leaves larger than ones below; fruits red globose, 6.5 mm (¼ in.) diameter, pedicels 6.5 mm (¼ in.) long; oval habit with fan shaped branches; hardy in zone 7; original tree 3 × 3 m (10 × 10 ft.) at 40 years;

'Gay Blade' (female; seedling discovered in the 1950s at Wight Nursery by J. Wight Sr.; introduced by Wight Nursery).

Leaves dark olive green, glossy, obovate to quadrangular, 4–5 cm (1⅝–2 in.) long, 3–4 cm (1³⁄₁₆–1⅝ in.) across upper lateral spines, margins typically with 2 basal spines, 2 apical spines and tip spine reflexed, older plants often with leaf bases rotund or with remote basal spines on one or both sides, petioles 5–6 mm (³⁄₁₆–⁷⁄₃₂ in.) long; fruits vivid red, globose, 8–10 mm (⁵⁄₁₆–⅜ in.) diameter; upright compact columnar habit. No longer in production but a few plants still found in home plantings around Cairo, Georgia.

'Glenwood' (female; seedling of *I. cornuta*; discovered around 1975 by C. F. Young; plants under evaluation in Philadelphia, Pennsylvania, but never reported).

Leaves bluish green, variable in shape; fruits larger than those of 'Burfordii'; broadly upright habit.

'Grandview' (male; original plant in garden of E. Vallot; named and registered H.S.A. 10-60 by S. Solymosy).

Leaves dark olive green, glossy, oval to obovate to obovate-oblong, convex, 4–6.5 cm (1⅝–2½ in.) long, 2.5–3.5 cm (1–1⅜ in.) wide, bases rotund, apices acuminate, tip spines, margins entire, slightly twisted; compact habit of growth with spreading branches. Good pollinator. Plate 129.

'Herta' (female; seedling raised in 1950; selected and registered H.S.A. 6-61 by W. Hopfensitz).

Leaves dark olive green, glossy, elliptic, 58 cm (2¼ in.) long, 2.5 cm (1 in.) wide, long tip spines depressed, usually 4 forward pointed spines on each side; fruits vivid red.

'Hody Wilson' (female; synonym 'Louisiana Selection No. 2'; old seedling plant at Southeast Horticultural Experiment Station, Hammond, Louisiana; named for Walter F. "Hody" Wilson, retired superintendent of the Station).

Leaves dark olive green, glossy, quadrangular, convex, 5–8 cm (2–3⅛ in.) long, 3–4 cm (1³⁄₁₆–1⅝ in.) wide, bases rotund, apices acuminate, tip spines reflexed, margins usually entire, occasionally 2 top marginal spines 4–5 cm (1⅝–2 in.) across, very rarely 2 basal spines, petioles 5 mm (³⁄₁₆ in.) long; fruits vivid red 45A, globose, 10 mm (⅜ in.) diameter, pedicels 13–16 mm (¼–⅝ in.) long, very heavy fruiting; original plant approximately 50–55 years old, 7 m (23 ft.) high, 8 m (26 ft.) wide. Reported to be perfect flowering.

'Hume' (male; seedling of 'Burfordii' raised at McLean Nursery; selected by S. H. McLean and named for H. Hume before 1960).

Leaves dark olive green, glossy, quadrangular, flat, 4–6 cm (1⅝–2⅜ in.) long, 2.5–3 cm (1–1³⁄₁₆ in.) wide, bases truncate or slightly rotund, apices short, acuminate, margins reflexed, spines small, 3 apical, 2 basal, usually 1 small spine on each side in center, petioles faintly purple, 2–4 mm (¹⁄₁₆–⁵⁄₃₂ in.) long; new branches purple; reported to be unusual and distinct; small compact habit; original plant 1.2 × 0.75 m (4 × 2½ ft.) wide.

'Ira S. Nelson' (female; seedling selected at Jungle Gardens in 1957 by A. Delcambre, I. S. Nelson, and J. Foret; named for the late I. S. Nelson, horticulturist at the University of Southwestern Louisiana, Lafayette).

Leaves dark olive green, margins with contrasting light yellow edges, extremely variable, oblong to quadrangular, convex, 6–10 cm (2⅜–4 in.) long, 3.5–6 cm (1⅜–2⅜ in.) wide, bases rotund, apices acuminate tip spines reflexed, 2 top apical spines to 8 cm (3⅛ in.) across, petioles 8 mm (⁵⁄₁₆ in.) long; fruits vivid red 45A, ellipsoid, 12–14 mm (¹⁵⁄₃₂–¹⁷⁄₃₂ in.) long, 10–12 mm (⅜–¹⁵⁄₃₂ in.) wide, pedicels 10–12 mm (⅜–¹⁵⁄₃₂ in.) long. Upright loose growing large shrub, with large unusual leaves. Plate 130.

'Jungle Gardens' (female; seedling selected in late 1940s and named by E. A. McIlhenny from a hedge row at Jungle Gardens; seed originally from U.S. Plant Introduction Station).

Leaves dark olive green, glossy, obovate-quadran-

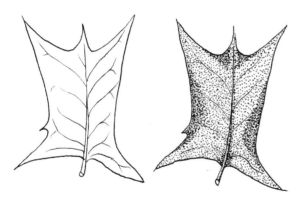

Figure 15-26. *Ilex cornuta* 'Ira S. Nelson'. Drawing by Randy Allen.

gular, slightly convex to nearly flat, 4–5.5 cm (1⅝–2⅛ in.) long, 2.5–4.5 cm (1–1¾ in.) wide, widest at apex, bases concave to truncate, apices sharp acuminate, tip spines reflexed, margins reflexed, 3 apical spines, 2 basal spines, petioles 4 mm (⁵⁄₃₂ in.) long; fruits red, globose, 6.5 mm (¼ in.) diameter; large shrub, semicompact habit.

'Karen Masteller' (female; chance seedling in Bethlehem, Pennsylvania; registered H.S.A. 12-67 by L. K. Ziegler at Lehigh Valley Nursery).
  Leaves glossy; fruits red, globose; broadly conical habit, original tree 3.7 × 3.7 m (12 × 12 ft.) in 15 years.

'Kingsville' (female; synonyms 'Kingsville No. 1', 'Kingsville Special No. 1'; selected by H. Hohman).
  Leaves dark olive green oblong, 6–9 cm (2⅜–3½ in.) long, 2.5–4.5 cm (1–1¾ in.) wide, bases rotund, apices acuminate, tip spines reflexed margins usually entire, occasionally 1 or 2 spines near apex, petioles 8 mm (⁵⁄₁₆ in.) long; fruits deep red 46A, globose, 10 mm (⅜ in.) diameter, pedicels 10 mm (⅜ in.) long.

'Lehigh Valley' (sex unknown; seedling selected and named by L. K. Ziegler at Lehigh Valley Nursery in the 1970s).
  Leaves dark olive green, sinuate, quadrangular.

'Leroy's Favorite' (female; origin from S. McLean, named for neighbor; plant at Scott Arboretum)
  Leaves dark olive green, glossy, quadrangular, 4.5–6.5 cm (1¾–2½ in.) long, 2.2–3.5 cm (1³⁄₁₆–1⅜ in.) wide, 3.8–4.5 cm (1½–1¾ in.) wide, bases truncate, apices acute, tip spines strongly reflexed, margins convex, 2 top spines, 2 basal spines 1 on each side, occasionally 1 small lateral spine on each side, petioles 8 mm (⁵⁄₁₆ in.) long; fruits red, globose,

8–10 mm (⁵⁄₁₆–⅜ in.) diameter, fasciculate, 1–5 in clusters; broadly upright, rounded habit.

'Little Leaf', see 'Small Leaf'.

'Lottie Moon' (female; selected and introduced by Tom Dodd Nursery in late 1950s).
  Leaves dark olive green, glossy, squarish to quadrangular, convex, 4–5 cm (1⅝–2 in.) long, 2.5–3 cm (1–1³⁄₁₆ in.) wide, bases rotund to truncate, apices acuminate, tip spines reflexed, margins nearly entire, 2 marginal near apex and 2 spines at base, petioles 3–4 mm (⅛–⁵⁄₃₂ in.); fruits deep red 46A, globose, 8 mm (⁵⁄₁₆ in.) diameter, 2–4 in clusters, pedicels 2–4 mm (¹⁄₁₆–⁵⁄₃₂ in.) long; compact habit.

'Matthew Yates' (male; plant at Callaway Gardens from Tom Dodd Nursery in 1964; not in production).
  Leaves dark olive green, glossy, squarish to quadrangular, convex, 4–6.5 cm (1⅝–2½ in.) long, 2.8–3.5 cm (1⅛–1⅜ in.) wide, bases rotund to truncate, apices acuminate, tip of spines reflexed, margins variable, entire to spiny, with 2 top corner marginal spines, 2 basal spines, occasionally 1 spine on each side in middle of leaf, petioles 5 mm (³⁄₁₆ in.) long.

'Medaillion' (male; seedling raised and selected at Grandview Nursery; registered H.S.A. 11-60 by S. Solymosy).
  Leaves dark olive green, glossy, oblong, 4–6 cm (1⅝–2⅜ in.) long, 2–2.5 cm (¾–1 in.) wide, bases rotund, apices acuminate, sharp tip spines, margins entire, usually flat, petioles 5 mm (³⁄₁₆ in.) long.

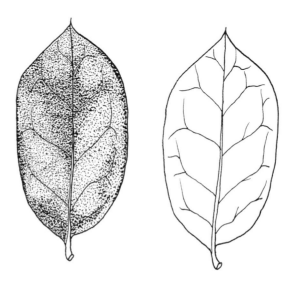

Figure 15-27. *Ilex cornuta* 'Kingsville'. Drawing by Randy Allen.

'Merry Berry' (female; selected seedling by K. Durio from seed planted before 1954; named by Durio; introduced by Louisiana Nursery).

Leaves dark olive green, glossy, variable, quadrangular to oblong, convex, 4–6 cm (1⅝–2⅜ in.) long, 2–3 cm (¾–1³⁄₁₆ in.) wide, top marginal spines 3–5 cm (1³⁄₁₆–2 in.) across, tip spines usually reflexed, apices truncate, bases obtuse to rotund, occasionally entire or with 1–2 apical marginal spines, petioles 8–10 mm (⁵⁄₁₆–⅜ in.) long; fruits vivid red 44A, flattened globose, 8–10 mm (⁵⁄₁₆–⅜ in.) diameter, 6–8 mm (⁷⁄₃₂–⁵⁄₁₆ in.) thick, fasciculate, 3–5 in clusters, abundant, pedicels 5 mm (³⁄₁₆ in.) long; large compact upright rounded shrub, original plant 7.3 m (24 ft.) high, 4.6 m (15 ft.) wide.

'National' (female; synonym 'Cornuta No. 2'; original tree at U.S. Botanic Gardens, Washington, D.C.; propagation started in 1918 at Glen Saint Mary Nursery, Glen Saint Mary, Florida).

Leaves dark olive green, convex, slightly bullate, oval-elliptic to obovate, 4.5–6 cm (1¾–2⅜ in.) long, 2.5–3 cm (1–1³⁄₁₆ in.) wide, bases acuminate, short sharp tip spines, petioles 5–8 mm (³⁄₁₆–⁵⁄₁₆ in.) long; fruits vivid red 45B, globose, 8–10 mm (⁵⁄₁₆–⅜ in.) diameter, 2–6 in cluster, abundant, pedicels 8–13 mm (⁵⁄₁₆–½ in.) long; compact upright rounded habit; hardy in zone 6b. Similar to 'Burfordii' but with smaller leaves and fruits.

'Needle Point' (a popular name in the trade for 'Anicet Delcambre', which see).

'Nickel' (female; sport of 'Burfordii'; selected in 1950 by H. R. Nickel, Greenleaf Nursery).

Leaves narrower and darker than 'Burfordii', margins silver, single spine at apex; fruits dark red, smaller; upright dense habit. Similar to 'Fine Line', may be the same.

'O. Spring' (male; seedling found by Otto Spring; plant given to T. Dodd Jr.; named for Spring and introduced in late 1950s by Dodd).

Leaves variegated, dark to moderate yellow green 138A and B, with irregular blotches of light yellow 11A and B, near margins and apex, oblong, to obovate-oblong, convex, 5–10 cm (2–4 in.) long, 2–3.5 cm (¾–1⅜ in.) wide, bases obtuse, apices acuminate, tip spines usually reflexed, margins 1–4 spines on each side, usually 2 spines at apex to 6 mm apart, petioles 6 mm (⁷⁄₃₂ in.) long; fruits red, rare. Red fruits reported in 1989 by P. Joseph. Interesting plant for accent and contrast in the landscape. Foliage winter burns at U.S. National Arboretum. Plate 131.

Figure 15-28. *Ilex cornuta* 'O. Spring'. Photo by Fred Galle.

'Olga' (female; origin about 1965 from seed collected at Shayne, Louisiana; selected and named by G. Posey; registered H.S.A. 2-77 by C. S. Britt; sibling of 'Aglo').

Leaves dark olive green, square-shaped, convex, 5–7.5 cm (2–3 in.) long, 3.8–5 cm (1½–2 in.) wide, strong tip spines reflexed down, 3 marginal spines on each side, upper marginal spines point forward, small middle spines lower ¼ of leaf, petioles 3 mm (⅛ in.); fruits vivid red 45A, globose, 10 mm (⅜ in.) diameter, in clusters, pedicels 1.8 cm (¹¹⁄₁₆ in.) long; compact columnar habit, original plant 2.3 m (7 ft.) tall, 1.8 m (6 ft.) wide in approximately 18 years.

'Pendula' (female; plant at Ebersole Gardens; origin from Southern States Nursery).

Leaves dark olive green, variable, triangular to quadrangular, 3–7 cm (1³⁄₁₆–2¾ in.) long; triangulate leaves 3 cm (1³⁄₁₆ in.) long, 5 cm (2 in.) wide at apex, tip spines reflexed; quadrangular leaves 6–7 cm (2⅜–2¾ in.) long, 7 cm (2¾ in.) wide at top, marginal spines, bases truncate, tip spines reflexed; 2 marginal basal spines, petioles 6–7 mm (⁷⁄₃₂–⁹⁄₃₂ in.) long; fruits red, globose, 8–9 mm (⁵⁄₁₆–⁹⁄₃₂ in.) diameter; upright spreading habit, branches arch down and then tip upward.

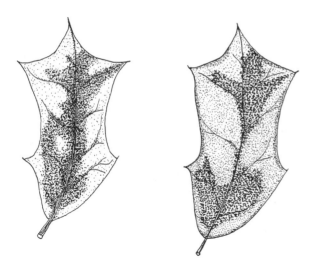

Figure 15-29. *Ilex cornuta* 'O. Spring'. Drawing by Randy Allen.

'Perkinston College' (female; plant on Perkinston College Campus, Perkinston, Mississippi; first observed in the 1960s).

Leaves dark olive green, oval to quadrangular, 5.5–8 cm (2⅛–3⅛ in.) long, 2.5–4 cm (1–1⅝ in.) wide, bases obtuse to rotund, apices acuminate, tip spines slightly reflexed, margins slightly convex, usually entire, occasionally 2 basal spines, petioles 5–8 mm (³⁄₁₆–⁵⁄₁₆ in.) long; fruits vivid red 45A, globose, 10 mm (⅜ in.) diameter, 1–5 in clusters, pedicels 5–8 mm (³⁄₁₆–⁵⁄₁₆ in.) long; upright spreading habit.

'Pyonsan Lyre' (female; collected from Pyonsan peninsula, Korea, by C. F. Miller; named by Miller; cultivar to be introduced to the United States).

Leaves dark olive green, glossy, oval, lyre shaped, 4.5–6 cm (1¾–2⅜ in.) long, 2.5–3.8 cm (1–2½ in.) wide, bases rotund, usually wider at base, 3 tip spines, flat, petioles 4–5 mm (⁵⁄₃₂–³⁄₁₆ in.) long; fruits vivid red, globose, large, abundant.

'Rotunda' (female; seedling selected in mid 1930s by E. A. McIlhenny; plants presented to U.S. Plant Introduction Station for distribution).

Leaves dark olive green, convex, oblong, 4–9 cm (1⅝–3½ in.) long, 2–2.5 cm (¾–1 in.) wide, bases rotund to truncate, apices short, triangular, acuminate, tip spines reflexed, margins undulate, 3–5 spines on each side of leaf, petioles 4–5 mm (⁵⁄₃₂–³⁄₁₆ in.); fruits vivid red 45A, ellipsoidal, 8 mm (⁵⁄₁₆ in.) diameter, pedicels 8 mm (⁵⁄₁₆ in.) long, often hidden by dense very spiny foliage. First reported sterile but mature plants approximately 25 years old and older are producing fruit. Compact, dwarf landscape plant, usually wider than high. Young rooted cut-

tings from mature fruiting stock plants are now producing fruits in 2- to 3-gallon-size plants. Plate 132.

'RPV Special' (female; synonyms 'Burford Sport', 'RPV'; sport of 'Burfordii'; introduced by Vermeulen Nursery; named for Raymond Patrick Vermeulen).

Leaves dark olive green, glossy, ovate to oval, 4–5.5 cm (1⅝–2⅛ in.) long, 2.5–3.5 cm (1–1⅜ in.) wide, bases rotund, apices acute, tip spines usually straight, rarely reflexed, margins recurved, usually entire, or very rarely 2 marginal spines at apex; fruits red, globose, 6–8 mm (⁷⁄₃₂–⁵⁄₁₆ in.) diameter; compact broadly pyramidal habit, faster growing than 'Dwarf Burford' and slower than 'Burfordii'.

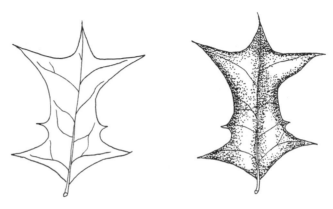

Figure 15-30. *Ilex cornuta* 'Rotunda'. Drawing by Randy Allen.

Figure 15-31. A hedge of *Ilex cornuta* 'Rotunda' (foreground) and masses of *I.* 'Nellie R. Stevenson' (left and right background) on the campus of Mississippi State University. Photo by Ed Martin.

'Ryan' (female; plant at Ebersole Gardens; origin Southern States Nursery).

Leaves dark olive green, glossy, elliptic, convex, 4.5–7 cm (1¾–2¾ in.) long, 2–3.5 cm (¾–1⅜ in.) wide, bases cuneate to obtuse, apices acuminate to single tip spine, margins entire, petioles 5 mm (³⁄₁₆ in.) long; fruits vivid red 45A, globose, 8 mm (⁵⁄₁₆ in.) diameter, pedicels 10–13 mm (⅜–½ in.) long; compact upright rounded habit.

'Sam Souder' (female; chance seedling selected by S. Souder about 1956 and given to J. Kassab; registered H.S.A. 1-79 by Kassab).

Leaves dark olive green, glossy, extremely variable from broadly elliptic to broadly and narrow strap-like or oblong, 5.8–12 cm (2½–4¾ in.) long, 3.2–9 cm (1¼–3½ in.) wide, bases rotund or truncate when spined, apices acuminate, long tip spines reflexed or straight, top marginal spines variable and pointed forward or outward, additional spines usually near middle and adjacent to base, usually weaker than tip and upper marginal spines, margins flat to undulate, petioles 6.5–10 mm (¼–⅜ in.) long; fruits dark red, globose, to 11 mm (⁷⁄₁₆ in.) diameter, 6–8 in clusters, pedicels 10 mm (⅜ in.) long; broadly conical habit, hardy in zone 6b; original tree 3.7 m (12 ft.) tall, 4.6 m (15 ft.) wide.

'Shangri La' (female; cross of large-fruited *I. cornuta* × small-leaved male made by J. W. Batchelor; selected and named by Batchelor; PP No. 1749).

Leaves dark olive green, glossy, quadrangular oblong, convex, 3.8–9 cm (1½–3½ in.) long, 2–3 cm (¾–1³⁄₁₆ in.) wide, bases rotund to truncate, apices broadly acuminate, tip spines reflexed, margins entire, 2 top marginal spines, 1–2 basal spines, petioles short 4–5 mm (⁵⁄₃₂–³⁄₁₆ in.) long; fruits vivid red 45A, globose, 10–16 mm (⅜–⅝ in.) diameter; hardy in zone 7a. Selected for its large fruit and vigorous dense pyramidal growth.

'Shiu-Ying' (female; selected seedling of 'Burfordii'; raised and registered H.S.A. 1-58 by S. H. McLean; named for Shiu-Ying Hu).

Leaves dark olive green, glossy, quadrangular, convex, to 6.5 cm (2½ in.) long, apices acuminate, tip spines reflexed, margins with 3 strong spines on each side, rarely 4; fruits vivid red 45A, 10–13 mm (⅜–½ in.) diameter, 7–8 in clusters.

'Sizzler' (female; seedling discovered in early 1940s by J. E. Brailsford in a shipment of *I. cornuta* liners from Fruitland Nursery; named by Brailsford; introduced by Shady Grove Plantation and Nursery).

Leaves dark olive green, oblong to slightly obovate-oblong, bullate, venation pronounced, 4–6.5 cm (1⅝–2½ in.) long, 2–3 cm (¾–1³⁄₁₆ in.) wide, bases rotund, apices acuminate, tip spines reflexed, margins entire, convex, occasionally slightly twisted, petioles 8 mm (⁵⁄₁₆ in.) long; fruits vivid red 45A, globose, 8 mm (⁵⁄₁₆ in.) diameter, fascicles 1–5 in clusters, pedicels 5–10 mm (³⁄₁₆–⅜ in.) long; symmetrical dense habit of growth. Brailsford believes plant superior to 'Burfordii' as it does not overfruit the way 'Burfordii' does; this makes it less vulnerable to cold and more tolerant to adverse sites.

'Slack' (female; origin Clarendon Gardens before 1960s).

Leaves dark olive green, oblong to quadrangular, 5–9 cm (2–3½ in.) long, 2.5–4.5 cm (1–1¾ in.) wide, bases rotund to truncate, apices acuminate, margins variable, entire to irregular small spines, giving odd-shaped leaves, petioles 6–8 mm (⁷⁄₃₂–⁵⁄₁₆ in.) long; fruits vivid red 45A, globose, 10–13 mm (⅜–½ in.) diameter, pedicels 8–10 mm (⁵⁄₁₆–⅜ in.) long, holds fruit longer than other *I. cornuta* cultivars; upright spreading habit.

'Small Leaf' (female; synonym 'Little Leaf'; origin Clarendon Gardens).

Leaves moderate olive green, quadrangular, keeled, convex, 2.5–4 cm (1–1⅝ in.) long, 1.5–2.5 cm (¹⁹⁄₃₂–1 in.) wide, bases truncate, apices acuminate, tip spines reflexed, 2 top marginal spines 3.5 cm (1⅜ in.) across, 2 basal marginal spines; fruits vivid red 45A, globose, 8 mm (⁵⁄₁₆ in.) diameter, very abundant; upright spreading habit.

'Spiny' (female; open-pollinated seedling grown at Cartwright Nursery; selected and named in 1961 by A. D. Cartwright Sr.; PP No. 2229);

Leaves dark olive green, glossy, quadrangular oblong, convex, 2.5–4.5 cm (1–1¾ in.) long, 1.5–2.5 cm (¹⁹⁄₃₂–2 in.) wide, bases rotund, apices acuminate, tip spines reflexed, margins entire 1 spine on each side of wide apex, petioles 6 mm (⁷⁄₃₂ in.) long; fruits vivid red 45A, globose, 6–8 mm (⁷⁄₃₂–⁵⁄₁₆ in.) diameter, 3–5 in clusters, pedicels 5–6.5 mm (³⁄₁₆–¼ in.) long; dense broadly upright habit; hardy in zone 6b.

'Sunrise' (female; synonyms 'Burfordii Variegated', 'Burford Yellowleaf'; found in Tom Dodd Nursery; named, introduced, and registered H.S.A. 1-90 by Dodd).

Leaves strong greenish yellow near tip, bases and margins green, often blotchy greenish yellow near tip and middle of leaf, oblong to obovate-oblong, 3.5–5 cm (1⅜–2 in.) long, 1.8–2.5 cm (¹¹⁄₁₆–1 in.) wide, bases cuneate to rotund, apices acuminate, small tip spined, entire, occasionally 2 spines near apex, petioles 5 mm (³⁄₁₆ in.) long; fruits deep red 46A, globose, 6–8 mm (⁷⁄₃₂–⁵⁄₁₆ in.) diameter, pedicels 6–8 mm (⁷⁄₃₂–⁵⁄₁₆ in.) long; dense habit. Plate 133.

'Tabletop' (female; seedling selected in late 1950s by A. D. Cartwright Sr.; discontinued).
Fruits red, borne freely; low broad spreading habit, transplants easily.

'Tall Stallion' (male; selected seedling by K. Durio, from seed planted before 1954; named by Durio; introduced by Louisiana Nursery).
Leaves dark olive green, glossy, oblong to slightly oval, convex, 6–7.5 cm (2⅜–3 in.) long, 3.2–4 cm (1–1⅝ in.) wide, margins entire, bases and apices obtuse to rotund, small tip spines, petioles 7–9 mm (⁹⁄₃₂–1¹⁄₃₂ in.) long; compact large shrub to small tree, original plant about 7.5 m (25 ft.) high, 4.6 m (15 ft.) wide. Good pollinator; one of few male *I. cornuta* plants available.

'Teretiformis' (male; chance seedling selected by Y. H. Reinsmith in Atlanta, Georgia, area in early 1960s; originally listed as a variety or form but never previously described; plant at Callaway Gardens; name illegitimate).
Leaves dark olive green, quadrangular, 6–9 cm (2⅜–3½ in.) long, 2–3 cm (¾–1³⁄₁₆ in.) wide, bases rotund, apices acuminate, tip spines reflexed, 2 strong top marginal spines, often 7 cm (2¾ in.) across, 2 strong basal spines, occasionally additional side spines, petioles 5 mm (³⁄₁₆ in.) long. Selected for upright habit.

'Walker' (female; origin unknown; plant at Callaway Gardens from Mr. Walker received in 1953).
Leaves dark olive green, glossy, quadrangular, convex, 6–7.5 cm (2⅜–3 in.) long, 3–4.5 cm (1³⁄₁₆–1¾ in.) wide, bases rotund, apices acuminate, tip spines reflexed, margins usually entire, occasionally small basal spines, petioles 5 mm (³⁄₁₆ in.) long; fruits vivid red 45A, globose, 10 mm (⅜ in.) diameter, pedicels 10–13 mm (⅜–½ in.) long; upright broadly pyramidal habit.

'Willowleaf' (female; originally reported as an open-pollinated seedling grown at Cartwright Nursery; selected and named in early 1960s by A. D. Cartwright Sr.; PP No. 2290; often confused with and considered by most authorities to be the same as 'Anicet Delcambre' and 'Needle Point').
Leaves dark olive green, glossy, elliptic oblong, usually widest above middle, convex, 3.8–6.5 cm (1½–2½ in.) long, 1.6–2.5 cm (⅝–1 in.) wide, bases obtuse, apices acuminate, tip spines small, margins

entire, slightly twisted, petioles 6–8 cm (⁷⁄₃₂–⁵⁄₁₆ in.) long; fruits vivid red 45A, globose to ellipsoid, 6.5–8 mm (¼–⁵⁄₁₆ in.) diameter, pedicels 10–16 mm (⅜–⅝ in.) long; dense broad habit; hardy to zone 6b.

'Yellow Edge' (female; origin unknown).
Leaves variegated, dark olive green with yellow margin; fruits red, globose; compact upright habit.

'Yellowleaf' (female; origin unknown).
Leaves strong greenish yellow 151A, oval to obovate-oblong, convex, 4–5.8 cm (1⅝–2¼ in.) long, 2–3 cm (¾–1³⁄₁₆ in.) wide, bases obtuse to rotund, apices acuminate, sharp tip spines, margins entire, rarely 1 small marginal spine near apex, petioles 4–5 cm (⁵⁄₃₂–³⁄₁₆ in.) long; fruits vivid red 45A, globose, 6–8 cm (⁷⁄₃₂–⁵⁄₁₆ in.) diameter, 6–8 in clusters, pedicels 8 mm (⁵⁄₁₆ in.) long.

Ilex crenata (Japanese Holly) Cultivars

Japanese (or boxleaf) hollies have been reported as cultivated plants in Japanese literature for several centuries. *Ilex crenata* was named by Carl Peter Thunberg (1743–1828), a Swedish physician who worked for the Dutch East India Company in Japan from 1776 to 1777. While in Japan, Thunberg collected data for his book *Flora Japonica* (1784). While using Thunberg's manuscript, J. A. Murray was the first authority to publish Thunberg's species name *I. crenata*. Murray's *Systema Vegelabilium*, published in May or June 1784, therefore has priority over Thunberg's *Flora Japonica*, which was published in August 1784. Thunberg and Murray were the first Western botanists to name and describe many Japanese plants which were collected by Thunberg and which are widely cultivated today. The list includes *I. crenata*, *I. integra*, *I. latifolia*, *I. rotunda*, and *I. serrata*.

Carl Maximowicz introduced *Ilex crenata* from Japan to the Russian czar's garden in St. Petersburg (Leningrad) in 1864, and it soon became available to other European countries. Charles S. Sargent made the earliest known introduction from Japan to the Arnold Arboretum, Jamaica Plain, Massachusetts, in 1898, followed by E. H. Wilson in 1900.

The Arnold Arboretum in the 1930s had a successful promotion and distribution of *Ilex crenata* that resulted in production and sales of the plant. Nursery growers soon found that the species was easy to propagate from cuttings, and the ease in growing seedlings led to a mass seedling population for testing and selection of new cultivars. Nurseries and landscape architects found the species and its cultivars adaptable and useful in the landscape as foundation plants, in mass plantings and hedges, and for general use. Today Japanese holly is one of the most popular landscape plants in the United States.

Japanese hollies are variable, multiple, densely branched shrubs to 5 m (16 ft.) tall with densely pubescent branches. The leaves are dark green, glossy or dull, obovate or ovate or oblong-elliptic, usually 1–2.5 cm (3⁄8–1 in.) long, occasionally longer, 0.5–1.5 cm (3⁄16–19⁄32 in.) wide, and punctate beneath. The mostly flat margins are occasionally convex, crenate or serrate, and generally have 6–10 teeth on each side. The petioles are short, 2–3 mm (1⁄16–1⁄8 in.) long. Male inflorescences are solitary, axillary, with 1- to 7-flowered cymes. Female inflorescences are axillary, solitary or rarely 2- to 3-flowered cymes, with 4 yellowish white petals. The fruits are black, rarely yellow, globose, 6–8 mm (7⁄32–5⁄16 in.) diameter. The 4 smooth pyrenes are striate esculate.

Ilex crenata is native to Japan, Korea, Fujian Province, The People's Republic of China, Kuril, Sakhalin Islands, Taiwan, the Philippines, and the Himalayas. The species is cold hardy usually to zone 7, and some cultivars are hardy to zone 6 and possibly to zone 5b.

'Convexa' (female), an early introduction from Japan in the 1900s, became a popular landscape item and is the parent of many cultivars. Several cultivars introduced in the late 1920s and 1930s are still popular today: 'Helleri', 'Green Lustre', 'Prides Tiny', 'Rotundifolia', and 'Stokes'. Following World War II the mass production and selection of Japanese holly seedlings became almost a fad in the nursery industry with many new cultivar names introduced (e.g., Bennett Hybrid Group, which see). More than 500 cultivars have been named and introduced. One of the early criteria in selecting seedlings was cold hardiness. Other criteria are plant habit and rate of growth, followed by variations in leaves and other qualities.

Ilex crenata and its many cultivars are well adapted to container production. They are among the leading broad-leaved evergreens grown by U.S. nurseries. A limited survey of the leading wholesale plants in 1990 included 'Cherokee', 'Compacta', 'Glory', 'Green Island', 'Green Lustre', 'Helleri', 'Hetzii', 'Hoogendorn', 'Petite Point', 'Prides Tiny', 'Rotundifolia', and 'Steed's Upright'.

Many of the new *Ilex crenata* cultivars are seedling selections and hybrids selected by nursery growers and hybridizers. One of the leading geneticists and hybridizers of *Ilex,* Elwin R. Orton Jr. at Rutgers University, has released numerous specialty cultivars (e.g., 'Beehive', 'Dwarf Pagoda', 'Green Dragon', 'Jersey Pinnacle', 'Midas Touch'). Norman H. Cannon, a nurseryman in Greenwood, Delaware, has introduced both dwarf and yellow fruited-cultivars (e.g., 'Butterball', 'Dwarf Cone', 'Delaware Diamond', 'Fairyland', 'Firefly', 'Forty Niner', 'Honeycomb', 'Ivory Hall', 'Ivory Tower', 'Miss Muffet', 'Piccolo', 'Pincushion', 'Sentinel', 'Topiary'). Tom Dodd Jr., a nurseryman in Semmes, Alabama, has made many seedling selections which he has named for various friends (e.g., 'Edwin Dozier', 'Curtis Askew', 'Luther Copeland', 'Tee Dee', 'Valeria Rankin', 'William Jackson'). For the future, new germ plasm introduced from Korea is being evaluated in the United States and Canada and may provide more cold hardy selections. Seed from the People's Republic of China has not been evaluated in the United States.

'Alan Seay' (male; synonym 'Nigra'; Bennett Hybrid Group; named and introduced around 1970 by Greenbriar Farms).

Leaves dark green, obovate, flat, 1.6–2 cm (5⁄8–3⁄4 in.) long, 8–10 mm (5⁄16–3⁄8 in.) wide, margins crenulate, upper half of leaf, petioles 3–5 mm (1⁄8–3⁄16 in.) long, good winter color; broadly upright pyramidal habit.

'Angelica' (introduced in late 1960s by Angelica Nursery; illegitimate name due to priority of *I. opaca* 'Angelica').

Leaves narrow-elliptic; low spreading habit.

'Angyo' (male; synonym 'Kiiro-fukurin', old form from Japan, collected by J. L. Creech at Nakada Nursery, Angyo, Japan, in 1956; U.S. PI 236021, NA 25700; renamed by T. R. Dudley and G. K. Eisenbeiss to commemorate the city Angyo; Japanese common name means yellow margins).

Leaves variegated, irregular yellow blotches, usually near apex, occasionally completely yellow, narrow-elliptic, to 2.8 cm (1 1⁄8 in.) long, 1 cm (3⁄8 in.) wide, bases and apices cuneate, margins crenate, 3–8 minute teeth on each side, pointing forward.

'Beehive' (male; controlled cross of 'Convexa' × 'Stokes' made in 1961 by E. R. Orton Jr.; selected from 21,000 seedlings; named and introduced in 1984; registered H.S.A. 11-84 by Orton).

Leaves dark green, variable, usually small, elliptic to obovate-elliptic, slightly wider near tip than base, 1.5–2.2 cm (19⁄32–13⁄16 in.) long, 5–6.5 mm (3⁄16–1⁄4 in.) wide, margins crenate, near apex, petioles 1.6 mm (1⁄16 in.) long; dense compact, mounding habit, original plant 1.12 m (42 in.) tall, 1.58 m (5 1⁄4 ft.) wide in 22 years; hardy in zone 6a.

Bennett Hybrid Group

Developed by E. L. Bennett, propagator for

Greenbriar Farms, in search for plants of superior winter hardiness, with the large leaf size of 'Rotundifolia' and the recurved foliage of 'Convexa'. 'Convexa' was planted between 2 rows of 'Rotundifolia', seed collected from 'Convexa' in Fall 1945 was stratified and sown in Fall 1946. Approximately 250,000–300,000 seedlings were obtained, but the winter of 1947–1948 reduced the number to 3000–4000. Fifty seedlings were selected and less than 20 were named: 'Alan Seay', 'Bennett's Compact', 'Compacta' (Tingle), 'Convexa Male', 'Fastigiata', 'Hadlock', 'Howard', 'Howard Compacta', 'Major', 'Maxwell', 'Nigra', 'Oleafera', 'Recurvifolia', 'Selene', 'Vaseyi', and 'Willowleaf'.

'Bennett's Compact' (male; synonyms 'Bennett's Compacta', 'Bennett's Compactum', 'Compacta'; Bennett Hybrid Group).

Leaves dark green, broadly elliptic, flat to remotely convex, 1.5–2.5 cm (¹⁹⁄₃₂–1 in.) long, 0.8–1.3 cm (⅝–½ in.) wide, distinct serrations on margin, upper two-thirds of leaf, petioles 3–4 mm (⅛–⁵⁄₃₂ in.) long; low compact habit. Popular landscape plant.

'Birmingham' (female; seedling selected in 1963; introduced 1980 by Styer Nursery; registered H.S.A. 3-84 by J. F. Styer).

Leaves dark green, lanceolate to broadly lanceolate, 2.8 cm (1⅛ in.) long, 8 mm (⁵⁄₁₆ in.) wide, petioles 2.5 mm (³⁄₃₂ in.) long; low flat compact habit, original plant 2 m (6½ ft.) tall, 2.75 m (9 ft.) wide. Named for Birmingham Township, Pennsylvania, locale of nursery plot.

'Black Beauty' (male; seedling selected in 1956–1958 by P. E. Girard Sr., after a long hard winter destroyed nearly 6000 mature seedlings; named and introduced in 1969 by Girard's Nursery; illegitimate name due to priority of *I. opaca* 'Black Beauty').

Leaves dark green, convex, obovate, 1.8–2.2 cm (1¹⁄₁₆–1³⁄₁₆ in.) long, 1–1.2 cm (⅜–¹⁵⁄₃₂ in.) wide, bases cuneate, apices obtuse, margins crenulate, upper one-third of leaf, petioles 3 mm (⅛ in.) long; low compact habit. Selected for hardiness.

'Border Gem' (male; seedling selected 1956–1958 by P. E. Girard Sr., after a long hard winter destroyed nearly 6000 mature seedlings; named and introduced in 1969 by Girard's Nursery).

Leaves dark green, broadly elliptic, 1–1.3 cm (⅜–½ in.) long, 6–7 mm (⁷⁄₃₂–⁹⁄₃₂ in.) wide, bases and apices acute, margins remotely crenulate, upper half of leaf, petioles 2–2.5 mm (¹⁄₁₆–³⁄₃₂ in.) long; dense compact habit, very hardy.

'Braddock Heights' (female; synonym 'Braddock'; selected by H. Hohman at Braddock Heights, Maryland).

Leaves dark green, obovate, 2–3 cm (¾–1³⁄₁₆ in.) long, 1–1.3 cm (⅜–½ in.) wide, bases cuneate, apices obtuse, margins crenulate, upper one-third of leaf, petioles 3–5 mm (⅛–³⁄₁₆ in.) long; upright spreading habit.

'Bruns' (female; selected by J. Bruns before 1959).

Broadly compact habit; winter hardy. Recommended for specimen planting and hedges.

Bullata

A name often misused in U.S. nurseries. Also a group name (Bullata Group) now rejected, for plants generally characterized by bullate convex leaves. *Ilex crenata* f. *bullata* Rehder was published in 1931 and soon invalidated and changed to f. *convexa* (Makino) Rehder, later to a cultivar or clone 'Convexa', which see. The name Bullata should be dropped from any association with any *I. crenata* plants as an invalid name per the Cultivated Code.

'Bullata Convexa' (illegitimate name), see 'Convexa'.

'Bullata Convexa Male' (illegitimate name), see 'Convexa Male'.

'Bullata Green Cone' (illegitimate name), see 'Green Cone'.

'Butler' (female; synonym 'Butler No. 1'; discovered by G. Butler in the 1950s; named and introduced by him, later by Green Biz Nursery).

Leaves moderate green, elliptic, 10–13 mm (⅜–½ in.) long, 4–6 mm (⁵⁄₃₂–⁷⁄₃₂ in.) wide, petioles 3–4 mm (⅛–⁵⁄₃₂ in.) long; fruits greenish yellow, globose, 6 mm (⁷⁄₃₂ in.), pedicels 5 mm (³⁄₁₆ in.) long, abundant; upright habit, spreading with age, good hedge.

'Butterball' (female; Watanabeana Group; selected by N. Cannon from about 400 sprouted seeds distributed by U.S. Plant Introduction Station, Glenn Dale, Maryland, in 1965; selected and named by Cannon).

Leaves light green, broadly elliptic, 1.3–2 cm (½–¾ in.) long, 6–8 mm (⁷⁄₃₂–⁵⁄₁₆ in.) wide, petioles 5 mm (³⁄₁₆ in.) long, margins crenate near apex; fruits yellow. Sister seedling to 'Forty Niner', ' Honeycomb', 'Ivory Hall', 'Ivory Tower', 'Sir Echo', and 'Starglow'.

'Buxifolia' (male; seedling selected 1950 by T. Dodd Jr.; named and introduced in 1954 by Tom Dodd

Nursery; name illegitimate due to priority of *I. aquifolium* 'Buxifolia').

Leaves dark green, elliptic, 1–1.5 cm (³⁄₈–¹⁹⁄₃₂ in.) long, 4–6 mm (⁵⁄₃₂–⁷⁄₃₂ in.) wide, bases and apices acute, margins crenulate, upper two-thirds of leaf, petioles 2–3 mm (¹⁄₁₆–¹⁄₈ in.) long; stiff, dense, compact habit.

'Buxifolia' (female; from Tingle Nursery), see 'Convexa'.

'Buxifolia' (selected and introduced about 1912 by Andorra Nursery).

'Buxifolia' (introduced around 1930 by Cottage Gardens).

'Buxifolia' (female; introduced 1924–1925 by Towson Nursery).

'Canton' (seedling about 1932; selected and named by J. F. Styer; introduced about 1947 by Styer Nursery).

Leaves light green, small; irregular medium, conical habit.

'Cape Fear' (male; introduced early 1970s by Robbins Nursery).

Leaves dark green, usually broadly elliptic, 2–3.5 cm (³⁄₄–1³⁄₈ in.) long, margins crenulate, upper half of leaf, petioles 4–6 mm (⁵⁄₃₂–⁷⁄₃₂ in.) long, stems brownish on top; broadly upright habit.

'Carefree' (female; from wild seed collected by J. L. Creech, Collection No. 1011, U.S. PI 275853, as *I. crenata* subsp. *radicans*; later identified as *I. crenata* var. *paludosa* (Nakai) Tatewaki; from open bog meadow on Mount O-take, Honshu, Japan; named and introduced by Clemson College; registered H.S.A. 4-82 by D. W. Bradshaw and L. R. Schmid).

Leaves dark green, broadly ovate, 1.8 cm (¹¹⁄₁₆ in.) long, 0.8 cm (⁵⁄₁₆ in.) wide; dwarf mound-shaped habit, open branched, numerous branchlets, original plant 61 cm (24 in.) tall, 107 cm (41 in.) wide in 14 years.

'Carolina Upright' (male; introduced in the 1970s by Robbins Nursery).

Leaves dark green, glossy, broadly elliptic, 2–2.5 cm (³⁄₄–1 in.) long, 8–10 mm (⁵⁄₁₆–³⁄₈ in.) wide, margins crenulate; upright pyramidal habit.

'Centennial' (male; selected by C. Orndorff in the 1980s).

Narrow to medium upright habit. Suitable for screens and hedges.

'Chandler' (male; seedling found and selected by J. Chandler in the late 1970s; grown and introduced by Norman Chandler Nursery).

Leaves dark green, elliptic, 1.3–2 cm (¹⁄₂–³⁄₄ in.) long, 7–10 mm (⁹⁄₃₂–³⁄₈ in.) wide, 3–5 small crenate teeth on each side, upper half of leaf, petioles 4–6 mm (⁵⁄₃₂–⁷⁄₃₂ in.) long; upright spreading habit of growth.

'Changsha' (female; seedling about 1932; selected and named by J. F. Styer; introduced about 1947 by Styer Nursery).

Leaves small; slow growing, upright irregular habit.

'Chengtu' (female; seedling about 1932; selected and named by J. F. Styer; introduced about 1974 by Styer Nursery).

Leaves small; slow growing, irregular habit.

'Cherokee' (male; synonym 'Upright Cherokee'; seedling selected at Commercial Nursery and introduced by it in early 1960s).

Leaves dark green, elliptic, 1.5–2.2 (¹⁹⁄₃₂–1³⁄₁₆ in.) long, 7–10 mm (⁹⁄₃₂–³⁄₈ in.) wide, bases cuneate, apices acute, margins crenulate, upper half of leaf, petioles 3–4 mm (¹⁄₈–⁵⁄₃₂ in.) long; upright pyramidal habit.

'Chesapeake' (origin unknown; introduced in the 1970s by Chesapeake Nursery).

Leaves dark green, broadly elliptic to obovate, slightly convex, 1.5–1.8 cm (¹⁹⁄₃₂–1¹⁄₁₆ in.) long, 8–10 mm (⁵⁄₁₆–³⁄₈ in.) wide, bases cuneate, apices obtuse, petioles 3 mm (¹⁄₈ in.) long; upright pyramidal habit.

'Clemson' A, B, C (cuttings from plants at Clemson Botanical Gardens; could be 'Carefree' = A, 'Crescent' or 'Gayle' = B, 'Tyke' = C; plants too small for definite identification).

'Cole's Hardy' (synonym 'Cole's Hardy Type'; origin unknown; introduced in the 1950s by Cole's Nursery).

Upright pyramidal habit; very hardy.

'Columnaris' (female; Bennett Hybrid Group; introduced by Greenbriar Farms; illegitimate name in Latin form, also invalid due to priority of *I. opaca* 'Columnaris').

Upright columnar habit.

'Compacta' (several plants introduced with this name, possibly the best known is a member of the Bennett Hybrid Group, 'Bennett's Compact', introduced by Tingle Nursery).

Compact habit.

'Conners' (synonym 'Crenata No. 1'; seedling selected about 1946 by C. H. Conners at J. Schmidt's Nursery).

Leaves dark green, elliptic to oval, 1.8–2 cm (11/16–3/4 in.) long, 1–1.3 cm (3/8–1/2 in.) wide, bases and apices obtuse, margins crenulate, upper two-thirds of leaf, petioles 3–5 mm (1/8–3/16 in.) long; narrow upright, columnar habit, about 3 times as tall as wide. Reported hardy to −20°C (−5°F).

'Convexa' (female; synonyms 'Bullata', 'Buxifolia' of Tingle; named from a cultivated plant in Japan; described by T. Makino as *I. crenata* var. *convexa* in 1928; recombined in a reduced rank f. *convexa* by A. Rehder in 1931; introduced in United States in 1919 by Arnold Arboretum).

Leaves moderate green, elliptic, convex, 10–22 mm (3/8–13/16 in.) long, 7–10 mm (9/32–3/8 in.) wide, bases obtuse to cuneate, apices obtuse, margins remotely serrate near apex; upright spreading habit. Very popular landscape plant. Numerous seedlings and selections of 'Convexa' have been introduced. Plate 134.

'Convexa Compacta', see 'Bennett's Compacta' and Bennett Hybrid Group.

'Convexa Compacta' (introduced by Wayside Gardens before 1966).

Dwarf habit.

'Convexa Horizontalis' (introduced by J. Dieckmann and Son before 1980).

Horizontal branching.

'Convexa Male' (male; Bennett Hybrid Group; introduced by Greenbriar Farms).

Very similar to 'Convexa' with good fall and winter foliage color due to lack of fruit.

'Convexa Nana' (introduced by Strander Evergreen Nursery).

Dwarf mounding habit.

'Convexa Upright' (possibly synonym of 'Fastigiata' of Bennett Hybrid Group; listed in auction in 1976 of Millcreek Landscape Division).

'Convexa Xanthocarpa' (introduced by Millcreek Landscape Division).

Fruits yellow.

'Crescent' (male; origin from wild seed collected by J. L. Creech, Collection No. 1049, U.S. PI 276112, as *I. crenata* subsp. *radicans*; later identified as *I. crenata* var. *paludosa*; from a cut-over area at 390 m (1300 ft.) elevation on Mount Shikotsu, Hokkaido, Japan; named and introduced by Clemson University; registered H.S.A. 5-82 by D. W. Bradshaw and L. R. Schmid).

Leaves elliptic to ovate, 1.4 cm (17/32 in.) long, 1 cm (3/8 in.) wide, terminal leaves usually smaller; dwarf mounding habit, with fastigiate compact branching, original plant 71 cm (28 in.) tall, 135 cm (52 in.) wide in 15 years.

'Dan's Gold' (synonyms 'Golden Microphylla', 'Variegated Microphylla'; mutation on 'Microphylla' discovered by D. G. Fenton; introduced about 1980).

Leaves variegated, irregular yellow blotches, spots to entirely yellow, elliptic to lanceolate, 1.8–2.2 cm (11/16–13/16 in.) long, 6–7 mm (7/32–9/32 in.) wide, petioles 3–5 mm (1/8–3/16 in.) long; upright spreading habit.

'Delaware Diamond' (male; synonym 'Elfin'; seedling selected by N. Cannon in the 1970s; introduced in the early 1980s but not promoted; to be registered with H.S.A.).

Leaves dark green, very small, elliptic, 6–8 mm (7/32–5/16 in.) long, 3–4 mm (1/8–5/32 in.) wide, petioles 1–1.5 mm (1/32–3/64 in.) long, stems dark; dense mounding habit, very dwarf, 30 cm tall × 50 cm wide, (12 × 20 in.) in more than 12 years. Excellent dwarf rock garden and bonsai plant; one of the smallest leaved Japanese holly cultivars. Plate 135.

'Dewdrop' (female; cross made in 1972 by N. Cannon; selected and named in 1973 by Cannon).

Leaves dark green, elliptic, 12–16 mm (15/32–5/8 in.) long, 4–6 mm (5/32–7/32 in.) wide, margins crenulate, upper half of leaf, petioles 2–3 mm (1/16–1/8 in.) long; very dwarf, slow growing, 20 cm (8 in.) wide, 10 cm (4 in.) tall in 7 years. Excellent dwarf plant for rock gardens and bonsai.

'Divaricata' (seedling selected 1950 by T. Dodd Jr.; introduced 1955 by Tom Dodd Nursery).

Leaves dark green, elliptic-obovate, 1.8–2.2 cm (11/16–13/16 in.) long, 6–9 mm (7/32–11/32 in.) wide, bases cuneate, apices acute, margins crenulate, upper two-thirds of leaf, petioles 3–4 mm (1/8–5/32 in.) wide; slightly upright, spreading habit, like *Juniperus* × *media* 'Pfitzeriana' (pfitzer juniper).

'Duncan' (male; seedling selected before 1962 by C. A. Rowland; introduced by Athens Landscape Service).

Leaves small; semi-spreading habit.

'Dwarf Cone' (male; O. P. seedling from F_2 population of 'Convexa' × 'Microphylla'; selected and named in 1964 by N. Cannon; registered H.S.A. 3-80 by Cannon).

Leaves dark green, narrow-elliptic, 1.5 cm (19/32 in.) long, 5.5 mm (7/32 in.) wide, bases and apices acute, petioles 5 mm (3/16 in.) long; upright broadly conical habit, cone shaped, semi-compact and spreading when young; original plant 1.8 m (6 ft.) tall, 1 m (3 ft.) wide in 16 years. 'Firefly' and 'Piccolo' have same origin in F1 cross.

'Dwarf Pagoda' (female; selected from 825 seedlings of controlled cross of 'Mariesii' × 'John Nosal' made in 1966 by E. R. Orton Jr.; named and registered H.S.A. 9-72 by Orton).

Leaves dark green, orbiculate to oval, 8–10 mm (5/16–3/8 in.) long, 6.5–8 mm (1/4–5/16 in.) wide, 1–2 remote teeth on each side, near apex, petioles 1–1.5 mm (1/32–3/64 in.) long; fruit black, very sparse to rare; branching habit irregular, essentially upright horizontal, internodes very short, giving very heavy foliage effect, average annual growth usually less than 5 cm (2 in.) long; excellent for rock gardens, bonsai, and, house plant; hardy in zone 6b. Sister seedling of 'Green Dragon'. Plate 136.

'Edwin Dozier' (male; synonym 'Edwin B. Dozzer'; Tom Dodd 56-342; seedling selected in 1956 by T. Dodd Jr.; named and introduced in 1966 by Dodd; discontinued).

Leaves medium green, lighter than 'William Jackson'; compact spreading, distinct horizontal branching, wider than tall.

'Elegans Maculata' (male; listed in Louis de Smet Nursery catalog).

Leaves extremely small, spotted yellow.

'Elfin' (invalid name due to priority of *I. opaca* 'Elfin'), see 'Delaware Diamond'.

'Ellipta' (discovered in 1979 by E. Stührenberg, Germany).

Leaves dark green, glossy, narrow-elliptic, 1–1.5 cm (3/8–19/32 in.) long, 3–6 mm (1/8–7/32 in.) wide, margins finely serrate, petioles long, leaves close together; young branchlets purplish; compact densely branched; hardy to −25°C (−13°F).

'Ellipta Convex' (sport of 'Ellipta'; discovered in E. Stührenberg Nursery; illegitimate name due to part in Latin form).

Leaves bright green, in sun yellowish green, slightly glossy, narrow-elliptic, 1–1.5 cm (3/8–19/32 in.) long, 4–6 mm (5/32–7/32 in.) wide, margins convex, finely serrate; compact densely branched shrubs; very hardy to −25°C (−13°F).

'Ellipta Gold' (sport of 'Ellipta'; discovered in E. Stührenberg Nursery; illegitimate name due to part in Latin form).

Leaves variegated, irregular mottling of yellow blotches or yellow spots, slightly glossy, narrow-elliptic, similar to 'Ellipta', leaves punctate beneath, top surface clear, margins finely serrate; young branchlets purple; compact, densely branched habit; very hardy to −25°C (−13°F).

Figure 15-32. *Ilex crenata* 'Ellipta Gold'. Photo by Hans-Georg Buchtmann.

'Fairyland' (female; cross made in 1972 by N. Cannon; selected and named in 1973 by N. Cannon; sister seedling to 'Dewdrop').

Leaves moderate olive green, elongate to elliptic, 8–13 mm (5/16–1/2 in.) long, 3–4 mm (1/8–5/32 in.) wide, curled and slightly twisted, margins very minutely crenulate, upper half of leaf, petioles 2–3 mm (1/16–1/8 in.) long; dwarf, 37.7 cm (15 in.) wide, 15 cm (6 in.) high in 7 years; grows faster than 'Dewdrop'. Excellent dwarf plant for rock gardens and bonsai.

'Fastigiata' (old selection from Japan; listed first as *I. crenata* var. *fastigiata* Makino 1917; later as f. *fastigiata* (Makino) Hara 1958, then as cultivar name; doubtful if introduced to the United States).

Upright growth habit. Habitat: Japan.

'Fastigiata' (selected by K. Wada Hakoneya Nursery, Numazu-Shi, Japan).

Pygmy form.

'Fastigiata' (female; Bennett Hybrid Group).
Leaves convex; narrow-fastigiate habit.

'Fiel's Upright' (Roslyn Nursery).
No description available.

'Firefly' (male; open-pollinated seedling selected in 1966 by N. Cannon from F3 population of 'Convexa' × 'Microphylla' made in 1954; F2 cross made in 1960 from a dwarf female × dark green male; named and registered H.S.A. 4-80 by Cannon).
Leaves dark green, glossy, elliptic to ovate, 2.5 cm (1 in.) long, 13 mm (½ in.) wide, petioles to 5 mm (³⁄₁₆ in.) long; spreading habit, moderate growth rate, original plant 1.2 m (4 ft.) tall, 2.5 m (8 ft.) wide in 29 years; compact plant with little shearing. Deserves wider distribution.

'Flushing' (male; introduced by Vermeulen Nursery).
Leaves large; compact upright habit, medium height.

'Fortunei' (possibly synonym of 'Latifolia'; originated as *I. fortunei* Miquel, then *I. crenata* var. *fortunei* Nicholson, and later f. *fortunei* Rehder).
Name difficult to establish and identify to one clone due to varying descriptions.

'Forty Niner' (female; Watanabeana Group; selected by N. Cannon from about 400 sprouted seeds distributed by U.S. Plant Introduction Station, Glenn Dale, Maryland, in 1965; selected and named by Cannon before 1975; sibling of 'Butterball').
Leaves light green, oval to oval-obovate, 1.5–1.8 cm (¹⁹⁄₃₂–²³⁄₃₂ in.) long, 8–9 mm (⁵⁄₁₆–¹¹⁄₃₂ in.) wide, petioles 5 mm (³⁄₁₆ in.) long, margins crenate near apex; fruits yellow.

'Foster No. 1' (male; seedling selected and introduced by E. Foster in early 1950s; name illegitimate due to priority of *I.* × *attenuata* 'Foster No. 1').
Leaves small, flat; low compact spreading habit.

'Foster No. 2' (seedling selected and introduced by E. Foster in early 1950s; name illegitimate due to priority of *I.* × *attenuata* 'Foster No. 2').
Low compact habit.

'Frierson' (female; selected and named by W. C. Frierson before 1963).
Leaves dark green, elliptic-obovate, 2.5–3 cm (1–1³⁄₁₆ in.) long, 1–1.3 cm (³⁄₈–½ in.) wide, bases cuneate, apices acute, margins crenulate, upper half of leaf, petioles 3–5 mm (⅛–³⁄₁₆ in.) long; vigorous, upright spreading habit, small tree to 8 m (26 ft.) tall in 25 years.

'Fukasawana' (female; see *I. crenata* subsp. *fukasawana*).

'Fulvo-Marginata' (old cultivar in Conder (1912); common name cha-fukurin-tsuge means "tea green margins"; the Latin name means "brownish yellowish green margins").

'Gable Dwarf' (possible synonym of 'Gable's'; origin unknown; listed in Watnong Nursery catalog before 1974).
Leaves dark green, small; very dwarf habit.

'Gable's' (male; possibly synonym of 'Gable No. 1'; origin unknown; plant at Scott Arboretum).
Leaves dark green, broadly elliptic to elliptic-obovate, 1.5–2 cm (¹⁹⁄₃₂–¾ in.) long, 7–9 mm (⁹⁄₃₂–¹¹⁄₃₂ in.) wide, bases cuneate, apices acute, margins remotely crenate near apex, petioles 2–3 mm (¹⁄₁₆–⅛ in.) long; upright rounded habit.

'Gayle' (female; origin from wild seed collected in 1961 by J. L. Creech, Collection No. 1054, U.S. PI 276080, as *I. crenata* subsp. *radicans*; later identified as *I. crenata* var. *paludosa*; from a cut-over area on Mount Shikotsu, Hokkaido, Japan; named and introduced by Clemson University; registered H.S.A. 2-82 by D. W. Bradshaw and L. R. Schmid).
Leaves dark green, broadly elliptic, 2.2 cm (1³⁄₁₆ in.) long, 9 mm (¹¹⁄₃₂ in.) wide, margins very small crenate near apex, petioles 2 mm (¹⁄₁₆ in.) long; very dense uniform spreading habit; original plant is 76 cm (2½ ft.) tall, 152 cm (5 ft.) wide in 16 years.

'Geisha' (female; NA 31369, U.S. PI 578192; controlled cross of yellow-fruited *I. crenata* from Japan (NA 10815, U.S. PI 231948) × *I. crenata* K 60-20-2 made in 1966 by W. F. Kosar at U.S. National Arboretum; final selection and name by G. K. Eisenbeiss in 1993; registered H.S.A. 7-94).
Leaves elliptic-ovate to obovate, small, to 15 mm (¹⁹⁄₃₂ in.) long, 6 mm (⁷⁄₃₂ in.) wide, strongly convex, very glossy, apices obtuse and mucronate, bases attenuate, strongly convex, margins crenate, 4 mucros on each side, on upper half to one-third of leaf, petioles 2 mm (¹⁄₁₆ in.) long; fruits brilliant yellow 10A, where shaded light greenish yellow 4B, globose, 6–7 mm (⁷⁄₃₂–⁹⁄₃₂ in.) diameter, borne singly or occasionally cymes of 2–3 fruits; 10-year plant 0.75 m (30 in.) tall and wide with spreading habit, not considered a dwarf plant; easily propagated; hardy in zone 7. Selection based on small convex leaves and yellow fruit.

'Glass' (male; possible synonym of 'Glass Upright'; seedling of f. *microphylla* introduced in 1947 by P. Glass and H. Hohman).

Leaves dark green, elliptic, 1–1.8 cm (3/8–11/16 in.) long, 4–6 mm (5/32–7/32 in.) wide, bases and apices acute, margins crenulate, upper two-thirds of leaf, petioles 2–3 mm (1/16–1/8 in.) long; compact upright habit.

'Globosa' (female; introduced around 1939 by Lindley Nursery; illegitimate name due to priority of *I. opaca* 'Globosa').
Leaves dark green, broadly elliptic to elliptic-obovate, 1.8–2.5 cm (11/16–1 in.) long, 1.3–1.5 cm (1/2–19/32 in.) wide, bases acute, apices obtuse, margins crenulate, upper two-thirds of leaf, petioles 3 mm (1/8 in.) long; dwarf, compact habit.

'Glory' (male; synonyms 'Compacta Nana No. 1', 'Green Glory'; seedling of 'Convexa' selected by J. Vermeulen; introduced in 1958 by Vermeulen Nursery).
Leaves dark green, 0.5–2 cm (3/16–3/4 in.) long, 3–9 mm (1/8–11/32 in.) wide, margins slightly serrate near apex; compact broadly rounded habit, 1.5 m (5 ft.) tall, 2.5 m (8 ft.) wide in 12 years; hardy in zone 6a to −30°C (−23°F). Considered to be one of most cold hardy clones.

'Glossy' (synonym 'Glossy Leaf'; seedling of 'Convexa'; introduced in 1960 by G. B. Klyn Nursery).
Leaves convex, glossy; habit similar to 'Convexa' but larger and more compact.

'Golden Gem' (female; selected seedling introduced by L. Kenijin and Company before 1971).
Leaves bright yellow, slightly convex to flat, lower leaves blotchy yellow to green, elliptic to elliptic-obovate, 1.3–1.8 cm (1/2–11/16 in.) long, 7–11 mm (9/32–7/16 in.) wide, bases cuneate, apices obtuse, petioles 2–3 mm (1/16–1/8 in.) long; dense habit, similar to that of 'Convexa'; reported very hardy.

'Golden Heller' (female; synonym 'Lancaster Yellow', mutation from 'Helleri' discovered in 1967 by R. Block; introduced in 1972 by Lancaster Farms Nursery).
Similar to 'Helleri' with yellow cast to leaves, many leaves green with yellow blotches. Plate 137.

'Golden Queen' (in R.H.S. Flower Show exhibited by Burkwood and Skipworth, of Elstead, England; introduced before 1969; illegitimate name due to priority of *I. aquifolium* 'Golden Queen').
Leaves yellow, glossy; very hardy.

'Golden Variegated' (origin unknown; introduced by Tingle Nursery).
Leaves green spotted and blotched yellow, some entirely green.

'Goldstaub'
Leaves variegated, many leaves yellowish green, elliptic.

'Grandifolia' (female; origin unknown; introduced by Vermeulen Nursery; illegitimate name due to priority of *I. aquifolium* 'Grandifolia').
Leaves rotund to oblong, glossy.

'Green Cone' (male; synonym 'Bullata Green Cone'; origin unknown, possibly seedling of 'Convexa'; introduced in late 1960s by Holly Creek Nursery).
Leaves convex; strictly upright habit. Described as a mate for 'Convexa'.

'Green Dragon' (male; selected from 825 seedlings germinated in 1966 from controlled cross of 'Mariesii' × 'John Nosal' made by E. R. Orton Jr.; named and registered H.S.A. 10-72 by Orton; sibling of 'Dwarf Pagoda').
Leaves dark green, orbiculate to broadly oblong, similar to 'Mariesii' but smaller, 8–13 mm (5/16–1/2 in.) long, 6.5–8 mm (1/4–5/16 in.) wide, slightly keeled, 1–3 remote teeth on each side, petioles 1–2 mm (1/32–1/16 in.) long; irregular branching habit, essentially horizontal when young, older plants more upright, 28 cm (11 in.) tall, 20 cm (10 in.) wide in 7 years; hardy in zone 6b. Excellent for rock gardens, bonsai, and house plants; very short internodes gives heavy foliage effect.

'Green Island' (male; seedling selected 1935 by J. F. Styer; named and introduced by Styer; PP No. 817).
Leaves dark green, oval to obovate, 1.3–2.2 cm (1/2–13/16 in.) long, 6.5–13 mm (1/4–1/2 in.) wide; low spreading, vigorous habit; hardy in zone 6a.

'Green Lustre' (female; synonym 'Green Luster'; seedling of 'Stokes' about 1935 given to O. S. Pride by Warren Stokes; named and introduced by Pride).
Leaves elliptic, 1.5–2.5 cm (19/32–1 in.) long, 0.7–1.1 cm (9/32–7/16 in.) wide, bases cuneate, apices acute, 5–7 minute teeth on each side, upper two-thirds of leaf; low compact dwarf habit. Popular landscape plant. Faster growing than 'Stokes' and 'Tiny Tim'.

'Greenpoint' (male; origin unknown; plant at Scott Arboretum obtained from Styer Nursery).
Leaves dark green, elliptic, 2–2.5 cm (3/4–1 in.) long, 8–10 mm (5/16–3/8 in.) wide, bases cuneate, apices acute, margins crenulate near apex, petioles 3–5 mm (1/8–3/16 in.) long; broadly upright spreading habit.

'Green Pygmy' (female; seedling of 'Convexa' in

1952; selected, named, and registered H.S.A. 3-60 by A. M. Shammarello; PP No. 2069).

Leaves dark green, slightly glossy, convex, 1–2 cm (⅜–¾ in.) long, 8–10 mm (5⁄16–⅜ in.) wide, bases acute, apices rotund, margins serrate, petioles 3 mm (⅛ in.) long; compact dwarf habit, slightly higher than wide.

'Green Splendor' (origin unknown; introduced in early 1980s by Angelica Nursery).

Leaves dark green, glossy; broadly pyramidal habit.

'Green Thumb' (female; selected in 1945 from convex-leaved seedlings; named and introduced in 1956; registered H.S.A. 2-61 by J. P. Vermeulen).

Leaves dark green, retains good winter color, broadly elliptic, 1.3–2 cm (½–¾ in.) long, 6–9 mm (7⁄32–11⁄32 in.) wide, bases acute to obtuse, apices obtuse, margins crenulate, upper one-third of leaf, petioles 2–3 mm (1⁄16–⅛ in.) long; dwarf compact habit; 72 cm (28 in.) tall, 76–92 cm (30–36 in.) wide in 15 years.

'Green Velvet' (female; seedling selected at Sheridan Nursery, Canada, before 1972, for hardiness).

Leaves small.

'Grier' (female; seedling selected and introduced by Mobjack Nursery).

Leaves dark green, convex; dense coarse habit.

'Hatfield' (synonym *I. hatfieldi*; selected by T. Hatfield as interspecific hybrid of *I. crenata* × *I. glabra*; later identified as cultivar of *I. crenata*; introduced in early 1950s by Framingham Nursery).

Leaves dark green, obovate, 1.8–3 cm (11⁄16–13⁄16 in.) long, 9–14 mm (11⁄32–17⁄32 in.) wide, bases cuneate, apices obtuse, margins crenulate, upper half of leaf, petioles 3–5 mm (⅛–3⁄16 in.) long; upright vigorous habit.

'Hayden' (female; synonym 'Haydeni'; seedling selected by P. Hayden at Athens Nursery before 1970).

Leaves dark green, slightly convex, 1.8–2.2 (11⁄16–13⁄16 in.) long, 8–12 mm (5⁄16–15⁄32 in.) wide, margins crenulate, upper half of leaf, petioles 3 mm (⅛ in.) long; compact upright pyramidal habit.

'Helleri' (female; synonym *I. crenata* f. *helleri,* seedling selected in 1934 by J. Heller, manager of Newport Nursery; named and introduced in late 1930s).

Leaves dark green, elliptic to broadly elliptic, 1.2–2 cm (15⁄32–¾ in.) long, 5–10 mm (3⁄16–⅜ in.) wide, bases cuneate to obtuse, apices obtuse to rotund, margins remotely crenulate; sparse fruiting; dwarf

dense mounding habit, to 1 m (3 ft.) tall, usually twice as wide as tall. Popular dwarf landscape plant; used as a standard to judge dwarf clones. 'Helleri' seedlings (e.g., 'Heller Green Cushion') have been named without descriptions. Plate 138.

'Hetzii' (female; synonyms 'Globosa Rotundifolia', 'Reflexa Supreme'; putative hybrid of 'Convexa' × 'Rotundifolia'; selected about 1940 by C. Hetz; named and introduced by Fairview Nursery).

Leaves dark green, broadly elliptic to oval, convex, 2–2.8 cm (¾–1⅛ in.) long, 1–1.5 cm (3⁄16–19⁄32 in.) wide, bases acute, apices obtuse to rotund, margins revolute, remotely crenulate, on upper half of leaf, petioles 3–4 mm (⅛–5⁄32 in.) long; upright spreading habit; hardy in zone 6a. Popular landscape plant; similar to 'Convexa' with larger leaves and faster growing.

'High Light' (male; branch mutation of 'Microphylla' discovered in 1956 by W. F. Kosar at U.S. National Arboretum; named, introduced, and registered H.S.A. 2-64 by Kosar).

Leaves dark green, elliptic, 1.5–2.3 cm (19⁄32–⅞ in.) long, 6–8 mm (7⁄32–5⁄16 in.) wide, bases and apices acute, margins crenulate, upper two-thirds of leaf, petioles 2–3 mm (1⁄16–⅛ in.) long; conical habit. Short internodes and boxwood-like texture effectively display highlights and shadows, thus name.

'Highlander' (male; 'Convexa' seedling selected by N. H. Cole; introduced in the 1960s by Cole's nursery; PP No. 2272; registered H.S.A. 16-60 by W. C. Frierson).

Leaves dark green, elliptic-obovate, 1.5–1.8 cm (19⁄32–11⁄16 in.) long, bases acute, apices obtuse, margins remotely crenulate, upper half of leaf; broadly upright pyramidal habit; hardy in zone 6a. Selected for hardiness.

'Hillier' (synonyms 'Hilleri', 'Hillieri'; origin 1917 in Netherlands; introduced from Hillier and Sons Nursery, England, to United States by Boulevard Nursery about 1920).

Leaves small; low dense mound.

'Historyland Upright' (plants originally from Robbins Nursery, now discontinued);

No description available.

'Honeycomb' (female; Watanabeana Group; selected by N. Cannon from about 400 sprouted seeds distributed by U.S. Plant Introduction Station, Glenn Dale, Maryland, in 1965; selected and named by Cannon; sister of 'Butterball').

Leaves light green, broadly elliptic to broadly elliptic-obovate, 1.5–2 cm ($^{19}/_{32}$–¾ in.) long, 7–9 mm ($^9/_{32}$–$^{11}/_{32}$ in.) wide, margins crenate near apex, petioles 6 mm ($^7/_{32}$ in.) long; fruits yellow.

'Hoogendorn' (male; synonym 'Compacta Hoogendorn'; seedling origin; cuttings from plant at Hoogendorn Nursery; named by T. Dodd Jr. for origin of cuttings).
    Leaves dark green, elliptic, 2–2.8 cm (¾–1⅛ in.) long, 0.8–1.8 cm ($^5/_{16}$–$^{11}/_{16}$ in.) wide, bases cuneate to obtuse, apices acute, margins serrate, petioles 3–5 mm (⅛–$^3/_{16}$ in.) long; vigorous, compact, upright, rounded habit; very cold hardy.

'Horizontalis' (selected, named, and introduced by A. M. Shammarello in the 1960s; illegitimate name due to Latin form).
    Dwarf compact prostrate, branching habit.

'Howard' (male; synonym 'Howard Compacta'; Bennett Hybrid Group).
    Leaves dark green, slightly convex, obovate-oblong, 13–20 mm (½–¾ in.) long; vigorous upright spreading habit. Popular plant.

'Hunt Selection' (male; seedlings from Le-Mac Nursery in late 1920s; selected by J. Le Jendre; selected again by W. L. Hunt; introduced by Camellia Forest Nursery).
    Leaves dark green, elliptic, 1.3–2.5 cm (½–1 in.) long, 6–10 mm ($^7/_{32}$–⅜ in.) wide, margins crenate upper half of leaf, stems light yellowish green; upright spreading, vigorous large shrub or small tree.

'Imperial' (female; selected seedling for winter hardiness, −25°C (−13°F); discovered, named, and introduced by Imperial Nursery before 1980).
    Leaves dark green, broadly elliptic to slightly obovate, 1.3–1.8 cm (½–$^{11}/_{16}$ in.) long, 8–12 mm ($^5/_{16}$–$^{15}/_{32}$ in.) wide, petioles 2–3 mm ($^1/_{16}$–⅛ in.) long; fruits black, 8 mm ($^5/_{16}$ in.) diameter, peduncles 5 mm ($^3/_{16}$ in.) long; vigorous upright habit almost fastigiate. Good for hedges.

'Integrifolia' (origin unknown; introduced by Kibble and Clare Nursery, Berkshire, England, before 1958; illegitimate name due to priority of *I. aquifolium* 'Integrifolia').
    Leaves dark green, obovate, 1.8–2.5 cm ($^{11}/_{16}$–1 in.) long, 1–1.8 cm (⅜–$^{11}/_{16}$ in.) wide, slightly keeled, curved, margins crenulate, upper one-third of leaf, petioles 3 mm (⅛ in.) long; fruits black, color up early; dwarf and slow growing, becoming more open with age.

'Irene Peters' (male; seedling discovered in 1959 by A. Peters at Arie Peters Nursery; named, introduced and registered H.S.A. 5-64 by Peters).
    Leaves narrow-elliptic; mounding shaped habit; original plant when discovered was 38 cm (15 in.) tall, 46 cm (18 in.) wide.

'Ivory Hall' (female; seedling selected from F1 population of *I. crenata* f. *watanabeana*, U.S. PI 231984, in 1965; named and registered H.S.A. 3-74 by N. Cannon; sibling of 'Butterball').
    Leaves light green, elliptic, 1–1.8 cm (⅜–$^{11}/_{16}$ in.) long, 6–13 mm ($^7/_{32}$–½ in.) wide, bases and apices obtuse; fruits clear yellow to greenish yellow, globose, 6–8 mm ($^7/_{32}$–$^5/_{16}$ in.) diameter, ivory color in greenhouse in January; original plant 43 cm (17 in.) tall and 71 cm (28 in.) wide in 9 years.

'Ivory Tower' (female; seedling selected from F1 sibling population of *I. crenata* f. *watanabeana*, U.S. PI 231984, in 1965; selected about 1972; named, introduced, and registered H.S.A. 4-74 by N. Cannon; sibling of 'Butterball').
    Leaves light green, elliptic, 1.3–1.8 cm (½–$^{11}/_{16}$ in.) long, 5–8 mm ($^3/_{16}$–$^5/_{16}$ in.) wide, apices usually obtuse; fruits greenish yellow, globose, 6.5 mm (¼ in.) diameter; vigorous broadly erect habit, 1.2 m (4 ft.) tall and 0.9 m (3 ft.) wide in 9 years, heavily sheared.

'Jackson', see 'William Jackson'.

'Jersey Pinnacle' (male; controlled cross of 'Green Lustre' × 'John Nosal' made in 1974 by E. R. Orton Jr.; selected, named, introduced, and registered H.S.A. 12-84 by Orton).
    Leaves dark green, broadly elliptic, usually broader at tip than at base, 1.8 cm ($^{11}/_{16}$ in.) long, 1 cm (⅜ in.) wide, slightly keeled, curved, margins serrate, upper half of leaf, petioles 3 mm (⅛ in.) long; upright dense habit, original plant 1.8 m (6 ft.) tall and 1.2 m (4 ft.) wide; upright pyramidal habit when young; hardy in zone 6b, −25°C (−13°F).

'John Nash' (male; possible synonym of 'John Nosal'; origin unknown; plant at North Carolina State University Arboretum).
    Leaves dark olive green, oval to broadly elliptic, 1.5–1.8 cm ($^{19}/_{32}$–$^{11}/_{16}$ in.) long, 8–10 mm ($^5/_{16}$–⅜ in.) wide, petioles 4–5 mm ($^5/_{32}$–$^3/_{16}$ in.) wide, margins 1–2 minute teeth near apex, stems brownish; compact columnar habit.

'John Nosal' (male; chance seedling discovered in 1939 by John Nosal; named, introduced, and registered H.S.A. 7-70 by M. A. Nosal).

Leaves dark green, elliptic to oval, usually 2 cm (¾ in.) long, and 1 cm (⅜ in.) wide, margins usually entire, occasionally 1–3 serrations on each side, leaves on older branches usually broader and more rotund at tip; columnar habit, fastigiate branches; original plant 1.7 m (5½ ft.) high, 0.5 m (1½ ft.) wide in 20 years.

'Kingsville Dwarf' (female; synonyms 'Kingsville', 'Kingsvale'; seedling of 'Microphylla' discovered in 1912 by W. Appleby in his garden, Baltimore, Maryland; named and introduced in 1940 by H. Hohman).

Leaves dark green, elliptic, 1.8–2.5 cm (11/16–1 in.) long, 6–12 mm (7/32–15/32 in.) wide, bases cuneate, apices acute, margins crenulate, upper half of leaf, petioles 3–5 mm (⅛–3/16 in.) long; dwarf compact habit, slightly faster growing and taller than 'Helleri'.

'Kingsville Green Cushion' (male; synonyms 'Green Cushion', 'Heller Green Cushion', 'Kingwood Green Cushion'; origin Kingsville Nursery; named, introduced and registered American Association of Nurserymen No. 364 by H. Hohman; thought by some to originate at McLean Nursery).

Leaves dark green, broadly elliptic, 1.2–1.8 cm (15/32–11/16 in.) long, 5–9 mm (3/16–11/32 in.) wide, bases cuneate, apices acute to obtuse, 2–3 small teeth on each side, petioles 2–3 mm (1/16–⅛ in.) long; twiggy, dense, low compact, upright, globular habit; hardy to −14°C (−6°F).

'Kunming' (female; seedling origin about 1932; selected and named by J. F. Styer; introduced about 1947 by Styer Nursery).

Leaves dark green, broadly elliptic, 1.2–1.8 cm (15/32–11/16 in.) long, 6–10 mm (7/32–⅜ in.) wide, minute crenulate, upper half of leaf; young stems reddish; open rapid growing, upright globose shape.

'Kuro Fukurin' (synonym 'Angyo'; origin Japan).

Leaves variegated, spotted yellow.

'Latifolia' (introduced to England by R. Fortune; still popular in Europe; illegitimate name due to priority of *I. aquifolium* var. *latifolia*).

Leaves elliptic to elliptic oblong to oval, 1.3–3.2 cm (½–1¼ in. long, bases and apices obtuse, leaves longer than those of 'Rotundifolia'; vigorous upright open large shrub or small trees.

'Latifolia Major' (one of the clonal forms often found listed under this name; may be the same or similar to one of the clonal forms of 'Major', which see).

Leaves dark green, oval, 1.5–2 cm (19/32–¾ in.) long, 1.2–1.6 cm (15/32–⅝ in.) wide, bases obtuse, apices obtuse to rotund, petioles 3–5 mm (⅛–3/16 in.) long; upright broadly pyramidal habit.

'Laurel Lake' (female; origin unknown; introduced in the 1960s by Laurel Lake Nursery).

Leaves dark green, obovate, 1.1–2 cm (7/16–¾ in.) long, 8–13 mm (5/16–½ in.) wide, bases cuneate, apices obtuse, margins crenulate, upper two-thirds of leaf, petioles 2–3 mm (1/16–⅛ in.) long; upright broadly spreading habit.

'Lindleyana' (male; selected seedling introduced in late 1940s by Lindley Nursery).

Leaves dark green, broadly elliptic to slightly obovate-elliptic, 2–2.8 cm (¾–1⅛ in.) long, 10–13 mm (⅜–½ in.) wide, bases and apices cuneate, margins coarsely crenulate, upper one-third of leaf, petioles 3–5 mm (⅛–3/16 in.) long; dense broadly spreading, vigorous habit.

'Lisa' (female; synonym 'Lisia'; a seedling named and introduced before 1978 by Athens Nursery).

Leaves dark green, broadly elliptic to obovate, 1.2–1.8 cm (15/32–11/16 in.) long, 8–10 mm (5/16–⅜ in.) wide, bases cuneate, apices obtuse, margins crenulate, upper two-thirds of leaf, petioles 2–3 mm (1/16–⅛ in.) long; dense globular habit.

'Little Gem' (male; origin unknown; introduced in early 1960s by Tingle Nursery).

Leaves elliptic, 1–1.3 cm (⅜–½ in.) long, 5–6 mm (3/16–7/32 in.) wide, petioles 1–2 mm (1/32–1/15 in.) long; low compact plants, broader than tall.

'Little Leaf' (synonym 'Littleleaf'; origin unknown, possibly introduced in late 1950s by Millcreek Nursery).

'Loeb' (origin unknown; introduced in late 1960s by Medford Nursery).

Compact spreading habit; hardy.

'Longboy' (male; selected and named in late 1950s by W. C. Frierson).

Leaves dark green, elliptic, 1.8–3.2 cm (11/16–1¼ in.) long, 8–11 mm (5/16–7/16 in.) wide, bases cuneate, apices acute, margins crenulate, upper half of leaf, petioles 5–7 mm (3/16–9/32 in.) long; vigorous upright spreading habit.

'Longfellow' (male; origin in the Netherlands in 1917; introduced about 1920 to United States by Boulevard Nursery).

Leaves dark green, elliptic, 1.3–2.2 cm (½–13/16

in.) long, 5–7 mm (3⁄16–9⁄32 in.) wide, bases crenate, apices acute, margins crenulate, upper half of leaf, petioles 3 mm (1⁄8 in.) long; upright spreading habit.

f. *longifolia* (Goldring) Rehder 1908 (first described as a var. from a cultivated plant, later including plants from the wild; confusing descriptions exist).

Leaves narrow-elliptic to lanceolate, 1.3–3.5 cm (1⁄2–1 3⁄8 in.) long.

'Longifolia' (male; origin in question and difficult to authenticate to f. *longifolia*).

Leaves narrow-lanceolate to oblong-elliptic, 3–5 cm (1 3⁄16–2 in.) long, 0.9 cm (11⁄32 in.) wide; young twigs dark reddish brown; large upright spreading habit.

'Loyce Nelson' (male; seedling origin; selected and named by T. Dodd Jr.; introduced in the 1960s by Tom Dodd Nursery).

Leaves dark green, ovate; low growing, distinct horizontal branching; plant twice as wide as tall.

'Lustgarten' (synonym 'Latifolia Lustgarten Strain'; seedling origin in 1946; named and introduced in the 1970s by Bauer Lustgarten Nursery).

Leaves deep green; upright habit; reported very hardy. Good evergreen hedge.

'Luteo-Variegata' (synonyms var. *luteo-variegata* f. *luteo-variegata,* var. *major* 'Microphylla Aureo-Variegata', var. *variegata*; original plant sent from Japan to Russia by C. Maximowicz in 1863; introduced to United States from Royal Botanic Gardens, Kew, in 1957 by F. Meyer).

Leaves spotted yellow, elliptic to lanceolate, to 2 cm (3⁄4 in.) long. 'Aureo-Variegata' has leaves longer than 2 cm (3⁄4 in.) with spotted and blotched leaves. Due to variation in variegation there is considerable confusion, and numerous names and variable plants.

'Luther Copeland' (male; seedling No. 1284; selected and named by T. Dodd Jr.; introduced around 1985).

Leaves dark green, broadly elliptic, 10–16 mm (3⁄8–5⁄8 in.) long, 5–9 mm (3⁄16–11⁄32 in.) wide, petioles 3–5 mm (1⁄8–7⁄32 in.) long, minutely crenulate upper one-third of leaf, stems green; compact globose habit; original plant approximately 25 years old, 1.5–1.8 m (5–6 ft.) tall and wide.

'Macrophylla' (female; several different clones introduced with same name; illegitimate name due to priority of *I. aquifolium* 'Macrophylla').

Leaves usually larger and broader than typical; large upright spreading shrubs.

'Magda' (male; seedling origin; named and introduced in late 1950s by Cartwright Nursery).

Leaves dark green, broadly elliptic to obovate, 1.2–2 cm (15⁄32–3⁄4 in.) long, 7–11 mm (9⁄32–7⁄16 in.) wide, margins crenulate, petioles 2–3 mm (1⁄16–1⁄8 in.) long; dense upright, globular habit.

'Magnolia' (No. 360, selected by N. Cannon, used in crossing, never introduced).

'Major' (female; synonyms var. *major,* f. *major*; origin unknown, from England; vary confusing background; see Dudley and Eisenbeiss (1992); several clones with same name).

Leaves oval, 1.3–3.8 cm (1⁄2–1 1⁄2 in.) long, 1.3–1.6 cm (1⁄2–5⁄8 in.) wide, margins crenate.

'Major' (male; Bennett Hybrid Group).

Leaves obovate, 1–2.3 cm (3⁄8–7⁄8 in.) long, 6.5–13 mm (1⁄4–1⁄2 in.) wide, bases acute, apices usually rotund; upright rounded shrubs.

'Major' (male; introduced from Royal Botanic Garden, Edinburgh, Scotland, in 1959 by F. Meyer; U.S. PI 276276 recorded as *I. latifolia* 'Major').

Leaves elliptic to obovate, 2.5 cm (1 in.) long, 1.8 cm (11⁄16 in.) wide, margins with large rounded crenations; large upright shrubs.

'Mariesii' (female; synonyms var. *mariesii,* f. *mariesii, I. mariesii, I. nummularioides, I. nummularioides* var. *nummularioides*; collected in Japan about 1890 by Charles Maries and sent to Veitch Nursery; frequently misidentified as *I. nummularia*; plant sent from Royal Botanic Gardens, Kew, in 1908 to Arnold Arboretum).

Leaves dark green, thick, stiff, ovate or orbiculate, rarely obovate, 3–16 mm (1⁄8–5⁄8 in.) long and wide, margins obscurely crenate, 1–4 teeth on each side, apices appear tridentate, 2 conspicuous shallow notches, petioles thick, 1–2 mm (1⁄32–1⁄16 in.) long; fruits black, usually globose, abundant; short internodes, branches stiff, upright; single to few stems. Interesting rock garden plant or small specimen. See Dudley and Eisenbeiss (1977) for the complex nomenclatural history of this plant. Plate 139.

'Marigold Glitters' (female; origin unknown, introduced in mid 1950s by Clarendon Gardens).

No description available; believed to have yellow fruits.

'Maxwell' (male; synonym 'Hadlock'; Bennett Hybrid Group).

Leaves dark green, slightly convex, similar to 'Convexa' elliptic, 1.3–2.2 cm (1⁄2–13⁄16 in.) long, 1–

1.3 cm (3/8–1/2 in.) wide, bases acute, apices obtuse, margins crenulate, upper two-thirds of leaf, petioles 3 mm (1/8 in.) long; vigorous upright spreading habit, ascending branches.

'Mentor Dense' (female; synonym 'Dense'; seedling of 'Convexa' in 1952; selected, named, introduced, and registered H.S.A. 4-60 by A. M. Shammarello; sibling of 'Green Pigmy').

Leaves dark green, convex, obovate, 1–1.5 cm (3/8–19/32 in.) long, 6–8 mm (7/32–5/16 in.) wide, bases acute to obtuse, apices obtuse, margins remotely crenulate, upper one-third of leaf, petioles 2–3 mm (1/16–1/8 in.) long; semidwarf compact habit, numerous short upright branches.

'Mentor Glossy' (male; seedling of 'Convexa' in 1945; selected, named, introduced, and registered H.S.A. 5-60 by A. M. Shammarello).

Leaves dark green, glossy, slightly larger than 'Convexa'; informal upright spreading bushy habit; very hardy.

'Micro Special' (origin unknown; introduced in the 1970s by Phyto Ecology Nursery; illegitimate name due to Latin form).

Leaves dark green, small, convex; dwarf, semi-upright habit.

'Microphylla' (synonyms var. *microphylla* Maximowicz ex Matsumura 1895 and 1897, without description, f. *microphylla* Rehder 1908; very confusing background; introduced as a variety and later as a forma; introduced from seed collected in Japan by C. Sargent in 1892 and sent to Arnold Arboretum; probably most U.S. clones are of the Arnold Arboretum 1892 seed origin; also introduced in 1868 to the Netherlands by Siebold, but not the same clone introduced by Sargent; name illegitimate due to priority of *I. aquifolium* 'Microphylla').

Leaves dark green, ovate-elliptic or narrow-elliptic, 0.8–1.3 cm (5/16–1/2 in.) long, 3–6 mm (1/8–7/32 in.) wide, margins crenate serrate; low compact densely branched shrubs; frequently used as a low hedge. Many 'Microphylla' selections (male and female) introduced without complete descriptions. Plate 140.

'Microphylla Aureo-Variegata' (old clone in Japan; introduced from Japan to Europe, then to United States).

Leaves yellow variegated. In Japan a variegated form is often intermixed in a mass planting.

'Microphylla Columnaris' (origin unknown; introduced in 1970 by Tankard Nursery).

Narrow columnar habit.

'Microphylla Compacta' (origin unknown; introduced in the 1960s by Laurel Lake Nursery).

No description available.

'Microphylla Erecta' (origin unknown; introduced in the 1960s by Gresham's Nursery).

Leaves small; narrow columnar habit.

'Microphylla Maculata' (female; said to have been introduced by E. H. Wilson).

Leaves yellow blotched, oval to obovate.

'Microphylla Nana' (origin unknown; introduced in the 1960s by Gresham's Nursery).

No description available.

'Microphylla Pyramidalis' (possible synonym of 'Microphylla Erecta'; origin unknown; introduced in the 1960s by Gresham's Nursery).

No description available.

'Microphylla Supreme' (female; origin unknown; introduced in the 1960s by Robbins Nursery).

Leaves dark green, glossy, obovate, 2–3 cm (3/4–1 3/16 in.) long, 1.3–1.6 cm (1/2–5/8 in.) wide, apices obtuse, margins crenulate, upper two-thirds of leaf, petioles 5 mm (3/16 in.) long; dense compact, globular habit.

'Midas Touch' (male; branch mutation discovered by E. R. Orton Jr. on 2-year seedling of population from controlled cross made in 1968 of *I. crenata* f. *watanabeana* × 'Microphylla'; named, introduced, and registered H.S.A. 10-84 by Orton).

Leaves variegated, broadly and variably marginal, light greenish yellow 8C and light yellow 10B, center of leaves light green, tip leaves with most variegation, elliptic to narrow-elliptic, 1–2.2 cm (3/8–13/16 in.) long, 5–7 mm (3/16–9/32 in.) wide, bases and apices acute, margins crenate, upper half of leaf, petioles 3 mm (1/8 in.) long; compact, broadly spreading habit; original plant 72.5 cm (2 1/2 ft.) tall, 84.5 cm (2 3/4 ft.) wide; hardy in zone 6b. Plate 141.

'Miss Muffet' (female; open-pollinated seedling of 'Convexa' × 'Microphylla' in 1954; named, introduced, and registered H.S.A. 4-70 by N. Cannon; sibling of 'Pincushion' and 'Sentinel').

Leaves elliptic, 1–1.6 cm (3/8–5/8 in.) long, 5–7 mm (3/16–9/32 in.) wide, margins crenulate, upper half of leaf, petioles 2–3 mm (1/16–1/8 in.) long; low compact twiggy dwarf, moundlike; 1 m (3 ft.) tall, 1.8 m (6 ft.) wide in 35 years.

'Mobjack Supreme' (synonym 'Mobjack'; origin unknown; introduced in the 1970s by Mobjack Nursery).

No description available.

'Monmouth' (synonym 'Manmouth'; origin unknown; introduced in the 1970s by Bobbink Nursery).

Compact, spreading, slow growing habit; hardy.

'Morris Dwarf' (male; origin unknown; introduced in the 1950s by Morris Nursery; reported to be clone of *I. crenata* f. *microphylla*).

Leaves dark green, elliptic, 1–1.3 cm (⅜–½ in.) long, 6–8 mm (⁷⁄₃₂–⁵⁄₁₆ in.) wide, crenulate near apex, petioles 1–2 mm (⅓₂–⅙₆ in.) long; very dwarf, compact, mounding habit.

'Mount Amagi' (female; seedling from seed collected by A. Teese on Mount Amagi, Honshu, Japan; selected, named, and introduced by Teese).

Leaves dark green, oval, 7–13 mm (⁹⁄₃₂–½ in.) long, 3.5–5 mm (⁹⁄₆₄–³⁄₁₆ in.) wide, bases cuneate to obtuse, apices obtuse, margins crenate, upper half of leaf, petioles 1–2 mm (⅓₂–⅙₆ in.) long; leaves close together, short internodes; dense compact, upright habit.

'Mount Halla' (female; synonym 'Halla'; discovered in the wild about 1977 by C. F. Miller on Mount Halla, Cheju Island, South Korea; named and introduced by Miller).

Leaves oval, 8–12 mm (⁵⁄₁₆–¹⁵⁄₃₂ in.) long, 5–7 mm (³⁄₁₆–⁹⁄₃₂ in.) wide, tip leaves smaller; branchlets very thick, rigid, uniquely tapering to spurlike tip; moderate growth habit, exceptionally wide angled branching, short right-angled branching. Could be interesting pot plant.

'Mr. C.' (male; chance seeding selected around 1948; named and introduced in the 1960s by Cartwright Nursery; named for A. D. Cartwright Sr.).

Leaves dark green, elliptic, broadly elliptic to slightly obovate, 2–2.5 cm (¾–1 in.) long, 0.8–1.3 cm (⅜–½ in.) wide, bases acute, apices acute to cuneate, margins crenate, upper half of leaf, petioles 1–2 mm (⅓₂–⅙₆ in.) long; compact, low horizontal habit; dense intergrowth.

'Muffin' (male; seedling of 'Convexa'; seed from Dr. Rukujo in 1965 in Japan; selected, named, and registered H.S.A. 7-77 by P. Hill).

Leaves dark green, glossy, oblong, 1.4 cm (¹⁷⁄₃₂ in.) long, 6.5 mm (¼ in.) wide, 5 crenulate teeth on each side, last near apex giving trident shape; slow growing, very low compact habit; original plant 37.7 cm (15 in.) tall, 76.7 cm (27 in.) wide in 12 years; reported hardier than 'Helleri'.

'Nakada' (male; discovered in 1955 by J. L. Creech in Nakada Nursery, Angyo, Japan; cuttings introduced in 1957 as *I. crenata* var. *nummularia*, U.S. PI No. 236233, NA 25701; first male clone of Nummularia Group; selected, named, and registered H.S.A. 5-77 by T. R. Dudley and G. K. Eisenbeiss).

Leaves dark green, broadly ovate-elliptic to obovate or distinctly orbiculate to suborbiculate, 5–16 (–25) mm (³⁄₁₆–⅝ (–1) in.) long and wide, bases truncate to obtuse, apices appearing tridentate, 2 conspicuous notches, margins slightly revolute, obscurely crenate, 1–4 minute mucronate teeth on each side, petioles thick, grooved, 2–5 mm (⅙₆–³⁄₁₆ in.) long; flowers fragrant, 4- to 10-flowered, often branched, axillary cymes, peduncles usually 5–10 (–20) mm (³⁄₁₆–⅜ (–¾) in.) long; upright habit, single to multiple stems, densely branched, close internodes; hardy in zone 7. Distinct from other clones and selections of *I. crenata* by the congested densely clustered leaves and deeply tridentate leaf apices. See Dudley and Eisenbeiss (1977).

'Nanking' (male; origin seedling about 1932; selected by J. F. Styer; introduced about 1947 by Styer Nursery).

Leaves dark green, elliptic-obovate, 1.8–2.8 cm (¹¹⁄₁₆–1⅛ in.) long, 8–10 mm (⁵⁄₁₆–⅜ in.) wide, bases acute, apices obtuse, margins crenulate, upper one-third of leaf, petioles 3–5 mm (⅛–³⁄₁₆ in.) long; upright dense, vigorous growth, soft texture.

'Nigra', see 'Allen Seay'.

'Noble Upright' (male; synonym 'Noble', 'Nobilis'; seedling named and introduced in the 1950s by Appalachian Nursery).

Leaves dark green, broadly elliptic to obovate, 1.5–2.5 cm (¹⁹⁄₃₂–1 in.) long, 6–8 mm (⁷⁄₃₂–⁵⁄₁₆ in.) wide, bases cuneate, apices obtuse, margins crenulate, upper half of leaf, petioles 2–2.5 mm (⅙₆–³⁄₃₂ in.) long; broadly upright pyramidal habit; hardy.

'North Star' (origin from Lincoln Nursery, Michigan; introduced by Roemer Nursery; received early 1970s, now discontinued).

Leaves dark green, elliptic-obovate, 1.3–2 cm (½–¾ in.) long, 7–11 mm (⁹⁄₃₂–⁷⁄₁₆ in.) wide, 7–11 mm (⁹⁄₃₂–⁷⁄₁₆ in.) wide, bases cuneate, apices obtuse; upright spreading habit.

'Northern Beauty' (male; origin unknown; introduced by Fairview Nursery before 1969).

Leaves dark green, oval, convex, 1.8–2.5 cm (1¹⁄₁₆–1 in.) long, 1.1–1.3 cm (⁷⁄₁₆–½ in.) wide; vigorous upright habit.

'Nummularia' (synonym *I. nummularia,* var. *nummularia,* and f. *nummularia;* not to be confused with 'Mariesii'; name for a cultivated plant in Japan).

Leaves obovate or round-edged, usually 1 cm (³⁄₈ in.) long and wide, bases obtuse to rotund, apices 3, rarely 5 dentations, triangular, pointed forward, usually 3 teeth on each side, petioles short, 1–2 mm (¹⁄₃₂–¹⁄₁₆ in.) long; dwarf habit, dense branches with dense leaf scars.

Nummularia Group

A group name for convenience to accommodate the close genetic and morphological relationship of five cultivars: 'Dwarf Pagoda', 'Green Dragon', 'Mariesii', 'Nakada', and 'Nummularia'. For additional information, see Dudley and Eisenbeiss (1977).

'Oconee River' (male; seedling of convex-leaved holly raised in 1950; selected, named, introduced, and registered H.S.A. 5-61 by C. A. Rowland; PP No. 1902).

Leaves dark blue-green, broadly elliptic, 1.5–2 cm (¹⁹⁄₃₂–¾ in.) long, 8–10 mm (⁵⁄₁₆–³⁄₈ in.) wide, bases acute to obtuse, apices obtuse, margins crenulate, upper half of leaf, petioles 2–3 mm (¹⁄₁₆–⅛ in.) long; dark purple winter twig color; vigorous globular habit.

'Oleafera' (female; Bennett Hybrid Group).

Leaves dark green, obovate or oblong-obovate; upright spreading habit.

'Orchard' (female; origin unknown, from Orchard Nursery before 1957).

Leaves dark green, oblong-obovate, 1.8–2.5 cm (1¹⁄₁₆–1 in.) long, 8–12 mm (⁵⁄₁₆–¹⁵⁄₃₂ in.) wide, bases acute, apices obtuse, margins remotely crenulate, petioles 3–5 mm (⅛–³⁄₁₆ in.) long; vigorous upright, spreading habit.

'Peconic' (male; selected seedling about 1945 by M. A. Nosal of Holly Heath Nursery; named, introduced, and registered 8-72 by Nosal).

Leaves dark green, narrow-elliptic, to 2.3 cm (⅞ in.) long, 1 cm (³⁄₈ in.) wide, slightly keeled, bases and apices acuminate; compact mounding habit; original plant 2 × 2 m (6 × 6 ft.) in 25 years.

'Peking' (female; seedling origin about 1932; selected by J. F. Styer; named and introduced in 1947 by Styer Nursery).

'Pendula' (not a correct cultivar name, possibly a clone of f. *pendula,* which see).

'Petite' (male; origin unknown; H. Elmore obtained plant from North River Garden Center, Chattanooga, Tennessee; illegitimate name due to priority of *I. aquifolium* 'Petite').

Leaves dark green, elliptic to broadly elliptic, 1.8–2 cm (1¹⁄₁₆–¾ in.) long, 8–10 mm (⁵⁄₁₆–³⁄₈ in.) wide, bases cuneate, apices acute to obtuse; upright pyramidal habit.

'Petite Point' (female; origin developed on Eastern Shore, Maryland; introduced in 1963 by Wight Nursery).

Leaves gray-green 137A, narrow-elliptic to nearly linear, slightly curved, 1.8–2 cm (1¹⁄₁₆–¾ in,) long, 4–7 mm (⁵⁄₃₂–⁹⁄₃₂ in.) wide, margins minutely crenate, petioles 3–4 mm (⅛–⁵⁄₃₂ in.) long; vigorous compact upright habit.

'Phyto Ecology' (seedling from N. Cannon; introduced in early 1980s by Phyto Ecology Nursery).

Leaves dark green, glossy, oblong to slightly obovate, 1.3–2.2 cm (½–1³⁄₁₆ in.) long, 5–10 mm (³⁄₁₆–³⁄₈ in.) wide, curved, bases cuneate to obtuse, apices obtuse, petioles 3–5 mm (⅛–³⁄₁₆ in.) long; dense compact, mushroom habit.

'Piccolo' (female; seedling in 1972 from F₃ seedling population of 'Convexa' × 'Microphylla' made in 1954; female parent F₂ back crossed with male selected from F₁; selected, named, and registered H.S.A. 5-80 by Cannon).

Leaves dark green, broadly elliptic, 1.3–1.6 cm (½–⅝ in.) long, 8–10 mm (⁵⁄₁₆–³⁄₈ in.) wide, apices rotund, margins crenate, upper half of leaf, petioles 2–3 mm (¹⁄₁₆–⅛ in.) long; fruits black, sparse; very dwarf, dense mounding habit, slightly wider than tall; 7-year plant 15 cm (6 in.) tall, 22.5 cm (8⅞ in.) wide; annual growth about 2.5 cm (1 in.), plants in low hedge 14 years old vary from 35 to 45.7 cm (14–18 in.) wide. Excellent for rock gardens. 'Dwarf Cone' and 'Firefly' have same origin in F₁ cross. Plate 142.

'Piedmont Pyramidal' (synonym 'Piedmont'; origin unknown; plants at Ebersole Gardens and Clemson Arboretum).

Leaves dark green, obovate, 2–2.5 cm (¾–1 in.) long, 1–1.3 cm (³⁄₈–½ in.) wide, petioles 4–5 mm (⁵⁄₃₂–³⁄₁₆ in.) wide; fruits black, 7 mm (⁹⁄₃₂ in.) diameter, 1–2 in clusters; broadly upright, pyramidal habit.

'Pincushion' (seedling of 'Convexa' × 'Microphylla'; origin before 1969; named by N. Cannon; introduced by Phyto Ecology Nursery; illegitimate name due to priority of *I. opaca* 'Pin Cushion').

Leaves small; dwarf, very dense globose habit; not winter hardy in zone 6. Not in production.

'Pinocchio' (sex unknown; obtained from nursery on west coast about 1992 as named cultivar, records misplaced; in production by Tom Dodd Nursery).

Leaves small, ovate to oval, 0.8–1 cm (5/16–3/8 in.), numerous small leaves 0.5–0.6 mm long, 4–6 mm (5/32–7/32 in.) wide, petioles very small, usually less than 2 mm (1/16 in.) long; low irregular, dwarf habit. Ideal for rock garden or as sheared low edging plant.

'Praecox' (female; old cultivar listed in 1938 catalog from Chugai Shokubutsuen Nursery, Kōbe, Japan; plant with white fruits, seed offered but seedlings not true to form; 'Praecox' at Henry Foundation probably a different clone).

No description available.

'Pride Dwarf' (seedling of 'Green Lustre'; selected and named in late 1950s by O. S. Pride).

Leaves dark green, slightly convex, broadly elliptic to obovate, 1.5–2 cm (19/32–3/4 in.) long, 8–13 mm (5/16–1/2 in.) wide, bases acute, apices obtuse, margins crenulate, upper two-thirds of leaf, petioles 2–3 mm (1/16–1/8 in.) long; dwarf compact habit.

'Prides Tiny' (female; synonyms 'Tiny', 'Tiny Tim'; seedling of 'Green Lustre'; selected by O. S. Pride in the 1970s).

Leaves elliptic to obovate-elliptic, 1.3–1.8 cm (1/2–11/16 in.) long, 0.7–1 cm (9/32–3/8 in.) wide, bases cuneate, apices obtuse, margins 3–4 crenate teeth on each side; compact low habit.

'Prostrata' (synonyms 'Repandens', 'Spreading'; several Prostrata forms introduced, all with prostrate spreading habits; illegitimate name due to Latin form).

'Pyramidalis' (origin unknown; introduced in 1959 by Angelica Nursery; a common name given to several pyramidal clonal plants; illegitimate name due to priority of *I. aquifolium* 'Pyramidalis').

Leaves dark green, glossy; broadly compact pyramidal habit; very hardy.

'Radicans' (plant at Clemson University; probably a seedling clone; origin from U.S. Plant Introduction Station, distributed as var. *radicans;* illegitimate name due to Latin form; plant should be renamed).

Large leaves; spreading, dwarf, dense compact habit. See *I. crenata* var. *paludosa.*

'Recurvifolia' (male; Bennett Hybrid Group; intended to replace 'Convexa'; may be under several different names).

Leaves dark green, convex; upright spreading habit.

'Red Lion' (male; origin unknown; selected 1934 by P. du Pont, Longwood Gardens; propagated and named by E. Hamilton, Red Lion Nursery; propagation discontinued).

Leaves dark green, elliptic to broadly elliptic, 1.3–1.8 cm (1/2–11/16 in.) long, 6–8 mm (7/32–5/16 in.) wide, 3–4 teeth on each side, petioles 2–3 mm (1/16–1/8 in.) long. Similar to 'Helleri' but not as compact plant.

'Repandens' (male; synonyms 'Prostrata', 'Spreading'; origin about 1940 by B. Howell).

Leaves dark green, flat, elliptic-obovate, 1.6–2.2 cm (5/8–13/16 in.) long, 6–8 mm (7/32–5/16 in.) wide, bases cuneate, apices obtuse, margins crenulate, upper half of leaf, petioles 3 mm (1/8 in.) long; very low spreading habit. Several different cultivars with same name.

'Robbins' (origin unknown; introduced by Robbins Nursery in late 1960s).

Leaves dark green, obovate, 1.8–2.5 cm (11/16–1 in.) long, 6–13 mm (7/32–1/2 in.) wide, bases cuneate, apices obtuse, margins crenulate, upper half of leaf, petioles 3–4 mm (1/8–5/32 in.) long; upright, globular habit.

'Robert Culpepper' (male; seedling origin; selected and named by T. Dodd Jr.; introduced by Tom Dodd Nursery).

Leaves dark green, curved, elliptic-obovate, 1.3–2.2 cm (1/2–13/16 in.) long, 8–10 mm (5/16–3/8 in.) wide, bases cuneate, apices obtuse, margins remotely crenulate, near apex, petioles 2–3 mm (1/16–1/8 in.) long; broadly upright spreading habit.

'Rocky Creek' (male; mutation discovered by O. Howell in 1982 on 'Compacta' of the Bennett Hybrid Group; parent plant from Wight Nursery; named and registered 3-89 H.S.A. by Howell; introduced in 1989 by Rocky Creek Nursery).

Leaves dark green, ovate, flat to convex, to 3.2 cm (1 1/4 in.) long, 1.3 cm (1/2 in.) wide, apices broadly pointed to rotund, margins finely crenate, petioles 3 mm (1/8 in.) long; twigs angulate, gradual to sharp, usually 6–8 per flush of growth, vary from 1.3–2.5

cm (½–1 in.) from straight alignment, each angulation in opposite direction from previous, sometimes curved to side different from previous angulation; broadly upright habit, vigorous erect stem; corkscrew effect is permanent, obvious on entire branches; hardy in zone 7a. Selected for distinct corkscrew stems.

'Rotundifolia' (male; synonyms var. *rotundifolia,* f. *rotundifolia,* 'Round Leaf'; doubtful if synonym of 'Latifolia'; origin not completely known, possibly a cultivated clone from Japan; illegitimate name due to priority of *I. aquifolium* 'Rotundifolia').

Leaves dark green, oblong or obovate-oblong, 1.6–3.2 cm (⅝–1¼ in.) long, 1–1.6 cm (⅜–⅝ in.) wide, obtuse at both ends, margins crenate, 11–16 teeth on each side; upright dense, compact, rounded habit. A very popular landscape plant. There are several clonal variations in the trade such as 'Rotundifolia Aurea' (female), 'Rotundifolia Aureo-Variegata', 'Rotundifolia Pyramidalis', 'Rotundifolia Suspensum', 'Rotundifolia Upright', and 'Rotundifolia Weeping'.

Rovex Hybrid Group

A group name originating before 1940 from a block of open-pollinated seedlings of 'Convexa' × 'Rotundifolia' at Fairview Nursery. Only two seedlings were selected and introduced: 'Hetzii', still popular, and 'Rovex Hybrid No. 32', discontinued.

'Schwoebel's Compact' (female; synonym 'Schwoebeli'; open-pollinated seedling in 1949 of 'Convexa' × 'Microphylla'; selected, named, and introduced in the 1960s by R. Schwoebel).

Leaves light green, small; similar to spreading habit of 'Helleri' but faster growing, more upright and hardier.

'Schwoebel's Upright' (synonyms 'Erecta', 'Excelsa', 'Excelsa Schwoebel', 'Excelsa Upright'; same origin as 'Schwoebel's Compact', which see; selected, named, and introduced in late 1950s by R. Schwoebel).

Leaves dark green, glossy, broadly elliptic; upright, compact habit.

'Sensation' (male; origin after 1954 from a cross made by N. Cannon; selected and named by Cannon; not sure if introduced by others; propagation discontinued).

Leaves dark green, small, curved; semi-dwarf, cone-shaped habit.

'Sentinel' (female; origin in 1955 from a group of 5000 seedlings; selected, named, introduced, and registered H.S.A. 3-63 by N. Cannon).

Leaves dark green, oval to obovate, slightly convex, 2.2–3 cm (13⁄16–1 3⁄16 in.) long, 1.2–1.5 cm (15⁄32–19⁄32 in.) wide, bases acute to slightly obtuse, apices obtuse, margins remotely crenulate, upper one-third of leaf, petioles 3 mm (⅛ in.) long; narrow conical habit; reported very hardy; original plant 2 m (66 in.) tall, 0.82 m (32 in.) wide in 8 years. Good hedge plant, 2.1 m × 1.5 m (7 × 5 ft.) wide in 30 plus years.

'Shanghai' (female; seedling origin about 1932; selected by J. F. Styer; named and introduced in 1947 by Styer Nursery).

Leaves dark green, elliptic, slightly keeled, curved, 1.8–2.2 cm (11⁄16–13⁄16 in.) long, 7–9 mm (9⁄32–11⁄32 in.) wide, 2–3 teeth on each side, near apex, petioles 2–3 mm (1⁄16–⅛ in.) long; upright globular habit.

'Shoul' (synonym 'Shouli'; probably introduced before 1957 by Towson Nursery; named for Lawrence Shoul).

Leaves gray green; compact, low spreading habit.

'Sir Echo' (female; Watanabeana Group; selected by N. Cannon from about 400 sprouted seeds distributed by U.S. Plant Introduction Station, Glenn Dale, Maryland, in 1965; named and introduced by Cannon before 1977; sibling of 'Butterball').

Leaves dark green, oval to slightly obovate, 1.0–1.6 cm (⅜–⅝ in.) long, 7–10 mm (9⁄32–⅜ in.) wide; fruits yellow.

'Sky Pencil' (female; discovered on Mount Dai-sen, Honshu, Japan, and named by N. Shibamichi; first introduced into United States in 1985 from a private collection in Japan; in commercial production in Japan; should be available in United States in the mid 1990s).

Leaves elliptic, 1.5–3.5 cm (19⁄32–1⅜ in.) long, 0.8–1 cm (5⁄16–⅜ in.) wide, curved, slightly keeled and convex, bases broadly acuminate, tips rounded, margins finely serrate, petioles 2–4 mm (⅛–5⁄32 in.) long; very unique, distinct narrow upright habit, at least ten times taller than wide. Plate 143.

'Snowflake' (female; synonyms 'Albo-Marginata' of Conder, 'Shiro Fukurin', 'Sirofukurin'; old clone from Japan; purchased by J. L. Creech in 1957 and 1966 from Nakada Nursery, Angyo, Japan; U.S. PI 236020 and 236234; sirofukurin is Japanese common name and means "white margin"; new name by T. R. Dudley and G. K. Eisenbeiss).

Leaves variegated, irregular yellowish white margin, dark green center with pale green streaking, broadly ovate, to 3 cm (1 3⁄16 in.) long, 1.1 cm (7⁄16 in.) wide; upright habit, moderate growth rate. Plate 144.

'Soft Touch' (synonym 'Soft Helleri'; origin unknown; named by D. Ellis; introduced by Magnolia Gardens and Nursery in the 1980s).

Leaves dark green, elliptic, 2–2.5 cm (¾–1 in.) long, 8–10 mm (5/16–⅜ in.) wide, in shade leaves often 3.5 cm (1⅜ in.) long with distinct light green midrib, 3–8 teeth on each side; compact spreading habit, branchlets not ridged, feel soft when touched.

'Starglow' (female; Watanabeana Group; selected by N. Cannon from about 400 sprouted seeds distributed by U.S. Plant Introduction Station, Glenn Dale, Maryland, in 1965; selected and named by Cannon; sibling of 'Butterball').

Leaves dark green, elliptic, 1.3–1.6 cm (½–⅝ in.) long, 5–7 mm (3/16–9/32 in.) wide; fruits yellow.

'Steed's Upright' (male; synonym 'Steeds'; seedling origin; named and introduced by W. Steed in the 1970s).

Leaves dark green, broadly elliptic to short oblong, 1.3–1.6 cm (½–⅝ in.) long, 8–10 mm (5/16–⅜ in.) wide, bases and apices obtuse, margins crenate, upper two-thirds of leaf, petioles 3 mm (⅛ in.) long; vigorous compact, upright habit.

'Stokes' (male; synonym 'Stokes Variety'; seedling origin; discovered about 1925 by W. E. Stokes; introduced about 1951 by Stokes Nursery; PP No. 877).

Leaves moderate green, elliptic to broadly elliptic, 1–1.5 cm (⅜–19/32 in.) long, 5–7 mm (3/16–9/32 in.) wide, margins crenulate, upper two-thirds of leaf, petioles 1–2 mm (1/32–1/16 in.) long; dwarf compact habit, branches slightly upright; very cold hardy.

'Stokes Sport' (mutation from 'Stokes'; introduced in the 1980s by Phyto Ecology Nursery; propagation discontinued).

Leaves dark green, small; low vigorous dense, globular habit; not cold hardy.

'Sunshine' (female; synonym 'Yellow Berry'; seedling origin by N. Cannon, from a collection of cultivars—'Butterball', 'Forty Niner', 'Honeycomb', 'Sir Echo', 'Starglow' and one unknown, name lost—sold to Parks Company; renamed and introduced as 'Sunshine' in the 1970s by George W. Parks Seed Company).

Leaves dark green, fruits yellowish green until Christmas, then turning yellow, turn brown at lower than −15°C (5°F) persistent; hardy in zone 6.

'T-One' (female; synonyms 'T 1', 'Tingle-One'; origin unknown; named and introduced in late 1950s by Tingle Nursery).

Leaves dark green, oblong elliptic, curves, occasionally slightly convex, 1.4–1.8 cm (17/32–11/16 in.) long, 8–10 mm (5/16–⅜ in.) wide, bases cuneate, apices rotund, margins crenulate, upper two-thirds of leaf, petioles 2–3 mm (1/16–⅛ in.) long; low compact habit.

'Tee Dee' (female; synonym 'Helleri Mutation'; mutation on 'Helleri' discovered in late 1960s by T. Dodd Jr.; introduced in late 1970s by Tom Dodd Nursery).

Leaves elliptic, narrower than 'Helleri', 1–1.8 cm (⅜–11/16 in.) long, 5–8 mm (3/16–5/16 in.) wide, 2–3 teeth on each side, near apex, petioles 1–2 mm (1/32–1/16 in.) long; very slow growing, dense, upright spreading habit.

'Tennyson' (female; origin the Netherlands in 1917; introduced to United States about 1920 by Boulevard Nursery).

Leaves dark green, obovate, 2–3 cm (¾–1 3/16 in.) long, 9–14 mm (11/32–17/32 in.) wide, bases acute, apices obtuse, margins crenulate, upper two-thirds of leaf, petioles 3–5 mm (⅛–3/16 in.) long; upright spreading habit.

'Tiny Tim' (a frequent name in the trade for 'Prides Tiny', which see).

'Topiary' (female; selected from a cross made in 1960 by N. Cannon; named and introduced by Cannon).

Leaves dark green, elliptic, 1.3–1.8 cm (½–11/16 in.) long, 6–8 mm (7/32–5/16 in.) wide, bases and apices acute, margins crenulate, upper two-thirds of leaf, petioles 1.5–3 mm (1/16–⅛ in.) long; dense stiff irregular growth, branching at all angles in which new buds are pointing, even downward. Plant suitable for topiary work.

'Totem Pole' (open-pollinated seedling of 'Convexa' × 'Microphylla' in 1954; named by N. Cannon, not introduced, original plant in Cannon's yard).

Leaves dark green; upright rangy habit; original plant 2 m (6 ft.) tall.

'Twiggy' (female; controlled cross of *I. crenata* yellow fruit (NA 10815) × *I. yunnanensis* (NA 21018) in 1960 by W. F. Kosar; later verified as *I. crenata* and not a hybrid; named and registered H.S.A. 1-81 by G. K. Eisenbeiss; NA 31352, U.S. PI 45226; introduced in 1981 by the U.S. National Arboretum).

Leaves dark green, elliptic to narrow-elliptic,

10–15 mm (⅜–¹⁹⁄₃₂ in.) long, 5–7 mm (³⁄₁₆–⁹⁄₃₂ in.) wide, margins indented, many prominent notches, petioles 2 mm (¹⁄₁₆ in.) long; compact growth, globose to broadly pyramidal, wide as tall, varying 1.2–1.8 m (4–6 ft.) tall in 15 years, main branching upright, outer twigs strongly divaricate branching. An excellent landscape plant. Plate 145.

'Tyke' (male; origin from seed collected in the wild in 1961 by J. L. Creech, Collection No. 1057, U.S. PI 276082, as subsp. *radicans,* a prostrate form with large leaves from Horomom, Hokkaido, Japan; named and introduced by Clemson University; registered H.S.A. 3-82 by D. W. Bradshaw and L. R. Schmid).

Leaves dark green, broadly ovate, to 13 mm (½ in.) long, 8 mm (⁵⁄₁₆ in.) wide,; extremely prostrate, dwarf, compact habit; 43 cm (17 in.) tall, 94 cm (37 in.) wide in 14 years.

'Upright' (several different clones introduced with upright habit of growth using the name Upright', 'Upright Helleri', 'Upright Hetzii', and others).

'Uprite' (origin unknown; introduced in the 1960s by Appalachian Nursery).

Leaves dark green; similar to var. *latifolia*; large upright bulky habit, extremely hardy.

'Valeria Rankin' (seedling selected by T. Dodd Jr.; introduced by Tom Dodd Nursery in the 1970s).

Leaves dark green, slightly convex and curved, broadly elliptic to obovate, 1.3–2.5 cm (½–1 in.) long, 8–14 mm (⁵⁄₁₆–¹⁷⁄₃₂ in.) wide, bases cuneate, apices obtuse to rotund, margins crenulate, upper two-thirds of leaf, petioles 2 mm (¹⁄₁₆ in.) long; upright compact, globular habit.

'Variegata' (several variegated plants listed, may be the same or different clones; see 'Luteo-Variegata').

'Vaseyi' (male; Bennett Hybrid Group).

Leaves dark green, oblong-obovate, slightly convex, bases obtuse, apices rotund; broadly upright spreading habit.

'Viridis' (seedling selected and introduced in late 1960s by H. van de Laar, Boskoop, Netherlands).

Leaves dark green, slightly glossy, elliptic to slightly elliptic-obovate, 1.5–2.5 cm (¹⁹⁄₃₂–1 in.) long, 5–10 mm (³⁄₁₆–⅜ in.) wide, margins occasional twisted, small teeth, upper one-third of leaf, branchlet dark purple, changing to grayish green; upright habit.

Watanabeana Group

A group name for *I. crenata* plants with yellow fruit, or of known yellow-fruited parentage, including 'Butterball', 'Forty Niner', f. *fructo-alba*, 'Gayle', 'Honeycomb', 'Ivory Hall', 'Ivory Tower', 'Praecox', 'Sir Echo', 'Starglow', 'Sunshine', f. *watanabeana*, 'Xanthocarpa', 'Yellow Berry', 'Yellow Fruit', and 'Yellowberry'. *Watanabeana* in Latin form should not be used as a cultivar name. See *I. crenata* f. *watanabeana* in Chapter 14.

'Wayne' (female; synonym 'Waynesii'; seedling selected in late 1950s by E. Quillen; named and introduced by Waynesboro Nursery).

Leaves dark green, elliptic to slightly elliptic oblong, 10–15 mm (⅜–¹⁹⁄₃₂ in.) long, 5–7 mm (³⁄₁₆–⁹⁄₃₂ in.) wide, petioles 2–3 mm (¹⁄₁₆–⅛ in.) long; low spreading habit, similar to 'Helleri'; plants 1.5–1.6 m (5–6 ft.) in 10 to 15 years. Selected for hardiness.

'Wier' (synonym 'Wier Upright'; selected before 1963 from a local garden by Millcreek Nursery).

Leaves oval; vigorous multistemmed, upright habit.

'Wiesmoor Silber' (female; sport of 'Convexa' discovered in 1975 in the Martin Zimmer Nursery).

Leaves attractively variegated, mottled with 3 colors, mainly gray-green, green and yellowish white (cream), young leaves attractive silvery color above, gray-green beneath, some leaves partially to completely yellow white, leaves distinctly convex, to 2 cm (¾ in.) long, 1 cm (⅜ in.) wide, majority of leaves smaller, margins finely serrate; fruits black, small, sparsely produced; branches gray-green to violet-gray; dense compact habit, wider than tall, not as vigorous as 'Convexa' but same winter hardiness.

'Wildwood' (male; chance 7-year-old seedling selected and registered H.S.A. 1-66 by R. E. Marvin; introduced by Wildwood Nursery).

Low spreading habit, similar to 'Helleri' but faster rate of growth; 1.2 × 1.5 m (4 × 5 ft.) wide in 7 years.

'William Jackson' (male; synonym 'Jackson', TD 56-332; seedling selected and named by T. Dodd Jr.; introduced by Tom Dodd Nursery in the 1970s).

Leaves dark green, elliptic, 1.3–2 cm (½–¾ in.) long, 6–10 mm (⁷⁄₃₂–⅜ in.) wide, bases cuneate, apices acute, petioles 2 mm (¹⁄₁₆ in.) long; vigorous horizontal branching habit, twice as wide as high.

'Willowleaf' (male; synonym 'Willow'; Bennett Hybrid Group).

Leaves dark green, slightly convex to flat, oblanceolate, 1.5–2.5 cm ($^{19}/_{32}$–1 in.) long, 8–10 mm ($^5/_{16}$–$^3/_8$ in.) wide, bases cuneate, apices acute, petioles 2–3 mm ($^1/_{16}$–$^1/_8$ in.) long; upright spreading habit.

'Wintergreen' (female; selected for winter hardiness from 3000 seedlings grown from seed collected in Japan; named and introduced by C. Orndorff; grown by Kalmia Farms Nursery, closed in the 1980s).

Leaves dark green, oval to broadly elliptic, 2–3 cm ($^3/_4$–1$^3/_{16}$ in.) long, 10–18 mm ($^3/_8$–1$^1/_{32}$ in.) wide, bases cuneate, apices broadly cuneate to obtuse, margins crenulate, upper one-third of leaf, petioles 2–4 mm ($^1/_{16}$–$^5/_{32}$ in.) long; narrow upright habit, vertical branching, 38 cm (15 in.) wide, 1–1.2 m (3–4 ft.) tall in 3–4 years, slow to make up pyramidal form. Good hedge and screen plant 0.6–1.8 m (2 × 6 ft.) tall.

'Winter King' (origin unknown; introduced in the 1960s by Angelica Nursery; illegitimate name due to priority of *I. aquifolium* 'Winter King').

Spreading habit; extremely hardy.

'Xanthocarpa' (female; name given to several different yellow-fruited clones; illegitimate name due to Latin form and also due to plants of other species with yellow fruit labeled 'Xanthocarpa', f. *xanthocarpa*, or var. *xanthocarpa*).

'Yellow Beam' (University of Delaware).

No information available.

'Yellow Berry' (female; synonym 'Sunshine'; Watanabeana Group; name given to several yellow-fruited clones).

'Yellow Fruit' (female; Watanabeana Group; name given to first yellow-fruited *I. crenata* plants introduced to the United States, U.S. PI 231948, NA 10815; one plant at University of Washington given this name).

No information available.

'Yunnan' (female; seedling about 1932; selected by J. F. Styer; introduced about 1947 by Styer Nursery).

Leaves large; branchlets yellow tinged; upright, dense columnar habit.

'Zwischenahn' (female; introduced in late 1950s by J. Bruns).

Leaves gray-green, elliptic to ovate, 1–2 cm ($^3/_8$–$^3/_4$ in.) long; fruits black, globose, 6 mm ($^7/_{32}$ in.) diameter; compact broad, upright habit; very hardy. Good for hedges.

Ilex glabra (Gallberry Holly) Cultivars

Inkberry (or gallberry) holly was first described in 1753 by Linnaeus as *Prinos glabra* and later changed to *Ilex glabra* by Asa Gray in 1856. It is an important broadleaf evergreen for areas with cold winters and is now being used as a replacement for many Japanese hollies (*Ilex crenata*), as it is more drought tolerant. Inkberry and its selected cultivars are excellent foundation plants, low hedges, and for mass plantings.

Inkberry hollies are small to medium size shrubs 1–3 m (3–10 ft.) tall, often stoloniferous, forming dense clumps. The leaves, vary in color from light to dark green; some have a reddish purple coloration in the winter. They are obovate to elliptical, 2–5 cm ($^3/_4$–2 in.) long and 1.5–2 cm ($^9/_{16}$–$^3/_4$ in.) wide, with margins sparsely toothed near apex. The male inflorescences are fasciculate, axillary on new growth. The fruits generally are solitary and black, occasionally purplish red changing to black, rarely white.

Ilex glabra is native from Nova Scotia south to Florida and west to Missouri. It often grows as a dense understory plant under pines and in sandy soils. It is hardy in zones 5 to 10 and, like *I. coriacea*, is a good source of a light clear honey.

'Bob Rappleye' (male; collected in 1966 by B. Rappleye in the wild dune area, Bethany Beach, Delaware, from a low compact plant, NA 28995).

Leaves elliptic to elliptic-obovate, 2.5–4 cm (1–1$^5/_8$ in.) long, 10–13 mm ($^3/_8$–$^1/_2$ in.) wide, petioles 5–7 mm ($^3/_{16}$–$^9/_{32}$ in.) long. Doubtful if this cultivar is available except in several arboreta and test gardens.

'Bronze' (female; native seedling discovered in New Jersey and named by E. C. White before 1960).

Leaves obovate or obovate-lanceolate, 2.5–4 cm (1–1$^5/_8$ in.) long, 10–13 mm ($^3/_8$–$^1/_2$ in.) wide; fruits black, globose, 5 mm ($^3/_{16}$ in.) diameter; compact habit. Winter foliage turns bronze in late fall and winter. Doubtful if this selected cultivar is still available.

'Chamzin' (female; Nordic®; seedling selected for dark green foliage and hardiness by J. Zampini from field of seedlings; introduced by Lake County Nursery Exchange, PP No. 6962).

Leaves dark green, elliptic, 3.5–4 cm (1$^3/_8$–1$^5/_8$ in.) long, bases cuneate, apices acute, margins nearly entire, petioles 6–8 mm ($^7/_{32}$–$^5/_{16}$ in.) long; fruits black, globose, 6–8 mm ($^7/_{32}$–$^5/_{16}$ in.) diameter; vigorous compact rounded habit; reported hardy in zone 3 at −29 to −33°C (−20 to −30°F). Plate 146.

'Compacta'

A common name for any compact form, often a selected seedling grown from seed or a cutting-grown plant of 'Princeton's Compact'. Name is illegitimate name, due to the Latin form. There are possibly 4–5 different "Compacta" cultivars in the trade. See 'Princeton's Compact'.

'Densa' (female; selected from 500 seedlings planted in 1938 by B. Flemer, introduced by F. and F. Nursery).

Leaves dark green, 4 cm (1⅝ in.) long, 2.5–3 cm (1–1³⁄₁₆ in.) wide; upright rounded habit, usually 2.5–3 m (8–10 ft.) tall.

'Emerald' (female; seedling selected by W. F. Kosar at U.S. National Arboretum; sent out for testing and later dropped; plants still found in test gardens but never officially released).

'Ivory Queen' (female; native seedling discovered in New Jersey; named and registered H.S.A. 3-61 by C. R. Wolf).

Leaves moderate green, lanceolate, 3–4.5 cm (1³⁄₁₆–1¾ in.) long, 10–13 mm (⅜–½ in.) wide; fruits white, globose, 6 mm (⁷⁄₃₂ in.) diameter, small black, stigma at apex; upright rounded habit, old plants open up with age. Plate 147.

'Nana' (female; U.S. National Arboretum received as cuttings, in 1958 from H. Hohman, origin unknown; plants need to be sent out for evaluation; name illegitimate).

'Nigra'

Hortus III reports a selection with purple leaves in winter; plant at Arnold Arboretum has dark green leaves in winter, not uncommon to find native seedlings in the wild with purplish foliage in the winter; doubtful if original named plant is available.

'Princeton's Compact' (female; synonyms 'Compacta', 'Squat', 'Squats'; seedling selected around 1935 by W. Flemer III; seed source from near Whitesbog, New Jersey, Pine Barrens, introduced and in catalog in 1948 as 'Compacta'. 'Princeton's Compact' is a new proposed name to distinguish this plant from other "compacta" forms and to eliminate the use of the Latin form).

Leaves dark olive green, elliptic, 2.5–3.5 cm (1–1⅜ in.) long, 8–10 mm (⁵⁄₁₆–⅜ in.) wide, bases and apices cuneate, margins nearly entire, 1–2 very small teeth near apex, petioles green to brownish 5–10 mm (³⁄₁₆–⅜ in.) long; fruits black, globose, 6–8 mm (⁷⁄₃₂–⁵⁄₁₆ in.) diameter, pedicels dark, 6 mm (⁷⁄₃₁ in.) long; compact, rounded habit; very hardy. Generally considered the best of the compact forms of *I. glabra*. A good hardy, compact evergreen, dwarf plant for the Midwest and Northeast. Plate 148.

'Shamrock' (female; synonym 'Tankard Strain'; chance seedling selected around 1963 by A. Lancaster according to C. Parkerson; named and introduced by John Tankard, Tankard Nursery).

Leaves dark olive green, bronze in winter, elliptic to slightly oblanceolate, curved, 2.5–3.5 cm (1–1⅜ in.) long, 8–10 mm (⁵⁄₁₆–⅜ in.) wide, bases and apices cuneate, margins nearly entire, 1–2 small teeth near apex, petioles 5 mm (³⁄₁₆ in.) long; fruits black, globose, 6–8 mm (⁷⁄₃₂–⁵⁄₁₆ in.); compact upright rounded habit.

'Virdis' (*Hortus III* reports a cultivar with green leaves through the winter; plants at Arnold Arboretum and Weston Nursery).

Leaves light green, 3.5 cm (1⅜ in.) long, 1 cm (⅜ in.) wide, broadly pyramidal habit, 1–2 m (3–6 ft.) tall.

***Ilex integra* 'Xanthocarpa'.** Kimi-no-mochi-no-ki (synonyms f. *xanthocarpa* (Matsumura & Nakai) Ohwi 1953, var. *xanthocarpa* Matsumura & Nakai). Fruits yellow.

Ilex latifolia 'Variegata' Makino 1940.

A variegated form collected in Japan, but not a botanical form or hybrid. Rare in the United States.

Ilex myrtifolia Cultivars

'Lowei' (female; synonym *I. myrtifolia* f. *lowei*; discovered about 1924 by S. F. Blake in South Carolina).

Leaves dark olive green, linear, 1.6–2.5 cm (⅝–1 in.) long, 4–5 mm (⁵⁄₃₂–³⁄₁₆ in.) wide, petioles 3 mm (⅛ in.) long, young stems and petioles purplish; fruits vivid yellow, globose, 6–8 mm (⁷⁄₃₂–⁵⁄₁₆ in.) diameter; small trees, upright spreading habit. Several yellow fruited forms have been reported and often listed as 'XC' or 'Xanthocarpa'.

'Sarah's Choice' (female; wild selection of *I. myrtifolia* discovered by S. Gladney about 1987 in Mississippi; named by Gladney; introduced by Magnolia Gardens and Nursery).
Leaves dark olive green, linear elliptic, 2.5–3.2 cm (1–1¼ in.) long; fruits vivid red, globose, 5 mm (³⁄₁₆ in. diameter); distinct upright spreading, layering habit of growth, branches at right angles to trunk, 2–2.5 m (6½–8 ft.) tall.

'Sebring' (male?; selection of *I. myrtifolia*; origin unknown; selection of *I. cassine* var. *angustifolia*).
Leaves moderate olive green, elliptic, 3–6.5 cm (1³⁄₁₆–2½ in.) long, 1.6–2.5 cm (⅝–1 in.) wide, bases cuneate, apices acuminate, margins nearly flat, 1–4 very small spines on each side, pointing forward, petioles dark, 6–10 mm (⁷⁄₃₂–⅜ in.) long; large shrub, multiple stems, upright spreading.

'Uncle Herb' (male; form of *I. myrtifolia*; a native seedling discovered by W. Steed and father in their nursery, Candor, North Carolina; named by Steed for his father; registered H.S.A. 15-91 by P. Joseph).
Leaves dark bluish green 131A, slightly glossy, linear, midrib depressed, 2.5–3.5 cm (1–1⅜ in.) long, 5–7 mm (³⁄₁₆–⁹⁄₃₂ in.) wide; young stems purplish; small tree, upright branching habit. Very distinct dark leaves with depressed midribs.

'Walker' (female; seedling of *I. myrtifolia* in garden of S. Reath; named by H. Elmore).
Leaves dark green, linear, 1.8–2.2 cm (¹¹⁄₁₆–¹³⁄₁₆ in.) long, 3–4 mm (⅛–⁵⁄₃₂ in.) wide; fruits red; hardy in zone 6.

Ilex opaca (American Holly) Cultivars

American holly is the most commercially important holly native to North America and, more specifically, to the eastern United States. It is native to a large part of the eastern United States from Massachusetts to Pennsylvania and West Virginia, south to Florida, and west to Texas, Missouri, Tennessee, and Indiana. Also known as white holly, this North American native was introduced to England in 1744 by Archibald, the duke of Argyle, at Inverary Castle in Scotland. *Ilex opaca* was described by A. T. Aiton in *Hortus Kewensis,* ed. 1, in 1789. For other synonym names prior to and following this publication, see the species description in Chapter 14.

American hollies are conspicuous medium to large trees, occurring as understory plants in many areas. They are tolerant of a wide variety of soil types ranging from upland forest to marshy hardwood bottoms in association with oaks, and among pines in the Coastal Plain areas. American holly also occurs as a coastal beach plant with a tolerance to high soil and atmospheric salts. The best growth is in deep rich, fertile, well-drained, acid soils. The ultimate size of American holly restricts the use of many cultivars except for large properties and large homes or large buildings. It is an excellent specimen on a lawn, as a screen or hedge planting, or as a background for a shrub or perennial border.

The evergreen leaves are extremely variable in size and shape, ranging from 2.5 to 13 cm (2 to 5 in.) long. The margins also vary from flat to wavy and are usually spiny to often entire. The entire-leaved plants from the northern range belong to *Ilex opaca* f. *subintegra,* while those from southern ranges belong to *I.* × *attenuata,* which includes natural hybrids of *I. opaca* × *I. cassine* and *I. opaca* × *I. myrtifolia.* Leaf color varies from light olive to dark olive green. Many leaves have a glossy shine. Two registered cultivars have variegated foliage—'Steward's Cream Crown' and 'Steward's Silver Crown'—and are more winter hardy than the variegated English holly which has more glossy attractive foliage.

The fruits are borne singly, one to a pedicel or occasionally 1–3 on a peduncle. The berries are typically rotund to elliptical and 8–13 mm (⁵⁄₁₆–½ in.) diameter. They are usually vivid red, but vary from various shades of orange to yellows.

The white flowers are borne in mid to late spring, axillary on new growth. While the pistillate flowers are solitary, the staminate flowers on separate plants are borne in cymose clusters.

The wood of American holly is very heavy, compact, white, and hard. The grain is fine and takes a fine polish. The wood is excellent for turning, cabinet making, inlaying, and carving. It is often stained for inlay work and for the black keys on pianos.

Selecting and propagating of superior American holly plants began in the late 1920s by Paul Bosley Sr., Earl Dilatush, Guy Nearing, Orlando Pride, Wilfred Wheeler, Elizabeth White, and others. A committee of the American Association of Nurserymen registered the first cultivated holly names from 1948 to 1958.

International registration of *Ilex* began in 1958 by the Holly Society of America, the International Registration Authority. Many of the first named cultivars were selected for winter hardness and good foliage. Following World War II and in the 1950s and 1960s it was very popular to name selected cultivars. More than 1000 selections of American holly have been given cultivar names but not all of these names have been registered with the International Registration Authority. The majority of American holly cultivars described below were introduced in the United States.

The chance of finding a yellow-fruited seedling of *Ilex opaca* is one in a million or more. There is no record of discovery of the first plant with yellow fruit instead of red. Undoubtedly yellow-fruited plants were collected by Native Americans and used in their decorations together with the red-fruited plants.

Alfred Rehder of the Arnold Arboretum officially described the form *Ilex opaca* f. *xanthocarpa,* possibly from North Carolina, in 1901. This botanical forma includes all the yellow-fruited selections. Yellow-fruited plants have now been reported from Virginia, Georgia, Alabama, and numerous other states. Many of the colorful fruited variations have been given fancy cultivar names and often have been registered; however, they are still overlooked and underutilized as an attractive landscape plant.

The Holly Society of America and its members are indebted to Jesse and Ruth Rankin, Salisbury, North Carolina, for the wealth of knowledge and plants which they shared with arboreta and holly friends across the country. Jesse often named his introductions for the wives, mothers, and daughters of his friends. Table 10 lists yellow-fruited American hollies with their introducers.

Table 11 lists American holly cultivars lacking complete descriptions. The names were gleaned from various publications of the Holly Society of America, *American Nurseryman Magazine,* and catalogs.

'Acuminata' (E. Schelle, in Beissner et al., *Handb. Laubh.—Benenn,* 1903).
No description available.

'Adams' (male; plant discovered by A. N. Adams near Clarkesville, Maryland; moved around 1937 to Ten Oaks Nursery).
Leaves dark olive green, oval, 3–5.5 cm (1³⁄₁₆–2⅛ in.) long, 2.2–3.5 cm (¹³⁄₁₆–1⅜ in.) wide, bases rotund, apices acute, slightly keeled, curved, margins recurved, 2–3 spines on each side, upper two-thirds of leaf, petioles 8 mm (⁵⁄₁₆ in.) long. Excellent pollinator.

'Albert King' (female; selected by A. King and W. C. Frierson around 1940 in Bristol, Tennessee, at about 545 m (1800 ft.) elevation).
Leaves dark olive green; fruits profuse, vivid red; broadly pyramidal.

'Albert Pride' (male; selected by O. S. Pride; Grace Hybrid Group).
Leaves moderate olive green, elliptic, slightly keeled, curved, 6–7 cm (2⅜–2¾ in.) long, 3.5–4.5 cm (1⅜–1¾ in.) wide, slightly wavy margins, 3–6 spines on each side, petioles 6–7 mm (⁷⁄₃₂–⁹⁄₃₂ in.) long; very hardy.

'Alice Steed' (female; introduced by W. Steed).
Leaves moderate olive green, elliptic, 4.5–6 cm (1⅝–2⅜ in.) long, 2.5–3 cm (1–1³⁄₁₆ in.) wide, keeled, curved, 2–5 spines on each side, margins reflexed, petioles 8 mm (⁵⁄₁₆ in.) long; fruits vivid red 45A, globose, 10 mm (⅜ in.) diameter, pedicels 6 mm (⁷⁄₃₂ in.) long.

'Allen' (female; W. Wheeler, 1939; introduced before 1953 by W. Phillips).
Leaves dark olive green, oval, 4–6 cm (1⅝–2⅜ in.) long, 2.5–3 cm (1–1³⁄₁₆ in.) wide, bases obtuse, slightly keeled, curved, 3–5 spines usually on upper two-thirds of leaf, petioles 8 mm (⁵⁄₁₆ in.) long; fruits vivid red 45A, globose, pedicels reddish, 6–8 mm (⁷⁄₃₂–⁵⁄₁₆ in.) long.

'Allison' (female; seedling origin 1938, Sussex County, Delaware; registered H.S.A. No. 1-65 by W. Phillips).
Leaves dark olive green, broadly elliptic, 5–7 cm (2–2¾ in.) long, 3–3.5 cm (1³⁄₁₆–1⅜ in.) wide, bases obtuse, keeled, curved, 3–4 spines usually on upper two-thirds of leaf, petioles stout, 5–7 mm (³⁄₁₆–⁹⁄₃₂ in.) long; fruits deep red, 46A, globose, 6–8 mm (⁷⁄₃₂–⁵⁄₁₆ in.) diameter, pedicels reddish, 8–10 mm (⁵⁄₁₆–⅜ in.) long.

'Alloway' (synonym 'Alloway Upright'; selected 1929 near Alloway, New Jersey, and introduced 1948 by E. Dilatush; only 25 cuttings produced to evaluate for form, foliage, and fruits, then discontinued; plant at Secrest Arboretum, Wooster, Ohio).
Leaves dark olive green, elliptic, 3.8–6 cm (1½–2⅜ in.) long, 2–3 cm (¾–1³⁄₁₆ in.) wide, bases cuneate, keeled, curved, margins recurved, wavy, 5–7 small spines on each side, petioles 8 mm (⁵⁄₁₆ in.) long; fruits reddish orange at first then vivid red 45A, globose, 8 mm (⁵⁄₁₆ in.) diameter, pedicels 8 mm (⁵⁄₁₆ in.) long.

'American Spineless' (female; synonym 'Spineless'; E. Dilatush before 1953; probably a clone of *I. opaca* f. *subintegra*; seedling purchased from Boyce Thompson Institute in late 1930s; discontinued due to spineless leaves).

'American Wreath' (female; selected by E. Dilatush before 1953).

Table 10. Yellow-fruited cultivars of *Ilex opaca* (American holly).

Name of cultivar	Introducer/namer
'Betty Nevison'	Named & introduced by J. Rankin
'Beverly Belin'	Introduced by J. Rankin
'Bladen Maiden'	Named by J. Rankin
'Blanche Morgan'	Selected & named by G. Morgan
'Blush'	Selected by R. L. Tomayer; introduced by Wavecrest Nursery
'Boyce Thompson Xanthocarpa'	Introduced by P. W. Zimmerman
'Calloway'	Selected by W. A. Roach; registered by S. Solymosy
'Canary'	Named & introduced by E. Dilatush
'Carrie'	Introduced by J. Rankin
'Cecil'	Introduced by J. Rankin
'Clatworthy'	Named & introduced by W. Hallenberg & T. Klein
'Clemson'	Named & introduced by F. Galle
'Cornett'	Named & introduced by T. Klein
'Corpening No. 1'	Introduced by J. Rankin
'Corpening No. 2'	Introduced by J. Rankin
'Corpening No. 3'	Introduced by J. Rankin
'Dengle Bells'	Named & introduced by J. Rankin
'Dunn No. 1'	Introduced by J. Rankin
'Dunn No. 2'	Introduced by J. Rankin
'Ermine Watson'	Named & introduced by J. Rankin
'Fallow'	Introduced by Jackson M. Batchelor
'Forest Nursery'	Named & introduced by F. Galle
'Francis Lewis'	Introduced by F. Lewis
'Fruitland Nursery'	Introduced by Fruitland Nursery
'Galyean Gold'	Introduced by W. Steiner
'Golden Valentine'	Introduced by T. Klein
'Goldie'	Selected by Mrs. W. K. du Pont; introduced by E. C. White
'Helen Mitchell'	Introduced by J. Rankin
'Jeannette Adanson'	Named by J. Rankin
'Jesse Taylor'	Introduced by J. Rankin
'Judy Kay'	Introduced by J. Rankin
'Julie Koehler'	Introduced by T. Klein

Leaves dark olive green, elliptic, 5–7.5 cm (2–3 in.) long, 2.5–3.5 cm (1–1⅜ in.) wide, slightly keeled, slightly curved, bases cuneate to obtuse, margins recurved, 5–7 strong spines on each side, very attractive leaves, petioles reddish, 8–10 mm (5/16–⅜ in.) long; fruits vivid red 44A, globose, 8 mm (5/16 in.) diameter, pedicels reddish, 10 mm (⅜ in.) long.

'Amy' (female; synonym 'Wheeler No. F-2'; selected 1939 and named 1948 by W. Wheeler; Wheeler received seed from New York Botanical Gardens, although the seed may have come originally from the Missouri Botanical Gardens).

Leaves dark olive green, glossy, elliptic, keeled, 5–7.5 cm (2–3 in.) long by 2.5–4 cm (1–1⅝ in.) wide, margins wavy from base to apex, spines 5–8 on each side, petioles 7–11 mm (9/32–7/16 in.) long; fruits large, abundant, vivid red, 10 mm (⅜ in.) diameter, pedicels 7 mm (9/32 in.) long; twigs slender, dark gray. Large upright tree and good specimen type.

'Andorra' (female; origin Andorra Nursery before 1953).

Leaves broadly elliptic, moderate olive green, curved, bases obtuse, 6.5–8 cm (2⅜–3⅛ in.) long, 3–4 cm (1³/16–1⅝ in.) wide, 4–5 spines on each margin, reflexed; petioles stout, 5 mm (³/16 in.) long; fruits red.

'Andover' (female; selected and named from trees in southern Pennsylvania; introduced by H. Rohrbach).

Leaves dark olive green; fruits red. Selected for superior hardiness.

'Anet' (female; seedling of 'Old Heavy Berry'; named by T. Klein).

Leaves dark olive green, oval, 5–6 cm (2–2⅜ in.) long, 3–3.5 cm (1³/16–1⅜ in.) wide, keeled, curved, 3–6 prominent spines on each side, petioles 8 mm (5/16 in.) long; fruits red, globose, 8–10 mm (5/16–⅜ in.) diameter. Similar to 'Old Heavy Berry' but more upright and leaves slightly elongated.

NAME OF CULTIVAR	INTRODUCER/NAMER
'Lady Blakeford'	Introduced by J. Rankin
'Lenape Moon'	Introduced by W. Phillips
'Longwash'	Plant at North Carolina State Arboretum
'Longwood Gardens'	Introduced by Longwood Gardens
'Maiden Blush'	Introduced by J. Rankin
'Margret Moran'	Named & introduced by J. Rankin
'Marion'	Introduced by H. H. Hume
'Mary Emily'	Named & introduced by J. Rankin
'Maryland'	Introduced by H. Hohman
'Mays Landing'	Introduced by D. Fenton
'Morgan Gold'	Introduced by Morgan & T. A. Darr
'Morris Arboretum'	Named & introduced by J. Rankin
'Mrs. Clark'	Named & introduced by J. Rankin
'Mrs. Davis'	Named & introduced by R. W. Pease
'Oak Grove No. 1'	Named & introduced by F. Galle & B. Pace
'Oak Hill'	Introduced by J. Rankin
'Old Gold'	Introduced by T. Klein
'Perfection'	Introduced by Tyler Arboretum
'Princeton Gold'	Named & introduced by Princeton Nurseries
'Saga Serene'	Named by J. Rankin; introduced by W. Steed
'Spring Grove'	Introduced by T. Klein
'24 Karat'	Named by A. Gould; introduced by J. Shaffer
'Valentine'	Introduced by T. Klein
'Villanova'	Introduced by P. Hill
'Virginia Giant'	Introduced by T. Klein
'Virginia West'	Named by J. Rankin
'Wilmat Yellow'	Introduced by Wilmat Nursery
'Winn Nursery'	Introduced by Winn Nursery
'Xanthawood'	Named by J. Rankin
'Yellow Berry Brownell'	Introduced by Brownell Nursery
'Yellow Jacquet'	Named & introduced by J. Rankin

'Angelica' (female; synonym 'Koles Angelica'; origin Angelica Nursery 1953).

Leaves dark olive green, oval to broadly elliptic, 5–8 cm (1–3⅛ in.) long, 3–4.5 cm (1³⁄₁₆–1¾ in.) wide, slightly keeled, curved, 3–5 spines on each side, petioles stout, 10–15 mm (⅜–¹⁹⁄₃₂ in.) long; fruits vivid red 44A, globose, 8–10 mm (⁵⁄₁₆–⅜ in.) diameter, pedicels 5 mm (³⁄₁₆ in.) long.

'Angustifolia' (synonym 'Willowleaf Holly'; origin Altex Nursery 1963).

No description, possibly *I. × attenuata* 'Foster No. 2'.

'Anne Arundel' (female; selected from trees in Anne Arundel County, Maryland; introduced by S. McLean, 1935).

Leaves dark olive green, broadly oval, 5.5–7.5 cm (2⅛–3 in.) long, 3–4 cm (1³⁄₁₆–1⅝ in.) wide, bases cuneate, very slightly keeled, curved, margins recurved, 2–3 spines usually on upper two-thirds of leaf; fruits vivid red 45B, globose, 7–8 mm (⁹⁄₃₂–⁵⁄₁₆ in.) diameter, pedicels 5–7 mm (³⁄₁₆–⁹⁄₃₂ in.) long.

'Aquapaca' (male; origin Angelica Nursery).

Leaves moderate olive green, oval, 4–5 cm (1⅝–2 in.) long, 2.5–3 cm (1–1³⁄₁₆ in.) wide, keeled, curved, 4–6 spines on each side, petioles 6–8 mm (⁷⁄₃₂–⁵⁄₁₆ in.) long.

'Arden' (female; Nearing 1922; discovered in Arden, Delaware; introduced by Arden Nursery, 1926).

Leaves dark olive green, reddish brown in fall, narrow-elliptic, slightly curved, keeled, 7–8 cm (⁷⁄₃₂–⁵⁄₁₆ in.) long, 2–3.5 cm (1–1⅜ in.) wide, margins wavy, 4–8 short spines on each side, petioles purplish 6–8 mm (⁷⁄₃₂–⁵⁄₁₆ in.) long; fruits single, vivid red 44A, ellipsoid, 10 mm (⅜ in.) long, 8 m (⁵⁄₁₆ in.) wide, pedicels slender 8–12 mm (⁵⁄₁₆–⁵⁄₃₂ in.) long, ripening early; easily rooted.

Table 11. Cultivars of *Ilex opaca* (American holly) without complete descriptions.

NAME	SOURCE
'Aaron' (male)	Holly Haven Nursery catalog 1955, New Lisbon, New Jersey, no description
'Acuminata'	E. Schelle in Beissner et al., *Handbook Laubh.— Benenn,* 1903, no description
'Aldridge Red' (female)	Aldridge Nursery, Van Ormy, Texas, no description
'Argentine' (female)	E. C. White, Holly Haven Nursery catalog 1953, habit robust, fruits large
'Aunt Mary' (female)	Tingle Nursery catalog 1954, origin Pennsylvania, good grower & foliage, heavy fruiting
'B. H.' (female)	Breeze Hill Gardens finding list 1940, no description
'Bailey' (female)	Kelsey Nursery catalog 1933, origin Florida, named by H. Hume in 1937, leaves large & spiny, fruits red
'Baker No. 1' (male; syn. 'Baker No. 2')	Selected & named by H. Hume at Glen Saint Mary Nursery, Glen Saint Mary, Florida, leaves glossy, dark olive green, elliptic to obovate, compact dense tree
'Big Leaf'	H.S.A. Bulletin No. 6, 1953, selected by E. Dilatush, no description
'Bill Comb' (female)	Selected 1947 by W. C. Frierson, near Bristol, Virginia, in Green Spring Community, 562 m (1800 ft). elevation, leaves dark olive green, spiny, fruits red
'Birdsnest'	Selected 1929 on coast of Massachusetts, introduced 1948 by E. Dilatush, similar to 'Christmas Hedge', very few plants produced, H.S.A. Bulletin No. 6, 1953
'Black Beauty' (male)	Selected 1929, introduced 1948 by E. Dilatush, catalog 1952, leaves dark to very dark olive green, dense upright, slow growing, hardy in zone 5
'Boggs' (female)	Selected 1947 by W. C. Frierson, Westminster, South Carolina, 281 m (900 ft.) elevation, leaves dark olive green, fruits red
'Bountiful Improved' (female)	Selected in New Jersey & introduced 1948 by E. Dilatush, old plants less attractive in fruit than 'Bountiful'
'Boyce Thompson No. 3' (female)	*Plant and Gardens* 12, 1956, no description
'Brigham Young' (male)	Selected about 1945 by P. Vossberg, near Setauket, Long Island, New York, H.S.A. Bulletin No. 6, 1953, no description
'Cape Christmas' (syn. 'Christmas Queen')	Tingle Nursery catalog 1958, no description
'Carter' (male)	Plant growing in Morris Arboretum, Philadelphia, Pennsylvania, no description
'Clarendon' (syn. 'Clarendon No. 1')	Origin Clarendon Gardens, H.S.A. Bulletin No. 6, 1953, no description
'Clarendon Satellite' (female)	Origin Clarendon Gardens, catalog 1957, leaves large
'Clarissa No. 2'	M. Baron & G. Parmelee, reported on Michigan State University campus, H.S.A. Letter 25, 1965, no description
'Clark's Valley' (female)	*National Horticulture Magazine* 26, 1947, selected by M. M. Fulton at Clark's Valley, Pennsylvania, leaves dark olive green, oval, flat, spines short & fine, fruits vivid red
'Collier' (female)	Fairfax Farm Nursery catalog 1926, Fairfax, Virginia, no description
'Convexa'	Tingle Nursery catalog 1960, no description
'Craighead'	H.S.A. Bulletin No. 6, 1953, selected by W. W. Steiner from U.S. Plant Introduction Station, Glenn Dale, Maryland, origin New York, no description
'Crimson Tide'	H.S.A. Bulletin No. 6, 1953, origin H. Hohman, Kingsville, Maryland, later discarded 1953, no description
'Darby' (female)	Wight Nursery catalog 1955, no description
'Dark Red' (female)	Clarendon Gardens catalog 1953, leaves dark olive green, well spined, fruits dark red
'Darkleaf' (male)	Selected 1925, introduced 1949 by E. Dilatush, catalog 1953, selected for dark green foliage & plant habit
'Dauphin'	H.S.A. Bulletin No. 6, 1953, selected from the wild near Dauphin, Pennsylvania, by W. J. Dauber before 1953, no description
'Deerfield' (syn. 'Deerfieldi')	Deerfield Nursery catalog 1961, no description.
'Deitz'	Hume & Owens in H.S.A. Letter 31, 1968, no description
'Drenning'	H.S.A. Bulletin No. 6, 1953, selected by W. J. Dauber, no description
'Eden'	H.S.A. Letter 25, 1965, no description
'Edith May' (female)	O. Pride, reported on Michigan State University campus but not found
'Excelsior' (male)	J. S. Wells Nursery catalog 1957, leaves good color, vigorous plant.
'Faulkner'	H.S.A. Bulletin No. 6, 1953, female, selected by J. R. Schramm near Faulkner, Maryland, no description, reported to be a big tree, fruits red

NAME	SOURCE
'15 Mile Hill'	Towson Nursery catalog 1957, no description, valid name
'Flat Leaf' (male)	Clarendon Gardens catalog 1962, leaves flat
'Francis Fruck'	Hume & Owens in H.S.A. Letter 31, 1968, no description
'Frederick'	J. Vermeulen Nursery catalog 1964, no description
'Full-O-Berries' (female; syn. 'Full O' Berries')	M. Baron & G. Parmelee, reported on Michigan State University campus, 1966 university list, no description
'Globosa'	E. Schelle, in Beissner et al., *Handbook Laubh.— Benenn,* 1903, no description
'Goliath' (male)	Hume & Owens in H.S.A. Letter 31, 1968, no description
'Gravatt' (female)	H.S.A. Bulletin No. 6, 1953, selected at Frederick, Maryland, by F. L. O'Rourke, named for G. F. Gravatt, U.S.D.A. Beltsville, Maryland, no description
'Halstead'	Origin E. C. White about 1930, from New Jersey, H.S.A. Bulletin No. 6, 1953, no description
'Hamlet'	Robins Nursery catalog 1972, Willard, North Carolina, no description
'Harry' (male)	Holly Haven Nursery catalog 1951, Whitesbog, New Jersey, leaves very spiny
'Hawkins' (female)	Jones Nursery catalog 1962, Nashville, Tennessee, no description
'Holloway' (female)	Clarendon Gardens catalog 1962, leaves waxy, convex, fruits red
'Holly-By-Golly' (male)	H.S.A. Bulletin No. 6, 1953, selected by K. Meserve, no description
'Holmes' (female)	Selected by M. Fulton in Pennsylvania, H.S.A. Bulletin No. 6, 1953, no description
'Holmes' (male)	Selected by W. J. Dauber, H.S.A. Bulletin No. 6, 1953, no description
'Holmes Red Berry Wonder' (female)	Holmes Nursery catalog 1951, Tampa, Florida, no description
'Hurst No. 1'	Wight Nursery catalog 1958, no description
'Indian Summer'	H.S.A. Bulletin No. 6, 1953, selected by W. Dauber about 1953, no description
'Ingleside Gold' (female)	Ingleside Nursery catalog 1964, fruits vivid yellow, not in production
'Iso'	H.S.A. Bulletin No. 6, 1953, selected before 1950 by W. Wheeler, no description
'January '36'	Selected by T. Windon & E. C. White, no description
'Jersey Golden' (male)	H.S.A. Bulletin No. 6, 1953, named in 1950 by C. Wolf, no description
'Jersey Special'	J. Vermeulen Nursery catalog 1961, no description
'Karen' (female)	*National Horticultural Magazine* 26 (3) 1947, selected 1935-1940 near Whitesbog, New Jersey, by T. Windon & E. C. White, fruits red, heavy bearer
'King Bountiful' (male)	Selected by E. Dilatush, catalog 1950, no description
'King Cardinal' (male)	Selected 1929 in New Jersey, introduced 1948 by E. Dilatush, catalog 1950, dense round crown or pyramidal
'Kingsville'	Hume & Owens in H.S.A. Letter 31, 1968, no description
'Lambert' (female)	*Plant and Gardens* 3 (4) 1947, selected at Lenior, North Carolina, by W. C. Frierson, fruits red, heavy annual bearing
'Langdon'	Cascio Nursery catalog 1958, no description
'Lanny' (male)	H.S.A. Bulletin No. 6, 1953, selected by O. Pride, leaves with good winter color, medium broad, compact habit
'Large Leaf No. 4'	Clarendon Gardens catalog 1957, no description
'Larry'	Hume & Owens in H.S.A. Letter 31, 1968, no description
'Latifolia'	E. Schelle, in Beissner et al., *Handbook Laubh.— Benenn,* 1903, no description
'Macrondon'	E. Schelle, in Beissner et al., *Handbook Laubh.— Benenn,* 1903, no description
'Magic'	H.S.A. Bulletin No. 6, 1953, selected about 1946 by E. Dilatush, no description
'Magothy'	H.S.A. Bulletin No. 6, 1953, selected by S. McLean, named for Magothy River, Maryland, no description
'Male No. 1' & 'Male No. 2'	H. G. Mattoon, no description
'Male No. 1'	Glen Saint Mary Nursery, Glen Saint Mary, Florida, no description
'Male No. 2'	Glen Saint Mary Nursery, Glen Saint Mary, Florida, early bloomer
'Male No. 3'	Glen Saint Mary Nursery, Glen Saint Mary, Florida, midseason bloomer
'Male No. 4'	Glen Saint Mary Nursery, Glen Saint Mary, Florida, late bloomer
'Martha Twitty' (female)	Introduced by Stephen's Nursery catalog 1954, leaves moderate yellow-green, spiny, fruits red
'Mary Snowell' (female)	Wyman Garden Center catalog 1961, leaves dark green, fruits red, abundant
'Matawan' (female)	J. S. Wells Nursery catalog 1957, origin Matawan, New Jersey, no description
'Mattoon'	*American Horticultural Magazine* 49 (11) 1970, no description

(continued)

Table 11. Continued.

NAME	SOURCE
'McKenny No. 1' & 'McKenny No. 2'	Selected by R. B. McKenny, no description
'Mitchell'	No description
'Monroe' (female)	Rocknoll Nursery catalog 1961, leaves large, spiny, fruits red
'Mossy' (male)	Introduced by O. Pride (?), leaves yellow-green, spiny, good winter color, compact habit
'Mr. Heavy Berry' (male)	J. S. Wells Nursery catalog 1957, habit similar to that of 'Old Heavy Berry'
'Mrs. John Bennett'	Hume & Owens in H.S.A. Letter 31, 1968, no description
'Mrs. S. D. Hunter' (female)	Selected 1957 by W. C. Frierson at Westminster, South Carolina, leaves good quality, fruits red
'Muller No. 2'	J. S. Wells Nursery catalog 1958, Red Bank, New Jersey, no description
'Muriel'	H.S.A. Bulletin No. 6, 1953, selected by W. Wheeler & E. C. White, no description
'Murphy' (male)	H.S.A. Bulletin No. 6, 1953, selected 1948 by O. Pride, no description
'Myles' (female)	Selected before 1947 by W. C. Frierson near Fayetteville, West Virginia, leaves good green, fruits red, in clusters, annually
'Nash' (male)	H.S.A. Proceedings, 1953, selected about 1940 by W. Wheeler & E. C. White, no description
'Nell' (synonyms 'Aalto No. 15', 'Alto No. 15)	H.S.A. Bulletin No. 6, 1953, selected by W. Wheeler & E. C. White, no description
'Nelson' (female)	Selected before 1947 by W. C. Frierson from Victory, Kentucky, fruits red, globose, annual bearing
'New Jersey'	H.S.A. Bulletin No. 6, 1953, selected by W. J. Dauber, no description
'Nicholson' (female)	Selected before 1947 by W. C. Frierson on Walhalla Highland Highway, Georgia, fruits red, abundant
'No. 1' through 'No. 6'	Tingle Nursery, Pittsville, Maryland, no descriptions
'No. 7' through 'No. 13', 'No. 21'	Grovatt's Nursery catalog, Burlington, New Jersey, no descriptions
'Norb' (male)	H.S.A. Bulletin No. 6, 1953, selected by O. Pride, named for Norb Garbish, leaves glossy, good winter color
'Norton Bigleaf'	G. Malinborg, origin North Carolina before 1947, no description
'Norton No. 3'	H.S.A. Letter 31, 1968, G. Malinborg, origin North Carolina, no description
'Old Glory' (female)	Fruits yellow; H.S.A. Letter 31, 1968, no description
'Old Gloss' (female)	Rocknoll Nursery catalog 1963, leaves glossy, fruits vivid red, upright, vigorous.
'Old Hale and Hearty' (male)	Selected about 1925 in New Jersey, introduced before 1949 by E. Dilatush, leaves dark green, very large, fast growing
'One-B' & 'One-D'	Hume & Owens in H.S.A. Letter 31, 1968, origin P. Bosley, no description
'Orange'	H.S.A. Letter 18, 1963, selected by W. Wheeler, no description
'Owens Strain'	Grandview Nursery catalog 1955, no description
'Perkins de Wilde No. 1', 'Perkins de Wilde No. 2', & 'Perkins de Wilde No. 4'	Catalog, no description
'Phoebe' (synonym 'Aalto No. 12')	H.S.A. Bulletin No. 6, 1953, selected by W. Wheeler & E. C. White, no description
'Pinehurst Special'	Clarendon Gardens catalog 1957, no description
'Pitman' (female)	Selected & introduced by Koster Nursery catalog 1938, fruits red, very large
'Pride'	Suncrest Nursery, Homer City, Pennsylvania, no description
'Prospect' (male)	H.S.A. Bulletin No. 6, 1953, by W. J. Dauber, no description
'Quinn'	H.S.A. Proceedings 3, 1948, selected in Massachusetts by W. Wheeler & E. C. White, no description
'Red Chief' (female)	Wayside Gardens catalog 1962, fruits vivid red, male & female forms
'Red Lady' (female)	Hoogendorn Nursery, New Port, Rhode Island, no description
'Regars'	Grovatt's Nursery catalog, Burlington, New Jersey, no description
'Richards V'	Holly-by-Golly catalog 1954, no description
'Roecker'	Selected by D. E. Felton on property of E. Roecker, Merchantville, New Jersey, H.S.A. Bulletin No. 6, 1953, no description
'Runyon Selection'	One or group, selected before 1970 by C. Runyon, Springhill Cemetery, Cincinnati, Ohio, no description(s)
'S. Lane' (female)	Holly Haven Nursery catalog 1955, no description

Name	Source
'Sagain'	No description
'Salem'	H.S.A. Bulletin No. 6, 1953, selected by W. Dauber, no description.
'Selected Heavy Fruiter' (female)	Wilmat Nursery, ad in *American Nurseryman Magazine* 1955, no description
'Selection No. 1' & 'Selection No. 2'	H. G. Mattoon, ad in *American Nurseryman Magazine* 1955, origin Connecticut, no description
'Sellars No. 2'	Selected by J. H. Schmidt, catalog 1954, leaves crinkled, no other description
'Sepers'	Grovatt's Nursery, ad in *American Nurseryman Magazine* 1964, no description
'September Glow'	Reported on Michigan State University campus, no description
'Shelia'	Holly Haven Nursery catalog 1955, no description
'Shreve'	H.S.A. Bulletin No. 6, 1953, selected about 1930 by E. C. White, no description
'Shreveport'	H.S.A. Proceedings 30, 1953, origin unknown, reported as good Christmas green in Atlanta, Georgia
'Sibyl' (synonym 'Aalto No. 10')	H.S.A. Bulletin No. 6, 1953, selected by W. Wheeler & E. C. White, no description
'Silver Fleece'	No description
'Snowball' (male)	H.S.A. Bulletin No. 6, 1953, selected by S. McLean, no description
'Snyder'	Grovatt's Nursery catalog, Burlington, New Jersey, no description
'Southcarpa'	Tingle Nursery catalog 1934, no description
'Speed'	Discovered near Clayton, Georgia, by J. Speed, named by W. C. Frierson before 1947, no description
'Stanley'	H.S.A. Bulletin No. 6, 1953, selected about 1930 by E. C. White, no description
f. *subintegra* 'Sullivan'	Grovatt's Nursery, ad in *American Nursery Magazine* 1964, no description
'Success'	H.S.A. Letter 19, 1963, introduced by Hess Nursery, no description
'Superberry'	H.S.A. Letter 25, 1965, O. Pride, no description
'Thomas'	Holly Haven Nursery catalog 1955, no description
'Thompson' (female)	Listed by Wilmat Holly Company catalog 1955, possibly a Boyce Thompson selection, fruits red, small, reported very hardy
'Tingle'	Possibly a Tingle Nursery numbered selection, no description available; also reported as 'Tingle Nursery XC' with yellow fruits
'Tom Cross' (male; syn. 'Cross')	Watnong Nursery catalog 1966, leaves dark olive green, large, good pollinator
'Turner (female)	Clarendon Gardens catalog 1957, leaves small, very broad, almost round, with 1–6 broad spines on each side
'Twisted Leaf' (male)	Clarendon Gardens catalog 1963, leaves twisted, dense upright habit
'University of Maryland'	H.S.A. Bulletin No. 6, 1953, no description
'Valley'	H.S.A. Bulletin No. 6, 1953, selected by W. Dauber, no description
'Van Sciver'	Grovatt's Nursery catalog, Burlington, New Jersey, no description
'Variegata'	Wilmat Holly Company, Narberth, Pennsylvania, no description
'Virginia Dare'	H.S.A. Bulletin No. 6, 1953, selected from Virginia Tree Farm by E. J. Jones, no description
'Vora Woods' (female)	Selected by W. C. Frierson before 1947 from Lookout Mountain, West Virginia, fruits orange, medium size, borne in profusion
'Waltemyer' (female)	H.S.A. Bulletin No. 6, 1953, discovered in southern York County, Pennsylvania, by W. Dauber, fruits red, compact pyramidal habit
'West Virginia Supreme'	H.S.A. Bulletin No. 6, 1953, selected by E. W. Jones, no description
'Westtown Male No. 2'	H.S.A. Proceedings 36, no description
'White Cottage' (female)	H.S.A. Letter 25, 1965, Appalachian Nursery, fruits red, heavy bearing
'Willie Prophet'	H.S.A. Letter, 25, 1965, no description
'Windchester'	H.S.A. Letter 31, 1968, no description
'Winddrift'	H.S.A. Bulletin No. 6, 1953, no description
'Winter Glory'	H.S.A. Letter 31, 1968, no description
'Yellow Berry' (female)	Angelica Nursery before 1956, fruits vivid yellow, upright pyramidal habit
'Yellow Berry No. 34'	H.S.A. Bulletin No. 6, 1953, no description
'Yellow Edge No. 34'	H.S.A. Bulletin No. 6, 1953, no description
'Yellowii' (female)	Wildacre Nursery catalog 1932, fruits deep yellow
'York'	H.S.A. Bulletin No. 6, 1953, selected 1936 by K. McDonald in York County, Virginia, no description
'Yost' (male)	H.S.A. Bulletin No. 6, 1953, selected by W. Dauber, no description
'Young Flowering Male'	No description

'Argentine' (female; E. White 1953; Rutgers?).
Robust plant; fruits large.

'Arlene Leach' (female; synonym 'Arlene'; O. S. Pride, 1960; Grace Hybrid Group).
Leaves large, dark olive green, free of leaf spot, broadly elliptic, 7–8 cm (2¾–3⅛ in.) long, 4–5.5 cm (1⅝–1¾ in.) wide, slightly keeled, margins slightly wavy with 5–6 prominent spines on each side, petioles 8 mm (5⁄16 in.) long; fruits deep reddish orange 43A, globose, 8 mm (5⁄16 in.) diameter, pedicels 5 mm (3⁄16 in.) long, persistent, heavy annual bearer. Narrowly pyramidal, compact; very hardy.

'Ashland No. 10' (female; Dawes Arboretum, Newark, Ohio).
Leaves moderate olive green, oval, 4–5.5 cm (1⅝–2⅛ in.) long, 2–3.5 cm (¾–1⅜ in.) wide, keeled, curved, 2–4 spines on each side, usually on upper two-thirds of leaf, petioles 7–8 mm (9⁄32–5⁄16 in.) long; fruits vivid red 45A, globose, 8–10 mm (5⁄16–⅜ in.) diameter, pedicels 6 mm (7⁄32 in.) long.

'Ashumet' (male; synonym 'Male Ashumet'; W. Wheeler, 1954; discovered in Lowell Woods, Mashpee, Massachusetts).
Leaves dark olive green, oval, 4.5–5.5 cm (1¾–2⅛ in.) long, 3–3.5 cm (1³⁄16–1⅜ in.) wide, keeled, curved, 1–2 spines on upper two-thirds of leaf, margins reflexed, stout petioles 8–10 mm (5⁄16–⅜ in.) long; heavy flowering. Compact ornamental with horizontal branches, cold resistant.

'Aunt Mary' (female; Tingle Nursery, 1954; originated in Pennsylvania).
Good grower with good foliage; heavy fruiting.

'Authur Pride' (male; O. S. Pride 1961; Grace Hybrid Group).
Leaves dark olive green, oval to broadly elliptic, 5.5–7.5 cm (2⅛–3 in.) long, 3–4 cm (1³⁄16–1⅝ in.) wide, bases obtuse to rotund, keeled, curved, margins undulate, 4–5 spines on each side, petioles 8 mm (5⁄16 in.) long; free of leaf spot, persistent to 3 years; heavy flowering; broadly pyramidal tree, rapid grower, very hardy. Suitable for orchard pollinator.

'Autumn Wine' (female; chance seedling selected by T. Klein).
Leaves moderate olive green, oval, 4–4.5 cm (1⅝–1¾ in.) long, 3–3.5 cm (1³⁄16–1⅜ in.) wide, bases truncate, 3–4 spines on each side, usually on upper two-thirds of leaf, petioles dark, stout, 6–8 mm (7⁄32–5⁄16 in.) long; fruits first dark black turning wine color, dark red 59A, ellipsoid, 10 mm (⅜ in.) long.

'Ayr-Way' (female; original tree at St. Matthews, Kentucky; introduced by T. Klein).
Leaves moderate olive green; fruits red, heavy producer.

'B.H.' (female; plant at Breeze Hill Gardens received from J. Gable around 1940).
No description available.

'B. & O.' (female; synonym 'Baltimore & Ohio R.R.'; origin in the wild adjacent to railroad tracks in Jackson, Harford County, Maryland; estimated to be more than 200 years old; known as "The Traveler's Christmas Tree" as it is decorated annually at Christmas; registered H.S.A. 11-70 by W. Pyne).
Leaves olive green, ovate-lanceolate, bases acuminate, tip narrow, curved, keeled, 5 small fine pointed spines on each side; fruits red, slightly ellipsoid to rounded; large tree, pyramidal habit. Plate 149.

'Bailey' (female; Kelsey Nursery 1933; named by H. Hume 1937; original tree at Glen Saint Mary Nursery, Glen Saint Mary, Florida).

Figure 15-33. *Ilex opaca* 'Ayr-Way'. This sole survivor from an old estate, now Ayr-Way shopping center at Westport and Hubbards Lane in St. Matthews, Kentucky, stands in a completely paved parking area on a 60-cm (2-ft.) raised mound. The tree is about 15 m (50 ft.) tall and has a trunk circumference of 16 m (5⅓ ft.) at 1.4 m (4½ ft.). Photo by Theodore R. Klein.

Leaves large, spiny, grayish green; fruit red; densely branched, broadly pyramidal tree. An "unusual male" per Hume.

'Baker' (male; H. Hume 1947).
Leaves oval to elliptic, flat to slightly curved, dull dark olive green above, grayish beneath, slightly reflexed spines usually 2 on each side, petioles small rounded 6–10 mm (⁷⁄₃₂–³⁄₈ in.) long; twigs small slender, gray.

'Baker No. 1' (male; synonym 'Baker No. 2'; selected and named by H. Hume at Glenn Saint Mary Nursery, Glen Saint Mary, Florida, 1947).
Leaves dark olive green, glossy, elliptic to obovate; compact dense tree.

'Barberry' (female; W. Wheeler, 1960).
Leaves dark olive green, broadly elliptic, 5–6.5 cm (2–2⅜ in.) long, 3–3.5 cm (1³⁄₁₆–1⅜ in.) wide, keeled, curved, 3–5 spines on each side, margins twisted, petioles 8 mm (⁵⁄₁₆ in.) long; fruits vivid red 45A, glossy, ellipsoid, 8 mm (⁵⁄₁₆ in.) long.

'Barbosa' (synonym 'Barbarosa'; selected by W. Wheeler in 1960 from plants collected in the wild by P. Barbosa).
Leaves dark olive green, oval to elliptic, 6–7 cm (2⅜–2¾ in.) long, 3–3.5 cm (1³⁄₁₆–1⅜ in.) wide, bases rotund, keeled, curved, convex, 2–3 spines on each side, on upper two-thirds of leaf, petioles 8 mm (⁵⁄₁₆ in.) long; fruits vivid red 45A, globose, 8–10 mm (⁵⁄₁₆–1⅛ in.) diameter, pedicels reddish, 10–15 mm (⅜–¹⁹⁄₃₂ in.) long.

'Barnard Luce' (female; discovered by P. Hill in wild near Barber, Talbot County, Maryland; registered H.S.A. No. 8-77 by Hill).
Leaves moderate olive green, glossy, broadly elliptic, 5–7.5 cm (2–3 in.) long, 3–4.5 cm (1³⁄₁₆–1¾ in.) wide, keeled, curved, 4–5 spines on each side, margins reflexed, slightly wavy, petioles 6–8 mm (⁷⁄₃₂–⁵⁄₁₆ in.) long, fruits vivid red 45A, globose, 8 mm (⁵⁄₁₆ in.) diameter, pedicels 8–10 mm (⁵⁄₁₆–³⁄₈ in.) long.

'Beautiful Ohio' (female; seedling selected in 1933 near Wakefield, Virginia; transplanted to Kent, Ohio; registered H.S.A. 12-69 by M. W. Staples).
Leaves dark olive green, oval to broadly elliptic, 5–5.5 cm (2–2⅛ in.) long, 3–4 cm (1³⁄₁₆–1⅝ in.) wide, keeled, curved, 3–4 spines on each side, margins wavy, petioles stout, 7 mm (⁹⁄₃₂ in.) long; fruits deep reddish orange 43A, globose, 8 mm (⁵⁄₁₆ in.)

diameter, pedicels short, 3–5 mm (⅛–³⁄₁₆ in.) long; hardy in zone 5.

'Betsy' (female; synonym 'Betzy'; selected by T. Windon and E. C. White 1935–1940; named 1947 and introduced by White in 1948).
Leaves dark olive green, elliptic, 4–4.5 cm (1⅝–1¾ in.) long, 2–2.5 cm (¾–1 in.) wide, keeled, curved, 2–3 prominent spines on each side, usually on upper two-thirds of leaf, margins reflexed, petioles 8 mm (⁵⁄₁₆ in.) long; fruits vivid red 45A, globose, 8 mm (⁵⁄₁₆ in.) diameter, pedicels 5–7 mm (³⁄₁₆–⁹⁄₃₂ in.) long, prolific; strong grower.

'Betty Ann' (selected by W. Wheeler before 1963).
Leaves moderate olive green, elliptic, 4.5–5 cm (1⅝–2 in.) long, 2–3 cm (¾–1³⁄₁₆ in.) wide, slightly keeled, curved, 2–4 spines on each side, margins reflexed, twisted, convex, petioles stout 8–10 mm (⁵⁄₁₆–³⁄₈ in.) long; fruits vivid red 45A, subglobose 10 mm (³⁄₈ in.) diameter, pedicels 5 mm (³⁄₁₆ in.) long.

'Betty Hills', see *I. × attenuata* 'Betty Hills'.

'Betty Nevison' (female; discovered in the wild and moved in the 1930s to Look Away Gardens, North Augusta, South Carolina; selected and named by J. D. Rankin, 1968; named for wife of F. Galle).
Leaves dark olive green, broadly elliptic, slightly keeled, curved, 8–10 cm (3⅛–4 in.) long, 5–5.5 cm (2–2⅛ in.) wide, obtuse bases, margins slightly wavy, 4–5 spines on each side; fruits brilliant greenish yellow, globose, 8 mm (⁵⁄₁₆ in.) diameter; slow growing, dwarf type.

'Betty Pride' (female; O. S. Pride 1960?; Grace Hybrid Group).
Leaves moderate olive green, broadly elliptic, keeled, curved, 6.5–7 cm (2⅜–2¾ in.) long, 3.5–4 cm (1⅜–1⅝ in.) wide, 4–5 spines on each side, margins reflexed and wavy; fruits vivid reddish orange 44A, globose, 10 mm (³⁄₈ in.) diameter. Reported very hardy.

'Beulah' (female; synonym 'Boyden No. 3'; selected by W. Wheeler and E. C. White before 1953).
Leaves dark olive green, oval, 5–6 cm (2–2⅜ in.) long, 2.5–3.5 cm (1–1⅜ in.) wide, bases rotund, keeled, curved, margins recurved, 1–3 spines on each side, usually on upper half of leaf, petioles 10 mm (³⁄₈ in.) long; fruits red, globose, 8 mm (⁵⁄₁₆ in.) diameter, pedicels reddish, 8–10 mm (⁵⁄₁₆–³⁄₈ in.) long.

'Beverly Belin' (female; origin in Washington, D.C.; purchased from a North Carolina nursery in the 1930s; introduced by J. D. Rankin).

Leaves dark olive green, broadly elliptic, 4–5 cm (1⅝–2 in.) long, 2.5–3 cm (1–1³⁄₁₆ in.) wide, keeled, curved, 3–5 spines on each side, margins reflexed, wavy, petioles 6–8 mm (⁷⁄₃₂–⁵⁄₁₆ in.) long; fruits vivid yellow 16A, with blush, globose, 6–8 mm (⁷⁄₃₂–⁵⁄₁₆ in.) diameter, pedicels 6 mm (⁷⁄₃₂ in.) long.

'Bickel' (female; selected by T. Klein; origin Cave Hill Cemetery, Louisville, Kentucky).
Leaves moderate olive green, elliptic, 5–7 cm (2–2¾ in.) long, 2.5–3.5 in. (1–1⅜ in.) wide, keeled, curved, usually entire, occasional 1 spine, margins reflexed, petioles 10–12 mm (⅜–½ in.) long; fruits vivid red 45A, ellipsoid, 10 mm (⅜ in.) long, pedicels 6–10 mm (⁷⁄₃₂–⅜ in.) long.

'Big Berry' (female; selected by E. Dilatush before 1953).
Leaves dark olive green, broadly elliptic, 6.5–8.5 cm (2½–3⅜ in.) long, 3.5–4.5 cm (1⅜–1¾ in.) wide, bases rotund or truncate, keeled, curved, 4–5 well-spaced spines on each side, petioles 8–10 mm (⁵⁄₁₆–⅜ in.) long; fruits deep reddish orange 43A, globose, 7–8 mm (⁹⁄₃₂–⁵⁄₁₆ in.) diameter, pedicels dark, 8–10 mm (⁵⁄₁₆–⅜ in.) long.

'Big Daddy' (male; selected by T. Klein).
Leaves dark olive green, oval to broadly elliptic, 5.5–6 cm (2⅛–2⅜ in.) long, 3.5–4.5 cm (1⅜–1¾ in.) wide, keeled, curved, 3–5 spines on each side, margins reflexed, petioles 8–10 mm (⁵⁄₁₆–⅜ in.) long; large spreading habit, fast growing.

'Big Ditch' (female; Tingle Nursery, 1957).
Leaves dark olive green, broadly elliptic, 6.5–7 cm (2⅜–2¾ in.) long, 3.5–4 cm (1⅜–1⅝ in.) wide, 3–4 spines on each side, margins reflexed; fruits vivid red 44A, globose, 10 mm (⅜ in.) diameter, pedicels 8 mm (⁵⁄₁₆ in.) long, heavy annual bearer.

'Big Leaf' (selected by E. Dilatush 1953?).
No description available.

'Big Mack' (female; selected from Frankfort, Kentucky; introduced by T. Klein).
Leaves moderate olive green, broadly oval, 7–8.5 cm (2¾–3⅛ in.) long, 4–4.5 cm (1⅝–1¾ in.) wide, curved, 4–5 spines on each side, margins reflexed, petioles 8–10 mm (⁵⁄₁₆–⅜ in.) long; fruits vivid red 45A, ellipsoid, 10 mm (⅜ in.) long, clustered.

'Big Red' (female; origin in southern New Jersey; selected and introduced by E. Dilatush 1937; registered American Association of Nurserymen No. 511 in 1956).
Leaves dark olive green, broadly elliptic, 7–7.5 cm

(2¾–3 in.) long, 4–4.5 cm (1⅝–1¾ in.) wide, bases obtuse, keeled, curved, 4–5 spines on each side, margins reflexed, petioles 8–10 mm (⁵⁄₁₆–⅜ in.) long; fruits vivid red 45A, globose, 10 mm (⅜ in.) diameter, pedicels 3–5 mm (⅛–³⁄₁₆ in.) long, singly to 2–3 in cluster, abundant.

'Bill Comb' (female; selected by W. C. Frierson, 1947, near Bristol, Virginia, in Green Spring community, at about 545 m (1800 ft.) elevation).
Leaves dark olive green, spiny; fruits red.

'Birdsnest' (selected 1929 on coastal Massachusetts; introduced 1948 by E. Dilatush).
Similar to 'Christmas Hedge'; very few plants produced.

'Bittersweet' (female; selected in Massachusetts by Boyce Thompson Institute in late 1930s).
Leaves moderate olive green, elliptic to oval, 4–5 cm (1⅝–2 in.) long, 3–4 cm (1³⁄₁₆–1⅝ in.) wide, bases obtuse to truncate, keeled, 3–6 spines on each side, margins reflexed, wavy, petioles 8 mm (⁵⁄₁₆ in.) long; fruits vivid reddish orange 41A, turning to red in winter, globose, 8 mm (⁵⁄₁₆ in.) diameter; heavy annual fruiting.

'Bivins' (female; synonym 'Bivinsi'; registered American Association of Nurserymen No. 606 by Perkins de Wilde Nursery).
Leaves dark olive green, oval, 5.5–6.5 cm (2⅛–2½ in.) long, 3–3.5 cm (1³⁄₁₆–1⅜ in.) wide, bases obtuse, curved slightly convex, 2–4 spines usually on upper two-thirds of leaf, petioles 8–10 mm (⁵⁄₁₆–⅜ in.) long; fruits vivid red; pyramidal free branching tree.

'Black Beauty' (male; selected 1929; introduced 1948 by E. Dilatush).
Leaves dark to very dark olive green; dense upright, slow growing habit. Hardy in zone 5.

'Bladen Maiden' (female; selected and named by J. D. Rankin in the 1960s; origin from Oakland estate, overlooking Cape Fear River, Bladen County, North Carolina).
Leaves dark olive green, elliptic, 5–7 cm (2–2¾ in.) long, 3–3.5 cm (1³⁄₁₆–1⅜ in.) wide, keeled, curved, 2–3 spines on upper two-thirds of leaf, some entire, petioles 10–15 mm (⅜–⁹⁄₁₆ in.) long; fruits vivid orange yellow 21A, ellipsoid, 11 mm (⁷⁄₁₆ in.) long, persisting 2 years, pedicels 5 mm (³⁄₁₆ in.) long.

'Blanche Morgan' (female; chance seedling in soil from R. D. Bailey Dam moved to G. Morgan's property near Hanover, West Virginia; selected and named by Morgan for his mother).

Leaves moderate olive green, oval, 5–7 cm (2–2¾ in.) long, 3–4 cm (1³⁄₁₆–1⅝ in.) wide, bases obtuse to truncate, keeled, curved, 4–6 prominent spines on each side, margins reflexed, slightly wavy, petioles 8–10 mm (⁵⁄₁₆–⅜ in.) long; fruits light orange, globose, 6–8 mm (⁷⁄₃₂–⁵⁄₁₆ in.) diameter.

'Boggs' (origin Westminster, South Carolina, at 272 m (900 ft.) elevation; selected by W. C. Frierson 1947).
    Leaves dark olive green; fruits red, regular bearer.

'Bountiful' (female; synonym 'Beverly'; original tree at Beverly, New Jersey; selected by E. Dilatush 1942).
    Leaves moderate olive green, broadly elliptic, 6.5–8.5 cm (2½–3⅜ in.) long, 3.5–5 cm (1⅜–2 in.) wide, bases obtuse, curved, margins wavy, 5–8 spines on each side, petioles slender 5–8 mm (³⁄₁₆–⁵⁄₁₆ in.) long; fruits vivid red 45A, single ellipsoid, 7–8 mm (⁹⁄₃₂–⁵⁄₁₆ in.), pedicels short 3–5 mm (⅛–³⁄₁₆ in.) long; compact symmetrical cone-shaped tree with graceful pendulous branches; heavy, annual fruiting.

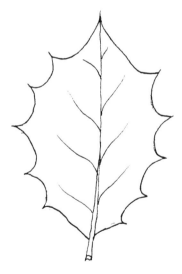

Figure 15-34. *Ilex opaca* 'Bountiful'. Drawing by Randy Allen.

'Bountiful Compacta No. 1' (name not valid).
    No description available.

'Bountiful Compacta No. 2' (name not valid).
    No description available.

'Bountiful Improved' (female; selected in New Jersey and introduced by E. Dilatush 1948).
    Leaves dark olive green, spiny; fruits red; heavy

fruiting; 10-year-old plants less attractive in fruit than 'Bountiful'.

Boyce Thompson Group
    Numerous hollies planted on the grounds of the Boyce Thompson Institute. Collected by B. W. Zimmerman and others. Plants named and introduced by the Institute's staff and others. All the Boyce Thompson numbers and names are badly confused in the literature as well as in the trade.

'Boyce Thompson No. 3' (female).
    No description available.

'Boyce Thompson No. 4' (female; origin Boyce Thompson Institute).
    Leaves dark olive green, oval, 4–5.5 cm (1⅝–2⅛ in.) long, 2.5–3.5 cm (1–1⅜ in.) wide, keeled, curved, 3–4 spines on each side, margins reflexed, petioles 6–8 mm (⁷⁄₃₂–⁵⁄₁₆ in.) long; fruits deep reddish orange 43A, ellipsoid, 10–12 mm (⅜–¹⁵⁄₃₂ in.) long, pedicels 5 mm (³⁄₁₆ in.) long.

'Boyce Thompson Selection' (female; synonyms 'Boyce Thompson', 'Boyce Thompson No. 1'; selected before 1952; introduced by E. Dilatush and E. H. Diehl; reported as one of the best Boyce Thompson selections).
    Leaves dark olive green, elliptic, 6–8.5 cm (2⅜–3⅜ in.) long, 2.5–3.5 cm (1–1⅜ in.) wide, keeled, curved, bases obtuse, apices acute, margins slightly wavy, 4–5 spines on each side, petioles dark, 5–7 mm (³⁄₁₆–⁹⁄₃₂ in.) long; fruits vivid red, globose, 6–8 mm (⁷⁄₃₂–⁵⁄₁₆ in.) diameter, pedicels dark, 6–8 mm (⁷⁄₃₂–⁵⁄₁₆ in.) long, early bearing; plant habit somewhat compact.

'Boyce Thompson Xanthocarpa' (female; synonym 'Boyce Thompson X.C.'; introduced by B. W. Zimmerman in late 1920s; reported as collected from Mount Vernon, Virginia).
    Leaves dark olive green, broadly elliptic, 6–7 cm (2⅜–3 in.) long, 3–3.5 cm (1³⁄₁₆–1⅜ in.) wide, keeled curved, 3–5 spines usually on upper two-thirds of leaf, margins reflexed, petioles 8 mm (⁵⁄₁₆ in.) long; fruits vivid yellow 15A, globose, 8 mm (⁵⁄₁₆ in.) diameter, conspicuous black spot, pedicels 6 mm (⁷⁄₃₂ in.) long; shapely plant.

Boyden Group
    A group of hollies selected by W. Wheeler and E. C. White. Introduced as numbered cultivars, later renamed:
    Boyden No. 1 = 'Zoe'
    Boyden No. 2 = 'Vera'
    Boyden No. 3 = 'Beulah'

Boyden No. 4
Boyden No. 6 = 'Perpetual'

'Bradshaw' (female; introduced by H. Hohman about 1935; reportedly a seedling of 'Delia Bradley').
Leaves moderate olive green, broadly oval, curved, 8–8.5 cm (3–3⅜ in.) long, 4.5–5 cm (1⅝–2 in.) wide, 5–7 spines on each side, margins slightly reflexed; petioles dark, 7–8 mm (⁹⁄₃₂–⁵⁄₁₆ in.) long; fruits red.

'Brigham Young' (male; origin at Setauket, Long Island, New York; selected by P. Vossberg about 1945).
No description available.

'Brilliance' (female; origin at Hillenmeyer Nursery in the 1950s).
Leaves dark olive green, glossy, broadly elliptic, curved, 7.5–8.5 cm (3–3⅜ in.) long, 3.5–4.5 cm (1⅜–1¾ in.) wide, 5–6 spines on each side, bases obtuse, margins reflexed and wavy, petioles 8–10 mm (⁵⁄₁₆–⅜ in.) long; fruits large vivid red.

'Brilliantissima', see 'George E. Hart'.

'Brooks' (female; selected by M. Brooks 1942).
Conflicting descriptions. According to F. L. S. O'Rourke: leaves large leathery, blunt end; fruits large, nearly 11 mm (⁷⁄₁₆ in.) diameter; coarse plant habit. Discovered in the wild on Irvin Farm near French Creek, Upshur County, West Virginia, at 515 m (1700 ft.) elevation.

Brown Group
A series of 32 numbered selections from the wild made around 1945 by the Holly Research Committee of Rutgers University at Holly Hill, on the estate of the late Judge Thomas Brown, Locust, New Jersey. Not all the plants have been published or otherwise designated. The best known is 'Jersey Knight' (synonym 'Brown #9'); best female selection is 'Brown #7'.

'Brown #5' (female).
Leaves dark olive green, oval elliptic, 6.5–8 cm (2⅜–3⅛ in.) long, 3.5–4 cm (1⅜–1⅝ in.) wide, bases cuneate to obtuse, keeled, curved, margins recurved, slightly wavy, 3–4 spines, usually on upper two-thirds of leaf, petioles 8 mm (⁵⁄₁₆ in.) long; fruits red, globose, 8 mm (⁵⁄₁₆ in.) diameter, pedicels 8–10 mm (⁵⁄₁₆–⅜ in.) long; borne in clusters.

'Brown #7', see 'Judge Brown'.

'Brown #9', see 'Jersey Knight'.

'Cain' (female; discovered by F. Cain near Westminster, South Carolina, at 272 m (900 ft.) elevation; introduced 1947 by W. C. Frierson).
Leaves small to medium, very dark olive green, elliptic, cuneate, curved, widely separated spines; fruits small, globose, vivid red, annually in great abundance.

'Callaway' (female; discovered by W. A. Roach in open pasture near Calhoun, Louisiana; registered H.S.A. 9-62 by S. Solymosy).
Leaves medium glossy; fruits yellow.

'Callaway Red' (female; cutting from Callaway Gardens; not named by Callaway Gardens; possibly distributed by J. D. Rankin).
Leaves moderate olive green, elliptic, 5–6 cm (2–2⅜ in.) long, 2–2.5 cm (¾–1 in.) wide, keeled, curved, 2–4 spines on each side, margins reflexed, wavy, petioles 8 mm (⁵⁄₁₆ in.) long; fruits vivid red 45A, globose, 8 mm (⁵⁄₁₆ in.) diameter, pedicels 3–5 mm (⅛–³⁄₁₆ in.) long.

'Camelot' (male; named by O. S. Pride, 1965; Grace Hybrid Group).
Leaves moderate olive green, broadly oval, slightly keeled, curved, 6–8 cm (2⅜–3⅛ in.) long, 3.5–4 cm (1⅜–1⅝ in.) wide, 4–5 spines on each side, reflexed; petioles stout, 6 mm (⁷⁄₃₂ in.) long.

'Canary' (female; introduced 1938–1939 from western North Carolina registered American Association of Nurserymen No. 512, 1956, by E. Dilatush).
Leaves dark olive green, keeled, curved, bases obtuse, 7–7.5 cm (2¾–3 in.) long, 3.5–4 cm (1⅜–1¾ in.) wide, 5–6 small spines on each side, margins reflexed, slightly wavy; fruits vivid orange yellow 17A, ellipsoid, 9 mm (¹¹⁄₃₂ in.) long, 7 mm (¼ in.) wide, abundant, 1–3 on short pedicels and peduncles. Plate 150.

'Cape Cod Dwarf' (female; synonym 'Cape Cod'; E. Dilatush 1941; found on Cape Cod, Massachusetts; original tree destroyed by storm).
Leaves moderate olive green, elliptic to oval, slightly keeled, curved, 5.5–7 cm (2⅛–2¾ in.) long, 3–4 cm (1³⁄₁₆–1⅝ in.) wide, 6–9 small evenly spaced spines on each side, margins reflexed, petioles stout

5–6 mm (³⁄₁₆–⁷⁄₃₂ in.) long; fruits deep red, globose, single, 10 mm (³⁄₈ in.) diameter, pedicels 9–10 mm (³⁄₈ in.) long; low growing, spreading habit.

'Cape Cod Dwarf Improved' (female; synonym 'Cape Cod Improved'; selected about 1932 at Boyce Thompson Institute; introduced 1937 by E. Dilatush).

Leaves moderate olive green; fruits large red, "the size being the result of a double ovary, which occurs in the manner of double-yolked eggs"; fruit size inconsistent, with the majority large in some years but a scattering of normal and small fruit; vigorous growing, bushy habit.

Cape Cod Group
Six selections made by Cornelius Van Tol Nursery. Apparently none are described or named; Cape Cod No. 1, No. 2, No. 3, No. 4, No. 5, No. 6 are doubtful names. Not to be confused with 'Cape Cod Dwarf' and Cape Cod Dwarf Improved'.

'Cape Queen' (female; Tingle Nursery, 1958).
Leaves dark olive green, elliptic, 6–7.5 cm (2³⁄₈–3 in.) long, 2.8–3.5 cm (1¹⁄₈–1³⁄₈ in.) wide, keeled, curved, bases obtuse to rotund, margins recurved, wavy, 2–4 spines on each side, tip spines reflexed, petioles 12–15 mm (¹⁵⁄₃₂–¹⁹⁄₃₂ in.) long; fruits vivid red 45A, globose, 8–12 mm (⁵⁄₁₆–¹⁵⁄₃₂ in.) diameter, pedicels reddish, 8–10 mm (⁵⁄₁₆–³⁄₈ in.) long.

'Cardinal' (female; selected in Massachusetts by E. Dilatush before 1942).
Leaves dark olive green, elliptic, keeled, curved, 7–8 cm (2³⁄₄–3¹⁄₈ in.) long, 3.5–4 cm (1³⁄₈–1⁵⁄₈ in.) wide, 5–6 spines on each side, margins reflexed, slightly wavy, petioles 7–8 mm (¼ in.) long; fruits light red, borne singly, globose, 8–9 mm (⁵⁄₁₆ in.) diameter; compact, slow habit of growth; early, heavy fruiting.

'Cardinal Compact' (female; selected 1929 in New Jersey; introduced 1949 by E. Dilatush).
More compact habit than 'Cardinal', but both clones lack outstanding features.

'Cardinal Hedge' (female; synonym 'Cardinal Improved'; selected about 1932 at Boyce Thompson Institute; introduced 1948 by E. Dilatush).
Leaves moderate olive green, elliptic, slightly keeled, curved, 5–6 cm (2–2³⁄₈ in.) long, 3–3.5 cm (1³⁄₁₆–1³⁄₈ in.) wide, 4–6 spines on each side, margins reflexed, slightly wavy, petioles stout, 5 mm (³⁄₁₆ in.) long; fruits vivid red 45A, globose, 8–9 mm (⁵⁄₁₆–¹¹⁄₃₂ in.) diameter, pedicels 4 mm (⁵⁄₃₂ in.) long; slow growing, nearly as wide as tall.

'Cardinal Supreme' (female; selected 1929 in New Jersey; introduced 1948 by E. Dilatush).
Leaves dark olive green, broadly oval, 6–8.5 cm (2³⁄₈–3¹⁄₈ in.) long, 3–4 cm (1³⁄₁₆–1⁵⁄₈ in.) wide, bases rotund to truncate, keeled, curved, 5–6 spines on each side, petioles 8–10 mm (⁵⁄₁₆–³⁄₈ in.) long; fruits vivid red 45A, globose, 8 mm (³⁄₈ in.) diameter, pedicels 10–12 mm (³⁄₈–¹⁵⁄₃₂ in.) long. Parent plant attractive, but clone reported by T. Dilatush as growing too fast with a stretched appearance.

'Carnival' (female; introduced 1962 by O. S. Pride; Grace Hybrid Group).
Leaves moderate olive green, broadly elliptic, keeled, curved, 6.5–7 cm (2½–2¾ in.) long, 3.5–4 cm (1³⁄₈–1⁵⁄₈ in.) wide, usually 5 spines on each side, margins reflexed, petioles stout, 5 mm (³⁄₁₆ in.) long; fruits vivid red 44A, globose, 8 mm (⁵⁄₁₆ in.) diameter, abundant, holds well through winter; broadly dense pyramidal habit, fast growing; very hardy to −34°C (−30°F), easily propagated.

'Carol' (female; synonym 'Carol Wheeler'; selected by W. Wheeler at Ashumet Farm, Falmouth, Massachusetts, before 1947).
Leaves dark olive green, broadly elliptic, 4.5–6 cm (1¾–2³⁄₈ in.) long, 2.5–3 cm (1–1³⁄₁₆ in.) wide, glossy, bases obtuse, keeled, curved, 3–4 spines usually on upper two-thirds of leaf, petioles 8–10 mm (⁵⁄₁₅–³⁄₈ in.) long; fruits strong red 45C, globose, 9 mm (¹¹⁄₃₂ in.) diameter, pedicels reddish, 8 mm (⁵⁄₁₆ in.) long

'Carolina' (female; synonym 'Carolina Large Leaf'; Clarendon Gardens, selected before 1955; parent tree at Carolina Hotel, Pinehurst, North Carolina).
Leaves dark olive green, slightly glossy, broadly elliptic, 6–9.5 cm (2³⁄₈–3½ in.) long, 3–4.5 cm (1³⁄₁₆–1¾ in.) wide, 5–6, usually 3–5, prominent spines on each side, margins reflexed, slightly wavy, petioles stout 6–8 mm (⁷⁄₃₂–⁵⁄₁₆ in.) long; fruits vivid red 45A, globose, 8 mm (⁵⁄₁₆ in.) diameter, pedicels 4–8 mm (⁵⁄₃₂–⁵⁄₁₆ in.) long.

'Carolina No. 2' (female; seedling selected in the 1940s by F. J. Aichele).
Leaves dark olive green, oval, 4.5–5 cm (1¾–2 in.) long, 2.5–3.5 cm (1–1³⁄₈ in.) wide, slightly keeled, curved, 1–3 spines on upper half of leaf, petioles 6 mm (⁷⁄₃₂ in.) long; fruits vivid red 44A, globose to oval, 8–9 mm (⁵⁄₁₆–¹¹⁄₃₂ in.) diameter, reddish pedicels 5 mm (³⁄₁₆ in.) long.

'Caroline Pearson' (female; plant at Bernheim Forest from H. Hohman).
Leaves moderate olive green, elliptic, 4–5.5 cm

(1⅝–2⅛ in.) long, 2–3.5 cm (¾–1⅜ in.) wide, keeled, curved, 3–5 spines on each side, petioles stout, 5 mm (³⁄₁₆ in.) long; fruits vivid red, ellipsoid, 8 mm (⁵⁄₁₆ in.) long.

'Carrie' (female; named and introduced by J. D. Rankin about 1958; discovered in the wild near Flat Creek Primitive Church, eastern Rowan County, North Carolina; named for wife of Ben Brown).
    Leaves dark olive green, elliptic to broadly elliptic, 6.5–9 cm (2½–3½ in.) long, 3–4 cm (1³⁄₁₆–1⅝ in.) wide, bases obtuse to rotund, keeled, curved, margins recurved, 3–6 spines on each side, petioles 6–8 mm (⁷⁄₃₂–⁵⁄₁₆ in.) long; fruits light yellow 12B, ellipsoid, 8 mm (⁵⁄₁₆ in.) long, 6 mm (⁷⁄₃₂ in.) diameter, pedicels reddish, 6–8 mm (⁷⁄₃₂–⁵⁄₁₆ in.) long.

'Cascade Inn' (female; plant at F. Ebersole garden).
    Leaves dark olive green, broadly oval to ovate, 4.5–7 cm (1¾–2¾ in.) long, 3–4.5 cm (1³⁄₁₆–1¾ in.) wide, keeled, curved, bases cuneate, margins recurved, 3–4 widely spaced spines on each side, petioles 8–10 mm (⁵⁄₁₆–⅜ in.) long; fruits red, ellipsoid, 10 mm (⅜ in.) long, 8 mm (⁵⁄₁₆ in.) diameter, pedicels 3–4 mm (⅛–⁵⁄₃₂ in.) long.

Cave Hill Group
    Three numbered plants originating at the Cave Hill Cemetery, Louisville, Kentucky: 'Cave Hill No. 1', 'Cave Hill No. 2', and 'Cave Hill No. 3'. Selected and introduced before 1940 by T. Klein.

'Cave Hill No. 1' (female; selected by T. Klein before 1940).
    Leaves dark olive green, oval, keeled, curved, bases obtuse, 5.5–6 cm (2⅛–2⅜ in.) long, 3.5–4 cm (1⅜–1⅝ in.) wide, 4–5 spines on each side, margins reflexed, petioles 8 to 10 mm (⁵⁄₁₆–⅜ in.) long; fruits vivid reddish orange 41A, globose, 8 mm (⁵⁄₁₆ in.) diameter.

'Cave Hill No. 2' (female; selected by T. Klein).
    Leaves moderate olive green, elliptic, 5–5.5 cm (2–2⅛ in.) long, 2–2.5 cm (¾–1 in.) wide, curved, convex, 2–3 spines on each side, petioles 8–10 mm (⁵⁄₁₆–⅜ in.) long; fruits red.

'Cave Hill No. 3' (female; introduced by T. Klein).
    Leaves dark olive green, oval, 5–6 cm (2–2⅜ in.) long, 3.5 cm (1⅜ in.) wide, keeled, curved, 3–5 spines on each side, margins wavy, petioles 7 mm (⁹⁄₃₂ in.) long; fruits red.

'Cecil' (female; original tree near Carthage, Texas; introduced by J. D. Rankin; named for wife of James S. Wells).

Leaves moderate olive green, broadly oval, 7–8 cm (2¾–3⅛ in.) long, 3.5–5 cm (1⅜–2 in.) wide, subentire to 1–3 spines on each side, upper half, petioles 8–10 mm (⁵⁄₁₆–⅜ in.) long; fruits brilliant orange-yellow 21B, ellipsoid, 10–12 mm (⅜–¹⁵⁄₃₂ in.) long.

'Charles' (male; synonym 'Ashumet No. 2'; selected and named by W. Wheeler before 1952).
    Leaves dark olive green, elliptic, 5–7 cm (2–2¾ in.) long, 2.5–3.5 cm (1–1⅜ in.) wide, slightly keeled, petioles dark, 5 mm (³⁄₁₆ in.) long. A good male with heavy branches and colorful dark foliage. Not to be confused with Pride selection invalidly referred to as 'Charles Pride'.

'Cheerful' (female; named and introduced by H. Hohman about 1928).
    Leaves dark olive green, slightly keeled, curved, 5–5.5 cm (2–2¼ in.) long, 3–4 cm (1³⁄₁₆–1⅝ in.) wide, 4–5 large spines on each side, margins wavy, petioles 7–8 mm (¼–⁵⁄₁₆ in.) long; fruits vivid red 44A, globose, 8 mm (⁵⁄₁₆ in.) diameter, borne singly, abundant.

'Cheerful No. 3' (selected by H. Hohman).
    Very similar to 'Cheerful'.

'Chesapeake' (female; plant at Dawes Arboretum, Newark, Ohio).
    Leaves moderate olive green, elliptic, 5–6 cm (2–2⅜ in.) long, 2–3 cm (¾–1³⁄₁₆ in.) wide, keeled, curved, 2–4 spines usually on upper two-thirds of leaf; fruits vivid red 45A, globose, 8 mm (⁵⁄₁₆ in.) diameter, petioles 6 mm (⁷⁄₃₂ in.) long.

'Chief Paduke' (female; original plant in cemetery in Paducah, Kentucky; selected in 1959; introduced and registered H.S.A. 2-63 by B. Hartline).
    Leaves dark olive green, broadly elliptic, 7–8.8 cm (2¾–3⅜ in.) long, 3–4 cm (1³⁄₁₆–1⅝ in.) wide, keeled, curved 1–3 spines on each side, on upper two-thirds of leaf, petioles 14–18 mm (¹⁷⁄₃₂–¹¹⁄₁₆ in.) long; fruits vivid reddish orange 44C, ellipsoid, 10–12 mm (⅜–¹⁵⁄₃₂ in.) long.

'Christmas Beauty' (female; chance seedling; introduced and registered H.S.A. 5-74 by R. V. Hearn, Tingle Nursery).
    Leaves dark olive green, broadly elliptic, 6–8 cm (2⅜–3⅛ in.) long, 3–4 cm (1³⁄₁₆–1⅝ in.) wide, keeled, curved, 4–6 prominent spines on each side, margins wavy, petioles 11 mm (⁷⁄₁₆ in.) long; fruits vivid red 44A, globose, 8 mm (⁵⁄₁₆ in.) diameter.

'Christmas Bouquet' (female; selected 1929 in New Jersey; introduced 1947 by E. Dilatush).

Leaves moderate olive green, broadly elliptic, curved, bases obtuse, 6.5–7 cm (2½–2¾ in.) long, 3–3.5 cm (1³⁄₁₆–1⅜ in.) wide, 2–4 spines each side, upper two-thirds of leaf, margins reflexed, petioles 8–10 mm (⁵⁄₁₆–⅜ in.) long; fruits vivid red 44A, globose, 8 mm (⁵⁄₁₆ in.) diameter, pedicels 5 mm (³⁄₁₆ in.) long; rapid informal growth.

'Christmas Carol' (female; selected seedling from Massachusetts; named by P. Bosley in 1953; listed as 'Pride of New England' by E. Dilatush).

Leaves dark olive green, elliptic, 4.5–7 cm (1¾–2¾ in.) long, 2.5–3 cm (1–1³⁄₁₆ in.) wide, bases cuneate to obtuse, keeled, curved, margins recurved, wavy, 5–6 spines on each side, petioles 8–10 mm (⁵⁄₁₆–⅜ in.) long; fruits deep reddish orange 43A, ellipsoid, 10 mm (⅜ in.) long, 8 mm (⁵⁄₁₆ in.) wide, often in clusters, pedicels 8–10 mm (⁵⁄₁₆–⅜ in.) long; compact, pyramidal at early age.

'Christmas Hedge' (female; origin Boyce Thompson Institute; selected and named by E. Dilatush, 1950).

Leaves dark olive green, elliptic, 7.5 cm (3 in.) long, 5.5 cm (2⅛ in.) wide, keeled, curved, slightly bullate, 5 spines on each side; fruits red, ellipsoid, erratic fruiting; low compact spreading habit.

'Christmas Snow' (female; synonym 'Silver Crown Improved'; variegated sport found about 1983 by L. Steward in his nursery; named and introduced by Steward).

Leaves variegated, elliptic to broadly elliptic, 5–7 cm (2–2¾ in.) long, 3–3.5 cm (1³⁄₁₆–1⅜ in.) wide, distinct yellow 5A, margin, 5–6 spines on each side, small tip leaves blotched and mottled grayish green. keeled, curved; fruits red, globose, 8 mm (⁵⁄₁₆ in.) diameter; upright pyramidal habit; hardy in zone 5. Attractive accent plant. Plate 151.

'Christmas Spray' (female; selected by E. Dilatush, before 1952).

Leaves moderate to dark green, elliptic, keeled, curved, spines prominent, petioles purplish; fruits red, globose-ellipsoid, heavy fruiting; rapid growth, awkward and leggy when small. Good for orcharding.

'Christmas Tide' (female; introduced by Hess Nursery 1954).

Leaves moderate olive green, broadly elliptic 4–5 cm (1⅝–2 in.) long, 2–3 cm (¾–1³⁄₁₆ in.) wide, keeled, curved, 4–5 spines on each side, petioles short, 5 mm (³⁄₁₆ in.) long, margins reflexed, slightly wavy; fruits vivid red 45A, ellipsoid, 10 mm (⅜ in.) long, pedicels 8 mm (⁵⁄₁₆ in.) long.

'Christmas Tree' (female; seedling selected by W. Flemer III; seed source from coastal Massachusetts; introduced by Princeton Nursery).

Leaves dark olive green, oblong elliptic, keeled, curved, 4–6 cm (1⅝–2⅜ in.) long, 2–3 cm (¾–1³⁄₁₆ in.) wide, bases obtuse to rotund, apices acute, margins slightly wavy, 4–6 spines on each side, on upper two-thirds of leaf, petioles 7 mm (⁹⁄₃₂ in.) long; fruits vivid red 44A, globose to slightly ovoid, 10 mm (⅜ in.) long, 8 mm (⁵⁄₁₆ in.) diameter, single, occasionally 3 in cluster, pedicels reddish, 8–10 mm (⁵⁄₁₆–⅜ in.) long; very dense compact, pyramidal habit, forms good central leader without staking; hardy in zone 5.

'Clarendon Large Leaf' (synonym 'Large Leaf'; origin Clarendon Gardens, where parent plant is; introduced before 1957).

Leaves large, heavily spined.

'Clarendon Spreading' (female; parent plant at Clarendon Gardens; introduced before 1957; registered H.S.A. 1-93 by P. Joseph).

Leaves moderate olive green, oval, slightly curved, 6.5–8 cm (2⅜–3⅜ in.) long, 4–5 cm (1⅝–2 in.) wide, 4–5 spines on each side, petioles 8–10 mm (⁵⁄₁₆–⅜ in.) long; fruits vivid reddish orange 33A, ellipsoid, 9 mm (¹¹⁄₃₂ in.) long, pedicels 8–10 mm (⁵⁄₁₆–⅜ in.) long, sparse fruiting; dense spreading habit, often 2.5–3.7 m (8–12 ft.) wide or larger. Plate 152.

'Clarissa' (female; named and introduced by O. S. Pride; registered H.S.A 6-67; origin from seed collected in Buckhannon, West Virginia).

Leaves moderate olive green, broadly elliptic, 6–8 cm (2⅜–3⅛ in.) long, 3–4 cm (1³⁄₁₆–1⅝ in.) wide, keeled, curved 2–5 prominent spines on each side, usually upper two-thirds of leaf, petioles 10 cm (⅜ in.) long; fruits deep reddish orange 43A, ellipsoid, 10 mm (⅜ in.) long; extremely hardy.

'Clark' (female; synonym 'White Hedge'; selected by J. J. White, around 1930; introduced by E. C. White).

Leaves dark olive green, slightly glossy, broadly oval, 7–8.5 cm (2¾–3⅜ in.) long, 4.5–5 cm (1¾–2 in.) wide, bases obtuse, 2–6 spines on each side, often on upper half of leaf, margins reflexed, slightly wavy, petioles 7–8 mm (⁹⁄₃₂–⁵⁄₁₆ in.) long; fruits vivid red, globose, 7 mm (⁹⁄₃₂ in.) diameter, pedicels long, 10–12 mm (⅜–¹⁵⁄₃₂ in.) long; compact habit with ascending branchlets.

'Clatworthy' (female; synonym 'Clatsworthy'; origin tree on property of Mrs. M. Clatworthy, Houghston, West Virginia; selected by W. Hallenberg and T. Klein).

Leaves moderate olive green, oval to broadly elliptic, 4.5–5.5 cm (1¾–2⅛ in.) long, 2.5–3.5 cm (1–1⅜ in.) wide, bases obtuse to rounded, keeled, curved, 1–2 sparse spines usually on upper one-third of leaf, margins reflexed, petioles 6–8 mm (7/32–5/16 in.) long; fruits vivid yellow 15B, some with slight blush, globose, 8 mm (5/16 in.) diameter, pedicels 3–5 mm (⅛–3/16 in.) long.

'Clemson' (female; synonym 'Clemson College'; origin about 15 miles from Clemson, South Carolina; introduced by F. Galle).

Leaves moderate olive green, elliptic, 6–7.5 cm (2⅜–3 in.) long, 2.5–3.5 cm (1–1⅜ in.) wide, keeled, curved, 1–5 spines on each side, margins reflexed, slightly wavy, petioles 8–10 mm (5/16–⅜ in.) long; fruits vivid yellow 15A, ellipsoid, 8–10 mm (5/16–⅜ in.) long, pedicels 6 mm (7/32 in.) long.

'Clifton' (female; selected 1965 by G. Clifton; origin Boyce Thompson Institute; plant at Planting Fields Arboretum).

Leaves moderate olive green, elliptic, 5.5–6.5 cm (2⅛–2⅜ in.) long, 3–3.5 cm (1 3/16–1⅜ in.) wide, bases cuneate to obtuse, keeled, curved, 3–4 spines on upper two-thirds of leaf, petioles 8 mm (5/16 in.) long; fruits vivid red 45A, globose, 8 mm (5/16 in.) diameter, pedicels 8–10 mm (5/16–⅜ in.) long.

'Cobalt' (male; selected by O. S. Pride 1948–1952; origin seed collected 1928 near Buckhannon, West Virginia).

Leaves dark olive green, slightly shiny; very hardy, survived −36°C (−32°F).

'Columbia' (female; collected seedling planted around 1936–1938 at Veterans Administration grounds, Columbia, South Carolina; cutting-grown plant by G. Wood for University of Alabama, Tanglewood Arboretum, Hale County, Alabama; named by Wood).

Leaves dark olive green, glossy, elliptic, 4.5–6 cm (1¾–2⅜ in.) long, 2–3 cm (¾–1 3/16 in.) wide, keeled, curved, bases acute, apices acuminate, tip spines reflexed, 1–3 spines on each side, often on upper half of leaf, petioles 8–10 mm (5/16–⅜ in.) long; fruits vivid red 45B, globose, 8 mm (5/16 in.) diameter, abundant, pedicels 5 mm (3/16 in.) long; columnar habit.

'Cornett' (female; origin tree on cliff near Cornettsville, Kentucky; found and introduced by T. Klein).

Leaves dark olive green, broadly elliptic, 5–5.5 cm

(2–2⅛ in.) long, 2.5–3.5 cm (1–1⅜ in.) wide, keeled, curved, 4–7 prominent spines on each side, margins wavy, petioles 8 mm (5/16 in.) long; fruits vivid yellow 15A, globose, 6–8 mm (7/32–5/16 in.) diameter; compact upright habit. Said to be only yellow-berried holly found in the wild in Kentucky.

Corpening Hollies

A group of three trees with yellow fruits. Found on Corpening property in western Caldwell County, North Carolina. Named and introduced as numbered plants: 'Corpening No. 1', 'Corpening No. 2', 'Corpening No. 3'.

'Corpening No. 1' (female; introduced by J. D. Rankin).

Leaves moderate olive green, elliptic, 4.5–6 mm (1⅗–2⅜ in.) long, 2–3 cm (¾–1 3/16 in.) wide, keeled, curved, 1–4 small spines on each side, many leaves entire, margins reflexed, twisted, petioles 8–10 mm (5/16–⅜ in.) long; fruits vivid yellow 15A, ellipsoid, 8–10 mm (5/16–⅜ in.) long, pedicels 6 mm (7/32 in.) long.

'Corpening No. 2' (female: introduced by J. D. Rankin).

Leaves moderate olive green, broadly elliptic, keeled, curved, 3–4 spines on each side, margins reflexed, wavy, petioles 8–10 mm (5/16–⅜ in.) long; fruits vivid yellow 15A, globose, 8 mm (5/16 in.) diameter, pedicels 3–5 mm (⅛–3/16 in.) long.

'Corpening No. 3' (female; introduced by J. D. Rankin).

Leaves moderate olive green, broadly elliptic, 5–6.5 cm (2–2½ in.) long, 3.5–4 cm (1⅜–1⅝ in.) wide, keeled, curved, 4–5 spines on each side, petioles 8–10 mm (5/16–⅜ in.) long; fruits brilliant orange yellow 21B, ellipsoid, 8–10 mm (5/16–⅜ in.) long.

'Crinkleleaf' (male; selected about 1932 at Boyce Thompson Institute; introduced 1948 by E. Dilatush).

Leaf margins unusually undulated. A novelty; very few propagated.

'Croonenberg' (female; original tree discovered and selected by W. Bennett and C. L. Sorg on the garden estate of Arislides Croonenberg, Lynnhaven Bay, near Norfolk, Virginia, then transplanted to Greenbriar Farms; plant reported to have been brought in from Europe, but Croonenberg family reported plant to be a hybrid between American and English holly; introduced by S. H. Thrasher in 1934).

Leaves dark olive green, slightly glossy, broadly

elliptic, 7–8.5 cm (2¾–3⅝ in.) long, 4.5–5 cm (1¾–5 in.) wide, bases truncate, 5–6 spines on each side, margins slightly wavy, petioles 7–8 mm (9/32–5/16 in.) long; fruits vivid red 45A, globose to ellipsoid, 10–12 mm (⅜–15/32 in.) long, borne singly; compact pyramidal tree, often does not fill out well as young plant, produces fruit profusely; reported to produce both female and male flowers at ratio of 10:1.

'Cullowhee' (female; origin east of Western North Carolina University in Macon County, North Carolina, and moved to the campus near the Science Building; named by D. Pittillo).

Leaves moderate olive green, oval, 4–7.5 cm (1⅝–2¾ in.) long, 3–5.7 cm (1 5/16–2¼ in.) wide, keeled, curved, 1–4 spines on each side, usually upper half of leaf, margins reflexed and slightly wavy; fruits vivid red 45A, broadly ellipsoid, 8–10 mm (5/16–⅜ in.) long, 6–7 mm (7/32–9/32 in.) wide. Reported to fruit abundantly with no male plant near. Plate 153.

'Cumberland' (female; selected and named in 1949 by C. R. Wolf; registered H.S.A. 7-74 by D. G. Fenton).

Leaves dark olive green, glossy, elliptic to oval, 5–6 cm (2–2⅜ in.) long, 2.5–4 cm (1–1⅝ in.) wide, bases usually truncate, keeled, curved, 4–6 small spines on each side, occasionally only 1–2 spines on upper one-third of leaf, short petioles 5 mm (3/16 in.) long; fruits vivid red 45A, globose or slightly ellipsoid, 10 mm (⅜ in.) diameter, pedicels 5 mm (3/16 in.) long, singly. Considered one of the glossiest-leaved American holly cultivars.

'Cup Leaf' (female; synonyms 'Cupleaf', 'Dilatush Cup Leaf', 'Merry Christmas Convex'; selected 1929; introduced 1947 by E. Dilatush).

Leaves dark olive green, oval, 6.5–7 cm (2½–2¾ in.) long, 3.5–4 cm (1⅜–1⅝ in.) wide, convex, curved, bases truncate, 3–4 spines on each side, margins reflexed, petioles 8–10 mm (5/16–⅜ in.) long; fruits vivid red 45A, globose, 8 mm (5/16 in.) diameter, borne singly on dark pedicels, 6–8 mm (7/32–5/16 in.) long.

'Dan Fenton' (female; controlled cross by E. R. Orton Jr. of 'Maurice River' × unnamed male; original tree at Rutgers University; selected and registered H.S.A. 6-87 by Orton; released at 40th anniversary H.S.A. meeting in honor of Dan G. Fenton).

Leaves dark olive green, glossy, ovate to broadly elliptic, 5–8.2 cm (2–3¼ in.) long, 3.5–5.6 cm (1⅜–2¼ in.) wide, bases cuneate to truncate, slightly keeled and curved, margins wavy, 6–8 spines on each side, petioles stout, dark, 8–10 mm (5/16–⅜ in.) long; fruits red, globose, 6 mm (¼ in.) diameter, pedicels 6 mm (¼ in.) long; broadly conical habit; 6 m (20 ft.) tall, 4.6 m (15 ft.) wide in 26 years; hardy in zone 6b to −25°C (−13°F).

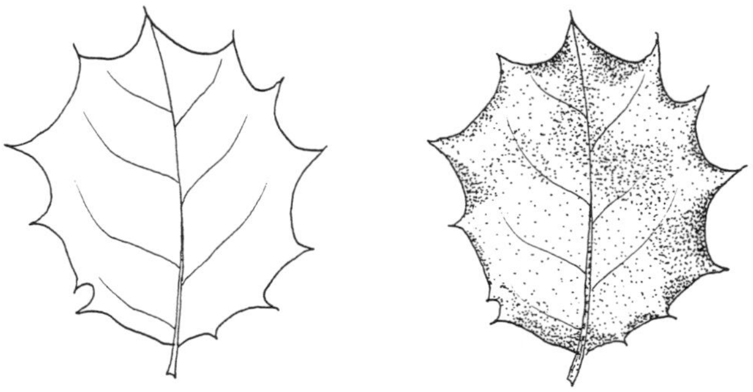

Figure 15-35. *Ilex opaca* 'Dan Fenton'. Drawing by Randy Allen.

'Danny Allen' (female; volunteer seedling, selected, named, and registered H.S.A. 3-87 by R. K. Peters).

Leaves dark olive green, oval to elliptic-obovate, 5 cm (2 in.) long, 2 cm (¾ in.) wide, slightly keeled, curved, veins depressed above, 2–8 spines on each side, tip spine often sharply reflexed, margins often curled or revolute; fruits vivid red 45B, elongate, 11 mm (7/16 in.) long, 10 mm (⅜ in.) diameter, abundant; conical habit; hardy in zone 5.

'Dauber' (female; selected in the 1950s by W. J. Dauber's nursery).

Leaves dark olive green, glossy, elliptic to obovate, 4–5.5 cm (1⅝–2⅛ in.) long, 2.5–3 (1–1 3/16 in.) wide, slightly keeled, curved, 3–5 prominent spines on each side, margins wavy, petioles 8–10 mm (5/16–⅜ in.) long; fruits deep reddish orange 43A, globose, 8 mm (5/16 in.) diameter, pedicels 6 mm (7/32 in.) long.

'David' (male; named by C. R. Wolf; selected near Millville, New Jersey; registered H.S.A. No. 17-74 by D. G. Fenton).

Leaves small, dark olive green, oval, 3–4 cm (1 3/16–1⅝ in.) long, 2.5–3 cm (1–1 3/16 in.) wide, keeled, curved, 3–4 spines on each side, margins reflexed, twisted, petioles 5 mm (3/16 in.) long.

'David G. Leach' (male; synonym 'David Leach'; introduced by O. S. Pride, 1965; Grace Hybrid Group).

Leaves moderate olive green, free of leaf spot,

slightly glossy, oval, 6–7 cm (2⅜–2¾ in.) long, 3–4 cm (1³⁄₁₆–1⅝ in.) wide, keeled, curved, 3–4 prominent spines on each side, stout petioles 6–8 mm (⁷⁄₃₂–⁵⁄₁₆ in.) long; broadly pyramidal, rapid grower; hardy to −37°C (−35°F). Good for orcharding.

'Delaware Red' (female; seedling grown and registered H.S.A. 9-65 by W. Phillips).
Leaves dark olive green, broadly elliptic, 6–7.5 cm (2⅜–3 in.) long, 3.5–4.2 cm (1⅜–1¹¹⁄₁₆ in.) wide, slightly keeled to flat, curved, 2–3 spines usually on upper half of leaf, petioles 6–8 mm (⁷⁄₃₂–⁵⁄₁₆ in.) long; fruits deep reddish orange, globose to ellipsoid, 6–8 mm (⁷⁄₃₂–⁵⁄₁₆ in.) long, 6 mm (⁷⁄₃₂ in.) diameter, pedicels reddish, 5 mm (³⁄₁₆ in.) long.

'Delia' (female; selected 1935–1940 by T. Windon and E. C. White).
Leaves dark olive green, elliptic, 5.5–6.5 cm (2–2½ in.) long, 2.6–3 cm (1–1³⁄₁₆ in.) wide, slightly glossy, bases obtuse to rotund, keeled, curved, 4–6 small spines, petioles 6–8 mm (⁷⁄₃₂–⁵⁄₁₆ in.) long; fruits vivid reddish orange 44B, ellipsoid, 10 mm (⅜ in.) long, 8 mm (⁵⁄₁₆ in.) diameter, pedicels 10–13 mm (⅜–½ in.) long. Often confused with 'Manig'.

'Delia Bradley' (female; selected about 1928 at Lorely, Maryland, and introduced about 1930 by H. Hohman).
Leaves dark green, elliptic to oval, 7–8 cm (2¾–3⅛ in.) long, 3.5–4 cm (1⅜–1⅝ in.) wide, tip curved, keeled, evenly toothed margins slightly wavy, petioles 5–7 mm (³⁄₁₆–⁹⁄₃₂ in.) long; fruits vivid red 45A, slightly ellipsoid, 8 mm (⁵⁄₁₆ in.) diameter, pedicels 6–8 mm (⁷⁄₃₂–⁵⁄₁₆ in.) long, abundant, 1–3 per peduncle.

'Dengle Belles' (female; found by W. F. Smith in wild, east of West End, North Carolina; selected 1958 and introduced 1959 by J. D. Rankin; named for daughters of H. Dengler).
Leaves dark olive green, oval, 4–5 cm (1⅝–2 in.) long, 2.5–3 cm (1–1³⁄₁₆ in.) wide, keeled, curved, 3–6 spines on each side, margins reflexed, petioles 8 mm (⁵⁄₁₆ in.) long; fruits strong orange 25B, sometimes with pink blush, globose, 8 mm (⁵⁄₁₆ in.) diameter, pedicels 6 mm (⁷⁄₃₂ in.) long.

'Diane' (female; selected by T. Klein; origin Cave Hill Cemetery, Louisville, Kentucky).
Leaves moderate olive green, elliptic to oval, 4.5–5.5 cm (1¾–2⅛ in.) long, 3–3.5 cm (1³⁄₁₆–1⅜ in.) wide, keeled, curved, 3–6 spines usually on upper two-thirds of leaf, petioles 8 mm (⁵⁄₁₆ in.) long; fruits deep reddish orange 43A, globose, 8 mm (⁵⁄₁₆ in.) diameter, pedicels 8 mm (⁵⁄₁₆ in.) long, abundant;

vigorous compact, wide spreading habit. One of first hollies to be stripped of fruit early by birds.

'Dias' (male; synonym 'Dias' No. 1'; selected and named in the 1950s by W. Wheeler).
Leaves moderate olive green, broadly elliptic, 4–6 cm (1⅝–2⅜ in.) long, 2.5–3 cm (1–1³⁄₁₆ in.) wide, keeled, curved, 3–6 spines on each side, margins reflexed, wavy.

'Dias No. 2' (female; selected and named by W. Wheeler).
Leaves moderate olive green, elliptic, 4.5–5 cm (1¾–2 in.) long, 2–2.5 cm (¾–1 in.) wide, keeled, curved, 1–3 spines usually on upper half of leaf, margins reflexed, convex, petioles 8–10 mm (⁵⁄₁₆–⅜ in.) long; fruits vivid red 45 A, globose, 8 mm (⁵⁄₁₆ in.) diameter, pedicels 5 mm (³⁄₁₆ in.) long, abundant.

'Dick' (male; synonym 'Wheeler No. 1'; selected and named by W. Wheeler).
Leaves dark olive green, elliptic, 4.5–6 cm (1¾–2⅜ in.) long, 2.5–3 cm (1–1³⁄₁₆ in.) wide, keeled, curved, bases obtuse to rotund, margins recurved, 2–3 spines on each side, usually on upper half of leaf, petioles 8–10 mm (⁵⁄₁₆–⅜ in.) long.

'Dorothy' (female; selected in West Barnstable, Massachusetts, before 1947 by W. Wheeler; moved to Ashumet Farm, Falmouth, Massachusetts).
Leaves dark olive green, obovate to elliptic, 4.5–5.5 cm (1¾–2⅛ in.) long, 2.5–3 cm (1–1³⁄₁₆ in.) wide, almost flat, keeled, curved, 1–3 prominent spines on each side, margins convex, twisted, petioles 8–10 mm (⁵⁄₁₆–⅜ in.) long; fruits vivid red 45A, subglobose, 8–10 mm (⁵⁄₁₆–⅜ in.) diameter, borne singly on pink pedicels 3–5 mm (⅛–³⁄₁₆ in.) long.

'Dorsey' (female; selected on Dorsey Farm, Howard County, Maryland, by A. N. Adams before 1950).
Leaves medium large, late flowering; fruits red, very large, borne in great profusion.

'Dr. Cribbs' (male; synonym 'Doctor Cribbs'; introduced by O. S. Pride, 1961).
Leaves moderate olive green, oval, 6.5–7 cm (2½–2¾ in.) long, 3.5–4 cm (1⅜–1⅝ in.) wide, curved, 4–5 prominent spines on each side, margins reflexed, stout petioles 6–7 mm (⁷⁄₃₂–⁹⁄₃₂ in.) long, free of leaf spot, good winter color; broadly pyramidal vigorous habit.

'Dr. S. Edwin Muller' (female; selected about 1944 at Bradshaw, Maryland; introduced by Kingsville Nursery).
Leaves moderate olive green, broadly elliptic, 4–

6.5 cm (1⅝–2⅜ in.) long, 2–3 cm (¾–1³⁄₁₆ in.) wide, keeled, curved, 2–3 spines on upper half of leaf, margins convex, slightly twisted, petioles 8 mm (⁵⁄₁₆ in.) long; fruits vivid red 45A, globose, 8–10 mm (⁵⁄₁₆–⅜ in.) diameter, pedicels 3–5 mm (⅛–³⁄₁₆ in.) long; almost fastigiate habit.

'Dr. T. B. Symons' (male; synonyms 'Big Boy', 'T. B. Symons'; selected 1959 by H. Dengler at St. Elizabeth Hospital, Washington, D.C.; registered American Association of Nurserymen No. 255).
Leaves dark olive green, unusually large; flowers abundantly.

'Draper' (female; selected 1948 at Chadds Ford, Pennsylvania, by H. G. Mattoon).
Leaves moderate olive green, oval, 6.5–7 cm (2½–2¾ in.) long, 3.5–4 cm (1⅜–1⅝ in.) wide, curved, 2–4 prominent spines on each side, margins reflexed, petioles 6–7 mm (⁷⁄₃₂–⁹⁄₃₂ in.) long; fruits vivid red 44B, globose to slightly ellipsoid, 8–10 mm (⁵⁄₁₆–⅜ in.) diameter.

'Dull Red' (female; introduced about 1938 by Kingsville Nursery).
Leaves moderate olive green, elliptic, 4.5–5 cm (1⅗–2 in.) long, 2–2.5 cm (¾–1 in.) wide, keeled, curved, 3–6 spines on each side, margins reflexed, petioles 6–8 mm (⁷⁄₃₂–⁵⁄₁₆ in.) long; fruits strong red 45C, globose to ellipsoid, 10 mm (⅜ in.) long, pedicels 5 mm (³⁄₁₆ in.) long.

'Dunn No. 1' (female; introduced by J. D. Rankin).
Leaves moderate olive green, elliptic, 4.5–5.5 cm (1¾–2⅛ in.) long, 2–2.5 cm (¾–1 in.) wide, keeled, curved, 2–5 spines on each side, margins reflexed, slightly wavy, petioles 6–8 mm (⁷⁄₃₂–⁵⁄₁₆ in.) long; fruits vivid yellow 15A, ellipsoid, 10 mm (⅜ in.) long, pedicels 5 mm (³⁄₁₆ in.) long.

'Dunn No. 2' (female; introduced by J. D. Rankin).
Leaves moderate olive green, broadly elliptic, 6–7 cm (2⅜–2¾ in.) long, 3–3.5 cm (1³⁄₁₆–1⅜ in.) wide, keeled, curved, 3–4 spines on each side, usually on upper two-thirds of leaf, petioles 8–10 mm (⁵⁄₁₆–⅜ in.) long; fruits vivid orange yellow 17A, globose, 8 mm (⁵⁄₁₆ in.) diameter.

'DuPre' (female; synonym 'El Durprey', 'Du Pre'; selected 1940 near Walhalla, South Carolina, and introduced 1946 by W. C. Frierson; registered American Association of Nurserymen No. 24).
Leaves moderate olive green, similar to those of 'Taber No. 3, flat, keeled, shallow sharp spines; fruits dark red, ellipsoid; broadly rotund spreading habit.

'DuPre No. 2' (female; selected by W. C. Frierson, presumably near same locality as 'DuPre').
Leaves cuneate to elliptic, dark olive green; fruits red, small to medium, ellipsoid.

'Earl' (female; selected about 1930 by O. C. White on property of R. Lippencott near Pemberton, New Jersey).
Leaves moderate olive green; fruits red, globose to obovate, small.

'Early Coloring' (selected in the 1950s by W. Wheeler).
Leaves dark olive green, elliptic, 5.5–6 cm (2⅛–2⅜ in.) long, 2.8–3.5 cm (1⅛–1⅜ in.) wide, bases cuneate, slightly keeled and curved, 4–5 spines on each side, petioles 5–7 mm (³⁄₁₆–⁹⁄₃₂ in.) long; fruits deep reddish orange 43A, depressed globose, 6 mm (⁷⁄₃₂ in.) thick, 8 mm (⁵⁄₁₆ in.) diameter, 1–5 in clusters, color early, pedicels reddish, 7–10 mm (⁹⁄₃₂–⅜ in.) long.

'Edith' (female; selected 1948–1952 by O. S. Pride; origin seed collected 1928 near Buckhannon, West Virginia).
Leaves moderate olive green; fruits vivid red; broad vigorous habit.

'Edna' (female; synonym 'Aalto No. 1; selected about 1950 by W. Wheeler and E. C. White at Barnstable, Massachusetts).
Leaves dark olive green, broadly elliptic to oval, keeled, curved, 5–7 cm (2–2¾ in.) long, 3–3.5 cm (1³⁄₁₆–1⅜ in.) wide, margins slightly wavy, 4–6 spine on each side, pedicels dark, 8 mm (⁵⁄₁₆ in.) long; fruits red, globose, 5–6 mm (³⁄₁₆–⁷⁄₃₂ in.) diameter, pedicels dark, 8–10 mm (⁵⁄₁₆–⅜ in.) long; upright pyramidal habit.

'Ed Thomas' (male; origin unknown; plant on Michigan State University campus).
Leaves moderate olive green 139A, oval, 4.5–5.5 cm (1¾–2⅛ in.) long, 3–3.5 cm (1³⁄₁₆–1⅜ in.) wide, keeled, curved, 3–5 spines on each side, margins reflexed, petioles 6–8 mm (⁷⁄₃₂–⁵⁄₁₆ in.) long.

'Eleanor' (female; selected 1939 by C. R. Wolf from Cumberland County, New Jersey; registered H.S.A. 8-74 by D. G. Fenton).
Leaves moderate olive green, broadly oval, 5.5–6 cm (2⅛–2⅜ in.) long, 3.5–4 cm (1⅜–1⅝ in.) wide, keeled, curved, bases obtuse, 3–6 short spines on each side, usually upper two-thirds of leaf, petioles 8 mm (⁵⁄₁₆ in.) long; fruits vivid red 45A, glossy, globose, 8 mm (⁵⁄₁₆ in.) diameter, abundant.

'Elegantissima' (female: grown on Long Island, New York; origin unknown).

Leaves dark olive green, broadly elliptic to obovate-elliptic, slightly keeled, curved, 5.5–8.5 cm (2⅛–3⅜ in.) long, 2.5–3.8 cm (1–1½ in.) wide, bases obtuse, apices acuminate, margins with 2–5 widely spaced spines on each side, often on upper two-thirds of leaf; fruits red.

'Elephant Berry' (female; selected by E. Dilatush at Bunting Nursery, Selbyville, Delaware; introduced 1949 by O. D. Diller and J. E. Ford).

Leaves moderate olive green, oval, 6-7 cm (2⅜–2¾ in.) long, 4–5 cm (1⅝–2 in.) wide, keeled, curved, 1–2 spines on upper half of leaf, petioles 8–10 mm (5/16–⅜ in.) long; fruits deep reddish orange 42A, globose, 12 mm (15/32 in.) diameter.

'Elfin' (female; selected in New Jersey in 1929 and introduced 1948 by E. Dilatush).

Leaves moderate olive green, elliptic, 6–7 cm (2⅜–2¾ in.) long, 3–3.5 cm (1 3/16–1⅜ in.) wide, curved, 3–5 spines on each side, margins reflexed, petioles 6–8 mm (7/32–5/16 in.) long; fruits very sparse, red, globose, 8 mm (5/16 in.) diameter.

'Elizabeth' (female; selected in 1945 by W. Makepeace and W. Wheeler; plant moved to Ashumet Farm, Falmouth, Massachusetts; named by Wheeler for Elizabeth C. White, a horticultural pioneer in blueberries and hollies).

Leaves widely spaced, dark olive green, broadly elliptic, 4.5–5.5 cm (1¾–2⅛ in.) long, 3–3.5 cm (1 3/16–1⅜ in.) wide, keeled, curved, convex, 3–4 small spines, margins reflexed, convex, slightly wavy, petioles 8–10 mm (5/16–38 in.) long; fruits vivid reddish orange 44B, globose, 8–10 mm (5/16–⅜ in. diameter, pedicels reddish, 5–7 mm (3/16–9/32 in.) long.

'Emily' (female; synonym 'Aalto No. 4'; selected in the 1940s by W. Wheeler from West Barnstable, Massachusetts, and named for his wife).

Leaves dark olive green, elliptic to oval, slightly bullate, 6–7 cm (2⅜–2¾ in.) long, 3.5–4 cm (1⅜–1⅝ in.) wide, keeled, curved, bases cuneate to rotund, apices acute, margins wavy, 2–6 spines on upper half of leaf, petioles dark, 8–10 mm (5/16–⅜ in.) long; fruits vivid red 42A, globose, 6–8 mm (7/32–5/16 in.) diameter, borne in clusters, heavy fruiting, pedicels dark, 8–10 mm (5/16–⅜ in.) long; fast grower and early bearing. Reported to be the best and most spectacular of W. Wheeler's selections.

'Ermine Watson' (female; named 1959 by J. D. Rankin for mother of H. Orr; origin in the wild in southern Davidson County, North Carolina; introduced by W. Steed).

Leaves dark olive green, oval 4.5–6 cm (1¾–2⅜ in.) long, 3–4 cm (1 3/16–1⅝ in.) wide, bases obtuse to rotund, keeled, curved, 3–6 spines on each side, petioles 8–10 mm (5/16–⅜ in.) long; fruits vivid orange yellow 17A, globose to ellipsoid, 8 mm (5/16 in.) long, 6–8 mm (7/32–5/16 in.) diameter, pedicels 5–6 mm (3/16–7/32 in.) long.

'Estes' (female; selected before 1947 by W. C. Frierson near Lenoir and Blowing Rock, North Carolina, about 606 m (2000 ft.) elevation).

Leaves dark green; fruits red; annual bearer.

'Evans' (female; selected at Greenville, Delaware, and introduced in 1948 by H. G. Mattoon).

Petioles and twigs wavy in growth; fruits red, large.

'Everberry' (female; selected by O. S. Pride 1948–1952; origin seed collected 1928 near Buckhannon, West Virginia).

Leaves good green color; fruits vivid red, persisting until next crop turns red.

'Exotic' (female; synonym 'Exotica'; selected and named before 1956 by Angelica Nursery).

Leaves dark olive green, broadly elliptic to oval, 5–5.5 cm (2–2⅛ in.) long, 2.5–3 cm (1–1 3/16 in.) wide, keeled, curved, 2–3 spines on upper half of leaf, margins reflexed and twisted, petioles 8 mm (5/16 in.) long; fruits vivid reddish orange 44B, globose, 8–10 mm (5/16–⅜ in.) diameter.

'Fair Lady' (female; selected before 1965 by O. S. Pride).

Leaves moderate olive green, broadly elliptic, 6.5–7.5 cm (2½–3 in.) long, 4 cm (1⅝ in.) wide, bases rotund, keeled, curved, 6–7 spines on each side, margins slightly wavy, petioles stout, 5 mm (3/16 in.) long; fruits red, pedicels 8–10 mm (5/16–⅜ in.) long.

'Fallaw' (female; discovered 1939 by J. W. Batchelor on Fallaw Farm, near Batesburg, South Carolina; one of three trees growing close together).

Leaves moderate olive green, oval to broadly elliptic, to 10 cm (4 in.) long, 5 cm (2 in.) wide, keeled, curved, 2–4 spines on each side, margins reflexed, petioles 8–10 mm (5/16–⅜ in.) long; fruits vivid yellow 15A, ellipsoid, 8 mm (5/16 in.) long, pedicels 5 mm (3/16 in.) long, profuse; compact upright, vigorous habit.

'Falmouth Powerhouse' (female; selected by W. Wheeler near Falmouth, Massachusetts).

Leaves moderate olive green, broadly elliptic, 4.5–5.5 cm (1¾–2⅛ in.) long, 3–3.5 cm (1³⁄₁₆–1⅜ in.) wide, keeled, curved, 2–5 spines on each side, petioles 6–8 mm (⁷⁄₃₂–⁵⁄₁₆ in.) long; fruits vivid red 45A, globose, 10 mm (⅜ in.) diameter, pedicels reddish 5 mm (³⁄₁₆ in.) long.

'Farage' (female; synonym 'Forage'; selected by E. C. White in the wild near New Lisbon, New Jersey, before 1942; moved to Whitesbog, New Jersey; one of first hollies used by White in rooting experiments).

Leaves dark olive green, broadly elliptic, 7.5–8.5 cm (3–3⅜ in.) long, 4.5–5 cm (1¾–2 in.) wide, curved, 3–4 small spines on each side, usually upper half of leaf, petioles long, 11 mm (⁷⁄₁₆ in.) long; fruits vivid red 44A, globose, 8–10 mm (⁵⁄₁₆–⅜ in.) diameter, pedicels 6 mm (⁷⁄₃₂ in.) long, fruits persistent; vigorous, broadly symmetrical habit of growth. Considered to be of superior quality.

'Fay' (female: synonym 'Aalto No. 14'; selected by W. Wheeler and E. C. White before 1953).

Leaves dark olive green, oval to broadly elliptic, 6.5–8.5 cm (2½–3⅜ in.) long, 3–4 cm (1³⁄₁₆–1⅝ in.) wide, bases cuneate, slightly keeled, curved, 2–5 widely spaced spines on each side, petioles 8–10 mm (⁵⁄₁₆–⅜ in.) long; fruits vivid red 45A, globose, 8–10 mm (⁵⁄₁₆–⅜ in.) diameter, pedicels reddish, 8 mm (⁵⁄₁₆ in.) long.

'Felten's Selection' (female; synonyms 'Felteni', 'Felton's Special'; seedling selected about 1945 by E. E. Felten; introduced by E. C. White).

Leaves dark olive green, broadly elliptic, 5–6 cm (2–2⅜ in.) long, 2.5–3.5 cm (1–1⅜ in.) wide, bases obtuse, keeled, curved, 3–5 prominent spines on each side, margins reflexed, slightly wavy, petioles 8–10 mm (⁵⁄₁₆–⅜ in.) long; fruits vivid red 45A, globose, 6 mm (⁷⁄₃₂ in.) diameter, pedicels 6–8 mm (⁷⁄₃₂–⁵⁄₁₆ in.) long.

'Felton No. 7' (female; selected by E. E. Felton; introduced around 1958 by P. Cascio Nursery).

Leaves dark olive green, broadly elliptic, 5–7 cm (2–2¾ in.) long, 3–4.5 cm (1³⁄₁₆–1¾ in.) wide, bases obtuse to rounded, keeled, curved, 3–5 spines on each side, margins reflexed, petioles 6–8 mm (⁷⁄₃₂–⁵⁄₁₆ in.) long; fruits vivid red 45A, globose, 7–9 mm (⁹⁄₃₂–¹¹⁄₃₂ in.) diameter, reddish pedicels 5–6 mm (³⁄₁₆–⁷⁄₃₂ in.) long.

'Fire Chief' (female; introduced by Hillenmeyer Nursery in the 1950s).

Leaves dark olive green, broadly elliptic, 6–7.5 cm (2⅜–7 in.) long, 4–4.5 cm (1⅝–1¾ in.) wide, slightly keeled, curved, 4–5 spines on each side, margins reflexed, slightly wavy, petioles 10 mm (⅜ in.) long; fruits reddish orange 42A, broadly oval, 7–8 mm (⁹⁄₃₂–⁵⁄₁₆ in.) long, 9–10 mm (¹¹⁄₃₂–⅜ in.) wide, borne singly; narrow upright pyramidal habit. Plate 154.

'Fire Chief' (male; listed in 1960 catalog of Light's Nursery).

Leaves moderate olive green, elliptic, 5–7 cm (2–2¾ in.) long, 3–4 cm (1³⁄₁₆–1⅝ in.) wide, curved, 3–4 spines on each side, petioles 5–7 mm (³⁄₁₆–⁹⁄₃₂ in.) long.

'Fisher' (male; plant at Dawes Arboretum, Newark, Ohio).

Leaves moderate olive green, elliptic to broadly elliptic, 4.5–5.5 cm (1¾–2⅛ in.) long, 2.5–3 cm (1–1³⁄₁₆ in.) wide, keeled, curved, 3–5 spines on each side, petioles 5–7 mm (³⁄₁₆–⁹⁄₃₂ in.) long.

'Fishing Creek' (female; selected near Dauphin, Pennsylvania, in the 1950s by W. J. Dauber).

Leaves narrow; compact plant; reported heavy fruiting.

'Floribunda' (female; discovered by R. Demcker near Navesink Highlands on Shrewsbury River, Massachusetts).

Fruits red, holding well in late winter; compact habit.

'Forest Nursery' (female; large tree near old house on Forest Nursery, Tennessee; selected in late 1950s by F. Galle; name for location not registered; original tree destroyed, plants at Callaway Gardens destroyed; G. Wood received cuttings from Callaway Gardens for University of Alabama, Tanglewood Arboretum, Hale County, Alabama).

Leaves dark olive green, broadly elliptic, keeled, curved, 4.5–6.5 cm (1¾–2½ in.) long, 2.5–3.5 cm (1–1⅜ in.) wide, bases obtuse to rotund, apices acuminate, tip spines reflexed, 2–3 spines on each side, upper two-thirds of leaf, petioles reddish brown, 6–8 mm (⁷⁄₃₂–⁵⁄₁₆ in.) long; fruits vivid yellow 15A, dark spot, globose, 6–8 mm (⁷⁄₃₂–⁵⁄₁₆ in.) diameter, pedicels dark, 5 mm (³⁄₁₆ in.) long; upright pyramidal habit. Excellent dark green foliage for a yellow-fruited plant.

'Formal' (female; R. Coleman; plant at Morris Arboretum, Philadelphia, Pennsylvania).

Leaves dark olive green, broadly elliptic, 4.5–6.5 cm (1¾–2½ in.) long, 2.5–3 cm (1–1³⁄₁₆ in.) wide, bases cuneate, keeled, curved, margins recurved, 2–4 spines on each side, petioles 6–8 mm (⁷⁄₃₂–⁵⁄₁₆ in.) long; fruits red, globose, 8 mm (⁵⁄₁₆ in.) diameter, pedicels reddish, 8–10 mm (⁵⁄₁₆–⅜ in.) long.

'France' (female; synonym 'Parkton Berry'; selected from Parkton, Maryland, by J. Gable about 1935).

Leaves dark olive green, elliptic, 5.5–7.5 cm (2⅛–3 in.) long, 3–3.5 cm (1³⁄₁₆–1⅜ in.) wide, keeled, curved, 1–3 spines usually on upper half of leaf, margins reflexed, petioles 7 mm (⁹⁄₃₂ in.) long; fruits vivid red 45B, globose, 8 mm (⁵⁄₁₆ in.) diameter; rapid grower.

'France Fink' (female; selected from Cave Hill Cemetery, Louisville, Kentucky, in the 1960s; introduced by T. Klein).

Leaves dark olive green, oval, 4.5–5 cm (1¾–2 in.) long, 3–3.5 cm (1³⁄₁₆–1⅜ in.) wide, keeled, curved, 4 spines on each side, margins reflexed and wavy, petioles 8–10 mm (⁵⁄₁₆–⅜ in.) long; fruits deep reddish orange 34A, globose, 8 mm (⁵⁄₁₆ in.) diameter.

'Frances Kern' (female; original seed collected in early 1950s by C. Orndorff, from group of trees discovered by A. L. Quaintance in 1932 near boundary line of Montgomery and Prince Georges counties, Maryland; selected in 1962 from 20 females selected in 1960; named by Orndorff and registered H.S.A. 10-89; first sold as unnamed self-fruiting selected by Kalmia Farms Nursery).

Leaves dark green, ovate, to 9.2 cm (3⅝ in.) long, 5 cm (2 in.) wide, curved, slightly keeled, bases cuneate, tip spines reflexed, margins wavy, 3–6 spines on each side, petioles 13 mm (½ in.) long; fruits vivid red 44A, globose to slightly subglobose, 8 mm (⁵⁄₁₆ in.) diameter, usually single, pedicels 8–11 mm (⁵⁄₁₆–⁷⁄₁₆ in.) long, reported self-fruiting, seed has low fertility; narrow conical habit, short dense horizontal branching; hardy in zone 6.

'Francis Lewis' (female; discovered 1972 near Sharptown, Maryland, on property of Ed Brummel; registered H.S.A 5-72 by F. Lewis).

Leaves olive green, oval, margins flat, 4 spines on each side; fruits brilliant yellow 20A, globose. Only yellow-fruited holly among a large population of red-fruited trees.

'Frank' (male; plant at Bernheim Forest; also listed as a female?).

Leaves dark olive green, oval, 4.5–5 cm (1¾–2 in.) long, 3–3.5 cm (1³⁄₁₆–1⅜ in.) wide, slightly keeled, curved, 2–3 spines on upper half of leaf, margins reflexed, stout petioles 10 mm (⅜ in.) long; broadly pyramidal habit.

'Frank Mack' (female; origin from H. Hohman before 1968).

Leaves moderate olive green, oval, 5–6 cm (2–2⅜ in.) long, 2.5–3 cm (1–1³⁄₁₆ in.) wide, bases obtuse to rounded, keeled, curved, 2–4 spines usually on upper two-thirds of leaf, margins reflexed, convex, petioles 8 mm (⁵⁄₁₆ in.) long; fruits 45A, globose, 8 mm (⁵⁄₁₆ in.) diameter, reddish pedicels 5 mm (³⁄₁₆ in.) long.

'Frank Thomas' (male; origin unknown; plant on Michigan State University campus, 1963).

Leaves dark olive green, elliptic, 4–4.5 cm (1⅝–1¾ in.) long, 2.5–3 cm (1–1³⁄₁₆ in.) wide, curved, usually 2–3 spines on each side upper half of leaf, petioles 8 mm (⁵⁄₁₆ in.) long.

'Fred Anderson' (male; volunteer seedling about 1975 in garden of R. K. Peters; selected, named and registered H.S.A. 9-89 by Peters).

Leaves dark green, glossy, ovate, occasionally obovate or elliptic, 9 cm (3½ in.) long, 3.8 cm (1½ in.) wide, bases cuneate, tip spines large, margins flat, 3–4 large spines on each side, petioles 13 mm (½ in.) long; male flowers, pollen abundant, peduncles to 13 mm (½ in.) long, 3 pedicels 5 mm (³⁄₁₆ in.) long; broadly conical habit; original tree 3.1 m (10 ft.) high and wide in 15 years; hardy in zone 5b.

'Freeman' (female; origin tree at Water Works Station, Falmouth, Massachusetts; named by W. Wheeler in 1940 and given to town of Falmouth; named for foreman of Falmouth parks).

Leaves dark olive green, oval, 5–5.5 cm (2–2⅛ in.) long, 3–3.5 cm (1³⁄₁₆–1⅜ in.) wide, keeled, curved, keeled, 1–3 spines usually on upper half of leaf, margins reflexed, slightly bullate, petioles 8–10 mm (⁵⁄₁₆–⅜ in.) long; fruits vivid red 45B, globose, 8 mm (⁵⁄₁₆ in.) diameter, pedicels 3–5 mm (⅛–³⁄₁₆ in.) long, abundant; long branched and rapid growing.

'Fruitland Nursery' (female; selected in the 1930s; named and introduced about 1933 by Fruitland Nursery; original tree from South Carolina).

Leaves moderate olive green, broadly elliptic, 6.5–8 cm (2⅜–3⅛ in.) long, 3–4 cm (1³⁄₁₆–1⅝ in.) wide, keeled, curved, 2–4 spines on upper two-thirds of leaf; fruits vivid yellow 15A, ellipsoid, 9–11 mm (¹¹⁄₃₂–⁷⁄₁₆ in.) long, pedicels 10–15 mm (⅜–¹⁹⁄₃₂ in.) long.

'Galyean Gold' (female; synonym 'Gallean Gold'; introduced by W. W. Steiner; origin on property of O. Galyean, Dobson, North Carolina; reported by J. D. Rankin; registered H.S.A. 4-94 by Steiner).

Leaves moderate olive green, oval, 6–7 cm (2⅜–2¾ in.) long, 3.5 cm (1⅜ in.) wide, keeled, curved, 3–4 prominent spines on each side, petioles 10 mm (⅜ in.) long; fruits vivid orange yellow 17A, globose, 8 mm (⁵⁄₁₆ in.) diameter.

'Gee' (female; introduced by O. S. Pride before 1965; Grace Hybrid Group).

Leaves moderate olive green, broadly elliptic, 5.5–6.5 cm (2⅛–2½ in.) long, 3.5–4 cm (1⅜–1⅝ in.) wide, bases obtuse, keeled, curved, 2–5 spines on each side, margins reflexed, convex, stout petioles 10–12 mm (⅜–½ in.) long; fruits vivid red 45A, globose, 8 mm (5⁄16 in.) diameter, reddish pedicels 6 mm (7⁄32 in.) long.

'George E. Hart' (female; synonyms 'Brilliantissima', 'Hart', 'Pyramidalis', 'Pyramidalis Brilliantissima'; selected from New York by P. Vossberg about 1945; original plant moved in the 1920s to nursery of G. E. Hart).

Leaves moderate olive green, broadly elliptic, 6–7.5 cm (2⅜–3 in.) long, 3.5–4 cm (1⅜–1⅝ in.) wide, curved, 3–4 spines on each side, reflexed wavy margins, petioles 8 mm (5⁄16 in.) long; fruits vivid red 45A, globose, 8 mm (5⁄16 in.) diameter, pedicels 5 mm (3⁄16 in.) long, heavy fruiter.

'Gertrude' (female; selected by O. S. Pride; Grace Hybrid Group).

Leaves dark olive green, broadly elliptic, 5–6.5 cm (2–2½ in.) long, 3–3.8 cm (1³⁄16–1½ in.) wide, bases obtuse, keeled, curved, margins recurved, slightly wavy, 3–5 small spines on each side, petioles 7 mm (9⁄32 in.) long; fruits vivid red 45A, globose, 8 mm (5⁄16 in.) diameter, 1–2 in cluster, pedicels 8–10 mm (5⁄16–⅜ in.) long.

'Girard's Male' (male; introduced by Girard's Nursery in the 1960s).

Leaves dark olive green, elliptic, 7–7.5 cm (2¾–3 in.) long, 3 cm (1³⁄16 in.) wide, keeled, curved, 2–3 spines on each side, petioles dark, 10–15 mm (⅜–19⁄32 in.) long; narrow upright habit.

'Gloucester' (female; collected in 1952 from a group of seedlings in hedgerow at public library, Gloucester, Virginia; selected and named in 1962; registered H.S.A. 1-88 by R. K. Peters).

Leaves dark olive green, glossy, ovate, keeled, curved, to 8.3 cm (3¼ in.) long, 2.5 cm (1 in.) wide, tip spines strongly reflexed, margins undulate, 3 spines evenly spaced on each side, petioles 8 mm (5⁄16 in.) long; fruits vivid red, globose, 8 mm (5⁄16 in.) diameter; narrow upright habit, horizontal branching; original tree 4.6 m (15 ft.) tall, 1.8 m (6 ft.) wide in 38 years; hardy in zone 5a.

'Golden Fleece' (female; synonym 'Frierson Golden'; selected in North Carolina around 1940 by A. Brownell and W. C. Frierson).

Leaves deep yellow green, irregularly blotched with vivid yellow 12A toward margins when in sun, green in shade, easily sunburned, elliptic, 5.5–7 cm (2⅛–2¾ in.) long, 3–3.5 cm (1³⁄16–1⅜ in.) wide, convex, curved, nearly entire or 2–6 small spines, petioles 8 mm (5⁄16 in.) long; fruits vivid reddish orange 41A, globose, 6 mm (7⁄32 in.) diameter, very sparse fruiting; broadly upright mounding habit, not a vigorous plant.

'Golden Valentine' (female; seedling from 'Valentine XC'; raised and introduced in the 1960s by T. Klein).

Leaves moderate olive green, oval, 3.5–5 cm (1⅜–2 in.) long, 2–3 cm (¾–1³⁄16 in.) wide, keeled, curved, 2–3 spines on each side, margins reflexed, petioles 8–10 mm (5⁄16–⅜ in.) long; fruits vivid yellow 15A, globose to ellipsoid, 8 mm (5⁄16 in.) long, pedicels 5 mm (3⁄16 in.) long.

'Goldie' (female; origin Wilmington, Delaware; discovered by Mrs. W. K. du Pont; introduced 1940 by E. C. White).

Leaves moderate olive green, obovate to oval, 5–6 cm (2–2⅜ in.) long, 3–3.5 cm (1³⁄16–1⅜ in.) wide, curved, keeled, bullate, 3–6 spines on each side, stout petioles 5 mm (3⁄16 in.) long; fruits vivid yellow 15A, ellipsoid, 10 mm (⅜ in.) long, abundant, borne singly.

'Good Will Park' (female; selected in 1942 by W. Wheeler from Good Will Park, Falmouth, Massachusetts).

Leaves dark olive green, oval to elliptic, 4–5.5 cm (1⅝–2⅛ in.) long, 2–3.2 cm (¾–1¼ in.) wide, bases cuneate to obtuse, keeled, curved, 1–3 spines usually on upper half of leaf, petioles 6–8 mm (7⁄32–5⁄16 in.) long; fruits red.

'Governor William Paca' (female; seedling selected 1960 in Sussex County, Delaware, by N. Cannon; named and registered H.S.A. 1-70 by L. S. Brigham; original plant moved to William Paca Garden, Annapolis, Maryland).

Leaves olive green elliptic, 5 spines on each side, wavy margins; fruits red, early ripening, retains well on cut branches; conical habit.

'Grace' (female; named and registered H.S.A. 11-76 by O. S. Pride; seedling selected 1948–1952 from seed collected near Buckhannon, West Virginia; Grace Hybrid Group).

Leaves moderate olive green, broadly elliptic to oval, 5–6 cm (2–2⅜ in.) long, 3–4 cm (1³⁄16–1⅝ in.) wide, bases cuneate to obtuse, keeled, curved, 3–4 spines on each side, margins reflexed, wavy, petioles 6–8 mm (7⁄32–5⁄16 in.) long; fruits vivid red 44A, globose, 8 mm (⁵⁄₁₆ in.) diameter, in large clusters; pyramidal, slow growing; hardy to −34°C (−30°F).

Grace Hybrid Group

A strain selected for hardiness, vigor, habit of growth, ease of culture, and early ripening of fruits. Originated and named by O. S. Pride. Both parents, 'Grace' being the female, were selected from many thousands of seedlings grown from seed collected near Buckhannon, West Virginia, and the results of more than 40 years of testing for winter hardiness, often down to −34°C (−30°F). Members of the group include 'Albert Pride' (male), 'Arlene Leach' (female), 'Arthur Pride' (male), 'Betty Pride' (female), 'Carnival' (female), 'David G. Leach' (male), 'Dr. Cribbs' (male), 'Edith May' (female), 'Gee' (female), 'Gertrude' (female), 'Grace' (female), 'Homer' (male), 'Ling' (female), 'Ling Close' (female), 'Marianne' (female), 'Mary Holman' (female), 'Mrs. F. J. Close' (female), 'Pride of Butler' (female), 'Red Flush' (female), 'Red Spice' (female), 'Sleigh Bells' (female), 'Thanksgiving' (female), 'Valentine' (female).

'Grace McCutchan' (female; original tree on McCutchan property in Evansville, Indiana; named and registered H.S.A. 1-80 by H. R. Schroeder Jr.).

Leaves moderate olive green, elliptic, 4.5–5.5 cm (1¾–2⅛ in.) long, 2.5–3 cm (1–1³⁄₁₆ in.) wide, keeled, curved, 3–4 spines on each side, petioles 6–8 mm (⁷⁄₃₂–⁵⁄₁₆ in.) long; fruits vivid red, ellipsoid, 1 mm (⅜ in.) long.

'Grandpappy' (male; introduced in 1969 by W. Steed; registered H.S.A. 1-71 by T. Eure).

Leaves moderate size, broadly ovate, curved, keeled, 3–4 spines on each side; narrow upright habit, with horizontal branching. The original tree was found in the wild 3 miles northeast of New Bern, North Carolina, on the property of J. W. Laughinghouse. In 1961 it was determined by the North Carolina Holly Commission to be the largest and oldest known specimen of *I. opaca*: circumference, 3.38 m (11 ft.); height, 22 m (72 ft.); spread, 13.3 m (45 ft.). To preserve the tree, in 1965 the state of North Carolina purchased the tree and 3 acres of land surrounding it for a state park. Unfortunately this old specimen was destroyed in 1978, at the age of 208 years, by a hurricane.

'Greaser' (female; discovered by G. Greaser; origin on Mount Lookout, West Virginia, at 760 m (2500 ft.) elevation; selected before 1947 by W. C. Frierson).

Good foliage and good everbearing fruits.

'Great Smoky' (female; selected about 1930 by E. Dilatush).

Leaves moderate olive green, broadly elliptic, 5.5–7 cm (2⅛–2¾ in.) long, 3.5–4 cm (1⅜–1⅝ in.) wide, keeled, curved, 3–8 spines on each side, margins wavy, petioles 10 mm (⅜ in.) long; fruits large, vivid red.

'Greenleaf', see *I.* × *attenuata* 'Greenleaf'.

'Greta' (female; selected before 1953 by Angelica Nursery).

Leaves dark olive green, elliptic, 4–5 cm (1⅝–2 in.) long, 1.5–2.5 (½–1 in.) wide, bases obtuse, keeled, curved, 3–5 prominent spines on each side, margins reflexed, petioles 6–8 mm (⁷⁄₃₂–⁵⁄₁₆ in.) long; fruits vivid red 45A, globose, 6–8 mm (⁷⁄₃₂–⁵⁄₁₆ in.) diameter, reddish pedicels 3–6 mm (⅛–⁷⁄₃₂ in.) long; pyramidal, slow growing.

'Griscom' (female; selected near Woodbury, New Jersey, by E. C. White and Griscom; introduced about 1930 by White; original tree hit by lighting in the 1980s and removed, probably largest *I. opaca* in that state).

Leaves moderate olive green, broadly oval, 7–8.5 cm (2¾–3⅛ in.) long, 4–4.5 cm (1⅝–1¾ in.) wide, convex, curved, midrib depressed, 4–5 small reflexed spines on each side, bases obtuse to truncate, petioles reddish, 8 mm (⁵⁄₁₆ in.) long; fruits vivid red 45A, globose, 7 mm (⁹⁄₃₂ in.) diameter, singly on short pedicels 2 mm (¹⁄₁₆ in.) long; also reported 1–3 per peduncles.

'Gunby' (female; synonyms 'Gumby', 'Gunbi'; selected at Marion Station near Crisfield, Maryland, by F. L. S. O'Rourke; introduced by Kingsville Nursery about 1935).

Leaves moderate to dark olive green, elliptic, 7.5–8 cm (3–3⅛ in.) long, 3.5 cm (1⅜ in.) wide, keeled, curved, bases obtuse, 6–8 spines on each side, margins reflexed, slightly wavy, petioles 6–8 mm (⁷⁄₃₂–⁵⁄₁₆ in.) long; fruits deep reddish orange 43A, ellipsoid, 8 mm (⁵⁄₁₆ in.) long, pedicels 10 mm (⅜ in.) long.

'H. L. Russell' (female; discovered before 1942 at Gunston, Virginia, by W. F. Smith and identified as a new "novelty" by P. Ricker, P. Coville, and W. A. Dayton; several wild trees were discovered about 1912 by E. P. Carpenter, but the name was applied to the first plant selected in honor of H. L. Russell, former dean at Wisconsin College of Agriculture; 'Firecracker' was suggested by Smith as an alternate name for all these everbearing trees).

Fruits everbearing, persisting for 2 years, with at least 1 set of fruits at all times.

'Halcyon' (female; selected by T. Windon and E. C. White 1935–1940; origin New Jersey).

Leaves moderate olive green, oval, 4–5.5 cm (1⅝–2⅛ in.) long, 2–3.5 cm (¾–1⅜ in.) wide, keeled, curved, 2–3 spines usually on upper two-thirds of leaf, petioles 6–8 mm (7⁄32–5⁄16 in.) long; fruits moderate reddish orange 35A, ellipsoid, 1 cm (⅜ in.) long, pedicels 6 mm (7⁄32 in.) long.

'Hamie' (female; collected seedling from northwestern Alabama, moved to home of Mrs. Hamie Stamps; cutting given to G. Wood for University of Alabama, Tanglewood Arboretum, Hale County, Alabama; named by Wood).

Leaves moderate to yellowish green, broadly elliptic to nearly globose, 5–6 cm (2–2⅜ in.) long, 3.5–4.8 cm (1⅜–1⅞ in.) wide, keeled, curved, bases obtuse to rotund, apices rotund, tip spines slightly reflexed, petioles 8–10 mm (5⁄16–⅜ in.); fruits vivid red 45A, globose, 8–9 mm (5⁄16–11⁄32 in.) diameter, pedicels 5 mm (3⁄16 in.) long; pyramidal habit.

'Hampton' (discovered in York County, Virginia, and introduced 1942 by K. McDonald).

Leaves dark olive green, 6–6.5 cm (2⅜–2½ in.) long, 3–4 cm (1 3⁄16–1⅝ in.) wide, curved, entire to 2 spines on each side, petioles 7–10 mm (9⁄32–⅜ in.) long; fruits vivid red 45B, ellipsoid, 8–10 mm (5⁄16–⅜ in.) long, pedicels 8 mm (5⁄16 in.) long.

'Harriet' (female; synonym 'Aalto No. 2'; selected 1942 by E. C. White and W. Wheeler in Massachusetts).

Leaves dark olive green, oval, 5–6 cm (2–2⅜ in.) long, 3–3.5 cm (1 3⁄16–1⅜ in.) wide, keeled, curved, 1–2 spines on each side, petioles 6 mm (7⁄32 in.) long; fruits vivid red 45B, globose, 8 mm (5⁄16 in.) diameter, pedicels reddish, 5 mm (3⁄16 in.) long.

'Hedgeholly' (female; synonyms 'Bosley Hedge', 'Hedge'; selected near Porterwood, West Virginia, before 1949 by P. Bosley).

Leaves very closely spaced, dark olive green, elliptic, 5–6 cm (2–2⅜ in.) long, 3–3.5 cm (1 3⁄16–1⅜ in.) wide, keeled, curved, 4–5 spines on each side, margins wavy, petioles 5 mm (3⁄16 in.) long; fruits vivid red 45A, globose, 8–10 mm (5⁄16–⅜ in.) diameter, dark pedicels; dense compact plant. Withstands shearing, excellent for hedges.

'Helen Hahn' (female; chance seedling discovered by Stephen Schroeder along road of his Holly Hills Lane Nursery; named for wife of H.S.A. past president Harold Hahn; registered H.S.A. 4-95 by Schroeder; evaluation by Roberts Landscape Nursery, Kentucky).

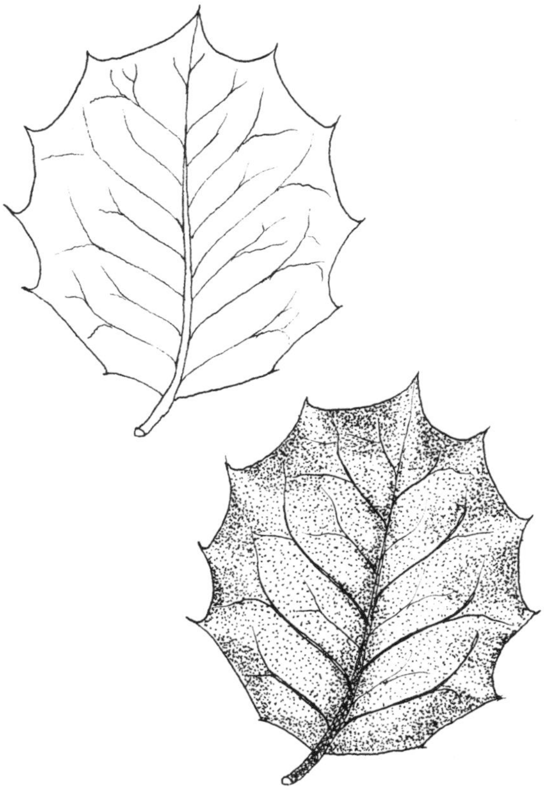

Figure 15-36. *Ilex opaca* 'Hamie'. Drawing by Randy Allen.

Leaves large, ovate, to 10 cm (4 in.) long, 5 cm (2 in.) wide, slightly curved, tips abruptly cuneate, margins wide, revolute, 1–3 lateral spines on each side, usually upper half of leaf, petioles 13 mm (½ in.) long; fruits vivid red 44A, globose to slightly elongate, borne singly, pedicels 8 mm (5⁄16 in.) long, ripen in early November; hardy in zone 5. Original tree 6 m (20 ft.) tall, 3 m (10 ft.) wide in 20 years. Selected for leaf gloss and shape.

'Helen Makepeace' (female; selected from West Barnstable, Massachusetts, before 1947 by W. Wheeler and W. Makepeace).

Leaves moderate olive green, oval, 4–5.6 cm (1¾–2⅜ in.) long, 3–3.5 cm (1 3⁄16–1⅜ in.) wide, keeled, curved, usually 1–2 spines on upper half of leaf, margins reflexed, convex, wavy, petioles 8 mm (5⁄16 in.) long; fruits vivid red 45A, globose, 8 mm (5⁄16 in.) diameter, in compact clusters, reddish pedicels 5 mm (3⁄16 in.) long; pyramidal upright habit. Resembles 'Griscom' but of different origin.

'Helen Mitchell' (female; named and introduced 1956 by J. D. Rankin for wife of Brian Mulligan;

original tree on a farm on Bringles Ferry Road near Salisbury, North Carolina).

Leaves moderate olive green, elliptic, 8–9 cm (3⅛–3½ in.) long, 3–3.5 cm (1³⁄₁₆–1⅜ in.) wide, bullate, curved, 3–4 spines on each side, petioles 8–10 mm (⁵⁄₁₆–⅜ in.) long; fruits vivid orange yellow 17A, distinct black spot, globose, 8 mm (⁵⁄₁₆ in.) diameter, pedicels 8 mm (⁵⁄₁₆ in.) long.

'Helvetia' (female; selected 1949 by S. B. Detwiller near Buckhann, Upshur County, West Virginia, at 515 m (1700 ft.) elevation; introduced by C. S. Britt and W. W. Steiner; U.S. PI 183819, 1949).

Leaves unusually large, to 10 cm (4 in.) long; fruits vivid red; easily rooted.

'Henry Clay' (male; original from Henry Clay property in Lexington, Kentucky; introduced by Hillenmeyer Nursery).

Leaves dark olive green, oval, 4–5 cm (1⅝–2 in.) long, 3–4 cm (1³⁄₁₆–1⅝ in.) wide, keeled, curved, 3–5 spines on each side, stout dark petioles 8–10 mm (⁵⁄₁₆–⅜ in.) long.

'Henry Hicks' (female; selected by W. C. Frierson near Clayton, Georgia, at 363 m (1200 ft.) elevation; named for outstanding nurseryman in Westbury, Long Island, New York).

Leaves dark green; fruits vivid red. Not to be confused with the yellow-fruited 'Henry Hicks'.

'Henry Hicks' (female; selected by J. D. Rankin).

Fruits yellow. Not to be confused with the red-fruited 'Henry Hicks'.

'Hibernia' (female; synonym 'Hybernia'; selected by H. Hume; named for a town on the St. John's River, Florida).

Leaves bright green, small spines; fruits large, dark red, abundant; broadly conical, open branches.

'Highway' (male; synonym 'Highway Male'; selected about 1925 and introduced 1949 by E. Dilatush).

Leaves dark olive green, oval to broadly elliptic, 4.5–5.5 cm (1¾–2⅛ in.) long, 2.5–4 cm (1–1⅝ in.) wide, bases obtuse to truncate, keeled, curved, 3–4 spines on each side, margins reflexed, wavy, petioles 6–8 mm (⁷⁄₃₂–⁵⁄₁₆ in.) long.

'Hoagland' (female; selected at Sea Girt, New Jersey, by New Jersey Holly Research Committee about 1948).

Leaves dark olive green, broadly elliptic, 5–6.5 cm (2–2⅜ in.) long, 3–3.5 cm (1³⁄₁₆–1⅜ in.) wide, bases obtuse, slightly keeled, curved, 3–5 spines on each side, petioles 8–10 mm (⁵⁄₁₆–⅜ in.) long; fruits vivid

red 45A, globose, 8 mm (⁵⁄₁₆ in.) diameter, reddish pedicels 10 mm (⅜ in.) long; robust grower.

'Holiday' (female; Angelica Nursery).

Leaves slightly spiralled; fruits subglobose in clusters; compact pyramidal, slow growing.

'Homer' (male; O. S. Pride; Grace Hybrid Group).

Leaves dark olive green, glossy; compact vigorous growth.

'Hopkins' (female; origin before 1949 in New Jersey by E. C. White).

Leaves dark olive green, oval to elliptic, 5.5–7 cm (2⅛–2¾ in.) long, 3–4 cm (1³⁄₁₆–1⅝ in.) wide, bases cuneate, keeled, curved, 3–4 widely spaced spines, usually on upper two-thirds of leaf, petioles 8–10 mm (⁵⁄₁₆–⅜ in.) long; fruits vivid red 45B, ellipsoid, 10 mm (⅜ in.) long, 8 mm (⁵⁄₁₆ in.) diameter, petioles 8–10 mm (⁵⁄₁₆–⅜ in.) long, pedicels reddish, 8 mm (⁵⁄₁₆ in.) long.

'Howard' (female). See *I.* × *attenuata* 'Howard'.

'Hume's Choice' (female; origin McLean Nursery; named and introduced about 1976 by B. Kuhl; H. Hume commented favorably on the plant).

Leaves moderate olive green, elliptic to broadly elliptic, 4.5–6.5 cm (1¾–2½ in.) long, 2.5–3 cm (1–1³⁄₁₆ in.) wide, keeled, curved, 2–5 spines on upper two-thirds of leaf, margins slightly wavy, petioles 7–10 mm (⁹⁄₃₂–⅜ in.) wide; fruits vivid red 44A, globose, 8–11 mm (⁵⁄₁₆–⁷⁄₁₆ in.) diameter, abundant, reddish pedicels 6–8 mm (⁷⁄₃₂–⁵⁄₁₆ in.) long.

'Hyde' (female; selected near Toms River, New Jersey, before 1929 by E. Dilatush; from a double-trunked tree, with 2 separate plants, the better plant named 'Jekyll', the other as a joke 'Hyde', meaning literally "ugly").

Leaves dull light green; fruits of poor quality.

'Illini' (female; seedling; original plant at Hartline Nursery; named by B. Hartline).

Leaves moderate olive green, oval, 4–5 cm (1⅝–2 in.) long, 2.5–3 cm (1–1³⁄₁₆ in.) wide, keeled, curved, 3–4 spines on each side, petioles 5–7 mm (³⁄₁₆–⁹⁄₃₂ in.) long; fruits vivid reddish orange 44B, globose, 6–8 mm (⁷⁄₃₁–⁵⁄₁₆ in.) diameter. No longer propagated.

'Indian Maiden' (female; synonym 'Indian Maid'; origin Steed Nursery, introduced by J. D. Rankin, 1958).

Leaves moderate olive green, oval, 5–6.5 cm (2–2½ in.) long, 3.5–4.5 cm (1⅜–1¾ in.) wide, slightly keeled, curved, 4–6 prominent spines on each side, petioles 8 mm (⁵⁄₁₆ in.) long; fruits vivid reddish orange 32A, globose, 10 mm (³⁄₈ in.) diameter, pedicels 8 mm (⁵⁄₁₆ in.) long.

'Indian Steps' (female; described by H. Hume; origin in Indian Steps Park, on the banks of the Susquehanna River near Collinsville, York County, Pennsylvania).

Leaves olive green, broadly elliptic, curved, not keeled, margins flat, 6 evenly spaced spines on each side; fruits red, borne singly.

'Ingleside Big Berry' (female; seedling discovered 1955 by C. Flemer Jr. on hedgerow at Ingleside Plantation; transplanted to an open site).

Leaves moderate olive green, broadly elliptic, 4–5 cm (1⁵⁄₈–2 in.) long, 2.5–3 cm (1–1³⁄₈ in.) wide, bases obtuse to cuneate, keeled, curved, convex, 3–5 prominent spines on each side, margins wavy, petioles 8 mm (⁵⁄₁₆ in.) long; fruits vivid red 44A, globose, 10–12 mm (³⁄₈–½ in.) diameter, pedicels 10 mm (³⁄₈ in.) long, abundant fruiting, persisting most of a year; upright pyramidal tree.

'Irene Smith' (female; chance seedling selected and introduced by T. Klein in the 1960s).

Leaves dark olive green, glossy, oval, 3–4.5 cm (1³⁄₁₆–1¾ in.) long, 2.2–3 cm (1¹⁄₁₆–1³⁄₁₆ in.) wide, keeled, curved, 4–8 prominent spines on each side, margins reflexed, twisted, stout dark petioles 5–7 mm (³⁄₁₆–⁹⁄₃₂ in.) long; fruits vivid red.

'Irene-Sophie' (female; origin from seedling selected on estate of I. du Pont, Wilmington, Delaware; registered H.S.A. 5-59 by E. C. Waddington Jr.).

Leaves retained for 2 years; fruits strong red, in bunches; branches horizontally.

'Iro' (female; synonym 'Wheeler No. 12'; selected by W. Wheeler before 1953).

Leaves dark olive green, elliptic to oblong, keeled, curved, 5–7.5 cm (2–3 in.) long, 2.5–4 cm (1–1⁵⁄₈ in.) wide, bases acute to rotund, 4–6 spines on each side, petioles 6 mm (⁷⁄₃₂ in.) long; fruits vivid red 45A, pedicels 6 mm (⁷⁄₃₂ in.) long.

'Isaiah' (male; selected and named by E. C. White before 1948 from tree in Whitesbog, New Jersey).

Leaves moderate olive green, oval elliptic, 6.5–7 cm (2½–2¾ in.) long, 3.5–4 cm (1³⁄₈–1⁵⁄₈ in.) wide, curved, midrib depressed, 3–7 spines on each side, reflexed, petioles dark, 7 mm (⁹⁄₃₂ in.) long; broadly conical habit.

'Janice Arlene' (female; chance seedling selected in 1960 by L. Steward Sr. and Jr., near Aura, New Jersey; moved to Steward residence in Pitman, New Jersey; registered H.S.A. 1-84 by D. Lansdale).

Leaves olive green, broadly elliptic, 4–7 cm (1⁵⁄₈–2¾ in.) long, 2–3.8 cm (¾–1½ in.) wide, bases obtuse to attenuate, tip spines reflexed, keeled, 2–5 stout long spines on each side, margins wavy, petioles 7 mm (⁹⁄₃₂ in.) long; fruits deep reddish orange 43A, globose to oblong, 11 mm (⁷⁄₁₆ in.) diameter, pedicels 4 mm (⁵⁄₃₂ in.) long. Selected for superior fruit production and shade tolerance; plant fairly resistant to holly berry midge.

'Jeannette Adamson' (female; synonym 'Janette Adamson'; selected by W. W. Steiner in the 1960s, near old Flint Hill School in east Rowan County, North Carolina; introduced by W. Steed).

Leaves moderate green, oval, 4.5–5.5 cm (1¾–2⅛ in.) long, 3–3.5 cm (1³⁄₁₆–1³⁄₈ in.) wide, keeled, curved, 2–4 spines on each side, margins reflexed, petioles 8–10 mm (⁵⁄₁₆–³⁄₈ in.) long; fruits vivid orange 25B, with blush, ellipsoid, 8 mm (⁵⁄₁₆ in.) long, pedicels 3–5 mm (⅛–³⁄₁₆ in.) long.

'Jekyll' (female; synonym 'Jeckle'; selected near Toms River, New Jersey, before 1929 and introduced 1948 by E. Dilatush; from a double-trunked tree, with 2 separate plants, the better plant named 'Jekyll', the "ugly" plant named 'Hyde').

Leaves moderate olive green, elliptic, 7–7.5 cm (2¾–3 in. long, 3.5–4 cm (1³⁄₈–1⁵⁄₈ in.) wide, bases obtuse keeled, curved, 3–4 spines on each side, margins reflexed, petioles 8 mm (⁵⁄₁₆ in.) long; fruits vivid red 45A, globose, 8 mm (⁵⁄₁₆ in.) diameter, pedicels 10–15 mm (³⁄₈–¹⁹⁄₃₂ in.) long.

'Jersey Delight' (female; controlled cross in 1956 of 'Old Heavy Berry' × 'Isaiah'; selected 1971, named 1988, introduced and registered H.S.A. 11-89 by E. R. Orton Jr.).

Leaves dark green, broadly ovate, 6.5–9 cm (2½–3½ in.) long, 3–5 cm (1³⁄₁₆–2 in.) wide, not keeled, slightly curved, bases broadly cuneate to rotund, tip spines short, slightly reflexed, margins 3–9 small spines on each side, upper two-thirds of leaf, petioles stout, 8–10 mm (⁵⁄₁₆–³⁄₈ in.) long; similar to 'Old Heavy Berry', deeply impressed veins above; fruits deep reddish orange 43A, globose, 11 mm (⁷⁄₁₆ in.) diameter, single to fasciculate, 2 pedicels; vigorous conical compact habit; original tree at 30 years old 5.78 m (19 ft.) high, 3.95 m (13 ft.) wide; hardy in zone 6a.

'Jersey Knight' (male; synonyms 'Brown #9', 'Judge Brown #9', 'Tom Brown'; selected from the wild

1945 by the Holly Research Committee of Rutgers University at Holly Hill, the home of the late Judge Thomas Brown, Locust, New Jersey; registered H.S.A. 8-65 by E. R. Orton Jr.).

Leaves dark olive green, semiglossy, elliptic to ovate, 5–8 cm (2–3⅛ in.) long, 2.5–4.5 cm (1–1⅗ in.) wide, flat, curved, margins recurved, 5–7 spines on each side, petioles 5–7 mm (3⁄16–9⁄32 in.) long. Very popular male plant: vigorous and winter hardy in zone 6a. When used in hybridization, transmits characteristics of dark green semiglossy foliage to a high percentage of the offspring. Is male parent of 'Jersey Princess', which see.

'Jersey Princess' (female; from controlled cross; male parent is 'Jersey Knight'; selected and registered H.S.A 13-76 by E. R. Orton Jr.).

Leaves dark olive green, glossy, oval to broadly elliptic, 5.5–6.5 cm (2⅛–2½ in.) long, 3.5–4 cm (1⅜–1⅝ in.) wide, slightly keeled, curved, 5–6 spines on each side; fruits vivid red 45A, globose, 8–10 mm (5⁄16–⅜ in.) diameter. Noted for glossy foliage, which is the darkest foliage of any *I. opaca*.

'Jersianna' (female; synonym 'Jessiana'; from the wild near Morristown, New Jersey; registered H.S.A. 1-68 by R. D. Chisholm).

Leaves dark olive green; fruits large red, abundant.

'Jesse Younce' (female; selected near Walhalla, South Carolina, by W. C. Frierson; registered American Association of Nurserymen No. 25, 1948).

Leaves dark olive green, medium size, elliptic, semiglossy; fruits reddish orange, globose, reported to be a heavy fruiter.

'Jessie Taylor' (female; origin from tree in a West Virginia state park; introduced by J. D. Rankin in the 1960s).

Leaves moderate olive green, broadly elliptic 6–8 cm (2⅜–3⅛ in.) long, 3.5–4.5 cm (1⅜–1¾ in.) wide, keeled, curved, 2–5 spines on each side, margins reflexed, petioles 8–10 mm (5⁄16–⅜ in.) long; fruits vivid orange yellow 23A, ellipsoid, 10 mm (⅜ in.) long, pedicels 6–8 mm (7⁄32–5⁄16 in.) long.

'Jingle Bells' (female; selected by P. Bosley from West Virginia before 1957).

Leaves dark olive green, semiglossy, broad, keeled; fruits very large, red, tinged orange; heavy fruiting.

'Joanne' (female; selected by A. Flemer about 1930; registered H.S.A. 4-59 by R. C. Jennings).

Leaves moderate olive green, elliptic, 4–5 cm (1⅝–2 in.) long, 2–3.5 cm (¾–1⅜ in.) wide, keeled, curved, 1–4 spines, some leaves nearly entire, mar-

gins reflexed, petioles 8–10 mm (5⁄16–⅜ in.) long; fruits vivid red 44A, globose, 8 mm (5⁄16 in.) diameter, short pedicels 5 mm (3⁄16 in.) long.

'Joe Stephens' (female; original tree from a limestone ridge in southwestern Virginia; collected before 1947).

Leaves dark olive green, medium size; fruits reddish orange, ovate, borne in clusters, annual bearing.

'John Banks' (male; synonym 'Wheeler No. 9'; origin in Cape Cod, Massachusetts; selected by W. Wheeler and E. C. White before 1947).

Leaves dark olive green, broadly oval, 5–6 cm (2–2⅜ in.) long, 3.5–4 cm (1 3⁄16–1⅝ in.) wide, bases obtuse, curved, 3–5 spines on each side, margins reflexed, petioles stout, 10 mm (⅜ in.) long.

'John Higgins' (male; selected before 1949 and introduced by E. C. White).

Leaves dark olive green, oval, 5–6 cm (2–2⅜ in.) long, 3.5–4 cm (1⅜–1⅝ in.) wide, bases obtuse to rotund, keeled, slightly curved, 2–3 spines on each side, petioles 7–8 mm (9⁄32–5⁄16 in.) long; dense bushy habit.

'John Wister' (male; seedling from Millcreek Nursery in 1964; named by J. Zuk; registered H.S.A 5-87 by A. Bunting; plant at Scott Arboretum; named for former director of the Arthur Hoyt Scott Horticultural Foundation, Swarthmore College, Pennsylvania).

Leaves dark olive green, glossy, broadly ovate, 5.5–8.2 cm (2–3¼ in.) long, 3.5–5.6 cm (1⅜–2½ in.) wide, bases rounded, slightly keeled and curved, 3–4 small spines on each side, tip leaves less spiny, stout petioles 6–8 mm (7⁄32–5⁄16 in.) long; broadly conical habit; tree 7.5 m (25 ft.) tall, 4.6 m (15 ft.) wide in 25 years.

'Johnson' (female; synonym 'Johnston'; selected 1934 by J. Gable from Johnson Farm near Sunnybrook, Pennsylvania, after surviving severe exposed winter of −32°C (−25°F)).

Leaves dark olive green, broadly elliptic to ovate, 4.5–6.5 cm (1¾–2½ in.) long, 2.5–3.5 cm (1–1⅜ in.) wide, curved, convex, 2–4 spines on each side, margins reflexed, petioles 8–10 mm (5⁄16–⅜ in.) long; fruits vivid red 44A, globose, 8 mm (5⁄16 in.) diameter, short pedicels 2–3 mm (1⁄16–⅛ in.) long; pyramidal habit.

'Joyce' (female; selected about 1935–1940 near Whitesbog, New Jersey, by T. Windon and E. C. White).

Leaves moderate olive green, elliptic, 6.5–8 cm (2½–3⅛ in.) long, 3–3.5 cm (1 3⁄16–1⅜ in.) wide, bases obtuse, keeled, curved, 4–6 spines on each side, margins reflexed, petioles 10 mm (⅜ in.) long; fruits deep reddish orange 43A, globose, 10 mm (⅜ in.) diameter, pedicels 6 mm (7⁄32 in.) long; upright, rapid growing.

'Judge Brown' (female; synonym 'Brown #7'; original tree at Holly Hill, home of the late Judge T. Brown, Locust, New Jersey; selected and named by the Holly Research Committee of Rutgers University; registered American Association of Nurserymen No. 419, 1954).
   Leaves dark olive green, glossy, oval elliptic, bases cuneate to obtuse, flat, curved, margins recurved, 2–4 spines on each side, petioles 8 mm (5⁄16 in.) long; fruits red, globose, 8 mm (5⁄16 in.) diameter, pedicels 5–6 mm (3⁄16–7⁄32 in.) long, borne singly, abundant.

'Judy' (female; synonym 'Bill Judd'; named in the 1960s for Bill Judd, propagator at Arnold Arboretum).
   Leaves dark olive green, broadly elliptic, 4.5–7 cm (1¾–2¾ in.) long, 2.5–3.5 cm (1–1⅜ in.) wide, bases obtuse to rotund, keeled, curved, margins recurved, 3–5 small spines on each side, petioles 8–10 mm (5⁄16–⅜ in.) long; fruits red, pedicels reddish, 7 mm (9⁄32 in.) long.

'Judy Evans' (female; origin Cave Hill Cemetery, Louisville, Kentucky; named and introduced by T. Klein around 1940).
   Leaves dark olive green, glossy, broadly elliptic, 4–6.5 cm (1⅝–2½ in.) long, 3–4.5 cm (1³⁄16–1¾ in.) wide, keeled, curved, 4–6 prominent spines on each side, dark petioles 8 mm (5⁄16 in.) long; fruits vivid red 45A, globose, 8 mm (5⁄16 in.) diameter.

'Judy Kay' (female; discovered in wild in Sussex County, Delaware, by Mrs. E. Lynch; introduced 1959 by J. D. Rankin).
   Leaves moderate olive green, oval, 4–5.5 cm (1⅝–2⅛ in.) long, 2.5–3 cm (1–1³⁄16 in.) wide, keeled, curved, 2–3 spines usually on upper half of leaf, margins reflexed, petioles 6–8 mm (7⁄32–5⁄16 in.) long; fruits vivid yellow 15A, with pink blush, globose, 8–10 mm (5⁄16–⅜ in.) diameter, pedicels 5 mm (3⁄16 in.) long.

'Julian' (male; seedling selected in the 1950s by T. Klein).
   Leaves dark olive green, oval to broadly elliptic, 5–6 cm (2–2⅜ in.) long, 2.5–4 cm (1–1⅝ in.) wide, bases obtuse to truncate, 2–5 spines on each side, margins reflexed, petioles 10–12 mm (⅜–15⁄32 in.) long.

'Julie Koehler' (female; selected by W. Hallenberg and T. Klein on property of I. L. Kinkead in Kesslers Cross Lanes, West Virginia, in the 1960s; named by Klein for his granddaughter).
   Leaves moderate olive green, elliptic to broadly elliptic, 6–7 cm (2⅜–2¾ in.) long, 2.5–3 cm (2–1³⁄16 in.) wide, bases cuneate, keeled, curved, 4–5 spines on upper two-thirds of leaf, margins reflexed; fruits brilliant orange yellow 21B, globose, 8 mm (5⁄16 in.) diameter, pedicels 5–8 mm (3⁄16–5⁄16 in.) long.

'Kate' (synonyms 'Aalto No. 3', 'Alto No. 3'; selected near Whitesbog, New Jersey, by W. Wheeler and E. C. White before 1953).
   Leaves moderate olive green, elliptic, 4.5–6 cm (1¾–2⅜ in.) long, 1.5–2.5 cm (½–1 in.) wide, keeled, curved, 2–5 spines on each side, margins reflexed, wavy, twisted; fruits deep reddish orange 43A, ellipsoid, 8 mm (5⁄16 in.) long, pedicels 6–8 mm (7⁄32–5⁄16 in.) long.

'Kathryn' (female; chance seedling selected and named by T. Klein in the 1960s).
   Leaves moderate olive green, oval, 5–5.5 cm (2–2⅛ in.) long, 3.5–4 cm (1⅜–1⅝ in.) wide, keeled, curved, 3–5 spines on each side, petioles 8 mm (5⁄16 in.) long; fruits vivid reddish orange 44B, globose, 8 mm (5⁄16 in.) diameter; upright vigorous grower.

'Katz' (female; found in garden in Covington, Louisiana, by S. J. Katz in the 1960s).
   Leaves dark green, oval to obovate, curved, spines sharp, petioles stout; fruits vivid red, ovoid, singly or in clusters of 2–3; branches pendant.

'Kentucky Gentleman' (male; plant at Bernheim Forest).
   Leaves moderate olive green, oval, 5–5.5 cm (2–2⅛ in.) long, 3–3.5 cm (1³⁄16–1⅜ in.) wide, keeled, curved convexed, 2–3 spines on upper half of leaf, stout petioles 6 mm (7⁄32 in.) long.

'Kentucky Smoothleaf' (female; origin tree on a school property in Louisville, Kentucky; selected and named by T. Klein in the 1960s).
   Leaves moderate yellow green, darker in shade, completely spineless, heavy texture; fruits red, heavy producer.

'Kerns' (female), see *I.* × *attenuata*.

'Kildare' (female; origin unknown, plant at Secrest Arboretum).
   Leaves dark olive green, oval to broadly elliptic, 5–5.5 cm (2–2⅛ in.) long, 3–4 cm (1³⁄16–1⅝ in.)

wide, bases obtuse, keeled, curved, margins recurved, 5–6 spines on each side, petioles 5–7 mm (3/16–9/32 in.) long; fruits deep reddish orange 43A, globose, 6–8 mm (7/32–5/16 in.) diameter, pedicels 5 mm (3/16 in.) long.

'King Midas' (female; plant at Bernheim Forest, origin unknown).
Leaves moderate olive green, broadly oval, 5–5.5 cm (2–2⅛ in.) long, 3–3.5 cm (1 3/16–1⅜ in.) wide, keeled, curved, convexed, 2–3 spines on upper half of leaf, margins wavy; dark petioles 8 mm (5/16 in.) long; fruits yellow changing to orange and than red, flat globose, 10 mm (⅜ in.) diameter.

'Klein Compact' (female; seedling of 'Klein No. 1'; introduced by T. Klein in the 1940s).
Leaves moderate olive green, oval, 4–4.5 cm (1⅝–1¾ in.) long, 2–3 cm (¾–1 3/16 in.) wide, keeled, curved, 3–4 spines on each side, margins twisted, dark petioles 5 mm (3/16 in.) long; fruits red; compact habit of growth.

'Klein No. 1' (female; origin about 1910; introduced 1940 by Klein Nursery).
Leaves dark olive green, oval, 6.5–7.5 cm (2½–3 in.) long, 3.5–4 cm (1⅜–1⅝ in.) wide, bases wide obtuse, keeled, curved, 4–5 spines on each side, margins reflexed, petioles 7–8 mm (9/32–5/16 in.) long; fruits deep reddish orange 43A, ellipsoid, 1 cm (⅜ in.) long.

'Knight' (female; selected before 1950 from wild between Beltsville and Fairland, Montgomery County, Maryland, by A. L. Quaintance; named in honor of Paul Knight).
Leaves moderate olive green, broadly elliptic, convex, 7.5–9 cm (3–3½ in.) long, 2.5–3.8 cm (1–1½ in.) wide, bases obtuse, apices acute, tip spines reflexed, margins 4–6 spines on each side; fruits vivid red 45A, globose, 8 mm (5/16 in.) diameter, pedicels 10–13 mm (⅜–½ in.) long, fruits retain until spring; upright pyramidal habit.

'La Bar No. 1' (male; selected 1950 by C. H. Conners).
Leaves dark olive green, elliptic, 5–7 cm (2–2¾ in.) long, 2.2–3.8 cm (13/16–1½ in.) wide, keeled, curved, margins recurved, 2–4 spines on each side, petioles 10–12 mm (⅜–15/32 in.) long.

'Lady Alice' (female; selected 1929 near Millville, New Jersey; named 1950 by C. Wolf; registered H.S.A. 9-74 by D. G. Fenton).
Leaves moderate olive green, broadly elliptic, 7.5–8 cm (3–3⅛ in.) long, 4–4.5 cm (1⅝–1¾ in.) wide, keeled, curved, 4–6 spines on each side, margins wavy, petioles 8–10 mm (5/16–⅜ in.) long; fruits vivid red 44A, ellipsoid, 10 mm (⅜ in.) long; easily propagated.

'Lady Blakeford' (female; selected in the 1930s by H. G. Mattoon near Blakeford, Pennsylvania; introduced 1959 by J. D. Rankin).
Leaves moderate olive green, elliptic, 4–5 cm (1⅝–2 in.) long, 2.5–3 cm (1–1 3/16 in.) wide, keeled, curved, 1–4 spines on each side, many entire, margins reflexed, wavy, petioles 8–10 mm (5/16–⅜ in.) long; fruits vivid yellow 15A, globose, 6–8 mm (7/32–5/16 in.) diameter, pedicels 4–6 mm (5/32–7/32 in.) long.

'Lady Esmee' (female; old tree discovered on W. Fairfax Griffith property, Westmoreland County, Virginia, around 1958; named by Frances Taylor in honor of Mrs. W. F. Griffith; registered H.S.A. 5-88 by W. F. Griffith).
Leaves dark olive green, ovate to obovate, to 8 cm (3⅛ in.) long, to 5.5 cm (2⅛ in.) wide, curved, slightly keeled, bases cuneate, apices acuminate, margins wavy, 2–4 spines upper one-third of leaf, petioles 11 mm (7/16 in.) long; fruits vivid red 44A, ovoid, 19 mm (¾ in.) long, 8 mm (5/16 in.) diameter, pedicels 11 mm (7/16 in.) long; original tree conical with horizontal branching, 9 m (30 ft.) tall, 4.8 m (16 ft.) wide; hardy to at least zone 7.

'Lamp Post' (female; chance seedling discovered 1960 by L. Steward Sr. and Jr., near Aura, New Jersey; moved to Steward residence, Pitman, New Jersey; registered H.S.A. 2-84 by D. Lansdale).
Leaves dark olive green, broadly oval, 7 cm (2¾ in.) long, 4.5 cm (1¾ in.) wide, bases broad, variably keeled, curved, 3–4 strong spines on each side, margins twisted near apex, petioles 7 mm (¼ in.) long; fruits vivid reddish orange 41A, slightly elongate, 10 mm (⅜ in.) long, 8 mm (5/16 in.) wide, pedicels 5 mm (3/16 in.) long; resistent to holly berry midge. Selected for compact conical habit, fruit quality, and resistance to midge.

'Laura' (female; selected 1935–1940 near Whitesbog, New Jersey, by T. Windon and E. C. White).
Leaves moderate olive green, broadly elliptic, 6–7.5 cm (2⅜–3 in.) long, 3–4 cm (1 3/16–1⅝ in.) wide, keeled, curved, 4–6 spines on each side, margins wavy, recurved, petioles 7–10 mm (9/32–⅜ in.) long; fruits vivid red 45A, ovate to ellipsoid, 10–12 mm (⅜–15/32 in.) long, 8–9 mm (5/16–11/32 in.) diameter, pedicels 8–10 mm (5/16–⅜ in.) long. There is

another 'Laura' male; name invalid, without origin or description.

'Laura Thomas' (female; selected 1941 in Osterville, Massachusetts, by W. Wheeler and E. C. White).

Leaves dark olive green, elliptic, 5.5–6.5 cm (2⅛–2½ in.) long, 2.5–3 cm (1–1³⁄₁₆ in.) wide, bases cuneate to obtuse, keeled, curved, 4–7 small spines on each side, petioles 6–8 mm (⁷⁄₃₂–⁵⁄₁₆ in.) long; fruits deep reddish orange 43A, globose, 8 mm (⁵⁄₁₆ in.) diameter, pedicels reddish, 6 mm (⁷⁄₃₂ in.) long.

'Laurel Lake' (female; selected by Laurel Lake Nursery).

Leaves moderate olive green, broadly elliptic, 8–11 cm (3⅛–4¼ in.) long, 4–4.5 cm (1⅝–1¾ in.) wide, curved, 5–8 spines on each side, margins slightly reflexed, petioles 8 mm (⁵⁄₁₆ in.) long; fruits vivid red 46B, globose, 10 mm (⅜ in.) diameter, pedicels 6–8 mm (⁷⁄₃₂–⁵⁄₁₆ in.) long.

'Laurie' (male; from twin trees growing together and moved from Boyden Farm, Sandwich, Massachusetts, to Ashumet Farm, Falmouth, Massachusetts; H. Hume said "it was remarkable, represents seed from same berry"; other twin is female 'Nora'; leaf characteristic not same as 'Laura').

Leaves dark olive green, elliptic, smooth.

'Lawrence' (female; synonym 'Lawrence No. 2'; selected in 1940 from West Barnstable, Massachusetts, by W. Wheeler).

Fruits large, red.

'Lenape Moon' (female; discovered 1932 in Sussex County, Delaware, by W. Phillips and registered H.S.A. 2-68).

Leaves dark olive green, broadly elliptic, 6.5–7.5 cm (2½–3 in.) long, 2.5–3 mm (1–1³⁄₁₆ in.) wide, slightly keeled, curved, bases cuneate, 2–3 spines usually on upper half of leaf, petioles 7–8 mm (⁹⁄₃₂–⁵⁄₁₆ in.) long; fruits vivid yellow 13A, faint pinkish blush, ellipsoid, 8 mm (⁵⁄₁₆ in.) long, pedicels reddish, 5–6 mm (³⁄₁₆–⁷⁄₃₂ in.) long.

'Lewis Swartz' (male; selected and named at Ivyland, Pennsylvania, by J. C. Swartley before 1957).

Leaves dark olive green, oval, 4.5–5.5 cm (1¾–2⅛ in.) long, 2.5–3.5 cm (1–1⅜ in.) wide, bases obtuse to rotund, keeled, curved, 2–4 spines usually on upper two-thirds of leaf, petioles 8–10 mm (⁵⁄₁₆–⅜ in.) long; abundant flowering male; compact habit.

'Ley' (male; introduced by Hillenmeyer Nursery in the 1950s).

Leaves moderate olive green, oval elliptic, 7–7.5 cm (2¾–3 in.) long, 4–4.5 cm (1⅝–1¾ in.) wide, keeled, curved, 4–6 spines on each side, margins reflexed, petioles 7 mm (⁹⁄₃₂ in.) long.

'Lida Lane' (female; chance seedling selected and introduced by H. Elmore in the 1980s; named for Elmore's maternal grandmother; not registered).

Leaves dark olive green, broadly obovate, 5–7 cm (2–2¾ in.) long, 3–4 cm (1³⁄₁₆–1⅝ in.) wide, bases cuneate, slightly keeled, nearly flat, 4–6 very small spines on upper two-thirds of leaf, stout petioles 8–10 mm (⁵⁄₁₆–⅜ in.) long; fruits red. Selected for unusual leaf form and pendulous growth habit.

'Lindsey' (female; origin from Hamlet, North Carolina).

Leaves with few dull spines; fruits red.

'Ling' (female; also called 'Ling-A-Ling'; introduced 1964 by O. S. Pride; Grace Hybrid Group).

Leaves moderate olive green, elliptic, 7–7.5 cm (2¾–3 in.) long, 3 cm (1³⁄₁₆ in.) wide, bases obtuse, keeled, curved, 6–7 prominent spines on each side, margins wavy, reflexed, petioles 8 mm (⁵⁄₁₆ in.) long; fruits vivid reddish orange 33A, globose, 8–10 mm (⁵⁄₁₆–⅜ in.) diameter, pedicels 10 mm (⅜ in.) long; vigorous, narrow pyramidal habit.

'Ling Close' (female; O. S. Pride; Grace Hybrid Group; thought by some to be same as 'Ling').

Leaves moderate olive green, elliptic, 4.5–6.5 cm (1¾–2½ in.) long, 2.5–3 cm (1–1³⁄₁₆ in.) wide, keeled, curved, 4–6 prominent spines on each side, margins reflexed, wavy, petioles 8 mm (⁵⁄₁₆ in.) long; fruits deep reddish orange 43B, globose, 8–10 mm (⁵⁄₁₆–⅜ in.) diameter, pedicels 6 mm (⁷⁄₃₂ in.) long.

'Ling No. 2' (female; origin unknown; plant at Secrest Arboretum).

Leaves dark olive green, broadly elliptic, 5.5–7 cm (2⅛–2¾ in.) long, 3–3.5 cm (1³⁄₁₆–1⅜ in.) wide, bases cuneate to obtuse, keeled, curved, margins recurved, wavy, 4–7 spines on each side, petioles 10 mm (⅜ in.) long; fruits red, pedicels 10 mm (⅜ in.) long.

'Lin's Gold' (male; seedling sport discovered in 1975 by L. Steward Jr. in his nursery).

Leaves variegated, yellow margins, with irregular yellowish blotches on the leaves; hardy in zone 5; upright pyramidal habit. Good pollinator and accent plant.

'Little's Cascade' (female; discovered in 1978 by Parker Lewis Little in Hanover County, Virginia;

named, introduced, and registered H.S.A. 4-96 by Little.

Leaves elliptic, 12.6 cm (4⁵⁄₁₆ in.) long, 9 mm (1¹⁄₃₂ in.) wide, convex curved, tips aristate, bases cuneate to attenuate, margins with 3–5 evenly spaced spines on each side, petioles to 1.1 cm (⁷⁄₁₆ in.) long; fruits scarlet-orange; hardy in zone 7. Original tree 7.2 m (24 ft.) tall, 4.2 m (14 ft.) wide. Selected for large, convex leaves with down-pointed tip spines, and showy scarlet-orange fruits. Available from Piping Tree Gardens, Beaverdam, Virginia.

'Little's Compact Red' (female; discovered in 1994 by Parker Lewis Little in Hanover County, Virginia; named, introduced, and registered H.S.A. 5-96 by Little).

Leaves broadly ovate, curved, 6.6 cm (2⁵⁄₁₆ in.) long, 4.8 cm (1⁷⁄₁₆ in.) wide, tips aristate, bases broadly cuneate, margins with 3–5 short lateral spines on each side, usually on upper two-thirds of leaf, petioles 1 cm (³⁄₈ in.) long; fruits vivid red 44A, globose to 9 mm (1¹⁄₃₂ in.) diameter; hardy in zone 7 to −10°C (13°F). Original tree 13 m (40 ft.) tall, 4.6 m (16 ft.) wide in 60 years. Selected for dense habit of growth, thick leaf texture, and compact fruit clusters. Good specimen, screen, or hedge plant. Available from Piping Tree Gardens, Beaverdam, Virginia.

'Little's Glossy Lady' (female; seedling discovered in 1995 by Parker Lewis Little; named, introduced, and registered H.S.A. 10-96 by Little).

Leaves glossy, flat, ovate, to 9.1 cm (3½ in.) long, 5.2 cm (2 in.) wide, tips aristate, bases cuneate, margins with 4–5 evenly spaced moderate spines on each side, petioles 1 cm (³⁄₈ in.) long; fruits vivid red 45A, slightly ovoid, 9 cm (1¹⁄₃₂ in.) diameter. Original tree 2.4 m (8 ft.) tall, 1.8 m (6 ft.) wide in 12 years. Selected for flat glossy leaves and vivid red fruit. Available from Piping Tree Gardens, Beaverdam, Virginia.

'Little's Glossy Princess' (female; discovered in 1996 by Parker Lewis Little; named, introduced, and registered H.S.A. 7-96 by Little).

Leaves oval, curved, keeled, to 8 cm (3⅛ in.) long, 4.2 cm (1⁵⁄₁₆ in.) wide, tips aristate, reflexed downward, bases cuneate, petioles to 9 mm (1¹⁄₃₂ in.) long, margins slightly wavy with 1–4 spines on each side; fruits vivid red 44A, ovoid, 9 mm (1¹⁄₃₂ in.) long, 8 mm (⁵⁄₁₆ in.) wide, borne singly, pedicels 10 mm (³⁄₈ in.) long; hardy in zone 7 to −10°C (13°F). Original tree 5.4 m (17 ft.) tall, 4.2 m (14 ft.) wide. Selected for deep glossy leaves and vivid red fruits. Available from Piping Tree Gardens, Beaverdam, Virginia.

'Little's Glossy Salmon' (female; seedling tree discovered in 1996 by Parker Lewis Little in Hanover County, Virginia; named, introduced, and registered H.S.A. 9-96 by Little).

Leaves large, ovate, to 10 cm (4 in.) long, 6.8 cm (2⅝ in.) wide, convex, slightly curved, tips bluntly aristate, reflexed downward, bases rounded, margins with 4–6 large evenly spaced spines on each side, petioles 8 mm (⁵⁄₁₆ in.) long; fruits vivid reddish orange 41A, subglobose, to 8 mm (⁵⁄₁₆ in.) diameter, borne singly, pedicels to 1 mm (³⁄₈ in.) long; hardy in zone 7. Original tree 2.7 m (8 ft.) tall in 22 years, with pyramidal habit, and horizontal branching. Selected for dark green leaves and glossy reddish orange fruits. Available from Piping Tree Gardens, Beaverdam, Virginia.

'Little's Red Bunch' (female; tree discovered in 1995 by Parker Lewis Little; named, introduced, and registered H.S.A. 11-96 by Little).

Leaves ovate, flat, to 9.2 cm (3⅝ in.) long, 5.2 cm (2¹⁄₁₆ in.) wide, tips aristate, bases cuneate, margins with 4–5 evenly spaced moderate spines on each side, some leaves entire, petioles 1 cm (³⁄₄ in.) long; fruits vivid red 45A, ovoid, to 9 mm (1¹⁄₃₂ in.) diameter, 1–3 in clusters on peduncles 9 mm (1¹⁄₃₂ in.) long; hardy in zone 7. Original tree 6.3 m (21 ft.) tall, 3 m (10 ft.) wide in 35 years. Selected for heavy fruit production, spineless leaves, and columnar habit. Available from Piping Tree Gardens, Beaverdam, Virginia.

'Little's Red Giant' (female; seedling tree discovered by Parker Lewis Little in Hanover County, Virginia; named, introduced, and registered H.S.A. 1-96 by Little).

Leaves glossy, ovate, keeled, strongly curved, to 8 cm (3⅛ in.) long, 4.3 cm (1⅝ in.) wide, margins cuneate with 3–4 moderate lateral spines on each side, petioles to 1 cm (³⁄₈ in.) long; fruits vivid red 44B, ovoid to obovoid, 10 mm (³⁄₈ in.) long, 8 mm (⁵⁄₁₆ in.) wide, borne singly, pedicels to 7 mm (⁹⁄₃₂ in.) long; vigorous habit; hardy in zone 7. Original tree 5.4 m (18 ft.) tall in 20 years. Selected for large fruit and glossy leaves.

'Little's Ruby Gem' (female; tree discovered in 1985 by Parker Lewis Little in Hanover County, Virginia; named, introduced, and registered H.S.A. 8-96 by Little).

Leaves broad, ovate, to 7.3 cm (3 in.) long, 4.8 cm (1¹³⁄₁₆ in.) wide, tips broadly aristate, bases rounded, margins with 1–3 evenly spaced short spines on each side of upper two-thirds of margin, petioles to 8 mm (⁵⁄₁₆ in.) long; fruits vivid red 45A, ovoid, to 10 mm (³⁄₈ in.) long, 9 mm (1¹⁄₃₂ in.) wide; hardy in zone 7 to −10°C (13°F). Original tree 10.5 m (35 ft.) tall, 3.3 m (11 ft.) wide, with conical shape and horizontal branching. Available from Piping Tree Gardens, Beaverdam, Virginia.

'Little's Scarlet' (female; discovered in 1994 by Parker Lewis Little in Hanover County, Virginia; named, introduced, and registered H.S.A. 2-96 by Little).

Leaves broad, ovate, slightly curved and keeled, to 8.7 cm (3⁵⁄₁₆ in.) long, 5.6 cm (2.25 in.) wide, tips aristate, bases cuneate, margins with 3–4 spines on each side, petioles 1 cm (³⁄₈ in.) long; fruits ovoid, vivid red 44A, 10 mm (³⁄₈ in.) long, 9 mm (¹¹⁄₃₂ in.) wide, borne singly on petioles; hardy in zone 7. Selected for glossy leaves, vivid red fruit, yellowish brown twigs, and dense habit. Available from Piping Tree Gardens, Beaverdam, Virginia.

'Little's Sparking Red' (female; discovered in 1994 by Parker Lewis Little in Hanover County, Virginia; named, introduced, and registered H.S.A. 6-96 by Little).

Leaves ovate, glossy, to 9.5 cm (3¾ in.) long, 5.2 cm (2¹⁄₁₆ in.) wide, curved, tips aristate, bases cuneate, tip spines strongly reflexed downward, margins revolute with 3–5 unevenly spaced spines on each side, some lateral spines deviated and curled under, upper lateral spines typically point outward, petioles to 1.9 cm (1⁵⁄₁₆ in.) long; fruits vivid red 45A, ovoid, 9 mm (¹¹⁄₃₂ in.) long, 8 mm (⁵⁄₁₆ in.) wide, borne singly, pedicels to 1 cm (³⁄₈ in.) long; hardy in zone 7 to −10°C (13°F). Original tree 5.4 m (18 ft.) tall, 2.7 m (9 ft.) wide in 20 years. Selected for glossy leaves and bright red fruit in large clusters. Available from Piping Tree Gardens, Beaverdam, Virginia.

'Little's Waxleaf' (female; seedling discovered by Parker Lewis Little in Hanover County, Virginia; named, introduced, and registered H.S.A. 3-96 by Little).

Leaves ovate, deep glossy green, to 8.8 cm (3⁵⁄₁₆ in.) long, 4.5 cm (1¾ in.) wide, tips aristate, bases cuneate, slightly keeled, curved, petioles 1.2 cm (1⁵⁄₃₂ in.) long; fruits vivid red 45A, globose, 9 mm (¹¹⁄₃₂ in.) diameter, borne singly, pedicels to 7 mm (⁹⁄₃₂ in.) long; hardy in zone 7 to −10°C (13°F). Original tree 23 years old. Selected for dense growth habit with numerous suckers and for glossy red fruit. Available from Piping Tree Gardens, Beaverdam, Virginia.

'Little's Weeping Mound' (female; tree discovered in 1996 by Parker Lewis Little in the woods in Henrico County, Virginia; named, introduced, and registered H.S.A. 12-96 by Little).

Leaves ovate, green, 8.5 cm (3⅜ in.) long, 5 cm (2 in.) wide, slightly convex, sometimes flat or even concave, tips aristate, bases cuneate, margins with 4–7 evenly spaced spines on each side, petioles 1 cm (³⁄₈ in.) long; fruits vivid red 45A, slightly ovate, 11 mm (⁷⁄₁₆ in.) long, 10 mm (³⁄₈ in.) wide, borne singly, pedicels 8 mm (⁵⁄₁₆ in.) long; hardy in zone 7 to −10°C (13°F). Original plant 2.85 m (9 ft.) tall, 6.6 m (22 ft.) wide in 45 years, with shrubby mound shape; some side branches have rooted and produced shoots, further extending the shrubby habit.

'Lombard' (female; discovered 1914 at Horse Hole, North Carolina, at 940 m (3100 ft.) elevation by E. G. Lombard).

Fruits red; heavy annual fruiting.

'Longwash' (female; origin unknown; plant at North Carolina State University Arboretum).

Leaves moderate olive green, elliptic to broadly elliptic, keeled, curved, 4–6.5 cm (1⅝–2½ in.) long, 2–3.5 cm (¾–1⅜ in.) wide, bases cuneate to obtuse, apices acuminate, tip spines often reflexed, margins undulate, often twisted, 5–7 spines on each side; fruits vivid yellow 14A, globose, 6–8 mm (⁷⁄₃₂–⁵⁄₁₆ in.) diameter, prominent black spot, pedicels dark, 8 mm (⁵⁄₁₆ in.) long.

'Longwood Gardens' (female; synonym 'Longwood'; from Longwood Gardens; original tree from Mount Vernon, Virginia).

Leaves moderate olive green, broadly elliptic, 5–6.5 cm (2–2⅜ in.) long, 3–4 cm (1³⁄₁₆–1⅝ in.) wide, keeled, curved, margins reflexed and twisted; fruits vivid yellow 16A, globose, 6–8 mm (⁷⁄₃₂–⁵⁄₁₆ in.) diameter.

'Louise' (female; listed in 1959 by Native American Holly Farm).

Leaves dark olive green, broadly elliptic, 5–6.5 cm (2–2½ in.) long, 3–3.5 cm (1³⁄₁₆–1⅜ in.) wide, keeled, curved, 4–6 spines on each side, petioles 1 cm (³⁄₈ in.) long; fruits vivid red 44A, globose, 6–8 mm (⁷⁄₃₂–⁵⁄₁₆ in.) diameter, reddish pedicels 8–10 mm (⁵⁄₁₆–³⁄₈ in.) long.

'Lowell' (female; selected 1948 from Lowell Woods, Mashpee, Massachusetts, by W. Wheeler).

Leaves moderate olive green, oval to broadly elliptic, 5–5.5 cm (2–2⅛ in.) long, 3–3.5 cm (1³⁄₁₆–1⅜ in.) wide, keeled, curved, 3–4 spines on each side, margins reflexed, slightly wavy, petioles 8–10 mm (⁵⁄₁₆–³⁄₈ in.) long; fruits deep reddish orange 43A, globose, 8–10 mm (⁵⁄₁₆–³⁄₈ in.) diameter, abundant, reddish pedicels 3–6 mm (⅛–⁷⁄₃₂ in.) long.

'Loyalton' (female; tree named by M. Fulton before 1947; said to have been planted by President Buchanan on Rumberger property in Loyalton, Pennsylvania).

Leaves dark green, obovate, flat, spines very small; fruits red, small.

'Lucille' (female; origin from seed of 'St. Mary'; named and registered H.S.A. 13-67 by L. B. Austin).

Leaves dark olive green, glossy; fruits red; broad, conical dense habit.

'Mae' (female; selected by T. Windon and E. C. White about 1935–1940 from woods near Whitesbog, New Jersey).

Leaves dark olive green, glossy, elliptic, 4–6 cm (1⅝–2⅜ in.) long, 2–3 cm (¾–1³⁄₁₆ in.) wide, often spineless, or 1–3 spines on upper one-third of leaf, petioles 9 mm (1¹¹⁄₃₂ in.) long, fruits red, globose, 8 mm (⁵⁄₁₆ in.) diameter, abundant, borne singly on short spurs.

'Magna Semen' (female; selected by E. W. Windsor before 1948; name means "large seed").

Leaves dark olive green elliptic, 8–9.5 cm (3⅛–3¾ in.) long, 3.5–4 cm (1⅜–1⅝ in.) wide, keeled, curved, convex, bases cuneate, margins recurved, slightly twisted, 2–4 small spines on each side, usually on upper half of leaf, petioles 8–12 mm (⁵⁄₁₆–¹⁵⁄₃₂ in.) long; fruits deep reddish orange 42B, globose, 8 mm (⁵⁄₁₆ in.) diameter, pedicels 10–16 mm (⅜–⅝ in.) long.

'Maiden Blush' (female; selected 1936–1937 by W. C. Frierson from Allen Dalton's garden in Seneca, South Carolina; named by J. D. Rankin; introduced by E. C. Clark, Appalachian Nursery).

Leaves moderate olive green, oval, 4.5–5 cm (1¾–2 in.) long, 3–3.5 cm (1³⁄₁₆–1⅜ in.) wide, keeled, curved, 2–3 spines usually on upper two-thirds of leaf, petioles 6–8 mm (⁷⁄₃₂–⁵⁄₁₆ in.) long; fruits vivid yellow 14A, globose, 8 mm (⁵⁄₁₆ in.) diameter, pinkish blush, no blush if fertilized.

'Makepeace' (male; synonym 'Ed Thomas'; selected by W. Wheeler and E. C. White before 1953).

Leaves dark olive green, oval, 5–6 cm (2–2⅜ in.) long, 3.5–4 cm (1⅜–1⅝ in.) wide, bases obovate, keeled, curved, 3–5 spines on each side, petioles stout, 5–7 mm (³⁄₁₆–⁹⁄₃₂ in.) long.

'Male' (male; Rocknoll Nursery, listed in 1963 catalog; name is ambiguous and rejected as a valid name).

Leaves large. A showy plant with a long flowering period.

'Male Aquapaca' (male; Angelica Nursery, 1956 catalog).

Leaves moderate olive green, oval, 4–5 cm (1⅝–2 in.) long, 2.5–3 cm (1–1³⁄₁₆ in.) wide, keeled, curved, 4–6 sharp spines on each side, twisted, petioles 6–8 mm (⁷⁄₃₂–⁵⁄₁₆ in.) long. A prolific flowerer and excellent pollinator.

'Mallory' (selected and named by J. C. Swartley at Ivyland, Pennsylvania, on property of Lewis Swartz).

Leaves dark olive green, oval to broadly elliptic, 5–7 cm (2–2¾ in.) long, 3–3.5 cm (1³⁄₁₆–1⅜ in.) wide, bases obtuse to rotund, 3–4 spines on each side, petioles 8–10 mm (⁵⁄₁₆–⅜ in.) long; fruits vivid red 45B, globose, 8 mm (⁵⁄₁₆ in.) diameter, pedicels 10–12 mm (⅜–½ in.) long.

'Mamie Eisenhower' (female; synonym 'Mamie'; named and introduced 1952 by C. R. Wolf; origin Cumberland County, New Jersey; registered H.S.A. 10-74 by D. G. Fenton).

Leaves dark olive green, broadly elliptic, 7–8 cm (2¾–3⅛ in.) long, 4–4.5 cm (1⅝–1¾ in.) wide, slightly heeled, curved, 2–3 spines on each side, on upper half of leaf, margins reflexed, petioles 10 mm (⅜ in.) long; fruits deep reddish orange 43A, oval, 12 mm (¹⁵⁄₃₂ in.) long, pedicels 10–12 mm (⅜–¹⁵⁄₃₂ in.) long; heavy fruiting.

'Manig' (female; selected by T. Windon and E. C. White; origin about 1935–1940 in New Jersey).

Leaves dark olive green, elliptic to ovate, 4–6 cm (1⅝–2⅜ in.) long, 2–3.5 cm (¾–1⅜ in.) wide, curved, heeled, spines 3–5 on each side evenly distributed; petioles 5–7 mm (³⁄₁₆–⁹⁄₃₂ in.) long; fruits reddish orange, globose to ellipsoid, 9 mm (¹¹⁄₃₂ in.) long, singly or 2–3 per peduncle, abundant, reddish pedicels 5 mm (³⁄₁₆ in.) long. Plate 155.

'Maple Swamp' (female: synonym 'Swamp Maple'; Tingle Nursery).

Leaves moderate olive green, elliptic, 7.5–8 cm (3–3⅛ in.) long, 3.5–4 cm (1⅜–1⅝ in.) wide, keeled, curved, 2–3 spines on each side, upper half of leaf, margins reflexed, petioles 10–12 mm (⅜–¹⁵⁄₃₂ in.) long; fruits vivid reddish orange 43A, globose, 6–8 mm (⁷⁄₃₂–⁵⁄₁₆ in.) diameter, pedicels 8–10 mm (⁵⁄₁₆–⅜ in.) long; compact habit.

'Margaret Moran' (female; selected and named by J. D. Rankin before 1961 from a private garden in Bowling Green, Virginia; named for wife of W. F. Kosar).

Leaves moderate olive green, oval, 4–5 cm (1⅝–2 in.) long, 2.5 cm (1 in.) wide, keeled, curved, petioles light green, 8 mm (⁵⁄₁₆ in.) long; fruits vivid orange yellow 17A, globose, 8 mm (⁵⁄₁₆ in.) diameter.

'Margaret Pride' (female; synonym 'Margaret'; selected by O. S. Pride; Grace Hybrid Group).

Leaves dark olive green, broadly elliptic, 6.5–9 cm (2½–3½ in.) long, 4–5 cm (1⅝–2 in.) wide, slightly keeled, curved, bases obtuse, apices acute, margins slightly wavy, 4–5 spines on each side, tip spines reflexed, petioles 7–8 mm (9/32–5/16 in.) long; fruits red, slightly pyriform, 8 mm (5/16 in.) diameter, pedicels 13–16 mm (½–⅝ in.) long; upright pyramidal habit.

'Margaret Smith' (female; selected from Randolph County, West Virginia, by R. W. Pease).

Leaves dark olive green, broadly oval, 6–7 cm (2⅜–2¾ in.) long, 3.5–4.5 cm (1⅜–1¾ in.) wide, keeled, curved, convexed, usually 2–3 spined on upper two-thirds of leaf, stout petioles 8 mm (5/16 in.) long; fruits vivid red 45A, globose, 8 mm (5/16 in.) diameter.

'Marianne' (female; introduced 1965 by O. S. Pride; Grace Hybrid Group).

Leaves moderate olive green, broadly oval, 4.5–5 cm (1¾–2 in.) long, 2.5–3 cm (1–1 3/16 in.) wide, keeled, curved, 5–7 spines on each side, margins twisted and wavy, stout petioles 5–6 mm (3/16–7/32 in.) long, persistent to third year, free of leaf spot; fruits reddish orange, globose, 8 mm (5/16 in.) diameter, abundant in large clusters; narrowly pyramidal; hardy to −34°C (−30°F).

'Marion' (female; synonym 'Merion'; introduced 1935–1936 by H. Hume from western Marion County, Florida).

Leaves yellow green, obovate, 5.5–7.5 cm (2⅛–3 in.) long, 3–3.5 cm (1 3/16–1⅜ in.) wide, slightly bullate, spines, widely spaced, usually 2–3 on each side, curved, margins recurved, twisted, petioles 12 mm (15/32 in.) long; fruits vivid yellow 15A, globose, 8–9 mm (5/16–11/32 in.) diameter; upright openly branched habit.

'Marsh' (female; original tree from Marsh plot in Spring Grove Cemetery).

Leaves moderate olive green, broadly elliptic, 4.5–6 cm (1¾–2⅜ in.) long, 2.5–3 cm (1–1 3/16 in.) wide, bases broadly cuneate, keeled, curved, 3–4 spines on each side, margins reflexed, wavy, petioles 6–8 mm (7/32–5/16 in.) long; fruits vivid red 45A, globose, 8 mm (5/16 in.) diameter, pedicels 5 mm (3/16 in.) long.

'Marsh Mutation' (female; plant at Bernheim Forest from Marsh plot in Spring Grove Cemetery; witches'-broom variable).

Leaves moderate olive green, elliptic, keeled, curved, 5–6 cm 5–2⅜ in.) long, 3–4 cm (1 3/16–1⅝

in.) wide, 3 spines on upper two-thirds of leaf; fruits vivid red 44A, globose, 8 mm (5/16 in.) diameter; has distinct tight upright habit of growth.

'Marta' (female; selected seedling from 'Cave Hill No. 1'; named by T. Klein for his wife).

Leaves moderate olive green, oval, small 3–6 cm (1 3/16–2⅜ in.) long, 1.3–2.5 cm (½–1 in.) wide, keeled, curved, 3–5 spines on each side, margins reflexed, petioles 6–8 mm (7/32–5/16 in.) long; fruits vivid red 45A, globose, 6–8 mm (7/32–5/16 in.) diameter, reddish pedicels 5 mm (3/16 in.) long.

'Martha's Vineyard' (female; origin seedling selected about 1960 by P. Hill, in Wilmington, Delaware; plant later moved to Hill's property on Martha's Vineyard, Massachusetts; registered H.S.A. 2-72 by Hill).

Leaves moderate olive green, elliptic, 4–5.5 cm (1⅝–2⅛ in.) long, 2.5–3 cm (1–1⅜ in.) wide, keeled, curved, usually 5 spines on each side, stout petioles 5 mm (3/16 in.) long; fruits vivid reddish orange 44B, globose, 8–10 mm (5/16–⅜ in.) diameter, pedicels 10 mm (⅜ in.) long; conical habit, vigorous, strong central leader.

'Mary Emily' (female; selected, named, and introduced 1956–1958 by J. D. Rankin; original on D. S. Hurley farm near Mount Gilead, North Carolina).

Leaves dark olive green, elliptic 6.5–7.5 cm (2½–3 in.) long, 4 cm (1⅝ in.) wide, bases obtuse, keeled, curved, 5–6 spines on each side, margins wavy reflexed, petioles about 6 mm (7/32 in.) long; fruits vivid orange yellow, globose, 6–8 mm (7/32–5/16 in.) diameter, pedicels 6 mm (7/32 in.) long.

'Mary Gable' (female; origin unknown, plant at Secrest Arboretum).

Leaves dark olive green, elliptic to broadly elliptic, 5–7 cm (2–2¾ in.) long, 3–3.8 cm (1 3/16–1½ in.) wide, bases cuneate to obtuse, keeled, curved, margins recurved, wavy, 4–7 spines on each side, petioles 8 mm (5/16 in.) long; fruits vivid reddish orange 33A, ellipsoid, 11 mm (7/16 in.) long, 8 mm (5/16 in.) diameter, pedicels 8–10 mm (5/16–⅜ in.) long.

'Mary Holman' (female; selected by O. S. Pride; Grace Hybrid Group).

Leaves moderate olive green, broadly elliptic 6.5–7 cm (2½–2¾ in.) long; 3.5–4 cm (1⅜–1⅝ in.) wide, keeled, curved, 4–6 spines each side, margins wavy, reflexed, petioles 6 mm (7/32 in.) long; fruits deep reddish orange 43A, globose, 8 mm (5/16 in.) diameter, pedicels 10 mm (⅜ in.) long; annual bearing.

'Mary P. Turner' (female; origin tree on Allen Jones residence, Pine Reach, Rehoboth Beach, Delaware; named and registered H.S.A. 3-90 by D. Turner; introduced by Patuxent Valley Nursery).

Leaves dark olive green, glossy, broadly elliptic, 6–9 cm (2⅜–3½ in.) long, 3–4.5 cm (1³⁄₁₆–1¾ in.) wide, keeled, curved, margins undulate, 3–6 spines on each side, petioles 10 mm (⅜ in.) long; fruits vivid red 45B, slightly pyriform, 10 mm (⅜ in.) long, 8–9 mm (⁵⁄₁₆–¹¹⁄₃₂ in.) diameter, single, pedicels 10–13 mm (⅜–½ in.) long; dense pyramidal habit; hardy in zone 6; no midge damage.

'Mary Woodward' (female; selected 1933 from southern Delaware and registered H.S.A. 6-59 by E. C. Waddington Jr.).

Fruit reddish orange, in bunches; horizontally branching.

'Maryland' (female; synonym 'Marylandica'; seedling selected in 1928 and introduced 1940 by H. Holman).

Leaves moderate olive green, broadly elliptic, 4.5–6 cm (1¾–2⅜ in.) long, 3–3.5 cm (1³⁄₁₆–1⅜ in.) wide, keeled, curved, 2–3 spines usually on upper two-thirds of leaf, margins reflexed, convex, petioles 8–10 mm (⁵⁄₁₆–⅜ in.) long; fruits vivid yellow 15A, globose, 6–8 mm (⁷⁄₃₂–⁵⁄₁₆ in.) diameter, pedicels 5 mm (³⁄₁₆ in.) long.

'Maryland Dwarf' (female; synonyms 'Dilatush's Spreading', 'Repandens', 'Repandens Spreading', 'Spreading'; selected and introduced 1942 by E. Dilatush from Bunting's Nursery).

Leaves dark olive green, oval, 4–5 cm (1¾–2 in.) long, 2.5–3 cm (1–1³⁄₁₆ in.) wide, keeled, curved, 3–4 small spines on each side; fruits vivid red 44A, globose, 8 mm (⁵⁄₁₆ in.) diameter, sparse fruiting; low spreading habit, broader than tall.

'Massachusetts Dwarf', see 'Cape Cod Dwarf'.

'Matriarch' (female; selected 1929; introduced by E. Dilatush).

Leaves dark green, oval, 3.5–4.5 cm (1⅜–1⅝ in.) long, 2–2.5 cm (¾–1 in.) wide, keeled, curved, bases cuneate to obtuse, 3–5 small spines on each side of leaf, petioles dark, 6 mm (⁷⁄₃₂ in.) long; fruits red, globose, 6–8 mm (⁷⁄₃₂–⁵⁄₁₆ in.) diameter, pedicels reddish, 6 mm (⁷⁄₃₂ in.) long. Reported slow growing in Ohio.

'Maureece' (female; seedling of 'St. Mary' and male plant from Maine; origin 1955, Plainsville, Massachusetts; registered H.S.A. 14-67 by L. B. Austin).

Fruits reddish orange, abundant; conical habit.

'Maurice River' (female; named 1949 by C. Wolf; origin 1939 from Cumberland County, New Jersey; registered H.S.A. 11-74 by D. G. Fenton).

Leaves dark olive green, broadly oval, 5–6 cm (2–2⅜ in.) long, 3.5–4 cm (1⅜–1⅝ in.) wide, curved, 4–6 spines on each side, margin reflexed, petioles stout, 6 mm (⁷⁄₃₂ in.) long; fruits vivid red 44A, globose, 8 mm (⁵⁄₁₆ in.) diameter.

'Maxwell Point' (female; selected from Maxwell Point, near Edgewood, Massachusetts, by H. Hohman).

Leaves dark olive green, elliptic, 6.5–7.5 cm (2½–3 in.) long, 3–3.5 cm (1³⁄₁₆–1⅜ in.) wide, midrib depressed, curved 4–5 spines each side, margins reflexed, petioles 8–10 mm (⁵⁄₁₆–⅜ in.) long; fruits vivid red, abundant.

'Mays Landing' (female; synonym 'Daniella'; found by a hunter near Mays Landing, Atlantic County, New Jersey; named by D. G. Fenton).

Leaves moderate olive green, elliptic, 5–7.5 cm (2–2¾ in.) long, 2.5–3 cm (1–1³⁄₁₆ in.) wide, bases cuneate, keeled, curved, 2–5 spines on each side, occasionally 1–2 spines on upper half of leaf, petioles reddish, 8–10 mm (⁵⁄₁₆–⅜ in.) long; fruits vivid orange yellow 17A, globose, 8 mm (⁵⁄₁₆ in.) diameter, prominent stigma, abundant, pedicels reddish, 8–10 mm (⁵⁄₁₆–⅜ in.) long.

'McDonald' (female; origin from McDonald residence, now Snyder residence, in Vincennes, Indiana; named by R. C. Simpson).

Leaves dark olive green, elliptic, 4–6 cm (1⅝–2⅜ in.) long, 3–3.5 cm (1³⁄₁₆–1⅜ in.) wide, keeled, curved, 2–5 spines on each side, usually on upper half of leaf, margins slightly wavy, petioles 6–8 mm (⁷⁄₃₂–⁵⁄₁₆ in.) long; fruits color very late, vivid red 44A, globose, 8–10 mm (⁵⁄₁₆–⅜ in.) diameter, reddish pedicels 8–10 mm (⁵⁄₁₆–⅜ in.) long.

'Menantico' (female; selected from Salem County, New Jersey; introduced 1949 by C. R. Wolf; registered H.S.A. 12-74 by D. G. Fenton).

Leaves dark olive green, elliptic, 5–5.5 cm (2–2⅛ in.) long, 2.5–3 cm (1–1³⁄₁₆ in.) wide, bases obtuse, keeled, curved, 5–6 short spines on each side, margins wavy, petioles short 5 mm (³⁄₁₆) long; fruits vivid red 44A, globose, 8–9 mm (⁵⁄₁₆–¹¹⁄₃₂ in.) diameter; resembles 'Slim Jane' but leaves are wider and fruits smaller.

'Merrimack' (female; origin by Heatherfells Nursery; selected and named from southern Pennsylvania by H. Rohrbach before 1958).

Leaves dark green; fruits red. Selected for superior hardiness.

'Merry Christmas' (female; origin tree discovered in the Catskill Mountains near Eldred, New York, by E. Dilatush).

Leaves moderate olive green, elliptic to oval, 6–6.5 cm (2⅜–2½ in.) long, 3.5 cm (1⅜ in.) wide, bases cuneate to rotund, 4–5 spines on each side, margins reflexed, petioles 10 mm (⅜ in.) long; fruits vivid red 45B, ovoid to globose, 9 mm (¹¹⁄₃₂ in.) long, pedicels 8 mm (⁵⁄₁₆ in.) long. Plate 156.

'Merry Christmas Improved' (female; selected about 1932 at Boyce Thompson Institute; introduced 1942 by E. Dilatush).

Leaves good green; fruits vivid red 45B; dependable.

'Mike Brown' (female; chance seedling found in 1972 by Mike Brown, along Pigeon Creek in Vanderburgh County, Indiana; moved to Brown's home in Evansville, Indiana; named and registered H.S.A. 3-95 by Jeanne and Ken Brown).

Leaves ovate to oblong, 7 cm (3¾ in.) long, 4.5 cm (1¾ in.) wide, curved, tips obtuse, bases cuneate, tip spines reflexed, lateral spines 3–4 on each side, petioles 8 mm (⁵⁄₁₆ in.) long; fruits red 44B, slightly elongate, 11 mm (¹¹⁄₃₂ in.) wide, borne singly; flowers in early May, fruits in November; hardy in zone 6. Tolerates drought; has moderate resistance to holly leaf minor. Available from Holly Hill Nursery in 1998.

'Mildred Brewer' (female; seedling tree at Mrs. M. Brewer home, Panson, Alabama; seed originally from old tree at Brewer family home, Ecola, in Tuscaloosa, Alabama; cuttings taken 1976; named by G. Wood, University of Alabama, Tanglewood Arboretum, Hale County, Alabama).

Leaves dark olive green, elliptic, 5–8 cm (2–3⅛ in.) long, 2–4 cm (¾–1⅝ in.) wide, keeled, curved, margins subentire to 2–4 spines on each side, bases obtuse, apices acuminate, tip spines reflexed, petioles dark, 8–10 mm (⁵⁄₁₆–⅜ in.) long; fruits vivid red 45A, ellipsoid, 9–10 mm (¹¹⁄₃₂–⅜ in.) long, 6–8 mm (⁷⁄₃₂–⁵⁄₁₆ in.) diameter, pedicels 4–6 mm (⁵⁄₃₂–⁷⁄₃₂ in.) long.

'Millville' (female; selected in Cumberland County, New Jersey; introduced 1954 by C. R. Wolf; registered H.S.A. 13-74 by D. G. Fenton).

Leaves moderate olive green, oval, 4–6 cm (1⅝–2⅜ in.) long, 2.5–3.5 cm (1–1⅜ in.) wide, keeled, curved, 2–4 spines on each side, petioles 8 mm (⁵⁄₁₆ in.) long; fruits deep reddish orange 43A, globose, 1 cm (⅜ in.) diameter, pedicels 5 mm (³⁄₁₆ in.) long.

'Minard Red' (female; seedling about 1959; selected and registered H.S.A. 6-74 by A. V. Motsinger; original tree presented to U.S. National Arboretum in 1973 as NA 35579; PP No. 3575, 1974).

Leaves olive green, broadly oval, 6.5 cm (2½ in.) long, 2.5–3.7 cm (1–1¼ in.) wide, slightly keeled, curved, 3–5 long spines on each side, margins wavy; fruits red, globose, 5 mm (³⁄₁₆ in.) diameter, short pedicels 2 mm (¹⁄₁₆ in.) long.

'Minute Man' (male; seedling about 1959; selected and registered H.S.A. 20-74 by A. V. Motsinger; original tree presented to U.S. National Arboretum as NA 35580).

Leaves olive green, ovate, 6.5 cm (2½ in.) long, 4.5 cm (1¾ in.) wide, bases distinctly abruptly acuminate, keeled, curved, 5 spines on each side, margins flat, petioles 6 mm (⁷⁄₃₂ in.) long; vigorous upright habit. Selected as a male companion to 'Minard Red'.

'Miss Angie' (female; selected by T. Klein from Cave Hill Cemetery, Louisville, Kentucky).

Leaves moderate olive green, broadly elliptic, 4.5–5.5 cm (1¾–2⅛ in.) long, 2.5–3 cm (1–1³⁄₁₆ in.) wide, keeled, curved, 2–5 spines on each side, margins reflexed, petioles 8 mm (⁵⁄₁₆ in.) long; fruits deep reddish orange 43A, oval 8 mm (⁵⁄₁₆ in.) long, pedicels reddish, 5 mm (³⁄₁₆ in.) long.

'Miss Bulter' (female; origin unknown; plant at Arnold Arboretum).

Leaves dark olive green, oval to broadly elliptic, 4.5–6 cm (1¾–2⅜ in.) long, 2.5–4 cm (1–1⅝ in.) wide, bases obtuse to rotund, keeled, curved, 4–6 small spines on each side, petioles 6–8 mm (⁷⁄₃₂–⁵⁄₁₆ in.) long; fruits vivid reddish orange 44B, ellipsoid, 11 mm (⁷⁄₁₆ in.) long, 8 mm (⁵⁄₁₆ in.) diameter, pedicels reddish, 7–9 mm (⁹⁄₃₂–¹¹⁄₃₂ in.) long.

'Miss Helen' (female; selected in 1936 south of Baltimore, Maryland, by S. H. McLean; registered H.S.A. 1-74 by McLean).

Leaves moderate olive green, elliptic to oval, 6–7 cm (2⅜–2¾ in.) long, 3–3.5 cm (1³⁄₁₆–1⅜ in.) wide, curved, keeled, 4–6 short spines on each side, petioles stout, 5–9 mm (³⁄₁₆–¹¹⁄₃₂ in.) long; fruits dark red, glossy, ellipsoid, 10 mm (⅜ in.) long, abundant; broadly pyramidal habit. Plate 157.

'Miss Liberty' (female; selected and introduced by Woodlanders Nursery in the 1980s).

Leaves olive green, elliptic, 10 cm (4 in.) long, 3 cm (1³⁄₁₆ in.) wide, keeled, curved, 7–8 uniform spines on each side, petioles 5 mm (³⁄₁₆ in.) long; fruits red.

'Miss Martha' (female; sibling of 'Pin Cushion'; selected by E. S. Wyckoff in J. H. Schmidt Nursery; registered H.S.A. 14-60 by Wyckoff).

Foliage good, spiny; fruits red; compact grower.

'Miss White' (female; Holly Haven Nursery, Lisbon, New Jersey, 1956 catalog);

Leaves moderate olive green, elliptic, 4.5–5.5 cm (1¾–2⅛ in.) long, 2–3.5 cm (¾–1⅜ in.) wide, keeled, curved, 3–5 spines on each side, margins reflexed, wavy, petioles 6–8 mm (7/32–5/16 in.) long; fruits vivid red 45A, globose to slightly ellipsoid, 8–10 mm (5/16–⅜ in.) diameter, pedicels 5–7 mm (3/16–7/32 in.) long.

'Montauk' (male; synonym 'Montauk Male'; discovered in the 1970s by M. Whipple near Montauk Point, Long Island, New York).

Leaves dark olive green, elliptic, 4–5 cm (1⅝–2 in.) long, 2–2.2 cm (¾–1 3/16 in.) wide, slightly keeled, curved, bases obtuse, apices acuminate, margins 3–5 widely spaced spines on each side, petioles dark, 5–7 mm (3/16–9/32 in.) long; compact, maximum height about 2 m (6 ft.). Good pollinator.

'Montclair' (female; origin 1929 from seed grown at Montclair, New Jersey; registered H.S.A. 6-69 by C. A. Glover).

Leaves olive green, oblong, 6.5 cm (2½ in.) long, 4 cm (1⅝ in.) wide, very spiny, 8 spines on each side, margins wavy; fruits red, elongate; dense fastigiate habit, outer branches droop slightly.

'Monticello' (female; reported from Pennsylvania by J. McDaniel and moved on Highway 23, only 1.6 km (1 mi.) from Monticello, Virginia; not known if plant still alive).

Leaves dark olive green, glossy, oval to elliptic, 4–5 cm (1⅝–2 in.) long, 2.5–3.5 cm (1–1⅜ in.) wide, keeled, curved, usually 1–3 spines on upper two-thirds of leaf, margins reflexed, petioles 5–7 mm (3/16–9/32 in.) long; fruits vivid red 44A, ellipsoid, 10 mm (⅜ in.) long, pedicels 6 mm (7/32 in.) long.

'Monty' (female; selected in Pennsylvania by W. J. Dauber; origin about 1937 in Alabama).

Leaves good color; fruits red; compact; fast grower.

'Morgan Gold' (female; discovered 1902 on Morgan Farm, Rowan Township, North Carolina; moved to private property in Lexington, North Carolina; selected and introduced 1959 by J. M. Morgan; registered American Association of Nurserymen No. 620 in 1959; registered H.S.A. 4-61 by Mrs. J. M. Morgan and Mrs. T. A. Darr).

Leaves moderate olive green, broadly oval, 7–8 cm (2¾–3⅛ in.) long, 3.5–4 cm (1⅜–1⅝ in.) wide, curves, 3–5 spines on each side, margins reflexed, petioles 8–10 mm (5/16–⅜ in.) long; fruits vivid yellow 15A, globose, 8–10 mm (5/16–⅜ in.) diameter.

'Morris Arboretum' (female; named and introduced by J. D. Rankin; discovered by Mrs. Spawn about 1920–1927 in south-central Bird Township in western North Carolina; first moved to Washington, D.C.; later presented to Morris Arboretum, Philadelphia, Pennsylvania).

Leaves moderate olive green, elliptic, 5–6.5 cm (2–2½ in.) long, 2.5–3 cm (1–1 3/16 in.) wide, keeled, curved, 2–4 prominent spines on each side, margins wavy; fruits vivid orange yellow 21A, globose, 8 mm (5/16 in.) diameter, long pedicels. Note: a male cultivar has been distributed.

'Mrs. Clark' (female; named and introduced by J. D. Rankin; origin 1956 on Hood Farm, Burke County, North Carolina).

Leaves dark olive green, broadly elliptic, 4.5–5 cm (1¾–2 in.) long, 2.5–3 cm (1–1 3/16 in.) wide, keeled, curved, 3–5 prominent spines on each side, margins reflexed, wavy, petioles 6–8 mm (7/32–5/16 in.) long; fruits vivid orange yellow 16A, with blush, globose, 8 mm (5/16 in.) diameter, pedicels 3–5 mm (⅛–3/16 in.) long.

'Mrs. Davis' (female; synonym 'Roaring Bill'; discovered by B. Kramer near Davis, West Virginia; named and introduced by R. W. Pease before 1953).

Leaves moderate olive green, broadly elliptic, keeled, curved, 3–4 spines on each side, petioles 6 mm (7/32 in.) long; fruits vivid orange yellow 23A, ellipsoid, 8–10 mm (5/16–⅜ in.) long, pedicels 5 mm (3/16 in.) long, good clusters.

'Mrs. E. D.' (female; synonym 'Mrs. Grace Dilatush'; selected by E. Dilatush and named for his wife).

Leaves moderate olive green, oval, 4.5–5 cm (1¾–2 in.) long, 2.5 cm (1 in.) wide, keeled, curved, 3–5 spines on each side, dark petioles, 8 mm (5/16 in.) long; fruits deep reddish orange 43A, globose, 10 mm (⅜ in.) diameter.

'Mrs. F. J. Close' (female; introduced by O. S. Pride; Grace Hybrid Group).

Leaves moderate olive green, broadly oval, 6–7.5 cm (2⅜–3 in.) long, 4–4.5 cm (1⅝–1¾ in.) wide; 6–7 spines on each side, margins reflexed, petioles 7–8 mm (9/32–5/16 in.) long; fruits deep reddish orange 43A, globose, 7 mm (9/32 in.) diameter; one of the hardiest of the Grace Hybrid Group.

'Mrs. Henry' (female; origin unknown).

Leaves moderate olive green, broadly elliptic, 6–7.5 cm (2⅜–3 in.) long, 3–4 cm (1 3/16–1⅝ in.) wide, keeled, curved, 3–6 spines on each side, petioles 8 mm (5/16 in.) long; fruits vivid red 45B, ellipsoid, 10 mm (⅜ in.) long, pedicels 6 mm (7/32 in.) long.

'Mrs. Lawrence' (female; synonyms 'Emily Lawrence', 'Wheeler No. 34'; from Emily Lawerence farm, West Barnstable, Massachusetts; collected by W. Wheeler; moved to Ashumet Farm, Falmouth, Massachusetts).

Leaves moderate olive green, broadly elliptic, 4.5–5.5 cm (1¾–2⅛ in.) long, 2.5–3 cm (1–1 3/16 in.) wide, keeled, curved, 4–5 prominent spines on each side, margins slightly convex, twisted, petioles 8–10 mm (5/16–⅜ in.) long; fruits vivid red 45A, flattened globose, 10 mm (⅜ in.) diameter, reported to 13 mm (½ in.) diameter, reddish pedicels 8–10 mm (5/16–⅜ in.) long.

'Mrs. McCormick' (female; origin unknown; plant at Tyler Arboretum).

Leaves dark olive green, broadly elliptic to oval, 6.5–8.5 cm (2½–3⅜ in.) long, 4–4.5 cm (1⅝–1¾ in.) wide, slightly keeled, curved, bases broadly cuneate, apices acute, margins spined, petioles dark, 8–10 mm (5/16–⅜ in.) long; fruits red, globose, 6 mm (7/32 in.) diameter, pedicels dark, 8–13 mm (5/16–½ in.) long; upright pyramidal habit.

'Mrs. Robb' (female; introduced by O. S. Pride; Grace Hybrid Group).

Leaves moderate olive green, broadly oval, 6–7 cm (2⅜–3 in.) long, 4.5 cm (1¾ in.) wide, 5–6 spines on each side, margin reflexed; fruits vivid red 45A, 8–10 mm (5/16–⅜ in.) diameter, pedicels 6 mm (7/32 in.) long.

'Mrs. Santa (female; selected about 1924 at Guyancourt Nursery, Guyancourt, Delaware, by G. G. Nearing from seedling; origin from Georgia; introduced about 1933).

Leaves dark olive green, elliptic to oval, 4.5–6.5 cm (1¾–2½ in.) long, 2.5–3 cm (1–1 3/16 in.) wide, curved, slightly keeled, 4–6 spines each side; fruits vivid red, elliptic, 8 mm (5/6 in.) long, abundant, 1–3 per peduncle; close pyramidal branching.

'Mt. Hood' (female; seedling selected, named, and registered H.S.A. 1-75 by J. S. Wieman; named for mountain in Cascade Range, Oregon; thought to be first cultivar of *I. opaca* selected and named in Oregon; originally registered as *I.* × *altaclerensis* hybrid).

Leaves moderate olive green, broadly elliptic, 4.5–6 cm (1⅝–2⅜ in.) long, 2.5–3 cm (1–1 3/16 in.) wide, slightly keeled, curved, 4–6 spines on each side, margins twisted, petioles 8 mm (5/16 in.) long; fruits red.

'Mt. Vernon' (female; selected 1941 at Mount Vernon, Virginia, by F. L. S. O'Rourke).

Leaves dark olive green, exceptionally long; fruits red, large.

'Muench' (female; origin Cave Hill Cemetery, Louisville, Kentucky; introduced by T. Klein).

Leaves moderate olive green, elliptic, 4.5–5.5 cm (1¾–2⅛ in.) long, 2.5–3 cm (1–1 3/16 in.) wide, keeled, curved, 2–4 spines on each side, margins reflexed, slightly wavy, petioles 8–10 mm (5/16–⅜ in.) long; fruits vivid red 45A, ellipsoid to broadly ovate, 10–12 mm (⅜–15/32 in.) long, pedicels reddish, 6 mm (7/32 in.) long.

'Nancy' (synonym 'Wheeler No. 13'; named and introduced by W. Wheeler before 1953).

Leaves moderate olive green, oval, 5–6 cm (2–2⅜ in.) long, 3–3.5 cm (1 3/16–1⅜ in.) wide, keeled, curved, 3–4 prominent spines on each side, margins reflexed, petioles 8 mm (5/16 in.) long; fruits vivid red 45A, globose, 8–10 mm (5/16–⅜ in.) diameter, reddish pedicels 5 mm (3/16 in.) long.

'Natale' (female; selected by P. Barbosa; named by W. Wheeler before 1947).

Leaves dark olive green, elliptic, 4.5–5.5 cm (1¾–2⅛ in.) long, keeled, curved, 3–6 spines on upper two-thirds of leaf, margins reflexed; fruits red, ellipsoid, 8 mm (5/16 in.) long, abundant, singly on short pedicels. Wheeler regarded this as one of the best American hollies.

'Natalie Webster' (female; seedling collected on Fire Island, New York, by Mr. Hicks in early 1930s; plant given to Mrs. Charles D. Webster around 1935; reported to do better in England than most other cultivars of *I. opaca*).

Leaves dark green, often entire or with few spines.

'Needlepoint' (female; selected 1929 and introduced 1948 by E. Dilatush).

Leaves dark olive green, oval, 4–5.5 cm (1¾–2⅛ in.) long, 2.5–3.5 cm (1–1⅜ in.) wide, bases rotund, keeled, curved, margins recurved, undulate, 3–5 prominent spines on each side, petioles 5–7 mm (3/16–9/32 in.) long; fruits vivid red 45A, ellipsoid, 10 mm (⅜ in.) long, 8 mm (5/16 in.) diameter, pedicels reddish, 10–13 mm (⅜–½ in.) long.

'Nelson West' (male; synonym 'Mrs. Peggy West'; discovered near New Lisbon, New Jersey, by Nelson and Peggy West; registered H.S.A. 7-64 by M. L. Hill).

Leaves moderate olive green, narrow-elliptic, 3–5 cm (1³⁄₁₆–2 in.) long, 1–1.5 cm (³⁄₈–½ in.) wide, slightly keeled, curved, deeply spinose, 5–7 spines on each side, petioles dark, 5 mm (³⁄₁₆ in.) long. Plate 158.

'New Smyrna' (female; origin New Smyrna Beach, Florida; selected and introduced by Howell Nursery).

Leaves moderate olive green, oval, 5–6 cm (2–2½ in.) long, 3–4 cm (1³⁄₁₆–1⅝ in.) wide, slightly keeled, curved, 2–4 prominent spines on each side, margins reflexed, petioles 8–10 mm (⁵⁄₁₆–³⁄₈ in.) long; fruits red, globose, 6–7 mm (⁷⁄₃₂–⁹⁄₃₂ in.) diameter; hardy to −31°C (−24°F).

'Nina Foster Searcy' (female; tree in front yard of University of Alabama, Systems Building, Tuscaloosa, Alabama, approximately 80 years old; selected by Joe Searcy; registered H.S.A. 8-94 by G. Wood).

Leaves dark green, broadly elliptic, 7–9 cm (2¾–3½ in.) long, 4.5–5 cm (1¾–2 in.) wide, bases obtuse to rotund, keeled tip spines reflexed, 2–3 spines on each side on upper half of leaf, petioles brownish, 13–15 mm (½–¹⁹⁄₃₂ in.) long; fruits vivid red 43A, ellipsoid, 13 mm (½ in.) long, 10 mm (³⁄₈ in.) diameter, abundant, petioles 8–10 mm (⁵⁄₁₆–³⁄₈ in.) long. Beautiful old tree, difficult to propagate from old wood.

'Nittany' (female; from Pennsylvania State University; plant at Tyler Arboretum).

Leaves dark olive green, broadly elliptic to oval, curved, 5.5–8 cm (2⅛–3⅛ in.) long, 3–3.5 cm (1³⁄₁₆–1⅜ in.) wide, bases obtuse, apices acute, 3–4 spines on each side, petioles dark, 8 mm (⁵⁄₁₆ in.) long; fruits red, globose, 6–8 mm (⁷⁄₃₂–⁵⁄₁₆ in.) diameter; upright pyramidal habit.

'Nora' (female; selected by W. Boyden, W. Wheeler, and E. C. White; two twin seedlings moved to Ashumet Farm, Falmouth, Massachusetts).

Leaves dark olive green, elliptic, 4.5–6 cm (1¾–2⅜ in.) long, 2–3 cm (¾–1³⁄₁₆ in.) wide, keeled, curved, 3–5 spines on each side, petioles reddish, 10 mm (³⁄₈ in.) long; fruits red, globose.

'Norfolk' (female; selected near Norfolk, Virginia, by W. J. Dauber before 1957).

Leaves large; fruits red, abundant; spreading habit. Good orchard type.

'North Wind' (male; volunteer seedling found in C. Richardson garden; selected 1986, named 1989, and registered H.S.A. 5-91 by Richardson; introduced by McLean Nursery).

Leaves dark green, flat, slightly reflexed, leaves thin, elliptic, to 6.5 cm (2½ in.) long, 3.2 cm (1¼ in.) wide, bases cuneate to acuminate, apex aristate, 3–6 large spines on each side; flowers very early, prolific; narrow compact, conical habit, original tree 3.7 m (12 ft.) high, 1.2 m (4 ft.) wide; hardy in zone 6a. Plate 159.

'Oachs' (female; selected by J. McDaniel who obtained it from Oachs Nursery).

Leaves dark olive green, elliptic, 6–6.5 cm (2⅜–2½ in.) long, 2.5–3 cm (1–1³⁄₁₆ in.) wide, keeled, curved, 2–4 spines often on upper two-thirds of leaf, margins reflexed, petioles 8–10 mm (⁵⁄₁₆–³⁄₈ in.) long; fruits deep reddish orange 43A, oval 11 mm (⁷⁄₁₆ in.) long, pedicels 8 mm (⁵⁄₁₆ in.) long.

'Oak Grove No. 1' (female; selected in 1960 by F. Galle and B. Pace near Oak Grove Community, Troup County, Georgia; moved to Callaway Gardens).

Leaves moderate olive green, oval, 4.5–5.5 cm (1¾–2⅛ in.) long, 3–4 cm (1³⁄₁₆–1⅝ in.) wide, keeled, curved, 2–3 spines on upper two-thirds of leaf, petioles 8 mm (⁵⁄₁₆ in.) long; fruits vivid yellow 15A, ellipsoid, 1 cm (³⁄₈ in.) long, pedicels 5–6 mm (³⁄₁₆–⁷⁄₃₂ in.) long. Differs from 'Oak Grove No. 2' by shape of fruit. Plate 160.

'Oak Grove No. 2' (found near 'Oak Grove No. 1', which see; plant destroyed).

Fruits yellow, globose.

'Oak Hill No. 1' (female; introduced by J. D. Rankin in the 1960s).

Leaves moderate olive green, elliptic to broadly elliptic, 4–4.5 cm (1⅝–1¾ in.) long, 2–2.5 cm (¾–1 in.) wide, keeled, curved, 3–5 spines on each side, margins reflexed, petioles 5 mm (³⁄₁₆ in.) long; fruits yellow, ellipsoid, 8 mm (⁵⁄₁₆ in.) long.

'October Glow' (female; selected about 1948 by H. Hohman).

Leaves moderate olive green, broadly oval, 5–6 cm (2–2⅜ in.) long 2.5–3.5 cm (1–1⅜ in.) wide, curved, slightly keeled, 4–5 spines on each side, petioles 6 mm (⁷⁄₃₂ in.) long; fruits dark red, globose to ellipsoid, 8 mm (⁵⁄₁₆ in.) diameter, abundant.

'Ohio King' (male; origin Gallipolis State Hospital grounds, Gallipolis, Ohio; selected, named, and registered H.S.A. 18-74 by O. D. Diller and H. F. Karenbauer).

Leaves moderate olive green, oval to obovate, 3.8

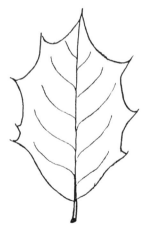

Figure 15-37. *Ilex opaca* 'October Glow'. Drawing by Randy Allen.

cm (1½ in.) long, 2.5 cm (1 in.) wide, flat, spines variable, 0–3 on each side, margins slightly wavy; abundance of male flowers.

'Ohio Queen' (female; origin Gallipolis State Hospital grounds, Gallipolis, Ohio; selected, named, and registered H.S.A. 19-74 by O. D. Diller and H. F. Karenbauer).
    Leaves moderate olive green, broadly ovate, 5 cm (2 in.) long, 2.5 cm (1 in.) wide, flat, spines variable, 0–3 on each side; fruits vivid red, globose.

'Okrent' (female; introduced by Okrent Nursery; specimen from T. Klein).
    Leaves moderate olive green, broadly elliptic, 4.5–6.5 cm (1¾–2½ in.) long, 2.5–4 cm (1–1⅝ in.) wide, keeled, curved, 1–3 spines on upper half of leaf, margins reflexed, petioles 8–10 (⁵⁄₁₆–⅜ in.) long; fruits vivid red 45A, globose, 10 mm (⅜ in.) diameter, single and 1–3 in clusters, abundant, pedicels 3–5 mm (⅛–³⁄₁₆ in.) long.

'Old Faithful' (female; selected 1929 and introduced 1947 by E. Dilatush).
    Leaves dark green, glossy, 4–6 cm (1⅝–2⅜ in.) long, 2.5–3.5 cm (1–1⅜ in.) wide, flat, curved, 3–6 spines on each side, petioles short 5–6 mm (³⁄₁₆–⁷⁄₃₂ in.) long; fruits dark red, globose, 9 mm (¹¹⁄₃₂ in.) diameter, abundant.

'Old Gold' (female; discovered 1947–1949 near Pioneer, Tennessee; introduced by Klein Nursery).
    Leaves moderate green, elliptic, 4.5–5.5 cm (1¾–2⅛ in.) long, 2–2.5 cm (¾–1 in.) wide, keeled, curved, 3–5 spines on upper two-thirds of leaf, petioles 6–8 mm (⁷⁄₃₂–⁵⁄₁₆ in.) long; fruits brilliant or-

ange yellow 23B, with blush, globose, 8 mm (⁵⁄₁₆ in.) diameter; slow growing, compact, rounded habit.

'Old Heavy Berry' (female; synonyms 'Hookstra', 'Hookstraw', 'Old Heavy Berry'; selected on Hookstra estate, Burlington, New Jersey, by E. Dilatush; introduced 1937; registered American Association of Nurserymen No. 513, 1956).
    Leaves dark olive green, broadly elliptic to oval, 7–10 cm (2¾–4 in.) long, 3.5–5 cm (1⅜–2 in.) wide, bases obtuse, keeled, curved, 4–6 spines on each side, petioles dark, 8–10 mm (⁵⁄₁₆–⅜ in.) long; fruits vivid red 46B, globose, 9 mm (¹¹⁄₃₂ in.) diameter; slow growing, round to conical habit. Popular commercial holly.

'Old Leather Leaf' (male; synonyms 'Happy New Year', 'King Christmas', 'Leatherleaf'; selected 1929 and introduced 1947 by E. Dilatush).

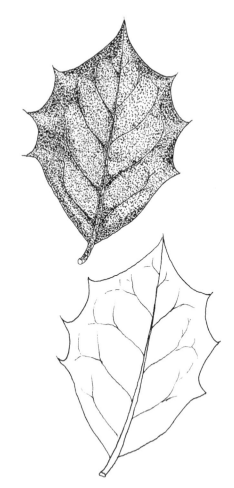

Figure 15-38. *Ilex opaca* 'Old Heavy Berry'. Drawing by Randy Allen.

Leaves dark olive green, heavy texture, broadly elliptic, 7.5–8.5 cm (3–3⅜ in.) long, 3–4 cm (1³⁄₁₆–1⅝ in.) wide, bases obtuse to truncate, keeled, curved, 4–7 spines on each side, margins reflexed, petioles stout, 8–10 mm (⁵⁄₁₆–⅜ in.) long. Reported to be very hardy.

'Old Science Big Leaf', see 'Southern Illinois University'.

'Orlando Pride' (female; plant at Planting Fields Arboretum).
Leaves broadly oval, 9.5–11 cm (3½–4⅜ in.) long, 4.5–5.5 cm (1¾–2⅛ in.) wide, keeled, curved, 4–6 spines on each side; fruits vivid red 45B, globose, 8 mm (⁵⁄₁₆ in.) diameter, pedicels green, 15 mm (¹⁹⁄₃₂ in.) long.

'Osa' (female; selected from New Jersey by T. Windon and E. C. White).
Leaves deep olive green, elliptic to oval, 4.5–7 cm (1¾–2¾ in.) long, 2.5–4 cm (1–1⅝ in.) wide, curved, almost flat, 4–8 short spines on each side; fruits vivid reddish orange 33A, ellipsoid, 9–10 mm (¹¹⁄₃₂–⅜ in.) long, pedicels 6–9 mm (⁷⁄₃₂–¹¹⁄₃₂ in.) long.

'Oyster Bay' (female; origin from the village of Oyster Bay, New York; moved to Planting Fields Arboretum in 1960).
Leaves moderate olive green, broadly elliptic, 6.5–8 cm (2½–3⅛ in.) long, 3.5–4 cm (1³⁄₁₆–1⅝ in.) wide, keeled, curved, 4–5 spines on each side, petioles stout, 8 mm (⁵⁄₁₆ in.) long; fruits vivid red 45B, globose, 8 mm (⁵⁄₁₆ in.) diameter, pedicels dark, 13–15 mm (½–¹⁹⁄₃₂ in.) long.

'Palmetto' (female; selected and named by T. Dodd Jr. in the 1970s).
Leaves dark olive green, obovate, keeled, curved, 4.5–5.5 cm (1¾–2⅛ in.) long, 2.5–3 cm (1–1³⁄₁₆ in.) wide, bases cuneate, apices obtuse, small tip spines, margins convex to wavy, 1–5 spines on each side, petioles 8–10 mm (⁵⁄₁₆–⅜ in.) long; fruits vivid red 45A, globose, 8–10 mm (⁵⁄₁₆–⅜ in.) diameter, pedicels reddish, 3 mm (⅛ in.) long; pyramidal habit.

'Pauline' (female; selected by W. Wheeler and E. C. White).
Leaves dark olive green, elliptic, 5–6.5 cm (2–2½ in.) long, 2.5–3 cm (1–1³⁄₁₆ in.) wide, slightly keeled, curved, convex, bases cuneate, margins recurved, 3–4 small spines on each side, usually on upper two-thirds of leaf, tip spine reflexed, petioles 7–10 mm (⁹⁄₃₂–⅜ in.) long; fruits vivid reddish or-ange 44B, globose, 7–8 mm (⁹⁄₃₂–⁵⁄₁₆ in.) diameter, abundant, pedicels 6–8 mm (⁷⁄₃₂–⁵⁄₁₆ in.) long, abundant; good display.

'Pawley's Island', see *Ilex × attenuata* 'Pawley's Island'.

'Peace', see *I. × attenuata* 'Greenleaf'.

'Pearle le Clair' (female; collected 1951 in Orange County, North Carolina, by F. J. LeClair; named for his wife; often misspelled as 'Perle LeClair').
Leaves dark olive green, broadly oval, 6.5–7 cm (2½–2¾ in.) long, 4–5.5 cm (1⅝–2⅛ in.) wide, curved, slightly keeled, 3–4 spines on each side, usually upper two-thirds of leaf, petioles 8 mm (⁵⁄₁₆ in.) long; fruits deep reddish orange 43A, elliptic, 10–13 mm (⅜–½ in.) diameter, heavy bearing, fruits without pollination. Noted for large fruit.

'Perfection' (female; selected 1929 in New Jersey and introduced 1948 by E. Dilatush).
Leaves dark olive green, elliptic, 5–7.5 cm (2–2¾ in.) long, 2.5–3.5 cm (1–1⅜ in.) wide, almost flat, curved tip, 3–5 spines on each side, petioles 6 mm (⁷⁄₃₂ in.) long; fruits vivid red 45A, ellipsoid, 8 mm (⁵⁄₁₆ in.) long.

'Perfection Xanthocarpa' (female; origin unknown; plant at Tyler Arboretum).
Leaves dark olive green, broadly elliptic, 6–8 cm (2⅜–3⅛ in.) long, 3–3.5 cm (1³⁄₁₆–1⅜ in.) wide, slightly keeled, curved, bases cuneate, apices acute, 5–8 spines on each side, tip spines reflexed, petioles dark, 5 mm (³⁄₁₆ in.) long; fruits yellow, 6 mm (⁷⁄₃₂ in.) diameter, pedicels 10–13 mm (⅜–½ in.) long.

'Perkins de Wilde No. 3' (male; selected by Perkins de Wilde Nursery).
Leaves olive green, ovate, flat, slightly curved, 7.5 cm (3 in.) long, 4.5 cm (1¾ in.) wide, petioles 5–6 mm (³⁄₁₆–⁷⁄₃₂ in.) long, 5–6 spines on each side.

'Perpetual' (female; synonym 'Boyden No. 6'; selected by W. Wheeler and E. C. White before 1953; origin Sandwich, Massachusetts).
Leaves dark olive green, broadly elliptic, 4.5–6 cm (1¾–2⅜ in.) long, 3–3.5 cm (1³⁄₁₆–1⅜ in.) wide, bases obtuse, slightly keeled, curved, 2–3 spines usually on upper half of leaf, petioles 8 mm (⁵⁄₁₆ in.) long; fruits deep reddish orange 43A, globose, 8–10 mm (⁵⁄₁₆–⅜ in.) diameter, reddish pedicels 5–8 mm (³⁄₁₆–⁵⁄₁₆ in.) long. Fruits annually in large clusters, persistent throughout the year.

'Perrine' (female; selected by A. Perrine before 1953).

Leaves dark olive green, elliptic to broadly elliptic, 5.5–7.5 cm (2⅛–3 in.) long, 3.5–4 cm (1⅜–1⅝ in.) wide, bases obtuse to rotund, keeled, curved, 2–5 spines on each side, petioles 6 mm (7/32 in.) long; fruits vivid red 45A, globose, 8 mm (5/16 in.) diameter, 3–6 in cluster, pedicels 10–15 mm (⅜–19/32 in.) long.

'Phillips' (female; selected at Wynnewood, Pennsylvania, before 1962 by H. G. Mattoon).
Leaves moderate olive green, elliptic, 4.5–5.5 cm (1¾–2⅛ in.) long, 2.5–3 cm (1–1 3/16 in.) wide, keeled, curved, margins reflexed, petioles 6–8 mm (7/32–5/16 in.) long; fruits vivid orange 25A, globose, 6–8 mm (7/32–5/16 in.) diameter, pedicels 3–5 mm (⅛–3/16 in.) long.

'Pin Cushion' (female; seedling at J. H. Schmidt Nursery; selected by H. Hohman; registered H.S.A. 1-60 by E. S. Wyckoff).
Leaves moderate olive green, elliptic, 7–7.5 cm (2¾–3 in.) long, 3–3.5 cm (1 3/16–1⅜ in.) wide, bases obtuse, curved, slightly keeled, 4–6 spines on each side, margins reflexed, slightly wavy, petioles stout, 5–7 mm (3/16–9/32 in.) long; fruits deep reddish orange 43B, globose, 8 mm (5/16 in.) diameter; dwarf compact habit, twice as wide as high.

'Podocarpa' (female; selected and named by E. Dilatush before 1956).
Leaves dark olive green, oval, 4.5–6 cm (1¾–2⅜ in.) long, 3–4 cm (1 3/16–1⅝ in.) wide, bases obtuse, slightly keeled, curved, 2–5 spines on each side, margins reflexed, petioles 8–10 mm (5/16–⅜ in.) long; fruits vivid red 45A, globose, 8 mm (5/16 in.) diameter, reddish pedicels 6–8 mm (7/32–5/16 in.) long.

'Polly' (female; synonyms 'Ashumet No. 45', 'Wheeler No. 5'; selected by W. Wheeler before 1963).
Leaves dark olive green, elliptic, 5–6.5 cm (2–2½ in.) long, 3–3.5 cm (1 3/16–1⅜ in.) wide, keeled, curved, 3–5 small spines on each side, usually upper two-thirds of leaf, pedicels 8 mm (5/16 in.) long; fruits reddish orange, 8 mm (5/16 in.) diameter, pedicels 3–4 mm (⅛–5/32 in.) long.

'Pomona' (female; selected in Alabama by J. A. Smith; registered H.S.A. 4-75 by Smith).
Leaves moderate olive green, broadly ovate, 8.9 cm (3½ in.) long, 4.5 cm (1¾ in.) wide, bases cuneate to obtuse, slightly convex, 0–3 spines usually upper half of leaf, margins wavy; fruits deep reddish orange 42A to vivid red 46B, globose, 11–13 mm (7/16–½ in.) diameter, peduncles 5 mm (3/16 in.) long, pyrenes large. Selected for large fruits.

'Pride Berry' (female; selected by O. S. Pride, 1948–1952).
Leaves dark olive green, good winter color, oval to broadly elliptic, 5–6 cm (2–2⅜ in.) long, 3–4.5 cm (1 3/16–1¾ in.) wide, bases obtuse to rotund, keeled, curved, margins recurved, wavy, 5–8 spines on each side, petioles 8–10 mm (5/16–⅜ in.) long; fruits vivid red, pedicels reddish, 6–8 mm (7/32–5/16 in.) long.

'Pride Dwarf' (female; selected by O. S. Pride; name illegitimate because predated by *I. crenata* 'Pride Dwarf' by Pride).
Leaves dark olive green, oval, 5–6 cm (2–2⅜ in.) long, 2.5–3.5 cm (1–1⅜ in.) wide, keeled, curved, 2–4 spines on each side, margins reflexed, petioles 8–10 mm (5/16–⅜ in.) long; fruits vivid red 45A, globose, 8–10 mm (5/16–⅜ in.) diameter, pedicels 3–5 mm (⅛–3/16 in.) long; compact growth.

'Pride Hedge' (female; selected by O. S. Pride; Grace Hybrid Group).
Leaves moderate olive green, good winter color, elliptic, 4–5 cm (1⅝–2 in.) long, 2–2.5 cm (¾–1 in.) wide, keeled, curved, convex, 2–4 spines on each side, petioles 8 mm (5/16 in.) long; fruits deep reddish orange 43A, ellipsoid, 8 mm (5/16 in.) long, pedicels 6 mm (7/32 in.) long.

'Pride of Butler' (female; selected by O. S. Pride; Grace Hybrid Group).
Leaves dark olive green, broadly oval, 7–8 cm (2¾–3⅛ in.) long, 4.5–5 cm (1¾–2 in.) wide, bases obovate, curved, 5–6 spines on each side, petioles stout, 7 mm (9/32 in.) long; fruits deep reddish orange 43B, globose, 8 mm (5/16 in.) diameter.

'Pride Orchard' (female; selected by O. S. Pride).
Leaves moderate olive green, broadly elliptic, 4.5–6 cm (1¾–2⅜ in.) long, 3–4 cm (1 3/16–1⅝ in.) wide, keeled, curved, 2–5 spines on each side, margins wavy, stout petioles 10 mm (⅜ in.) long; fruits vivid red 45A, globose, 8 mm (5/16 in.) diameter, pedicels 5 mm (3/16 in.) long.

'Prince Ed' (male; sibling of 'Pin Cushion'; selected at J. H. Schmidt Nursery; named by H. Hohman; registered H.S.A. 6-60 by E. S. Wyckoff).
Leaves moderate olive green, broadly oval, 6–7 cm (2⅜–2¾ in.) long, 3.5–4 cm (1⅜–1⅝ in.) wide, bases truncate, 5–6 short spines on each side, margins slightly reflexed, petioles stout, 5 mm (3/16 in.) long; reported as heavy flowering at a young age.

'Princeton Gold' (female; seedling grown by Princeton Nursery about 1948; selected and named by W. Flemer III; introduced in the 1980s).

Leaves dark olive green, elliptic, 5–6.5 cm (2–2⅜ in.) long, 2–3 cm (¾–1³⁄₁₆ in.) wide, keeled, curved, bases cuneate, apices acuminate, tip spines reflexed, margins revolute, usually 2–5 small spines on each side, occasionally only 1–2 spines, petioles dark, 6–8 mm (⁷⁄₃₂–⁵⁄₁₆ in.) long; fruits vivid yellow 14A, globose, 6–8 mm (⁷⁄₃₂–⁵⁄₁₆ in.) diameter, abundant, pedicels 7–10 mm (⁹⁄₃₂–⅜ in.) long, persistent, are not readily eaten by birds; vigorous, pyramidal habit. Selected for good dark green winter foliage and persistent yellow fruit.

'Rake Pond' (male; seedling origin near New Lisbon, New Jersey, about 1910; registered H.S.A. 11-59 by F. R. Genard).

Leaves moderate olive green, elliptic, 3.5–5 cm (1⅜–2 in.) long, 1.5–2.5 cm (1–1⅜ in.) wide, keeled, curved, 4–7 prominent spines on each side, margins reflexed, wavy, dark petioles, 8–10 mm (⁵⁄₁₆–⅜ in.) long; very heavy flowering male.

'Red Bird' (female; introduced Light's Nursery).

Leaves dark olive green, elliptic, 4–5 cm (1⅝–2 in.) long, 2–2.5 cm (¾–1 in.) wide, keeled, curved, 3–6 spines on each side, margins reflexed, slightly convex, dark petioles 6–8 mm (⁷⁄₃₂–⁵⁄₁₆ in.) long; fruits vivid red 45A, ellipsoid, 8 mm (⁵⁄₁₆ in.) long, pedicels 5 mm (³⁄₁₆ in.) long.

'Red Flush' (female; synonym 'Red Flash'; selected by O. S. Pride; Grace Hybrid Group).

Leaves dark olive green, elliptic, 6.5–7 cm (2½–2¾ in.) long, 3.5–4 cm (1⅜–1⅝ in.) wide, bases obtuse to cuneate, curved, slightly keeled, 7–8 spines on each side, margins reflexed, wavy, petioles stout, 5–7 mm (³⁄₁₆–⁹⁄₃₂ in.) long; fruits vivid red 45A, globose, 8 mm (⁵⁄₁₆ in.) diameter, pedicels 5 mm (³⁄₁₆ in.) long.

'Red Spice' (female; selected by O. S. Pride; Grace Hybrid Group).

Leaves moderate olive green, oval, 6–6.5 cm (2⅜–2½ in.) long, 3.5–4 cm (1⅜–1⅝ in.) wide, keeled, curved, 4–7 spines on each side, margins reflexed, petioles stout, 5 mm (³⁄₁₆ in.) long; fruits vivid red 45A, globose, 8–10 mm (⁵⁄₁₆–⅜ in.) diameter.

'Red Tower' (female; Tingle Nursery, before 1958).

Leaves moderate olive green, oval, 5–6 cm (2–2⅜ in.) long, 3–3.5 cm (1³⁄₁₆–1⅜ in.) wide, slightly keeled, curved, convex, 2–4 small spines usually on upper two-thirds of leaf, petioles 8–10 mm (⁵⁄₁₆–⅜ in.) long; fruits vivid red 45A, globose, 8 mm (⁵⁄₁₆ in.) diameter, abundant, close together, persistent, pedicels 3–5 mm (⅛–³⁄₁₆ in.) long; pyramidal habit.

'Red Velvet' (female; selected 1953 by C. R. Wolf, Millville, New Jersey; registered H.S.A. 14-74 by D. G. Fenton).

Leaves dark olive green, oval to broadly elliptic, 6–7 cm (2⅜–2¾ in.) long, 3.5 cm (1⅜ in.) wide, keeled, curved, 3–5 spines on each side, margins reflexed, slightly wavy, petioles 8–10 mm (⁵⁄₁₆–⅜ in.) long; fruits vivid red 45A, globose, 8 mm (⁵⁄₁₆ in.) diameter, pedicels 5 mm (³⁄₁₆ in.) long; low pyramidal habit.

'Reeve East' (female; selected 1953 by E. C. White).

Leaves dark olive green, broadly elliptic, 5.5–7 cm (2⅛–2¾ in.) long, 2.8–4 cm (1⅛–1⅝ in.) wide, bases obtuse to rotund, slightly keeled and curved, margins recurved, wavy, 3–5 spines on each side, tip spine reflexed, petioles 8–10 cm (⁵⁄₁₆–⅜ in.) long; fruits vivid red 45B, globose to slightly ellipsoid, 8–10 mm (⁵⁄₁₆–⅜ in.) diameter, pedicels reddish, 5–7 mm (³⁄₁₆–⁹⁄₃₂ in.) long.

'Reeve West' (female; selected 1953 by E. C. White).

Leaves moderate olive green, elliptic to broadly elliptic, 5–6.5 cm (2–2½ in.) long, 3–4 cm (1³⁄₁₆–1⅝ in.) wide, bases cuneate to obtuse, slightly keeled, curved, margins recurved, 2–3 spines on each side, on upper two-thirds of leaf, tip spines reflexed, petioles 8–10 mm (⁵⁄₁₆–⅜ in.) long; fruits vivid red 45B, globose, 10 mm (⅜ in.) diameter, long reddish pedicels, 12–18 mm (½–1¹⁄₁₆ in.) long.

'Reynolds' (female; discovered 1946 by H. Shadow on property of L. L. Reynolds; introduced by Reynolds, J. McDaniel, and H. Shadow; registered H.S.A. 62-48 by McDaniel).

Leaves moderate olive green, elliptic, 6.5–8 cm (2½–3⅛ in.) long, 3–3.5 cm (1³⁄₁₆–1⅜ in.) wide, bases obtuse to rotund, curved, 4–5 spines on each side, margins reflexed, wavy, petioles 8 mm (⁵⁄₁₆ in.) long, fruits vivid red 45A, globose, 10–12 mm (⅜–¹⁵⁄₃₂ in.) diameter, pedicels reddish, 8–10 mm (⁵⁄₁₆–⅜ in.) long.

'Richards' (female; discovered by S. B. Detwiller near Tammany Hall, Maryland; introduced by C. S. Britt and W. W. Steiner).

Leaves dark olive green, broadly elliptic, 7.5–9.5 cm (3–3¾ in.) long, 4.5–5 cm (1¾–2 in.) wide, bases nearly truncate, curved, slightly keeled, 5–8 spines on each side, petioles dark, stout, 8–10 mm (⁵⁄₁₆–⅜ in.) long; fruits deep reddish orange 43A, globose, 10 mm (⅜ in.) diameter, in clusters, pedicels 5 mm (³⁄₁₆ in.) long.

'Rick' (male; synonym 'Wheeler No. 2M'; selected by W. Wheeler before 1953).

Leaves dark olive green, oval, 4–4.5 cm (1⅝–1¾ in.) long, 2.5–3 cm (1–1³⁄₁₆ in.) wide, bases cuneate to rotund, keeled, curve, margins recurved, slightly wavy, 2–5 spines on each side, tip spines reflexed, petioles reddish, 6–8 mm (⁷⁄₃₂–⁵⁄₁₆ in.) long.

'Ridgeway' (female; selected by D. Hales, in Monongalia County, West Virginia; introduced by R. W. Pease before 1957).

Leaves small; fruits red; very upright, throws many lateral branches, needs staking when young.

'Robbinsville' (male; chance seedling selected 1956 and registered H.S.A. 5-67 by E. Dilatush).

Leaves dark olive green; original plant 2.3 m (7 ft.) high when registered. A good pollinator; easily propagated.

'Robin Tree' (female; selected by W. Wheeler before 1963).

Leaves dark olive green, oval to broadly elliptic, 4–5 cm (1⅝–2 in.) long, 2.5–3 cm (1–1³⁄₁₆ in.) wide, bases obtuse, keeled, curved, 4–7 spines on each side, petioles 8 mm (⁵⁄₁₆ in.) long; fruits strong red 45C, globose, 8 mm (⁵⁄₁₆ in.) diameter, pedicels 5 mm (³⁄₁₆ in.) long; fruits mature early, not stripped by robins in late fall.

'Rosalind Sarver', see *I.* × *attenuata* 'Rosalind Sarver'.

'Rotunda' (female; Clarendon Gardens before 1962).

Leaves olive green, glossy, margins entire; fruits red; vigorous upright habit.

'Rotundifolia' (female; selected 1930–1940 by Vermeulen Nursery).

Leaves dark olive green, oval, 6.5–8 cm (2½–3⅛ in.) long, 4–4.5 cm (1⅝–1¾ in.) wide, slightly keeled, curved, 5–7 spines on each side, margins reflexed, petioles 8–10 mm (⁵⁄₁₆–⅜ in.) long; fruits vivid red 45A, globose, 8 mm (⁵⁄₁₆ in.) diameter, abundant, reddish pedicels 6–8 mm (⁷⁄₃₂–⁵⁄₁₆ in.) long.

'Roundleaf' (male; selected 1925 and introduced 1947 by E. Dilatush).

Leaves dark olive green, oval, 4–5 cm (1⅝–2 in.) long, 2.8–3.2 cm (1⅛–1¼ in.) wide, bases obtuse to rotund, slightly keeled, curved, margins recurved, 2–4 spines on each side, tip spines reflexed, petioles reddish, 6–8 mm (⁷⁄₃₂–⁵⁄₁₆ in.) long; abundant male flowers.

'Ro Val', see *Ilex* × *attenuata* 'Ro Val'.

'Ruby Red' (female; 250-year-old tree in Richmond, Virginia, introduced in late 1940 by O. Gresham; named for wife of Gresham; original tree destroyed).

Leaves dark olive green, oval, 6–8 cm (2⅜–3⅛ in.) long, keeled, curved, 4–4.5 cm (1⅝–1¾ in.) wide, bases rotund, apices acuminate, 2–3 widely spaced spines on each side, usually upper two-thirds of leaf, petioles 10 mm (⅜ in.) long; fruits vivid red 45A, globose to slightly ellipsoid, 8–9 mm (⁵⁄₁₆–¹¹⁄₃₂ in.) diameter, abundant, pedicels 5–8 mm (³⁄₁₆–⁵⁄₁₆ in.) long; compact pyramidal habit.

'Rumson' (female; synonyms 'Muller', 'Muller No. 1'; introduced by Wells Nursery before 1957; was one of largest hollies in state, along with 'Seaville' and 'Shoemaker', which see; circumference of 2.31 m (7½ ft.) in Rumson, Monmouth County, New Jersey; felled by windstorm about 1988).

Leaves dark olive green, fruits red, abundant.

'Ruston' (female; selected by H. Hohman).

Leaves dark olive green, broadly elliptic, 4.5–5.5 cm (1¾–2⅛ in.) long, 2.5–3 cm (1–1³⁄₁₆ in.) wide, bases obtuse, keeled, curved, 3–5 spines on each side, margins reflexed, petioles 8 mm (⁵⁄₁₆ in.) long; fruits vivid red 45A, globose, 8 mm (⁵⁄₁₆ in.) diameter, pedicels 5 mm (³⁄₁₆ in.) long.

'Ruth' (female; selected by W. Wheeler before 1963).

Leaves dark olive green, elliptic, 8–8.5 cm (3–3⅜ in.) long, 4–4.5 cm (1⅝–1¾ in.) wide, curved, keeled, 5–6 spines on each side, margins reflexed, slightly wavy, petioles stout, 8 mm (⁵⁄₁₆ in.) long; fruits deep reddish orange 43A, globose, 8 mm (⁵⁄₁₆ in.) diameter, pedicels 8 mm (⁵⁄₁₆ in.) long.

'Saga Serene' (female; introduced by W. Steed; discovered 1956 on J. W. Parson's property near Norman, North Carolina; named by J. D. Rankin for wife of T. Klein).

Leaves moderate olive green, oval, 5–5.5 cm (2–2⅛ in.) long, 2.5–3 cm (1–1³⁄₁₆ in.) wide, curved, convexed, twisted, petioles 7 mm (⁹⁄₃₂ in.) long; fruits vivid yellow 15A, globose, 8 mm (⁵⁄₁₆ in.) diameter.

'Salem Compact' (female; synonym 'Salem Compacta'; discovered southern New Jersey by W. J. Dauber before 1958).

Leaves dark olive green, elliptic to oval, 5–6.5 cm (2–2½ in.) long, 2.5–4 cm (1–1⅝ in.) wide, slightly keeled, curved, 3–5 spines on each side, margins reflexed, petioles 7 mm (⁹⁄₃₂ in.) long; fruits vivid red 44A, globose, 7 mm (⁹⁄₃₂ in.) diameter.

'Sallie' (female; synonyms 'Aalto No. 2', 'Sally', 'Wheeler No. 2'; selected in New Jersey by E. C. White before 1948).

Leaves dark olive green, elliptic to obovate, 4.5–6 cm (1¾–2⅜ in.) long, 2.5–3.5 cm (1–1⅜ in.) wide, bases obtuse, curved, keeled, 2–4 spines on each side, margins reflexed, slightly twisted, petioles dark, 7–9 mm (9/32–11/32 in.) long; fruits vivid red 44A, globose, 10–11 mm (⅜–7/16 in.) diameter.

'Sallie Seedling' (female; seedling of 'Sallie' introduced by T. Klein).

Leaves dark olive green, oval, 4–4.5 cm (1⅝–1¾ in.) long, 2.5–3 cm (1–1 3/16 in.) wide, keeled, curved, 3–4 prominent spines on each side, upper two-thirds of leaf, petioles 6–8 mm (7/32–5/16 in.) long; fruits red, glossy, globose, 8–10 mm (5/16–⅜ in.) diameter.

'Sambeau' (female; discovered around 1970 in Atlanta, Georgia, by S. Gray; propagated and named by Tom Dodd Jr. in Gray's memory).

Leaves dark olive green, broadly elliptic, 6–8 cm (2⅜–3⅛ in.) long, 3–4 cm (1 3/16–1⅝ in.) wide, bases cuneate to obtuse, tip spines reflexed, slightly keeled, convex, 5–9 spines on each side, petioles brown, stout, 8–10 mm (⅝–⅜ in.) long; fruits red, globose, reported very large, 10–13 mm (⅜–½ in.) diameter.

'Santa Claus' (male; selected by P. Bosley before 1957).

Leaves moderate olive green, elliptic, 5–6 cm (2–2⅜ in.) long, 2.5–3 cm (1–1 3/16 in.) wide, curved, keeled, 5–6 spines on each side, margins reflexed, wavy, petioles 5–7 mm (3/16–9/32 in.) long; profuse male flowers.

'Sara Higgins' (female; synonym 'Sara Higgens'; introduced by Holly Haven Nursery, New Jersey, before 1952).

Leaves dark olive green, elliptic, 6.5–8 cm (2½–3⅛ in.) long, 3–3.5 cm (1 3/16–1⅜ in.) wide, bases cuneate to obtuse, keeled, curved, 2–5 small spines usually on upper two-thirds of leaf, petioles dark, 8 mm (5/16 in.) long; fruits vivid red, 45A, globose to slightly ellipsoid, 8 mm (5/16 in.) diameter, pedicels reddish, 8–10 mm (5/16–⅜ in.) long.

'Satyr Hill' (female; volunteer seedling selected and introduced by S. McLean, registered H.S.A. 3-70 by McLean).

Leaves dark olive green, oval, 5–6 cm (2–2⅜ in.) long, 4.5–5 cm (1¾–2 in.) wide, slightly keeled, 5–6 spines on each side, margins reflexed, petioles stout, 7 mm (9/32 in.) long; fruits red, globose, 10 mm (⅜

in.) diameter, pedicels 10 mm (⅜ in.) long, borne singly, well spaced.

'Scarlet Sue' (female; selected 1950 near Aldine, New Jersey; registered H.S.A. 7-59 by E. C. Waddington Jr.).

Leaves dark olive green, persist more than 2 years, broadly elliptic, 4.5–7 cm (1¾–2¾ in.) long, 3–4 cm (1 3/16–1⅝ in.) wide, keeled, curved, 4–6 spines on each side, margins wavy, petioles 8 mm (5/16 in.) long; fruits vivid red 44A, globose, 10 mm (⅜ in.) diameter, pedicels 8 mm (5/16 in.) long.

'Scott' (male; plant at Planting Fields Arboretum received from Dilatush Nursery in 1978).

Leaves dark olive green, elliptic, 6–7.5 cm (2⅜–2¾ in.) long, 2.5–3 cm (1–1 3/16 in.) wide, bases rotund, slightly keeled, curved, 3–5 spines usually on upper two-thirds of leaf, petioles 8 mm (5/16 in.) long.

'Seaville' (second largest holly in New Jersey, with circumference of 2.28 m (7½ ft.); located between Route 9 and Parkway about 300 m (1000 ft.) north of Dennis Township line and south of Smith Lane; see 'Rumson' and 'Shoemaker' for other large hollies).

'Secrest' (female; origin from seed obtained from Forest Nursery and Seed Company; planted 1922 in Secrest Arboretum; registered H.S.A. 10-69 by O. D. Diller).

Leaves moderate olive green, broadly elliptic, 6–7.7 cm (2⅜–3 in.) long, 3–4.5 cm (1 3/16–1¾ in.) wide, keeled, curved, 4–5 prominent spines on each

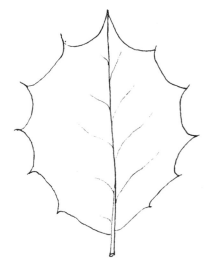

Figure 15-39. *Ilex opaca* 'Satyr Hill'. Drawing by Randy Allen.

side, margins reflexed, petioles 7 mm (⁹⁄₃₂ in.) long; fruits vivid red 44A, oval, 9 mm (¹¹⁄₃₂ in.) long.

'Seminary' (female; original tree on Seminary Street, Florence, Alabama, now dead; cuttings taken by G. Wood in 1976 for University of Alabama, Tanglewood Arboretum, Hale County, Alabama).

Leaves dark olive green, broadly elliptic, 5.5–7 cm (2⅛–2¾ in.) long, 3–4 cm (1³⁄₁₆–1⅝ in.) wide, keeled, curved, bases acute, apices acute, tip spines reflexed, margins undulating, 4–6 spines on each side, petioles 8–10 mm (⁵⁄₁₆–⅜ in.) long; fruits vivid red 45A, ellipsoid, 8–10 mm (⁵⁄₁₆–⅜ in.) long, 6–8 mm (⁷⁄₃₂–⁵⁄₁₆ in.) diameter, fruit abundant, pedicels 8–10 mm (⁵⁄₁₆–⅜ in.) long; pyramidal habit.

'September Fire' (female; volunteer seedling selected, named, and registered H.S.A. 2-87 by R. K. Peters; sibling of 'Danny Allen').

Leaves dark olive green, ovate, 7.5 cm (3 in.) long, 4.5 cm (1¾ in.) wide, bases obtuse, keeled, curved, margins occasionally twisted, 2–5 long slender spines on each side and reflexed down, tip spines reflexed, petioles 11 mm (⁷⁄₁₆ in.) long; fruits vivid red 45A, globose to elongate, 11 mm (⁷⁄₁₆ in.) long, 10 mm (⅜ in.) diameter, pedicels 10 mm (⅜ in.) long, ripens early in mid September; conical habit; hardy in zone 5.

'Sewell' (female; synonym 'Tilghman'; selected 1953 by H. G. Mattoon on Gillespie estate near Sherwood, Tilghman's Island, Maryland).

Leaves dark olive green, elliptic, 6.5–8 cm (2½–3⅛ in.) long, 3–3.5 cm (1³⁄₁₆–1⅜ in.) wide, convex, curved, midrib depressed, 5–9 spines on each side, margins reflexed, wavy, wrinkled, petioles 10 mm (⅜ in.) long; fruits deep reddish orange 43A, elliptic, 10 mm (⅜ in.) long.

'Shawsheen' (female; selected from southwestern Pennsylvania and named by H. Rohrbach before 1958).

Leaves dark olive green; fruits red. Selected for superior hardiness.

'Sherman' (female; Holly Hill Farms, Earleville, Maryland, before 1963).

Leaves moderate olive green, elliptic, 5–7 cm (2–2¾ in.) long, 2.5–3.5 cm (1–1³⁄₁₆ in.) wide, bases cuneate, keeled, curved, 3–5 prominent spines, margins reflexed, wavy, petioles 8 mm (⁵⁄₁₆ in.) long; fruits vivid red 44A, globose, 8–10 mm (⁵⁄₁₆–⅜ in.) diameter, pedicels 4 mm (⁵⁄₃₂ in.) long.

'Shirley' (female; selected by W. Wheeler; tree moved from Mashpee, Massachusetts, to Ashumet Farm, Falmouth, Massachusetts).

Fruits red, small, globose, 6.5 mm (¼ in.) diameter, pedicels about 1½–2 times as long as fruit.

'Shoemaker' (female; large holly at Mile 22 on Garden State Parkway, New Jersey; plaque beneath tree reads, "In 1953 the route of the Garden State Parkway was changed for a distance of 120 yards in order to preserve this rare, centuries-old American Holly Tree"; fourth largest holly in state, with circumference of 2.23 m (7⅓ ft.); see also 'Rumson' and 'Seaville').

Figure 15-40. *Ilex opaca* 'Shoemaker' at Garden State Park, New Jersey, the fourth largest holly in New Jersey, with a circumference of 2.23 m (7⅓ ft.). Photo by Franklin West.

'Silica King' (male; named 1949 by C. R. Wolf; registered H.S.A. 15-74 by D. G. Fenton).

Leaves dark olive green, glossy, elliptic to oval, 6.5–8 cm (2½–3 in.) long, 3–4.5 cm (1³⁄₁₆–1⅝ in.) wide, curved, slightly keeled, 5–6 spines on each side, margins recurved, petioles 10–15 mm (⅜–¹⁹⁄₃₂ in.) long; abundant male flowers.

'Simpson' (female; plant at Planting Fields Arboretum received from Dilatush Nursery 1978).

Leaves dark olive green, broadly elliptic, 6–8 cm (2⅜–3⅛ in.) long, 3–4 cm (1³⁄₁₆–1⅝ in.) wide, keeled, curved, 5–7 spines on each side, petioles stout, 5 mm (³⁄₁₆ in.) long; fruits vivid red 45A, globose, 6–8 mm (⁷⁄₃₂–⁵⁄₁₆ in.) diameter, pedicels 6–8 mm (⁷⁄₃₂–⁵⁄₁₆ in.) long.

'Simpson No. 3' (female; seedling from Simpson Nursery; plant at Bernheim Forest).
Leaves dark olive green, oval, 4.5–5 cm (1¾–2 in.) long, 3 cm (1³⁄₁₆ in.) wide, keeled, curved, 2–3 spines on upper two-thirds of leaf; fruits vivid red 45A, globose, 8 mm (⁵⁄₁₆ in.) diameter; upright pyramidal habit of growth. Similar in form to 'Cheerful'.

'Sims' (female; origin Winchester, Tennessee; selected and introduced by H. Templeton in the 1960s).
Leaves dark olive green, broadly elliptic, 4.5–5.5 cm (1¾–2⅛ in.) long, 2.5–3 cm (1–1³⁄₁₆ in.) wide, slightly keeled, curved, 1–3 spines on upper two-thirds of leaf, margins reflexed, petioles 6–7 mm (⁷⁄₃₂–⁹⁄₃₂ in.) long; fruits red.

'Skookum' (female; Kingsville Nursery, Kingsville, Maryland, before 1947).
Leaves moderate olive green, elliptic, 7–7.5 cm (2¾–3 in.) long, 3.5–4 cm (1⅜–1⅝ in.) wide, convexed, curved, midribs depressed, 2–3 spines on each side, upper half of leaf, margins reflexed; fruits vivid red 45A, globose, 8 mm (⁵⁄₁₆ in.) diameter, pedicels 8 mm (⁵⁄₁₆ in.) long.

'Sleigh Bells' (female; selected by O. S. Pride; Grace Hybrid Group).
Leaves moderate olive green, broadly elliptic, 7.5–9 cm (3–3½ in.) long, 3.5–4.5 cm (1⅜–1¾ in.) wide, slightly keeled, curved, 5–8 spines on each side, deeply scalloped, margins reflexed, petioles 8 mm (⁵⁄₁₆ in.) long; fruits dark red, globose, 8 mm (⁵⁄₁₆ in.) diameter.

'Slim Jane' (female; named 1949 by C. R. Wolf; registered H.S.A. 16-74 by D. G. Fenton).
Leaves dark olive green, glossy, very narrow elliptic, 5.5–7 cm (2⅛–2¾ in.) long, 2.3–3 cm (⅞–1³⁄₁₆ in.) wide, flat, curved tip, 4–7 prominent spines on each side, petioles 5–7 mm (³⁄₁₆–⁹⁄₃₂ in.) long; fruits vivid reddish orange 41A, globose, 10 mm (⅜ in.) diameter, pedicels 3–5 mm (⅛–³⁄₁₆ in.) long. Resembles 'Slim Jim'.

'Slim Jim' (male; selected about 1940 by T. Windon and E. C. White).
Leaves moderate olive green, narrow-elliptic, 6–6.5 cm (2⅜–2½ in.) long, 2.5–3 cm (1–1³⁄₁₆ in.) wide, keeled, curved, 4–6 spines on each side, margins reflexed, wavy, petioles stout, 7 mm (⁹⁄₃₂ in.) long.

'Snipatuit' (female; chance seedling, discovered 1985 by Arthur A. Allen on his property in Snipatuit, North Rochester, Massachusetts; registered H.S.A 4-90 by Allen; 'Snipatuit' is a Native American word for "rocky water").
Leaves dark olive green, broadly elliptic, 6.5–10 cm (2½–4 in.) long, 3–4 cm (1³⁄₁₆–1⅝ in.) wide, curved, slightly keeled, bases cuneate to obtuse, apices acute, margins slightly convex, slightly wavy, 4–5 spines on each side, petioles dark, 8–12 mm (⁵⁄₁₆–¹⁵⁄₃₂ in.) long; fruits vivid red 44A, slightly ellipsoid, 10 mm (⅜ in.) long, 8 mm (⁵⁄₁₆ in.) diameter, petioles reddish, 8–10 mm (⁵⁄₁₆–⅜ in.) long; narrow pyramidal habit, 6 m (20 ft.) tall, 1.8 m (6 ft.) wide in about 20 years.

'Snowden' (female; selected by A. N. Adams on estate of Colonel Snowden near Fort Meade, Maryland; introduced by Ten Oaks Nursery before 1953).
Leaves dark olive green, heavy texture; fruits red, large.

'Somerset' (female; introduced by Tingle Nursery, before 1958).
Leaves moderate olive green, broadly elliptic, 5–6.5 cm (2–2½ in.) long, 2.5–3.5 cm (1–1⅜ in.) wide, keeled, curved, 3–6 spines on each side, margins reflexed, petioles 10 mm (⅜ in.) long; fruits deep reddish orange 43A, globose, 10 mm (⅜ in.) diameter, pedicels 5 mm (³⁄₁₆ in.) long.

'Southern Illinois University' (female; synonym 'Old Science Big Leaf'; on Southern Illinois University campus near old Science Building; named and introduced by B. Hartline).
Leaves dark olive green, thick, leathery, oval to broadly elliptic, 6.5–8.5 cm (2⅜–3⅜ in.) long, 3–5 cm (1³⁄₁₆–2 in.) wide, keeled, curved, 4–6 spines on each side, margins wavy, stout petioles 8 mm (⁵⁄₁₆ in.) long; fruits vivid red 45A, ellipsoid, 1 cm (⅜ in.) long.

'Splendorberry' (female; introduced 1959 by Vermeulen Nursery).
Fruits dark red, large; strong straight growing habit.

'Sprig' (female; selected 1929 and introduced 1947 by E. Dilatush).
Leaves moderate olive green, oval, 4–4.5 cm (1⅝–1¾ in.) long, 3 cm (1³⁄₁₆ in.) wide, midrib depressed, 3–5 spines on each side, margins reflexed, wavy, petioles 6–7 mm (⁷⁄₃₂–⁹⁄₃₂ in.) long; fruits red, annually. Initially used to provide cut fruiting sprigs for florists.

'Spring Grove XC' (female; origin seedling from

nursery of Spring Grove Cemetery; introduced by T. Klein).

Leaves moderate olive green, broadly elliptic, 6.5–7.5 cm (2½–3 in.) long, 3–3.5 cm (1³⁄₁₆–1⅜ in.) wide, keeled, curved, 3–4 spines on each side, margins reflexed, petioles 8 mm (⁵⁄₁₆ in.) long; fruits vivid orange yellow 23A, globose, 8 mm (⁵⁄₁₆ in.) diameter, pedicels 6 mm (⁷⁄₃₂ in.) long.

'Springhill' (female; introduced by Springhill Nursery).

Leaves dark olive green, elliptic, 4.5–5 cm (1¾–2 in.) long, 2.5–3 cm (1–1³⁄₁₆ in.) wide, keeled, curved, 1–3 spines usually on upper two-thirds of leaf, margins reflexed, petioles 8–10 mm (⁵⁄₁₆–⅜ in.) long, fruits deep reddish orange 43A, globose, 8–10 mm (⁵⁄₁₆–⅜ in.) diameter, reddish pedicels 4–6 mm (⁵⁄₃₂–⁶⁄₃₂ in.) long.

'St. Ann' (female; origin St. Mary Island in Oyster Bay Harbor, Massachusetts; selected about 1934 and introduced by W. Wheeler).

Leaves dark olive green, broadly elliptic, 6.5–7.5 cm (2½–3 in.) long, 3.5–4 cm (1⅜–1⅝ in.) wide, bases obtuse to rotund, keeled, curved, slightly twisted at apex, usually 6–8 spines on each side, petioles dark, 10–12 mm (⅜–½ in.) long; fruits vivid red 44A, globose, 8 mm (⁵⁄₁₆ in.) diameter, pedicels reddish, 11–15 mm (⁷⁄₁₆–⁹⁄₁₆ in.) long; open spreading habit with long sweeping branches.

'St. John's' (female; origin St. John's College, Annapolis, Maryland; named and registered H.S.A. 6-77 by A. Kungle Jr.).

Leaves dark olive green, oval, 5–7 cm (2–2¾ in.) long, 3.5–4.5 cm (1⅜–1¾ in.) wide, keeled, curved, 1–6 spines on each side, usually on upper half of leaf, margins reflexed, petioles 8–10 mm (⁵⁄₁₆–⅜ in.) long; fruits deep reddish orange 43A, ellipsoid, 8–10 mm (⁵⁄₁₆–⅜ in.) long, pedicels 4–6 mm (⁵⁄₃₂–⁷⁄₃₂ in.) long. Tree about 135 years old.

'St. Mary' (female; synonym 'Saint Mary'; collected West Barnstable, Massachusetts; moved and named for St. Mary Island in Oyster Bay Harbor, Massachusetts; introduced by W. Wheeler before 1947).

Leaves dark olive green, broadly elliptic, 6–6.5 cm (2⅜–2½ in.) long, 3–3.5 cm (1³⁄₁₆–1⅜ in.) wide, keeled, curved, 4–5 spines on each side, margins reflexed, wavy, petioles 8–10 mm (⁵⁄₁₆–⅜ in.) long; fruits deep reddish orange 42A, globose, 8 mm (⁵⁄₁₆ in.) diameter, pedicels 6 mm (⁷⁄₃₂ in.) long.

'St. Stephens' (female; selected about 1928, introduced 1945 by Kingsville Nursery, Kingsville, Maryland; sibling of 'Delia Bradley').

Leaves moderate olive green, oval, 5–5.5 cm (2–2⅛ in.) long, 3–3.5 cm (1³⁄₁₆–1⅜ in.) wide, keeled, curved, 3–4 spines on each side, margins reflexed, petioles 5 mm (³⁄₁₆ in.) long; fruits vivid red 45A, globose, 6–8 mm (⁷⁄₃₂–⁵⁄₁₆ in.) diameter, pedicels 6 mm (⁷⁄₃₂ in.) long.

'Steward's Cream Crown' (female; origin as a single bud mutation and first reported as leaf variegation of *I. opaca*; named and registered H.S.A. 1-63 by L. Steward Jr.).

Leaves with yellow white marginal variegation, without yellowish pink cast; fruits red; upright conical habit. Foliage variegation unstable, new growth not pink; plant propagation stopped, plant not sold commercially.

'Steward's Silver Crown' (female; bud mutation of 7-year-old plant discovered by L. Steward Jr. in his nursery in Pitman, New Jersey, 1956; variegated mutation occurred on a single leaf; registered H.S.A. 3-78 by Steward; PP No. 4367).

Leaves variegated, center of leaves dark green 137A to light yellowish green 145C, margins irregular variegation of off white, new spring growth tinged yellowish pink, which disappears as leaves mature, mature summer foliage with light yellow 4B, irregular margins, centers of leaves marbled with gray-green blotches and swirls, undersides of leaves yellow green 147C and 145B, with yellow margins; leaves oval-elliptic, 5.2–8 cm (2¹⁄₁₆–3⅛ in.) long, 3.5–4.5 cm (1⅜–1¾ in.) wide, keeled, curved, 5–8 spines each side, petioles 5 mm (³⁄₁₆ in.) long; fruits globose, glossy, deep red 46A, 8–9 mm (⁵⁄₁₆–¹¹⁄₃₂ in.) diameter, good fruit retention, pedicels reddish, 5 mm (³⁄₁₆ in.) long; hardy to −18°C (0°F). First sold in 1978. Excellent accent plant. Plate 161.

'Stinking Creek No. 1' (female; found by W. C. Edds in Tennessee in the 1970s).

Leaves moderate olive green, broadly elliptic, 5–6 mm (2–2⅜ in.) long, 2.5–3 cm (1–1³⁄₁₆ in.) wide, bases obtuse, keeled, curved, 3–4 spines on each side, margins reflexed, petioles 8 mm (⁵⁄₁₆ in.) long; fruits vivid red 45A, globose, 6–8 mm (⁷⁄₃₂–⁵⁄₁₆ in.) diameter, pedicels 4–6 mm (⁵⁄₃₂–⁷⁄₃₂ in.) long.

'Stumphouse' (female; selected from property of Mrs. S. Vissage, Stumphouse Mountain, Walhalla, South Carolina, by W. C. Frierson before 1948).

Leaves dark olive green, elliptic, 6.5–7.5 cm (2½–3 in.) long, 3.5–4 cm (1⅜–1⅝ in.) wide, bases obtuse to rotund, slightly keeled, curved, 2–3 spines usually on upper half of leaf, petioles dark, 10 mm (⅜ in.) long; fruits vivid red 45A, globose, 7–8 mm (⁹⁄₃₂–⁵⁄₁₆ in.) diameter, pedicels reddish, 10–12 mm (⅜–½ in.) long. Possibly *I. × attenuata* hybrid.

'Sunset Glow' (female; selected about 1925 and introduced 1948 by E. Dilatush).

Leaves dark olive green, elliptic, 6.5–7 cm (2½–2¾ in.) long, 4–4.5 cm (1⅝–1¾ in.) wide, bases obtuse, slightly keeled, curved, usually 4 spines, occasionally only 2 spines on each side, upper half of leaf, margins reflexed, petioles dark, 6–8 mm (7⁄32–5⁄16 in.) long; fruits vivid red 44B, globose, 8 mm (5⁄16 in.) diameter, pedicels 5 mm (3⁄16 in.) long; slow dense habit.

'Suntan' (female; chance seedling introduced by T. Klein before 1968).

Leaves dark olive green, oval, 3.5–4 cm (1⅜–1⅝ in.) long, 2–3 cm (¾–1 3⁄16 in.) wide, keeled, curved, 2–3 spines on upper half of leaf, margins reflexed, petioles 1 cm (⅜ in.) long; fruits vivid reddish orange 33B, ellipsoid, 8–9 mm (5⁄16–11⁄32 in.) long, pedicels 6–9 mm (7⁄32–11⁄32 in.) long; upright open habit of growth. Unusual fruit color.

'Susan' (female; origin near New Lisbon, New Jersey; selected 1920–1923 by E. C. White).

Leaves dark olive green, elliptic to broadly elliptic, 4.5–6 cm (1¾–2⅜ in.) long, 2.5–3 cm (1–1 3⁄16 in.) wide, bases obtuse, keeled, curved, 3–4 spines on each side, petioles 8 mm (5⁄16 in.) long; fruits vivid reddish orange 44B, globose, 8 mm (5⁄16 in.) diameter, produces fruit at young age, occasionally 2 fruits per peduncle, peduncles 10–12 mm (⅜–15⁄32 in.) long, pedicels 3–5 mm (⅛–3⁄16 in.) long.

'Susan Gregory' (female; original on Kinead property, Kesslers Cross Lanes, West Virginia; selected by W. Hallenberg and T. Klein; named for Klein's granddaughter; introduced by Klein in the 1960s).

Leaves moderate olive green, broadly elliptic, 4.5–6 cm (1¾–2⅜ in.) long, 3–3.5 cm (1 3⁄16–1⅜ in.) wide, bases cuneate to obtuse, keeled, curved, 2–5 spines on each side, margins twisted, wavy, petioles 8 mm (5⁄16 in.) long; fruits strong orange 24A, with slight blush, ellipsoid, 10 mm (⅜ in.) long, reddish pedicels 8–10 mm (5⁄16–⅜ in.) long.

'Sussex Orange-Red' (female; discovered 1948 in a swamp in Sussex County, Delaware; registered H.S.A. 2-67 by W. Phillips).

Leaves olive green, semiglossy; fruits brownish red, maturing reddish orange, early ripening, good keeping quality after cut.

'Swarthmore' (female; chance seedling moved 1957 to J. R. Frorer holly collection, Swarthmore College Campus; named by Frorer; registered H.S.A. 4-87 by A. Bunting).

Leaves dark olive green, broadly elliptic 8–12.7 cm (3⅛–5 in.) long, 5–6.6 cm (2–2⅝ in.) wide, bases obtuse, keeled, slightly curved and keeled, margins revolute, slightly wavy, 4–7 spines on each side, stout petioles 8–20 mm (5⁄16–¾ in.) long; fruits vivid red 44A to 45A, elongate 11 mm (7⁄16 in.) long, 10 mm (⅜ in.) diameter, pedicels 10 mm (⅜ in.) long; conical habit, 7.5 m (25 ft.) tall, 3.7 m (12 ft.) wide in 30 years. One of the unusual hollies in the Swarthmore collection with large broad leaves.

'Taber', see I. × attenuata 'Taber'.

'Taber No. 2', see I. × attenuata 'Taber No. 2'.

'Taber No. 3', see I. × attenuata 'Taber No. 3'.

'Taber No. 4', see I. × attenuata 'Taber No. 4'.

'Ten Oaks' (female; origin near Clarkesville, Maryland; introduced by Ten Oaks Nursery before 1950).

Leaves deep olive green, large; fruits reddish orange, large, oblong.

'Terry' (female; discovered 1939 in Sussex County, Delaware, by W. Phillips; registered H.S.A. 2-65 by Phillips).

Leaves dark olive green, elliptic to broadly elliptic, 5–7 cm (2–2¾ in.) long, 2.5–4 cm (1–2¼ in.) wide, slightly keeled, curved, veins above light in color, usually 2–3 spines on each side of the leaf, petioles 8–12 mm (5⁄16–15⁄32 in.) long; fruits vivid red 45A, slightly ellipsoid, 10 mm (⅜ in.) long, 8 mm (5⁄16 in.) diameter, pedicels reddish, 5–7 mm (3⁄16–9⁄32 in.) long.

'Thanksgiving' (female; introduced 1963 by O. S. Pride; Grace Hybrid Group).

Leaves dark olive green, oval, 4.5–5 cm (1¾–2 in.) long, 2.5–3 cm (1–1 3⁄16 in.) wide, keeled, curved, 3–4 spines on each side, petioles 8 mm (5⁄16 in.) long, persistent to third year; fruits vivid red 45A, globose, 8 mm (5⁄16 in.) diameter, heavy bearer; dense broadly pyramidal habit, hardy to −34°C (−30°F).

'Thompson No. 2' (male; plant at Callaway Gardens from Wilmat Nursery).

Leaves dark olive green, broadly elliptic, 7.5–9 cm (3–3½ in.) long, 4–4.5 cm (1⅝–1¾ in.) wide, bases obtuse, curved, 4–5 spines on each side, usually upper two-thirds of leaf, margins reflexed, petioles stout, 7–8 mm (9⁄32–5⁄16 in.) long; fruits vivid red 45A, globose, 10 mm (⅜ in.) diameter, pedicels 10 mm (⅜ in.) long.

'Thunderbird' (female; origin seedling from Forest Nursery about 1940; registered H.S.A. 13-61 by H. Walter).

Leaves dark olive green, glossy; fruits reddish orange; compact conical habit.

'Tinga' (female; chance seedling selected and introduced by Tinga Nursery before 1956).

Leaves dark olive green, elliptic, 5–5.5 cm (2–2⅛ in.) long, 2–2.5 cm (¾–1 in.) wide, usually entire margins, 1 spine at apices; fruits red, globose, 5–8 mm (¼–5⁄16 in.) diameter.

'Tiny' (female; synonyms 'Ashumet No. 23', 'Petite'; selected by W. Wheeler and E. C. White before 1953).

Leaves dark olive green, elliptic, keeled, curved, 4.5–5.5 cm (1¾–2⅛ in.) long, 2.5–3 cm (1–1 3⁄16 in.) wide, bases obtuse to rotund, 3–5 spines on each side, petioles 8 mm (5⁄16 in.) long; fruits vivid red 45A, globose, 5 mm (3⁄16 in.) diameter, pedicels 8 mm (5⁄16 in.) long.

'Tiny Tim' (male; selected 1939 from Cumberland County, New Jersey; introduced 1956 by C. R. Wolf).

Leaves unusually small; dense habit.

'Tom Brown' (male; synonym of 'Brown #4'; introduced 1945 by New Jersey Holly Research Committee; registered American Association of Nurserymen No. 420, 1959, by C. H. Conners).

Leaves dark olive green, elliptic, 4–5 cm (1⅝–2 in.) long, 2.2–2.5 cm (13⁄16–1 in.) wide, bases obtuse to rotund, keeled, curved, margins recurved, wavy, 3–6 spines on each side, tip spines reflexed, petioles 5–7 mm (3⁄16–9⁄32 in.) long. Less vigorous, with smaller and lighter green foliage, and less desirable than 'Jersey Knight'; uncommon in the trade.

'Tom Rivers' (female; Simpson Nursery; plant at Dawes Arboretum, Newark, Ohio).

Leaves moderate olive green, oval, 4–6 cm (1⅝–2⅜ in.) long, 2.5–3 cm (1–1 3⁄16 in.) wide, bases cuneate to truncate, keeled, curved, 3–4 prominent spine on each side, margins reflexed, wavy, petioles 6–10 mm (7⁄32–⅜ in.) long; fruits vivid red 44B, globose, 8–10 mm (5⁄16–⅜ in.) diameter, pedicels 8–10 mm (5⁄16–⅜ in.) long.

'Toner' (female; selected 1935–1942 near Toner Hall at St. Elizabeth Hospital, Washington, D.C., by F. L. S. O'Rourke).

Leaves moderate olive green, elliptic, 7–8 cm (2¾–3⅛ in.) long, 3.5–4 cm (1⅜–1⅝ in.) wide, bases obtuse, slightly keeled, curved, 4–5 spines on each side, margins reflexed, petioles 7 mm (9⁄32 in.) long; fruits vivid red 45A, globose, abundant.

'Torchbearer' (female; synonym 'Torch Bearer'; selected 1939 and introduced 1947 by E. Dilatush).

Leaves dark olive green, elliptic, 4.5–6 cm (1¾–2⅜ in.) long, 2–2.5 cm (¾–1 in.) wide, bases cuneate, keeled, curved, margins recurved, 3–5 small spines on each side, petioles 10 mm (⅜ in.) long; fruits vivid red 45A, ellipsoid, 10 mm (⅜ in.) long, 8 mm (5⁄16 in.) diameter, 1–3 in clusters, abundant, pedicels reddish 10 mm (⅜ in.) long; rapid growing, branches stiff.

'Trisco' (female; selected in the wild 1935–1945 and named by F. L. S. O'Rourke; introduced by Kingsville Nursery).

Leaves dark olive green, broadly elliptic, flat, slightly curved; fruits vivid red, large clusters.

'24 Karat' (female; seedling of unknown origin selected and named in 1989 by Anthony Gould; registered H.S.A. 4-89 and introduced by J. G. Shaffer; original tree at Shaffer residence, Potomac, Maryland).

Leaves dark green, broadly elliptic to oval, sometimes ovate, to 9 cm (3½ in.) long and 4.2 cm (1 11⁄16 in.) wide, curved, slightly keeled, bases cuneate to attenuate, strong tip spines reflexed, margins wavy, subentire, to 5 small spines on each side, upper two-thirds of leaf, petioles 8 mm (5⁄16 in.) long; fruits vivid yellow 15B, prominent residual black stigma, globose, 9.5 mm (⅜ in.) diameter, single, pedicels reddish, 6.5 mm (¼ in.) long; original tree 10 years old, columnar habit, 2.4 m (8 ft.) high, 0.9 m (3 ft.) wide. Subentire leaves with attenuate bases suggest some *I. cassine* influence.

'Ulla' (female; chance seedling discovered in Voorhees Township, Camden County, New Jersey; moved to Magnolia, New Jersey, in 1926 by U. E. Bauers; registered H.S.A. 4-78 by B. Bauers Sr.).

Leaves dark olive green, elliptic, 7 cm (2¾ in.) long, 3.2 cm (1¼ in.) wide, bases oblique, keeled, curved, 5–6 spines on each side, margins slightly wavy, petioles 8–10 mm (5⁄16–⅜ in.) long; fruits vivid red, globose, 9 mm (11⁄32 in.) diameter, pedicels 7–8 mm (9⁄32–5⁄16 in.) long, heavy annual fruit crop, good resistance to berry midge.

'Uncle Tom' (female; reported from Hess Nursery before 1955).

Leaves dark olive green, elliptic, 5.5–8 cm (2⅛–3⅛ in.) long, 2.5–3 cm (1–1 3⁄16 in.) wide, convex, bases cuneate to obtuse, keeled, curved, margins recurved, slightly wavy, 3–5 small spines on each side, petioles 8–10 mm (⁵⁄₁₆–³⁄₈ in.) long; fruits vivid red 45A, globose, 8 mm (⁵⁄₁₆ in.) diameter, pedicels 8 mm (⁵⁄₁₆ in.) long.

'Valentine' (female; introduced by O. S. Pride; Grace Hybrid Group).

Leaves dark green, broadly elliptic, 6.5–7.5 cm (2½–3 in.) long, 4–4.5 cm (1⅝–1¾ in.) wide, keeled curved, 5–6 spines on each side, margins reflexed, wavy, petioles 8–10 mm (⁵⁄₁₆–³⁄₈ in.) long; fruits vivid red 44A, globose, 8 mm (⁵⁄₁₆ in.) diameter, pedicels 10 mm (³⁄₈ in.) long.

'Valentine XC' (female; purchased from Valentine Nursery; moved to Kentucky and introduced by T. Klein; original tree died in the 1960s).

Leaves moderate olive green, oval to broadly elliptic, 5–6 cm (2–2⅜ in.) long, 3–3.5 cm (1³⁄₁₆–1⅜ in.) wide, keeled, curved, 2–3 spines on upper half of leaf, stout petioles 8–12 mm (⁵⁄₁₆–¹⁵⁄₃₂ in.) long; fruits yellow.

'Valley Evergreen' (female; unnamed seedling purchased about 1956 from Valley Evergreen Nursery, Hagerstown, Maryland; selected in 1978, named, introduced, and registered H.S.A. 2-88 by R. K. Peters).

Leaves dark olive green, small, ovate, to 6.5 cm (2½ in.) long, 3.8 cm (1½ in.) wide, slightly curved, keeled, margin with 3–4 evenly spaced spines on each side, often only on upper half of leaf, petioles 13 mm (½ in.) long; fruits vivid red 45A, ovoid, 11 mm (⁷⁄₁₆ in.) long, pedicels 16 mm (⅝ in.) long; conical habit, original tree 6 m (20 ft.) tall, 3 m (10 ft.) wide in 36 years; hardy in zone 5a.

'Vera' (female; synonym 'Boyden No. 2'; selected from wild on Cape Cod, Massachusetts, by W. Wheeler and E. C. White before 1953).

Leaves dark olive green, elliptic, 4–4.5 cm (1⅝–1¾ in.) long, 2–2.5 cm (¾–1 in.) wide, keeled, curved, apex down, 1–2 spines upper half of leaf, margins twisted; fruits deep reddish orange 43A, globose, 8–9 mm (⁵⁄₁₆–¹¹⁄₃₂ in.) diameter, abundant, pedicels reddish, 5–6 mm (³⁄₁₆–⁷⁄₃₂ in.) long, fruits at end of branches; compact upright habit with branchlets and leaves appearing clustered and giving very distinct appearance with curly leaves. Good for cut sprigs and wreaths.

'Victory' (female; selected by F. C. Crooks; origin in New Jersey before 1953).

Leaves dark olive green, broadly elliptic, 6–7.5 cm (2⅜–3 in.) long, 3–4 cm (1³⁄₁₆–1⅝ in.) wide, bases obtuse, keeled, curved, 4–5 prominent spines on each side, petioles 6–8 mm (⁷⁄₃₂–⁵⁄₁₆ in.) long; fruits dark red, globose, produced at young age.

'Villanova' (female; selected and named by P. Hill on residence of H. Butcher III in Villanova, Pennsylvania; first observed 50 years ago by Butcher; registered H.S.A. 5-84 by Hill).

Leaves olive green, glossy, broadly ovate, 8.9 cm (3½ in.) long, 5.1 cm (2 in.) wide, bases obtuse, flat, curved, 5 spines on each side, margins recurved; fruits brilliant orange yellow 17B, subglobose, 7 mm (¼ in.) long, 10 mm (⅜ in.) wide, pedicels 8 mm (⁵⁄₁₆ in.) long; tall pyramidal habit.

'Virginia Giant' (female; original tree by Chickahominy River on Hog Island near Williamsburg, Virginia; found and reported by R. Mahone; introduced by T. Klein).

Leaves moderate olive green, glossy, broadly elliptic, 7–9 cm (2¾–3½ in.) long, 3.5–4.5 cm (1⅜–1¾ in.) wide, keeled, curved, 5–7 spines on each side, margins wavy, petioles 6 mm (⁷⁄₃₂ in.) long; fruits brilliant orange yellow 21B, globose, 10 mm (⅜ in.) diameter. Reported to be the largest yellow-berried holly in Virginia.

'Virginia West' (female; origin unclear; reported to be collected in wild in West Virginia; small tree planted at Carnifax Ferry Battlefield State Park, West Virginia; named by J. D. Rankin and released to several nurseries and arboreta; registered H.S.A. 6-91 by C. Suk).

Leaves dark green, keeled, curved, ovate, to 6 cm (2⅜ in.) long, to 4.5 cm (1¾ in.) wide, bases cuneate, tip spines aristate, reflexed, 1–4 spines evenly spaced on each side, when less than 3 spines on upper half of leaf, petioles 6 mm (⁷⁄₃₂ in.) long; fruits deep reddish orange 42A, globose, 7 mm (⁹⁄₃₂ in.) diameter, usually single, occasionally 2–3, pedicels 5 mm (³⁄₁₆ in.) long; pyramidal habit, branches slightly pendulous with fruit, 29-year-old tree 4.6 m (15 ft.) tall, 4 m (13⅓ ft.) wide; hardy in zone 6.

'Vissage' (female; synonym 'Mrs. Vissage'; origin on property of Mrs. J. Vissage at Walhalla, South Carolina; selected by W. C. Frierson before 1947).

Leaves dark olive green, elliptic, 5–7 cm (2–2¾ in.) long, 2.2–3 cm (¹³⁄₁₆–1³⁄₁₆ in.) wide, bases cuneate to obtuse, keeled, curved, 3–6 spines on each side, petioles 10–12 mm (⅜–½ in.) long; fruits vivid red 45B, slightly ellipsoid, 9 mm (¹¹⁄₃₂ in.) diameter, pedicels reddish, 8–10 mm (⁵⁄₁₆–³⁄₈ in.) long.

'Vivian' (female; selected about 1935–1940 near Whitesbog, New Jersey, by T. Windon and E. C. White).

Leaves dark olive green, elliptic to broadly elliptic, 5–7 cm (2–2¾ in.) long, 3–4 cm (1³⁄₁₆–1⁹⁄₁₆ in.) wide, bases cuneate to obtuse, keeled, curved, margins recurved, 2–4 spines on each side, on upper two-thirds of leaf, petioles 8–10 mm (⁵⁄₁₆–³⁄₈ in.) long; fruits deep reddish orange, 43B, globose to ellipsoid, 10 mm (³⁄₈ in.) long, 8 mm (⁵⁄₁₆ in.) diameter, pedicels reddish, 5–8 mm (³⁄₁₆–⁵⁄₁₆ in.) long.

'War Woman' (female; selected near Clayton, Georgia, on War Woman Creek by W. C. Frierson before 1947).

Leaves dark olive green, large; fruits vivid red, large, 3–5 in cluster.

'Warren Orange' (female; introduced by Warren Nursery).

Leaves moderate olive green, broadly elliptic, 4.5–6 cm (1¾–2³⁄₈ in.) long, 2.5–3 cm (1–1³⁄₁₆ in.) wide, keeled, curved, spines rare, usually entire, margins reflexed, petioles 10–13 mm (³⁄₈–½ in.) long, fruits deep reddish orange 34A, ellipsoid, 10 mm (³⁄₈ in.) long, pedicels 7 mm (⁹⁄₃₂ in.) long.

'Warrior' (male; selected by B. Hartline before 1968).

Leaves moderate olive green, oval, 4–4.5 cm (1⁵⁄₈–1¾ in.) long, 2–3 cm (¾–1³⁄₁₆ in.) wide, keeled, curved, 4–5 spines on each side, petioles 6–8 mm (⁷⁄₃₂–⁵⁄₁₆ in.) long.

'Webber' (female; synonym 'Weber'; origin Cave Hill Cemetery, Louisville, Kentucky; introduced by T. Klein before 1968).

Leaves moderate olive green, elliptic, 4–4.5 cm (1⁵⁄₈–1¾ in.) long, 2 cm (¾ in.) wide, keeled, curved, 3–6 spines on each side, petioles 6 mm (⁷⁄₃₂ in.) long; fruits vivid red 45B, globose, 7–9 mm (⁹⁄₃₂–¹¹⁄₃₂ in.) diameter.

'Westcroft' (female; synonym 'Westcroft No. 1'; selected in West Virginia by Westcroft Nursery; named before 1957).

Leaves moderate olive green, oval, 5–6 cm (2–2³⁄₈ in.) long, 3.5–4 cm (1³⁄₈–1⁵⁄₈ in.) wide, slightly keeled, curved, convex, 1–2 spines upper half of leaf; fruits vivid red 44B, ellipsoid, 8–10 mm (⁵⁄₁₆–⁵⁄₈ in.) long, pedicels 3–5 mm (⅛–³⁄₁₆ in.) long.

'Westcroft' (male; origin unknown; plant at Bernheim Forest).

Leaves moderate olive green, broadly elliptic, 5–6 cm (2–2³⁄₈ in.) long, 3–3.5 cm (1³⁄₁₆–1³⁄₈ in.) wide, keeled, curved, 1–2 spines on upper half of leaf, petioles 8 mm (⁵⁄₁₆ in.) long.

Wheeler Selections

Wilfred Wheeler made many holly selections. Some were grown as numbered plants that were later named:

'Wheeler No. 1' = 'Dick'
'Wheeler No. 2 = 'Sallie'
'Wheeler No. 2M' = 'Rick'
'Wheeler No. 5' = 'Polly'
'Wheeler No. 12' = 'Iro'
'Wheeler No. 13' = 'Nancy'
'Wheeler No. F-2' = 'Amy'

Other numbered Wheeler selections without descriptions are ambiguous, such as Wheeler No. 7, No. 40, No. 50.

'Wheeler No. 4' (female; origin Cape Cod, Massachusetts; plant at Klein Nursery).

Leaves dark olive green, oval, 3.5–4.5 cm (1³⁄₈–1¾ in.) long, 2.5 cm (1 in.) wide, keeled, curved, 2–3 spines on upper half of leaf, margins reflexed, petioles 8–10 mm (⁵⁄₁₆–³⁄₈ in.) long; fruits deep reddish orange 43A, globose, 8 mm (⁵⁄₁₆ in.) diameter, pedicels 5 mm (³⁄₁₆ in.) long.

'Wheeler No. 20' (female; origin unknown; selected by W. Wheeler; plant at Klein Nursery).

Leaves moderate olive green, oval, 4.5–5 cm (1¾–2 in.) long, 2.5–3 cm (1–1³⁄₁₆ in.) wide, keeled, curved, 3–5 small spines on each side, margins reflexed, petioles 6–10 mm (⁷⁄₃₂–³⁄₈ in.) long; fruits vivid red 45A, globose, 8 mm (⁵⁄₁₆ in.) diameter, pedicels 5 mm (³⁄₁₆ in.) long.

'Wheeler No. 25' (female; origin unknown; selected by W. Wheeler; plant at Klein Nursery).

Leaves moderate olive green, oval, 4–5.5 cm (1¾–2⅛ in.) long, 2.5–3 cm (1–1³⁄₁₆ in.) wide, keeled, curved, 2–4 spines on each side, margins reflexed, dark petioles 8 mm (⁵⁄₁₆ in.) long; fruits deep reddish orange 43A, globose, 8 mm (⁵⁄₁₆ in.) diameter, pedicels 5 mm (³⁄₁₆ in.) long.

'Wheeler No. F-1' (female; origin unknown; selected by W. Wheeler; plant at Klein Nursery).

Leaves dark olive green, oval elliptic, 5–7 cm (2–2¾ in.) long, 3–3.8 cm (1³⁄₁₆–1½ in.) wide, bases rotund, keeled, curved, 3–6 spines on each side, petioles dark, 6–8 mm (⁷⁄₃₂–⁵⁄₁₆ in.) long; fruits red, globose, 8 mm (⁵⁄₁₆ in.) diameter, pedicels reddish, 8–10 mm (⁵⁄₁₆–³⁄₈ in.) long.

'Wilfred' (male; synonyms 'Ashumet No. 1', 'Wheeler No. 43', 'Wilford'; named and selected by W. Wheeler before 1953).

Leaves moderate olive green, oval, 4–6 cm (1⁵⁄₈–2³⁄₈ in.) long, 2.5–3 cm (1–1³⁄₁₆ in.) wide, curved, bases acute to obtuse, 2–3 spines on upper half of leaf, margins wavy, petioles 7–10 mm (⁹⁄₃₂–³⁄₈ in.) long; broadly pyramidal habit.

'William Hawkins' (male; synonym 'Mentone'; a witches'-broom on *I. opaca* discovered about 1979 by wildflower enthusiast William Hawkins near Little River Canyon, Alabama; scion wood given to T. Dodd Jr. for grafting; named and introduced by Dodd).

Leaves dark olive green, linear, 3–5.5 cm (1³⁄₁₆–2⅛ in.) long, 0.5–1 cm (³⁄₁₆–³⁄₈ in.) wide, bases cuneate, apices long tapered to tip spines, margins usually with 3 (rarely 4) evenly spaced spines on each side, petioles 5–8 mm (³⁄₁₆–⁵⁄₁₆ in.) long; compact pyramidal habit. Very distinct, attractive leaves. Good bonsai or container plant. Plate 162.

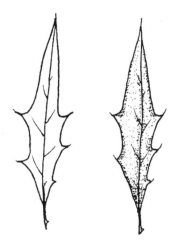

Figure 15-42. *Ilex opaca* 'William Hawkins'. Drawing by Randy Allen.

Figure 15-41. *Ilex opaca* 'William Hawkins'. Photo by Fred Galle.

'Wilmat Yellow' (female; introduced by Wilmat Nursery).

Leaves moderate olive green, broadly elliptic, 6.5–7 cm (2½–2¾ in.) long, 3.5–4 cm (1⅜–1⅝ in.) wide, keeled, curved, 3 widely spaced spines on each side, margins reflexed, petioles stout, 8 mm (⁵⁄₁₆ in.) long; fruits vivid yellow 15A, globose, 8–10 mm (⁵⁄₁₆–³⁄₈ in.) diameter.

'Winn Nursery' (female; selected by Winn Nursery before 1968).

Leaves moderate olive green, elliptic, 5–5.5 cm (2–2⅛ in.) long, 2.5–3 cm (1–1³⁄₁₆ in.) wide, keeled, curved, 2–4 spines on each side, margins wavy, petioles 8–10 mm (⁵⁄₁₆–³⁄₈ in.) long; fruits vivid orange 25A, ellipsoid, 8 mm (⁵⁄₁₆ in.) long.

'Wyetta' (female; synonym 'Wyatta'; selected in wild near Medford, New Jersey; named and registered H.S.A. 6-64 by E. T. Harbaugh; named for a relative of the owner of Medford Nursery).

Leaves dark olive green, glossy, broadly elliptic, 4.5–5 cm (1¾–2 in.) long, 2.5–3 cm (1–1³⁄₁₆ in.) wide, keeled, curved, 3–4 spines on each side, petioles 5 mm (³⁄₁₆ in.) long; fruits deep reddish orange 43A, globose, 8–10 mm (⁵⁄₁₆–³⁄₈ in.) diameter, pedicels 4 mm (⁵⁄₃₂ in.) long; compact pyramidal, densely branched.

'Xanthawood' (female; discovered by W. Hallenberg and T. Klein on property of A. Woods near Mount Lookout, West Virginia).

Leaves dark olive green, broadly elliptic, 5–6 cm (2–2⅜ in.) long, 3–3.5 cm (1³⁄₁₆–1⅜ in.) wide, keeled, curved, 2–3 spines on upper two-thirds of leaf, margins reflexed, petioles 8–10 mm (⁵⁄₁₆–³⁄₈ in.) long; fruits vivid orange 25A, slight blush, globose, 8 mm (⁵⁄₁₆ in.) diameter; pedicels 3–5 mm (⅛–³⁄₁₆ in.) long; upright habit of growth.

'Yellow Berry Brownell' (female; sold by Brownell Nursery).

Leaves dark olive green, broadly elliptic, 7–9 cm (2¾–3½ in.) long, 4.5–5 cm (1¾–2 in.) wide, keeled, curved, margins wavy, 5–7 spines on each side, petioles 8–10 mm (⁵⁄₁₆–³⁄₈ in.) long; fruits yellow, globose, 6.5 mm (¼ in.) diameter, pedicels 8–10 mm (⁵⁄₁₆–³⁄₈ in.) long.

'Yellow Jacquet' (female; synonym 'Yellow Jacket'; discovered between 1953 and 1956 on J. W. Parson's property near Norman, North Carolina; selected, named, and introduced by J. D. Rankin; named for wife of H. Dengler).

Leaves moderate olive green, oval, 6–7 cm (2⅜–2¾ in.) long, 3–4 cm (1³⁄₁₆–1⅝ in.) wide, bases obtuse, slightly keeled, curved, 3–5 spines upper half of leaf margins reflexed, petioles 8–10 mm (⁵⁄₁₆–⅜ in.) long; fruits brilliant orange yellow 17B, ellipsoid, 8 mm (⁵⁄₁₆ in.) long.

'Yule' (female; believed to be a Boyce Thompson Institute selection; introduced by P. Bosley).

Leaves moderate olive green, broadly elliptic, 6.5–7.5 cm (2⅜–2¾ in.) long, 3.5–4 cm (1⅜–1⅝ in.) wide, bases obtuse, keeled, curved, 3–5 spines on each side, margins reflexed, petioles 10 mm (⅜ in.) long; fruits vivid red 45A, globose, 8 mm (⁵⁄₁₆ in.) diameter, pedicels 8–10 mm (⁵⁄₁₆–⅜ in.) long, abundant; fruits persist as they are reported to be unappetizing to birds; broadly pyramidal habit.

'Zoe' (female; synonym 'Boyden No. 1'; selected by W. Wheeler and E. C. White).

Leaves moderate olive green, elliptic, 5–7 cm (2–2¾ in.) long, 3–3.5 cm (1³⁄₁₆–1⅜ in.) wide, bases cuneate to obtuse, keeled, curved, 2–4 spines on each side usually on upper two-thirds of leaf, petioles reddish, 10 mm (⅜ in.) long; fruits deep reddish orange 43A, globose, 8–10 mm (⁵⁄₁₆–⅜ in.) diameter, 1–3 in clusters, pedicels reddish, 10 mm (⅜ in.) long.

Ilex pedunculosa (female; selected from New York Botanical Gardens, not a hybrid).

Leaves dark green, glossy, more rounded than species; fruits red, on long peduncles. Selected for attractive more rounded foliage.

Ilex pedunculosa 'Aurantiaca'. Kiwi-soyogo (synonyms *I. pedunculosa* var. *aurantiaca* Koidzumi 1934, *I. pedunculosa* f. *aurantiaca* (Koidzumi) Ohwi 1953).

Fruits yellow.

Ilex pedunculosa 'Variegata'. Kimi-soyogo (synonyms *I. pedunculosa* var. *variegata* Nakai ex Makino 1925, *I. pedunculosa* f. *variegata* (Nakai) Ohwi 1953).

Leaves variegated.

Ilex vomitoria (Yaupon Holly) Cultivars

Yaupon holly with its numerous cultivars is a popular landscape plant in the southeastern United States. The species is usually confined to the coastal plains in hammocks and places protected from fires from southeastern Virginia to Florida, west to Texas, southwestern Arkansas, and southeastern Oklahoma, in soils ranging from pure sand to limestone.

Ilex vomitoria was introduced to England in 1700, and the name was published by A. T. Aiton in 1789 in *Hortus Kewensis*. Aiton's material was grown in the Royal Botanic Gardens, Kew. It was first cultivated by Leonard Putkenet, a doctor in Westminster who published a description under *Cassine vera Floridanorum*. Over the years *I. vomitoria* has been called cassena, cassiana, emetic holly, evergreen cassine, South-Sea tea, and various spellings of yaupon such as yapon and youpon. To avoid confusion with *I. cassine,* it is suggested that yaupon be used as the standard common name for *I. vomitoria*.

Ilex vomitoria has no close relatives in North America. It is of more tropical origin and a relict species. It has small, crenulate-serrate evergreen leaves and fasciculate inflorescences produced on the previous season's growth. Hu said, "*Ilex vomitoria* is a highly specialized species in the genus *Ilex*."

Yaupon hollies are evergreen shrubs 2–4 m (6–13 ft.) tall or small trees 7–9 m (23–29 ft.) tall, usually with multiple trunks and a smooth light gray bark (see Figure 15-43). The leaves are dark green, often with a bluish cast, ovate to oblong or elliptic, 1.5–4.5 cm (1⅜–1¾ in.) long, 1–2 cm (⅜–¾ in.) wide, with rounded or obtuse bases, and obtuse to cuneate apices. The margins are crenulate-serrate, each tooth terminated by a callose mucro that turns black on drying and is visible with a hand lens. The fruits are red, glossy, semitranslucent, globose, 5–8 mm (³⁄₁₆–⁵⁄₁₆ in.) diameter.

One orange-fruited cultivar has been named ('Dare County'), and there are several yellow-fruited

Figure 15-43. *Ilex vomitoria* tree form on the campus of Mississippi State University. Photo by Ed Martin.

cultivars ('Otis Miley', 'Wiggins', 'Yawkey'). Pistillate inflorescences are 3–4 fasciculate; male fascicles have many more flowers. The fascicles are axillary on previous season's growth and older branches.

The leaves possess stimulant properties and contain more caffeine than any other North American plant. In this respect *Ilex vomitoria* is a near relative of *I. paraguariensis* (commonly called mate or Paraguay tea) and *I. guayusa*. It is well known to the Native Americans, who made a beverage known as black tea or black drink. The drink was used in various ceremonies and, when drunk to excess, had emetic properties; thus the species epithet *vomitoria*. The drink is prepared by collecting small twigs (usually in the spring), chopping them up with the leaves, and drying the material rapidly so the leaves are scorched. When needed the dried material is put in water and heated indefinitely until the drink is needed. For additional information, see Hudson (1979).

Yaupon holly does not cross readily with other North American species, but there are numerous selected cultivars of various sizes and habits suitable for the southern landscape as foundation plantings, hedges, screening, and specimen plants. There are at least three dwarf types, the female 'Dwarf' and the male 'Stokes Dwarf' being the most common. 'Dwarf' was first reported sterile; however, red fruit has been reported on old plants.

Weeping forms such as 'Folsom's Weeping' make attractive specimen plants with their long pendulous branches. Seedlings of pendulous plants give a high percentage of plants with varying degrees of weeping habit. 'Jewel' has an open mounding habit with right-angled branching. 'Gray's Little Leaf', male, has very small leaves. 'Gray's Greenleaf' produces a large display of red fruits. 'Tricolor' has attractive variegated foliage, and 'Wildwood Blue' has attractive bluish green foliage in the winter. Most of the yaupon cultivars are hardy in zone 7a. Both 'Hoskin Shadow' and 'Nanyehi' are hardy in zone 6b.

'Arlington' (female; chance seedling discovered and named by Tom Dodd Jr.; to be introduced in 1996).

More shrubby than 'Dorothy Gray', 'Elsie Gray', and 'Louise Gray'. No description available.

'Aurea' (female; introduced by Fruitland Nursery; given cultivar name in *Hortus III*).

Fruit yellow; doubtful if any plants exist.

Bordeaux™ (male; a sport of *I. vomitoria* 'Stokes Dwarf'; discovered by James Pittman at Flowerwood Nursery in 1988; PP No. 8779, June 1994, named 'Condeaux'; selected for unique foliage).

Leaves and new growth purplish red 59D, old growth grayish yellow-green 148D, older growth gray-green 194A; leaves oval to elliptic, 13 mm to 2.5 cm (½–1 in.) long; habit similar to 'Stokes Dwarf', dense, 1.2–1.5 m (4–5 ft.) tall, 1.5–1.8 m (5–6 ft.) wide.

'Buchanan' (female; plant received from University of Southwestern Louisiana, Lafayette, planted at Callaway Gardens in 1963).

Leaves moderate to dark olive green, purplish in winter, oval-elliptic, 1.8–3.8 cm ($^{11}/_{16}$–1½ in.) long, 1–1.6 cm (⅜–⅝ in.) wide; fruits vivid red 45A, globose, shiny, 6 mm ($^{7}/_{32}$ in.) diameter, abundant; vigorous, upright spreading tall shrub or small tree.

'Dare County' (female; synonym 'Virginia Dare'; discovered in the wild in Dare County, North Carolina, in 1978 by B. Bauers Sr.; named and registered H.S.A. 6-85 by Bauers).

Leaves dark olive green, slightly glossy, ovate, to 6.5 cm (2½ in.) long, and 3.75 cm (1½ in.) wide; fruits orange, globose, 7 mm ($^{9}/_{32}$ in.) diameter, 2–3 in clusters, abundant; upright habit with stiff divergent branching, 2.5 m (8 ft.) tall in 15 years; hardy in zones 7 to 9. Selected for the attractive orange fruit; first orange-fruited yaupon to be reported and named.

'Dewerth' (male; plant in "Doc" Dewerth garden, College Station, Texas; propagated and named by T. Dodd Jr. in the 1970s).

Leaves narrow-elliptic, 0.6–1.6 cm ($^{7}/_{32}$–⅝ in.) long, 2–3 mm ($^{1}/_{16}$–⅛ in.) wide; upright spreading habit. Very similar to 'Gray's Little Leaf' and possibly the same.

'Dodd's Suspensa' (female; seedling of 'Folsom Weeping'; grown selected, and named by T. Dodd Jr.).

Leaves dark olive green, ovate to elliptic, 2.5–4 cm (1–1⅝ in.) long, 1–1.6 cm (⅜–⅝ in.) wide; fruits vivid red 45A, shiny, globose, 6 mm ($^{7}/_{32}$ in.) diameter; upright weeping habit.

'Dorothy Gray' (female; chance seedling discovered and named by Tom Dodd Jr.; to be introduced in 1996).

No description available.

'Dwarf' (female; synonym 'Nana', dwarf yaupon; confusion between this and 'Nana', both considered the same; several seedlings collected in 1936 in Louisiana, evaluated and named by S. Stokes and Tom Dodd Jr.; introduced by Stokes).

Leaves moderate olive green, elliptic, 2.5–3.5 cm (1–1⅜ in.) long, 1–1.6 cm (⅜–⅝ in.) wide, fruits vivid red 45A, glossy, globose, 6 mm ($^{7}/_{32}$ in.) diameter, dwarf compact habit. Popular landscape plant due to dwarf habit. Often reported sterile; however, large (1.8–2.5 m or 6–8 ft.) plants approximately 33 plus years are fruiting. Fruit often hidden by dense foliage. Plate 163.

'Elsie Gray' (female; chance seedling discovered and named by Tom Dodd Jr.; to be introduced in 1996).
No description available.

'Field's' (female; native plant collected in North Carolina in late 1950s by F. Field; moved to office in Pinehurst, North Carolina; named by F. Ebersole).
Leaves moderate olive green, oval to elliptic, 2–4 cm (¾–1⅝ in.) long, 1.2–2.2 cm (¹⁵⁄₃₂–¹³⁄₁₆ in.) wide; fruits vivid red 44A, globose, 6–7 mm (⁷⁄₃₂–⁹⁄₃₂ in.) diameter; upright compact habit.

'Folsom's Weeping' (female and male forms; synonym 'Gray's Weeping'; collected in 1952 in Folsom, Louisiana, by J. A. Foret; named by T. Dodd Jr.; not registered).
Leaves moderate olive green, elliptic, 2–2.5 cm (¾–1 in.) long, 0.8–1 cm (⁵⁄₁₆–⅜ in.) wide; fruits vivid red 45A, globose, 6–7 mm (⁷⁄₃₂–⁹⁄₃₂ in.) diameter, single, abundant; upright weeping habit.

'Goodyear' (female; seedling discovered by L. Lowery at fence row around Goodyear Blimp hanger in Houston, Texas; named and introduced by T. Dodd Jr. in the 1980s).
Leaves dark olive green, elliptic, 1–1.6 cm (⅜–⅝ in.) long, 6–8 mm (⁷⁄₃₂–⁵⁄₁₆ in.) wide, petioles brownish, young twigs purplish brown at ends, contrasting with older light gray stems; fruits vivid red 45A, globose, 5–8 mm (³⁄₁₆–⁵⁄₁₆ in.) diameter, pedicels 4 mm (⁵⁄₃₂ in.) long; lateral branches at distinct right angles to stems, twigs thicker than average, distinct taper in small branchlets, pendulous with a semiweeping, loose open habit.

'Gray's Greenleaf' (female; seedling selected by O. Gray in Texas, named by T. Dodd Jr.).
Leaves dark olive green, elliptic, 2–25 cm (¾–1 in.) long, 0.8–1.3 cm (⁵⁄₁₆–½ in.) wide; fruits vivid red 45A, glossy, globose, 6–7 mm (⁷⁄₃₂–⁹⁄₃₂ in.) diameter, very heavy fruiting; upright compact habit. Plate 164.

'Gray's Little Leaf' (male; seedling selected by O. Gray in Texas, named by T. Dodd Jr.).
Leaves dark olive green, narrow-elliptic, 0.7–2.2 cm (⁹⁄₃₂–¹³⁄₁₆ in.) long, 2–3 mm (³⁄₃₂–⅛ in.) wide, often very close together, petioles reddish; young twigs reddish brown in contrast to older gray stems; upright spreading habit.

'Gray's Weeping', see 'Folsom Weeping'.

Figure 15-44. *Ilex vomitoria* 'Dwarf' on the campus of Mississippi State University. Planted in a raised box with a western exposure in 1965 as a one-gallon container plant, this specimen has never been pruned. Photo by Ed Martin.

'Hoskin Shadow' (female; synonyms 'Round Leaf', 'Shadow'; seedling selected by H. Shadow at Howell Nursery in late 1970s).
Leaves dark olive green, elliptic to ovate, 2–4 cm (¾–1⅝ in.) long, 1–1.6 cm (⅜–⅝ in.) wide, bases cuneate to obtuse, apices cuneate to obtuse, margins serrulate, pedicels 3–5 mm (⅛–³⁄₁₆ in.) long; fruits red 7–8 mm (⁹⁄₃₂–⁵⁄₁₆ in.) compact upright spreading habit; hardy to zone 6. Selected for large dark green foliage and hardiness.

'Huber's Compact' (female; selected by the late Fritz Huber at Jennings Nursery; registered H.S.A. 12-60 by S. Solymosy).
Leaves moderate olive green, elliptic, 2–3 cm (¾–1³⁄₁₆ in.) long, 1–1.3 cm (⅜–½ in.) wide; fruits vivid red 45A, globose, 5–7 cm (³⁄₁₆–⁹⁄₃₂ in.) diameter, abundant, ripening in October, persisting until March; dense upright habit.

'Intermedia' (female; origin Clarendon Gardens; doubtful if still available).
Leaves moderate olive green, elliptic to oval elliptic, 2.5–4 cm (1–1⅝ in.) long, 1.5–2 cm (¹⁹⁄₃₂–¾ in.) wide; fruits deep reddish orange 42A, glossy, globose, 6–7 mm (⁷⁄₃₂–⁹⁄₃₂ in.) diameter, ripening late; upright compact, irregular open habit.

'Jewel' (female; seedling discovered by S. Solymosy at Cornelius Nursery in the 1960s; plant at Callaway Gardens).

Leaves dark olive green, ovate to oval, 1–1.5 cm (⅜–¹⁹⁄₃₂ in.) long, 0.8–1 cm (⁵⁄₁₆–⅜ in.) wide; fruits vivid red 45A, globose, 6–7 mm (⁷⁄₃₂–⁹⁄₃₂ in.) diameter; open mounding habit, right-angle branching of gray stems in good contrast with leaves.

'Kathy Ann' (female; native, discovered in Stone County, Mississippi, in 1985 by D. Batson; named by Batson for his wife and registered H.S.A. 1-92).

Leaves dark green, broadly elliptic to ovate-elliptic, 2–3.3 cm (¾–⅞ in.) long, 1–1.5 cm (⅜–¹⁹⁄₃₂ in.) wide, bases cuneate to obtuse, apices cuneate, 5–7 crenulate-serrate teeth on each side, petioles 4–5 mm (⁵⁄₃₂–³⁄₁₆ in.) long, branches gray; fruits red vivid 45A, shiny, single to 3 in cluster, 6–8 mm (⁷⁄₃₂–⁵⁄₁₆ in.) diameter. abundant; multistemmed, upright spreading habit, 3–4.6 m (10–15 ft.) high.

'Louise Gray' (female; chance seedling discovered and named by Tom Dodd Jr.; to be introduced in 1996).

No description available.

'Lynn Lowery' (female; synonym 'Lynn's Large Leaf', seedling selected by L. Lowery around Rock Port, Texas; named and introduced by Tom Dodd Jr.).

Leaves dark olive green, oval, curved, 2–4.2 cm (¾–1⅝ in.) long, 1.3–2.5 cm (½–1 in.) wide, bases obtuse to rotund, apices obtuse, petioles dark; fruits deep red 46A, globose, 5–6 mm (³⁄₁₆–⁷⁄₃₂ in.) diameter, pedicels 2–3 mm (¹⁄₁₆–⅛ in.) long; upright spreading habit.

'Nana', see 'Dwarf'.

'Nancy' (female; origin Athens Nursery in the 1970s);

Leaves dark olive green, elliptic, 2.2–4.5 cm (¹³⁄₁₆–1¾ in.) long, 1–2.5 cm (⅜–1 in.) wide; fruits vivid red 45A, glossy, globose, 6–7 mm (⁷⁄₃₂–⁹⁄₃₂ in.) diameter; vigorous upright habit.

'Nanyehi' (female; selected at Don Shadow Nursery; named by H. Elmore in the 1980s).

Leaves dark olive green, glossy, ovate to elliptic, 1.8–3 cm (¹¹⁄₁₆–1³⁄₁₆ in.) long, 1–1.5 cm (⅜–¹⁹⁄₃₂ in.) wide, bases rotund to cuneate, apices obtuse, petioles reddish, 3 mm (⅛ in.) long; fruits red; stems gray; hardy in zone 6.

'Otis Miley' (female; discovered in 1956 by F. Woods, west of Bogalusa, Louisiana; plant moved to Callaway Gardens; named and registered H.S.A. 2-60 by F. Galle).

Leaves moderate olive green, elliptic, 2.5–3.5 cm (1–1⅜ in.) long, 1.3–1.6 cm (½–⅝ in.) wide; fruits vivid orange–yellow 17A, globose, 6 mm diameter, abundant; upright spreading habit; hardy in zone 8a. Selected for its attractive yellowish fruit.

'Poole's Best' (female; origin unknown, from Harold Poole Nursery; named and introduced by K. Durio in the 1980s).

Leaves elliptic to slightly ovate-elliptic, 1–2 cm (⅜–¾ in.) long, 5–8 mm (³⁄₁₆–⁵⁄₁₆ in.) wide, margins minutely crenulate, petioles 3 mm (⅛ in.) long; fruits red; upright spreading habit, stiff ridged branching.

'Pride of Houston' (female; synonyms 'City of Houston', 'Pride of Texas'; seedling discovered at Cornelius Nursery; named by S. Solymosy in the 1970s).

Leaves dark olive green, elliptic, 2–3.5 cm (¾–1⅜ in.) long, 1–1.6 cm (⅜–⅝ in.) wide; fruits vivid red 45A, glossy, 6 mm (⁷⁄₃₂ in.) diameter, abundant; vigorous upright spreading habit.

'Pyramidalis' (listed in *Hortus III*).

No description available.

'Royal' (male; origin Grandview Nursery).

Leaves dark olive green, oval elliptic, 1.6–2.8 cm (⅝–1⅛ in.) long, 0.8–1.6 cm (⁵⁄₁₆–⅝ in.) wide; upright open habit.

'Saratoga Gold' (female; discovered in Saratoga, Texas, by Laniar Rosier in 1951; named and introduced by L. Lowery for good display of yellow fruit).

Leaves dark green, broadly elliptic to ovate-elliptic, 1.8–2 cm (¹¹⁄₁₆–¾ in.) long, 0.8–⅜ in.) wide, petioles 3 mm (⅛ in.) long, margins remotely crenulate, upper half of leaf; fruits brilliant yellow, glossy, 6–8 mm (⁷⁄₃₂–⁵⁄₁₆ in.) diameter, 2 to 3 in clusters, abundant, good display; vigorous upright spreading habit of growth, single or multistemmed, for group plantings or specimen plants. Plate 165.

'Schilling's Dwarf', see 'Stokes Dwarf'.

'Steed's Dwarf' (origin Steed Nursery).

Leaves dark green, broadly elliptic to slightly ovate-elliptic, 1.3–1.8 cm (½–¹¹⁄₃₂ in.) long, 8–10 mm (⁵⁄₁₆–⅜ in.) wide, bases obtuse to rotund, apices obtuse, margins crenulate, petioles reddish brown, 3–4 mm (⅛–⁵⁄₃₂ in.) long, branches light gray, tips of young branches reddish brown; upright habit of growth. See also *I. crenata* 'Steed's Upright'.

'Stokes Dwarf' (male; synonym 'Shillings Dwarf', one of 3 dwarf yaupon seedlings—'Dwarf', 'Schillings Dwarf', and 'Stokes Dwarf'—discovered at S. Stokes Nursery; registered H.S.A. 1-61 by S. Solymosy).

Leaves moderate olive green, new foliage pink, elliptic, to slightly obovate-elliptic, 1.2–1.8 cm (¹⁵⁄₃₂–1¹⁄₁₆ in.) long, 6–8 mm (⁷⁄₃₂–⁵⁄₁₆ in.) wide; low dwarf compact plant, 33 × 38 cm (12 × 15 in.) wide in 4–5 years. Popular dwarf landscape plant, container plants stack well for shipping.

'Straughan's Dwarf' (male; synonyms 'Soft Dwarf Yaupon', 'Straughan's Soft'; a sport of 'Schilling's Dwarf' discovered in early 1970s; introduced and named by Straughan Nursery).

Leaves elliptic, 1.3–2.5 cm (½–1 in.) long, soft textured; branches limber; dwarf habit. Plants not the same as 'Dwarf Yaupon' and 'Stokes Dwarf'.

'Tricolor' (male; discovered in 1955 at Cornelius Nursery; registered H.S.A. 13-60 by S. Solymosy).

Leaves variegated, moderate green, irregular blotched yellow, often covering ½ of leaf to midrib, some leaves entirely yellow, purplish margin in winter, ovate to ovate-elliptic, 2.5–3.8 cm (1–1½ in.) long, 1–1.6 cm (⅜–⅝ in.) wide; vigorous upright spreading, habit. Distinct foliage, leaves color best in full sun.

'Wiggins' (female; synonym 'Wiggins Yellow'; collected near Wiggins, Mississippi; named and introduced by T. Dodd Jr. in the 1970s).

Leaves dark olive green, elliptic, 2.5–3.5 (1–1⅜ in.) long, 0.8–1.8 cm (⁵⁄₁₆–1¹⁄₁₆ in.) wide; fruits vivid yellow 15A, globose, 6 mm (⁷⁄₃₂ in.) diameter; upright spreading habit.

'Wildwood Blue' (female; wild seedling discovered about 1974 in Colleton County, South Carolina, by E. Marvin; named and introduced by Marvin in the 1970s).

Leaves dark olive green, developing distinct bluish cast in winter, elliptic to slightly broadly elliptic, 1.3–3.2 cm (½–1¼ in.) long, 0.8–1.5 cm (⁵⁄₁₆–1⁹⁄₃₂ in.) wide, bases cuneate, apices acute, margins serrulate, petioles 3 mm (⅛ in.) long, stems light gray; fruits deep red 46A, globose, 6 mm (⁷⁄₃₂ in.) diameter, abundant; dense compact pyramidal habit. Selected for bluish winter foliage and abundant fruit.

'Will Fleming' (male; synonym 'Will's Upright'; discovered by W. Fleming; named and introduced by T. Dodd Jr. in the 1970s).

Leaves dark olive green, elliptic, 1–1.8 cm (⅜–1¹⁄₁₆ in.) long, 0.5–1 (³⁄₁₆–⅜ in.) wide, stems light gray; narrow upright habit, branches fastigiate.

'Yawkey' (female; synonym *I. vomitoria* var. *yawkeyi*; discovered by F. G. Tarbox Jr. in Georgetown County, South Carolina, on T. A. Yawkey Plantation; introduced by Brookgreen Gardens).

Leaves dark olive green, elliptic to ovate-elliptic, 2–3 cm (¾–1³⁄₁₆ in.) long, 1–1.3 cm (⅜–½ in.) wide, fruits vivid orange-yellow 21A, depressed globose, 6–7 mm (⁷⁄₃₂–⁹⁄₃₂ in.) diameter, abundant; upright spreading habit. Selected for colorful yellow fruits.

'Yellow Berry' (female; origin unknown).

Fruits yellow.

CHAPTER 16

Interspecific Evergreen Holly Hybrids

The first reported controlled interspecific cross in the genus *Ilex,* and the first registered cross of *I. cornuta* × *I. pernyi,* was made by the late Henry Skinner in 1948 while working at Morris Arboretum, Philadelphia, Pennsylvania. The cross, between *I. cornuta* 'Burfordii' and *I. pernyi* yielded two seedling plants that were named for founders of the Arboretum: 'Lydia Morris' and 'John T. Morris'. After Skinner became director of the U.S. National Arboretum, Washington, D.C., the plants were given Plant Introduction (PI) numbers for distribution and registered: 'Lydia Morris' H.S.A. 7-61, Plant Introduction No. 267824, and 'John T. Morris' H.S.A. 8-61, Plant Introduction No. 267825. Both clones are still found in the trade.

In the 1950s the late Henry Hohman, noted plantsman and nurseryman of Kingsville Nursery, Kingsville, Maryland, made the same cross (*Ilex cornuta* 'Burfordii' × *I. pernyi*) and introduced 27 or more named cultivars. We can assume that the plants were selected from around 50 or more seedlings, for one of the introduced plants was numbered #49. These hybrids were also known as CB hybrids for "Cornuta Burfordii."

While at Callaway Gardens, Pine Mountain, Georgia, I received 21 of these hybrids in 1961 from Hohman, losing only one 'Pyris'. As often happens when a large number of similar plants are introduced into the trade, some get lost or overlooked. While all are good landscape plants many are no longer available. 'Cetus' is still found in the trade, and occasionally 'Red Robe', 'Red Delight', and 'Indian Chief' are found, possibly because of the attractive names. 'Doctor Kassab' is a popular plant in Philadelphia, Pennsylvania, due to friendly holly enthusiasts Dr. and Mrs. Joseph Kassab.

The hybrids are intermediate and show great resemblance to both parents. The glossy leaves are in-termediate in size and attractively spined. The fruiting habit, size, and clusters are more similar to those of *Ilex cornuta* plants. In plant shape and habit, the plants are compact, usually pyramidal or upright mounding and slower growing than *I. cornuta* or *I. cornuta* 'Burfordii', but less rank and open as is characteristic of *I. pernyi*. All the cultivars are attractive landscape plants and hardy in zone 7, possibly in protected areas in zones 6b and 6a. A list of the hybrids of *I. cornuta* × *I. pernyi* follows.

'Aquila'	'Lydia Morris'
'Aries'	'Lyra'
'Atlas'	'Mercury'
'Audrey'	'Moon Glow'
'Beacon'	'Phoenix'
'Brighter Shines'	'Pyris'
'Cetus'	'Red Delight'
'Doctor Kassab'	'Red Princess'
'Drace'	'Red Robe'
'Fernax'	'Security'
'Good Taste'	'Sextans'
'Hydra'	'Starlight'
'Indian Chief'	'Taurus'
'John T. Morris'	'Titan'
'Lacerta'	'Virgo'
'Lepux'	

Ilex 'Accent' (male; *I. integra* × *I. pernyi* cross made by W. F. Kosar at U.S. National Arboretum; named and registered H.S.A. 7-66 by Kosar; sibling of 'Elegance').

Leaves moderate olive green, ovate, 2.5–3.5 cm (1–1⅜ in.) long, 1.6–2 cm (⅝–¾ in.) wide, bases rotund, apices acute, margins nearly flat, 3–5 small spines on each side, petioles 3–5 mm (⅛–3⁄16 in.) long; upright pyramidal habit. Introduced as a pollinator for 'Elegance'.

Ilex 'Adonis' (male; controlled cross ((*I. aquifolium* × *I. cornuta*) 'Nellie R. Stevens') × *I. latifolia*, U.S. National Arboretum No. 28313 by W. F. Kosar; selected and named by F. S. Santamour and G. Eisenbeiss; registered H.S.A. 9-91 by Eisenbeiss; brother seedling to 'Venus'; released in 1992).

Leaves dark green, glossy, ovate to broadly lanceolate, slightly convex, curved, slightly keeled, to 11.9 cm (4.7 in.) long, 5.7 cm (2¼ in.) wide, tips aristate, reflexed and twisted, margins wavy, 11–13 uniform blunt spines on each side, petioles 12 mm (¹⁵⁄₃₂ in.) long. Introduced as a pollinator for 'Venus'. Original plant 22 years old, compact broadly pyramidal, 6.1 m (20 ft.) tall, 5.4 m (17¾ ft.) wide, can be grown single or multistem; hardy zone 7. Plate 166.

Ilex 'Agena' (female; U.S. National Arboretum received 10 cm (4 in.) seedling in 1962, U.S. PI 282427, U.S. National Arboretum No. 19791, from Duncan and Davies Nursery, New Zealand, as *I. paraguariensis*, later identified as *I.* × *koehneana*; selected and named by F. S. Santamour and G. Eisenbeiss; registered H.S.A. 10-91 by Eisenbeiss; released in 1992).

Leaves dark green, glossy, flat, slightly curved, broadly lanceolate, to 12 cm (4¾ in.) long, 6.4 cm (2½ in.) wide, bases cuneate, small tip spines aristate, slightly reflexed, margins with to 12 uniformly spaced small prickly spines on each side, pedicels 6.4 mm (¼ in.) long; fruits vivid red 45A, elongate, 15.9 mm (⅝ in.) long, 8 mm (⁵⁄₁₆ in.) diameter, fasciculate 11 per axil, pedicels 6.4 mm (2½ in.) long; vigorous pyramidal tree, 21 years old 10 m (33 ft.) tall, 6 m (20 ft.) wide; hardy to zone 7, tolerates poor soil and poor drainage. Plate 167.

Ilex 'Ajax' (male; U.S. National Arboretum received small plant 28–35 cm (11–14 in.) tall from Hillier and Sons Nursery, England, as *I. perado*, later identified as *I.* × *koehneana*; selected by F. S. Santamour and G. Eisenbeiss; registered H.S.A. 11-91 by Eisenbeiss; released in 1992).

Leaves dark green, glossy, broadly lanceolate, to 12.6 cm (5 in.) long, 7.8 cm (3⅛ in.) wide, flat, bases broadly cuneate, tips aristate, slightly curved downward, margins with 14 small uniform stiff spines on each side, petioles 1.6 cm (⅝ in.) long; vigorous pyramidal habit, plant 31 years old 10 m (33 ft.) tall, 6 m (20 ft.) wide, tolerates poor soil and poor drainage; selected as pollinator for 'Agena'.

Ilex 'Albert Close' (female; *I. cornuta* (U.S. PI 65860) × *I. ciliospinosa* (U.S. PI 78144); cross made in 1952 at U.S. Plant Introduction Station, Glenn Dale, Maryland; named and registered H.S.A. 1-69 by W. L. Ackerman and J. L. Creech).

Leaves dark olive green, oval, to 12 cm (4¾ in.) long, 1.6–2.5 cm (⅝–1 in.) wide, margins flat, usually 2 spines on each side; fruits red; conical shape, horizontal branching, short internodes resulting in dense twiggy growth, 1.8 × 1.3 m (6 × 4½ ft.) wide in 16 years.

Ilex 'Aquila' (female; synonym CB26; *I. cornuta* 'Burfordii' × *I. pernyi* cross; named and introduced by H. Hohman).

Leaves dark olive green, glossy, squarish to oblong, long reflexed, wide tapered apical spines, 3.5–5 cm (1⅜–2 in.) long, 1.6–2.5 cm (⅝–1 in.) wide, bases rotund to slightly truncate, margins convex, 2 strong spines on each side, occasionally 1–2 small spines near base, between larger spines, petioles 3–5 mm (⅛–³⁄₁₆ in.) long; fruits vivid red 45A, globose, 6–8 mm (⁷⁄₃₂–⁵⁄₁₆ in.) diameter, 1–5 in clusters, pedicels 3 mm (1.8 in.) long; compact broadly pyramidal habit.

Ilex 'Aquipern' (female; cultivar name given to *I.* × *aquipernyi* (*I. aquifolium* 'Pyramidalis' × *I. pernyi*) discovered by J. B. Gable in 1933; W. B. Clarke Nursery listed seedlings of *I.* × *aquipernyi* in 1937, no source but possibly the same as Gable).

Leaves dark olive green, glossy, 3–5 cm (1³⁄₁₆–2 in.) long, 1.5–2.5 cm (¹⁹⁄₃₂–1 in.) wide, margins undulate, resembles *I. pernyi*, fruits red, globose, 7 mm (⁹⁄₃₂ in.) diameter; small upright shrub.

Ilex 'Aries' (female; synonym CB14; *I. cornuta* 'Burfordii' × *I. pernyi* cross; named and introduced by H. Hohman).

No description available.

Ilex 'Arthur Bruner' (male; chance seedling of *I. cornuta* 'Burfordii' × *I. latifolia*; synonym 'Bruner Boy'; sibling of 'Emily Bruner'; selected and named by Emily Bruner in late 1980s; released and to be registered).

Leaves dark olive green, oval, 4.5–6 cm (1⅝–2⅜ in.) long, 2.5–3.5 cm (1–1³⁄₁₆ in.) wide, bases obtuse, 7–9 uniform spines on each side; upright pyramidal habit; good pollinator; hardy in zone 7.

Ilex 'Atlas' (female; synonym CB5; *I. cornuta* 'Burfordii' × *I. pernyi* cross, named and introduced by H. Hohman).

Leaves dark olive green, oblong, 2.5–4.5 cm (1–1¾ in.) long, 1.3–2 cm (½–¾ in.) wide, bases obtuse to rotund, apices acute, tip spines slightly reflexed, margins convex, undulate, 2–4 spines on each side, petioles 5 mm (³⁄₁₆ in.) long; fruits vivid red 44A, globose, 6–8 cm (⁷⁄₃₂–⁵⁄₁₆ in.) diameter, 1–3 in clusters, pedicels 3 mm (⅛ in.) long; compact upright pyramidal habit.

Ilex 'Audrey' (female; chance seedling, putative hybrid *I. cornuta* × *I. pernyi;* selected and registered H.S.A. 12-76 by A. C. Patterson).

Leaves dark olive green, nearly squarish, to 6.5 cm (2½ in.) long 3.8 cm (1½ in.) long, strong apical spines, usually reflexed, margins flat, 2 prominent spines on each side, 1 near base, 1 near apex, occasionally smaller spines between, petioles 2–3 mm (⅟16–⅛ in.) long; fruits red, globose, 8 mm (⁵⁄16 in.) diameter, pedicels 5 mm (³⁄16 in.) long, abundant fruiting; compact, slow mounding habit. In 24 years 1.7 × 2.1 m (5½ × 7 ft.) wide.

Ilex B 51517 or B 51517 (female; *I. cornuta* × *I. ciliospinosa* seedling; cross by W. L. Ackerman and J. L. Creech; plant at Ebersole Garden from Tingle Nursery; doubt if plant or seed were officially released by U.S. Plant Introduction Station, Glenn Dale, Maryland; name not valid, new name suggested).

Leaves dark olive green, glossy, quadrangular, convex, 4–5 cm (1⅝–2 in.) long, 1.5–2 cm (¹⁹⁄32–¾ in.) wide, 1–3 spines on each side, tip spines reflexed; fruits red, globose, 8–10 mm (⁵⁄16–⅜ in.) diameter; pyramidal habit.

Ilex 'Bancroft' (female; selected seedling of *I. integra* originally from U.S.D.A., questionable hybrid, plant near Bancroft Hall, University Southeastern Louisiana, Hammond, Louisiana).

Leaves obovate-elliptic, margins usually serrate; fruits orange to reddish orange; bisexual, many male flowers observed; upright compact habit.

Ilex 'Beacon' (male; synonym CB18; *I. cornuta* 'Burfordii' × *I. pernyi* cross; named and introduced by H. Hohman).

Leaves dark olive green, glossy, oblong to slightly rectangular, 3.5–5.5 cm (1⅜–2⅛ in.) long, 2–2.8 cm (¾–1⅛ in.) wide, bases rotund to slightly truncate, apices acute, tip spines reflexed, margins convex, 2 strong spines on each side, 1 near base, 1 near apex, occasionally 1–2 small spines near base on each side, petioles 3 mm (⅛ in.) long; compact broadly pyramidal habit. Plant had winter damage at Callaway Gardens, Pine Mountain, Georgia.

Ilex Becky Stevens™ (female; 'Wyebec', PP name, discovered by N. G. Fischer at Wye Nursery, Hillsboro, Maryland, PP No. 8792; superior hybrid of Nellie Stevens, male unknown, assumed *I. ciliospinosa*).

Leaves dark green 139A, narrow-elliptic 5.5–5.8 cm (2⅛–2¼ in.) long, 2.3–2.5 cm (⅞–1 in.) wide, 3–4 small spines on each side; petioles 6–8 mm (⁷⁄32–⁵⁄16 in.) long; fruits deep reddish orange 43A, elliptic-oblong 10–11 mm (⅜–⁷⁄16 in.) long, 5–9 mm (⁵⁄16–

¹¹⁄32 in.) diameter, produced abundantly; narrow upright habit with 1 or more strong leaders, 6-year-old plant 1.5 m (6 ft.) tall, 0.75 m (3 ft.) wide, 18-year-old plant 3.6 m (12 ft.) tall, 1.8–2.1 m (6–7 ft.) wide; good foundation plant; winter hardy to −26°C (−15°F). Plate 168.

Ilex 'Bessie Smith' (female; *I. cornuta* × *I. latifolia* discovered by Hal Elmore, in mid 1980s).

Leaves moderate olive green, elliptic, 8–9 cm (3⅛–3½ in.) long, 3–3.5 cm (1³⁄16–1⅜ in.) wide, bases cuneate, margins slightly convex, 7–8 small spines on each side, tip spines reflexed, petioles reddish 8–10 mm (⁵⁄16–⅜ in.) long, stems green to reddish.

Ilex 'Betty Zane' (female; *I. ciliospinosa* × unknown male species, records lost, controlled cross in 1959 by O. M. Neal, named and registered H.S.A. 6-76 by Neal; named for revolution war heroine).

Leaves dark olive green, glossy, elliptic, curves, to 7.3 cm (2⅞ in.) long, 3.2 cm (1¼ in.) wide, bases broadly cuneate to rotund, tip spines strongly reflexed, margins extremely variable, 1–3 small ciliate spines each side, margins strongly notched, adjacent to first spines below apex, petioles 5 mm (³⁄16 in.) long; fruits red, globose, 10 mm (⅜ in.) diameter; pyramidal habit, pendulous branches. Original tree 3.1 m (10 ft.) tall in 10 years; hardy in zone 4.

Ilex 'Bill's', see 'Loch Raven'.

Ilex 'Bisex' (female; thought to be *I. aquifolium* × *I. pernyi,* looks more like *I. cornuta* × *I. pernyi,* plant at McLean Nursery, Towson, Maryland; name not valid).

Leaves dark olive green, broadly elliptic, 3.5–4.5 cm (1⅜–1⅝ in.) long, 2–2.5 cm (¾–1 in.) wide, curved, slightly keeled, bases obtuse to rotund, apices acuminate, reflexed, 2 spines on each side, petioles 4 mm (⁵⁄32 in.) long; fruits vivid red 45A, oval, 8 mm (⁵⁄16 in.) long, 6–7 mm (⁷⁄32–⁹⁄32 in.) diameter, pedicels 5 mm (³⁄16 in.) long; upright pyramidal habit, slow growing.

Ilex Blue Angel® (female; *I.* × *meserveae* controlled crosses of (*I. rugosa* × *I. aquifolium*) × *I. aquifolium;* made in 1958 and selected in 1963 by K. K. Meserve; introduced in 1975 by Conard-Pyle Company; PP No. 3662; Blue Holly Group).

Leaves dark olive green, elliptic to oval elliptic, 3–4.5 cm (1³⁄16–1¾ in.) long, 1.6–2.2 cm (⅝–¹³⁄16 in.) wide, bases obtuse to rotund, apices acuminate, tip spines reflexed, margins undulate, 4–6 spines on each side, occasionally subentire, petioles 5 mm (³⁄16 in.) long, stems purplish; fruits vivid red 45A, glo-

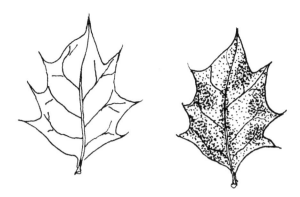

Figure 16-1. *Ilex* 'Bisex'. Drawing by Randy Allen.

bose, 8–10 mm (⁵⁄₁₆–³⁄₈ in.) diameter, abundant; compact upright habit; not as hardy as other Blue Hollies, hardy in zone 7. Plates 169, 170.

Ilex 'Blue Boy' (not trademarked, male; *I. × meserveae* controlled crosses of *I. rugosa* 'Long Island' × *I. aquifolium* 'Lawrence White' by K. K. Meserve; introduced in 1963 by Perkins de Wilde; PP No. 2435; Blue Holly Group).
    Leaves dark green, ovate, 4–5 cm (1⅝–2 in.) long, 2.5–2.8 cm (1–1⅛ in.) wide, bases obtuse to rotund, apices acute, tip spines reflexed, margins undulate, 5–6 spines on each side, spines pointing forward, petioles 4–5 mm (⁵⁄₃₂–³⁄₁₆ in.) long; stems purplish; compact upright habit; hardy in zone 7. Plate 171.

Ilex 'Blue Bunny' (female; 'Meseal' *I. × meserveae*, discovered by G. Hoogenroad, Boskoop, Netherlands; silver medal in Netherlands; published in *Dendroflora* 1992; Blue Holly Group).
    Leaves dark green oblong-elliptic to 7 cm (2¾ in.) long, 2.5 cm (1 in.) wide, smooth, wavy, twisted, margins, entire to toothed, to 8 small spines on each side; vigorous, upright, narrow pyramidal habit; very winter hardy. No information in the United States.

Ilex 'Blue Girl' (not trademarked, female; *I. × meserveae* controlled cross of *I. rugosa* 'Long Island' × *I. aquifolium* 'Lawrence White' by K. K. Meserve; introduced in 1963 by Perkins de Wilde; PP No. 2434; Blue Holly Group).
    Leaves moderate olive green, ovate, slightly curved and keeled, 2.5–3.5 cm (1–1⅜ in.) long, 1.3–1.8 cm (½–1¹⁄₁₆ in.) wide, bases rotund, apices acute, margins 4–6 small forward pointing spines, petioles 5 mm (³⁄₁₆ in.) long, stems purplish; fruits vivid red 45A, globose, 6–8 mm (⁷⁄₃₂–⁵⁄₁₆ in.) diameter, pedicels reddish, 6 mm (⁷⁄₃₂ in.) long; broadly upright spreading habit; hardy in zones 6a to 9a.

Blue Holly Group
    A group name for *I. × meserveae* hybrids of *I. rugosa* × *I. aquifolium* first developed by Kathleen K. Meserve, a dedicated horticulturist and hybridizer of St. James, Long Island, New York. In the early 1950s, Meserve made the first cross of *I. rugosa* with *I. aquifolium*. This cross was first described and given the name *I. × meserveae* by S.-y. Hu in 1970 (*Arnoldia* 30 (2)).
    The Blue Hollies are popular cold hardy landscape plants suitable for planting in Zone 6, except for Blue Angel®, which is only hardy to Zone 7. The glossy dark green leaves are elliptic or acute depending upon the cultivar, margins are spinose with dentate teeth and conspicuous impressed veins on the upper surface. All the plants I have observed have white flowers; however, the Plant Patent descriptions indicate that the flowers are said to be pale pink 46D.
    There is confusion in popular literature and even with the Plant Patent descriptions as to the correct parentage. The seed parent is *Ilex rugosa*. The correct parentage of the Blue Hollies is *I. × meserveae* and most of the cultivars are *I. rugosa* × *I. aquifolium*, unless noted. Blue Angel® is (*I. rugosa* × *I. aquifolium*) × *I. aquifolium*. Nonetheless, the epithet *I. × meserveae* can be applied to *I. rugosa* × *I. aquifolium* or *I. aquifolium* × *I. rugosa*.
    Meserve used two different plants of *Ilex rugosa* for the seed parents which she called 'Long Island' and 'Arnold Arboretum'. The Arnold Arboretum introduced *I. rugosa* from Japan; six plants were given to Westbury Rose Company on Long Island, and Paul Vossberg gave Meserve one plant. The other plant we can assume came from the Arnold Arboretum. For the male plants three different selections of *I. aquifolium* were used: 'Lawrence White', 'Fisher's Island' and 'Goliath'. It is unfortunate that there is little to no information as to the complete origin of the parent plants and their present disposition.
    The Blue Hollies are important plants in the nursery and landscape business and will continue to grow in popularity as they become better known. Unfortunately, as new plants are propagated, sources of cutting and labeling can be a problem. For example, there are three different plants in the nursery trade sold as 'Blue Maid'. See plant descriptions of Blue Maid®, 'Blue Maid No. 2' and 'Blue Maid Sport'.
    In the future we can expect to see seedlings and F₂ hybrids of *Ilex × meserveae* plants being grown. It is hoped they will be tested and evaluated with the presently named Blue Hollies. Golden Girl®, a yellow fruited *I. × meserveae*, was introduced in 1989 and there is a very compact small leaf sport being tested in the West for possible future introduction.
    China Boy®, China Girl®, and Dragon Lady®,

also developed by Meserve, are not Blue Hollies or hybrids of *I.* × *meserveae.* They are of different parentage. S.-y. Hu in 1964 examined and made herbarium specimens for the Arnold Arboretum of the *I.* × *meserveae* hybrids. These specimens for the most part are still identified by Meserve's nursery numbers.

Group A: F1 hybrids of *I. rugosa* 'Long Island' × *I. aquifolium* 'Lawrence White'.

S.-y. Hu 7792: 'Blue Girl', female, leaves ovate, spinose, flowers white, compact plant 1.5 m (6 ft.) high. Plant Patent 2434.

S.-y. Hu 7793: 'Blue Girl 2', female, same hybridization as above.

S.-y. Hu 7794: 'Blue Boy', male, leaves ovate, spinose, flowers white. Plant Patent 2435.

S.-y. Hu 7796: male, leaves elliptic, 5–8 spines each side.

S.-y. Hu 7797: 'Yellow Boy', male, leaves ovate, spinose.

S.-y. Hu 7798: nursery #4-53, male, leaves ovate, spinose, 3–3.5 cm (1³⁄16–1⅜ in.) long, 1.7–2.3 cm (²¹⁄32–⅞ in.) wide, bases rotund.

S.-y. Hu 7799: nursery #1-57, male, leaves elliptic, 2–3 cm (¾–1³⁄16 in.) long, 1.2–1.6 cm (¹⁷⁄32–⅝ in.) wide.

Group B: F1 hybrids of *I. rugosa* 'Long Island' × *I. aquifolium* 'Fisher's Island'.

S.-y. Hu 7795: nursery #F-1, female, M-3 male, leaves elliptic, spinose, compact shrubs.

S.-y. Hu 7780: nursery #2-57, male, leaves small, elliptic, 1.8–3 cm (¹¹⁄16–1³⁄16 in.) long, 0.7-1.5 cm (⁹⁄32–¹⁹⁄32 in.) wide, bases acute, very compact.

S.-y. Hu 7802: nursery #F-1, female, leaves green with purplish tint, elliptic, spinose, 1.3-3.3 cm (½–1⁵⁄16 in.) long, fruit abundant, pyrenes fertile.

S.-y. Hu 7803: nursery #F-2, female, leaves elliptic, spinose, 2.5-3.5 cm (1–1⅜ in.) long, 1.3–2 cm (½–¾ in.) wide, bases acute or obtuse, fruits in cymose clusters.

S.-y. Hu 7804: nursery #M-5, male, leaves elliptic, weakly spinose, 3.5–4.5 cm (1⅜–1¾ in.) long, 1.4–1.9 cm (½–¾ in.) wide, similar to *I. ciliospinosa.*

S.-y. Hu 7805: 2 branches, separate plants, male = M-4; female = F-2, leaves elliptic, spinose, 3.5 cm (1⅜ in.) long, 1.7–2.5 cm (²¹⁄32–1 in.) wide.

Group C: F1 hybrids of *I. rugosa* 'Arnold Arboretum' × *I. aquifolium* 'Lawrence White'.

S.-y. Hu 7801: nursery #2-58, male, leaves elliptic or oblong, spinose, 2.5–3 cm (1–1³⁄16 in.) long, 1.1–1.8 cm (⁷⁄16–¹¹⁄16 in.) wide, bases acute or obtuse.

Group D: F1 hybrids of *I. rugosa* 'Long Island' × *I. aquifolium* 'Goliath'.

S.-y. Hu 7806: female, leaves elliptic, weakly spinose, loosely arranged, 3–4.5 cm (1³⁄16–1¾ in.) long, 1.3–2 cm (½–¾ in.) wide, bases acute, rarely obtuse, similar to *I. ciliospinosa,* fruit pedicels long (equal to diameter of fruit).

S.-y. Hu 7807: female, leaves elliptic, spinose, 5–5.3 cm (2–2³⁄32 in.) long, 1.8–2.3 cm (¹¹⁄16–⅞ in.) wide, bases obtuse, 5–10 spines each side, shy flowering, vigorous habit.

Group E: F1 hybrids of *I. rugosa* 'Arnold Arboretum' × *I. aquifolium* 'Fisher's Island'.

S.-y. Hu 7808: nursery #1-58, male, leaves elliptic, strongly spinose, 3–4 cm (1³⁄16–1⅝ in.) long, 1.1–1.6 cm (⁷⁄16–⅝ in.) wide, bases obtuse or acute.

Group F: Parent Plants

I. rugosa: low shrubs 0.5 m (19 in.) high, glabrous stems and pedicels, leaves elliptic or ovate-elliptic, margins crenulate, serrate.

I. rugosa 'Long Island', female.

I. rugosa ' Arnold Arboretum', female.

I. aquifolium 'Lawrence White', male, small tree 3 m (9¾ ft.) high, branches purplish puberulent, pedicels and peduncles pilose, calyx lobes ciliate, leaves oblong, sinuate strongly spinose.

I. aquifolium 'Fisher's Island', male.

I. aquifolium 'Goliath', male, branchlets puberulent, leaves elliptic or rarely obovate, 5–8 cm (2–3⅛ in.) long, 2–4.3 cm (¾–1¾ in.) wide, strongly spinose, 4–8 spines on each side.

Note: China Boy®, China Girl®, and Blue Hollies are patented plants (i.e., trademarked plant names) with fancy cultivar names on all the plant patents. The Cultivated Code does not recognize or deal with trademark names because they are not cultivar names. Accordingly both names are listed in the Blue Holly descriptions—the registered trademarked plant name and the corresponding cultivar name. The Blue hollies described here include Blue Angel®, 'Blue Boy', 'Blue Bunny', 'Blue Girl', Blue Maid®, 'Blue Maid No. 2', 'Blue Maid Sport', 'Blue Mist', Blue Prince®, Blue Princess®, and Blue Stallion®.

Ilex Blue Maid® (female; synonym Mesid; *I.* × *meserveae* controlled crosses of *I. rugosa* × *I. aquifolium* by K. K. Meserve; introduced in 1978 by Conard-Pyle Company; PP No. 4685; Blue Holly Group).

Leaves dark olive green, glossy, elliptic, slightly keeled, curved, 4–6 cm (1⅝–2⅜ in.) long, 2–3.5 cm (¾–1⅜ in.) wide, bases acute, rarely obtuse, apices acute, tip spines reflexed, margins wavy, occasionally slightly undulating, 4–6 small spines on each side, pointing forward, usually on upper two-thirds of leaf, petioles larger, 5–8 mm (3⁄16–5⁄16 in.) long, stems green; fruits vivid red 45A, globose, 8–10 mm (5⁄16–3⁄8 in.) diameter, 1–5 in clusters, pedicels reddish; compact upright spreading habit; hardy in zones 5b to 9a. Plate 172.

Ilex 'Blue Maid No. 2' (female; synonym 'Old Maid'; an unknown *I.* × *meserveae* plant mislabeled in nurseries and holly test gardens; mixed (as late as 1990) and sold as Blue Maid®; suggest eliminating renaming plants or keeping them as 'Blue Maid No. 2'; Blue Holly Group).

Leaves moderate olive green, glossy, ovate, slightly keeled, 4–5.5 cm (1⅝–2⅛ in.) long, 2.5–3 cm (1–1 3⁄16 in.) wide, bases rotund, apices acute, tip spines reflexed, margins undulate, 6–7 spines on each side, pointing forward, petioles 3–5 mm (⅛–3⁄16 in.) long, stems green; fruits vivid red 45A, globose, 8–10 mm (5⁄16–⅜ in.) diameter, 1–5 in clusters, pedicels reddish; upright spreading habit. Compared to Blue Maid®, leaves ovate, petioles shorter and less compact. Hardy in zones 6a to 9a. Plants set numerous fruits and may account for the lighter leaf color.

Ilex 'Blue Maid Sport' (female; synonym 'New Maid'; narrow-elliptical leaf sport of Blue Maid®; presently sold as Blue Maid®; should be dropped, renamed, or registered as a sport of Blue Maid®; Blue Holly Group).

Leaves dark olive green, narrow-elliptic, keeled, 4–5.5 cm (1⅝–2⅛ in.) long, 1.3–1.8 cm (½–11⁄16 in.) wide, bases cuneate, apices acute, margins slightly wavy, 4–6 small spines on each side, pointing forward, usually on upper two-thirds of leaf, petioles 5–8 mm (3⁄16–5⁄16 in.) long; fruits red. Compared to Blue Maid® has narrow-elliptic leaves. Conard-Pyle Company reports licensee damaged plants with spray of Benelate™ (atrozine) applied in 1988–1989; however, the narrow leaf sport was noted about 3 years before.

Ilex 'Blue Mist' (*I.* × *meserveae,* plants at Holly Haven Nursery obtained from Pallack Nursery, Pennsylvania; possibly a seedling or one of named Blue Holly Group).

Leaves dark olive green, ovate to slightly elliptic, 2.5–3.5 cm (1–1⅜ in.) long, 1.6–2 cm (⅝–¾ in.) wide, bases obtuse to rotund, apices acute, tip spines reflexed, margins undulate, 5–6 spines on each side, pointing forward, petioles 5 mm (3⁄16 in.) long; stems purplish.

Ilex Blue Prince® (male; *I.* × *meserveae* controlled cross of *I. rugosa* × *I. aquifolium* made 1959 and selected 1964 by K. K. Meserve, introduced 1972 by Conard-Pyle Company; PP No. 3517; cultivar name not included in patent; Blue Holly Group).

Leaves dark olive green, glossy, ovate, 2.5–4.5 cm (1–1¾ in.) long, 2–2.5 cm (¾–1 cm) wide, bases rotund, apices acute, margins nearly flat, 4–8 small spines on each side, pointing forward, petioles 6–8 mm (7⁄32–5⁄16 in.) long, stems purplish; upright compact habit; hardy in zones 6a to 9a. Plate 173.

Ilex Blue Princess® (female; *I.* × *meserveae* controlled cross of *I. rugosa* × *I. aquifolium;* made in 1952 and selected in 1958 by K. K. Meserve; introduced in 1974 by Conard-Pyle Company; PP No. 3675; cultivar name not included in patent; Blue Holly Group).

Leaves dark olive green, glossy, ovate, keeled, 2–3.8 cm (¾–1½ in.) long, 1.6–2 cm (⅝–¾ in.) wide, bases obtuse to rotund, apices acute, petioles 5 mm (3⁄16 in.) long, stems purplish; fruits vivid red 45A, globose, 6–8 mm (7⁄32–5⁄16 in.) diameter, abundant, pedicels reddish, 6 mm (7⁄32 in.) long; compact rounded habit; hardy in zones 6a to 9a. Plate 174.

Ilex Blue Stallion® (male; synonym 'Mesan'; *I.* × *meserveae* controlled cross of *I. rugosa* × *I. aquifolium* by K. K. Meserve; introduced in 1979 by Conard-Pyle Company; PP No. 4804; Blue Holly Group).

Leaves moderate to dark olive green, ovate, 4.5–5 cm (1¾–2 in.) long, 2–3 cm (¾–1 3⁄16 in.) wide, margins flat, 5–7 small spines, pointing forward, petioles 5–6 mm (3⁄16–7⁄32 in.) long, stems purplish; vigorous upright spreading habit; hardy in zones 6a to 9a. Plate 175.

Ilex 'Bob Bruner' (male; sibling of 'Emily Bruner', which see; selected and named in late 1980s by Emily Bruner; named for Bruner's son; to be registered).

Leaves dark olive green, broadly elliptic to oval, 5.5–7.5 cm (2⅛–2¾ in.) long, 3–4 cm (1 3⁄16–1⅝ in.) wide, bases obtuse to rotund, 9–10 uneven spines on each side, usually alternating, medium and small spines.

Ilex 'Brighter Shines' (male; synonym CB2; *I. cornuta* 'Burfordii' × *I. pernyi* cross; named and introduced by H. Hohman).

Leaves dark olive green, glossy, oblong, 3.5–4.5 cm (1⅜–1¾ in.) long, 1.3–2.5 cm (½–1 in.) wide, bases rotund to truncate, apices acute, tip spines reflexed, margins convex, 2 moderate spines on each side, occasionally 1–2 very small spines, 1 near base, 1 between larger spines; compact pyramidal habit.

Ilex 'Brilliant' (female; *I. ciliospinosa* × *I. sikkimensis,* A.A.N. registered; developed in 1935 and named by

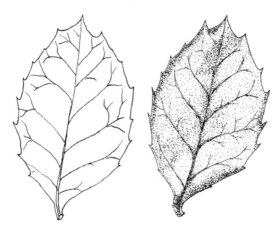

Figure 16-2. *Ilex* 'Bob Bruner'. Drawing by Randy Allen.

W. B. Clarke; not *I. aquifolium* 'Golden Beauty' × *I. sikkimensis* or *I. pernyi* as first reported, possibly *I. ciliospinosa* × *I. pernyi*).

Leaves dark olive green, ovate-elliptic, slightly curved, 3–5 cm (1³⁄₁₆–2 in.) long, 1.6–2.2 cm (⁵⁄₈–1³⁄₁₆ in.) wide, bases obtuse rotund, apices acute, margins slightly wavy, usually 3–4 spines on each side, petioles 5 mm (³⁄₁₆ in.) long; fruits vivid red 44A, globose, 8–10 mm (⁵⁄₁₆–³⁄₈ in.) diameter, abundant, pedicels 3–4 mm (¹⁄₈–⁵⁄₃₂ in.) long; upright pyramidal habit.

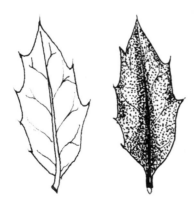

Figure 16-3. *Ilex* 'Brilliant'. Drawing by Randy Allen.

Ilex 'Brilliant' (female; *I. ciliospinosa* × *I. pernyi* plant at Washington Park Arboretum, Seattle; very similar to Clarke's 'Brilliant' described above).

Ilex 'Brooklyn Queen' (female; possibly a hybrid with *I. ciliospinosa* as one parent, origin unknown).
Leaves dark olive green, elliptic, 3.8–5 cm (1½–2

in.) long, 1.3–2 cm (½–¾ in.) wide, bases and apices acute, 3–5 small weak spines on each side; fruits red, globose, reported pyrenes sterile.

Ilex Buttercup™ (female; 'Hefcup', PP name, variegated sport of (*I. aquifolium* × *I. cornuta*) 'Nellie R. Stevens' discovered by Randy B. Hefner, in his nursery, Conover, North Carolina; PP No. 8537).
Leaves variegated, elliptic-oblong to oblong-rectangular, 5–8 cm (2–3¹⁄₈ in.) long, 3–4 cm (1³⁄₁₆–1⁵⁄₈ in.) wide, margins entire to spinose, revolute, curving down, 1–3 small spinose teeth on each side, apices spinose-acute, bases broadly cuneate, variegations extremely variable, new juvenile leaves brilliant orange-yellow 23A, maturing to vivid yellow 9A, apical tips to marginal variegations with green bases; flowers 4-merous, fasciculate, lobes white; fruits in summer light yellow, maturing to reddish orange 42A, ovoid 7–10 mm (⁹⁄₃₂–³⁄₈ in.) long, 5–8 mm (³⁄₁₆–⁵⁄₁₆ in.) wide; pyramidal upright habit; mature plants similar to 'Nellie R. Stevens', but slower growing to 5.5–6 m (18–20 ft.) tall, 2.5 m (8 ft.) wide; hardy in zone 7, adult foliage may have some winter damage at −22°C (−8°F); excellent specimen, accent plant, screen or tall hedge, or interplanted with other hollies or evergreen plants. Plate 176.

Ilex 'Byam K. Stevens' (female; selected seedling of *I. pernyi* × *I. ciliospinosa;* named and registered H.S.A. 11-67 by T. Dilatush).
Leaves dark olive green, glossy, elliptic, slightly curved, 3.5–5 cm (1³⁄₈–2 in.) long, 1.6–2 cm (⁵⁄₈–¾ in.) wide, bases obtuse, apices acute, tip spines reflexed, 2–4 small spines on each side, petioles 6 mm (⁷⁄₃₂ in.) long; fruits vivid red 45A, globose to ellipsoid, 8 mm (⁵⁄₁₆ in.) diameter, upright, conical habit 1.2 × 0.6 m (4 × 2 ft.) wide in 7 years.

Ilex 'Calina' (female; putative hybrid *I. aquifolium* × *I. cornuta*; origin unknown, possibly from seedlings purchased from LeMac Nursery by W. Edingloh; selected and named around 1938 by Edingloh; name is a contraction of Carolina).
Leaves moderate to dark olive green, oval to broadly elliptic, keeled, 5–6.5 cm (2–2³⁄₈ in.) long, 2.5–3.5 cm (1–1³⁄₈ in.) wide, bases obtuse to rotund, apices acute, tip spines often reflexed, margins variable, subentire to 1–5 spines on each side, petioles 8 mm (⁵⁄₁₆ in.) long; fruits vivid red 45A, globose, 8 mm (⁵⁄₁₆ in.) diameter, 1–5 in clusters, abundant; compact upright pyramidal habit; attractive plant and heat tolerant in southeastern United States; hardy in zone 7. Plate 177.

Ilex Cardinal™ (female; Red Holly Hybrid).
Leaves large, similar to 'Mary Nell', new growth

reddish, pyramidal habit 4.5 m (15 ft.) tall. Plate 178.

Ilex 'Carolina Cone' (sex unknown; *I. dimorphophylla* × *I. cornuta,* first hybrid of this parentage made in 1982 by G. Eisenbeiss at U.S. National Arboretum; cuttings given to J. C. Raulston, North Carolina State University Arboretum, in 1980s; rooted cuttings given to North Carolina nurseries for testing and evaluation; plant named and introduced by L. Edwards, Turtle Creek Nursery, in 1992).

Leaves dark green, glossy, narrow, rectangular, typically 3 stout spines on each side, occasionally with smaller spines on each side, tip spines elongated and reflexed, 2–3 cm (¾–1³⁄₁₆ in.) long, 7–9 mm (⁹⁄₃₂–¹¹⁄₃₂ in.) wide, petioles 3–5 mm (⅛–³⁄₁₆ in.) long; no fruit observed on 6-year plants and no adult entire foliage. Upright habit, narrow, spreading; vigorous pruning required to keep tight compact form; hardy in zone 9. Other seedlings of this cross (U.S. National Arboretum) are producing small red fruits. Still under observation and may be released later. Plate 179.

Ilex cassine var. *angustifolia* × *I. vomitoria* (sex unknown; controlled cross made by E. E. Orton Jr., Rutgers University; named and introduced by Tom Dodd Nursery, Semmes, Alabama).

Young stems green, brown on upper side; leaves dark green, glossy, elliptic, 3–4 cm (1⅜–1⅝ in.) long, 1.5–1.8 cm (¹⁹⁄₃₂–⅝ in.) wide, slightly keeled and curved, bases cuneate, apices blunt to obtuse, margin appears entire with very minute spurs, petioles 5–7 mm (³⁄₁₆–⁹⁄₃₂ in.) long; upright spreading habit. Hardiness unknown, possibly zone 7a or lower. Short, good background plant, screen, or hedge.

Ilex 'Centennial Girl' (female; PPAF; *I. centrochinensis* × *I. aquifolium* by K. K. Meserve; named and introduced in 1997 by Conard-Pyle Company).

Leaves dark green, glossy, elliptic, 6 spines on each side; fruits vivid red, persistent until spring; broad, pyramidal upright habit. Good specimen, hedge, or screen plant in the landscape.

Ilex 'Cetus' (female; synonym CB25; *I. cornuta* 'Burfordii' × *I. pernyi* cross; named and introduced by H. Hohman).

Leaves dark olive green, glossy, slightly squarish, 3–4.5 cm (1³⁄₁₆–1¾ in.) long, 1.6–3 cm (⅝–1³⁄₁₆ in.) wide, bases truncate, apices acute, tip spines reflexed, margins convex, usually only 2 spines on each side, petioles 3–5 mm (⅛–³⁄₁₆ in.) long; fruits vivid red 45A, globose, 6–8 mm (⁷⁄₃₂–⁵⁄₁₆ in.) diameter, good heavy clusters, pedicels 2–4 mm (¹⁄₁₆–⁵⁄₃₂ in.) long; compact upright mounding habit to upright broadly pyramidal. Plate 180.

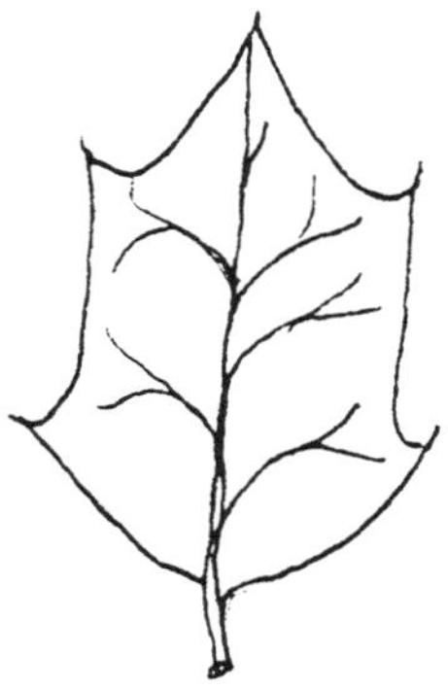

Figure 16-4. *Ilex* 'Cetus'. Drawing by Randy Allen.

Ilex 'Chestnut Leaf' (female; synonym *I. castaneifolia* Hort.; old cultivar from France).

Leaves moderate olive green, elliptic to oblong lanceolate, 10–15 cm (4–6 in.) long, 2.5–5 cm (1–2 in.) wide, margins with 10–15 spines on each side; fruits red, globose, fasciculate; vigorous upright pyramidal habit. Unknown in the United States. Reported hardier than most *I.* × *koehneana* in Germany by H.-G. Buchtmann.

Ilex 'Chieftain' (male; *I.* × *koehneana,* seedling of putative hybrid *I. latifolia* × *I. aquifolium;* found about 1955; named and registered H.S.A. 1-67 by S. H. McLean).

Leaves moderate to dark olive green, elliptic to ovate-elliptic, 6–9.5 cm (2⅜–3¾ in.) long, 2.5–4 cm (1–1⅝ in.) wide, 6–10 small spines on each side, pointing forward, petioles stout, 10–13 mm (⅜–½ in.) long, stems green; habit upright, broadly pyramidal. Valued as a flowering ornamental, flowers yellowish white, thick clusters of flowers around stem.

Ilex China Boy® (male; synonym 'Mesdob'; controlled cross of *I. rugosa* × *I. cornuta* by K. K. Meserve; introduced in 1979 by Conard-Pyle Company; PP No. 4803).

Leaves moderate olive green, semiglossy, oblong to quadrangular, 3.5–6 cm (1⅜–2⅜ in.) long, 2.1–3.5 cm (¾–1⅜ in.) wide, bases obtuse to truncate, apices acute, 2–3 prominent spines on each side, upper two-thirds of leaf, tip spines at apex; compact upright rounded shrubs; hardy in zones 6a to 9b; good pollinator. Plate 181.

Ilex China Girl® (female; synonym 'Mesog'; controlled cross of *I. rugosa* × *I. cornuta* by K. K.

Leaves dark olive green, oval to oval oblong, 5–7 cm (2–2¾ in.) long, 2–3 cm (¾–1³⁄₁₆ in.) wide, appears entire, 2–4 minute spines on each side, petioles 8–10 mm (⁵⁄₁₆–³⁄₈ in.) long; fruits vivid red 45A, globose, 6–8 mm (2³⁄₈–⁵⁄₁₆ in.) diameter, pedicels reddish, 8 mm (⁵⁄₁₆ in.) long, large clusters around the stems; habit pyramidal. Plate 183.

Figure 16-5. *Ilex* 'Chestnut Leaf' in the botanical garden in Hamburg, Germany. Photo by Hans-Georg Buchtmann.

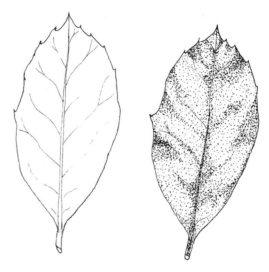

Figure 16-6. *Ilex* 'Clusterberry'. Drawing by Randy Allen.

Ilex 'Compacta' (female; *I.* × *aquipernyi,* plant at Callaway Gardens, Pine Mountain, Georgia, from Wilmat Nursery in 1954).

Leaves dark olive green, ovate, keeled, curved, 3.5–4.5 cm (1³⁄₈–1¾ in.) long, 1.6–2.8 cm (⁵⁄₈–1¹⁄₈ in.) wide, bases rotund, apices acute, margins slightly undulate, usually 3–4 spines on each side, petioles 5 mm (³⁄₁₆ in.) long; fruits vivid red 45A, ovoid, 8 mm (⁵⁄₁₆ in.) long, 6 mm (⁷⁄₃₂ in.) diameter, sparse fruiting, pedicels 3 mm (¹⁄₈ in.) long; habit slow, compact, pyramidal.

Ilex 'Coronet' (female; controlled cross ((*I. aquifolium* × *I. cornuta*) 'Nellie R. Stevens' × (*I. ciliospinosa* × *I.* × *aquipernyi*)) by W. F. Kosar; selected by Kosar; named and registered H.S.A. 12-91 by G. Eisenbeiss).

Leaves dark green, ovate to lanceolate, to 6.7 cm (2.7 in.) long, 3.8 cm (1¼ in.) wide, slightly rugose, curved, bases cuneate, tips aristate, sometimes twisted, large tip spines, 4–5 large, soft, slightly divaricate spines, on each side, petioles 6.4 mm (¼ in.) long; fruits vivid red 45B, subglobose, 10 mm (³⁄₈ in.) long, 12 mm (¹⁵⁄₃₂ in.) diameter, fasciculate to 7 in axil, pedicels 6.4 mm (¼ in.) long, parthenocarpic

Meserve; introduced in 1979 by Conard-Pyle Company; PP No. 4878).

Leaves moderate olive green, semiglossy, oblong to quadrangular, small leaves often ovate, 3.1–5.4 cm (1³⁄₈–2¹⁄₈ in.) long, 2.1–3.1 cm (¾–1³⁄₁₆ in.) wide, bases obtuse to truncate, apices acute, margins twisted, tip spines reflexed, 2–3 prominent spines on each side, petioles 4–10 mm (⁵⁄₃₂–³⁄₈ in.) long; fruits vivid reddish orange 44B, globose, 7–9 mm (⁹⁄₃₂–¹¹⁄₃₂ in.) diameter, pedicels average 9 mm (¹¹⁄₃₂ in.) long; compact upright rounded shrubs; hardy in zones 6a to 9a to −26°C (−15°F). Plate 182.

Ilex 'Clusterberry' (female; ((*I. aquifolium* × *I. cornuta*) 'Nellie R. Stevens') × *I. leucoclada;* cross made in 1961; selected, named, and introduced by W. F. Kosar at U.S. National Arboretum; registered H.S.A. 3-66 by Kosar).

without pollination; hardy to zone 7. Original tree dead, broadly columnar, compact habit, 15-year plant 3.7 m (12.2 ft.) tall, 2 m (6.5 ft.) wide. Tested in California, Oregon, and several states on East Coast. Selected for soft spiny leaves; heavy fruiting without pollination. U.S. National Arboretum released in 1992.

Ilex 'Cousin' (female; cross made by K. K. Meserve in 1950s, possibly *I. ciliospinosa* × *I. rugosa;* introduced by Roslyn Nursery).

Leaves dark olive green, elliptic, slightly keeled, 3–5.5 cm (1³⁄₁₆–2⅛ in.) long, 1–1.9 cm (⅜–¾ in.), 4–6 small spines on each side, tip spines reflexed; petioles purplish, 5 mm (³⁄₁₆ in.) long; compact pyramidal habit. Reported to have yellow fruit.

Ilex 'Dangerfield' (female), see 'Wirt L. Winn'.

Ilex 'Doctor Kassab' (female; *I. cornuta* × *I. pernyi* selected from seedlings purchased from Davenport Nursery in 1948 by Joseph Kassab; registered H.S.A. 7-65 by Kassab; first registered as *I. aquifolium* × *I. cornuta*).

Leaves dark olive green, glossy, bullate, oblong, 4–5 cm (1⅝–2 in.) long, 2–2.2 cm (¾–1³⁄₁₆ in.) wide, bases rotund, apices acute, tip spines slightly reflexed, margins nearly flat, 2 margin spines, one on each side, near apex, occasionally 2 very small spines near base, petioles 5–7 mm (³⁄₁₆–⁹⁄₃₂ in.) long; fruits vivid red, globose, 6–8 mm (⁷⁄₃₂–⁵⁄₁₆ in.) diameter, fasciculate, 3–5 in clusters, abundant; upright compact, pyramidal habit; hardy in zone 6a. Popular plant. Plate 184.

Ilex 'Dorothy Lawton' (female; seedling of *I.* × *aquipernyi* 'Brilliant'; grown in 1967 at Tom Dodd Nursery, Semmes, Alabama; T. Dodd No. 6789190; selected and named by T. Dodd Jr.).

Leaves dark olive green, glossy, oblong, curved, 4–6 cm (1⅝–2⅜ in.) long, 1.8–3 cm (¹¹⁄₁₆–1³⁄₁₆ in.) wide, bases rotund, apices acute, tip spines reflexed, margins convex, usually 2 small spines on each side, upper two-thirds of leaf, occasionally 1 very small spine between, petioles 6–8 mm (⁷⁄₃₂–⁵⁄₁₆ in.) long; fruits vivid red 45A, globose, 8 mm (⁵⁄₁₆ in.) diameter, fascicles 1–5 in clusters, pedicels 6–8 mm (⁷⁄₃₂–⁵⁄₁₆ in.) long; compact pyramidal habit.

Ilex 'Drace' (female; synonym CB34; *I. cornuta* 'Burfordii' × *I. pernyi* cross; named and introduced by H. Hohman).

Leaves dark olive green, glossy, slightly squarish, long tapered reflexed apical spines, 3–4.5 cm (1³⁄₁₆–1¾ in.) long, 1.3–2 cm (½–¾ in.) wide, bases truncate, margins convex, 2 strong spines on each side,

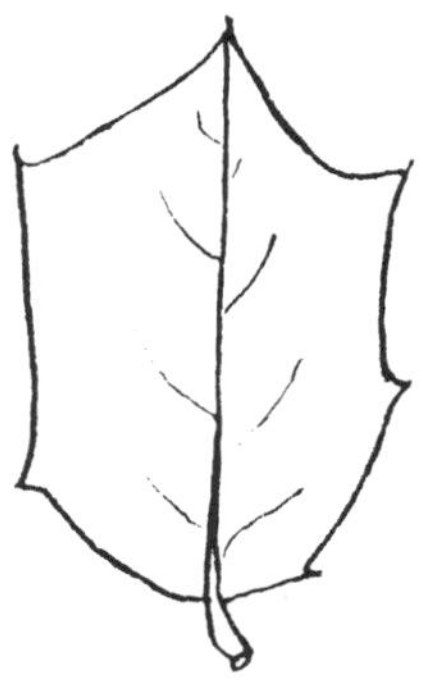

Figure 16-7. *Ilex* 'Doctor Kassab'. Drawing by Randy Allen.

occasionally 1 additional small spine on each side, petioles 5 mm (³⁄₁₆ in.) long; fruits vivid red 45A, globose, 8 mm (⁵⁄₁₆ in.) diameter, 1–3 in clusters, pedicels 5 mm (³⁄₁₆ in.) long; compact pyramidal habit.

Ilex Dragon Lady® (female; synonym 'Meschick'; controlled cross of *I. pernyi* × *I. aquifolium* made by K. K. Meserve; introduced by Conard-Pyle Company; PP No. 4996).

Leaves moderate olive green, glossy, obovate to ovate-quadrangular, keeled, curved, 3–5 (1³⁄₁₆–2 in.) long, 1.6–3 cm (⅝–1³⁄₁₆ in.) wide, bases rotund to truncate, apices cuneate, tip spines reflexed, margins entire to 4–6 spines on each side, petioles 5 mm (³⁄₁₆ in.) long, stems dark; fruits vivid red 44A, globose to slightly flattened, 6–8 mm (⁷⁄₃₂–⁵⁄₁₆ in.) diameter upright pyramidal habit; hardy in zones 6b to 9a to −26°C (−15°F). Plate 185.

Ilex 'Dr. Hu' (female; *I. pernyi* × *I. ciliospinosa,* plant at Ebersole Gardens; reported to be a cross of A. Brownell, Oregon).

Leaves dark olive green, oval to oval elliptic, 3–4.5 cm (1³⁄₁₆–1¾ in.) long, 1.6–2 cm (⅝–¾ in.) wide, slightly keeled, curved, bases rotund, apices acuminate, tip spines slightly reflexed, slight grainy surface, 3–4 small spines on each side, petioles 1–2 cm (⅜–¾ in.) long; fruits vivid red 45A, flat globose, 10 mm (⅜ in.) diameter, 5 in cluster, pedicels 3–5 mm (⅛–³⁄₁₆ in.) long.

Ilex 'Dwarf Semala' (female; sport of 'Semala' discovered by Tom Dodd Jr., at his Semmes, Alabama, nursery in early 1980s and named by him).

Leaves smaller than those of 'Semala'; very dwarf habit, rare in trade.

Ilex Ebony Magic™ (female: open-pollinated seedling, discovered in Ohio by L. L. Demaline; PP No.

5004 in 1983, name not in patent; propagated by Monrovia Nursery, Azusa, California).

Leaves dark olive green, elliptic to oblong elliptic, 4.5–6 cm (1⅝–2⅜ in.) long, 2–2.5 cm (¾–1 in.) wide, bases obtuse, to slightly truncate, margins wavy, 7–11 spines on each side, tip spines reflexed, petioles 8–10 mm (5⁄16–⅜ in.) long, stems distinctly purplish to nearly black 202A; fruits deep reddish orange 43A, globose, 10 mm (⅜ in.) diameter, abundant; pedicels 8–10 mm (5⁄16–⅜ in.) long; hardy in zone 5. Thought by some to be a Blue Holly seedling.

Ilex 'Ed Adams' (female; putative hybrid of *I. opaca* × *I. aquifolium*; chance seedling discovered in 1984 by J. S. Wieman, at his residence, under a female *I. opaca;* selected and named for his son-in-law in 1989; original plant moved to San Mateo, California).

Leaves light green, ovate, glossier than *I. opaca,* 5 cm (2 in.) long, 3.5 cm (1⅜ in.) wide, tips moderately aristate, bases cuneate, margins with 4–8 fairly uniform short spines on each side, many slightly depressed veins, appearance nearly rugose, leaves more similar to parent *I. opaca* than *I. aquifolium,* petioles 4 mm (5⁄32 in.) long; fruits globose, slightly depressed 1 cm (⅜ in.) in diameter, vivid red 45A, borne fasciculate, 4–6 on pedicels 3 mm (⅛ in.) long; flowers produced on previous season's growth. First fruited in 1992. Hardiness not determined, only evaluated in Oregon and San Mateo, California. Original tree 42 cm (16 in.) tall, 60 cm (21 in.) wide, rounded shrubby habit. Selection based on *I. opaca* leaf shape with *I. aquifolium* leaf gloss.

Ilex 'Edward Goucher' (female; controlled cross of *I. cornuta* (U.S. PI 65860) × *I. ciliospinosa* (U.S. PI 78144); made in 1952 at U.S. Plant Introduction Station, Glenn Dale, Maryland; named and registered H.S.A. 4-69 by W. L. Ackerman and J. L. Creech).

Leaves dark olive green, oblong, to 9.5 cm (3¾ in.) long, 2–2.5 cm (¾–1 in.) wide, margins flat, usually 3 spines on each side; fruits red; narrow columnar shape, herring-bone habit of branching. Plant 16 years old 2.9 × 1.2 m (9½ × 3¾ ft.) wide.

Ilex 'Edward J. Stevens' (male; synonyms 'Male Nellie', 'Mr. Stevens'; putative hybrid of *I. cornuta* × *I. aquifolium* from seed of *I. cornuta* obtained about 1900 by Nellie R. Stevens in Oxford, Maryland, from U.S. National Arboretum; brother seedling to 'Maplehurst' and 'Nellie R. Stevens'; introduced in 1958 and registered H.S.A. 9-67 by G. A. Van Lennep Jr.).

Very similar to 'Nellie R. Stevens' (which see), usually with 1 less spine on each side.

Ilex 'Edward Nosal' (male; cross of *I. pernyi* × *I. aquifolium* 'Little Bull' made in 1956; selected, named, and registered H.S.A. 4-71 by M. A. Nosal).

Leaves dark olive green, glossy, intermediate in shape between 2 parents, to 4.5 cm (1¾ in.) long, 2 cm (¾ in.) wide, margins undulate, 3–4 strong spines on each side, twigs purplish; conical habit. Original tree 2.1 × 0.8 m (7 × 2.6 ft.) wide. Good pollinator for English holly.

Ilex 'Elegance' (female; controlled cross of *I. integra* × *I. pernyi* by W. F. Kosar; named and registered H.S.A. 6-66 by Kosar; sibling of 'Accent').

Leaves moderate olive green, ovate-elliptic, curved, 2.5–3 cm (1–1 3⁄16 in.) long, 1.6–2 cm (⅝–¾ in.) wide, bases rotund, apices acute, margins nearly flat, 1–3 small spines on each side, usually upper half of leaf, petioles 3–5 mm (⅛–3⅙ in. long; fruits red, globose, 8 mm (5⁄16 in.) diameter; upright pyramidal habit. Plate 186.

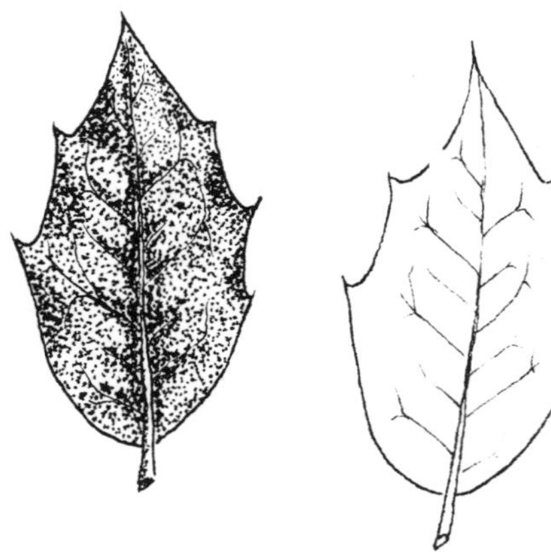

Figure 16-8. *Ilex* 'Elegance'. Drawing by Randy Allen.

Ilex 'Emily Bruner' (female; open-pollinated chance seedling of *I. cornuta* 'Burfordii' × *I. latifolia* discovered in 1960 on Swan Bakery grounds in Knoxville, Tennessee, by Emily Bruner; one of six seedlings (2 female, 4 males) moved to her garden; named in 1972 by Don Shadow; registered H.S.A. 3-83 by Bruner).

Leaves dark olive green, glossy, broadly ovate to broadly lanceolate, 7–11 cm (2¾–4⅜ in.) long, 4–5.5 cm (1⅝–2⅛ in.) wide, curved, slightly keeled, veins depressed above, bases rotund, apices obtuse, tip spines slightly reflexed, usually 10–13 spines on each side, occasionally alternating large and small, petioles 7–8 mm (9⁄32–5⁄16 in.) long, stems green; fruits vivid red 45A, ovoid, 8 mm (5⁄16 in.) long, 6.5 mm (¼ in.) diameter, 2–8 in clusters, abundant, pedicels 6 mm (⁷/₃₂ in.) long; broadly pyramidal habit, distinct horizontal branching. Original tree 3.7 m (12 ft.) tall and 2.5 m (8 ft.) wide. Distinct from male sibling 'James Swan' by smaller curved and keeled leaves, spines larger and more irregular. Very popular landscape plant in southeastern United States. See "Bruner Hollies," *Holly Society of America Journal* 1 (1), 1982. Plate 187.

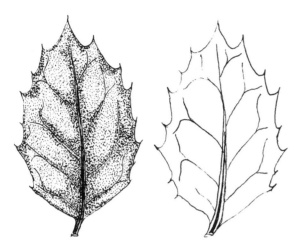

Figure 16-9. *Ilex* 'Emily Bruner'. Drawing by Randy Allen.

Ilex 'Fernax' (male; synonym CB46; *I. cornuta* 'Burfordii' × *I. pernyi* cross; named and introduced by H. Hohman).

Leaves moderate olive green, glossy, ovate, 2–3.5 cm (³/₄–1³/₈ in.) long, 1.6–2.5 cm (⁵/₈–1 in.) wide, bases rotund, apices wide acute, margins nearly flat, 2–3 small spines on each side, petioles 3–5 mm (¹/₈–³/₁₆ in.) long; compact pyramidal habit.

Ilex Festive™ (female; Red Holly Hybrid).
Leaf shape unusual. Plate 188.

Ilex 'Gable's Male' (male; putative hybrid of *I.* × *aquipernyi* discovered and introduced by J. Gable in 1960s).

Leaves dark olive green, ovate to ovate-elliptic, 3–4.5 cm (1³/₁₆–1⁵/₈ in.) long, 1.3–2 cm (¹/₂–³/₄ in.) wide, keeled, curved, bases rotund to truncate, apices tapered to sharp reflexed spines, margins undulate, usually 3–4 spines on each side, petioles 5 mm (³/₁₆ in.) long, stems green.

Ilex 'Gene' (female; sport of *I. dimorphophylla,* discovered at Monrovia Nursery, Azusa, California, in late 1980s; tentative name).

Dwarf compact habit; slower reverting to adult rotund foliage; hardy in zone 9. Doubtful if commercially available.

Ilex 'Ginny Bruner' (female; sibling of 'Emily Bruner'; selected and named by Emily Bruner in late 1980s; named for daughter-in-law; to be registered);

Leaves dark olive green, oval, 4.5–7 cm (1³/₄–2³/₄ in.) long, 2.5–3.5 cm (1–1³/₈ in.) wide, bases obtuse, 9–11 uneven spines on each side, alternating medium and small; fruits red, in fascicles, good fruit display on young plants; hardy in zone 7.

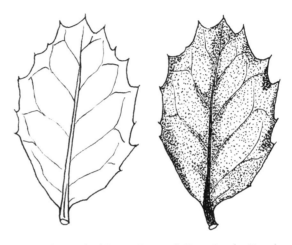

Figure 16-10. *Ilex* 'Ginny Bruner'. Drawing by Randy Allen.

Ilex 'Golden Angel' (female; sport of Blue Angel, discovered in 1989 in Ernst Stührenberg Nursery, Wiesmoor, Germany).

Leaves variegated, dark green, with vivid yellow margins, to broad yellow margins with narrow green strip along midrib.

Ilex Golden Girl® (female; synonym 'Mesgolg', *I.* × *meserveae* controlled cross of *I. rugosa* × *I. aquifolium* by K. K. Meserve, introduced 1989 by Conard-Pyle Company, PP No. 7652).

Leaves dark olive green, elliptic, 3.5–5.5 cm (1³/₈–2¹/₈ in.) long, 1.7–2.2 cm (²¹/₃₂–1³/₁₆ in.) wide, bases cuneate, apices acute, tip spines reflexed, margins wavy, 3–5 spines pointing forward, on each side, usually upper two-thirds on leaf, petioles 8–10 mm (⁵/₁₆–³/₈ in.) long; fruits brilliant yellow 14B, usually brilliant orange 29A on underside, globose, 6–8 mm (⁷/₃₂–⁵/₁₆ in.) diameter, 1–5 in clusters, pedicels orange-yellow, 5–6 mm (³/₁₆–⁷/₃₂ in.) long; compact upright spreading habit; hardy in zones 5 to 9. Plate 189.

Ilex 'Goliath' (female; *I.* × *meserveae* = *I. rugosa* × *I. aquifolium,* origin McLean Nursery, Towson, Maryland, in 1970s not *I. aquifolium* 'Goliath').

Leaves dark olive green, elliptic, keeled, 4.5–5 cm (1¾–2 in.) long, 2–2.5 cm (¾–1 in.) wide, bases cuneate, apices acute, 4–5 small spines on each side; fruits red, globose, 8–10 mm (5⁄16–⅜ in.) diameter, pedicels 10 mm (⅜ in.) long; compact, pyramidal habit.

Ilex 'Good Taste' (female; synonym CB1; *I. cornuta* 'Burfordii' × *I. pernyi* cross; named and introduced by H. Hohman).

Leaves dark olive green, glossy, squarish, long tapered, reflexed apical spines, 3–4.5 cm (1³⁄16–1¾ in.) long, 1.6–2.5 cm (⅝–1 in.) wide, bases truncate, apices acute, margins convex, 2 strong spines on each side, occasionally 1 very small spine on each side, petioles 3 mm (⅛ in.) long; fruits vivid red 45A, flattened globose, 8–10 mm (5⁄16–⅜ in.) diameter, heavy clusters around stem, pedicels 1–2 mm (1⁄32–1⁄16 in.) long; compact pyramidal habit.

Ilex 'Green Shadow' (female; synonym Furi machi no ki; variegated *I. integra* Collection No. 712; collected 1984 by Barry Yinger at Kiraku-En Nursery Mito, Iharaki, Japan; introduced to United States and named in 1985; registered H.S.A. 2-89 and introduced by Brookside Gardens).

Leaves variegated, variable, moderate dark green 137B in center, broad irregular streaks or blotches of light greenish gray 191B margins, irregular and broken streaks of light yellow 10A often extending to midrib; ovate, to 7.4 cm (2⅞ in.) long, 3.9 cm (1¼ in.) wide, bases and apices attenuate, margins entire, distortion of margin due to undevelopment of variegated tissues, petioles strong greenish yellow 151A on both surfaces, 8 mm (5⁄16 in.) long; 1-year twigs strong greenish yellow 151A, 2- to 3-year twigs strong yellow-green 144A; fruits vivid red 45B, globose to slightly truncate, 9.5 mm (⅜ in.) diameter, fasciculate, pedicels 8 mm (5⁄16 in.) long; habit upright to broadly rounded shape, to small tree; hardy in zone 8, thought to be less hardy than species. Six variegated or contorted leaved selections mentioned in classic Japanese publications, *Somuku kiayoshi* 1928, but 'Green Shadow' appears to be different.

Ilex 'Guenter Horstmann' (male; selected seedling of Blue Maid® discontinued 1985; discovered in Guenter Horstmann Nursery, Schneverdingen, Germany; named by H.-G. Buchtmann).

Young leaves bright green, glossy, margins dark bluish green, later dark green; leaves very distinct, partially trifoliate, 1–5 cm (⅜–2 in.) long, 0.5–2 cm (3⁄16–¾ in.) wide, margins undulate, 5–9 small spines on each side, mostly lobate to odd cutlike or tattered pattern, young stems somewhat purplish, stems slightly squarish.

Figure 16-11. *Ilex* 'Guenter Horstmann' from Germany. Photo by Hans-Georg Buchtmann.

Ilex 'Hale' (male; putative seedling of *I.* × *aquipernyi* discovered in nursery in Huntington, West Virginia; selected and registered H.S.A. 3-76 by O. M. Neal; named for the late Randolph Hale, descendant of Nathan Hale).

Leaves dark olive green, narrow-elliptic, to 9.5 cm (3¾ in.) long, 3.8 cm (1½ in.) wide, convex, apices acuminate, tip spines slightly reflexed, margins flat, 2–3 stout spines on each side; conical habit, hardy in zone 4, roots easily. Original tree 3.7 × 1.5 m (12 × 5 ft.) in 15 years.

Ilex 'Harry Gunning' (male; controlled cross of *I. cornuta* (U.S. PI 65860) × *I. ciliospinosa* (U.S. PI 78144); made in 1952 at U.S. Plant Introduction Station, Glenn Dale, Maryland; named and registered H.S.A. 5-69 by W. L. Ackerman and J. L. Creech).

Leaves moderate olive green, oblong, 3.2–4.5 cm (1¼–1¾ in.) long, 1.3 cm (½ in.) wide, bases cuneate, tip spines reflexed, margins convex, 3 spines on each side, petioles 3–5 mm (⅛–3⁄16 in.) long; globular to broadly columnar shape, horizontal branching, 1.6 × 2.3 m (5½ × 7 ft.) wide in 16 years. Good pollinator.

Ilex 'Hohman' (female; (*I. cornuta* × *I. pernyi*) × *I. latifolia*; origin possibly from H. Hohman, Kingsville Nursery, Kingsville, Maryland; plant from McLean Nursery, Towson, Maryland).

Leaves dark olive green, ovate to ovate-elliptic, 6–10 cm (2⅜–4 in.) long, ⅗–4.5 cm (1⅜–1¾ in.)

wide, bases obtuse to rotund, 7–14 small spines on each side, pointing forward, petioles 8 mm (⁵⁄₁₆ in.) long; fruits vivid red 45A, globose, 8 mm (⁵⁄₁₆ in.) diameter; upright pyramidal habit. Plate 191.

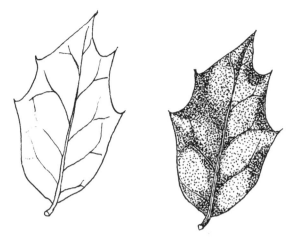

Figure 16-13. *Ilex* 'Hollowell'. Drawing by Randy Allen.

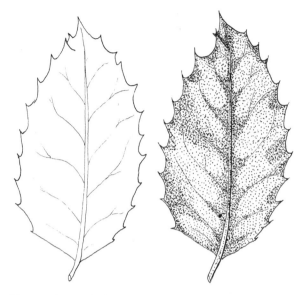

Figure 16-12. *Ilex* 'Hohman'. Drawing by Randy Allen.

Ilex 'Hohman's Weeping' (female; probably *I.* × *aquipernyi* hybrid from H. Hohman; plant at Tom Dodd Nursery, Semmes, Alabama).

Leaves dark green, glossy, ovate-elliptic, keeled, curved, 4–7.5 cm (1⅝–2¾ in.) long, 2.5–3 cm (1–1⅜ in.) wide, bases obtuse to nearly rotund, apices acute, tip spines reflexed, margins slightly wavy, 5–8 irregular spines on each side, petioles 8 mm (⁵⁄₁₆ in.) long; fruits vivid red 44A, globose, 8 mm (⁵⁄₁₆ in.) diameter, 1–4 in fascicles; pyramidal habit, branches slightly drooping.

Ilex 'Hollowell' (male; chance putative seedling of *I. aquifolium* × *I. cornuta* found on estate of E. A. Hollowell; named and registered H.S.A. 1-64 by D. F. Beard).

Leaves dark olive green, broadly elliptic, curved, keeled, 4.5–8 cm (1¾–3⅛ in.) long, 2–3.5 cm (¾–1⅜ in.) wide, bases obtuse to rotund, apices acute, tip spines reflexed, margins convex, 1–3 sharp spines on each side, usually upper half of leaf, petioles 5–6 mm (³⁄₁₆–⁷⁄₃₂ in.) long; stems green, ridged.

Ilex 'Honey Jo' (female; variegated branch mutation on 'Blue Girl'; discovered by E. O. Mills Jr. in 1979 on a plant at Winslows Nursery, Mashpee, Massachusetts; named for honey-colored leaves and for Jo

Ann Gumbert, who accompanied Mills at plant's discovery; registered H.S.A. 1996).

Leaves soft, finely rugose on upper surface, ovate, to 4.5 cm (1¾ in.) long, 2.8 cm (1⅛ in.) wide, margins wavy, with 5–7 short spines pointed forward, keeled, curved, tips aristate, bases cuneate, variegated with no consistent borders or pattern, sometimes blotching centrally located to concentrating at tips or bases, occasionally entire green, attractive greenish yellow 6D to deep yellowish green 141A, on under surface light yellowish green 144D, yellow leaves more intense in full sun; petioles 7 mm (⁹⁄₃₂ in.) long, young branches sometimes purplish; fruits vivid red 44A, globose to 8 mm (⁹⁄₃₂ in.) diameter, borne singly or fasciculate in twos; pedicels 4 mm (⁵⁄₃₂ in.) long. Original plant 10–12 years old, 0.91 m (34 in.) tall, 1.2 m (39.4 in.) wide. New excellent low shrub for accent, small hedge, specimen plant, and in rock garden. Plate 190.

Ilex 'Howard Dorsett' (female; controlled cross of *I. cornuta* (U.S. PI 65860) × *I. ciliospinosa* (U.S. PI 78144); made at U.S. Plant Introduction Station, Glenn Dale, Maryland; named and registered H.S.A. 3-69 by W. L. Ackerman and J. L. Creech).

Leaves moderate olive green, oblong to 10.2 cm (4¼ in.) long, 3.2–3.8 cm (1¼–1½ in.) wide, margins convex, average 4 spines on each side, new growth purplish pink before turning green; fruits red; conical habit, fastigiate branching, 2.3 × 1.25 m (7 × 4½ ft.) wide in 16 years.

Ilex 'Hydra' (sex unknown; synonym CB41; *I. cornuta* 'Burfordii' × *I. pernyi* cross; named and introduced by H. Hohman).

No description available.

Ilex 'Indian Chief' (female; synonym CB19; *I. cornuta* 'Burfordii' × *I. pernyi* cross; named and introduced by H. Hohman).

Leaves dark olive green, glossy, slightly squarish, wide tapered reflexed apical spines, 3–4.5 cm (1³⁄₁₆–1¾ in.) long, 1.6–2.5 cm (½–1 in.) wide, margins convex, usually 2 strong spines on each side, rarely extra small spines, petioles 5 mm (³⁄₁₆ in.) long; fruits vivid red 44A, globose, 8 mm (⁵⁄₁₆ in.) long, 1–3 in clusters, pedicels 3–5 mm (⅛–³⁄₁₆ in.) long; compact pyramidal habit.

Ilex 'Jade' (male; *I.* × *koehneana*; controlled cross of *I. aquifolium* 'Whitney' × *I. latifolia* by W. F. Kosar; named and registered H.S.A. 4-67 by Kosar).

Leaves ovate to broadly elliptic, 7–10 cm (2¾–4 in.) long, 3–4 cm (1³⁄₁₆–1⅝ in.) wide, 13–15 spines on each side; exhibits purple pigmented stem and petioles. Original tree 2.3 m (7 ft.) tall in 9 years. Introduced as pollinator for sibling 'Ruby'.

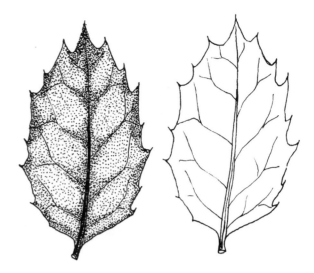

Figure 16-15. *Ilex* 'James Swan'. Drawing by Randy Allen.

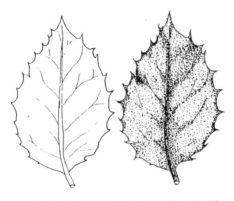

Figure 16-14. *Ilex* 'Jade'. Drawing by Randy Allen.

Ilex 'James Swan' (male; 1 of 6 open-pollinated seedlings of *I. cornuta* 'Burfordii' × *I. latifolia* discovered in 1960 on Swan bakery property by Mrs. E. C. Bruner; named and registered H.S.A. 4-83 by Mrs. Bruner).

Leaves dark olive green, glossy, broadly ovate, to 12 cm (4½ in.) long, 6.7 cm (2⅝ in.) wide, bases rotund to truncate, apices obtuse, tip spines, margins flat to slightly convex, mid-veins depressed above, 8–12 short uniform spines on each side, petioles to 8 mm (⁵⁄₁₆ in.) long; male flowers prominent 28–30 in clusters; upright mounding habit, pendulous branches, original tree 4.3 × 3.4 m (14 × 11 ft.) wide; hardy in zone 7. Popular in southeastern United States. See 'Emily Bruner'.

Ilex 'Jermyns Dwarf' (female; voluntary seedling prior to 1955; reported as putative hybrid seedling

with *I. pernyi* as one parent; named and registered H.S.A. 2-71 by Hillier and Sons Nursery, England).

Leaves long and narrow, 3.2 cm (2¼ in.) long, 2.5 cm (1 in.) wide, bases cuneate, long narrow pointed tip, larger and thinner than *I. pernyi,* margins undulate, 4 spines on each side; fruits red, oblong and depressed to triangulate in cross section; prostrate habit, wider than high. In 16 years 32 cm (13 in.) tall, 1 m (39 in.) wide.

Ilex 'Jersey Globe' (female; synonym #152; *I. opaca* 'Brown #18' × *I. aquifolium*).

Leaves dark green, glossy, elliptic, 3–3.5 cm (1³⁄₁₆–1⅜ in.) long, 1.5–1.7 cm (¹⁹⁄₃₂–²¹⁄₃₂ in.) wide, 3 large lobes, 3 moderate spines on each side, slightly keeled, apex elongated, petioles 5 mm (³⁄₁₆ in.) long; fruits rare, red; very dwarf, mature plant, 14 plus years, 18 cm (7 in.) tall, 20 cm (8 in.) wide. Good rock garden plant, bonsai, and collector's garden. See Jersey Pigmy for more information.

Ilex 'Jersey Jewel' (female; synonym H627-3; *I.* × *aquipernyi* 'San Jose' × (*I.* × *aquipernyi* × 'San Jose' × *I. rugosa*)).

Leaves dark green, glossy, elliptic 2.5–3 cm (1–1³⁄₁₆ in.) long, 1.5–1.7 cm (¹⁹⁄₃₂–²¹⁄₃₂ in.) wide, slightly curved, 2–3 small spines on each side, on upper two-thirds of leaf; petioles 3–5 mm (⅛–³⁄₁₆ in.) long; fruits red, rare; dwarf plant, short stubby growth. Good rock garden plant, bonsai, connoisseur's plant. See Jersey Pigmy for more information.

Ilex 'Jersey Midget' (female; synonym 159; *I. opaca* 'Hedgeholly' × *I. aquifolium*).

Figure 16-16. *Ilex* 'Jersey Globe' (left) and *I.* 'Jersey Sprite' (right). New in 1995. Very slow growing. Photo by Fred Galle.

Figure 16-17. *Ilex* 'Jersey Midget' (left) and *I.* 'Jersey Moppet' (right). New in 1995. Small plants 3 to 5 years old. Photo by Fred Galle.

Leaves moderate dark green, keeled and twisted, elliptic 3–4 cm (1³⁄₁₆–1⅝ in.) long, 1.7–1.8 cm (¹⁹⁄₃₂–¾ in.) wide, curved, 5–6 small to moderate spines on each side, petioles 5 mm (³⁄₁₆ in.) long; fruits red, rare; growth habit, low stout spreading. Good for rock gardens, bonsai, connoisseur's plant. See Jersey Pigmy for more information.

Ilex 'Jersey Moppet' (female; synonym H189; *I. opaca* 'Hedgeholly' × *I. aquifolium*).
Leaves moderate dark green, flat to slightly curved, elliptic, 2–4 cm (¾–1⅝ in.) long, 1.3–2 cm (½–¾ in.) wide, 5–6 moderate spines on each side; petioles 5–6 mm (³⁄₁₆–⁷⁄₃₂ in.) long; fruits red, rare; growth stout, spreading. Good rock garden, bonsai, connoisseur's plant. See Jersey Pigmy for more information; see also Figure 16-17.

Jersey Pigmy Group
A new proposed name, for a group of genetic dwarfs, selected by Elwin R. Orton, Rutgers University, who, in his intensive work in hybridizing hollies, has also selected out dwarfs such as *I. crenata* 'Dwarf Pagoda', *I. crenata* 'Green Dragon' and *I.* 'Rock Garden'. The new dwarfs were first numbered for observation and evaluation. Jim Cross of Environmental Inc., Cutchogue, New York, and the late Don Smith and Hazel, Watnong Nursery, obtained plants in the mid to late 1970s for evaluations. The five plants described here have been selected by Cross and named by Cross and Orton. Orton will register them with the Holly Society of America in 1996.

Ilex 'Jersey Sprite' (female; synonym H1112-17; (*I.* × *aquipernyi* × *I. rugosa*) × *I.* × *aquipernyi* 'Accent').
Leaves dark green, small, broadly elliptic 1.5–1.7 cm (¹⁹⁄₃₂–²¹⁄₃₂ in.) long, 8–10 mm (⁵⁄₁₆–⅜ in.) wide, slightly curved, 3–4 small spines, pointing forward on each side, on upper half of leaf, petioles 3–4 mm

(⅛–⁵⁄₃₂ in.) long; fruits red, rare; very dwarf, old plant 12 in. tall × 24 in. wide. Good rock garden plant, bonsai, a real gem in a collector's garden. See Jersey Pigmy for more information; see also Figure 16-16.

Ilex 'Joe McDaniel' (male; controlled cross of *I.* × *aquipernyi* 'San Jose' × *I. cornuta* 'Cairo' made in 1964 by J. C. McDaniel; selected by McDaniel and J. Bon Hartline; named and registered H.S.A. 3-77 by Hartline).
Leaves dark olive green, glossy, quadrangular, 3.5 cm (1⅜ in.) long, nearly as wide, keeled, margins strongly curved, twisted, 2 deep indented spines near base on each side, occasionally additional small spine near base, tip spines moderate, petioles 3 mm (⅛ in.) long; compact upright habit; hardy to −26°C (−15°F). Original tree 2.1 m (7 ft.) tall, 7.6 cm (2½ ft.) wide in 10 years.

Ilex 'John T. Morris' (male; *I. cornuta* 'Burfordii' × *I. pernyi* cross; made in 1948; named and registered H.S.A. 8-61 by H. Skinner, U.S. PI 267825).
Leaves dark olive green, glossy, slightly squarish, 2.5–4.5 cm (1–1¾ in.) long, 1.8–2.8 cm (¹¹⁄₁₆–1⅛ in.) wide, bases rotund to slightly truncate, apices acute, tip spines reflexed, petioles 3–5 mm (⅛–³⁄₁₆ in.) long; compact upright pyramidal habit; companion to 'Lydia Morris' but larger. Plate 192.

Ilex 'Kurly Koe' (female; synonym 'Whipple No. 1'; putative hybrid seedling of *I.* × *koehneana;* discovered, named, and introduced in 1980s by M. S. Whipple).
Leaves dark olive green, ovate, 10–12 cm (4–4¾ in.) long, reported to 30 cm (more than 11 in.) tall, 4.5–5 cm (1¾–2 in.) wide, bases rotund, margins

wavy to undulate, 10–14 strong spines on each side, petioles 13–15 mm (½–¹⁹⁄₃₂ in.) long; fruits red, globose, fasciculate; upright pyramidal habit.

Ilex 'Lacerta' (female; synonym CB29; *I. cornuta* 'Burfordii' × *I. pernyi* cross; named and introduced by H. Hohman).

Leaves dark olive green, oblong to slightly squarish, 2.5–4 cm (1–1⅝ in.) long, 1.3–2 cm (½–¾ in.) wide, bases truncate, apices long tapered reflexed spines, margins convex, undulate, 2–3 strong spines on each side, occasionally smaller spines, petioles 3–5 mm (⅛–³⁄₁₆ in.) long; fruits vivid red 44A, ellipsoid, 10 mm (⅜ in.) long, 8 mm (⁵⁄₁₆ in.) diameter, 1–5 in clusters, pedicels 3–5 mm (⅛–³⁄₁₆ in.) long; compact pyramidal habit.

Ilex 'Lassie' (female; *I.* × *koehneana*; putative hybrid of *I. aquifolium* × *I. latifolia;* volunteer seedling discovered in McLean Nursery, Towson, Maryland; named and registered H.S.A. 2-70 by S. H. McLean).

Leaves dark olive green, broadly lanceolate, 7–10 cm (2¾–4 in.) long, 3–4 cm (1³⁄₁₆–1⅝ in.) wide, bases obtuse to rotund, apices acuminate, margins flat, 7–12 small spines, pointing forward, petioles 8–10 mm (⁵⁄₁₆–⅜ in.); fruits vivid red 45A, globose, 8 mm (⁵⁄₁₆ in.) diameter, single, abundant, pedicels short; pyramidal habit, horizontal branches. Good female for 'Chieftain'.

Ilex 'Lepux' (female; synonym CB49; *I. cornuta* 'Burfordii' × *I. pernyi* cross; named and introduced by H. Hohman).

Leaves dark olive green, ovate, 2–3.5 cm (¾–1⅜

in.) long, 1.6–2.5 cm (⅝–1 in.) wide, bases truncate, apices acute, tip spines slightly reflexed, 1–4 small spines on each side, petioles 5 mm (³⁄₁₆ in.) long; fruits vivid red 45A, globose, 8 mm (⁵⁄₁₆ in.) diameter; compact habit.

Ilex 'Lib's Favorite' (female; synonym 'Libby's Favorite'; putative hybrid of *I. latifolia* × *I. cornuta*; seedling grown in late 1960s; selected by T. Dodd Jr.; named by T. Dodd and T. R. Dudley for Dodd's wife).

Leaves dark olive green, oval to broadly elliptic, keeled, curved, 5–8 cm (2–3⅛ in.) long, 2–4 cm (¾–1⅝ in.) wide, bases rotund, apices acute, margins with 2–5 small spines on each side, petioles stout, 8–10 mm (⁵⁄₁₆–⅜ in.) long; fruits vivid red 45A, globose, 10–13 mm (⅜–½ in.), fascicles 1–5 in clusters; vigorous compact pyramidal habit.

Ilex Little Red™ (female; Red Holly Hybrid).

Globose habit, responds to shearing, new growth reddish; 3–3.5 m (10–12 ft.) tall.

Ilex 'Live Oak' (female; *I. latifolia* hybrid, plant at Live Oaks Gardens; plant received from U.S. Plant Introduction Station, Glenn Dale, Maryland; Live Oaks Gardens records unavailable; named and introduced by Louisiana Nursery).

Leaves dark olive green, ovate, 6.5–9.5 cm (2½–3¾ in.) long, 3.5–5.5 cm (1⅜–2⅛ in.) wide, bases obtuse to rotund, apices acute, margins with 7–9 spines on each side, petioles 10–16 mm (⅜–⅝ in.) long; fruits red, globose, 8 mm (⁵⁄₁₆ in.) diameter; upright pyramidal habit.

Ilex 'Loch Raven' (male; synonym 'Bill's'; putative hybrid seedling discovered by S. McLean, named by Bill Kuhl).

Leaves dark olive green, ovate-elliptic, 8–10 cm (3⅛–4 in.) long, 2.5–4 cm (1–1¾ in.) wide, bases rotund, apices acute, margins slightly twisted, 12–16 moderate spines on each side, pointing forward, petioles purplish, 10–13 mm (⅜–½ in.) long, stems purplish. Pollinator for 'Lassie'.

Ilex 'Lord' (female; selection of *I. rotunda;* original plant from U.S.D.A. in 1950s, planted in E. L. Lord's property, North Gainesville, Florida).

Leaves dark olive green, oval or broadly elliptic, 6–8.5 cm (2⅜–3⅜ in.) long, 2.5–4 cm (1–1⅝ in.) wide, bases obtuse, apices acute, margins entire, petioles channeled, branchlets purplish brown; fruits vivid red 45B, fasciculate umbellate, 4–15 in clusters, oblate, 5–6 mm (³⁄₁₆–⁷⁄₃₂ in.) long, 4 mm (⁵⁄₃₂ in.) wide; upright broadly spreading habit, pendent branches; hardy in zone 8b.

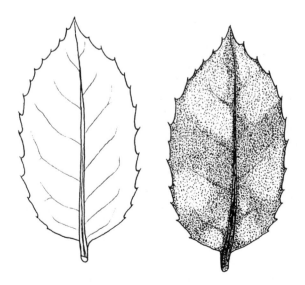

Figure 16-18. *Ilex* 'Lassie'. Drawing by Randy Allen.

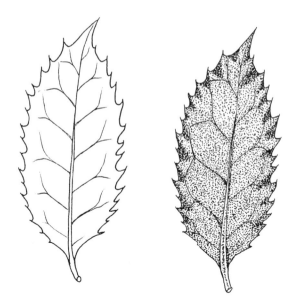

Figure 16-19. *Ilex* 'Loch Raven'. Drawing by Randy Allen.

Ilex 'Lydia Morris' (female; *I. cornuta* 'Burfordii' × *I. pernyi* cross; made in 1948; named and registered 7-61 by H. Skinner, U.S. PI 267824).

Leaves dark olive green, glossy, quadrangular, 2.5–4 cm (1–1⅝ in.) long, 1.6–2.5 cm (⅝–1 in.) wide, bases rotund to truncate, apices acute, tip spines reflexed, margins convex, 2 spines on each side, 1 near base, 1 near apex, occasionally small spines between, petioles 3–5 mm (⅛–³⁄₁₆ in.) long; fruits vivid red 45A, globose to oval, 8–10 mm (⁵⁄₁₆–⅜ in.) diameter, 1–5 in clusters, pedicels 5 mm (³⁄₁₆ in.) long; compact upright pyramidal habit. Plants smaller than 'John T. Morris'.

Ilex 'Lyra' (male; synonym CB23; *I. cornuta* 'Burfordii' × *I. pernyi* cross; named and introduced by H. Hohman).

Leaves dark olive green, glossy, oblong, 3–4.5 cm (1³⁄₁₆–1¾ in.) long, 1.3–2 cm (½–¾ in.) wide, bases rotund, apices acute, tip spines reflexed, margins convex, usually 2 small spines on each side, petioles 3–5 mm (⅛–³⁄₁₆ in.) long; compact pyramidal habit.

Ilex 'Malcolm S. Whipple' (male; putative hybrid of *I. aquifolium* × *I. cornuta;* chance seedling obtained in 1964 by M. S. Whipple; named and registered H.S.A. 7-73 by Whipple).

Leaves dark olive green, glossy, ovate, 4.5–5 cm (1¾–2 in.) long, 2.5–4.5 (1–1¾ in.) wide, bases cuneate to truncate, apices acute, tips spines, margins flat, 2–3 evenly spaced spines on each side; flowers fasciculate, axillary, to 7 flowers in cluster, pedicels 4

mm (⁵⁄₃₂ in.) long; broadly conical habit, original tree 1.7 m (5½ ft.) tall × 1.1 m (3½ ft.) wide; hardy in zone 7.

Ilex 'Mao Hostess' (female; *I.* × *meserveae,* seedling introduced in the 1980s by Hanno Hardijzer B. V., Boskoop, Netherlands).

Leaves dark green; fruits red to bright (vivid) red; upright shrub.

Ilex 'Mao Man' (male; *I.* × *meserveae*; seedling introduced in the 1980s by Hanno Hardijzer B. V., Boskoop, Netherlands).

Leaves fresh (bright) green, margins twisted or undulate; vigorous upright shrub.

Ilex 'Mao Wife' (female; *I.* × *meserveae*; seedling introduced in the 1980s by Hanno Hardijzer B. V., Boskoop, Netherlands).

Leaves fresh (bright) green, margins wavy, undulate; vigorous upright shrub.

Ilex 'Maplehurst' (male; putative hybrid of *I. cornuta* × *I. aquifolium* from seed obtained about 1900 by Nellie R. Stevens from a plant of *I. cornuta* at U.S. National Arboretum; brother seedling to 'Edward J. Stevens' and 'Nellie R. Stevens'; introduced and registered H.S.A. 10-67 by G. A. Van Lennep Jr.).

Leaves dark olive green; slightly more narrow, strongly curved and twisted, giving distinct linear shape, tip spines strongly reflexed.

Ilex 'Martha Berry' (female; *I.* × *koehneana* hybrid, seed collected in 1979 by Tom Dodd III from *I. latifolia* plant at Auburn University Horticulture Greenhouse; propagated by Flowerwood Nursery, Loxley, Alabama; named by Dodd for wife of Jim Berry at Flowerwood Nursery; two plants planted at Auburn University Arboretum entrance; registered in 1993).

Leaves dark olive green, glossy, elliptic to slightly ovate-elliptic, 9–12 cm (3½–4¾ in.) long, 4–5 cm (¾–2 in.) wide, slightly wavy, bases cuneate to ovate, apices cuneate, 16–18 variable, sharp spines, on each side, petioles stout, canaliculate, 12–15 mm (¹⁵⁄₃₂–¹⁹⁄₃₂ in.) long; fruits vivid red, globose, 8–11 mm (⁵⁄₁₆–¹¹⁄₁₆ in.) diameter, persistent, good clusters; compact pyramidal habit. Original plant 5.7–6.1 m (18–20 ft.) tall, 3–3.5 m (10–12 ft.) wide in 12 years. Plate 193.

Ilex 'Mary Nell' (female; controlled cross of (*I. cornuta* 'Burfordii' × *I. pernyi* 'Red Delight') × *I. latifolia* made in 1962 at Tom Dodd Nursery, Semmes, Alabama, by Joe C. McDaniel; selected and named in 1981 by T. H. Dodd Jr., for McDaniel's wife; registered H.S.A. 5-85 by Dodd).

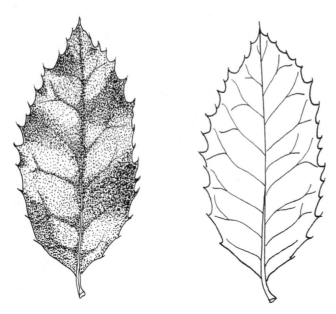

Figure 16-20. *Ilex* 'Martha Berry'. Drawing by Randy Allen.

Leaves dark olive green, glossy, ovate to broadly lanceolate, slightly convex, to 8.5 cm (3½ in.) long, 4.5 cm (1¾ in.) wide, bases rotund, apices acuminate, margins uniformly spined, 8–10 short distinct spines on each side, petioles 10–13 mm (⅜–½ in.) long; fruits vivid red 44A, globose, 8–10 mm (5⁄16–⅜ in.) diameter, abundant; upright pyramidal habit. Popular landscape plant in southeastern United States. Plate 194.

Ilex 'Mary Nell Sibling' (female; young 2-in. seedling, sibling of 'Mary Nell', given to J. Bon Hartline by Joe C. McDaniel, in 1963; named and introduced by Hartline).

Leaves dark olive green, glossy, elliptic to ovate-elliptic, 5–7.5 cm (2–3 in.) long, 2.2–3 cm (13⁄16–1⅜ in.) wide, bases obtuse to slightly rotund, apices acute, margins flat, with 9–14 sharp spines on each side, petioles 8–10 mm (5⁄16–⅜ in.) long, stems brown on top; fruits red, globose, 8–10 mm (5⁄16–⅜ in.) diameter; upright compact, pyramidal habit; not winter hardy in zone 6. Tom Dodd Jr., has grown more than a thousand seedlings of 'Mary Nell', some very similar to the parents, others extremely variable. Many of these have been selected by others and are often labeled and sold as 'Mary Nell Sibling' but should be renamed or listed as 'Mary Nell' seedling.

Ilex 'Mercury' (female; synonym CB3; *I. cornuta* 'Burfordii' × *I. pernyi* cross; named and introduced by H. Hohman).

Leaves moderate olive green, glossy, slightly squarish, 3.5–5 cm (1⅜–2 in.) long, 2.5–3.5 cm (1–1⅜ in.) wide, bases truncate, apices widely acute, tip spines slightly reflexed, margins convex, usually 2 spines on each side, rarely additional spines, petioles 3–5 mm (⅛–3⁄16 in.) long; fruits vivid red 45A, slightly ellipsoid, 8 mm (5⁄16 in.) diameter, 1–4 in clusters, pedicels 6 mm (7⁄32 in.) long; compact broadly pyramidal habit.

Ilex × *meserveae*, see description in Chapter 14.

Ilex 'Meserve No. 3-50' (female; seedling from Holly-by-Golly Nursery around 1950s; seedling of *I.* × *meserveae*).

Leaves dark olive green, glossy, ovate-elliptic, 4–4.5 cm (1⅝–1¾ in.) long, 2–2.5 cm (¾–1 in.) wide, bases rotund, apices acumen, tip spines reflexed, margins undulate, 8–9 spines on each side, petioles 5–8 mm (3⁄16–5⁄16 in.) long; stems green.

Ilex 'Miniature' (female; controlled cross (*I. aquifolium* × *I. cornuta*) 'Nellie R. Stevens' × *I. pernyi*; made in 1961 by W. F. Kosar, National Arboretum No. 28362; selected and named by Kosar; registered H.S.A. 13-91 by G. Eisenbeiss).

Leaves dark green, glossy, almost square-shaped, to 4.5 cm (1¾ in.) long, 1.25 cm (17⁄32 in.) wide, slightly curved and keeled near tips, bases broadly cuneate, 2 stout lateral spines on each margin, tips acute, sometimes reflexed, leaves larger than *I. pernyi*; fruits vivid red 44A, globose to subglobose, 9.5 mm (⅜ in.) diameter, fasciculate 1–4 in each axil, pedicels pinkish, 6.4 mm (¼ in.) long; compact broadly conical habit; hardy to zone 7. Original tree died, 14 years old 1.8 m (6 ft.) tall, 2.4 m (7.9 ft.) wide. Plate 195.

Ilex 'Moon Glow' (female; synonym CB9; *I. cornuta* 'Burfordii' × *I. pernyi* cross; named and introduced by H. Hohman; also listed as 'Moonglow').

Leaves dark olive green, glossy, oblong to slightly squarish, long tapering reflexed tip spines, 4–4.5 cm (1⅝–1¾ in.) long, 1.8–2.5 cm (11⁄16–1 in.) wide, bases rotund to slightly truncate, margins convex, 2 strong spines on each side, occasionally 1–2 small spines near base and on side, petioles 3–5 mm (⅛–3⁄16 in.) long; fruits vivid red 45A, globose, 6–8 mm (7⁄32–5⁄16 in.) diameter, good clusters, pedicels 3 mm (⅛ in.) long; compact upright mounding habit.

Ilex 'Nellie R. Stevens' (female; putative hybrid of *I. cornuta* × *I. aquifolium* from seed obtained about 1900 by Nellie R. Stevens from a plant of *I. cornuta* at U.S. National Arboretum; one of 3 original seedlings (the other 2, both male, were named 'Edward J.

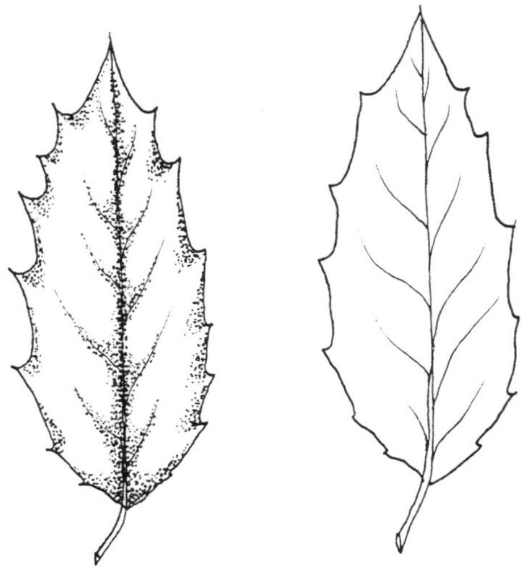

Figure 16-21. *Ilex* 'Mary Nell'. Drawing by Randy Allen.

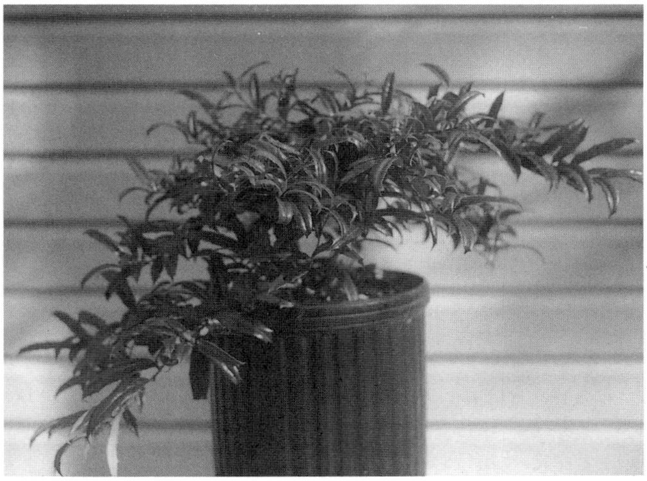

Figure 16-22. Open-pollinated seedling of *Ilex* 'Mary Nell' selected by Tom Dodd; sex unknown; interesting upright arching habit of growth. Photo by Fred Galle.

Stevens' and 'Maplehurst' and grow in garden of "Maplehurst," Oxford, Maryland) observed in 1952; named and introduced in 1954 by G. A. Van Lennep Jr.; registered H.S.A. 8-67 by Van Lennep).

Leaves dark olive green, elliptic to oblong, 7–9 cm (2¾–3½ in.) long, 3–6 cm (1³⁄16–2⅜ in.) wide, bases obtuse to rotund, apices acuminate, tip spines slightly reflexed, margins convex, nearly entire, occasionally 1–2 spines, on upper two-thirds of leaf, veins conspicuously depressed above, petioles 12–16 mm (⅜–⅝ in.) long; fruits vivid red 45A, globose, 8–10 mm (5⁄16–⅜ in.) diameter, 1–3 in cluster; upright broadly pyramidal habit. Original tree more than 88 years old. Popular landscape plant in southeastern United States from the Mid Atlantic South. Plates 196, 197.

Ilex Oak Leaf™ (female; Red Holly Hybrid).

Leaves large; tall pyramidal habit. Plate 198.

Ilex 'Patricia Varner' (female; (Tom Dodd No. 6789913) seedling of *I.* × *aquifolium* × *I. ciliospinosa* 'Brilliant'; grown in 1967 at Tom Dodd Nursery, Semmes, Alabama; selected and named by T. Dodd Jr.).

Leaves dark olive green, glossy, elliptic to broadly elliptic, curved, 2–4 cm (¾–1⅝ in.) long, 1.3–2 cm (½–¾ in.) wide, bases obtuse, apices acute, tip spines reflexed, margins recurved, 1–3 small spines on each side, petioles 3–4 mm (⅛–5⁄32 in.) long; fruits vivid red 45A, globose, 8–10 mm (5⁄16–⅜ in.) diameter, fascicles 1–6 in clusters, pedicels 5–8 cm (3⁄16–5⁄16 in.) long; compact pyramidal habit.

Ilex 'Patrick Smith' (male; seedling of *I. cornuta* × *I. latifolia*; named and introduced by H. Elmore in 1995).

Leaves similar to those of 'Bessie Smith'; upright pyramidal habit. Good pollinator for *I.* × *koehneana* hybrids.

Ilex 'Pendleton Miller' (male; seedling *I.* × *meserveae* from private garden in Japan received about 1980 by Mrs. P. Miller among dwarf oak seedlings; named for husband of Elisabeth C. Miller; registered H.S.A. 2-90 by Mrs. Miller; introduced by Briggs Nursery in 1992).

Leaves dark green, narrow to broadly ovate, to 6 cm (2⅜ in.) long, to 3.8 cm (1½ in.) wide, dorsal surface distinctly rugose, bases cuneate, apices aristate, tip spines reflexed, almost mucronate, margins wavy, 9–11 soft forward pointed spines on each side, petioles 6.4 mm (¼ in.) long, prominently grooved; dwarf prostate habit. Original plant 45.5 cm (1½ ft.) tall, 2.4 m (8 ft.) wide.

Ilex 'Pernella' (female; putative hybrid of (*I. cornuta* × *I. pernyi*) × *I. aquifolium;* chance seedling discovered about 1976 by Mrs. J. W. Hill; plant moved in 1984 to Styers Nursery, Concorville, Pennsylvania; named and registered H.S.A. 4-84 by Mrs. Hill).

Leaves dark olive green, broadly ovate, stiff, to 6 cm (2⅜ in.) long, 3.5 cm (1⅜ in.) wide, curved, keeled, bases sometimes truncate, apices acute, tip spines long, and stout, margins with 3 sharp spines on each side, petioles 5 mm (3⁄16 in.) long; fruits deep reddish orange 43A, globose, 13 mm (½ in.) diameter, 3 in fascicles, pedicels 5 mm (3⁄16 in.) long; upright conical habit; hardy in zone 6b. Original plant 1.5 m (5 ft.) tall, 0.92 m (3 ft.) wide.

Ilex 'Phoenix' (sex unknown; synonym CB47; *I. cornuta* 'Burfordii' × *I. pernyi* cross; named and introduced H. Hohman).
No information available.

Ilex 'Pyris' (sex unknown; synonym CB4; *I. cornuta* 'Burfordii' × *I. pernyi* cross; named and introduced by H. Hohman).
No information available.

Ilex 'Red Delight' (female; synonym CB10; *I. cornuta* 'Burfordii' × *I. pernyi* cross; named and introduced by H. Hohman).
Leaves dark olive green, glossy, slightly squarish, 2.5–4.5 cm (1–1¾ in.) long, 1.6–2.5 cm (⅝–1 in.) wide, bases rotund to truncate, apices wide acute, tip spines reflexed, margins convex, 2–3 spines on each side, petioles 3–5 mm (⅛–³⁄₁₆ in.) long; fruits vivid red 44A, globose, 8 mm (⁵⁄₁₆ in.) diameter, 1–5 in heavy clusters, pedicels 3 mm (⅛ in.) long; compact broadly pyramidal habit.

Red Holly Hybrids
A new group of open-pollinated seedlings of 'Mary Nell'; selected by Mitch Magee in Poplarville, Mississippi; made in 1980s; to be introduced by Evergreen Nursery and Flowerwood Nursery in 1994 or 1995. Includes Cardinal™, Festive™, Little Red™, Oak Leaf™, and Robin™.

Ilex 'Red Princess' (sex unknown; synonym CB48, *I. cornuta* 'Burfordii' × *I. pernyi* cross; named and introduced by H. Hohman).
No description available.

Ilex 'Red Robe' (female; synonym CB17; *I. cornuta* 'Burfordii × *I. pernyi* cross; named and introduced by H. Hohman).
Leaves dark olive green, slightly squarish to quadrangular, 3.5–4.5 cm (1⅜–1¾ in.) long, 1.6–2 cm (⅝–¾ in.) wide, bases truncate, apices long tapered, reflexed spines, margins convex, usually 2 spines on each side, top spines 3 cm (1³⁄₁₆ in.) across, petioles 5 mm (³⁄₁₆ in.) long; fruits vivid red 45A, globose, 8–10 mm (⁵⁄₁₆–⅜ in.) diameter, 1–3 in cluster, pedicels 5 mm (³⁄₁₆ in.) long; compact broadly pyramidal habit.

Ilex River Queen™ (female; 'Wyeriv' is PP name, discovered by N. G. Fischer in 1972 at Wye Nursery, Hillsboro, Maryland, PP No. 8793, putative hybrid of (*I. aquifolium* × *I. cornuta*) 'Nellie R. Stevens × *I. cornuta*).
Leaves evergreen, dark green 139A, 6.2–6.8 cm

(2⅜–2⅝ in.) long, 2.3–5 cm (¾–1⅜ in.) wide, broadly elliptic, slightly convex, apical spine 2 mm (¹⁄₁₆ in.) long, turned downward margins, to 4 very small spines on each side; fruits red 44A, oblate-globose, 7–8 mm (⁹⁄₃₂–⁵⁄₁₆ in.) wide, 10–12 mm (⅜–¹⁵⁄₃₂ in.) diameter, in clusters, ripens early, mid October, persists through February–March; upright, broad, mounding habit; hardy in zone 6, 21–24°C (−5 to −10°F) with minimal stem damage, hardier than *I. cornuta* cultivars. Good for foundation plantings and thick hedges or screens. A 15-year-old tree, 3 m (10 ft.) tall, 2.5 m (8 ft.) wide, is estimated to reach an ultimate height of 3–4.6 m (10–15 ft.) tall. Plate 199.

Ilex Robin™ (female; Red Holly Hybrid).
Leaves similar to those of 'Nellie R. Stevens', new growth reddish.

Ilex 'Rock Garden' (female; controlled cross of *I.* × *aquipernyi* × (*I. integra* × *I. pernyi* 'Accent'); made in 1971 by E. R. Orton Jr.; selected, named, and introduced in 1984; registered H.S.A. 1-88 by Orton).
Leaves moderate olive green, elliptic to broadly elliptic, 3–4.2 cm (1³⁄₁₆–1¹¹⁄₁₆ in.) long, 1.1–1.7 cm (⁷⁄₁₆–²¹⁄₃₂ in.) wide, slightly keeled, curved, bases cuneate, apices acute, margins 3–4 very small spines on each side, petioles 5–7 mm (³⁄₁₆–⁹⁄₃₂ in.) long; fruits red, globose, 6–8 mm (⁷⁄₃₂–⁵⁄₁₆ in.) diameter, creased vertically, compact clusters, pedicels 3 mm (⅛ in.) long; dense, low spreading habit; hardy in zone 6a. Original plant 36 cm (14 in.) tall, 55 cm (22 in.) wide in 14 years. One of first true dwarf compact hollies, excellent for rock gardens, facing plants, and bonsai. For other unnamed miniature hollies from E. R. Orton, see Table 15 in Chapter 20. Plate 200.

Ilex 'Romal' (male; selection of *I. rotunda,* plant from U.S.D.A. not a hybrid in 1950s, original plant at Glen Saint Mary Nursery, Glen Saint Mary, Florida:
Leaves dark olive green, oval 5–8.5 cm (2–3⅜ in.) long, 3–5 cm (1³⁄₁₆–2 in.) wide, margins entire, bases

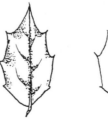

Figure 16-23. *Ilex* 'Rock Garden'. Drawing by Randy Allen.

obtuse, apices acute, petioles channeled; upright broadly spreading habit; hardy in zone 8b. Good pollinator for 'Lord'.

Ilex 'Rosendo' (male; discovered 1982 in a mixed bed of (?) Blue hollies by Rosendo Avila at Monrovia Nursery, Azusa, California; possibly a sport of 'Blue Boy'; plant patent pending).

Leaves dark olive green, ovate, glossy, 2.8–3.2 cm (1⅛–1¼ in.) long, 1.3–1.7 cm (½–11/16 in.) wide; bases obtuse to rotund, apex curved, 10–11 teeth on each side, soft texture, petioles dark, 4–5 mm (5/32–3/16 in.) long, stems purplish; flower buds pink open to white; dwarf compact plant. Original plant 0.5–0.6 m (19–24 in.) tall, 0.6–0.92 m (24–36 in.) wide. In a block of 1000 three-gallon plants, approximately 10 had scattered red fruits. Excellent for container or low hedge.

Ilex 'Ruby' (female; *I.* × *koehneana* controlled cross made in 1958 of *I. aquifolium* 'Whitney' × *I. latifolia* by W. F. Kosar; named and registered H.S.A. 3-67 by Kosar).

Leaves dark olive green, ovate, 6.5–8 cm (2½–3⅛ in.) long, 3–4.5 cm (1 3/16–1¾ in.) wide, keeled, bases obtuse to rotund, apices acute, margins flat to slightly wavy, 8–14 spines on each side, petioles 10–12 mm (⅜–15/32 in.) long, petioles and stems purplish on outer surface; fruits red, 10–12 in fascicles ripen early December; compact pyramidal habit. Plate 201.

Ilex 'San Jose' (female; *I.* × *aquipernyi* origin of plant and name unknown, possibly a Henry Skinner hybrid but never verified; not to be confused with 'San Jose' below).

Leaves dark olive green, ovate to broadly elliptic, 4–5 cm (1⅝–2 in.) long, 2–2.5 cm (¾–1 in.) wide, keeled, curved, bases rotund to truncate, apices tapered to long spine, 2–3 spines on each side, upper two-thirds of leaf, petioles 4–8 mm (5/32–5/16 in.) long, stems green; fruits vivid red 44A, ellipsoid, 10 mm (⅜ in.) long, 8 mm (5/16 in.) diameter, single to fasciculate, pedicels slightly reddish, 5 mm (3/16 in.) long; upright pyramidal habit; hardy in zone 6b.

Ilex 'San Jose' (female; first reported as a putative hybrid of *I.* × *altaclerensis* 'Wilsonii' × *I. sikkimensis;* introduced in 1940s by W. B. Clarke; later identified as *I.* × *koehneana*).

Leaves dark olive green, elliptic to broadly elliptic, slightly keeled, 5–12 cm (4¾ in.) long, 2.5–5.5 cm (1–2⅛ in.) wide, bases cuneate to obtuse, apices acute, tip spines often twisted, margins slightly wavy, 9–12 spines on each side, petioles 12–16 mm (15/32–⅝ in.) long; fruits vivid red 45A, globose, in fascicles 3–10 in clusters, pedicels 8–10 mm (5/16–⅜ in.) long; broadly pyramidal habit; hardy in zone 7b.

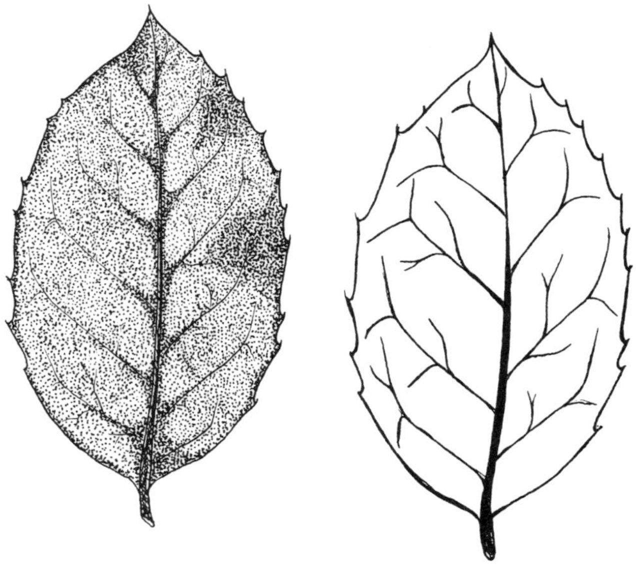

Figure 16-24. *Ilex* 'Ruby'. Drawing by Randy Allen.

Ilex 'Scepter' (female; U.S. National Arboretum No. 28237, U.S. PI 578191 originated from a controlled cross of *I. integra* (U.S. National Arboretum No. 3245); plant received from Washington Park Arboretum × *I.* × *altaclerensis* 'Hodginsii', U.S. National Arboretum No. 10891, U.S. PI 231703 (scions received from W. Fromow and Sons, Windlesham, Surrey, England); cross was made in 1960 at the U.S. National Arboretum by W. F. Kosar, who also made the initial selection as pedigree number K60-20-18 in 1968; final selection and naming by G. Eisenbeiss in 1993).

Leaves dark green, broadly ovate, to 8 cm (3⅛ in.) long, 1–4 cm (⅜–1⅝ in.) wide slightly curved and keeled, bases cuneate, tips aristate, short tip spines, sometimes twisted, margins mostly entire, occasionally 1–4 inconspicuous, short, spines on each side, upper half of leaves, petioles 1 cm (⅜ in.) long; fruits vivid reddish orange 41A, globose, to 1 cm in diameter, borne fasciculate in clusters of 2–10 in leaf axil of previous season's growth, pedicels 1 cm (⅜ in.) long; hardy in zone 7. Original plant 16 years old, 6 m (20 ft.) tall, 4.5 m (14½ ft.) wide. Plant compatible with many species. Selection based on vigorous, pyramidal, compact habit, with large soft leaves, generally spineless. Plate 202.

Ilex 'Security' (female; synonym CB11; *I. cornuta* 'Burfordii' × *I. pernyi* cross; named and introduced by H. Hohman).

Leaves dark olive green, glossy, slightly squarish to oblong, 2–4 cm (¾–1⅝ in.) long, 1.3–2 cm (½–¾ in.) wide, bases rotund to slightly truncate, apices acute, tip spines reflexed, margins convex, usually 2 strong spines on each side, occasionally 1–2 additional small spines on each side, petioles 3–5 mm (⅛–³⁄₁₆ in.) long; fruits vivid red 45A, globose, 6–8 mm (⁷⁄₃₂–⁵⁄₁₆ in.) diameter, 1–3 in clusters, pedicels 2–3 mm (¹⁄₁₆–⅛ in.) long; compact habit.

Ilex 'Semala' (female; hybrid × *I. integra* × *I. cornuta*; cross made by Joe C. McDaniel at Tom Dodd Nursery, Semmes, Alabama, in late 1970s or early 1980s; selected and evaluated by T. Dodd Jr.; named and registered H.S.A. 4-85 by Dodd).

Leaves dark olive green, elliptic to ovate, slightly keeled, curved, 5.8–8.1 cm (2¼–3¼ in.) long, 3.2–3.8 (1¼–1½ in.) wide, tip spines reflexed, 1 small spine on each side near apex, occasionally 1–3 very small unindentated spines on upper one-third of leaf, petioles 6.5 mm (¼ in.) long; fruits vivid reddish orange 42A, subglobose, 5 mm (³⁄₁₆ in.) long, 8 mm (⁵⁄₁₆ in.) diameter, depressed stigmas, in fascicles 1–4 in clusters, pedicels 5 mm (³⁄₁₆ in.) long; broadly pyramidal, vigorous compact habit; hardy in zone 7.

Ilex 'September Gem' (female; controlled cross of *I. ciliospinosa* × *I.* × *aquipernyi* made in 1957 by W. F. Kosar; named and registered H.S.A. 1-78 by Kosar).

Leaves dark olive green, glossy, elliptic, slightly keeled, 5–7 cm (2–2¾ in.) long, 1.3–2 cm (½–¾ in.) wide, bases obtuse, apices tapered to sharp spines, margins curved, 3–4 spines on each side, petioles 8–10 mm (⁵⁄₁₆–⅜ in.) long; fruits vivid reddish orange 44B, globose, 8–10 mm (⁵⁄₁₆–⅜ in.) diameter, ripen early in September, persist; pedicels 8–10 mm (⁵⁄₁₆–⅜ in.) long; compact, upright pyramidal habit; hardy in zone 7a. Noted for early ripened red fruit. Plate 203.

Ilex 'Sextans' (sex unknown; synonym CB40; *I. cornuta* 'Burfordii' × *I. pernyi* cross; named and introduced by H. Hohman).

No description available.

Ilex 'Shin Nien' (male; synonym 'New Year'; reputed controlled cross of *I. opaca* 'Chief Paduke' × *I. cornuta* made in 1966 by Joe C. McDaniel; registered H.S.A 2-74 by McDaniel; first cultivar named from this species combination; new study needed to verify parentage as plant shows no characters of *I. opaca*).

Leaves dark olive green, glossy, elliptic, to 6.5 cm (2½ in.) long, 3.8 cm (1½ in.) wide, margins undulate, 5–8 strong spines on each side, tip spines reflexed; pollen viable, inflorescences fasciculate like *I.*

Figure 16-25. *Ilex* 'September Gem'. Drawing by Randy Allen.

cornuta but fewer in number; hardy to −18°C (0°F). Original plant 1.2 m (4 ft.) tall, 0.76 m (2½ ft.) wide in 7 years. See *Holly Society of America Letter* 39.

Ilex 'Sid Burns' (male; open-pollinated seedling, putative parentage of *I.* × *aquipernyi* 'San Jose × *I.* × *aquipernyi* 'Gable's Male'; original plant dead, selected from 60 plus seedlings; named and registered H.S.A. 4-92 by R. Emmerich, H. C. Gehnrich, and R. Murcott; named for founder and president of the first chapter of the Holly Society—started on Long Island, New York).

Leaves dark olive green, lanceolate, curved, slightly keeled, more typical of *I. pernyi*, 3.3 cm (1⁵⁄₁₆ in.) long, 2 cm (¾ in.) wide, bases broadly cuneate, tips broadly aristate, margins with 3 strong, finely tipped evenly spaced spines on each side; 15 year plant, compact, very dwarf, globose habit, 45 cm (18 in.) tall, 62.5 cm (24¼ in.) wide; hardy in zone 7.

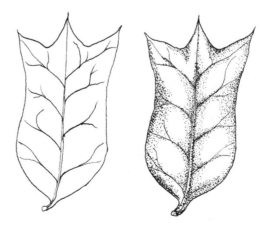

Figure 16-26. *Ilex* 'Shin Nien'. Drawing by Randy Allen.

Ilex 'Starlight' (sex unknown; synonym CB32, *I. cornuta* 'Burfordii' × *I. pernyi* cross; named and introduced by H. Hohman).
No description available.

Ilex 'Taurus' (male; synonym CB45; *I. cornuta* 'Burfordii' × *I. pernyi* cross; named and introduced by H. Hohman).
No description available.

Ilex 'Titan' (female; synonym CB6; *I. cornuta* 'Burfordii' × *I. pernyi* cross; named and introduced by H. Hohman).
Leaves dark olive green, glossy, quadrangular, to slightly squarish, 2.5–3.5 cm (1–1⅜ in.) long, 1.3–1.8 cm (½–11/16 in.) wide, bases rotund to truncate, apices acute, top spines reflexed, margins convex, 2–4 spines on each side, petioles 3–4 mm (⅛–5/32 in.) long; compact mounding habit.

Ilex 'Tom Dodd Hybrid' (sex unknown; temporary name for selection of 'Mary Nell' seed grown in mid 1980s by T. Dodd).
Leaves dark olive green, new spring leaves brownish, 7–8 cm (2¾ in.) long, 1.5–1.8 cm (19/32–⅝ in.) wide, glossy, 3–5 small spines on each side, petioles 5 mm (3/16 in.) long; upright arching habit. Could prune to 0.9–1.2 m (3–4 ft.) high.

Ilex 'Venus' (female; controlled cross of (*I. aquifolium* × *I. cornuta*) 'Nellie R. Stevens' × *I. latifolia* by W. F. Kosar, U.S. National Arboretum No. 28358; selected and named by F. S. Santamour and G. Eisenbeiss; registered H.S.A. 8-91 by Eisenbeiss; sister seedling to 'Adonis').
Leaves dark green, slightly convex, ovate, to 13 cm (5⅛ in.) long, 6.5 cm (2⅜ in.) wide, bases cuneate, apex obtuse, tips slightly turned down, margins to 13 very uniform, short, blunt and prominent, but not incised spines on each side, petioles to 2 cm (¾ in.) long; fruits vivid red 45 B, glossy, slightly elongate, 11 mm (7/16 in.) long, 9 mm (11/32 in.) diameter, fasciculate usually 14 in cluster, to 50 in mass around stems, fruits larger and more glossy than those of *I. latifolia,* persistent until next season, pedicels to 11 mm (7/16 in.) long; broadly pyramidal habit, single or multistemmed; hardy in zone 7. The 29-year-old plant is 6.1 m (20 ft.) tall, 5.4 m (17¾ ft.) wide. Plate 204.

Ilex 'Virgo' (male; synonym CB22; *I. cornuta* 'Burfordii' × *I. pernyi* cross; named and introduced by H. Hohman).
Leaves dark olive green, glossy, slightly squarish, long tapered reflexed tip spines, 3–4.5 cm (1 3/16–1¾ in.) long, 1.3–2 cm (½–¾ in.) wide, bases truncate, margins usually 2 strong spines on each side, top spines to 3 cm (1 3/16 in.) across, petioles 3–5 mm (⅛–3/16 in.) long; compact broadly pyramidal habit.

Ilex 'Vleck' (female; selection of *I. pedunculosa* discovered in garden of Bessie Vleck in Cleveland, Ohio; named and introduced by H. Elmore; to be registered by Elmore).
Leaves and habit similar to the species; selected for hardiness in Cleveland, Ohio (zone 5).

Ilex 'Washington' (female; hybrid of *I. cornuta* (U.S. PI 65860) × *I. ciliospinosa* (U.S. PI 78144); cross made in 1952 at U.S. Plant Introduction Station, Glenn Dale, Maryland; named and introduced in the Netherlands from seedlings (B515?) sent from Glenn Dale).
Leaves dark olive green, glossy, elliptic, 4–6 cm (1⅝–2⅜ in.) long, 2–3 cm (¾–1 3/16 in.) wide, 2–3 spines on each side; fruits dark red, globose, 8 mm (5/16 in.) diameter; pyramidal habit.

Ilex 'Whipple Seedling No. 5' (female; open-pollinated seedling, possibly of *I.* × *altaclerensis,* discovered by M. Whipple in his garden in 1980s; name pending).
Leaves dark olive green, ovate-oval, 5.5–7.5 cm (2⅛–3 in.) long, 4 cm (1⅝ in.) wide, bases truncate, apices acuminate, tip spines reflexed, margins undulate, 4–5 widely spaced spines on each side, petioles 7–10 mm (9/32–⅜ in.) long, stems purple; fruits red, globose, 8–10 mm (5/16–⅜ in.) diameter.

Ilex 'Wieman's Oriental Queen' (female; putative hybrid of *I.* × *aquipernyi*; chance seedling discovered about 1970 by J. Wieman in his nursery; named and registered H.S.A. 7-84 by Wieman).
Leaves dark olive green, glossy, broadly ovate, to 5 cm (2 in.) long, 3.5 cm (1⅜ in.) wide, keeled, curved, bases truncate, apices acute, tip spines reflexed, margins undulate, 3–4 large spines on each side, petioles 6.5 mm (¼ in.) long; fruits deep reddish orange 43A, globose, 10 mm (⅜ in.) diameter, fasciculate 1–4 in clusters, pedicels 6.5 mm (¼ in.) long; columnar, pointed habit; reported heat tolerant. Original tree 3.7 m (12 ft.) tall, 2.1 m (7 ft.) wide.

Ilex 'Wieman's Pacific Queen' (female; putative hybrid of *I.* × *aquipernyi;* chance seedling discovered about 1970 by J. Wieman in nursery of C. F. Moyer, Roseburg, Oregon; moved to Wieman Nursery, Portland, Oregon; named and registered H.S.A. 6-84 by Wieman).
Leaves dark olive green, glossy, ovate to ovate-lanceolate, curved, to 4.8 cm (1⅞ in.) long, 2.8 cm

(1⅛ in.) wide, bases cuneate to truncate, tip spines reflexed and occasionally twisted, margins flat to slightly keeled, 4–5 large, strong spines on each side, petioles 5 mm (³⁄₁₆ in.) long; fruits vivid reddish orange 43A, globose, 10 mm (⅜ in.) diameter, fasciculate 1–3 in clusters, pedicels 8 mm (⁵⁄₁₆ in.) long; compact columnar habit; reportedly heat tolerant. Original tree 3 m (10 ft.) tall, 1.7 m (5 ft.) wide.

Ilex 'Willburg' (male; *I.* × *aquipernyi* from McLean Nursery, Towson, Maryland, in 1970s).

Leaves dark olive green, obovate, 3.5–4 cm (1⅜–1⅝ in.) long, 1–1.5 cm (⅜–¹⁹⁄₃₂ in.) wide, bases rotund to truncate, tip spines reflexed, margins with 3–4 spines on each side.

Ilex 'William Cowgill' (female; *I. cornuta* (U.S. PI 65860) × *I. ciliospinosa* (U.S. PI 78144); cross made in 1952 at U.S. Plant Introduction Station, Glenn Dale, Maryland; named and registered H.S.A. 2-69 by W. L. Ackerman and J. L. Creech).

Leaves moderate olive green, elliptic to oblong, 3–4.5 cm (1³⁄₁₆–1¾ in.) long, 1.6–2 cm (⅝–¾ in.) wide, bases rotund, apices acuminate, tip spines reflexed, margins convex, slightly undulate, 3 spines on each side, petioles 3–5 mm (⅛–³⁄₁₆ in.) long; fruits vivid red 45A, globose, fasciculate, abundant, pedicels 3–5 mm (⅛–³⁄₁₆ in.) long; conical habit, horizontal branching. Plant 1.8 × 1.3 m (6 × 4½ ft.) wide in 16 years.

Ilex 'Wirt L. Winn' (female; putative hybrid of *I.* × *koehneana* seedling in Winn's nursery; named and registered H.S.A. 5-66 by W. Winn; described by T. R. Dudley and G. Eisenbeiss).

Leaves dark olive green, oblong elliptic, 7–10 cm (2¾–4 in.) long, 3–4.5 cm (1³⁄₁₆–1¾ in.) wide, bases obtuse to rotund, tip spines reflexed, margins flat to slightly wavy, 8–12 small spines on each side, petioles stout, 10–13 mm (⅜–½ in.) long, stems dark green; fruits vivid red 45A, globose, 8–10 mm (⁵⁄₁₆–⅜ in.) diameter; broadly pyramidal habit. Very good plant. Plate 205.

◆ PART IV

CHAPTER 17

Planting and Care of Hollies

Hollies are adapted to a wide range of acidic soils from heavy loam to sandy soils. Soil pH can range from 5.5 to 7.0, with 6.0 being ideal. Hollies do not require as much acidity as azaleas or rhododendrons, but will adapt and are good companion plants. They are best in light humus loam that is well drained, so heavy clay soils will require provisions for draining and additional humus. Sandy soil, too, requires additional humus.

Soil tests are important for new plantings and should be taking annually for the first couple of years and then every five years unless fertilizer problems occur. Soil tests can be taken at any season, but for quick results and to avoid the rush, take samples in the fall or very early spring. To obtain a chemical analysis of soil nutrients and pH, collect soil samples from at least 3 to 10 locations on the site. Use a soil probe in planting beds, getting samples 4 to 6 inches below the surface. One or two tablespoons of soil from each location is sufficient. Mix the samples together for the test. If you have different soil types in your garden, be sure to test each area separately. Send the test sample(s) to your local County Agent (who can also test the chemicals in your water if you send a water sample) or to a soil laboratory with specific instructions regarding the analysis needed and the type of plants to be grown. Most laboratories do not evaluate nitrogen levels unless specifically requested.

The test report will indicate if lime- or acid-forming materials are needed to adjust the pH of your soil. To lower the pH, add ground sulfur (flowers of sulfur) or ferrous sulfate, but not aluminum sulfate. Approximately 1.5 pounds of ground sulfur per 100 square feet mixed into the soil will lower the pH 0.5 point (e.g., from 6.0 to 5.5). Sandy soils will require less sulfur, 0.5 pounds per 100 square feet, while heavy clay soils may require up to 3 pounds or a mixture of equal parts of sulfur and ferrous sulfate.

Soils below a pH of 5.0 may indicate low levels of calcium and magnesium for plant growth. Adding lime or calcium carbonate will raise the pH. If magnesium is low adding dolomite (about 20 percent calcium and 10 percent magnesium carbonate) will raise the pH. Occasionally gypsum (calcium sulfate) is required if the calcium is low and the pH is relatively high (5.5 to 6.0). Adding gypsum will have little effect on the soil pH, but will increase the calcium and not tie up the micronutrients.

Soil testing kits are available for home use, but the results can often be misleading, due to deterioration of the chemical reagents. It is best to send samples to a lab.

Drainage is of major importance no matter what the soil type. A simple test can be done to check the internal soil drainage. Dig a hole 10 to 12 inches deep, fill it with water twice in the same day, and check the water level 24 hours after the last filling. If water is still present in the hole, extra drainage must be provided.

The newest recommendation from many universities regarding the planting of trees and shrubs is to NOT add or mix soil amendments with the backfill soil. This is CONTRARY to the old practice of adding peat moss, shredded pine bark, or other organic materials to the backfill soil before planting. The key, from my perspective, is to have "good field soil." If, however, the soil at your site is poor, add soil amendments or replace the existing soil. Check with your local County Agent if you have any questions on your soil and revise or adjust their recommendations to fit your site. From personal experience planting on an old, abandoned farm site covered with a mix of pines and hardwoods and a very shallow top soil, I have found that adding soil amendments to the backfill soils brings good success.

In preparing a site for a group of plants, whether a row for a hedge or a circular planting, rototill the entire area before digging individual holes. Incorporate fertilizer in the soil during the soil preparation. All planting holes should be at least three times as large as the root ball or container plant and only as deep as the root ball. Whether the hole is round or square is a matter of personal preference. Some gardeners feel that square holes reduce the circling of root growth. The bottom of the planting hole should be firm (not tamped) to keep the ball from sinking after planting. Back fill with the local soil or an amended soil and firm (but not compact) it by stamping with your feet or pressing down with a shovel handle. It is important to support the plant with fill soil but not compact the soil around the root ball. Soil aeration is important for active root growth.

Most hollies today are grown in containers from one to fifteen gallons or larger. The plants must be removed from the container before planting. If the plants are balled-in-burlap, the burlap or plastic wrap should be removed from around the side of the ball along with the binding rope. If the ball is wrapped with a close-knit wire, the wire should be removed or cut off to prevent any root girdling later.

Before planting, all container-grown plants should be checked for root girdling or circling of roots inside the container. With a small hand tool, screw driver, or closed hand pruners, rake or tease the ball lightly to pull out the circling roots. Do not cut the base of the root ball in two or more sections to flair the roots, as is sometimes recommended; this is harsh treatment and a good way to kill plants. Check the root at the bottom of container-grown plant and separate or spread out the individual roots. The first inch or two of soil near the top of the container often has no roots and can be removed before planting. Plant immediately, and do not allow the roots to dry out.

Water hollies thoroughly after planting and repeat in several hours; this settles the soil around the root ball and eliminates air pockets. Proper watering is critical in establishing new plantings. Take care not to drown the roots. Water weekly the first year, based on rainfall received. If drainage is slow, excessive watering may be detrimental. It is helpful to build a small rim around the plants to catch and hold water; a rim is especially helpful when planting on a slope but be sure to build it on the lower side.

Fertilize hollies with a slow-release material or, if phosphorus, potash, and other slow-leaching amendment were added to the backfill soil (because a soil test indicated they were needed), fertilize only with a slow-release nitrogen. The standard recommendation for fertilizer is one pound of nitrogen per 900 square meters (1000 square feet) of soil surface. If you use a 30-percent formulation of nitrogen, this is about three pounds of material per 1000 square feet of surface.

I usually fertilize young and newly planted hollies for several years until firmly established with a 2–1–1 fertilizer mix containing 10 to 12 percent nitrogen. I fertilize in late February or early March using 1 lb per caliper inch, spreading the dry fertilizer by hand 60–90 cm (2–3 ft.) or more around the shrub. Plants often require a second application of fertilizer around midsummer at half strength. Heavily fruited plants will benefit in late summer with a light application of urea to reduce the yellowing of the foliage and retain a good green color.

Super adsorbents or hydrogels are commercially available as an aid in planting. They hold 50 times more water than peat moss and up to 200 to 5000 times their own weight. While these materials are great to play with, I have found no visible evidence that they aid in transplanting or as a root dip. Tests conducted at many universities have gotten similar negative results. Having a regular watering schedule of one inch of water per week will give better results.

Use a well-aerated mulch, such as ground pine bark, shredded leaves, or pine straw, over the exposed soil. Both peat moss and rotted saw dust tend to cake over and shed water when dry, thus they are better mixed in the soil as an amendment. Apply 5 to 10 cm (2 to 4 in.) of organic material. Porous weed barriers can be applied under the mulch, but do not use black or clear plastic materials. Mulching has many good benefits such as protecting the root ball, conserving moisture, and controlling soil temperatures. When used to excess, however, a "grave yard mulching" of 25 cm (10 in.) or more is unattractive and wasteful of good mulch and can be damaging to the base of the plant.

Container-grown plants can be planted year-round in many areas, and fall planting is popular. For the southeastern and northwestern parts of the United States, this means late September through mid-November. For the midwestern and northeastern parts of the country, hollies should be planted a month or more before the ground begins to freeze (i.e., September through October). Again, check with your County Agent or with the horticultural department of your state university about fall planting.

Small seedling hollies can be transplanted bare root. Seedlings usually have a tap root and very few lateral roots, but grown plants have a deep tap root and should be dug and planted immediately. For best success, cut off a portion of the tap root, prune or cut back some of the branches, and reduce the leaf surface by cutting the leaves in half. Wrap bare roots in wet burlap, then place them in plastic bags, and store in a cool location if they cannot be planted immediately.

Larger hollies also can be successfully transplanted (Plate 206). In the early 1960s we moved more than 80 large trees of *Ilex cornuta* 'Burfordii' at Callaway Gardens, Pine Mountain, Georgia, to make room for a new road. Each tree was 2.8–3 m (8–12 ft.) tall and had a 1.5- to 8-m (5- to 6-ft.) wide root ball. The trees were given a moderate to heavy rejuvenation pruning, and the rounded masses of bare branches resembled "coatracks" or "hatracks" (see Chapter 18, "Pruning Hollies", for more details on this type of pruning).

CHAPTER 18

Pruning Hollies

Pruning is an important part of the proper care of hollies. Although it is not required annually, it is just as essential as watering, fertilizing, mulching, and pest control.

Pruning to maintain the natural form of a species or cultivar is called informal pruning. It is the best kind of pruning for our present-day landscaping. Most hollies can receive corrective pruning and light pinching or cutting back at any season of the year. Pruning to "green gum drop" forms, however, is very unnatural and seldom relates to the general architecture and design of the garden.

Fortunately, hollies adjust to various and often unnatural environmental conditions. With proper selection of the right species or cultivar for a particular situation, little pruning is required other than to train a true leader or remove a dead, diseased, or damaged branch. Unlike rejuvenation or heavy pruning, general pruning should not be noticeable. The tree or shrub should look natural (see Figure 18-1).

Young Japanese hollies (*Ilex crenata*) are often very vigorous, sending out long leggy shoots of new growth. If these are distracting, they can be removed by cutting below the general shape of the plant. This results in a denser, more compact plant. Light tip pruning throughout the growing season is a common practice. Young rooted cuttings of American holly *Ilex opaca*) and English holly (*I. aquifolium*) are often sprawling with no apparent leading shoot. The most promising branch should be selected and tied upright to a stake. Cutting back the tips of side shoots or lateral shoots will hasten the filling out of the young trees. Often two or more upright shoots will develop. Select the one most favorable, preferably the one closest to the main axis, and cut back the others. A crook may be noted where the leader joins the trunk of the small tree. This will be noticeable, but as the plant develops the lateral branches will hide any deformity.

Multistemmed tree hollies are often preferred by some gardeners. I prefer single-trunked trees, though I have no objection to multistemmed, bushy plants. Many nursery growers root two to three cuttings in a gallon container, then transfer the rooted plant in late summer or the following spring to a 2- or 3-gallon unit, and sell it in the fall as a multistemmed plant.

Large overgrown, multistemmed hollies, such as *Ilex cornuta* 'Burfordii', can be pruned to beautiful multitrunked small trees. Limbing up the lower branches exposes the beautiful trunk formation. This may require sawing off some lower branches at the branch collar, close to the main trunk so as to leave no stubs. While tree paints are generally not recommended, for aesthetic purposes with this type of sculpture pruning they should be used. A second option is to wrap the pruned area with a 5- to 10-cm (2- to 3-in.) wide strip of 4-mil black plastic starting below the wound and wrapping upward. The wrapping can be secured with black plastic electrical tape and should be removed in one year.

Because terminal leader shoots are often damaged by frost, insects, or other causes, they need to be trimmed back to live wood. Surrounding side branches should also be pruned. Large

Figure 18-1. *Ilex cassine* and *I. cornuta* 'Rotunda' on the grounds of Mississippi State University. Photo by Ed Martin.

established hollies often send out vigorous upright shoots 60–120 cm (2–4 ft.) in length. These, too, need to be cut back.

Yellow-bellied sapsuckers often cause damage to tree trunks by drilling row after row of small holes so they can feed on the inner bark and sap of hollies. The trunk of a tree can be weakened by this girdling. Vigorous upright shoots usually occur below and along the damaged trunks; they can be removed completely or trimmed back to promote branching in the damaged area.

Mature deciduous hollies should be thinned of old dead wood and headed back to bushier shapes without changing the natural form of the plant. Because deciduous hollies flower on old wood and on short spur growth along a stem, they can be pruned by renewal pruning.

Renewal pruning is practiced in late winter and involves removing or cutting back one-third of the stems at the ground, leaving stems 36–54 cm (12–18 inches) long. This can be done throughout the plant and not just on one side. Follow-up pruning involves removing another one-third of the old stems the second spring, and the final third the third spring.

Evergreen hollies also benefit from renewal pruning, but it is more drastic than the renewal pruning of deciduous hollies. Again, it is done in late winter or early spring (before new growth appears) and involves removing all stems and branches close to the ground, leaving stems 10–54 cm (4–18 inches) long. The strong vegetative growth that subsequently develops in late spring will require thinning and cutting back to encourage lateral branching and to develop compact plants.

An alternate to complete rejuvenation is called *hatracking* or *coatracking* (Plates 207 to 209). This kind of pruning is often used on large pyramidal trees such as *Ilex opaca* or *I. aquifolium* and on large, rounded shrubs such as *I. cornuta* 'Burfordii'. Using loppers and pruning saws, cut off the outer 0.9–1.3 m (3–4 ft.) of each branch 2–3.8 cm (¾–1½ in.) diameter starting from ground level. As you work up the tree, angle in to produce a narrow conical "hatrack" of leafless branches. Leave several short branches 13–20 cm (5–8 in.) long at the top. Although the branches are severely cut back in this type of pruning, the tree still retains its original shape.

Hatracking is best done in early spring, so new growth soon begins to cover the bare stems the first season. Do not prune any branches back to the main trunk or flush with the tree trunk or you will stimulate shoots from the main trunk, which will grow straight up parallel to the trunk; the final result will be a mess of upright shoots instead of well-balanced new horizontal-growing branches. In two years the plants will show no signs of being severely pruned.

Hedges should be shaped with tapering sides, so the top of the hedge is narrower than the base. This allows sufficient light, air, and moisture to the lower branches. Some shrubs, such as boxwood and barberry, can be sheared with vertical sides, but hollies do not tolerate this type of pruning and soon become thin and open at the base.

Most holly hedges are sheared with a flat top; however, in Japan there are beautiful scalloped-top hedges made following temporary templates as shearing guides. To get the height of a 0.9- to 1.5 m (3- to 5-ft.) tall hedge even, tight lines of heavy cord or rope make good shearing lines. Wooden templates can also be used. At Brookgreen Gardens, Murrells Inlet, South Carolina,

Figure 18-2. *Ilex crenata* topiary in Japan. Photo by Fred Galle.

a beautiful low border hedge of *I. vomitoria* is pruned several times a year using a 54-cm (18-in.) tall wooden template frame as guide.

Holly hedges require several shearings per year. The last shearing of the season is best done in late summer to early September to develop a fringe of new growth and eliminate a sheared winter appearance.

Pruning fruit-bearing holly branches in December provides material for holiday decorations. Keep in mind that some hollies produce fruit on old wood; thus, removing flower buds on branches in the fall or winter will reduce the floral and fruit development the following spring. Hollies in this group include *Ilex × altaclerensis, I. aquifolium, I. cornuta, I. latifolia,* the many hybrids of *I. cornuta* 'Burfordii' × *I. pernyi* such as 'Cetus' and 'Lydia Morris, and *I. vomitoria.* Heavy pruning of these hollies in the winter will reduce the abundance of fruit the next season.

Fortunately, most hollies produce fruit on the current season's growth. In this group are several hollies indigenous to the United States and their cultivars: *I. × attenuata, I. cassine, I. myrtifolia,* and *I. opaca. Ilex vomitoria* is the only North American evergreen holly that produces flowers and fruits on old wood.

Several introduced holly species produce fruit on new growth, including *Ilex pedunculosa* and *I. purpurea. Ilex crenata* and *I. glabra* both flower on new growth but have relatively inconspicuous black fruits, save for the yellow-fruited and white-fruited forms. These can be pruned in late summer and touched up once or twice during the growing season as needed, especially if used as hedges.

Figure 18-3. *Ilex crenata* topiary in Japan. Photo by Fred Galle.

Figure 18-4. Sculpture *Ilex crenata* in Japan. Photo by Fred Galle.

Sculpture pruning is often seen in Japan, where various forms of *Ilex crenata* are shaped into frogs, turtles, mushrooms, and large stylized green trees (Figures 18-2 to 18-4). In parks and street plantings in Tokyo, large irregular-shaped green mounds are sculptured by planting *I. crenata* cultivars of different sizes close together to become one large beautiful massive, green mound, which is then sheared or clipped to perfection. A similar type of green sculpture was seen at The Cloister, Sea Island, Georgia, where a large specimen of *I. vomitoria* 'Dwarf' 1.8 m (6 ft.) in diameter was planted next to a smaller holly 0.9 m (3 ft.) tall by 1.3 m (4 ft.) wide; the two were growing together as one large irregular closely sheared, "green pillowy" mass. Similar mounds with a different texture might be made by planting *I. cornuta* 'Dwarf Burford' and *I. cornuta* 'Carissa' close together. More details on using holly for topiary can be found elsewhere in this volume.

Pruning is a fun and relaxing gardening activity. An old nursery adage advises, "Prune when the knife and hand pruners are sharp."

CHAPTER 19

Holly Propagation

Hollies can be propagated by seed, cuttings, divisions, and grafting. Each method has its advantages and difficulties, and all are not used for every species. Interested readers are referred to the many specialized books and articles on holly propagation. An overview is presented here.

SEED PROPAGATION

In nature *Ilex* species are propagated by seed. In cultivation, germination of holly seed is variable and often requires one to two years or more. This is due to the immature embryos characteristic of most species and to the variety of seed coverings (endocarps) in the genus, from stony to woody to leathery. *Ilex aquifolium, I. cornuta, I. decidua, I. opaca, I. serrata,* and *I. verticillata* have very hard stony seed coats nearly impervious to water. *Ilex rotunda* and *I. pernyi* have subligneous to woody endocarps. *Ilex amelanchier, I. cassine, I. crenata, I. glabra,* and *I. myrtifolia* have leathery endocarps and generally require 6 months for germination if properly handled. *Ilex vomitoria* and *I. × attenuata* require 6 to 12 months for germination.

Seed should be collected in the fall and not allowed to dry out but cleaned free of the fleshy pulp. The pulp is easily removed by crushing the fruits, then soaking them for several days to remove the exocarp or skin. Large quantities of seed can be cleaned in a blender or by washing seed in a screen or sieve under water to discard the pulp. Seeds that float are usually not viable, due to many causes including midge damage, and therefore should be discarded.

A practical way to handle small quantities of seed is to plant it in a sterilized medium of 1 part sharp sand and 2 parts peat, or equal parts of peat, fine pine bark, and sand. Use clean clay or plastic pots and cover the pots with plastic or place them in a plastic bag. The seed label should include the name, source, and date. Sterilizing the rooting medium by heat or steam is important to control weeds and fungi.

Hard exocarp-coated seed can be stratified for storage before mixing clean seed with sterilized sand and peat and placing the mixture in plastic bags or wide-mouth jars. The medium should be moist but not soaking wet. The unit should be stored in a cool place for 6 to 12 months.

Seeds planted in pots should be placed in a cool area at 13 to 21°C (55 to 70°F). Little attention is necessary until the seedlings appear, except to watch for mold and fungi growth. Stratified seed after a year or more of treatment should be planted outdoors in prepared beds of soil, peat, and sand or in flats and kept in a greenhouse. The beds or flats should be protected from rodents by enclosing them with wire mesh. If a natural shaded area is not available, it is advisable to place a shadecloth over a wire-enclosed bed. Seed can be broadcast in shallow rows and covered with a fine layer of peat or fine pine bark.

Seedlings can be left in the seed beds until they are large enough for transplanting, or they can be potted or replanted when approximately 2.5–3.8 cm (1–1½ in.) high. The young transplanted seedlings should be shaded and lightly moistened (not soaked) frequently until established.

Growing seedlings is a challenge that requires at least 3 to 5 years or longer to select desired plants. Seedlings will vary as to size and shape of leaves, luster, and other qualities. The longest waiting period, however, is for flowering so that plant sex as well as fruit size, shape, and color can be determined. Evaluating winter hardiness cannot be done in one year. It often requires 20 to 30 years of observation to determine hardiness and the true value of a plant (Tony Shammarello and Orlando Pride, pers. comm.).

Seeds collected from open-pollinated plants produce variable plants. The ratio of female to male plants is about equal, along with size, shape of leaves, and other characteristic. No two plants are alike. The sex ratio of seedling plants, however, has been reported as 1 female to 3 to 4 males, and as low as 1 female to 10 males, but long-term studies of 8 to 9 years have shown the ratio is about equal. Seedling male plants usually produce flowers in three to four years while female plants may not develop flowers until six to eight years or longer. This may account for the varied reports on the ratio of male to female plants.

For seed collected from an arboretum or garden with many different species, where natural hybridization occurs between plants flowering at the same time, the variability increases. Seeds collected from open-pollinated yellow-fruited plants will generally produce all red-fruited seedlings. In one case, crossing pollen from a male seedling of *Ilex cornuta* 'D'Or' with 'D'Or' (yellow fruited) produced all red-fruited plants. Raising seedling of *I. crenata* 'Convexa' might be considered a waste of time and energy, unless you wanted to prove that you could do it. Many thousand seedlings of this cultivar have been raised in the past in the search for more hardy selections. Collecting seed from dwarf forms of *I. crenata*, such as 'Dwarf Pagoda', 'Piccolo', 'Mariesii', or from other dwarf plants such as *I.* 'Rock Garden' might prove more interesting. Collecting seed of less-known species such as *I. integra, I. purpurea, I. rugosa, I. spinigera, I. sugerokii*, and *I. yunnanensis* would be a challenge.

In the late 1950s and 1960s there were several reports on embryo culture of holly seed. Cleaned seeds are sterilized in alcohol and then cut lengthwise with a sterilized razor to release the tiny embryo (⅕₀ in.) which must be dissected under a microscope. The immature embryos are transferred to test tubes containing germ-free agar jelly medium with added minerals, sugars, and vitamins. The tubes are plugged to keep out mold and bacteria and placed in the dark for 2 weeks, then under continuous florescent lights. The entire operation take place under sterile conditions. Usually the embryos begin to enlarge within two weeks. Adenine sulfate, when added to the agar at 40 to 80 ppm, speeds up germination and growth. In 4 to 6 weeks the small seedlings are 13–20 mm (½–¾ in.) tall. After several weeks they can be transferred to a sterilized medium in plastic-covered containers. This is a very tedious procedure that must be done under *sterile conditions*. Even dedicated propagators find it difficult and seldom repeat the procedure.

Raised seedlings are very important for the plant breeder and hybridizer, who with dedication and patience take up the challenge to produce new and better hybrids.

PROPAGATION BY CUTTINGS

Propagation of hollies by cuttings is the best method for cultivars and most species as the selected plant characteristic is carried over to the new plants. Not all plants root with the same ease, however, and some are very difficult such as *Ilex decidua* 'Byer's Golden' and some cultivars of *I. aquifolium, I. latifolia, I. opaca, I. purpurea*, and *I. rotunda*. Other hollies root with little difficulty, including *I.* × *attenuata, I. cornuta, I. crenata, I. glabra*, most cultivars of *I. opaca, I. vomitoria*, and most deciduous holly cultivars.

Before taking cuttings, select a site, unit, or method of rooting cuttings. Talk with other holly enthusiasts about their methods of propagating plants and then adapt their system to fit your needs. Cuttings can be rooted in a glass or plastic greenhouse or outdoors with a mist or fog system. The home system may be very simple or very elaborate depending on the needs and interest of the gardener. Commercial nurseries also have varied propagating systems to fit their area and method of operation (Plate 210). In mild climates it may be a mist system under a lath or shade cloth house, or an open-topped but enclosed wind-free area using mist.

The time of taking cuttings and the condition of the wood at the time of cutting vary from propagator to propagator. The old adage says to take the cutting when the knife is sharp and new growth from the current season's growth is beginning to firm up. For many plants this would mean from mid to late June to late January and February. Cuttings are best taken in the morning and placed in moistened plastic bags until they can be worked up. If the cuttings can not be worked up the same day, they should be stored in moist sealed plastic bags in a cool place or overnight in a refrigerator. Wilted cuttings stored over night will regain turgidity and root better than their counterparts stuck directly into the rooting media.

The length of cuttings depends on the plants. Cuttings of cultivars of *Ilex crenata* such as 'Beehive', 'Delaware Diamond', 'Dwarf Pagoda', and 'Piccolo' may be very short if just taking new growth—less than 5 cm (2 in.)—or they may be much larger if cuttings are taken into second- and third-year branched growth. The average cutting length is 15–20 cm (6–8 in.), depending on the ease of rooting and space in the propagation unit. Long cuttings 20–30 cm (8–12 in.) each are feasible, but take up more space. More attention is required to keep moisture and media in good condition.

The leaves on the bottom third or half of the cutting should be removed. On some small-leaved cuttings the lower leaves can be stripped with the fingers, while on cuttings with larger leaves it will be necessary to cut off the leaves.

Wounding the base near the end of the cutting helps induce root formation. The wound, 13–20 mm (½–¾ in.), can be single, double, or done on two sides. It can be made with the thumb when removing the lower leaves, or by cutting off a thin slice with a sharp knife. The cut should be through the outer bark and cambium layer to just expose the white inner wood. On cuttings of *Ilex crenata*, wounding induced by removal or stripping of lower leaves may be sufficient; however, I prefer a small wound on the dwarf cultivars for better root development. The wound calluses over, and from the callus area roots are initiated.

Reducing leaf surface is often advised for large-leaved cuttings of *Ilex latifolia* and *I. purpurea* and for various hybrid cultivars such as *I.* 'Emily Bruner'. Cutting the leaves in half rather than reducing the number of leaves allows more cuttings per unit space. This practice is used with success on rhododendrons.

For some difficult plants such as *Ilex aquifolium,* some cultivars of *I. opaca, I. purpurea,* and *I. rotunda,* cuttings from juvenile growth are preferred over cuttings from mature growth. In these instances, mature plants are cut back to induce new growth, called "water sprouts."

The use of root-promoting chemicals or hormones is important. Indolebutyric acid (IBA) at high concentrations (8000 to 20,000 ppm) is essential to obtain rooting of some cultivars and species. Combinations of IBA and NAA (naphthaleneacetic acid) are used. For easy-to-root types, a 1000- to 3000-IBA solution or talc is generally used. (The use of a powder versus a quick-dip solution is a matter of personal preference.) Boron at 50 to 200 ppm, in combination with IBA, has increased quality of rooting in cuttings of *Ilex aquifolium.* Table 12 lists four common commercial root-inducing substances with their ingredients and sources.

For higher concentrations of rooting substances, it is necessary to mix your own solution using IBA and NAA crystals. Table 13 lists several sources of the crystals, and Table 14 gives the procedure for making a solution.

The rooting media varies with propagators. A standard media is 2 parts fine pine bark, 1 part

Table 12. Ingredients and sources of common plant hormones and root-inducing substances.

Dip N' Grow®
Alpkem Corporation
P.O. Box 1260
Clackamas, Oregon 97015

Active ingredient:	Indole-3-butyric acid	1.0 %
	1-naphthaleneacetic acid	0.5 %
Inert ingredient:	Alcohol	98.5 %

Combination of 10,000 milligrams IBA per liter and 5,000 milligrams NAA per liter of alcohol. It can be diluted with 1:1 solution of water and alcohol to desired concentration.

Hormex No. 8®
Brooker Chemical Corporation
P.O. Box 9335
N. Hollywood, CA 91609

Active ingredient:	Indole-3-butyric acid	0.8 %
Inert ingredient:	Talc	99.2 %
Hormex No. 16®:	1.6 % IBA	
Hormex No. 30®:	3.0 % IBA	

Hormodin 8®
MSD-AGVET
Division of Merck & Company
Rahway, New Jersey 07065

Active ingredient:	Indole-3-butyric acid	0.8 %
Inert ingredient:	Talc	99.2 %
Hormodin 1®:	0.1 % IBA	
Hormodin 3®:	0.3 % IBA	

Wood's Compound®
Earth Science Products Corporation
P.O. Box 327
Wilsonville, Oregon 97070

Active ingredient:	Indole-3-butyric acid	1.03 %
	1-naphthaleneacetic acid	0.51 %
Inert ingredient:	Ethanol SD 3A	78.46 %
	Dimethylformamide	20.00 %

Dimethylformamide added as a penetrant to allow active ingredients to reach root initiation area more effectively.

peat, and 1 part perlite by volume. Under a mist system, where drainage is essential, the media may include sand in the above mix or be composed of equal parts of fine bark and sand or peat and sand. If rooting is done in a closed unit, care should be taken to have a moist media that is not soaking wet. The major problem with plastic boxes and covered outdoor frames is soaking wet media. With enclosed outdoor frames, I prefer to root cuttings in small plastic pots 2¼ to 3 inches square, which are then placed in trays. This helps in transplanting later.

Rooting requires 6 to 8 weeks before shifting the rooted cuttings from the flats or small pots to larger units. It is not uncommon to apply a light weekly application of liquid fertilizer to the young rooted cuttings before shifting or transplanting. In the early fall, small potted plants should be transplanted to prepared soil beds or larger containers. Young plants require protection for the winter. Roots of holly and most plants are less cold hardy than the top of the plant and thus must be protected. The pH of the soil in the prepared bed and potting media should range from

Table 13. Suppliers of IBA and NAA.

Aldrich Chemical Company
949 E. Saint Paul Avenue
Milwaukee, Wisconsin 07043
(414) 273-3850

Research Organics
4353 East 49th Street
Cleveland, Ohio 44125
(800) 321-9322

Sigma Chemical Company
P. O. Box 14508
Saint Louis, Missouri 63178
(800) 325-3010

Table 14. Procedure for making rooting solutions with IBA and NAA.

Liter

20,000 milligram concentration 20 %
20 grams dissolved in 1:1 solution distilled water & alcohol

500 CC

20,000 milligram concentration 20 %
10 grams dissolved in 1:1 solution distilled water & alcohol

Dissolve the IBA crystals in pure alcohol, add an equal amount of distilled water. The solution can be used at full strength (20 %) or diluted as needed. It should be stored under refrigeration. Shelf life is unknown (short).
    Caution: Chemicals are corrosive and poisonous (IBA - LD 50 100 mg/kg: NAA - LD 50 1.0) g/kg). **Handle with extreme care.**

5.5 to 6.0. Plants can be stored in cold frames enclosed with glass or plastic plus insulated matted outdoor covers.

Winter cuttings rooted under enclosed bottom-heated beds in cool greenhouses are ready to transplant or shift up to larger containers in the very early spring. This results in an early flush of growth before moving plants outdoors to ground beds in a lath or shade house, or to containers. Adding a complete slow-release fertilizer to the prepared soil beds and to potting media is advised.

Deciduous Hollies

Of the three deciduous holly species commonly propagated by cuttings, *Ilex decidua* and its cultivars are usually more difficult to propagate than are *I. serrata* and *I. verticillata*. *Ilex decidua* 'Byer's Golden', a yellow-fruited cultivar, is very difficult. Bon Hartline (pers. comm.) found that fall rooting is preferred for *I. decidua* using 20- to 25-cm (8- to 10-in.) long cuttings taken after the first or second frost in mid October. Leaves are stripped before cuttings are stuck in plastic-covered greenhouse beds with bottom heat 20 to 24°C (68 to 75°F) in a medium of peat and perlite. Cuttings are wounded and treated with Hormodin No. 3 or a quick dip. Rooting is slow, and new growth usually appears in 6 to 8 weeks, the same time small roots appear. By spring, cuttings are shifted to gallon containers. If dormant cuttings are taken later in the winter, top growth starts before rooting and mortality is very high.

Ilex serrata, I. verticillata cultivars, and other deciduous species are variable but generally root from soft wood cuttings taken in late June or July. Long new vegetative shoots up to 61 cm (24 in.) are cut into segments 13–15 cm (5–6 in.) long, then wounded and treated with a quick dip or Hormodin powder. Cuttings are rooted under glass or plastic with mist or fog in beds, flats, or individual pots. Various media or combinations of fine pine bark, peat and perlite are recommended. Rooting requires about 6 weeks before the young plants can be transferred from flats or small pots to a well-mixed soil (peat and bark mix with a pH of 5.5–6.0) in beds or larger pots. Plants are grown under shade or lath with mist or fog until fall. Plants should be overwintered in the same area, with winter covers, if required. In spring the young plants are ready to shift up to larger containers or spaced out in shaded beds to grow on for another season. Water and slow-release fertilizers should be applied as needed.

GRAFTING HOLLY

Grafting of many plants is a lost art and seldom taught in horticultural schools. Although it is not a common practice with hollies, it often is the only method of propagating some difficult-to-root species and cultivars.

Grafting is the placing of a scion or portion of a plant to be propagated onto the stock (root portion) of another plant. There are many types of grafts, but the best for holly are the cleft and side grafts. T-budding, seldom used with holly, might be useful for a nursery wanting to produce more plants from a single branch than just one cutting. It is best done in early spring or mid to late summer.

The general practice is to graft the scion onto a similar stock plant. I would not recommend grafting a plant with a single trunk onto a plant with multiple trunks. I have grafted a hybrid plant of *Ilex opaca* onto a seedling of *I. decidua,* but I would not advise grafting it onto a multi-trunked plant such as *I. verticillata.*

The stock plants are often seedlings or plants grown from rooted cuttings. I have not observed any incompatibility between scion and stock as often observed in other plant genera. The understock has a great influence on the scion or top portion of the grafted plant. For example, *Ilex aquifolium* 'Angustifolia', the beautiful small narrow-leaved English holly, on its own roots is very slow growing in the South, but when grafted on *I. cornuta* 'Burfordii', it shows good seasonal growth. *Ilex cornuta* 'Ira S. Nelson' is a large-leaved, vigorous growing plant that reaches 4.6–6.2 m (15–20 ft.) in 25 years, but when James Foret of Southwestern Louisiana University grafted it onto *I. cornuta* 'Dwarf Burford', in 25 years the grafted plants averaged 1.2 m (4 ft.) tall.

Ilex opaca seedlings are good understock for its cultivars. The best understock for *I. aquifolium* and *I.* × *altaclerensis* are *I. cornuta* seedlings, including *I. cornuta* 'Burfordii' where hardy.

By grafting one can develop larger plants of a new sport or mutation and seedling hybrids faster than by rooted cuttings. The slow-growing dwarf *Ilex* 'Rock garden' could be grafted onto *I. cornuta* 'Dwarf Burford' or *I. cornuta* 'Burfordii' to produce vigorous stock plants (a source of cuttings) for a nursery.

Grafting can be done in a greenhouse in the late fall and winter or outdoors with container-grown and established plants in the field. Seedling stock plants are often recommended over cutting-grown stock plants. Both are good, but if potted seedlings are used, the end of the tap root should be cut off to help the plant develop more lateral roots. The stock plants should be established in pots from 4 in. to 1 gallon in size for ease in handling. The stock plants should be brought indoors in the late fall or winter to get new root growth started before grafting. The scion wood should be dormant, not in active growth, but not frozen.

After the grafts are completed the plants can be individually sealed in plastic bags, with a wire hoop placed over the scion, or plunged in moist peat-filled benches under a plastic tent. A major problem with plastic-covered grafts is removing the covers too early. Wait until new growth has started on the scion, then cut a small hole in each bag, and weekly enlarge the hole; after 5 to 6 weeks the entire bag can be removed. Where grafted plants are placed under tents that cover an entire bench, ventilation also should be increased gradually.

Sharp knives are very important in grafting, so keep a sharpening stone handy. In cleft grafting the top 2.5–5 cm (1–2 in.) of the potted understock above soil level is cut off with shears or a saw. The stock is split with a knife (or, if very large, with a sharp wedge) in the middle to a depth of about 25–38 mm (1–1½ in.). The split is held open with a small wedge (e.g., small screw driver) to ease insertion of the scion. The scion is cut to a wedge about 16–25 mm (⅝-1 in.) long with one side a little thicker than the other. The scion is carefully inserted in the split of the stock, carefully matching the cambium layers and wrapping the union with waxed twine or rubber banding stripes. Cut rubber bands will also work. If the stock is 6 mm (¼ in.) in diameter or larger, two scions can be used on opposites sides of the split. The cleft graft can be used with larger stock up to 25 mm (1 in.) or more in diameter. If done outdoors in late winter, use a large-mouth gallon jar to cover the graft and place a paper bag over the jar to prevent sun scalding. After the scion begins to grow, place a small stick or stone under one edge of the jar to ventilate; in several weeks the jar can be removed.

Side grafts are used with potted stock that is smaller than ¼ inch in diameter, often matching the size of the scion. The top of the scion is not removed until the union has taken place. A cut 2.5 cm (1 in.) long is made near the base of the stock and slanting inward on the side of the potted stock. The scion, which is cut into a 2-cm (¾-in.) wedge with both sides even, is inserted in the cut, matching the cambiums at least on one side. The graft union is tied with a rubber strip or waxed twine. The new grafts are handled the same way as recommended for the cleft grafts. The top of the stock is gradually reduced and cut completely off after the union has firmed.

Both cleft and side grafted plants are best grown for at least one season under lath or shade cloth in the same pot or transplanted in a prepared soil bed. Care should be taken to not damage the scion the first season. Plants can be supported by tying them to a small stake.

PROPAGATION BY DIVISION

Several *Ilex* species that tend to have stoloniferous systems can be propagated by division. For example, *I. glabra* and *I. coriacea* produce stems from shallow underground roots. I have also produced plants from root pieces of *I. cornuta, I. decidua,* and *I. vomitoria.* Plants that naturally spread and propagate themselves by vegetative shoots can be dug up and divided. The root systems are usually poor, so the stems should be cut back to compensate for the poor root system. Dividing plants is best done in late winter and early spring.

Propagation by root pieces can be done at any season, but best in late winter and early spring. Roots 6–13 mm (¼–½ in.) in diameter are preferred. Cut them in 10-cm (4-in.) lengths, lay them horizontally in a rooting media, and lightly cover them. New roots will develop, and new shoots will soon follow.

CHAPTER 20

Hybridizing, Evaluating, Selecting, and Introducing Hollies

The majority of the 2000 plus named holly cultivars are plants selected from the wild, chance seedlings, or controlled hybrids and sports. Many of the sports and seedlings of *Ilex aquifolium* (English holly) were selected in the early to mid 1800s, while interest in the variations of *I. opaca* started in the early 1900s. Many of the cultivars were named without being tested widely or placed in a performance trial for evaluation with other cultivars. The test gardens at arboretums are a starting point, but some of them are limited, by facilities, in the number of plants they can grow (Plate 211).

HOLLY BREEDERS

Numerous dedicated holly enthusiasts and nursery growers have selected and introduced outstanding hollies and other plants. Among them are hands-in-the-soil or with-pruners-in-their-hand gardeners, with a keen eye always looking for the unusual plant. The list of enthusiastic gardeners is endless.

One of the first was Earl L. Bennett, propagator for Greenbriar Farms nurseries at Chesapeake, Virginia. He planted a long row of *Ilex crenata* 'Convexa' between two rows of *I. crenata* 'Rotundifolia'. Seeds were collected in the fall of 1945 and stratified, with the resultant seedlings planted in 1946. The original seedling population of 250,000–300,000 plants was reduced by the winter of 1947–1948 to 3000–4000. Fifty seedlings were then selected, but less than thirty were named. Some of them are still popular today, including 'Bennett's Compact', 'Howard', 'Vaseyi', 'Willowleaf', and others of the Bennett Hybrid Group of *I. crenata*.

Tom Dodd Jr. of Tom Dodd Nurseries, Semmes, Alabama, is well known as a dedicated plantsman, nursery grower, and naturalist. He has one of the largest wholesale inventories of *Ilex* species and cultivars. Every year he collects seed, mainly open-pollinated fruit and seed sent by his friends for growing and evaluating. Tom has a keen eye for good plants and, of the tens of thousands of seedling plants which he has grown, has only named and registered about 25 hollies. Some of his selections include *I.* × *attenuata* 'Nasa', *I. cornuta* 'Lottie Moon', *I. crenata* 'Luther Copeland', *I. crenata* 'William Jackson', *I.* 'Lib's Favorite (a hybrid named for his wife), *I. opaca* 'William Hawkins', *I. vomitoria* 'Will Fleming', and *I. vomitoria* 'Wiggins'. He named and introduced *I.* 'Mary Nell' from a cross made at his nursery by the late Joe McDaniel.

Norman H. Cannon of Cannon Plants, Greenwood, Delaware, has selected and introduced excellent dwarf cultivars of *Ilex crenata* as well as yellow-fruited selections. Most of these are open-pollinated seedling selections; several are controlled crosses. His dwarf introductions of *I. crenata* include 'Dwarf Cone', 'Firefly', 'Miss Muffet', 'Piccolo', 'Pincushion', and two very dwarf selections to be registered—'Dewdrop' and 'Delaware Diamond'. His selections with yellow fruits are 'Butterball', 'Ivory Hall', and 'Ivory Tower'.

In the mid 1950s I visited the late E. E. Foster at his nursery in Bessemer, Alabama, and learned about his *Ilex × attenuata* Foster seedlings. Of the five plants he named, 'Foster No. 2' is still very popular today.

Wendell Winn of Norfolk, Virginia, introduced in 1966 a collected female seedling of *Ilex × koehneana,* later named and registered as *I.* 'Wirt L. Winn'. This plant was slowly accepted, but now, in the 1990s, is popular though hard to find.

John S. Wieman, noted for his work with nursery growers in Oregon and his dedicated interest in improved selections of English hollies, named and introduced more than 20 of his own colorful seedling selections and hybrids. Among them are *Ilex × altaclerensis* 'Adaptable', *I. aquifolium* 'Beacon', *I. aquifolium* 'Wieman's Moonbrite', *I. aquifolium* 'Night Glow', and *I. aquifolium* 'Yellow Beam'. Some are growing in test gardens, but are not yet readily available commercially.

Robert (Bob) Simpson, of Simpson Nursery Company, Vincennes, Indiana, has worked with *Ilex verticillata* and other deciduous hollies. He has named and introduced many excellent selections including *I.* 'Bonfire', *I. verticillata* 'Winter Red', and *I. verticillata* 'Winter Gold'. In the 1940s it was difficult to sell a deciduous holly, but with Simpson's dedication and persistence, there is now a constant demand for the named selections of deciduous hollies.

Others who have named and introduced deciduous hollies include Bon Hartline, Anna, Illinois; Polly Hill, Martha's Vineyard, Massachusetts; and R. K. Peters, Bendersville, Pennsylvania. The list is endless, but should include Paul Bosley, the late Orlando Pride, Tony Shammarello, and Malcolm S. Whipple (see Appendix 5 for a complete list of holly breeders and hybridizers). Behind every named holly is a person or persons who have selected and named the plant. Every new plant should be tested and evaluated in the holly test gardens throughout the country and then promoted through the Holly Society of America and other media.

Many early holly breeders are not well known. Henry T. Skinner, while a graduate student at Cornell University, Ithaca, New York, in 1935–1936, reported unsuccessful attempts in crossing *Ilex aquifolium, I. cornuta, I. opaca,* and *I. verticillata.* By 1949, while at the Morris Arboretum, Philadelphia, Pennsylvania, with greenhouses and flowering potted plants he reported on 33 crosses. The successful ones include *I. aquifolium × I. opaca, I. cornuta* 'Burfordii' *× I. pernyi, I. cornuta × I. aquifolium × I. pernyi, I. opaca × I. aquifolium, I. opaca × I. × aquipernyi, I. opaca × I. ciliospinosa,* and *I. pernyi × I. ciliospinosa.* From these early studies it was learned that *I. pernyi* crosses readily with *I. aquifolium, I. cornuta,* and *I. opaca.* The suggestion of Jonathan A. Wright that *I. pernyi* can perhaps serve as a bridge in inter-crossing the evergreen species was confirmed. Following Skinner's move to the U.S. National Arboretum, Washington, D.C., as director, he found records of Oliver Freeman's 1940 crosses of *I. aquifolium × I. cornuta, I. opaca × I. aquifolium,* and *I. opaca × I. cornuta.* Skinner doubted that the Freeman plants of *I. opaca × I. aquifolium* were true hybrids because of their close resemblance to *I. opaca,* which he interpreted as a possible case of apomixis. (It was far more likely, however, that the bull got over the fence.)

Other American holly enthusiasts involved in holly breeding include William L. Ackerman and John L. Creech, formerly director of the U.S. Natural Arboretum, Washington, D.C.; Gene K. Eisenbeiss, U.S. National Arboretum, Washington, D.C.; the late Henry Hohman, nurseryman, Kingsville, Maryland; the late William F. Kosar, geneticist; the late Joseph C. McDaniel, University of Illinois; Kathleen K. Meserve, St. James, New York, now retired in Florida; O. M. Neal, West Virginia University; the late Matthew A. Nosal, nurseryman, New York; Elwin R. Orton Jr., Rutgers University; and R. B. Rypma, Ohio University. See Tables 15 and 16 for a list of their attempted crosses and the results.

It was a fortunate day in 1955 when William F. Kosar was transferred from his lettuce breed-

Table 15. U.S. holly breeders and the results of their crosses.

Name of breeder Plants used in cross	Results of cross[1]
Wt. L. Ackerman & John L. Creech *I. cornuta* × *I. ciliospinosa*	'Albert Close', 'Edward Goucher', 'Harry Gunning', 'Howard Dorsett', 'William Cowgill'
J. M. Willard Batchelor *I. cornuta* (large fruit) × *I. cornuta* (small leaves)	'Shangri-La'

Norman Cannon
  I. crenata
  I. crenata × *I. crenata*
	Open-pollinated seedlings
	'Fairyland'

Gene Eisenbeiss
  I. dimorphophylla × *I. aquifolium*
  I. dimorphophylla × *I. ciliospinosa*
  I. dimorphophylla × *I. cornuta*
	H
	H
	H

Oliver M. Freeman
  I. aquifolium × *I. cornuta*
  I. opaca × *I. aquifolium*
  I. opaca × *I. cornuta*
	P
	?
	?

Henry Hohman
  I. aquifolium × *I. latifolia*
  I. cornuta 'Burfordii' × *I. pernyi*
	P
	'Aquila', 'Aries', 'Atlas', 'Beacon', 'Brighter Shines', 'Cetus', 'Drace', 'Fernax', 'Good Taste', 'Hydra', 'Indian Chief', 'Lacerta', 'Lepux', 'Lyra', 'Mercury', 'Moon Glow', 'Phoenix', 'Pyris', 'Red Delight', 'Red Princess', 'Red Robe', 'Security', 'Sextans', 'Starlight', 'Taurus', 'Titan', 'Virgo'

William F. Kosar
  I. aquifolium × *I. latifolia*
  I. aquifolium × *I. pernyi*
  I. aquifolium × *I. ciliospinosa* (× *I. pernyi*)
  I. aquifolium × *I. latifolia*
  I. aquifolium × *I. cornuta*
  I. aquifolium × *I. perado*
  I. aquifolium × *I. vomitoria*
  I. cassine × *I. ciliospinosa*
  I. cassine × *I. crenata*
  I. cassine × *I. glabra*
  I. cassine × *I. latifolia*
  I. cassine × *I. myrtifolia*
  I. ciliospinosa × *I. rugosa*
  I. coriacea × *I. glabra*
  I. coriacea × *I. sugerokii*
  I. cornuta × *I. aquifolium*
  I. cornuta × *I. ciliospinosa*
  I. cornuta × *I. integra*
  I. cornuta × *I. latifolia*
  I. cornuta × *I. leucocarpa*
  I. cornuta × *I. pernyi*
  I. cornuta × *I. vomitoria*
  I. crenata × *I. coriacea*
  I. crenata × *I. purpurea*
  I. crenata × *I. sugerokii*
  I. crenata × *I. yunnanensis*
  I. cumulicola × *I. aquifolium*
  I. decidua × *I. aquifolium*
	'Adonis' (male), 'Venus' (female)
	'Miniature'
	'Coronet'
	H
	F
	P
	P
	F
	F
	P
	F
	P
	H
	H
	H
	H
	P
	H
	H
	H
	H
	P
	P
	P
	H
	F
	P
	H

Name of breeder Plants used in cross	Results of cross[1]
I. decidua × *I. latifolia*	H
I. decidua × *I. opaca*	H
I. glabra × *I. coriacea*	H
I. glabra × *I. crenata*	H
I. glabra × *I. purpurea*	H
I. glabra × *I. serrata*	H
I. glabra × *I. sugerokii*	H
I. integra × *I. aquifolium*	H
I. integra × *I. cornuta*	H
I. integra × *I. leucoclada*	H
I. integra × *I. cornuta*	H
I. integra × *I. latifolia*	P
I. integra × *I. leucoclada*	H
I. integra × *I. pernyi*	H
I. integra × *I. vomitoria*	F
I. latifolia × *I. pernyi*	P
I. leucoclada × *I. integra*	H
I. leucoclada × *I. pernyi*	H
I. myrtifolia × *I. glabra*	F
I. myrtifolia × *I. opaca*	H
I. myrtifolia × *I. purpurea*	F
I. opaca × *I. aquifolium*	F, H
I. opaca × *I.* × *aquipernyi*	F
I. opaca × *I. cassine*	H
I. opaca × *I. centrochinensis*	F
I. opaca × *I. coriacea*	F
I. opaca × *I. crenata*	F
I. opaca × *I. glabra*	F
I. opaca × *I. integra*	F
I. opaca × *I. latifolia*	F
I. opaca × *I. pedunculosa*	F
I. perado × *I. aquifolium*	H
I. perado × *I. latifolia*	P, H
I. perado × *I. cornuta*	P
I. pernyi × *I. aquifolium*	H
I. pernyi × *I. coriacea*	P
I. pernyi × *I. integra*	H
I. pernyi × *I. latifolia*	H
I. pernyi × *I. perado*	H
I. pernyi × *I. vomitoria*	P
I. purpurea × *I. crenata*	P
I. purpurea × *I. sugerokii*	P
I. rugosa × *I. aquifolium*	P
I. rugosa × *I. cornuta*	P
I. rugosa × *I. coriacea*	P
I. rugosa × *I. integra*	H
I. rugosa × *I. latifolia*	P
I. rugosa × *I. leucoclada*	P
I. rugosa × *I. pernyi*	P
I. rugosa × *I. vomitoria*	P
I. sugerokii × *I. crenata*	H
I. vomitoria × *I. aquifolium*	P
I. vomitoria × *I. cornuta*	H
I. vomitoria × *I. crenata*	H
I. vomitoria × *I. integra*	F

(continued)

Table 15. (continued).

Name of breeder Plants used in cross	Results of cross[1]
I. vomitoria × *I. latifolia*	F
I. vomitoria × *I. pernyi*	F
I. vomitoria × *I. rugosa*	P
I. yunnanensis × *I. aquifolium*	P
I. yunnanensis × *I. cornuta*	F
I. yunnanensis × *I. crenata*	F
I. yunnanensis × *I. glabra*	P
I. yunnanensis × *I. latifolia*	F
I. yunnanensis × *I. pernyi*	F
I. yunnanensis × *I. sugerokii*	H
Joseph C. McDaniel	
I. × *aquipernyi* 'San Jose' × *I. cornuta*	'Joe McDaniel'
(*I. cornuta* 'Burfordii' × *I. pernyi* 'Red Delight') × *I. latifolia*	'Mary Nell'
I. opaca 'Chief Paduke' × *I. cornuta*	'Shin Nien'
Kathleen K. Meserve	
I. aquifolium × *I. opaca*	H
I. aquifolium × (*I. rugosa* × *I. aquifolium*)	P
I. aquifolium × *I. yunnanensis*	P
I. × *aquipernyi* × *I.* × *aquipernyi*	P
I. centrochinensis[2] × *I. aquifolium*	P
I. centrochinensis[2] hybrid × *I.* × *aquipernyi*)	P
I. centrochinensis[2] hybrid × (*I. ciliospinosa* × *I. aquifolium*)	P
I. centrochinensis[2] hybrid × *I. fargesii*	P
I. ciliospinosa hybrid × (*I. rugosa* × *I. aquifolium*)	P
I. cornuta × *I.* × *aquipernyi*)	P
I. cornuta × *I. fargesii*	P
I. cornuta × *I. pernyi*	P
I. cornuta × *I. rugosa*	P
I. opaca × *I. aquifolium*	P
I. pernyi × *I. aquifolium*	'Dragon Lady'
I. pernyi × *I. cornuta*	P
I. pernyi × (*I. rugosa* × *I. aquifolium*)	P
I. rugosa × *I. aquifolium*	'Blue Boy', 'Blue Girl', 'Blue Maid', 'Blue Prince', 'Blue Princess', Blue Stallion', 'Golden Girl'
I. rugosa × *I.* × *aquipernyi*	P
I. rugosa × *I. centrochinensis* hybrid	P
I. rugosa × *ciliospinosa* hybrid	P
I. rugosa × *I. cornuta*	'China Boy', 'China Girl'
I. rugosa × *I. fargesii*	P
I. rugosa × *I. latifolia*	P
I. rugosa × (*I. rugosa* × *I. aquifolium*)	P
(*I. rugosa* × *I. aquifolium*) × *I. aquifolium*	P
(*I. rugosa* × *I. ciliospinosa*) hybrid × *I. aquifolium*	P
(*I. rugosa* × *I. aquifolium*) × (*I. rugosa* × *I. aquifolium*)	P
O. M. Neal	
I. × *attenuata* × *I. opaca*	'Erma Byrd'
I. ciliospinosa × male lost	'Betty Zane'
I. collina collected plant	—
I. myrtifolia × *I. opaca*	'Monongahelia', 'Mountain State'
I. verticillata collected plants	—
Mathew A. Nosal	
I. aquifolium 'Cottage Queen' × *I. aquifolium* 'Little Bull'	'Barbarosa'

Name of breeder Plants used in cross	Results of cross[1]
I. pernyi × *I. aquifolium*	'Edward Nosal'
Elwin R. Orton, Jr.	
I. aquifolium × *I. opaca*	Winter injury to seedling
I. × *aquipernyi* × (*I. integra* × *I. pernyi* 'Accent')	'Rock Garden'
I. cassine var. *angustifolia* × *I. sugerokii*	P
I. crenata 'Convexa' × *I. crenata* 'Stokes'	'Beehive'
I. crenata 'Green Lustre' × *I. crenata* 'John Nosal'	'Jersey Pinnacle'
I. crenata 'Mariesii' × *I. crenata* 'John Nosal'	'Dwarf Pagoda' (female), 'Green Dragon' (male)
I. crenata 'Mariesii' × *I. yunnanensis*	P
I. decidua × *I. serrata*	—
I. decidua × *I. verticillata*	—
I. glabra × *I. crenata*	H
I. integra × *I. pernyi*	P
I. opaca × *I. aquifolium*	H
I. opaca 'Hedgeholly' × *I. aquifolium*	P
I. opaca 'Maurice River' × *I. opaca* male	'Dan Fenton'
I. opaca 'Old Heavy Berry' × *I. opaca* 'Isaiah'	'Jersey Delight'
I. opaca × *I. opaca*	'Jersey Princess'
I. serrata × *I. verticillata*	'Autumn Glow' (male), 'Harvest Red' (female)
I. sugerokii × *I. yunnanensis*	—
I. verticillata × (*I. verticillata* × *I. serrata*)	'Raritan Chief'
R. P. Rypma	
(*I. serrata* × *I. verticillata*) 'Sparkleberry' × *I. serrata*	'Hopewell Grenadier', 'Hopewell Myte'
Henry T. Skinner	
I. aquifolium × *I. opaca*	P
I. cornuta 'Burfordii' × *I. pernyi*	'John T. Morris', 'Lydia Morris'
I. opaca × *I. aquifolium*	P, F
I. opaca × *I. cornuta*	F
I. opaca × *I. verticillata*	F
Francis de Vos	
I. glabra × *I. pedunculosa*	F
John S. Wieman	
I. aquifolium 'Flavescens' × *I. aquifolium* 'Duke'	'Wieman's Moonbrite'

[1]F = failure, no seed produced; P = possible seeds produced or no germination; H = hybrids, verified cross
[2]Probably *I. centrochinensis*

ing work at the U.S.D.A. Beltsville Agricultural Plant Center to the U.S. National Arboretum, Washington, D.C. In collaboration with Dr. Francis de Vos in 1955, he carried out exploratory holly hybridization. Interspecific hybrids achieved that year were *Ilex cornuta* × *I. latifolia, I. glabra* × *I. serrata, I. opaca* × *I. aquifolium,* and several tri-specific combinations. This initial experimentation and evaluation of holly hybridizing lead to the first formal breeding project with holly, which Kosar led from 1957 until his retirement in 1971. During the 16 years with the holly project he assembled an amazing collection of holly germ plasm, including 64 species and 695 horticultural varieties and cultivars. Holly hybridizing is a long-range project and his first cultivars, registered in 1964 and 1966, included 'Tanager' (female), 'Oriole' (female), 'Clusterberry' (female), 'Elegance' (female), 'Accent' (male), 'Ruby' (female), and 'Jade' (male). Kosar was the first scientist to explore interspecific hybridizing in holly and the first to achieve *Ilex* hybrids containing more than two parental species (e.g., [*I. aquifolium* × *I. cornuta*] × *I. latifolia*). He left a legacy of new holly hybrids, some just registered in 1991 after his death in 1985.

Table 16. Interspecific crosses and their results.

PLANTS USED IN CROSS	RESULTS OF CROSS[1]
Primary interspecific crosses involving deciduous species	
I. ambigua × *I. pubescens*	P
I. aquifolium × *I. decidua*	P
I. crenata × *I. decidua*	P
I. decidua × *I. aquifolium*	H
I. decidua × *I. crenata*	P
I. decidua × *I. glabra*	F
I. decidua × *I. latifolia*	H
I. decidua × *I. opaca*	H
I. glabra × *I. serrata*	H
I. glabra × *I. verticillata*	F
I. laevigata × *I. glabra*	P
I. laevigata × *I. verticillata*	P
I. nipponica × *I. pubescens*	P
I. nipponica × *I. serrata*	P
I. serrata × *I. verticillata*	H
I. sugerokii × *I. serrata*	P
I. sugerokii × *I. verticillata*	F
Crosses involving species of different sections	
I. anomala × *I. latifolia*	P
I. ciliospinosa × *I. fargesii*	P
i. corallina × *I. aquifolium*	F
I. cumulicola × *I. myrtifolia*	P
I. cumulicola × *I. opaca*	P
I. georgei × *I. aquifolium*	P
I. paraguariensis × *I. vomitoria*	P
I. perado var. *platyphylla* × *I. aquifolium*	P
I. perado var. *platyphylla* × *I. colchica*	P
I. rugosa × *I. corallina*	P
I. vomitoria × *I. corallina*	F
Crosses with no fruit or no seed germination	
I. aquifolium × *I. fargesii*	F
I. aquifolium × *I. pernyi*	F
I. bioritsensis × *I. yunnanensis*	F
I. cornuta × *I. rugosa*	F
I. cornuta × (*I. rugosa* × *I. aquifolium*)	F
I. cornuta × *I. yunnanensis*	F
I. latifolia × *I. aquifolium*	F
I. rugosa × *I. pernyi*	F
I. rugosa × (*I. centrochinensis* hybrid × *I. aquifolium*)	F
Other species used in interspecific crosses	
I. cornuta	—
I. georgei	—
I. crenata var. *thompsonii*	—
I. melanotricha	—
I. myrtifolia	—
I. pernyi	—
I. rugosa	—
I. vomitoria	—

[1]F = failure, no seed produced; P = possible seeds produced or no germination; H = hybrids, verified cross

With more than 30 years of experience, Elwin R. Orton Jr., geneticist and research professor of ornamental horticulture at Rutgers University, is recognized as the world's leading breeder of woody ornamental plants, including more than 25 *Ilex* species. It is difficult to appreciate the patience required and the frustrations endured by Orton and his staff in crossing plants. The intraspecific cross of *Ilex crenata* 'Convexa' × *I. crenata* 'Stokes' required intense evaluation of 40 seedlings from an initial population of 21,000. Criteria for selection included winter hardiness, semi-dwarf habit, mite resistance, and glossy green, year-round foliage. This work resulted in the selection and naming of *I. crenata* 'Beehive'. Two dwarf Japanese hollies, *I. crenata* 'Dwarf Pagoda' (female) and *I. crenata* 'Green Dragon' (male), were selected by Orton from 800 seedlings of the cross *I. crenata* 'Mariesii' × *I. crenata* 'John Nosal'.

Crossing *Ilex aquifolium* × *I. opaca* to develop winter hardy plants with useful characteristics of both species required true dedication. The first cross involved 3-m (10-ft.) tall *I. opaca* 'Jersey Knight' (male), which was dug up and moved into a greenhouse to force early; later it was moved outdoors to a block of 10 specimens of *I. aquifolium* enclosed in a large cheesecloth-covered frame. A hive of bees was introduced to the enclosure for pollination of approximately 20,000 flowers. Within two days the new growth of the female English holly plants suddenly wilted as a result of extreme winter damage; it was soon apparent that the plants were dead to within 18 inches above the soil level.

Work continued using a large male specimen of English holly from the greenhouse to pollinate a female American holly that normally flowers at least 3 to 4 weeks later. A large plant of *Ilex opaca* 'Hedgeholly' was selected in the nursery as the female parent, enclosed in a 2.4-m (8-ft.) high solar house built from coldframe sash to accelerate flowering. The daytime temperature of the solar house was 21 to 24°C (70 to 75°F), dropping often to −23 to −26°C (−10 to −15°F), but the plant withstood the temperature variation and flowered early to coincide with the male English holly. Before the female plant flowered, the solar house was covered with cheesecloth and sprayed to prevent introduction of insect-borne foreign pollen. Approximately 10,000 female flowers were pollinated by hand-application of pollen from the male English holly, but only 500 very small seeds were produced (under complete fertility, approximately 40,000 seeds would have been expected). Some of the small hybrid seeds did germinate and produced a range of normal to very dwarf seedlings. None of the F1 plants possessed the desirable characteristics of both parents, and 8 to 10 years are required before these seedlings will flower and, if fertile, produce an F2 generation.

During the winter and spring months of 1980, 1981, and 1982, a total of 657 controlled crosses were attempted involving 45,438 hand pollinations. In Dr. Orton's words, "That's a lot of tweezers'-directed anther activity while looking through a 5× head magnifier." Each new cross offers endless challenges—germinating seed, maintenance, fertilizing, watering, labeling, evaluating, selecting, and introducing new plants. The role of a plant hybridizer deals with frustrations, patience, and dedication.

The future for new holly hybrids is still great with the introduction of new and old species from around the world. It is hoped that someone in a university or research facility will follow Kosar and Orton and devote his or her career to the hybridization and selection of hollies and other woody ornamentals for the future. For the devoted holly enthusiast, holly breeding and the searching and selection of unusual seedlings are fascinating adventurist hobbies. A review of the crosses made by others will suggest directions to take in the future.

OBJECTIVES IN HOLLY BREEDING

The objectives in holly breeding are numerous and include producing good plants with good annual crops of berries; developing hardier cultivars of English holly for the hot, dry conditions of the U.S. Southeast; developing plants resistant to root rot and humid conditions, and faster-growing plants with a good show of fruit and foliage in a few years; developing new leaf shapes and sizes as well as large fruits colored orange, yellow, and red; and developing semidwarf shrubs 1.2–1.8 m (4–6 ft.) high with medium to large leaves and good colorful fruit displays. Although the hybrids of *Ilex×koehneana* (*I. aquifolium × I. latifolia*) and *I. cornuta × I. latifolia* are grand, they are all trees or large shrubs. A small shrub with attractive evergreen foliage and persistent colorful fruits developing early would be useful as a container plant for the patio and porch or as a facing plant before a display of larger shrubs. The potential for developing superior new cultivars of holly in a well-planned hybridization program is very good.

Jonathan W. Wright (1950) and others have suggested that the species within the same section and series based on morphological information are more compatible than species from different sections and series. *Ilex aquifolium* and *I. opaca,* for example, are in different sections or series and have proven to be difficult to cross. Species within the same section or from related series have been more receptive (e.g., *I. aquifolium × I. cornuta, I. aquifolium × I. latifolia, I. aquifolium × I. rugosa*). There are natural hybrids and crosses between *I. aquifolium* and *I. pernyi,* and between *I. pernyi* and *I. opaca,* indicating that *I. pernyi* may form a bridge between sections. The potential for other species serving as a bridge between sections should be investigated.

The deciduous-leaved species in subgenus *Prinos* section *Prinos,* such as *Ilex serrata* and *I. verticillata,* cross well. *Ilex geniculata* should be included in future crosses. Species in section *Prinoides* (e.g., *I. decidua*), however, do not cross readily with species in section *Prinos.*

INTRASPECIFIC AND INTERSPECIFIC HYBRIDIZATION

Intraspecific hybridization (the crossing of clones and cultivars of the same species) is usually very simple and sterility barriers are uncommon. Within a given species of *Ilex* is an array of morphologically and physiologically diverse genetic types, with a similarity of genes maintained between individuals within the species. Selection of good parental forms is important, followed by a critical evaluation (in 5 to 10 years) of large populations of seedlings to select superior plants (e.g., *I. opaca* 'Jersey Princess', *I. opaca* 'Dan Fenton'). The selected superior plants should be asexually propagated, primarily by stem cuttings, and those plants evaluated in other habitats and climatic zones before final naming and introduction.

Interspecific hybridization (the crossing of different genetic species with very different genetic complements) is usually more difficult than intraspecific hybridization because the F_1 hybrids may be highly sterile. Of major concern with interspecific origin is the restriction on the exchange of genes from the different species in the F_1 hybrid plants and eventual derivatives (e.g., *Ilex opaca × I.* 'Shin Nien').

Chromosome numbers of the various species are often a basis for deciding which interspecific crosses might be successful. As shown with other plants, crosses made with plants of the same chromosome number are more successful than when the parents have different chromosome numbers. Earlier studies showed the haploid set of chromosomes to be 18 or 20. Later studies by John L. Frierson (1959) and others showed that the somatic chromosome number is 40. Cells containing 80 (4n) chromosomes are infrequent.

One would anticipate, on the basis of the chromosome numbers on the facing page, that crosses of *Ilex pedunculosa* would be unsuccessful with plants with a lesser number of chromosomes. Plants with 40 somatic chromosomes offer no assurance that any two species will produce viable F_1 hybrids. This, as reported by Dr. Orton, can be determined only by a trial-and-error approach. The initial cross may be compatible, but the F_1 hybrid plants may be sterile. The degree of sterility may bear little or no relationship to morphological similarities of parent plants or to the vigor of the F_1 seedlings.

Interspecific hybrid sterility may be categorized as genic or chromosomal, or both, in nature.

Species of *Ilex*	Somatic chromosome number (2n)	Species of *Ilex*	Somatic chromosome number (2n)
I. aquifolium	40	*I. montana*	40
I. × attenuata	40	*I. myrtifolia*	40
I. cassine	40	*I. opaca*	40
I. ciliospinosa	40	*I. paraguariensis*	40
I. cornuta	40	*I. pedunculosa*	110 triploid (3n)?
I. crenata	40	*I. pernyi*	40
I. decidua	40	*I. purpurea*	40
I. dumosa	40	*I. rotunda*	40
I. glabra	40	*I. serrata*	40
I. integra	40 80? (4n)	*I. theezans*	40
I. latifolia	40 80? (4n)	*I. verticillata*	40
I. liukiensis	40	*I. vomitoria*	40

Even the different species may have similar genic material but the arrangement of the genic material may be quite different. The normal meiotic process may be interfered with in the hybrids that possess nonhomologous parental chromosomes, resulting in sterility considered as chromosomal in origin. Genetic sterility results in a disturbance or breakdown of the harmonious gene combinations achieved within the genetic system of each species over many thousands of years. It is important to recognize that sterility, labeled chromosomal or genic in nature, is not uncommon in interspecific hybrids since these hybrids bridge a natural barrier or system of barriers of reproductive isolation.

Interspecific hybridization has made and will continue to make important contributions to the list of commercial hollies and other ornamental plants. Hybridizers should review the holly crosses made by others and select parental species carefully.

PROCEDURE

The dioecious condition of holly, with rare exception, results in exclusively male or female plants and cross-pollination is the rule. The habit of flowering and floral structure differ within the various species of holly. Male floral inflorescences usually have more flowers than those on female plants. The female flowers are borne singly or in small fascicular clusters, while the male flowers are more numerous, usually borne 2 to 3 on a stalk or in large fascicular clusters (see Chapter 9, "Morphological Characteristics of the Genus *Ilex*").

The female flowers consist of a well-developed pistil (small yellow greenish knob) terminated by a conspicuous stigmatic surface and surrounded by four or more petals and an equal number of short aborted stamens without conspicuous yellow anthers (sacs). The male flowers have a poorly developed pistil, which is much smaller than its female counterpart. The male flowers have well-developed anther sacs and, when the flowers open, display a sticky mass of yellow pollen. The yellow anther is supported by a thin whitish filament, which arises between the petals.

The dioecious condition of holly simplifies the breeding techniques of controlled pollination. It also insures cross-pollination in nature. Thus, the plants possess tremendous genetic variability, which is what holly breeders work with in their attempts to achieve new and desirable combinations of the genetic material. Controlled pollination essentially is the placing of pollen from a male flower onto the stigmatic surface of the pistil of a female flower protected against natural pollination by insects or foreign pollen. The steps required are as follows:

1. Bag male and female flowers before the female flowers open.
2. Collect pollen.
3. Apply the pollen to the stigmatic surface of the pistil.
4. Unbag the female flowers after the time for natural pollination is past.
5. Bag the nearly ripened fruits to protect them from birds and animals.
6. Collect the ripened berries.

Large female plants outdoors are bagged (Step 1) by enclosing them in a screen tent, while smaller container-grown plants can be caged to use outdoors or in the greenhouse. Screen the greenhouse and cover the air intake vents with cheesecloth to exclude insects. With large field-grown or garden plants, individual selected flowering branches should be enclosed in netted bags or water resistant kraft bags to exclude insects. It is important to bag both male and female flowers. Any female flowers that open before bagging should be removed. Nonabsorbent rayon or cotton is wrapped around the stem just inside the open end of the bag. Tie the bag to prevent insects from entering. Tag the bag with date, number of flowers enclosed, and number of the cross. The cross number is usually preceded by the year of the cross (e.g., 96-5 indicates the fifth cross of 1996).

The netted cage, which is placed over the flowers a few days before they open, should be removed after the flowers have opened to permit detachment of the male flowers (Step 2). Pollen collecting should be done at anthesis when flowers open. Unopened female flowers should be removed. The pollen can be brushed onto waxed paper or picked off an entire stamen. With care, 20 or more female flowers can be pollinated with one male flower. The fresh male flowers can be used as a pollinating brush by grasping the filament of a stamen with tweezers or forceps. With some species, due to the difference in flowering time, it may be necessary to force the later-flowering parent plant in a warm greenhouse to obtain coincident periods of bloom. For example, when crossing female English holly with male American holly it is necessary to force the American holly plants about 4 to 6 weeks early due to the difference in blooming time.

Viability of holly pollen has not been studied extensively nor have the best storage conditions for the pollen. Pollen can be kept in a refrigerator within a desiccator for weeks with the relative humidity between 25 to 75 percent. Freezing of holly pollen, like rhododendron pollen, has not been reported. Frozen pollen of some plants remains viable for a year or more. Stored pollen can be tested by placing the pollen in a drop of 10-percent sugar in a 2-percent agar solution, keep it moist and warm about 27°C (80°F) for 2 to 3 days, then observe it under a microscope for germinating pollen tubes.

Lightly touch or brush the pollen-bearing anthers to the viscid stigmatic surface of the pistil of each female flower (Step 3). After pollination the bags should be replaced over the flowering branch and kept intact for 7 to 10 days, until the female flowers are no longer receptive. At this stage the petals will discolor and the stigmatic surface of the pistil will appear dry and darkened in color. Fresh flowers remaining at the time of unbagging should be removed.

The plants are recaged for a week or 10 days until all danger of insect contamination is past (Step 4). Additional precautions to eliminate insects are to screen the greenhouse and fumigate with a pesticide before starting pollination. Pistils are receptive to pollen as soon as the flowers open. The receptive period is reportedly short, usually two or three days and often a week or more under conditions of cool temperatures but may vary with species and cultivars. Daily observation of bagged flowers is important since they usually open earlier than flowers outside the enclosure.

Be sure to record the number of pollinated flowers, cross number, date, and other information for future reference. Labeling and keeping notes of your work is very important. Label the cross with plastic or a durable vinyl plastic label. The label may only have the cross number or include the female and male parent plants and the date. Take notes for a permanent record file of number of flowers pollinated, condition of flowers (e.g., fresh or nearly opened). Notes on pollen should include condition, stored or fresh, abundance or limited in amounts. In late summer or early fall collect information on fruit development, harvest time, size (e.g., small, medium, or large) and color. Also make note of seed count and condition and, after cleaning, the number of floating and viable seeds that sink. The date of seed emergence of first seedlings from each cross is important to record. For collected seedlings, notes should include information on the area or site, condition of the plant, and a list of other hollies in the area. Without good records it is often difficult to guess or establish parentage.

COLLECTING SEED AND EVALUATING SEEDLINGS

Seed from the hybridizer's crosses should be collected in the fall after the fruits mature and are well colored. Bagging the fruiting branches in the early fall is important to prevent birds and animals from pilfering the fruit (Step 5). Some fruits ripen very early, such as that of *Ilex wilsonii* and several deciduous species and cultivars. To be on the safe side the fruits of these early ripening plants should be protected and harvested early. Record the number of fruits collected from each cross.

Clean the seed from the pulp soon after harvesting (see Chapter 19, "Holly Propagation"). Viable seed, free of the pulp will sink in water and should be planted immediately; nonviable seed that floats can be discarded. Seedlings should be transplanted after the first true leaves appear to pots 2¼ to 3 inches in diameter filled with a light soil mixture; for better moisture control, use 4-inch porous clay pots. When larger, move plants to 6-inch containers. If the hybrid objectives are expected in F1 seedlings, the plants can be field-planted directly from the 6-inch containers. If the F1 plants are not winter hardy and need to be grown on to obtain future generations, they should be grown under greenhouse conditions or given extra winter protection outdoors (e.g., wrapped in burlap) or moved to an overwintering structure (e.g., deep coldframe, plastic-covered greenhouse, pots mulched in a lath house).

The major concern with seedling hybrids in the field is selection of the better plants. Winter hardiness, insect resistance, vigor, plant size and shape, and any plant characteristic such as leaf size, shape, and color are points to consider. This requires repeated evaluation of the seedlings to eliminate the least desirable plants as soon as possible. Each additional evaluation of the remaining seedlings must be progressively more critical. The newly selected hybrid seedlings should be equal to and preferably superior to plants already available in the trade. Only then should limited propagation begin to obtain plants to send out for additional testing. Each new test location should offer different soil types, exposure, and climatic conditions, and plants should again be compared with standard cultivars known to perform well in that area.

Of major concern within some plant societies is the naming of every new hybrid seedling. This floods the literature and registration with many new names, and often mediocre plants. New cultivars should only be introduced after all evaluations are in and the new plant is *equal to* or *superior to and distinctly different from* standard cultivars. Future success in holly hybridization will, in many instances, result from controlled interspecific crosses. It is important to recognize that sterility is not uncommon in interspecific hybrids.

A majority of the new holly cultivars in the trade are collected or controlled interspecific F1 hybrids, and are usually intermediate in appearance to the parental species. Considerable variation may be present among the seedlings as evidenced by the number of hybrids belonging to *Ilex × koehneana* (*I. aquifolium × I. latifolia*), *I. aquifolium × I. cornuta*, *I. cornuta* 'Burfordii' *× I. pernyi*, *I. pernyi × I. ciliospinosa*, *I. cornuta × I. ciliospinosa*, *I. × meserveae* (*I. rugosa × I. aquifolium*).

The transfer of genes conditioning a specific characteristic can be achieved by the selection of fertile or partially fertile hybrids, followed by backcrossing to one of the parent plants or to a different plant of one of the parent species. This method is being utilized by breeders to incorporate the red fruit characteristic of various species into plants of *Ilex crenata* and *I. glabra*. When backcrossing with plants that have a high degree of sterility, it is better if the hybrid plants are used as the female parent, since female gametogenesis is less often upset by chromosomal disharmonies than is male gametogenesis.

Sibling crosses (brother-sister mating) of relatively fertile F1 hybrids can be utilized to obtain large F2 populations. Plants of the F2 generation should be extremely diverse in appearance due to the extreme heterozygosity of the F1 interspecific hybrids, with the possibility that novel types unlike either parent will occur. The possible variations resulting in F2 populations may be similar to the seedling resulting from a backcross mating to one or the other parent. This situation can occur if a high proportion of the male gametes are nonviable. It may be that a few functional male gametes will be genotypically similar to the gametes produced by a female plant of one or the other parent species.

New hybrids involving three or more species of *Ilex* are being produced and tested as a result of the hybridization of F1 interspecific hybrids with plants of a third species. Some examples are listed here:

'Adonis' (M)	(*I. aquifolium* × *I. cornuta* 'Nellie R. Stevens') × *I. latifolia*
'Clusterberry' (F)	(*I. aquifolium* × *I. cornuta* 'Nellie R. Stevens') × *I. leucoclada*
'Coronet' (F)	(*I. aquifolium* × *I. cornuta* 'Nellie R. Stevens') × (*I. ciliospinosa* × *I. × aquipernyi*)
'Miniature' (F)	(*I. aquifolium* × *I. cornuta* 'Nellie R. Stevens') × *I. pernyi*
'Venus' (F)	(*I. aquifolium* × *I. cornuta* 'Nellie R. Stevens') × *I. latifolia*

POLLINATION AIDS

Interspecific hybridization with plants that flower at different times of the year requires storing pollen or using container-grown plants that can be shifted from one environmental condition to another. Early flowering species can be delayed by holding dormant plants at 3 to 5°C (38 to 41°F). Conversely, flowering can be advanced by moving small plants to a warmer temperature. Usually small male holly plants are manipulated in this fashion, since a small male plant will produce sufficient pollen to pollinate a large, field-grown plant.

Incompatibility between species such as *Ilex opaca* and *I. aquifolium* might possibly result from chemical or mechanical difficulties involving either pollen germination or penetration of the stigma by the pollen tube. A method used with success on rhododendrons and other plants involves cutting horizontally through the stigma with a sterilized razor blade and pollinating the cut surface. Skinner reported that using this method resulted in good seed using *I. opaca* pollen on *I. aquifolium*. He also stated that cutting the stigmatic surface may not be necessary if compatible combinations of male and female parents within the two species can be discovered.

Mutation breeding using various chemical mutagens and high energy radiation have been used in breeding programs with other plants to induce additional genetic variability. Orton reported that natural occurring genetic variability within each holly species is so great that breeders have scarcely begun to study the diversity of forms which can be obtained through standard techniques of intraspecific hybridization.

Introducing polyploidy with the use of colchicine to cause chromosome doubling, and thereby obtain tetraploid or octoploid plants, has been reported on herbaceous plants. Inducing polyploidy may also have value in the production of novel holly cultivars. With the increasing use of interspecific hybridization, the greatest value of induced polyploidy may be in the doubling of sterile interspecific hybrids to produce fertile amphidiploids.

Pollen culture has produced haploid plants (n) of tobacco and tomato plants grown from pollen grains cultured on nutrient agar. Treating these haploid plants with colchicine induces chromosome doubling, producing diploid (auto-diploid) plants with two identical sets of chromosomes and a high degree of homozygosity. This technique has not been highly developed for woody plant species but would be a powerful tool to develop homozygous plants from seed in one generation.

Biotechnology or genetic engineering is standing in the wings to become the new tool in plant breeding. Already research is changing agriculture (food crops and livestock) and pharmaceuticals. Developing a genetically improved plant (e.g., red fruit on *Ilex crenata* or *I. coriacea*) through biotechnology involves three basic steps:

1.   A complete understanding of the desired trait or characteristic to isolate the gene governing that property.
2.   Transferring the desired genetic material from the host or donor to the recipient or target plant.
3.   Growing the recombinant cells of the recipient (containing the desired gene) in tissue culture to develop a genetically modified plant. The new plant can be cloned in tissue culture or by conventional asexual propagation.

Each stage is a major step in the future, but failure in any one will be a stumbling block in the development of a new cultivar. The tools exist and the techniques, but the funding is presently lacking for such work with ornamental plants. Once success in such procedures is achieved with high-value food crops, geneticists may devote such efforts to genera such as *Ilex.*

CHAPTER 21

Holly Pests and Diseases

Hollies are relatively free of insect and diseases. Gardeners and growers of hollies need, however, to be alert to recognize problems and to be prepared to use control measures when necessary rather than a preventive program.

INSECT PESTS

Two excellent reference books on the subject of insect pests have been written by McComb (1986) and Smith (1982). The latter is generally available in major libraries and found as a reference in garden centers and county agent offices. Your local county agent is a food source for identification of pests and recommended control measures. Most state agriculture colleges publish an agricultural chemical handbook and are a good source of information for use in their respective states.

McComb (1986) divided the insects attacking holly into six groups: leaf miners, insects with sucking mouth parts, chewing insects, adult beetles that feed on various plant parts, midges, and scale insects. Most insects have four stages in their life cycle: eggs, nymphs, pupa, and adults or complete metamorphosis. Incomplete metamorphosis is the reduction or elimination of the nymphs, larvae, and/or pupa stages. Some scale insects give birth ovoviviparously (i.e., to living young). The life history of each insect pest is important for learning the optimum time for control.

Leaf miners

Leaf miners are the most serious pest with seven different species attacking hollies. They make the foliage unattractive and may cause premature leaf drop (Plate 212). The adult insects are small, 2.5- to 3-mm (3/32- to 1/8-in.) long, black flies. They belong to the genus *Phytomyza*, which is a member of the large order Diptera. The young adults appear in mid spring and may be early or delayed by weather conditions and by the stage of growth of new holly leaves. They can be expected to appear at about the same time each season, usually around the flowering time of the particular holly species. This, then, is the optimum time for control. There are usually one or two generations in the spring and again in mid summer to early fall, depending upon the species. The adults mate and live only a few days. When laying eggs, the female inserts her ovipositor into young leaf tissue, causing small puncture wounds. Frequent punctures can cause deformed leaves. Eggs are deposited usually into the underside of leaves and hatch in about 3 to 4 days. Young maggots or larvae immediately start to mine the leaves.

460

Phytomyza ilicicol Loew., native or American holly leaf miner (Figures 21-1, 21-2)
Ilex opaca (American holly) is the preferred host of this pest which rarely attacks *I. aquifolium.* Irregular mines become large and wide, eventually developing into a large blotch. There can be more than one mine per leaf, and premature leaf drop may occur on heavily infested trees.

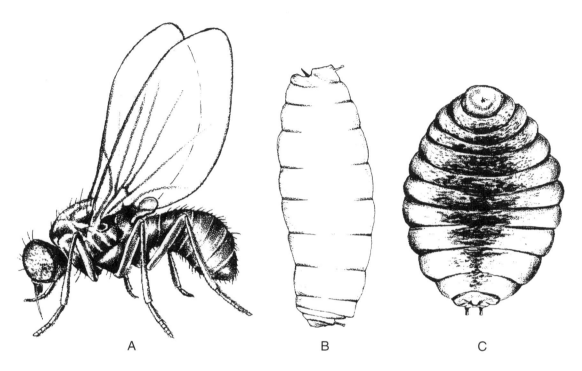

Figure 21-1. Native holly leaf miner. A: adult, B: maggot, C: pupa. Drawing by North Carolina Coop Extension Service.

Phytomyza ilices Curtis, English or holly leaf miner
This leaf miner was introduced from England with its host *Ilex aquifolium* (English holly). It is the major leaf miner on the West Coast from British Columbia to Washington and Oregon. The female oviposits in the midrib of the leaf. By midsummer the blotches developed by the larvae become light colored and are about 13 mm (½ in.) in diameter.

Phytomyza opacae Kulp, linear holly leaf miner
This is the only holly leaf miner forming linear mines in all its three larval stages. The mines are up to 2 mm (1/16 in.) wide and usually transverse the leaf several times. The host plants are *I. aquifolium* cultivars, *I. cumulicola,* and *I. opaca.* The distribution of this leaf miner is from New Jersey, Maryland, Delaware, and District of Columbia to Florida. The damage it causes leaves is usually not as severe as the damage caused by *Phytomyza ilicicol* (American holly leaf miner).

Phytomyza glabricola Kulp, inkberry holly leaf miner
The only host for this species is *Ilex glabra.* Infected leaves develop yellowish brown to reddish brown linear blotches. The insect usually produces two generations a year, overwintering in the pupal stage within the leaves. The distribution of this species has been reported from Connecticut, Massachusetts, New Jersey, New York, and Ohio. There are none from the South and Southeast.

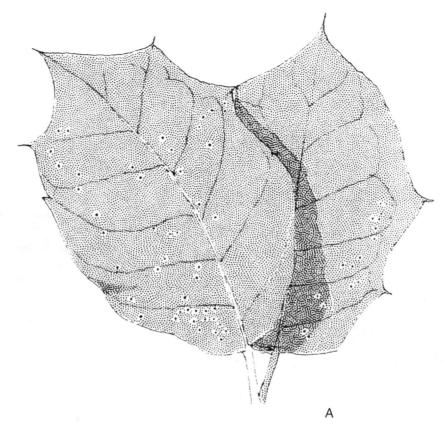

A

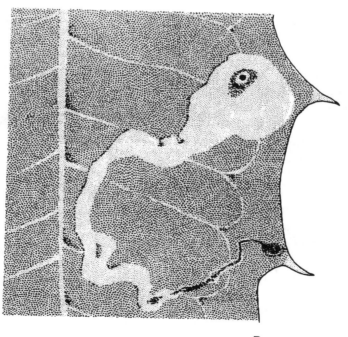

B

Figure 21-2. Native holly leaf miner. A: egg scars, B: damage. Drawing by North Carolina Coop Extension Service.

Phytomyza ditmani Kulp, deciduous holly leaf miner
The first mines occur in the spring and are obscure, being on the under sides of the leaf, small, and blotchy. Later mines, from a second generation, occur in the summer and are serpentine blotches in the upper layer of the leaf. Pupae overwinter in fallen leaves. *Ilex decidua* and *I. serrata* are the only known hosts of this insect found in the District of Columbia area.

Phytomyza verticillatae Kulp, winterberry leaf miner
Ilex verticillata is the only known host of this leaf miner, whose pupae overwinter in fallen leaves. Irregular linear blotchy mines occur on both the upper and lower epidermis of the leaf. There are probably two generations per year with pupae found from May to November. This species is reported only from the District of Columbia, Florida, and Maryland.

Phytomyza vomitoria Kulp, yaupon holly leaf miner
Ilex vomitoria is the only known host of this insect with distribution reports from California, Florida, and Georgia. The larvae form irregular linear mines, and the pupae protrude their pro-thoracic spiracles through the upper epidermis of the leaves.

Sucking Insects

Oligonychus ilicis McGregor, southern red mite (Figure 21-3)
This is the most common mite attacking hollies in the eastern United States. While insects have three pairs of legs, mites have four pairs of legs, 0.5 mm (1/64 in.) long, nearly as long as the body. The small adult mites are usually reddish brown. The adults and larva feed on the underside of leaves, sucking juices with their sucking parts. The foliage becomes discolored, turning grayish brown or a dirty brownish green, and falls prematurely. The mites overwinter in the egg stage in cold climates, but in warm areas may be active year-around. While they feed on many hollies, *Ilex crenata* 'Convexa' is the host most commonly damaged. Other species of mites are found on numerous woody ornamentals. The population of mites is greater in the spring and fall and lowest during the hot summers. Check for mites in early spring by examining the underside of leaves. Shaking branches over white paper is a good way to observe the minute active mites. Six generations of mites per season are not uncommon. Mites are distributed throughout the eastern United States and also reported in California.

Brevipalus californicus, Banks, Tenuipalidae mite
The Tenuipalidae mites are very small, less than half the size of red mites, with very short stubby legs. The life cycle is not known, but probably several generations are produced per year. These mites feed on the leaves, stems, and fruits of many woody ornamentals including hollies. They are distributed in California, Florida, Kansas, Louisiana, Maryland, and Texas.

Eriphyid Mites
At least two species of Eriphyid mites are known from the Pacific Northwest. Their feeding is restricted to the underside of leaves. The two species reported are *Acaricalus hederae* Keifer and *Diptacus swensini* Keifer. They are much smaller than spider mites and often very abundant on leafs, ranging from 500 to more than 2000 mites per single leaf.

Aphids
Aphids are a common pest feeding on tender young shoots of numerous plants including hollies. The rose aphid (*Macrosiphum rosae* L.) is reported on *Ilex aquifolium, I. cornuta, I. opaca,* and *I. verticillata* (Figure 21-4). Adult aphids are winged, the nymphs are wingless; the bodies of both

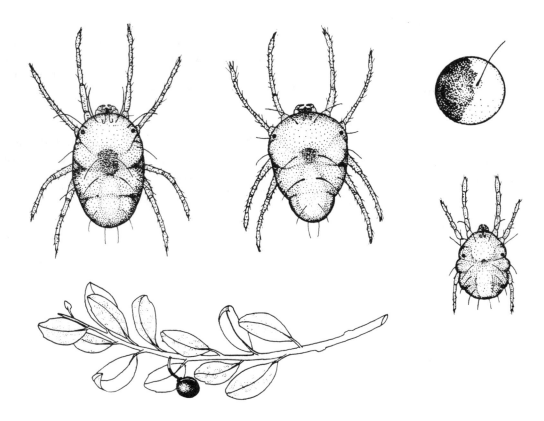

Figure 21-3. Southern red mite. Drawing by North Carolina Coop Extension Service.

may be pink or green. The entire life cycle is often spent on one host plant. Throughout the growing season, reproduction is by birth of living young, all female. In late fall a generation of male and female aphids is produced. The female lays eggs in the fall that overwinter. In the spring eggs hatch and young nymphs begin to feed by sucking plant juices. Secretion or honeydew produced by aphids, followed by a black fungus, is often as objectionable as the aphids.

Pseudococcus comstocki, Comstock mealy bug
Mealy bugs are closely related to scale insects. They are small oval-shaped, soft, and white. There are usually two generations per year, and the eggs overwinter. Mealy bugs have many host plants and feed on leaves and young stems.

Tetraleuroudes mori, mulberry white fly
The small dark elliptical nymphs, with white fringe, resemble scale insects and usually feed on the underside of the leaves. The white adults fly from the leaves in a flurry, when a branch or shrub is shaken.

Chewing Insects

Normally leaf chewing insects are not a major problem on holly; however, larvae or caterpillars are usually ravenous feeders that cause various degrees of leaf damage if not controlled. Leaf-feeding insects are members of the large order Lepidoptera, which includes moths and butterflies having

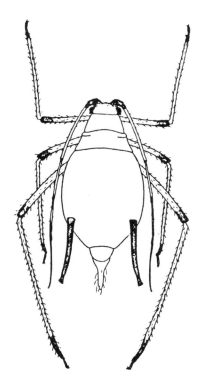

Figure 21-4. Rose aphid. Drawing by North Carolina Coop Extension Service.

two pairs of wings. The female adults lay eggs, which normally hatch into larvae in a few days. The larvae pupate, a resting stage, before transforming into adults. The pupal stage may last only a few days or as an over wintering stage near the host plant.

Thysanopyga intractata Walker, holly looper
This pest is common in the Southeast. The preferred host is *Ilex opaca,* but *I. aquifolium, I. cornuta,* and *I. vomitoria* are also affected. The light green larvae are 2 cm (¾ in.) long and feed on leaves. Damage is manifested as a distinct irregular notched-out blotch on the leaf.

Rhopobota unipunctana Haworth, holly bud moth
This pest was first reported on *Ilex verticillata* in North Carolina. The light gray green larvae feed on new growth and web together newly developing leaves. The common host is *I. aquifolium* in the Pacific Northwest (including British Columbia, Washington, Oregon), Massachusetts, New Jersey, and North Carolina. There is only one generation each year in the Northwest.

Choristoneura rosaceana Harris, obliquebanded leafroller
This pest is a member of the family Tortricidae, commonly known as the leafrollers. The brownish to yellowish green larvae come forth in the spring and bore into open buds. They also are found in a tuberal chamber or "nest" of young leaves. The mature larvae fold leaves lengthwise and distinctly eat a small portion of the leaf at each end. When disturbed, the larvae spin down on a strand of silk. The larvae overwinter in cocoons, and the females are prolific egg producers, laying up to 900 eggs. The leafroller is found in southern Canada and throughout the temperate areas of the United States. It feeds on many different deciduous trees and shrubs as well as holly, and it is reported in the Pacific Northwest as a pest of English holly.

Adult Beetles That Feed on Various Plant Parts

Callirhopalpus bifasciatus Roelofs, two-banded Japanese weevil (Figure 21-5). Confined primarily to the eastern United States, this pest attacks numerous plants including the Japanese and English hollies. The parthenogenetic females (no males reported) are pear-shaped, light brown, 4–7 mm (5/32–9/32 in.) long. Eggs are deposited along folds of leaf margins. Larvae feed on roots, and female adults feed during the day on new leaves and stems.

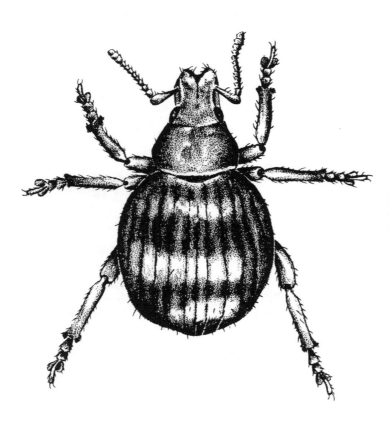

Figure 21-5. Two-banded Japanese weevil. Drawing by North Carolina Coop Extension Service.

Popillia japonica, Japanese beetle
This noted pest was discovered in New Jersey in 1916. The metallic green adults, 2–2.5 cm (¾–1 in.) long are omnivorous on woody plants, and the larvae feed on roots of grasses.

Otiorhychus sulcatus F., black vine weevil (Figures 21-6, 21-7)
This weevil is a pest in nurseries in the northeastern United States, and it is reported in the Pacific Northwest. It is found on many woody plants, including rhododendrons and hollies. The brownish black beetles, about 10 mm (⅜ in.) long, are night feeders and seldom seen. The parthenogenetic females are very active, depositing 200 to more than 800 eggs. Interior mature foliage is preferred over new growth. Damage is evidenced by a distinct marginal notching of chewed leaves.
    The larvae feed by girdling and striping bark from the roots. The adult beetles cannot fly but spread by crawling. They are moved from one part of the country to another in soil.

Pantomorus cervinus Boheman, Fuller rose beetle (Figure 21-8)
This pest is found in California and the South Atlantic states. The light brown adults, 7–9 mm (9/32–11/32 in.) long, feed on many different plants, while the larvae are more restricted, feeding on roots of roses, citrus, and cane fruits.

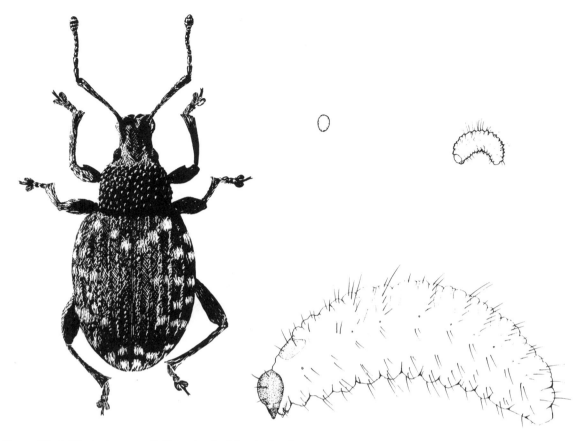

Figure 21-6. Black vine weevil. Drawing by North Carolina Coop Extension Service.

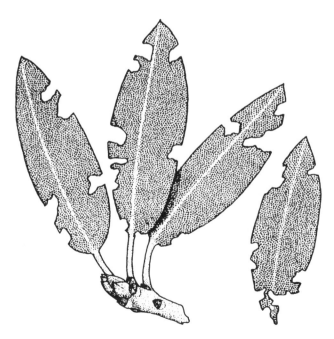

Figure 21-7. Black vine weevil damage. Drawing by North Carolina Coop Extension Service.

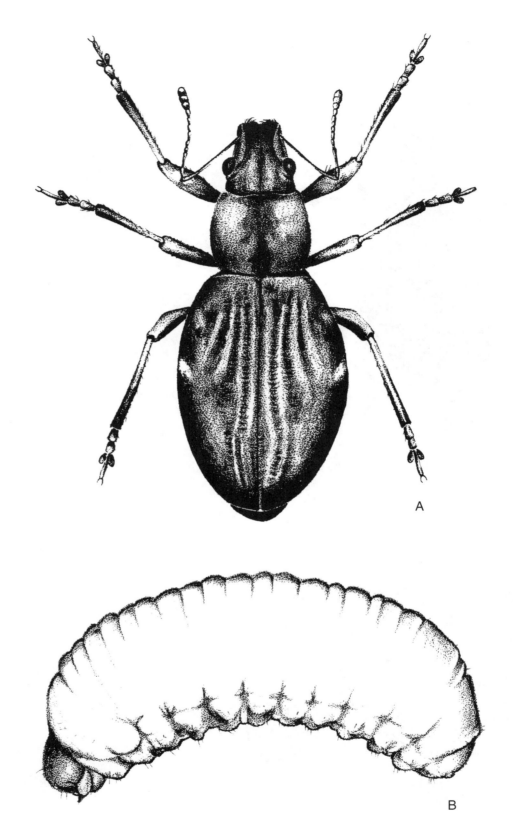

A

B

Figure 21-8. Fuller rose beetle. A: adult, B: grub. Drawing by North Carolina Coop Extension Service.

Otiorhychus rugostriatus Goeze, rough strawberry root weevil
This pest feeds on many different plants and is found from New York south to Georgia, in Michigan, and in the western United States. The larvae feed on the roots of the host plant, and the adult weevil feeds on the foliage.

Otiorhychus cribricollis Gyllenhal, Cribrate weevil
The larvae feed on wormwood (*Artemisia*), while the adult beetles feed on foliage of many different plants including hollies. This pest is distributed in the western states—California, Texas, Arizona, Nevada, and New Mexico.

Other feeding insects
Additional feeding insects on holly are *Epicauta pennsylvanica* (black blister beetle gypsymoth), *Porthetria diapar,* and various species of grasshoppers.

Midges

Ashondylia iliciola Foote, holly berry midge
This is an unwelcome pest of fruiting *Ilex opaca* and its cultivars. The adult midge is a small brown mosquito-like fly, 1.5–2.3 mm (3/64–5/64 in.) long that emerges from the pupal case, housed in old fruit, about the time of flowering in mid to late May. The adult midges are weak fliers and stay close to the original host. The females lay eggs in the small fruit while flowers are still present. The tiny young larvae are confined to the capillary cavity of the fruit with up to 3 larvae per berry. One generation is produced per year. This midge overwinters in the larvae stage.

Brown pupal cases protrude from old mature green fruits in the spring. This affects the esthetic value of specimen female holly trees. Up to 100 percent of the berries may fail to turn red in the fall and thus remain green. This midge is found only on the East Coast from North Carolina to Connecticut and was originally thought to be confined to American hollies. McComb (1986), however, reported the rearing of midges from berries of *Ilex glabra* and *I. vomitoria* collected in 1984 by Barton Bauers at Manns Harbor, North Carolina. Control spraying should be done when 60 percent of the flower petals have dropped.

Miscellaneous Pests

Gyrropsylla ilicis Ashmead, yaupon psyllid
This pest is confined to *Ilex vomitoria* (yaupon holly) in the southeastern United States. The adults are small, yellowish but variable, winged insects 5–6 mm (3/16–7/32 in.) long. They lay eggs in late February to April on terminal leaf buds, with one generation per year. The nymphs feed on young leaves, causing them to be stunted and deformed into galls. Up to 19 nymphs may be found in one gall. Plants infected with gall are unattractive, but fortunately the galls appear to be generally confined to individual plants rather than spread throughout an entire planting. Distribution of this pest is presently confined to Georgia and Florida.

Megaatigmus floridanus Milliron
A new pest was discovered in 1982 when a small, yellow, seed-feeding wasp emerged in the spring from fallen mature fruit of *Ilex opaca* in Beltsville, Maryland. The wasp was identified by E. Grissell, but had been first described in 1949 from a single specimen taken in Osceola County, Florida. There is one generation per year, and the female adults emerge in the spring to oviposit into mature fruits. One larvae develops per pyrene. Although each fruit of *I. opaca* has four pyrenes, it was uncommon to find 3–4 larvae per fruit. Most fruits had one or two infested seeds. Each larva feeds on a single seed with no outward change in the fruit. Mature larvae overwinter within the

seed, pupating in late spring at flower bud formation. The wasp has been reared from seed of *I.* × *attenuata* collected in Florida, but not from *I. cassine,* and only from *I. opaca* in Maryland.

Scale Insects

More than fifty different scale insects feed on hollies (see Table 17, Figures 21-9 to 21-15, Plate 213). Some cause serious damage but are easily detected and generally easy to control. They can be controlled in the crawler stage in the spring with weekly applications of a pesticide or with a dormant spray in the winter. I have only seen one case where a group of plants was neglected to the point that scales were so numerous on the stems and leaves that the plants were severely weakened. With a good spray program, however, the infested plants were completely controlled in two years.

Scale insects belong to the order Homoptera and are small with long needlelike mouth parts that attach to plants and suck out plant juices. The adult scales are usually less than 10 mm (⅜ in.) long and most are 1.5–5 mm (³⁄₆₄–³⁄₁₆ in.) long. Species differ in appearance, many have a scale-like covering, others are cottony or resemble a drop of whitish wax. Some produce "honey dew," a by-product of feeding, and the sugary substance attracts other insects and becomes a host for unsightly black sooty mold fungi. Scales come in various shapes from oval to elliptical to rectangular. The scale adults attach to leaves or stems and become immobile.

Scale insects have many hosts including holly. They also have similar life histories and overwinter as mature females or eggs (males are rare). The overwintering mature females lay eggs in early spring under the scales, which hatch to nymphs or "crawlers," and then move out to new feeding sites. The young nymphs have legs for mobility but usually lose them at the first molt and develop an outer covering into a protective scale. Some female scales are ovoviviparous, giving birth to living young. Others are very productive and lay up to 3000 eggs.

ABIOTIC AND NONPATHOGENIC DISEASES

In contrast to insect damage, most holly pathogens are not aggressive and generally not serious. Some diseases, however, can be serious when perishable environmental conditions are present. Many organisms on holly are secondary or weak pathogens on weak or dead portions of the plant; often these organisms are not direct but follow abiotic or non-pathogenic problems through wounds or mechanical injuries.

Biotic or Pathogenic Diseases

More than 15 genera of fungi on holly are known. Many of these genera include more than one species. Biotic plant diseases are pathogenetic or infectious diseases caused by living organisms, fungi, bacteria, nematodes, and viruses.

Leaf Problems

Fungal leaf spots are usually small and regular in size and shape. Most are brownish in color, with small rings or borders, but often range from white to black depending on the host and disease.

Tar spots. This disease is found mainly in the southern United States and along the coast to New England. Yellow spots occur in early summer often turning reddish brown. By fall the small tar-like spots are easily recognized in the discolored areas. *Phacidium curtisii* Luttell is the general cause of tar spot, plus four other *Phacidium* species and three species of the fungus *Rhytisma.*

The yellow spot disease is more common in wet seasons and in high humid areas, overwin-

Table 17. Scale insects, their hosts, and their distribution.

Scale	Comment	Host	Distribution
Cyanophyllum scale *Abgrallaspis cyanophylli* Signoret	Oval or triangular, whitish	Numerous, *I. cassine*, *I. cornuta, I. myrtifolia*	U.S.A., greenhouses
Howard scale *Abgrallaspis howardi* Cockerell	Oval, whitish	*I. crenata, I. opaca*	Southern U.S.A. from Florida to Texas, eastern & midwestern states
Townsend scale *Abgrallaspis townsendi* Cockerell	Round, grayish white	*I. opaca*	Alabama, Arkansas, District of Columbia, Florida, Georgia, Louisiana, Maryland, Massachusetts, Mississippi, Missouri, Ohio, Pennsylvania, Tennessee, Virginia
Red bay scale *Acutaspis perseae* Comstock	Circular, red-brown to brown	*I. crenata, I. glabra,* *I opaca, I. vomitoria*	District of Columbia, Florida, Georgia, Louisiana, Mississippi, Missouri, Oklahoma, South Carolina, Tennessee, Texas
Yellow scale *Aonidiella citrina* Coquillett	Circular, flat, yellow or whitish	*I. cornuta*	California, Florida, Texas
Oleander scale *Aspidiotus nerii* Bouche	Circular to irregular, flat to convex, white to light brown	*I. cornuta, I. crenata*	Warm areas of U.S.A.
Spinose scale *Aspidiotus spinosus* Comstock	Circular, convex, light brown	*I. opaca, I. cassine*	Alabama, California, Florida, Georgia, Louisiana, Mississippi, Texas
Puteanum scale *Asterolecaniun* *puteanum* Russell	Convex, yellow-green	*I. crenata, I. vomitoria* *I. opaca, I. cornuta*	Florida
Indian wax scale *Ceroplastes ceriferus*	Waxy, produces honeydew	Numerous, *I. cornuta*	Texas to Maryland
Barnacle scale *Ceroplastes* *cirripediformis* Comstock	Waxy, produces honeydew	Numerous, *I. aquifolium*	Caribbean, North Carolina to Texas, Arizona to California
Florida wax scale *Ceroplastes floridensis* Comstock	Waxy, produces honeydew	Numerous, *I. glabra,* *I. cornuta, I. vomitoria,* *I. crenata*	Southeastern U.S.A. to Maryland, west to New Mexico
Red wax scale *Ceroplastes rubens* Maskell	Pink to reddish wax	Numerous, citrus	Australia, Florida

(continued)

Table 17 (continued).

SCALE	COMMENT	HOST	DISTRIBUTION
Chinese wax scale *Ceroplastes sinensis* Del Guerico	Waxy	Numerous, *I. aquifolium,* *I. crenata, I. vomitoria*	California, southeastern Virginia
Florida red scale *Chrysomphalus* *aonidum* L.	Circular, convex, dark reddish brown to black	Numerous, *I. cornuta,* *I. crenata, I. glabra*	Most states, greenhouses in colder areas
Dictyospermum scale *Chrysomphalus* *dictyospermi* Morgan	Circular, slightly convex, light brown	Numerous, *I. cassine,* *I. cornuta, I. crenata,* *I. glabra, I. latifolia,* *I. pernyi*	Alabama, Arizona, California, Florida, Georgia, Louisiana, Maryland, Massachusetts, Michigan, New Jersey, Ohio, Pennsylvania, South Carolina, Texas, Utah, Virginia
Brown soft scale *Coccus hesperidum* Linn	Convex, yellow-green to yellow-brown	Numerous, *I. cornuta,* *I. crenata* in Virginia (produces honeydew), *I. aquifolium* in Oregon & Florida	Eastern U.S.A. to Pacific Northwest, greenhouses
Green scale *Coccus viridis* Green	Oval, pale green	*I. cornuta, I. paraguariensis,* *I. vomitoria*	Florida
Camellia mining scale *Duplaspidiotus claviger* Cockerell	Circular, slightly convex, grayish	*I. opaca, I. vomitoria*	Florida
Holly scale *Dynasoidiotus* *britannicus* Newstead	Oval, yellow	*I. aquifolium,* evergreen *Prunus* & *Buxus*	Pacific Northwest
Tessellated scale *Eucalymnatus tesselatus* Signoret	Ovate, dark brown	*I. cassine, I. cornuta,* *I. glabra, I. integra,* *I. latifolia, I. vomitoria*	Florida, greenhouses
Tea scale *Fiorinia theae* Green	Elongate-oval, light yellow to brown	Numerous, *I. aquifolium,* *I. cassine, I. crenata,* *I. vomitoria*	Southern U.S.A. from Arizona north to Maryland
Latania scale *Hemiberlesia* Signoret	Circular, convex, dirty white	Very numerous: *I. cassine,* *I. cornuta, I. crenata,* *I. integra, I. opaca*	Southern U.S.A. from California to Florida, East Coast to New England
Greedy scale *Hemiberlesia rapax* Comstock	Circular, convex, gray to whitish	*I. cornuta, I. crenata*	Alabama, California, District of Columbia, Florida, Georgia, Idaho, Illinois, Indiana, Louisi- ana, Maryland, Michigan, Mississippi, New Jersey, New York, Ohio, Oregon, Pennsylvania, South Carolina, Texas, Virginia, Washington

SCALE	COMMENT	HOST	DISTRIBUTION
Mining scale *Howardia biclavis* Comstock	Circular, convex, whitish to yellow	Numerous, *I. vomitoria*	Florida, Maryland, Missouri, Pennsylvania
Glassy scale *Inglisia vitrea* Cockerell	Round or oval, glassy wax	*I. cassine*	Florida
Black thread scale *Ischnaspis longirodtris* Signoret	Threadlike, black	*I. opaca*	District of Columbia, Florida, Georgia, Maryland, Missouri, New Jersey, New York, Ohio, Oklahoma, Pennsylvania
Acuminata scale *Kilifia acuminata* Signoret	Triangular, pale green	*I. aquifolium, I. cassine, I. coriacea, I. glabra, I. myrtifolia, I. rotunda, I. vomitoria*	District of Columbia, Florida, Georgia, Missouri, New York, Texas
Purple scale *Lepidosaphes beckii* Newman	Oystershell-shaped, purplish	*I. cornuta, I. glabra, I. integra, I. latifolia, I. opaca*	Alabama, Arkansas, California, Florida, Georgia, Louisiana, Mississippi, Texas
Camellia scale *Lepidosaphes camelliae* Hoke	Oystershell-shaped, convex, brown	*I. cornuta, I. crenata*	Alabama, Arkansas, Connecticut, Delaware, Florida, Georgia, Louisiana, Maryland, Massachusetts, Mississippi, Missouri, New York, North Carolina, Oklahoma, Oregon, South Carolina, Texas, Virginia
Japanese maple scale *Lopholeicaspis japonica* Cockerell	Elongate, whitish, purple hue	*I. crenata, Pyracantha & Acer*	Connecticut, Delaware, District of Columbia, Maryland, New Jersey, New York, Pennsylvania, Rhode Island
Smilax scale *Melanaspis smilacis* Comstock	Circular to oval, convex, dark brown to black	*I. vomitoria* in Florida	District of Columbia, Florida, Georgia, Louisiana, Maryland, Massachusetts, South Carolina, Texas, Virginia

(continued)

Table 17 (continued).

SCALE	COMMENT	HOST	DISTRIBUTION
Gloomy scale *Melanaspis tenebricosa* Comstock	Circular, convex, dark gray to black	*I. glabra*	Delaware, District of Columbia, Florida, Georgia, Louisiana, Maryland, Mississippi, Missouri, New Jersey, New York, North Carolina, Ohio, Oklahoma, Pennsylvania, South Carolina, Tennessee, Texas, Virginia, West Virginia
Terrapin scale *Mesolecanium nigrofasciatum* Pergande	Round, red to black	Numerous, *I. opaca*	Every state east of the Mississippi River except Massachusetts, New Hampshire, Vermont. Also in Arizona, Iowa, Louisiana, Minnesota, Mississippi, New Mexico, Texas
Harper Scale *Neopinnaspis harperi* McKenzie	Elongate, convex, whitish	*I. myrtifolia, I. opaca*	Florida, Georgia
Chaff scale *Parlatoria pergandii* Comstock	Oval to irregular, brownish	*I. latifolia*	Florida, Georgia, Kansas, Louisiana, Maryland, Mississippi, New York, Oklahoma, Pennsylvania, South Carolina, Texas
Proteus scale *Parlatoria proteus* Curtis	Elongate ovale, green to greenish yellow	Numerous, *I. cornuta*	District of Columbia, Florida, Louisiana, Maryland, New York, Pennsylvania, Tennessee, Texas
Lesser snow scale *Pinnaspia strachani* Cooley	Irregular, flat, whitish	*I. glabra*	Alabama, Florida, Georgia, Louisiana, Mississippi, Texas
Mango shield scale *Protopulvinaria mangiferae* Green	Triangular, flat, light green	Mangoes, *I. cassine*	Florida, Texas
Pyriform scale *Protopulvinaria pyriformis* Cockerell	Pyriform, light brown to reddish brown	*I. vomitoria*	East Coast, New Hampshire to Texas, California

SCALE	COMMENT	HOST	DISTRIBUTION
Camphor scale *Pseudaonidia duplex* Comstock	Circular, convex, brownish	*I. cassine, I. vomitoria*	Florida, Georgia, Louisiana, Mississippi, Texas, Virginia
False oleander scale *Pseudaulacaspis cockerelli* Cooley	Pyriform, convex, white	Numerous, *I. latifolia*	Florida, Georgia, Louisiana, Missouri, South Carolina, Tennessee, Texas
White peach scale *Pseudaulacaspis pentagona* Targioni-Tozzetti	Circular, convex, whitish	Numerous, *I. opaca*	Southern U.S.A., Texas, East Coast to Connecticut
False parlatoria scale *Pseudiparlatoria parlatorioides* Comstock	Circular, usually flat, yellowish brown	*I. vomitoria*	Florida, Georgia, Maryland, New Jersey, Texas
Cottony camellia scale *Pulvinaria floccifera* Westwood	Oval, cream to light brown	*I. aquifolium, I. opaca*	East & West Coasts, midwestern states, Texas
Cottony maple scale *Pulvinaria innumerabilis* Rathvon	Convex, ovate, variable gray to brown	Many, including *Ilex*	U.S.A.
Green shield scale *Pulvinaria psidii* Maskell	Oval, deep-green to light green	*Ilex*	Alabama, Florida, Georgia
Urbicola soft scale *Pulvinaria urbicola* Cockerell	Oval, convex, light or dark yellow-green	*I. purpurea*	Florida
Forbes scale *Quadraspidiotus forbesi* Johnson	Circular, flat to convex, dirty gray	*I. opaca, I. vomitoria*	U.S.A.
Walnut scale *Quadraspidiotus juglansregiae* Comstock	Circular, flat, gray to reddish brown	Numerous, *I. crenata, I. glabra, I. opaca*	U.S.A.
Hemispherical scale *Saissetia coffeae* Walker	Hemispherical, oval, yellow brown to dark brown	*I. cassine, I. cornuta, I. glabra*	Warm areas of U.S.A., greenhouses
Mexican black scale *Saissetia miranda* Cockerell & Parrott	Oval, brown to black-brown	*I. × attenuata, I. glabra, I. paraguariensis, I. vomitoria*	Southwestern & southern U.S.A., greenhouses

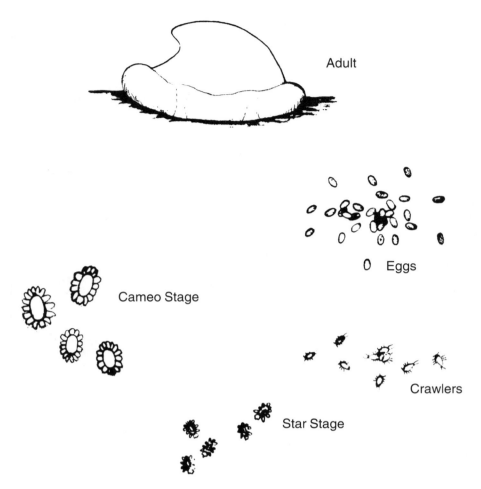

Figure 21-9. Lifecycle of Indian wax scale (*Ceroplastes ceriferus*). Drawing by North Carolina Coop Extension Service.

tering in old infected leaves and spores spread by wind to young leaves in the spring. General control is sanitation, removal of old leaves from the area, and pruning to improve air circulation and overcrowding. The following hollies are host to various tar spot fungi species: *I. ambigua*, *I. cassine*, *I. cumulicola*, *I. decidua*, *I. monticola*, *I. opaca*, *I. verticillata*, and *I. vomitoria*.

***Phyllosticta ilicis* Sacc., leaf spot.** This disease is common in the Gulf states and reported from other areas in the United States. It can be serious on susceptible species and cultivars. The leaf spot symptoms vary with holly species, but usually appear as irregular yellowish white spots with reddish borders on the upper surface of the leaf. Infected areas begin near the leaf apex, enlarging and coalescing until often covering the entire leaf. The presences of pycnidia (flesh-like body containing conidia or spores) is an important diagnostic characteristic of the leaf spots. Six hollies are hosts to this disease: *Ilex aquifolium*, *I. coriacea*, *I. cornuta* 'Burfordii', *I. crenata*, *I. opaca*, and *I. verticillata*. Control involves removing infected leaves and keeping plants in a vigorous condition with proper fertilizer and irrigation in dry seasons. Fungicide sprays should be applied in late summer and early fall.

***Elsinoe ilicis* Plakidas, spot anthracnose or scab.** This disease was first reported in Louisiana on *Ilex cornuta*, but has been observed in other southern states. Small black spots appear, enlarging

Figure 21-10. Underside of Indian wax scale (*Ceroplastes ceriferus*). Drawing by North Carolina Coop Extension Service.

Figure 21-11. Brown soft scale (*Coccus hesperidum*). Drawing by North Carolina Coop Extension Service.

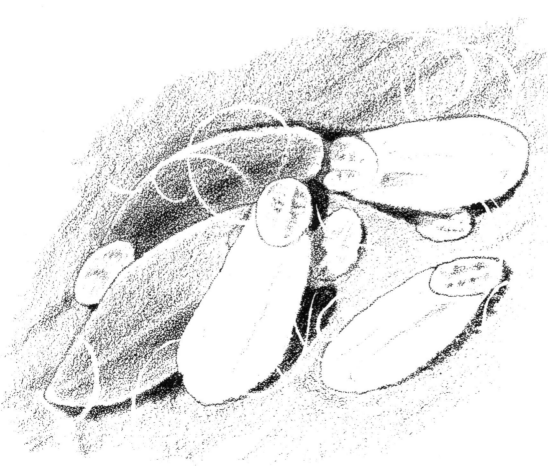

Figure 21-12. Tea scale (*Fiorinia theae*). Drawing by North Carolina Coop Extension Service.

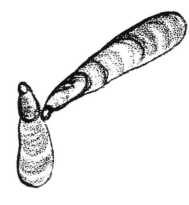

Figure 21-13. Camellia scale
(*Lepidosaphes camelliae*). Drawing by
North Carolina Coop Extension Service.

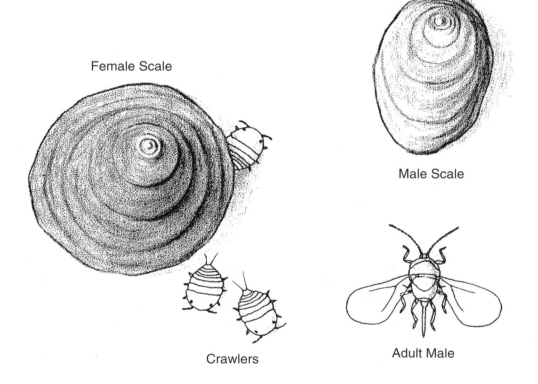

Female Scale

Male Scale

Crawlers

Adult Male

Figure 21-14. Gloomy scale (*Melanaspis tenebricosa*). Drawing by North Carolina Coop
Extension Service.

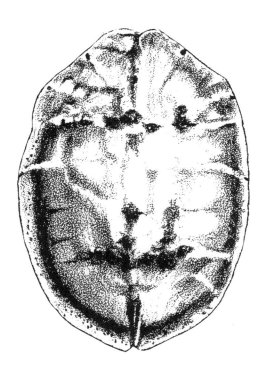

Figure 21-15. Two views of hemispherical scale (*Saissetia coffeae*). Drawing by North Carolina Coop Extension Service.

to 1–2 mm (¹⁄₃₂–¹⁄₁₆ in.) spots at the apex or throughout the leaf. Spots may coalesce, but are confined to the upper leaf surface as observed in the fall. A second symptom appears in early fall: chlorotic areas followed by lesions on the leaf surface, which may become visible on the lower surface. Fungicide should be used when symptoms are noted.

***Cylindrocladium avesiculatum*, leaf spot.** This serious disease attacks container-grown hollies and was first reported in 1970 in Georgia and Florida on *Ilex cornuta, I. crenata, I. opaca,* and *I. vomitoria*. It manifests itself as small chlorotic spots that become purplish black with light green borders. Mature lesions may be 16 mm (⅝ in.) in diameter, with purplish black margins and grayish to light brown centers. In humid weather entire leaves become affected along with twig dieback and plant death. Sanitation of fallen leaves is an important control measure as is using a fungicide.

***Sclerophoma*, holly scab.** This disease is reported on *Ilex aquifolium* in the Pacific Northwest and should not be confused with spot anthracnose. Small dark spots usually appear on the lower leaf surface, aggregating to spots 10 mm in diameter. A fungicide may be effective plus selecting resistant cultivars.

***Gloesporium aquifolii*, leaf spot or anthracnose.** This disease is reported in scattered areas throughout the United States on *Ilex aquifolium*. Light brown spots appear on the leaves, but twigs and branches also can be affected. Pink to salmon colored spores appear on necrotic areas and defoliation can occur. Sanitation is important and a fungicide should be applied if necessary. Other anthracnose fungi include *Gloesporium ilicis*, which has been reported on *I. cassine, I. cornuta,* and *I. opaca.*

***Cerocospora*, leaf spot.** Three fungi species are reported on several species of holly in the Gulf states and north to New Jersey. The symptoms vary with the fungi and the host. The leaf spots range from 1 to 3 mm (¹⁄₃₂ to ⅛ in.) in diameter up to large blotches. The spots are light to dark brown, some with purple borders or ridges. *Cerocospora ilicicola* Maubl. is reported on *Ilex opaca, C. ilicis* on *I. cornuta, I. decidua. I. glabra, I. opaca,* and *I. vomitoria.* A fungicide spray is warranted.

Blights

There are two major blight diseases that kill young leaves, fruits, and twigs of holly. These blights spread rapidly and effect a side or entire tree.

***Phytophthora* leaf and twig blight.** This disease is a major problem in the Pacific Northwest for *Ilex aquifolium.* First reports were from the cool wet coastal areas, but the blight was later found in the warm dry areas of the Willamette Valley. The first symptoms are black areas on lower leaves followed by defoliation of blighted leaves and continuing with twig dieback and cankers on the stems. Air movement is important as is selection of orchard site. The site should be open with well-drained soil and with adequate spacing between trees to increase air movement. Pruning also helps air flow. The blight can be retarded with protective fungicides in the cool rainy fall season.

***Botrytis cinerea* Per. ex. Fr., blight or gray mold.** This common disease on many plants is found on the flowers of the host *Ilex opaca* in wet seasons. It continues as a grayish brown fungal growth on twigs in humid weather. Blighted twigs should be pruned to reduce spread of the disease, and fungicides should be used after plants flower.

Mildews. Powdery mildew and black mildew are generally not serious but can distract from the foliage. A fungicide is generally not required, although it can be used for control.

Sooty Molds. Sooty molds are brownish black superficial fungus growths that are usually distracting on leaves and fruits. The fungi live on bird and insect droppings or on the "honeydew" usually associated with aphids. Insecticides applied to overhanging trees that harbor the aphids will reduce sooty mold.

***Corynebactium ilicis* Mandel & Guba, bacterial leaf and twig blight.** This disease was first reported in 1957 in Massachusetts on *Ilex opaca.* It is not common on all cultivars. The symptoms are dried twigs, appearing scorched or dark, then drooping. Black lesions are bordered by a yellow-green halo and soon drop from the wilted stems. Heavily fertilized trees are more susceptible to this disease, and a secondary organism, often *Fusarium,* invades the damaged tissue. A bactericide is recommended for control.

Viruses or yellow leaf spot. This disease is not common or well known. It was first observed in 1973 in Maryland on *Ilex crenata* 'Rotundifolia'. The disease is caused by the tobacco ring spot virus. Alfalfa mosaic virus has also been isolated on Japanese holly. Chlorotic spots are found on infested leaves and usually on all new growth. Irregular yellow leaf margins are common symptoms on older leaves. The disease spreads slowly and is not considered a serious problem.

Green Algae. Green scum is not parasitic, but may be distracting on the holly leaves. It is a problem in orchards in the Pacific Northwest and in Florida. An algicide is recommended.

Twig and Branch Diseases.

Twig blights are often secondary following a leaf spotting organism. Other organisms causing a blight or die-back directly invade the twigs and young branches. Cankers are localized disease areas with cracking bark, a depressed area, or an open wound. Canker wood usually has a brown discoloration. It begins at a twig scar or wound and completely girdles a branch or trunk. Numerous fungi are reported as agents of twig blight, but many are secondary organisms found in lesions caused by other organisms. Often 3 to 4 different organisms are isolated from a single canker. Plants in good healthy condition are usually free of twig and canker problems.

Botryosphaeria **canker.** This disease is common on stressed plants and is isolated from blighted twigs and cankers. It is associated with the death of twigs followed by browning and dead leaves. The symptoms are the cankers appearing on branches and trunks as depressed areas and cracking and numerous black fruiting bodies. The cankerous wood is brown and can completely girdle the branches and stems, causing death above the canker.

 Botryosphaeria organisms are common on many ornamentals. Three species have been reported on hollies: *B. ribis* Gross & Dug on *Ilex crenata* and *I. opaca*; *B. dothidea* Ces. & de Not. on *I. crenata*, *I. glabra*, and *I. opaca*; and *B. philoprina* Arx & Muller on *I. opaca*. The fungus overwinters on infected wood. Numerous nursery-grown plants can be host to the fungus and serve as a source of inoculum. Good cultural practices are important. Healthy plants usually have few cankers. Prune dead cankerous branches 3 in. below the cankers and destroy them. Fungicides are usually not effective.

Fusarium solani **App. & Wr., die-back.** This disease was first reported in New Jersey in 1941 on drought-stressed specimens of *Ilex opaca*. *Fusarium solani* is the casual agent, but other *Fusarium* species have been isolated. Leaves appear frost-damaged, turning black and defoliating. Brown discoloration of cortex and pith is typical with the xylem lighter. Removal of diseased twigs is advised, and the use of a fungicide is questionable.

Gloesporium, **canker and die-back.** This disease was first reported in Alabama in 1971 on container-grown *Ilex cornuta* 'Burfordii'. First symptoms are discoloration of terminal twigs and defoliation, followed by sunken lesions and exuding of pink spore masses from the twigs. Pruning (and destroying) diseased wood is an effective control, but use of fungicide is questionable.

Root Rots

With the extensive use of container culture, root rots have become more important and a problem in propagating beds. Several different fungi are the organisms causing root rots. The symptoms of root rot are plant decline, yellowing, die back, and poor growth. Root rot organisms are usually secondary and present symptoms initiated by unfavorable growing conditions such as excessive soil moisture, poor drainage, unfavorable pH, and adverse soil environmental factors.

Rhizoctonia solani **Kuhn, root rot or damping off.** This disease is found on many plants including hollies and often is serious on seedlings and cuttings in propagating beds. Seedlings are affected at the media level, and the young stems turn black with rot. Cuttings rot at the base and on young developing roots. Poor drainage and poor aerated media offer favorable conditions for damping off. It is not uncommon in very moist propagating beds for the fungus to grow on the cuttings following leaf drop. All hollies are host to this disease. Sanitation of the propagating area and benches is important. Use a fungicidal drench to clean the benches and entire area. Media should be changed after each batch of cuttings and replaced with clean sterilized media if possible. The media should be porous (25 to 35 percent air-filled pore space), a mix of 1 part peat, 1 part fine pine bark, and 2 parts coarse perlite or other lightweight neutral aggregate. The media should be moist but not soaking wet.

Cylindrocladium scoparium **Morgan, cutting rot.** Cutting rot afflicts *Ilex crenata* cuttings, and its symptoms are similar to those of *Rhizoctonia* rot. Leaves appear water-soaked and darkened and soon drop. The base of the cutting turns dark brownish black and rots. In the advance disease stage, in high humidity, a brownish mycelium spreads rapidly, covering the leaves and media. Control of moisture in the propagation house and media is important.

***Pythium* root rot.** *Pythium* root rot is similar to *Rhizoctonia* root rot in that it attacks plants and cuttings of *Ilex crenata*. The symptoms also are similar: plants develop poorly, leaves yellow and drop prematurely. *Pythium* is common in excessive moisture on cuttings and container plants and associated with nematodes causing root damage. Sanitation and control of soil or media moisture is important. Using a fungicide drench on propagation benches and containers will give control.

***Thielaviopsis basicola* Ferr., root rot.** Container-grown *Ilex crenata* is the host of this fungus in Virginia. The fungus is saprophytic in the soil causing deep lesions and rotting of new holly rootlets. The symptoms of infected plants are poor growth. Good cultural practices will reduce the disease as will use of a fungicide soil drench.

***Phymatotrichum omnivorum* Dug., root rot.** This fungus is common in the southern states on many plants and is reported on holly in Texas. Holly hosts include *Ilex ambigua, I. cassine, I. decidua, I. opaca,* and *I. vomitoria*. Characteristic summer symptoms are wilting of plants followed by dying. The fungus is found in heavy, alkaline soils. Adding organic matter and heavy fertilization is helpful in reducing the disease.

Graft Failure

The failure of callus formation on grafts and cuttings is caused by the fungus *Chalaropsis thielavioides* Peyronel, reported in New Jersey. The development of callus on the cut surfaces is prevented by a white mycelium. Sanitation is important: remove infected plants and decontaminate grafting benches and beds.

Nematodes

Nematodes are seldom seen due to their microscopic size. They live in organic matter in the soil or on roots and other parts of living plants. Most parasitic nematodes feed by a stylet, sucking juices from plants cells. They injure plants by direct feeding or wounding tissue, making entrance for other disease organisms. Plant decline is often the only symptom, followed by gradual stunting, chlorosis, and leaf drop, all of which make diagnosing difficult. *Ilex crenata* is the host of ring, stunt, and root-knot nematodes, and its various cultivars are susceptible to root-knot.

Four *Meloidogyne* species cause small identifiable root-knots on holly; one *Criconemoides* species causes ring nematode; and one *Tylenchorhynchus* species is known as stunt nematode. Some soil fungicides and nematocides are effective in controlling nematodes. For container-grown plants of *Ilex crenata* it is important to use nematode-free and sterilized soils.

Abiotic or Non-Pathogenic Diseases

Abiotic diseases are usually the results of environmental or handling conditions. These include winter injury, drought, excessive moisture, nutritional deficiencies, plant weaknesses, and mechanical damage.

Loss of leaves

Many species of holly are evergreen and, depending upon species, may retain their leaves one or more years. The older leaves turn yellow and fall off. This leaf drop normally occurs in early spring just before new growth develops; however, in a dry season a premature yellowing and dropping of some leaves may occur in the fall. This is a normal occurrence but may vary with species, cultivars, and adjacent plants.

Weather and mechanical injuries

Selecting species and cultivars hardy in your area is important. Hardiness zone ratings are based on an average minimum temperature. In severe winters, however, plants may suffer: snow-covered lower branches or protected sides of a tree may remain green while exposed leaves turn brown.

Sudden drops in temperature may kill plants that were not hardened off before the sudden drop occurred. In 1991 a very mild October and early November was followed, in many areas, by the first killing frost, with lows of −11°C (12°F) repeated for several nights. Plants that normally withstand such temperatures were killed to the ground.

Symptoms of winter damage may be browning of leaves, marginal leaf scorch, defoliation, twig and limb death, and death of entire plants. Planting hollies in non exposed or protected areas helps to reduce winter damage from sudden changes in temperature and prolonged, extreme cold periods.

Drought Damage

Holly leaves often turn yellow or brown during a sudden drought period. This is more noticeable on newly planted material or after a spring of excessive rain followed by an extreme drought during a long dry summer. Newly planted hollies should be watered once a week during the summer and early fall, and not allowed to go into the dormant winter season in a dry condition.

Leaf Scald

Sun-scalded leaves have light brown to yellowish spots 2.5 cm (1 in.) in diameter on the upper surface, with well-defined margins. Direct, hot sunlight drys the exposed tissue of succulent leaves. As the spots enlarge, they may be noted on the lower surface. The unsightly scald spots are often first observed on glossy leaves (e.g., *Ilex aquifolium, I. cornuta* 'Burfordii'). Secondary fungi, often thought to be the cause, will invade the spots. The spots are not injurious to the plant but are distracting.

Edema

Small, brown corky or wartlike spots may appear on the lower leaf surface. Each spot is an outgrowth at or near a stomata and more common on container plants during high humidity and when soils are extremely wet. Edema usually occurs in late summer and is not associated with the wet conditions earlier in the season. The spots are not considered objectionable, and no control is recommended.

Spine Spots

Various small purplish spots with a gray center are caused by leaf spines puncturing adjacent leaves. Young tender leaves are easily punctured, when rustled in the wind, by spines on older leaves. The tiny punctures may be visible on both sides of the leaves and are most common on cultivars of *Ilex aquifolium* and *I. opaca*. The tiny punctures should not be confused with the non-purplish spots caused by the feeding and egglaying adult leaf miner insects.

Girdling roots

This problem is common for many container-grown plants. When plants are left too long in the container and not shifted, the roots begin to encircle one another to the point of strangulation (Plate 214). If not corrected, girdling roots can kill a plant: the roots encircle the main trunk or large lateral roots causing a disruption of translocation of nutrients from the affected area. Similar damage is seen when wires or heavy string are left around a limb or trunk. Affected trees have poor vegetative growth and usually die. The best control is to check the roots when first removing the plant from the container. Remove the encircling roots and loosen other roots from the mass. If heavy root pruning is done, thin out the top of the plant to compensate for the removed roots. The treated root-girdled plants usually respond favorably.

Mower and Tractoritis

Damage from mowers and tractors is a common problem around plants. Anyone working with this type of equipment should avoid hitting the trunks. A mulch at the base of the trunk helps to control weeds and grasses, but high heavy rings of mulch (often 30 cm/12 in. or more) are distracting and not advised.

Purple leaf blotch

Purple leaf blotch is not caused by insects or a disease organism, but is an inherent genetic weakness in some cultivars and selections of *Ilex opaca*. Do not propagate trees showing the purple blotch for the symptoms can be perpetuated in cuttings.

Nutritional Deficiencies

Boron deficiency in *Ilex aquifolium* will display irregular-shaped reddish or purplish spots on the upper leaf surface. The spots on deformed leaves enlarge to a pattern of concentric rings bordered by yellow tissue. Fertilizing holly to avoid deficiencies should be based on soil conditions, soil test, time of year, and the cultivar being grown.

Air Pollution

Air pollution damage to holly is not a serious problem. Ozone levels up to 0.5 ppm for 7 hours at different temperature and humidity levels showed no adverse effect. High levels of sulfur dioxide (SO_2) caused a few small necrotic areas on terminal leaves. Holly escaped damage from SO_2 levels normally injurious to other plants. Both *Ilex crenata* and *I. opaca* are reported quite resistant to ozone under experimental conditions.

Salt Injury

Holly grown near the seashore often shows scorch or marginal leaf burn. The tips and margins become gray or burned following periods of high winds. High salt content in underground water can cause burning of the roots and salt deposit on the leaves, which leads to scorching and death of the leaves. Nonetheless, hollies have a high salt tolerance and survive salt concentrations that kill many other plants.

Spray Injury

Many pesticides applied at high concentrations (i.e., above recommended dosage rate) and at temperatures above 32°C (90°F) can cause more damage than the pest to be controlled. Improper use of herbicides for weed control can cause damage or kill holly. Contact your local county extension service or state university for any pesticides toxic to holly.

Wildlife Damage

Vole and Rabbit Protection. Both rabbits and voles consume succulent green forbs and grasses during the growing season and move to woody ornamentals in the fall and winter when other foods are scarce. Voles leave small irregular girdled patches on the trunks. Rabbits neatly clip stems at a smooth 45 degree angle and gnaw bark, causing severe damage.

Young holly plants in liner beds need protection by inclosing them within a 6- to 13-mm (¼- to ½-in.) hardware-cloth. Cylinders of hardware-cloth encircling the trunks of small plant will exclude both voles and rabbits. To prevent vole damage the wire should be buried 10 to 15 centimeters (4 to 6 inches); for rabbits, at least 45 centimeters (18 inches) of wire is needed above ground (more in snow areas). Plastic pipe (split once lengthwise) can be placed around trunks for protection.

Voles can be trapped or fed pellet form toxic baits. Baits are usually applied by hand to burrows, trails, and in bait stations at the base of trees. There are no registered toxicants for rabbit control, and the available repellents are usually of limited use. Hunting (where allowed) and both live and lethal trapping are the final resorts to reduce rabbits. Trapping is best done in the winter months.

Deer Protection. Deer have increased rapidly in the eastern United States and have adapted to the present land development practices of a mosaic of crops (home properties, with ornamental plantings) and wooded areas that provide food and shelter in close proximity. This habitat is referred to as the "edge effect" and is a good urban habitat for deer. From personal observation, deer prefer the foliage of oriental holly species and cultivars over native species, but do not eat the fruit (Figures 21-16, 21-17).

Repellents are best used in a complete program including fencing, scare devices, and herd

Figure 21-16. *Ilex × koehneana* 'Chieftain' at Tyler Arboretum, Lima, Pennsylvania, showing deer browse damage. Photo by Franklin West.

management. Contact repellents are applied best on dormant plants and repel deer by their unpleasant taste. Area repellents are applied near but not on the plant, repelling by their odor. Many repellents do not weather well, particularly when it rains, and require frequent applications. Unwashed hair or dried blood, if used as a repellant, should be in a net sack and hung in an inverted open-bottom plastic container. Small bars of wrapped fragrant hand soap can be placed on plants with wire hooks. Some repellents contain thiuram; others contain ammonium soaps, paradichloro-benzene, capsaicin, putrescent whole egg solids, or bonetar oil. When applying repellents follow label instructions for legal protection and maximum success.

Fencing may be the only major effective method of an Integrated Pest Management program to minimize damage. A standard 2.4- to 3-m (8- to 10-ft.) high fence is very expensive and requires a minimum of 3 m (10 ft.) cleared around the perimeter. Plastic netting is less expensive to install, but requires the perimeter clearing and continual follow up and repair.

There are many different types of electric fencing ranging from a single strand for small plots to seven-strand fences for large areas and high populations of deer. High-tension fences are easier and cheaper to install but require more maintenance. Chargers must be monitored and weeds must be controlled along the fence line. In areas of high snow, accumulations can short-circuit fencing, leaving plants vulnerable to deer damage. Electric fencing is a behavioral barrier, not a physical barrier. Deer can penetrate an electric fence, but they learn to associate a shock with it and thus to avoid it.

For assistance with wildlife damage, contact county agents, state and game biologists, and representatives of the U.S.D.A. Animal Damage Control program. Reducing a deer population is a short-term control. For long-term control managing the habitat to make it less attractive to wildlife pests and less supportive of their reproduction is much more economical.

DIAGNOSING AND CONTROL

Diagnosing plant diseases, insect injuries, and wildlife damage require knowledge of the symptoms of the injury, including signs of evidence and patterns of occurrence. Good diagnosis should lead to a knowledge of the disease or pest. Among the things to note are the following (Peterson 1982):

1. Observe the part of plant affected (e.g., leaves, branches), its position, and the entire plant.
2. Keep track of the pattern of disease occurrence.
3. Check for any varietal or cultivar susceptibility.
4. Look for mechanical damage to the trunk or branches.
5. Check for evidence of actual fungal bodies.
6. Observe the entire plant and examine the roots.
7. Determine if the problem is seasonal or year around.
8. Review the cultural practices, fertilization, use of herbicides, irrigation, and general maintenance.
9. Check your observations with county or state agricultural agents.

Gardens, orchards, and plants should be monitored on a weekly or monthly basis. Begin in early spring when the first pest emerges and continue every week or two; in the summer check once a month, less frequently in winter months. One of the first steps in monitoring is to take a soil sample. The soil analysis should determine the levels of calcium, nitrogen, potassium, phosphate, and pH to aid in understanding the growing conditions.

Monitoring and keeping records will give the widest array of options for controlling pests and minimizing risks to the environment. For any group of pests you monitor there is usually a

Figure 21-17. *Ilex aquifolium* 'Laura Barnes' at Tyler Arboretum, Lima, Pennsylvania, showing deer browse damage. Photo by Franklin West.

"key plant" or plants that are attacked early. For example, tea scale, if found on a camellia or a Chinese holly, would indicate a problem that should be checked for on other potential hosts. For holly orchardists, many different pheromone traps are available and useful in snaring pests for identification.

Integrated Pest Management (IPM)

Rabbits, voles, and deer are major pests of ornamental plants throughout the United States. In some areas woodchucks and pocket gophers are also troublesome pests. Population reduction, the first reaction, addresses only the pest, not the entire problem. Voles and rabbits, for example, have high reproductive rates, so the benefits of reducing the population are short term.

Effective control should be long term and involves strategies affecting the pest both direct and indirectly. Integrated Pest Management (IPM) includes habitat modification, good cultural practice, animal behavior management, and population reduction (see below).

Good cultural practices include things like weed control and selection of an appropriate ground cover. Weed control reduces the food available to voles and reduces brush piles and undergrowth to expose rabbits to predators, thus lowering the survival rate of rabbit litters. Crown vetch makes a good ground cover as it is unpalatable to voles and it reduces growth of forb species, which are the preferred food of voles.

As a decision-making process, IPM is based predominantly on processes found in the natural ecosystems. In the natural environment, something keeps potential pests in check. Identify these natural factors that keep pests under control and encourage or develop them in your own garden.

The IPM system is based on an understanding of plants and pest biology. The long list of potential biotic and abiotic problems of holly does not warrant the use of a weekly spray or control program. Less than 1 percent of the insects in existence pose potential problems to people and their gardens. We can and often do tolerate some pests on our plants. The important criterion when considering a control measure is the economic damage if the control is not applied.

Pesticides

There are many alternatives to toxic pesticides and many good reasons for not using harmful chemicals. Using Sevin in the spring to control caterpillars also kills beneficial mites that control pest mites in the summer, but using *Bacillus thuringiensis* (which only kills caterpillars) in the spring leaves the beneficial insects to control the mites in the summer. Scale insects can be effectively controlled with horticultural oil rather than with a more toxic material that may be damaging to the environment and to the operator. Timing is important, however, to control scale during the young crawler stage in the early spring.

Female flowers of holly plants depend on honey bees and other insects to produce fruits, but many pesticides are highly toxic to honey bees and other beneficial insects. To protect these insects it is essential to use the safest recommended material, to carefully plan the timing of the application, and to be aware of pesticide toxicity to bees.

Pesticide use for insect and disease control is carefully regulated by the United States government. Giving specific recommendations is difficult because of regional differences. It is best to contact your local county agricultural office or the state extension service at a land grant university for current pesticide recommendations that apply to your particular locality.

It is important to the holly grower to determine the following before using pesticides:

1. The exact pest (biotic or abiotic).
2. Can this disease or pest be controlled by cultural methods?
3. Does the disease warrant time and expense in using a pesticide?
4. Is the pesticide legally cleared for use in your area?

Pesticides by their very nature are poisonous to people, animals, and sometimes plants. Poisonous or toxic compounds become dangerous when improperly or carelessly used, but can be used safely when following recommendations for concentrations, rates, and methods of application. Table 18 lists some chemical controls for various holly pests and diseases.

Use the recommended materials according to the labeled instructions. Read pesticide labels carefully. It is illegal to use any pesticide for the control of any pest or on any host plant for which it is not labeled. Store pesticides in their original labeled containers in a locked storage area out of reach of children, pets, and livestock. Dispose of empty containers promptly, safely, and according to the law.

Table 18. Chemical controls for various holly pests and diseases.

PEST OR DISEASE	CHEMICAL CONTROL	
	BRAND NAME	GENERIC NAME
Southern red mites	Cygon™[1]	Dimethoate
	Diazinon™	Diazinon
	Di-Syston™	Disulfoton
	Dursban™	Chlorpyrifos
	Insecticidal soaps	—
	Isotox™	—
	Kelthane™	Dicofol
	Morestan™	—
	Orthene™	Acephate
Leaf miner	Cygon™[1]	Dimethoate
	Diazinon™	Diazinon
	Di-Syston™	Disulfoton
	Isotox™	—
	Orthene™	Acephate
Scale	Cygon™[1]	Dimethoate
	Di-Syston™	Disulfoton
	Dursban™	Chlorpyrifos
	Orthene™	Acephate
	Superior oils	×××
General chewing & sucking insects	Orthene™	Acephate
	Sevin™	Carbaryl
Crown & root rot	Banrot™	Etridiazole & thiophanate-methyl
	Daconil™	Chlorothalonil
	Subdue™	Metalaxyl
	Terrazole™	Etridiazole
	Topsin™	Thiophanate-methyl
	Truban™	Etridiazole
Nematodes	Oxamyl™	Oxamyl
	Vydate™	—

[1]Do not use Cygon™ on *I. cornuta* cultivars such as 'Burfordii' or *I. cornuta* hybrids such as *I.* 'Nellie R.Stevens'.

✦ APPENDICES

APPENDIX 1

The Holly Society of America

Plant societies often have slow and difficult roads to clear and follow in the process of becoming organized. They frequently evolve around people who have a common interest with a "catalyst" of one or more individuals to pull everyone together.

In the 1930s an unknown number of people in the Northeast were interested in hollies, although they were unaware of others who shared their interest in their own and adjacent states. Uniting these people who were interested in holly was a major challenge.

Jackson (Jack) Batchelor, horticulturist with the Hillculture Division of Soil Conservation Service, U.S.D.A., had the interesting task of introducing woody and herbaceous plants into "hillculture" farming suitable for marginal land and to improve the income of farmers. In 1936 Jack was investigating the beach plum on a trip to Cape Cod when he met Wilfred Wheeler of Ashumet Farm, Hatchville, Massachusetts. There he learned of Wheeler's interest in woody plants as they explored the Cape hunting for beach plum. In 1937 Wheeler inoculated Jack with the "holly bug," specifically with the plight of American holly which at that time was being ruthlessly stripped of branches for holiday greens. Throughout Massachusetts, Maryland, Virginia, New Jersey, and other states in its natural range, American holly was getting the same tragic treatment. When Jack received the blessings of Samuel Detwiller, chief of the Hillculture Division, the selection and evaluation of American holly became a project of the Division. Commercially potential holly selections were propagated and evaluated by a Dr. Stoutmeyer and F. S. L. (Steve) O'Rourke.

In the early 1940s Jack Batchelor met the young, enthusiastic Harry Dengler, Extension Forester at Maryland University, and together they expanded their mutual interest of holly and friendship. Harry was encouraged to get involved and form a Maryland Holly Society. Steve O'Rourke also urged Harry to do something actively about holly, stating that "we in federal service can help, but you in the Maryland Extension Service can get things going." The ball started rolling with Harry pushing and pulling.

Holly was on the back burner during World War II; however, in 1944 Jack and Harry attended a meeting in Eastern Shore, Maryland, where they met Elizabeth White and Earl Dilatush, Robbinsville, New Jersey. The latter two convinced Harry to set his sights on American holly. In a meeting with T. R. Symons, Director of the Maryland Extension Service, Harry received their "blessing" and the green light to form a Maryland holly organization.

In 1945 Dengler wrote letters to every one who might be interested in forming a Maryland Holly Society, and Steve O'Rourke talked with everyone he met about holly. Later in the year a meeting was called with 60 people attending. Harry was authorized to form a committee to draw up a constitution, bylaws, and a slate of officers. Many people were interested in a holly society, but there were no takers for the president. Plans lay dormant for nearly two years. On 30 June

1947 a questionnaire was distributed by Harry to ask for a count of people interested in holly, and a meeting was called for 18 April 1947 in Baltimore.

While all this was going on in Maryland, similar interest groups were meeting in New Jersey. At the College of Agriculture, Rutgers University, there was interest in holly and a research program was placed under the direction of Charles H. Conners, chairman of the section of ornamental horticulture. P. P. Pirone, plant pathologist and Richard Farnham of the Agriculture Extension Service attended these planning meetings, but a "spark" was still needed, to move forward.

Later both Pirone and Farnham were witnesses in a legal case involving natural gas injury to plants. The trial took place in Jersey City and was long and drawn out. After three days the presiding judge, Thomas Brown, asked for a brief recess to question the second witness, Dr. Farnham, about an attractive subject. The jury smilingly granted permission. Judge Brown ask Farnham if he knew any thing about holly. The witness pleaded guilty. Judge Brown told of writing for assistance with holly from the New Jersey Experiment Station, but received no reply. Dr. Farnham asked Judge Brown, before the judge passed sentence, for permission for he and Dr. Pirone to meet with the Judge after court to find out how they could assist him. Permission was granted and the trial finished. Later on 4 November 1944 they visited Judge Brown's beautiful home site to view a large collection of excellent native American hollies. Others invited to view this holly collection were G. G. (Guy) Nearing, Elizabeth White, and Charles Conners. Unfortunately, Wilfred Wheeler was unable to attend. With their shared interest in American holly, the New Jersey Holly Research Committee came into being with Judge Brown as chairman and Dr. Conners as vice chairman. In 1946, a holly collection was established at Rutgers University under Dr. Conners, and an experimental holly orchard was started.

Correspondence continued between White and Wheeler and others in their interest in holly. The private 27-hectare (68-acre) holly orchard of Clarence Wolf, Millville, New Jersey, was discovered. Wolf, who was president and co-founder of the New Jersey Silica Sand Company, sent more than 40 tons of berried cut holly to his customers and friends as Christmas gifts. Soon holly was coming from his own orchard, the most famous private orchard of American holly in the world.

Following the 1945 visit to his home, Judge Brown invited a group of twelve to a dinner at the Rumson Club, Rumson, New Jersey: General Ostram, Major Anderson and Colonel Parks from Fort Monmouth; Charles Conners, H. H. Cox, Wesley Davidson, Richard Farnham, P. P. Pirone, Guy Nearing, Mr. Dilatush, and Elizabeth White. Naturally they talked about holly and forming a holly society. Pirone sent copies of the two meetings of the Holly Research Committee to all the members and to Harry Dengler and Steve O'Rourke.

Most of the people mentioned in this story were the early pioneers interested in holly and were responsible for naming selected American holly or had plants named in their honor, such as 'Judge Brown', 'Elizabeth' and others. Harry Dengler is best referred to as a "catalyst," never giving up the challenge to form an American holly society.

A meeting of the Maryland Holly Society was called by Harry Dengler on 18 April 1947 in Baltimore, Maryland. He fortunately invited the new Holly Research Committee of New Jersey and Clarence Wolf. The formation of a permanent organization on a national level was discussed and officers were elected. Charles A. Young, park forester for the city of Baltimore, presided at the busy morning meeting, and Clarence R. Wolf was tentatively nominated president (a position he held for twelve years), Harry Dengler became vice-president, and Mr. and Mrs. Charles Young Jr. were secretary-treasurer. The afternoon program was very busy with three talks and extended discussions, and the meeting was adjourned without the election of officers. Fortunately, a motion had been unanimously passed in the morning session that the Maryland Holly Society and the New Jersey Holly Research Committee combine forces and form the Holly Society of America (HSA). The tentative officers were authorized to incorporate the proposed society as soon as possible, draw up a constitution and a set of bylaws, and arrange for the society's first meeting.

The officers were considered as trustees. To make the board a more proportionately representative group, Daniel G. Fenton of Millville, New Jersey, was selected as the fifth trustee. On 24 June 1947 the five trustees met in Wolf's office, where they approved and signed the Articles of Incorporation of the Holly Society of America and made tentative plans for the society's first meeting to be held in New Jersey in mid-November of 1947. The officers nominated at the April 18th meeting were deemed elected; the only change being that Mr. Young was designated treasurer and Mrs. Young became secretary.

The Holly Society of America became the organization for the promotion of holly, with the slogan "More people knowing and growing more holly." The Society has played a major role in popularizing holly and in the development of scientific knowledge about holly. Officers and trustees for 1996 are as follows:

PRESIDENT
Mr. Charles R. Anderson
11801 Greenspring Avenue
Owings Mill, Maryland 21117

EXECUTIVE VICE-PRESIDENT
Ms. Barbara Taylor
3758 Dunn
Memphis, Tennessee 38111

ADMINISTRATIVE VICE-PRESIDENT
Mr. Dan Turner
11018 Berrypick Lane
Columbia, MD 21044

TREASURER
Mrs. Eren Rose
R.R.3, Box 110
25398 Learman Road
Chestertown, Maryland 21620

SECRETARY
Mrs. Linda R. Parsons
11318 West Murdock
Wichita, Kansas 67212

EDITOR
Mrs. Eleanor K. Ford
6 East Brookhaven Road
P.O. Box 52
Wallington, Pennsylvania 19086

By 1994 the Holly Society of America had more than 800 members, 11 overseas members, and seven chapters. Annual meetings are held in late October or early November in different regions of the country. There are tours scheduled to public and private gardens, nurseries, arboreta, and botanic gardens in the area. A full day of talks and demonstrations are held with an annual holly plant auction, where new and unusual plants are available. Each of the regional holly chapters has one- or two-day functions within their area.

The Society has a number of active committees pertaining to various holly problems and actives. The Editorial Committee has a major role of publishing the quarterly *Holly Society Journal* with reports on the Society and articles written by members or others on holly.

The Research and Development Committee provides grants to universities, arboreta, and experiment stations for research on and testing of holly. In 1992 six active research grants were in progress.

The Arboreta Committee has the responsibility of assisting and selecting the present 26 holly test gardens in the United States and the Bokrijk Arboretum holly garden in Belgium (see Appendix 4). The committee's annual report is published in the *Holly Society Journal*.

The Taxonomy Committee keeps the Society and its membership informed of new holly species and nomenclature problems, such as name changes and others. This is done by publishing articles and papers in the *Holly Society Journal*, learned technical journals, and books.

The International Registration Committee assists hybridizers and introducers of holly selection cultivars to register their plant names and publish detailed reports in the *Holly Society Journal*.

The Insect and Disease Committee reports on holly problems and their controls. Papers are presented at annual meeting, and written reports are published in the *Holly Society Journal*.

For information on membership in the HSA, a Holly Source List, and general information write to the Society's secretary (name and address given above).

Holly Sources

The sources listed below are located in North America. For information on plant sources in the British Isles, see *The Plant Finder,* published by Royal Horticultural Society, London. For information on plant sources elsewhere in Europe, see *PPP Index: The Europlant Finder,* by Anne Erhardt & Walter Erhardt, published by Moorland Publishing Company, Moor Farm Road, Airfield Estates, Ashbourne, Derbyshire DE6 1HD, England.

RETAIL SOURCES IN NORTH AMERICA

Appalachian Nurseries
P.O. Box 82
Waynesboro, Pennsylvania 17268

Bovees Nursery
1737 S.W. Coronada
Portland, Oregon 97219

Bull Valley Rhododendron Nursery
214 Bull Valley Road
Aspers, Pennsylvania 17304

Calloway's Nursery
4800 Blue Mount Road
Fort Worth, Texas 76106

Camellia Forest Nursery
125 Carolina Forest Road
Chapel Hill, North Carolina 27516

Carroll Gardens
444 E. Main Street
P.O. Box 310
Westminster, Maryland 21157

Carter Seed
475 Mar Vista Drive
Vista, California 92083

Eastern Plant Specialties
P.O. Box 226
Georgetown, Maine 04548

Fairweather Gardens
P.O. Box 330
Greenwich, New Jersey 08323

Five Star Gardens
Route 2, Box 252-B
Forest Grove, Oregon 97118

Forestfarm
990 Tetherow Road
Williams, Oregon 97544

Girard Nurseries
P.O. Box 428
Geneva, Ohio 44041

Gossler Farms Nursery
1200 Weaver Road
Springfield, Oregon 97478

Greer Gardens
1280 Goodpasture Island Road
Eugene, Oregon 97401

Holly Haven Hybrids
136 Sanwood Road
Knoxville, Tennessee 37923

Holly Hills
1216 Hilldale Road
Evansville, Indiana 47711

Kel Brothers
220-15 Horace Harding Boulevard
Bayside, New York 11364

Louisiana Nursery
Route 7, Box 43
Opelousas, Louisiana 70570

McLean Nurseries
9000 Satyr Hill Road
Baltimore, Maryland 21234

Mellinger's
2310 W. South Range Road
North Lima, Ohio 44452

Piping Tree Gardens
Scotchtown Road
Beaverdam, Virginia 23015

Richter's
Goodwood, Ontario L0C 1A0
Canada

Roslyn Nursery
211 Burr's Lane
Dix Hills, New York 11746

Schumacher Company
36 Spring Hill Road
Sandwich, Massachusetts 02563

Shady Oaks Nursery
700 19th Avenue N.E.
Waseca, Minnesota 56093

Sheffield's Seed Company
273 Auburn Road, Route 34
Locke, New York 13092

Trees by Touliatos
2020 Brook Road
Memphis, Tennessee 38116

Vineland Nurseries
P.O. Box 98
Vineland Station, Ontario L0R 2E0
Canada

Wallingford Gardens
P.O. Box 52
Wallington, Pennsylvania 19086

Washington Evergreen Nursery
P.O. Box 125
South Salem, New York 10590

Waynesboro Nursery
Route 664, Box 987
Waynesboro, Virginia 22980

Wayside Gardens
1 Garden Lane
Hodge, South Carolina 29695

Weston Nurseries
Route 135, Box 186
Hopkinton, Massachusetts 01748

White Flower Farm
Litchfield, Connecticut 06759

Woodlanders
1128 Colleton Avenue
Aiken, South Carolina 29801

WHOLESALE SOURCES IN NORTH AMERICA

The following nurseries provide plants for other nurseries and are not equipped to deal directly with the gardening public. If you desire a plant that is available only from a wholesale source, please ask your local nursery to order for you.

Aldridge Nursery
P.O. Box 1299
Von Ormy, Texas 78073

Angelica Nursery
RD 1, Box 174
Kennedyville, Maryland 21645

Baier Lustgarten Nurseries
Route 25
Middle Island, New York 11953

Bailey Nurseries
1325 Bailey Road
St. Paul, Minnesota 55119

Byers Nursery Company
6001 Moores Mill Road
Huntsville, Alabama 35811

Carter Seed
475 Mar Vista Drive
Vista, California 92083

Coles Nurseries
Route 1, Box 118
Forest Hill, West Virginia 24935

Conard-Pyle Company
372 Rose Hill Road
West Grove, Pennsylvania 19390

Crestwood Nursery
Crestwood, Kentucky 40041

Tom Dodd Nurseries
P.O. Drawer 45
Semmes, Alabama 36575

Dodd & Dodd Wholesale Nursery
P.O. Box 439
Semmes, Alabama 36575

Environmentals
P.O. Box 730
Cutchogue, New York 11935

Flowerwood Nursery
Daupin Island Parkway
Mobile, Alabama 36605

Foxborough Nursery
3611 Miller Road
Street, Maryland 21154

Gilmore Plant & Bulb Company
Julian, North Carolina 27283

Greenbriar Farms
201 Hickory Road W.
Chesapeake, Virginia 23322

Greenleaf Nursery Company
Route 1, Box 163
Park Hill, Oklahoma 74451

Hartline Holly Nursery
Anna, Illinois 62906

Hines Nursery
P.O. Box 42284
Houston, Texas 77242

Hines Wholesale Nursery
P.O. Box 11208
Santa Ana, California 92711

Holly Haven Hybrids
136 Sanwood Road
Knoxville, Tennessee 37923

Homestead Nurseries
4262 Wright Road
Clayburn, British Columbia V0X 1E0
Canada

Ingleside Plantation Nurseries
P.O. Box 1038
Oak Grove, Virginia 22443

McLean Nurseries
9000 Satyr Hill Road
Baltimore, Maryland 21234

Mellinger's
2310 W. South Range Road
North Lima, Ohio 44452

Monrovia Nursery Company
P.O. Box Q
Azusa, California 91702

Patuxent Valley Nurseries
11018 Berrypick Lane
Columbia, Maryland 21044

Princeton Nurseries
P.O. Box 191
Princeton, New Jersey 08540

Schumacher Company
36 Spring Hill Road
Sandwich, Massachusetts 02563

Simpson Nursery Company
1504 Wheatland Road
P.O. Box 2065
Vincennes, Indiana 47591

Trees by Touliatos
2020 Brook Road
Memphis, Tennessee 38116

Triangle Nursery
Route 2, Box 229
McMinnville, Tennessee 37110

Warren County Nursery
Route 2, Box 204
McMinnville, Tennessee 37110

Waynesboro Nursery
Route 664, Box 987
Waynesboro, Virginia 22980

Weston Nurseries
Route 135, Box 186
Hopkinton, Massachusetts 01748

Wick Nurseries
Brenford Road
RD 2, Box 750-A
Smyrna, Delaware 19977

Woodbourne Cultural Nurseries
301 Colonial Springs Road
Melville, New York 11747

Wye Nursery
Hillsboro, Maryland 21641

Zelenka Nursery
16127 Winans
Grand Haven, Michigan 49417

APPENDIX 3

Holly Fossils

The study of fossil records of *Ilex* and other plants is rarely available to dedicated students of horticulture and general botany students.

GEOLOGICAL TIME CHART FOR THE CENOZOIC ERA

PERIOD	EPOCH	COMMENT
	RECENT 12,000	Development and spread of human culture.
QUATERNARY	PLEISTOCENE 600,000	Great glaciers cover much of North America and northwestern Europe.
TERTIARY	PLIOCENE 10,000,000	Western North America uplifted.
	MIOCENE 25,000,000	Renewed uplift of Rockies, great lava flows in western United States, manlike apes appear.
	OLIGOCENE 35,000,000	Many old mammals become extinct.
	EOCENE 55,000,000	Mountains raised in Rockies, Andes, Alps, and Himalayas.
	PALEOCENE 65,000,000	Development of primitive mammals.

HOLLY FOSSIL RECORDS

North America (Lamotte 1952)

I. barillensis Berry 1919; Toyahvale, Texas; EOCENE.

I. calvertensis Berry 1934; Good Hope Hill, Washington D.C.; MIOCENE.

I. coloradensis Brown 1934; Green River, Debeque, Colorado; EOCENE.

I. dissimilis Lesquereux 1878; Sage Creek, Montana; OLIGOCENE.

I. dura Heer 1880; Atanekerdluk, Greenland; PALEOCENE.

I. eolignitica Berry 1916; Holly Springs, Marshall County, Mississippi; EOCENE.

I. florissantensis Knowlton & Cockerell 1919; Florissant, Colorado; OLIGOCENE.

I. fulva MacGinitie 1937; Redding Creek Trinity County, California; OLIGOCENE.

I. furcinervis Jennings 1920; White River, Missoula, Montana; OLIGOCENE.

I. glabra (Linnaeus) A. Gray 1917; Vero Beach, Florida; RECENT, PLEISTOCENE.

I. grandifolia Lesquereux 1883; Florissant, Colorado; OLIGOCENE.

I. insiginis M. 1869; O. Heeb, Alaska; EOCENE.

I. integrifolia (Elliott) Chapman; Chalky Banks, Mississippi River; RECENT. Also Columbus, Kentucky; PLEISTOCENE.

I. knightiaefolia Lesquereux 1883; Florissant, Colorado; OLIGOCENE.

I. leonis Cockerell 1906; Florissant, Colorado; OLIGOCENE.

I. lomensis Condit 1938; Contra Costa Company, California; MIO-PLIOCENE.

I. longifolia Sismonda 1865; Atanekerdluk, Greenland; PALEOCENE.

I. macrophylla Heer 1869; Atanekerdluk, Greenland; PALEOCENE.

I. opaca Aiton 1892; Yellow Gravels, Bridgeton, New Jersey. Berry 1907; PLEISTOCENE. Also Neuse River, Wayne County, North Carolina, and Abercrombies Landing, Russell County, Alabama.

I. opacoides Condit 1944; Buchanan Tunnel, Tuolmne County, California; MIO-PLIOCENE.

I. oregona Chaney & Sanborn 1933; Goshen, Lane County, Oregon; EOCENE.

I. (?) ovata Knowlton 1930; Green Mountain, Golden, Colorado; PALEOCENE.

I. prunifolia Lesquereux 1878; Table Mountain, Tuolumne County, California; TERTIARY.

I. pseudocassine Hollick 1924; Abra del Jumari, Matanza, Cuba; MIOCENE.

I. pseudomyrtifolia Hollick 1924; Abra del Jumari, Matanza, Cuba; MIOCENE.

I. pseudostenophylla Lesquereux 1883; Florissant, Colorado; OLIGOCENE.

I. (?) reticulata Heer 1868; Atanekerdluk, Greenland; PALEOCENE.

I. sclera Mac Ginilie 1973; Wyoming; EOCENE.

I. sonomensis Dorf 1930; Petrified Forest; Calistoga, California; PLIOCENE. Also Matamzas Creek, Santa Sonoma County, California.

I. subdenticulata Lesquereux 1884; Florissant, Colorado; OLIGOCENE.

I. triboleti Heer 1883; Atanekerdluk, Greenland; PALEOCENE.

I. verticillata (Linnaeus) A. Gray 1857; Waterville, Mississippi; PLEISTOCENE.

I. vomitoria Aiton 1789; RECENT. Berry 1933; Bridgeton, New Jersey, and Port Royal, Virginia; PLEISTOCENE.

I. vomitoriadolia Berry 1916; Holly Springs, Marshall County, Mississippi; EOCENE.

Bergheim, Germany

I. ahrensi Mai; MIDDLE PLIOCENE.

I. aquifolium Linnaeus; PLIOCENE.

I. bilinica Unger; PLIOCENE.

I. brachyptera J. Van Der Burgh 1978; PLIOCENE.

I. cassinites Wessel & Weber 1956; PLIOCENE.
I. dubia Weber 1948; PLIOCENE.
I. falsani Saportat & Marion 1847; PLIOCENE.
I. fortunensis J. Van Der Burgh 1979; PLIOCENE.
I. jonkeri J. Van Der Burgh 1978; PLIOCENE.
I. parschlugiana Unger 1847; PLIOCENE.
I. rhomboifolia Wessel & Weber.
I. rottensis Wayland 1938; PLIOCENE.
I. sphanophyllum Unger 1847; PLIOCENE.

Poland

I. lusatica Menzel & Mai 1970; MIOCENE.
I. saxonica Mai 1964; MIOCENE.

Romania

I. pseudocanariensis R. Givulescu 1982; PLIOCENE.

Japan

I. pedunuculosa Miquel 1868; PLIOCENE.
I. subcornuta Huzioka & Uemura 1973; LOWER MIOCENE.

REPORTS OF AQUIFOLIACEAE IN NORTH AMERICA (TAYLOR 1990)

Fossil genus	Organ	Age	Locality	Reference
Ilex	Pollen	Upper Miocene	Vermont	Traverse 1955
Ilex	Pollen	Upper Miocene	Puerto Rico	Graham & Jarzen 1969
Ilex	Leaves	Lower Oligocene	Montana	Becker 1960
Ilex	Pollen	Lower Oligocene	Mississippi	Frederiksen 1980
Ilex pollenites	Pollen	Eocene	Nevada	Wingate 1983
Ilex pollenites	Pollen	Eocene	Tennessee to Texas	Fairchild & Elsik 1969
Ilex	Pollen	Upper Eocene	British Columbia (Canada)	Hopkins 1969
Ilex	Leaves	Upper Eocene	Alaska	Wolfe 1977
Ilex pollenites	Pollen	Upper Eocene	Mississippi	Tschudy & Van Loen 1970
Ilex	Pollen	Upper Eocene	Mississippi	Frederiksen 1980
Ilex	Pollen	Upper Eocene	Panama	Graham 1985
Ilex	Pollen	Upper Eocene	British Columbia (Canada)	Rouse et al. 1970
Ilex pollenites	Pollen	Middle Eocene	Northwest Territories (Canada)	Doerenk 1976
Ilex	Pollen	Middle Eocene	British Columbia (Canada)	Rouse & Math. 1988

Fossil genus	Organ	Age	Locality	Reference
Ilex	Pollen	Middle Eocene	Wyoming	Leopold 1974
Ilex	Pollen	Middle Eocene	Wyoming	MacGinitie 1974
Ilex	Pollen	Middle Eocene	Wyoming	Fisk 1976
Ilex	Pollen	Middle Eocene	Wyoming	Love et al. 1978
Ilex	Pollen	Middle Eocene	California	Frederiksen 1983
Ilex	Pollen	Middle Eocene	California	Penny 1969
Ilex	Pollen	Middle Eocene	Tennessee	Elsik & Dilcher 1974
Ilex pollenites	Pollen	Middle Eocene	Tennessee	Taylor 1987
Ilex	Pollen	Middle Eocene	Alabama	Frederiksen 1980
Ilex pollenites	Pollen	Middle Eocene	Mississippi	Engelhardt 1964
Ilex pollenites	Pollen	Middle Eocene	Louisiana	Tschudy 1973
Ilex pollenites	Pollen	Middle Eocene	Texas	Elsik 1974
Ilex pollenites	Pollen	Lower Eocene	Northwest Territories (Canada)	Doerenk et al. 1976
Ilex pollenites	Pollen	Lower Eocene	Virginia	Frederiksen 1979
Ilex pollenites	Pollen	Lower Eocene	Mexico	Martinez-Hernan 1980
Ilex	Leaves	Paleocene	Colorado	Brown 1962
Ilex pollenites	Pollen	Lower Paleocene	California	Drugg 1967
Ilex pollenites	Pollen	Lower Paleocene	Alabama	Jarzen 1978
Ilex pollenites	Pollen	Upper Cretaceous	Alabama	Leopold & Pakis. 1964
Ilex pollenites	Pollen	Campanian to Maestrichtian	Alberta (Canada)	Srivast. 1966
Ilex pollenites	Pollen	Cennomania	Wyoming	Stone 1973

APPENDIX 4

Holly Arboreta and Collections

Listed below are organizations with official (i.e., designated by the Holly Society of America) collections of holly. A few unofficial collections are also listed here. The USDA zone in which the collection grows is listed below the address of the organization.

Bernheim Forest Arboretum
Clermont, Kentucky 40110
Zone 6a

Blue Ridge Community College
Asheville, North Carolina 28806
Zone 7a

Bokrijk Arboretum
Stationstraat 70
3530 Houthalen, Belgium
Zone 8

Callaway Gardens
Pine Mountain, Georgia 31822
Zone 7b

The Chicago Botanical Garden
P.O. Box 400
Glencoe, Illinois 60022
Zone 5b

Clemson University Botanical Garden
Clemson, South Carolina 29634
Zone 7b

The Dawes Arboretum
7770 Jacksontown Road S.E.
Newark, Ohio 43055
Zone 5b

Denver Botanic Gardens
909 York Street
Denver, Colorado 80206
Zone 4b

Ebersole Holly Garden
Sandhills Community College
2200 Airport Road
Pinehurst, North Carolina 28374
Zone 7b

Highland Botanical Garden
180 Reservoir Avenue
Rochester, New York 14620
Zone 6a

The Holden Arboretum
9500 Sperry Road
Mentor, Ohio 44060
Zone 5b

Holly Haven Hybrids
136 Sanwood Road
Knoxville, Tennessee 37923
Zone 7a

Missouri Botanical Garden
4344 Shaw Boulevard
St. Louis, Missouri 63110
Zone 6a

Morris Arboretum
University of Pennsylvania
9414 Meadowbrook Avenue
Philadelphia, Pennsylvania 19118
Zone 7a

New Jersey Agricultural Experiment Station
Rutgers-The State University
New Brunswick, New Jersey 08903
Zone 6b

North Carolina State University Arboretum
NCSU Box 7609
Raleigh, North Carolina 27695
Zone 7b

Ohio University
Department of Botany, Porter Hall
Athens, Ohio 45701
Zone 6a

Planting Fields Arboretum
Planting Fields Road
Oyster Bay, Long Island, New York 11771
Zone 7a

The Scott Arboretum
Swarthmore College
Swarthmore, Pennsylvania 19711
Zone 7a

Secrest Arboretum
Ohio State University
Wooster, Ohio 44691
Zone 5b

Taylor University Arboretum
Upland, Indiana 46989
Zone 5b

The Tyler Arboretum
515 Painter Road
P.O. Box 216
Lima, Pennsylvania 19037
Zone 7a

U.S. National Arboretum
3501 New York Avenue N.E.
Washington, District of Columbia 20002
Zone 7a

University of Alabama Arboretum
338 Thomas Street
P.O. Box 870176
Tuscaloosa, Alabama 35487
Zone 7b

University of British Columbia Botanical
    Garden
6501 North West Marine Drive
Vancouver, British Columbia V6T 1W5
Canada
Zone 8b

University of Delaware
Department of Plant Science
Newark, Delaware 19717
Zone 7a

University of Tennessee Arboretum
901 Kerr Hollow Road
Oakridge, Tennessee 37830
Zone 7a

Vandusen Botanical Garden
5251 Oak Street
Vancouver, British Columbia V6M 4H1
Canada
Zone 8b

Washington Park Arboretum
University of Washington XD-10
Seattle, Washington 98195
Zone 8b

APPENDIX 5

Holly Breeders and Introducers

* indicates defunct or deceased.

Ackerman, W. L.; Glenn Dale, Maryland, U.S.A.
Adams, A. N.; Clarkesville, Maryland, U.S.A.
Aichele, F. J.; Charleston, South Carolina, U.S.A.
Albert, M. H.; Oak Ridge, Tennessee, U.S.A.
Allen, Arthur E.; Jamaica Plains, Massachusetts, U.S.A.
* Anderson, Edgar; Missouri, U.S.A.
Andrews, Susyn; Surrey, Richmond, England.
Altex Nursery; Alvin, Texas, U.S.A.
* Andorra Nursery; Conshohocken, Pennsylvania, U.S.A.
Angelica Nursery; Mohnton, Pennsylvania, U.S.A.
Appalachian Nursery; Waynesboro, Pennsylvania, U.S.A.
Appleby, W.; Baltimore, Maryland, U.S.A.
Arden Nursery; Arden, Delaware, U.S.A.
Austin, L. B.; Plainsville, Massachusetts, U.S.A.
Avila, R.; Azusa, California, U.S.A.
Bailey Arboretum; Locust Valley, New York, U.S.A.
Bailey Orchard; Gladstone, Oregon, U.S.A.
* Baker, R. L.; College Park, Maryland, U.S.A.
Barbosa, Peter; West Barnstable, Massachusetts, U.S.A.
* Batchelor, J.; Willard, North Carolina, U.S.A.
Batson, Dan; Perkinston, Mississippi, U.S.A.
Bayley Orchard; Gladstone, Oregon, U.S.A.
Bauers Jr., Bart; Hatteras Island, North Carolina, U.S.A.
Bauers Sr., Bart; Manns Harbor, North Carolina, U.S.A.
* Beadle, C.; Ashville, North Carolina, U.S.A.
Beard, D. F.; England.
Bears, R.; Cairo, Georgia, U.S.A.
Bennett, E. L.; Chesapeake, Virginia, U.S.A.
Bennett, W.; Norfolk, Virginia, U.S.A.
Bernheim Forest and Arboretum; Clermont, Kentucky, U.S.A.
Berryhill Nursery; Springfield, Ohio, U.S.A.
Blake, S. F.; Brookgreen, South Carolina, U.S.A.
Blanken, B.; Boskoop, Netherlands.

Blanken, Arie; Boskoop, Netherlands.
Bleeg, H. F.; Portland, Oregon, U.S.A.
Block, R.; Virginia, U.S.A.
* Bobbink Nursery
Bock, G.; Vancouver, British Columbia, Canada.
Bodley, R. M.; Portland, Oregon, U.S.A.
Bos and Hoogeboom Nursery; Boskoop, Netherlands.
* Bosley, Paul: Mentor, Ohio, U.S.A.
Bostic, Mrs. L.; St. Francisville, Louisiana, U.S.A.
Boulevard Nursery; Massachusetts, U.S.A.
Boyce Thompson Institute; Yonkers, New York, U.S.A.
Bradshaw, D. W.; Clemson, South Carolina, U.S.A.
Brailsford, J. E.; Orangeburg, South Carolina, U.S.A.
Breeze Hill Gardens, Harrisburg, Pennsylvania, U.S.A.
Brewer, Mrs. Millard; Panson, Alabama, U.S.A.
Briggs Nursery; Olympia, Washington, U.S.A.
Brigham, L. S.; Annapolis, Maryland, U.S.A.
Britt, C. S.; Clarkesville, Maryland, U.S.A.
Brockley, B. H.; Earleville, Maryland, U.S.A.
Broetje, J. F.; Portland, Oregon, U.S.A.
Brookgreen Gardens; South Carolina, U.S.A.
Brooks, M.; Morgantown, West Virginia, U.S.A.
Brookside Gardens; Wheaton, Maryland, U.S.A.
* Brosemer, Philip; Huntsville, Alabama, U.S.A.
Brown, Jeanne and Kenneth; Evansville, Indiana, U.S.A.
Brown, Peter; North Newton Nursery, Somerset, England.
* Brownell, Ambrose; Milwaukee, Oregon, U.S.A.
Bruner, E. C.; Hilton Head, South Carolina, U.S.A.
Bruns, Heinz; Westerstede, Germany.
Bruns, John; Bad Zwischenahn, Germany.
Buchtmann, Hans-Georg; Varel, Germany.
Bull Valley Nursery; Aspers, Pennsylvania, U.S.A.
Bunting, A.; Scott Arboretum, Swarthmore, Pennsylvania, U.S.A.
Bunting's Nursery; Selbyville, Delaware, U.S.A.
* Burford, T. W.; Atlanta, Georgia, U.S.A.
Butler, Gordon; Fayetteville, North Carolina, U.S.A.
Byers, M. D.; Huntsville, Alabama, U.S.A.
Callaway Gardens; Pine Mountain, Georgia, U.S.A.
Camellia Forest Nursery; Chapel Hill, North Carolina, U.S.A.
Cannon, Norman H.; Greenwood, Delaware, U.S.A.
Cannon Plants; Greenwood, Delaware, U.S.A.
Carstens, Berno; Varel, Germany.
* Cartwright Sr., A. D.; Collierville, Tennessee, U.S.A.
Cartwright Nursery; Collierville, Tennessee, U.S.A.
Casico Nursery, P.; West Hartford, Connecticut, U.S.A.
Cattison, N. A.; Sherwood Forest Holly Farm, Pauls, Washington, U.S.A.
Chandler Nursery, Norman; Florence, Alabama, U.S.A.
Chesapeake Nursery; Salisbury, Maryland, U.S.A.
* Chestnut Nursery; West St. Paul, England.
Chisholm, R. D.; Moorestown, New Jersey, U.S.A.

* Clarendon Gardens; Pinehurst, North Carolina, U.S.A.
* Clarke Nursery, W. B.; San Jose, California, U.S.A.
Clemson University; Clemson, South Carolina, U.S.A.
Clifton, G.; Huntington, New York, U.S.A.
Coleman Nursery, R.; Mechanicsburg, Pennsylvania, U.S.A.
Cole, Norman H.; Forest Hills, West Virginia, U.S.A.
Commercial Nursery; Winchester, Tennessee, U.S.A.
Conard-Pyle Nursery; West Grove, Pennsylvania, U.S.A.
Conners, C. H.; Rutgers University, Brunswick, New Jersey, U.S.A.
Corbit, J. D.; Narberth, Pennsylvania, U.S.A.
Cordes, Hinrich; Hamburg, Germany.
Cornelius Nursery; Houston, Texas, U.S.A.
* Cornelius Van Tol Nursery; East Falmouth, Massachusetts, U.S.A.
Cottage Gardens; Queens Village, New York, U.S.A.
Creech, John L.; Hendersonville, North Carolina, U.S.A.
Crooks, F. C.; Narberth, Pennsylvania, U.S.A.
* Cross, Jim; Cutchogue, New York, U.S.A.
Cunnington Nursery; England.
Darr, Mrs. T. A.; Lexington, North Carolina, U.S.A.
Darthuizer Nursery; Leersum, Netherlands.
Dauber, W. J.; York, Pennsylvania, U.S.A.
Davenport Nursery; Kennett Square, Pennsylvania, U.S.A.
Davis, Dr.; Gig Harbor, Washington, U.S.A.
de Mille, Paul; Gig Harbor, Washington, U.S.A.
de Smet Nursery, Louis; Ledeberg-Lea-Gand, Belgium.
* de Wilde Rhodo-Lake Nursery, Perkins; Robbinsville and Shiloh, New Jersey, U.S.A.
Deerfield Nursery; Deerfield, New Jersey, U.S.A.
Delcambre, Anicet; Avery Island, Louisiana, U.S.A.
Demaline, L. L.; Willoway Nursery, Avon, Ohio, U.S.A.
Demcker, R.; U.S.A.
Dengler, Harry; Hyattsville, Maryland, U.S.A.
Descanso Nursery; Chino, California, U.S.A.
Detwiller, S. B.; Washington, DC, U.S.A.
Dewerth, A. F. "Doc"; College Station, Texas, U.S.A.
Dieckmann, John, and Son; Wheeling, West Virginia, U.S.A.
* Dilatush, Earl; Robbinsville, New Jersey, U.S.A.
Dilatush, Tom; Robbinsville, New Jersey, U.S.A.
* Diller, O. D.; Wooster, Ohio, U.S.A.
Dodd Jr., Tom O.; Semmes, Alabama, U.S.A.
Dodd III, Tom O.; Semmes, Alabama, U.S.A.
Dodd Nursery, Tom; Semmes, Alabama, U.S.A.
* Dudley, Theodore R.; Washington DC, U.S.A.
Duncan and Davies; Christ Church, New Zealand.
du Pont, P.; U.S.A.
du Pont, Mrs. W. K.; Wilmington, Delaware, U.S.A.
Durio, Ken; Opelousas, Louisiana, U.S.A.
Eagleson, T.; Port Arthur, Texas, U.S.A.
Ebersole, Fred; Newton, North Carolina, U.S.A.
Ebersole Gardens; Sandhills Community College, Pinehurst, North Carolina, U.S.A.
Edds, W. C.; Louisville, Kentucky, U.S.A.

Edingloh, William; New Bern, North Carolina, U.S.A.
Eisenbeiss, Gene K.; Washington, DC, U.S.A.
Ellis, D.; Evergreen, Alabama, U.S.A.
Elmore, Hal L.; Holly Haven Nursery, Knoxville, Tennessee, U.S.A.
Emmerich, R.; Huntington, New York, U.S.A.
Environmentals; Cutchogue, New York, U.S.A.
* Erickson, Archie M.; Portland, Oregon, U.S.A.
Esson, James G.; New York, U.S.A.
Esveld, C.; Boskoop, Netherlands.
Eure, T.; Raleigh, North Carolina, U.S.A.
Everett, Tom H.; New York, U.S.A.
Evergreen Nursery; Poplarville, Mississippi, U.S.A.
F. and F. Nursery; Pennsylvania, U.S.A.
* Fairfax Farm Nursery; Fairfax, Virginia, U.S.A.
Fairview Nursery; Erie, Pennsylvania, U.S.A.
Felton, D. E.; U.S.A.
Felton, E. E.; Merchantville, New Jersey, U.S.A.
* Fenton, Dan G.; Millville, New Jersey, U.S.A.
* Ferger, James; Wilmington, North Carolina, U.S.A.
Fields, Fred; Pinehurst, North Carolina, U.S.A.
Finch, Bill; Selma, Alabama, U.S.A.
Fischer, Norman G.; Hillsboro, Maryland, U.S.A.
Fisher and Holmes; Handsworth, England.
Fisher, Son, and Sibray; Sheffield, England.
Flemer, A.; Long Island, New York, U.S.A.
Flemer Jr., Carl; Ingleside Plantation, Westmoreland County, Virginia, U.S.A.
Flemer III, William; Princeton Nursery, Princeton, New Jersey, U.S.A.
Fleming, R. J.; Horticulture Research Institute, Ontario, Vineland Station, Canada.
Fleming, Will; U.S.A.
Flowerwood Nursery; Mobile, Alabama, U.S.A.
Forest Nursery; McMinnville, Tennessee, U.S.A.
* Forest Nursery and Seed Company; Virginia, U.S.A.
Foret, James; Lafayette, Louisiana, U.S.A.
Foster, E.; Foster Nursery, Besemer, Alabama, U.S.A.
Frederick, William; Hockessin, Delaware, U.S.A.
Frierson, J. L.; Denmark, South Carolina, U.S.A.
* Frierson, W. C.; Denmark, South Carolina, U.S.A.
* Frorer, James R.; Wilmington, Delaware, U.S.A.
Fromow and Sons Nursery, W.; Windlesham, Surrey, England.
* Fruitland Nursery; Augusta, Georgia, U.S.A.
Fulton, M.; Dauphin, Pennsylvania, U.S.A.
* Gable, J.; Stewartstown, Pennsylvania, U.S.A.
Galle, Fred C.; Hamilton, Georgia, U.S.A.
* Geddes, Douglas; Brentwood, Tennessee, U.S.A.
Gehnrich, A. C.; Huntington, New York, U.S.A.
Genard, F. R.; New Lison, New Jersey, U.S.A.
Germain, W.; Horsham (near Willow Grove), Pennsylvania, U.S.A.
Germer, Paul; Wietmarschen, Germany.
Giordano, John; Eight Mile, Alabama, U.S.A.
* Girard Sr., Peter E.; Geneva, Ohio, U.S.A.

Girard's Nursery; Geneva, Ohio, U.S.A.
Gladney, Sarah; Gloster, Mississippi, U.S.A.
Glass, P.; U.S.A.
Gloster Arboretum; Gloster, Mississippi, U.S.A.
Glover, C. A.; Upper Montclair, New Jersey, U.S.A.
Goldsworth Nursery; Woking, Surrey, England.
Goochland Nursery; Pembroke, Virginia, U.S.A.
Grandview Nursery; Youngville, Louisiana, U.S.A.
* Gray, Sam; Hickory Hill Nursery, Atlanta, Georgia, U.S.A.
Gray, Osea; Arlington, Texas, U.S.A.
Green Biz Nursery; Fayetteville, North Carolina, U.S.A.
Greenbriar Farms; Chesapeake, Virginia, U.S.A.
Green Forest Nursery; Perkinston, Mississippi, U.S.A.
Greenleaf Nursery; Park Hill, Oklahoma, U.S.A.
Gresham's Nursery, O.; Richland, Virginia, U.S.A.
Griscom; Griscom, New Jersey, U.S.A.
Grovatt's Nursery; Burlington, New Jersey, U.S.A.
* Gulf Stream Nursery; Wachapreague, Virginia, U.S.A.
Hachmann, Hans; Barnstedt, Holstein, Germany.
Hale, H. D.; Pennsylvania, U.S.A.
Hales, D.; Monongahela County, West Virginia, U.S.A.
Hallenberg, H.; Anchorage, Kentucky, U.S.A.
Hampden Nursery; Hampden, Massachusetts, U.S.A.
* Handsworth Nursery; England.
Harbaugh, E. T.; Eayrestown, Medford, New Jersey, U.S.A.
Harbaugh's Holly Farm; Eayrestown, New Jersey, U.S.A.
Hart Nursery, George E.; Malvern, New York, U.S.A.
Hartline, Bon; Anna, Illinois, U.S.A.
Hatfield, T.; U.S.A.
* Hayden, Pappa; Athens, Alabama, U.S.A.
Hawkins, Williams; Fort Paine, Alabama, U.S.A.
Hearn, R. V.; Pittsville, Maryland, U.S.A.
* Heatherfells Nursery; Andover, Massachusetts, U.S.A.
Hefner, Randy B.; Concover, North Carolina, U.S.A.
Heller, J.; U.S.A.
Henderson, Mrs. P. F.; Aiken, South Carolina, U.S.A.
Hendrix, B. R.; Crosby, Mississippi, U.S.A.
Hess Nursery; Cedarville (Mountain View), New Jersey, U.S.A.
Hetz, Charles; U.S.A.
Hickory Hill Nursery; Atlanta, Georgia, U.S.A.
Hill, Polly; Hockessin, Delaware, U.S.A.
Hillenmeyer Nursery; Lexington, Kentucky, U.S.A.
Hillier and Sons Nursery; Winchester, England.
* Hillier, Harold G.; Winchester, England.
* Hills Nursery; Georgetown, South Carolina, U.S.A.
Hodgins, T.; Wicklow, Ireland.
* Hohman, H.; Kingsville Nursery, Kingsville, Maryland, U.S.A.
* Hollowell, E. A.; Port Republic, Maryland, U.S.A.
Holly Creek Nursery; Feller, Virginia, U.S.A.
Holly Haven Nursery; Knoxville, Tennessee, U.S.A.

* Holly Haven Nursery; New Lisbon, New Jersey, U.S.A.
* Holly Hill Farms; Earleville, Maryland, U.S.A.
  Holly Hills Nursery; Evansville, Indiana, U.S.A.
* Holmes Nursery; Tampa, Florida, U.S.A.
* Hoogendorn, Cass; Connecticut, U.S.A.
  Hopfensitz, W.; Hummelstown, Pennsylvania, U.S.A.
  Hopperton, J.; Warsaw, Kentucky, U.S.A.
  Horstmann, Gunter; Schneverdingen, Germany.
* Howe, Frances W.; Pinehurst, North Carolina, U.S.A.
  Howe, Tom; Pinehurst, North Carolina, U.S.A.
* Howell, Bruce; Tennessee, U.S.A.
  Howell, Owen; Lucedale, Mississippi, U.S.A.
  Howell Nursery, S. R.; Knoxville, Tennessee, U.S.A.
  Hubbard, Sally F.; Mechanicsville, Pennsylvania, U.S.A.
  Huber, Fritz; Jennings, Louisiana, U.S.A.
* Hume, H. Harold; Glen St. Mary, Florida, U.S.A.
  Hume, E. P.; Edwardsville, Illinois, U.S.A.
  Hunt, William L.; Chapel Hill, North Carolina, U.S.A.
  Hunt's Nursery; Eureka, California, U.S.A.
  Hutton, R. J.; Westgrove, Pennsylvania, U.S.A.
  Ingleside Plantation; Oakgrove, Virginia, U.S.A.
  Irvine, Paul; Corvallis, Oregon, U.S.A.
* Jenkins, C. A., and Sons; Mitchellville, Maryland, U.S.A.
  Jennings, R. C.; Short Hill, New Jersey, U.S.A.
  John James Audubon Foundation Arboretum; Gloster, Mississippi, U.S.A.
* Jones Nursery, Nashville, Tennessee, U.S.A.
  Jones, E. W.; Woodlawn, Virginia, U.S.A.
  Jones, J. A.; Wilmington, North Carolina, U.S.A.
  Joseph, Patricia; Ebersole Gardens, Pinehurst, North Carolina, U.S.A.
  Jungle Gardens; Avery Island, Louisiana, U.S.A.
  Kale, Herb; New Jersey, U.S.A.
  Karenbauer, H. F.; Canton, Ohio, U.S.A.
  Kassab, Elizabeth; Wallingford, Pennsylvania, U.S.A.
* Kassab, J.; Wallingford, Pennsylvania, U.S.A.
  Katz, S. J.; Conington, Louisiana, U.S.A.
* Kelsey Nursery; Highlands, New Jersey, U.S.A.
  Kenijin and Company, L.; Raenwijk, Netherlands.
  Kibble and Clare Nursery; Berkshire, England.
  King, Albert; U.S.A.
* Kingsville Nursery; Kingsville, Maryland, U.S.A.
* Kinser Jr., S. J.; Wytheville, Virginia, U.S.A.
  Klehm Nursery; South Barrington, Illinois, U.S.A.
  Klein Nursery, T.; Crestwood, Kentucky, U.S.A.
  Klijn and Company, C.; Boskoop, Netherlands.
  Klyn Nursery, G. B.
  Kordes, H; Germany.
* Kosar, W. F. (Bill); Corvallis, Oregon, U.S.A.
* Koster Nursery; Bridgeton, New Jersey, U.S.A.
* Koster and Son Nursery; Boskoop, Netherlands.
  Kramer, B.; U.S.A.

Kuhl, W. N. Bill; Baltimore, Maryland, U.S.A.
Kungle, A.; Annapolis, Maryland, U.S.A.
Lake County Nursery Exchange; Perry, Ohio, U.S.A.
Lancaster, Art; Suffolk, Virginia, U.S.A.
Lancaster, Roy; England.
Lancaster Farms Nursery; Suffolk, Virginia, U.S.A.
Lansdale, D.; Media, Pennsylvania, U.S.A.
Laurel Lake Nursery; Salemburg, North Carolina, U.S.A.
* Lawson Nursery; Edinburgh, Scotland.
LeFeher and Company; Boskoop, Netherlands.
Le Jendre, Jacque; Wachapreague, Virginia, U.S.A.
Le-Mac Nursery; Hampton, Virginia, U.S.A.
Leach, Ray; Aurora, Oregon, U.S.A.
LeClair, F. J.; Pittsboro, North Carolina, U.S.A.
Lehigh Valley Nursery; Bethlehem, Pennsylvania, U.S.A.
Lewis, Francis; Bridgeville, Delaware, U.S.A.
Light's Nursery; Richland, Michigan, U.S.A.
Lilly III, J. K.; West Falmouth, Massachusetts, U.S.A.
Lindley Nursery; Greensboro, North Carolina, U.S.A.
Little, Parker Lewis; Beaverdam, Virginia, U.S.A.
* Livingston, L. F.; Cecilton, Maryland, U.S.A.
Longwood Gardens; Kennett Square, Pennsylvania, U.S.A.
Lousiana Nursery; Opelousas, Louisiana, U.S.A.
Lowery, Lynn; Houston, Texas, U.S.A.
Lustgarten Nursery, Bauer; Germany.
Magee Evergreen Nursery; Poplarville, Mississippi, U.S.A.
Magnolia Gardens and Nursery; Chunchula, Alabama, U.S.A.
Mahone, R.; Williamsburg, Virginia, U.S.A.
Makepeace, W.; West Barnstable, Massachusetts, U.S.A.
Malmborg, Gustav; Elizabethtown, Pennsylvania, U.S.A.
Marvin, Earle; Wildwood Nursery, Walterboro, South Carolina, U.S.A.
Marvin, Robert E.; Wildwood Nursery, Walterboro, South Carolina, U.S.A.
* Mattoon, H. G.; Wellesley, Massachusetts, U.S.A.
* McDaniel, Joseph C.; Urbana, Illinois, U.S.A.
McDonald, K.; Hampton, Virginia, U.S.A.
McKees Nursery; Covington, Louisiana, U.S.A.
McKenney, R. B.; Newton, Pennsylvania, U.S.A.
* McLean Nursery, S. H.; Baltimore, Maryland, U.S.A.
McLean Nursery; Towson, Maryland, U.S.A.
McIlhenny, E. A.; Jungle Gardens, Avery Island, Louisiana, U.S.A.
McQuage, Kenneth; Baltimore, Maryland, U.S.A.
* Medford Nursery; Medford, New Jersey, U.S.A.
Merian, Dr.; Harvard University, Massachusetts, U.S.A.
Meserve, Kathleen; St. James, Long Island, New York, U.S.A.
* Millcreek Nursery; Newark, Delaware, U.S.A.
Miller, Elizabeth (Betty); Seattle, Washington, U.S.A.
Miller, Paul; Corvallis, Oregon, U.S.A.
Missouri Botanical Gardens; St. Louis, Missouri, U.S.A.
Mobjack Nursery; Virginia, U.S.A.
* Monroe, W. L.; Atlanta, Georgia, U.S.A.

Monrovia Nursery; Azusa, California, U.S.A.

Morgan, M.; Lexington, North Carolina, U.S.A.

Morris Nursery; U.S.A.

Morgan, G.; Hanover, West Virginia, U.S.A.

Motsinger, A. V.; Mitchell, Indiana, U.S.A.

Moyer Nursery; Roseburg, Oregon, U.S.A.

Munas, J.; England.

Munford, Curtis; Corvallis, Oregon, U.S.A.

Murcott, R.; East Norwich, New York, U.S.A.

Murray, Neil; Dundrum, England.

* Native American Holly Farm; Manheim, Pennsylvania, U.S.A.

North Carolina Holly Arboretum Committee; Raleigh, North Carolina, U.S.A.

North Carolina State University Arboretum; Raleigh, North Carolina, U.S.A.

Neal, O. M.; Morgantown, West Virginia, U.S.A.

* Nearing, G. G.; Ulster, Pennsylvania, U.S.A.

* Nelson, Ira S.; LaFayette, Louisiana, U.S.A.

* New Jersey Holly Research Committee; Rutgers, New Jersey, U.S.A.

Nissen, H. and D.; Wuppertal Aprath, Germany.

Nissen, J.; Netherlands.

* Nosal, E. A.; New York, U.S.A.

Nosal, M. A.; Calverton, New York, U.S.A.

Oachs Nursery; Illinois, U.S.A.

* Okrent Nursery; Cincinnati, Ohio, U.S.A.

Ooster, Wijk P.; Boskoop, Netherlands.

Orchard Nursery; Oregon, U.S.A.

* Orr, Henry; Opelika, Alabama, U.S.A.

* O'Rourke, F. L.; Michigan, U.S.A.

Orton Jr., Elwin R.; Sommerville, New Jersey, U.S.A.

Orndorff, Carl C.; Clarkesville, Maryland, U.S.A.

Osgood Holly Orchard; Aurora, Oregon, U.S.A.

Owens, P.; Edwardsville, Illinois, U.S.A.

* Pace, Ben; Pine Mountain, Georgia, U.S.A.

Parkerson, Charles; Suffolk, Virginia, U.S.A.

Parks Seed Company, George; Greenwood, South Carolina, U.S.A.

Patuxent Valley Nursery; Columbia, Maryland, U.S.A.

* Paul, W; Waltham, England.

Peace, S.; Arkansas, U.S.A.

Pederson, Eric; Bogense, Denmark.

Patterson, A. C.; Lutherville, Maryland, U.S.A.

Patterson Nursery; Albany, Georgia, U.S.A.

Pease, R. W.; West Virginia, U.S.A.

Perkins de Wilde Nursery; Shiloh, New Jersey, U.S.A.

Perrine, A.; Cranbury, New Jersey, U.S.A.

Peters, Arie; Skillman, New Jersey, U.S.A.

Peters, R. K.; Bendersville, Pennsylvania, U.S.A.

Peyran, P. H.; Hollycroft Gardens, Gig Harbor, Washington, U.S.A.

Phillips, W.; Selbyville, Delaware, U.S.A.

Phyto Ecology Nursery; Ridgley, Maryland, U.S.A.

Phytotektor Nursery; Winchester, Tennessee, U.S.A.

Pittillo, J. D.; Cullowhee, North Carolina, U.S.A.

Pittman, James; Mobile, Alabama, U.S.A.
Planting Fields Arboretum; Oyster Bay, New York, U.S.A.
Posey, G.; Washington, DC, U.S.A.
Pounders, C.; Decatur, Alabama, U.S.A.
* Pride, Orlando S.; Butler, Pennsylvania, U.S.A.
Princeton Nursery; Princeton, New Jersey, U.S.A.
Proefstation voor de Boomwerkerij; Boskoop, Netherlands.
Pyne, W.; Baltimore, Maryland, U.S.A.
* Quaintance, A. L.; Silver Spring, Maryland, U.S.A.
Rainbow Nursery; Decatur, Alabama, U.S.A.
* Rankin, Jesse D.; Salisbury, North Carolina, U.S.A.
* Rappleye, Bob; University of Maryland, Maryland, U.S.A.
Ravenstein, W., and Son; Netherland.
Reath, Sally; Pennsylvania, U.S.A.
Reams, Mrs. R. N.; Rockwood, Tennessee, U.S.A.
Red Lion Nursery; Pennsylvania, U.S.A.
Reinsmith, Y. H.; Atlanta, Georgia, U.S.A.
Reynolds, L. L.; Belvedere, Tennessee, U.S.A.
Richardson, Catherine; Baltimore, Maryland, U.S.A.
Roach, Wiley A.; Calhoun, Louisiana, U.S.A.
Robbins Nursery; Willard, North Carolina, U.S.A.
Robertson, W. H.; Savannah, Georgia, U.S.A.
Rocknoll Nursery; Hillsboro, Ohio, U.S.A.
Rocky Creek Nursery; Lucedale, Mississippi, U.S.A.
Roemer Nursery; Madison, Ohio, U.S.A.
Rohrbach, H.; Andover, Massachusetts, U.S.A.
Roller Holly Farm; Salem, Oregon, U.S.A.
Rosel, T.; Florida, U.S.A.
Roslyn Nursery; Dix Hills, New York, U.S.A.
Rowland, C. A.; Athens, Georgia, U.S.A.
* Runyon, C.; Cincinnati, Ohio, U.S.A.
* Rutgers University, Holly Research Committee; Rutgers, New Jersey, U.S.A.
Rypma, R. B.; Athens, Ohio, U.S.A.
Santamour Jr., F. S.; Washington, DC, U.S.A.
Sawyer, Ken; Sherwood, Oregon, U.S.A.
Scherff, Al; Athens, Alabama, U.S.A.
Schiphorst; Wageningen, Netherlands.
Schmid, L. R.; Clemson, South Carolina, U.S.A.
Schmidt Nursery, J. H.; Millburn, New Jersey, U.S.A.
Schramm, J. R.; Philadelphia, Pennsylvania, U.S.A.
Schroeder Jr., H. R.; Evansville, Indiana, U.S.A.
Schroeder, Stephen; Evansville, Indiana, U.S.A.
Schwoebel Nursery, R.; Ardmore, Pennsylvania, U.S.A.
Scudder, Sadie; Mill Neck, New York, U.S.A.
Seligmann, E. B.; Frederick, Maryland, U.S.A.
Shaffer, J. G.; Potomac, Maryland, U.S.A.
Shadow Nursery, Don; Winchester, Tennessee, U.S.A.
Shady Grove Plantation and Nursery; Orangeburg, South Carolina, U.S.A.
Shadow, H.; Winchester, Tennessee, U.S.A.
* Shammarello, A. M.; Euclid, Ohio, U.S.A.

Shibamichi, Norihiro; Japan.
Sicbaldi, L. J.; Hampden, Massachusetts, U.S.A.
Simpson Nursery, R. C.; Vincennes, Indiana, U.S.A.
* Singletary, Mrs. Carl; Columbus, Georgia, U.S.A.
* Skinner, Henry T.; Hendersonville, North Carolina, U.S.A.
Slocock, W. C.; Working, Surrey, England.
Smith, H. B.; Plainfield, New Jersey, U.S.A.
Smith, J. A.; Chunchula, Alabama, U.S.A.
* Solymosy, S.; Lafayette, Louisiana, U.S.A.
Sorg, C. L.; Norfolk, Virginia, U.S.A.
Souder, Sam; Narberth, Pennsylvania, U.S.A.
Sparkes, Ted; Lymington, Hampshire, England.
Speed, J.; Clayton, Georgia, U.S.A.
Spring, Otto; Okmulgee, Oklahoma, U.S.A.
Spring Grove Cemetery; Cincinnati, Ohio, U.S.A.
Springhill Nursery; Troy, Ohio, U.S.A.
Stamps, Hamie; Florence, Alabama, U.S.A.
Staples, M. W.; Kent, Ohio, U.S.A.
Steed, Warren; Candor, North Carolina, U.S.A.
Steed Nursery; Candor, North Carolina, U.S.A.
Steiner, W. W.; U.S.A.
Stephens Nursery; Semmes, Alabama, U.S.A.
Steward, Lin T.; Pitman, New Jersey, U.S.A.
Stokes Nursery, Sam; Forest Hills, Louisiana, U.S.A.
Straughan Nursery; Lorganer, Louisiana, U.S.A.
Stührenberg Nursery, Ernst; Wiesmoor, Germany.
Styer Nursery, J. F.; Media, Pennsylvania, U.S.A.
Suk, Carl; Clermont, Kentucky, U.S.A.
* Swartley, J. C.; Pennsylvania, U.S.A.
* Taber, G. L.; Florida, U.S.A.
Tankard Nursery; Exmore, Virginia, U.S.A.
Taylor's Nursery; Raleigh, North Carolina, U.S.A.
* Tarbox and Blake; Brookgreen, South Carolina, U.S.A.
Teese, A.; Yamina Rare Plants, Victoria, Australia.
* Templeton, H.; Winchester, Tennessee, U.S.A.
Ten Oaks Nursery; Clarkesville, Maryland, U.S.A.
Teufel, G.; Portland, Oregon, U.S.A.
* Teufel Nursery; Portland, Oregon, U.S.A.
Thacher, Mrs. A. B.; Long Island, New York, U.S.A.
Thrasher, S. H.; Greenbriar Farms, Chesapeake, Virginia, U.S.A.
Tilt, Ken; Auburn University, Auburn, Alabama, U.S.A.
Tinga Nursery; Castle Hayne, North Carolina, U.S.A.
* Tingle Nursery; Pittsville, Maryland, U.S.A.
Tomayer, R. L.; Fennville, Michigan, U.S.A.
Towson Nursery; Cockeysville, Maryland, U.S.A.
Turner, Daniel; Columbia, Maryland, U.S.A.
Turtle Creek Nursery; Huntsville, North Carolina, U.S.A.
Tyler Arboretum; Lima, Pennsylvania, U.S.A.
University of Southwestern Louisiana, Lafayette, Louisiana, U.S.A.
U.S. National Arboretum; Washington, DC, U.S.A.

Valentine Nursery; Cosby, Tennessee, U.S.A.
Vallot, Earl; Grandview Nursery, Youngville, Louisiana, U.S.A.
Van de Laar, H. L.; Boskoop, Netherlands.
Van Houtte, L.; Belgium.
Van Lennep Jr., G. A.; Saint Michaels, Maryland, U.S.A.
Van Tol, J. C.; Netherlands.
Van Wilgen, D.; Boskoop, Netherlands.
Vermeulen Nursery, J. P.; Neshanic Station, New Jersey, U.S.A.
* Virginia Tree Farm; Woodlawn, Virginia, U.S.A.
* Vossberg P.; Westbury, New York, U.S.A.
Waddington Jr., E. C.; West Grove, Pennsylvania, U.S.A.
Walder, Mr.; Fresno, California, U.S.A.
Waldman, Philip; Dix Hills, New York, U.S.A.
Walter, H.; Oklahoma City, Oklahoma, U.S.A.
Walters, E.; Neptune, New Jersey, U.S.A.
Warren Nursery, Otis; Oklahoma City, Oklahoma, U.S.A.
Warren; Bureau Parks, Victoria, British Columbia, Canada.
Wavecrest Nursery; Fernville, Michigan, U.S.A.
Wayside Gardens; Daniesville, South Carolina, U.S.A.
Webb, J. A.; Huntsville, Alabama, U.S.A.
Webber, B.; Covington, Kentucky, U.S.A.
Webster, Charles D.; Islip, New York, U.S.A.
Wells Nursery, James S.; Red Bank, New Jersey, U.S.A.
West View Cemetery; Atlanta, Georgia, U.S.A.
* Westbury Rose Company; Westbury, New York, U.S.A.
* Wheeler, Wilfred; Falmouth, Massachusetts, U.S.A.
* Whipple, Malcolm S.; St. James, New York, U.S.A.
* White, J. J.; Whitesbog, New Jersey, U.S.A.
* White, Elizabeth C.; Whitesbog, New Jersey, U.S.A.
Wieman, John S.; Portland, Oregon, U.S.A.
Wight Sr., John; Cairo, Georgia, U.S.A.
Wight Nursery; Cairo, Georgia, U.S.A.
Wills Jr., Elwood O.; East Falmouth, Massachusetts, U.S.A.
* Wilmat Nursery; Narberth, Pennsylvania, U.S.A.
Wildacre Nursery; Colliersville, North Carolina, U.S.A.
Wildwood Nursery; Walterboro, South Carolina, U.S.A.
Windon, T.; New Jersey, U.S.A.
Windsor, E. W.; Farmingdale, New Jersey, U.S.A.
Winn, W.; Norkfolk, Virginia, U.S.A.
* Wister, J. C.; Swarthmore, Pennsylvania, U.S.A.
* Wolf, C. R.; Millville, New Jersey, U.S.A.
Wood, George; Northport, Alabama, U.S.A.
Woodlander's Nursery; Aiken, South Carolina, U.S.A.
Woods, Franch; Durham, North Carolina, U.S.A.
Wye Nursery; Hillsboro, Maryland, U.S.A.
Wyman, D.; Weston, Massachusetts, U.S.A.
Wyman's Garden Center; Framingham, Massachusetts, U.S.A.
Yamina Rare Plant Nursery; Victoria, Australia.
Yinger, Barry; Lewisberry, Pennsylvania, U.S.A.
* Young, C. F.; Baltimore, Maryland, U.S.A.

Zampini, James; Ohio, U.S.A.
Ziegler, L. K.; Bethlehem, Pennsylvania, U.S.A.
Zimmer Nursery, Martin; Wiesmoor, Germany.
* Zimmerman, B. W.; Yonkers, New York, U.S.A.
Zuk, Judy; Brooklyn Botanic Garden, Brooklyn, New York, U.S.A.

Glossary

Abort. Fail to develop; stay rudimentary.

Abortive. Defective, barren, or imperfectly developed.

Adaxial. On the side of axil or stem.

Actinomorphic. Regular, symmetrical.

Acumen. A point or sharp tip.

Acuminate. An acute apex with sides somewhat concave and tapered to a protracted point.

Acute. Sharp, ending in a point, sides of taper essentially straight.

Alternate. Any arrangement of leaves or other parts not opposite or whorled on the axis.

Amphidiploid. Having complete set of diploid chromosomes, resulting from doubling chromosomes.

Angulate. Having angles or corners.

Anther. The pollen-bearing part of the stamen.

Anthesis. The act of flowering, when pollen is released. Also when pollination takes place.

Apex. The tip or distal end.

Apiculate. Terminated by an *apicule,* a short sharp, flexible point.

Appressed. Closely and flatly pressed.

Areolae. Small dark area, as a dark ring around a nipple.

Aristate. Tipped by an awn or stiff bristle, tapered to a very narrow elongated apex.

Attenuate. Showing a long gradual taper, applied to bases or apices.

Awn. A bristlelike part or appendage.

Axil. Upper angle formed by a petiole or peduncle with the stem.

Axillary. Situated in the axil.

Bacco-drupe. Berrylike drupe or multiseeded drupe.

Basionym. Original use of a name especially when the status or rank of a name is changed to another name or new name.

Belize. Formerly British Honduras.

Berry. Pulpy, indehiscent few or many seeded fruit, originating from a single pistil, as the tomato or grape.

Bisexual. Having both sexes present in one flower.

Blade. The extended portion of a leaf.

Borneo. Now part of Indonesia and Malaysia.

Bract. A much reduced leaf, small or scalelike leaves in a flower cluster, subtending petals, morphologically a foliar organ.

Bracteole. A secondary bract; a bractlet.

British New Guinea. Now Papua, New Guinea.

British North Borneo. Now Sabah, Malaysia.
British West Borneo. Now Borneo, Indonesia.
Bullate. Blistered or puckered.
Burma. Now Myanmar.

Caducous. Falling off early or prematurely.
Callose. Presence of callus.
Callus. A mass of undifferentiated tissue growing over a wound or at the base of a cutting.
Calyx. The collective term for the sepals of a flower, calyces plural.
Campanulate. Bell-shaped.
Canaliculate. With channels or grooves.
Capitate. Headed, headlike, in heads or compact cluster.
Carnose. Fleshy, soft but firm.
Carpel. One of the foliar units of a compound pistil or ovary.
Cartilaginous. Tough and hard but not bony.
Caudate. Bearing a tail-like appendage.
Celebes. Now Celebes, Indonesia.
Ceylon. Now Sri Lanka.
Chartaceous. Of papery texture.
Choripetalose. Having separate and distinct petals.
Cilia. Fringe of small hair.
Ciliate. Fringed with hairs, as on a margin.
Clone. A plant, originally spelled clon, propagated by asexual or vegetative means that is genetically identical to the plant from which it was propagated.
Compound. Of two or more parts in one organ.
Connate. United or joined.
Convex. Curved outward on the dorsal surface; like the surface of a sphere.
Cordate. Heart-shaped.
Coriaceous. Of leathery texture.
Corolla. The inner series of floral envelopes, consisting of either connected or separated petals.
Costate. Having ribs or riblike ridges.
Crenate. Toothed with rounded or shallow teeth.
Crenulate. Finely or shallowly crenate.
Cristate. Crested.
Cultivar. A horticultural or cultivated variety when reproduced (sexually or asexually) retains its distinguishing characteristics and is given a name. The name is at a lower rank than any botanical name.
Cuneate. Wedged-shaped; triangular, with narrow end at point of attachment as the base of a leaf.
Cuneiform. Wedge-shaped.
Cuspidate. Sharp-pointed, an apex constricted into an elongated, sharp-pointed tip.
Cyme. A convex or flat-topped flower cluster, central flowers opening first.
Cymose. Arranged in cymes; cymelike.

Dbh. Diameter at breast height, 1.37 m (4½ ft.).
Deciduous. Falling at end of one season's growth, not persistent.
Decumbent. Reclining or laying on the ground, but with ends ascending.
Decussate. Leaves opposite, growing at right angles to those above and below.
Decurrent. Extending down and united with the stem.
Deltoid. Triangular.
Dentate. With sharp coarse teeth pointed outward or perpendicular to the margin.

Diam. Diameter.

Dichotomous. Forked in one or more pairs.

Dimorphic. Two stages of growth, having juvenile and adult foliage types.

Dioecious. Staminate and pistillate flowers on different plants.

Diploid. Cells having two sets of chromosomes in their nuclei, 2n.

Divaricate. Spreading very far apart, extremely divergent.

Divergent. Spreading broadly, but less so than divaricate.

Dorsal. Relating to the back or outer surface of a part such as a leaf or a pyrene.

Downy. Covered with very short hairs.

Drupe. A fleshy indehiscent fruit with seed enclosed in a stony endocarp (a pyrene); such as holly, cherry and peach.

Dutch Guiana. Now Surinam.

Dutch New Guinea. Now Irian Jaya.

E- or Ex-. In Latin-formed words, denoting as a prefix, part missing or without as: estriate, without stripes.

Ellipsoid. A solid body, such as a fruit, elliptic in the longitudinal section.

Elliptic. Oblong with narrow to rounded ends and widest at or about the middle, about two times as long as wide.

Elongate. Lengthened or stretched out.

Emarginate. With a shallow notch at the apex.

Endemic. Native or confined naturally and usually restricted to a particular area or region.

Endocarp. The inner layer of the pericarp or fruit wall.

Endosperm. Nutritive tissue adjacent to the embryo in a seed.

Entire. With a continuous margin with no indentations.

Epiphytic. Plants growing on one another, not parasitic.

Erose. A margin appearing gnawed, having irregular notched edge.

Estriate. Without longitudinal lines or ridges.

Esulcate. Without sulcate groves or furrows.

Evergreen. Remaining green for a full year or longer. Applied to plants and not leaves, but due to persistence of leaves.

Excrescent. Forming an abnormality or excrescence.

Exocarp. The outer layer of the pericarp or fruit wall.

Explanate. Spread out or flat.

Falcate. Sickle-shaped.

Farinose. Mealy.

Fascicle. Condensed cluster of flowers.

Fasciculate. Congested in close clusters.

Fastigiate. Tapering to a point, conelike.

Ferruginous. Having the color of rust; reddish brown.

Filament. The stalk of an anther.

Fimbriate. Fringed.

Furrowed. With longitudinal channels or grooves.

Gamete. A reproductive cell that is haploid (1n) and can unite with another gamete to form a new cell (2n) zygote.

Gametogenesis. Entire process of consecutive cell division and differentiation by which mature eggs or sperm are developed.

Gamopetalous. With a corolla of one piece, the petal united, at least at the base.

Geniculate. Bent, like a knee.
Genotype. A type (plant or population) determined by genetic characters.
Glabrous. Not hairy.
Glaucous. Covered with a bloom, or whitish substance that rubs off.
Guiana. Now Guyana.
Guyana. Formerly British Guiana.

H.S.A. Holly Society of America.
Haploid. Half the number of chromosomes in a somatic cell, 1n.
Hastate. Having a triangular shape, like an arrowhead.
Heterozygosity. Plants having different chromosomes or genes, not breeding true to type; hybrid.
Histogenic. A group of cells that develop and differentiate into new tissue, such as cambium.
Hirsute. With rather rough or coarse hairs.
Hirtellous. Softly or minutely hirsute or hairy.
Holotype. Single herbarium specimen as a type species, designated as nomenclatural type.
Homonym. Different plants having the same name.
Hyperaccumulate. Excess accumulation.

I.C.B.N. International Code of Botanical Nomenclature. The Code.
I.C.N.C.P. International Code of Nomenclature for Cultivated Plants.
IBA. Indole-3-butyric acid, synthetic type plant hormone.
Indehiscent. Not regularly opening, as a seed pod or anther.
Indigenous. Growing naturally in a region or country, as a native.
Indochina. Now Vietnam and Laos.
Indonesia. Formerly Dutch East Indies.
Indumentum. Hairy or pubescent covering.
Inflorescence. The arrangement of flowers on a stem or axis.
Infructescence. Fruiting florescence.
Internode. The part of an axis between two nodes.
Interspecific. Between species.
Intraspecific. Within a species.
Irian Jaya. Formerly Dutch New Guinea.
Isotype. Duplicate, such as a duplicate specimen of a holotype.

Keeled. Ridged like the bottom of a boat.

Lanceolate. Lance-shaped; much longer than broad; widening above the base and tapering to the apex.
Lectotype. Specimen selected as type, when holotype is missing.
Lenticel. Corky spot on young branches, corresponding to leaf epidermal stomata.
Ligneous. Woody.
Linear. Long and narrow, the sides parallel or nearly so.
Locule. Compartment or cell of an ovary.

Mammiform. Breastlike.
Median. The middle.
-merous. Referring to the number of parts; as a 4-merous flower.
Mesocarp. Middle layer of pericarp tissue of a fruit with exocarp outside and endocarp inside.
Midrib. The main vein or rib of a leaf.
Monoecious. With separate staminate and pistillate flowers on the same plant, as opposite from dioecious.

Monotypic. In reference to a genus having only one species.
Mucro. A short and sharp abrupt spur or spiny tip.
Mucronate. Terminated abruptly by a distinct and obvious mucro.
Multiflorous. Many flowers.
Myanmar. Formerly Burma.

NAA. Naphthaleneacetic acid, synthetic type plant hormone.
Neotype. Replacing a specimen, when lost or damaged.
Nerves. Slender unbranched rib or vein.
Node. A joint where a leaf is produced.

Obcordate. Deeply lobed at the apex.
Oblanceolate. The reverse of lanceolate, broadest at the upper third near the apex.
Oblique. Slanted, unequal sided.
Oblong. Longer than broad, sides nearly parallel.
Obovate. The reverse of ovate, the terminal half broader than the basal.
Obtuse. Blunt or rounded.
Octoploid. Eight times the haploid number.
Orbiculate. Circular or disc-shaped.
Oval. Broad elliptic, about half as long as broad and rounded at the ends.
Ovate. Outline like an egg, the broadest end below the middle.
Ovoid. A solid that is oval.
Ovoviviparous. Giving birth to living young as some scale insects.

Paleobotany. The study of plants of previous geological periods, as evidenced by fossils, cast, impression, or other preserved parts.
Palynology. Study of fossil spores and pollen.
Pandurate. Shaped like a violin.
Panicle. A compound inflorescence of a racemose type with pedicelled flowers.
Paniculate. Borne in or resembling a panicle.
Papua New Guinea. Formally British New Guinea.
Paratype. Specimen for comparing with original description.
Parthenocarpic. Development of ripe fruit without fertilization.
Perianth. The flora envelope, consisting of a calyx and corolla when present.
Patelliform. Plate or saucer-shaped or flattened cone.
Paucifasciculate. Few fascicles.
Pedicle. The stalk of one flower in a cluster.
Peduncle. The lower stalk of a flower cluster, or of a solitary flower.
Pendulose. Drooping, hanging downward.
Penultimate. After or next to last.
Pericarp. Wall of ripened ovary, or wall of pyrene.
Persistent. Remaining attached, not falling off.
Petal. One of the units of the corolla of a flower.
Petiole. The leaf stalk.
Phenotype. A type (plant or population) determined by its appearance.
Phylogenetic. The evolutionary development of a species.
Pilose. Shaggy with soft hairs.
Pistil. The seed-bearing organ of the flower consisting of the ovary, style (when present), and stigma.
Pistillate. Having pistils and no functional stamens; female.

Pistillode. Rudimentary pistil.
Pistilloidia. Rudimentary or abortive ovaries.
Pitted. Having little depressions, or cavities.
Plicate. Folded or plaited, having parallel folds like a fan.
Polygamodioecious. Functionally dioecious but having a few flowers of the opposite sex.
Polymorphic. Having different forms; variable.
Polyploids. Having three or more times the haploid chromosome number.
Pomiform. Apple-shaped.
PP. Plant Patent.
Prophylla. A bracteole, scales on pedicels.
Prostrate. Low spreading habit.
Pseudoracemose. False racemose.
Puberulent. Minutely pubescent, scarcely visible.
Pubescent. Covered with soft hairs, downy.
Pulvinate. Having a pad or cushion shape.
Punctate. With translucent or colored dots or depressions or pits.
Putative. Considered to be, or reported.
Pyrene. The nutlet in a drupe, a seed and bony endocarp.
Pyriform. Pear-shaped.

Quadrangular. Four angled.

®. Indicates name is a registered trademark.
Raceme. A simple elongated inflorescence with pedicelled or stalked flowers.
Racemose. Having flowers in a racemelike inflorescence.
Rachis. Axis bearing flowers or leaflets.
Recurved. Curved downward.
Reg. Registered.
Relict. Species living on in isolation in a small local area as a survival from an earlier period.
Repand. Having a wavy margin.
Reticulate. Netted.
Retuse. Notched at the rounded apex.
Revolute. Rolled backward, to lower side.
Rhomboid. Parallelogram with oblique sides.
Rhombate. Shaped like a rhomboid.
Rostellate. Having a beak.
Rotund. Nearly circular.
Rudimentary. Incomplete, very little developed.
Rugose. Wrinkled.

Sabah, Malaysia. Formally British North Borneo.
Sarawak. Now state of Malaysia.
Scabrous. Rough, or gritty to the touch.
Scion. The upper or shoot portion of a graft.
Scurfy. Scales like dandruff.
Sensus. Opinion of; "sensu Engler," for example, means "in the opinion of Engler."
Serrate. Saw-toothed margin with teeth pointing forward.
Serrulate. Minutely serrate.
Sessile. Not stalked.
Setulose. Covered with bristles.

Sinuate. With a strong wavy margin.
Smooth. Surface with no hairiness, roughness, or pubescence.
Somatic. Cells that are diploid, 2n, as opposed to germ cell or gamete which is haploid or 1n.
Spathulate. Spoon-shaped.
Spiciform. Spikelike.
Spine. A strong and sharp pointed tip at end of leaf or from a stem.
Spinose. Having spines.
Spinulose. With small spines.
Spurs. Short modified stem; spurlike.
Sri Lanka. Formally Ceylon.
Stamen. The pollen bearing male organ of the flower.
Staminate. Having stamens and no pistil; male.
Stigma. The part of the pistil that receives the pollen.
Stipule. A basal appendage of a petiole.
Stock. The root portion of a graft.
Stoloniferous. A runner with stems under ground.
Striate. With fine longitudinal lines, channels, or ridges.
Striolate. Slightly striate.
Strigose. With sharp, appressed straight hairs.
Style. The part of the pistil between the ovary and the stigma.
Sub-. As a prefix, usually signifying somewhat, less, beneath, or below.
Subglobose. Slightly or almost globose.
Subobtuse. Slightly or almost blunt or rounded.
Succose. Juicy.
Sulcate. Grooved or furrowed lengthwise.
Sumatra. Now midland of Indonesia.
Surinam. Formerly Dutch Guiana.
Sympatric. Closely related species occurring in the same geographic area.
Sympetalous. The petals united, at least at the base.
Syncarpous. Having carpels united.
Synonym. Plant with like meaning or same name.
Syntype. In lieu of holotype, when no holotype was designated.

Taxon (plural, taxa). Applied to a taxonomic group at any rank such as species, genus, or family.
Terete. Circular in transverse section.
TM. Trademark.
Tomentose. With dense woolly pubescence.
Tonkin. Now northern part of Vietnam.
Trichotomous. Three parted, three forked.
Tricuspidate. Three pointed.
Trigonous. With 3 angles and 3 plane faces between.
Triploid. Three times the haploid number, 3n.
Tristriate. With 3 longitudinal lines or channels.
Truncate. Ending abruptly, as if cut off straight across at the end.
Tuberculate. Having tubercles, small rounded projections, knobs, or warts.
Turbinate. Inversely conical, or top shaped.

Umbel. Often flat-topped inflorescence with pedicels arising from the same point.
Umbellate. Borne in umbels.
Umbelliform. Umbel-like, resembling an umbel.

Undulate. With wavy (up and down, not in and out) surface or margin.
Unisexual. Of one sex, staminate or pistillate only.
Unsinuate. Without a wavy margin.
U.S.D.A. United States Department of Agriculture.

Venation. Arrangement of veins.
Verrucose. Having wartlike or nodular surface.
Vietnam and Laos. Formerly Indochina.

Whorl. Three or more leaves or flowers at one node, in a circle.

Zygote. A cell formed by the union of a male and female gametes; fertilized egg cell.

Bibliography

Adams, C. D. 1972. *Flowering Plants of Jamaica.* Mona, Jamaica: University of the West Indies.

Airy-Shaw, H. K. 1932. Additions to the flora of Borneo and other Malay Islands 14. *Oxford University Expedition to Sarawak.*

Alain, Bro. 1951. Aquifoliaceae: *I. victoriana* and *I. turquinensis.* Havana: Museum of U.S. History 12.

———. 1962. Novelties in the Cuban flora 14. *Phytologia* 8(7).

Alikarides, F. 1987. Natural constituents of *Ilex* species. *Journal of Ethnopharmacology* 20: 121–144.

Amshoff, G. J. H. 1951. Aquifoliaceae. Flora of Suriname (Netherlands Guyana). *Koninkljke Vereeniging Indisch Onstiuut, Amsterdam.* Mededling, No. 11.

Andrews, S. 1983a. A new species of *Ilex* (Aquifoliaceae) from Bahia, Brazil. *Kew Bulletin* 37.

———. 1983b. *Ilex × altaclerensis* not *altaclarensis* (Aquifoliaceae). *Taxon* 32(4): 625–626.

———. 1984. More notes on clones of *Ilex × altaclerensis. The Plantsman* 6(3): 157–166; and in *Holly Society Journal,* 1986, 4(3).

———. 1985. A reappraisal of *Ilex aquifolium* and *I. perado* (Aquifoliaceae). *Kew Bulletin* 39.

———. 1986a. The *Ilex fargesii* complex. *The Kew Magazine* 3(1).

———. 1986b. Notes on some *Ilex × altaclerensis* clones. *The Plantsman* 5(2) 65–81; and in *Holly Society Journal,* 1986, 3(3).

———. 1986c. The clones of *Ilex × altaclerensis. Acta Horticulturae,* p. 182.

———. 1989. A checklist of the Aquifoliaceae of Bahia. *Rodriguésia* (Rio de Janeiro) 37(63): 34–44.

———. 1990. Aquifoliaceae, notes on East Himalayan *Ilex Eden. Journal of Botany* 47(3): 351–360.

———. 1991. Family 100. Aquifoliaceae. *Flora of Butan* 2(1).

Angely, J. 1965. *Flora Analitica do Parana.* Institute Paranaense de Botany.

Arber, A. 1938. *Herbals, Their Origin and Evolution.* Cambridge, England: University Press.

Backer, C., and R. C. B. van der Brink Jr. 1963–1968. *Flora of Java.* Groningen, The Netherlands: N. V. P. Noordhoff.

Bailey, L. H. 1941. *Standard Cyclopedia of Horticulture.* New York: Macmillan.

Baker, J. R. 1972. *Eastern Forest Insects.* USDA Forest Service, Miscellaneous Publication No. 1174. Washington, D.C.: Government Printing Office.

Barrett, R. E. 1959. Genetics in layman's terms. *Proceedings of the Holly Society of America* 26.

Bartholomew, B., T. R. Dudley, S. C. Sun. 1980. Sino-American botanical expedition to western Hubei Province, China. *Journal of the Arnold Arboretum* 64(1).

Batchelor, J. A. 1970. Orcharding in the South. *American Horticultural Magazine* 49(4).

Bauers, B. M., Sr. 1993. *A Guide to Identification of Cultivated Ilex*. Holly Society of America.

Bean, J. W. 1976. *Trees and Shrubs Hardy in the British Isles*. 8th ed., rev., 4 volumes. London: John Murray.

Beissner et al. 1903. *Handb. Laubh.—Benenn.*

Bentham, G., and J. D. Hooker, eds. 1862–1883. *Genera Plantarum*. 3 volumes. London: Lovell Reeve.

Borhidi et Muniz. 1976. Aquifoliaceae. *Acta Botanica Academiae Scientiarum Hungaricae*. Budapest.

Borland, H. 1969. *Plants of Christmas*. New York: HarperCollins Children's Books.

Brandegee, T. S. 1901. Plantae Mexicanae Purpusianae. *University of California, Publications in Botany* 4(3): 85–95.

———. 1989. The vascular flora of Isla Socorro, Mexico. Memoir 16, Department of Botany, San Diego Natural History Museum, California.

Brickell, C. D., et al., eds. 1980. *International Code of Nomenclature for Cultivated Plants—1980*. Volume 104. Utrecht, The Netherlands: Bohn, Scheltema, and Holkema.

Britton, N. L. 1920. Descriptions of Cuban plants new to science. *Memoirs of the Torrey Botanical Club* 16(2).

Britton, N. L., and C. F. Millspaugh. 1962. *The Bahama Flora*. New York: New York Botanical Garden.

Brown, F. B. H. 1935. Flora of Southeastern Polynesia. *Bernice P. Bishop Museum Bulletin* 130.

Brown, N. E. 1901–1905. Iliaceae. *Transactions of the Linnean Society of London*, 2nd ser., botany, 6.

Brummitt, R. K., and C. F. Powell. 1992. *Authors of Plant Names*. Kew, England: Royal Botanic Garden, Kew.

Candolle, A. P. de. 1813. *Theorie elementaire de la botanique*. Paris.

Capitaine, L. 1910. Aquifoliaceae, *Ilex celedensis*. *Bulletin de la Societe Botanique de France*. 4th ser., volume 10. Paris.

Cast. 1986. *Genetic Engineering in Food and Agriculture*. Council Agriculture Science Technology Report No. 110.

Chma, P. C., ed. 1978. *Flora of Taiwan*. 6 volumes. Taipei, Taiwan: Epoch Publishing Company.

Chun, W. Y. 1963. Material for the flora of Hainan (II). *Acta Phytotaxonomica Sinica* 8(4).

Cole, W. 1657. *History of Plants*.

Conder, J. 1990. *Landscape Gardening in Japan*. 2nd ed. New York: Dover.

Cook, A. D., ed. 1984. Propagation for the home gardener. *Brooklyn Botanic Garden Record, Plant and Gardens* 40(1).

Coombes, A. J. 1987. *Dictionary of Plant Names*. Portland, Oregon: Timber Press.

Coville, P. 1933. *Growing Christmas Holly on the Farm*. USDA Farmers Bulletin No. 1693.

Cronquist, A. 1968. *The Evolution and Classification of Flowering Plants*. Boston: Houghton Mifflin.

———. 1981. *An Integrated System of Classification of Flowering Plants*. New York: Columbia University Press.

Cuatrecasas, J. 1948. Studies in South American plants. *Lloydia Library and Museum* 11(3).

———. 1955. Studies in South American plants—3. *Fieldiana* (botany) 27.

Culpeper, N. 1653. *A Physical Directory*. London.

Dale, I. R., and P. J. Greenway. 1961. *Kenya Trees and Shrubs*. Nairobi: Buchanan's Kenya Estates.

Dallimore, W. 1908. *Holly, Yew and Box*. London: John Lane Company.

Darke, R. 1991. The horticultural dilemma—trademarks, patents, royalties, and cultivars: colloquium, American Society of Horticulture Science, Northeast Regional Meeting, January, 1990. *HortScience* 26(4).

Darlington, D. D., and Janaki Ammal, E. K., 1945. *Chromosome Atlas of Cultivated Plants*. London.

Dengler, H. W., ed. 1957. Handbook of hollies. *National Horticulture Magazine*, special issue, 36: 1–139.

Dirr, M. A. 1990. *Manual of Woody Landscape Plants.* Champaign, Illinois: Stipes Publishing Company.

Dirr, M. A., and C. W. Heuser Jr. 1987. *The Reference Manual of Woody Plant Propagation: From Seed to Tissue Culture.* Portland, Oregon: Timber Press.

Dreilinger, S., ed. 1990. *Indoor Bonsai.* New York: Brooklyn Botanic Gardens.

Dudley, T. R. 1980. Two new variants of *Ilex* (Aquifoliaceae) from Eastern Asia and the Philippines. *Feddes Repertorium,* sp. nov., 91(9–10): 577–579.

———. 1981. The native *Ilex* (Aquifoliaceae) of Turkey, Transcaucasia, Iran, the Georgian Caucasus and Bulgaria. *Mitt. Dtsch. Dendr.* Ges. 72: 97–128.

———. 1983. A new species of *Ilex* (Aquifoliaceae) from Sumatra. *Feddes Repertorium* 94(3–4): 165–172.

———. 1984a. *Holly Society Journal* 2(2): 12–18.

———. 1984b. New taxa of *Ilex* from the People's Republic of China. *Acta Botanica Yunnanica.*

———. 1985. New taxa of *Ilex* from Guangxi and Yunnan Provinces of the People's Republic of China. Trans. C.-y. Hu.

———. 1986. The story of hollies. Part 1: diversity and history. *Holly Society Journal* 4(3).

———. 1991. New taxa of *Ilex* (Aquifoliaceae) from China: *I. serrata* subsp. *cathayensis, I. lihuaiensis,* and *I. suichangensis. Holly Society Journal* 4.

Dudley, T. R., and G. K. Eisenbeiss. 1973. *International Checklist of Cultivated Ilex, Part 1, Ilex opaca.* U.S. National Arboretum Contribution No. 3, USDA Agricultural Research Service. Washington, D.C.: Government Printing Office.

———. 1977. *The Coin-Leaved Japanese Hollies.* Holly Society of America Bulletin No. 16.

———. 1992. *International Checklist of Cultivated Ilex, Part 2, Ilex crenata Thunberg ex J. A. Murray.* U.S. National Arboretum Contribution No. 6, USDA Agricultural Research Service. Washington, D.C.: Government Printing Office.

Durbin, R. D., ed. 1965. *Nicotiana: Procedures for Experimental Use.* USDA Technical Bulletin No. 1956. Washington, D.C.: Government Printing Office.

Dutcher, R. 1988. Application of genetic engineering in horticulture: a practical perspective. *Proceedings of the International Plant Propagators' Society* 38.

Edwin, G. 1965a. Botany of the Guayana Highlands, *Ilex* (Aquifoliaceae). *Memoirs of The New York Botanical Garden* 12(3).

———. 1965b. New Peruvian *Ilex. Brittonia* 17: 284–285.

Eisenbeiss, G. K. 1973. "Ashe's holly: what is it?" *Proceedings of the Holly Society of America* 50.

———. 1987. Holly by another name, sources of name confusion. *Holly Society Journal* 5(1).

———. 1994. *International Ilex Cultivar Registration.* 3 parts. Wichita, Kansas: Holly Society of America.

———. 1995. *Ilex* cultivar registration list, 1985–1993. *Holly Society Journal* 13(3): 1–37.

Eisenbeiss, G. E., and T. R. Dudley. 1983. *Ilex Cultivar Registration List, 1958–1983.* Holly Society of America Bulletin No. 20.

Eisenbeiss, G. E., and F. S. Santamour Jr. 1973. Holly hybridization at the National Arboretum. *Holly Society of America Letter* 47.

Elmer, E. 1908. A century of new plants. *Leaflet of Philippine Botany* 1(16).

Emsweller, S. L. 1974. Fundamentals of plant breeding. *Brooklyn Botanic Garden Record, Plant and Gardens* 30(1).

Engler, A., and K. Prantl. 1897. *Die Natürlichen Pflanzenfamilien.*

Evelyn, J. 1662. *Sylva or a Discourse on Forest-Trees.* London.

Fawcett, W. 1926. *Flora of Jamaica.* Vol. 5.

Fenton, D. G. 1966. In Memoria 1886—Clarence R. Wolf—1966. *Holly Society of America Letter* 28.

———. 1970. Orcharding in the Middle Atlantic Area. *American Horticultural Magazine* 49(4).

Fernald, M. L. 1950. *Gray's Manual of Botany.* 8th ed. Portland, Oregon: Dioscorides Press.

Frierson, J. L. 1959. *Cytotaxonomic Study of Selected Indigenous and Introduced Species of the Genus Ilex Commonly Grown in the United States.* Ph.D. Thesis, University of South Carolina.

Geistlinger, L. 1994. Guess who is coming to dinner? *American Nurseryman* (1 August).

van Gelderen, D. M. 1988. *Ilex aquifolium* en *Ilex × altaclerensis. Dendroflora.*

Girarde, J. 1597. *The Herbal or General Historie of Plants.* London: John Norton.

Gleason, H. A., and A. Cronquist. 1991. *Manual of Vascular Plants of Northeastern United States and Adjacent Canada.* 2nd ed. Bronx: New York Botanical Garden.

Godfrey, R. K. 1988. *Trees, Shrubs, and Woody Vines of Northern Florida and Adjacent Georgia and Alabama.* Athens, Georgia: The University of Georgia Press.

Griffiths, M. 1994. *Index of Garden Plants.* Portland, Oregon: Timber Press.

Grisebach, A. H. R. 1965. Flora of the British West Indian Islands. *Historiae Naturalis Classica.* Reprinted by J. Cramer, Weinbeim, Wheldon and Lesley, and Hefner Publishing Company, New York.

Grissell, E. E. 1989. Discovery of a holly seed-feeding wasp. *Holly Society Journal* 7(4): 3–8.

Hahn, L. C. 1986. A dirt farmer's method of rooting holly. *Holly Society Journal* 4.

Hahn, W. J. 1988. A new species of *Ilex* (Aquifoliaceae) from Central America. *Annals of the Missouri Botanical Garden* 75(2).

Hanbury, W. 1770. *Complete Book of Gardening.* Multivolume.

Hansell, D. E. 1969. The beginning of the Holly Society of America. *Proceedings of the Holly Society of America* 46.

Hansell, D. E., T. R. Dudley, and G. K. Eisenbeiss, eds. 1970. Handbook of hollies. *American Horticulture Magazine* 40(4).

Hansen, A., and P. Sunding. 1930. Flora of Micronesia, checklist of vascular plants. Publication 278. *Field Museum of Natural History,* bot. ser., 8(2).

Hara, H. 1954. *Enumerato Spermatophytarum Japonicarum.* (A Bibliographic Enumeration of Flowering Plants indigenous to or long cultivated in Japan and its adjacent Islands.) Tokyo: Iwanami Shoten. Reprinted 1972 by O. K. Antiquariat, Korenigstein—Ts. B.R.D.

Hartmann, H. T., and D. E. Kester, 1984. *Plant Propagation: Principles and Practices.* 3rd ed. Englewood Cliffs, New Jersey: Prentice-Hall.

Hayata, B. 1911. Flora of Formosa. *Journal of the College of Science, Imperial University of Tokyo* 44.

————. 1913. Ilicineae. *Icones Plantarum Formosanarum.*

Heer, O. 1869. *Fossile Flora Von Alaska.* Konge Svenska Vetenskaps-Akadrmiens Handlingar Branden 8(4). Stockholm, Sweden.

Hermano, A. 1960. Aquifoliaceae. *Flora Cubana,* XIII.

Hilliers' Manual of Trees and Shrubs. 1974. Newton Abbot, Great Britain: David Charles.

Ho, P.-h. 1992. *Cayco Vietnam.* An Illustrated Flora of Vietnam. Santa Ana, California: Mekong Printing.

Hooker, J. D., ed. 1872–1897. *The Flora of British India.* 7 volumes. London: Reeve.

Hooker, W. J. 1837. New or rare plants. *Icones Plantarum.* Volume 2. London: Longman.

Howard, R. A. 1986. Notes on *Quiina* (Quiinaceae) and *Ilex* species (Aquifoliaceae) in Cuba. *Brittonia* 38(1): 13–16.

Hu, C.-y. 1977a. Advances in *Ilex* embryo culture. *Proceedings of the Holly Society of America* 54.

————. 1977b. Embryo culture: a technique to shorten holly breeding cycle. *Holly Society of America Letter* 57.

————. 1978. Holly embryo culture: materials and methods. *Holly Society of America Letter* 62.

Hu, H.-H., and T. Tang. 1936. Notes on five new and several other known species of *Ilex* of China. *Bulletin Fan Memorial Institution Biology, Botany Service,* 15.

Hu, S.-y. 1949. *Ilex* in Taiwan and the Liukiu Island. *Journal of the Arnold Arboretum* 30(14).

———. 1950. The genus *Ilex* in China. Reprinted from *Journal of the Arnold Arboretum* 30 (1949): 233–387; 31(1950): 39–80, 214–240, 241–263.

———. 1951. Notes on the flora of China, I. *Journal of the Arnold Arboretum* 32.

———. 1959. Chinese hollies. *Tsing Hua Journal of Chinese Studies* (Peking, China), special no. 1, natural science, December.

———. 1964. Fruit characters in holly. *American Horticultural Magazine* (January).

———. 1967. The evolution and distribution of species of Aquifoliaceae in the Pacific Area. *Journal of Japanese Botany* 42(1): 13–27.

Hudson, C. M., ed. 1979. *Black Drink: A Native American Tea*. Athens, Georgia: The University of Georgia Press.

Humbert, H. 1956. Nouvelles Especes de L'Amerique sud Recoltees par le Professeur Henri Humbert. Notulae Systematicae. *Muséum national d'Histoire naturelle*. Volume 15, fascicle 2. Paris.

Hume, H. H. 1953. *Hollies*. New York: Macmillan.

———. 1959. *Holly Pyrenes (Seeds)*. Holly Society of America Bulletin No. 10.

Huse, R. D., and K. L. Kelly. 1984. *A Contribution Toward Standardization of Color Names in Horticulture: Application of Universal Color Language to the Royal Horticultural Society's Colour Chart*. American Rhododendron Society.

Huzioka, K., and K. Uemura. 1973. The Late Miocene Miyata flora of Akita Prefecture, Northeast Honshu, Japan. *Botanical Natural Science Museum* (Tokyo) 15(3).

Jackson, B. D., et al. 1895. *Index Kewensis Plantarum Phanerogamarum: Covering the Period from Linnaeus up to the Year 1885*. 2 volumes plus supplements. Oxford: Clarendon Press. Reprinted 1977 by Koeltz Scientific Books, Königstein, Germany.

Jacobs, P. L. 1988. Propagation on a shoestring. *American Nurseryman* (15 August).

Jensen, N. F. 1990. *Plant Breeding Methodology*. New York: John Wiley.

Johnson, A. T., and H. A. Smith. 1931. *Plant Names Simplified*. Reprinted 1986 by Landsmans Bookshop, Herefordshire, England.

Johnson, I. M. 1938. *Ilex quercetorum sp. nov. Journal of the Arnold Arboretum*.

Johnson, W. T., and H. H. Lyon. 1990. *Insects that Feed on Trees and Shrubs*. 2nd ed. Ithaca, New York: Cornell University Press.

Johnston, J. R. 1938. Species from Mexico and Guatemala. *Journal of the Arnold Arboretum* 19.

Jones, S. B., Jr., and A. E. Luchsinger. 1986. *Plant Systematics*. 2nd ed. New York: McGraw-Hill Book Company.

Kan, Y., and D. Mao-bin. 1987. A new species of *Ilex* Linn. (Aquifoliaceae) from Anhui. *Acta Phytotaxonomica Sinica*.

Karow, G. A. 1989. *A Systematic Study of Ilex ambigua, Ilex decidua, and Related Taxa*. M.Sc. Thesis, University of Georgia, Athens.

Kelsey, H. P., and W. A. Dayton. 1942. *Standardized Plant Names*. 2nd ed.

Kiew, R. 1978a. Notes on the System of Malayan Phanerogams. XXV Aquifoliaceae. *Gardens' Bulletin Singapore* 28: 231–234.

———. 1978b. A new species of *Ilex* (Aquifoliaceae) from Malaya. *Kew Bulletin* 32(3).

Kitamura, F., and Y. Ishiza. 1963. *Garden Plants in Japan*. Tokyo: Koousa Bunka Shinkokai.

Koreshoff, D. R. 1984. *Bonsai: Its Art, Science, History, and Philosophy*. Portland, Oregon: Timber Press.

Kosar, W. F. 1957. Holly hybridizing: techniques and results. *Proceedings of the Holly Society of America* 22.

———. 1957. Hybridizing hollies. *National Horticulture Magazine*, special issue, 36.

Krüssmann, G. 1983–1986. *Manual of Cultivated Broad-Leaved Trees and Shrubs*. 3 volumes. Portland, Oregon: Timber Press.

Kunkel, G. 1976. The *Ilex* complex in the Canary Islands and Madeira. *Cuadernos de Botanica Canaria* 28: 17–29.

Kunth, R. 1928. Repertorium Specierum Novarum Regni Vegetabilis Beitefte/ Bd. XLIII. Initia Florae Venezuelensis. *Dahlem Bei Berlin Verlag Des repertoriums.*

Lace, J. H. 1914. Aquifoliaceae. *Ilex englishii. Kew Bulletin.*

Lamotte, Robert S. 1952. Catalogue of the Cenozoic plants of North America through 1950. *The Geological Society of America Memoir* 51.

Lawrence. G. H. M. 1951. *Taxonomy of Vascular Plants.* New York: Macmillan.

Lemee, A. 1952. De la Guyane française. Volume 2. Brest Imp. Com and Adm.

Li, H.-L. 1970. Aquifoliaceae. In *Flora of Taiwan.* Ed. P. C. Chma. Taipei, Taiwan: Epoch Publishing Company.

Li, Y.-K. 1986. A new series of *Ilex* L. *Acta Phytotaxonomica Sinica.*

Liberty Hyde Bailey Hortorium. 1976. *Hortus Third.* New York: Macmillan.

Linnaeus, C. 1735. *Systema Naturae,* Lugdoni: Batavorum.

———. 1737. *Genera Plantarum.* Lugdoni: Batavorum.

———. 1753. *Species Plantarum.* 2 volumes. Stockholm. Facsimile edition, 1957–1959, London.

Little, E. L., and R. G. Skolman. 1989. *Common Forest Trees of Hawaii (Native and Introduced).* Agriculture Handbook 679, USDA Forest Service. Washington, D.C.: Government Printing Office.

Loesener, T. 1901. *Monographia Aquifoliacearum, Part 1.* Nova Acta Acad. Caes. Leop.-Carol. Nat. Cur., 78: 1–589.

———. 1908. *Monographia Aquifoliacearum, Part 2.* Nova Acta Acad. Caes. Leop.-Carol. Nat. Cur., 89: 1–313.

———. 1913. In I. Urban, Nova genera et species VI. *Symbolae Antillane seu Fundamental Florae Occidentalis* 7: 516–519.

———. 1919. Über die Aquifoliaceen, besonders über *Ilex. Mitt. Dtsch. Dendr.* Ges. 28: 1–66.

———. 1923. Aquifoliaceae. *Plant cubensis Ekman.* I.

———. 1924. Die Aquifoliaceen Papuasiens. Lauterbach, Beitr. zur Flora van Pap. XI. in Eng. *Botanische Jahrbücher für Systematik, Pflanzengeschichte und Pflanzengeographie* 59: 80–83.

———. 1942. Aquifoliaceae. In *Die Natürlichen Pflanzenfamilien,* 2nd ed., A. Engler and K. Prantl, eds. Volume 20b: 38–86.

———. 1964. Urban. *Symbolae Antillanae seu Fundamenta Florae Indiae Occidentalis.* 1st ed. Volume 9.

Loudon, J. C. 1844. *Arboretum et Fruticetum Britannicum (The Trees and Shrubs of Britain).* London: Longman, Brown, Green, and Longmans.

Loudon, J. C., and Wise. 1706. *The Retired Gardener.*

Lundell, C. R. 1970. Studies of American plants. *Wrightia* 4(4).

MacGinitie, H. D. 1974. *An Early Middle Ecocene Flora from the Yellowstone Absaroka Volcanic Province, Northwestern Wind River, Wyoming.* Berkeley: University of California Press.

Maguire, B., J. A. Steyermark, and J. J. Wurdack. 1957. Botany of the Chimanta Massif, I: Grana Sabana, Venezuela. *Memoirs of The New York Botanical Garden* 9(3): 393–439.

Maguire, B., and J. Wurdack, eds. 1958. The botany of the Guayana Highland—Part 4. *Memoirs of The New York Botanical Garden* 10(1).

Makino, T. 1913. Observations on the flora of Japan. *Botany Magazine* (Tokyo Botany Society) 27: 313–324.

———. 1917. A contribution to the knowledge of the flora of Japan. *Journal of Japanese Botany* 1(6).

———. 1987. Section *Stigmatatophorae stat. nov.* and *Ilex maximowicziana* Yamazaki *comb nov. Journal of Japanese Botany* 62(6).

McComb, C. W. 1986. *A Field Guide to Insect Pests of Holly.* Wichita, Kansas: Holly Society of America.

McDaniel, J. 1970. Fertile foster hybrids. *Holly Society of America Letter* 37.

———. 1973. Notes on holly breeding. *Holly Society of America Letter* 46.

McIvor, D. E., and M. Conover, 1991. Uninvited guests. How to keep deer from dining on your valuable nursery stock. *American Nurseryman* (15 September).

Meikle, R. D. 1980. *Draft Index of Author Abbreviations.* Compiled at the Herbarium, Royal Botanic Gardens, Kew. London: Her Majesty's Stationery Office.

Merrill, E. D. 1915. New or noteworthy Philippine plants, XII. *The Philippine Journal of Science.*

———. 1923. Aquifoliaceae. *Enumeration of Philippine Plants.* Manila: Bureau of Science.

———. 1925. New species of Philippine plants collected by A. Loher. *The Philippine Journal of Science* 26(4); 27(1).

———. 1934. *New Sumatran Plants. I.* Papers of the Michigan Academy of Science Arts and Letters 19. Ann Arbor: University of Michigan Press.

———. 1939. Two new species of opposite-leaved *Ilex* from Borneo. *Journal of the Arnold Arboretum* 20.

Merrill, E. D. 1910. Aquifoliaceae. *The Philippine Journal of Science* 5(4).

Merrill, E. D., and J. Perry. 1939. Plantae Papuanae Archboldianae. *Journal of the Arnold Arboretum.*

———. 1941. Plantae Archboldianae VI. *Journal of the Arnold Arboretum.*

Meserve, Mrs. F. L. 1958. Progress report of controlled interspecific breeding of holly. *Proceedings of the Holly Society of America* 24.

Metcalf, F. P. 1932. Botanical notes on Fukien and Southeast China. *Lingnan Science Journal* 11(1).

Miller, P. 1731. *The Gardeners Dictionary, Containing Methods of Cultivating and Improving the Kitchen, Fruit, and Flower Garden.* London.

Moore, J. W. 1933. New and critical plants from Raiatea. *Bernice P. Bishop Museum Bulletin* 102.

Munson, R. H. 1988. A crisis in cultivar nomenclature. *Proceedings of the International Plant Propagators' Society* 38: 504–509.

Murray, J. A. 1784. *Systema Vegelabilium.* 14th ed.

Murthy K. R. K., S. N. Yoganarashimham, and K. Vasudevan Nair. 1987. A new species of *Ilex* (Aquifoliaceae) from Karnataka. *Current Science* 56(6).

Nakai, T. 1935. Notulae ad Plantas Japoniae and Koreae XLVI. *Plantae Boninenses Novae Vel Criticae* II.

Nelson, P. K. 1956. Embryo culture of English holly. *Proceedings of the Holly Society of America* 20.

Ohwi, J. 1965. *Flora of Japan.* Eds. F. R. Meyer and E. H. Walker. Washington, D.C.: Smithsonian Institution.

Orton, E. R., Jr. 1965. Hybridization of American and English holly. *Proceedings of the Holly Society of America* 39.

———. 1970a. Hybridizing holly. *Journal of the American Horticulture Society* 49(4).

———. 1970b. Breeding new cultivars of holly (a progress report). *Proceedings of the Holly Society of America* 47.

———. 1974. Holly hybridizing program. *Brooklyn Botanic Gardens Record, Plant and Gardens* 30(1).

———. 1983. Holly breeding at Rutgers University. *Holly Society of America Journal* 2.

———. 1984. Holly cultivars developed at Rutgers University. *Holly Society of America Journal* 3(1).

Parkinson, J. 1640. *Theatrum Botanicum, or an Herball of a large extent.*

Perry, L. R. 1964. *Bonsai: Trees and Shrubs—A Guide to the Methods of Kyuzu Nurat.* New York: Ronald Press.

Peterson, J. L. 1982. *Diseases of Holly in the United States.* Holly Society of America Bulletin No. 19.

Pinto Da Silva, A. R., and G. Quiteria. 1974. Ferns and flowering plants of the Azores. *Agronomia Lusitana* 36(1).

Pott, R. 1990. Die Nacheiszeitliche Ausbreitung and Heutigue Pflanzensoziologische Stellung von *Ilex aquifolium* L. *Tuexenia* 10: 497–512.

Purkayastha, C. S. 1938. Four new species from Assam. *Indian Forester* 64.

Reisseck, S. 1840–1906. *Ilex* section. In *Flora Brasiliensis.* C. F. P. von Martius, ed. Munich.

Rehder, A. 1940. *Manual of Cultivated Trees and Shrubs Hardy in North America.* Reprinted in 1987 by Dioscorides Press, Portland, Oregon.

Reveal, J. L., and C. R. Broome. 1980. Autonyms and new confusion in the international code. *Taxon* 29: 495–498.

Ridley, H. N. 1920. New and rare species of Malayan plants. *Journal of the Straits Branch of the Royal Asiatic Society.*

———. 1931. Iliaceae. *Kew Bulletin.*

———. 1967. *The Flora of the Malay Peninsula.* Volume 1, *Polypetalae.* Reprinted.

Roberts, A. N. 1959. Problems in growing holly commercially in the Pacific Northwest. *Proceedings of the Holly Society of America* 27.

Roberts, A. N., and C. A. Boller. 1957. Orcharding in the Pacific Northwest. *National Horticultural Magazine,* special issue, 36.

Roberts, A. N., and R. L. Ticknor. 1970. Commercial production of English holly in the Pacific Northwest. *American Horticultural Magazine* 49(4).

Roberts, A. N., R. L. Ticknor, and O. C. Compton. Boron deficiency evident in Oregon holly orchards. *Plant Distribution Report* 45(8): 634–635.

Rock, J. F. 1975. *The Indigenous Trees of the Hawaiian Islands.* Lawai, Kauai, Hawaii: Pacific Tropical Botanic Garden.

Rolfe, R. A. 1886. Ilicineae. Flora from the Philippine Islands. *Botanical Journal of the Linnean Society* 21.

Roxburgh, W. 1980. *Flora Indica or Description of Indian Plants.* 3 volumes. New York: State Mutual Book.

Royal Horticulture Society. 1990 *R.H.S. Colour Chart.* London: The Royal Horticultural Society.

Sanchez, J. A. 1911. Descripcion de Plantas Nuevas. *Annales de la Sociedad Cientifica Argentina* 72.

Segal, B. 1991. *The Holly and the Ivy, A Celebration of Christmas.*

Shufunotomo, Editors of. 1982. *The Essentials of Bonsai.* Portland, Oregon: Timber Press.

Simpson, R. C. 1983. Propagating deciduous holly. *Proceedings of the International Plant Propagators' Society* (1980)30; and *Holly Society Journal* 1(1).

Sinclair, W. A., and W. T. Johnson. 1990. *Diseases of Trees and Shrubs.* Ithaca, New York: Cornell University Press.

Skinner, H. T. 1952. Holly breeding. *Proceedings of the Holly Society of America* 11.

Smith, M. D. 1982. *The Ortho Problem Solver.* San Francisco, California: Ortho Information Service.

Stafleu, F. A. 1967, 1971. *Taxonomic Literature.* Kew.

———, ed. 1972. *International Code of Botanical Nomenclature.* Volume 82.

Stahl, A. 1936. Estudios Sobre la Flora de Puerto Rico. *Publ. de la Fed. Em., Rel. Adm.* San Juan de Puerto Rica.

Standley, P. C. 1893. Flora of Cost Rica, part II. *Field Museum of Natural History,* bot. ser., 58.

———. 1926. The flora of Costa Rica. *Journal of the Washington Academy Science* 16:481; *Field Museum of Natural History,* bot. ser., 15(21); 16(18).

———. 1931. Studies of American plants. *Field Museum of Natural History,* bot. ser.

————. 1940. Aquifoliaceae. *Field Museum of Natural History,* bot. ser., 22.

Stearn, W. T. 1992. *Botanical Latin.* 4th ed. Portland, Oregon: Timber Press.

Steyermark, J. A. 1938. Flora of Venezuelan Guayana-IV. *Annals of the Missouri Botanical Garden* 75(1).

————. 1954. Una Nueva Especie de *Ilex* de Venezuela.

Stilwell Jr., G. R. 1985. IBA quick-dip for cuttings. *Holly Society Journal* 3(3).

Stone, B. C., and R. Kiew, 1984. A new endemic species of *Ilex* (Aquifoliaceae) from Gunung Ulu Kali, Pahang, Peninsular Malaysia. *Malayan Nature Journal* 37: 193–198.

Stowe. 1568. *Survey of London.*

Suplee, Frank. 1985. Highlights of the past. *American Holly Society Journal* 3(1).

Taylor, D. W. 1990. Paleobiogeographic relationship of abeioperms from Cretaceous and Early Tertiary of the North America Area. *Botanical Review* 56(4): 279–417.

Theophrastus (370–285 B.C.). 1961. *Enquiry into Plants.* 2 volumes. Trans. A. Hort. London: W. Heinemann.

Thunberg, P. C. 1784. *Flora Japonica.* Germany.

Ticknor, R. L., R. N. Roberts, and O. C. Compton. Nutrition of English holly (*Ilex aquifolium*) in Oregon. *American Horticultural Magazine* 48(2): 67–69.

Tilt, K., D. Williams, W. Witte, and M. K. Gaylor. 1995. *Hollies for the Landscape in the Southeast.* Circular, A N R-837. Alabama Cooperative Extension Service, Auburn University.

Tjia, B. 1983. Rooting *Ilex rotunda. Holly Society Journal* 1(2).

Toogood, A. 1991. *The Hillier Guide to Connoisseur's Plants.* Portland, Oregon: Timber Press.

Tseng, C.-j. 1981. Contributions to the Aquifoliaceae of China. *Bulletin of Botanical Research* 1(1–2): 1–44.

————. 1989. New taxa of *Ilex* from Fujian. *Bulletin of Botanical Research* 9(4).

Turczaninow, N. S. 1858. Secundam Partem Herbarii Turczaninowiani, Nunc Univ. Caesareae Charkowiensis. *Bulletin of the Society of Natural History,* Moscow.

Turner, W. 1551. *A New Herball.* London.

Tuyama. 1935. Aquifoliaceae. *Botany Magazine* (Tokyo) 49.

U.S. Department of Agriculture. 1960. *Index of Diseases in the United States.* Agriculture Handbook 165. Washington, D.C.: Government Printing Office.

U.S. Forest Service. 1974. *Seeds of Woody Plants in the United States.* Agriculture Handbook No. 450, USDA Forest Service. Washington, D.C.: Government Printing Office.

Van Der Burgh, J. 1978. The Pliocene flora of Fortuna-Garddorf I. of Angiosperms. *Review of Palaeobotany and Palynology* 26: 173–211. Amsterdam, Netherlands: Elsevier Scientific Publishing Company.

Walker, E. 1976. *Flora of Okinawa and the Southern Ryukyu Islands.* Washington, D.C.: Smithsonian Institution.

Weiser, C. J., and L. T. Blaney. 1960. The effects of boron on the rooting of English holly cuttings. *Proceedings of the American Society of Horticulture Science* 75: 704–710.

Wells, J. S 1964. *Plant Propagation Practices.* New York: Macmillan.

Weston, R. 1775. *Flora Anglicana.* London, England.

Whitcomb, C. E. 1991. *Establishment and Maintenance of Landscape Plants.* Rev. ed. Stillwater, Oklahoma: Laceback.

Wieman, J. S. 1961. *History of English Holly (Ilex aquifolium) in Oregon and the Northwest.* Published in cooperation with the Oregon Holly Growers Association.

Wijnands, D. O. 1990. Correct author citation for the species described in material collected by Thunberg in Japan. *Thunbergia* 12: 1–48.

Williams, D. E. 1989. Prevention and control of wildlife damage in ornamental planting. *Holly Society Journal* 7(1): 6.

Wolfe, J. A., and W. Wehr 1987. Middle Eocene dicotyledonous plants from Republic, Northeastern Washington. *U.S. Geological Survey Bulletin* 1567: 1–25.

Wright, J. W. 1950. *Holly Hybridizing Techniques*. Holly Society of America Bulletin No. 4.

Wunderland, R. P., and J. E. Poppleton. 1977. *The Flora Species of Ilex (Aquifoliaceae)*. Department of Biology, University of Florida, Tampa.

Yamamoto, Y. 1925. *Supplementa, Icones Plantarum Formosanarum*. Cum descip. novarum spec., 20-figuris et 1-tabula. Published by the Department of Forestry Government Research Institute, Taihoku, Formosa.

Yamazaki, T. 1987. New Aquifoliaceae species. *Journal of Japanese Botany*.

Yashiroda, K., ed. 1989. *Bonsai: Special Techniques*. New York: Brooklyn Botanic Gardens.

Yoshimura, Y., and G. M. Halford. 1976. *The Japanese Art of Miniature Trees and Landscapes*. Vermont: Charles E. Tuttle Company.

Yuncker, T. G. 1938. Flora of Honduras. *Field Museum of Natural History,* bot. ser., 17(4).

Yunhua, H. 1988. *Chinese Penjing: Miniature Trees and Landscapes*. Portland, Oregon: Timber Press.

Botanical Summary of
Nomenclatural Changes

Ilex alainii T. R. Dudley, *nom. nov.*
Ilex atabapoensis T. R. Dudley, *nom. nov.*
Ilex buswellii f. *channellii* (Edwin) T. R. Dudley, *comb. nov.*
Ilex charrascosensis T. R. Dudley, *nom. nov.*
Ilex chimantaensis T. R. Dudley, *nom. nov.*
Ilex chimantaensis var. *pygmaea* (Edwin) T. R. Dudley, *comb. nov.*
Ilex decidua var. *mulleri* Edwin *ex* T. R. Dudley, *var. nov.*
Ilex discolor var. *tolucana* (Hemsley) Edwin *ex* T. R. Dudley, *comb. & stat. nov.*
Ilex fuertensiana (Loesener) T. R. Dudley, *comb. nov.*
Ilex longipes f. *hirsuta* (Lundell) T. R. Dudley, *comb. & stat. nov.*
Ilex megalophylla (Hemsley) Edwin *ex* T. R. Dudley, *comb. & stat. nov.*
Ilex nuculicava f. *brevipedicellata* (S.-y. Hu) T. R. Dudley, *comb. & stat. nov.*
Ilex pseudoumbelliformis T. R. Dudley, *nom. nov.*
Ilex repanda var. *hypaneura* (Loesener) Edwin *ex* T. R. Dudley, *comb. & stat. nov.*
Ilex reisseckiana T. R. Dudley, *nom. nov.*
Ilex rugosa f. *hondoensis* (Yamazaki) T. R. Dudley, *comb. & stat. nov.*
Ilex tamii T. R. Dudley, *nom. nov.*
Ilex tardieublotii Tran Dirh Dai, *nov. nom.*
Ilex urbaniana var. *riedlaei* (Loesener) Edwin *ex* T. R. Dudley, *comb. & stat. nov.*
Ilex vietnamensis T. R. Dudley, *nom. nov.*
Ilex zippeliana T. R. Dudley, *nom. nov.*
Series *Spicatae* T. R. Dudley, *stat. nov.*

Common Names of Hollies Belonging to the Genus *Ilex*

Common and colloquial names are often favored by gardeners as an easy way to avoid pronouncing and spelling of scientific names. Some plants have five or more common names, and some names apply to more than one plant!

There are no rules or guidelines for assigning common names to a plant, and common names are neither universal nor necessarily recognized by other gardeners in the same city or state. Scientific names, however, are universal, and they are recognized throughout the world. Furthermore, they provide information about the generic and family relationships that are so important and very interesting.

Many garden publications, such as *Plant Names Simplified* by A. T. Johnson, give guidelines to the pronunciation and meaning of Latin names. The importance of plant nomenclature is stressed to the students in botany, but often not to the students in horticulture and landscape design, who soon realize this loss and find it difficult to obtain and to use properly. It is hoped that this situation might change and that we can begin to stress the importance of Latin names when discussing plants.

Common names are written in lower case unless they are based on a proper name, person or place, and they are always written in roman (not italic or underline as is proper for scientific plant names).

Common Name	Scientific Name
acebino	*I. canariensis*
acebo desierra	*I. macfadyenii*
agrifolio	*I. aquifolium*
aka-mizuki	*I. micrococca*
aka-tsuge	*I. sugerokii*
akami-no-inu-tsuge	*I. sugerokii*
American holly	*I. opaca*
andun-wenna	*I. zeylanica*
ao-hada	*I. macropoda*
appalachian tea	*I. vomitoria*
areno	*I. tectonica*
arisan	*I. glomeratifolia*
atuba-motinoki	*I. percoriacea*

<u>Common Name</u>	<u>Scientific Name</u>
bacho	*I. rotunda*
bakrabakaro	*I. ovalifolia*
bay gall bush	*I. coriacea*
bead bush	*I. monticola*
bearberry	*I. decidua*
bearbush	*I. glabra*
belize	*I. tectonica*
black alder	*I. verticillata*
black holly	some selections of *I. aquifolium*
black Irish holly	some selections of *I. aquifolium*
bois Fourni	*I. sideroxyloides*
bois gris	*I. sideroxyloides*
bois petit Jean	*I. nitida*
boise-citron	*I. sideroxyloides*
bony thorn (Chinese)	*I. cornuta*
boxleaf holly	*I. crenata*
boxwood	*I. opaca*
buckbush	*I. longipes*
bui	*I. fabrilis, I. harmandiana, I. wallichii*
bui havo	*I. fabrilis*
bui hova	*I. thorelii*
buiba vo	*I. thorelii*
bulan	*I. macrophylla*
Buswell's possumhaw holly	*I. buswellii*
caa-chiri	*I. dumosa*
caa-na	*I. caaquazuensis, I. theezans* var. *fertilis*
caachiriri	*I. amara, I. crepitans*
caaquazu	*I. paraguariensis*
caerode sapo	*I. urbaniana*
caholina tea	*I. ambigua, I. vomitoria*
camibar	*I. tectonica*
can-hoop	*I. laevigata*
cassena	*I. vomitoria*
cassena-bush	*I. cassine*
cassina	*I. vomitoria*
cassine	*I. cassine*
cassinea	*I. vomitoria* subsp. *vomitoria*
catuabe do mato	*I. conocarpa*
cassioberrybush	*I. vomitoria*
cat thorn (Chinese)	*I. cornuta*
caulah	*I. dipyrena*
caunina	*I. amara*
cauna amarga	*I. amara, I. integerrima, I. theezans* var. *fertilis*
cauna de folhas largas	*I. theezans* var. *fertilis*
caybui	*I. fabrilis*
cerezo	*I. anodonta*
Chinese holly	*I. cornuta, I. purpurea*
Chinese horned holly	*I. cornuta*

Common Name	Scientific Name
Chinese spiny holly	*I. cornuta*
Christmas holly	*I. aquifolium, I. opaca*
christdorn	*I. aquifolium*
citronnien	*I. nitida*
citronnier	*I. sideroxyloides*
citronnier-montagne	*I. dioica*
cogolin	*I. sideroxyloides*
common holly	*I. aquifolium*
congonha	*I. affinis, I. conocarpa, I. cuyabensis, I. paltorioides,* *I. paraguariensis, I. vitis-idaea*
congonha do campo	*I. affinis*
congonhas minda	*I. dumosa*
congonhinha	*I. chamaedryfolia, I. congonhinha*
congoroba	*I. amara*
cueri de sapo	*I. urbaniana*
cuero de sapo	*I. nitida*
Curtiss's holly	*I. curtissii*
Cuthbert's holly	*I. cuthbertii*
dahoon holly	*I. cassine*
deciduous holly	*I. decidua*
deciduous yaupon holly	*I. decidua*
deer-berry	*I. vomitoria*
diusa	*I. dipyrena*
dogberry	*I. verticillata*
droopbead holly	*I. geniculata*
dune holly	*I. cumulicola*
Dutch holly	a group within *I.* × *altaclerensis*
Dutch-English holly	a group within *I.* × *altaclerensis*
dwarf box holly	*I. crenata*
eastern holly	*I. opaca*
Egham holly	*I. aquifolium* 'Heterophylla Aureomarginata'
eight-angled thorn (Chinese)	*I. cornuta*
emetic holly	*I. vomitoria*
English holly	*I. aquifolium*
European holly	*I. aquifolium*
evergreen cassena	*I. vomitoria*
evergreen cassine	*I. vomitoria*
false alder	*I. verticillata*
fan cha shu	*I. corallina*
farmer variegated holly	*I. aquifolium* 'Variegated'
feverbush	*I. verticillata*
fuiri-inu-tsugi	*I. crenata* f. *luteo-variegata*
fuiri-soyogo	*I. pedunculosa* f. *variegata*
furin Holly	*I. geniculata*
furin-ume-modoki	*I. geniculata*
furi machi no ki	*I.* 'Green Shadow'
gading	*I. macrophylla*
gallberry	*I. glabra*

<u>Common Name</u>	<u>Scientific Name</u>
gallberry, bitter	*I. glabra*
gallberry, large	*I. coriacea*
garliewood	*I. anomala*
gayaun	*I. crenata*
Georgia long-stalked holly	*I. longipes*
Godajam	*I. godajam*
gold-blotched	*I. aquifolium* 'Crispa Aurea-Picta'
gold porcupine	*I. aquifolium* 'Ferox'
graines vertes	*I. montana*
gray holly	*I. cinerea*
green porcupine holly	*I. aquifolium* 'Ferox'
guayusa	*I. guayusa*
gumshing	*I. dipyrena*
hai-inu-tsuge	*I. crenata* var. *paludosa*
Hawaiian holly	*I. anomala*
hedgehog holly	*I. aquifolium* 'Ferox'
heitzu-shu	*I. macrocarpa*
Himalayan holly	*I. dipyrena*
hime mochi	*I. leucoclada*
hizen Mochi	*I. buergeri*
holme	*I. aquifolium*
hoopwood	*I. laevigata*
horned holly	*I. cornuta*
hosoba-tsuru-tsuge	*I. rugosa*
hosoba-ume-modoki	*I. nipponica*
hulst	*I. aquifolium*
hulver	*I. monticola*
Indian black drink	*I. vomitoria*
India tea	*I. vomitoria*
inkberry	*I. glabra*
inu-mochi	*I. integra* f. *ellipsoidea*
inu-tsuge	*I. crenata*
inu-ume-modoki	*I. serrata*
Irish black holly	some selections of *I. aquifolium*
jagua negro	*I. nervosa* var. *glabrata*
jaloto on	*I. cymosa*
Japanese box holly	*I. crenata*
Japanese curled-leaf holly	*I. crenata*
Japanese dwarf holly	*I. crenata*
Japanese holly	*I. crenata*
Japanese tree holly	*I. crenata*
Japanese winterberry	*I. serrata*
Jesuit's tea	*I. paraguariensis*
kakotaro	*I. martiniana*
kalatan	*I. crenata*
kanial	*I. hypotricha*
kashi	*I. purpurea*
katagdo	*I. wenzelii*

Common Name	Scientific Name
katagio	*I. wenzelii*
katotara	*I. martiniana*
kaula	*I. dipyrena*
kawan	*I. anomala*
keebino	*I. canariensis*
ke-nashi-ao-hada	*I. macropoda*
kikko Inu-tsuge	*I. crenata*
kimi-no-mochi-no-ki	*I. integra*
kimi-ume-Modoki	*I. serrata*
kimi-soyogo	*I. pedunculosa*
kimino-kurogane mochi	*I. rotunda*
kisekkal	*I. cymosa, I. spicata*
koawan	*I. anomala*
kowan	*I. anomala*
korharatu	*I. gardneriana*
koshobai	*I. serrata*
Krug's holly	*I. krugiana*
kundar	*I. dipyrena*
kunyatangbukit	*I. laurocerasus*
kuro-soyogo	*I. sugerokii*
kurogane-mochi	*I. rotunda*
kuta-mutcha-gara	*I. liukiensis*
Kwangtung holly	*I. kwangtungensis*
large gallberry	*I. coriacea*
large-leaved holly	*I. monticola*
limoneillo	*I. discolor*
little-leaf Japanese holly	*I. crenata*
long-stalked holly	*I. pedunculosa*
lusterleaf holly	*I. latifolia*
macoucou	*I. guianensis*
Madeira holly	*I. perado*
magnolia-leaved holly	*I. latifolia, I. verticillata*
malagidia	*I. cymose*
mapirinoeloe	*I. martiniana*
marintok	*I. pulogensis*
maruba-tsuru-tsuge	*I. rugosa*
masaliksik	*I. antonii*
mate	*I. paraguariensis*
meadow holly	*I. decidua*
mensirah	*I. cymosa*
medang	*I. macrophylla*
Michigan holly	*I. verticillata*
Minnesota holly	*I. verticillata*
miyama-ume-modoki	*I. nipponica*
mochi-no-ki	*I. integra*
mountain holly	*I. ambigua, I. montana, I. verticillata*
mountain privet	*I. monticola*
Mt. Fuji holly	*I. crenata*

Common Name	Scientific Name
mountain winterberry	*I. ambigua*
mucha gira	*I. maximowicziana*
munin-inu-tsuge	*I. matanoana*
mushroom holly	*I. crenata*
muttcha-gara	*I. crenata*
muttchagii	*I. cinerea*
myrtle-leaf Dahoon	*I. myrtifolia*
myrtleleaf holly	*I. myrtifolia*
nagaba inu tsuge	*I. maximowicziana*
nagaha-nindo-machinoki	*I. hakkuensis*
nan-chiao	*I. tamii*
nanami-no-ki	*I. purpurea*
naranjillo	*I. dugesii*
naranjero salvage	*I. perado*
naranjo salvage	*I. perado*
narihira-mochi	*I. × kiusiana*
narrow-leaf Dahoon	*I. myrtifolia*
noko giri	*I. latifolia*
noko-ko	*I. latifolia*
northern holly	*I. verticillata*
o-tsuru-tsuge	*I. × makinoi*
Okinawan holly	*I. dimorphophylla*
okumo-furin-ume-modoki	*I. geniculata*
Oregon holly	*I. aquifolium*
orelha de burro	*I. paraguariensis*
orelha de mico	*I. brevicuspis*
orlo	*I. wightiana*
ostrolist	*I. aquifolium*
pala de yuba	*I. argentina*
palo mulato	*I. kunthiana*
pao d'azeile	*I. theezans*
Paraguay tea	*I. paraguariensis*
papatak	*I. pulogensis*
Perny's holly	*I. pernyi*
petit citronnier	*I. montana*
pidgeon-berry	*I. verticillata*
possumhaw holly	*I. decidua*
privet	*I. decidua*
quinti	*I. myricoides*
red thunderberry	*I. monticola*
roble	*I. argentina*
ryukyu-mochi	*I. liukiensis*
saisa swa	*I. excelsa*
San Juan arenillo	*I. tectonica*
San Juan campano	*I. tectonica*
San Juan macho	*I. tectonica*
sarvis holly	*I. amelanchier*
sas swa	*I. excelsa*

Common Name	Scientific Name
saw-leaved	*I. aquifolium crassifolia* 'Holly'
seiyo hiiragi	*I. aquifolium*
sekrepatoe-wiwirie	*I. guianensis* var. *elliptica*
serviceberry holly	*I. amelanchier*
screw-leaf holly	*I. aquifolium* 'Crispa'
shii-mochi	*I. buergeri*
shima inu-tsuge	*I. crenata* var. *mutchagara*
shiny inkberry	*I. glabra*
shiro-ume-modoki	*I. serrata* 'Leucocarpa'
shu cha tze	*I. yunnanensis*
sibuc che	*I. tectonica*
small leaves holly	*I. viridis*
small-leaf holly	*I. crenata*
smooth winterberry	*I. laevigata*
smudge holly	*I. aquifolium* 'Aurifodina'
southern holly	*I. opaca*
South-Sea tea	*I. paraguariensis*
soygo	*I. pedunculosa*
St. Bartholomew's tea	*I. paraguariensis*
striped holly	*I. verticillata*
swamp holly	*I. amelanchier*
sweet gallberry	*I. coriacea*
Tajaro	*I. latifolia*
takane-soyogo	*I. pedunculosa* var. *senjoensis*
tall gallberry	*I. coriacea*
tama-mizuki	*I. micrococca*
tara-yo	*I. latifolia*
tarebi-yek	*I. karuaiana*
tawnyberry holly	*I. krugiana*
Texas holly	*I. vomitoria*
thunderberry	*I. monticola*
thunderwood	*I. decidua*
tiger spine tree (Korean)	*I. cornuta*
tiger thorn (Chinese)	*I. cornuta*
timah-timah	*I. cymosa*
tisitron	*I. sideroxyloides*
topal holly	*I.* × *attenuata*
trambui	*I. eugeniaefolia*
true cassena	*I. vomitoria*
tsuge-mochi	*I. goshiensis*
tsukushi inu-tsuge	*I. crenata*
tsuru-tsuge	*I. rugosa*
tulok	*I. macrophylla*
tumari	*I. excelsa*
tun-ching	*I. purpurea*
turkeyberry	*I. decidua*
upright silverstriped holly	*I. aquifolium* 'Argenta Marginata Erecta'
ume-modoki	*I. serrata*

Common Name	Scientific Name
usaba-arisan-aoyogo	*I. arisanensis*
Virginia winterberry	*I. verticillata*
wajam moesesamoer	*I. guianensis* var. *elliptica*
wan-sho-hong	*I. purpurea*
weeping English holly	*I. aquifolium* 'Pendula'
white holly	*I. opaca, I. verticillata*
willow-leaved holly	*I. myrtifolia*
wilpeer	*I. mitis*
winterberry	*I. verticillata*
woho-sandzuki	*I. micrococca*
yapon	*I. cassine, I. vomitoria*
yaupon	*I. vomitoria*
yerba	*I. theezans*
yerba de maté	*I. paraguariensis*
yerba maté	*I. paraguariensis*
youpon	*I. vomitoria*

Common Names of Hollies
Not Belonging to the Genus *Ilex*

The word *holly* is often used in the name of plants that do not belong to the genus *Ilex*. These plants may have holly-like foliage or resemble holly in some other way, or they may simply make use of the word *holly* to create an interesting common name such as hollyhock.

Common Name	Scientific Name
African holly	*Solanum giganteum*
Arizona holly	*Photinia serratifolia*
box holly	*Ruscus aculeatus*
Braun's holly fern	*Polystichum braunii*
California holly	*Heteromeles arbutifolia, Photinia arbutifolia, Rhamnus* sp.
California holly grape	*Mahonia lomariifolia*
Chinese holly	*Osmanthus heterophyllus*
Chinese holly grape	*Mahonia japonica*
Cuban holly	*Atriplex hymenelytra*
desert holly	*Atriplex hymenelytra*
dwarf holly	*Malpighia coccigera*
false holly	*Osmanthus heterophyllus*
holly berry vine	*Lycium chinensis*
holly cherry	*Prunus ilicifolia*
holly fern	*Polystichum falcatum, P. lonchitis*
holly grape	*Mahonia aquifolium*
holly oak	*Quercus chrysolepis, Q. ilex*
holly scale	*Atriplex hymenelytra*
holly xylosma	*Xylosma heterophylla*
hollyhock, sea	*Eryngium maritimum, Hibiscus palustris*
holly-leaved ashberry	*Mahonia bealei*
holly-leaved barberry	*Berberis ilicifolia*
holly-leaved cherry	*Prunus laurocerasus*
holly-leaved olive	*Osmanthus aquifolium*
holly-leaved osmanthus	*Osmanthus heterophyllus*
Japanese holly	*Mahonia japonica*
miniature holly	*Malpighia coccigera*

Common Name	Scientific Name
mountain holly	*Nemopanthus mucronatus*
Oregon holly	*Mahonia aquifolium*
Oregon grape holly	*Mahonia aquifolium*
Pursh's holly fern	*Polystichum braunii* var. *purshii*
Scotch holly	*Osmanthus heterophyllus*
sea holly	*Eryngium alpinum, E. amethystinum, E. maritimum, E. planum*
Singapore holly	*Malpighia coccigera*
West Indian holly	*Leea coccinea*

Index of Botanical Names

Index of Cultivar Names

Boldfaced page numbers indicate pages of primary entries.

Key

alta	= *I. × altaclerensis*	*gla*	= *I. glabra*	*opa*	= *I. opaca*
aqu	= *I. aquifolium*	*hyb*	= Interspecific hybrid	*ped*	= *I. pedunculosa*
att	= *I. × attenuata*	*int*	= *I. integra*	*per*	= *I. pernyi*
cass	= *I. cassine* and *I. cassine*	*lae*	= *I. laevigata*	*perad*	= *I. perado*
	var. *angustifolia*	*lat*	= *I. latifolia*	*rot*	= *I. rotunda*
col	= *I. collina*	*long*	= *I. longipes*	*ser*	= *I. serrata*
cor	= *I. cornuta*	*myr*	= *I. myrtifolia*	*vert*	= *I. verticillata*
coria	= *I. coriacea*	NA	= Plant still under test at	*vom*	= *I. vomitoria*
cr	= *I. crenata*		the U.S. National		
dec	= *I. decidua*		Arboretum,		
			Washington, D.C.		

'Aalto No. 1' *opa*, 363
'Aalto No. 2' *opa*, 369, 390
'Aalto No. 3' *opa*, 373
'Aalto No. 4' *opa*, 364
'Aalto No. 14' *opa*, 365
'Accent' *int × per*, 414, 419, **404**, 451
'Acuminata' *opa*, **345**
'Adams' *opa*, **345**
'Adaptable' *alta*, 36, **261**, 447
'Adonis' *hyb*, **405**, 458; Plate 166
'Afterglow' *vert*, 49, **148**; Plate 46
'Agena' *hyb*, **405**; Plate 167
'Aglo' *cor*, **313**
'Ajax' *hyb*, **405**
'Alagold' *att*, 38, 60, **304**, 305, 306; Plate 110
'Alan Seay' *cr*, 40, **324**, 325
'Alaska' *aqu*, **269**, 283, 287
'Albert Close' *hyb*, **405**
'Albert King' *opa*, **345**
'Albert Pride' *opa*, **345**, 368
'Albo-Marginata' *aqu*, 271
'Albo-Marginata' *cr*, 339
'Albomarginata Pendula' *aqu*, 271
'Albo Picta' *aqu*, 295

'Alcicornis' *aqu*, **269**
'Alfred Anderson' *vert*, **148**
'Alice' *aqu*, **269**, 299
'Alice Steed' *opa*, **345**
'Allen' *opa*, **345**
'Allison' *opa*, **345**
'Alloway' *opa*, **345**
'Alloway Upright' *opa*, **345**
'Altaclerensis' *alta*, 261, 264, **269**
'Alto No. 3' *opa*, 373
'Amber' *aqu*, 37, **270**
'American Spineless' *opa*, **345**
'American Wreath' *opa*, **345–346**
'Ammerland' *aqu*, **270**
'Amy' *opa*, 41, **346**, 397
'Ananassifolia' *aqu*, **270**
'Andover' *opa*, 41, **346**
'Anet' *opa*, **346**
'Angelica' *cr*, **324**
'Angelica' *opa*, 324, **347**
'Angustifolia' *aqu*, 31, 37, 69, **270**, 273, 278, 283, 286, 287, 291, 292, 297, 444; Plate 86
'Angustifolia' *opa*, **347**
'Angustifolia Albo-Marginata' *aqu*, **270**

'Angustifolia Aurea Marginata' *aqu*, 270
'Angustifolia Minor' *aqu*, 288
'Angustimarginata Aurea' *aqu*, **270**
'Angyo' *cr*, **324**, 333
'Anicet Delcambre' *cor*, 26, 39, **313**, 320, 323; Plate 121
'Anna Mae' *cor*, **313–314**
'Anne Arundel' *opa*, **347**
'Apollo' *ser × vert*, 48, **152**
'Aprather' *aqu*, **269**
'Apricot' *aqu*, **270**
'Apricot Glow' *aqu*, 37, **270**, 291
'Aquapaca' *opa*, **347**
'Aquila' *cor × per*, **405**
'Aquinnah' *vert*, **148**
'Aquipern' *hyb*, **405**
'Arbutifolia' *aqu*, **270**
'Arden' *opa*, 59, **347**
'Argentea Erecta' *aqu*, **271**
'Argentea Latifolia' *aqu*, 295
'Argentea Longifolia' *aqu*, **270–271**
'Argenata Marginata' *aqu*, 37, **271**, 292, 294, 295, 296; Plate 87